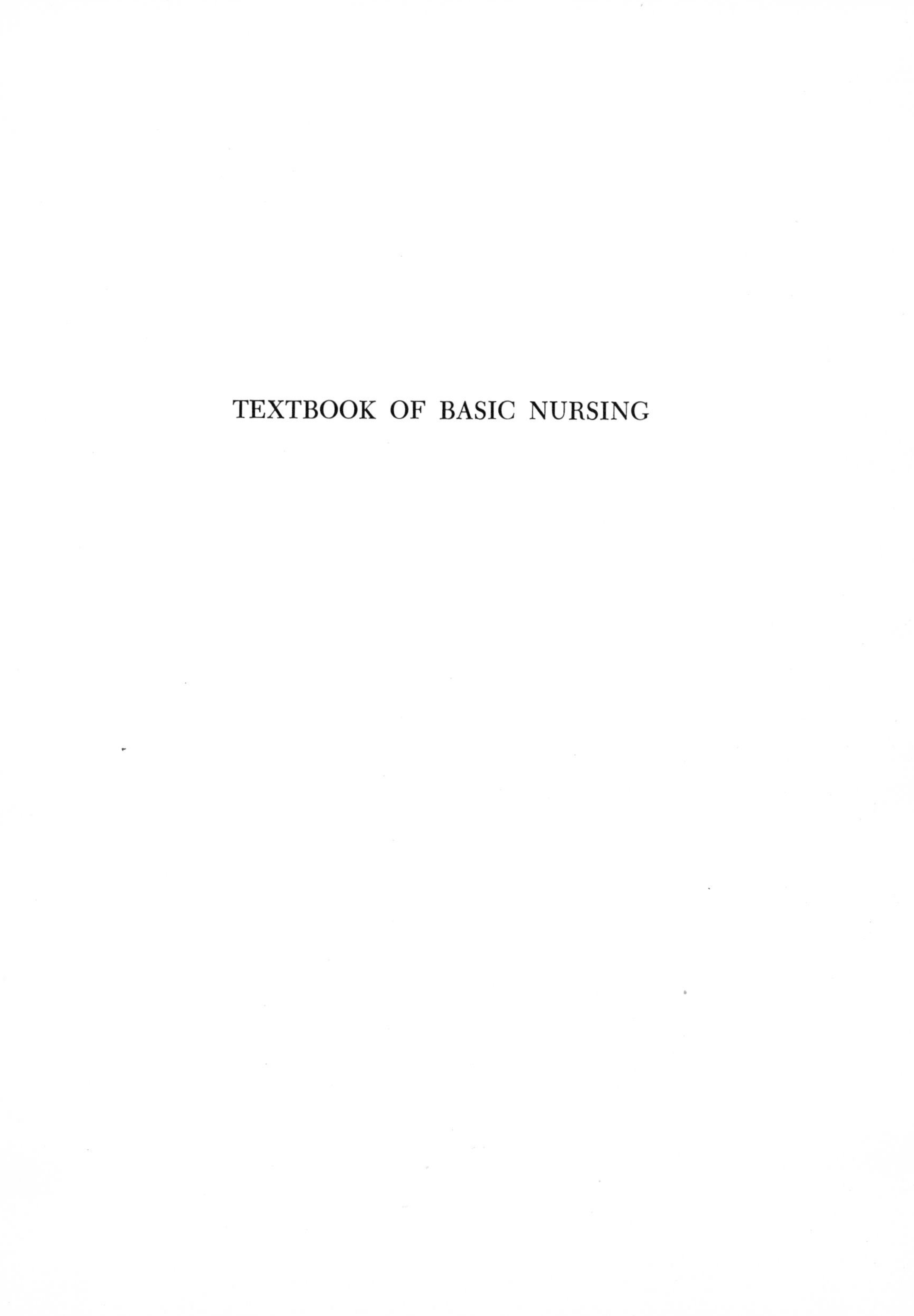

TEXTBOOK OF BASIC NURSING

Textbook of Basic Nursing

ELLA M. THOMPSON, R.N., B.S.

Field Consultant, National Association for Practical Nurse Education and Service, Formerly Associate Executive Director, National Association for Practical Nurse Education and Service; Formerly Member, Job Analysis Committee and Chairman, Production Committee of the Curriculum Committee, United States Office of Education

CONSTANCE MURPHY, R.N., B.S.

Director, Mercy Central School of Practical Nursing, Springfield, Ohio; Supervisor, Health Occupations, Springfield and Clark County Joint Vocational School.

J. B. LIPPINCOTT COMPANY

Philadelphia Toronto

EIGHTH EDITION

The 1st and 6th editions were published with Florence Dakin as senior author.

Distributed in Great Britain by
Pitman Medical Publishing Co., Limited, London

Library of Congress Card No. 66-11671

Printed in the United States of America

PREFACE

In the beginning was *Simplified Nursing*, a textbook that grew and matured with practical nursing; that served and was served by successive generations of students over four decades. Midway in the course of revision, its authors were struck by the realization that the sort of nursing that they were teaching was simplified no longer. Whereupon the decision was made to create an offspring of the parent text which would more truly reflect the enormous strides made in recent years by practical nurse educators, as well as the enhanced status and responsibilities of the graduate practitioner. With both books now free to pursue their respective destinies, the authors wish to introduce the first edition of *Textbook of Basic Nursing*.

Five general considerations were foremost in their minds in planning this book.

· Approaching the patient as a person with psychological as well as physical needs, with emphasis on total patient care

It no longer suffices for the nurse to be able to make the patient physically comfortable; she must also be able to make him psychologically comfortable in his environment, an aspect of care that goes beyond the "illness and cure" approach. In Chapter 3 the student learns the importance of understanding herself as a basis for understanding her patient and being able to work harmoniously with others as a team member.

· Presenting accurate scientific data and the application of scientific principles to nursing practice

Although the authors have followed the current trend in emphasizing the psycho-social approach to nursing care, they are aware that in order to practice efficiently the practical nurse must be well grounded in basic scientific principles, signs and symptoms, treatment, nursing care and complications of illness conditions. These areas are fully covered in Units 4 and 7. Pharmacology, diet therapy, rehabilitation and mental health are discussed as they apply to each condition, even though they are given separate consideration in other chapters. In order to better understand the cause and the control of disease, a separate chapter is devoted to the study of microbiology.

· Considering the normal condition before the abnormal, and proceeding from the simple to the more complex situation

The necessity for a sound working knowledge of normal body function and structure becomes increasingly important as the practical nurse assumes more responsibility for assisting with the care of the acutely ill patient. Unit 4, in addition to treating each body system in a separate chapter, contains a chapter describing the normal body as an integrated whole. Elementary principles of chemistry and physics as they apply to body function are discussed here. Clinical applications are made which will introduce the student to the concept of understanding illness and disease as a deviation from the normal.

· Incorporating the sociological implications and community health aspects of nursing, with preventive as well as restorative care

A full chapter is devoted to community health in Unit 2, while the broad concept of the family as a unit and the nurse-patient-family relationship forms the core of Unit 3. Developmental tasks of the healthy child at various age levels are discussed, and considerable attention is also given to the adolescent, an age often neglected in student texts. The role of the father as an integral part of the family group and the part he plays in the child bearing and child rearing cycles are also incorporated in the unit on Maternal and Child Care.

· Including content which the student will find applicable from the time of her (or his) orientation, through the period of actual experience in clinical areas and later, as a graduate practitioner

The five chapters which compose the first and last units have been devoted to the orientation of the student as an undergraduate and later, as a graduate practical nurse. Additional learning aids, such as an extensive glossary, a bibliography and a list of agencies distributing health information are found at the back of the book.

Despite the massive revision of content and the addition of much relatively advanced material, the authors have striven to preserve this book's heritage of readability and informality of presentation, plus an approach that is essentially practical. They have not hesitated to include suggested methods and procedures wherever appropriate, recognizing the value of such in reinforcing the student's self-confidence besides providing a point of departure for action. In all such instances the authors have furnished the rationale of each step, with the object of promoting essential understanding and the flexibility of mind that goes with it. It is hoped that *Textbook of Basic Nursing*, with its immensely broadened base of theory from many disciplines coupled with a practical orientation, will help to develop in the student that coordination of head, hands and heart which is the touchstone of the superior bedside practitioner.

ACKNOWLEDGMENTS

Of the many people whose assistance and encouragement have been vital to the completion of this task, the authors would like to single out the following for special thanks: Mr. Ray PeConga for his excellent photography; Mrs. Jeanne Bookwalter for her special consultation in the nutrition area; the Sisters of Mercy of Springfield, Ohio, for generously offering the use of their facilities, and in particular Sister Mary Camille, R.S.M., for her encouragement and understanding; Mr. David Miller, Nursing Editor, J. B. Lippincott Company, for his unfailing support, and Miss Anna May Jones, Associate Editor, J. B. Lippincott Company, for her competent editorial supervision. The authors are further indebted to the faculty and students of the Pennsylvania Hospital School of Nursing for their cooperation in arranging for photographs to illustrate clinical nursing care.

CONTENTS

Unit One: Orientation

Unit Two: Personal and Environmental Health

Unit Three: The Family

Unit Four: The Living Body

Unit Five: Normal Nutrition

Unit Six: Fundamentals of Nursing

Unit Seven: Conditions of Illness

Unit Eight: Maternal and Child Care

UNIT NINE: THE GRADUATE PRACTICAL NURSE

TEXTBOOK OF BASIC NURSING

Unit One:

Orientation

1. *Practical Nursing—Its Growth and Development*
2. *Guides to Effective Learning*
3. *Personality Adjustment*

1

PRACTICAL NURSING—ITS GROWTH AND DEVELOPMENT

Starting out on a new career is like going to a strange town—you have to learn your way around before you feel at home. You find out how the town began and how it grew; you know the monuments and the parks and the buildings that mark important points in its history. Practical nursing has a history, too; in fact, it has been making history since the end of World War II. When you know about the past and see what is happening today, you begin to feel at home in your new career.

You are very welcome as a prospective addition to the corps of nurses that this country needs—the demand for competent nurses is so much greater than the supply. Practical nursing today is a recognized vocation for both

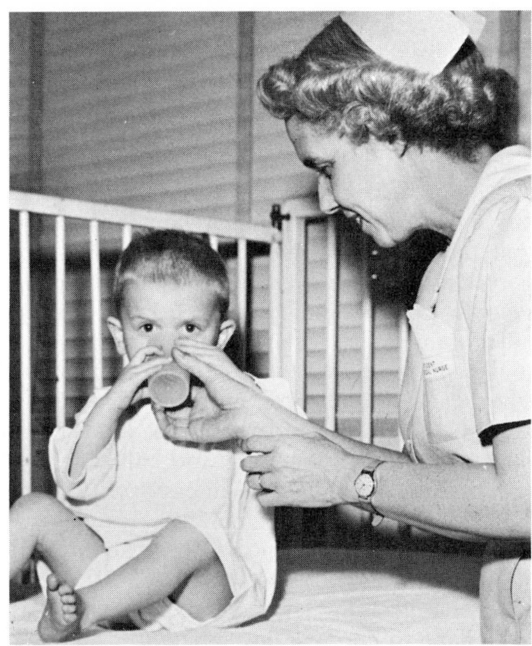

Fig. 1. Practical nursing includes a variety of experiences—one of them is taking care of sick and convalescent children.

men and women, and practical nurses have earned a respected place on the nursing team—your place will be waiting for you when you are ready for it. What could be more satisfying than to know you are needed? Your instructors are looking forward as eagerly as you are to the next months. Together, you will be writing another chapter in the success story of practical nursing.

PRACTICAL NURSING AS A CAREER

How Practical Nursing Began

The first practical nurses were the people who took over when one of the family was sick. Usually it was the mother; sometimes it was the unmarried aunt or the grandmother; perhaps one of the neighbors came in to help. Often there was someone in the town who liked to take care of sick people and found time to do it. Perhaps it was a widow with growing children to bring up. She used experience to earn a living for them. Or a woman looking for something to keep her busy after her children grew up and left home found that she could be useful, and the money helped her small income. Maybe it was a daughter who took care of her sick mother for 3 years. When her mother died and she was alone, it was wonderful to find that other people needed her too.

You know people like these women, who used what they had learned about running a house and making people comfortable. There are thousands like them. Always remember that they did not have your educational opportunities. There were no practical nursing schools. Doctors and sympathetic professional nurses taught them some things, but they had to depend mostly on their own common sense. They gave all practical nurses something to live up to. However, you should know, too, that some women thought (and still do) that practical nursing would be an easy way to earn a living; they were too ignorant or careless to care about what happened to the patient, and sick people were not safe with them. When we talk about licensing laws, you will see what has been done to improve this situation.

How It Is Today

How many practical nurses are there? We do not know exactly, but they number well above 200,000. More than 125,000 practical nurses are working in hospitals alone. In addition, many thousands more, many of them not trained, are practicing in other situations. It gives you some idea of how many sick people there are when you know that we have over 500,000 professional nurses, too, but we still cannot give a nurse to everybody who needs one. We need more professional nurses and trained practical nurses to give people the kind of care they need.

Her Title and Her Job

The practical nurse has had a number of titles such as *trained attendant, nurses' aide, nursing attendant. Practical nurse* is the recognized title today because it is the title that people know best, and practical nurses themselves seem to prefer it. (The exceptions are in California and Texas, where the word *vocational* is used instead of *practical.*) These titles also have the word *nurse* to indicate what this worker does. Do not confuse the person who is called a *nurses' aide* with the trained practical nurse. Today the *nurses' aide* or helper means a person who is taught on the job to do the work that makes good nursing possible. For example, when aides answer the telephone, run errands, or make empty beds, nurses have more time to take care of patients.

The National Association for Practical Nurse Education and Service gives this definition for the practical nurse: *A trained practical nurse is a person prepared by an approved educational program to share in the care of the sick, in rehabilitation and in the prevention of illness, always under the direction of a licensed physician and/or a registered professional nurse.*

Trained practical nurses do many of the same things that professional nurses do for patients—the choice of nurse depends on how sick the patient is. For example, a patient might be so ill that a practical nurse would not even make her bed or give her a bath; yet, we usually think these are simple nursing procedures that people can learn to do without being nurses at all.

People gradually are learning what the practical nurse's job is. We are teaching families who employ practical nurses that the nurse is coming to do *nursing*. Common sense tells you, though, that the patient will get well faster if she knows the house is running smoothly. Therefore, the practical nurse does some things that are not nursing but are necessary to keep patients comfortable and contented. This applies to the professional nurse, too.

What a Professional Nurse Does

Professional nurses spend from 2 to 5 years learning how to do the things they need to know. They have special training that teaches them how to be public health nurses and how to be specialists in the care of psychiatric, tuberculosis, medical or surgical patients. They are responsible for the care of the acutely ill patients; they teach professional and practical nurse students; they direct nurses and other people who work in hospitals; they are in charge of hospital wards. Professional nurses also perform many duties today that only doctors did 25 years ago.

Why We Need Practical Nurses

This is why we need practical nurses: in the first place, there are not enough professional nurses to go around. Then we have learned that not everyone needs a professional nurse; trained practical nurses can take care of those patients who are not acutely ill. Since medical science has lengthened life, people live longer than they did in our grandparents' day, and many of the patients are older people. By 1980, we are told, 1 person out of every 10 will be 65 or older. This means that more people are going to need nursing care. In any town there is a wide variety in the kinds of nursing people need. Sometimes they must go to hospitals; sometimes they can be at home. Some illnesses are short; others last for months and even years. Hospitals discharge many patients who still need nursing care. Placement bureaus and doctors help people to decide whether they need a professional or a practical nurse.

NURSING SCHOOLS

Professional nurses have always been taught that nursing is responsible work; many of them sincerely believed only professional nurses could do it. The practical nurses they knew were not trained; some of them were obviously not fit to be nurses at all. Nobody seemed to realize that there were places for two kinds of nurses; no one thought of training the practical nurse for her work. Yet all the time people who needed nurses had to turn to anyone who was willing to help them. They knew that some practical nurses did very poor work, but they appreciated the good ones all the more. They did not realize how dangerous it might be to let an untrained person take care of sick people.

However, a few professional nurses believed there was a place for the practical nurse, too. They saw there were not enough professional nurses to take care of the people who were sick at home. They knew how satisfactory a practical nurse could be if she were responsible and intelligent. They thought she should be trained and were sure intelligent women would rather be taught how to do their work properly than try to carry on as best they could.

Public-spirited citizens knew how hard it was to obtain care for a sick person; they agreed with these interested professional nurses and found the money to open the first practical nursing schools.

The Pioneer Schools

The Ballard School. In 1893, the first of these schools was opened in New York City by the YWCA. It was one of several other courses for women that together were named the Ballard School; Miss Lucinda Ballard, an interested New York woman, gave money for this venture. It was a 3-months' course to train women to give simple nursing care to people in their own homes.

The Thompson Practical Nursing School. The next course started with money that was given originally to help poor sewing women in Brattleboro, Vermont. Mr. Thomas Thompson, a wealthy man who lived there during the Civil War, was disturbed about the women who were making shirts for the Army at a dollar a dozen. The pay was wretched, but they had to support their families somehow while the men were away at war. He left money in his will to help them. Mr. Richard Bradley, the executor, was a public-spirited man who saw that Brattleboro citizens needed nursing service, too. He thought that women could be taught to do some of the nursing that people with moderate incomes needed and could pay for. Why not do two things—help needy women to earn a living and provide nursing care? So finally, in 1917, some of the money for the poor sewing women was used to open a practical nursing school.

The Household Nursing School. In Boston, a group of women were determined that something should be done to get nursing care for people who were sick at home. They called on Mr. Bradley for advice; he was only too glad to tell them about the school in Brattleboro and encouraged them to follow Brattleboro's example. So, in 1918, the Household Nursing Association School of Attendant Nursing* was opened. The Brattleboro and the Boston schools are in existence today. The Ballard School closed in 1949 because of YWCA reorganization plans.

These were the *pioneer practical nursing schools.* All of them have trained hundreds of women the community could not do without. Each school was quite different, but all were set up for the same thing—training for practical nurses. They planned regular classwork and experience that would teach the practical nurse how to take care of her patients. They took an important step to give sick people safe nursing care.

* Later renamed the Shepard-Gill School of Practical Nursing, in honor of Katharine Shepard Dodge, the first director, and Helen Z. Gill, her associate and successor.

The Schools Today

We have come a long way since those early days. Today there are over 700 approved practical nursing schools in different parts of the country—you notice that all 3 of the first schools were in the East. There are other changes. The first schools were under private agencies. Schools today are also sponsored by hospitals and by local boards of education in the public schools—the latter group has increased rapidly. These courses are under the vocational education division of a school system and give qualified adults an opportunity for further education. The schools follow much the same pattern in the things they teach practical nurses, and the courses are approximately the same in length.

Approved Schools

When you plan to be a practical nurse, you want to be sure you will learn what you need to know and how to do what will be required of you. Here is an important thing about nursing: a nurse works with human beings, and we must be sure people are safe with her. You can learn to sew by reading a book. Your mistakes will not harm anybody; at the worst you might run a needle through your finger or spoil the material. You cannot afford to make mistakes with human lives. This is why we must have *approved* practical nursing schools.

When a school is on the approved list, it means that a nursing authority has visited it and is satisfied that the students are having the kind of training they need. *Approved* tells you that a school (1) teaches the specific things a practical nurse must know; (2) provides experience with the kind of patients she will take care of when she is practicing nursing; (3) employs qualified instructors to teach and supervise the students' practice in the classroom and on the hospital wards.

It means, too, that the course is at least 12 months long. A few courses are longer and include experience with patients who are sick at home. All the schools would like to give this valuable experience before the student is graduated; some schools have found ways to do it.

Students are selected carefully. They are men and women who range in age from 18 to 50. Applicants under 25 are asked for proof that they have completed 2 years of high school—proof of graduation from the 8th grade is accepted for women over that age. Students must have good health and good grooming and must be responsible people. Schools may vary in some of these requirements, but, in general, they follow the same pattern.

Most of the practical nursing courses are given in the daytime for 5 days a week. However, there are some approved courses in which the student attends classes in the evening, 2 or 3 times a week, for 4-hour sessions during the first part of the course. It will take her about twice as long to complete this part of the work, but it allows her to go on working in the daytime for this period. When she begins the hospital experience part, she must give full time to it for 32 weeks.

THE GUIDE FOR TRAINING THE PRACTICAL NURSE

Setting Up Standards

How do we know what a practical nurse should learn? In 1941, a small group of directors and instructors in the practical nursing schools, together with some interested citizens, organized the National Association for Practical Nurse Education (NAPNE). They wanted to improve the education of the practical nurse and to set up standards for her instruction and service. They were looking ahead to the time when the practical nurse could take her place in nursing with dignity and confidence. The trouble was that no one was sure what she (or he) could or should do. The number of schools was increasing: some public school systems were giving practical nursing courses as a part of vocational training. The NAPNE appealed to the U.S. Office of Education for their cooperation in solving this problem.

Practical Nursing Possibilities

The result of this appeal was that in 1945, the U.S. Office of Education appointed a committee to study the possibilities of the practical nurse. Professional nurses, teachers, physicians, hospital administrators, vocational educators and a practical nurse worked together for 2 years to define practical nurse duties. The result was a manual* which gave the schools something to go by in training practical nurses. A second committee produced further suggestions† to guide directors and instructors in planning a teaching program. These 2 gray-covered books became milestones in practical nursing history.

Many changes have been made since these guides were published, and there will be more. Every day we know more about what the trained practical nurse can learn and do, so of course we must try to find the best ways to give her the best possible instruction—interested groups are working on this all the time.

The Course Plan

The course has been planned carefully to give students the information that they need about the human body, health, various illnesses and their treatment and the nursing skills used in the care of patients. The importance of a pleasing personality and of the nurse's personal development is emphasized. Above all, the student learns to center her attention on doing what is best for the individual patient.

Early in the course the students begin to work with patients, at first for a limited time each week and in a limited way. Hospital practice gradually increases, and during the last 6 months students spend most of their time giving nursing care. Instructors are with them constantly supervising their work and conducting classes planned to help them apply to the care of patients what they have learned. You can see why this is important—it protects the patients and helps each student. She always

* Practical Nursing—An Analysis of the Practical Nurse Occupation, U.S. Government Printing Office, 1947.

† Practical Nursing Curriculum, U.S. Government Printing Office, 1950.

has a teacher to guide her and correct her mistakes until she is efficient and the patients are safe with her.

Since practical nursing students will be working with patients, they should choose a school carefully—it should provide training which will meet standards adequately and will be acceptable anywhere.

LICENSING FOR NURSES

What a License Means

Licensing for any group of workers is important. *Licensing laws* protect the public from unqualified workers; they establish standards for any profession or occupation. A license helps people to tell the difference between a qualified and an unqualified worker in any kind of work.

Both professional and practical nurses are licensed to practice nursing. Every state, as well as the District of Columbia, Puerto Rico, Guam, Samoa and the Virgin Islands, has a licensing law for practical nurses. When a student (professional or practical nurse) has been graduated from an approved school, she is eligible to take the state licensing examination set up for her group.

The Registered Nurse

The professional nurse who passes the examination and pays the required registration fee becomes licensed under the title *registered nurse*, or *R.N.*

The Licensed Practical Nurse

The practical nurse who passes the examination and pays the required registration fee becomes licensed under the title *licensed practical nurse*, or *L.P.N.* There are 2 exceptions—in California and Texas the legal title is *licensed vocational nurse*, or *L.V.N.*

The Licensing Laws

There are some differences in the licensing laws from state to state. For instance, in some states it is illegal for any nurse to practice nursing for pay without a license. If she does, she can be prosecuted. This is a *mandatory* law. In some states this affects only professional nurses.

In other states the law does not forbid practicing nursing without a license but does forbid using the title "licensed practical nurse" if you do not have a license. Actually you would not be considered as being reputable without one, even though a state has this permissive type of law.

Does this mean that you have a choice between being licensed or unlicensed? Not really, because today a license is the passport to employment as a reputable practical nurse. It tells any prospective employer that you are a qualified person. Naturally, you cannot afford to be without this important credential, and the time is sure to come when a license will be essential in order to work in any state.

NURSING ORGANIZATIONS

The NAPNES, Inc.

The National Association for Practical Nurse Education and Service was the first national nursing organization to concentrate all its efforts on the development and the improvement of practical nurse education, together with advancing the interests of practical nurses themselves. It was organized in 1941, with 20 members—membership now approximates 25,000. Originally organized as the *NAPNE*, in 1959 it became the *NAPNES* with the addition of the words "and Service" to the title, to give recognition to the assistance that the Association gives to state practical nurse associations through its Department of Services. The chairman of the Department is a practical nurse.

Practical nurses take an active part in the affairs of the Association. The third vice-president is a practical nurse, and there are 5 practical nurses on the board of directors; all Association committees have practical nurse members.

Membership. The NAPNES has 3 types of membership:

1. Individual—open to professional nurse instructors and directors of practical nursing schools, licensed practical nurses, representatives of hospital, health and education groups and citizens interested in helping practical nursing to grow and to improve.

2. Per capita—open to members of state practical nurse associations voting a per capita assessment of dues.

3. Future (student)—open to students in approved practical nursing schools on a divided payment basis while they are in the school. Full membership is continued for a year after graduation at no extra cost.

Members receive the official monthly magazine of the Association, *The Journal of Practical Nursing* without extra cost.

This national nursing association has helped practical nursing grow. These are some of the things it does: it has a national office in New York City that answers inquiries about practical nursing; it sends a consultant to a state or group to help set up a practical nursing school; it publishes helpful leaflets and booklets; it publishes a list of the approved schools; it approves practical nursing schools that meet NAPNES standards and wish to have national approval; it publishes the magazine, *The Journal of Practical Nursing*, every month. It has helped practical nurses to organize their own state associations. It has a convention every year with special sessions for practicing practical nurses and for students. The NAPNES prepared the outlines used for the extension and the Education Units courses.

The NFLPN, Inc.

The National Federation of Licensed Practical Nurses was organized in 1949. It is the official membership organization for licensed practical nurses in the United States; membership is open to licensed practical nurses who are members in the individual state associations. These organizations set aside a certain amount of each person's dues for national membership dues. Provision is made also for individual and associate membership. The stated objectives of the NFLPN are:

To work actively with allied groups and the public to help meet the health needs of our country.

To continue to work for state laws which would provide mandatory licensure for all who nurse for hire.

To continue to work for licensed practical nurse representation on state boards of nursing.

To seek recognition in all employing agencies for the legal title "Licensed Practical Nurse" and the recognition of practical nursing as a distinct vocation separate from that of auxiliary personnel.

To encourage state associations to promote group insurance plans for their members to provide protection in cases of illness or disability.

To encourage all employing agencies to provide in-service programs for the licensed practical nurses.

To strive to increase the quality and the quantity of well-prepared licensed practical nurses.

To formulate a plan on public relations to interpret the field of practical nursing to allied groups and the lay public.

To strive to improve communications to every member.

To work to improve leadership within the organization.

The Federation works with the state practical nurse associations to help them in organizational matters through institutes and workshops; also, it holds an annual convention for its thousands of members. Its official bimonthly publication is the *American Journal of Practical Nursing*.

The NLN

The National League for Nursing has accepted practical nurses as members since 1952. In 1956 a consultant in practical nursing was employed, and in 1957 a Council on Practical Nursing was established. In 1961 the Council was replaced by the creation of the Department of Practical Nursing. The NLN, through its Department of Evaluation Service, has developed a number of tests which are used widely by the practical nursing schools. Among these tests are a pre-entrance test used as one indication of an applicant's eligibility for admission and achievement tests to be used during the course and on its completion. The

Evaluation Service has developed also the state licensing examination currently used by the majority of state boards of nursing. The NLN is discussed further in Chapter 53.

The State Practical Nurse Associations

Practical nurses can be very proud of the work that they have done in starting their state associations. There is a state association of practical nurses in every state, in the District of Columbia and in Puerto Rico and the Virgin Islands. Each state association conducts an annual convention; most of them publish their own magazine every month. They have worked to get licensing laws if none existed and to improve existing laws. They have promoted workshops for their members and have provided scholarships for attendance at summer courses for selected members, to train for organizational leadership.

Extension Courses. One of the outstanding accomplishments of the state practical nurse associations has been the promotion of extension courses for their members, many of whom are licensed practical nurses without training. These extension courses are open only to licensed practical nurses who have been doing practical nursing without benefit of formal training; they are not open to men or women who never have done nursing. Thousands of women have taken the 64-hour course and progressed to the 240-hour Education Units course. The outlines for these courses were prepared by the NAPNES; the teachers are professional nurses. The state associations promote and handle registration of classes, arrange for the instructors and classroom facilities and see that the essential records are on file in the state office.

MAIN IDEAS OF THIS CHAPTER

Practical nursing is a recognized vocation for both men and women.

Practical nurses take care of patients who are not acutely ill and assist with the care of seriously ill patients.

We need more professional and practical nurses.

Approved schools meet recognized standards for practical nurse training.

Licensing laws protect the public and raise practical nurse standards.

Practical nurses have their own associations.

ADAPTING SKILLS TO SITUATIONS

Find out all you can about your state law for licensing practical nurses.

Is there a state practical nurse association in your state? Get information about it.

Where do practical nurses work in your city?

2

GUIDES TO EFFECTIVE LEARNING

GETTING YOUR BEARINGS

Why do you want to be a practical nurse? To earn your living? To help humanity? To work with people? Whatever your reasons, you wonder what will be expected of you. Here are some guides to help you get your bearings so that you will "get off on the right foot" in your new career. First, let us begin with a description of what a practical nurse does:

The trained practical nurse takes care of people who are sick at home, in hospitals or other institutions. She is qualified in the home-making skills which are necessary for her patient's comfort and recovery. The practical nurse assists the professional nurse and is a member of the nursing team. She is directed by and is responsible to either a doctor or a registered professional nurse.

Naturally, this sounds like a great amount of responsibility, but physicians and professional nurses will guide you—you will not carry it alone.

The Next 12 Months

Secondly, in the next 12 months you will be learning many things: the technics of nursing; scientific facts about the human body and how it behaves in health and illness; rules and regulations of a hospital; observing the patients under your care, which includes noting the patient's behavior, appearance and the effects of treatments; and how to get along with people—to mention only a few. Learning means getting and using information, and this means that you must study to master the facts you will need to know and to master a definite amount of knowledge to be a nurse with whom patients are safe. You cannot risk somebody's life with guesses about what to do—you must know. You will also be learning by putting into practice with patients the information that you get in your classes and study. Altogether, this means that you are continually using and adding to your store of information to perfect your skill as a nurse.

One question you may have is what are the specific subjects that you will need to know. Some of the subjects to be covered include anatomy and physiology, personal and community health, personal and professional relationships, illness conditions and nursing technics. This is really not such a large order as it might seem, for the subjects are closely related. In health, for example, to understand illness you must know what constitutes being well, which naturally ties in with information about health protection. Since the condition of the body affects health, you must know how the body is built and how it functions, including the effect of mental attitudes on health. Illness is a disturbance of body and mind; a nurse must know about such disturbances and why certain treatments and medications help.

Food plays such an important part in health and illness that you must have information about normal nutrition and about the modifications of a normal diet that may be required in treating certain illness conditions.

A patient depends on you to protect him from infection, which means that you must know the technics used for his protection. He relies on you to understand his problems and take his weaknesses in your stride. Throughout the course, the importance of understanding each patient as a person will be emphasized, and ways for doing this will be suggested.

TO GET THE MOST FROM YOUR TRAINING

Get the Facts

A textbook gives you essential information, but your instructors will refer you to other books, pamphlets and magazine articles which will add to your knowledge. Radio and TV programs are additional sources of information. You can find other reliable sources, but how will you know that the information is reliable? First, look at the source of the information: an expert or a recognized organization in any field speaks with authority and has the latest information. For instance, there is a difference between accepting what Dr. Edwards, director of the health department, says about constipation, and an advertiser's claim for his cathartic.

Learn by Observation

Observation means understanding as well as seeing. You observe for a purpose—to note the effects of a medicine or a treatment or the patient's physical and mental reactions. To do this effectively, you must know why a medicine or a treatment is given and note whether or not it accomplishes its purpose, as well as observe any other effects that it may have. In addition to being a "seeing eye" you must have the knowledge you need to make correct judgments. The nurse's observations of a patient's reactions and behavior are important as signs of the patient's progress toward recovery and may indicate the need for changes in his medical and nursing treatment.

Learn by Practice

You learn nursing skills by observing the instructor's demonstrations of nursing procedures and then by practicing these procedures, first in the classroom with your fellow students, then with actual patients in the hospital—always under the helpful supervision of an instructor. At the same time, she will be showing you how to apply what you are learning in every subject to the care of each individual patient. This means that you must constantly practice putting together many different kinds of information.

Learn by Listening

Your instructors give you much information in classroom lectures (see How To Take Notes, p. 13). To get the most out of a lecture, come to class with your lesson assignment completed. Put everything else out of your mind and concentrate on the subject being discussed. Look at the instructor with interest. A class that looks alert and interested inspires her to do a better job of teaching. A class period is give-and-take between instructor and students. The instructor interprets information and adds to it; she highlights important points and puts them in the right order; she ties them in with other facts that you have learned. Class discussion provides an opportunity to get facts straight and to ask for an explanation of puzzling points. Most people need to ask questions about an unfamiliar subject—if you feel shy about asking, very likely your classmates are feeling the same way. But keep to the subject —do not bring up points or tell rambling personal stories that have no relation to it. We all have had experience with the class pest who wants to talk continually and wastes valuable time.

Aids to Learning

The Field Trip. A field trip shows you some process at work. It may be a market, a health department, milk pasteurization or physical therapy. You get a clearer impression by seeing an operation than you do by reading about it. To make the most of a field trip, you must have some information before you go. Then you must know what to look for or you may not get the information you need. For instance, if you spend all your time watching the people in a market, you will not learn much about the vegetables.

You will be asked for a report of the trip. Be curious but do not be a nuisance—sometimes there is no opportunity to ask questions, but make notes of what you see and write your report of the trip before you forget the details. Try to analyze what you got out of the trip and why. Students' opinions about a field trip help the instructor to decide whether it will be worthwhile for other students.

A Word About Films. Films, too, give you clearer impressions than reading. They show you people and action. Wartime instructors in the services and in industries found that films helped people to learn new operations faster and more thoroughly. Films show you places and things that are too far away to visit or impossible to observe firsthand. Companies, health organizations and health departments prepare films and film strips that schools can purchase or rent reasonably. Many schools have their own film libraries and projectors. You will need to know why a film is shown to you and what to look for. Like a field trip, a film strengthens impressions you already have.

How To Study

Study Time and Place. You are going to have a very full schedule for the next 12 months, so you will have to plan to use your study time to the best advantage to avoid falling behind in your work. You will have a limited time for study in your daytime schedule, but it will not be enough. You must plan to do the rest at night unless you are the type that finds that morning is the best time for study—then go to bed early and set your alarm!

If you have been out of school for some time and are no longer in the habit of studying, it may be a little difficult at first to re-establish the habit. Or if you live at home, it may be hard to find a quiet place away from the family. A suitable place is important. It should be well-lighted, with space to write and to spread your books out conveniently, and a place where you will not be distracted by the radio or TV or easily interrupted by questions or audible conversations.

Assemble everything that you need to work with before you settle down. Take time out for a "breather" now and then. Finally, remember that your mind can absorb only so much at one sitting. After 3 hours of concentrated reading at the most, you will have "had it," so to speak, and the longer you go on after that, the less you will retain.

How To Take Notes

You fix information more firmly in your mind by making notes during your reading. The most logical way to do this is to follow an outline form with main headings and notations under each heading. Except for definitions, try to put the main ideas in your own words. Some guides for taking reading notes are:

1. Put down the topic heading. Under it note the main points, using subheadings if necessary, with enough information about each point to explain it.
2. Write down the title and the page of the reference in case you desire to refer to it again.
3. Include additional information that you have not found in any other reference.
4. Make a note of anything that puzzles you; this will serve as a reminder to yourself to bring it up in class or to ask your instructor about it.
5. Look up unfamiliar words in the dictionary; use your medical dictionary for technical terms. You will also find a glossary of medical terms and a list of combining forms (prefixes and suffixes) in your textbook. Make a list of such words and their definitions and use it as a quiz for yourself.

You will also take notes in class lectures. Some guides for these are:

1. Try to follow an organized outline by making notes of the topics and the important points under each one. Your instructor will make this easier for you by emphasizing them or by writing them on the chalkboard as she talks.
2. Try to take down the "sense" of what the instructor is saying. If you try to include every word you may miss the point entirely.

3. Put a question mark after anything that is not clear to you so you can ask about it before the class is over.

4. If necessary, rewrite your notes after taking them in class. This will help also to establish the information firmly in your mind.

5. Check your notes for usefulness. They should help you to review a subject and by that standard should give you correct information and enough information. They should be arranged in a logical order—a notebook full of disorganized writing is a waste of time.

How To Solve a Problem

You are sure to meet situations from time to time in which you are undecided about what to do. In other words, you have a *problem* to solve. How do you go about it? In your haste to do something, you might take the first solution that occurs to you, which, 9 times out of 10, is only a partial answer. Or you could hastily try one thing after another with only partial success. Or you might even give up the whole thing and try to ignore the problem altogether.

There are guides that you can use in solving a problem. The first one is to be sure that you know exactly what the problem is. Examine the facts critically and try to define the difficulty and its causes. Then think of all the possible answers and what each one holds for accomplishing your purpose. Try to determine which solution will be the most satisfactory with the least disturbance to anyone else. Use your reasoning powers and put your emotions aside. Consider the other person's side and try to imagine how each possible solution will affect others.

You must be wise enough also to know when you are confronted with a problem that you cannot handle alone. You may not have the necessary authority to carry out the solution, or there may be angles that you do not understand fully. It may be that you need the help of your head nurse or your instructor. At this point, you can take your problem to the proper person for assistance.

Remember, then, that it requires both logical thinking and imagination to solve a problem, using what you have learned from your past experience and being able to know when you cannot solve a particular problem without help.

Tests and Examinations

Tests and examinations are required in the course. Some are the short "quickie" type to review a previous lesson; others are longer examinations given after completing a subject, or detailed and comprehensive ones to cover all you have learned up to that point. At the end of your course, there will be a final examination.

These tests are the written or "paper and pencil" type of test and require very little writing but a great deal of thinking. The written examination most commonly used today is the *objective* type, which is answered by checks or fill-ins. It consists of various forms of questions or statements and includes the following:

Multiple choice—you select the answer from a list of several, only one of which is correct.

Example: The recommended method for losing weight is to_____
1. Avoid eating breakfast.
2. Go on a banana diet.
3. Consult your doctor about a diet.
4. Limit your diet to 500 calories a day.

True-false—you are given a statement which you check as right or wrong.

Example: The pancreas is part of the urinary system. T___ F___

Completion—you fill in the missing word or words in a sentence to make it a true statement.

Example: The temperature of the water for a hot-water bag should not be higher than _____ degrees.

Matching—you are given 2 columns of words or phrases and asked to match each item in the first column with the related item in the second column.

These examples may not mean much now since you do not have the information neces-

FIG. 2. Who worries about tests?

sary to answer the questions, but they show you the form of examination to expect.

One other type of question should be mentioned—the essay. For example, you may be asked to write in a few sentences or in a paragraph how you would handle a certain nursing problem in a given situation. This type of question requires the ability to express ideas clearly and briefly.

In addition to written tests, observations and ratings will be made on performance in carrying out nursing procedures and on attitudes: reactions to criticism, efforts to improve, ability to get along with people, appearance, health habits and day-by-day responses in class. The final grade is based on a composite of all these ratings. Be thankful for tests and ratings! They are the checks and balances that steady you: they indicate strengths, weaknesses and areas for improvement.

Cramming for an Examination. If you have crammed correct information into your memory storage system, it may be permanent enough to get you through the examination. However, the chances are the memory of the information will not last if nothing is done to strengthen the impression. Instructors review the results of an examination with the class to strengthen true impressions and correct false ones. Always remember, though, that the practice of cramming gives information only temporarily; it may leave you without important knowledge when you need it most as a practicing nurse. This would mean that patients would not be in safe hands since a nurse must be sure of doing the right thing in the right way and so must be able to recall the correct information.

PROCESSES USED IN LEARNING

Communications

Communication means giving information and sharing thoughts and ideas. To be proficient in the art of communication means being able to convey what you mean to others so that it will be understood. It also means being sensitive to what others are trying to tell you, verbally or otherwise. We are apt to think of communication as mainly verbal but a great deal of communication goes on by means of gestures, actions, manner and facial expressions. A nurse needs to be especially sensitive to such communications from her patients. For instance, a patient may not *say* anything when you explain a treatment you are about to give, yet his eyes may tell you he is afraid.

Effective Speech

Since we do depend on *speech* to a great extent to put an idea across, its effectiveness is influenced not only by *what* we say but also by *how* we say it. Try to answer a patient's questions or to explain a procedure in plain, everyday language, using as few technical terms as possible. Your medical and nursing vocabulary will be unfamiliar to him.

Pay him the courtesy of addressing him as "Mr. Wright"—don't call him "grandpa" or "dear," even if he is 80 years old and seems like a dear old man to you. Above all, avoid the habit (which seems all too common) of phrasing your questions in the plural, such as "How are *we* feeling this morning?" or "*We* didn't eat all of *our* breakfast, did *we*?" Sound as if you were really interested in how he feels and in what he tells you. If you are hurried (as you easily may be), try not to let the pressure show in your voice or actions.

Effective Writing

Writing is a means of communication you will use often in recording your observations of patients, taking notes and writing reports. Therefore, you must be able to say what you mean clearly and concisely. An adequate vocabulary and a command of simple English will help you here. Legible writing is a necessity, since you will be required to fill out forms and record your observations on patients' charts. Most hospitals have adopted printing as the acceptable form for keeping patients' records.

How We Remember

The average person literally stores volumes of information in his brain. This is his *memory stock* which consists of lifetime, or permanent memories, such as his name and address, the multiplication tables, rules of grammar, important events in his life and knowledge he uses everyday in his job. He also has a short-term memory made up of passing bits of information, such as the name of someone he is introduced to casually, which he makes little or no effort to remember beyond the moment. Then there is an in-between kind of memory peculiar to people with brain damage—it can only be partially recalled.

Opinions differ about how memory operates. One school of thought believes that every impression the brain receives makes a tiny pathway in the brain; another says chemistry or electricity enter into it. They believe that electrical impulses pass along a memory path from time to time, even when we are not trying to stimulate them, and help to strengthen it. Time, then, would also strengthen it. This could explain why elderly people often remember things that happened to them in childhood more clearly than they remember recent events. Whatever the process, we have reliable proof that everything we hear, see or experience leaves some sort of impression on the brain. The problem is, how to get it off the shelf!

The situation is not hopeless—learning to remember is a skill, like learning to write; like any skill it takes perseverance and practice to develop it, but there are rules to help you. To begin with, your memory of anything depends largely on the strength of the impression it made on your brain. This, in turn, will depend on how interested you were in remembering, how much you needed to remember, the effect it had on your life or if it was striking or unusual. Any one or a combination of these conditions will tend to make the impression deep and lasting.

If we look at many ordinary things without really seeing them because we are not consciously observing them, the impression is not very strong. So the *first* rule is to observe carefully. The *second* rule is to pay attention to directions by looking at the person giving them and listening carefully. The *third* rule is to decide what is important to remember. We remember what we wish to remember. Deciding something is important helps to fix it in the mind. The *fourth* rule has to do with repetition: the more you go over an idea, the better your memory of it will be. The best time for doing this is immediately after a new fact is presented because forgetting is also going on even as you learn.

Take into account the things that make you forget. If you are tired, worried or out-of-sorts, your memory lags—this is no time to study. People devise tricks to help themselves remember. This is permissible as long as the devices do not become so complicated that you cannot remember what they were supposed to remind you of!

How Do You Read?

Coleridge,* possibly in an irritated moment, classified readers by 4 types: (1) *sponges*, who absorb all they read and return it in nearly the same state, only a little dirtied; (2) *sandglasses*, who retain nothing and are content to get through a book for the sake of getting through the time; (3) *strainbags*, who retain merely the dregs of what they read; and (4) *Mogul diamonds*, equally rare and valuable, who profit

* Nursing Outlook, April, 1963.

by what they read and enable others to profit by it also.

Reading Speed. Naturally, studying involves a great deal of reading—many people waste their reading time because they do not know how to read profitably. Two things affect your reading—the rate or speed with which you read, and your comprehension, or understanding, of what you read. Eye movements affect reading speed—rapid readers fix their eyes once on a line and seldom go back over it; slow readers move their eyes from word to word and keep going back over words. Some people actually form every word with their lips as they read. You can work on improving your reading speed by consciously trying to reduce the number of times you shift your eyes when reading a single line. Practice first with your light reading.

Reading Comprehension. A new field requires that you learn the terms and expressions peculiar to it. Make notes of anything you do not understand or anything about which you want to ask your instructor. Since you are reading or studying to obtain factual information that is important in your work, you will need to be sure that you understand facts correctly. Your background of general knowledge will help you to understand what you are reading.

Reading for a Purpose. Reading for pleasure and reading for information are quite different. You can read a murder mystery and hardly notice what is going on around you, but your anatomy lesson requires a different type of concentration. Beyond the moment, it is not important to remember how the murderer was caught but you *must* remember how the digestive system functions. Therefore, different reading methods are necessary according to your purpose. Technical material requires more time because you will have to look up and learn technical terms. You will also need to make notes of important points if you are reading to get additional information about an assigned topic.

The system you use for going over a topic is important too. You can (1) read it over quickly once, to get the general idea; (2) read it again, paying close attention to each part, asking yourself questions about it as you go along, making sure you understand it; and (3) make a brief summary of the whole in your own words. Do steps 2 and 3 several times until you have mastered the sense of it. It will stay in your memory longer if you space the last 2 combined steps over several days instead of depending on a "cram job" the night before an examination.

THE NURSING CARE STUDY

A nursing care study is a report about a selected patient for whom you have cared. It is the story of your observations of a person throughout his illness—it includes such things as treatments, tests, diet, medicines, x-rays, nursing care—and tells how they affected the patient. A nursing care study will show how well you understood the reasons for specific treatments or medications. It will also show how keenly you were aware of the patient as a person in trouble.

To begin with, give the patient a name. If you must invent one, avoid such old perennials as "Smith" or "Jones." Much of your information is taken from the patient's chart, and to really make him a person this information must be personalized and put into phrases and sentences, otherwise, he will seem like a robot, operated by push buttons. Compare these 2 beginnings for a nursing care study:

This?

"A male, aged 52, admitted by ambulance. Patient weak, pale, skin cold, pulse rapid, heat applied."

Or This?

"Mr. Daly, a 52-year-old farmer, was admitted to Ward D by ambulance, after falling from a ladder in his barn. He was unable to help himself in getting into bed, he was pale and his skin was cold; his pulse was 130 and slightly irregular. Hot-water bags and warm blankets were applied at once and he was given 1/6 gr. of morphine, since he was having a great deal of pain."

Which is the more interesting? Which sounds as if it were about a real person? The first example is an accurate record of the facts, and it might have been copied word for word from the chart, but it is the record of a faceless male. In the second example, the "male, aged 52," comes to life as "Mr. Daly." You can picture this middle-aged man. Perhaps you know someone like him; you are interested in what happens to him. You want to know how he felt—did he get warm, did his pulse slow down, was his pain relieved? Did the nurse have any problems in giving him nursing care and how did she handle them? Did he improve—slowly, rapidly or not at all? How long was he hospitalized? Who would look after him when he was discharged? Did this person have instructions about his care? From whom?

Finally, your nursing care study may be read by other nurses who hope to find in it some suggestions to help them in their care of patients. It is doubly important, then, that you make them want to read it, and that you tell them the things they want to know. The surest way to do this is to make them feel that you are writing about a *person*.

Your instructor may give you an outline to use as a guide in writing a nursing care study. It might include such points as:

1. The patient's *background* (his age, occupation, family situation, economic status, past experience with illness)
2. His *present illness* (how it developed, the symptoms, treatments and medications and their effects, any complications that developed and what was done about them)
3. His *nursing care* (reassurance of the patient, problems that came up and how they were handled, restorative nursing measures used)

INTERPERSONAL RELATIONSHIPS

Understanding Yourself

Your success as a nurse (and as a person) will depend on your ability to get along with people; you begin to develop this ability by learning to understand your own behavior and the reasons for it. Take a good honest look at your actions and the motives behind them—it will help you to understand similar actions and motives in others. This is hard to do because it means being willing to admit your imperfections, no matter how much it makes you squirm. Then you must make up your mind you will change and set about doing it.

Patients are understandably apprehensive about what may happen to them; they want (and need) a nurse who is steadfast, kind and reassuring—one who appreciates their problems and is someone they can lean on and trust. This does not mean that you will agonize with the patient in his suffering, for if you become so emotionally involved that you suffer too, you will be useless in helping him.

The Patient's Point of View

Many of the services a nurse gives to a patient are highly personal; some of them might seem personally distasteful if you did not know they are essential to his recovery and a necessary part of nursing care. What about the patient? No doubt he is embarrassed and humiliated because you must bring him a bedpan and change his bed if he is incontinent. His distress is lessened when he sees that you do not seem to find such services distasteful. He will be grateful also for your consideration in dealing with such handicaps as blindness or deafness. Your attitude toward the patient is reflected to the patient's family, who need the reassurance provided by your genuine interest in the patient and your skillful nursing care.

Patients Are People

It is always a great temptation to place the blame on a patient or to label him "difficult" if he resists your efforts to carry out the orders prescribed for him. There are 2 sides to this picture. First of all, the patient is a person—illness is one more problem added to those he may have already. He may seem uncooperative, but he is doing only what seems natural to him. Think of the adjustments he is expected to make: to let himself be waited on, to change his eating habits, to put up with pain and discomfort. These are problems he must handle in addition to his personal worries—his job, the payments on the house or rent, the care of children, his new expenses—is it any wonder that he seems to be difficult?

Another thing—it is quite possible that the patient thinks that you are the one who is being difficult. You give him baths he does not want, bring him milk when he longs for beer, stick him with needles every day and interfere with his life in a dozen ways. Does he stop to think that you are only following the doctor's orders? On the contrary, it seems logical to him that you are to blame because you are the one who does the things that upset him, yet at the same time he must depend on you to help him. Or if there is a language problem, he might think it is your fault that he does not understand what you are saying, rather than his because he may not have an adequate understanding of English.

ONE LAST WORD

Try to make these next 12 months a happy experience, warmed by new friends and new interests. Learn to understand yourself so you can better understand other people. Make the most of this opportunity to know your classmates and give them a chance to know you. If you wonder what all this has to do with you as a nurse, remember the reason for being a nurse in the first place—the patient. The kind of person you are will matter as much to him as the nursing care you give him. The more you put into your new career, the more you will get back. The observation of the little daughter of the itinerant minister, on seeing the meager contents of the collection plate, sums it up: "I guess if you want to get something out, you have to put something in." One of the most successful practical nurses we know illustrated this when she told the job placement director: "If Mrs. Craig likes music, I'll like it too."

MAIN IDEAS OF THIS CHAPTER

Develop an understanding of the principles which will guide you.

Remember that everything you learn is associated with health and can be applied in actual situations as well as classroom work.

In order to get the most from your training, you must make a concentrated effort to get the facts, take useful notes and form proper and effective study habits.

Learn how to participate actively and intelligently in class discussions as well as to conscientiously observe and accurately report on field trips.

Be able to give an honest appraisal of yourself.

Become better acquainted with the person that friends, classmates and patients will come to know.

ADAPTING SKILLS TO SITUATIONS

Has this chapter changed your ideas about practical nursing?

Practice writing a short paragraph about something you read or saw recently.

Bring to class a book or an article that you chose yourself and liked; ask to have your judgment checked.

Make a point of talking to one of your classmates whom you do not know at all.

3

PERSONALITY ADJUSTMENT

Perhaps one of the reasons you gave for wanting to be a nurse is the desire to "work with people." Life is not easy, and people often are hard to understand, but you have to take both as you find them. When working with people, it is necessary to know how to get along with them. Why do some people succeed and others fail? Because the successful ones know how to make people feel comfortable, and the others do not. We all have to change to fit ourselves in. Your personality can help or hinder you.

THE KIND OF PERSON YOU ARE

What Personality Is

Suppose we begin with a little sketch of the kind of person who does get along with people. First, she knows what she is doing and why; second, she likes her life and the people in it; and third, she wants people to like and trust her—and people do. What made her this kind of person? The same things that help to make every kind of personality—including yours.

Personality begins when a baby is conceived—the parents give a child physical characteristics and mental ability. Nature has a part in it—a body defect, such as blindness, for example, will influence personality. As soon as the baby is born, he begins to shape his personality as he struggles with his small world. Food, illnesses, playmates, experiences at school and contacts with religion affect him all his life. His personality will show how successfully he has handled his problems. His home life and the personalities of his parents affect him more than anything else. He needs to be safe, with people who care about him, feed him and keep him comfortable and happy in a pleasant, friendly place where people like each other.

It amounts to this: to understand people, you have to think of all the possible influences on their lives. People get along as best they can; sometimes they learn the wrong ways—ways that irritate and antagonize everybody. We all need to be loved, to have success and to feel safe. Because we need these things so much, naturally we try to get them—if one way doesn't work, we try others. Finally, each one of us works out a pattern of behavior. Your personality is your behavior, formed by your ability, successes and failures. A psychiatrist or a psychologist helps a person to make better adjustments to life by finding out about his experiences and how he met them. People often need help to see why they formed poor behavior habits. Information about a person will tell you about his personality. What can he do? Is he always changing jobs? Does he go to pieces when the going gets hard? What does he do in his leisure time? What is he interested in? How does he get along with the boss, with his co-workers, with people under him? (See Fig. 3.)

Two Personalities

Jean says her head nurses are nice to work with; everybody helps her to learn her way around, and she appreciates that. The ward

Fig. 3. Emotions are feelings expressed in behavior ways.

PERSONALITIES - UNDERSTANDING PEOPLE

ALWAYS JOLLY

WRAPPED UP IN ONE'S SELF

SHARP TONGUE

WHEN THE GOING GETS HARD

BEHAVIOR WAYS

maid is obliging, too. She laughs about spelling prostate *prostrate*—she will not make that mistake again! She thinks she is lucky to meet so many interesting people. Jean has lunch with a group of her classmates every day. She told them about her swimming classes at the "Y," and since then several of them have gone with her.

Esther wants to be first in everything; if she gets a low mark she is devastated. She has a sharp tongue, but somebody is always hurting *her* feelings. She can't stand Helen and Frances and doesn't care much about any of her classmates except Laura—she is devoted to Laura and doesn't want her to be friendly with anyone else. Esther expects everyone to make friendly gestures to her but never goes out of her way to be pleasant. She always has an excuse for her mistakes: the teachers do not like her; she had a headache the day of the nutrition test; she could not see the temperature demonstration very well. She laughed heartily when Mrs. Haines said the femur was in the arm but stayed away from school the day after she herself put sugar in the white sauce—she had a headache! Esther can't make up her mind which reference to read first; she forgot that she was to practice giving a hypodermic—the teacher had to wait while she got her equipment ready. She is always jittery and thrown off by any change of plans.

We say people like Esther are *neurotic*—so wrapped up in themselves that they pay no attention to anybody else. You know people like Jean and Esther—after the same things, but what different ways they use to get them!

What Maturity Is

As an adult you are expected to behave like one. Laws set an age when you are permitted to drive a car, get married or vote. This means it is taken for granted that people grow wiser as they grow older. Maturity or grown-upness is showing judgment, keeping your head, taking the knocks with the boosts and settling your problems like an adult, not like a child.

What Behavior Is

As we said before, life is full of problems. They become more complicated as we grow up; if we learn to handle them as we go along, we are ready to do what is expected of grown-up people. How, then, do people get on the wrong track? For a number of reasons: all of them are tied in with the 3 needs—affection, security and success. Our ways of behaving grow out of trying to satisfy these needs. We try one thing, then another and another; sometimes we are successful and sometimes not. We do not like to fail—failure makes us feel tense and uncomfortable. You try to avoid these tense feelings and keep a good opinion of yourself. Here is what you may do: Dodge every responsibility—if you do not try you cannot fail! Keep away from people, then you will not have to wonder whether they like you. Try to get out of doing unpleasant things. However, will these methods work?

Emotions

Emotions are feelings; emotions give you all your pleasant or unpleasant moments: you express them in your behavior. Feelings make life interesting and exciting, help you to get things done, give you individuality. Your body and its functions become full-grown; your mind can learn more complicated things; you learn to meet and associate with people. This is maturity or being grown-up. But you are not mature if you still express your emotions as a child or an adolescent. We try to work toward emotional maturity from childhood on, so we will gradually learn to control and direct our emotions to match our adult bodies and minds.

When a baby is hungry, or a pin sticks him, or he kicks off the covers, he expresses his feelings by movements or howls. He can not wait, he wants attention *now*—he screams until someone makes him comfortable again. We put up with this kind of behavior in babies but not in grownups—we expect adults to control their feelings. Learning to do so is a gradual process. We learn to bear pain without screaming; to keep our tempers when we are crossed; we learn not to be afraid; we manage to keep from being always either depressed or wildly happy. A baby *demands* and *accepts*—he gives little or nothing in return. An adult *gives* and is not too greatly concerned about the return.

The endocrine glands (the glands of internal secretion such as the thyroid) affect our emotions. If they are sluggish, we become dull or depressed; if they are overactive, we become restless or excitable.

Stress

Stress is one of the factors which affects our behavior. Medical authorities recognize that the stress and the strain of modern life affect people's health and well-being and as a result their behavior. It is the wear and tear that is part of being alive. We feel stress every day as we exert ourselves to get our work done, deal with our problems at home, attend classes or drive a car. A certain amount of stress is necessary and indispensable because it spurs us on to our best efforts and makes life more colorful and exciting. Increasing tension temporarily helps to get a job done, alerts the body's defenses against disease or danger and helps us to meet an emergency or a difficult situation. Stress becomes a problem only when we are unable to handle it constructively.

Stress may be due to physical pain, discomfort or to emotional pressures such as fear, anxiety, affection or hate. It creates tensions which may be harmful if they recur frequently or are allowed to persist. Prolonged tension affects both behavior and health. In caring for patients it is important to know the kinds of tensions that are likely to develop and how to relieve them. Sick people are under physical stress, but often it is the emotional stress which is more discouraging. We help to relieve these pressures by explaining nursing procedures as we prepare to carry them out and by performing them efficiently with the least possible amount of discomfort. We help to prevent and reduce tensions also by letting a patient talk about his fears and worries, by placing his call signal within easy reach, by answering his signal promptly, by assuring privacy during nursing treatments and by encouraging him to help himself as much as possible.

Remember, though, that you too are under stress whether you are learning a new kind of work, taking on responsibilities or adjusting to people and to new routines. Avoid letting stress affect the kind of person you are by having unnecessary tensions affect your work. Concentrate on doing one thing at a time instead of worrying about everything that has to be done. Do not waste time in rebelling against people or things that you cannot change. There is nothing abnormal about an occasional upset, but frequent "blow-ups" are danger signals of pressure build-ups. If things seem to be getting you down, try letting off steam by some physical activity. Take a brisk walk, go bowling, do your laundry. Take time for some recreation. A change gives you time for a new look at your problems. Talk over your problems with a sympathetic friend or member of your family. Keep physically fit. Your physical condition affects your attitude toward people and toward life. You must be able to handle your own tensions successfully before you can help patients to handle theirs.

EMOTIONS AND PERSONALITY

Our feelings give liveliness and color to personality. People who never let themselves feel strongly about anything are likely to be dull and uninteresting. However, it is just as true that uncontrolled emotions lead to the kind of behavior that makes people disliked.

Let us look at Marion and Donna. Marion is shy and self-conscious; if anyone criticizes her, her eyes fill with tears. She never has an opinion about anything; she is mousy and timid; her clothes are drab and unbecoming. Marion is about as uninteresting a person as you can imagine. She never talks about people but she never talks *to* them either. She really has no friends.

Donna seems exactly the opposite. Donna is always telling people what to do, always rushing off to an important date; she reels off stories about her conquests and the important jobs she has had. She buys extreme clothes—always tells you how much they cost, too. If you say complimentary things about Gretchen, Donna comes right back with a little gossip about her. If you admire Marge's sweater, Donna says, "Of course that shade of blue is terribly *hard.*" People stare at her when she goes to a restaurant for dinner, but Donna never seems to mind—she goes on talking and laughing loudly. Donna knows a lot of people—she is always telling you about them. She does not seem to have many *friends.*

Now here is the point: Marion and Donna are really very much alike. They behave differently, yes, but both are insecure, afraid people will not like them, dissatisfied with their lives.

It adds up to this: if you mingle with other people, go out of your way to be friendly; face facts and make up your mind; learn to do something well that amuses or helps you in your relations with others, then your personality rating goes up; you will also be happier.

Good Manners Come First

First impressions are strong, and people feel kindly toward the person who is thoughtful and friendly. Courtesy means being thoughtful of other people—your patients, their families and your co-workers. Good manners tell you to come forward to speak to a doctor, your head nurse, your instructor or a visitor if they are in need of assistance. On a hospital ward or in your patient's room you are more or less a hostess, as you would be in your own home. You will help bewildered visitors to find their way around; you will lend a helping hand to the people you work with. You will be tactful and make allowances for occasional sharp words and quick tempers. After all, you have known what it means to be rushed and worried.

A courteous, considerate person has no worries about manners, for good manners are a habit. When friends asked Mrs. Moore if she was uncertain about how to act when she was presented to the King and Queen of Sweden, she answered: "Why, no—I have only one set of manners and I use them all the time."

Quiet, Please!

Rules direct and remind you to do the right things. They are courtesies that you are expected to obey. Your respect for rules will affect your success.

The rules begin with your obligations to your patients. Gossip is always a waste of time—it can be dishonorable. You are in a position to know very personal things about people—they must be able to trust you not to discuss these personal matters with anyone. So don't be tempted to awe your friends with a description of Mrs. Hobart's dressing or a recital of the details of Mr. Cain's painful nights.

Your patient's doctor is your "officer-in-charge." Loyalty and good taste forbid any discussion or criticism of him before your patient or the family.

The Hospital Family

Every institution has its own rules about meals, laundry and living quarters. There are ward rules about linen and supplies; daily routines and time schedules are posted. Follow these rules—they help everybody. You are one of the hospital family. The care of patients is team work—as a member of the nursing team you work with professional nurses (graduates and students), practical nurses (graduates and students), and many other people, including the ward aides or helpers. This last group does not have nursing duties, but their work is indispensable to good nursing. They can answer the telephone, run errands, take care of flowers and keep the ward tidy so nurses have more time to take care of patients.

Inferiority Feelings

Most of us have some inferiority feelings, but it is dangerous to let them dominate us. How do people behave who let inferiority feelings rule them? They build themselves up by tearing others down (or the opposite); say that luck is always against them; build up imaginary situations where they always do spectacular things and are admired; become overreligious; often have headaches or other complaints; think too much about the past. When these things no longer bring even a little satisfaction, some people turn to drink or drugs for comfort. Sometimes suicide seems the only possible way out of what seems to be an unbearable life.

Habits are hard to change: if you want to improve yours you must begin by *wanting* to change them; behind that is the hardest thing of all—admitting that you are wrong. You must come out of your shell, think about other people and forget yourself. Think about the fix you are in as being funny instead of tragic. Put your spare time into a hobby instead of wasting it feeling sorry for yourself. It works for other people—why not for you? Wake up to the things you are missing; you will probably find that some of the things you wanted so badly are really not so important after all.

Worry Does Not Help

Do you worry a lot? It only makes you more tense. Talk your problem over with somebody who can see both sides. Face the worst and get it over with. Perhaps you are making mountains out of molehills. Get advice from somebody who knows more than you do. If it is impossible to do anything to change things, make the most of the pleasant parts of your life. It is natural to have *up* days and *down* days. Maybe you know when you are likely to have the blues—maybe they just descend on you for no reason that you can see. Try this on a blue day: say nothing about your feelings to anybody; wear your new hat; remember that perfect bed your instructor praised yesterday; turn in a good report on today's field trip. Behave as if you were on top of the world. You can carry this off and fool everybody—including yourself!

How To Improve

We do not *have* personalities; we *are* personalities. Since heredity and environment help to make you what you are, it is unfair to pass judgments on people about whom you know very little. You also need to know how they behave when the going is hard as well as when things run smoothly. It is encouraging to know that we can improve our personalities if we are willing to work at it. Learn to have fun with a group—not always with one person or alone. Do things you do not like, such as serving on committees, or taking part in the Christmas program; be friendly to people you really dislike; finish a job, even if it interferes with pleasure; take it for granted that people are friendly underneath, even if they seem reserved—if you feel self-conscious remember that other people are shy and self-conscious, too; learn how to do something well; get into the habit of making decisions, even in little things.

It Adds Up to This. You are going to be a nurse, true, but a nurse is a person first. You find your way of life by living. You cannot know all the answers in advance, but you can find them day by day as the problems come up.

People do not like us necessarily because we are neat and honest and do our work. People like us because of the feelings we arouse in them. If you make people feel happy and smart and wonderful, they will like you. You have to work at it and you will find you haven't much time left to think about yourself. Here are some *do's* for making people like you: listen to them, be easy and friendly, give them credit for good work, appreciate their help, notice what they do. There are *don'ts* too: don't act bored or interrupt; don't tell your own troubles; don't boast about *your* success or manage to bring in flattering things about yourself; don't pry into things that are none of your business; don't repeat confidences. It all amounts to this: you get along with people when you understand them and know how to make them feel comfortable. You learn how by understanding yourself.

The main point is that personality is not necessarily a gift with which you were born. It is comforting to know that you can improve yours if you are willing to work at it. Since this will mean changing your behavior you need to know some of the common ways of behaving and what is right or wrong about them. The discussion of emotional and mental health (Chap. 4) explains more fully different types of behavior.

MAIN IDEAS OF THIS CHAPTER

Heredity and environment affect personality—it is not fair to form opinions about people whom you do not know very well.

Behavior includes all the ways we take to satisfy our needs for affection, success and security.

The mature person shows judgment in his behavior.

Inferiority feelings can be dangerous.

Each one of us is a personality. People like or dislike us for the way we make them feel.

There are no special manners for nurses—there are rules that direct you.

ADAPTING SKILLS TO SITUATIONS

Think of the most likable person you know—can you tell why he or she is likable?

How do you rate in comparison?

How has your life affected your personality? Has it helped you to understand other people better?

What hobbies have you? What do you read? What do you do with your leisure time?

How will understanding yourself help you to understand patients?

What would you do if your head nurse gave a poor report on your work?

Unit Two:

Personal and Environmental Health

4

OVER-ALL HEALTH ASPECTS

If Americans had to choose between health and money, they would choose health although many of them would not know what health really is. Of course everybody wants bright eyes, firm muscles and that "on top of the world" feeling. These are only the signs of health. Many people think that health is not being sick. Health education teaches us what good health is and how to make the most of our individual possibilities. It is important to know what good health is before you begin to work with sick people; you can understand illness only by knowing first what being well is. This part of the book gives you information about health that you need as a citizen, a person and a nurse.

THE WORLD HEALTH ORGANIZATION (WHO)

WHO was established in 1948 as an auxiliary branch of the United Nations to which 100 countries now belong. WHO carries on a world-wide fight against disease; its health workers help these countries to establish health and sanitation practices and to fight disease epidemics. It also helps more than 20 small countries that are too poor to afford full membership. It issues warnings to countries all over the world when a disease epidemic breaks out. At one time, an epidemic in Calcutta was of no immediate threat to other countries, but today a typhus louse picked up by a tourist in a bazaar can be in New York, London or Paris within a few hours by jet. In 1918 an influenza epidemic swept the world, taking more than 15 million lives. There was no organization at that time ready to warn nations to prepare for it. In 1957, an outbreak of influenza in North China swept down into India. WHO officials in Singapore notified the International Influenza Centers who alerted drug manufacturers in this country and abroad to produce quantities of vaccine. As a result, although 80 million Americans had respiratory ailments, there was only a slight rise in the normal death rate. This was also true in other countries. WHO is concentrating on eliminating some of the diseases, such as malaria, trachoma and leprosy, which plague underdeveloped nations.

A DEFINITION OF HEALTH

The World Health Organization was set up on the principle that the health of every nation is part of the foundation in building the kind of world we want. This is how it defines health:

> Health is a state of complete physical, mental and social well-being and not merely the absence of disease or infirmity.
>
> The enjoyment of the highest attainable standard of health is one of the fundamental rights of every human being without distinction of race, religion, political belief, economic or social condition.
>
> The health of all people is fundamental to the attainment of peace and security and is dependent upon the fullest cooperation of individuals and states.

You can see that proper food, good living conditions, disease prevention, and education are important in every country. Some countries are far ahead of others in improving the health of people; although there is still much to be done, the United States has made great progress in improving the health of its citizens. Statistics show a lowered death rate and a marked decrease in some kinds of illness. People live longer, too. Other countries are less fortunate because their problems have been, and still are, many. War, disease, lack of food and money and large populations have hindered health protection and health education and have increased illness in many countries.

HEALTH AND HEREDITY

Your health equipment is given to you by your parents. They passed on to you materials received from their fathers and mothers. In the father and the mother cells that you came from were the genes, or determiners, that influenced your development. These genes are in bundles called chromosomes; you received 23 chromosomes from your mother and 23 from your father, a total of 46. The genes from one parent were paired with similar ones from the other. The gene that takes charge in each pair is called the *dominant* gene; the other has little, if any, effect on development and is called the *recessive* gene (see Chap. 11).

Disease and Inheritance

Comparatively few diseases are known to be inherited. It is true that it is possible to inherit a susceptibility to disease of certain parts of the body, such as the lungs, kidneys or heart, or a predisposition to allergies.

Sickle Cell Anemia

Recent medical research has revealed that the fatal blood disease sickle-cell anemia is transmitted by heredity. Every year approximately 2,000 children, mainly Negroes, inherit this disease. If only 1 parent carries this gene, the children will not be affected, but as carriers they could pass it on to their children. If both parents have the gene, some of their children are sure to develop the disease. It can be detected by a simple blood test* which could be included in premarital blood tests. (See also PKU, p. 32.)

Inherited Defects

Certain abnormalities and unusual conditions such as color blindness, deaf-mutism and Mongolian idiocy are known to be inherited. *Hemophilia,* a strong tendency to bleed, is transmitted by an inherited trait that causes a deficiency in a blood-clotting substance. Hemophilia, incidentally, only afflicts the males in a family, but the gene is transmitted through the females. The *Rh factor,* which is present in the red blood cells of 85 per cent of the white race, is hereditary (see p. 156). Fortunately, most of the troublesome genes are recessive; a person would have to inherit 2 of them to be defective.

Congenital Defects

It is well to point out here that some babies are born with defects that are not due to heredity but are the result of some interference with the baby's prenatal development. These congenital defects may be due to infectious diseases of the mother during pregnancy.

Inherited Mental Ability

Mental ability is inherited, but if it is not used, it does not develop to its fullest extent. A person with a high degree of mental ability may not be as successful in life as his friend who works harder and so makes the most of a less brilliant mental inheritance.

Heredity is complicated, but scientists believe that the human race can be improved by preventing defectives from marrying each other and by making the most of inheritance.

* Developed by Dr. Linus Pauling, Nobel prize winner and an authority in the field of genetics.

A good inheritance starts you off with a nice balance in your health bank account.

People Are Different. You can see that individual possibilities for health are not alike for everybody. The best health of which you are capable may be less or more than your sister's possibilities. It is well known that people pay too little attention to their individual health capacities. Say, for example, that you can do your work efficiently, take difficulties in your stride and not feel overtired if you get 8 hours' sleep every night. Do you still stay up late every night talking to Edith, who is as efficient with 7 hours' sleep as you are with 8? And look at Mrs. Harris and Mrs. Graves—Mrs. Harris has diabetes, follows a diet and takes insulin, but manages her house, belongs to a bridge club and is active on a church committee. Mrs. Graves, her neighbor, can eat everything she wants, does not take medicine and belongs to 5 committees. They have different health possibilities, but Mrs. Harris, who has a difficulty, still keeps her health at its best by knowing what her limitations are and keeping within them. She would soon fall below her *best* health if she ate the chocolate ice cream cake dessert at her bridge club or forgot to take her insulin.

KINDS OF HEALTH

Total Health

Health is much more than brushing your teeth, taking baths and vitamins. It includes your thoughts and feelings; it influences your efficiency and your relations with other people. This applies to your patients too. So we must consider health in its broadest meaning, or *total health*, which includes:

Social Health: A sense of responsibility for the health and welfare of others

Physical Health: Physical fitness—the body functioning at its best

Mental Health: A mind that grows, reasons and adjusts

Emotional Health: Feelings and actions that bring satisfaction

Spiritual Health: Inner peace and security in spiritual faith

Social Health

By *society* we mean the world we live in, with all its people, customs and conditions. As a member of society you have a social responsibility to be concerned about the welfare of the other members. Unfavorable conditions reflect on you even if indirectly. If your town has disgraceful slum areas and inadequate health protection, some of the discredit is yours since you are a part of the town and share in the social responsibility for health conditions.

Social Changes. We live in a time of rapid social changes which creates new social problems and often aggravates the old. Some social problems are nation-wide; one is technical progress that replaces men with machines; another is the threat of war. The speed of living and the pressure of competition in an atomic age create strains that end in mental illness. Moral standards are threatened. Authorities are alarmed about the "softness" of our youth, the increase in juvenile delinquency and the number of school drop-outs. If a factory comes to a community, this solves the unemployment problem but brings new difficulties as more people move in, creating problems of housing, transportation, water supply, medical and hospital care.

Our attitudes and concern about the general welfare are a measure of our social health. Like it or not, we are involved with our fellow men—in the words of the poet, John Donne, ". . . no man is an island."

Physical Health

To begin with, health depends on a smoothly running body. People have vague and erroneous notions about what goes on in their bodies. A truck driver knows what makes his truck work, but his body remains a mystery to him. He knows why he does not put water in the gas tank or oil in the radiator, but does he know why he should eat vegetables? He knows the engine will rebel unless he changes to low gear on a steep hill, but does he know why he is short of breath when he lifts those heavy logs? The human body is like a machine in many ways, and health depends on understanding how it is put together and how to handle it.

The normal structure and the functions of the human body are explained in Unit 4; Unit 5 discusses the food elements essential to maintain a healthy body and to promote the growth and repair of its parts.

Mental Health

A mentally healthy person uses her mind effectively. Mind is the reasoning part of you—the ability to know 2 and 2 equals 4, knowing that you cannot spend your money and have it too, learning not to make the same mistakes twice. The brain is capable of learning a wide variety of things; reasoning power should grow as the body grows. While all normal people can learn, not everyone will learn the same thing equally well.

Intelligence. The ability to learn and reason is called intelligence. Reasoning ability is determined by heredity, but a person is also shaped by his home, his education and his opportunities for development. His accomplishment depends on the mental equipment with which he has to work.

Intelligence Tests. Reliable tests have been worked out that measure ability to learn and to reason. Your score on a *psychometric* (intelligence) test indicates this ability as your mental age. This score, divided by your chronological or actual age and multiplied by 100 is your intelligence quotient or *IQ*.

Degrees of Intelligence. There are many degrees of intelligence. A person may be born with a high ability to learn and reason and by developing it may be a genius. Albert Einstein, one of the greatest scientists of all times, was an example of native intelligence developed to the utmost. Yet another person, with less native endowment will also achieve his ambitions by making the most of his abilities.

Kinds of Intelligence. There are different kinds of intelligence, and tests will show how good you are at work that requires such abilities as reading and reasoning, quick and clever hands, a friendly, even disposition and so on. A combination of tests will indicate whether or not you should choose nursing as a career. There are no right or wrong answers. These tests are intended to show your strengths and your weaknesses.

The Mentally Retarded

In another class altogether are the people who are born with defective mental equipment—the feebleminded. Their capacity for normal development is definitely limited. Lowest on the scale is the *idiot*, whose mental age will always be less than that of a normal 3-year-old. (An idiot may be 10 years old but unable to dress himself.)

Slightly higher on the scale is the *imbecile*, whose mental age will never be more than that of a normal child 5 to 7 years old.

The highest grade mental defective, the *moron*, can achieve a mental age equal to that of a normal child of 12. This group is the most difficult to cope with because they are self-sufficient to a considerable extent but, left to themselves, are ripe for trouble. They are easily influenced, get into bad company and run afoul of the law. With guidance and suitable vocational training under interested supervision, they can become self-supporting, acceptable members of the community.

PKU and Mental Retardation

It has been found that because of a defective gene inherited from both parents, some babies are unable to use the substance *phenylalanine*, which is found in most protein foods. As a result poison accumulates in the baby's body and damages the brain. This condition, *phenylketonuria* (known as PKU), can be discovered by a blood test; if it is detected early enough, a special diet will prevent brain damage. In one state,* a new law makes this test mandatory for every newborn baby on leaving the hospital. It is known as the *heel test* because it is made by taking drops of blood from a puncture in the baby's heel. The mother is

* Massachusetts is reportedly the first state to pass such a law. No doubt by the time you read this, other states will have followed Massachusetts' example.

given a leaflet which explains the purpose of the test and tells why she should have it repeated when the baby is a month old—babies usually leave the hospital in 5 days and this is too early to be absolutely sure about PKU in every case.

Hope for the Retarded

We know now that the mentally retarded child can be taught much more than we once thought possible, if he is allowed to learn at his own speed and in keeping with his mental ability. This is why these children should be taught as a group separate from normal children. If they are forced to compete with normal children, they soon become discouraged and lose interest. The situation then becomes hopeless for both pupils and teacher. Physical handicaps, such as defective hearing or eyesight, if they are not discovered and corrected may be mistaken for retarded mentality. This means that any program for the retarded should begin with a thorough physical check-up.

Emotional Health

Emotional health and mental health are closely related. Emotions are not physical feelings, such as pain and hunger, but are rather the way we feel *about* people and things. When you say, "I'm afraid of big dogs," "I'm afraid I won't pass my nutrition test," or "I like Betty," "I can't stand Laura," "I'm sorry your head aches," you express emotions—fear, love, dislike, sympathy. The strength of emotions varies—you may be *terrified*, or just *worried*; you are *fond* of a friend, or *in love* with your fiancé.

Emotional Responses

Emotions influence the motives for our actions. We consciously recognize some of them, but others are inborn or the result of the experiences stored in our unconscious mind. Our emotional responses vary according to our physical feelings. Good physical health tends to make us feel hopeful, secure and on top of the world. Fatigue or ill health tend to make us discouraged, uncertain and sorry for ourselves. Strong emotions affect us physically—fear or anger speed up the pulse, raise the blood pressure and send more adrenalin into the blood stream, preparing the body for action. These physical responses are automatic and not controlled by the mind. (The lie detector, used in securing legal evidence, is based on this principle.)

Effects of Emotions

Emotions can have favorable or harmful effects on your behavior or success. Strong feelings about accomplishing something can drive you on to achieve it. On the other hand, your emotions can rush you into making rash decisions or lead you into judging people unfairly. For example, a strong desire to be a top-flight nurse may impel you to study faithfully and bring you to the top of your class, but a quick temper may keep you continually in hot water.

As one more example of the effect of certain emotions on the body and the mind, suppose you fail in a test. You go home to dinner that night, but you cannot eat—your stomach feels "twitchy." You sit down to do tomorrow's lessons—you cannot concentrate. You do poorly in class the next day and worry about being dropped from the course. You can see how it goes—the emotions affect the body, the body affects the mind and the mind affects the emotions (see Fig. 4).

PSYCHOLOGY AND BEHAVIOR

Psychology is the study of the mental processes that direct behavior. Our mental and emotional health is measured by our behavior. Psychologists have taught us that a person uses both his conscious and his subconscious mind to direct his actions. By studying the ways people do behave, it has been found that there are certain patterns people follow to satisfy essential basic needs of the body, mind and spirit.

FIG. 4. Emotions affect the body, the body affects the mind, the mind affects the emotions.

Our Basic Needs

These essential basic needs are for affection, success and security. They take various forms —wanting people to like you can mean desiring this kind of acceptance from a person or from a group. Success can mean making good in your job, passing a test or making the bowling team. Security can mean money enough to live on, a job, or confidence in yourself. These basic needs can mean many things to many people, and everyone has his own ideas about what they mean to him.

Making Decisions

This is where the difficulties begin, for needs create problems in deciding how to satisfy them. We are influenced in making decisions by the strength of our desires, by our reasoning powers and by the patterns we have followed in the past. If these influences are well-balanced we come out on top—if not, we are in trouble. For example, we may be so anxious to be liked that we go along with standards of behavior which we do not really approve, just to be accepted by a group we happened to be associated with or to which we want to belong. Then we are uncomfortable because secretly we feel guilty for letting others take over and for shirking any personal responsibility for our acts.

We have to make choices constantly—where to live, what to eat, what to wear. Some of them are easy to make. When the Thrift Shop called to ask Ann what she did with her old clothes, she said: "I wear them!" She solved that problem without thinking because the reasons for her choice were obvious. Others are not so easily solved, especially if they involve one's conscience.

Mental Mechanisms

We bury many things in the unconscious mind. If they refuse to stay buried and work up to the surface, they bother us. Then we resort to the tricks which we have learned for pushing them down again. These *mental mechanisms* are very common—certainly we all have used them at one time or another. Some are helpful, but others are not. Knowing how these mechanisms work helps us to understand people better and, what is even more important, to understand ourselves.

Rationalization. To begin with a common example: you may try to justify something you have done that makes you feel uncomfortable. Let us say you are definitely on the "hefty" side and spend your Saturday nights at home with a good book. You try to get rid of your guilty feelings about eating that big piece of chocolate cake on the table beside you with "I certainly have to have *some* pleasure in life!" This is *rationalization.*

Repression. Suppose you have a nursing care study coming due. The last one you handed in was hastily prepared and received a poor grade. The thought of it brings unpleasant feelings so you "forget" you were going to spend Tuesday night in the library and go to the movies instead. This is *repression*—trying to push uncomfortable memories back into your unconscious mind.

Projection. If you excuse your poor showing on your monthly ward report by telling everybody "Miss Zeller (the head nurse) doesn't like me," you are using *projection*—making yourself look better by shifting the blame for your shortcomings to someone else.

Compensation. Perhaps you had always dreamed of being a nurse, but when you asked about professional nursing you found it would take 3 years. You needed to prepare yourself to earn a living as soon as possible and found out that a practical nursing course would take only 1 year. So you decide that you can realize your ambition by going into practical nursing. You exchange one ambition for another that is equally respected and approved and you will satisfy your wish to help others. This is *compensation*—changing an impossible goal for one that you can achieve.

Identification. You may admire and look up to someone and try to be like her. This is *identification* and is excellent if your idol is a fine person with high ideals, but it can also get you in trouble if you choose to imitate the wrong people.

Regression. Sometimes the going becomes difficult when you find you really are on your own and must be up on time, do your studying and be responsible for yourself. You long for the good old days when mother assumed much of this responsibility, so you decide to give up the course and go back to that comfortable life. This is *regression*—an attempt to side-step being an adult and to go back to childhood.

Frustration

When our efforts to satisfy our basic needs are unsuccessful, we are worried and uncomfortable. This is *frustration.* People meet frustrations in various ways. One is to give up trying to overcome them, "what's the use, I can't win." Another is to refuse to acknowledge a need. For example, a person may be in dire need of friends, but because he has none he keeps to himself and limits his interests entirely to his work. This cuts him off still further from satisfaction. Or he may try to develop some outside interests so he can share in the interests of others—a step in the right direction toward satisfying his need for friends.

Frustrations are to be expected as part of the normal process of growing up. They stimulate us to redouble our efforts to find healthy ways of satisfying our needs.

Spiritual Health

The spirit is sometimes described as the divine spark within us which is sustained and strengthened by religious faith and a belief in the innate worth of all men. Spiritual health could be defined as inner peace which comes from the conviction that our lives have a worthy purpose which we have an obligation to fulfill, with a genuine concern for the welfare of others.

MENTAL ILLNESS

People with difficulties that affect the mind are sick people, as truly as if they had physical ailments. It is old-fashioned today to think that mental illness is mysterious and unusual. Thousands of people in the United States are in mental hospitals for special treatment; many of them recover and go back to normal lives. Modern medicine recognizes the difficulties that people meet and has devised ways of helping people to adjust to a complicated world. This special field of medicine is called *psychiatry.* The doctor is called a *psychiatrist.*

The *mind* is the part of us that makes decisions. People who are unable to make the decisions that help them to carry on as independent human beings and to fit into the world are mentally ill. There are different kinds of mental illness. The feeble-minded person has defective reasoning power—he inherited this defect, or it was the result of an injury and is incurable. Tumors and injuries destroy brain tissues; syphilis organisms have the same effect. As people age, brain tissue sometimes loses its normal qualities. During the menopause, disturbances of the hormone balance in the body may cause mental disorders.

Effect of Emotions

Another type of mental illness is caused by emotional disturbances. The psychologist is concerned with finding the reasons for emotional difficulties, for when a person's behavior becomes so abnormal that he cannot lead a reasonably normal life or may injure other people, he is mentally ill. There are degrees of this kind of mental illness and many people we work with and know, while they are not ill, are not mentally healthy. Some of the people with poor mental health become mentally ill; others continue leading unsatisfactory lives. The United States could save millions of dollars by improving mental health; as it is, much is being done, but the trouble is that it is difficult to find and help all the people with poor mental health before they become really mentally ill. We also need more psychiatrists to treat mentally ill patients. Most of us probably could improve our mental health—as we said before, the difference between poor mental health and mental illness is just a difference in the degree of satisfactory adjustment to life.

POSITIVE HEALTH

Good health means that your body, your mind and your emotions are working efficiently, in proper balance, with no one of them dominating the others harmfully. In Chapter 3 we discussed the wrong and the right ways people take to fit into life. You can see how wrong adjustments have important effects on health. Doctors give a great deal of attention to the effects of mental and emotional attitudes on the body. They find that some people complain of pain which can be traced to emotional difficulties. A doctor's business is to keep the body in working order, but, to correct physical difficulties, he must first discover their cause. This means that he must consider everything about the patient. This kind of treatment is not new, but it has a comparatively new name: *psychosomatic medicine.* (*Psycho* means mind, *somatic* means body.) Remember that this principle applies to nursing, too, and think of your patients as *people*, not as *cases.*

Effects of Environment

Health is affected by personal attitudes and habits which we can try to control. Proper food and clothes, clean and pleasant homes, good working conditions, opportunities for fun and new interests make it easier to have good health. The lack of these things has the opposite effect. Most of these things are associated with money, and poor people are likely to be less healthy. This is not completely true if people learn good health habits—a millionaire who knows nothing about nutrition can be as poorly nourished as the child in the slums. The atmosphere of a home affects health; quarrels, unnecessary criticism and lack of affection can counteract the effects of good clothes, perfect meals and a spotless house.

Health Education

Health education is one of the strongest weapons in the fight for better health. Ingenious advertising will sell a product—it works by appealing to needs that people feel strongly. For example, the cosmetic industry knows every woman wants to be attractive and so finds it hard to resist a cream that promises a skin like velvet. This is equally true of medicine, for people *desire* health. The trouble is they do not know what it is and how to get it. Quacks and patent medicine manufacturers take advantage of the general ignorance to make glowing (and false) claims for their services and products. A determined and continuous campaign to inform people about good health practices and proper care goes on in newspapers and magazines and over the radio and television. Health organizations and health departments publish health information in pamphlets which are available to anyone. Health teaching begins with school children and goes on among all age groups.

A nurse has many opportunities for teaching health. For example, by tactfully explaining the reasons for a balanced diet and good personal health practices, a patient learns why health habits are desirable. At the same time, this is an opportunity to correct erroneous and superstitious beliefs about health and illness.

Health Habits

Your family circumstances, your work, your ambitions, illness and injuries mold your health habits. They are closely related to the body and its functions. You will find information about them in Chapter 5.

The body works less perfectly as you grow older. It slows down—the damages of illness or injuries and the wear and tear of living begin to show. It is sensible to change working and living habits with the years to keep your health at its best—exchange tennis at 20 for golf at 50, take milder exercise and get more rest. Every day the papers carry notices that men in their fifties have died of heart disease. Some of them would still be alive if they had worried less and modified their way of living. We all hate to admit that there are some things we no longer can do, but is it not rather shortsighted to deliberately shorten our lives? Aunt Rachel knew the secret. Somebody asked her how she kept so young. This was her answer: "When I works I works easy, when I sits I sits loose, when I worries I goes to sleep."

MAIN IDEAS OF THIS CHAPTER

Health is the sum of the condition of your body, your mind and your emotions. When in good health, a person has a feeling of physical, mental and social well-being.

Everyone should know what his or her "best" health can be as well as how to maintain it.

Your heredity, your health habits and the effects of illness or injuries influence your state of health.

A person's reasoning and learning power determines his intelligence.

There are varying degrees of mental retardation. Many retarded individuals can be trained and guided into being self-supporting, acceptable members of the community.

Your mental and emotional health is measured by your behavior, which in turn is influenced by how adequately you satisfy your basic needs—the need for affection, the need for success and the need for security.

There is hope for the mentally ill person if his illness is recognized and treatment is started in the early stages.

ADAPTING SKILLS TO SITUATIONS

Do you or do you not have health problems? If so, what can you do to curtail them?

Name some of the problems countries face in trying to promote their health programs. What part has WHO played in helping them?

What new responsibilities must the public health nurse assume for the peoples' health if a new factory opens in a community, which brings in a hundred new families?

What guidance would you give to the parents of a mentally retarded child who has been classified as an imbecile or moron?

Give an example of how a student nurse might rationalize in her reply to the head nurse when asked why, when she had adequate time, she neglected to tidy the patient's bedside table during morning care.

5

PERSONAL HEALTH HABITS

You may think that already you have heard enough about personal health to last the rest of your life, but good health habits are worth emphasizing, even more so in a career like nursing where they can seriously affect your efficiency and the impression you create. They can help or hinder you physically—nursing is hard work; and also mentally—you are sure to be upset if you do not make a good impression on the people whom you meet and with whom you work. Good health habits count heavily in obtaining and keeping a job. A nurse is in such close personal contact with patients that she must be doubly careful not to offend by careless health practices. She is also a health teacher and should be an example of practicing what she preaches.

YOUR ATTITUDE

One thing is certain: unless you really want to keep in good condition and are convinced that your health affects how you feel and look, any amount of health advice will be useless. If you choose to disregard known facts about health and are unwilling to make changes in your health habits, you do not want *health*—you only want temporary relief from your health problems. You will still turn to anything that promises fast relief, rather than work for the lasting improvement that takes longer and requires more effort. Such an attitude would be unthinkable for a nurse—people expect a nurse to improve and protect health, including her own.

Once you recognize your faults, you need to know how to correct them. It takes will power and persistence to uproot a poor habit and establish a better one, and it can not be done without a struggle. Your weapon for this battle is *knowledge:* knowing what your problems are, why one method of correcting a problem is sound, why another is useless and why still another may actually be harmful. You may find that some of your pet beliefs about health and beauty aids will have to be disregarded.

HEALTH AND APPEARANCE

Health might be given more serious attention if people realized how much it affects the way they look. Admit it or not, everybody wants to be attractive. Personal attractiveness begins with good grooming, which is based on good health habits. The most expensive cosmetics will not offset the impression left by dull and dirty hair, greasy skin and slouching posture. Good health habits can help you to make the most of your assets—knowing that you look and feel your best will give you poise and confidence. It will also help to give others confidence in you, for everyone likes to be with people who are well groomed. Attention to your health habits will pay dividends in popularity.

Posture

The way you stand, sit or move affects your efficiency and the impression you create. Good posture improves your health—you breathe better, your circulation and muscle tone are improved, you save energy and prevent muscle strain. These are only part of the benefits. Good posture makes you look taller and slimmer, pulls you in at the waist, lifts your chest and keeps the parts of your body in balance. It gives you poise and grace; one of the first things a professional model learns is how to stand, sit and move gracefully and easily.

Posture is the position of your body—the way its parts are lined up when you stand, sit, move or when you are lying down. You use your muscles to keep your body in good alignment. Think of your spine as a set of building blocks (*the vertebrae*) set one above the other, held together by strong bands of elastic tissue (*the muscles*) which can be made to stretch or contract to keep your body in line. Correct use of muscles is the secret of good posture. Nature has provided the appropriate muscles for every body movement but the use you make of them is up to you. Poor posture overstrains some muscles and over-relaxes others. One authority* compares good and poor posture in this way: (see Fig. 5)

Good Posture (Fig. A)	Poor Posture (Figs. B, C, D)
Head erect with chin drawn in	Head projecting forward
Chest lifted	Chest flat
Shoulders back resting on spine	Shoulders curved forward
Lower abdomen flat, upper abdomen full	Abdomen protruding
Natural curves of back	Exaggerated natural curves
Toes pointing straight ahead, weight on outer borders of feet	Weight carried on inner borders of feet, toes pointing too far inward or outward

The Way You Sit

To sit slouched in your seat, head down, chest collapsed, abdomen protruding, is very tiring. This position interferes with your breath-

* Stearn and Stearn: College Hygiene, Philadelphia, Lippincott, 1961.

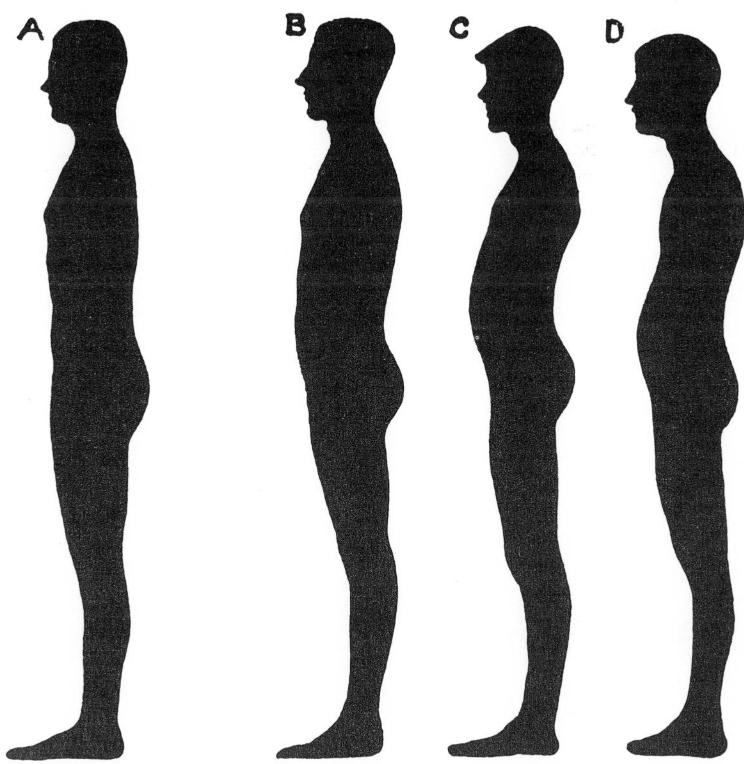

Fig. 5. Posture. **A** shows the body in good posture; **B, C** and **D** in increasingly poorer posture. (Harvard University Chart)

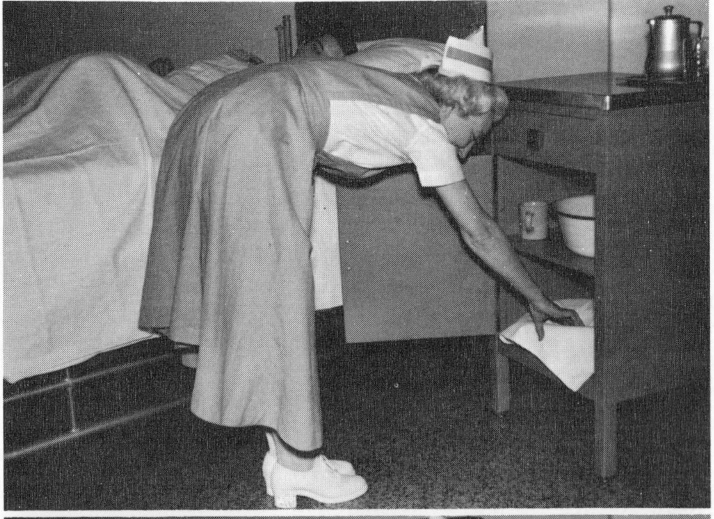

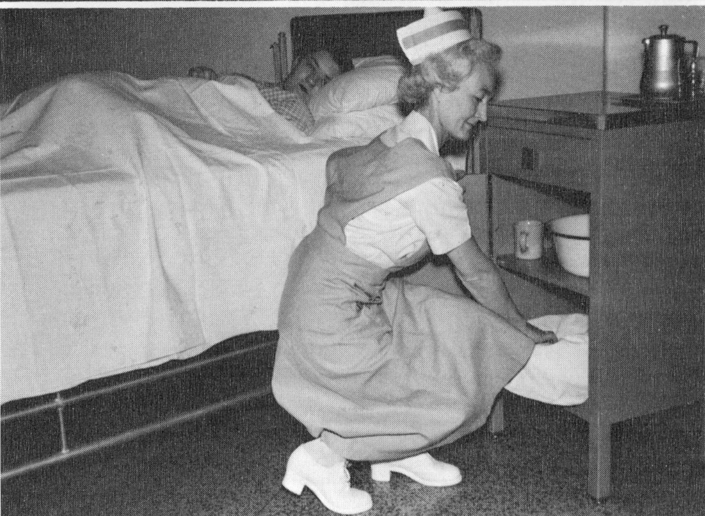

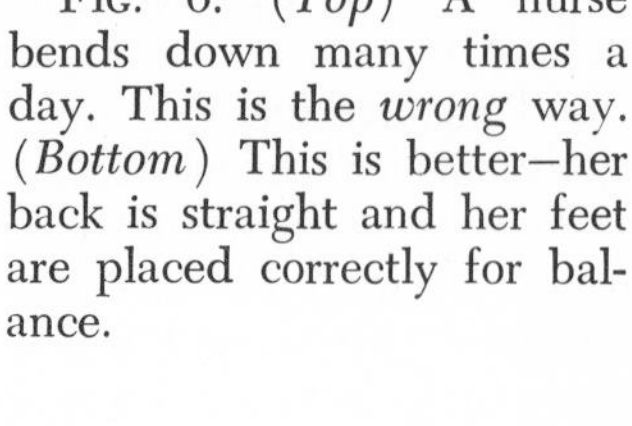

FIG. 6. (*Top*) A nurse bends down many times a day. This is the *wrong* way. (*Bottom*) This is better—her back is straight and her feet are placed correctly for balance.

ing, strains neck and back muscles and throws your weight on the end of your spine. Good posture is considerably more restful once it becomes a habit. Try sitting well back in your chair, with your spine straight, your head erect and your feet flat on the floor. Naturally, it will take time and perseverance to change a bad habit, but the improvement in the way you look and feel will be worth it.

Body Mechanics

The human body is like a machine with many parts—to be efficient these parts must work together. The operation of this machine, the way you use your body in any activity, is equally important. Since you want to move with the least amount of strain, you must use your muscles effectively, making the longest and the strongest muscles do the work. For example, a look at the anatomy charts will tell you there are no long, strong muscles in the lower part of the back, but you do find such muscles in the arms and legs. Therefore, to avoid back strain you lift with your arms and legs (see Fig. 6).

Lifting and Moving

Lifting, moving and carrying are daily activities that can be very tiring if we do not know how to save energy. Some methods are more effective than others because they are based on physical laws that never change. From these laws we learn that:

It is easier to pull, push or roll an object than it is to lift it.

Reason: *In lifting, you have to overcome the pull of gravity.*

It takes less effort to lift or move an object if you work as close to it as possible. Use your leg muscles as much as possible, and your back muscles as little as possible.

Reason: *This brings your center of gravity and that of the object closer together, and the stronger muscles are in the legs.*

Rocking backward or forward on your feet uses your body weight as a force for pulling or pushing.

Reason: *This lessens the strain on your arms and back.*

A nurse is expected to be able to help her patients to use good body mechanics. The first step is to practice good body mechanics herself.

FOOD HABITS

Food and Health

Food is important for health since life could not go on without it. In Chapter 22 of this book you will learn about essential foods and the use of food in the body. Study it carefully for it applies to you personally as well as to patients. You will learn that individual nutritional needs vary in some respects, depending upon body build, age or activity; and that people's eating habits (including your own) are affected by their work habits. In spite of these variations, everyone needs certain food materials to keep the body functioning and in good repair. Certainly, to work effectively and as a health teacher, a nurse should understand and practice good nutrition.

Your Weight

Too fat? Too thin? A sad commentary about overweight people is that although they are left out of activities because they are fat, they continue overeating because food seems to be their only satisfaction. Being overweight and underweight can be symptoms of such conditions as tuberculosis and thyroid or other glandular disturbances. However, someone has said that the only glands responsible for overweight conditions are the salivary glands!

Do you take up diet fads? Weight reduction should be gradual. It is risky to experiment with a drastic reducing diet without the advice of a physician; drugs can be either dangerous or useless. Go to a doctor if you have a serious weight problem. You can keep your weight under control and meet your nutrition needs, too, if you choose the right foods and regulate the amounts.

How Water Counts

The average adult loses about 2 quarts of water a day. If you take a glass of water with every meal, plus the water you get in beverages, soups, vegetables and fruits, you probably will have a sufficient amount. If you perspire a lot in hot weather, you need to drink more water. Body fluids contain a certain amount of salt, some of which is lost through perspiration, so you also may need extra salt in your diet.

Eating Habits

Once you know what good nutrition is, some changes in your eating habits may be indicated. For example, breakfast is a meal people often neglect. You can see that a cup of black coffee is obviously inadequate to supply the necessary energy for a typical morning's activities such as getting to school, participating in a class session or practicing nursing procedures. You ought not to start the day without an adequate nutritionally balanced breakfast.

Snacks, those between meal indulgences that build up excess poundage, may also interfere with adequate nutrition. "Cokes" and candy bars, too many and too often, can spoil your appetite for food your body needs. So watch the habit of munching between meals or nibbling while you study at night. Occasionally reach for a carrot instead of candy.

Regular eating hours give your intestinal tract a chance to digest and to absorb food in an orderly way. The time and the number of meals are not the same for everyone. Perhaps you can balance your diet more easily if you eat more often and eat less each time.

Be alert for the feelings that make you say: "Too tired to eat," "Too excited," or "Too upset." If you are overworking or emotionally disturbed, these feelings interfere with nutrition. Forcing yourself to eat will only upset your digestion.

Eating should be more than a duty—it should be fun, and it can be if food tastes and looks good. Your appetite is affected by the way food is cooked and served. Color helps—so do china, silver and glass, when they are clean and attractive. Surroundings make a difference. Try on yourself some of the devices that you use to make patients' food attractive.

Elimination Habits

Your intestinal tract works efficiently to get rid of waste if you cooperate. The intestine has to be stretched to start the motions that push out waste. The woody fibers in vegetables and fruits supply waste, or roughage, so you need both vegetables and fruits in your diet. When the nerve impulses in the rectum indicate that waste is ready to be emptied, they should be heeded. The habit of emptying the rectum at a definite time every day helps to prevent constipation. There is nothing to worry about if you regularly do this as infrequently as every 2 or 3 days—some people's intestines move more slowly than others.

Laxatives. Laxatives and cathartics are irritants that stimulate contractions of the intestines. If you use these irritants habitually, roughage gradually ceases to have any affect on the intestinal walls. In spite of advertising claims for the rejuvenating and cleansing effects of a cathartic, the surest road to healthy elimination is through a balanced diet and regular toilet habits. Cathartics are a crutch that you should not need. Many people think that mineral oil is harmless, but doctors tend to discourage its use because it is thought to interfere with the use of vitamin A by the body.

Fluids. You can help your kidneys to do their work efficiently by drinking enough fluids to keep up your body's water supply. Periodic health examinations, including urinalysis, are checkups to discover disturbances early enough to prevent serious damage. You should consult a doctor immediately if any symptoms of disturbance show in the urine itself or in connection with voiding. Unusual swelling in any part of the body, headaches, dizziness or sight disturbances, or shortness of breath are danger signals that you should report to your doctor at once.

DENTAL HEALTH

A Serious Health Problem

In spite of the advances in knowledge of the causes of dental health problems, dental services to correct or prevent them are not reaching many of the people who need them most. Young people, especially, seem to be the victims of dental neglect—the percentage of high school pupils with dental caries is far too high for comfort. School health programs should include dental examinations but many times do not. A recently released government report tells us that *one half* of the children in the United States under the age of 15 have *never* been to a dentist. Furthermore, by no means are all of the other half receiving the complete dental care they need. This is especially serious when we consider how important it is to begin dental care early, that is, with the baby teeth. A child uses these first teeth for chewing. Their loss through decay or accident and their position in the mouth affects the evenness and position of the permanent teeth.

Tooth Decay

No one knows exactly what causes *dental caries* (tooth decay), but several things are known to contribute to it: among them are lack of certain minerals (fluorine, phosphorus, calcium) and lack of vitamin D in the diet; low concentration of fluorine in drinking water; bacteria in the mouth that react with food particles to form an acid that is harmful to the teeth. Dental caries is largely responsible for the staggering amount of dental work we see in people's mouths—it is estimated that 15 out of every 100 adults wear complete artificial dentures, to say nothing of the number with partial dentures and fillings. Nature provided good equipment for biting and grinding food, but the tooth covering is often not hard enough to resist the acids that our diets produce.

Decay begins with sticky food particles accumulating in spots that are hard to keep clean: then bacteria appear and form acids, the acids destroy the enamel and eat through the dentin into the pulp cavity where the nerves and blood vessels are. This opens the door to organisms that cause infection. An acid-making organism which is always present in the mouth has an affinity for sugars and starches. Since the average American eats about 50 pounds of sugar a year, we candy-loving citizens are practically inviting dental troubles. Research has shown that people in war-torn countries who receive limited amounts of sugar in their food have remarkably little tooth decay.

Water Fluoridation

The effects of fluorine in preventing tooth decay first became known in 1902, when a dentist in Colorado Springs became curious about the brown stains on the teeth of some of his patients. As he studied this condition of "mottled enamel," as he called it, he discovered that it was caused by excessive fluorine in the drinking water. However, the interesting thing was that he found also that the people with the brown stains had less tooth decay. As a result of his study and of other research, it has been proven also that a dilute solution of sodium fluoride swabbed on children's teeth aids resistance to tooth decay.

An important outcome of this discovery is the water fluoridation program. A community can test its water supply, and if it is deficient in fluorine, fluorides can be added. It is estimated that 1 part fluoride to a million parts of water is an effective amount. Fluorides are available in toothpaste, bottled water or in tablets. However, the cheapest and most effective way to supply them is by fluoridation of a community water supply.

The Fluoridation Controversy. Approximately 51 million Americans are now drinking fluoridated water. Fluoridation has been approved by such outstanding authorities as the U.S. Public Health Service, the American Public Health Association, the World Health Association, the American Medical Association and many more. However, its acceptance as desirable is far from unanimous. About two-thirds of the population are still without fluoridated water. The decision to fluoridate is the individual community's, and this program is hotly debated. Efforts to pass federal or state laws to compel fluoridation meet with considerable resistance usually on the grounds that this is a matter for the individual community to decide or that fluoride may have harmful effects on the body that are not yet known.

Effects of Diet

Diet is very important when the teeth are forming. For the first 6 to 8 years of life, the minerals, calcium and phosphorus, and the vitamins A, C and D are essential to form normal teeth. Once the teeth are formed, starches and sugars are the only foods that have any effect on them—unfortunately, that effect is harmful. Diet also affects the gums and the jaws. If the vitamin and the mineral supply are inadequate, the jaw bones become porous and the teeth loosen; the gum tissues may become diseased.

Nutrition for young children may be inadequate if they belong to low-income families; the enormous consumption of candy bars and other sweets interferes with nutrition in teenage and older groups.

A Preventive Program

We have about half as many dentists as we need in the United States, which certainly is one reason for the poor state of dental health. The act of making an appointment with a dentist can be such a struggle that people resort to it only when something is wrong. This is not helpful to the growing belief that there should be far more emphasis on *preventive dentistry*, which recognizes the need for preventing dental ailments. In spite of the need in this field, only a small number of dentists go into public health dentistry. The public health-minded dentist encourages frequent cleaning of teeth by a dentist, emphasizes restricting sweets for children and keeps in touch with the patient's doctor to be informed about the patient's general health.

Progress in Dentistry

The improvements in dental technics have been many and satisfying. One of the most recent is success in transplanting a healthy tooth from one person's mouth to another's. This means that if for any reason a healthy tooth is knocked out accidentally or must be removed, it can be salvaged and replanted. Dentists report encouraging success with this technic.

Progress in Dental Health

Notwithstanding the technical improvements in dentistry and the growing change in attitude toward preventing dental health problems, progress is slow. A recent study indicates that in spite of 40 years of effort in dental health education over 100 million people never brush their teeth.

Dental Health for You

A ready smile is a valuable asset and nothing adds to its charm like gleaming white healthy teeth. Since one enemy of dental health is tooth decay your first concern will be about brushing your teeth. Of course, ideally, this always should be done after eating. Since it rarely is possible or convenient to do this, there is all the more reason for a thorough brushing morning and evening. Incidentally, it is well to remember that sticky sweets are the most active promoters of tooth decay.

Dentifrices

A dentifrice is a pleasant tasting powder or paste which acts as a mild abrasive in removing food particles from the teeth. In spite of each manufacturer's glowing claim for special ingredients in his product, one nationally advertised brand will probably do this as well as another. It should be used with a dry toothbrush with fairly stiff bristles. This means you will need at least 2 brushes. The electric toothbrush is a recent innovation which does the same work as the manual type—it just does it faster.

Halitosis

Of all the possible causes of social ostracism, *halitosis*, or breath odor, is well up on the list. This offense can seriously affect your working life, even to the extent of obtaining and keeping a job. It is up to you to make sure you are not an offender. The chances are the time-worn slogan "Even your best friend won't tell you" still holds true.

Persistent breath odor in itself is not a disease, but it may be a symptom of conditions that are a serious health hazard, such as tooth decay, pyorrhea or stomach or intestinal disorders. You need to know how to recognize these signs of dental trouble.

Dental Disorders

Dental *caries* is disintegration of the enamel and the dentin of the teeth. *Gingivitis* is inflammation of the gums. When gum tissues recede leaving spaces at the bases between the crowns of the teeth, particles get into those spaces and irritate the gums. Inflamed gums and gums that bleed easily are danger signs. The dentist removes the particles and applies an antiseptic to the broken surface. Dental examinations and cleaning of the teeth at least twice a year, a good diet and thorough tooth brushing help to prevent gingivitis.

Pyorrhea is destruction of the tissues around the teeth. Neglected gingivitis leads to pyorrhea. Tartar and food particles accumulate inside the gum line, the tissues shrink away from the teeth and pockets form. Organisms get into these pockets and set up infection that spreads and finally involves the bone; this weakens the support of the teeth so they become loose in their sockets. Improper bite also causes pyorrhea. Pyorrhea can be cured; if taken early enough, treatment prevents loss of teeth and jaw-bone damages. Pyorrhea does not always show bleeding gums or pockets. In some people, the teeth suddenly begin to separate, and within a year the bone around the teeth begins to disappear.

Mouthwashes

A word about mouthwashes, those products that figure so prominently in radio and television advertising with their alluring claims. One well-known product is said to have a $35 million market. However, users should realize that a mouthwash is useful mainly in removing food particles from the mouth. No mouthwash contains ingredients that of themselves can be guaranteed to prevent tooth decay or dental disease conditions; in fact, a normal mouth does not need the medications so highly advertised as beneficial. Nor will a mouthwash do more than "clean your breath" temporarily of a persistent breath odor. It may disguise the symptoms, but it does not remove the cause.

See Your Dentist

See your dentist at least twice a year, preferably more often, for the kind of thorough cleaning that only a dentist can give your teeth. If you need to choose a dentist, here are some pointers to help you to recognize a good one.

Choosing a Dentist. A good dentist is a graduate of a recognized dental school. He keeps up with developments in dentistry by belonging to his local and state dental associations, by reading his professional journals and by attending professional meetings.

He examines your teeth thoroughly and takes x-ray pictures of them. These pictures help to find difficulties that he could not otherwise see, and show pyorrhea and tooth abnormalities.

He consults with your physician about removing infected teeth that seem to be the cause of some other condition. He fits and matches dentures carefully and adjusts them. He advises you about preventive measures and reminds you by mail or telephone when it is time to see him again.

The *exodontist* is a specialist in tooth extraction. The *orthodontist* corrects dental defects such as protruding teeth or malocclusion (poor bite).

YOUR OWN EYES

Two things are important: know the signs of eye difficulty and consult an eye specialist for help. He is an *ophthalmologist*, or *oculist*, a physician especially trained in the care of eye disorders and the correction of vision difficulties. Because he is a physician also, he considers eye problems in relation to the body as a whole. He is the top authority, as compared to the *optician*, who grinds lenses and fills prescriptions for glasses, and the *optometrist*, who is qualified only to test for and correct errors in refraction.

Signs of Trouble

Danger signs that should send you to an ophthalmologist are persistent headaches, painful, watery, inflamed or discharging eyes and visual disturbances. To take chances with your eyesight is to risk serious interference with your career. General good health helps to keep your eyes bright and your sight keen. Diet deficiencies, lack of sleep and poor lighting have the opposite effect. Vitamin A, going to bed early and a 150-watt bulb will help to take care of these problems. Light falling on your book should measure about 15-foot candles, which is a 150-watt bulb. Bulbs should be shaded and frosted to eliminate glare; light rays should come from above and behind your shoulder. This applies both to studying and to reading in bed, and remember when reading to look up and away from the page occasionally—it rests your eyes.

Precautions To Take

Wash your hands before touching your eyes to avoid introducing infection. If something gets into your eye, do not rub it—you may only scratch your eyeball or embed a particle in the tissue. If tear secretions do not wash it out, do not ask the corner druggist to remove it; consult a doctor. Oculists discourage the use of an eye cup because of the danger of infection; the preparations advertised as effective in brightening and rejuvenating the eyes are probably harmless in themselves. One danger in using eyewashes is that you may be harming your eyes by using them as a substitute for needed medical attention.

Glasses

Fortunately, glasses are now so designed that they can enhance your appearance instead of detracting from it; many people actually look better with glasses than without them. If you must wear glasses, find the type that is most becoming; although you may yearn for the glamorous look, you should think twice before settling on over-bright colored frames encrusted with rhinestones unless you can afford 2 pairs!

Contact Lenses

If you are intrigued by the idea of contact lenses (the tiny lenses that fit over the eyeball), your first step should be to consult an ophthalmologist to determine if you can be fitted properly. This depends somewhat on the shape of your eyeball. In any case, you should know that contact lenses require adjustment too; they are expensive and can be irritating. They are most commonly used by entertainers or models for cosmetic reasons, or by athletes when eyeglasses would be hazardous.

Sun Glasses

Dark glasses that are carefully ground and do not distort vision are safe to use. For a person who already wears glasses, it is best to have dark glasses made to prescription.

SKIN, HANDS, HAIR AND FEET

Your Skin

A thorough understanding of body structure and functions is your best information in dealing with health problems. The next thing is to apply this knowledge. For example, the skin is one of the chief agents in eliminating waste products from the body. These wastes accumulate on the skin, and it requires soap and water to remove them. Use warm water and a mild soap. Do not use strong soaps if your skin is very dry. In fact, some people with very dry skins cannot use soap at all. If your skin tends to be oily, soap is essential. Do not forget that BO (offensive odor) is found especially in spots where perspiration tends to be excessive. Shave off underarm hair—it retains odors. Then use an antiperspirant—a deodorant only affects perspiration odor. It is not harmful to check perspiration in limited areas because your skin has countless other pores for elimination.

Your Face

Naturally, your first concern is your face. We have mentioned skin dryness and excess oil; another problem of the too oily skin is blackheads which may degenerate into pimples. Blackheads are collections of dead skin cells, oil and bacteria in the pores. Pimples are infected blackheads. If they go deep down into the skin (acne) they destroy the tissues and leave ugly scars. Again, first aid for these afflictions is cleanliness—thorough washing with soap and water several times a day. Avoid eating fried foods and an excess of candy bars in spite of the temptation to indulge in "snacks" in your off hours. A stubborn case of acne calls for medical advice.

Cosmetics. Cosmetics are big business in this country. Women spend millions of dollars every year searching for beauty. The trouble is that they are apt to rely on toilet preparations to do the job, and they overlook the importance of such health measures as cleanliness, a proper diet and elimination, exercise and rest. The extravagant claims which manufacturers make for their products are often misleading or downright false. For example, face creams can not "feed" the deeper layers of the skin although they can help to soften the outer layer. "Cover-up" preparations may partially conceal acne spots but they will not remove the cause. What it adds up to is that your health does affect the way you *look*.

Make-up. Most people look better with some make-up to bring out their good points and play down the less desirable ones. This is especially true as they grow older and lose some of the freshness and color that go with a younger skin. Powder, rouge and lipstick skillfully applied do have a tonic effect on your morale; when you look better you feel better. It is all a part of the impression you create. Naturally, you do not want to look so tired and worn out that patients hesitate to ask you for anything. Using a little care, you can find the shades of cosmetics that are right for you. Of course you will use these aids with discretion whether you are in or out of uniform. Although you may consider your off-duty appearance your personal affair, you will want to keep within the boundaries of good taste on any occasion.

Your Hands

Do not neglect your hands. Water tends to dry the skin, and a nurse has her hands in water often. A dry skin is susceptible to cracks and breaks that give easy access to bacteria and infection, so use a hand lotion that contains some fat or oil. A word about nails here—long nails break easily and could scratch your patients when you give baths and back-rubs. Bizarre or vivid nail polish is inappropriate with a uniform; it shows chips easily and there is nothing attractive about spotty nails. A neutral polish will solve this problem.

Your Hair

For sanitary reasons, certain restrictions are necessary about the arrangement of your hair. Therefore, you may be required to wear a hair net. Loose, flying locks or flakes of dandruff can be a menace to your patients' health. An over-elaborate hairdo is not appropriate with a uniform and will probably take more time to arrange than you have to give. You can follow prevailing hair styles without going to extremes. If you are tempted to experiment with the color of your hair, many harmless rinses are available. These rinses are not permanent and if you do not like the result you are not "stuck" with it. In any case, choose the new color to suit your skin and avoid making yourself appear ridiculous, whatever your age. Above all, depend on frequent shampoos and consistent brushing to keep your scalp and hair clean and shining.

Your Feet

"My feet are killing me!" And they could be—killing your chances of success because they interfere with your efficiency. Toeless shoes and barefoot sandals have made us conscious of how our feet look, but what is even more important, how do they feel? When your feet hurt, you hurt all over; your facial expression shows your distress, and yet the truth is most foot troubles can be prevented.

Arch Trouble. The foot bones are held together by ligaments and tendons. The foot framework forms 2 arches—the *lengthwise* arch from heel to toes and the *crosswise* arch across the ball of the foot. Weak muscles and ligaments let these arches down; they flatten out and cause *flatfoot*. This may happen suddenly or it may be such a gradual process that you hardly notice it at first; the first sign may be that your shoes seem too short. Look at your wet footprint—a nearly complete impression of your foot probably means flattened arches.

Your body weight should be distributed evenly between the heel and the toe. When you walk, you shift your metatarsal arches with every step. If your metatarsal arches are weak, your weight is carried by a few metatarsal bones instead of by all of them. This eventually causes discomfort and makes calluses on the soles of your feet.

Overweight puts extra strain on foot ligaments and muscles—so does poor posture. Poor muscle tone affects foot efficiency. Improper shoes cause so much foot trouble that we discuss them in detail.

Corns and Calluses. Corns and calluses are

caused by pressure or rubbing on some part of the foot, usually on the toes and soles. Corns are painful when the thickened epidermis presses on a nerve. The *chiropodist* is the person trained to treat corns and calluses; if you try to treat them yourself with razor blades or medications, you run the risk of infection. Shoes that do not fit properly are the usual cause of this foot problem.

Your Shoes. To begin with, your shoes should be suitable for your activities. Nurses are on their feet most of the time, so your "on-duty" shoes should give you the comfort and support your need. This means shoes long enough and wide enough to allow you to move your toes freely, with a sole at least ¼ inch thick, a heel with a broad base and not more than 1¾ inches high. Pointed-toed shoes crowd the toes and may cause a distortion (bunion) of the great toe. Very high, narrow heels throw the body off balance if you stand or walk on them constantly. You can wear spike heels and thin-soled shoes for occasions when you are not on your feet as much, but do not work in them.

If you have shoe-fitting difficulties, consult an orthopedist. The shoe salesman is not qualified to advise you about arches, lifts or pads for your shoes.

Athlete's Foot. Athlete's foot is a type of ringworm caused by a mold that infects the skin and nails. It flourishes in warm, moist places such as the floors around swimming pools and showers. As a foot infection it causes itching, watery blisters and peeling of the skin between the toes. Treatment should be prescribed by a physician since it usually includes medication of some kind as well as directions for observing precautions to prevent spreading the infection.

Foot Care. Foot care begins with cleanliness and extends to proper shoe selection with orthopedic advice on serious problems. Above all, remember the old saying that "an ounce of prevention is worth a pound of cure!"

SEX EDUCATION

Primitive peoples were matter-of-fact about sex; civilization has set up the walls that put sex information out of bounds. The result is a hodgepodge of wrong ideas, superstitions and self-consciousness about a relationship that is vital to our very existence. We have paid for this mistake in money, illness and unhappiness. Because sex relationships are emotional as well as physical, it has seemed difficult to discuss the reproductive organs or the process of pregnancy. The mental and the spiritual aspects of sex put sex experience on a higher plane than that of the physical relationship alone. On the other hand, ignorance of the physical side of sex disturbs spiritual and emotional relationships and leads to unhappiness.

The community accepts certain rules about sex relationships. The family unit is founded on marriage, and the rules protect it. Many people break the rules because they do not understand the body processes of fertilization or the strength of sex urges; they are equally as ignorant of the emotional and the spiritual effects. The sex urge is strong enough to outweigh reason temporarily, but society is hard on the person who breaks the rules and threatens the accepted family pattern.

Sex education begins by creating, in a child's mind, healthy attitudes about his body. As he grows up, give him honest answers to his questions and sound information about his body and its functions. Give him the right names for the parts of the body. Never appear shocked by his curiosity. Often parents are self-conscious about explaining sex because they do not understand body processes and do not know the rights words to use.

Sex consciousness begins with puberty; the hormones become active and increase emotional drives which must find ways to express themselves. Young people who do not understand the possible results of sexual intercourse are exposed to the dangers of venereal disease and to the social and the economic problems presented by pregnancy outside of marriage. Petting, necking and the use of alcohol and some drugs can stimulate the sex urges to a point beyond the individual's control. People should understand that intimate physical relations have definite consequences, because the body does carry out its functions. Salutary sex relations are built on a belief that sex has an emotional and spiritual side, on an acceptance of social conventions and understanding of the structure and the functions of the reproductive system.

MENSTRUAL HEALTH HABITS

Menstruation is a normal process.* During your menstrual period you should be able to exercise, take baths and live as you normally would. In fact, doctors recommend following the usual routine with special attention to cleanliness to prevent body odor. They also endorse using vaginal tampons (instead of pads), provided they are changed often enough to prevent irritation. As a rule, they do not recommend douches after menstruation as vaginal irrigation is not necessary for a normal, healthy vagina. So if you have been thinking of your condition during your menstrual period as "delicate" and requiring special treatment, you may be relieved to learn that it is old-fashioned to take to your bed as a semi-invalid every month.

Try to relax when your menstrual period is due and avoid the "cramps" caused by tense muscles. Heat over the pelvic area relieves minor discomforts. Of course it is possible for an anatomical or functional irregularity to cause menstrual difficulties. If pains or backache are persistent or severe enough to incapacitate you, consult a doctor for examination and advice.

The Menopause

The *menopause* marks the end of reproductive functions, and this may be a matter of relief or regret to the individual woman. In any event, certain physical changes are taking place which may be accompanied by unpleasant feelings. As ovulation gradually stops, such symptoms as fatigue, irritability and hot flashes appear. Feelings of depression are not unusual; a woman may feel she is unwanted or unneeded and that nothing really matters any more. Her children no longer need all of her attention and time hangs heavy on her hands, especially if she has few outside interests. Her mirror reminds her of her age, she gains weight and feels hopelessly unattractive.

Taken under a doctors' direction, small doses of hormones are effective in relieving these unpleasant symptoms. An extra effort toward good grooming, becoming clothes and attention to diet may be necessary at this time and it will be worthwhile. Many women do not know that the menopause does not bring an end to sex life; normal sexual relations can continue for many years.

Consult a Doctor

Consult your doctor about any of the following irregularities:

1. Vaginal bleeding between periods
2. Vaginal bleeding after the menopause
3. Excessive menstrual flow
4. Absence of menstruation before the usual time menopause would be expected. (Exceptions are during pregnancy and sometimes while breast-feeding a baby.)

And remember, after 35, a yearly gynecological examination should be routine for *every woman* for early discovery and treatment of actual or potential malignant conditions.

EXERCISE AND REST

Exercise

If body tissues are not used they atrophy and die. One of the reasons for exercise is to maintain muscle tone so we need some variety in exercise to benefit muscles in different parts of the body. An individual's age, occupation and general condition help to determine the amount and kind of exercise that is best for him; one man's meat may be another man's poison. Sports provide exercise, fun and relaxation at the same time. However, walking, gardening and household activities also exercise both large and small muscles. Nursing activities—bending, lifting, stretching, walking—provide exercise every day. A moderate amount of daily exercise is better than occasional spurts of strenuous activity. In general, we are told that up to 40 exercise should be enough to promote

* See Chapter 19.

muscle growth, and after that enough to maintain muscle tone.

The Physical Fitness Program

The late President Kennedy, disturbed by the number of draftees rejected for military service for physical reasons, appointed a Council on Physical Fitness whose job it is to urge people to work with school officials and community groups to encourage a program of physical fitness for everybody. The Council has prepared a booklet "Adult Physical Fitness,"* which describes a series of exercises for men and women that can be carried out in the home. It begins with gentle exercises and gradually works up to more challenging ones—a program that the Council says will make people "feel better, look better and perform more efficiently."

Sleep, Rest and Relaxation

Everyone does not need the same amount of sleep. You can tell if you are getting enough if you wake up rested and ready to go. You can expect some fatigue after a healthy day's work, but it should be normally nothing that a good night's sleep will not cure. If you are chronically tired, something is wrong, and you need medical advice. Sometimes after a day's work, rest is needed rather than sleep. Try lying relaxed and letting your thoughts drift. A change of activity is also restful, or watching television, listening to the radio or reading.

* Available from the Superintendent of Documents, Government Printing Office, Washington, D.C. 20402 (a best-seller at 35¢).

IF YOU HAVE A COLD

Your best cold preventive is good general health, which means among other things, a balanced diet and the right proportion of rest and recreation. Then keep away from people with colds; do not handle things they touch. Avoid sudden changes in temperature—this means drafts or going from a hot room into the cold outside air without a coat.

If you do catch a cold, stay away from other people. Go to bed and stay quiet. Eat balanced meals, take fruit juices and plenty of water; scald your dishes with boiling water; isolate

Fig. 7. This photograph, taken under a very short exposure (1/30,000 of a second), shows a cloud of minute droplets from the nose and throat at the climax of a sneeze. The moisture evaporates, leaving many germ-laden particles of matter floating in the air for other people to breathe. (American Society of Bacteriology)

your towels and toilet articles. Use disposable tissues instead of handkerchiefs; do not put used ones into your handbag or pockets. Wash your hands often, especially after blowing your nose. Cover your mouth when you cough or sneeze. Once you have a cold, you are responsible for protecting other people. The sneezing, dripping individual who refuses to stay at home is a menace to himself and to everyone else (see Fig. 7).

Call your doctor if cold symptoms persist or new symptoms appear. Severe aches and pains, a considerable elevation of temperature or continued coughing are signs of more serious conditions. Consult your doctor if you have one cold after another.

If you are under 45, periodic chest x-ray pictures are important, especially if you feel tired all the time, lose weight or have a cough. Tuberculosis organisms get in their deadly work during these years. Have physical conditions, such as infected tonsils or enlarged adenoids, corrected. Avoid forcibly drawing in solutions up the nostrils; blow your nose gently, with both nostrils open. Be careful about getting water in your nasal passages when you swim.

Colds and other infectious diseases pave the way for ear infections. Wax tightly packed in the auditory canal affects hearing—enlarged tonsils, adenoids or nasal trouble can damage it permanently. Protect your ears when you swim, especially if you dive or swim under the water. If your hearing becomes seriously impaired, consult an ear specialist to find out whether or not a hearing aid will help you.

MAIN IDEAS OF THIS CHAPTER

Your personal health habits can help or hinder you physically and mentally. Every nurse wants to be able to withstand the physical exertion involved in nursing and to feel at ease mentally, knowing that she is liked by her patients and by those with whom she works.

Personal attractiveness can be attained only if poor health habits are recognized as such and a conscious persistent effort is made to correct them.

Your posture, the way you sit and the way you use your body all play a part in your health and efficiency.

Balanced nutrition is essential for good health. Overweight and underweight people usually consume too much or too little food although a glandular disturbance may sometimes be the cause.

Proper eating and elimination habits not only contribute to good health, but also enable you to attain more efficiency in your work.

Many eye and teeth problems can be prevented if signs of abnormalities are recognized early and care is given immediately. Although fluoridation of water is endorsed by most of our national public health organizations as a preventative measure in tooth decay, there is still some controversy, and about two-thirds of the population are still without fluoridation.

The condition of your skin, hands, hair and the discretion with which you use cosmetics all affect the impression you make on those around you.

A healthy understanding and acceptance of sex relationships develop only if a child receives the proper sex education.

The necessary amount of exercise, sleep, rest and relaxation varies with individuals. Adequate amounts of each plus a balanced diet are your best protection against physical and mental illness.

ADAPTING SKILLS TO SITUATIONS

Unless ordered by the doctor, why would you not insist that a patient eat his regular full meal immediately following a lengthy treatment which caused much pain, some of which still persisted?

What would your reply be to the patient who complained that his bowels moved only every 2 or 3 days?

Is the water in your community fluoridated? If so, what is the purpose of the fluoridation?

List the procedures your dentist might take in giving you routine preventive dental care.

What are the abnormal patterns of vaginal bleeding that would indicate the necessity for a consultation with a doctor?

6

COMMUNITY HEALTH

HEALTH PROTECTION

We used to think of disease as the main cause of poor health. It still is responsible, but not so much as it used to be. The health of people in the United States has improved rapidly in the last 50 years. Improvement began when we realized that it was important to prevent disease—that this was the responsibility of national, state and local authorities. For instance, citizens in the city must use the water the city provides from a water supply. If sewage contaminates the water, the health of the entire community is endangered; certain infectious diseases are easily communicated from one person to another. A town or a city is responsible for protecting the health of its residents, and this health protection means keeping the city clean and providing safe water, uncontaminated food, safe buildings and health services as well. It also means health education.

Public Health Problems

Health problems are not exactly the same in every community. To begin with, they are related to the country, the climate, the food habits and the living standards of the people who live there. Some racial groups have large families and are accustomed to living in crowded quarters; others will eat only a few types of food. Illiterate people are influenced by superstitions and fears that lead to poor health habits and the wrong kind of medical care. In an industrial city, lay-offs and shut-downs increase health problems. Depressions, wars, housing shortages and rising costs of living also affect health.

Health Agencies

Group action is the most effective way of dealing with health problems. In this as in every country, health problems increase with the population. This leads to a need to organize groups to deal with these problems by setting up measures for health protection. Today we have many such groups on national, state and local levels. Some of them are official agencies of the federal, state or municipal governments, known as public health departments and are supported by public funds. Others are independent or voluntary agencies such as the American Heart Association or the National Tuberculosis Association, supported by voluntary contributions from individuals and groups.

Federal Agencies. On the national level, the federal government agency concerned with health is the United States Public Health Service (USPHS), one of several agencies under the Department of Health, Education and Welfare. The other agencies are the Food and Drug Administration, the Social Security Administration, the Office of Vocational Rehabilitation and the Office of Education.

The USPHS has many responsibilities for health protection, including the investigation and control of all diseases, protection from diseases carried by immigrants, control of sanitation on trains, ships and aircraft in interstate commerce, control of the manufacture and sale of biological products and the cooperation with state health departments in disease control. It is also responsible for publishing and distributing health information.

Many other departments of the federal government have a hand in health protection; for example, the Department of Agriculture through its various bureaus is concerned with the control of insect and animal-borne diseases, with meat and other food inspection, and the Bureau of Internal Revenue enforces the anti-narcotic laws.

State Health Departments. State health departments, through their divisions or bureaus, are responsible for health protection within a state. Their services are concerned with sanitation, food and water inspection, maternal and child health, public health nursing, laboratory services, vital statistics and others. State health laws must conform to federal laws, but states also have the right to make their own health laws as necessary to protect the health of the people.

City Health Departments. City health departments are concerned with the health protection within a city. Sometimes this interest is extended to provide health services to the county as well—which thus enables health services to reach more people and make more services possible. Usually the health department operates under a Board of Health which sets up policies and regulations which are carried out under the direction of a health officer, preferably a doctor with public health training. A city health department provides services in relation to conditions that affect everyone: it inspects places where food is sold, food handlers, water and milk supply, housing, sewage and other waste disposal, and provides services regarding air pollution. It provides school health services and health education, clinics, hospital and nursing care. Health protection in a large city is big business.

Local Health Services. Health protection in

FIG. 8. This health center serves a rural community in Maine.

rural areas and in towns and villages is provided by county, district or local health units (see Fig. 8). Each unit has its own health department which aims to provide the same basic services as those supplied by a city health department. The state health department supervises and gives consultant services to health units.

HEALTH MENACES

This atomic age we live in with its rapid advance in chemical discoveries and industrial development has intensified our health problems; the chemicals used in insecticides and detergents and the smoke from industrial plants and the fall-out from nuclear testing poison the air we breathe, the water we drink and the food we eat. Evidence of harmful effects is piling up and we are increasingly exposed to them in our everyday lives by air and water pollution.

Air Pollution

Air pollution is greatest in industrial areas, but every large city has some air pollution problems, even though it may have comparatively few industries, as is the case in Washington, D.C. Another source of air pollution is the exhausts from automobiles. The smog situation in Los Angeles is the result of the combined action of fog, smoke and automobile exhaust gases which produces substances harmful to health. Smog also causes crop damage.

Air pollution has been shown to be responsible for increases in respiratory infections such as chronic bronchitis, asthmatic attacks and emphysema. Heavy air pollution will cause irritation of the eyes, nose and throat, which may possibly have further serious effects not yet known on health. Air pollution also damages plant growth and affects buildings.

The Air Pollution Control Act in 1955 authorized the Surgeon General of the U. S. Public Health Service to look into the problem of air pollution. Five million dollars a year for 4 years was appropriated by Congress for a research program which included aid to states and cooperation with private agencies concerned with this problem.

Water Pollution

Water pollution is a serious health hazard that is increasing. A number of diseases are transmitted by contaminated water. Typhoid fever, dysentery and infectious hepatitis are noted examples. Water pollution not only affects people, but it is also a menace to wildlife and fish and recreation areas. It is estimated that 45 million fish were killed in the United States last year by polluted water. Increasing demands on the national water supply make it necessary to reuse water, and this calls for treatment of waste water to make it safe for reuse. In many areas this treatment is inadequate. In 1963 it was found that over 1,500 communities were discharging untreated sewage into their streams; more than 2,000 small towns had no sewer or treatment facilities at all.

Water pollution from detergents is a growing problem. It causes difficulties in sewage treatment plants, puts foam in drinking water and kills fish also. This leads to questions about the harmful effect of detergents on human health. This subject is being considered as part of the federal government's increased concern about water pollution by sewage and insecticides.

The federal government has a responsibility for insuring a safe water supply for the people in this country. Until recently, our national government had little or no authority to do this; it was left up to state and local governments. Legislation now gives the Public Health Service the authority and the funds to establish waste treatment projects.

Safe Water. Every community uses large quantities of water for drinking, cooking, bathing, cleaning and many manufacturing processes. Therefore, precautions must be taken to inspect the water supply at its source and to make sure that the water is not contaminated before it is used. Some famous examples of epidemics were traced to contaminated water. The best and safest water is clear, odorless, free from poisonous metals, disease germs and particles of sand or soil; it is soft enough to lather easily with soap.

Water Supply. Water comes from 2 sources: surface water and ground water. *Surface water* is the rain that falls into rivers and lakes. Because they are fed by small streams that run over the earth and contain plants and animals, surface water is often full of impurities. *Ground water* is the water that soaks into the earth just below the surface. Ground water passes through layers of sand and soil that filter out many of the impurities but can be contaminated if waste from stables and outside toilet facilities seeps into it. Well water is ground water. Water from a deep well is usually safer than water from a surface well, but this is not true if the soil around it is polluted.

Purifying Water. Trained workers in health departments analyze samples of water and test them for disease organisms. Water that comes from thickly populated districts and washes down slopes is more likely to be contaminated than water that comes from places where only a few people live, where there is therefore less animal and human waste. If the water supply is not safe for use, it can be purified by artificial means, such as aeration, filtration through sand, or by adding chemicals to it. Cities have reservoirs and filtration plants to purify the water supply. In camps or in the country where you are not certain that the water is safe, boil it for 10 minutes. Chlorine tablets can also be used to purify water. The public health engineer or the water chemist determines how much chlorine is needed to purify a water supply. You can send a sample of water to a local or a state health department to have it analyzed.

Insecticides

The rapid rise in the use of insecticides to kill insects is just beginning to be recognized as a serious threat to health. It was known that they can have harmful effects on vegetation and wildlife, but we now have evidence of their harmful effects on human beings through pollution of the air, food and water. Drift from plant spraying can cause poison seepage into nearby streams which contaminates fish and shellfish which are used for food. Spraying of crops that are used as food sources, such as cotton, where the seeds are a source of cooking oil, can endanger health. Articles contaminated by insecticides are other death-causing sources. One chemical that is widely used in vaporizers in spraying homes, restaurants and offices is reported to have profound and lasting damaging effects on the central nervous system.

A former government biologist warned us of a grim future when all birds and wildlife will have been destroyed unless something is done to curb the extensive and often irresponsible use of insecticides.* Her testimony before a Senate committee alerted government authorities to the need for stricter regulations. The United States Public Health Service has about 250 air sampling stations throughout the country, including Alaska, Hawaii and Puerto Rico.

The Department of Agriculture is the federal agency responsible for setting up regulations about the use of insecticides. One of the requirements is adequate warning on insecticide labels of the dangers in their use. Health authorities are asking that warnings about dangers to health from the use of pesticide sprays be more plainly emphasized on the product label.

Fall-Out

Another by-product of the atomic age that threatens health is fall-out from nuclear testing. The firing of nuclear test bombs (radiation in the air) releases the chemical *strontium-90*; particles falling upon the earth contaminate vegetation which is used for food by animals and man. Amounts of strontium-90 above a certain level are known to have harmful effects on the organs of reproduction and on the bone marrow. According to the Federal Radiation Council, which keeps a close watch on the amount of fall-out in the atmosphere, the amount found in food up to the present time is not enough to be dangerous to human health. Growing foods that are exposed to the air such as wheat grains, salad greens and apples are highest in fall-out contamination. The human body will absorb calcium in preference to strontium-90, so foods containing calcium are

* *Silent Spring* by Rachel Carson.

a protection against harmful radiation. Milk itself actually contains a great deal of strontium, but it is also so high in calcium that it is one of the safest foods.

A recent treaty (1963) banning nuclear bomb tests above the ground for the present alleviates the worry about a dangerous increase in fall-out.

CONTROLLING THE PROBLEMS

The FDA

The Food and Drug Administration (FDA) under the Food, Drug and Cosmetic Act, is the Federal agency responsible for seeing that the people of the United States have pure food, safe and effective drugs and safe cosmetics. This is a mammoth job in the face of the rapid increase in the use of chemicals and in the number of new drugs presented for approval. FDA regulations apply to all foods, drugs and cosmetics that are imported or shipped from one state to another.

Food Protection

FDA food protection is concerned with the safety and purity of foods. The regulations apply to commercially processed and prepared foods and include protection from possible dangers in the use of food "additives" such as coloring, nutrients and preservatives. They also require true and accurate labeling of food products. The manufacturer must present proof that the product meets FDA standards for safety. For example, the statement that food is "artificially colored" is not enough without assurance that the coloring matter has been used in a safe amount.

States and cities make their own laws about foods sold within their boundaries. These laws include regulations about places that serve food, such as hotels, restaurants, lunchrooms, soda fountains, shops and markets. They also require health examinations for food handlers.

Milk Protection

Some foods are so widely used as a part of the daily diet that it is doubly important to make sure they are of good quality and safe to use. One of these foods is milk; it is an essential food, and people use it in large quantities.

Milk is contaminated easily and is a carrier for the organisms that cause tuberculosis, undulant fever, typhoid fever, paratyphoid fever, scarlet fever, dysentery, diphtheria and infantile paralysis. Health regulations protect the milk supply by requiring inspection of dairy animals for Bang's disease and tuberculosis, inspection of dairy barns, health examinations for all milk handlers and clean utensils.

Pasteurization is the greatest protection against milk-borne disease. Pasteurization kills harmful organisms and makes milk safe to use. The process does not affect the taste and does

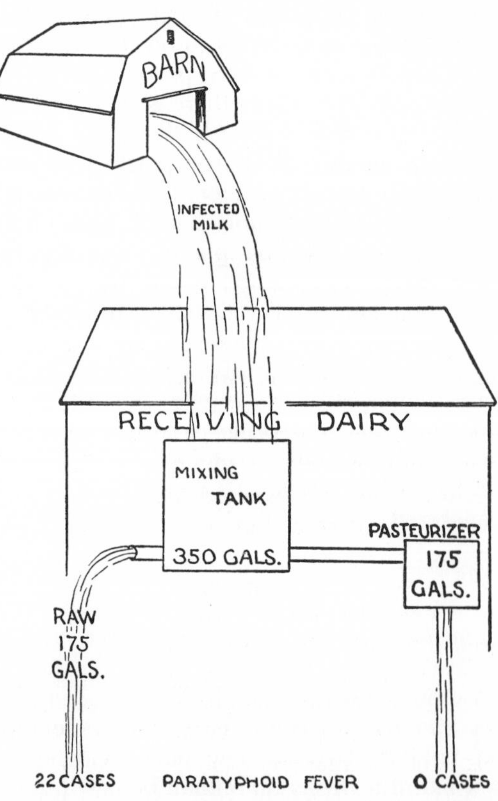

FIG. 9. Occurrence of paratyphoid fever from infected milk and absence when such milk is pasteurized. (Broadhurst, J.: Home and Community Hygiene, Philadelphia, Lippincott)

not destroy the harmless bacteria that make the milk sour. A commonly used method of pasteurization is the process of heating milk to 161°F. for at least 15 seconds.

Certified milk means that a milk commission has certified that the milk has been produced under the best conditions and is of high quality.

Milk is *graded* in some cities, and the ratings are published so that people may know the kind of milk they are getting. The grades show the differences in the bacterial count. For your own information, find out what the practice is in the city where you live.

The United States Public Health Service, under its Milk Ordinance Code, has established requirements for milk supplies. People should insist that the milk they are using meets these requirements. Even in this country, some people still are using unpasteurized milk.

Meat Protection

Meat is another food that is used in large quantities. Federal, state and local health departments make and enforce regulations about preparing and distributing meat; they inspect and supervise slaughterhouses to be sure that the buildings are clean, that the meat is handled carefully and that the workers are free from communicable disease. Animals are inspected for organisms that cause dysentry, tularemia, undulant fever, trichinosis, tapeworm, tuberculosis and enteritis—all diseases that can be contracted through infected meat.

Inspectors from a bureau of the U.S. Department of Agriculture examine every carcass that is shipped from one state to another and also inspect the places where the meat is prepared for distribution. Meat that has been approved is stamped "U.S. Inspected" in purple letters. It is somewhat appalling to note that a large number of states have no inspection controls over the marketing of meat *within* their borders, in spite of the fact that uninspected meat cannot be considered safe to use.

Food Poisoning

In spite of precautions, outbreaks of food poisoning occur periodically and can be traced to unsanitary preparation and careless handling of food. Among the foods most often affected are poultry, meat, custard-filled pastries, fish and potato salads and frozen eggs. A recent outbreak of food poisoning caused by *salmonella* bacteria was traced to the use of cracked eggs, sometimes sold as "seconds." *Botulism* is a disease caused by an organism in soil, and if it is not killed in the proper cleaning and processing of garden produce it produces a virulent poison in the body.

Drugs and Health

The Federal Drug Administration is the national agency charged with the responsibility of protecting the public from harmful drugs and from false claims about the efficiency of a drug. The first attempt at this kind of protection was the Federal Food, Drug and Cosmetic Act passed in 1938. In 1951 the law was amended to curb abuses in the use of additional dangerous drugs, such as sleeping pills, thyroid pills, sex hormones and antibiotics. The amendment required pharmaceutical companies to label all drugs that were considered potentially dangerous, with the caution to druggists that the drugs were not to be dispensed without a doctor's prescription.

FDA Approval. Since 1951, the many new discoveries in the treatment of disease have led to the production of a vast number of new drugs. It is estimated at more than 400 every year. Before the FDA approves a drug, it requires evidence that the drug does what it claims to do, and that it has been clinically tested on a sufficient number of patients for an adequate length of time to prove it is safe for use.

To obtain this evidence, the pharmaceutical companies' chemists first test the effects of a new drug on laboratory animals; then samples of the drug are sent to doctors throughout the country with the information about these effects. Doctors use the drug in treating patients (clinically test it) to observe its effects on human beings—it takes months and sometimes years to get enough accurate and reliable information to evaluate the effects of a drug and to publish reports of its approval or nonapproval in medical journals for the information of every doctor.

AMA Council on Drugs. The American Medical Association's Council on Drugs gives information to doctors about drugs and releases an annual list of new drugs. The Council is also establishing a central registry in Chicago to provide up-to-date information about unfavorable effects of drugs and chemicals. It is estimated that approximately 1 million people suffer every year from the side effects of drugs they have taken to make them well.

Worthless Remedies. Unfortunately, the market is flooded with an endless number of worthless and unapproved remedies: they claim to bring sleep, remove pain, lengthen life and cure arthritis, cancer and dozens of other ailments ranging from dental caries to athlete's foot. One preparation listed 18 conditions for which it was effective. The fly-by-night companies that bring out these products are interested only in making money, and, unfortunately, people always can be found who are willing to furnish testimonials about the benefits that they think they have received. The FDA frequently finds it necessary to file judgments against such companies for making false claims about their products. Why are so many people taken in by claims for a drug? For one thing, they do not know how to tell the difference between true and false claims. Also, as one victim remarked: "on your bed of pain, you will try anything, at any cost."

Tighter Control

The mounting number of reports of harmful effects from the use of drugs now on the market is arousing health authorities to the necessity for more stringent control over the sale of drugs. The need for an alert federal watchdog was demonstrated by a recent and much publicized controversy over the drug thalidomide, a tranquilizer, the use of which in Europe caused hundreds of pregnant women to give birth to deformed babies. A medical member of the FDA staff, Dr. Frances Kelsey, steadfastly refused to approve this drug for use in the United States, in spite of pressure from the manufacturer.* Her grounds for refusal were based on the failure of the pharmaceutical company to present sufficient evidence, through testing, that the drug was safe to use.

Waste Disposal. Waste is rubbish, garbage and animal and human body waste. All waste is a possible source of disease if it is not disposed of safely. Disease organisms lie in wait in dust and dirt, in remnants of food and in material eliminated from the body. Sanitation laws prevent the spread of disease through waste; in cities, the health department makes definite regulations and provides trucks and a working crew to collect and dispose of garbage and rubbish. Incinerators and garbage disposal plants take care of it.

In villages and on farms, people need to be equally careful, but they have to work out their own methods. This means burning garbage and refuse and keeping it in covered containers.

Cities build sewage systems, and home plumbing connects directly with them. Health regulations say that all garbage should be placed in closed cans and that it should be destroyed promptly; flies and other insects breed in garbage and body wastes and spread disease. Mechanical garbage disposal units are now available for home use.

HEALTH ENEMIES

Controlling Communicable Diseases

Since one of the primary purposes in controlling communicable disease is to prevent it from developing in the first place, immunization programs play an important part in health protection. It is now possible to protect people against an increasing number of diseases by giving them injections of a specific vaccine, antitoxin or serum (see Chap. 7). These preparations give protection for varying lengths of time. The National Institute of Health is the federal agency that controls the approval of these products and sets up standards that the manufacturer must meet.

* Dr. Frances Kelsey later was awarded the nation's highest honor for federal civilian service.

Spreading of Disease

In spite of precautions to prevent disease, people do get sick, so health authorities have another responsibility—they must keep disease from spreading. This is how the diseases that spread by person-to-person contact, the communicable diseases, are controlled: (1) state laws require physicians to report specific cases to the local health department, (2) the health department sees that persons sick with a communicable disease are isolated. It also puts persons exposed to a communicable disease under restrictions for the length of time that it takes the disease to develop. *Quarantine* means that no one may enter or leave a house where there is a communicable disease; *isolation* means that no one enters the room of a sick person except the person who is taking care of him. Regulations are not identical for every disease. You will learn how to isolate a patient to protect others and yourself.

Some communicable diseases affect large numbers of the population because some people do not take precautions, do not recognize the symptoms or fail to have treatment. You should know what some of these diseases are because they are health problems in every community.

Venereal Diseases

Syphilis and *gonorrhea,* the most common venereal diseases, disable many people every year and cost taxpayers thousands of dollars. These diseases are acquired usually through sexual intercourse, and, in the early stages, people are not disabled. Therefore, these diseases are called *hidden.* Infected persons often do not have treatment soon enough to protect their own health and they continue to infect others.

Early treatment will cure syphilis and gonorrhea, in most instances; if these diseases progress without treatment, they may affect the entire body of the victim, and in the case of syphilis, the mind as well. Some become disabled and may require so much care that they have to be placed in institutions. The U.S. Public Health Service and state and local health departments work tirelessly to prevent the spread of venereal disease. They make venereal disease reportable, provide laboratory and consultant services, set up treatment centers and distribute information explaining the symptoms and the dangers. They urge a blood test as a part of every health examination and also for every hospital patient and for every pregnant woman. Some states now require a physical examination and a blood test before granting a marriage license. The American Social Hygiene Association is active in the campaign against venereal disease. Penicillin has proved to be a powerful factor in the cure of syphilis and gonorrhea.

A Teenage Problem. We are always concerned about health problems that affect many people, especially the young people, who will carry on the human race and do the world's work in the future. Since 1957, the syphilis rate in America has risen more than 130 per cent, with a shocking increase in the incidence of venereal disease in the teenage group. This problem is not confined to slum areas or juvenile delinquents. It also appears in good neighborhoods and in nice families.

The rapid rise in venereal disease among teenagers is attributed to a number of causes: for one thing, families move frequently. This means that the children's circle of friends changes constantly and they find themselves in groups with varying standards of right or wrong; mothers work outside the home—young people return from school to a home where there is no adult; grandparents are no longer apt to be near to consult (even if young people today would think of consulting them, which is doubtful); and children are forced into a premature maturity. They have more money, cars make it easy to get away from supervision, they see sex constantly emphasized in the movies and on television, drinking is common and chaperones almost extinct. In short, their moral standards are confused or even nonexistent.

The discovery of penicillin brought such a rapid drop in venereal disease that federal funds for public health venereal disease clinics and health education were sharply reduced. Authorities agree that accurate and honest sex and health education are vitally needed to protect adolescents against venereal disease. In one large city, a study of teenagers showed that only 10 per cent knew what venereal disease is or that it is practically always contracted through sexual intercourse. Aside from the moral implications of promiscuous sexual intercourse, young people should know that venereal disease can blind, cripple and kill, cause insanity and sterility and damage unborn children.

The Common Cold

More than half of the people in the United States have 2 colds every year—one quarter of them have 3 colds or more. Having colds costs people a considerable amount of money. The cost runs into big figures in a year, counting the cost of drugs and medical care and the amount of wages lost. The health cost is also high, because colds pave the way for more serious illnesses, such as sinus and ear infections, arthritis, pneumonia and tuberculosis. Schools, industry, business, and federal, state and local health departments provide information about preventing colds; health services are trying to keep people from spreading the infection by sending them home from work and prescribing rest and isolation. Scientists have not discovered any one sure way to prevent and treat colds; although some discoveries benefit some people, colds are still a major health problem.

Tuberculosis

Tuberculosis kills thousands of people in the United States every year. It is a serious threat to health because it is communicable, and many people with tuberculosis do not know that they have it. Tuberculosis renders wage earners useless; it attacks young people. Such devices as making chest x-ray pictures on a mass basis with groups of school children and with groups of workers, such as food handlers, together with special hospitals for tuberculous patients and improved treatment, have pushed the tuberculosis death rate down. Fifty years ago, tuberculosis ranked 1st on the list of all causes of death in the United States. Public health agencies train and find jobs for people who have had tuberculosis, provide laboratory services and pay for the care of patients. The U.S. Public Health Service gives state and local health departments millions of dollars every year and supplies consultants to states to help in the fight against tuberculosis. The National Tuberculosis Association has been fighting this disease since 1904 through state and local associations. They raise the money for their work through the sale of the familiar Christmas seals.

It is true that fewer people are dying from tuberculosis. The drugs *isoniazid* and *streptomycin* arrest the development of the tubercle bacillus, the causative organism, but these drugs may not kill all of the bacilli in the patient. Therefore, continued treatment is important to control the disease and protect others. There is less tuberculosis infection in the school age group today, but the number of infections in people past middle age has increased. Tuberculosis is still a major health problem.

Heart Disease

Heart disease is our greatest health enemy. As a cause of death in the United States, it leads the list and kills and disables millions. It accounts for 2.25 times as many deaths as does cancer, which is second on the list. It is estimated that more than 5 million people in this country have some form of heart disease. It afflicts the young as well as the older age group.

Fortunately, medical progress in understanding and in treating heart disease holds strong hope for a brighter picture in the future. A great deal of research is going on to find out more about the causes and treatment of heart disease and high blood pressure. Special attention is being given to discovering the relation of fats in the diet to heart disease and to perfecting advances in heart surgery.

The American Heart Association and its branches encourage research, the education of both medical and lay people and cooperation between all health groups in the fight against heart disease. Films, exhibits, magazine articles and pamphlets tell the story of this public enemy. Every community is urged to make special efforts to distribute this information, especially during National Heart Week. Some cities have established heart clinics, and the American Heart Association is determined to make heart care soon available to everyone.

Medical Quackery

Millions of people spend countless dollars every year on supposedly sure cures for every imaginable ailment. False claims for food supplements, drugs, treatments and various devices induce people to spend money which they may actually need for food. More serious still, people who turn to quacks for help instead of to reputable physicians may be delaying vital treatment until it is too late. One study of people who had been admitted to a hospital after being in the hands of quacks, showed that nearly half of those who died could have been saved by earlier medical treatment.

Cancer and arthritis "cures,"* machines purporting to give off healing "z" rays (there is no such thing as a "z" ray), and so-called electrotherapy treatments also entrap people with real or imaginary ailments. The sale of many of these devices has been made illegal, but new ones keep turning up. Although the Federal Trade Commission has the power to crack down on false advertising, there are ways of getting around such action. For example, there is no way to prevent books from advocating any practice in the name of health so long as they do not commercialize a specific product.

Alcoholism

Alcoholism is a disease that makes people drink to such an extent that they cannot carry on normal lives. It causes so much human suffering and loss of ability and costs so much in crime and accidents and care that it is a national health and economic problem (one of the top 4), for which the nation pays over a billion dollars a year. Estimates put the number of alcoholics in the United States at more than 5 million. Some of these alcoholics are the town drunkards; a great many more are able to maintain the appearance of normal behavior most of the time. Yet it is said that 1 out of every 16 of the 65 million people who drink alcoholic beverages is a problem drinker. He, or she (there are a great many women alcoholics), has trouble holding a job, causes family suffering and gradually deteriorates mentally and physically.

Alcohol acts on the brain and spinal cord; it dims unpleasant feelings, but increased amounts of it bring confusion and stupor. The effects on an individual depend on his sensitivity to it and on the amount he takes. It has certain poisonous effects upon the body—in excess, it lowers body resistance and interferes with body nutrition because alcoholics substitute alcohol for food; it leads to personality changes and mental illness; it slows up and confuses brain responses; there are far too many examples of driving accidents and industrial injuries and illicit sex conduct occurring because people were temporarily unable to use good judgment when under the influence of alcohol.

The Symptoms of Alcoholism. Certain symptoms of alcoholism are easily recognized; an alcoholic will often drink alone; need a drink the first thing in the morning; and go on periodic drinking sprees. Drinking will interfere with his work in time lost and inability to think straight. As his illness progresses, people begin to avoid him; he feels remorseful and guilty and tries to stop drinking. He may even seek medical help, but his drinking steadily increases and gets to the point where blackouts and hallucinations follow drinking bouts. All the while he offers what seem to him to be good reasons for his drinking. It is now generally agreed that no one thing is responsible for alcoholism. People become alcoholics as a result of both mental and physical influences.

The Treatment of Alcoholism. The modern approach to treating alcoholism is to recognize it as a disease and to treat alcoholics as sick people who are using alcohol as a drug to get relief from tensions and pressures that are too much for them. Doctors can prescribe drugs to relieve tension and diet and vitamins to im-

* So far, no cure for cancer or arthritis has been found.

prove physical conditions. Psychotherapy can help to uncover hidden worries. More hospital facilities are being made available for the treatment of alcoholics since alcoholism has come into the open as an illness. Industry is beginning to take a hand in preventing alcoholism. Several large industries have set up programs for their employees to rescue the heavy drinker before he becomes a confirmed alcoholic.

Medical groups are studying the problem and are trying to educate people to seek help. Alcoholics Anonymous, an organization of former alcoholics, has helped to restore thousands of alcoholics to normal living through group therapy. One fact is inescapable: doctors recognize that to stay cured of addiction to alcohol, the former alcoholic can never again take even one drink. There is something in the alcoholic's makeup that will compel him to take more. Nothing seems to cure an addict so that alcohol will not have this effect on him.

The moderate use of alcohol is an age-old social custom that goes with pleasant talk and social occasions. Its use is a matter of personal preference, but it does affect individuals differently. Because we live in an age of pressures, perhaps alcohol has come to mean escape rather than pleasant relaxation and has turned social drinking into a business instead of a pleasure. Whatever the cause, more and more Americans are becoming alcoholics.

Drug Addiction

Narcotics. Narcotics are drugs that bring sensations of well-being and relief from pain or anxiety. When properly used, they are valuable aids in the treatment of illness. Prolonged use can lead to addiction. A drug addict is a person who has taken a narcotic drug continuously until he has built up a tolerance for it and is physically and emotionally dependent upon it. By tolerance, we mean that he must keep increasing the dose to get the desired effect. The most common addicting drugs are opium and its derivatives, morphine and heroin.

The life of a drug addict is both pitiful and appalling. His craving drives him to any lengths to procure the drug. Since he cannot obtain it legally, he must resort to a "pusher"* and pay him what he asks, no matter how exorbitant the price or how diluted the drug. Unable to hold a job, without money and tormented by the need for ever-increasing doses, an addict will steal and even kill to get money to buy drugs.

Harrison Narcotic Act. The Harrison Narcotic Act, passed in 1914, regulates the legitimate sale of narcotics in the United States. It limits the sale to doctors' prescription only and requires an accounting to the federal government by doctors, pharmacists and hospitals for every dose of narcotics prescribed and administered. Although the sale of heroin is illegal in this country, it is the drug most widely used by addicts, especially young people. Estimates are that, of a probable 40,000 to 100,000 addicts, one-third are not yet 21 years old.

The Size of the Problem. Drug addiction in the United States has increased rapidly in the last 10 years. Opium makes its way into this country mostly through the Orient, usually being smuggled in by merchant seamen through ports on the west coast. A pound of raw opium which costs the smuggler $25, when refined to an ounce of heroin may bring close to $1,000 when channeled into illegal drug traffic. Italy, France, Turkey and Germany are the world's largest producers of heroin and are the main sources of this country's illegal supply. Drugs are transported illegally by air, by train and by private car, carried by people from all walks of life who conceal them in such unlikely places as hollowed-out oranges, women's brassieres and children's dolls.

Barbiturates. Some barbiturates are known to be habit forming; their increasing use by such large numbers of people led to the restriction of their sale in some states to prescription only. Their habitual use can be highly dangerous and may lead to overdosage. Combined with alcohol, the effects may be fatal.

Marijuana. Marijuana (hashish, Indian hemp) is a drug obtained from the flowers of the Indian hemp plant. It does not cause true addiction but does produce exaggerated feel-

* A person who sells narcotics illegally.

ings of recklessness and excitement that lead to reckless behavior, such as dangerous driving, criminal assault or even murder. Marijuana cigarettes ("reefers") are often sold illegally in the neighborhood of high schools or places where young people congregate, thus taking advantage of the adolescent tendency to experiment.

Treatment. Tapering off the addicting drug is the most successful method of treating drug addiction. During this period, a similar drug, *Methadone,* is administered which has the characteristics of opium and helps to lessen withdrawal symptoms. The United States Public Health Service maintains 2 hospitals for the treatment of drug addicts—one in Lexington, Kentucky and the other in Fort Worth, Texas. Treatment of drug addiction is not as successful as we would like it to be, perhaps because it not only involves withdrawal of the drug but also must include finding and removing the reason for the person becoming an addict. Unless we are successful in dealing with social and emotional problems, an addict released as cured is likely to return to addiction. Efforts are being made toward establishing "halfway houses" for discharged addicts where they can be supervised and helped during the interval of finding a job and a place to live.

Look for Change. A presidential commission appointed to investigate the drug addiction problem has recommended some changes in the regulation of narcotics and marijuana. If this recommendation is carried out it will mean replacing the Harrison Narcotic Act with appropriate regulations. The Commission also recommended an intensive program to educate the public about narcotic addiction, with research to learn more about who becomes an addict, how addiction operates, what the best treatment is and whether or not most addicts can really be cured. They also would like to see a national reporting system set up, listing known drug addicts.

A Changing Attitude. The medical profession is beginning to recognize drug addiction as a form of illness. Some authorities believe that drug addicts under treatment in clinics should be able to obtain regulated amounts of narcotics legally. They believe that this is a safer and more effective treatment of the drug habit than placing an addict into jail, which does not cure anything. It would certainly curb the activities of the underworld drug "pushers." Need for the drug now often drives users to become criminals—they steal and sometimes murder to get the money to buy the drug they desperately need.

Plans are under way to establish 2 experimental outpatient clinics for treating narcotic addicts—one in New York and the other in California. The addicts will receive drugs in gradually decreasing doses and will also have psychiatric help and assistance in finding jobs. This experiment will provide an opportunity to try to find out why people become drug addicts; nobody knows now exactly what addiction is. We do know that addicts are sick people who need help, not punishment. Even if it is not possible to cure every addict, we may be able to find out how to control his addiction so that he does not become a criminal and so that he can still lead a comparatively normal life.

Smoking

Day by day, evidence piles up of the alarming effects of cigarette smoking on health. Statistics indicate that smoking is directly connected with 2 diseases that are among the top 4 as causes of death in the United States—heart disease and cancer, especially lung cancer. The death rate from lung cancer has risen sharply along with the rise in the consumption of cigarettes. Between 1920 and 1960, this figure rose from a yearly average of 750 cigarettes to nearly 4,000 for each adult American. Another serious and incurable lung condition, emphysema, has also been directly traced to smoking. Cigarette smoke contains irritating and poisonous tobacco tars, nicotine, arsenic and benzpyrene. The amounts of these substances inhaled from one cigarette exceed the limit considered safe to be allowed in food.

As a result of the growing alarm about this national health problem, Congress is now considering an amendment to the Food, Drug and Cosmetic Act to give the Federal Drug Administration some control over the sale of cigarettes and other smoking products. The amendment would give the FDA authority to set up regulations about the labeling of tobacco products and people would at least be warned of the poisonous effects of smoking products, just as they are warned about poisons in food and drugs.

Effects on Young People. Medical authorities are especially concerned about smoking as it affects youth. Smoking among young people has increased steadily. A recent survey of 22,000 high school students showed that more than 1 out of every 3 boys and more than 1 out of every 4 girls were smoking by the time they were seniors.

Medical groups in this country are urging action to limit tobacco advertising, especially in appeals directed to young people that link smoking with manliness, status, heroism and romance. Some state medical societies are using anti-smoking campaigns to warn people about the harmful effects of smoking. In one city, the druggists are cooperating with the American Cancer Society in an educational campaign to discourage smoking among teenagers. Other proposed restrictions would prohibit cigarette advertising on television until after 9 P.M. There is no doubt that a great deal needs to be done to inform the public about the dangers of smoking.

BLINDNESS

Help for the Blind

Approximately 500,000 persons in the United States are either totally blind or so nearly blind that they cannot carry on normal activities. About half of these people are 65 or older.

Fig. 10. A page of Braille. Note the raised dots and the placement of the fingers on the page. Note also the special watch with dots in place of numerals. It has no crystal, and the user can tell the time by feeling the relationship of the hands and the dots. (American Foundation for the Blind, Inc., New York City)

Many of their sight difficulties are due to the effects of aging or to diseases that go with the older years, such as cataract, arteriosclerosis (hardening of the blood vessels) or high blood pressure. The other half of our population were either born blind or have lost their sight as the result of infectious disease or accidents.

Some public health measures that help to protect eyesight and prevent blindness are: eye protection for workers, medication in the eyes of newborn babies and blood tests for expectant mothers. Improved lighting conditions, eye examinations for school children and sight-saving classes also help. Today, more and more blind people are leading happy, useful lives because of the public interest in their education and training. Blind students on college campuses are no longer a novelty; we find them preparing for teaching and other occupations requiring specialized skills. Federal laws provide such assistance as social security benefits, training and placement services and aid in setting up a business. Seeing Eye dogs, trained to guide their masters through city streets meet a special need. Materials in Braille make reading possible. (Braille is a system of raised dots arranged to represent the letters of the alphabet which the blind person can feel with his fingertips. See Fig. 10.)

Interested Organizations

Organizations to help the blind are plentiful. The Library of Congress provides information about securing talking books (recordings of books and magazines) and books in Braille. The American Foundation for the Blind and state agencies for the blind help people to find teachers of Braille and have information about special equipment for the use of blind people, such as Braille watches or Braille typewriters.

The partially sighted are an in-between group, with special needs which are not the same as those of the blind, and this group often is not given the kind of attention that will be most helpful. For example, they may be able to read with special magnifying glasses and do not need to learn Braille. On the side of prevention, the National Society for the Prevention of Blindness works with many groups in planning sight-saving programs. We are stressing the use of every means for helping the blind or the partially sighted to live and work as members of the community and not as an isolated group.

HEALTH SERVICES

Prenatal and Postnatal Health

Proper care of mothers before, during and after childbirth protects their health and helps to ensure healthy babies. As these babies grow up, they, in turn, need protection against disease and other conditions that harm growth; they need opportunities to become healthy, happy citizens, equipped with a good health heritage to pass on to their children. Governmental and private public health agencies provide information about prenatal and postnatal care; if necessary, they pay for medical and nursing services and provide food for the expectant mother and clothing for the baby. Classes for expectant mothers and fathers, such as those at the Maternity Center Association in New York City, teach prospective parents how to prepare for their baby and how to take care of him after he is born. The death rate for mothers and infants has gone down spectacularly in the last 30 years.

The community is interested in protecting the child's health before he goes to school. Care in nurseries and nursery schools, immunization programs and training in good health habits lay the foundations for good citizenship.

The School Years

Children and young people spend more time in school than at home. In most states, the law requires health examinations for school children to discover defects or conditions that need correction and to call their parents' attention to them. The community helps by finding ways to provide such things as food, medical attention, glasses and similar necessities when parents cannot afford them.

The health of school children is affected by ventilation, heating, lighting, seating arrangements, toilet and handwashing facilities, gymnasiums and playgrounds connected with their school buildings. Today you will find the schools using physicians, nurses, dentists, nutritionists, psychologists, psychiatrists and health teachers. You will not find all of these specialists in every school, but most school systems have some of them. Educators know that physical and mental defects interfere with education; a child may have difficulty with his lessons because he is deaf or needs glasses or is poorly fed or is unhappy at home.

Health in Industry

The modern employer pays attention to the health of his employees. He knows that they are more efficient if his factory is well-lighted and airy and has adequate rest rooms, toilet facilities and lunch rooms. Industries provide health services, recreational programs, shower and locker rooms and drinking fountains for employees. They install safety devices on machines, provide equipment to protect workers from chemical fumes, from sharp or molten glass and metals or from flying particles. The health programs of industries include medical and nursing services and health education. Laws and labor unions have done a great deal to safeguard the health of industrial workers. Some of the larger unions have their own health programs that provide for health examinations, medical care and vacation facilities for their members. The 40-hour week and the 8-hour day, minimum wage laws and protective labor laws for women and children safeguard health.

Social Security

People have to slow down as they grow older; older workers in the hazardous occupations sometimes have disabling accidents, or body conditions may appear that interfere with or restrict the older worker's activities. Many employing agencies and corporations make retirement compulsory at the age of 65. The federal government, under the Social Security Act, provides a plan for financial security. For a more detailed discussion of Social Security, see page 109.

Workmen's Compensation

Now, in every state workmen's compensation laws protect the worker who becomes ill or is injured as a result of his work. This means that such workers are given funds to pay for medical or surgical care and that they receive a part of their salaries while they are unable to work. If they are disabled permanently, they receive a lump sum in cash; if the worker dies, his family receives a cash allotment.

Rehabilitation

Federal and state governments supply funds to help incapacitated people to work again and to help them find jobs. This rehabilitation program provides medical care; equipment, such as crutches, braces, artificial limbs; and training that will fit handicapped people for work for which they can be paid. Many handicapped people and many accident and illness victims and wounded war veterans are successfully earning livings as a result of this program.

Public Safety

The National Safety Council and the state councils promote safety by analyzing the causes of accidents and suggesting ways to prevent them. They distribute information about accident prevention in industry, in the home and on the public highways. Highway and traffic laws protect everyone by requiring inspection of motor vehicles, driving licenses, speed regulation and highway markings. A number of states now require seat belts as standard equipment for motor vehicles. Building regulations and inspection reduce fire, accident and health hazards. Education programs, such as the Red Cross First Aid and Home Safety programs, teach people how to act in emergencies and how to prevent accidents and injuries in their homes.

Group Health Plans

Group health plans help everyone to pay for medical and hospital care. Being ill is expensive. The very poor are taken care of by public funds, and the very rich can afford to pay for care, but the people of the middle class find it hard to meet the cost of a long illness. Under group insurance plans, people pay a comparatively small sum every year to an insurance group which, in turn, pays a specific amount for illness care. These plans provide definite medical or hospital services for a specific period. Employers sometimes pay all or part of the premiums for their employees.

Private Organizations

Many private organizations are interested in specific health problems. We know the diseases that are the leading causes of death in the United States. Organizations are trying to learn more about these diseases to improve the treatment of them and to prevent them. Heart disease, tuberculosis and poliomyelitis are some of these diseases. At the end of this book, before the Index, we have listed some of the organizations concerned with them. They prepare a great deal of printed material about their specialties. You can write for a list of their publications and order those you want. There is a small charge for some; others are free.

Peacetime Blood Banks

Blood is so important to life that doctors and hospital and health officials consider blood banks a public health necessity. In 1948, the Red Cross began a gigantic program to set up blood donation centers over the entire country. These centers are still operating in many states, and new ones are being opened as the need arises. They supply blood when it is needed in community emergencies, such as accidents and disasters, or for treatment in certain illnesses. This is a contribution of the American people to life and health. Every drop of blood is donated and costs the recipient nothing. A donor may even have his donation of blood credited to another center. The Red Cross stresses the significance of a blood donation in its *Thank You* leaflet to blood donors, by saying:

"You can be proud all of your life of what you have done today. At least one other person will be grateful for it all of his life. For to him or her, this pint of blood that you have given can mean the difference between life and death."

HOSPITALS, NURSING HOMES AND HEALTH

Hospitals provide care for sick people, but they go further—they also nurse them back to health and teach them how to prevent illness. It requires a staff of highly qualified persons to give all the services that a modern hospital provides—doctors, professional nurses, dietitians, laboratory technicians, radiologists and druggists are essential. Hospitals also use cooks, housekeeping helpers, ward aides, laundry workers, engineers and other maintenance workers. Hospitals give care to people, in and out of the hospitals, by providing patient beds, outpatient clinics and other services.

Home Care Programs

Some hospitals arrange to give care to selected patients at home. Most patients are happier at home, and this plan releases beds for patients who must have hospital care.

Kinds of Hospitals

Hospitals may be tax-supported (federal, state, county or city), or they may be voluntary and supported by private funds, contributions (a share of the contributions to a Community Chest) and patient fees. These hospitals are nonprofit. Another type of hospital, known as proprietary, is privately owned and operated for profit.

Hospitals are classified also according to the types of patients: they may be general, caring for many types of patients; or specialized, caring for mental, tuberculosis, pediatric patients, etc. The tendency today is to do away with specialized hospitals and to include the care of special groups in an organized medical center. Other institutions, the nursing homes, take care of convalescents or people with long-term illness. Some nursing homes are affiliated with nearby hospitals which insures closer medical supervision for the patients.

Hospitals are greatly increasing their facilities through the aid of federal funds which are available if they are matched by money raised in local communities (Hill-Burton Act). In spite of the tremendous increase in the number of hospital beds, we still do not have enough to take care of all the people who need hospital care.

Nursing Services

Hospitals provide nursing care with a staff of professional and practical nurses assisted by nurses' aides and attendants who carry out services supplemental to nursing. Many public health agencies (official and voluntary) maintain a staff of public health nurses to give care to patients at home at a price which the patient can afford to pay. If the patient is unable to pay anything, the service is free. These visiting public health nurses make periodic visits to the patients assigned to them to give nursing care and to teach the patient and family good health practices. An increasing number of public health agencies are employing trained licensed practical nurses as nursing staff members.

Nursing Homes

The nursing homes in this country perform a much-needed service in providing nursing care for the convalescents and the older people in our population who need some degree of nursing care. This varies all the way from simple custodial care to care in a long-term illness with special attention to rehabilitative procedures.*

The need for nursing homes has been steadily increasing as the number of elderly people in the population has increased. In past generations, many people died of various ailments before the weaknesses of old age caught up with

* The branch of medicine which deals with problems of the aged or aging is called geriatrics.

Fig. 11. The public health nurse is deeply aware of her role in the total family group as she cares for her patients in their homes. (Department of Public Health Nursing, National League for Nursing)

FIG. 12. Happy, elderly people in a nursing home.

them. As a result of medical progress in the treatment of disease, people live longer today. In many cases, relatives can no longer take care of those who survive destructive diseases, nor can they be taken care of in welfare homes at public expense. Many who live in rented rooms eventually need more care than a boarding home can provide. If their sole means of support is relief payments, their funds are inadequate to meet the costs of a first class nursing home, even if one is available. Good nursing care is expensive and the need to reduce costs is responsible for the existence of many inferior homes, and less than half of the convalescent and rest homes are able to provide nursing care.

Many families face the problem of how to provide care for a parent who is no longer able to live alone and who needs more care than they can give in their own home. You may think a nursing home is the answer, but it is not that simple. The truth is that a pleasant, well-run nursing home often is hard to find at a price the patient or his family can afford to pay. Some so-called nursing homes are a disgrace, with poor food, inadequate equipment and indifferent service which may amount to neglect. No attempt is made to make life more pleasant, and the occupants sit or lie staring into space with no encouragement to help themselves. Some homes are actually unsafe places in which to live because of fire and accident hazards, and the care of patients is in the hands of an untrained or inadequately trained staff.

However, this picture has a brighter side and is improving. Good nursing homes do exist, where patients live pleasantly and have competent care, including the restorative nursing that is so important to prevent mental and physical deterioration. With this kind of care, some patients get to the point of being able to look after themselves well enough to be discharged to boarding homes. Organizations such as the American Nursing Home Association have driven forward steadily to obtain improved legislation in the individual states to upgrade standards for nursing homes. The federal government has made funds available for constructing and equipping modern facilities.

In some communities, public housing projects provide part-time arrangements for services needed by elderly people. These services include home nursing, homemaker services and sometimes "Meals on Wheels" which are delivered to the home and eliminate the need for cooking. They also set up recreation and rehabilitation programs that provide companionship and some degree of independence for the elderly.

MAIN IDEAS OF THIS CHAPTER

Every citizen has a responsibility for improving the public health in his own community. Federal, state and local laws protect health; health departments see that these laws are enforced; organizations promote health.

Health laws protect the community supplies of water, milk, meat and other foods. Sanitation laws and services protect people against disease and control its spread. Communicable diseases present special problems because they spread through person-to-person contacts.

Air pollution, the rapid rise in the use of insecticides and fall-out are growing health menaces which are being studied extensively by the United States Public Health Service.

The Federal Drug Administration is the national agency which is responsible for the protection of the public against harmful drugs and false claims about the efficiency of a drug. Drug addiction is a problem for which we have inadequate treatment.

There has been a marked increase in alcoholism, venereal disease and smoking in recent years, particularly in the teenage group.

Our blind and partially blind people are participating more in community activities as a result of the efforts of many interested organizations.

Conditions that affect mothers, babies and young people need special attention.

Public and private hospitals provide care for sick people of all ages and with all types of conditions. However, there are insufficient hospital beds, and many who are in need are not getting medical care. The elderly group presents special problems. Efforts are being made to increase the number of nursing homes in addition to improving their prevailing conditions.

Inexpensive and reliable information as well as free literature is available from many sources to keep you informed on new developments in the health field.

ADAPTING SKILLS TO SITUATIONS

How does the National Foundation of Infantile Paralysis obtain money for its work?

How would you treat water for drinking if you were camping in an isolated area where there is some question about the source of the water?

Give some reasons why the country may or may not be a healthier place in which to live than the city.

Where can you obtain information about heart disease?

Look at the reports of accidents and deaths given in your daily newspaper. Could any of them have been prevented? If so, how?

How are we assured that the milk we buy is safe for consumption?

What steps are being taken to alleviate the shortage of hospital beds in our communities?

7

MICROBES AND MAN

In addition to the visible world in which we live, there is another world around us which we cannot see by ordinary means. Plants, animals and as yet unclassified organisms flourish in our invisible surroundings. Because these living things cannot be seen without the aid of magnifying lenses, they are called microorganisms, also microbes (from the Greek *micros*, small; and *bios*, life). Men were puzzled for centuries by the actions of microorganisms. Everyday happenings could not be explained: Where do living things originate? Why does food spoil and other matter decay? Why do wounds become inflamed and pus appear? Why, and how do diseases spread—sometimes across continents?

Thinkers in early days accepted the belief that living things created themselves or were made from nonliving matter. Flies were thought to originate from putrefying food and animal manure; lice came from dirty clothes and bed covers. Some accepted the idea that evil spirits entered the body, that sickness was a punishment for sin, or that the "humours" of the body were in mysterious imbalance. In spite of today's proofs that none of these things makes us sick, you can still see signs of this nonsense. There are people who still wrap a soiled stocking around their neck to cure a sore throat; eat celery to improve their brains; and eat bread crusts to make their hair curly.

EARLY CONTRIBUTIONS

Invention of the Microscope

Other scientists of the early centuries believed that there were invisible living things, but they had no way of proving or disproving their theories since they had no tools for observation. However, with the growth of science in the 16th century, men began to experiment with glass magnifying lenses. *Anton von Leeuwenhoek* (1632–1723), a Dutch businessman, contributed to the early development of lenses. His hobby was grinding lenses and making simple microscopes. In the course of his investigations, Leeuwenhoek saw many types of living creatures invisible to the naked eye and excitedly wrote to the Royal Society of London of these discoveries of "little animals." He described and drew pictures of the 3 types of bacteria as well as of other microbes.

The early microscopes were crude and inadequate. During the early 1800's the compound microscope (containing several lenses) was developed and improved, and *microbiology*, the study of organisms too small to be seen without the aid of a microscope, began its golden age. The work of Louis Pasteur (1822–1895) on fermentation indicated the causes of spoilage of food and drink.

Immunology

In addition to disproving the age-old theory of spontaneous generation of microorganisms, Pasteur further developed the science of *immunology*, popularized by Jenner and his cowpox *vaccine*, to form the foundation of the preventive medicine programs of today. Smallpox was a disease greatly feared—200 years ago 1 out of every 10 deaths was caused by this scourge. Edward Jenner, a physician of the

1700's learned that dairy maids who contracted cowpox were free from the risk of infection of smallpox. In 1796 cowpox broke out on a farm near Jenner's home, and a dairy maid, Sarah Nelmes, was infected with the cowpox from her employer's cows. Jenner inoculated a healthy 8 year old, James Phipps, with some of the material from a sore on Sarah's hand. After several days the sores from James Phipps' inoculation healed without mishap. In order to prove that the boy was protected against smallpox, Jenner later inoculated him several times with matter from a smallpox patient, but no symptoms of the disease occurred. We call this protection against smallpox "vaccination," from the Latin word *vacca*, meaning cow.

Robert Koch (1843–1910) developed a method for obtaining pure growths of microorganisms (cultures) and was then able to prove that a specific organism was the cause of a specific disease. Baron Joseph Lister (1827–1912) introduced antiseptic technics in surgery, greatly reducing wound infections.

The Filtrable Viruses

These early scientists in the field of microbiology suspected the existence of other, much smaller microorganisms that were still invisible. Eventually their existence was proven, and they were called viruses. Because they passed through the finest laboratory filters, they were named the filtrable viruses. Not only were they invisible, but it was also impossible to culture them by commonly used means. Although many men worked on disease problems caused by the filtrable viruses, and their presence was definitely established, no one knew anything about the organisms themselves until it was found that they would grow only in living matter. Viruses were successfully cultured in living tissues and chick embryos. With the development of the powerful electron microscope, viruses were finally visible. Modern microbiology has made huge strides in the study of the virus.

THEN AND NOW

Because of the work of these pioneers in the development of microbiology, modern medicine is now able to look for and find the cause of a disease, to treat its source rather than its symptoms, and to cure rather than to palliate. An understanding of the methods of transmission of disease has given us the modern concept of preventing it before it starts by teaching good personal and community health practices to individuals, groups and entire nations.

As a student of practical nursing, you will learn the basic facts of this science. When you understand the use of its principles in the protection of patients from infection by environmental control, you will learn the reasons for certain technics employed in nursing practice. How well you understand and apply principles of microbiology will determine to a large extent how safe a nursing practitioner you will be.

Believing Without Seeing

Before undertaking the study of the details of microbiology, you must first accept the fact that microorganisms exist. We know they are simple forms of living substance composed of 1 cell or several simple cells, and that they are everywhere around us, on us and in us—in the air we breathe, in the soil, in the food we eat. Many of them live on our skin and even inside our bodies, where those that are called "natural inhabitants" help us to function.

These unseen inhabitants of our world are comparable in many ways to our familiar, visible every-day world. Just as we know there are hundreds of species of plants and animals, we will find there are hundreds of different microorganisms with varying shapes, sizes and characteristics.

CHARACTERISTICS OF ORGANISMS

Organisms Are Active

Each individual microorganism is able to carry out some or all of the vital functions characteristic of living organisms, such as: (1) metabolism, (2) growth, (3) reproduction, (4) irritability, and (5) motion.

All living organisms take in oxygen and use

it to burn food for energy and growth, and also excrete wastes—a total process called *metabolism.* The microbes have this ability; they increase in size, or grow; they produce new members of their species (under ideal conditions, a single bacterium will produce almost 17 million descendants in 12 hours).* They react in varying ways to changes in their environment, thus showing irritability or response to the stimulus of changing conditions. Many of the microorganisms are able to move under their own power, as animals do.

Of the thousands of species of microbes in existence, most of them are harmless, and many are directly beneficial to man. Man's "staff of life," the bread we eat daily, is raised by the action of the microorganisms, the gas-generating yeast cells, within it. Beer and wine are made with microorganisms that cause fermentation. The sharp pungent cheeses some people consider the most delicious owe their flavor to the molds. The decomposition of animal and vegetative wastes is dependent on microbes. The soil would not be fertile without them. Thus all higher forms of life, ourselves included, could not exist without the microorganisms. Comparatively few types of microbes are harmful to man. These are the pathogens (Greek *pathos*, disease and *gennan*, to produce), and are the ones we will be concerned with in nursing.

How They Are Studied

To facilitate the study of microorganisms, scientists have developed various methods for growing them within the laboratory. A growth of microorganisms for laboratory study is called a *culture.* The cultures are grown usually in test tubes or on small flat covered plates called petri dishes. The material on which the microbes are spread or planted is the culture medium, and there are various types of culture media for different purposes. The earliest used was *agar*, a gelatin-like substance developed from sea weed (see Fig. 13). This has been modified in many ways by the addition of blood or certain salts or sugars to promote better growth and easier identification of certain microorganisms in the laboratory. Beef broth, blood and certain body tissues (i.e. kidney tissue for growth of the polio virus) are also used as culture media.

To see and study the individual characteristics of microorganisms grown in cultures, a small amount of the material to be examined is placed on a clean oblong piece of glass called a *slide.* This slide is then prepared in several ways for viewing under the microscope. The organisms may be stained by drops of *dye* or viewed in their living, moving state in a drop of liquid culture placed in a hollow spot on a slide. Some forms are seen best in an arrangement in which they appear light against a dark background.

How Microorganisms Grow

Certain factors in the environment promote the growth of microbes. These are darkness, warmth, moisture, food and a suitable oxygen supply. If you remove any one of these, the microbial population decreases. Here, then, is the beginning of the microbial control technics that are so important in nursing practice.

The green plants we see daily need light to grow. The microorganisms, many of which are very low forms of plant life, do not contain the green pigment *chlorophyll*; that is, they are colorless and grow well in darkness. Most microorganisms are killed when exposed to the ultraviolet rays of the sun. Moderately diffuse light usually does not affect them.

The temperature at which a specific microorganism grows best is said to be its optimum temperature. Most of the microorganisms with which we are concerned grow best at temperatures ranging from that of a cool room to slightly above normal human body temperature.

All microorganisms require water for growth. The matter in or on which they grow must contain available moisture (such as jellies), or they may grow in liquids (such as milk).

Since the microorganisms do not contain chlorophyll, they cannot manufacture their own food from raw materials and, therefore, must

* An experiment at the University of Nebraska indicated that underclothing worn for 6 days contained 10,000,000 bacteria *per square inch.*

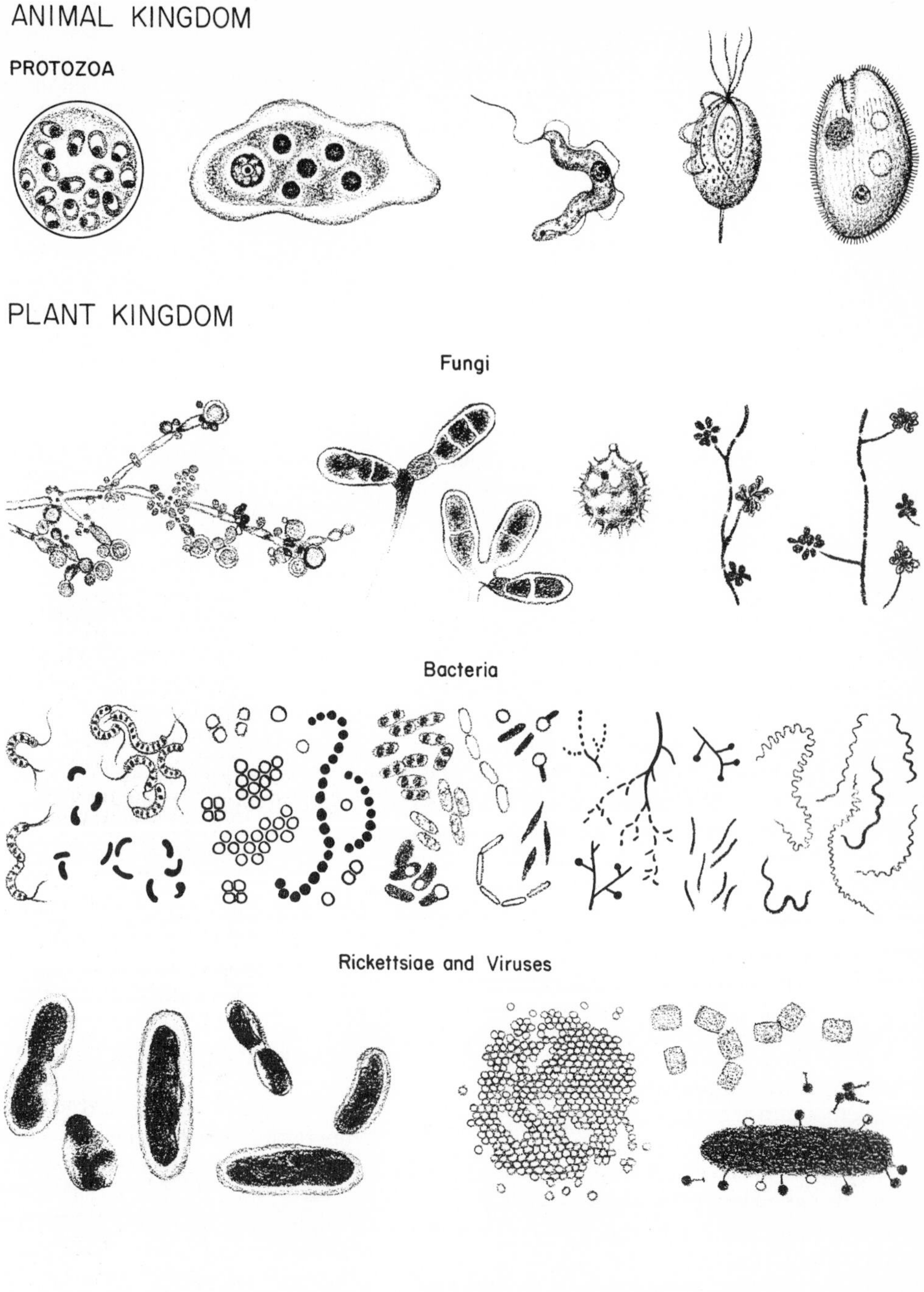

ANIMAL KINGDOM

PROTOZOA

PLANT KINGDOM

Fungi

Bacteria

Rickettsiae and Viruses

Fig. 13. Representative types of microorganisms. Not drawn to scale. (Von Gremp, Z., and Broadwell, L.: Practical Nursing Study Guide and Review, ed. 2, p. 50, Philadelphia, Lippincott) find it ready-made. Some organisms live within or at the expense of another living creature, called its *host*; these are the *parasites*. Others live on the dead remains of plants and animals; these are the *saprophytes*.

Some chemicals check the growth of microorganisms, or kill them outright, by injuring the cell and thus interfering with their life processes. These are known as *antiseptics* and *disinfectants*. Generally speaking, antiseptics slow down the growth of microorganisms, but may or may not destroy them. Disinfectants try to destroy disease organisms.

Kinds of Organisms

Just as we classify the plants and animals with which we are familiar into various groups, so do we differentiate the microorganisms. Because of their differences in form, size, rates of growth and other characteristics, we are able to classify them into the following general groups:

1. protozoa
2. fungi, including molds and yeasts
3. bacteria
4. rickettsiae
5. viruses
6. parasitic worms

Although strictly speaking parasitic worms are not microorganisms, they are generally included in the study of microbiology because they are microscopic in certain stages of their life cycles, and cannot be studied without the use of the microscope.

Protozoa are 1-cell forms of animals. They are all able to move by various means. Some of the diseases in man caused by pathogenic protozoa are amoebic dysentery and malaria.

The *fungi* include the molds and yeasts, which are low forms of plant life. We are all familiar with the common molds: a fuzzy patch on jelly and fruits, a sooty appearance on breads, or the blue veins interspersed through sharp cheeses. They grow best at room temperature and have a characteristic musty smell. They send extensive threads or branches called *hyphae* throughout the material on or in which they are growing. Some of the hyphae extend beyond the surface of the host material, and when mature produce at their tips rounded cases containing microscopic *spores*. The spores give the molds their characteristic colors. The spores are wafted about by the slightest currents of air and when they find suitable conditions, they attach themselves and begin another growth of mold. Ringworm and athletes foot are common fungus diseases. *Yeasts* reproduce by budding. Each parent cell grows or produces a bud (daughter cell) which eventually breaks off and grows in the same manner. Yeasts require sugars in solution as their food; and as the yeasts use the sugar, a chemical change called *fermentation* occurs, during which the sugar is changed to alcohol and carbon dioxide. Many industries use controlled

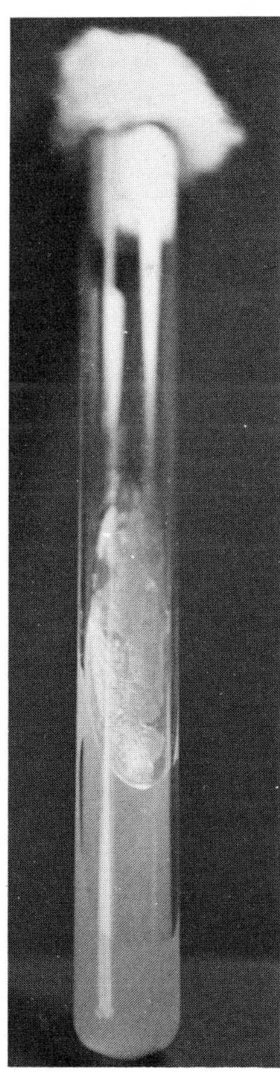

Fig. 14. Agar slant culture of bacteria (*E. coli*). (Wheeler, M., and Volk, W.: Basic Microbiology, p. 89, Philadelphia, Lippincott)

fermentation in the process of preparing their products. Thrush (moniliasis) is a disease caused by pathogenic yeasts.

Bacteria are single-cell organisms considered to be microscopic, colorless plants (see Fig. 14). They are divided into 3 groups according to their form. If the bacterium is spherical, it is called a *coccus* (pl. cocci) from the Greek word meaning "berry"; if rod shaped, a *bacillus* (pl. bacilli) from the Latin word meaning "little stick"; and if curved, or spiral shaped, a *spirillum* (pl. spirilla). Some spirillum-like microorganisms are also called spirochetes.

How Organisms Multiply

Most of the pathogenic bacteria are parasites. Bacteria reproduce by simply splitting into 2 parts. As each bacterium matures and reaches its maximum growth, it divides across the middle to form 2 new cells like the first. This type of reproduction is called *fission.* A very few types of bacilli are spore-formers; that is, when conditions are unfavorable for their growth, a protective covering (spore) is developed and the bacillus goes into a non-active phase. This spore is like a suit of armor; it survives light, drying, boiling, most chemicals and other ordinarily destructive conditions. When favorable conditions again develop, the spore will "sprout" or germinate. Because of their added protection, spore-forming pathogens are more difficult to control and destroy than any others.

Most bacteria move by means of one or more whip-like projections (flagella) which propel them through liquids. The cocci do not have flagella.

Different species of bacteria have their own optimal temperatures for growing; however, most pathogens grow best at human body temperature. All pathogens are killed at 212° F., the boiling point of water, *except* the spore-formers. The lowest temperature at which pathogenic bacteria can survive varies. To assure that certain articles used in the hospital are sterile, that is, free from the presence of any microorganisms including spore-formers, steam under pressure is used for sterilizing. This is provided in an apparatus called an *autoclave.*

Organisms and Disease

Some of the infections caused by nonspore-forming species of bacteria include boils, tuberculosis, and syphilis. Two examples of in-

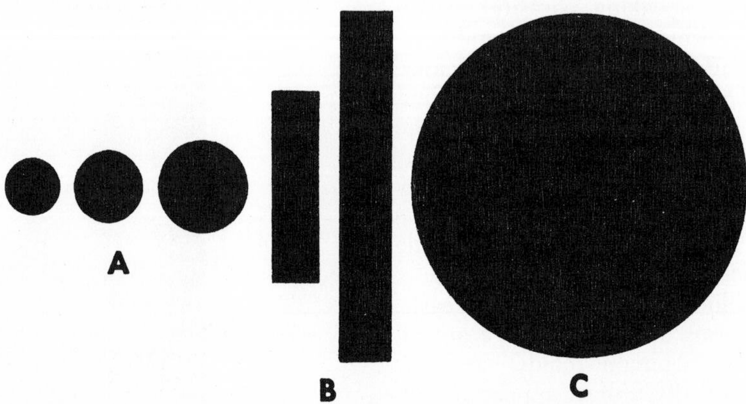

Fig. 15. Relative size of bacteria and a red blood cell. The small spheres at the left are cocci. The rod-shaped organisms are bacilli. The large sphere at the right is a red blood cell. If a pinhead were included in this picture, drawn to the same scale, it would have to be about 17 feet in diameter! (Adapted from Lutman: Microbiology, New York, McGraw-Hill.)

fections caused by spore-forming bacteria are tetanus (lockjaw) and gas gangrene.

Rickettsiae are microscopic forms of life in size between the bacteria and the virus. They are nonspore-forming and are readily killed by heat. Like the viruses, they can grow only in living tissue within the cells of their host. Rickettsiae are transmitted to man only through the bite of insects which carry them, and the effects of the infection vary from minor discomfort to fatal disease. A typical rickettsial infection is Rocky Mountain spotted fever, transmitted by ticks.

Viral Diseases. Viruses are protein substances which show certain properties of living things and are too small to be seen with the ordinary microscope. It is very difficult to culture certain viruses, and our limited knowledge of them has been gained mostly within the last 2 decades. The physiology of the virus cannot be studied by direct observation since they cannot be seen by usual laboratory methods, and most information about the virus has been gained by studying their effects, rather than by observing the virus itself. Known methods of destroying viruses are not satisfactory, nor are drugs for control of virus infections. The most satisfactory method for preventing such virus infections as smallpox and polio is by vaccination. Vaccines for other virus diseases are presently being developed; among the newest is a vaccine effective against measles.

Worm Infestations. Worms are called by the more scientific name of *helminths.* Man is infested with worms by either eating food contaminated by larva (immature, microscopic forms) of the helminths, or by being bitten by an insect that deposits the larva at the site. Usually symptoms are not apparent unless the infestation is massive. Tapeworms and hookworms are examples of helminths that infest man.

Communicable Diseases. Many diseases caused by the microorganisms are communicable; that is, they spread from one individual to another. Microbes have several avenues of spread (transmission), one of which is by direct contact. This means by touching or body contact, as in shaking hands, kissing or sexual relations. Another direct method of spread is by *droplet infection*—the spread of pathogens via microscopic drops of moisture expelled from the mouth or nose when talking, laughing, coughing or sneezing. Colds and other respiratory infections are easily spread by droplet infection in crowded places. Indirect contact implies that there is an intermediary object which harbors the microbes from the infected person and carries the microorganisms to the new victim. Nonliving carriers of pathogens, such as water, food, air dust, soil and various objects are called *fomites.* Living carriers of disease organisms (rats, fleas, lice, etc.) are *vectors.* A *human carrier* is a person who exhibits no signs or symptoms of a disease, but who carries disease pathogens in his body and transmits the disease to others. The carrier may transmit disease by direct or indirect contact.*

Disease Prevention. Knowledge of how pathogens enter and leave the body is essential to the prevention of spread of disease (prophylaxis). They enter through: (1) the respiratory system, (2) the gastrointestinal system, (3) the urinary and reproductive systems, and (4) breaks in the skin or mucous membrane.

Microorganisms may leave the body in any of the natural body discharges—mucus, sputum, saliva, urine and feces, as well as in vomitus and exudate from surface lesions.

Infection. Whether or not the pathogens will produce an active infection once they have gained entry to the body, depends both on the infecting agent and on the host. An *infection* is a condition in which the body is invaded by pathogens which then increase in number, causing injurious effects and their symptoms. Within the body, pathogenic microorganisms produce 2 possible effects: they either destroy the tissues in which they are living, or they produce substances that are poisonous. These poisons are called *toxins.* Some infections produce both effects. Whether or not the pathogen or the affected person is the victor in the battle that takes place when pathogens enter the body depends on several factors: (1) the route by which the pathogens enter the body; (2) the number of invading organisms; (3) the viru-

* A famous carrier was "Typhoid Mary," a cook who infected scores of people with typhoid fever without contracting the disease herself.

lence (strength) of the invaders; and (4) the resistance of the body that is, the effectiveness of its defenses against disease organisms.

For specific microorganisms to cause disease within the body, they must enter by an effective route. The typhoid bacillus must enter the digestive tract; the meningococcus uses the nose as its chief portal of entry. Their presence in other systems of the body would produce no disease effects.

If the number of pathogens entering the body is small, they are easily overcome by the natural defenses of the body. The greater the number of pathogens present, the greater their opportunity to set up a stronghold of disease within the body of the host.

The virulence or strength of the pathogens is subject to chance, sometimes for reasons unknown. If the microbes have been weakened, the body will overcome them before they produce disease. If the pathogen is extremely virulent, the defenses of the body may be overcome, at least temporarily. Strength is always the victor.

THE BODY'S DEFENSES. The body's natural defenses are many; it is well able to protect itself from the daily onslaughts of the pathogens. Intact skin covering the body surface and intact mucous membranes lining its cavities (those which open to the outside) serve as barriers for the microbes. In addition, the sticky mucus secreted by the mucous membranes in some cavities traps the organisms and prevents their journey further into the body.

The mucous membranes of the respiratory tract are covered with *cilia*, hairlike projections which are in constant motion. This wavelike motion, which resembles a soft breeze passing through tall grass, pushes a constant flow of mucus and the foreign particles trapped within it up and out of the lungs. If you consider the dust particles and other contaminants we inhale daily, you can appreciate the protection the cilia offer.

Some of the natural secretions of the body are responsible for protection in addition to their primary function. Saliva, tears, gastric secretions and others prove to be foes of the microbes. Tears and saliva are now believed to have antiseptic qualities and can "float away" or wash out microbes by purely mechanical means as well. The gastric secretions, particularly hydrochloric acid, are so potent that they easily destroy most ingested pathogens.

The increase in body temperature in the presence of pathogens is an automatic defense. In most infections the higher temperature checks the growth of microbes until the more effective defenses of the body are martialed.

SUSCEPTIBILITY TO INFECTION. Many factors determine an individual's susceptibility to infection. The general state of health is important; chronic fatigue and poor nutrition weaken seriously the body's defenses. Age also plays a part; the normal degeneration processes of aging make a person more vulnerable to disease processes. Emotional factors such as anxiety may also influence his chance of developing illnesses by altering the body's physiology and metabolic balance.

We have already said that some microorganisms use our bodies as their natural home. These microbes are called the "normal flora" of the body and play a necessary role in resistance to disease. The ability of some species of microbes to live together is called *symbiosis*. An association in which one species of microorganisms prevents the growth of another, or actually destroys members of another species, is termed *antibiosis*. Many of the normal body flora have an antibiotic relationship to the enemy pathogens and contribute immeasurably to the maintenance of health.

ANTIBIOTICS. The process of antibiosis has given us our most recent and powerful weapons for treating infection—the drugs we call *antibiotics*. An antibiotic is described as a chemical substance, produced by one living organism, which inhibits or kills another. The antibiotics are called miracle drugs because of their spectacular actions against pathogens. Antibiotics are discussed in more detail in Chapter 30.

The white blood cells and the lymphatic system play a major part in the natural body defenses. When pathogenic microorganisms enter the body, the white blood cells (leukocytes) increase in number and engulf the invaders at or near their point of entry. Other microbes which have passed beyond the normal barricades of the body are shunted into the lymphatic vessels in the lymph and carried to the nodes where they are destroyed by *phagocytosis*, the process of engulfing (or ingesting) and destroying bacteria and other foreign particles. Body cells which have this ability are *phagocytes.*

IMMUNITY. A person who cannot acquire a certain disease is said to be immune to it. Immunity is either *inborn* (inherited) or *acquired.* Inborn immunity is the resistance with which man has been endowed through inheritance from his forefathers. There is a difference in susceptibility of various species: man is *naturally* immune to the "hoof and mouth disease" of cattle. Different races have developed varying degrees of immunity to specific infections. For example, Negroes have a greater immunity to malaria than do white people.

Generally speaking, *inborn* immunity seems to depend on the general defense mechanisms of the human species. *Acquired* immunity results from the development of specific antibodies in the person's blood. An antibody is a specific substance formed in response to the presence of a specific *antigen.* An antigen is any substance whose presence in the living body provokes the formation of an antibody. Antigens characteristically are substances derived from living matter, usually protein in nature, whose presence is normally foreign to the body. Since the body regards the antigen as an invader, you can assume that the resultant production of antibodies is a defense mechanism of the body—an attempt at protection.

Each antigen stimulates formation of its own antibodies, and each kind of antibody is specific for one type of antigen only. Because microorganisms are living matter, you will understand that every microorganism (or its toxic secretions) acts as an antigen. (The substance produced in reaction to microbial toxins is called an antitoxin.)

Acquired immunity is either active or passive.

Active immunity is resistance to disease as a result of the development of antibodies within the body of the individual. It is developed in several ways: (1) by actually having the disease; (2) by injections of vaccines, which are preparations consisting of attenuated living microbes, dead pathogens, or weakened toxins prepared from cultures of pathogens (*toxoids*). (See cow pox vaccine, p. 71.)

Passive immunity occurs when a person is given a substance containing antibodies or antitoxins that have been developed in another person or animal. This substance is called either a *serum* or an *antitoxin.* The resultant immunity from a serum or antitoxin is said to be passive because the body of the recipient plays no active part in response to an antigen. Newborn babies have passive immunity to certain diseases from the antibodies of their mothers. This and other types of passive immunity offer only temporary protection. The value of passive immunity lies in the immediate resistance offered to a person exposed to, or already ill from, a dangerous infection.

Very dangerous results can occur if errors are made in the production of vaccines or immune sera. All companies who manufacture them must meet exacting specifications outlined by the United States government (see Chap. 6).

MAIN IDEAS OF THIS CHAPTER

The invention of the microscope enabled man to visualize the invisible "living things" called microorganisms and laid the foundation for the science of microbiology.

The science of immunology developed from the discovery of the cowpox vaccine which was found to protect a person against smallpox.

Some of the early scientific advances in microbiology were the identification of a specific organism as the cause of a specific disease, the introduction of antiseptic technics in surgery and the proven existence of the filtrable viruses.

Each individual microorganism is able to carry out some or all of the vital functions characteristic of living organisms, such as metabolism, growth, reproduction, irritability and motion.

In order to exist and grow, microorganisms need darkness, warmth, moisture, food and a suitable oxygen supply.

Antiseptics and disinfectants are chemicals that inhibit the growth of (or kill) the microorganism by injuring the cell.

According to differences in form, size and other characteristics, microorganisms are classified as protozoa, fungi (including molds and yeasts), bacteria, rickettsiae, viruses and parasitic worms.

Some of the ways communicable diseases are spread are by direct body contact, droplet infection, indirect contact (fomites, vectors) and human carriers.

Pathogens enter the body by way of the respiratory system, the gastrointestinal system, the urinary and reproductive systems and breaks in the skin or mucous membranes.

Whether or not a pathogen will cause an infection depends on how it enters the body, the number of invading organisms, their virulence and the body resistance.

Some of the body's natural defenses against infection are an intact skin and mucous membranes and body secretions, such as tears and saliva.

Age, sex and the general state of health are a few of the factors which determine an individual's susceptibility to infection.

Antibiosis led to the discovery of the "miracle drugs," antibiotics.

Immunity is classified as inborn (inherited) or acquired. Acquired immunity is further classified as active or passive.

ADAPTING SKILLS TO SITUATIONS

Name some of the useful activities of microorganisms in everyday living.

Why would the process of boiling milk destroy some of the microorganisms it contains?

Why is the autoclave rather than boiling used in the hospital as a method to make certain articles sterile?

What is responsible for "grayish blue" color on moldy bread?

What is the danger in not covering your nose when you sneeze?

What "natural" defenses against infection does everyone have?

How would you classify the type of immunity developed following an attack of measles? Following an injection of diphtheria toxoid?

Unit Three:

The Family

8

CHILD GROWTH AND DEVELOPMENT

Children are a country's stake in the future; as the adults of tomorrow, they will be its responsible citizens. Every 10 years the President of the United States calls together key people for the White House Conference on Children and Youth.* In 1960 more than 7,000 persons came to Washington "as representatives of many thousands of persons and organizations throughout the nation whose work and interests relate to the wholesome growth and development of our children."† The purpose of the conference was to consider how they could help children and young people grow up to become healthy, happy, responsible citizens.

Adults are responsible for preparing the child to take his place in the adult world, to make friends, to find and hold a job and usually to marry and have a family. As a nurse, you will share responsibility for his health, but also you must be concerned about his personality. Unless you consider the whole of him, you may not help his body at all.

THE NEEDS OF CHILDREN

A child's needs are only human needs that persist all his life. Adults help to meet these needs, and as the child grows older, he will find ways of his own. He must have the sense of security supplied by his parents' love, his family world and his playmates. His health needs must be met; he must have rest, nourishing food and recreation. It is also important that the child have the feeling of satisfaction earned by learning to use his mind and body in work and play.

Home is the child's first world. Gradually, this enlarges to take in the neighborhood, the school, the church and social activities. He meets more and more people with whom he must learn to get along. Thus, he makes friends, learns to share and learns to take responsibility. He meets people who behave differently from him, whose skin is a different color, who have different customs and religions. You may be the first nurse that the child-patient has ever seen. All of these experiences are necessary in the growing up process.

Parental Discipline

Some years ago much emphasis was placed on letting a child be "himself," which many parents took to mean permitting him to do entirely as he pleased. We have learned that absence of all discipline threatens the child's sense of security by forcing him to make decisions that he is incapable of making, with no one to turn to for guidance. Today child guidance authorities believe that if we begin early and gradually to help a child to become self-reliant, we begin to teach him how to manage his life when he is grown up.

Parental Authority

What parents regard as "being bad" is often

* The first conference was called by President Theodore Roosevelt in 1909.

† From Children in a Changing World, a book of charts, printed and distributed by the golden anniversary White House Conference on Children and Youth.

FIG. 16. The child who is loved and knows it has the inner security to keep working on his developmental tasks.

only the child's way of trying to meet his needs. We know that spanking will not cure bedwetting and that bribes and threats and coaxings are only temporary tricks to persuade children to cooperate with us. There are 3 basic methods by which adults attempt to guide or teach children to act in a fashion acceptable for our society. As you can see from the following examples, they are variously successful.

Dianne's father believes that his child should recognize and accept authority from the time she is able to understand the spoken word. His usual answer to requests is "No," and he punishes his child with spankings and other physical measures. Dianne may be a well-behaved child in her family circle, but her rebellion is shown in many ways when she is outside her parents' reach.

Patrick's parents are "permissive," with the result that he makes the majority of his own decisions. Sometimes Pat's decisions are satisfactory, and sometimes they are not. Occasionally, he wants to participate in activities that are beyond his abilities and development, and when he is unable to manage these experiences, he is frustrated and disappointed.

Tony's parents base his discipline and their "Yes" or "No" on his developmental level. They endeavor to understand his abilities and his lack of them and to adapt their disciplinary technics to this stage. At 2 years of age, Tony was not permitted to cross the street because he did not comprehend its dangers; during his fourth year, because he would soon be walking to kindergarten alone, he was taught safety measures that he could then understand and remember.

Parents need considerable knowledge and understanding of the behavior of their child as he develops through various stages and ages in order to apply their philosophy of discipline. Their plan to motivate him toward the behavior they desire, to channel or discipline his actions concurrently with his growth cycles, is called *developmental technics*, and his achievements and subsequently his altered behavior are his personal *developmental tasks*.

Growing and Learning

The developmental tasks of an individual are those new activities he learns to do at certain stages of his development. Developmental tasks are constant. Throughout his entire lifetime, each person grows and changes. He accepts and develops new psychological and physiologic abilities, discards old ones and endeavors to overcome weaknesses from the previous stages.

The developmental tasks of various ages are fairly characteristic and predictable. For instance, within our culture, we expect a child to be able to talk, walk, discard his bottle and be toilet-trained by the time he has reached a certain age.

A child, like anyone else, wants to build up a satisfying picture of himself. Every time he accomplishes something, he feels that he is a person who can do things. If you know what is reasonable to expect of a child at his different ages, if you understand and sympathize with his efforts to adjust to new undertakings in his growth stages, you will be more effective in your attempts to share his enthusiasm in his endeavors to learn and to guide him to satisfactory maturity. Wise parents will understand that there is no "average" child, that a real child has growth spurts and lags and that their first concern is each child's unique individuality. Even though their son and the boy next door are approximately the same age, the variations in their growth patterns will contribute to the development of each one as a distinct personality.

STAGES OF GROWTH

A newborn infant is a totally dependent creature, but he already conforms to several averages. He weighs about 7 pounds and is about 20 inches long. He cries lustily, kicks vigorously and often sucks even when he is not eating. (Authorities feel that some infants suck their thumbs before they are born.) The nervous system with which a child is born is his for a lifetime; his reactions to internal and external sensations and stimuli help to shape his physical, intellectual, emotional and social growth. His head is tucked forward, and his knees bend up to his chin. Indeed, all of him is curled into a ball, even his infant fists. He sees very little, focuses his eyes not at all, but he hears well and is easily startled, and sometimes he is disturbed by loud noises.

By the time 4 weeks have passed, the baby has made considerable progress. He may be able to stare directly in front of him for a short time, but his lack of head control is still marked. He cries to signal his needs and his desires and stops crying when comforted and satisfied. He has a preferred sleeping position, and although sleeping habits vary widely, he may average 18 or more hours a day.

Many babies have a routine "crying time" within their day, often in the evening. This makes suppertime very trying for new mothers and fathers (old experienced ones, too) for most people are tired at this time of day. If parents realize this is a common trial that will usually disappear after baby's third month, the frustration and dismay of not being able to "help" this crying baby will be endured more peacefully.

At this stage a baby's progress can almost be seen from day to day. By the time he is 4 months old, he is on his way to social success; he speaks soft noises, smiles and sometimes laughs aloud. He not only sees but also reaches for objects, although he is unable to grasp them. He holds his head with fair stability, likes to be held and to sit up or to be propped up to view the world.

The First Let-Up

Now the parents are more comfortable with the baby, and they feel that things are going better. They have had time to recognize that the new member of the family has many demands that alter their schedule—indeed, these demands use most of the mother's day. Feeding times are smoother as the baby eats with greater ease. He even allows his parents to eat while he sits propped up close by—a great relief from several weeks of dinner-hour crying. Among the other unconscious considerations he extends to his parents, he will wait quietly while being held for the short time his food is being prepared, and he now permits a blessed unbroken night's sleep.

Success Balances Failure

Between the ages of 4 to 7 months, the infant undertakes many new activities (developmental tasks). The inevitable failures as he makes every effort to succeed in these new tasks lead to frustration. As he goes through these stages, as physical development hastens on, he begins to achieve success in many of his undertakings and becomes happy and satisfied. Gesell calls this "equilibrium"; the total personality is in balance. Temporarily at least, he is able to do the things he tries to do; his abilities are equal to his efforts, and he is generally pleased with his success. His growth, desires, emotions and accomplishments are balanced. At 7 months, a child can not only grasp the reached-for object but he can put it in his mouth.* (This includes his own toes.) He is very pleased with his accomplishment of

* This "reached-for" object is frequently the most minute piece of thread on the arm of a chair or the floor and is immediately devoured.

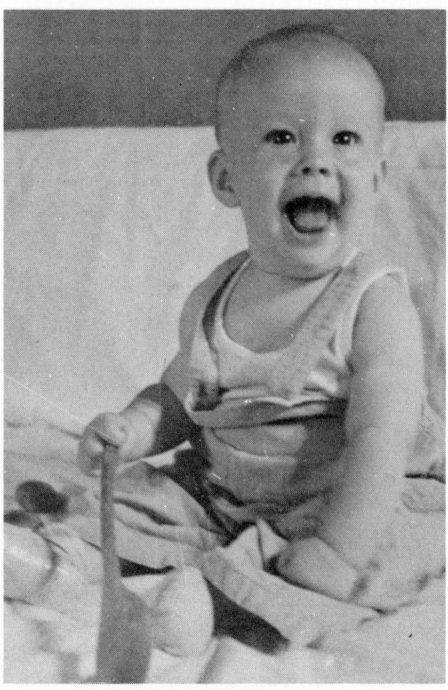

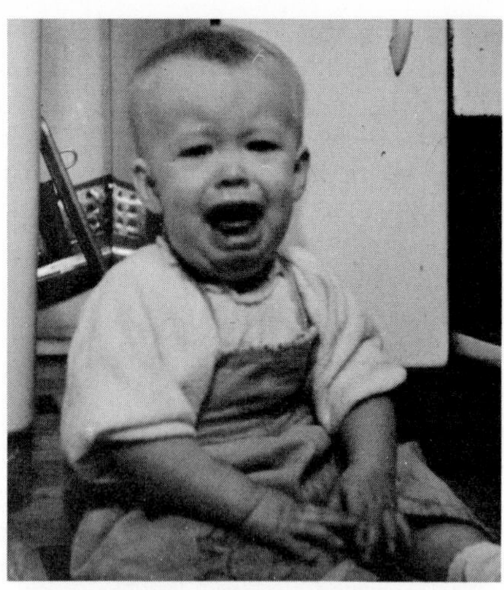

FIG. 18. The thwarting of his wishes is incomprehensible to the 1-year-old child. (Blake, F. G., and Wright, F. H.: Essentials of Pediatric Nursing, ed. 7, p. 436, Philadelphia, Lippincott)

FIG. 17. This 6-month-old baby revels in sitting and in the sound of her laughter. (Mr. and Mrs. Gene Birchfield)

transferring objects from one hand to another and will happily entertain himself at this task. He also enjoys what is to him the purposeful activity of bouncing or banging—he can control his muscles to follow his will to do this. He makes many different sounds, and although he can amuse himself for long intervals, he enjoys the company of others and is very friendly.

However, growth is by its nature a continuous process, and the happy satisfied child

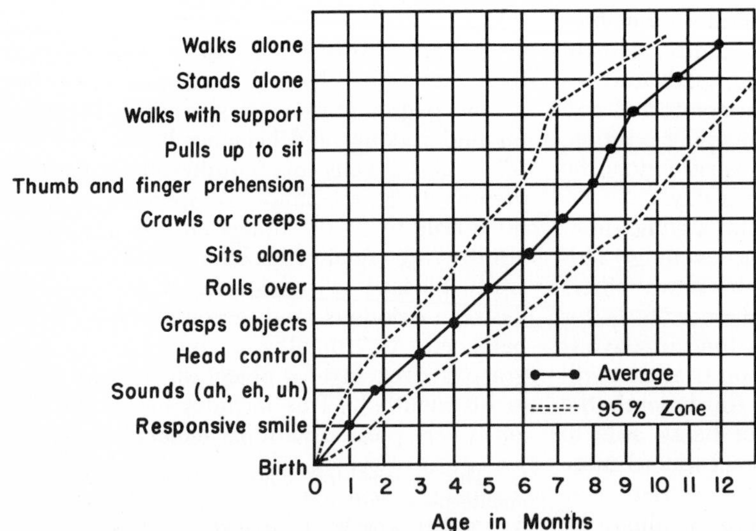

FIG. 19. A developmental graph for the first year, showing the average age for the beginning of the achievements selected and the zone in which 95 per cent of the infants' developmental graphs fell. (After Aldrich and Norval: J. Pediat. 29:304)

senses new fields to conquer. He tries to move toward desired objects, but he may be unable to reach them. He is able to know that some people are strangers and cries at the unfamiliar. Thus *equilibrium* changes to disequilibrium; *disequilibrium* soon passes to another period of good adjustment at 10 months.

Ages 1 to 10

Age 1. The happy mobile 1-year-old has passed through several peak stages of accomplishment (equilibrium) and several stages where he met frequent frustrations (disequilibrium). His growth rate is slowing, and his social, physiologic and psychological functions will advance also at a slower rate. This does not mean that new skills do not appear; the creeping or beginning-to-walk 1-year-old is a dashing, climbing explorer at 15 months; but the peak periods of accomplishment are further apart.

Age 18 Months. A day in the life of the 18-month-old (and of his parents) is far from smooth. He is a "no" creature in all respects and usually rejects all demands. He is a "now" creature who has no ability to wait. Sharing is beyond his comprehension, and he takes all to and for himself. He seems to derive his greatest consolation and pleasure from being the opposition in every situation.

Age 2. The change to the balance of the 2-year-old is very welcome in most households. He begins to explore his surroundings with interest, and he moves with more sureness and safety; he is able to talk well enough to make his wants understood. At 2, the child is a good-natured, warmly affectionate, easily pleased joy to his family.

Six Months Later. Parents should heed the warning that the charming, pleasant 2-year-old becomes the "Terrible Tommy" of 2½. When he decides to pour his milk from the large pitcher, no one may help; if he insists on putting on his own pants and ends up with both legs in one pant leg, it cannot be changed: he is the boss. If Mother kissed him twice before lifting him from his crib on Monday, she must kiss him twice on Tuesday—his routines are rigid! He resists any change, even in such details as demanding one specific glass or dish over and over. With all his rigidity, the child of this age is unable to make a choice. "I will—I won't" becomes a frequent and exasperating experience. However, patient parents find to their relief that the active, persistent, enthusiastic, ritualistic 2-year-old soon enters the balanced calm area of 3.

Fig. 20. The happy, inquisitive 2-year-old who delights in exploring his surroundings requires close parental supervision.

Age 3. The child at this age is in a stage of happy conforming equilibrium. His "No" changes to "Yes." His routines have become more flexible. His increased motor and language skills enable him to accomplish the developmental tasks; the play and growth activities of the 3-year-old proceed with ease and delight. His wants and his ability to carry out his desires are well balanced: he is pleased with himself and his associates. He is very friendly and willing to share. His friendliness, his interest in words and in sharing his thoughts and knowledge make him an enjoyable and entertaining companion.

Six Months Later. At age 3½ there is a great alteration in the behavior; again, disequilibrium appears in many phases. The smooth motor functions of 3 may be replaced by clumsy actions or falling. Children frequently stutter at this age; they may seem to be tense and insecure; they may suck their thumb more, seem to be jittery and whiny. This new, uncertain child is in continual need of the usually unreserved attention lavished on the affectionate 3-year-old.

Age 4. At 4, the pendulum swings to the opposite extreme. Uncertainty and insecurity are traded for the most brash self-confidence. He looks at a wider world (even if it does extend only to the corner of the block), and he is quite sure he can conquer it. It is hoped that his parents will be able to preserve some of this confidence while firmly controlling it. Ilg and Ames, authorities on child development, describe the 4-year-old as "out of bounds in most every direction. He breaks things . . . runs away . . . Laughter alternates with fits of

FIG. 21. The play and growth activities of the 3-year-old proceed with ease and delight.

rage . . . A terrible toughness seems to come over him . . . he swears, swaggers, boasts and brags."

As he leans toward 5, he again begins to assemble his abilities and control his skills. At 4½ he likes to draw and build with a purpose in mind. Interest in numbers and letters begins. He wants to be sure that things are "real" and enjoys talking about what he thinks and knows.

Age 5. Many parents find it difficult to believe that their frustrating 4-year-old could be transformed into their angel of 5. He is quite comfortable within himself and in his relations with others. He is satisfied with his world of home and family. The developmental tasks which he has mastered are sufficient for the moment. He is a good child, temporarily pleased with the balance and the equilibrium of his interests and his skills.

Age 6. "And now I am six and as clever as clever. I hope I'll be six now forever and ever" goes A. A. Milne's description of the psychology of the 6-year-old.

Parents and family have been ousted from first place; the 6-year-old thinks that he is the most important and the best. Because he always has to be first, he is difficult to live with. The eruption of the smooth behavior of the 5-year-old into the volcanic behavior of the 6-year-old is sometimes incomprehensible to parents. A squashy, squeezing "I love you" may be followed by "I hate you" 2 minutes later. (Gesell says "Six" is at his worst with his mother.) He recognizes no needs of others and demands that everyone give in to him.

The 6-year-old's saving grace is his eagerness to try new situations and his enthusiasm for learning and adventure. If his self-development and reaching out from the family can be accepted by parents as a big step forward, understanding will soften the difficulties.

Age 7. The child of this age is sensitive and presents a changed picture. He is described by some authorities as "moody." He observes, listens, reads—this is an age of learning. His sense of touch becomes a source of knowledge. He loves to feel things, to explore by touching, rubbing and crumbling. The 7-year-old girl has a reasonable enjoyment of life, but she seems to enjoy unhappiness: "You don't love me"; "I'm going to run away"; "You're mean to me." She wants a retreat of her own for "mooding."

Age 8. If the 7-year-old is quiet and withdrawn, the 8-year-old bounces back into life. New facts and difficult tasks—these are joyful challenges for the child. Enthusiasm and energy often allow the 8-year-old to undertake too much, and he recognizes his failures. Guidance is needed to prevent constant new projects from being repeated failures. Fortunately, at this age the child now appreciates how others treat him and also is concerned about how he affects them. A child of 8 is good for Mother's ego: although to the sensitive 7-year-old, his mother is a real trial, "Eight" enjoys, needs and wants his mother's company.

Age 9. The 9-year-old is a new story—independent and individual. At 7, he needed to investigate and to learn about himself. At 8, he needed to assure relationships with the outside world. "Nine" gives evidence of beginning to coordinate the developmental patterns of age 7 and 8. Being self-reliant, he proves himself able to make most decisions pertaining to the usual activities. The family circle may seem to be too constricting and he tends to want to become involved in interests and activities outside the family. However, in spite of all evidences of self-reliance, the 9-year-old worries a great deal and complains about developmental tasks in which he must assume responsibility—studies and home tasks alike.

Age 10. At age 10 there is a great improvement—a more mature version of the delightful child of 5. The typical 5-year-old accepted himself and others and was pleased with his world. The typical 10-year-old is a satisfied child, also. He enjoys his family, his school and life in general. He enjoys being obedient because it is reasonable and pleasing. He is friendly, realistic and accepts himself and life as it comes. Never again will his mother and father enjoy such complete approval and acceptance of themselves as parents and people as is offered by their agreeable 10-year-old.

The Same But Different

The various ages present many behaviors

which make them average for a specific stage of growth and development. It is the variations from average which make each child an individual. Even in everyday needs, such as food and rest, children show individuality. Some children, like some adults, love to sleep late; others truly enjoy waking to a new day's interests; still others find it difficult to get to bed and equally difficult to get up in the morning. Sleeping can show us variations within the same family. One child goes to bed easily, sleeps quietly and awakens easily and feeling rested. Another stays up as late as possible, goes to sleep quickly, moves constantly but with seeming restlessness and also awakens refreshed.

Recognition of these individual differences is nothing new. The old nursery rhyme tells us that people saw them long ago:

> "To bed, to bed," said Sleepy Head.
> "Tarry awhile," said Slow.
> "Put on the pan," said greedy Nan,
> "We'll sup before we go."

As the rhyme tells us, eating and other behavior show the same variation. Many "feeding problems" are slender children who do not particularly enjoy eating, prefer small portions and eat rapidly. These children are usually quite healthy. Another child may be round and plump and love to eat. Food is a real pleasure. If a girl, as an adult she will probably talk about food, enjoy exotic tastes, experiment with recipes and be a good cook with a plump family—except, perhaps, for the slender slight eater whom she considers her "feeding problem!"

Other Concerns

Other areas of behavior which are known to be of concern to parents are discontinuing bottle feedings, toilet training, bed wetting, thumb sucking, rocking and head banging. As in all decisions relating to child care, these "problems" must be handled on an individual basis. And, as in all things human, authorities differ about preferred methods. From 1911 to the present time, first at the Yale Clinic of Child Development and then at its successor, the Gesell Institute of Child Development, developmental research and studies have concentrated on the "analysis, interpretation and management of relatively normal manifestations" of childhood. The results of these studies furnish a suggested middle-of-the-road solution for many of the concerns of parents and reemphasize the need for recognizing the pace of development, as well as the ability of each child.

Mountains From Molehills. If the wide divergence in physical growth alone is considered—the rate of development of the various groups of muscles or the development of the nervous system—then the wise parents will be less disturbed about the child who hangs on to the habits which are mainly disturbing to them.

Many infants are ready to relinquish the bottle at the end of their first year. If a mother feels the child will not get enough milk, she may substitute custards, cheeses, ice cream, etc. Changing the color or style of the bottle or nipple at 15 months may encourage a child to drink from a pretty cup, but a reluctant child may want a bedtime bottle until he is 2 or 3 years old. It helps his active little body and mind to relax for sleep. As his third birthday draws near, he is usually willing to exchange it for a colorful toy beside his bed.

Masturbation. Even a year-old infant likes to touch things and handle them; he finds as he grows older that touching some parts of his body gives him pleasant sensations. The preschool child sometimes finds that handling his genitals relieves tensions rising from conflict with his parents. There is nothing abnormal or shameful about this; but if the child is shamed or threatened or punished it may have an injurious effect on his sexual expression later in life. The happy, busy child is not likely to seek comfort in masturbation. If he is encouraged to become independent, he learns to control his impulses and does not feel the need for sexual stimulation.

Fact and Fantasy. The imaginative child may often confuse fact with fiction. Tommy's mother, reproving Tommy for what she thought was an untruth, asked him if he remembered what happened to Annanias and Sapphira.

"Sure," he said, "They were struck dead for lying, and I saw them carried into the drug store." Quite likely at some time, he had seen some unconscious person carried into the drug store. Children try to make what is sense, for them, out of things they hear. Jean rushed home from Sunday School to report that Jesus is sneaking through Humboldt Park. This remarkable statement originated from the words of the hymn: "Jesus is seeking the humble heart."

Toilet-Training. Toilet-training is also an individual matter. Certainly we can see that nervous system development as well as muscular response and control are vital clues in this parental puzzle. Around 9 to 10 months, Kathy had established a fairly regular routine for bowel movements following her evening meal. Kathy's mother was overjoyed, for again it is mainly to the parent that early toilet-training is important. However, the problem here may be that Mother, not Kathy, has recognized the habit time, and Mother may be frustrated by irregular habit times in the future. As pointed out by Jeans, Wright and Blake, Mother must watch instead for "signs that indicate readiness to learn" rather than regularity. In many fortunate children, "readiness to learn" occurs around 2 years of age.

Bowel-training is usually accomplished with less effort than bladder-training, but this may not be true for some children (usually boys). Some perfectly normal children still do not have total conscious control by 5 years of age. Lane and Beauchamp in *Understanding Human Development* point out that "Under severe emotional strain or fatigue, children will loose control of their bladders for many years after they begin school." But, most parents are relieved to find that toilet-training, barring occasional accidents, is well under way by 3 years of age.

Bed-Wetting. Bed-wetting (enuresis) is another problem, usually for parents of boys. Most children who are unable to master this developmental task are unable to do so because of physiologic immaturity. For example, Danny, at age 4, exhibits excellent bowel control as well as pretty good daytime bladder control. However, it can be observed that he urinates at frequent intervals and occasionally is not dry after a nap. He is often wet an hour after he is asleep at night.

Danny evidently has a very limited bladder capacity, and his parents will have to accept the fact that Danny will be wetting his bed for a long time. At this time, the best answer may be plastic pants and enough pants or padding to let him sleep through the night.* When Danny is a little older and can sleep 3 hours or more without wetting, perhaps getting him up during the night will furnish a better solution. Restricting fluids between the evening meal and bedtime sometimes helps.

If the bed-wetting persists (and physical and psychological problems have been eliminated), there are other measures that can be tried. Some children have an "irritable" bladder, a condition in which a small amount of urine in the bladder produces the desire to urinate. In this case, the physician may order a drug such as one of the atropine derivatives to decrease the irritability. The child also can be encouraged to withhold the urine voluntarily during the daytime. This gradually distends the bladder, increasing its size and promoting retention. At the same time, a drug such as dexedrine may be ordered to produce lighter sleep.

Another measure which has proved to be successful, particularly with the older child, is to arrange for him to sleep overnight at the home of a friend. The fear of embarrassment overcomes the involuntary bedwetting and his satisfaction from the experience is often the stimulus needed to begin the cure of the problem.

Thumb-sucking, rocking, head-banging and masturbation are all classified as behavioral outlets† by many students of child development. Careful study of children with such habits indicates that the needs for tensional outlets often wax and wane with the equilib-

* The other children should not be permitted to ridicule the plastic pants or a child will resist wearing them.

† Others include whining, pulling out their own hair, etc.

rium and the disequilibrium of their growth cycles.

Thumb-sucking. Thumb-sucking usually begins around 3 or 4 months of age. Most infants are interested in popping everything into their mouths by the time they reach 7 months, and their thumb is a handy object. Usually by the time the child is 2 years of age, he sucks his thumb only when he is tired or hungry. The 3-year-old has a strong affection for his thumb and for his favorite blanket or soft toy. At 4 he is often ready to give up the blanket and sucks his thumb when going to sleep only. At 5 he will begin to drop the habit and often will be interested in planning ways to help—wrapping adhesive around the thumb or putting on a soft glove.

Many times parents have been told that thumb-sucking alters the shape of the mouth, with resultant "poor bite" and distorted teeth. Dentists strongly disagree as to whether or not this is true. Some definitely feel that it alters the structure of the mouth, while others have conducted studies which indicate that it is a harmless tensional response.

This controversy deprives the parent of a clear-cut guide to follow. However, most authorities agree that it does not affect the structure of the mouth and teeth *if* it is stopped before the second teeth appear. Usually by this time sucking his thumb has ceased to be important to the child, if the parents have not objected too strenuously in earlier ages.

Rocking. Rocking and head-banging are also habits that usually lose their usefulness to the child as other outlets become more available. If bed-rocking has not stopped by the time a child is 3 or 4, moving him to a bigger bed is usually an automatic cut-off. Head-banging sometimes causes bruises and, therefore, is worrisome to parents. Children who do this have many similar characteristics such as sleeping restlessly, having strong likes and dislikes, and resisting if not permitted to have their own way. Spanking, scolding and other punishments do not stop head-banging. Picking up the child will distract him momentarily. These children usually enjoy music, and a record player or radio playing softly in their room will sometimes help them to relax.

Parents Should Know

Parents will see that each one of their children differs from the others in the same behavior at the same age. But, most parents will enjoy the developmental progress of their children if they have a greater perception of the general direction of their growth. An understanding of a child's need to resist will not always relieve the stress and the distress of the moment but will greatly assist Mother and Dad in guiding him toward the next stage in which he usually yields to reason.

Parents are happier if they see changes in their children as signs of growth and progress. The instinctive curiosity of children, as well as their physical growth, carries them to new fields to conquer. C. Anderson Aldrich and Mary M. Aldrich in *Babies Are Human Beings* state: "The greatest educator of all time will be the person who shows us the way to conduct children through the preschool years so that this baby eagerness to learn is maintained."

Sincere concern for long-range development of their children leads many parents to seek knowledge which will foster greater understanding and happy parent-child relationships. This knowledge and understanding will not eliminate the need for parental discipline and guidance. Rather, it enhances it. It encourages a "mutual respect" approach to a balanced family relationship. Each family member can "practice the skills and preserve the satisfactions of his age level." Understanding the needs and the problems of children will supply parents with clues to more effective methods of control or discipline for each stage and age. It will offer support to both parent and children in working toward their mutual goal of increased abilities, skills, self-knowledge and self-discipline: all signposts of maturity.

If you know the physical and the psychological development characteristics of the different ages and stages, if you know what needs are stronger at one time than another, you will know what behavior is reasonable to expect. Through your knowledge of the child's possible and probable achievements and abilities, you will be able to establish a richer relationship with the children for whom you will be caring as a nurse.

MAIN IDEAS OF THIS CHAPTER

Adults must meet the child's basic needs until he is old enough to find ways of his own.

The seeds of adult success are planted in childhood.

Every child goes through stages of growth and development during which he undertakes new developmental tasks.

The various age groups present behaviors which make them average for every stage; however, it is the variations from average which make each child an individual.

Discontinuing bottle-feedings, masturbation, bed-wetting, toilet-training, thumb-sucking, rocking and head-banging are all problems of concern to the parents which must be handled on an individual basis, recognizing the speed of development, as well as the ability of the child.

An understanding of a child's need to resist makes it easier for parents to guide the child to the next stage in which he usually yields with reason.

As a nurse, you will enjoy your relationship more with the sick child, and you will give better care if you know the physical and the psychological characteristics of the different ages and stages.

ADAPTING SKILLS TO SITUATIONS

Five-year-old Peter slapped his baby sister, so his mother sent him to his room. When she went to tell him he could come out, she found that Peter had cut all the buttons from his coat and thrown the bedclothes out of the window. Is Peter a "bad" boy? Give reasons for your answer.

Virginia wants to hide her own toys when other children come to play with her. How would you handle this situation?

9

ADOLESCENCE

The previous chapter has provided a basis for understanding the behavior traits which mark the stages of growth from infancy to the age of 10: the earlier years of childhood. The alterations in the child's growth pattern proceed according to his individual timing, and growth does take time. However, no matter what the speed, growth tends to follow a pattern. The developmental tasks within the growth pattern are recognizable, and the mastery of these permits and encourages progress within the child's own growth picture.

Understanding helps to place problems in their proper perspective. If parents recognize the frustrations, the struggles and the achievements inherent in growth and development, they will be able to look beyond the suffering resulting from the changes and observe and enjoy their children.

THE STEP INTO PREADOLESCENCE

The amiable, approving 10-year-old has reached a milestone—a decade of tremendous developmental energy and accomplishment behind him. The almost imperceptible change from the early years to what some authorities call the middle years of childhood and others term pre-adolescence is in effect.

The enjoyment of "togetherness" is a predominant characteristic of the middle years. The 10-year-old finds and extends affection and pleasure in his family group. A tolerant and protective attitude is prevalent in his relationship with his younger brothers and sisters.

Ten-year-olds also enjoy friends but are most comfortable in groups of their own sex. The boys and the girls "cannot stand each other," but the hair-pulling, chasing and hating of "silly boys" seem to be a necessary stage in the maturing of relations between the sexes. Because the 10-year-old has such wide interests, he enjoys school and is often "a friend" of his teacher. He has a strong conscience in his awareness of what is "fair," but his questions indicate he knows that in some areas his conscience has a long way to grow.

A child of 10 shows anger in brief explosive episodes; his 10-year-old maturity does not permit him to assume blame without excuses. Tears are common at these times. Anger and hurt are short-lived, and the pleasant equilibrium of the disposition characteristic of 10 soon comes to the fore; he is casual, matter-of-fact, very liberal, relaxed and content.

Adolescent in the Making

The slow swing to age 11 brings more indications of the progress to maturity (although parents find the intensive 11-year-old somewhat jarring after the casual 10-year-old). The often difficult and restless qualities of the child are not regressions to earlier stages. He is an "adolescent in the making." His negativeness is a form of self-assertion, a beginning step in the establishment of the mature "I." His unending talk and arguments, his seeming impudence and rudeness indicate his inexperience in mastering new developmental tasks.

Physically as well as psychologically, age 11 characterizes a state of change. Most boys at

11 do not show the changes of puberty. Only 25 per cent have started to grow more rapidly, but many appear to have a heavier or more marked skeletal structure. There is a great variation in the physical structure and the sexual development of girls. The average 11-year-old girl has reached a period of rapid growth and shows signs of impending sexual maturity. Interest and occasional embarrassment accompany awareness of female curves; only a few girls of 11 menstruate.

The child of 11 is a dynamo, physically and psychologically. Energy bursts forth at every seam. Even while apparently sitting still, he is in constant motion: he stretches, wiggles, jiggles, waves his arms, clicks his feet together and generally finds it impossible to remain still.

Rebellions against parents, noisy and fault-finding quarrels with brothers and sisters and constant evasion of helping at home are irritating to live with. Patience is necessary, and the child needs to be handled with understanding and firmness. Although many of his new undertakings are to test independence and self-reliance, he still needs strong support and guidance from parents. The fact that he behaves best away from home gives clues to his self-discipline and other possibilities in his future growth pattern.

Shadows of Adult Potential

The gradual change to 12 shows improvement in meeting the challenges of maturity. The 12-year-old is more organized emotionally and is improved in his ability to see situations in total perspectives. He is not adult; but relative to his age, he indicates his positive capacities toward adulthood.

The psychological awareness of age 12 has broadened beyond self. He has gained more objectivity in his approval of self and others. This, plus his expanding sense of humor, makes his family associations much more pleasant.

Because the child of 12 is so enthusiastic, he brings spirit and buoyancy to all his undertakings. Extensive projects in school show initiative and effort. However, this high pitch of enthusiasm and initiative may get out of hand. Planned parties and social events need adult supervision, or the boisterous group activity of this age can wreck the party.

There is a slight improvement in attitude toward chores that he now regards as a necessity to be endured, but he still needs frequent reminding by parents, and he realizes it. As one 12-year-old wrote in an essay: "I think I should pick up my good clothes after church. I think parents should punish when necessary." At age 12 renewed interest is shown in working for money as a means to his extras.

Most girls at 12 are in a stage of rapid gains in both height and weight. Breast development is definite, and menstruation most commonly begins during the 12th year. Early periods are frequently irregular.

Variation in physical growth is marked in 12-year-old boys; the average boy shows some incipient pubertal changes by the end of this year. Spontaneous erections without external cause occur and are confusing to the 12-year-old. Boys are often more interested in sex from the view of their own development rather than from the view of adult sexual activity.

Twelve-year-olds are often concerned with appearance. Style, color and fit of clothing are important. They also take baths with less resistance and may enjoy soaking in the tub. However, both boys and girls may soak for hours, only to emerge not much cleaner than before the bath—they just forgot to wash!

Following only gradually upon the imbalances of age 11, age 12 shows shadows of adult potentials. The enthusiasm, the occasional self-discipline, the humor, the intelligence and the self-knowledge are clues to the constitutional treats and cultural moldings which will mature within the coming decade.

The Over-all Needs of the Preadolescent

Although the middle years or preadolescent years of childhood show specific trends of their own, there are general characteristics which can be summarized. The need to be part of a group or gang emerges, both as an inclusive and an exclusive force. Boys are more tolerant and informal in groups, and at this stage their "gang" is broadly inclusive. Girls are more choosy.

Physical development is variable, but in all preadolescent children some signs of sexual growth appear. They want biologic sex facts, and these can be enhanced by good attitude formation if the information is provided by the right people. If the parents, the teachers, or the counselors do not give the information that the child seeks, he will find misinterpretation and unwholesome attitudes in jokes, stories, immoral books, and perhaps the "wise" older teenager.

Because of the widened horizons of interest as well as the physical growth, children in these years work at many new skills. Sports become a great interest. Cooking may appeal to both boys and girls. It is hoped that adults will give them room to grow. Family relations may be delicate at this age. The attitude toward younger brothers and sisters is either protective or one of annoyance; the attitude toward parents is variable and extends from annoyance and criticism to genuine understanding. A wholesome family relationship at this time can influence lifetime interpersonal success, for it fosters respect of self and of others. The parents' respect for the child's need for self-assertion, privacy, information, recognition and acceptance, experimentation and growth in all developmental areas and for understanding adult imperfections furnishes a firm foundation for guidance and pleasure in coming years. As stated by Lane and Beauchamp: "The cement of mental health is self-respect." Self-respect is nourished by respect for and from others.

The Period of Reflection. As in other stages of maturity, the 13-year-old brings many and new forms of behavior. In contrast with the open spirit of middle years of childhood, the

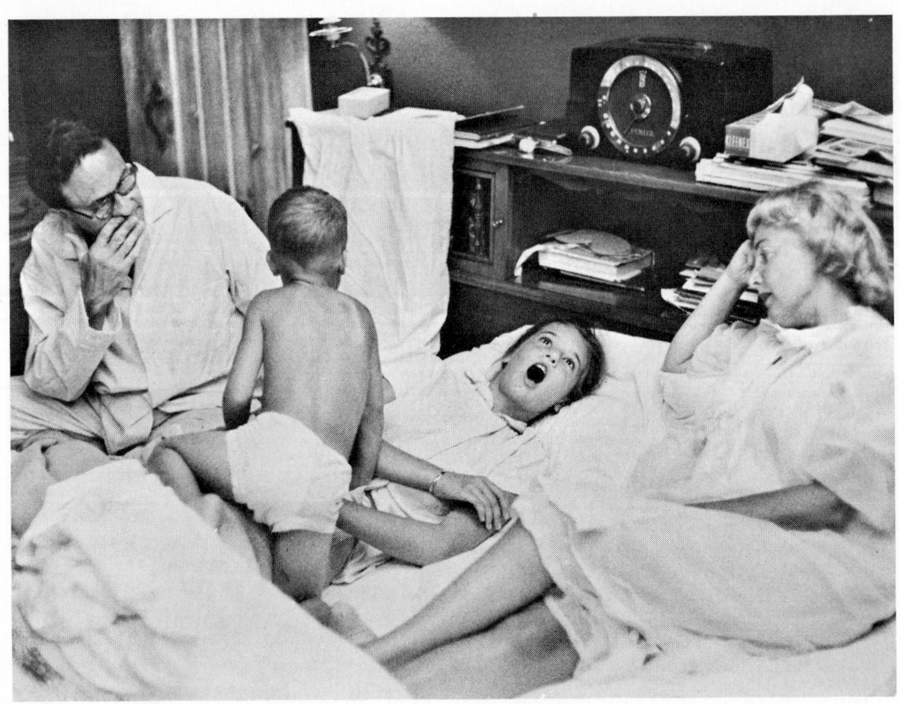

FIG. 22. Sustained parental interest during early adolescence when the youngster is hardest to live with because he is so unsure of himself is a boost to his self-esteem. Gathering together before bedtime to discuss the day's events help to further the family's understanding of each other. (Photographer Ken Heyman)

early adolescent shows tendencies to seclusion and moodiness.

Gesell and Ilg call worry the "cardinal maturity trait at this stage of adolescent development . . .the major key to the psychology of the 13-year-old." He has become aware of and takes pleasure in this emerging reasoning ability. He reflects on self and others and assesses new experiences. Appraisal of interaction between self and the world needs a place as well as time, so the 13-year-old tends to spend more time alone.

His measurings naturally include his family. His criticisms plus his withdrawal are often a source of puzzlement as well as hurt to parents. Both girls and boys have long associations with the mirror. They use the mirror as a prop for their role-playing, testing and measuring themselves in the situations they imagine.

By the completion of their 13th year, most girls have about reached their adult height and have established menstrual periods. Boys have begun their rapid growth and experience erections. Only about half have had nocturnal emissions (release of semen while sleeping), although most know about them.

Social Awareness. The child of 13 has taken further steps to maturity in the social area. Table manners are improved. Washing hands, taking baths, brushing teeth are becoming part of the routine. Appearance and selection of clothes are important, but care of clothing leaves much to be desired.

Authorities feel that at no other stage of development is there such need for conformity to their group, while at the same time, such development of individuality. Through this year as well as all those of adolescence, the maturing teenager takes frequent flights of independence but has a strong need to return to the nest for guidance and encouragement.

As always in developmental progression, patterns are tempered and adjusted by individuality.

Coming to Terms With Reality

The introspection of age 13 permits the child of 14 to move forward with relaxation of inner and outer tensions. Laughter is heard once more; he has achieved self-assurance. Glandular changes, alterations in body chemistry, the challenges of his age plus the continuing unbelievable capacity to consume food provide a great supply of energy.

The 14-year-old is more accepting of other people as individuals and is discriminatingly aware of personalities. His sense of humor releases tensions that previously have taxed family relationships. He is less critical and more tolerant of his parents, although he still has tendencies to regard them and their ideas as truly antique. He likes his brothers and sisters "more than he thought he did." "Talk, talk, talk, talk" is many an adult's version of this age. Authorities state this is a true growth characteristic and a developmental achievement of 14-year-olds. They show increased natural ability in perceiving more than one side of situations and are no longer frustrated by being unable to express or verbalize their own ideas. They are able to say what they think—a task of maturity.

The Introduction of Sex Boundaries. By the age of 14 most girls have the physical figure and appearance of young women. Few will add further height; breast and other secondary sex characteristics are adult.

Most boys grow more at 14 than at any other age. A strong muscular appearance and continued deepening of the voice add to the impression of maturity. Nocturnal emissions have begun for most; if the boys are properly informed, they accept it as a natural occurrence.

Further sex education is needed and accepted. Although dating is not yet a routine practice, boys and girls are interested in each other. They need to know that controls are necessary and why the controls need to be developed. They seem to accept this information if presented accurately and forthrightly. They are not yet ready to make decisions on their own. Parents must help to establish reasonable and sensible boundaries. These are accepted best by the 14-year-old if he is forewarned and forearmed with knowledge and understanding.

Toward Independence

These middle years of childhood are baffling to many adults. They have been described as the "phase when the nicest children behave in the most awful way." The physical alterations, the brash self-assertion, the preoccupation with self, the rapid change from streaks of independence to the dependent attitude of the child, the gay blithe spirit, the moody introspection—all are real challenges to the most interested and conscientious parent.

In the panorama of growth, these characteristics show that the child is growing away from childhood; and, in accord with the orderly pattern this permits the advancement to the next stage of maturity—growth to adulthood.

Traces of the outgoing 14-year-old, friendly and enthusiastic, are sometimes difficult to find in sensitive, indifferent or resisting 15-year-olds. Fifteen-year-olds are afflicted with a development that a knowing mother called "sophomoritis." (The word is combined from *sophos* meaning wise and *moros* meaning foolish.) This perceptive mother also stated that the 15th year of each of her children were the "worst years in being a parent."

The teenager is pulling away from childhood. He feels that he should be self-reliant. Although he values the dependencies of home and school, he feels a need to counterbalance these with independence. Since he is searching for a method of balance, his immaturity frequently produces withdrawal, belligerence or defiance. Because of the characteristics of 15, this may be an age of beginning juvenile delinquency. He views all parental directions as control and he sometimes seeks guidance away from home.

Fifteen has some ideas concerning his future; he has begun to plan for more than present interests and activities. His maturing has improved his relationship with brothers and sisters. Because he has vague ideas of marrying, having a home and, a career of his own, he scrutinizes home and parents closely. Parents may feel that they have been rejected because of their failure to meet the perfectionist standards of their observing 15-year-old.

In most girls, adult physical characteristics have already developed, and changes are concerned in bringing these characteristics toward the fuller blossom of womanhood. The menstrual cycle has become more regular.

Fifteen-year-old boys are approaching full growth. Reproductive organs are adult size; secondary sex characteristics are marked. Sexual response is more directed and less subject to stimuli such as fear. Authorities feel that masturbation increases at 15 and that calm reassurance from Father will help some boys to channel activities. These authorities suggest that keeping active does not reduce the tendency to masturbation but increases control.

Increased independence brings more interest and responsibility in self-care. Boys especially have huge appetites, but occasionally the 15-year-old loses or gains for a specific purpose. He also recognizes sleep needs and plans to "catch up" if he is tired. All continue to improve in cleanliness, and although boys may need reminders, girls are generally interested in baths, deodorants, shampoos and nail care.

At age 15, he likes to choose his own clothing and usually makes more purchases. There is general improvement in care of his clothes as well as of the care of his room. However, as part of the home relationship, the 15-year-old does not prove to be a good helper. Interest is shown in work away from home because it provides money. If the 15-year-old recognizes that his own money comes to him as a result of his own efforts, he may even become very interested in saving as well as earning.

Problems Along the Way. Because the 15-year-old is mentally attempting to graph his place in life in the present and the future, he may find this struggle plus the pressures of school too great. The psychological withdrawing from the family may be accompanied or followed by the dropout from school as well. (Most teachers give much time and effort to the prevention of dropouts.)

Although most find the problems at school an enjoyable challenge, hostilities sometimes arise between the child and the school. Recognition of the inborn drive to independence will enable the understanding teacher to overlook the occasional obvious impertinence in order to maintain authority based on mutual respect. At age 15 there is more awareness of the wider world of adults; he needs this time to observe and to analyze this world, his relationship to it, and how he can find himself comfortable in it. With restless disdain for the well-known, he is leading himself out to the unknown and to the further maturity of 16.

FIG. 23. Testing their power to be attractive to one another is characteristic of early adolescence. (Blake, F. G., and Wright, F. H.: Essentials of Pediatric Nursing, ed. 7, p. 759, Philadelphia, Lippincott)

Independence Sprouts

The true actions and attitudes of maturity are beginning to be obvious in the 16-year-old. In his interpersonal relations, he is friendly and self-confident. Gesell, Ilg and Ames state: "Wholesome *self-assurance* is his cardinal trait, and a symptom of his potentials. It was not so at the 15-year maturity level, when he often seemed to be dissatisfied, uncertain and even rebellious. He then had a *spirit* of independence—now he has achieved, instead, a *sense* of independence."

The informal interest in people and awareness and acceptance of social responsibilities make 16 a companionable age, one with many friendships of both sexes. Family relationships improve. The 16-year-old acts so much more grown up that most parents automatically accept the attitude of independence from him. He has so many interests and associations outside home that time spent with the family is limited; but he consults parents about problems (if parents are willing to discuss them at this early adult level), and he likes to feel free to have home as a base for his friends.

Further physical development is not marked in girls, and most boys have reached close to adult height. The finishing touches seem to be the smoothing and the toughening appearance of boys.

The girl of 16 is often ready to accept menstruation as part of adult biology. Some boys find increased difficulty in sexual control. Petting is more common, and children need to be warned of the problems to which this may lead. Girls should be counseled in how to handle these situations, and boys require instruction about their responsibilities and need for self-control.

Although a boy may still have a heavy appetite, the food consumption at this age is balanced with his needs. The 16-year-old usually sets his own sleep habits according to need.

Those who have jobs may now buy their own clothes, and they have definite opinions about how they want to look. Many are saving, particularly for a car.

Boys are concerned with their future—work, college or military service. They do not think too much about marriage or the qualities they will want in a marriage partner. Girls, on the other hand, are very marriage-minded but

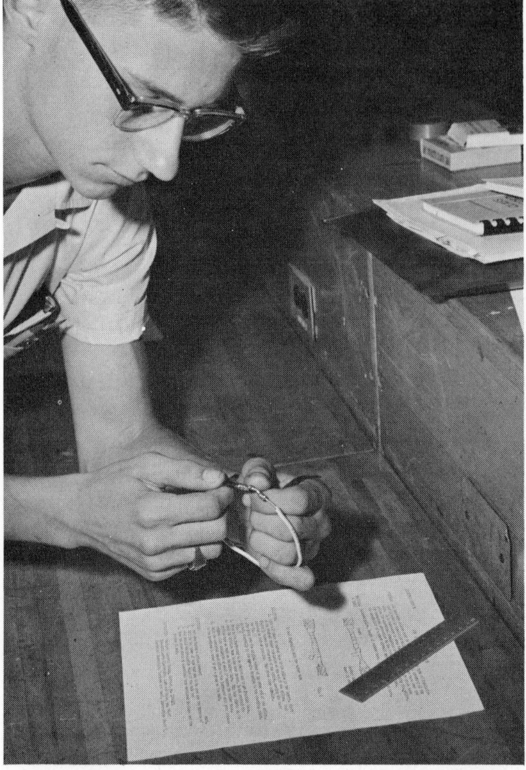

FIG. 24. Problems at school help the adolescent to test his aptitudes, find his special interests and consider them in terms of the opportunities they present for a career. (Blake, F. G., and Wright, F. H.: Essentials of Pediatric Nursing, ed. 7, p. 748, Philadelphia, Lippincott)

often plan work or further schooling. (As a contrast to previous culture orientations, many girls today plan to work after they are married.) Many 16-year-old girls have considered qualities that they desire in future mates and have given thought to what values form a solid foundation for marriage.

Toward Adulthood

The 16-year-old has made strides in maturing intellectually as well as physically and emotionally. His judgment ability has been stimulated and developed through his accomplishing the tasks of the preceding years. He, as well as his peers, usually finds the ensuing years of adolescence happy and fruitful.

We can find reason to study the adolescent from the point of view of numbers alone, for the estimated 1965 adolescent population is 14.3 million. However, there are other more appealing reasons to interest us in the teenager. The cycles of growth can be seen in strong clarification: the realization of the possibility of further accomplishments; the curiosity, the challenge, the thrust, effort and frustration in this further development; and the enjoyment and the satisfactions of the achievement.

The next few years are those of further transition from adolescence through young adulthood, but there is no sharp area of demarcation to divide these years. They bring further progress to maturity. The natural progress and ultimate task of the adolescent is to "grow up." The attitude and the success of each child in his progress to maturity is determined by his heredity and environment, the culture in which he lives and the self-determination as well as the perceptions of the individual child.

Various authorities define the components of achieving maturity in various ways but generally agree on certain important steps. Lane and Beauchamp define the developmental tasks of adolescents as achieving independence from home and the development of satisfactory heterosexual relationships. They quote Frankwood Williams as follows: "He begins life entirely dependent, egocentric, irresponsible; he should become fully independent, altruistic, responsible. He has to pass from the completely filial to the completely parental attitude."*

Other authorities break the broad goals into more defined tasks, but all tasks ultimately involve independence from parental domination and the acceptance of individual responsibility. For instance, emancipation from parental ties is seen to be intellectual, emotional and economic independence. Further, in order to initiate and maintain satisfactory interper-

* Williams, F. E.: *in* Lane, Howard, and Beauchamp, Mary: Understanding Adolescence, p. 313, Englewood Cliffs, N. J., Prentice-Hall, 1959.

sonal relations with both sexes the adult must have developed wholesome concepts of self-identity, self-respect and self-control. In assuring the adult's freedom to decide upon a course of action, the mature adult must develop and recognize the purpose of his action and will willingly accept personal responsibilities and social duties.

The contribution of a wholesome family life is strongly supported by evidence. Schneider states that the "adolescent's family is the most important single determination of his growth pattern, his mental health and his adjustments."

Homes are happy in which family relationships are based on mutual respect and affection. Mutual respect recognizes the task of the parent to discipline the child, and the task of the child to adjust to discipline. The gradual growth to independence demands the development of self-discipline of the mature adult; children agree themselves that they need firm disciplinary measures, fairly imposed according to their age and the extent of their misbehaviors. Many students of child behavior believe that strict "discipline for discipline's sake" stirs rebellion and undermines the child's self-respect.

The freedom of the child to use his home for his own friends and own activities, the use of family conferences for planning or for solving problems, wholesome companionship within the family and recognized moral standards all furnish guide lines for learning to respect one's self and others and to live with others.

"When the teen-ager is loved, accorded a measure of freedom and responsibility, disciplined in a sensible and respectful manner, encouraged to grow up and to achieve self-identity, he, in turn, will love and respect his parents, enjoy family life and achieve a healthy, mature adulthood. In this way, the circle of parent-child relationships is successfully completed, and the dynamics of the relationships oriented to a skillful and intelligent solution of the adolescent problem as well as the problems of adolescence."*

MAIN IDEAS OF THIS CHAPTER

From the age of 10 through adolescence, the growing child goes through definite stages of development which are characterized by specific developmental tasks.

These years present many frustrating problems to both the child and the parents; understanding on the part of the parents can help guide the child into young adulthood.

Parents, teachers and counselors are responsible for giving the preadolescent clear biologic sex facts so that he will avoid the serious sex problems that sometimes occur in the adolescent years.

The intellectual, physical and emotional maturing in girls proceeds at a slightly faster rate than in boys, but by 16 both have reached a state of maturity upon which they can continue to build in young adulthood.

Successful progress to maturity is determined by the child's heredity and environment, the culture in which he lives, his self-determination and his individual perceptions.

Family relations should be based on mutual respect and affection between the child and the parents, and both should recognize the need for parental discipline until the child develops the self-discipline of maturity.

ADAPTING SKILLS TO SITUATIONS

Twelve-year-old Mary's mother recognizes the great strides towards maturity that her daughter has made since the rebellious 11-year-old stage. To encourage Mary and help her develop a sense of responsibility, she feels, that she should be permitted to have an unchaperoned party for 10 of her friends. Her husband is not in agreement. Which of the two do you think is right and why?

Mrs. Davis complains to you that she is depressed and upset because her 16-year-old son is "beginning to spend less and less time at home and is always on the go with friends." How would you explain the son's behavior to Mrs. Davis?

* Steimel, Raymond J., Ph.D., editor: Psychological Counseling of Adolescents, p. 79, Washington, D.C., Catholic University of America Press, 1962.

10

FAMILY LIVING

You will use your own experience to understand how other people and patients feel about their homes and families. Successful relationships throughout your lifetime will depend in part on your ability and willingness to understand the other fellow. Your job begins with understanding people, extends to understanding the patient and includes helping him and his family adjust to his illness.

THE FAMILY UNIT

All of living centers around the home and the family. The family is the basic unit of successful society. The most primitive of people had rigid customs regarding the establishment of a family and rules for maintaining its integrity. History records that as family responsibility and relationships to great nations deteriorated and decayed, their civilizations crumbled from within.

The primary purpose of marriage, the socially approved relationship between the sexes, is the establishment of a family for the procreation and the education of children. The ideal family relationship is characterized by mutual affection and respect. This chapter will help to guide you to the realization that every patient is a person *before* he is a patient; he has a home of some kind that is his base. You cannot separate him from this tie merely because he

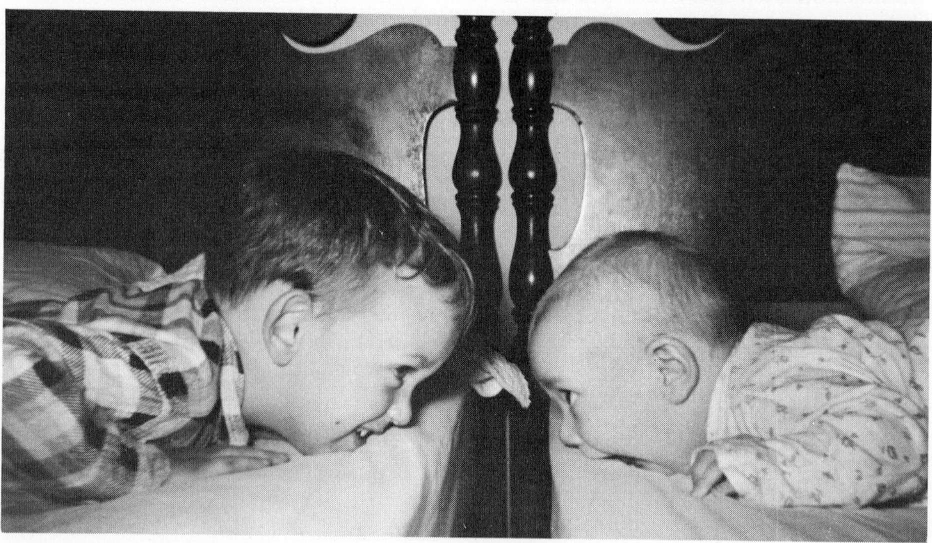

FIG. 25. Good brotherly relations

happens to be sick. Sometimes his home life is not satisfactory—he may be unhappy at home and not at all eager to go back. On the opposite side of the picture is the mother of a family who longs to look after her children and her house as soon as possible. Either way, you can see that family life affects *everyone* and that home is an important place.

Changes Within the Family

As an individual develops from infancy on into maturity and eventually old age, so the development of the normal family can be similarly traced through various stages and cycles. As the child has ages and stages which demand effort and energy on his part, so the family development cycle indicates growth through phases of greater and lesser effort and responsibility; through periods of hectic activity and times of relative calm; times for tasks and duties compensated for by breathing spells to enjoy the fruits of the efforts. The rhythm of the family life cycle is almost as predictable as the rhythm of the tides.

Sociologists divide the family cycle into different phases, the number of phases varying from 2 to 22. However, generally speaking, starting with *marriage* and the *establishment period,* the family moves into the *childbearing stage.* As the child grows, the family makes new adjustments, and the child responds; the coming of each new child makes new adjustments necessary in the childrearing stage. As the children mature and are allowed or encouraged to leave the family group, the family goes through another part of the cycle, the *childlaunching stage.* Eventually, the family returns to its original size (a couple) and at this time further adjustments have to be made. Successful acceptance of the roles of the *aging family* is frequently the most difficult adjustment of all.

Each of the stages of family life has its own pleasures and rewards to compensate for its sacrifices and duties. Socially acceptable behavior in any area and aspect of life follows the belief or the philosophy that rights bring corresponding duties, and duties bring corresponding rights. If you are a loyal citizen, you not only enjoy the rights and the privileges of your citizenship, but you also accept the duties of obeying the laws and respecting others. Members of families who reap the benefits of living within the group solidify family relationships by assuming a share of the problem-solving and the duties as well. The duties and the rewards of members of a family through the various phases of its cycle are called *developmental tasks.*

What a Family Is

The family is a group of related people (by marriage, birth, or adoption) whose purpose is to establish and maintain a unit which promotes the total development of its members.

The family developmental tasks which have been defined as essential for growth and success of American families are basically as follows:*

1. Supplying a home, food, clothing and other physical needs such as health care, etc.
2. Providing material requirements and facilities—as well as respect, affection and discipline—according to the needs of individual family members
3. Dividing the responsibility for and assigning the work load within the family group
4. Guiding and directing the desires of the members into socially acceptable channels in various areas related to eating, elimination, sex, interpersonal relations, etc.
5. Bearing or adopting children; including new members by marriage; allowing members of the family to leave the group
6. Establishing standards for communication, affection, disagreement, etc., as well as sanctions or punishments for actions that are out of bounds
7. Guiding members to establish healthful relationships in the community through the church, the school and other sources
8. Maintaining motivation and morale by recognition, affection, encouragement and family loyalty

Each person within a successful family must

* Freely adapted from Duvall, Evelyn M.: Family Development, pp. 27-28, Philadelphia, Lippincott, 1962.

maintain his individuality, establish a contributing role in his relationship with each of its members and interact compatibly within the total group.

The roles or parts that each individual plays within the family are many and vary with the relationship and the situation at hand. The father is husband and companion to his wife. He may be the confidant, teacher, playmate and disciplinarian to his children. The ability to carry out the developmental tasks demanded by each role is seldom exactly the same even for the same individual. As each person grows, changes and ages, he is expected to undertake those developmental tasks suited to his various roles, capacities and abilities. The happiness and the satisfaction of successful achievement in the various roles necessitated by the family development tasks stimulate continued growth through the family life cycle.

Marriage and Establishment Stage

The family development tasks begin with marriage and the establishment of the family. The new husband is typically about 22 years of age, his bride about 20. The change in responsibility from the child-parent relationship to the husband-wife relationship is usually drastic. Up to this point in life the energies of two *single* people have been directed toward the development of their own distinct personalities. Now the direction changes. The primary goal of the developmental tasks of the newly married is to establish a strong unit from the union and continued growth of *two* persons.

No matter how long two people have known one another or how long their engagement, adjustment to "living as one" involves flexibility with give and take on both parts. Recognizing that no two people, however devoted, will agree about all things, that differences of opinion are inevitable, will bring much comfort to the saddened bride who had anticipated the unending bliss of a story-book "happily ever after."

Some of the developmental tasks of the establishment phase include setting up a home, working out a system of finance and economy and dividing the work and the routine chores which are a responsibility of family life. Where to live is usually one of the easier tasks for newlyweds. Typically, their first home is rented, close to their work and often near family and friends. The budget is not always as simple. The average young couple today is accustomed to the comforts of their parents' home, to the niceties for which parents have worked and sacrificed and enjoyed giving, and the couple is not used to "doing without" the extras. The constant sales enticements for the luxuries of living make them seem like necessities, and the average young married couple either makes tremendous sacrifices to live like the "Joneses" or wonders how the "Joneses" can manage all the extras and they cannot.

In today's new family there are several common methods of adding to the family income. Some couples are helped by their parents, but this is not always satisfactory and is usually temporary. Most frequently, the young wife works outside the home, or the husband undertakes a part-time job in addition to his full-time occupation. However the income is padded, the extent of its stretch is eventually reached, and the couple must accept the reality of their own economic picture. As in other developmental tasks, working together to establish sound financial plans and budget habits makes the job easier and helps to weave a good design for the future.

Traditionally, the duties of the roles of the husband and the wife were as explicitly "his" and "hers" as the embroidered towels. The husband "worked from sun to sun," and the wife's "work was never done." Today the trend to share responsibilities and to decide who will do what according to individual interests, abilities, time and a sense of "sharing the load" is more familiar to the majority of families. Many men enjoy the variety of products to be seen while marketing or shopping in attractive stores and find relaxation puttering in the kitchen.

This is not to say that this aspect of modern marriage is without problems. The person who said that we should choose our parents carefully was thinking about the effect of home life on the children. The husband may have emerged from a household where both parents felt that housework was totally women's work.

Or perhaps the wife's parents always enjoyed Sunday breakfast which her father planned and prepared; he also often helped with household tasks, varying from waxing floors to doing the supper dishes.

Reconciling the attitudes created by two different backgrounds may prove to be a minor or major adjustment. However, it is the individual reactions to problems that create flavor or flaws in a marriage.

The adjustment problems of the first phases of marriage are many; for a high percentage of marriages they constitute a real hazard. The percentage of divorces rises steadily after the first months of marriage, increases to a peak in the third year and steadily decreases through further years. Some couples do not accept the problems to be solved or the responsibility for solving them; others realize that problems in certain developmental areas such as social activities, religion and in-law relationships will pursue them for their lifetime together.

Other developmental tasks of the establishment phase which carry over into following phases of marriage include: achieving an effective system of communication; building sexual relationships which are mutually satisfactory; forming understanding relationships with relatives; and developing a philosophy together which can recognize both individuality and "togetherness" in daily living and can give aim and purpose to married life. The task of problem-solving is usually divided into several steps which follow a general pattern as follows: Recognize the problem, analyze its causes, develop possible solutions and apply the solutions in the order in which they seem to be most acceptable and effective until a satisfactory conclusion of the problem is reached.

Childbearing Stage

The developmental tasks achieved in the establishment phase of marriage must now be changed to fit the new family phase. This demands considerable willingness to continue in growth with the courage to face the problems which are inherent in family development.

FIG. 26. Young couples today work out their own systems of who does what; they enjoy joint planning, consultation, and working together on mutually agreed projects. (Photographer George Woodruff)

There is seldom a relationship so fulfilling as that of parent to child. No matter what the couple felt about the initial certainty of pregnancy, the arrival of a first child is usually an occasion of wonder and joy. The father, done with the tensions of waiting, relaxes and exults. The mother, tired but relieved after her ordeal, basks in a serene sense of accomplishment. Every day brings new pleasures to parenthood.

As the days pass, there arise new responsibilities for this phase of the family cycle. The developmental tasks achieved in the establishment phase of marriage must be altered to the new family phase: housing must be rearranged for the caring of children; relationships with relatives must be reassessed, particularly for grandparents who are closely involved emotionally with the new offspring and sometimes have the tendency to interfere; social and recreational activities have to conform to the realities of the changed family picture. New and continuing parent responsibilities must be realized and accepted. The needs vary for children of different ages—providing space for each child, assuring clean bodies, clothes and surroundings and a balanced diet, reorganizing family routines to accommodate the infant and toddler, toilet training, being interested in and guiding the growth tasks of several—all this while maintaining a helpful satisfying relationship with her husband, relatives and community is the wife's undertaking, one which sometimes becomes overwhelming.

A recent survey concerned with fatigue and homemakers indicated that 70 per cent of tired housewives had toddlers. Another study showed that college athletes at the peak of their physical fitness were unable to duplicate the constant activities of the toddler or produce their continual energy output for 12 hours.

The father has new problems of his own. He finds financial demands ballooning while his income increases at a slower pace. Children's schedules destroy leisurely mealtime pleasures and sometimes menace sleep and rest as well. His job responsibilities and community contacts are usually increasing as well in this active time of life. Yet, he must find time to encourage growth tasks of all members of his family into a family design or plan.

Communication between husband and wife, including sexual communication and recreational opportunities, may be sharply displaced as their family grows. Private conversation is difficult. Children are omnipresent; the baby jabbers, the preschooler talks loudly and endlessly; the school child has many confidences and jokes to be appreciated—who can think, let alone communicate in such confusion? However, at this stage of the family cycle, communication is a family developmental task for all members, and if the jabbers and jokes are enjoyed at least a good part of the time, it all contributes to a happy family life. Wise parents keep their avenues of communication as clear as possible, spread responsibilities for household tasks and arrange for some adult stimulation outside the home as well.

Families in the childbearing stage are sometimes so pressured that they need more than 24 hours in a day. The average family of today has 3 or 4 children. The average mother of today has her first child at 22 years of age, her last at 26. Her first child enters school when she is 28, becomes a teenager when she is 35 and marries when she is 42 to 45. Her last child marries before she is 50 and she shares her now childless home with her husband until she is widowed in her 60's. She lives as a widow for about 16 years.

The average father has his first child at 25 years of age, his last around 28. When he is 38 his first child is a teenager. When he is in his mid-40's, his first child marries and his last child is married by the time he is 50. He usually lives to be about 65.

Decisions in day-to-day living are steps toward the goals set by individual family members for themselves. Helping a child to achieve a sense of orderliness and organization within a framework of social and emotional growth requires daily attention and effort to create attitudes of responsibility. Developing respect for authority and continuing to allow freedom of expression is another important responsibility. Families who face the stresses of life resourcefully and react casually to its many powerful pressures find living an endless satisfaction, with children opening windows and avenues to fresh pleasures.

Parents Must Learn

Many of the developmental tasks of children are aimed toward their growing independence. Although parents have mixed feelings about realizing that some day the children will be grown, responsible parents try to equip them to make their own way in the world. No apron strings which cannot be untied are attached to these children as they approach maturity. Parents will begin to prepare for children's future life outside the family if they are able to accept the first "teacher says" as one of the initial tugs on the apron strings.

Mutual respect and understanding within the family assist members at this stage of the family cycle in fostering the development which leads to a background of family solidarity. Although the maturing child needs the guidance, the acceptance and the favor of his family, he is ready and eager to establish his role of independence and free himself from the security they offer. If each adult member has accepted himself and his role realistically, the maturing children will have a satisfactory pattern to follow.

The social and emotional growth of adolescents depends on interaction within a group of their own age, and teenagers must explore associations outside the family. It is at this stage that rebellion explodes against the parent who believes that his most important relationship to his offspring is unquestioned authority. It is true that this child must continue to practice obedience and discipline, but his recognition of authority should be based on respect rather than on a demand for submission regardless of whether it is right or just. Because the child has met family standards for developmental tasks in the past, the father's concern for him should take the form of careful guidance and trust.

Give Him a Chance. Teenagers need the affection, the trust and the respect of their parents to help them in their growth toward maturity. Parents feel that the need of the love, the confidence and the respect of their children is a return on their investment of many years and it gives them courage for the next developmental phase, childlaunching.

Childlaunching

As this stage of the family cycle begins, the family is at its maximum size. As each child leaves home for college, military service, a job or to marry, the parental task is reorganization of the family from the household full of children (for some, one child is a full household) to the house again occupied by the parental couple alone.

As education has become more highly valued, and as the unskilled occupations become fewer, both the family and the schools help to stimulate the interest of young men and women in college preparation. However, a realistic appraisal of the person's capabilities must be made. Aspirations beyond a possible achievement level can result in disappointment for both the parent and the child. However, most young people should be able to prepare themselves vocationally today when there are an estimated 50,000 vocations from which to choose.

As the children reach adulthood, the developmental tasks of other stages, such as financial obligations, budgeting and sharing work responsibilities continue. The philosophy of life which the parents have built through two or more decades of rearing their children will provide them with feelings of achievement.

As the older children marry, the new in-law relationships enter the picture, and the family development tasks go on. A major one is to accept, even if they do not always approve, and to appreciate the differences in ideals, habits and philosophies in the new generation. These changes in ways of living are inevitable.

The typical family picture shows the last child leaving home before his parents leave their 40's. This allows a "seventh inning stretch" for parents in their middle years.

Life Goes On at 40

Failure to adjust to the "empty nest" leads to unhappiness and depression. Habits of pressure—time, work, finances—may be so ingrained that leisure and recreation are difficult adjustments. In our present society the husband and father who has devoted himself entirely to progressing in business may be regarded by his peers as eminently successful; but his own and his family's opinion of his success may be less satisfactory than that of the man who has enjoyed closer involvement within the family group.

Couples find the middle years a comfortable and serene period; fewer demands allow more time for them to be together and to enjoy life. Financial projects for children shrink, and time for shared activities expands. Grandchildren provide pleasure; grandparents must help without interfering, love without smothering and be available without being intrusive. The middle-aged man and wife find the rewards of time allow them to come to terms with themselves, as well as to find satisfaction in opportunities still available. The middle years prove to be a fine time to plan for financial security in the aged years: the expense of childrearing is lifted; the husband's income is usually at its peak; the wife may wish to work, as do about one third of the wives in the age group of 45 to 54.

Financial planning for the older years accepts the statistical fact that wives live longer than husbands; therefore, both husband and wife should be fully aware of the status of their finances.

Age Is Relative

People who are growing older cannot be lumped together and treated alike any more than can those of any other age. As in other phases of the life cycle, the husband and the wife, together and as individuals, must themselves undertake the developmental tasks of this period to make it successful.

Present society is too eager to estimate age in years instead of in a person's ability to make the most of any time of life. As Marie Dressler, an actress of former years, once said: "It's not how old you are but how you are old."

Another contemporary problem is that Americans are so determined to glorify youth and a pretty face that people are ashamed to admit their age. Beauty parlors prosper as women struggle to stop the clock. Men, too, resist the sands of time as they seek remedies for receding hairlines and enlarging waistlines. Many men are also faced with an employer's plan of enforced retirement which makes continued

FIG. 27. Maintenance of a close relationship with her husband is especially important now that the children have grown and gone. (Standard Oil Co.)

working impossible and decreased income inevitable.

Robert Browning said:

> Grow old along with me!
> The best is yet to be.
> The last of life, for which the first was made . . .

According to the latest statistics, this is just what our population is doing—growing old. Nearly 10 per cent of our citizens are over 65 years of age (see Table following). The average life span has increased 20 years since 1900. "The older American has nearly 18 million faces."* This aging population brings economic and social adaptations within the family group as well as in wider society. Those basic needs —security, affection and the need to be useful and wanted—still are important, and problems arise because many older people are denied these satisfactions.

INCREASE OF THE MIDDLE-AGED AND OLDER POPULATIONS

Year	Middle-aged and Older People in the Population		
	Total Population	45-64years	65 years and over
Both sexes			
1850	23,200,000	2,300,000	600,000
1900	76,000,000	10,400,000	3,100,000
1950	150,700,000	30,600,000	12,300,000
1975 (est.)	235,000,000	43,810,000	21,800,000

(Adapted from Tibbitts, C., and Donahue, W.: Aging in Today's Society, p. 13, Englewood Cliffs, N.J., Prentice-Hall, 1960.)

Happily, some attempts are being made to use the valuable abilities of retired people. As an example, Hastings College of Law, affiliated with the University of California, will not hire anyone under 65 years of age. It has 17 faculty members who average 73 years of age with an average of 42 years in teaching law. David Snodgrass, dean, reports: "We are extremely happy with our older faculty. They know their business and over the years have gotten rid of all their bad habits."

* The Older American, p. 1, Washington, D.C., Superintendent of Documents, 1963.

Financial Security. We have already mentioned the plan for providing money for older years during the earlier years of family life. True, money is not everything—millionaires have problems, too. However, it is a fact that money is a wonderful cushion for older years. According to Clark Tibbitts in *Aging in the Modern World*, "Social inventions designed to satisfy the needs of . . . older people have been slow in coming . . . although within our lifetime we have seen an unparalleled development of our material culture."

Social Security. In 1935, Congress passed the Social Security Act to provide financial security in old age. This guarantees a specified income to men over 65 and women over 62 who have made regular contributions to the program through payroll deductions from their salaries. The employer contributes an equal amount, but self-employed people make the entire contribution. Practical nurses are eligible for Social Security benefits.

The amount of money that a person receives in Social Security payments per year is based on the amount of money he received as salary during the period of contribution to the Social Security fund. Maximum earnings on which this can be calculated are $6,600 per year. At present, after retirement and up to 72 years of age, the maximum amount a person is allowed to earn and also receive Social Security payments is $1,500 per year. After 72 there is no restriction on the amount he is allowed to earn.

An insured person who becomes totally and permanently disabled at the age of 50 or over will receive payments in the amount he would have received at retirement age. On the death of an insured person, the widow or the widower or the person who paid the burial expenses will receive a lump sum payment.

The newly enacted Medicare law will assure medical care for many of our elderly people and will enable the younger group to plan for their future years with an increased sense of security.

Old-Age Assistance. The Old-Age Assistance Program is also part of the Social Security Act. This program operates in the individual states, and the funds come from federal and state governments. To receive this help, people must be over 65, must meet the requirements for residence in their state and must prove that they have no other income.

In addition to Social Security and Old-Age Assistance, there are annuities (life insurance plans) and pensions to ease the financial problems of the elderly. Information from the President's Council on Aging in 1963 states that in 1935 only about 1,100 employers had pension plans. Today there are more than 25,000 plans covering 23 million workers, and Social Security benefits are being collected by 12.6 million Americans.

Housing

Many times the aging couple remains in the family house because this is home. The loss of one of the loved ones calls for a change in the habits of a lifetime of living. Careful planning may allow a widow to remain in her long-time home, lessening the immediate emotional bereavement, or a widower may find that smaller quarters will be more suitable. On the other hand, a person may be forced into moving in with his children. A report from one study of homes which houses 3 generations states this is a "hazardous type of family living in which combined virtues of diplomat, statesman and saint are needed." In the past 15 years great interest has been shown in housing units adapted especially to the older person—efficient, dignified and easy to maintain. In addition to private housing for older people, the federal and state programs have increased tremendously since 1960.

Assistance for the older citizens to prepare them for the adjustments necessary at this phase of the family cycle is available from many sources. The development of retirement preparation began with universities and was followed by employers, unions, civic and government leaders. Their purpose is two-fold:

> To tell the people nearing retirement about the adjustments they will have to make and to help change their attitudes about retirement giving them factual information about social security, health, housing, social welfare, investments, recreation, civic activities, legal matters, community resources and other matters with which they may have had no previous experience.*

Your Own Plans

Does old age have to be an unhappy time? Many older people find life very enjoyable; they seem to be the ones who form the habit of making the most of everything. They enjoy "the best" of the "yet to be." The well-adjusted oldster has several decisive characteristics such as a philosophy which allows reason for their being; which values wisdom more than physical agility; which encourages flexible mental attitudes and enjoys expanded interests beyond earlier duties and roles. When Michelangelo, already well along in years, was discussing life with an old friend, the latter commented, "Yes, after such a good life, it's hard to look death in the eye." "Not at all!" contradicted Michelangelo. "Since life was such a pleasure, death coming from the same Source cannot displease us."

What are your plans for the later years? You cannot begin planning too soon for the years which young people think are far away. Provide yourself with financial security; provide for emotional security, make friends and keep your friendships in repair.

The Patient Is Part of the Family

Now that you know the "person" you will begin to understand the "patient." Your first step in this cooperative job is important. You must try to see hospital patients as people who have homes, families and friends. Their likes and dislikes, their belongings and their visitors will tell you many things about them. You must remember first that no two people are exactly alike. What does the patient think about? One is the illness itself. Another is the family, especially if the patient is the one responsible for the housekeeping. If the patient is the wage-earner, money will be a worry. If the illness is long and expensive, this can be a worry in itself.

* The Older American, p. 27, Washington, D.C., Superintendent of Documents, 1963.

With these things as a start, how do you fit in? First, as a nurse, of course, to make your patient comfortable and to do what the physician prescribes. Next, you must remember that the patient will get well faster if he is contented. He will be relieved to know that you are interested in and aware of his family and his life with them.

You Work Together

If the patient is ill at home, you also might be stepping into the household as a manager to keep the household on an even keel and plan each day so that it will run smoothly. You should be able to help the family with the changes that they need to make because there is a sick person in the house. You can accomplish this by making the family realize that this is a job to be done together. If the patient must have quiet, you can help with plans to keep the children amused or out of the way. Explain why they may not be allowed to see the patient or why visits must be short. This can be tricky, because people cannot always see how members of the family or friends could tire the patient or upset him. This can be especially difficult if one of the family was taking care of the patient before you came. This person may not want to see you take over. Let her help in any way possible until she learns to have confidence in you.

Illness Can Be Expensive

Discuss with the family the equipment which you will need for the patient. See what can be used from the home, and when purchases are necessary, explain what is needed and help the family to obtain them as economically as possible. For example, you would not recommend Monel metal basins and bedpans unless the family could afford them—you would suggest a less expensive type. You must be guided by the kind and the length of the illness as well as the family pocketbook when you choose or recommend specific equipment.

In many communities there are volunteer agencies which will supply equipment for the home patient at little or no cost. You can find out about these services through your Health and Welfare Council, your local Red Cross chapter, or from an agency directly concerned with your patients' illness, such as the Heart Association, the American Cancer Society and the National Society for Crippled Children and Adults.

Time for You

If you are on resident duty, explain to the family why you must have some hours to yourself every day. You must decide who will stay with your patient when you are away. If you are not getting sufficient rest at night, tell the physician and the family. Explain how this affects your care of the patient. If the patient is the one who normally runs the house, perhaps you can get help from her concerning household routines. If she is unable to help you, then you must use your common sense in deciding which plan will be best. This is the executive side of your work and will give you a chance to prove that you are equal to any situation.

Conclusion

It is very important that you know much about the patient—his anatomy and physiology, his personality and his place in the family and the larger community. You must remember that the patient is an individual as well as an integral part of a family group. In helping the patient and his family during illness, you will get better results if you understand the influences that make them behave as they do. You will have more patience with children when you understand and appreciate their development patterns, their family background and their training. You will be more tolerant of older patients when you appreciate the economic and the emotional pressures that affect them, their nationality and religious backgrounds and the things they hold dear. The patient must always be considered in his family setting.

Finally, you must remember that one of the most important things to a patient is your friendliness and your personal interest in him. This remark from a patient points this out: "I wanted somebody to talk to me—to take a few minutes to chat. You know. Not just patient-nurse talk but to be interested in *me*." He said he knew nurses were probably too busy to do that in a hospital, but he wished they had time, because it did so much good. You would never guess how lonely many people are and how much they need friendliness.

MAIN IDEAS OF THIS CHAPTER

There are 4 major phases in a family cycle: marriage and establishment; childbearing; child-launching; and the aging family.

The home and the family are the centers for life.

Every patient comes from a home and a family of some kind; remember that money, nationality, religion and family customs affect family life.

You are expected to know how to carry out housekeeping procedures in ways that are safe and efficient.

A child's start in life depends on how well his needs for security, health and success are met.

Most of the problems of the older years are concerned with the loss of independence, finding social satisfactions, keeping health and finding something for which to live.

Help the family to adjust to the illness of a family member.

Remember to consider the family setting when trying to understand the patient.

ADAPTING SKILLS TO SITUATIONS

Jane and John, with their first newborn, invited John's mother to visit them for 2 weeks. The doting grandmother, feeling sorry for her busy daughter-in-law, has insisted that she care for the baby while she is there to give Jane a rest. Jane has strongly resisted and has asked you as a friend and a nurse to speak to her mother-in-law about the situation. What would you say?

Your elderly grandmother comes to live with you in your home. How could you make her feel needed and welcome?

Unit Four:

The Living Body

II

THE BODY AS AN INTEGRATED WHOLE

In recent years science has produced such a profusion of miracles that we have almost lost our capacity to wonder at them. Even so, anybody—even the most learned scientist—who looks within the human body continues to be awed by its marvels of engineering, architecture, efficiency and economy. As we study the structure and the function of the body, we learn to appreciate even more the intricate patterns which enable each of us to perform as a miraculously integrated human being.

THE UNIT OF LIFE

In a brick building, the unit of structure is "one brick." The unit of structure and organization of the body is "one cell"—the building block of the body. This fact was first established by two German biologists, Schleiden and Schwann, and it has been the foundation from which all biologic sciences have developed. *All* living things, plants and animals alike, are made up of cells. The smallest of them, the microorganisms, are composed of a single cell. The human body is made up of millions of cells.

PROTOPLASM

The cells of all living creatures are composed of a substance called protoplasm (meaning "original substance"). Protoplasm has been analyzed in the laboratory, and we know which chemicals it contains—ordinary materials that we see around us in varying forms every day. However, we have not been able to make protoplasm in the laboratory. Apparently, it is the organization of the material in the cells, and not some exclusive chemical, that gives it that property which we call life.

Although the *quality* of life remains elusive, the "*stuff*" of life is familiar—all part and parcel of that fixed reservoir of matter composing the interior of our planet, its surface and the atmosphere enveloping it.

MATTER

Matter is said to be anything that occupies space and has weight. All the matter in the world, living and nonliving, can be broken down into slightly over 100 different elements. Elements are not *the* simplest form of matter, but only the simplest form obtainable by ordinary chemical means. Some common elements are carbon, iron, sulfur, copper, oxygen, hydrogen and nitrogen.

The smallest unit of any element is the atom. Atoms in turn are composed of subatomic particles, which only rather recently have been subjected to intensive study. As far as we are concerned, the main subatomic particles are electrons, protons and neutrons, which are arranged in relation to one another in somewhat the same manner as the earth and the other planets are around the sun. An atom of one element differs from that of another element in the arrangement of its subatomic particles. For instance, a hydrogen atom has 1 proton with 1 electron whirling around it. However, an atom of oxygen has 8 electrons revolving about a central mass composed of 8 protons and 8 neutrons. Each element has its own characteristic atom.

Compounds

Atoms of 2 or more elements can combine to form an enormous variety of substances called compounds. In every compound, the atoms of its elements combine in definite proportions. For example, the most common compound found on the surface of the earth is water. Water is formed when 2 atoms of hydrogen are combined with 1 atom of oxygen. In chemical shorthand, water is expressed as H_2O.

Suppose you were able to take a knifeblade and cut a drop of water in two, and then divide one of these halves. If you continued to divide each half into smaller and smaller fractions, finally you would come to a particle which you could not divide and still have water left. This single particle of water is called a *molecule,* which consists solely of the 2 hydrogen atoms and the 1 oxygen atom. Therefore, a molecule is the least quantity of atoms needed to form a particular compound.

Physical and Chemical Changes

Water has a definite chemical structure, H_2O. Normally, it is a liquid. Freeze water, and it changes to a solid, ice; boil it, and it becomes water vapor, steam. The water has undergone a *physical* change—that is, a change in its outward properties. However, it is still water, H_2O, no matter which of these 3 states it is in. Its chemical structure remains unchanged. However, if you pass a direct electric current through a sample of water, a more fundamental change occurs. The water gradually disappears because the electric current breaks it down into the 2 invisible gases of which water is composed—hydrogen and oxygen. In this instance, the chemical structure of the water has been changed; the water molecules have been made to disintegrate into their respective elements. A *chemical* change has occurred. Familiar types of chemical change are the processes of burning (called combustion) and the rusting of iron. In all chemical changes, compounds are broken down into substances that no longer have the same chemical structure of the original compound. Completely rusted iron no longer has the same characteristics of iron; burned wood is no longer wood but ashes and gases instead.

Mixtures

Not all elements or compounds will combine chemically when brought together. A *mixture* is a class of matter in which 2 or more substances are mixed together without forming a new compound. Salt water is an example of a mixture. Both the salt and the water remain 2 separate compounds. They can be brought together in any proportion, and they can be separated by a physical change such as boiling. In a true compound, the elements combine in definite proportions, and they cannot be separated except through a chemical change.

Energy

Speaking practically, energy is the ability to do work. It takes many forms: light energy, heat energy, mechanical energy, chemical energy, etc. One type of energy can be converted into another. For instance, energy from the sun (heat, light and other types of radiation) is stored in natural fuels such as oil and coal. These contain chemical energy, which is transformed into mechanical energy in engines. Engines can turn generators, producing electrical energy; electricity in turn can be transformed into light and heat.

The chemical combining of elements and compounds is called a *chemical reaction.* All chemical reactions are accomplished by a transfer of energy. For example, the cells of the body receive energy from food materials (see p. 142). Chemical reactions that take place in protoplasm result in the release of heat energy, mechanical energy and other forms which are all a part of the so-called "life processes."

LIVING MATTER

Protoplasm is a semiliquid substance which resembles the white of an egg. It is composed mostly of water (about 70%), and protein compounds, which "build up" the cell and supply it with energy when combined with oxygen. Protoplasm contains mineral elements (calcium, sodium, sulfur, etc.), carbohydrates (sugars and starches) and lipids (fats and fatty substances). Protoplasm in its simplest form has 5 general characteristics: irritability, motility, metabolism, growth and reproduction. These 5 characteristics are used to distinguish living from nonliving matter.

Irritability means that protoplasm responds to a change in its environment, that is, it reacts in some way to a stimulus. An example of this is the action of a nerve cell of the body. When a nerve is stimulated, an electrical impulse is touched off and travels along the nerve as though a fuse had been lighted.

Motility is the ability to move. The protoplasm moves within the cells of both plants and animals. Sperm cells, the male reproductive cells, are capable of rapid self-propulsion. Some cells are capable of ameboid movement ("ameboid" referring to the tiny 1-celled animal called an ameba which can move about by itself). The protoplasm of these cells bulges out into footlike processes called pseudopodia ("false feet"), and then the entire cell follows the foot. An example of this type of cell is certain white blood cells which travel by ameboid movement through the blood vessel walls to sites of inflammation and infection in the body.

Another type of motion is contractility, which is the ability of a cell to become shorter and thicker in response to a signal sent out by a nerve. This property is most highly developed in cells that make up the muscles.

Metabolism is the process by which the cells build protein and produce energy. It is the sum total of all the physical and chemical processes that take place within a cell. Food and oxygen which enter the cell in dissolved forms react chemically and liberate the energy necessary for the cell to carry on its work. At the same time, the cell uses some of the products of these reactions for its own nourishment, for the manufacture of more protoplasm and for certain specialized activities such as secreting. (A secretion is a cell discharge useful to another body part.) Another phase of metabolism involves the removal of the waste products following the chemical reactions. The factors controlling the passage of food and oxygen into and the waste products out of the cell will be considered later in this chapter.

Growth and *reproduction* produce an increase in the total amount of protoplasm as a result of an increase in the number of cells. Through a complicated process called mitosis, cells can divide into 2 parts and reproduce themselves. Each of the "daughter" cells is an exact genetic duplicate of the original or "mother" cell from which it came. If the body is thought of as a group of cells, mitosis is responsible for its growth as well as the repair and the replacement of injured and dead tissues. The speed with which cells reproduce varies, but many thousands are formed daily in the skin alone to compensate for those lost by shedding or destroyed by injury or disease. Reproduction also refers to division of the ovum (the egg cell) which is responsible for the creation of new individuals and the preservation of the race.

THE CELL

Cells are too small to be seen without a microscope (the sole exception in the body is the ovum). Although cells may be of different sizes, shapes and types having only a vague resemblance to each other, their general plan of structure is the same. They all have a *cell membrane* (also called the cell wall) which is a firm boundary resembling a delicate film. Within the membrane is the *cytoplasm,* the material which makes up the body of the cell. Suspended in or near the center of the cell is the *nucleus* enveloped by its nuclear membrane. The nucleus is responsible for the reproduction (division) of the cell and the coordination of certain cell activities. The nucleus also contains a tiny globule known as the *nucleolus* which is particularly important in reproduction. A secondary nucleolus is also present in some cells. Usually, the nucleus is filled with a network of fine strands (linen fibers) on and between which are globules of a material called *chromatin*. All of these structures, of course, are part of the protoplasm.

The cytoplasm is a miniature chemical laboratory involved in many complicated processes vital to the life of the cell. It is here that the work of the cell such as absorption, secretion, etc., is carried on.

Two of the important structures in the cytoplasm are the *mitochondria*, rod-shaped bodies active in the production of power and energy, and granules of *ribonucleic acid* (RNA), which is related to the production of protein, the important constituent of all protoplasm. The *centrosomes* (centrioles) are small paired bodies also important in cell division. Many other less important structures have been identified in the cytoplasm, particularly since the invention of the electron microscope with its tremendous magnifying powers. A typical cell is seen in Figure 28.

Within the cell nucleus are small chromatin granules called *chromosomes* which contain the genes (see p. 119). Although human reproductive cells are known to have 23 pairs of chromosomes (46 total), the genes are present in the thousands. Genes transmit specifications for the characteristics of a species. They determine whether a living organism is male or female; whether it has blue or brown eyes; whether it has light or dark skin. In other words, in human reproduction, the genes transfer from one generation to the next all the characteristics which are inherited. If there were no organization to this process of cell division, known as *mitosis*, each new cell would not have the same charac-

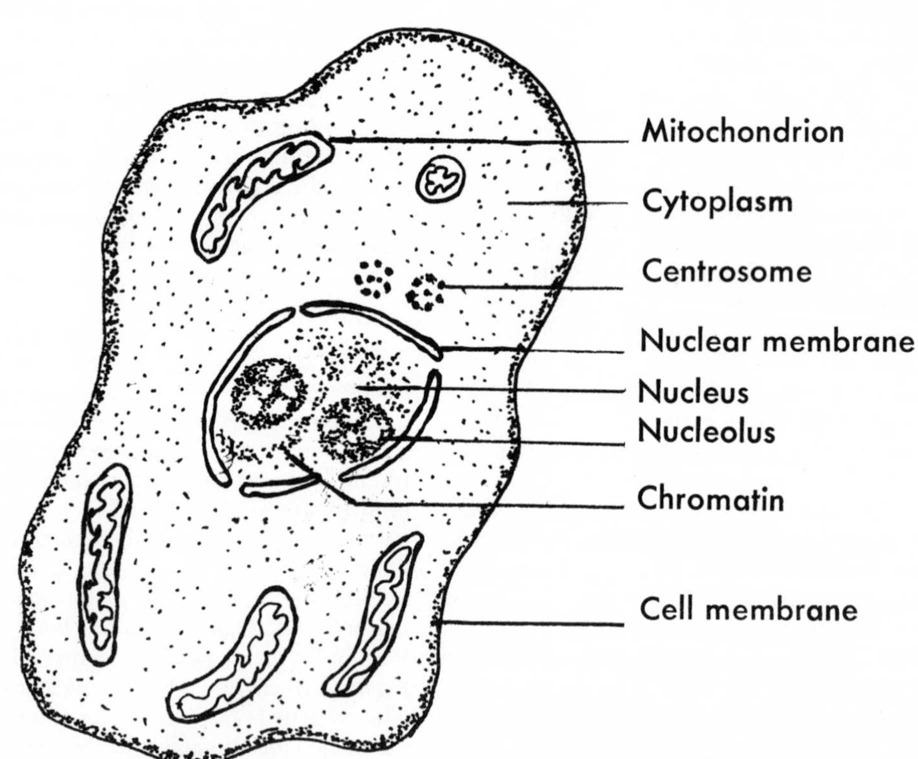

Fig. 28. A typical cell showing some of its components (diagrammatic). (Adapted from Chaffee, E. E.: Laboratory Manual in Physiology and Anatomy, ed. 2, p. 9, Philadelphia, Lippincott)

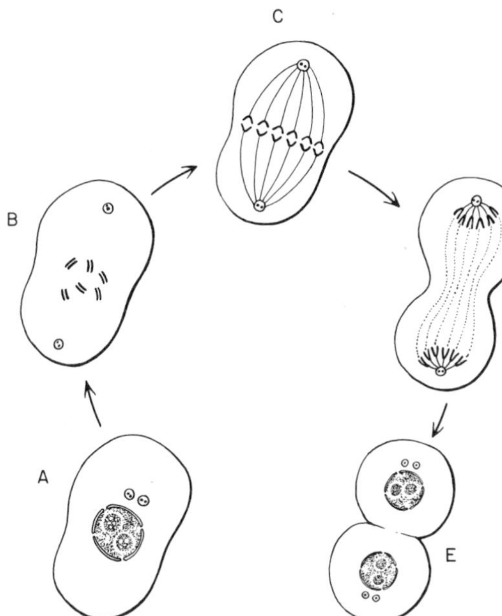

Fig. 29. Diagram of a cell undergoing mitosis. (A) Typical cell. (B) The nuclear membrane disappears and the chromosomes come together in pairs. The centrosomes separate and are drawn towards opposite ends of the cell. (C) The chromosomes split, so that half move towards each centrosome. (D) The cell begins to elongate, thinning in the middle with the cell wall following the same shape. (E) The cell splits into two parts with half the cytoplasm, nuclear material and cell wall in each of the two new cells.

teristics as the original. As it is, because of the genes, each of the 2 new cells is genetically identical with the original from which it was formed.

This amazing process of mitosis occurs as a result of a rearrangement of the particles in the nucleus. Briefly, what happens is that the centrosomes separate and are drawn toward opposite ends of the cell. The nuclear membrane then disappears, and the chromosomes split so that half move toward each centrosome. The cell then begins to elongate, thinning in the middle with the cell wall following the same shape. It finally splits into 2 parts with half the cytoplasm, the nuclear material and the cell wall in each of the 2 new cells (see Fig. 29).

Scientists do not know exactly how the process of cell division and the resulting duplication of cells is carried out. However, they have found within the chromosomes a nucleic acid known as DNA. DNA is a giant molecule, of which the genes are probably segments, which will duplicate itself if provided with the proper raw materials. Evidence shows that DNA is the cell substance that provides the "blueprint" for the succeeding generations.

The cell membrane plays an important role in regulating cell activities, since it controls what passes into and out of the cytoplasm. It contains tiny openings (pores) which act more or less like filters, allowing the passage of some molecules and rejecting others. There are many factors influencing this mechanism, but before discussing them, it is necessary to understand something about the water (body fluids) in which all cells are bathed.

Body Fluids

There is a large amount of water in all living material. Life cannot exist for long without it, since it is the medium which holds the various components of protoplasm in solution, both solids and gases, and is necessary for all of the chemical reactions which occur in the cell. Water comprises about 70% of our body weight. About three fourths of this water is found within the cells, and this is called *intracellular fluid* ("intra" means "within"). The remainder is found outside of the cells and is called *extracellular fluid* ("extra" means "outside"). About one fourth of the extracellular fluid is found in the blood vessels as plasma—the liquid portion of the blood—and the remaining three fourths is in the spaces between the blood vessels and the cells. The latter is known as *intercellular* fluid ("inter" means "between"), *tissue* fluid or *interstitial fluid*. It acts as a vehicle for the exchange of substances between the blood stream and the cells. For example, oxygen is carried by the blood and eventually passes through the walls of the capillaries (the smallest of the blood vessel network) into the intercellular fluid. It then circulates in this fluid and is ready to enter the cells for use in metabolism. The waste materials of metabolism pass through the cell membranes in the opposite direction, circulating through the intercellular fluid into the blood or lymph vessels, which transport them to the systems of excretion. This is illustrated diagrammatically on page 161.

Many elements such as sodium, potassium, magnesium and calcium *ionize* when they are dissolved in water; that is, they acquire electrical charges. Hence, we have given them the name *electrolytes.* Electrolytes may take the form of acids, alkalies (bases) or salts. In order for the body to function normally, electrolytes must be present in precisely the right quantities in both the intracellular and the extracellular fluids. Electrolyte balance is extremely critical; if the fluid is too acid or too alkaline, it may have highly destructive effects on the cells. Normally, this balance is maintained automatically by various mechanisms, chiefly by the action of the kidneys. Many illnesses and surgical procedures disturb this balance, but fortunately we can usually control it by injecting solutions containing electrolytes into the body. Maintenance of fluid and electrolyte balance is discussed in greater detail in Chapter 33.

Tissues

We have said that the body is organized in a definite pattern. Cells of the same type and structure join together to form tissues, each of which has a special function. The list below tells what tissues do and where they are located:

Epithelial: Covers body surfaces and lines cavities (skin, nails, hair, lining of parts of the body such as the nose and the throat)

Connective: Anchors and holds other tissues together

Muscular: Contracts and stretches, causing motion

A. *Skeletal*—attached to bones

B. *Smooth (visceral)*—found in the walls of blood vessels and internal organs such as the stomach

C. *Cardiac*—found in the walls of the heart

Nervous: Receives stimuli and conducts impulses to and from all parts of the body

Blood: Carries food and oxygen to the cells, removes wastes and fights infection and poisons. (NOTE: The presence of cells places this liquid in the category of a tissue. Blood is really a form of connective tissue, but it has so many special characteristics that we study it separately.)

Membranes. Certain kinds of epithelial and connective tissues act together, serving in a very special function as membranes. We have already spoken of the cell and nuclear membranes which really are considered parts of a single cell. However, "tissue" membranes are made up of many cells. Both tissues and membranes will be discussed in the next chapter.

In discussing cells and tissues we have considered normal structure and growth. Occasionally, a cell or group of cells will grow into an abnormal mass of tissue called a *tumor,* which has no function whatever. Research has shown that these growths are usually the result of some kind of irritation to the tissues, such as continued exposure of the skin to x-rays or chemicals, oversecretion of some glands of the body or old scars. Heredity has also been found to be a factor. However, the direct cause for tumor formation is still unknown. Those tumors which do not spread to other tissues are called *benign* or *innocent;* those which do are called *malignant,* a condition known as cancer.

Organs and Systems

Different kinds of tissues form organs. For example, the heart is a combination of muscle, nerve, blood and epithelial tissue. An organ is defined as a part of the body which performs a definite function. It does not work independently but is associated with other organs and may have many functions. These group associations are called *systems*—groups of organs in which each contributes its share to the function of the whole. Systems do specialized work in the body. Your understanding of the structure and the functions of the systems is the basis for your own health habits and your care of patients. Here is a bird's-eye view of the systems, showing how organs are grouped together for specific purposes:

Skeletal: Bones, which are the body framework

Muscular: Muscles, attached to bones, which make the body movements possible

Circulatory: Heart, blood and blood vessels, lymph and lymph vessels. These organs carry food, water, oxygen and wastes in the body.

Digestive: Mouth, salivary glands, pharynx, esophagus, stomach, intenstines, liver and pancreas. These organs take in food and convert it into substances the cells can use.

Respiratory: Nose, pharynx, larynx, trachea, bronchi and lungs. This system supplies the body with oxygen, and eliminates carbon dioxide as waste.

Urinary: Kidneys, ureters, urinary bladder and urethra. They eliminate waste products from the body. Sometimes this system is discussed under the classification of the *excretory system*, which includes the respiratory and the digestive systems and the skin.

Reproductive: Ovaries, fallopian (uterine) tubes, uterus, vagina and mammary glands (breasts) in the woman; testes, accessory glands and penis in the man. This system makes possible the perpetuation of the race.

Endocrine: Ductless glands (pituitary, thyroid, parathyroids, adrenals, testes, ovaries, thymus, pineal, and islands of Langerhans in the pancreas). These glands secrete hormones that regulate various body processes, such as growth, cell metabolism, etc.

Nervous: Brain, spinal cord and nerves, which control and coordinate the activities of the body.

Sensory: Eyes, ears, taste buds, organs of smell, touch, pain, etc. These organs operate in special ways to bring stimuli from the outside to the brain.

The next 10 chapters will be devoted to a description of each of these systems.

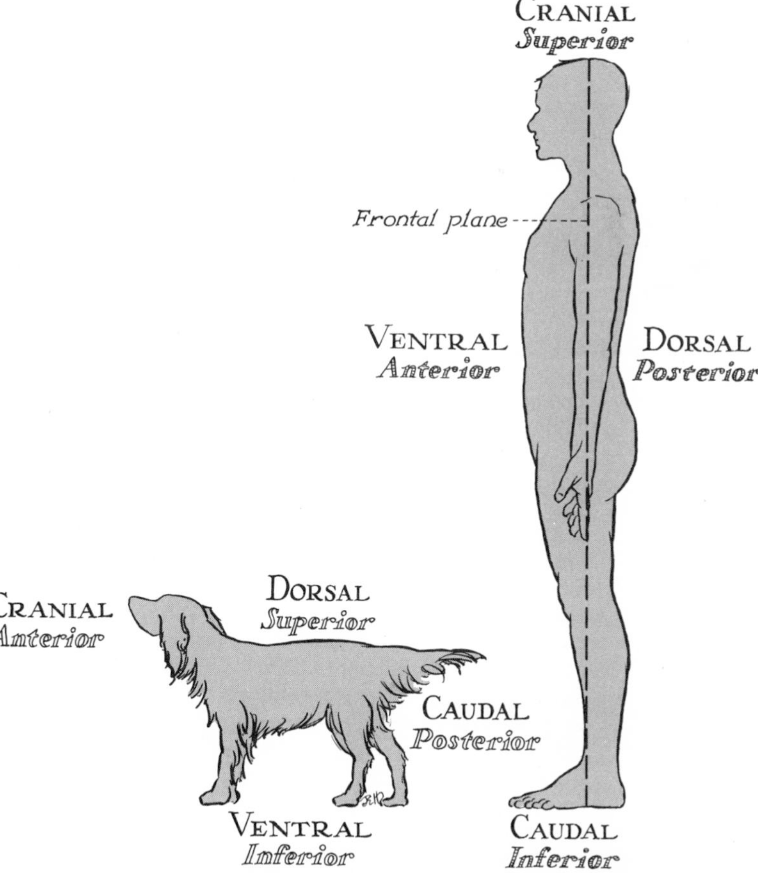

FIG. 30. Comparative terminology in quadruped and man, for location or position; frontal plane is indicated by broken line. (Greisheimer, E. M.: Physiology and Anatomy, ed. 8, p. 5, Philadelphia, Lippincott)

BODY DIRECTIONS

A number of terms are used to designate certain areas and directions of the body. They help to specify the location of an organ or system in studying anatomy and physiology and also give the doctor and the nurse a guide in noting and recording signs and symptoms. As we discuss some of these terms, it is important to remember that they refer to the body in the "anatomic position" (i.e., the body is erect with arms at the sides and palms turned forward).

Superior: "Above" or in a higher position
Inferior: "Below" or in a lower position
Examples: The head is superior to the neck. The chest is inferior to the neck.

Cranial: Near the head
Caudal: Near the lower end of the body (i.e., near the end of the spine)
Examples: The brain is in the cranial cavity. The buttocks, the muscles upon which we sit, are located at the caudal end of the body.

Anterior or ventral: Toward the front or "belly" surface of the body
Posterior or dorsal: Toward the back of the body
Examples: The nose is on the anterior, or ventral, surface of the head. The calf is on the posterior, or dorsal surface of the leg.

Medial: Nearer the midline
Lateral: Farther from the midline, toward the side
Examples: The nose is medial to the eyes. The ears are lateral to the nose.

Internal: Deeper within the body
External: Toward the outer surface of the body
Examples: The stomach is an internal body organ. The skin covers the external surface of the body.

Proximal: Nearest the origin of a part
Distal: Farthest from the origin of a part
Examples: In the upper extremity (arm), the upper arm above the elbow is proximal to the lower arm below. In the lower extremity (leg), the lower leg below the knee is distal to the thigh.

Central: Situated at or pertaining to the center

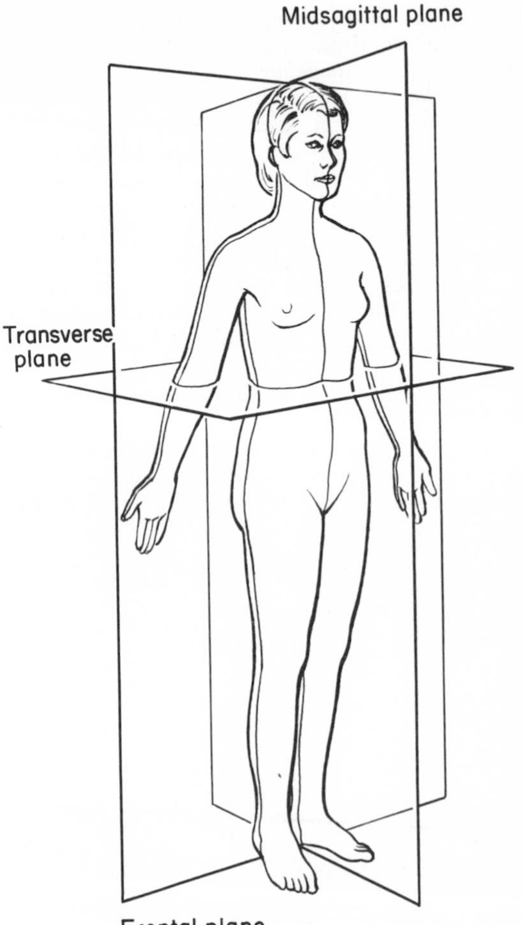

FIG. 31

Peripheral: Situated at or pertaining to the outward part of surface
Examples: The brain and the spinal cord are part of the central nervous system. The peripheral nerves go out to the body parts and return to the central nervous system.

Parietal: Pertaining to the sides or the walls of a cavity
Visceral: Pertaining to the organs within a cavity
Examples: The abdominal cavity is lined with a membrane called the parietal peritoneum. The stomach and the intestines are visceral organs in the abdominal cavity.

In order to show a better relation of the position of the body structures to each other, the following imaginary planes are used to divide the body into sections (also see Fig. 31):

The Midsagittal Plane: Divides the body into right and left halves by passing through the midline from top to bottom.

The Frontal (Coronal) Plane: Divides the body into front and back parts by passing through longitudinally from head to toes.

The Transverse (Horizontal) Plane: Divides the body into upper (superior) and lower (inferior) parts by passing through horizontally.

Body Cavities

Within the body are 2 groups of spaces (or cavities) which contain various organs. They are the *dorsal* and the *ventral cavities.*

The dorsal cavity consists of the cranial portion, which houses the brain and the vertebral portion, which houses the spinal cord.

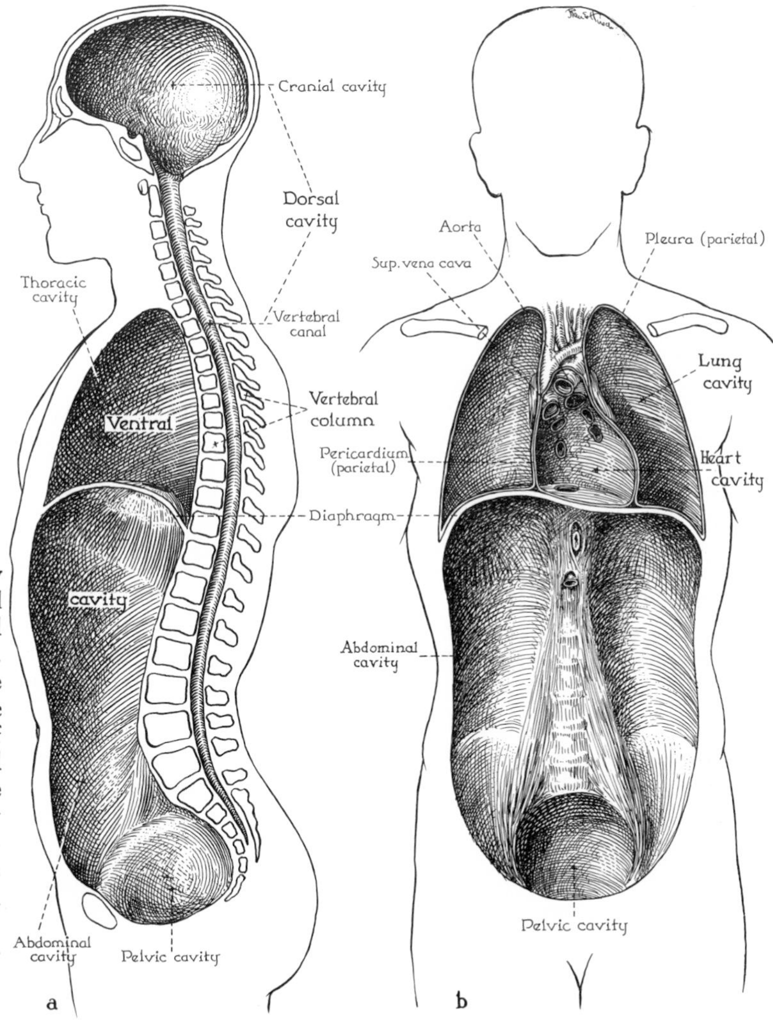

FIG. 32. Diagram of body cavities. (a) The vertebral column, the dorsal cavity and the ventral cavity are shown. The diaphragm separates the abdominal from the thoracic portion; the lower portion of the abdominal cavity is called the pelvic cavity. (b) The divisions of the ventral cavity are shown. The thoracic division of the ventral cavity is subdivided into the pleural and the pericardial cavities. (Greisheimer, E. M.: Physiology and Anatomy, ed. 8, p. 9, Philadelphia, Lippincott)

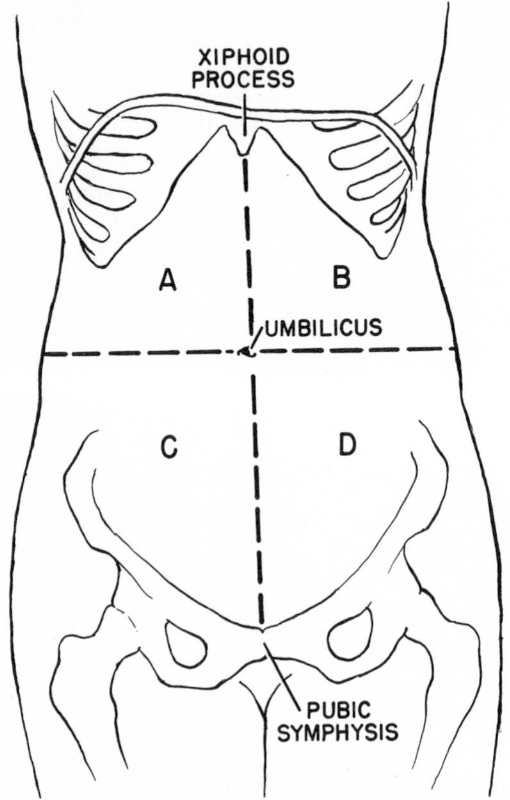

FIG. 33. Quadrants of the abdomen:
(A) The right upper quadrant–RUQ
(B) The left upper quadrant–LUQ
(C) The right lower quadrant–RLQ
(D) The left lower quadrant–LLQ
(Fuerst, E. V., and Wolff, L.: Fundamentals of Nursing, ed. 3, p. 197, Philadelphia, Lippincott)

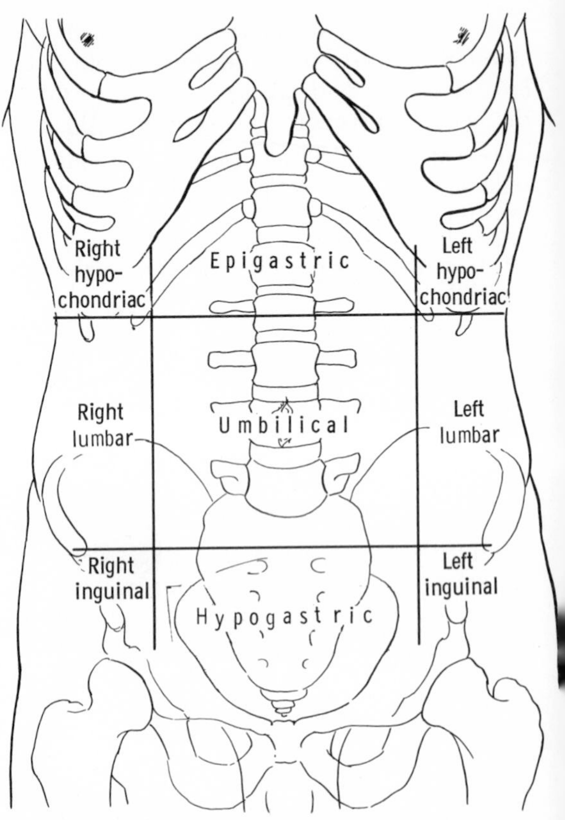

FIG. 34. Regions of the abdomen. (Greisheimer, E. M.: Physiology and Anatomy, ed. 8, p. 619, Philadelphia, Lippincott)

The ventral cavity consists of the thoracic and the abdominal portions which are separated by a large muscle called the diaphragm. (The diaphragm will be discussed in Chapter 13.) The thoracic cavity comprises the pericardial cavity, which contains the heart, and 2 pleural cavities, each of which contains a lung. In addition to the heart, the space between the lungs (called the mediastinum) also contains structures such as the large blood vessels, the trachea, the esophagus and the thymus gland.

The upper part of the abdominal cavity contains the stomach, most of the intestines, the liver, the gallbladder, the pancreas, the spleen, the kidneys, the adrenal glands and the ureters. The lower portion, called the pelvic cavity, contains the urinary bladder, the remaining part of the intestines, the rectum and the internal reproductive organs. The body cavities are shown in Figure 32.

Regions in the Abdominal Cavity

The abdominal cavity has been divided into quadrants to help in describing signs and symptoms and locating the viscera from the surface. These are the right upper, the left upper, the right lower and the left lower quadrants as shown in Figure 33. In addition, there is another division which divides it into 9 regions. These are illustrated in Figure 34.

12

THE BODY'S CELL PATTERN: TISSUES AND MEMBRANES

TISSUES

Cells which are grouped together according to their functions are called tissues. The following give further descriptions of the kinds of tissues within the body and their functions.

Epithelial Tissues

Epithelial tissues are those which cover the body surfaces or line the cavities of the body. An important characteristic of epithelial tissue (also called *epithelium*) is that the cells are packed closely together with very little intercellular material between them. This arrangement enables them to protect other parts of the body.

Some epithelial cells have fine hairlike processes on them called *cilia,* which move in waves, carrying or transporting materials, such as mucus. Other epithelial cells are heavily supplied with nerve endings, like those found in the fingertips.

Groups of epithelial cells shaped like tiny goblets have the ability to form secretions; these are called *glands.* They release their secretions either into a duct or directly into the bloodstream. Another kind of epithelium is especially adapted to the function of absorption, like that found in the intestines.

Because the outer layers of the epithelial cells are constantly being worn off at the surface, the bottom layers of epithelium are continually producing new cells. The epithelium is in a continuous state of regeneration.

Connective Tissues

Connective tissues are found everywhere in the body. They do what their name suggests—bind or tie together other cells, tissues or organs of the body and anchor organs in place. One type of connective tissue, the blood, is active in protecting the body from infection by producing antibodies to immunize against reactions to disease.

Connective tissue, unlike epithelium, has few cells for a given amount of tissue. Material between cells is a nonliving substance called *intercellular substance.* It varies in nature from the liquid found in the blood to the hard compound of bone. The intercellular substance in connective tissue is abundant, whereas the cells are few.

There are several different kinds of connective tissue. *Adipose* tissue is fatty in substance; *cartilage* tissue serves as a shock absorber between bones; and *elastic* tissues, which are found in the walls of the various tubes of the body, are more flexible due to the presence of a network of elastic fibers in its intercellular substance.

Muscle Tissue

Muscle tissue contracts or extends to provide motion. Skeletal (striated) muscle looks like the meat we eat—red and soft, sometimes stringy, and usually held in large bundles and shaped into muscle masses. This is the muscle tissue that is attached to bone to provide body movements. It is called *voluntary muscle* because its movements originate in an act of will. Smooth (visceral) muscle tissue makes up the walls of the intestines and the blood vessels. This is known as *involuntary muscle* because it acts independently of the will; that is, we cannot voluntarily control the action of smooth muscle tissue. A third kind of muscle tissue is cardiac, the muscle of the heart.

Nerve Tissue. This will be discussed in Chapter 14.

MEMBRANES

A membrane is a thin soft sheet of tissue that may be very fragile. Membranes cover surfaces, line body cavities or divide organs. All have protective and secretory functions. Some membranes absorb or excrete.

Mucous membranes line cavities of the body which open to the exterior, such as the mouth, the nose, the intestinal or the urinary tracts. They secrete a substance called mucus and form a protection against bacterial invasion as well as other foreign particles.

Serous membranes line the cavities that do not open to the exterior; they cover organs such as the lungs, the stomach and the heart. These membranes secrete a thin fluid which prevents friction when organs are in contact with one another.

Synovial membranes line joint cavities between bones and cover tendons and bursal sacs. They also provide for smooth motion without friction.

Fascia is a *fibrous membrane* which underlies the skin and attaches it to underlying structures. Deep fascia surrounds the muscles and the internal organs.

THE SKIN

The skin, sometimes classified as a membrane, is one of the largest and most important organs of the body. It is generally soft and elastic with a resistive outer layer that serves as a protection.

The skin has several important functions. Its function as a protection serves the body in several ways. It prevents the entrance of microorganisms or other foreign substances; it also prevents injury to more fragile organs within the body and usually keeps the body from suffering from too great a loss of water.

The skin contains many nerve endings or receptors for the nervous system and, therefore, serves as an organ of sensation. Along with our sense of touch, we can perceive warmth, cold, pain, etc.

One of the important duties of the skin is the regulation of body temperature. In hot weather, the blood vessels dilate, bringing the blood to the surface of the skin for cooling. If the blood vessels constrict (that is, become smaller), the amount of heat lost through the skin is reduced. The evaporation of water through the sweat glands also cools the body. The skin has the powers of absorption and excretion. Some medications are applied to be absorbed through the skin. Because the sweat glands excrete excess water and salts, some authorities classify the skin as part of the excretory system.

The skin is composed of 2 layers: the dermis and the epidermis. Directly under the dermis, but not part of the skin, is the subcutaneous tissue. The epidermis (outer layer) protects the layer beneath. It is thicker over the soles of the feet and palms of the hands—places that undergo considerable wear and tear. The cells on the outside or the top layer are constantly being rubbed off by the friction of movement, bathing, etc. The live inner cells continually replace these cells by mitosis; these live cells push up to the surface to replace the dead cells. The living cells contain pigment, the coloring matter of the skin. The amount of pigment varies in races and individuals—the Nordic peoples and other blondes have less pigment than the Asiatic people and other brunettes. Skin color is inherited; however, exposure to the sun increases the amount of pigment in the skin. There are no blood vessels in the epidermis.

The dermis (inner layer), usually called the true skin, is composed entirely of live cells enclosed in a network of lymph vessels, capillaries and nerves projecting out to form ridges (papillae) in the epidermis. These ridges make the individual pattern of fingerprints and footprints that are used for identification. The nerve endings provide us with a sense of touch. The cells in this layer give the skin elasticity, allowing it to stretch. There are also fat cells in this layer which give the skin a smooth appearance. As aging occurs, the loss of subcutaneous fat and elastic tissues causes wrinkles to appear.

The hair, the nails, the sebaceous (oil) glands and the sweat glands are called the "appendages" of the skin.

The skin is covered with hairs except in a few areas such as the palms of the hands and the soles of the feet. The part of the hair seen above the skin is the shaft; the part lying below is the root. The shaft runs slantwise from the body. The organs of touch lie in the true skin, close to the hair follicle, so that only a slight movement of the hair will cause the sensation of touch. The skin hairs have their roots in tiny sacs, called the hair *follicles.* Each follicle contains a single hair root, which, as long as it is alive, will continue to grow a hair that projects above the skin. (Two gray hairs cannot come in for everyone that is pulled out!) Diseased or injured follicles destroy hair roots.

The hair obtains its nourishment entirely from the blood stream serving living cells at its roots. Since hair growth takes place here, cutting or trimming the ends will not stimulate growth. However, brushing the hair or massaging the scalp may be effective. The color of the hair is due to pigment that is deposited in a layer of the hair; when hair turns gray, there is a reduction of pigment and an increase in the light-reflecting air spaces between the cells. Baldness may be associated with the endocrine system, or it may be due to a factor of heredity. Constriction of the scalp by tight hat bands may contribute to baldness.

Surrounding each hair follicle are small muscles called the *arrectores pilorum.* If you become cold and the body wants to generate heat rapidly by widespread muscle action, these small muscles contract and the hairs stand erect. This is commonly called "goose flesh."

The sebaceous, or oil glands, lie close to the hair follicles into which they empty oil (sebum). The oil travels from there to the surface of the skin. These glands provide a natural oil to keep the skin soft and make the hair glossy. Overactive oil glands make your skin

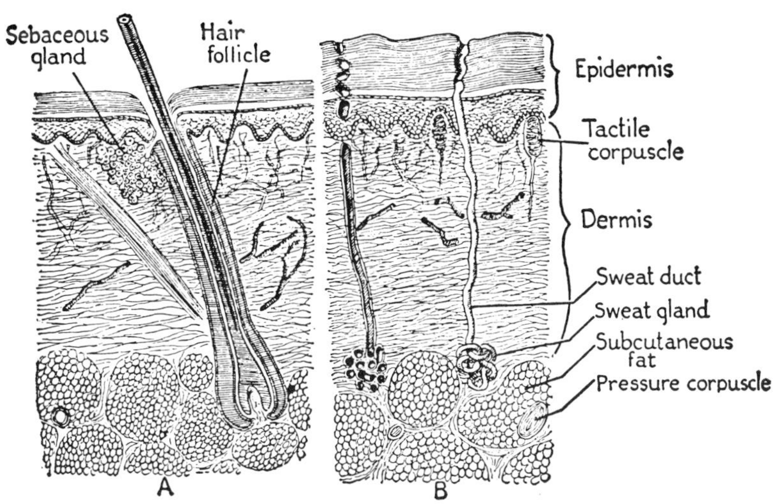

Fig. 35. Section through skin: (A) with hair follicle; (B) with sweat glands and nerve endings. (Baillif and Kimmel: Structure and Function of the Human Body, p. 213, Philadelphia, Lippincott)

and hair unattractive. Pimples are caused by inflamed or infected oil glands.

The sweat glands remove waste from the body in the form of perspiration. They extract water and salt wastes from the blood and discharge them through the tiny outlets on the skin surface called the *pores.* These openings are countless—there are millions in the skin of an adult—especially in the hands, the feet, the forehead and the axillae (armpits). Perspiration also helps to control the temperature of your body. If your body becomes too warm, the dermal capillaries expand, and more blood flows to the surface. The sweat glands then have more blood from which to take water and other materials; therefore, they pour out more perspiration. Greater evaporation increases the cooling effects on the body, just as wetting the porch roof or the sidewalks makes the surrounding air cooler on a hot summer day.

The nails are tightly packed cells of the epidermis that protect the tips of the fingers and the toes and help in handling and picking up objects. Their roots are live cells, but the outer ends are dead. An injured nail will grow again if the root cells are still alive. After middle age, the nails usually become thicker and more brittle.

13

THE ERECT AND MOVING BODY: THE MUSCULOSKELETAL SYSTEM

THE BODY'S FRAMEWORK

The skeleton is the living bony framework for the rest of the body. It supports and gives shape to the body and protects vital organs and delicate soft tissues. It serves also as an anchor for the skeletal muscles by providing attachments for tendons, parts of the muscles, and thereby allows motion. In addition to these functions of the skeletal system, the bone marrow manufactures red blood cells, some white blood cells and the platelets—the solid elements of the blood tissue.

Structure of the Bones

There are more than 200 bones in the body. (The total usually given for an adult is 206.) Long bones provide support; short bones facilitate greater motion within parts; and flat bones give protection. Some bones are classified as irregular, either because they vary in size and shape to accommodate other structures or simply because they do not fit into other categories. Bones contain cavities of various types. A *sinus* is a hollow area within a bone; a *foramen* is an opening through which the nerves or the blood vessels pass. Hollows and projections on bone surfaces provide attachment points for the muscles.

Although the tissue is hardened by deposits of calcium and phosphorus, bones are made up of living cells. The *periosteum,* a membrane that covers every bone, contains the blood vessels that supply the oxygen and the nutrition to the bone cells to keep them alive. The blood vessels also bring the bone building materials and minerals that harden the bone by filling the intercellular spaces.

Bones are living active organs that change greatly in the lifetime of an individual. Although the bone structure and size are altered primarily to accommodate growth, change continues into later life when most growth has stopped. The hardening process of bones is gradual: a baby's bones are partly cartilage, which is soft bone tissue. Bones grow both in diameter and in length and are not completely hardened until the individual's growth is complete, which usually occurs between the ages of 18 and 21. Ossification, or the increase in calcified tissue, extends from the middle of the shaft outward, while the cartilagenous ends also continue to extend the length of the bone.

Two types of osseous (bone) tissue enter into the construction of the long bones of the extremities. The shaft, or *diaphysis,* is a hard compact portion, while the end, or *epiphysis,* is spongelike and covered by a shell of harder bone. The diaphysis and the epiphysis do not fuse until full growth is reached. Bone cells multiply rapidly in the growing years, but thereafter new cells are formed only to replace dead or injured ones and to repair breaks. Bones become harder and more brittle, breaking more easily as they grow older.

The outside surface of the bones is hard;

the hollow inner part is filled with a soft substance called marrow. There are 2 kinds of marrow: the yellow kind, which we have seen in "soup bones," is found in the central cavities of the long bones; and the red marrow, which is found in the ends of long bones as well as in the bodies of the vertebrae and the flat bones. Red marrow is responsible for the manufacture of red blood cells, white blood cells and probably also of blood platelets.

Joints

The points at which the bones are attached to each other are called joints or articulations. Because of the way the bones are attached the

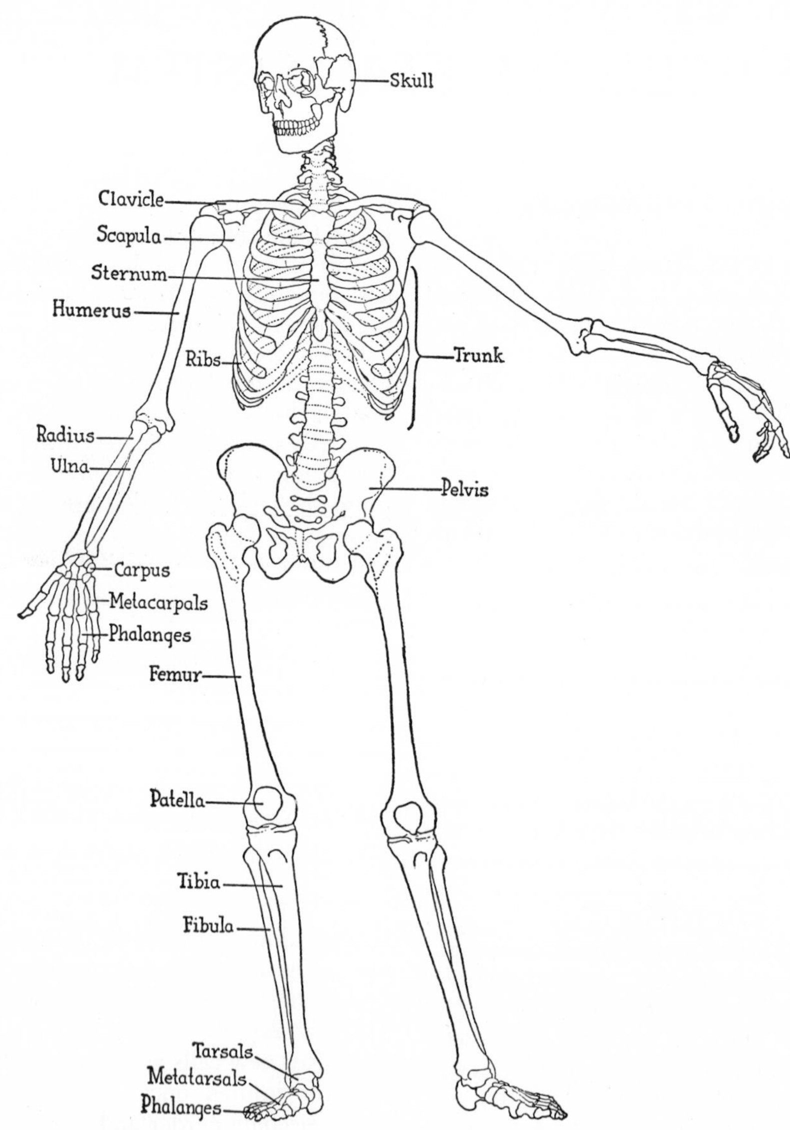

Fig. 36. The skeleton, front view.

body position can be changed, and hundreds of motions are possible.

Kinds of Joints. The joints are primarily of 3 different kinds. The first is that type in which there is no motion at all, as in the bones of the skull which are fitted together with interlocking notches. Within the second kind, there is a slight degree of motion or flexibility, as is found in the vertebral column. The third type of joint is classified as "freely movable" and can be found in many parts of the body such as the shoulder.

The freely movable joints are of several different kinds. Your finger and knee joints move like a door on its hinges and are appropriately called hinge joints. In the shoulders and the hips, ball-and-socket joints allow rotating motions—the rounded end of one bone (the ball)

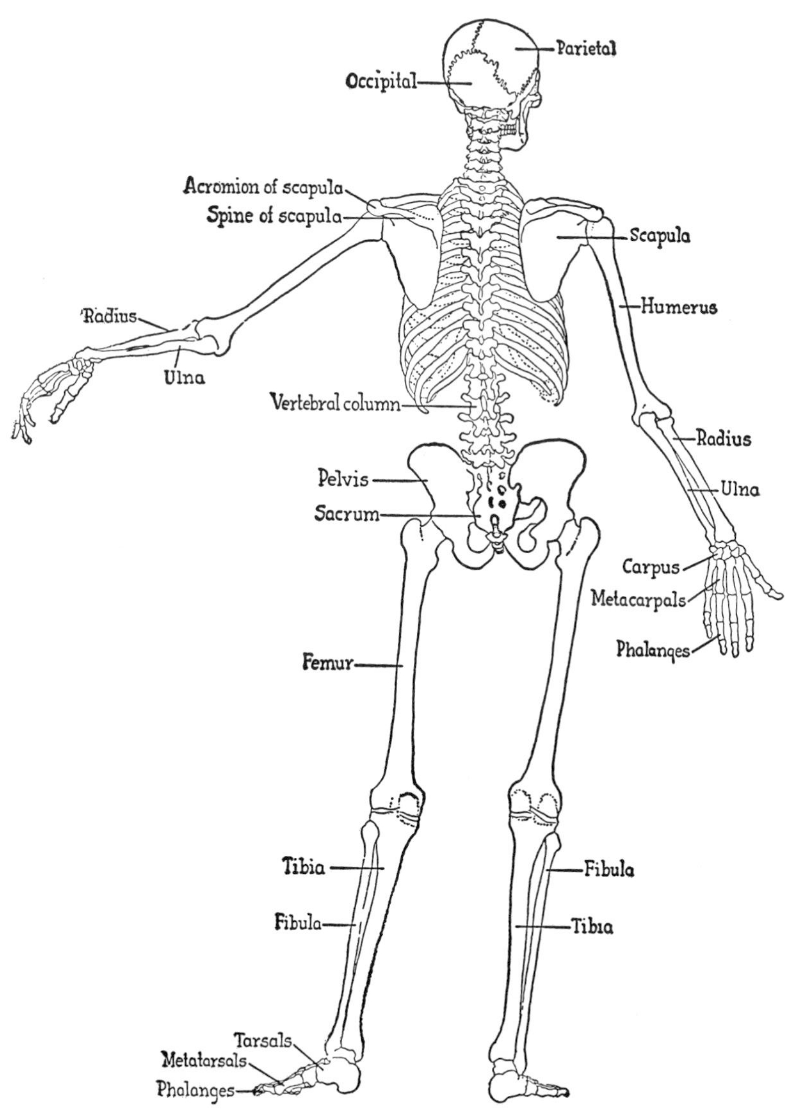

Fig. 37. The skeleton, back view.

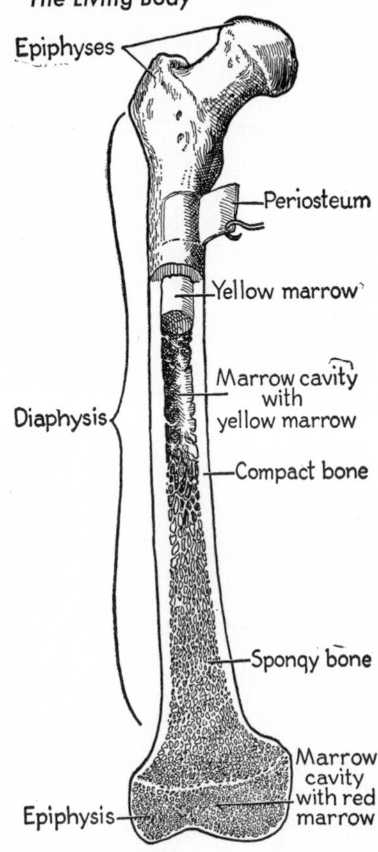

Fig. 38. Bone as an organ. (Baillif and Kimmel: Structure and Function of the Human Body, p. 84, Philadelphia, Lippincott)

fits into the hollowed-out end of the other (the socket). The elbow is an example of a pivot joint, which makes it possible for you to turn your forearm as you do in turning a doorknob (see Fig. 39).

Ligaments

Strong, fibrous bands, called ligaments, hold bones together, and the moving joints are lined with a membrane that secretes a fluid called synovial fluid which keeps them lubricated and working smoothly. Cartilage plates on the ends of bones make a slick surface for rotation and absorb shocks and jars.

Bursae

The body contains sacs called *bursae*, which are also lined with synovial membrane. These act as cushions between the ends of the bones and also are found between muscles and bones or between tendons, wherever motion is likely to produce friction.

Movements

Some of the many different motions that the body can perform have definite names so far as function is concerned. *Flexion* decreases the angle between 2 bones or bends a part on itself, as in bending the elbow; *extension*, or straightening, is the opposite. *Abduction* is movement away from the midplane of the body; *adduction*, the opposite, is movement toward the midplane. If you hold your arm out straight and then move it around in a circle, all these movements are combined; the resulting motion is *circumduction*. A different kind of motion is *rotation*, which is twisting one part with respect to that which joins it, but without changing the angle between the two. An example of rotation is twisting the head in the familiar gesture of saying "No."

Some joined structures have special movements. If you stand with your arms hanging down and your palms facing forward, the movement that brings the forearm into this position is *supination*. Now, if you reverse your hands so that the backs of them face forward, the movement is called *pronation*. These movements are special because, as you reverse your hands, the 2 bones in the forearm actually cross one another (see Fig. 39).

The ankle joint also has special movements. If you bend your ankle so that the sole of the foot faces the opposite foot, the motion is called *inversion*. If you bend your ankle the opposite way, with the sole facing outward, the movement is known as *eversion*.

THE SKULL

The 3 main parts of the skeleton are the skull, the trunk and the extremities. The skull has 2 parts: the thin, flat bones of the *cranium*, which protect the brain, and the facial bones. The facial bones are light and irregularly shaped, and most of them are small; the lower jaw bone, the mandible, is the only movable facial bone. The cranial and the facial bones give the face its individual shape.

Figures 41 and 42 show the bones of the skull. The list on page 134 is the simplest way of describing their arrangement.

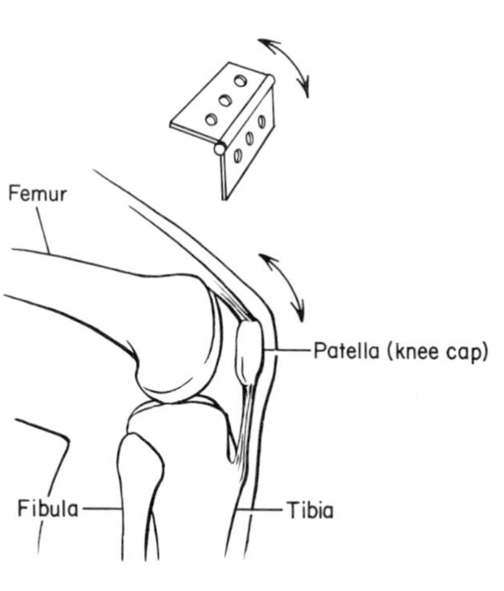

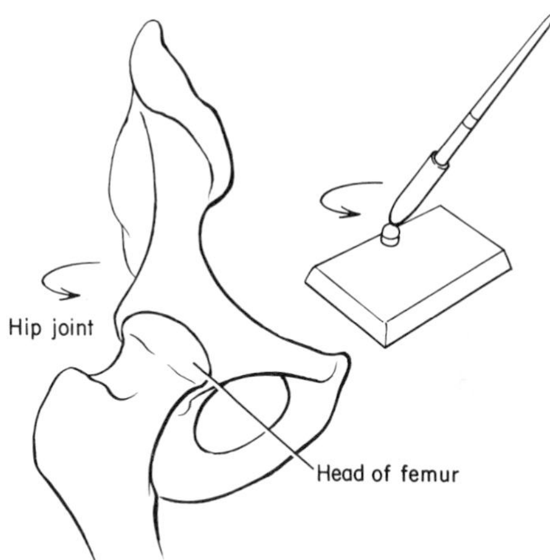

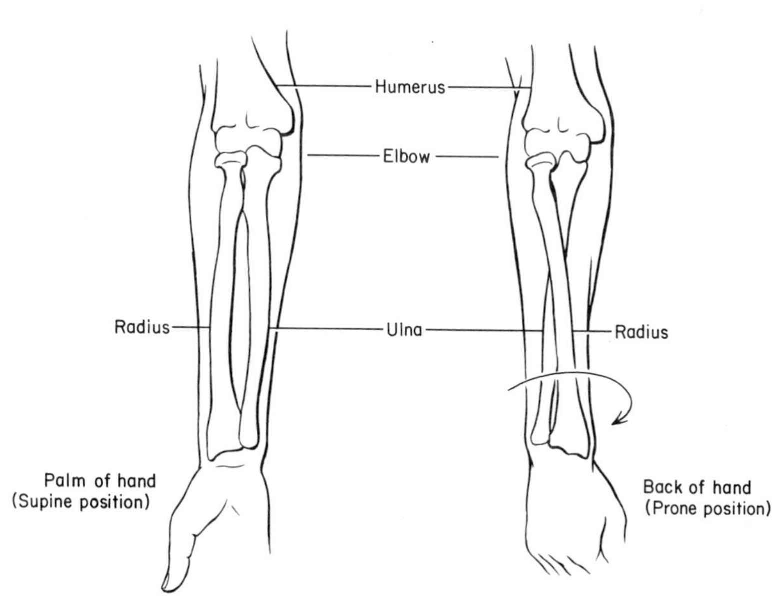

FIG. 39. Some freely movable joints.

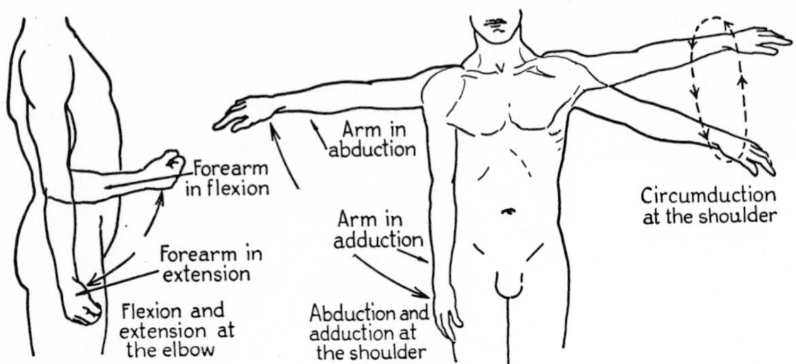

Fig. 40. Movement types. (Baillif and Kimmel: Structure and Function of the Human Body, p. 110, Philadelphia, Lippincott)

BONES OF THE CRANIUM

2 parietal
top and sides of head
1 occipital
back of head
1 frontal
forehead
2 temporal
contain ear cavities, mastoid cells in tip
1 sphenoid
center of base of skull
1 ethmoid
roof of nasal cavity

BONES OF THE FACE

2 nasal
bridge of nose
1 vomer
divides nasal cavity (as part of nasal septum)
2 inferior turbinates (conchae) in the nostrils
2 lacrimal
front part of eye sockets
2 zygomatic
prominent part of cheeks
base of eye sockets
2 palate
roof of mouth

BONES OF THE FACE—(*Cont.*)

2 maxillae
upper jaw
1 mandible
lower jaw

A small horseshoe-shaped bone, the *hyoid*, lies just behind and below the mandible; the tongue muscles are attached to it.

Four pairs of cavities in the cranial bones make your skull lighter and give back the sound of your voice. They are the *sinuses* and are named for the bones in which they lie: the frontal, the ethmoid, the sphenoid and the maxillary. These sinuses are lined with mucous membrane continuous with the nasal mucosa and drain into the nasal cavity.

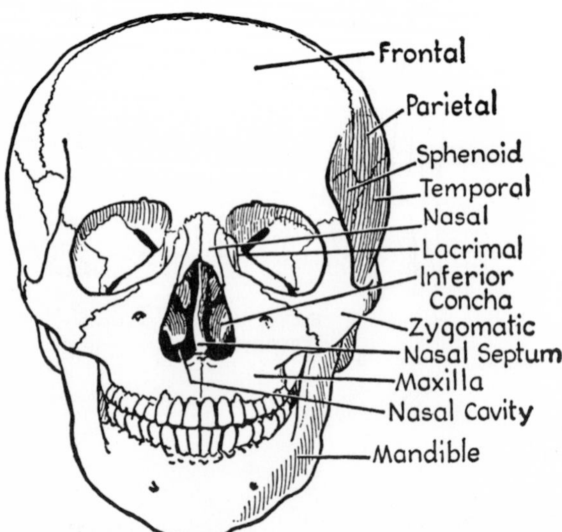

Fig. 41. Anterior view of the skull. (Baillif and Kimmel: Structure and Function of the Human Body, p. 87, Philadelphia, Lippincott)

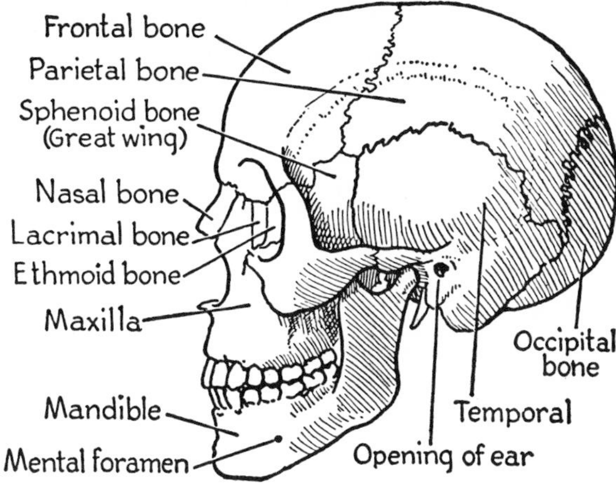

FIG. 42. Lateral view of the skull. (Baillif and Kimmel: Structure and Function of the Human Body, p. 88, Philadelphia, Lippincott)

THE TRUNK

The Vertebral Column

The vertebral column, or spine, holds the head, stiffens and supports the midportion of the body and provides attachments for the ribs and the pelvic bones. It protects the spinal cord, which passes from the brain down through the bony rings which make up the spinal canal. The vertebrae are constructed on a common plan; there are slight variations in their structure, but each one is made to adjust to the one beneath. They are separated from each other by plates of cartilage called *intervertebral disks*, which act as shock absorbers when you walk, jump or fall. On the inner side of the vertebra is a bony structure called the *arch*, which forms an opening or spinal foramen through which the spinal cord passes. Jutting from the arch are several fingerlike extensions, or *processes*, on which ligaments and tendons of the muscles of the bank are anchored. (See Figs. 43 and 44.) The muscles, the ligaments and the cartilage disks help to make the vertebral column strong yet flexible: we can bend forward, backward and to either side and can accomplish a considerable rotation of the central portion of our body as well.

The spine has 4 normal curves that help to balance the body. Disease or injury and poor posture distort these curves. Increased abnormal thoracic curvature of the lumbar spine is called *lordosis* or *swayback*. An increased lateral curvature is called *scoliosis*.

Division of the Vertebrae

The 26 vertebrae are divided into groups: the top 7, or cervical, are located in the neck—the first (the *atlas*) supports the skull, and the second (the *axis*) has an especially wide surface so that the head can be turned freely; the next 12 are the thoracic, to which the ribs are attached; and the next 5, the lumbar, are in the small of the back. The 5 sacral vertebrae form 1 solid bone, the *sacrum*, which anchors the pelvis; and the last 4 vertebrae, small and incomplete, form the *coccyx*.

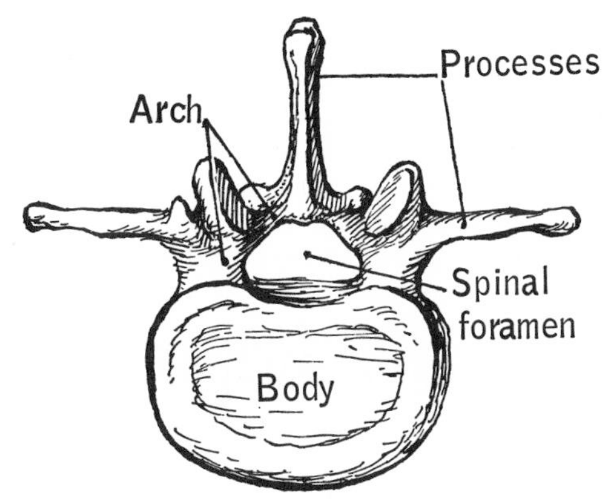

FIG. 43. Transverse section of a vertebra.

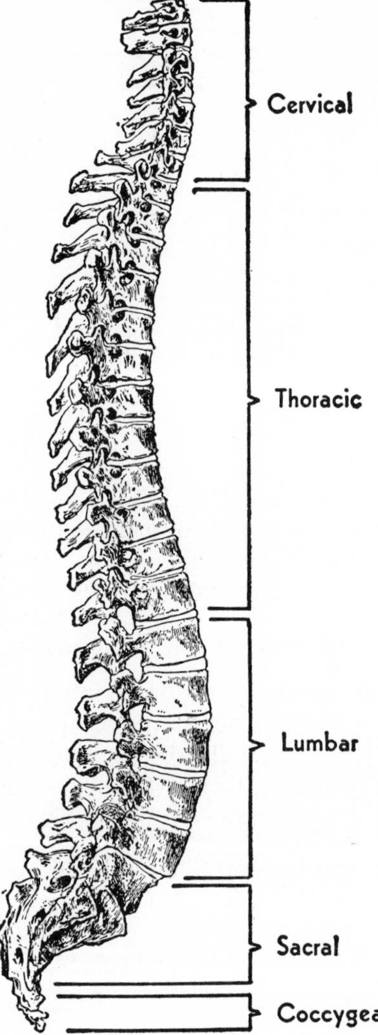

FIG. 44. Lateral view of an adult vertebral column, showing the curves and the divisions of the columns with reference to the spaces from which the spinal nerves emerge. Note the cartilage disks in the spaces between the bodies of the vertebrae.

The Thorax

The *thorax* is a cavity formed by the ribs, attached anteriorly to the sternum and posteriorly to the thoracic vertebrae. The thorax protects the heart, the lungs and the great thoracic blood vessels. It is also a supportive structure for the bones of the shoulder girdle. The floor of the thorax is the diaphragm.

The front boundary of the upper part of the thorax is the *sternum* (or breast bone), a flat, sword-shaped bone in the middle of the chest opposite the thoracic vertebrae in the back.

The ribs make the cage that supports the chest and protects the heart and the lungs. These flat, narrow bowed bones are arranged in pairs, 12 on each side. From their attachment to the spine at the back, the ribs curve out and to the front like barrel hoops. The upper 7 pairs are attached to the sternum in front, the next 3 pairs are attached to each other and indirectly to the sternum, and the last 2 pairs are free in front. These "floating ribs" are shorter than the rest. The relatively elastic cartilage on the ends of the ribs allows leeway for the chest and the abdomen to expand.

THE EXTREMITIES

The Pelvis

Although it is not considered a part of the extremities, the pelvic girdle is discussed here because it anchors the legs to the central part of the body. It is formed by the 2 large, irregularly shaped *innominate* (hip) bones attached posteriorly to the sacrum. These bones spread outward at the top and become narrow at their front lower edges. In fetal development, the innominate bone develops as 3 separate bones known as the *ilium,* the *ischium* and the *pubis,* which usually fuse by the time growth is completed. The ilium is the upper flaring portion that one usually identifies as his hip bone. The ischium is the lower, stronger portion, which you may be conscious of only after horseback riding. The pubic bones meet in front and are joined by a pad of cartilage. This juncture is called the *symphysis pubis.* Connected to the sacrum and the coccyx posteriorly, these bones form your pelvic cavity, which houses the urinary bladder, the rectum and, in a woman, the reproductive organs. A woman's pelvis is larger and wider than a man's, which is Nature's way of providing room for the development and birth of a baby. (See

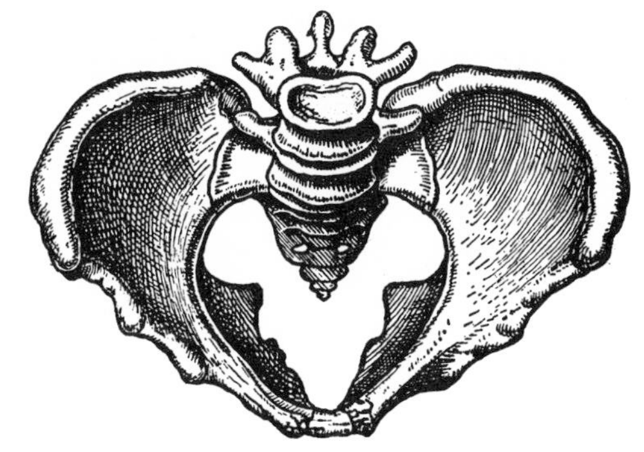

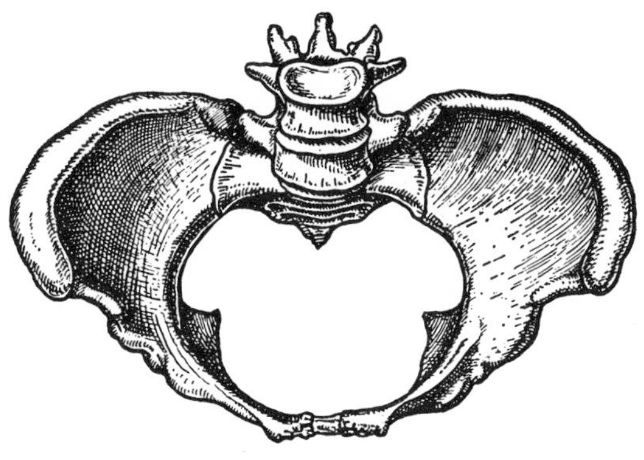

FIG. 45. Pelvic girdles viewed from above. (*Top*) Male pelvis. (*Bottom*) Female pelvis. (Baillif and Kimmel: Structure and Function of the Human Body, p. 102, Philadelphia, Lippincott)

Fig. 45.) A hollow on the outer side of each innominate bone makes a socket for the upper end of the femur and provides attachments for thigh and abdominal muscles.

The Leg

The *femur,* the upper bone of the leg, supports the weight of the trunk and is the longest and strongest bone of the body. Its upper end is attached to the pelvic bone in a ball-and-socket joint, where its rounded end (the head) fits into the depression on the outerside of the innominate bone; the other end is attached to the tibia in the lower leg. The head of the femur joins the shaft (the cylindrical long portion) by a short length of bone called the neck. This area is a common site of fractures in the elderly. Elevations on either side of the junction of the shaft and the neck are called the *trochanters,* which serve as points of attachment.

There are 2 bones in the lower leg; the *tibia,* or "shin bone" and the *fibula.* The upper end of the tibia is attached to the lower end of the femur in the knee joint. The front of this joint is protected by a small bone, the *patella,* or "knee cap," which is buried in a tendon that passes over the joint. The other bone in the lower leg, the fibula, is smaller than the tibia and is attached to it at the upper end. The lower ends of these bones meet the bones of the ankle to form the ankle joint.

The Shoulders and the Arms

The shoulder girdle, which anchors the arms, is formed by 4 bones. Two long, thin bones, the *clavicles,* or "collar bones," are attached to the sternum and extend outward at right angles to it on either side. Opposite the clavicles at the back are the *scapulae,* the "shoulder blades." They are flat, triangular bones attached to the outer ends of the clavicles and to the humerus in the upper arm. Look at these bones on the skeleton. You can see that they are attached to the trunk of the body at only one place—the sternum. This is why you can move your shoulders and arms so freely.

The *humerus* is the single long bone in the upper arm; the upper end is attached to the scapula, and the lower end meets the larger of the 2 forearm bones, the ulna, to form the elbow joint.

There are 2 bones in the forearm. The larger, the *ulna,* has 2 hollows in its upper end; the lower end of the humerus fits into one of these depressions, and the upper end of the second forearm bone, the *radius,* fits into the other. The radius lies beside the ulna and is attached to it at the upper end; both the radius and the ulna are attached to the wrist bones to make the wrist joint. The arrangement of these bones lets you turn your palm forward (supine position) or backward (prone position), and the radius and the ulna move so freely with the wrist bones and each other that, when you turn your palm down, the radius crosses the ulna. The relationship of these bones in movement is shown in the illustration of a pivot joint on page 133.

The Hand

The bones of the hands and the feet are especially structured for their unique functions. One of the differences between man and the other animals is his ability to use his hands.

More than one fourth of the total number of bones in the human body are found in the hands and the wrists. Because of the many small bones which allow for a great range of motions—twisting, bending, grasping, squeezing—you can do such things as play a violin, write your name and pick up minute objects with your thumb and forefinger.

The 8 *carpal,* or wrist, bones are small, irregular bones that support the base of the palm and are attached to the radius, the ulna and to the 5 long, slender and slightly curved *metacarpal* bones that form the palm of the hand. The other ends of the metacarpal bones are attached to the *phalanges,* or finger bones. There are 3 phalanges in each finger and 2 in the thumb.

The Foot

The foot is constructed to hold the weight of the entire body, and at the same time, give flexibility and resilience to our motions. The 7 *tarsal* bones of the ankle are compact and shaped irregularly; the largest of these bones is in the heel. They join the 5 *metatarsal,* or "instep bones," to form 2 arches: the longitudinal, which extends from the heel to the toe; and the transverse, or metatarsal arch, which extends across the foot. The body weight falls on these arches, and the many joints spring and give when you walk. Weak muscles lessen this "spring," and high, spiky heels and poor posture upset the body balance, flattening the arches. The 14 bones of the toes, the *phalanges,* are attached to the metatarsal bones. The great toe has 2 phalanges; each of the other toes has 3.

In general, the hands and the feet are built alike, but in the hands, the bones are finer and the joints more numerous (there are 29 in the wrist and the hand). The hands are designed for fine and flexible movements; the feet, for support. Together these bones number about half of those in the body.

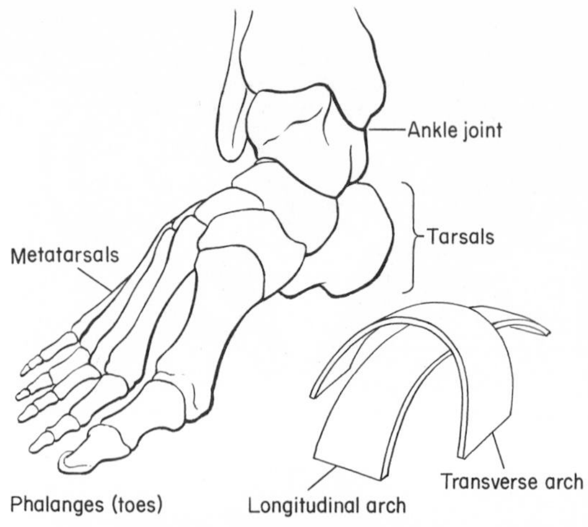

Fig. 46. Bones of the right foot and ankle. The longitudinal and the transverse arches are illustrated diagrammatically.

MUSCLES

Although the functions of the skeleton include giving shape to the body and providing joints for the purpose of allowing body motion, neither of these functions is carried out without the aid of other body systems, including the muscles. Muscles lie in sheets and cords beneath the skin and cover the bones. The skeleton determines the size of the framework, but the muscles (plus fat!) determine the body shape.

Muscles and tendons move the bones. Muscle cells are like millions of little motors moving your body, just as a motor moves an automobile. Without muscles your body would be as stationary as the classroom skeleton.

The muscles are arranged in fine elastic threads, or *fibers.* Each fiber is comparable in size with a human hair and will hold about 1,000 times its own weight. The fibers are wrapped together in *bundles,* and several bundles form a muscle.

Each muscle is covered by a sheath of connective tissue called *fascia,* the ends of which lengthen into tough cords called *tendons.* The muscles are attached to bones by means of these tendons. The tendons have sheaths lined with a synovial membrane which permits a smooth gliding movement. The thick meaty portion of the muscle is called the body or the *belly* of the muscle.

To understand the anatomy of a muscle and its tendon, place your hand on the thick muscle at the calf of your leg. Here are located some of the strongest muscles in the body. Move your hand toward your ankle and you will find that as both the leg and the muscles become narrower, the tissues become tough, fibrous and ropelike. (Flex and extend your foot to emphasize this.) This occurs because approximately halfway to the ankle the muscle is attached to a tendon, the tendon of Achilles, which extends down to the heal and attaches to the calcaneus (the large bone of the heel). It is interesting to note that the Indians understood the function of this tendon in walking, and therefore frequently cut it in their prisoners in order to prevent them from escaping.

All living cells have certain characteristics,

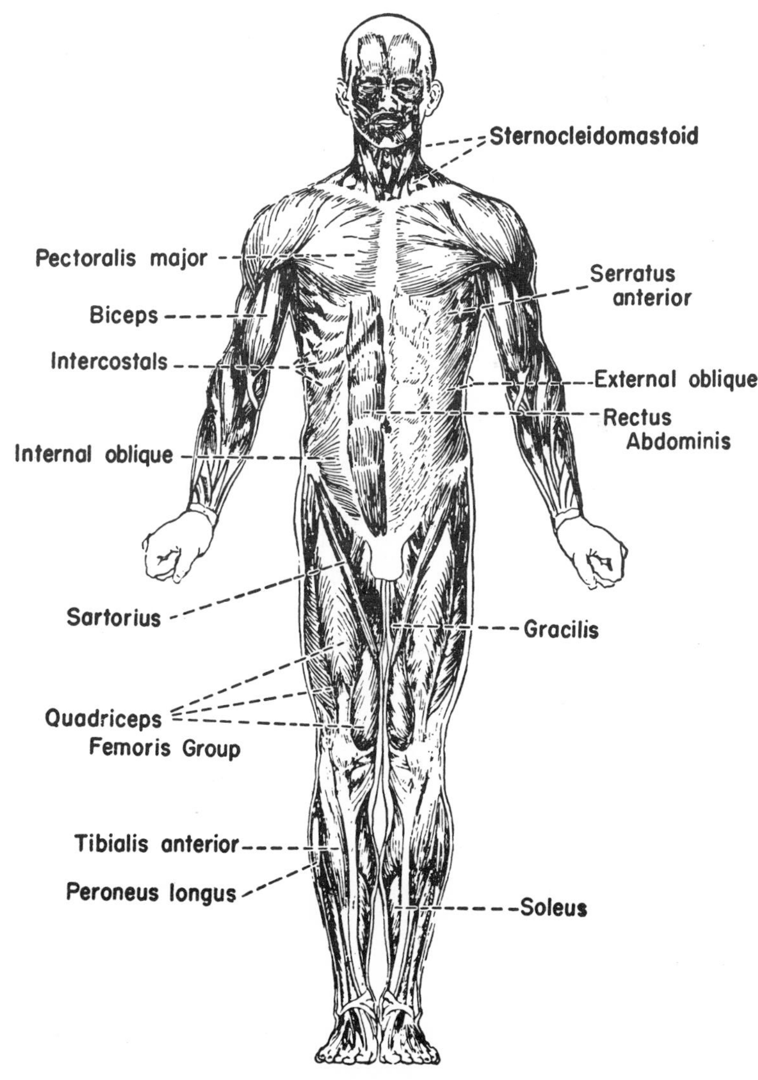

Fig. 47. Muscles of the body, front view. The deeper muscles are shown on the right side of the abdomen.

such as *excitability*, or the ability to react to a stimulus. Specialized cells exhibit special characteristics. The specialized muscle cells have the characteristic of *contractility*—the ability to shorten and become thicker—which is how the muscles accomplish their work. Muscle tissue is also said to have the property of *extensibility*, or the ability to stretch. Because it possesses *elasticity*, the muscle tissue returns to its normal length after it has been used. Some of the characteristics of muscle tissue can be observed by using a heavy rubber band, which exhibits many similar traits.

Muscles are attached to bones at points which will bring about the most effective motions. Since muscles work by contracting or shortening (and thereby pulling), most muscles attach one bone to another or extend from one part to another. One end of the muscle, the *origin*, is attached to the nonmoving or less-movable bone or part, while the other end, the *insertion*, is attached to the part or bone being moved.

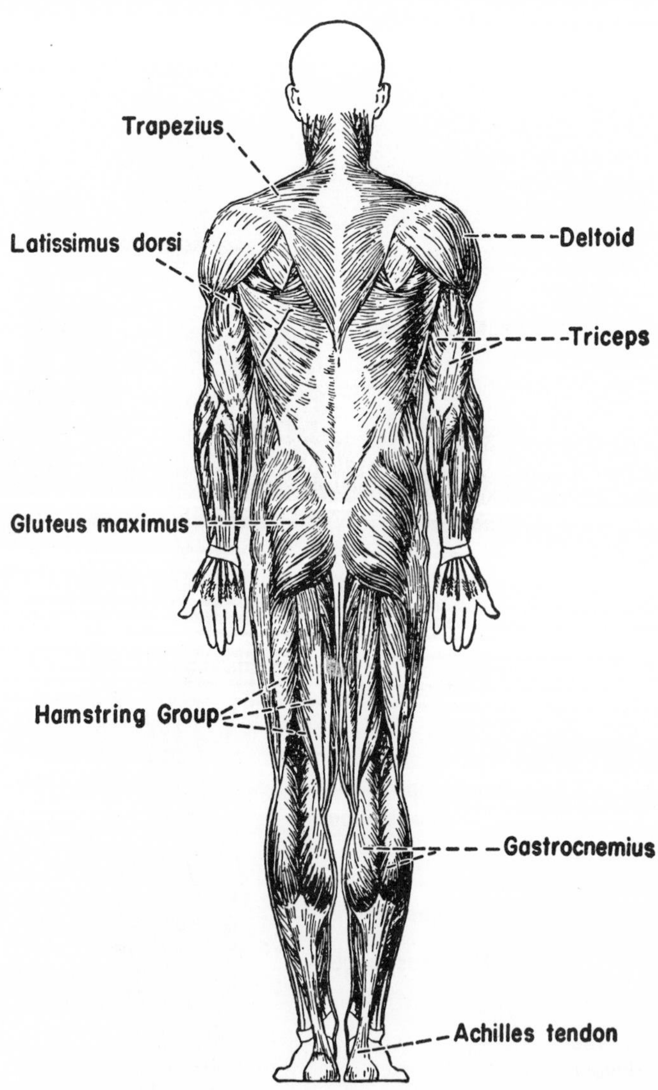

FIG. 48. Muscles of the body, back view.

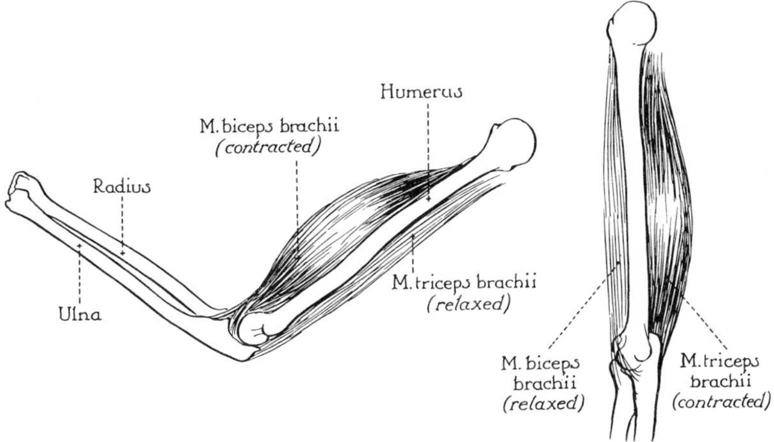

FIG. 49. Diagram of co-ordinated movement. (*Left*) In flexion of the forearm the biceps brachii is contracted (note the bulging), and the triceps is relaxed. (*Right*) In extension, the reverse condition holds. (Redrawn from Keith; Greisheimer, E. M.: Physiology and Anatomy, ed. 8, p. 152, Philadelphia, Lippincott)

Muscles are elastic and work in pairs having opposite actions—when one muscle contracts, the other relaxes. When you bend your elbow (flexion), you can feel the muscle in your upper arm contract, grow hard and thicken as the muscle fibers shorten to raise the forearm. At the same time, the muscles on the back of your upper arm relax, lengthen and pull against the front muscles. If you permit it, they will pull your forearm straight (extension). These paired muscles whose motions are opposing are called antagonistic (see Fig. 49).

Types of Muscles

When you examine muscle tissue through a microscope, you find 3 different kinds. Those which you can control consciously are called *voluntary muscles*. They are made of special types of cells that are long and give the appearance of being striped; therefore, they are also known as *striated* muscles. Since it is the voluntary striated muscles which control the skeletal movements (they are attached to the bones), they are also called *skeletal* muscles.

The second kind is not striped like the vol-

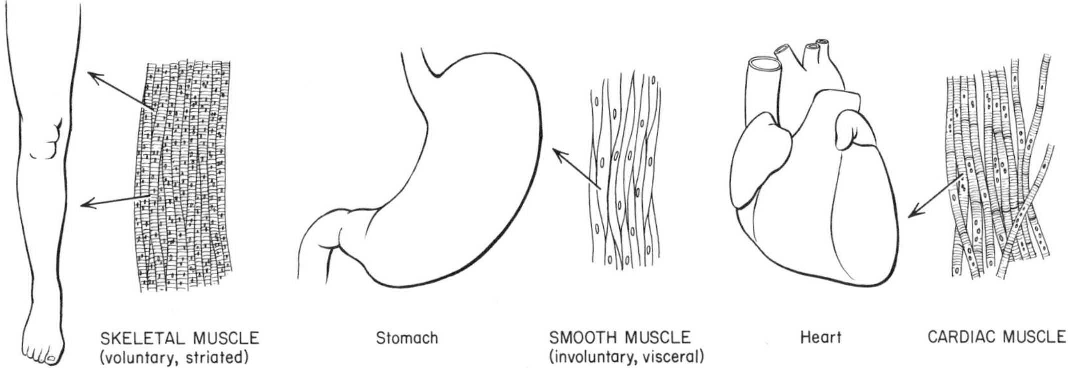

FIG. 50. The 3 types of muscle in the human body.

untary muscle and is called *smooth muscle.* It is also called *involuntary* because these muscles work automatically; you do not control their actions. The involuntary muscles control motion inside body organs (the viscera). For example, they move food along the digestive tract, make eye adjustments and dilate and contract the blood vessels to assist the circulation of the blood.

The third type of muscle tissue is found in the heart and is called *cardiac muscle.* It works automatically but looks like the striped or striated muscle. However, these fibers are formed in a continuous network rather than being wrapped in sheaths. Since you do not control cardiac muscle, it is referred to as involuntary muscle.

Power Source

Muscles need energy to move any part of the body. The foods we eat furnish carbon, hydrogen and oxygen from which the body makes glycogen, a special form of carbohydrate used by the body for fuel. (It is also called animal starch.) Oxygen and glycogen (sugar), brought to the muscle cells by the blood, react with each other, and the result of this oxidation or burning process is energy and heat. In fact, most of the heat that is produced in the body originates from muscle activity. When muscles are very active they draw on the reserve glycogen stored in their cells. The body makes use of our muscles' ability to produce heat rapidly by the automatic device of general muscle action or shivering when we are cold. To produce a great amount of necessary heat in an emergency, the body produces the more violent exercise of chilling.

Waste Products. Carbon dioxide and lactic acid are waste products produced in the process of oxidation. The blood carries carbon dioxide to the lungs, and it is removed in breathing; lactic acid is removed through the urinary system and the sweat glands. Vigorous or prolonged muscle action produces such a quantity of waste products that the blood cannot carry it away fast enough, and some of it accumulates in the muscle cells. This is why your muscles are fatigued, ache or feel sore after violent exercise or prolonged use. A simple formula might help you to summarize the action of muscles:

MUSCLE CELL + FOOD AND OXYGEN

↓

HEAT AND ENERGY

↓

BY-PRODUCTS: LACTIC ACID AND CARBON DIOXIDE

Muscle Tone

Because man stands erect against the constant pull of gravity, many of his muscles are constantly in a mild state of contraction to help him to maintain his balance. Even relaxed muscles are always ready to go into action if they are in good condition. This state of slight contraction and this ability to spring into action is called *muscle tone.* When muscle tone is good you feel springy and alive: your walk is firm, your head erect, your eyes wide open and alert. Poor muscle tone makes you feel dragged out: your head droops, your body sags. Physical exercise improves the tone of the muscles and builds them up. An idle muscle loses its tone and wastes away. This is why it is important for children who sit in school all day to have an opportunity for vigorous play after school; their muscles need such stimulation. If a patient does not use certain muscles or uses them very little, they become flabby and weak.

Pressure on the nerves in muscles makes them sore; patients who must lie on their backs most of the time complain of aches and pains in these muscles. Strains or inactivity also affect them. For these reasons, a back rub is comforting and you are taught to adjust the patient's body to positions that do not cause strain, to change his position frequently and to support him the first time he stands on his feet after a lengthy illness.

Rehabilitation. An injured or inactive muscle can be retrained to do its work. Retraining usually requires working with more than one muscle because muscles work in groups, except for the simplest movements. Fine work is being done today in helping people to recover the use of injured or inactive muscles. Rehabilitation activities are prescribed by physicians, and trained physiotherapists carry them out. Nurses work under the direction of these specialists to help the patient with selected exercises. Reeducating muscles is sometimes a long process; improvement is likely to be so gradual that it is hardly noticeable from day to day, and the patient often needs encouragement to persevere. The general principles of rehabilitation will be considered in more detail in Chapter 31.

Important Muscles

Neck and Shoulders. The sternocleidomastoid is the strong muscle on the side of the neck which helps to hold the head erect. When it becomes diseased or injured (which sometimes occurs during the birth process), the head is permanently drawn to one side, a condition known as torticollis or wry neck.

From the nurse's standpoint, the most important muscle of the shoulder is the deltoid. It is used as a site for intramuscular injections and moves the upper arm outward from the body.

Arm and Anterior Chest. The triceps and the biceps are used to extend and flex the forearm. The biceps is located on the front of the upper arms; the triceps, posteriorly to it. The pectoralis major and minor and the serratus anterior are large anterior chest muscles. The pectoralis helps to bring the arm across the chest.

Respiration. One group of muscles assists in the process of breathing. A large, flat dome-shaped muscle, the *diaphragm*, lies between the abdominal and the thoracic cavities. When the diaphragm contracts, it moves downward, making the chest cavity larger and forming a partial vacuum about the lungs, which causes air to rush into the lungs. As the diaphragm relaxes, it pushes up and the air is forced out of the lungs. An easy way to check this change in the size and the shape of the rib cavity is to place a tape measure around the chest at the nipple line and inhale and exhale. Notice the difference in your chest measurements. The intercostal muscles located between the ribs also aid in respiration by helping to enlarge the chest cavity.

Abdomen. The abdominal muscles are the flat bands that stretch from the ribs to the pelvis and support the abdominal organs. The main muscles found here are the internal and the external oblique, the transversus abdominis and the rectus abdominis. These are arranged to give support by overlapping in layers from various angles. Any opening in a muscle creates an area of weakness within it because the opening may stretch or enlarge. There are weak places within the abdominal muscles where a hernia (rupture) may occur with pressure from or protrusion of part of the intestine. These weak places are areas where blood vessels, nerves, ligaments and cords extend through the muscles. The inguinal rings, the femoral rings and the umbilicus are common sites for hernias.

Healthy abdominal muscles "give" just enough to permit the organs to move when you breathe; when they lose some of their contracting power, the abdominal organs drop out of place or bulge outward against the muscles.

Back and Posterior Chest. Large muscles lie across the back and the posterior chest, two of which are the trapezius and the latissimus dorsi. The trapezius is also called the "swimming muscle" and helps to lift the shoulder area. The latissimus dorsi and other muscles of the back often work in groups to help you to stand erect, balance when you carry heavy objects and turn or bend your body.

Gluteal Muscles. The large muscles forming the buttocks are called gluteal muscles (gluteus maximus, medius and minimus). You use these muscles in changing from sitting to standing positions, as well as in walking. These muscles are frequently used as a site for intramuscular injections.

Thigh and Lower Leg. A large group of muscles on the front of the thigh is called the quadriceps femoris group. On the posterior surface, another group called the hamstring group flexes and extends the leg and the thigh. The gracilis and the sartorius are thigh muscles. The latter is called the "tailor's muscle," since it allows a person to sit crosslegged.

The tibialis anterior is located in the front of the lower leg. The gastrocnemius, the soleus and the peroneus longus give the rounded appearance to the calf of the leg. The Achilles tendon is a name taken from Grecian mythology to designate the tendon which attaches the calf muscle to the heel bone. The calf muscles allow you to extend your foot to give you the "spring in your step" when walking or running.

The Muscles and the Tendons of the Hands and the Feet

The muscles and the tendons of the hands and the feet are planned in a slightly different manner than those of the rest of the body. There are many bones in the hands and the feet to permit their more intricate functions, and many muscles and tendons are necessary to move them. However, bulky muscles would make clumsy motions, so the larger muscles that move the hands and the feet are located in the forearm and the lower leg. When you flex your fingers to clench your fist, you can feel the muscles move and tighten in your forearm. Some muscles begin from the wrist. These muscles extend into long thin tendons that attach to the bones of the fingers, permitting accuracy as well as a wide range of motion (see Fig. 51).

You can stand on your toes, your heels and the ball of your foot. Consider the many motions of the dancer, and you will understand that to accomplish such fine movements, the structure of the foot is similar to that of the hand. Their variance in design allows a difference in function.

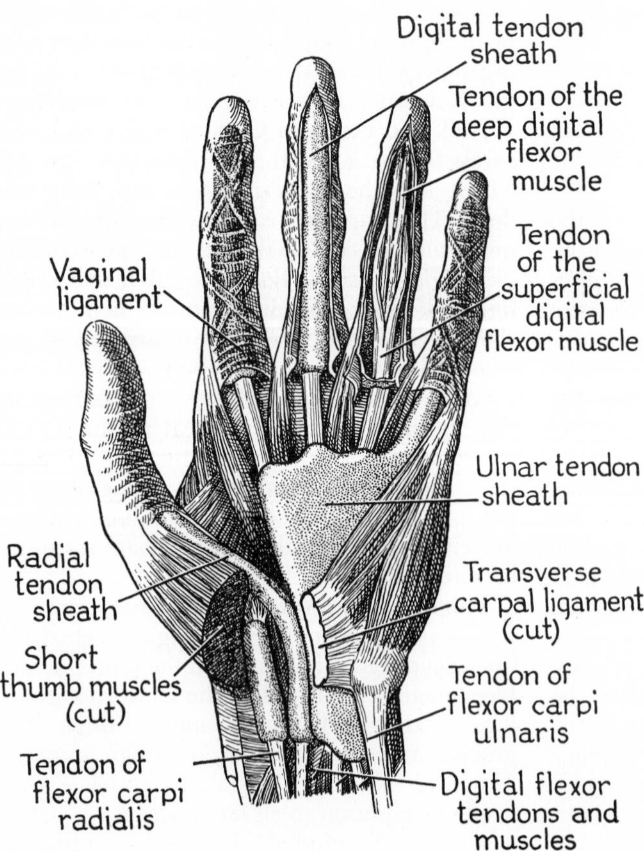

Fig. 51. Deep structures in palm and wrist. (Baillif and Kimmel: Structures and Function of the Human Body, p. 120, Philadelphia, Lippincott)

14

THE BODY'S CONTROLLER: THE NERVOUS SYSTEM

Our bodies are made up of billions of cells, divided into systems according to either their structure or the functions they perform. None of these systems functions alone; their activities are interrelated, integrated and coordinated by messages carried from one system to another. The hormones and the enzymes of the body act as chemical messengers, but our major system of communication from both within and without is the nervous system.

The nervous system brings us all the impressions and the information that we have from the world outside us. It stores this information for future reference and application; it serves as the center that coordinates the messages from the internal body systems, and it makes it possible for us to readjust constantly to both our internal and our external environment. The nervous system is the director of all body activities.

The nervous system is often likened to the operations of a telephone exchange. Through a network of wires, messages come into the central switchboard, where the necessary connections are made to direct them to the right places. Your nervous system is organized to bring messages into a center which relays them to certain parts of the body. The brain and the spinal cord are the switchboard. Anatomically, this functions as the *central nervous system*. The nerves are the wires that carry incoming and outgoing messages and make up what is called the *peripheral nervous system*.

The Nerves

The nervous tissue is made up of special cells called *neurons*. The neuron consists of a cell body containing a nucleus, granular cytoplasm and threadlike projections of the cytoplasm called nerve fibers. Scattered throughout the cytoplasm are Nissl bodies concerned with the nutrition of the cell. The fibers which bring the impulses to the cell are called *dendrites*; those which carry the impulses away are called *axons*. Each neuron has one axon and several dendrites. (See Fig. 53.)

There are 3 types of neurons: *sensory, motor* and *connecting*. Sensory neurons receive messages from all parts of the body and transmit them to the central nervous system. Motor neurons transmit messages from the central nervous system to all parts of the body, either to alter muscle activity or to cause glands to secrete. The impulse is carried through pathways between the sensory and the motor neurons by the connecting neurons.

Because of their fibers or processes, the neurons are able to carry out their unique activity of transmitting signals from one neuron to the next. The nerve fiber is an axon or a dendrite that extends from the central nervous system out into the body. Some of these fibers are several feet in length.

When one neuron receives a signal, it sends it on to the next neuron across a small space or junction between the axon and the dendrite called a *synapse*. The sensory neurons begin to

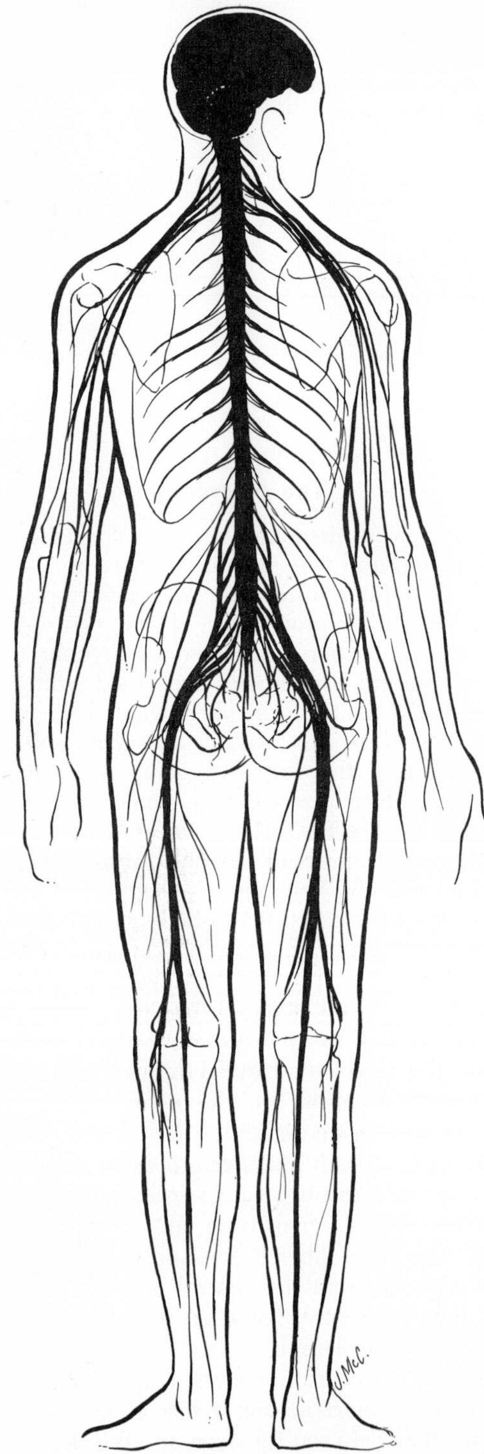

Fig. 52. Diagram illustrating the brain, the spinal cord and the spinal nerves.

bring information to the brain by means of *receptors* (end organs which are the initial receivers of sensations). Then the sensation is carried to the central nervous system via the fibers of the sensory neurons; it is sent through the connecting neurons through complex pathways for interpretation and decision for action. If a corresponding action is required, further impulse is sent via the fibers of the motor neurons to bring about the proper response. For example, the sting of the bite of a mosquito is made known to the brain by a sensory neuron; the brain interprets the sensation for what it is; the connecting neurons carry the message via the proper paths to the motor neuron; the brain sends the order to slap the insect away, by means of a motor neuron to the appropriate muscles. (A similar illustration is shown in Fig. 54.)

The nerve fibers dispatch messages to the brain by electricity manufactured by and in the neurons. Recordings of the impulses have been made, and the electrical impulses, no matter what the sensation or its source, all sound the same. However, the various areas of the brain decipher the signals and relay them to the proper channels.

The nerve fibers outside the brain and the spinal cord are covered with a myelin sheath which might be likened to the insulation of electric wires. An outer thinner covering over this myelin sheath is called the *neurilemma*. Its function is to serve in the regeneration of nerve fibers. Regeneration of nerve fibers is very slow, so that the symptoms of nerve injury (paralysis, numbness, tingling) may persist for months.

Nerve tissue is very fragile and easily subject to injury. For this reason, the central nervous system has top priority on the oxygen supply from the circulatory system. It is also well protected by the skull bones and by the surrounding structures of the vertebral column. If the nerve fiber is injured, eventually it may repair itself. If the neuron itself is destroyed, it will never be replaced. When the nucleus of a neuron is destroyed, it is lost forever.

End organs (receptors) bring sensations to the nerve fibers which flash messages along to the nerve cells that send these messages out again to the body. There are many possible

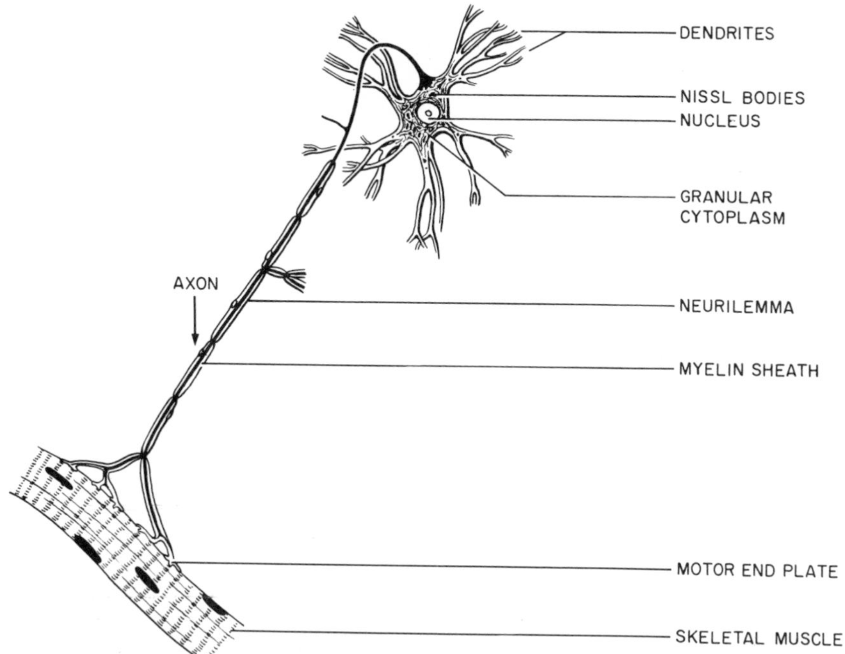

FIG. 53. Diagram of a typical neuron showing the motor end plate, the point of contact between the axon and the skeletal muscle.

pathways that messages can take. It is amazing that they take the quickest route (the body is very thrifty in its use of body products and its automatic activities) and that the same kind of messages tend to follow the same paths every time. This helps you to do things quickly—for example, getting dressed in the morning or going to school or work. These motions that you repeat become more or less automatic habits. Habits are patterns that you have built up by using the same nerve pathways over and over. "Changing your ways" is sometimes difficult because it involves breaking one habit pattern thoroughly established through nerve pathways and building another.

You have some activities which are considered as *reflex acts*. For example, you close or blink your eyes to protect them from danger. You do this before any conscious stimulus reaches the brain; the stimulus enters and leaves at the level of the spinal cord. It is a simple entrance of the stimulus through the sensory nerve, across the connecting neurons in the spinal cord and out via the motor neuron.

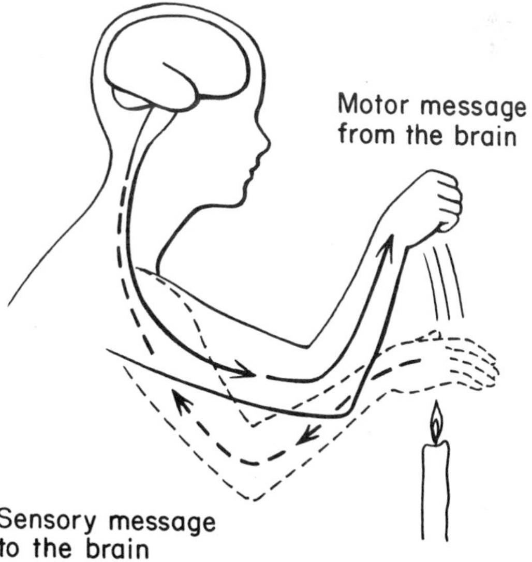

FIG. 54. Sensory and motor processes involved when the hand is held over a flame.

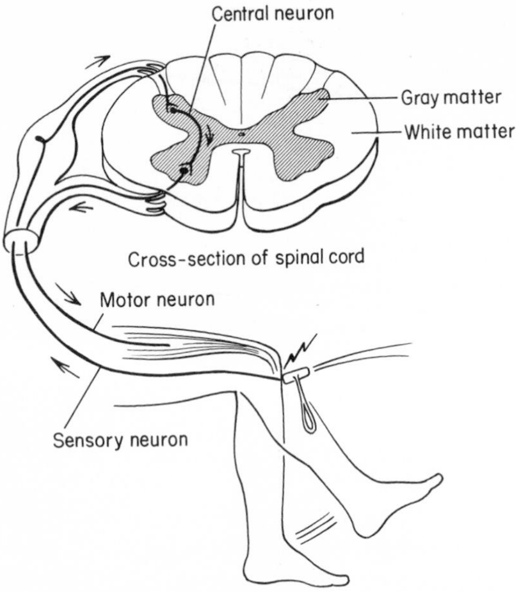

FIG. 55. Diagrammatic section of the lower part of the spinal cord to illustrate a simple reflex arc as elicited by the knee jerk. When the tendon of the patella (knee cap) is tapped, the receptors in the tendon are stimulated. The impulses pass over the sensory neurons to the spinal cord where they are transmitted over the central neurons to the motor neurons leaving the cord. The effectors of the motor neurons are in the anterior thigh muscles which, when stimulated, contract and extend the leg.

The simplest "reflex arc" in man is the knee jerk triggered by a light blow to the knee. (See Fig. 55.)

Although the nervous system is complicated, you are relieved of some of the responsibility in the operations of your body. You choose and direct the actions that make life pleasant; you can protect yourself from dangers; you can think and feel. However, one part of your nervous system works on its own and requires no planning from you. It directs such things as the digestion of food and circulation of the blood.

The nervous system has 2 sections—one that you control, and the other, though closely related, an automatic one called the *autonomic* nervous system.

Autonomic Nervous System

The autonomic nervous system has 2 divisions: the *sympathetic* and the *parasympathetic* which regulate the action of the glands, the smooth muscles and the heart. These structures receive their stimuli from both divisions; however, their effects are opposite. For example, the sympathetic nerves speed up the heart rate, constrict the blood vessels and dilate the pupil of the eye; the parasympathetic nerves constrict the pupil of the eye, dilate the blood vessels and slow the heart rate.

Knowledge of the actions of the autonomic nervous system is important in giving medications which affects one or the other division. To illustrate, atropine, a drug used in examining the eye, inhibits (slows down) the action of the parasympathetic division and thus causes a dilation of the pupil of the eye. On the other hand, pilocarpine, which is used in certain disease conditions such as glaucoma, stimulates the parasympathetic division and causes the pupil to become more constricted.

The close relationship between the two parts of the nervous system (that controlled consciously and the autonomic system) can be illustrated if you visualize a large, juicy, sizzling steak. If it is an idea which stimulates your appetite, your mouth will water—saliva and other digestive juices will flow. The flow of digestive juices is a function controlled by the autonomic nervous system which works automatically. However, you know that control of the appetite by the individual is a conscious function, and you can decide not to supply the food for the juices to digest if you wish.

The Brain

As stated previously, the central nervous system is made up of the brain and the spinal cord. The human brain is the center for thought. It weighs about 3 pounds, it has 3 divisions, and it is located within the skull. The largest division of the brain is the *cerebrum,* which fills the upper part of the cranium. The cerebrum is divided into halves (*hemispheres*), one on either side of the cranium. The outside of the cerebrum (the *cerebral cortex*) is made of soft grayish matter that is mostly nerve cells. Underneath this is the white matter, which contains the nerve fibers that connect with the cells. (The myelin sheaths which cover the nerve fibers give the white appearance.) The cerebral cortex is wrinkled and folded upon itself many times. This gives a greater surface in a small area. It is divided into 4 *lobes* which are named from the overlying cranial bones—frontal, parietal, temporal and occipital. A number of special centers in the cerebrum enable it to carry out the work of associating impressions and information, which becomes our knowledge. After comparing and combining knowledge, we think and arrive at judgments, the highest function of the human mind. While it has been suggested that our mental faculties of memory, reasoning and intelligence involve the cerebral cortex, exactly where or how these processes are performed is not known.

Other centers in the cerebrum are related to hearing, seeing, moving, speaking and other activities. There are duplicate motor control centers in the right hemisphere and the left hemisphere of the brain. The right center controls the muscles on the left side of the body, and the left center controls the muscles on the right side of the body. Some of the functional areas of the cerebrum are shown in Fig. 57.

Directly beneath the cerebral hemispheres and covered by them are 2 centers called the *thalamus* and the *hypothalamus*. The thalamus is a relay station for nerve stimuli. It receives impulses from every part of the body and relays them to appropriate parts of the cortex. Investigations indicate that the thalamus may contain a center for interpreting whether or not actions or sensations give us pleasure.

The hypothalamus contains centers that control many of the autonomic functions, as well as heat regulation and food and water metabolism. Some authorities think that the center for appetite control as well as our "waking center" is located here. The hypothalamus also is involved in the expression of certain emotions and is closely associated with pituitary activities.

The *cerebellum* is the second largest part of the brain and is concerned with muscle tone, coordination and equilibrium. It helps keep you balanced when you walk, makes your movements graceful and affects your skill in sports and other muscle activities.

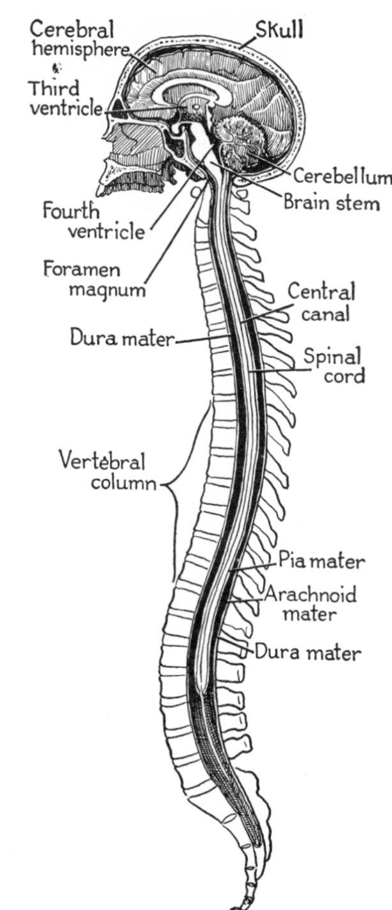

Fig. 56. The central nervous system. (Baillif and Kimmel: Structure and Function of the Human body, p. 73, Philadelphia, Lippincott)

The brain stem includes the *midbrain*, the *pons* and the *medulla*. The midbrain is located at the very top of the brain stem and functions as an important reflex center. The word "pons" means "bridge," and the pons has nerve tracts within it which carry messages between the cerebrum and the medulla.

The medulla lies just below the pons and rests on the floor of the skull. It is continuous with, but not a part of, the spinal cord. Mes-

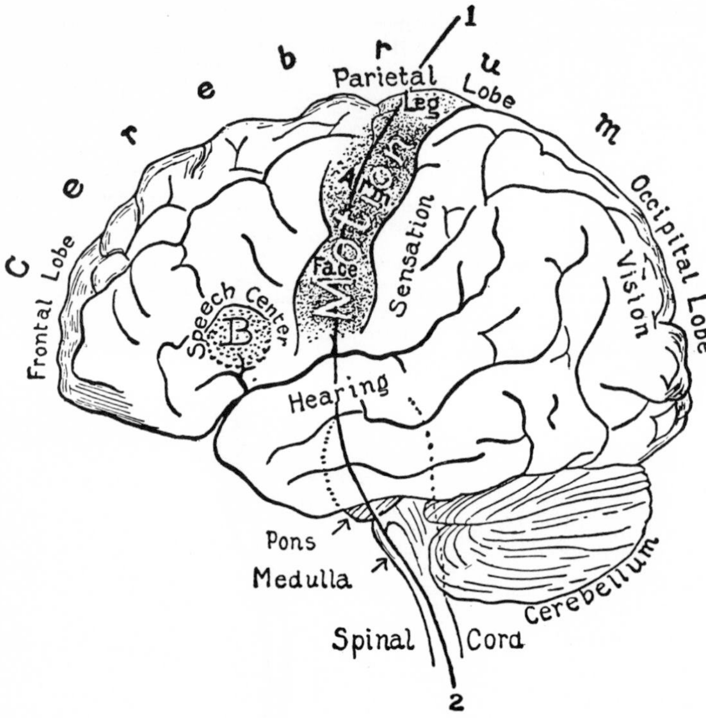

FIG. 57. Side view of the brain, showing some of the functional areas of the cerebrum. (Emerson and Bragdon: Essentials of Medicine, ed. 17, p. 602, Philadelphia, Lippincott)

sages go to and from the cerebrum through the medulla. It also contains centers for many vital body functions: the rate of the heart beat, the constriction of blood vessels, a respiratory center, and control of swallowing are all part of its activities. Other activities are concerned with such reflexes as coughing, sneezing and laughing.

The Spinal Cord

The *spinal cord* is a long mass of nerve cells and fibers extending through a central canal from the medulla to the approximate level of the 1st or the 2nd lumbar vertebra. It is well protected from shocks and injuries by its position within the vertebral column. The spinal cord has 2 main purposes: it acts as a conductor of impulses to and from the brain and is a reflex center. The reflex centers in the cord receive and send out messages through the nerve fibers. They act as substations for messages and relieve the brain of routine work. Some nerve fibers in the cord are sensory, that is, they carry messages to the brain, while other nerve tracts are motor—they carry messages away from the brain. The nerve fibers of the spinal cord do not regenerate after an injury.

The Peripheral Nervous System

The peripheral nervous system is made up of 2 groups: the cranial nerves and the spinal nerves. There are 12 pairs of cranial nerves which attach directly to the brain. Most of them carry impulses to and from the brain and various structures about the head (the sensory organs, the organs of swallowing and speech, the facial muscles, etc.). However, other cranial nerves act on the organs of the thorax and the abdomen.

The spinal nerves attach to the spinal cord. They carry such impulses as temperature, touch, pain, muscle tone and balance. They also transport motor impulses to the skeletal muscles.

The Meninges

The brain and the spinal cord (the central nervous system) are covered with 3 protective membranes called the *meninges*. The outer one (*dura mater*) is a tough, fibrous covering which adheres to the bones of the skull. The inner layer (*pia mater*) lies closely over the brain and the spinal cord. It is a thin vascular layer containing many blood vessels which bring oxygen to nourish the nervous tissue. The middle layer is a delicate weblike tissue called the *arachnoid*. The space between the middle layer and the inner layer (*subarachnoid space*) is filled with *cerebrospinal fluid*. Cerebrospinal fluid is produced constantly, mainly by filtration from the blood in the capillaries of the brain, but it is also produced in the brain in spaces called ventricles. This liquid circulates around the brain and the spinal cord, maintaining an even pressure and acting as a cushion or shock absorber for these delicate structures. In order for the amount to remain constant it is continuously absorbed into the blood vessels in the brain.

15

THE BODY'S HIGHWAYS: THE CIRCULATORY SYSTEM

The circulatory system is a meticulously organized plan for communication of each of the cells with various other parts of the body. Even though a cell may be located in the tip of your toe or at the end of your fingers, it gets oxygen from the lungs, food from the intestines, and sends its wastes back to the kidneys. The circulatory system is composed of the blood, the heart and the tubes or vessels (arteries, veins, capillaries) which are the routes over which the blood travels. The blood carries the necessary products to the cells and carries away wastes; the heart provides the force to pump the blood through the body; and the arteries, the veins and the capillaries contain the blood.

FUNCTIONS

The circulatory system has many functions, some of which you already know. The following is a list of its more important duties:

It carries oxygen from the lungs to the cells.

It carries carbon dioxide from the cells to the lungs.

Food is picked up (absorbed) from the small intestine and brought to the cells by the blood.

Certain waste products of the work of the cells are transported by the blood to the kidneys to be eliminated from the body.

The products of the endocrine glands, the hormones, are carried to their destinations by the blood.

The blood and the blood vessels contribute to the regulation of body temperature. If the body needs to become cooler, surface blood vessels dilate, giving off heat. For example, the flushed face which occurs after strenuous exercises is a result of the dilation of the facial blood vessels. If the body needs to conserve heat or energy, the surface blood vessels constrict, thereby reducing heat loss.

The blood assists in maintaining the acid-base balance of the body. There are alkaline products in the blood which constantly work against (buffer) the acids formed by metabolism within the body; the acids also guard against excessive alkalinity by buffering the alkaline (base) substances in the blood.

The circulatory system helps to maintain the fluid balance of the body. As was stated in Chapter 11, within and surrounding all cells is body fluid. In a healthy person this fluid remains fairly constant in amount. Although we take in extra liquid every day, the body eliminates an approximately equal quantity through the evaporation of perspiration and through the kidneys. The circulatory system serves as a transport medium for this fluid.

The circulatory system defends the body against disease by means of its white cells. It also produces antibodies and antitoxins, important in immunity and disease control.

THE BLOOD

If you wish to consider the marvels of your body, the blood alone can be a source of wonder. The blood is a liquid within the body, but it can coagulate quickly to form a solid clot, but under normal conditions coagulation does not take place within the body. It is a *liquid tissue*, because the fluid portion, called plasma, contains many cells and other substances. Within this watery intercellular substance are the formed elements which consist of white blood cells, red blood cells and platelets.

Blood Plasma

It is interesting to note that scientists speculate that the concentration of salts in the blood is similar to the salt content of the sea when life on earth first began. This is one of the theories which leads them to believe that life originally arose in the warm currents of the sea. (Chapter 33 has more information on this topic.) The salts contained in the plasma are sodium, calcium, potassium and magnesium, as well as the ions of other elements in the forms of bicarbonates, sulfates, chlorides and phosphates. These salts are absorbed by the plasma from the foods we eat and are used by the cells. The maintenance of these salts within the plasma (in special quantities to act as neutralizers or buffers to each other) controls the chemical and acid-base balance of the blood, as well as contributing to the chemical and fluid balance of the entire body.

The plasma also contains antibodies, foods, nitrogenous waste products such as urea and ammonium salts, and small amounts of gases such as oxygen, carbon dioxide and nitrogen. Hormones are carried in the plasma, as well as the chemicals involved in the process of the clotting of blood. Some of the plasma proteins are albumin, a main constituent of cells; serum globulins, which are related to disease protection; and fibrinogen, one of the clotting substances.

Red Blood Cells

Although the red blood cells (*erythrocytes*) give blood its red color, they appear under the microscope as faintly pink disks, thinner in the center than at the edges. These cells are different from other cells of the body in that they have no nucleus when they are mature. There are so many red blood cells that the blood appears to be packed solid with them, but they are so tiny that approximately 3,000 of them could be placed side by side within the distance of 1 inch. There are about 25 trillion red blood cells in the whole body.

The erythrocytes get their color from an iron compound which they contain called *hemoglobin* (heme: iron; globin: protein). As the blood passes through the lungs, the iron in the hemoglobin picks up oxygen in a loose chemical combination, and carries it to the body cells. When hemoglobin is saturated with oxygen, it is bright red. As the erythrocytes circulate through the capillaries in the tissues, the hemoglobin gives its oxygen to the cells and picks up their carbon dioxide. Carbon dioxide makes the blood darker red.

Often a count of the blood cells is made to determine if the body is producing the normal amount. The average number of the red blood cells (R.B.C.) is 4½ to 5 million per cubic millimeter, the amount of blood in a tiny drop. It is believed that erythrocytes survive for about 3 to 4 months. They are made in the red marrow of the bones at the rate of about 1 million per second. They wear out and are destroyed at the same rate in the liver and the spleen, an organ of the lymphatic system sometimes referred to as the "graveyard of the red blood cells" (see p. 163).

White Blood Cells

White blood cells (*leukocytes*) are colorless cells that defend the body against disease organisms, toxins or irritants. They have a nucleus and are larger and far fewer in number than the red cells. The normal white blood count (W.B.C.) is 5,000 to 10,000 per cubic millimeter of blood.

There are 2 subgroups of white cells: the granular and the nongranular leukocytes. The 3 types of granular leukocytes—basophils, eosinophils and neutrophils—are characterized by a speckled or grainy cytoplasm. They are also produced in the bone marrow and function by surrounding and dissolving the body's invaders. The nongranular leukocytes, classified as lymphocytes and monocytes, are produced in lymphatic tissue, such as lymph nodes and the spleen, and have relatively clear cytoplasm. Their exact function is unknown, but some believe that they have a relationship to antibody formation in producing immunity to certain diseases.

Unlike the red blood cells which remain inside the blood vessels to do their work, the leukocytes leave the blood stream to travel to the affected site. They can move by changing shape, a process known as ameboid movement. They push or squeeze themselves through the capillary wall and rush to the threatened spot. They increase in number, engulf and devour the invaders and assist in repairing the damaged tissues.

Since the white blood cells increase in number (a condition called leukocytosis) in certain diseases, a white cell count is a valuable aid to diagnosis. A drop of blood is viewed under the microscope, and the number of white cells is estimated. The normal white count of 5,000 to 10,000 may increase to 25,000 or higher when infection is present. In some diseases, the relative proportion of the kinds of white blood cells may vary, and therefore a differential count is made, in which the number of granular leukocytes is compared with the number of nongranular leukocytes. This count gives further diagnostic clues to the doctor.

RED BLOOD CELLS (in capillary)

Basophil Eosinophil Neutrophil

GRANULAR LEUKOCYTES

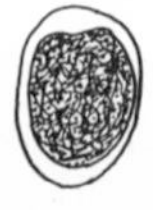

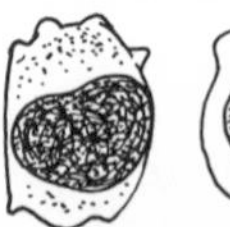
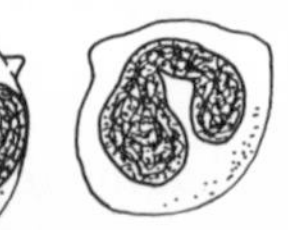

NONGRANULAR LEUKOCYTES

BLOOD PLATELETS

FIG. 58.

Platelets

The blood platelets, sometimes called *thrombocytes*, are smaller than erythrocytes and leukocytes. They are thought to be manufactured in the red bone marrow, as are the other formed elements of the blood. There is a wide variance in the normal count, but 250,000 to 500,000 per cubic millimeter of blood could be considered as being normal. They assist in the clotting of blood. Figure 58 diagrammatically illustrates the red and the white blood cells and the platelets.

Blood Pressure

The blood in the arteries always exerts some pressure against their walls, as water does when running through a garden hose. When the heart muscle contracts to pump the blood (a phase known as *systole*), the force increases the pressure against the blood vessel walls, as it would against the garden hose if you had the water pressure up to full. When the heart relaxes (a phase known as *diastole*), the pressure decreases as it would if the water pressure were turned down; then the water would trickle through the hose. When you take a person's blood pressure, both pressures are recorded with the figure of the higher or systolic pressure reading written over the lower or diastolic pressure reading. For example, a normal blood pressure (B.P.) reading for some individuals might be $\frac{120}{80}$.

Children normally have lower blood pressures than adults. Some people have lower than average blood pressure and, unless this is caused by disease, their prospects for a long life are good. The statement that your blood pressure should be "your age plus 100" is not true.

Blood pressure varies from time to time, depending on activity, emotion and strain. Such changes are normal and are only temporary. However, if the arteries are not in good condition, any strain puts an added burden on them. If their walls become hardened and lose their elasticity (arteriosclerosis), the blood needs extra force to be pushed through them. This increases the blood pressure. When the pressure in the arteries remains high (hypertension), the heart must work harder, the muscle becomes thicker, and the heart enlarges.

There are many factors other than the force of the pumping of the heart which are related to the control of blood pressure, such as the muscles in the capillary walls, kidney function and hormones. The arteries naturally become less elastic with age, but this condition begins much earlier in some people than in others. The reasons for this are not known completely, but scientists believe that diet, physical and emotional stress, plus heredity are responsible. (Blood pressure and the method of measuring it will be described in more detail in Chapter 29.)

The Clotting of Blood (Coagulation)

The blood protects the body from losing vital plasma fluid and blood cells by sealing off broken blood vessels through a process of clotting called *coagulation.* Otherwise, we would not survive minor cuts and wounds. The process in clot formation is not a simple one but is the result of a number of activities within the blood, some of which are not totally understood. Calcium must be present for clotting to occur. When the tissue is injured, the platelets break down and release a chemical, thromboplastin. This interacts with prothrombin, a protein substance in the blood, which further reacts with fibrinogen in the blood to form threads of fibrin. The threads of fibrin form a net which entraps the cells which build up to form the clot. The clot acts like a plug in a hole and tends to draw the injured edges together. Coagulation is a complicated mechanism and will not take place if any of the necessary elements are missing.

A clot that forms within a blood vessel and remains at the formation site is called a *thrombus.* One that moves from its original site is called an *embolus.*

Hemorrhage and Blood Types

Literally, the definition of hemorrhage is the escape of blood from blood vessels, but we usually think of a hemorrhage as the loss of a considerable amount of blood. A cut or torn blood vessel allows blood to escape. As soon as a clot forms, the bleeding stops. Therefore, once a blood vessel is broken, the clotting of the blood becomes very important. Severe hemorrhage is serious because the body loses fluid and the oxygen-carrying red blood cells which can result in death. The strength of the force behind the flow of blood (as in a severed artery), the size of the wound and the volume of blood, or a deficiency in any of the coagulant substances can prevent clotting.

Severe hemorrhage is treated by replacing the blood lost with blood from another person. This replacement of blood is called *transfusion.* First, tests must be made to determine if the blood of both the donor (the one who donates) and the recipient (the one who receives) will mix safely. Blood types which will mix safely are said to be compatible. Blood usually falls into 1 of 4 main groups: A, B, AB and O, which are determined largely by the type of protein in the red blood cell. Usually blood from the same group or type can be given in a transfusion. Incompatible blood causes blood cells to clump or stick together (agglutinate) in groups or small clotlike formations in the recipient's blood vessels and can cause death. Blood group O can be given safely to any other group and is known as the *universal donor.* About 40 percent of all people have Type O blood. Likewise, group AB can receive the blood of any other group and is known as the *universal recipient.* Plasma transfusion is always safe and is quicker than a transfusion of whole blood; but blood plasma does not contain red and white blood cells, so a doctor may prefer that whole blood be used.

Some people have mistaken notions about blood and blood transfusions. It is important to remember that, except for the usual blood type variations, there is no difference in the blood of healthy persons of different races. Blood does not carry or transmit mental, emotional or racial characteristics; these are genetically determined traits which can be transmitted only through heredity.

Since the value of transfusions has proved itself beyond doubt, almost every community has established blood banks to cover emergency needs. The American National Red Cross Blood Donor Service is known all over the world and serves all communities.

The Rh Factor

The Rh factor is another red-cell protein which is inherited just as our blood types A, B, AB or O are inherited. About 85 per cent of white Americans have this factor in their blood, and they are said to be Rh positive (expressed Rh+). Those who do not have this factor in their blood are said to be Rh negative (Rh—). The percentage of Rh-negative people is lower in some races than in others. For instance, only 7 per cent of the Negro race and 1 per cent of Oriental peoples are found to be Rh negative.

People worry needlessly about the effect of the Rh factor in marriage and pregnancy. The only possibility of trouble is in the case of pregnancy between an Rh+ husband and an Rh— wife. Only a small percentage of marriages have this problem. Even in this group, trouble may occur (but does not always) only if a baby inherits the father's Rh-positive blood factor. If the mother's body reacts to the baby's Rh factor as a foreign agent within her, since it is not normally present in her blood, she may produce antibodies to destroy this intruder, the Rh factor. The antibodies enter the baby's bloodstream and destroy its red blood cells. Usually, there are not sufficient antibodies to bother the first baby, but they may produce increasing effects in later pregnancies. As a rule, such a baby is born successfully, but its life is threatened by the destruction of its red blood cells (a condition called *erythroblastosis fetalis*). If necessary, the baby can be given one or more transfusions to replace the blood which is being destroyed. Recent developments indicate this can be done even before the baby is born if its condition is severe enough to warrant such intervention.

Shock

Shock accompanies about 80 per cent of all severe injuries. This is known as *traumatic shock* and is not to be confused with the electric shock treatments sometimes used for the mentally ill (which is discussed in Chapter 44). Traumatic shock is caused by a loss of fluid in the body and the general circulation. Loss of blood means that less blood goes to the brain, the heart and the other vital organs of the body; the oxygen supply is cut down, and the body cells suffer. Transfusions of whole blood or plasma are given to elevate the blood pressure and to replace the loss of fluids. The treatment of shock is discussed in further detail in Chapters 33 and 48.

THE HEART

The Heart Chambers

The heart is a strong muscular pump, about the size of a doubled-up fist, which lies in the lower left part of the chest cavity. Its shape is that of an irregular and slightly flattened cone. The base of the cone is directed upward and to the right. The apex (the pointed part) is directed downward, anteriorly and to the left. It is hollow and made of thick strong muscles that contract to force the blood into the arteries. The heart is covered by a thin sac, the *pericardium*. The membrane that lines the heart is the *endocardium*, and the muscular part of the heart is known as the *myocardium*. The heart is divided into 4 chambers. The 2 upper chambers, the *atria* (auricles), receive the blood; and the 2 lower chambers, the *ventricles*, pump the blood out. Between the atria and the ventricles are "one-way" flaps of tissue (valves), whose purpose is to prevent the backflow of the blood. The valve between the right atria and the right ventricle is called the *tricuspid* valve, because it is formed of 3 flaps of tissue. The valve between the left auricle and the left ventricle is called the *mitral* or bicuspid valve, since it has only 2 flaps of tissue.

The heart does its work by opening and closing the hollows within it at an average rate of 72 times per minute, or 100,000 times a day. The blood is literally squeezed out of the heart's chambers. This squeezing or pumping drives 5 to 6 quarts of blood per minute through thousands of feet of blood vessels in the body. Each pumping is called the heart beat.

The heart is divided into a right and a left half by a complete muscular wall, the *septum*. The 2 sides are completely separated with no communication from the right to the left side.

The atria fill between beats, when the heart is resting. When the heart contracts, the atria squeeze down to force the blood through the mitral and the tricuspid valves into the ventricles below. The wave of contraction continues to the ventricles and forces the blood from the left ventricle through the aortic valve into the *aorta* (the large artery leading to all body parts) and from the right ventricle through the pulmonary semilunar valve into the pulmonary artery leading to the lungs. After blood is squeezed from the atria into the ventricles, the mitral and tricuspid valves close to prevent the blood from flowing back into the atria when the ventricles contract. The semilunar valves close after the blood has been forced into the aorta and pulmonary artery. Because the left ventricle must contract with sufficient force to send the blood to the entire body, its muscle walls are thicker than the other chambers of the heart. The contraction which pumps the blood from the heart is called the systole, and the period when the heart is relaxed or at rest is called the diastole.

Blood that has delivered its food materials and oxygen to the cells and has accumulated waste products from the body flows into the right atrium, goes down into the right ventricle and is pumped through the pulmonary artery to the lungs to get rid of the carbon dioxide and to pick up a supply of oxygen. This phase is designated as pulmonary circulation. The blood has now exchanged its carbon dioxide waste for oxygen and returns to the heart at the left atrium, enters the left ventricle and is pumped into the aorta, carrying the precious oxygen supply to all the body cells. The circulation of oxygenated blood from the left ventricle to the body cells and back again to the right atrium is designated as *general circulation*. The oxygenated blood on the left is sep-

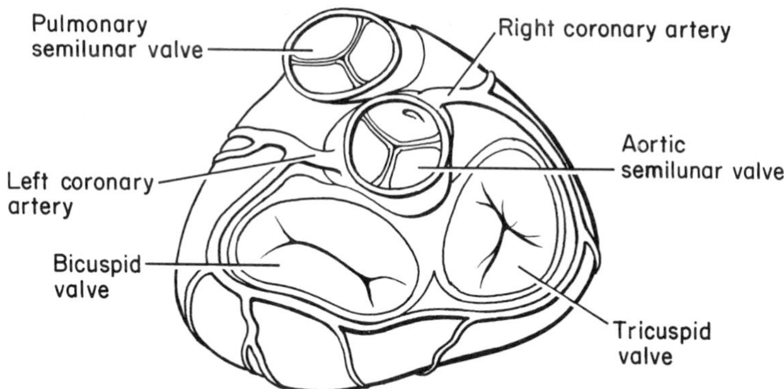

Fig. 59. Valves of the heart, viewed from above toward the ventricles. The atria and the greater part of the aorta and the pulmonary artery have been removed. Note the flaps of tissue which form the tricuspid and the bicuspid valves. Each semilunar valve is formed by a set of 3 pocketlike flaps. The right and the left coronary arteries which branch from the aorta to supply the heart muscle with oxygen and nourishment are also shown.

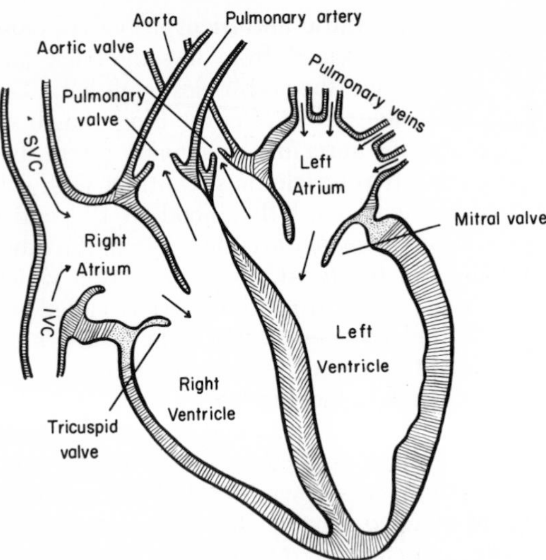

FIG. 60. These points will help in remembering how the heart and the circulation operate:

1. The auricles (atria) are receiving stations only.
2. The ventricles are dispensing stations only.
3. The right side of the heart contains only "blue" (deoxygenated) blood.
4. The left side of the heart contains only "red" (oxygenated) blood.
5. All arteries carry blood **away from** the heart.
6. All veins carry blood **to** the heart.
7. All arteries carry red blood
   Except the pulmonary artery.
8. All veins carry "blue" (deoxygenated) blood
   Except the 4 pulmonary veins.

(After Kimber, Gray, Stackpole and Leavell: Anatomy and Physiology, New York, Macmillan)

arated from that carrying carbon dioxide on the right by the solid wall of the septum.

The Nerve Supply of the Heart

The nerve supply of the heart is a part of the autonomic nervous system. It is a complex distribution possessing both accelerating and braking devices. This results in an accurate and delicate control of the rate. The vagus nerves are the "brakes." Their function is to slow the heart and reduce the force of its beats. The fibers of the accelerator nerve have the opposite action to that of the vagus; they increase the rate and the force of the heart beat. The result of both actions is a delicate balance. If the action of the vagus is reduced and the accelerator action is increased, then faster than normal acceleration of the heart is brought about.

There are special bundles of unique tissue in the heart—a combination of muscle and nerve tissue. The first of these bundles is embedded in the wall of the right atrium at the junction of the superior and the inferior venae cavae. It is called the *sino-atrial node* or the S.A. node and is the "pacemaker" of the heart. The other bundle is found in the lower part of the septum between the atria. This bundle is the *atrioventricular* or A.V. node. Originating from this area is a bundle of fibers, the *bundle of His.* It is called the co-ordinator.

It is in the S.A. node that the heart beat originates. It sets the pace, and the rest of the heart follows its bidding. The swift message is sent out through the muscular tissue of the atrium, which contracts; then the A.V. node picks up the message like a receiving station and relays the message on to the muscle fibers of the ventricle, which contracts in turn. The heart then rests for a short period between beats.

THE BLOOD VESSELS

The Arteries

The blood is carried through the body in a set of tubes or blood vessels: *arteries, capillaries* and *veins.* The arteries carry blood away from the heart, the capillaries serve as "in-between" channels, and the veins carry blood to the heart. As the blood leaves the left ventricle of the heart, it surges into the aorta, the largest artery of the body. The arteries have in their walls smooth muscle cells, one layer of which runs lengthwise and another layer of which is circular. As in all muscle cells of the body, the contraction of these cells (and therefore the size of the opening in the arteries) is controlled by the nervous system. The arterial walls are strong and elastic, and they expand as the heart pumps the blood out to be carried *away* to the cells of the body. From the aorta the arteries branch into smaller and smaller vessels, just as do the branches from the central trunk of a tree. The smallest of the arteries are called arterioles. From the arterioles the blood flows into the smallest blood vessels of all, the capillaries.

The Capillaries

The *capillaries* are so small that the minute red blood cells must pass through them in single file. Their walls are 1 cell layer thick. The capillaries must be plentiful, since it is through their walls that the oxygen and the food finally are supplied to the individual cells. (One estimate of the total length of the blood vessels of the body is 70,000 miles, most of

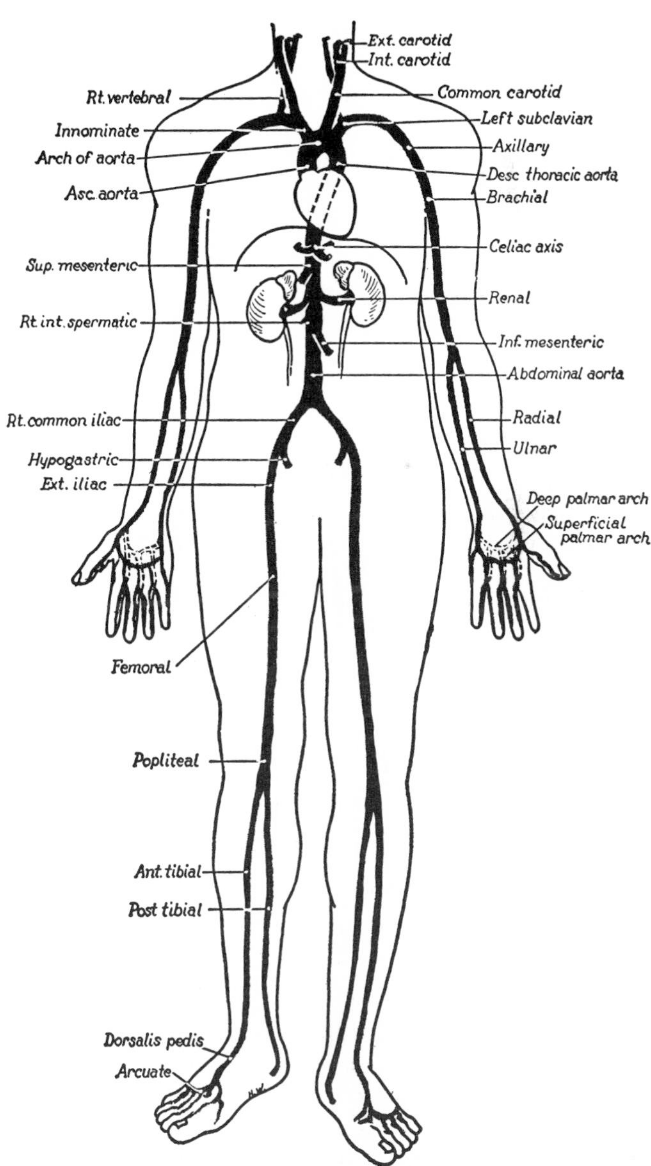

FIG. 61. The main arteries of the body. (Anthony, C. P.: Textbook of Anatomy and Physiology, St. Louis, Mosby)

which is made up of capillaries.) The blood flow into each capillary from the arteriole is guarded by a sphincter muscle. This slow single file passage of the blood through the capillaries allows time for the oxygen, the food and the white blood cells to leave the blood vessels and enter the tissues. Part of the plasma of the blood, the lymph, which is the intercellular fluid that surrounds all body cells, also seeps through the capillary walls, as do the salts and other materials necessary for the health of the tissues.

The Veins

At the same time that materials are being delivered to the cells, waste products are being picked up from the cells by the capillaries.

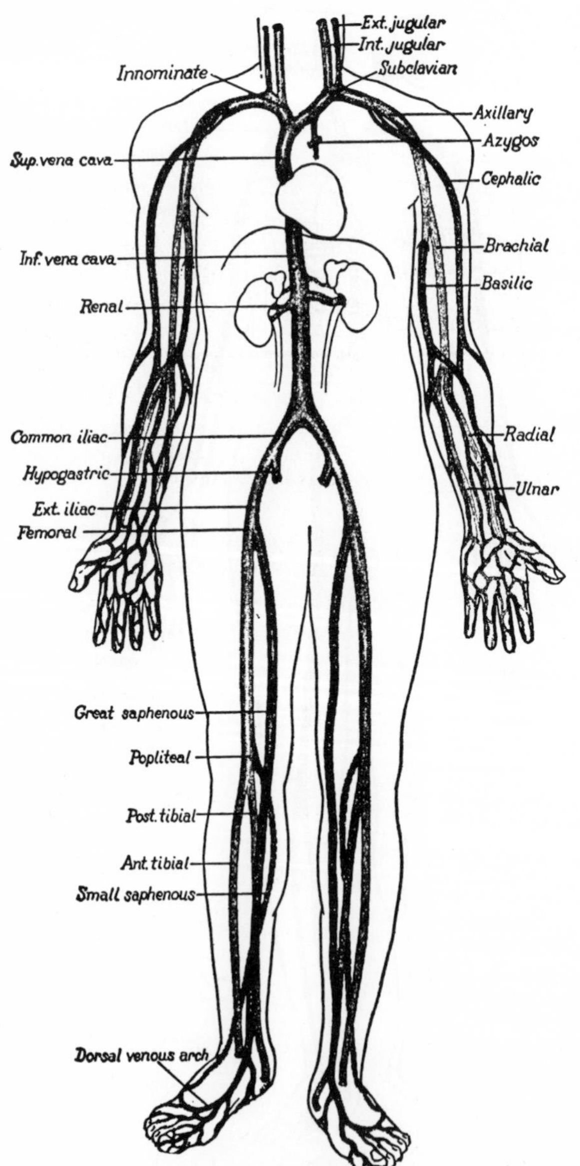

Fig. 62. The main veins of the body. (Anthony, C. P.: Textbook of Anatomy and Physiology, St. Louis, Mosby)

The blood starts traveling back to the heart through the venules, the smallest veins. The branches of the veins grow larger and fewer as they near the heart, until finally the blood reaches the superior and the inferior venae cavae, the 2 large veins that deliver the blood to the right atrium. (This blood is dark red because the oxygen has been replaced with carbon dioxide waste.)

The blood in the veins has lost the force from the contractions of the heart during the slow journey through the capillaries. Our bodies provide an extra push for venous blood because the veins are located between skeletal muscles. The contractions of the skeletal muscle squeeze the blood forward. In addition to this help, a backflow of blood in the veins is prevented by a system of valves that permits the blood to flow in one direction only. These valves contribute to the efficient venous flow from the extremities.

The Circulatory Route

The route of the blood through the entire system is as follows: The blood leaves the left ventricle of the heart through the largest artery, the aorta. It travels through smaller and smaller arterial branches to all parts of the body. From the smallest arteries, the arterioles, the blood enters the capillaries where the oxygen and the food is exchanged for waste products. The blood then begins its journey back to the heart from the capillaries to the venules, the larger veins, and through the inferior and the superior venae cavae to the right atrium (Fig. 63). The route thus far is the general circulation. The blood now begins the pulmonary circulation to the lungs to rid itself of the carbon dioxide.

From the right atrium the blood flows into the right ventricle; from the right ventricle the blood is pumped into the pulmonary artery. The blood goes to the capillaries in the lungs where the carbon dioxide carried in the hemoglobin is exchanged for the oxygen. The blood in the lung capillaries is collected by small veins that combine eventually into the 4 pulmonary veins, which pour the oxygenated blood into the left atrium. From here the blood again begins to travel through the general circulation.

The Coronary Arteries

The heart muscle itself must have its own supply of blood, since none of the blood which flows through the heart chambers is absorbed for use by heart tissue itself. The first branches from the aorta are those which return to supply the heart tissue with oxygen and nourishment. They are called the *coronary* arteries because they fit over the heart like a crown (corona). A narrowing of these arteries or an obstruction from a blood clot interferes with the heart's own blood supply, resulting in coronary artery disease (see Fig. 59).

The Portal System

Another area of the circulatory system is called the portal system. The veins from the stomach, the intestine, the spleen and the pancreas all empty into a common vessel, the *portal vein*, which leads to the liver. The liver extracts food materials from this blood for storage and chemical modification (including removal of toxins). Then the blood leaves the liver by way of the *hepatic veins* and empties into the inferior vena cava. It is through the

FIG. 63. Diagrammatic view of an artery, arteriole, capillary, venule and vein. The arrows indicate the passage of oxygen and food from the capillary through the tissue fluid, into the body cell, and in reverse, from the body cell through the tissue fluid, into the capillary.

portal system that the digested foods from the intestine reach the general circulation for distribution to the tissues.

THE LYMPHATIC SYSTEM

The body cells normally are bathed in tissue fluid. Some of this fluid drains into the blood capillaries which go directly to the veins. However, there is another group of vessels called the *lymphatic system* which also drains this fluid. The first group of these vessels is a network of tiny lymph capillaries in which excess fluid and certain other waste products collect to form the thin watery liquid known as lymph.

Since lymph originally is derived from plasma, its composition is much the same ex-

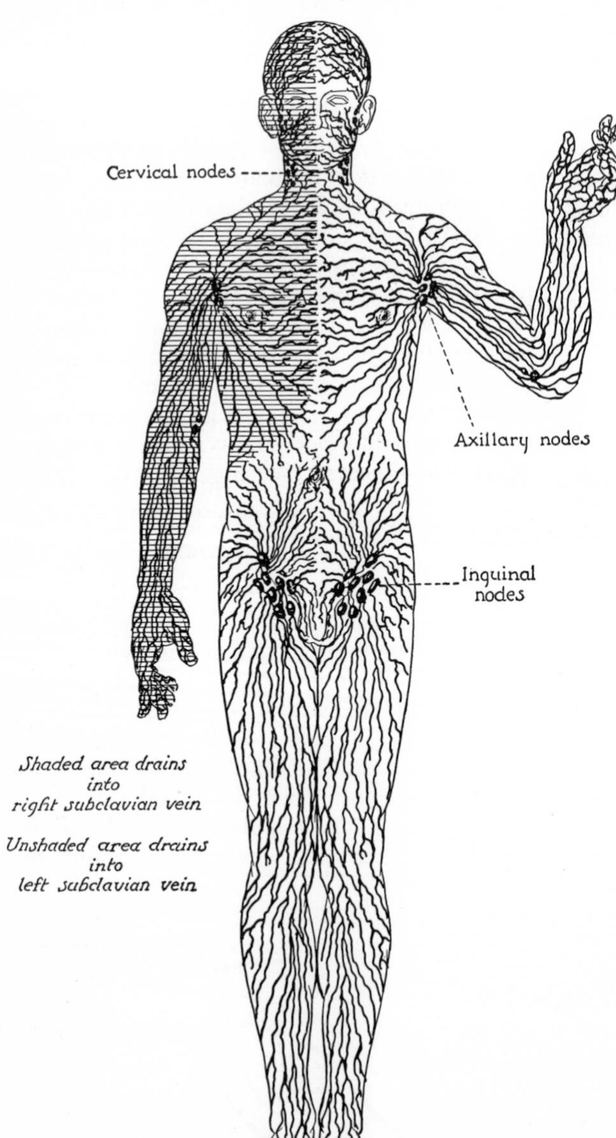

Fig. 64. Diagram of the superficial lymphatic vessels and the cervical, axillary and inguinal nodes. (Greisheimer, E. M.: Physiology and Anatomy, ed. 7, p. 468, Philadelphia, Lippincott)

cept that it is lower in protein content. Lymph that is drained from the intestinal area may contain large amounts of fats after a fatty meal, which gives this lymph a milky white appearance. The lymph capillaries empty into progressively larger vessels that finally end in 2 main channels: the thoracic duct and the right lymphatic duct. These 2 ducts enter the veins at the base of the neck where the lymph mixes with the blood plasma and becomes part of the general circulation. It is through these 2 vessels that the digested fats from the small intestine finally reach the bloodstream. The lacteals in the villi (the small projections in the lining of the intestine) are small lymphatic capillaries which absorb digested fats and eventually empty into the thoracic and the right lymphatic ducts.

Lymph flows very slowly in the lymphatic system of channels. As in the venous system, it is aided by pressure from the contractions of muscles which keep the lymph moving, as well as by valves which prevent the backward flow.

Small bundles of special lymphoid tissue called *lymph nodes* are situated at various points in the lymphatic system. Many of these nodes appear in the neck, the groin and the armpits (Fig. 64). Before the lymph reaches the veins, it passes through the nodes traveling through passages lined with cells which devour bacteria and filters waste products and other foreign substances. Another function of the nodes is to manufacture lymphocytes and monocytes and add them to the lymph for transportation to the blood.

The Spleen

The *spleen*, another mass of lymphoid tissue, is often classified as part of the lymphatic system. It is a somewhat flattened dark-purple organ about 6 inches long and 3 inches wide located directly below the diaphragm, above the left kidney and behind the stomach. Its functions are somewhat of a mystery, but it is known to act as a blood storage reservoir, to destroy red blood cells, and to manufacture one type of white blood cells, the lymphocytes. It also produces antibodies which give us an immunity to certain diseases. Although the functions of the spleen are very important, it can be removed without ill effects. The tonsils and the adenoids are also organs composed of lymphoid tissue.

FETAL CIRCULATION

Circulation in the body before birth differs from the circulation in the body after birth. The unborn infant, the fetus, secures oxygen and food from the mother's blood instead of using its own lungs and digestive system. Since the fetal and the maternal blood are in separate capillaries and, do not mix, there must be some place where the interchange of gases, food and wastes can take place. This occurs in the *placenta*, sometimes called the *afterbirth*, since it is cast out of the uterus following the birth of the baby. Fetal capillaries in the placenta are surrounded by maternal blood, and the exchanges take place across the capillary membranes.

The fetal heart drives the deoxygenated blood to the placenta through 2 vessels, the *umbilical arteries*. The oxygenated blood is returned to the fetus from the placenta by a single vessel, the *umbilical vein*. This is another exception to the classification that all arteries carry oxygenated (bright red) blood, and all veins carry deoxygenated (bluish) blood (see p. 158). These 3 vessels are intertwined and covered by a soft jellylike substance, the whole system making up the *umbilical cord*. The cord enters the body of the fetus at approximately the middle of the abdomen at the *umbilicus* (naval). Some of the oxygenated blood from the umbilical vein passes through the liver and some enters the inferior vena cava by way of the ductus venosus, passing on into the right atrium. The great bulk of blood is shunted to the arterial (left) side of the heart by 2 short cuts. These short cuts are an opening between the 2 atria called the *foramen ovale* and a vessel known as the *ductus arteriosus*, which connects the pulmonary artery and the aorta. Normally, with the first few respirations of the newborn child,

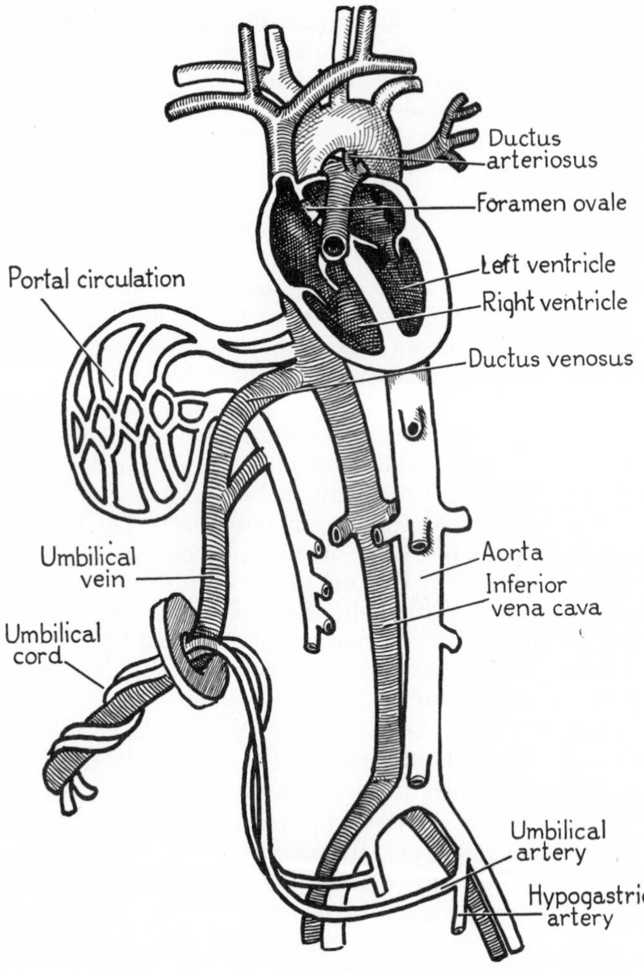

Fig. 65. Diagram of fetal circulation. (Baillif and Kimmel: Structure and Function of the Human Body, p. 141, Philadelphia, Lippincott)

the lungs are expanded. The foramen ovale then closes, and the ductus arteriosus becomes obliterated. Sometimes these circulatory adjustments do not take place, causing abnormalities. The fetal circulation will be mentioned again in later chapters.

16

OXYGEN FOR THE BODY: THE RESPIRATORY SYSTEM

Your body cells must have oxygen in order to survive. If you are without oxygen for more than a few minutes, the brain cells are injured, and the rest of the body slowly begins to fail. The air you take in through your respiratory system is about 20 per cent oxygen and provides a more than ample supply for your needs.

Respiration consists of taking oxygen into the body through the lungs and eliminating the waste product, carbon dioxide. Breathing the air in is called *inspiration* (inhaling), and breathing it out is called *expiration* (exhaling).

The Nose

The air begins its journey into the body through the nose, which is divided into 2 sides or cavities by the *nasal septum*, a structure consisting of bone and cartilage. The nerve endings in the septum and the nasal passages are responsible for the sense of smell. The nasal cavities are lined with mucous membrane richly supplied with blood vessels which aid in warming and moistening the air before it reaches the lungs. The mucus is sticky and traps within itself the dust, the dirt and the microorganisms from the air within the mucus secretions. The hairs at the entrance of the nostrils and the tiny hairlike projections (cilia) on the membrane serve as filters to remove some foreign particles that otherwise might be carried to the lungs.

Three small bones, the *turbinates* (*conchae*), project into the nasal cavity to increase the surface lining of the nose. The *nasolacrimal* (*tear*) *ducts* open into the upper nasal cavities, which explains the "runny nose" that occurs when crying. Also communicating with these cavities are the sinuses in the frontal, the maxillary, the ethmoid and the sphenoid bones. (These were described in Chapter 13.) The lining of the sinuses is continuous with the mucous membrane of the nose and therefore is subject to infection from the nasal cavity.

The Pharynx

Air travels from the nose to the *pharynx* (pronounced *fair′ inks*), a tube-shaped passage for both air and food. The section of the pharynx which lies behind the nose is called the *nasopharynx* and contains a mass of lymphoid tissue called the adenoids. The part behind the mouth is the *oropharynx*, commonly called the throat. The tonsils, also masses of lymphoid tissue, are in the back of the oropharynx. Both the tonsils and the adenoids serve as filters for microorganisms and other foreign substances. The *eustachian tubes* open into the pharynx; they are passageways which connect the middle ear with the pharynx in order to equalize the pressure in the middle ear.

The Larynx

From the pharynx, the air passes into the *larynx* (*lair′ inks*), a boxlike structure made

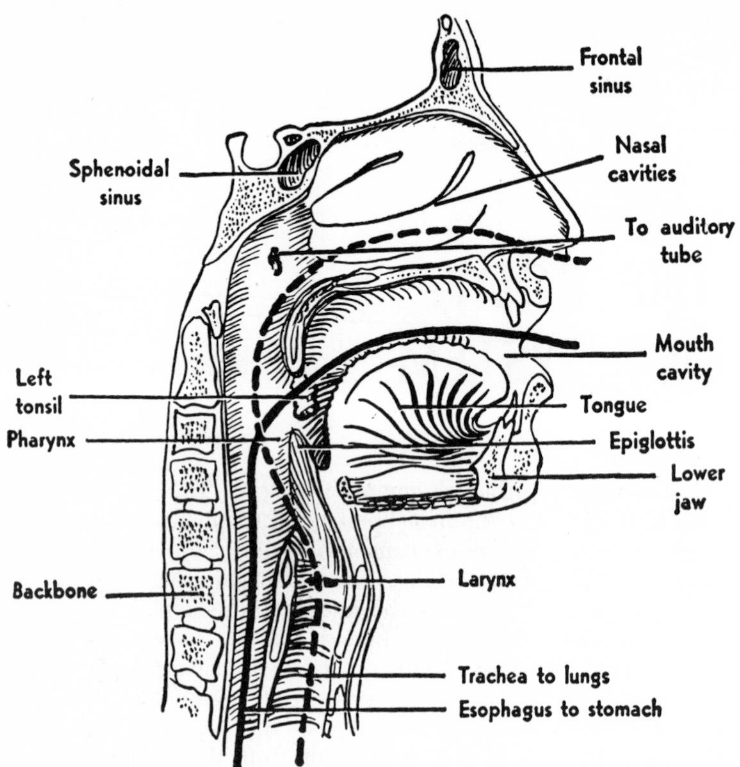

FIG. 66. Section through the middle plane of head, neck and thorax. The air path is indicated by the dotted line, the food path by the solid line. The 2 paths cross in the lower pharynx.

of cartilages held together by ligaments. It is located in the midline of the neck.

The pharynx is a dual passageway for air and food, but only air is allowed to pass into the larynx. The entrance to the larynx is guarded by a lid or cover called the *epiglottis*. This cover to the larynx automatically closes when you swallow and therefore prevents food from entering the lower respiratory passages. If, by accident, a portion of food becomes lodged in the larynx, usually it can be dislodged by coughing. If not, the air passage may be blocked and prove to be fatal to the individual unless proper emergency treatment is rendered.

Within the larynx or voice box are the *vocal cords*, 2 triangular-shaped membranous folds which extend from front to back. As air leaves the lungs and passes over the vocal cords, the cords vibrate and produce sounds. The size of the vocal cords and the size of the larynx vary in different individuals, which causes the difference in voices. A man has a larger larynx and therefore a deeper voice than a woman. Your voice becomes louder and stronger when you rapidly force out a large amount of air.

The Trachea and the Bronchi

The air passes from the larynx into the *trachea*—a tube made of horseshoe-shaped rings of cartilage and connective tissue, which extends from the lower end of the voice box into the chest cavity behind the heart. Immediately posterior to the larynx and the trachea is the tube called the esophagus which transports the food from the pharynx to the stomach. The cartilaginous rings of the trachea provide sufficient rigidity to keep it open at all times for the air to pass through, and yet they are flexible enough to permit bending the neck. The trachea is lined with ciliated mucous membrane. As in the nose, the mucus in the trachea traps inhaled foreign particles, which the waves of cilia carry out of the respiratory tract through the pharynx.

As the trachea enters the chest cavity, it

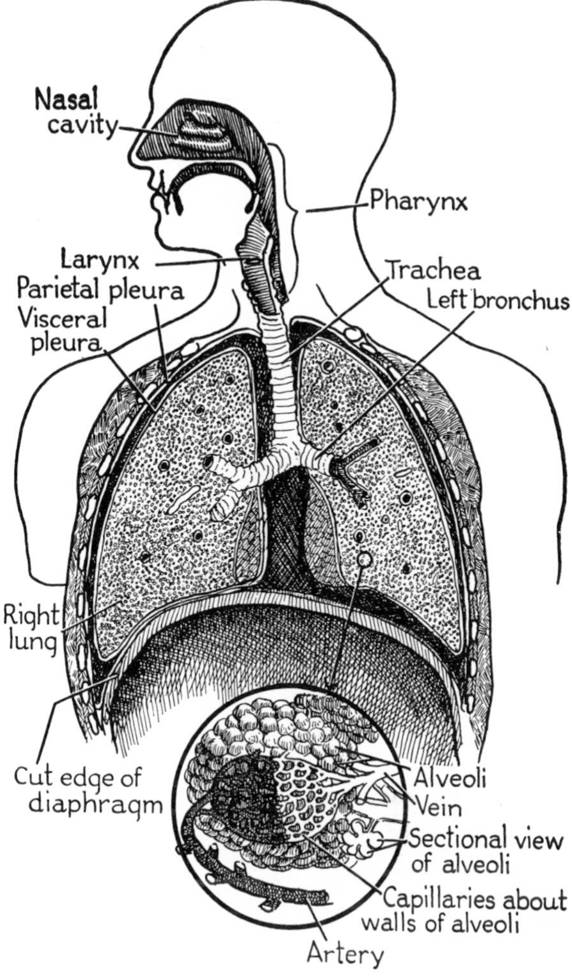

FIG. 67. The respiratory system showing nasal cavity, pharynx, larynx, trachea, lungs, bronchi and alveoli. Note the enlarged diagram of the alveoli with surrounding blood capillaries through which the exchange of gases takes place between the inspired air and the blood. (Baillif and Kimmel: Structure and Function of the Human Body, p. 58, Philadelphia, Lippincott)

divides into 2 smaller tubes called the *bronchi.* The bronchi enter the lungs and divide into smaller and smaller branches to form what is commonly called the "bronchial tree" which is spread throughout the lung tissue. As the bronchi become smaller and smaller their walls become thinner, and they are called *bronchioles.* The bronchi and the bronchioles continue to be lined with ciliated mucous membrane. The bronchioles terminate in microscopic balloonlike structures or air sacs called *alveoli,* which somewhat resemble a bunch of grapes. These microscopic "balloons" give the lungs their spongy appearance.

It is through the alveoli that the exchange of gases (oxygen and carbon dioxide) takes place. The walls of the alveoli are 1 cell layer thick. They are surrounded by the equally thin blood capillaries. When oxygen enters the lungs it travels through the walls of the alveoli into the capillaries, where it combines with hemoglobin, the main chemical component of the red blood cells. In this manner the oxygen is distributed to the body cells by the bloodstream. After it gives up its oxygen, hemoglobin combines with carbon dioxide, a waste product of cells. This carbon dioxide is released into the lungs for removal by exhalation in exchange for oxygen. An enlargement of the alveoli is shown in Figure 67.

The Lungs

The *lungs* are the stations where the blood picks up oxygen and drops off its load of carbon dioxide. The lungs are 2 cone-shaped organs which fill the chest cavity. The term *apex* is given to the top of the triangular cone. The lower wide portion which fits over the diaphragm is called the *base*. The lungs are spongy tissue, filled with alveoli, nerves and blood and lymph vessels. They are separated by the heart, the large blood vessels, the esophagus and other contents of the *mediastinum*, the area which lies between the lungs in the thorax.

The lungs are divided into sections called lobes. On the inner surface of the lungs is an indented area called the *hilum*. The arteries, the veins, the bronchi and the nerves enter the lungs at the hilum.

The lungs are covered with a smooth double-layered sac called the *pleura*. One layer covers the lungs, and the outer layer lines the chest cavity. Their surfaces are in constant contact and are moist, allowing the lungs to move without pain or friction against the chest wall.

The Mechanics of Breathing

As mentioned previously in Chapter 13, the lungs do not move by themselves during the process of breathing—they are inflated and deflated by the muscles which surround them. The intercostal muscles contract to lift the ribs when you inhale, and they relax when you exhale. The diaphragm, the dome-shaped muscle which separates the thorax and the abdominal cavities, contracts and flattens to increase the chest space. The resulting partial vacuum inflates the lung as the air rushes in. When the diaphragm relaxes, it curves upward into the thorax, presses against the lower surface of the lungs and pushes the air out of them (Fig. 68).

The respiratory center which controls breathing is in the medulla in the brain. Breathing is also affected by the amount of carbon dioxide in the blood. Therefore, if you take deep breaths and breathe in a large amount of oxygen, you do not need to breathe as often. When you exercise strenuously, your muscles need more energy for power, and you breathe more rapidly to supply more oxygen.

Even when you have exhaled all the air you can from your lungs, there is still slightly more than a quart (1,100 ml.) of residual air remaining constantly in the alveoli. If filled to capacity the lungs will hold approximately 1 gallon (4,000 + ml.) but the intake and the output with every normal breath is about 500 ml. or 1 pint. Adults usually average between 14 to 20 respirations per minute. The rate is much higher for children.

There are 2 kinds of respirations: the external and the internal. The exchange of oxygen for carbon dioxide within the alveoli of the lungs is called external respiration. The trade of oxygen for carbon dioxide within the cells is called internal respiration.

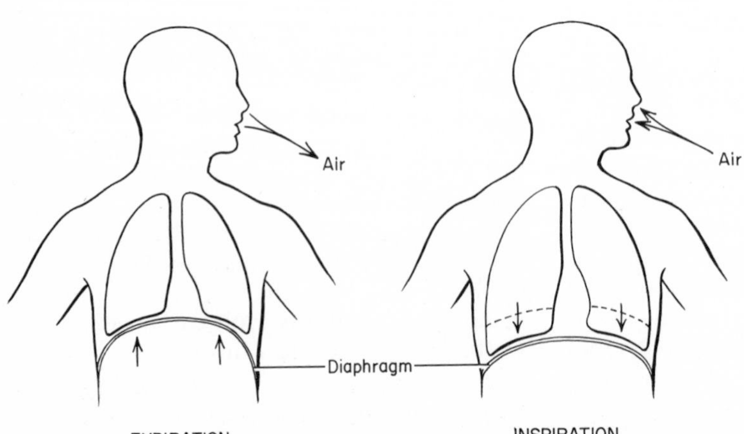

Fig. 68. The mechanics of breathing. (*Left*) Chest space and lung size when air is exhaled and the muscles of respiration are relaxed. (*Right*) Expansion of the lungs in the vacuum created by an increase in the size of the chest upon inhalation. The ribs are lifted and the diaphragm contracts.

17

FUEL FOR THE BODY: THE DIGESTIVE SYSTEM

FOOD MATERIALS AND ENZYMES

Because the body must have energy to perform its many tasks, it has to have a supply of fuel. You are able to breathe, your heart beats, you talk and laugh and move because your digestive system supplies you with food which gives you the fuel for your energy demands.

The foods that provide fuel for the body are carbohydrates (starches and sugars), proteins and fats. Some of their main sources are listed on page 203. These organic food materials are made up of carbon, hydrogen and oxygen. The proteins also contain nitrogen. The function of the organs of the digestive system is to break down the food into its most simple forms—small units or molecules—that can be carried by the circulatory vessels and pass through cell membranes to be used by the cells. The cells use the simple forms of food molecules for energy as well as to build, maintain and repair body tissues.

This wonderfully efficient machinery which your body uses for processing food to be supplied to body cells is called the digestive tube. (It is also called the alimentary canal, the GI tract, or the gastrointestinal system.) The conversion of the mass of food to the basic food materials is called digestion. The chemicals that accomplish most of the digestive processes are called *enzymes.* An enzyme is a substance produced by the body to aid or speed a chemical reaction. Enzymes act only on specific substances; for instance, some act only on proteins, others on fats, and still others on carbohydrates.

THE ORGANS OF DIGESTION

The Mouth (Oral Cavity)

Food is taken into the body through the mouth, where digestion begins. The teeth cut, chop and grind the food so that the particles become smaller and more food surface is exposed to the actions of the digestive juices and enzymes.

The Teeth

The teeth are set in spaces called sockets in the upper and the lower jaw bones, the *maxilla* and the *mandible.* Humans have 2 sets of teeth: the deciduous or baby teeth and a permanent or adult set. A baby's deciduous teeth usually begin to erupt when he is from 6 to 8 months old, and the total of 20 is usually complete by the time he is 2½ years old. When the child is about 6, the permanent teeth begin to put in an appearance. As they grow in, they push out the deciduous teeth, replace them and fill in the spaces in the jaw. There are 32 teeth in the permanent set. The front and the side teeth are biters and cutters; the back teeth or molars are grinders. The last permanent teeth, the *wisdom teeth,* sometimes do not appear before adulthood. If the jaw is small and the jaw space limited, they may not have room to erupt and may have to be removed surgically.

A tooth has 3 parts: the exposed part, the *crown;* the narrowed *neck* at the gumline; and the *root* in the bony socket. The crown is covered by enamel, which is the hardest structure in the body. Covering the root is another substance called cement. Beneath the enamel and the cement is a hard bonelike substance called dentin which is the bulk of the material of the tooth. The center of the tooth is the pulp cavity. The pulp contains many nerves and blood vessels which enter from a canal through the roots from the sockets. The teeth are imbedded in and nourished by bone.

The Tongue

The tongue is muscular and flexible and has many functions. The rough upper surface is sprinkled with taste buds, small organs containing nerve endings that distinguish between salty, bitter, sweet and sour tastes. The tongue also helps us to know whether food is hot or cold, and whether it is smooth, lumpy, or stringy. The tongue mixes food with saliva and moves the food beneath the teeth to be

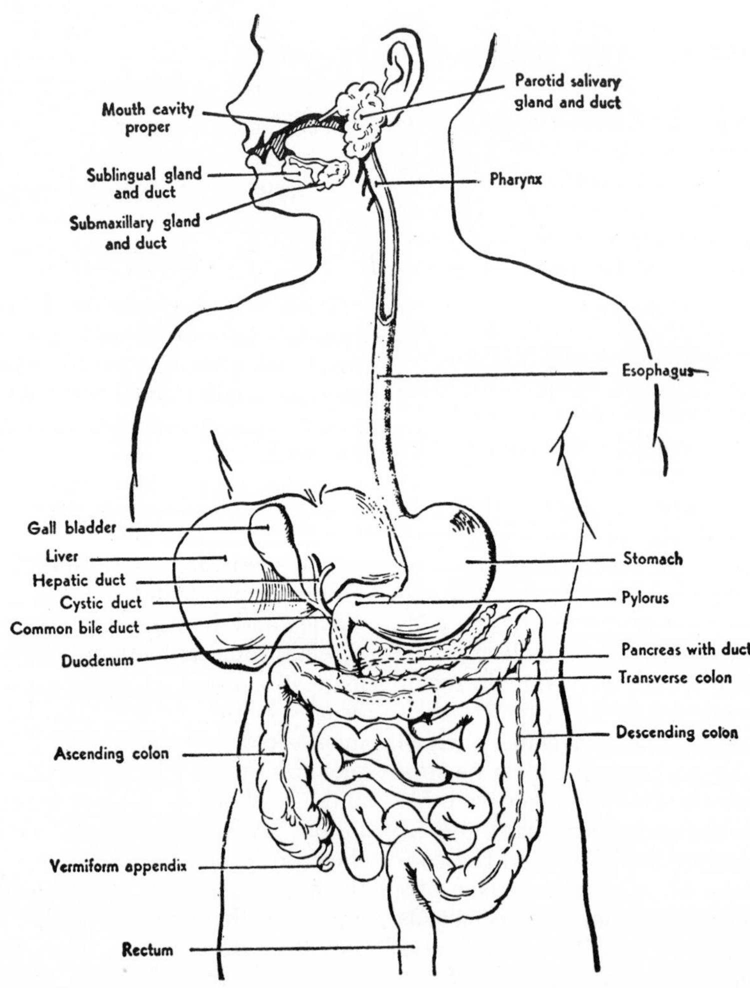

FIG. 69. Diagram of the digestive system.

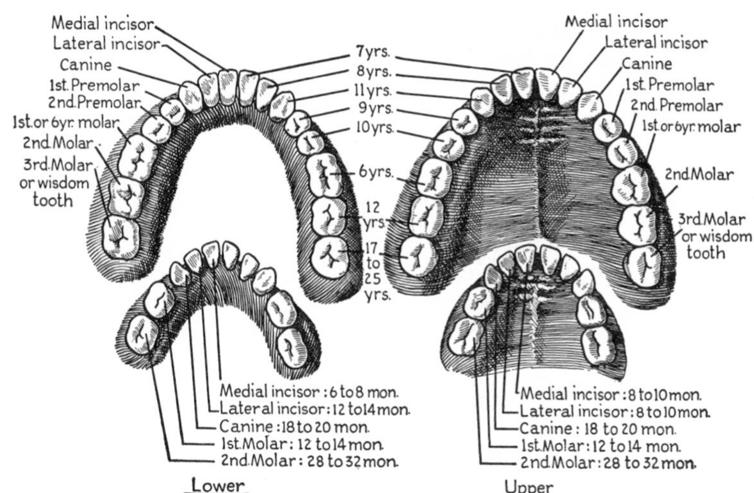

FIG. 70. Permanent and deciduous teeth. (Baillif and Kimmel: Structure and Function of the Human Body, p. 160, Philadelphia, Lippincott)

chewed. It begins the swallowing process by pushing the food into the pharynx, the next portion of the tube.

Three pairs of salivary glands from the mouth, the cheek and the jaw pour saliva into the mouth. Saliva is a thin watery fluid that contains ptyalin. Ptyalin is also called *salivary amylase* (*amyl:* starch; *ase:* pertaining to enzymes). Saliva moistens the food particles, which stimulates the taste buds, makes the food easier to swallow, and through the action of the enzyme begins the breakdown of starch into smaller sugar molecules. The salivary glands also excrete other substances, including some viruses, so that saliva can be a source for the spread of disease.

The Pharynx and the Esophagus

The tongue lifts the ball of food (called a *bolus*) which it has mixed with saliva into the muscular tube behind the mouth, the *pharynx.* Contractions of the pharynx continue the act of swallowing and push the food into the esophagus. The *epiglottis* covers the larynx and prevents the food from entering the respiratory tract. The contractions in the pharynx begin the automatic journey of the food through the digestive tract. The smooth or involuntary muscles pass the food along by waves of contractions called *peristalsis.* Peristalsis is the alternate relaxation and contraction of the muscles to push the food through the digestive tube. Figure 71 shows a peristaltic wave in a portion of the small intestine, the tube which follows the stomach.

From the pharynx, the food passes down the muscular *esophagus.* The esophagus averages about 10 inches in length and extends from the pharynx into the neck and the thorax and, through an opening in the diaphragm, to the stomach. Its role in digestion is merely to serve as a passageway. The stomach opening, the *cardiac orifice,* is guarded by a muscle called

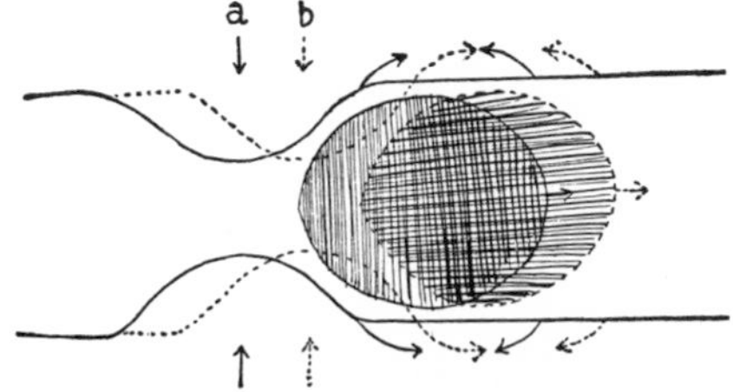

FIG. 71. Diagram of a peristaltic wave. In the intestine is a mass of food. The solid line (a) represents the beginning of the wave; the dotted line (b) represents the wave a moment later. (From Brunner, L. S., et al.: Textbook of Medical-Surgical Nursing, p. 569, Philadelphia, Lippincott, 1964)

the *cardiac sphincter*. As the waves of peristalsis push the food through the lower esophagus, the cardiac sphincter opens and allows the food to enter.

The Stomach

The *stomach* is a muscular collapsible pouch-like sac which is capable of great distention. It is located in the upper left side of the abdominal cavity. The rounded portion at the top of the stomach is called the *fundus*. The central portion is called the *body*; the lower portion, which attaches to the small intestine, is called the *pyloric portion*.

The strong walls of the stomach consist of 3 layers of smooth muscle: a circular layer, a longitudinal layer and an oblique layer. This spread of the muscles in all directions allows great motion in stirring and churning the food and breaking it into small particles.

The stomach is lined with mucous membrane. In addition to the glands that secrete mucus, the gastric lining also secretes gastric juice, which consists mostly of water, enzymes and hydrochloric acid. The hydrochloric acid activates some enzymes and also destroys organisms. The enzymes in the stomach are mostly concerned with the digestion of protein. The enzyme pepsin begins the breakdown of proteins, and rennin curdles the protein in milk, making it more easily digestible. Some authorities state that lipase, another enzyme, is present in small quantities and acts on emulsified fats (those that have already been broken down into tiny droplets). However, most of the fat digestion takes place later in the small intestine.

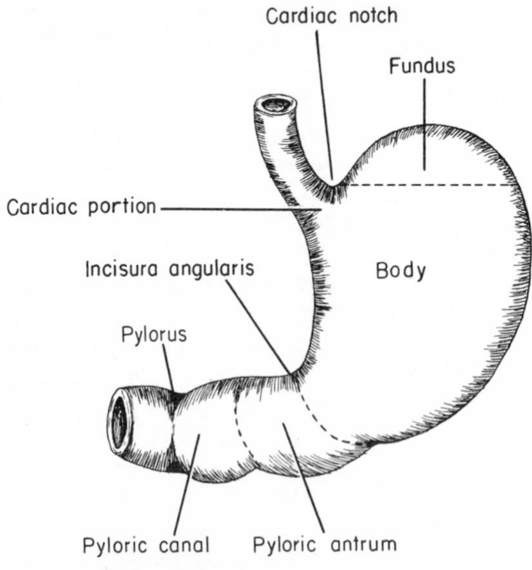

FIG. 72. Diagram of the parts of the stomach. (From Grant, J. C. B.: A Method of Anatomy, ed. 5, Baltimore, Williams & Wilkins)

In the stomach, all foods are mixed with the gastric juices and churned until they are in a semiliquid form called chyme. This process usually takes from 3 to 5 hours. Peristalsis in the smooth muscles of the stomach normally moves the food toward the pyloric outlet, and the pyloric sphincter at the lower opening contracts to keep the food in the stomach until it is thoroughly mixed. It then relaxes to let the peristaltic waves push the food in small amounts into the small intestine. If the stomach is irritated or overfull, sometimes the direction of the waves of peristalsis reverses and forces the material back into the lower end of the esophagus. Reverse peristalsis within the stomach plus contractions of the abdominal muscles and the diaphragm force the food back through the esophagus and out through the mouth, causing vomiting.

The actions of the digestive system are subject to the control of the nervous system. It is known that there are also hormones (chemical messengers carried in the bloodstream) which control certain actions. For instance, gastrin is a hormone of the stomach which appears to be related to the control of gastric secretions. There are many other known hormones of the digestive system and others which are being investigated.

The Small Intestine

The small intestine is about 23 feet long, 1½ inches in diameter and lies coiled upon itself in the abdominal cavity. It is about 18 feet longer than the large intestine which follows it. The first portion is the 10 to 12 inch "C"-shaped *duodenum*. As the chyme enters the duodenum, more digestive juices are added. *Bile*, a greenish-brown liquid which is manufactured by the *liver* and stored in the *gallbladder*, pours in through the *common bile duct* to emulsify fats in preparation for further digestive action. The *pancreas* is a glandular organ behind the stomach which adds 3 enzymes in the secretions it sends through the *pancreatic duct*: protease for proteins, amylase for carbohydrates and lipase for fat digestion. The common bile duct and the pancreatic duct enter the duodenum a short distance beyond the pyloric sphincter of the stomach. The small intestine itself secretes enzymes for the digestion of all foodstuffs. Together these juices break up the fats, the carbohydrates and the proteins into materials that the cells can use.

In order to be absorbed by the blood and the lymph capillaries, the carbohydrates must be in the form of the simple sugars: glucose, fructose and galactose. The proteins must also be digested to their simplest state, amino acids, and the fats to fatty acids and glycerol. The table at the bottom of the page summarizes the action of the enzymes in preparing food for absorption.

The chyme travels on through the remaining portions of the small intestine, the *jejunum* and the *ileum*. Like the rest of the alimentary canal, the entire intestinal tract is lined with mucous membrane. Throughout the whole length of the small intestine are tiny fingerlike projections called *villi*. These villi projecting from the walls add a tremendous area for absorption to the intestines, just as deep pleats in a skirt add to the amount of material needed to make it. They wave to and fro to keep the food molecules thoroughly mixed with digestive juices. It is through the villi that about 85 per cent of the food is absorbed as it flows over their surfaces.

The villi are heavily supplied with blood capillaries. In the center of each villus there is also a lymph capillary called a *lacteal*. The

ENZYMES AND THEIR ACTIONS

Area of Digestive System	Secretion	Enzyme	Action
Mouth	Saliva from the salivary glands	Amylase (also called ptyalin)	Begins digestion of starches
Stomach	Gastric juice from the stomach lining (includes hydrochloric acid—HCl)	Pepsin	Begins digestion of proteins
		Lipase	Acts on emulsified fats
		Rennin	Acts on casein in milk (a protein)
Small intestine	Bile from the liver	No enzyme	Emulsifies fats
	Pancreatic juice from the pancreas	Trypsin (Protease)	Digests proteins to amino acids
		Amylopsin (Amylase)	Digests starches to sugars
		Steapsin (Lipase)	Digests fats to simplest forms—fatty acids and glycerol
	Intestinal juice from the intestinal lining	Erepsin (Proteases)	Digests proteins to amino acids
		Lactase Maltase Sucrase	Digests sugars to simplest forms—glucose, fructose and galactose
		Enterokinase	Activates trypsin to act on proteins

digested carbohydrates and proteins pass into the villi and are absorbed by the blood capillaries, while most of the digested fat is absorbed into the lacteals and is carried in the lymph. The fats eventually reach the bloodstream by way of the thoracic and the right lymphatic ducts in the region of the neck. The completely digested foods are then ready for distribution to the various body tissues. We have already mentioned the processes by which the food needed by cells passes through the capillary walls into the surrounding tissue fluid and then through the cell membrane into the body of the cell.

As the food passes on into the large intestine, all that remains of it are water and waste products. A sphincter muscle, located where the large and the small intestine meet, acts as a valve to prevent the backflow of material to the small intestine and also regulates the forward flow. It is called the *ileocecal valve* from the names of the 2 joining parts, the ileum in the small intestine and the cecum in the large.

The Large Intestine

The large intestine (sometimes called the *large bowel*) is much wider than the small intestine (diameter about 2½ inches) but is only about 5 feet long. It has no villi, does not coil or lie in folds, and is divided into different areas by name.

The first portion is the *cecum*, a blind pouch about 2 to 3 inches long. A small fingerlike projection of the cecum is the *vermiform appendix*, which has no known function. It has some of the same lymphoid tissue as the tonsils and, like the tonsils, frequently becomes infected, a condition called *appendicitis*. The cecum and the appendix are located in the right lower quadrant of the abdominal cavity.

The next and longest portion of the large intestine is the *colon*, a continuous tube divided into 3 parts, taking their names from the course they follow: the *ascending colon* travels up the right side of the abdominal cavity; the *transverse colon* crosses to the left side in the upper part of the cavity; the *descending colon* goes down the left side into the pelvis. The next and last portion, which is called the *sigmoid* (sigma: Greek letter for S) ends at the *rectum*. The rectum is about 5 inches in length and terminates at the *anal canal*. This is the terminal portion of the large intestine. It is about 1 to 1½ inches long, and its opening to the outside, the *anus*, is guarded by internal and external sphincter muscles. The external sphincter is under the control of the will and can be consciously contracted and relaxed.

Since most of the valuable food products are absorbed in the small intestine, the main function of the large bowel is the absorption of water. As the contents move along, most of the water is absorbed through the walls of the large intestine into the circulation to assist in maintaining the body's fluid balance. As the water leaves, the cellulose left from food masses together and passes into the rectum. This solid waste, the feces, also contains bacteria, mucus and a small amount of water. As the feces enter the rectum they stimulate sensory nerve endings, causing the sensation of accumulating bulk. The peristaltic waves push the contents against the anal muscles as a signal to empty the rectum. Relaxation of the external sphincter muscle, the pressure from peristalsis plus that consciously exerted by the diaphragm and the abdominal muscles brings about defecation, the emptying of the rectum. If the sensation for defecation is ignored, the impulse dies.

The Liver

The digested food which has reached the blood through the villi in the small intestine passes through the *liver* and undergoes vital changes. The liver is the largest glandular organ in the body and lies just below the diaphragm in the upper right quadrant of the abdominal cavity. In man, it weighs about 3 pounds and resembles in color and texture the calf liver that we eat. The liver plays such an important part in our over-all bodily functions that a person cannot live long if it is severely diseased or injured. It can be likened to:

A filtration plant. The phagocytic cells lining the sinusoids of the liver engulf bacteria and other particles.

A chemical laboratory. It breaks down digested fats and proteins into substances which can be

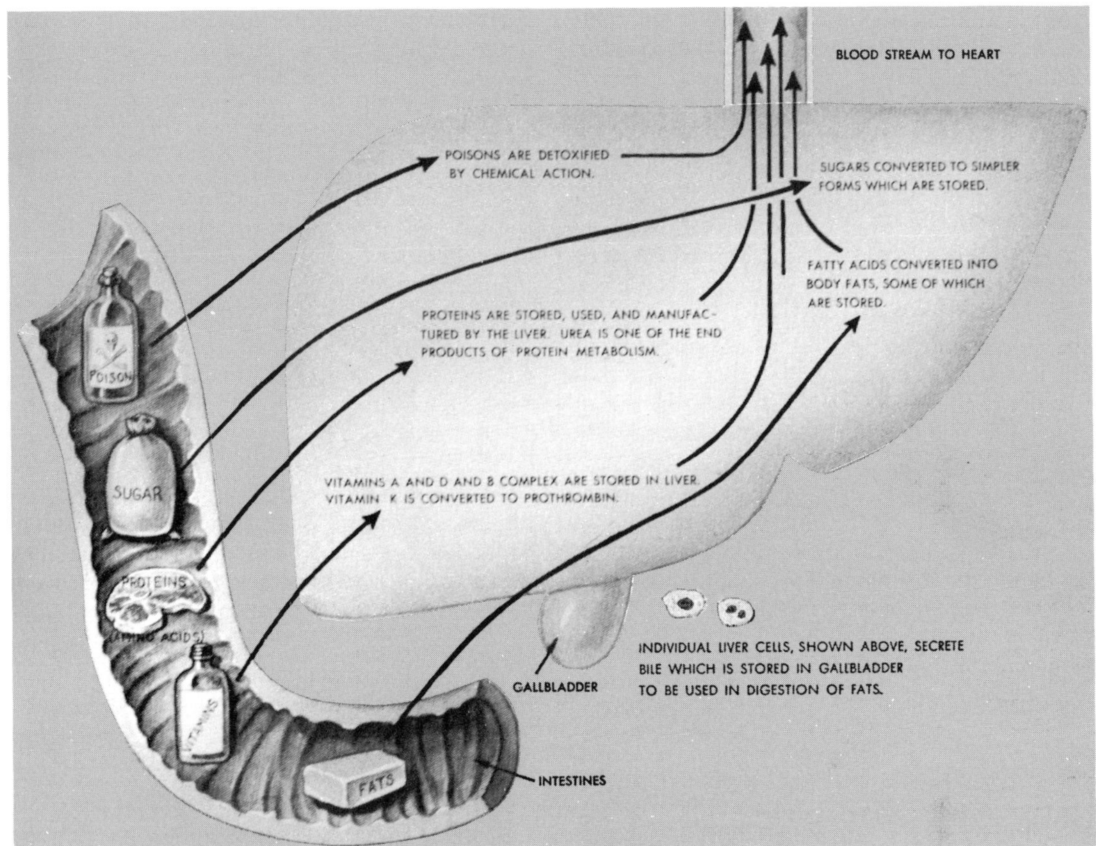

FIG. 73. (Diagrammatic) Some functions of the liver. (*Today's Health*, p. 42, June, 1961)

used or stored by the liver or elsewhere in the body. It prepares products from the breakdown of red blood cells for further use by the body and detoxicates bacterial and other poisons such as alcohol and drugs that have gained entrance into the blood stream.

A manufacturing plant. The liver produces bile, glycogen (a form of stored sugar) and a substance called heparin which prevents the clotting of blood in the blood vessels. It also produces most of the blood proteins, such as albumin, prothrombin and fibrinogen.

A warehouse. It stores carbohydrates, fats and proteins as well as vitamins and minerals, releasing them to the body as needed.

A waste disposal plant. It prepares many substances for excretion, including urea, the chief waste product from the utilization of amino acids.

A heating plant. The burning of the simple sugars, the amino acids and the fatty acids in the liver produces body heat second only to the amount produced by the skeletal muscles.

The Gallbladder

The *gallbladder* is a muscular sac resembling a small pear located on the undersurface of the liver. Some authorities regard it as an enlargement of the cystic duct through which it drains. Its main function is to store and release bile as it is needed in the small intestines to emulsify fats.

Cells within the liver manufacture bile. Small ducts from these cells emerge and join to form the hepatic duct which then joins the cystic duct coming from the gallbladder. At this point it is called the common bile duct which, with the pancreatic duct, empties into the duodenum at the major duodenal papilla, an opening a small distance beyond the pyloric portion of the stomach. This was mentioned earlier in this chapter in discussing digestion in the small intestine. As bile is produced, it flows down the hepatic duct and up into the cystic duct for storage in the gallbladder. With the appearance of fats in the intestines, the hormone cholecystokinin activates the gallbladder to release the bile; then it flows through the cystic duct into the common bile duct for deposit in the duodenum. This system of passageways for the transport of bile from the liver to the gallbladder to the intestines is known as the *biliary apparatus* and is shown diagrammatically in Figure 74.

When the biliary apparatus is not functioning properly, the bile may "back up" and be absorbed into the bloodstream instead of emptying into the intestines. This produces a condition known as *jaundice* (icterus) which is characterized by a yellow pigmentation in the skin. Unused bile is normally excreted through the gastrointestinal and the urinary systems, but when jaundice occurs, the feces lack bile pigments and often are pale instead of the normal brown. Sometimes substances solidify in the bile forming *gallstones.* They may stay in the gallbladder or become lodged in the ducts, interfering with the bile flow and causing severe pain (biliary colic). The usual remedy is surgical removal of the stones. These conditions will be discussed in Chapter 38.

The Pancreas

The *pancreas,* a long fish-shaped gland behind the stomach, has tissues for 2 distinct functions. Certain cells secrete pancreatic juice for food digestion. These enzymes, which were

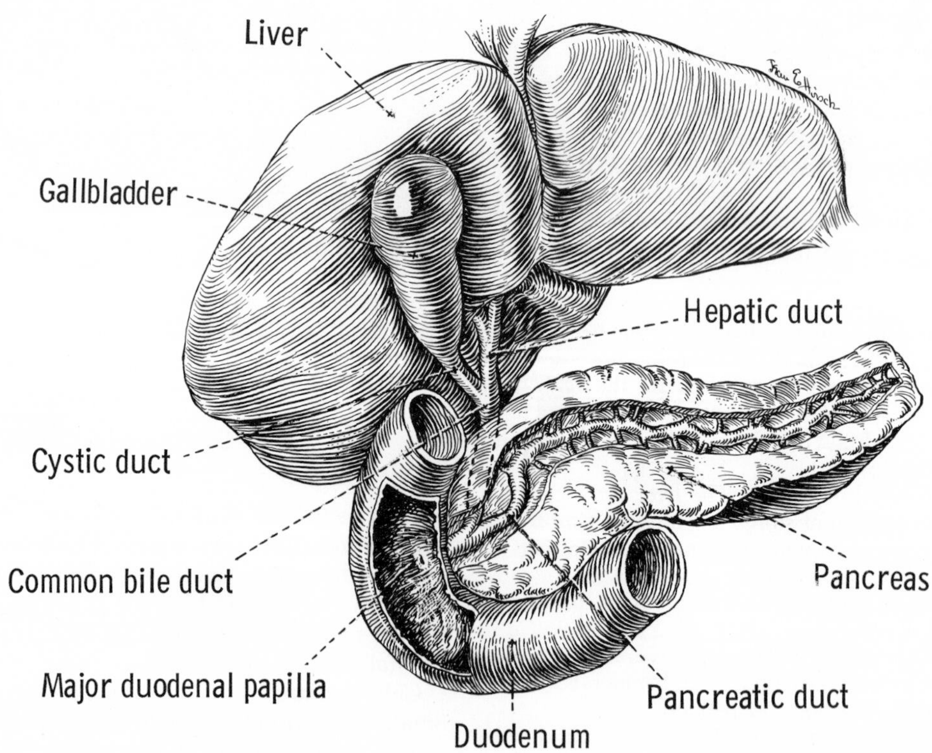

FIG. 74. Gallbladder, showing location. Bile ducts, pancreatic ducts and the entrance of the ducts into the duodenum are shown. (Greisheimer, E. M.: Physiology and Anatomy, ed. 8, p. 618, Philadelphia, Lippincott)

discussed previously, are carried to the small intestine by way of the pancreatic duct. Cells of other tissues, called the *islets of Langerhans*, secrete *insulin* which the body cells must have to utilize sugar. Without adequate insulin, the blood sugar (the blood glucose) level rises from a normal of 80 to 120 milligrams per 100 milliliters of blood to several hundred milligrams per 100 milliliters. This condition is called *diabetes mellitus*, commonly known as diabetes.

The Peritoneum

Lining the walls of the abdominal cavity is a large sheet of serous membrane called the *peritoneum* which reflects itself (turns itself back) to cover all of the abdominal organs. The peritoneal cavity is the very small space between the layer covering the organs and the layer lining the walls. It contains a small amount of fluid which permits the organs to glide freely against each other and against the wall without friction. Because of the continuity of this membrane, an infection which reaches it from a diseased organ can spread very rapidly and be very serious. Such an infection is known as *peritonitis*; fortunately, it can usually be controlled by the use of antibiotic drugs.

Folds of the peritoneum which support the intestines are called the *mesentery*. Between the folds are the blood and the lymph vessels and the nerves which supply the intestines. Another large fold of peritoneum, the *greater omentum*, lies anteriorly over the abdominal cavity like an apron, serving as an insulator and a protective covering. The *lesser omentum* extends from the stomach to the liver.

Basal Metabolism

The digestive system prepares food for the cells, and the circulatory system delivers it. The chemical changes involved in the utilization of the food in the cell body were discussed in Chapter 11 as a part of metabolism. This process of changing food into new tissues and oxidizing it into energy for use in body functions is carried out at a specific daily rate in each individual and is known as the *basal metabolic rate* (BMR). The body's use of energy and the BMR are discussed in more detail in Chapter 22.

18

THE BODY'S FILTER: THE URINARY SYSTEM

FUNCTIONS

As the body builds and repairs tissues and produces energy for the life processes, the food supplied by the digestive system is burned to waste in the cells. The respiratory system and the skin remove some of the water, the carbon dioxide and the nitrogenous wastes in breathing and perspiration, and the digestive system removes the bulk wastes of food in the feces. However, the urinary system is vital in eliminating other wastes of metabolism. Since these wastes are carried by the circulating blood from the cells to the kidneys for elimination in the urine, the urinary system has been called the body's filtration and removal plant.

In addition to being the primary source for eliminating protein wastes and other toxic material from the body, the urinary system provides the life-saving process of maintaining the steady composition of the blood:

The degree of acidity and alkalinity of the blood and the fluid in the tissues must be balanced. The kidneys aid in this control by eliminating excess acid or alkaline substances from the blood.

The amount of water in the body must remain at a fairly constant level. The kidneys maintain this water balance by excreting excess water or by conserving it according to body needs.

The salts in the body fluids are present in specific amounts. The kidneys balance the body salts by regulating their excretion from the body.

The Kidneys

The *kidneys* are 2 reddish brown bean-shaped organs located in the small of the back at the lower edge of the ribs on either side of the vertebral column. They are about 4 inches long, 2 inches wide and 1 inch thick; they are very vascular (heavily supplied with blood vessels). Each kidney is embedded in fatty tissue and is surrounded by a fibrous tissue covering called the *renal fascia.* The fatty pads plus the renal fascia, which is anchored to surrounding tissues, help to hold the kidneys in place. On the medial surface of each kidney is an indented area called the *hilum,* through which the blood vessels and the nerves, plus the structure known as the ureter, enter.

If the kidney is cut in half longitudinally, you can see that it is divided into 2 parts: the outside, the *cortex,* and the inner portion, the *medulla.* The cortex is smooth and solid in appearance. The greater portion of the nephron, the unit of function of the kidney which filters the waste products from the blood, is located in the cortex.

The medulla consists of 12 *pyramids,* cone-shaped structures which drain the wastes and the excess water into the basin of the kidney. This receiving space is called the *renal pelvis* (the word pelvis means *basin*). The pyramids are composed of tiny collecting tubules which give the kidneys a striped appearance. At the tip or apex of the pyramids are the *papillae,* with openings through which the urine passes

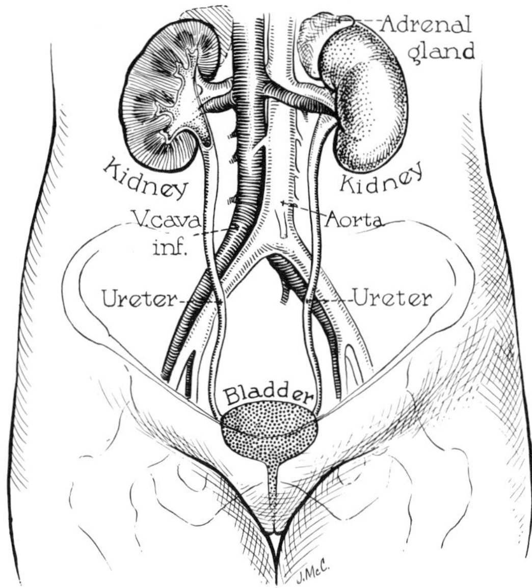

FIG. 75. The urinary system.

into the *calyces*, which are bell-shaped cups continuous with the renal pelvis.

There are over 1,000,000 functional units or *nephrons* in each kidney. These microscopic structures are composed of a cluster of capillaries, the *glomerulus*, partially enclosed in a funnel-shaped structure called the *Bowman's capsule*. The blood with its filterable products enters the glomerulus through the afferent arteriole which divides to form the capillary loop. Water, wastes, glucose and salts filter through the thin walls of the capillaries and into the Bowman's capsule in a very dilute solution. The capillaries unite to form the efferent arteriole through which the remaining blood leaves the glomerulus.

Extending from the Bowman's capsule is a long twisted tube called the *convoluted tubule*. The first portion is called the *proximal convoluted tubule*; the next, the *loop of Henle*, and the final portion, which is the end of the nephron unit, the *distal convoluted tubule*. The water with its dissolved contents travels the length of this tubule. It is surrounded by capillaries whose job it is to reabsorb the water and the salts needed by the body, as well as all of the glucose. (There is normally no sugar in the urine.) The remaining concentrated mixture of waste products and water is *urine*. The end of the proximal convoluted tubule is attached to a *collecting tubule*. These collecting tubules join in the renal pyramids and dump their contents, the urine, into the renal pelvis (Fig. 76).

The kidneys receive their generous blood supply from the renal arteries. Since these are

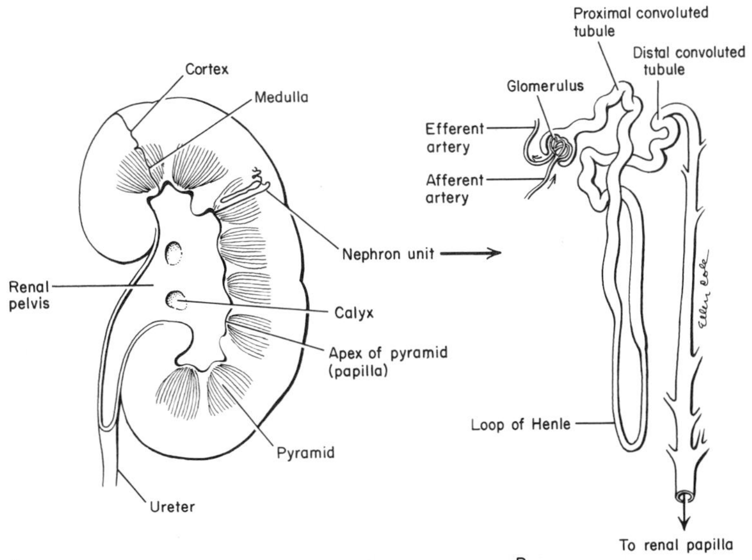

FIG. 76. (A) Longitudinal section of the kidney showing portion of an enlarged nephron. (B) Diagram of an enlarged nephron. The horseshoe-shaped Bowman's capsule surrounding the glomerulus connects with the convoluted tubule.

one of the early branches from the aorta, the blood enters at high pressure and thus can be spread throughout the glomeruli. It circulates at much lower pressure after it leaves the glomeruli and travels around the tubules for reabsorption of the necessary products. It leaves the kidneys through the renal veins which enter the inferior vena cava. The kidneys have a definite influence on blood pressure.

The Ureters

Urine travels from the pelvis of the kidneys into the *ureters*. The ureters are narrow tubes about one fifth inch in diameter and about 10 to 12 inches long. They are attached to the kidney at the renal pelvis and carry the urine from the kidneys down to the urinary bladder. In the walls of the ureters are smooth muscles which contract in peristaltic waves (similar to the peristalsis in the intestines) to carry the urine, drop by drop, to the bladder.

The Bladder

The *bladder* is a hollow muscular sac which when empty lies behind the symphysis pubis. When full, it may extend well up into the abdominal cavity. It is lined with mucous membrane, as is the entire urinary tract. The capacity of the bladder varies, but usually the desire to empty the bladder (void) is present when it fills to about 200 to 250 cc. Since the bladder is the reservoir where urine is stored, the muscles in its walls distend as it fills with urine and contract as it empties itself. A moderately full bladder holds about 500 cc. of urine.

The Urethra

The bladder wall contains 3 openings: 2 from the ureters and 1 from the *urethra*, the tube through which the urine passes to the outside. In the male, the urethra is about 8 inches long. It passes through the prostate gland where 2 ducts from the male sex glands join it and then through the length of the penis, the male organ of copulation (Fig. 77). The female urethra is short, about 1½ inches long, and opens to the outside at the urinary meatus. The female urethra is a passageway for urine only. In the male, the urethra serves the reproductive system as well and is the passageway for both urine and sperm, the male sex cells.

Voiding

The release of urine from the body is called *voiding* or *micturition*. (Involuntary voiding is called *incontinence*.) The urine flows from the collecting tubules into the renal pelvis, down the ureters and slowly enters the bladder. This sac, which is flat when empty, slowly fills. As the urine distends the bladder, it stimulates the nerve endings in the bladder walls. The brain interprets the message that soon the bladder will have to be emptied. The internal and the external sphincter muscles which control the opening to the urethra are stimulated by the nervous system to relax. However, the external sphincter can be controlled voluntarily. Therefore, when the person wills, the external muscular ring relaxes, the muscles in the bladder wall contract, and the urine which has accumulated within the bladder is forced out.

The Urine

About 1,000 to 1,500 cc. (2 to 3 pints) of urine are eliminated from the body daily. However, the quantity is influenced by many things: the amount of fluid taken into the body, perspiration, hemorrhage, fever, various diseases and many other factors. This clear amber liquid has a very characteristic odor. It is acid in reaction but upon standing may become alkaline as certain substances within it break down into ammonia bodies.

Certain wastes are always present in urine, but careful analysis will show whether or not other materials are present that normally should not be there. The composition of urine is:

Water, about 95 per cent. The water serves as the solvent.

Nitrogenous waste products from the breakdown of proteins. Common protein wastes are urea, uric acid and creatinine.

Excess minerals from the diet such as sodium, potassium, chlorides, etc.

Toxins

Hormones

Yellow pigment from certain bile compounds

Abnormal products such as blood, glucose and albumin may be present and indicate disease or malfunction.

You will notice in Figure 75 that there is a structure called the *adrenal gland* located on top of each kidney. These are a part of the endocrine system and will be considered in Chapter 20.

19

HOW LIFE BEGINS: THE REPRODUCTIVE SYSTEM

You know that cells within the body wear out and that these cells are constantly replacing themselves by a process of cell division. That the millions of body cells can accomplish this feat in such a systematized and routine manner is wonderful enough—but the function of the reproductive system in man is the most awesome and impressive of all. From the union of 2 small cells, the total being of another person develops, whose millions of body cells perform their individual and intricate functions; a being who can think, reason and plan—an entire human organism.

The general body structures of boys and girls are similar until they reach the stage of puberty, which occurs around 12 years of age in girls and 14 years in boys. At this time the sex glands become active, and the organs of the reproductive systems begin to function. *Secondary sex characteristics* appear.

The boy develops the hard musculature of the adult male. His glands of perspiration become more active. He develops a beard, pubic and axillary hair, and there is a general increase in hair growth all over his body. His body outline changes to the broader shoulders and the narrow hips, and a change in voice to the deeper tones is marked. The development of these secondary sex characteristics in the male is dependent upon the hormone testosterone, which is secreted by the testes, the male sex glands.

The girl at puberty exhibits many changes as well. The curved feminine contour appears; breast tissue develops; and fat deposits accumulate which alter the angular shape of childhood to a more rounded appearance. The glands of perspiration become active, and hair appears in the pubic and the axillary areas. Although voice changes are not as marked as those in the male, there is a deepening and maturing in voice tone and quality. As the glands of reproduction become active, menstruation appears. All secondary sex characteristics in the female are dependent upon the secretions of the hormones, estrogen and progesterone, which are produced in the ovaries, the female sex glands.

MALE REPRODUCTIVE SYSTEM

The Testes

The gonads or sex glands in the male are called the *testes* (singular = *testis*). These are 2 almond-shaped glands which are composed of long lengths of convoluted (*seminiferous*) tubules whose function is to produce the male reproductive cells called *spermatozoa*, commonly known as sperm. The testes also secrete the main part of the *semen* or seminal fluid in which the sperm are carried. The sperm are very small cells which look like tadpoles under the microscope; they have a "head" and a whiplike "tail" which provides them with motility—they swim very rapidly in the semen. Sperm are produced in very large numbers: millions of sperm can be found in 1 drop of seminal fluid. Between the seminiferous tubules are small groups of cells which secrete the male hormones.

The testes develop before birth in the abdominal cavity. Usually by the time a male infant is born, the testes have descended into a sac called the *scrotum*, which is composed of skin and muscle and is suspended below the groin between the thighs. Occasionally, the testes remain inside the abdominal cavity; undescended testes do not usually produce sperm, although they do manufacture male hormones. It is believed that the testes lie outside the body cavity because they are very sensitive to heat, and the higher temperature within the body is unfavorable to the production of sperm. The descent of the testes from the abdominal cavity makes a weak spot in the muscle wall of the abdomen. This is thought to account for the frequent number of inguinal hernias which occur in males.

The Epididymis

The sperm travel from the testis to a tightly coiled tube called the *epididymis*. This tube is approximately 20 feet long but is so tiny that it can barely be seen with the naked eye. It lies along the top and the posterior surface of each testis.

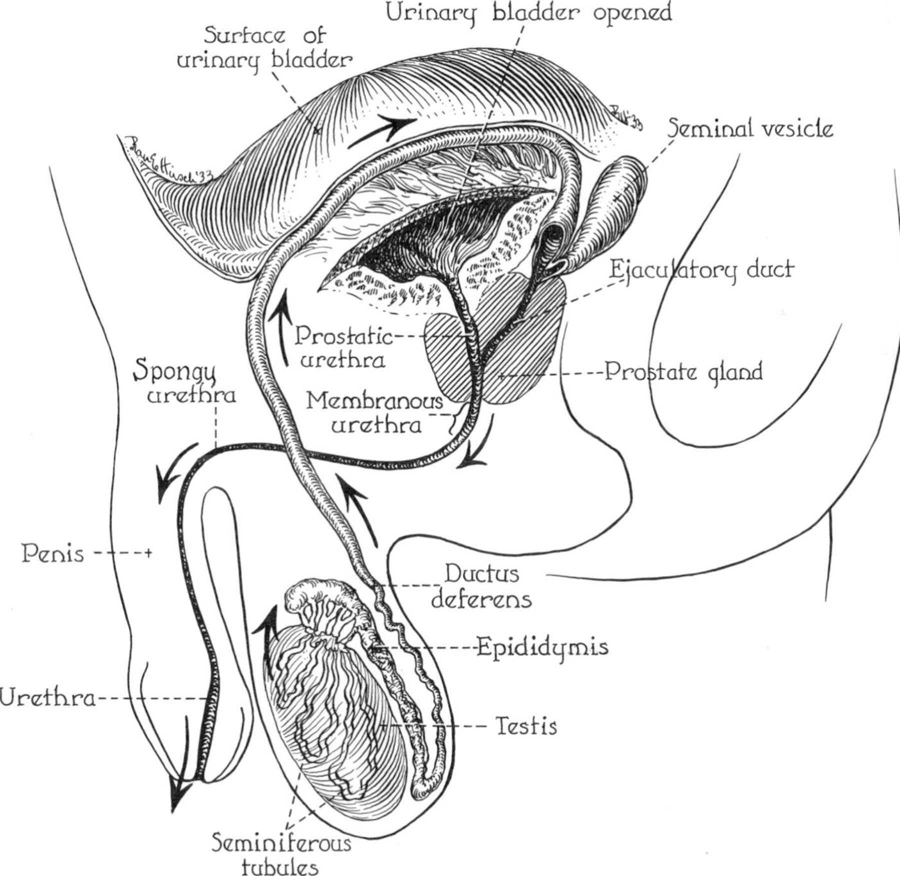

FIG. 77. Male reproductive system. The various organs of the male reproductive system are shown. The path of the spermatozoa from the time they leave the testis until they leave the body is indicated. (Greisheimer, E. M.: Physiology and Anatomy, ed. 8, p. 762, Philadelphia, Lippincott)

The Ductus Deferens. The sperm continue their journey through a tube called the *ductus deferens* (vas deferens) which is actually an enlarged continuation of the epididymis. The ductus deferens passes through the inguinal canal in the muscles of the abdominal wall into the abdominal cavity and continues over the top and down the posterior surface of the bladder, into the pelvic cavity. Each joins a duct from the seminal vesicles, and together with blood vessels, lymphatic vessels, nerves and covering, makes up a *spermatic cord.*

The Seminal Vesicles. The 2 *seminal vesicles* are pouches which store sperm and secrete a fluid which adds to the semen. Each vesicle has an excretory duct, which joins with 1 of the 2 ductus deferens to form the *ejaculatory duct.*

The Prostate Gland

The *prostate gland* is a doughnut-shaped gland lying just below the bladder, surrounding the neck of the bladder and the urethra. It adds an alkaline secretion to the semen, which is thought to increase the motility of the sperm. The urethra runs through the prostate gland and joins the 2 ejaculatory ducts. This passageway continues through the length of the penis, and the urethra serves as the outlet tube for both urine and semen. Any swelling or growth in the prostate gland causes pressure on the urethra and can easily stop the flow of urine, which is a fairly common condition in elderly men.

At the base of the penis and emptying into the urethra are 2 small glands called the *bulbourethral glands* (*Cowper's glands*). Their function is to secrete an alkaline substance into the urethra. Since the urine is usually acid in its reaction, this alkaline secretion tends to neutralize the urethral environment. Sperm survive better in an alkaline than in an acid medium.

The Penis

The penis is a cylinder-shaped organ located externally immediately above the scrotum. It is made up of *erectile tissue* with cavernlike spaces in it. At the time of sexual excitement, blood fills these spaces, changing the soft, limp penis to an enlarged rigid erect organ. The smooth cap of the penis is called the *glans penis* and is covered by a fold of loose skin which forms the hoodlike *foreskin* or prepuce. Removal of this foreskin (circumcision), is a frequently performed operation and has a special religious significance for the people of the Jewish faith. This operation will be discussed in more detail in Chapter 51, on care of the newborn. The penis and the scrotum are referred to as the external genitalia in the male.

Copulation

Sexual intercourse or sexual union between the male and the female is also called copulation or coitus. The erect penis is inserted within the vaginal canal, and sperm are deposited or ejaculated within the vagina by means of waves of contractions of the ducts through which the semen travels. The amount of semen in each ejaculation is about 3 to 5 milliliters. There are about 120,000,000 sperm per milliliter. If the sperm count falls below 60,000,000 per milliliter, the individual is considered to be infertile.

THE FEMALE REPRODUCTIVE SYSTEM

The female reproductive system includes the paired *ovaries*, the paired *fallopian* (*uterine*) *tubes*, and the single *uterus* and *vagina*, with their associated structures, the *external genitalia* and the *mammary glands* (*breasts*).

The Ovaries

The ovaries are 2 almond-shaped glands about 1½ inches in length located within the brim of the pelvis, one on either side of the uterus, the hollow organ in the center of the pelvic cavity where the unborn infant grows. The ovaries are composed of connective tissue and are covered with a special epithelium in which are imbedded thousands of microscopic structures called *graafian follicles.* Ova (egg cells) develop and mature within the follicles. From the time of puberty until menstruation ceases, at approximate monthly intervals, a follicle ripens and pushes its way to the surface of the ovary. It is during the ripening of the follicle that estrogen is released. The mature ovum then ruptures the surface of the follicle and is discharged into the pelvic cavity. This release of the ovum is called *ovulation*. Ovulation usually occurs about halfway between the average 28-day menstrual cycle, or about 14 days before the onset of the next menstrual period. Although the ovary produces many ova, usually only one ovum at a time is released. However, it is believed that some females ovulate more than once during their menstrual cycle. The menstrual cycle will be discussed on page 187.

After ovulation, the follicle is replaced by a yellowish substance called the corpus luteum. The corpus luteum then secretes the hormone, progesterone, to thicken and enrich the uterine lining in preparation for pregnancy. If the ovum is not penetrated (fertilized) by the sperm, the corpus luteum degenerates after approximately 2 weeks and forms scar tissue. If the ovum is fertilized, it remains for about 3 months and aids in the development of the fertilized egg cell.

The Fallopian Tubes

As the mature ovum bursts from the ovary into the pelvic cavity, it is picked up by the open fringed ends of the fallopian (uterine) tubes. There are 2 of these tubes, one attached to either side of the uterus. They are lined with cilia which help guide the ovum to the uterus, which takes about 5 days.

Fertilization of the ovum (i.e., the meeting of the sperm and the ovum) usually takes place about midway in the fallopian tube. From here the fertilized ovum travels to the uterus where it becomes embedded in the uterine lining in preparation for growth. The development of the fertilized ovum is discussed in Chapter 49.

The Uterus

The uterus is a hollow, muscular, pear-

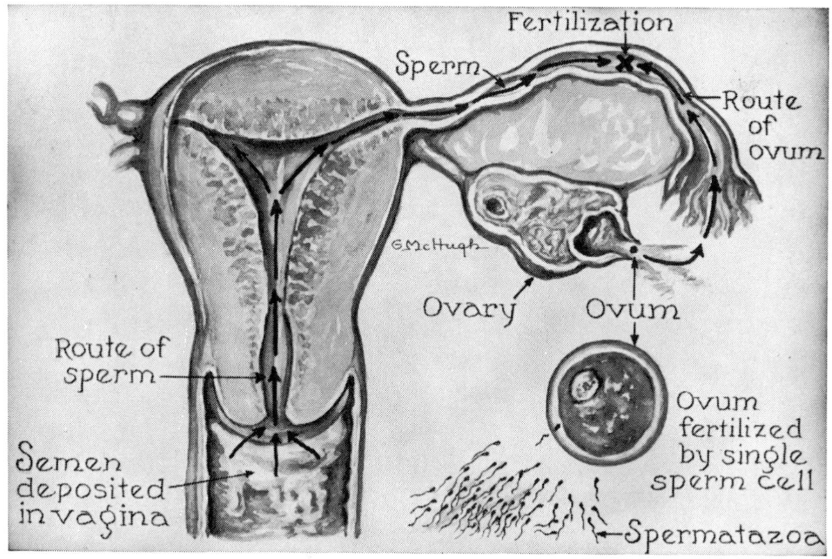

FIG. 78. The process of fertilization. Note the ovum leaving the ovarian follicle and its subsequent course into the tube. Sperm deposited in the vagina travel upward through the cervix and the uterus into the outer end of the tube, where fertilization takes place. The insert shows the relative sizes of the sperm and the ovum. (DeLee, S. T.: Safeguarding Motherhood, ed. 3, p. 22, Philadelphia, Lippincott)

shaped organ in the center of the pelvic cavity, immediately posterior to the bladder. It is about 3 inches long and usually lies tipped slightly forward over the bladder. The broader section above is called the *body*, and the narrower section below is called the *cervix*. The round surface which bridges the level where the tubes enter is the *fundus*. The myometrium is the thick smooth muscle layer of the uterine wall. The inside is lined with a tissue called the *endometrium*, a mucous membrane containing many blood vessels. The uterus is held in position by strong structures called the broad and the round ligaments.

The function of the uterus is to receive the fertilized ovum and to provide housing and nourishment for the developing baby. The uterus must be capable of great expansion, since it is the organ in which the baby develops.

The Vagina

The neck of the uterus projects into a muscular canal, the vagina, which extends from the cervix and opens to the outside of the body. The vagina is the female organ of intercourse and is part of the birth canal. It lies behind the urethra, and its inner surface is moistened by the secretions of many glands from the mucous membrane lining its walls. A fold of membrane, the *hymen*, is sometimes found closing the external opening of the vagina, but since it can be injured in various ways, it is not considered too reliable a sign of virginity.

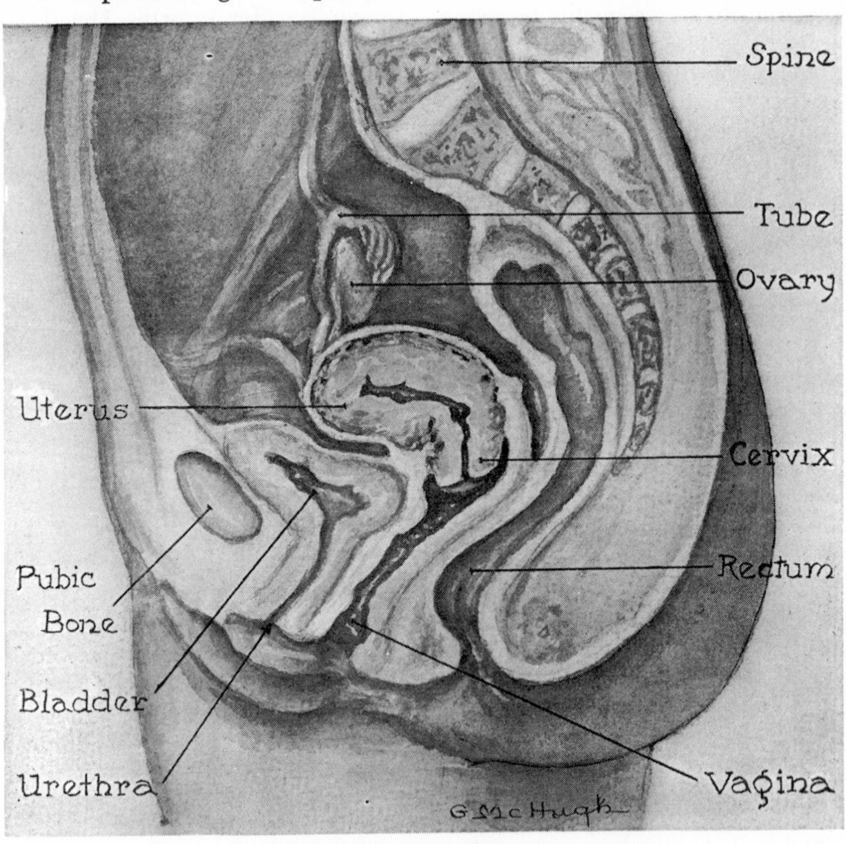

Fig. 79. Midline section through the pelvis viewed from the side, showing the relationship of the uterus to the bladder and the rectum. (DeLee, S. T.: Safeguarding Motherhood, ed. 3, p. 15, Philadelphia, Lippincott)

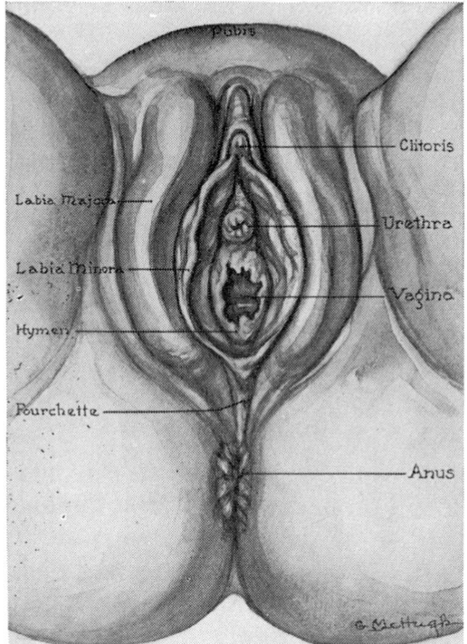

FIG. 80. External genitalia viewed from below. (DeLee, S. T.: Safeguarding Motherhood, ed. 3, p. 14, Philadelphia, Lippincott)

The External Genitalia

The external genitalia (vulva) of the female consists of the *mons pubis* (*veneris*), the *labia majora*, the *labia minora*, the *clitoris* and the *vestibule*. The mons pubis is a fatty pad over the symphysis pubis which is covered with pubic hair after the age of puberty. Posterior to the mons pubis are the other external organs. The labia majora are 2 large outer folds of fat and skin which extend backward almost to the anus. Under and between the labia majora are the labia minora which do not have pubic hair but contain many glands. At the anterior junction of the labia is the clitoris, a very small structure comparable with the penis in the male. It is composed of erectile tissue which is stimulated by sexual sensations. Posterior to the clitoris and between the labia minora is the space called the vestibule. Within the vestibule is found the urinary meatus and the vaginal opening, referred to as the vaginal orifice. The vestibule also contains the *Bartholin's glands*, which are considered to be glands of lubrication.

The space between the vaginal orifice and the rectum is called the *perineum*. It is made up of strong muscles which act as slinglike supports for the pelvic organs. These are the muscles that are sometimes torn during childbirth.

The Mammary Glands (The Breasts)

The mammary glands (breasts) are usually classified as organs of the reproductive system because they are stimulated by hormones to secrete milk after childbirth. These 2 glands, on the outside of the chest wall, are composed of glandular tissues and varying amounts of fat covered by rather thin skin. Each breast is divided into 16 to 20 separate lobes that secrete milk. The duct from each lobe converges toward the nipple, like the spokes of a wheel, and terminates in small openings through the nipple. The breasts enlarge during pregnancy due to the stimulation of estrogen and progesterone, and the skin around the nipples, the areola, becomes more heavily pigmented. After the termination of pregnancy, the production of milk by the mammary glands is stimulated by a hormone of the anterior pituitary gland.

MENSTRUATION

Throughout the universe we find many examples of Nature's "rhythms" or cycles. The phases of the moon change regularly; the ocean tides have a rhythm of their own. The human body has several of these built-in clocks; for instance, you sleep and eat in fairly regular cycles. Another of these cyclic activities is menstruation in the female. This rhythmic series of changes which occurs about every 28 days is called the *menstrual cycle*. Menstruation, which is the flow of blood from the vagina caused by the shedding of the lining of the uterus, usually begins between the ages of 10 and 14. The first menstrual period is called the *menarche*. The various changes that occur are brought about through the action of several hormones.

The onset of menstruation is the beginning of the cycle, i.e., the first day of menstruation is the first day of the cycle. The menstrual flow usually lasts from 3 to 5 days. During the next phase of the cycle, the graafian follicle in the ovary ripens, and the ovum within begins to mature. It finally ruptures about the 14th day, and the ovum is released, a process called ovulation, which was discussed earlier in this chapter. The anterior pituitary gland in the brain secretes the hormones which stimulate this action in the ovary.

The level of the ovarian hormones (estrogen and progesterone) is now high, and their action has caused the endometrium to become greatly thickened and vascular, preparing itself for possible pregnancy. Toward the end of the menstrual cycle, if the enriched uterine lining is not needed, the action of the hormones decreases. This affects the blood supply of the endometrium so that it begins to degenerate. The capillaries within the uterine wall begin to bleed, and the endometrium is sloughed off. The menstrual flow, consisting of blood, mucus and cells, then occurs.

Authorities differ in their ideas of the time during which the ovum can be fertilized following ovulation, opinions varying from 15 minutes to 72 hours. The length of time that sperm survive after intercourse is also debated. However, for fertilization to occur, the sperm must meet and penetrate the ovum in the fallopian tube. Their 2 nuclei then join to form the 23 pairs of chromosomes, the beginning of a new individual. The average time for ovulation to occur is 14 days before the next menstrual period, regardless of the length of the cycle. For example, in a 35-day cycle, the 21st day is the probable time of ovulation. This can be calculated if the menstrual periods occur at regular intervals. This method of computation is called the rhythm method and is used both for planning and for preventing pregnancy. If intercourse is avoided for 5 days before and 5 days following ovulation, fertilization of the egg cell is not likely to occur. If pregnancy is desired, sexual relations at the probable time of ovulation will enhance such a possibility. It is obvious that this method of calculating the time of ovulation is not suitable if menstrual periods are irregular.

The Menopause

Menstrual cycles continue as long as ovarian hormones stimulate the uterine lining. Normally, when a woman is between 40 and 50, her ovaries become less active and cease producing both ova and hormones. Menstruation may terminate abruptly, but it is usually a gradual process. The cessation of the menstrual cycles is called the *menopause*, and the period during which the ovaries are undergoing these changes is called the *climacteric.*

The menopause is a normal process and may be so gradual that the body adjusts to it without difficulty. However, since many hormonal changes are involved, some unpleasant symptoms such as headaches and sensations of heat (*hot flashes*) may occur. If too severe, usually these can be treated satisfactorily with temporary hormonal therapy (see Chap. 30). Men experience a similar period, but it is a much slower process, and usually there is no sharp demarcation of beginning or end as there is in the female. However, some authorities refer to it as the *male climacteric.*

20

THE BODY'S SPECIAL MESSENGERS: THE ENDOCRINE SYSTEM

FUNCTIONS

The endocrine system comprises a group of glands located in various parts of the body. Because they do not send their secretions through pipes or ducts but pour them directly into the blood stream instead, endocrine glands are also called the ductless glands or the glands of internal secretion. The chemical substances which they manufacture are called *hormones.*

The hormones are chemical regulators. They not only speed up or slow down the activities of entire body organs, but some affect the rate of various activities of individual cells of the body. Hormones also affect each other: too much or too little of a particular hormone not only affects an organ but also interferes with the actions of other hormones. There is a fine balance within the endocrine system that promotes normal body functions.

Some authorities feel that there is a close relationship between the endocrine system and the nervous system, since both have the function of stimulating as well as controlling actions of the body. However, the effect of nerve stimuli is immediate and lasts only as long as the stimulation is present; the action of the endocrine glands is slower and is a more prolonged stimulation and regulation.

Little was known about the endocrines before 1900. Research is still being conducted to learn more about their function.

The Pituitary Gland

The *pituitary* gland is a small gland about the size of a pea, located in a saddlelike hollow in the sphenoid bone at the base of the brain. It is made up of 2 parts: the *anterior lobe* and the *posterior lobe*; for this reason sometimes it is classified as 2 separate glands.

The anterior lobe secretes a large number of hormones. Five of these control the action of other endocrine glands; therefore, the pituitary is often referred to as the "master gland." One of these hormones, ACTH, stimulates the adrenal cortex; another regulates the thyroid hormone. Three other hormones stimulate the testes and the ovaries, as well as the mammary glands following pregnancy.

The 6th hormone secreted by the anterior pituitary is called the *growth hormone* (somatotropic hormone or STH). If the pituitary secretes too much growth hormone in childhood, it causes gigantism. The bones in the face, the hands and the feet enlarge to abnormal size, a condition called acromegaly. Too little of this hormone in childhood results in dwarfism.

The posterior lobe has entirely different functions. It secretes 3 hormones: oxytoxin (pitocin), vasopressin (pitressin) and the antidiuretic hormone (ADH). Oxytoxin stimulates contractions of the uterine muscles. Vasopressin stimulates smooth muscles in the walls of blood vessels and in the gastrointestinal tract. The antidiuretic hormone stimulates the reab-

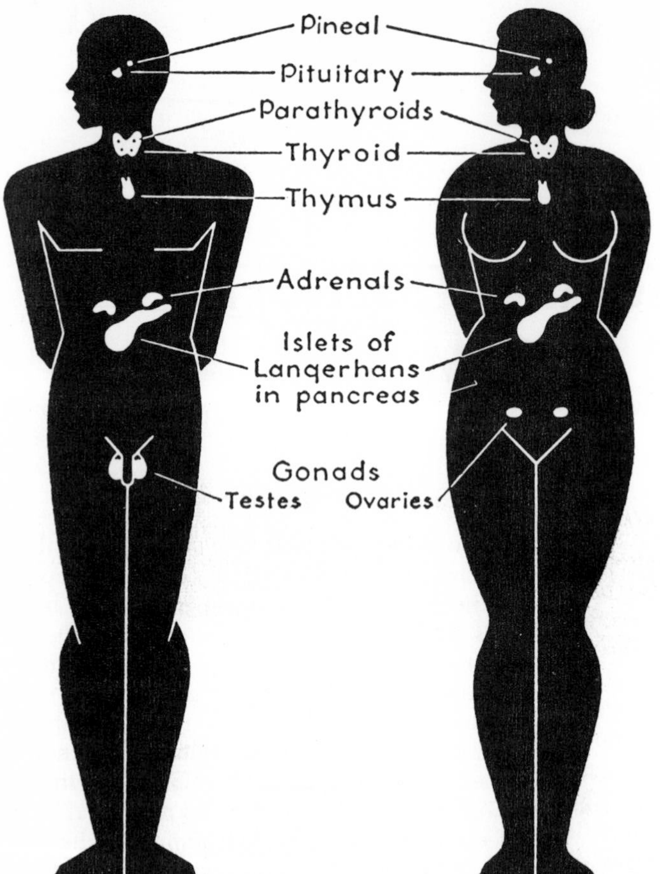

Fig. 81. The endocrine glands. (Hirsch, J.: Minnesota Department of Health; Todd and Freeman: Health Care for the Family, Philadelphia, Saunders)

sorption of water in the kidney tubules, thus affecting water balance.

The Thyroid Gland

The *thyroid* gland, the largest of the endocrine glands, lies in front of the neck just below the larynx, with a wing (lobe) on either side of the trachea. The thyroid secretes the hormone *thyroxin*, which it manufactures from iodine absorbed from the blood. Thyroxin regulates the metabolism of the body; that is, it controls the rate at which each of the individual cells carries on its work, building and repairing itself, producing energy, etc. It regulates the rate at which the cells burn food. If the thyroid does not secrete enough thyroxin (hypothyroidism), the cells oxidize food too slowly. This interferes with the cells' activities and slows down body functions. If the hypothyroidism is severe, the person may be retarded physically and mentally, a condition known as cretinism. If the thyroid secretes too much thyroxin, all body functions are speeded up. The cells burn food too rapidly and produce more energy than is needed. This is termed hyperthyroidism and causes such symptoms as nervousness, hyperactivity, irritability, and protrusion of the eyeballs (exophthalmia).

The thyroid removes iodine from the blood to make thyroxin. This iodine must be supplied through the diet. If the diet lacks iodine, the thyroid grows larger in overworking to make more thyroxin. An enlarged thyroid gland is called a goiter. In areas of the country where the soil lacks iodine, sufficient quantity in the diet is assured by the use of iodized salt.

The proper functioning of the thyroid gland is measured by a basal metabolism test, which measures the amount of oxygen needed to carry out basic body functions (see Chapters 11 and 22). Another test called a PBI (protein-bound iodine) measures the amount of iodine in the blood and is considered by some to be more nearly accurate.

The Parathyroid Glands

The *parathyroids* are small glands, each about the size of a pea, which lie on either side of the under part of the thyroid gland. They are 4, 6 or 8 in number; despite their size, they are essential to health and to life itself. The parathyroids secrete a hormone that regulates the amount of calcium and phosphorus in the blood, which in turn affects nerve and muscle irritability. Too little calcium causes muscle spasms and convulsions and can cause death within a few hours, a condition called tetany (not to be confused with the infection called tetanus or lockjaw). If the parathyroids secrete too much of the hormone, the diet cannot supply enough calcium, and the calcium salts are drawn from the bones, making them soft and unable to support weight.

The Adrenal Glands

The 2 *adrenal* glands (also known as the suprarenal glands) sit like hats on top of each kidney. Like the pituitary gland, the adrenal glands have 2 parts which produce different hormones. (In some animals other then men, they occur as 2 separate glands.) The central portion, called the *medulla*, secretes the hormone epinephrine (Adrenalin) which brings many body processes into action quickly. Epinephrine makes the heart beat faster, contracts blood vessels, raises blood pressure and increases muscle power by causing the liver to release glucose for energy. The adrenals are active in emergencies: emotions of fright, anger, love, or grief stimulate them. They are said to prepare us for "flight or fight." The functions of the medulla are important to life, in that they apparently help us adapt to stress.

The outer part of the adrenals, the *cortex*, is now known to secrete many compounds and probably more will be discovered. Their actions are so widespread and so complex that they are difficult to enumerate. The hormones of the adrenal cortex are called steroids. Some of the functions of adrenocortical secretions are to sustain the ability of the individual to withstand stress and infections, to regulate the behavior of salts in the body, to control water retention and to control carbohydrate, protein and fat metabolism. Male and female hormones are also secreted by the adrenal cortex, and hyperactivity can hasten sexual development in boys or cause masculine sex characteristics (such as facial hair and deeper voice, lack of menstruation) to appear in girls.

The hormones of the adrenal cortex are necessary for life. Many are available commercially, such as cortisone, and prospects are good for others to be available in the future.

The Pancreas

The pancreas is located behind the stomach, between the duodenum and the spleen. Within its tissue are cells called the *islets of Langerhans*, which secrete the hormone insulin. Without insulin, cells are unable to utilize glucose. This sugar then accumulates in the blood above the normal level, which is 80 to 120 mg. per 100 milliliters of blood. As the amount of sugar in the blood increases, the kidneys begin to excrete it through the urine, and the glucose reserves of the body are lost. This is called diabetes mellitus, and is controlled in one way by injections of insulin.

The Gonads

The *gonads* are the glands of reproduction: the testes of the male and the ovaries of the female. In addition to producing sperm, the testes produce testosterone, the male sex hormone. Testosterone controls the development of the sex organs of the male as well as influencing such characteristics as male body form, hair distribution and voice. There are

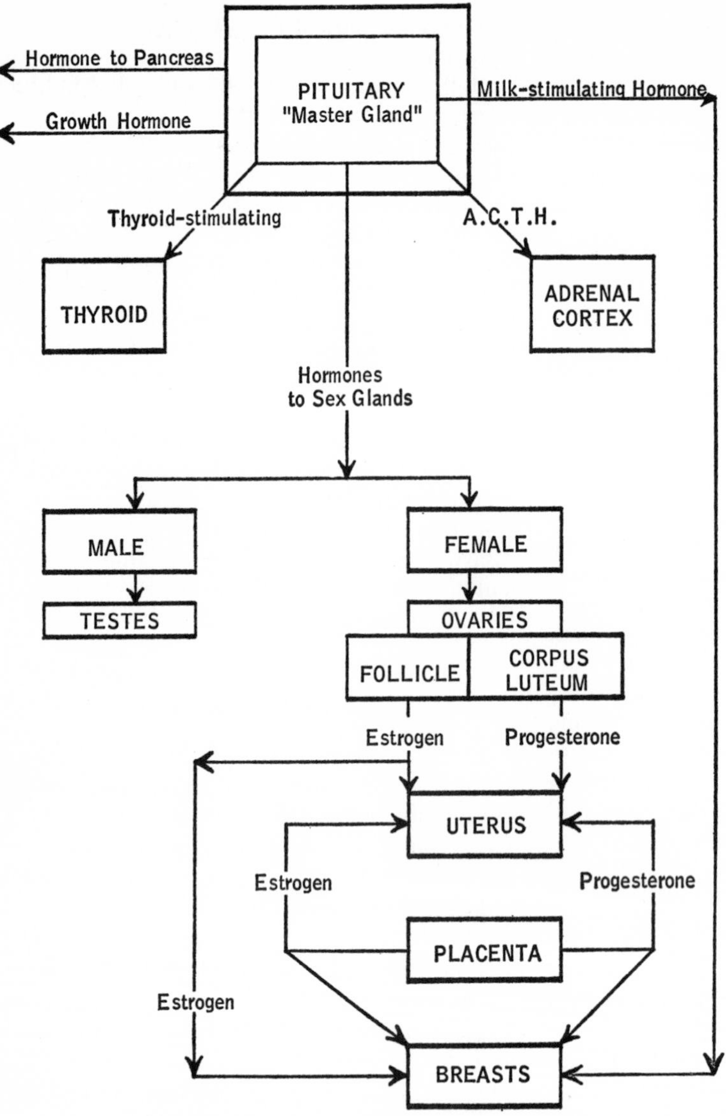

FIG. 82. Endocrine relationships (simplified) in the human body. Note the many functions of the pituitary gland and its effect upon both the male and the female reproductive systems. (After Cole and Elman: Textbook of General Surgery, ed. 6, New York, Appleton-Century-Crofts, 1952)

also other steroid hormones which produce masculinizing effects. As a group they are called androgens.

The ovaries produce estrogen and progesterone, hormones which stimulate maturing of the female sex organs. These hormones also influence development of secondary sex characteristics such as breast development, voice quality, and the broader pelvis of the female body form. Menstruation is established because of the hormone production of the ovaries. Estrogen is responsible for most of these changes. Progesterone apparently is concerned primarily with body changes that favor the implantation of the fertilized ovum and continuation of pregnancy. Both hormones seem to influence the mood changes and the emotional climate of the female.

The Thymus

The *thymus* gland lies behind the sternum

(breastbone). Efforts to discover any definite contribution of the thymus to the endocrine system have not yet been successful. It is made up of lymphoid tissue and is known to produce lymphocytes. Recent studies indicate that the thymus, which is comparatively large in infants, has an important role in establishing antibody formation in the newborn. It supposedly continues its functions related to immunity reactions through puberty but atrophies by the time of adulthood.

The Pineal Gland. The *pineal* gland, another endocrine puzzle, is attached to the brain. No secretion has been discovered, and its function is unknown.

Other Hormones

There are other hormones known and others being investigated and discovered. The stomach wall secretes a hormone, gastrin, that stimulates the secretions of the gastric glands. The lining of the upper part of the small intestine secretes the hormone secretin, which stimulates the pancreatic juices, and also another hormone that causes the gallbladder to contract. The placenta is also a temporary endocrine gland that secretes hormones that help to maintain pregnancy. The presence of high levels of these hormones in the body provides the basis for the commonly used tests for pregnancy.

21

AVENUES TO THE MIND: THE SENSORY SYSTEM

An often-repeated statement is that "all knowledge comes to us through our senses." The obvious sensory perceptions you think of are those of seeing, hearing, smelling, tasting and feeling. There are many more. You can receive impressions of warmth, pressure, softness and pain. A very important impression is your sense of equilibrium: you know whether or not you are moving and the posture and the position of your body.

From your study of the nervous system, you know that to be aware of information from the world around you, you must have receptors which receive the stimuli, nerve routes which carry the sensation or stimuli to the brain, and centers in the brain to interpret the stimuli, such as "red," "sweet," or "loud."

THE EAR

The ear is the special sense organ for hearing. It is an especially adapted apparatus for bringing the vibrations in the air to your nervous system for interpretation as sound. For instance, a piano being played produces vibrations or sound waves in the air which cause thousands of hairlike cells in the ear to carry a pattern to the brain which you translate as music.

The ear has 3 parts: the *external* (*outer*), the *middle* and the *inner* ear. These lead to the acoustic nerve and then to the center for hearing which is located in the temporal lobe of the cerebrum.

The external ear, called the *pinna* or *auricle*, is the only readily visible part. It is composed mostly of cartilage and is shaped like a funnel to gather and guide sound waves into its small opening, which extends into a tube called the *auditory canal*. The lining of the auditory canal is covered with tiny hairs and secretes a waxy substance called *cerumen*, both of which aid in protecting the ear from foreign objects. The auditory canal is very short, about 1 inch in length, and extends to the ear drum, a thin membrane called the *tympanum*. This tympanic membrane separates the external and the middle ear.

On the other side of the tympanum is the middle ear, a small cavity in the temporal bone. Within this cavity, between the ear drum and the inner ear, are 3 small bones called the *malleus* (hammer), the *incus* (anvil) and the *stapes* (stirrup). These 3 bones are called *ossicles* and are so small that sound waves can set them in motion. The sound waves start vibrations of the ear drum and the malleus or hammer which is attached to it. The malleus stimulates vibrations in the incus, which in turn moves the stapes. As the vibrations pass through the middle ear, the effect of the vibrations is magnified.

Extending from the middle ear are an opening into the mastoid cells behind it, and another into the eustachian tube which communicates with the nasopharynx. The eustachian tube opens during swallowing or yawning. Its function is to equalize the pressure in the middle ear with atmospheric pressure. By this means, the pressure on both sides of the drum membrane is equalized, and the drum can vibrate freely. The middle ear, the eustachian tube and the passage to the mastoid cells are lined with a continuous coat of mucous membrane.

The inner ear has 2 parts. One is the *cochlea*, which is shaped like a hollow snail shell and is filled with fluid. Along the cochlea are hairlike processes which are thought to be the receptors for the *organ of Corti*. The organ of Corti is said to be the true organ of hearing, because this is where the transmission of nerve stimuli begins.

The base of the stapes fits into an opening between the middle and the inner ear. This opening is covered by a thin membrane and is called the *oval window*. The stapes vibrates against the membrane, setting the fluid in the cochlea in motion. The fluid in motion passes the vibrations on to the tiny hairlike nerve endings or receptors in the organ of Corti which transmits the impulses to the *acoustic nerve*. The acoustic nerve sends them to the center for hearing in the brain, which then interprets these impulses as sounds (Fig. 83).

Another section of the inner ear is the *semicircular canals*. Shaped like horseshoes, they lie beside the cochlea. They also contain hairlike nerve endings which are set in motion by fluid within the canals. Motion in the fluid is caused by head or body movements. The receptors lead to the acoustic nerve, but the pathway of this section of the acoustic nerve goes to the cerebellum and is concerned with balance and coordination.

THE EYE

The eye is constantly compared with a camera, and although this analogy is not totally correct, there are many parts to each which have corresponding functions. One marked difference is that the camera shows 1 image, but the eye registers 2, which the brain combines into a single image. This binocular vision is possible because coordinated muscles move the eyeballs. The eye also automatically perceives depth, whereas in photography, this is an illusion.

The eye lies in a protective bony orbit in the skull. Between the eye itself and its bony surroundings is a cushion of fat. The eyelids, the brows and the lashes serve as further protection for the eye. The eyelid is the cover for the anterior surface of the eye which is deprived of the protection of the skull. Also covering

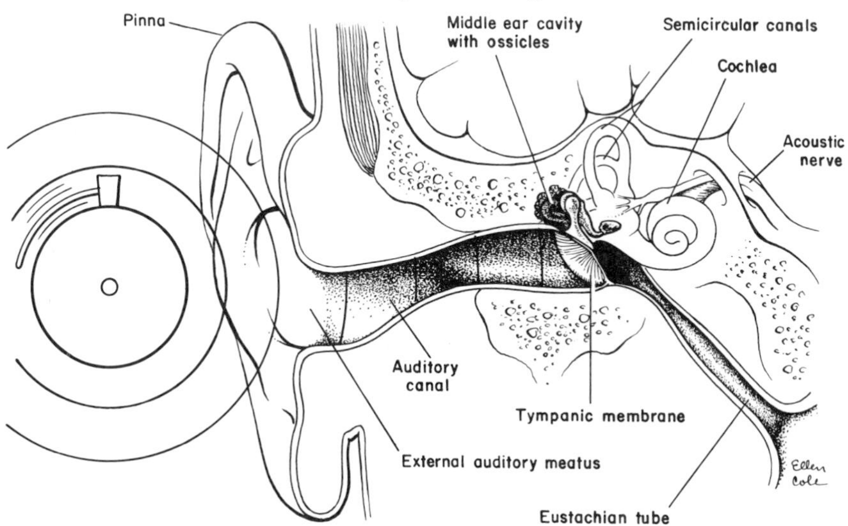

FIG. 83. How we hear.

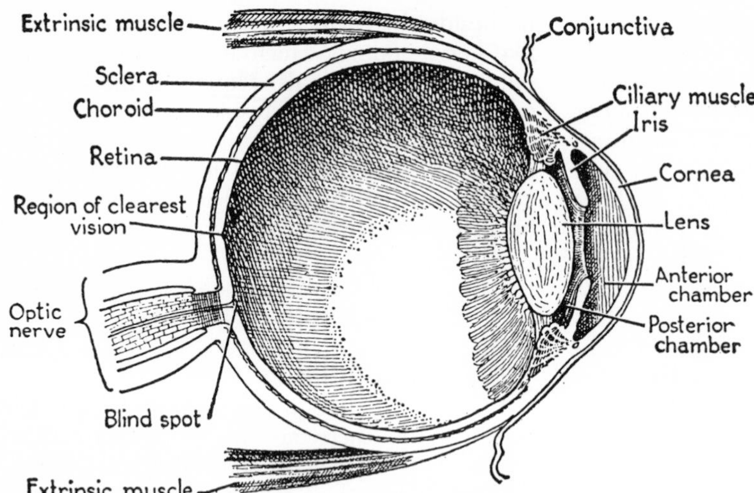

FIG. 84. Section through the eyeball. (Baillif and Kimmel: Structure and function of the Human Body, p. 281, Philadelphia, Lippincott)

the anterior eye, beneath and lining the eyelids, is a thin transparent mucous membrane called the *conjunctiva* which is well supplied with blood vessels and nerve endings.

In order to keep the surface of the eye moist, it is supplied with the *lacrimal glands* which produce tears. The lacrimal glands are located at the outer edge of the corner of the eye. Tears drain through a small opening in the inner canthus or corner of the eye, the nasolacrimal duct, into the nose. The tears are slightly antiseptic in their effect.

The eyeball is a hollow sphere made up of 3 layers of tissue. The tough protective outer layer is the *sclera* or white of the eye. In order to allow light rays to enter the front of the eye, the sclera has a transparent section over the front of the eyeball; this transparent section is called the *cornea*. The middle layer, or the *choroid*, is a vascular layer which brings oxygen and nutrients to the eye. The choroid extends to the ciliary body which helps to control the shape of the lens. Over the front of the eyeball, the choroid develops into a pigmented section, the *iris*, which gives the eye its individual color. Within the iris are muscles which control the size of the opening within its center, the *pupil*. The pupil regulates the amount of light traveling through the eye. It always appears black because it looks into the dark inner chambers of the eye.

The *lens* is a structure immediately behind the iris. This is a transparent body whose function is to bring the light rays into focus to allow a clear image. Then the image is reflected on the *retina*, which is the nerve center of the eye. Parallel rays of light, passing through the lens, are refracted or bent so that they focus on the retina. This adjustment by the lens to make a sharp clear image is called *accommodation*. If the eyeball is too short, the light rays are focused behind the retina instead of on it. This causes *farsightedness* (*hyperopia*). In *nearsightedness* (*myopia*), the eyeball is too long or the lens too strong, and the light rays are focused in front of the retina.

The space between the cornea and the lens is filled with a liquid called the *aqueous humor*; the space behind the lens is filled with a gelatinlike material called the *vitreous humor*.

The inner layer of the eyeball is the *retina*, which contains the receptors of the optic nerve. Some of the neurons of the retina cells are shaped as rods and cones. The cones permit perception of color; the rods are concerned with the perception of light and shade.

Light must pass through the cornea, the aqueous humor, the lens and the vitreous humor before coming into focus on the retina. The receptors in the retina send the nerve impulses through the nerve fibers to the nerve of sight, the *optic nerve*. The optic nerve carries the stimuli to the occipital area of the brain where visual images are interpreted.

Smooth muscles in the eye control the size of the pupil and the action of the lens in accommodation. Three pairs of muscles, attached to its outer coat, move the eyeball. Another muscle attached to the upper eyelid holds the eye open; when the eyelids shut, this muscle is relaxed.

Other Special Senses

The nerves of taste provide you with 4 taste sensations: sweet, salty, bitter and sour. The receptors for taste, located on the tongue, are what we commonly call the taste buds. Many foods are combinations of more than one taste sensation.

The nerve of smell is the *olfactory nerve,* and the receptors for the sense of smell are located in the upper nasal cavities. The sense of taste and the sense of smell work very closely together. Many times it is the odor of a food that makes it pleasant to eat. Think how tasteless your food is when you have a head cold. Smell and taste combine to give foods flavor.

Your touch receptors are constantly receiving nerve impulses, allowing you to feel pain, as well as the pleasures of softness and warmth, and the dangers of too much heat or cold. There are many more touch receptors in some areas, such as the fingertips and around the lips, than are found in other areas.

These special senses are as interesting and as useful as your eyes and ears, but because they are not so often involved in illness or disease, they are not studied in such detail.

Unit Five:

Normal Nutrition

22

FOOD FOR GROWTH AND ENERGY

FOOD AND HEALTH

Food plays a vital part in our lives. Although it is natural to eat because we enjoy food, it is also necessary to eat to live and be healthy. People today are healthier than people were in previous times; this is partly due to increased knowledge about food and to the greater availability of foodstuffs. In America food is plentiful —people in the United States are probably better fed than any other people in the world. Yet we are told that half of our population do not eat enough of the essential foods, such as milk, vegetables, meats and fruit. It has been estimated that 20 per cent of school age young people are malnourished.

Inadequate Diets

What are some of the reasons for this inadequacy in the midst of plenty? Sometimes no attention is paid to the needs of a family for an adequate diet. Many people eat only the foods they like and either do not know or care to learn what a well-balanced diet should be. Sometimes an inadequate diet is due to religious or nationality backgrounds. In some instances it is due to ignorance of true food facts or to superstitious beliefs or fads. Some of these beliefs have been handed down in families for many years. "Babies can eat gravy but should never have meat"—"Toasted bread has fewer calories than fresh bread"—"Fish and milk should never be eaten at the same meal." Any one or all of these things may be responsible for an inadequate diet.

One great menace to health today is the promotion of so-called "health" foods by food faddists. This has become big business for certain manufacturers, even to the extent of their sending out a flock of door-to-door canvassers who talk food nonsense to a trusting public. In spite of the fact that we still have many undernourished people in this country, our food supply is *nutritionally* adequate and the best in the world. Yet this does not prevent 10 million people from spending over a billion dollars every year on food fads.

Food misinformation is spread by some of the high-powered advertising, and manufacturers capitalize on it. Often false notions take root in people's minds—sprays are poisoning all our fruits, dark bread is superior to enriched white bread, aluminum cooking utensils are deadly. One fallacy some people believe is that the American soil is worn out; yet, authorities say that there is no scientific proof that vegetables grown in poor soil are deficient in nutrients. It is true that such vegetables may be smaller and fewer in number, but the essential nutrients will be there.

Another fallacy is the belief that one specific food will cure a disease or that another food will aggravate it. This can be serious in that it may prevent sound medical treatment and actually lead to poor nutrition. Food quacks' recommendations of their products as cures for almost everything would be laughable except that too many people take them seriously.

Lack of money and of food supplies also plays an important part in creating the existing malnutrition in this and in other countries. Yet, surprisingly enough, it may not always be actual poverty that prevents a family from maintaining good nutrition so much as it is the spending of most of their income for expensive cars, elaborate home furnishings, or other luxuries, and the skimping on necessary foodstuffs. It has been noticed by school nurses that many of the undernourished children are driven to school in new cars from expensively furnished homes but are not given the milk, the vegetables, the meat and the fruit that they need to keep them healthy.

Fortunately, we have a national watchdog whose job it is to protect us from dangers from the food we do eat. The Food and Drug Administration must always be on the alert to prevent violations of food regulations and to insist on safe processing and marketing methods. Local health authorities are responsible for enforcing regulations that ensure safe food for the community. Finally, you and I, the consumers of food, should be informed about food regulations and insist that all authorities carry out their responsibilities.

NUTRITION

Normal nutrition is the science concerned with the use of food by the body to (1) provide energy, (2) build and repair tissues and (3) regulate body processes. The benefits of good nutrition are obvious: health, happiness, enjoyable and productive work and play, and a long life relatively free from illness.

The person whose nutrition is good exhibits certain characteristics that are easy to recognize. His body is well developed with his weight in proportion to his body build. His skin has a healthy color and is elastic. His hair is smooth and glossy. His eyes are clear and are free from dark circles. He eats and sleeps well, and his posture is good. Usually, he appears to be enjoying life.

You may not realize that sometimes a person who does not look well may be showing many of the signs of poor nutrition: an undersized and poorly developed body, or overweight with flabby, soft fat; loose, pale skin, pasty or sallow; the posture of fatigue—rounded shoulders, protruding abdomen, head thrust forward; irritability or depression. Such a person is likely to have a poor or finicky appetite, appear listless and have a low resistance to infection.

What can be done to improve poor nutrition? Teach people the facts about nutrition—this kind of education is going on constantly in our schools, the logical place to begin it. It is also carried on in homes, industries, clubs, and agencies associated with clinics and hospitals. This is where the nurse comes in—as a teacher she can give her patients and their families information about nutrition and help them to improve poor eating habits. Guided by the doctor, the professional nurse and the dietitian, the practical nurse can accomplish much toward bringing about good nutrition.

Essential Nutrients

You think of food as including cereals, vegetables, meat, fish, eggs, milk, cheese, desserts, from which you choose your 3 meals a day and the snacks in between. However, the body cells are interested only in extracting from food, as you understand it, the materials they can use. These materials are called *nutrients*, from the word *nutrire* meaning to *nourish* or to *feed*. We list them here, with their uses in the body:

1. Carbohydrates (starches and sugars): provide heat and energy.
2. Fats: provide heat and energy; build fatty tissue.
3. Proteins: build and repair tissues; provide heat and energy.
4. Minerals: build and repair tissues; regulate body processes.
5. Vitamins: regulate body processes.
6. Water: regulates body processes.

The amounts of these nutrient materials present in individual foods vary considerably. Some foods contain large amounts of one nutrient and small amounts of others; other foods contain small amounts of several nutrients. The combinations are numerous. The purpose in planning meals is to provide the essential nutrients in the amounts necessary to keep the body healthy. These food combinations make up an adequate diet. But you also want meals to be appetizing and attractive; so, to make the plan complete, you need to know which foods provide the nutrients. The foods which provide for the needs of the body in the greatest measure are called "protective foods."

GENERAL CLASSIFICATIONS OF THE SOURCES OF NUTRIENTS

CARBOHYDRATES	PROTEINS	FATS
Provide fuel for energy	Build and maintain body tissues	Provide fuel for energy
Flour	Lean meats	Cooking fats
Breads	Fish	Salad oils (mayonnaise, French dressing)
Cereals	Poultry	
Sugar	Eggs	
Sweets (honey, jelly, syrups, candy)	Milk	Butter
	Cheese	Margarine
Vegetables (potato)	Legumes (dried peas, beans)	Animal fats (bacon, lard, salt pork, suet)
Fruits (dates)	Nuts (particularly peanuts)	
Carbonated beverages		Bitter chocolate

The Basic 4

The Daily Food Guide (see p. 204) shows the protective foods, in 4 groups essential for good nutrition, that should be included in the daily food plan.* Each group contributes to the essential nutrients—no one group will provide all of them.

1. *Milk group:* includes some milk every day in the following amounts:

Children	3 to 4 cups
Teen-agers	4 or more cups
Adults	2 or more cups
Pregnant women	4 or more cups
Nursing mothers	6 or more cups

Part of the milk can be replaced by cheese or ice cream.

2. *Meat group:* 2 or more servings of beef, pork, veal, lamb, fish, poultry or eggs. Alternates can be dry beans, peas, lentils or nuts.

* Essentials of an Adequate Diet, Agricultural Research Service, Washington, D. C., U. S. Department of Agriculture, ARS-62-4, June, 1956.

3. *Vegetable-fruit group:* 4 or more servings to include:

A. A dark-green or deep-yellow vegetable at least every other day.

B. A citrus fruit or other fruit or vegetable every day.

C. Other fruits and vegetables—including potatoes.

4. *Bread-cereals group:* whole-grain, enriched or restored.

This gives you the foundation for a good diet. Other foods not mentioned in these groups will be used to make meals more appetizing, such as butter, margarine, oils and sugars—especially when combined with baked dishes and desserts and as flavoring for vegetables. Some people will also use more of the basic foods to satisfy their individual requirements.

Carbohydrates*

The carbohydrates are the most economical and available sources of energy. The body uses carbohydrates more completely and readily than any of the other nutrients, and they are widely distributed in nature. Next to water they make up the greatest amount of bulk in plants. Carbohydrates are valuable because they supply energy quickly and provide roughage and give satisfaction in the diet; they are low in cost, and can be stored easily without spoiling.

The important sources of carbohydrates are the sugars and the starches in our diets. In relation to sugars, it may surprise you to learn that there is more than one kind of sugar. Starches are the more complex forms of sugars. Some forms are found in the foods we eat; others are made in the body in the process of digestion. Sugar is of no use to the tissues of the body until it is in the form that the body can use readily. This means that some sugars must be changed within the body into this usable form called *glucose.*

Sugars. 1. *Glucose* is the only form of sugar that can be absorbed and carried in the blood stream ready for use by the body tissues. All

* It is suggested that you refer back to Chapter 17 for a review of the digestion of carbohydrates, fats and proteins.

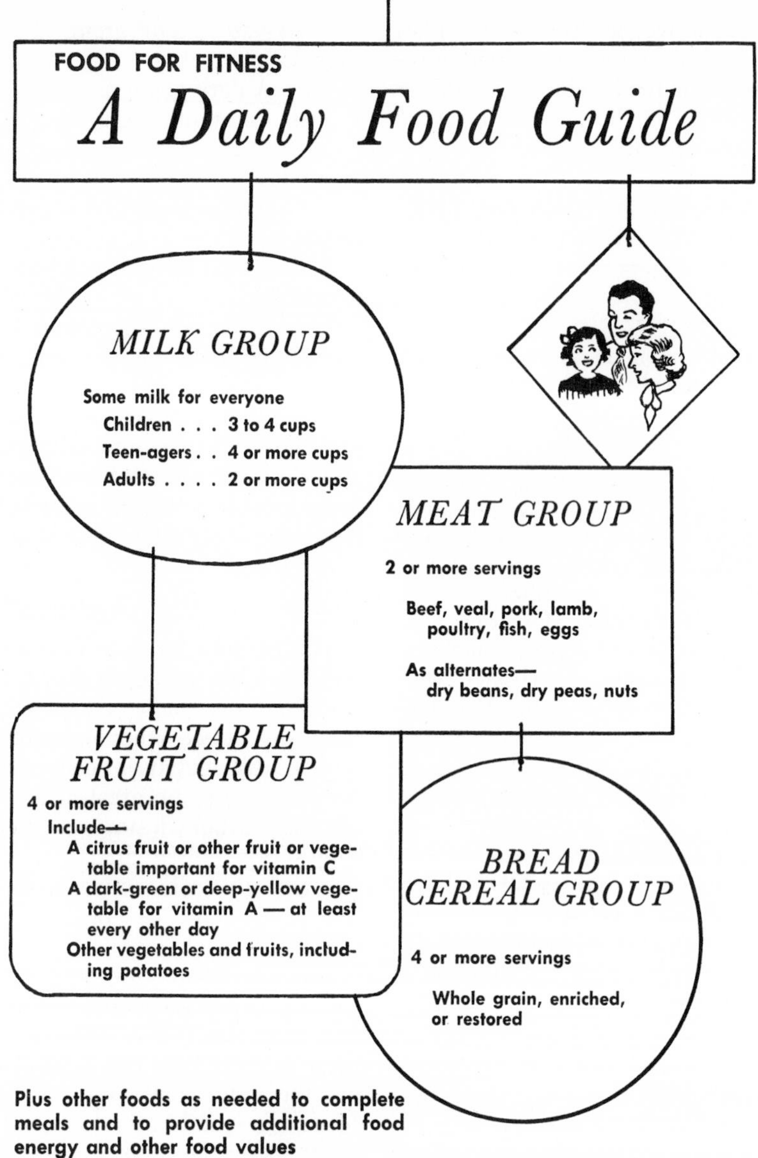

FIG. 85. (Leaflet 424. Institute of Home Economics, U.S. Department of Agriculture, Washington, D. C.)

the other forms of sugar must be changed into glucose, the sources of which are natural glucose, which is found in honey, fruits and most vegetables, and other sugars and starches which are changed into glucose within the body.

2. *Sucrose* is the form of sugar that probably is the most familiar to you. It tastes sweet; as crystallized sugar, it is used on the table and in cooking. The sources of sucrose are sugar beets, sugar cane and the sap of the maple tree.

3. *Fructose* is another form of sugar which is found mostly in honey and fruits and in some plants. It tastes almost twice as sweet as sucrose.

4. *Lactose* is the sugar which is found in

milk. It is neither as soluble nor as sweet as sucrose. It encourages the growth in the intestine of certain bacteria which aid in the use of vitamin K and niacin.

5. *Galactose* is not found naturally but is a product of the digestion of milk.

6. *Maltose* is the product of sprouting grain and of the digestion of starch within the body. It is readily soluble and easily changed into glucose, so it is often used in infant formulas in preference to other sugars.

Starch. Starch is the form of carbohydrate that is found in plants; the main sources are grain, roots, bulbs, tubers and seeds. The starch grains are encased in a tough covering which is broken down in the process of digestion. The cooking of foods containing starch speeds up digestion. Enzymes in the saliva can act on cooked starch but have no effect on raw starch.

Cellulose. Cellulose is classified as a carbohydrate, but it has no actual food value; it consists of the fibers of plant framework, which are insoluble and indigestible. However, it does have a definite use in providing bulk which helps in the elimination of food residue from the intestine. Bran, whole-grain cereals, fibrous vegetables and fruits are the main sources of this roughage.

Absorption and Digestion. Simple sugars are ready to pass into the blood stream without any digestive change. The more complex sugars have to be carried through several stages of digestion before they are ready for use. We have already mentioned the various enzymes in the saliva and the intestinal tract that carry out this breakdown.

Too much sugar in the diet takes away the appetite for other essential foods; also, it may ferment in the digestive tract and irritate it. The waste products from the use of carbohydrates by the body are carbon dioxide and water.

Glycogen. The body can store a reserve of carbohydrate in the liver in the form of glycogen; it can be changed into glucose and released into the blood stream as it is needed.

Carbohydrates taken into the body in excess of its immediate needs for heat and energy will be changed into fatty tissue. This can serve as a source of fuel stored for future use. If the intake of food is lowered, the body can call upon stored carbohydrates for energy. Carbohydrates also aid in the consumption of fats to keep them from burning up too rapidly.

Fats

Fats furnish a concentrated form of energy. Deposits of fat in the body guarantee a large and lasting supply of fuel. Certain fats are important in the function and the structure of body tissues, especially nerve tissue. Fat also serves as protection from mechanical injury and as a padding around vital organs; a layer of fat underneath the skin conserves body heat. Like carbohydrates, fat also can be used by the body for energy when the protein intake is low. It lubricates the intestinal tract to help in elimination. Fat makes the diet more attractive and tasteful and prevents hunger, since it remains in the stomach longer than other nutrients. Another important function of fats is to aid in the utilization of vitamins A, D, E and K.

The sources of fats are plants or animals. Fats are composed of carbon, hydrogen and oxygen and vary in consistency. They are classified as *saturated* or *unsaturated* fats. The saturated or solid fats (animal fats, butter, lard, hydrogenated shortenings) already contain their full complement of hydrogen, in their natural form or because hydrogen has been added by hydrogenation.

The unsaturated fats (soft or liquid fats or oils) are capable of taking on more hydrogen. Manufacturers add hydrogen to the oily fats to make them solid. The relatively inexpensive vegetable oils, such as corn, cottonseed, soybean and coconut oils, are used for this purpose. Margarine, which is also made in this way, is processed with cultured milk to give it a butter flavor with vitamins A and D added. Fortified margarine has approximately the same nutritional and caloric values as butter.

Fats are insoluble in water. There is no digestion of fats in the mouth and very little in the stomach. When fats reach the small intestine, bile secreted by the liver breaks them up into tiny droplets (emulsifies them). Then the intestinal and pancreatic juices can break up these droplets into fatty acids and glycerol—

simple forms that the body cells can use. Three of the fatty acids essential for the body (linoleic, linolenic and arachidonic) come from fats that are found only in butter, meats, egg yolks, soybean, cottonseed, corn and olive oils. Therefore, some of these fat sources must be included in the daily food supply.

As the body uses fatty acids, it breaks them down into other substances called acetone or ketone bodies. These substances are further broken down into carbon dioxide and water and are excreted as waste products.

Cholesterol, a combination of fatty acids and alcohols, is found in all body tissues, especially in the liver, the blood, the brain and the nerve tissue. Studies have shown that a high intake of certain fats may produce an abnormal storage of cholesterol in the blood, causing fat deposits in the lining of the blood vessels leading to atherosclerosis and heart disease. There is as yet no absolute proof that this is true, but much research is being done in this field. Among the foods that contain substantial amounts of cholesterol are butter, meat fats, poultry, shellfish and egg yolks.

Fats vary in digestibility. Foods fried in fat, especially at high temperatures, digest more slowly than if foods were boiled or baked. Although fats will produce about twice as much energy as equal amounts of carbohydrate, they are much more expensive as energy sources.

The average person in this country consumes more fat than the necessary amount which is 20 to 25 per cent of his diet. His diet consists of about 33 per cent fat which may have some bearing on the prevalence in the United States of heart and blood vessel difficulties, as well as overweight problems.

Proteins

Every animal, man included, must have protein to remain alive and to grow. Protein is the foundation element of every body cell. It is the only nutrient that will build tissue; it is the chief substance of muscles and glands, internal organs, brain, nerves, skin, hair and nails, and of essential enzymes and hormones. "*Protein*" comes from the Greek word that means "to take first place" and seems to be unquestionably the most important of all food substances.

Proteins come from both animal and plant food sources. Like carbohydrates, they contain carbon, hydrogen and oxygen but, in addition, they contain nitrogen; some proteins also contain phosphorus, sulfur and iron.

Protein digestion starts in the stomach where an enzyme (pepsin) breaks down the proteins, to be further acted upon in the intestines by another enzyme (erepsin) and the pancreatic juice. The end products of these processes of digestion are chemical compounds called *amino acids*. Twenty-two amino acids are known at present—10 of them are essential for growth and body maintenance. Many years ago experiments to determine the value of proteins in the body showed that rats would not grow properly or even stay alive if some of the amino acids were omitted from their diet (see Fig. 86).

The number of amino acids and the amounts of each in individual proteins vary widely. Accordingly, proteins are classified as *complete*,

Fig. 86. Adequate (*left*) and inadequate (*right*) protein diet. These rats are from the same litter. The stunted rat had a 4 per cent protein diet as against the 18 per cent diet of the normal rat. (Cooper, Barber, Mitchell, and Rynbergen: Nutrition in Health and Disease, ed. 12, p. 42, Philadelphia, Lippincott)

partially complete and *incomplete.* The complete proteins contain the essential amino acids in sufficient quantities for maintenance and normal growth; milk, meat, fish, poultry, eggs and cheese are complete proteins. Partially complete proteins will maintain life but will not promote normal growth; they are found in cereals and vegetables and are important in the diet to supplement the complete proteins. Incomplete proteins alone will neither maintain life nor promote growth; the proteins in corn and gelatin are in this group. Because we usually combine a variety of foods in every meal, we obtain a combination of proteins that supplement each other. However, every meal should provide some form of complete protein.

Your daily selection of protein foods should allow an intake well above your needs to ensure an adequate supply of the essential amino acids. The daily requirement for good nutrition for a healthy person varies with age and body weight. The Food and Nutrition Board recommends about 10 to 15 per cent of the total daily calories for men and women, estimated as 1 gm. per Kilogram of body weight; growing children need more per unit of weight. Pregnant women and nursing mothers need a higher percentage because they are supplying 2 people. In body conditions involving tissue damage or loss, the protein allowance is increased to help in tissue repair.

The blood stream carries the unneeded amino acids to the liver where they are changed into urea that is excreted by the kidneys and into sugarlike compounds that are used to provide energy. One of these compounds, glycogen, is stored in the liver, and others are changed into fatty tissue.

The waste products from the use of protein by the body are nitrogenous wastes including urea, as well as carbon dioxide and water.

Energy

Although science does not know exactly what energy is, it has been defined as the ability to do work. We can understand and measure several of the forms that energy assumes, such as light, heat, motion, sounds and electricity.

The human body uses these different forms of energy in its many activities: for breathing, for circulating the blood, or transmitting nerve stimuli; for moving the body or any part of it; and for the processing involved in digestion, absorption and the utilization of food.

The process of using food to produce energy for the total activities of the body is called metabolism (mentioned already in previous chapters). Even an inactive person continually uses some energy for the work of the heart, the lungs and all the tiny muscles in the body systems. The rate of this burning or oxidation process in the tissues producing the energy required just to keep him alive, to sustain only those activities fundamental or basic to living, is called the "basal metabolic rate" (BMR).

In diagnosing certain illness conditions, it is sometimes necessary to determine the patient's BMR. One method of doing this involves the use of a special machine which measures the amount of oxygen he consumes during a specified period prior to which he has rested and fasted. Briefly, the BMR test is given as follows: the patient breathes into a special chamber through a rubber tube leading to his mouth, with his nose clamped off; the amount of oxygen remaining in the chamber is measured after a certain period of time and is the basis for calculating the rate at which oxidation proceeds in the cells.

The amount of energy (measured in calories) which a normal individual needs depends on age, sex, weight and the make-up of his body. It also is influenced by the kind of work he does. Children need a great deal of energy for growing, and also because they are very active. Older people use less energy. People at desk jobs need less than day laborers, who are using their muscles a great deal. Men need more energy than women; large people use more than small people. Some people use a great deal of energy in the things they do for fun, such as walking or taking part in sports and games. Some household jobs take more energy than others—for example, sweeping takes more than mending. Certain body disturbances, such as fever or exophthalmic goiter, increase the amount of energy the body uses. It all amounts to this: the energy requirements of an individual is the sum of the amounts necessary to keep his body processes going and to carry on his activities. He provides this energy by the food he eats.

The unit of measurement for food energy is called a *calorie*, and the caloric value of foods can be determined in the laboratory. In this process an apparatus is used which measures the increased temperature of water as heat given off by the burning of test food passes into it. Consequently, the definition of calorie is "the amount of heat required to raise the temperature of 1 kilogram of water 1° centigrade." A calorie is designated sometimes by a large "C." The caloric values of the energy-producing foods have been determined as follows:

1 gram of protein will yield 4 calories
1 gram of fat will yield 9 calories
1 gram of carbohydrate will yield 4 calories

The table lists the calorie allowances for individuals of various body weights and ages.

Guides have been worked out naming the foods and estimating the amounts of each that a normal individual needs for light, moderate or heavy work.

Calorie charts, giving the number of calories in a serving of the foods we use, are available without cost from a number of sources. The National Dairy Council puts out an excellent booklet† which you can get from your local dairy council.

Minerals

Minerals are vital to the body for building bones and teeth; they help to maintain muscle tone, to regulate body processes and to maintain the acid-base balance in the body. Some minerals are used more readily by the body than others, and foods vary considerably in the amount of minerals which they contain. Some minerals are lost in cooking, and some are lost in body wastes.

Calcium. Calcium, the mineral which the body needs the most, is the one most likely to be left out of the ordinary diet. Most of the calcium in the body is in the bones and the teeth. It has other important uses in keeping the body fluids balanced, helping with the clotting of the blood as well as regulating heart and muscle and nerve responses. Calcium deficiencies cause poor teeth, rickets, damage to a mother's teeth and bones both before and after a baby is born, slow clotting of the blood and disabilities of the muscles and nerves.

Milk contains more calcium than any other

† Your Caloric Catalog, National Dairy Council, Chicago 6, Ill., 1957.

CALORIE ALLOWANCES FOR INDIVIDUALS OF VARIOUS BODY WEIGHTS AND AGES*

(At Mean Environmental Temperature of 20° C. and Assuming Moderate Physical Activity)

Men					Women				
Desirable Weight		Calorie Allowances			Desirable Weight		Calorie Allowances		
Kg.	Lbs.	25 Yrs.	45 Yrs.	65 Yrs.	Kg.	Lbs.	25 Yrs.	45 Yrs.	65 Yrs.
50	110	2,500	2,350	1,950	40	88	1,750	1,650	1,400
55	121	2,700	2,550	2,150	45	99	1,900	1,800	1,500
60	132	2,850	2,700	2,250	50	110	2,050	1,950	1,600
65	143	3,000	2,800	2,350	55	121	2,200	2,050	1,750
70	154	3,200	3,000	2,550	58	128	2,300	2,200	1,800
75	165	3,400	3,200	2,700	60	132	2,350	2,200	1,850
80	176	3,550	3,350	2,800	65	143	2,500	2,350	2,000
85	187	3,700	3,500	2,900	70	154	2,600	2,450	2,050
					75	165	2,750	2,600	2,150

* National Research Council: Recommended Dietary Allowances, Pub. 589, Washington, D. C., 1958.

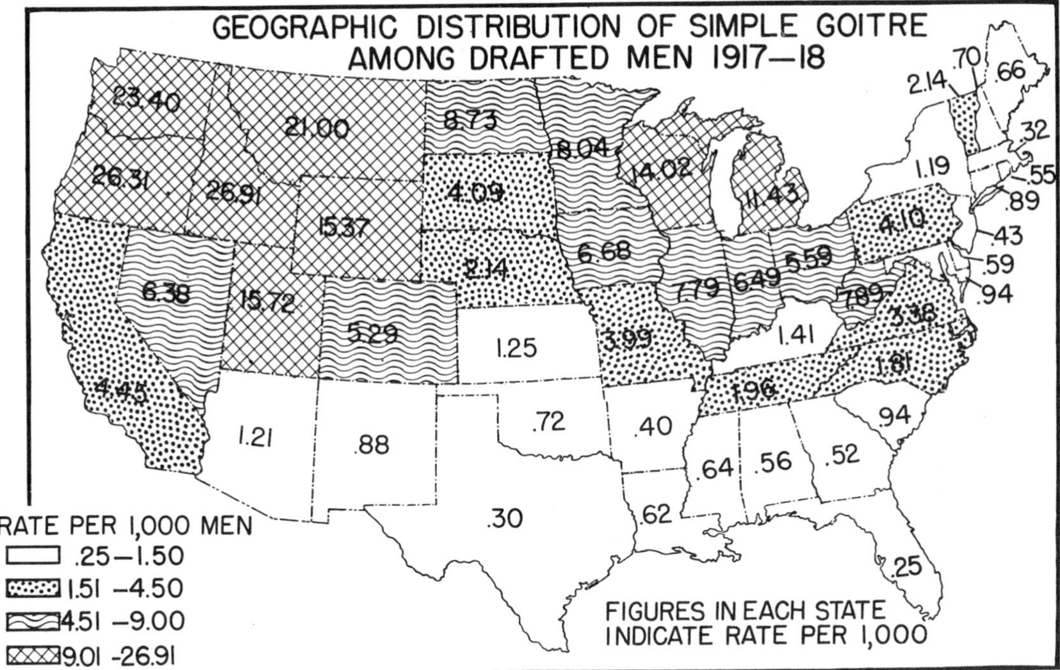

Fig. 87. Geographic distribution of simple goiter among men drafted for World War I. These goitrous areas are naturally low in iodine. (U.S. Department of Public Health)

food. A quart of milk for a child and a pint for an adult will supply the body with its daily calcium requirement. Milk products are also high in calcium. Vegetables contain varying amounts of calcium, but some of them in a form that the body cannot use readily. The richest vegetable sources are broccoli, kale, turnip and collard greens; other good sources are cheese and molasses.

Phosphorus. Phosphorus is a constituent of every body cell, but most of it is in the bones and the teeth. It helps the cells to use proteins, fats, carbohydrates and vitamins and regulates the acid-base balance in the blood. So many ordinary foods contain phosphorus that the body is almost certain to get enough of it. The best food sources are milk, fish, poultry, cereals, cheese, nuts, dried beans and peas.

Iron. The body needs a relatively small amount of iron, but this amount is vitally important because it is an essential part of every body cell and a constituent of hemoglobin in the red blood cells. The body is very thrifty with its supply of iron and uses it over and over by salvaging the iron from worn-out red blood cells. The best sources of iron are liver, meat, legumes, whole or enriched grains, green leafy vegetables and dried fruits. Molasses and raisins are rich in iron but are used in the diet in such small quantities that they are not practical sources.

Sodium, Potassium, Magnesium and Chlorides. These minerals work together in a very close relationship and have many similar functions. They are essential for maintaining the osmotic pressure balance between the cells and the surrounding cell fluids; they also help to maintain the normal acid-base balance in the body. *Sodium chloride* is readily available in common table salt; sea food is another good source. Cereals, legumes, meats and vegetables provide *potassium.* Since the amount required daily is relatively small and this mineral is found in so many foods, the ordinary diet provides adequate amounts.

Magnesium serves as a regulator of the action of other minerals and lack of it increases muscular irritability. It is present in large amounts in many foods, particularly in green vegetables; therefore, the ordinary diet provides an adequate amount.

Sulfur. Sulfur is a necessary constituent of the amino acids and is most highly concentrated in the bones, the hair and the nails, although it is present in all body cells. Good food sources are liver, chicken, bluefish, dried beans and peanuts, but it is widely available in protein foods.

Iodine. Although the amount of iodine in the body is small, the thyroid gland cannot function properly without it. The sources of iodine are sea water and sea salt, and water in localities where the soil contains iodine. Some parts of the United States have almost no iodine in the soil, especially near the Great Lakes and in parts of the Rocky Mountain regions. Food products from these areas also lack iodine, and goiter is common. This deficiency can be remedied by using *iodized salt*—a recommended practice in parts of the country where iodine is lacking.

Trace Elements. Some minerals are present in the body in very small amounts but are important in body processes. These elements are arsenic, aluminum, bromine, cobalt, copper, fluorine, manganese, nickel, silicon, selenium and zinc. The ordinary diet provides an adequate supply.

Copper is an essential agent in the process of changing iron into hemoglobin.

Cobalt and *manganese* play some part in blood formation.

Fluorine is essential in forming tooth enamel.

Zinc is associated with enzyme activity.

No functions are known for the other trace elements although they are present in plant and animal tissues.

Diet Planning

The problem is to plan for an adequate mineral supply and yet keep the diet interesting. For example, the body needs a considerable amount of calcium. Turnips contain calcium, but the amount is so small that you would have to eat a great many turnips to supply your body needs for only 1 day. However, there is more calcium in milk than in other food, and milk is easy to incorporate into the diet because you can use it in so many ways.

In choosing foods to supply the minerals select: (1) foods with the greatest amount of the mineral; (2) foods with the mineral in the form the body can use readily; (3) foods with minerals that will remain in the body and (4) foods high in minerals that can be used appetizingly in quantity.

Water

Except for oxygen, nothing is more essential to life than water. Man can survive for weeks without food but not without water.

We noted in Chapter 11 that about 70 per cent of the body's weight is water. Ordinarily the body excretes about 2½ quarts per day—in perspiration, in urine and in the breath. In order to maintain the fluid balance in the cells of the body, the amount lost must be replaced. Food provides us with some fluid intake, but we must supplement this amount by drinking water and other liquids. Most authorities say the average adult needs 6 to 8 glasses of fluid every day.

The importance of water in the diet is evident. In studying the cells of the body, we learned that water was part of their major make-up. The nutrients are distributed to the body cells by the blood, of which water is one of the essential components. The presence of water within the body allows vital chemical changes to take place, and it is necessary in the control of body temperature. No organ of the body can function without water. Water is so necessary to life that Nature has provided man with an inborn safety device: thirst is his strongest appetite.

The Vitamins

The word *vitamin* is a key to the importance of these substances in foods—*vita* is the Latin word for life. Vitamins have been recognized since 1911; they were discovered one after another, and new information is continually appearing. The body, with a few exceptions, cannot produce vitamins, but an adequate supply is essential for health and growth.

Foods are the natural sources of vitamins and should supply our vitamin needs. (Vitamins are available in concentrated form and physicians prescribe them for marked deficiencies.) Because some of the vitamins are not stored in the body, it is doubly important to ensure a daily supply; an all-around vitamin deficiency may not be the cause of a specific disease, but it does impair general health and efficiency.

Foods differ greatly in the amount and the number of vitamins they contain. Vitamins vary as to their solubility in fat (fat-soluble) or in water (water-soluble) and also in the degree to which they are affected by cooking temperatures. The following information applies to vitamins in general:

Some vitamins are lost by exposure to the air. They also may be lost in the storage of food. Frozen foods are second to fresh foods for retaining vitamins; canned foods retain a higher vitamin value if they are canned carefully and are not stored too long.

Some vitamins are soluble in fats and are stored in the body in this form. This means that the diet must include a sufficient amount of fat to provide an adequate supply of these vitamins.

Some vitamins are soluble in water. Therefore, foods should be cooked in a small amount of water and the cooking water should be used, if possible, in gravies and sauces.

High temperatures destroy vitamins; food should not be overcooked and should be served at once in order to preserve vitamin content.

In some foods, the vitamin content is in the portion that is likely to be thrown away, such as the outer leaves of lettuce and the peelings of vegetables.

Fat Soluble Vitamins

Vitamin A. Vitamin A (carotene) promotes growth, sustains normal vision, supports normal reproduction and maintains healthy skin and mucous membrane, promoting resistance to infection.

The best sources of vitamin A are liver, spinach and green and yellow vegetables. A bright yellow color identifies fruits and vegetables as being good sources. It is found also in cream, butter and egg yolk, in highly concentrated forms.

Surplus amounts are stored in the body; it is not destroyed by cooking.

Vitamin D. Vitamin D (calciferol) is essential in regulating the use of calcium and phosphorus in the body. A marked deficiency in vitamin D hampers growth and affects the hardness of bones. This deficiency, plus an inadequate supply of calcium and phosphorus, causes rickets—a condition in which the bones do not harden as they should and they bend into deformed positions; for example, bowlegs. Before and after a baby is born, a mother must provide herself with enough vitamin D to prevent rickets from developing in the baby and to preserve her own bones and teeth. However, recent studies show that an overdose of vitamin D can have toxic effects, such as abnormal calcification of growing bones and the hardening of soft tissues, and may develop other serious complications. Therefore, large supplemental dosages should be given only under the guidance of a physician, especially when the pregnant mother and the growing child are concerned.

The best sources of vitamin D are the fish-liver oils. Vitamin D is formed in the body by the action of sunlight on the cholesterol products in the skin. Milk is not high in vitamin D, but the content is increased by irradiation and by adding vitamin D concentrate. Infants and children need supplemental amounts, but under normal conditions it is not usually considered necessary to provide supplemental vitamin D for adults. It is not stored in the body to any extent.

Vitamin E. Vitamin E is called the reproductive or the antisterility vitamin. So far, there is no proof that vitamin E is necessary for human beings, but it has been proved that some animals definitely require this vitamin to reproduce successfully. It is found in many foods, especially in wheat-germ oils and green, leafy vegetables; it is present in egg yolks and margarine. Heat seems to have little effect on it.

Vitamin K. The body extracts vitamin K from its food sources via the same route that it absorbs fats from the small intestine. Any interference with fat absorption may result in a poor supply of any of the fat soluble vitamins, including vitamin K.

FAT-SOLUBLE VITAMINS*

	A	D	E	K
ACTIVE CHEMICAL FORMS	(Provitamin) Carotenes α, β, and γ	Calciferol	Tocopherols α, β, and γ	Vitamin K_1 and K_2 and Naphthoquinones
IMPORTANT FOOD SOURCES	Liver Egg yolk Butter, cream, margarine Green and yellow vegetables Apricots Cantaloupe	Irradiated foods Small amounts in Butter Egg yolk Liver Salmon Sardines Tuna fish	Wheat germ Leafy vegetables Vegetable oils Egg yolk Legumes Peanuts Margarine	Cabbage Cauliflower Spinach Other leafy vegetables Pork liver Soybean oil and other vegetable oils
CONCENTRATES OR PHARMACEUTICAL SOURCES	Fish-liver oil Beta-carotene	Fish-liver oil Viosterol	Wheat-germ oil	Synthetic
STABILITY TO COOKING, DRYING, LIGHT, ETC.	Gradual destruction by exposure to air, heat and drying, more rapid at high temperatures	Stable to heating, aging and storage Destroyed by excess ultraviolet irradiation	Stable to all methods of food processing Destroyed by rancidity and ultraviolet irradiation	Stable to heat, light and exposure to air Destroyed by strong acids, alkalis and ox. agents
FUNCTION:	Maintains function of epithelial cells, skin, bone, mucous membranes, visual purple	Calcium and phosphorus absorption and utilization in bone growth	Maintains function of reproductive and muscular tissues, antioxidant in tissues, related to action of selenium	Necessary in formation of prothrombin, essential for clotting of blood
DEFICIENCY MANIFEST AS	Night blindness Glare blindness Rough, dry skin Dry mucous membranes Xerophthalmia	Rickets Soft bones Bowed legs Poor teeth Skeletal deformities	Sterility in males (rats) Resorption of fetus (females) Muscular dystrophy in rats and rabbits	Slow clotting time of blood Some hemorrhagic disease of newborn Lack of prothrombin
ADULT HUMAN REQUIREMENT	5,000 I. U. when over ½ from plant sources	Children and adolescents, 400 I. U.	Needed but amount unknown	Unknown

* Cooper, Barber, Mitchell, Rynbergen and Greene: Nutrition in Health and Disease, Philadelphia, Lippincott, 1963.

Vitamin K is essential in the formation of *prothrombin*, a substance necessary for the clotting of blood.

The average diet supplies an adequate amount of vitamin K, as it is found in a variety of foods. Good sources are liver, cauliflower, cabbage, spinach and other green leafy vegetables. Margarine, soybean and other vegetable oils are also sources. The limited amount stored in the body is found in the liver.

Deficiencies of vitamin K produce hemorrhagic symptoms. Intramuscular administration is often used to overcome hemorrhagic tendencies in the newborn.

Water Soluble Vitamins

VITAMIN C. Vitamin C is probably equally well known by its other chemical name, *ascorbic acid.* Its function has been recognized for many years, but further uses are still being discovered.

One of the contributions of vitamin C to our vital processes is the maintenance of the intercellular substances of the body. Since these are everywhere in our bodies, vitamin C contributes to healthy tissues and proper functioning of the blood vessels, skin, gums, bones, joints and muscles—indeed, all tissues and organs of the body. Maintenance of these healthy organs helps to provide us with additional resistance to disease.

At present it is thought that vitamin C is related to both the formation and the hemoglobin content of the blood cells. Patients treated by surgery are frequently given large doses of ascorbic acid, since it is essential to and promotes healing of wounds.

The century-old classic disease of vitamin C deficiency is *scurvy,* a disease marked by bleeding gums, loose teeth, sore stiff joints, tiny hemorrhages, and great loss of weight. Lesser deficiencies affect health by causing listlessness, irritability and lowered resistance to disease.

Vitamin C is probably the most unstable of the vitamins. It is destroyed by exposure to the air, drying, heating and storing. Because vitamin C survives longer in acid surroundings, baking soda should not be added to foods in cooking, since it counteracts acids. Tomatoes retain vitamin C better than other vegetables because they contain acid. Freezing fruits and vegetables helps to preserve their vitamin C content, but they should be used immediately after thawing. Fruits and vegetables canned commercially retain this vitamin because the air is excluded during the canning process.

Since vitamin C is destroyed by heat as well as being water-soluble, cooking should be done in as little water as possible (using the cooking water or juices for other preparations). Overcooking should be avoided also.

VITAMIN B COMPLEX. At first, the group of vitamins presently known as the vitamin B complex was thought to be a single entity and was named vitamin B. Further research with the so-called vitamin B led to the discovery of several vitamins within the one, and each was given a name.

The B complex vitamins share the characteristics of being widely distributed in foods and soluble in water, but each of the members is chemically distinct. Each has functions which can be isolated, and each produces its own deficiency symptoms.

Thiamine (B_1). Thiamine promotes general body efficiency. It is necessary for growth, stimulates the appetite, aids the digestion, regulates the nervous system and aids reproduction and lactation. Signs of a deficiency of thiamine are poor appetite, fatigue, irritability, listlessness, loss of weight and strength, depression and poor intestinal tone. A very great deficiency causes *beriberi,* a disease of the nervous system which leads to paralysis and then to death from heart failure.

The best food sources of thiamine are the whole grain and enriched products: peas, beans and soybeans, pork, liver, meats from the glandular organs and dried yeast. Some of the thiamine in milk is lost in pasteurization.

Thiamine is not stored in the body to any extent; it is soluble in water and is destroyed by heat.

Riboflavin (B_2). Riboflavin is essential for growth and plays a part in protein metabolism. A deficiency leads to skin and eye irritations. Riboflavin is not stored in the body to any extent; therefore, a steady supply must be provided.

Riboflavin is available in a wide variety of foods but only in small quantities. The best sources are liver, meats, milk and milk products, eggs, green leafy vegetables, whole grain or enriched bread and cereals. Also, if it is exposed to light while in solution, it disintegrates.

Niacin. Niacin (nicotinic acid) is essential to metabolism. A marked niacin deficiency in the body leads to the disease *pellagra.* The mucous membrane of the mouth and of the digestive tract become red and inflamed; lesions appear on the skin. The victims lose their appetite and lose weight; they experience vomiting and diarrhea and become weak and irritable; they also may become mentally disturbed. A lesser defi-

WATER-SOLUBLE VITAMINS*

ACTIVE CHEMICAL FORMS	C	FRACTIONS OF THE VITAMIN B COMPLEX					
	Ascorbic Acid	Thiamine (B_1)	Riboflavin (B_2)	Niacin and Niacinamide (Precursor Tryptophan)	Pantothenic Acid	Vitamin B_6, Pyridoxine, Pyridoxal, Pyridoxamine	Folacin, Folinic acid and vitamin B_{12} (cyanocobalamine)
Important food sources	Citrus fruits Strawberries Cantaloupe Tomatoes Sweet peppers Cabbage Potatoes Kale, parsley Turnip greens	Pork Liver Organ meats Whole grains Enriched cereal products Nuts Legumes Potatoes	Liver, milk Meat, eggs Enriched cereal products Green, leafy vegetables	Liver, poultry Meat, fish Whole grains Enriched cereal products Legumes Mushrooms	Liver Organ meats Eggs, peanuts Legumes Mushrooms Salmon, whole grains	Pork Organ meats Legumes, seeds Grains Potatoes Bananas	Liver and other organ meats, milk, eggs Folacin in green, leafy vegetables
Concentrates or pharmaceutical sources	Synthetic	Yeast, wheat germ, extracts Synthetic	Yeast Liver concentrates Synthetic	Yeast Liver concentrates Synthetic	Yeast, wheat germ, liver concentrates	Yeast, wheat germ, liver concentrates	Yeast and liver concentrates
Stability to cooking, drying, light, etc.	Unstable to heat and oxidation, except in acids Destroyed by drying and aging	Unstable to heat and oxidation	Stable to heat in cooking, to acids and oxidation Unstable to light	Stable to heat, light and oxidation, acid and alkali	Unstable to acid, alkali, heat and certain salts	Stable to heat, light and oxidation	Probably unstable to heat and oxidation
Function: Essential in	Formation of intercellular substance, cellular oxidation and reduction	Carbohydrate metabolism, component of tissue enzyme cocarboxylase	Carbohydrate and amino acid metabolism, component of enzyme system	Carbohydrate and amino acid metabolism, component of enzyme system	Growth and health of all animals Active as coenzyme A	Metabolism of fats and amino acids	Growth, blood formation, choline synthesis amino acid metabolism
Deficiency manifest as	Scurvy Sore mouth Sore and bleeding gums Weak-walled capillaries	Beriberi (man) Polyneuritis (animals) Poor appetite Fatigue Constipation	Eye sensitivity Cataract Cheilosis (man) Alopecia (rats)	Pellagra (man) Blacktongue (dogs)	Dermatitis (chicks) Graying of hair (rats)	Acrodynia (rats) Microcytic anemia (dogs)	Macrocytic anemias, sprue & pernicious anemia
Adult human requirement	Men 75 mg. Women 70 mg.	Men 1.3-1.6 mg. Women 1.0-1.2 mg.	Men 1.8 mg. Women 1.5 mg.	Niacin equivalent Men 18-21 mg. Women 17 mg.	Not yet established	Probably 2-3 mg. for adults	Unknown

* Cooper, Barber, Mitchell, Rynbergen and Greene: Nutrition in Health and Disease, Philadelphia, Lippincott, 1963.

ciency brings on these same symptoms in a milder form.

The best sources of niacin are lean meat, liver, whole grain and enriched products, and fresh and dried peas and beans.

Niacin is a water soluble vitamin, not readily destroyed by heat and is stored in the body to a limited extent.

Biotin. Biotin is thought to be involved in the metabolism of amino acids. Although its exact function has not yet been established definitely, it is often included in multiple vitamin preparations. Food sources are liver, organ meats, whole grain cereals and leafy vegetables.

Folacin (Folic Acid). Folic acid is an essential component of tissues and seems to be necessary in the formation of red blood cells. A deficiency causes certain types of anemia (a decrease in the number of red blood cells). It is a recent addition to the B complex group, and its use in the body has not been fully determined. Good sources of food are liver, meat, eggs, fish and green leafy vegetables.

B_{12}. Vitamin B_{12} is related to folic acid but is far more potent. It also is involved in the formation of red blood cells. A deficiency leads to anemia and to retarded growth in children. Food sources are the same as for folacin.

Inositol. The function of this vitamin is not known for human beings although it seems to be necessary for animals. It is abundant in the average diet.

Choline. Choline is associated with the metabolism of fat and its storage in the liver. It is manufactured in the body, and since it is widely available in animals and plants, the average diet supplies it also.

B_6 (Pyridoxine). Vitamin B_6 is one of 3 closely related chemical compounds which function in the cellular metabolism of amino acids. A deficiency causes retarded growth and nervous irritability. Although the exact requirement is not yet known, a sufficient quantity is assured in the average diet.

Pantothenic Acid. Pantothenic acid is involved in a number of metabolic processes in animals—especially in the metabolism of carbohydrates and of fats. Its importance in human nutrition has not been established yet, and although the requirement has not been determined, it is thought that the average diet supplies a sufficient amount.

Para-Aminobenzoic Acid (PABA). There is no evidence of deficiency of this vitamin in man. Its functions are not yet verified, but it has been shown to be necessary for growth and for prevention of the graying of hair in certain experimental animals. Food sources are yeast, liver, whole grains and molasses.

MAIN IDEAS OF THIS CHAPTER

Health and efficiency depend on food.

Nutrition is the use of food for growth, body upkeep and repair to provide energy and to regulate the processes in the body.

The nutrients, or the food materials, which the cells must have are carbohydrates, fats, proteins, minerals, vitamins and water.

An adequate diet includes food materials necessary for health; if possible, these materials should be supplied by natural foods.

A deficiency in one or more of these food materials may cause specific disease or affect the general health, depending on how great the deficiency is.

Work is going on continually to determine whether other substances in foods are essential for us.

Most of the vitamins are not stored in the body and must be supplied every day in the diet.

Proper cooking and storage preserve the nutrient value of food.

The amount of energy an individual needs to keep his body going and active depends on age, sex, weight, body build, occupation and recreational activities.

ADAPTING SKILLS TO SITUATIONS

Which essential foods, if any, are you leaving out of your diet?

Check your diet for the foods that give you resistance to disease. Do you think you are likely to have colds this winter?

Why do experts say that a child needs twice as much milk every day as an adult?

If you wanted a quick supply of energy, which would you eat, a cracker or a piece of candy? Why?

Why is it important to have a doctor's advice about a reducing diet or about taking vitamins?

Are you doing light, moderate or heavy work? Is your diet suitable? How would you change it?

From your personal experience, bring up for class discussion 1 or 2 problems connected with including the necessary nutrients in the 3 daily meals.

23

SPECIAL DIETS FOR SPECIAL CONDITIONS

At this point, you put your knowledge to work to provide your patient with the diet prescribed as an important part of his treatment, but any diet is useless unless the patient eats the food prepared for him. You understand the patient's illness and you have the doctor's orders to guide you; on the other hand, you have the patient's own food habits, influenced perhaps by his nationality and certainly by his prejudices. As you learn something about the requirements for special, or modified, diets discussed in this chapter, you will see that you really need all your knowledge of nutrition and personality quirks. You may have to sell the idea of eating salads to the meat-and-potatoes addict, or substitute fruit for a cream puff or introduce milk into the diet of a patient who thinks that milk is for babies.

DIET TACTFULNESS

It will be easier to satisfy a finicky patient if you have a considerable margin of choice in the diet he is allowed, but many patients are on a diet prescribed as a part of the treatment of more than one body disturbance. For example, a patient with a heart condition also may be underweight; a convalescent surgical patient also may be a diabetic.

You can help a patient to like his diet by using color, variety and camouflage. Many a milk hater has had his daily allowance of milk in soup, ice cream or pudding, without being any the wiser. Attitudes about food are hard to change, especially if nutrition is a completely new idea to your patient, who may believe firmly that his stomach will tell him what is good for him. People also have many other ideas about food that simply are not true, for example that the acid in tomatoes sears the stomach, or that a sick person will "lose his strength" if he does not have solid food. Sometimes it is difficult to make people see that the intestinal tract welcomes a rest after it has been upset. So you must persevere with a diet until the improved condition of the patient speaks for itself.

KINDS OF DIETS

You will find that the patient is far more amenable to diet restrictions if he is not constantly reminded of his particular disease or condition by having diets classified according to the name of a disease. For instance, referring to the diabetic patient's diet as "controlled carbohydrate" deemphasizes diabetes and concentrates attention on dietary habits you want him to develop. The following classifications tell how diets are modified in the treatment of patients:

Diets with modification according to consistency

Liquid, soft, light, full, bland, high residue, low residue

Diets with modification according to energy value

High calorie, low calorie

Diets with modification of 1 or more of the nutrients

High iron (anemia), controlled carbohydrate (diabetic), controlled fat (cardiac), high protein (liver), low sodium (cardiovascular), acid-alkaline (kidney), low purine (gout), high vitamin (arthritis)

These titles show the kind of diet prescribed, although the amounts or the specific nutrients may be varied for an individual patient according to the doctor's orders. If there are no restrictions or special requirements, the patient may have any of the foods listed on his type of diet; you will be expected to know, generally, the kinds of food that will be allowed. Although the individual trays are checked carefully in a hospital, mistakes can happen. You should be able to recognize each type of diet and examine each tray with the patient in mind.

Consistency Modifications

Liquid Diets. These diets consist of liquids only. They are given as a patient's first steps toward taking solid foods after an operation; they are given during an acute illness, or they may be the sole diet in specific body disturbances, such as irritation of the intestinal tract. According to the individual patient's needs, they may be *full* or *limited* liquid diets and are often used progressively. Feedings may be given every 2, 3 or 4 hours, as prescribed.

CLEAR LIQUID DIET

Fat free meat broth
Tea, coffee (without sugar, milk or cream)
Gelatin
Carbonated beverages

FULL LIQUID DIET

Soup—clear, strained or milk
Milk, cream
Milk sherbet
Plain ice cream
Well-beaten eggs in beverages
Cereal gruels
Strained vegetable or fruit juices
Tea, coffee

A full liquid diet can be used for long periods to supply adequate amounts of protein, fat and carbohydrate if the patient is confined to bed. A limited or clear liquid diet is sufficient to replace body fluids but does not meet other nutrient requirements. For this reason, the patient progresses to a full liquid diet as soon as possible.

Soft Diet. A soft diet includes semisolid foods and is often supplemented with between-meal feedings; usually it is high in calories and is easily digested. The foods included are:

Soups—clear, strained vegetable, cream
Eggs—except fried
Milk, cream, butter, cottage cheese, cream cheese, mild cheddar cheese
Baked or mashed potato, milky flavored or sieved vegetables
Cooked or refined ready-to-eat cereals, refined rice, macaroni
Refined bread, crackers
Ground meats, white meat of poultry, fish
Milk puddings, plain ice cream, custards, gelatin desserts, sherbets, sponge or angel food cake
Sugar—a small amount
Tea, coffee

The doctor may order a modification of this diet that does not allow all of the foods listed above.

Light Diet. The light diet is sometimes called the *convalescent diet* and is the diet for preoperative and postoperative patients. It is more varied than the soft diet and precedes the full-diet stage. Usually it includes a liberal amount of calories, and the foods allowed are easily digested. The foods which are permitted are:

Soft diet foods
Broiled lamb chops, ground beef, liver, bacon
All but strongly flavored vegetables, dried beans or gas-forming vegetables
All fruits
Salads and salad dressings
Macaroni, spaghetti, noodles; all cereals but bran products
Any kind of bread but bran
All desserts except rich pastries
Small amounts of concentrated sweets, such as jam, jelly, honey
Butter, cream
Tea, coffee

Full Diet. The full diet is really a normal diet; sometimes it has to be modified to meet individual needs, but it allows a wide choice of foods and includes everything but rich pastries and foods likely to cause digestive disturbances. Since all patients are comparatively inactive, the number of calories should be kept within the requirements for an inactive person.

The full diet is the most frequently used of all hospital diets. It is given to all ambulatory and bed patients whose condition does not require a special diet.

DIETS AS TREATMENT

Diet plays an important part in the treatment of many diseases and in the correction of nutrition disorders. These special (therapeutic) diets will be discussed as a part of the treatment in the various conditions of illness. Some of the purposes of therapeutic diets are:

To regulate the amount of certain food constituents in disorders of metabolism (diabetes).

To increase or decrease body weight by adding or limiting calories (overweight or underweight).

To reduce or prevent edema, an accumulation of fluid in the tissues, by restricting salt (cardiac conditions).

To aid digestion by avoiding foods that irritate the alimentary tract or that interfere with stomach action (ulcer).

To help an overburdened organ to regain its normal function (nephritis).

These dietary adjustments may be made by increasing or decreasing the amount of protein, fats, carbohydrates or minerals; by providing or eliminating fiber foods; by increasing the water content of the body by "forcing" fluids or decreasing it by limiting them.

Bland Diet

Diarrhea is a symptom of such intestinal disturbances as food poisoning, colitis or typhoid fever, or it may be the result of improper eating or of taking laxatives. The diet prescribed depends on the cause of the diarrhea, but usually it is limited at first to clear broth and weak tea, then increased gradually. It is safer to give too little food rather than too much until the symptoms disappear.

This diet is designed to prevent stimulation of peristalsis and the flow of gastric secretions caused by chemical or mechanical irritation and also to reduce inflammation. It is employed in the treatment of ulcers, diarrhea and colitis (inflammation of the colon).

In spastic constipation, the nerve endings in the intestines become oversensitive and irritated; this causes spasms and pain. Smooth, nonirritating food is given to soothe and rest the intestine until the spasms are relieved.

The diet of the patient with a severe ulcer may consist at first of one half milk and one half cream (*Sippy diet*). Later, this is increased by adding puréed vegetables and fruits, strained cereals, eggs and tender meats. Spiced or salty foods, tea, coffee, gravies or broths are not allowed. The feedings are small and given frequently to keep the gastric juice in the stomach diluted and so reduce irritation of the ulcer. The temperature of the food served should not be extremely hot or extremely cold. This type of diet is called a *bland* diet.

High Fiber Diet

A poorly balanced diet may be one of the causes of *atonic* constipation. The intestines need bulky waste to stimulate movement, so the diet for constipation, caused by a lack of bulk, includes plenty of the vegetables high in cellulose; fruits except blackberries; whole-grain cereals; plenty of water, milk, cream and butter. Fats in the diet serve to oil and soften the contents of the intestines.

Low Residue or Residue-Free Diet

This diet is made up of foods which can be absorbed completely so that there is no residue left for the formation of feces. It may be used in cases of severe diarrhea, colitis, before and after surgery on the lower intestine and the rectum, and in partial obstruction. Foods may be included such as tender meat, fish and poultry, fruit juices, gelatin desserts, rice, clear soups and hard-cooked eggs. Coarse breads, cheese, milk, fried foods, fruits and vegetables and tough meats are to be avoided. This diet is deficient in both vitamins and minerals, and so it should be used for as short a time as is possible.

High Calorie Diet

Science has changed the old saying: "Feed a cold and starve a fever." Studies have proved that the body cells burn food rapidly in fevers; therefore, the body needs *more* instead of *less* food in the case of a fever. The prescribed diet (high calorie) for a fever is usually high in fats, carbohydrates and proteins. A fever interferes with the appetite, so you may need to give smaller feedings and give them more often. Unless there is a definite reason for excluding it, the patient is usually allowed solid food if he can chew and digest it easily. The high calorie diet also may be used whenever it is necessary to replace lost weight, as in cases of hyperthyroidism. It is used for weight-gaining in general undernutrition.

Underweight may vary, from a few pounds to a dangerous state of malnutrition. It is caused by a lack of food, the wrong kind of food or by body disturbances. The diet must include more fat-making foods than the body normally needs and may include increased amounts of protein if the muscles are wasted or shrunken. The opposite of the reducing diet, it is high in butter, cream and milk and in the carbohydrate foods such as jams, jellies, cereals, candy, breads, potatoes and plain sugar. The patient is usually given small portions 4 to 6 times daily—including between meal and bedtime snacks.

Low Calorie Diet

When the body weight is more than 10 per cent above the average weight for height and age, this type of diet can be used.

The standard tables for *normal weight* according to height and age will not apply to everyone because some people have larger bones and are more active than others—this is why a reducing or a weight-increasing diet should be prescribed by a physician. He allows for these differences and for body disturbances.

A low calorie diet is especially important in diabetes mellitus, cardiac and kidney disturbances with overweight, hypertension, gout and gallbladder disease.

Overweight comes from an oversupply of fat in the body tissues when a person takes in more food than he uses for energy. A safe reducing diet provides the necessary amounts of proteins, vitamins and minerals and cuts down on the fat-making foods. Extreme diets followed by faddists are dangerous because these diets are usually completely unbalanced.

A diet of from 1,200 to 1,800 calories per day brings a weight loss of from 1 to 3 pounds a week—gradual enough to be safe. Here are some important points about this diet:

1. The normal amount of protein is allowed; 1 pint of milk, 1 egg, 2 servings of lean meat, poultry, fish or cottage cheese will supply it.
2. The rest of the calorie allowance is divided between fruits, vegetables, butter and whole grain cereals to supply minerals and vitamins. Liberal servings of low calorie vegetables and fruits help also to allay feelings of hunger.
3. Cream and sugar are not allowed, and the amount of butter is limited to 1 teaspoon per meal.
4. Water and salt are not restricted unless there is a special reason for cutting down the amounts.
5. If the diet is cut to 1,000 calories or less, the vitamin content becomes dangerously low, and concentrates should be prescribed and taken.

High Iron Diet

The high iron diet is prescribed for patients with *anemia*, a condition in which either there is not enough blood (as a result of hemorrhage) or the red cells are deficient in quantity or quality. Iron is a necessary element in normal red cells. If it is deficient in the body, it can be supplied in the diet.

The diet given in anemia will depend on the type of anemia that the patient has. Before liver extract was developed, the diet for anemia included substantial amounts of liver to supply the body deficiency in iron and in the blood-forming substances. It was a difficult and monotonous diet, especially if the patient disliked liver. Today, doctors prescribe liver extract, to be given intramuscularly; the patient still may have some liver in his diet, but the amount required is less. The advantage of natural liver is that it contains iron, which liver extract does not. The diet for anemia also includes large amounts of red meat (kidneys, gizzards, sweetbreads and brains), green vegetables and fruits (peaches, apricots, prunes, raisins, apples and grapes) and cuts down the amount of fats, sweets and salt.

Low Carbohydrate Diet

The low carbohydrate diet is used mainly by the diabetic patient in controlling his disease. Diabetes mellitus is a disease of metabolism in which the body is either partially or completely unable to utilize sugar (glucose), owing to the failure of the pancreas to produce enough of the hormone *insulin*, which regulates the amount of sugar used by the tissues. There are 2 main aspects of the treatment of diabetes. One is by giving doses of insulin. The other is to modify the diet so that no more carbohydrates are given than are necessary for the patient to maintain health and carry on normal activities.

The diabetic's diet is calculated in relation to his weight and activities; usually, it is based on the tables of average weights that have been worked out in relation to sex, age and height. Then the total number of calories required is estimated. It must be enough to supply sufficient energy for the work, the play, the exercise and the household activities of the individual patient. A man of average build doing light work will need from 2,000 to 2,400 calories a day. If he does heavy work, he will need from 300 to 450 more. Women need somewhat fewer calories. Suitable allowance also must be made for the inactive patient with a severe diabetic condition.

Every diabetic diet must provide enough proteins, fats, carbohydrates, minerals and vitamins to maintain health. The protein requirement usually is considered first; the remaining calorie allowance is divided between the fat and the carbohydrate requirements, choosing those foods that also furnish minerals and vitamins. Tables have been worked out showing the percentages of carbohydrates in fruits and vegetables.

A general idea of these classifications is given below:

5 per cent vegetables—the leafy vegetables
10 per cent vegetables—the root vegetables
15 and 20 per cent vegetables—such as potatoes, corn and navy and lima beans
10 per cent fruits—a medium-sized orange or ½ cup of juice

You would be giving an equal amount of carbohydrate if you served any of the following fruits:

½ grapefruit	1 slice pineapple
½ apple	2 small dates
½ banana	10 large strawberries
½ pear	½ cup blueberries
2 small prunes	½ cup raspberries
2 small tangerines	1 small slice watermelon
2 plums	3 halves dried apricots
1 peach	

Fruits can be used fresh or cooked—without sugar. Canned or frozen fruits usually are not allowed because sugar has been added. Pure cane sugar is 100 per cent carbohydrate and will affect the diet if given in any quantity. Sugar substitutes are often used.

Low Sodium Diet

The low sodium diet is one which, while otherwise normal, has a decreased sodium content. This diet is given to patients with cardiovascular diseases, as well as certain kidney diseases such as nephritis and nephrosis, among others.

These patients sometimes are unable to excrete normal amounts of water and salts, with the result that these accumulate in the tissues and cause swelling (particularly in the extremities). This swelling is called *edema*.

If the sodium intake is reduced, the sodium and the water already in the tissues tend to flow back into the blood, where they are excreted. At the same time, the edema is relieved.

The diet for chronic heart disease is usually given in 5 or 6 small meals and omits gas-forming or bulky foods. Bland, easily digested foods are given. Carbohydrate and protein are given in sufficient amounts; but such foods as milk, meat, eggs, fish and fowl, all of which are high in sodium content, are limited. There is no restriction on whole-grain cereals, bread, fruits, vegetables and unsalted butter. In this diet, no salt is added to foods, and foods preserved with salt are not allowed.

The overweight cardiac patient is usually on a reducing diet as well, since weight adds to the work of the heart. In arteriosclerosis and hypertension, the diet regimen is one that prohibits excessive amounts of fluid, alcoholic beverages, carbohydrate, protein and fat.

Acid-Alkaline Diet

If this diet is planned carefully, it can meet the requirements for normal nutrition. It is used in such conditions as kidney stones and edema to adjust the reaction of urine so that salts will be held in solution. Neutral foods such as butter, sugar, oils and fat can be included. If an *alkaline urinary reaction* is desired, fruits, milk and vegetables are emphasized. If an *acid reaction* is desired, flesh meats, eggs, cereals, breads, plums, prunes and cranberries are served in large quantities. Supplementary vitamin A is usually given to reinforce the deficiency in this diet.

Low Purine Diet

This diet is usually a normal diet with restriction of foods containing purine and usually is given in cases of gout. (Purine, one of the products of protein metabolism, further breaks down into simpler products, one of which is uric acid.) Since there is a disturbance of purine metabolism in gout (see Chap. 35) foods such as meats—especially organs—fish, gravies, whole grain cereals, breads, such vegetables as spinach, cabbage, onions and asparagus are restricted. Excessive seasonings, relishes and alcoholic beverages are also eliminated. Obesity is frequently present; therefore, the patient may be placed on a low calorie diet as well (see Low Calorie Diet).

High Vitamin Diet

A well-balanced diet, plus food high in vitamins, is indicated in arthritis, pernicious anemia, hyperthyroidism, malnutrition, pregnancy and lactation. Foods to be included are: liberal amounts of eggs, milk, butter, liver, pork, whole grain cereals, citrus and other fruits and green and yellow vegetables. If the deficiency is severe, vitamins should be given in concentrated amounts. Refer to the charts on pages 212 and 214 for information about deficiency diseases and the foods which will supply the needed vitamins.

DIET IN FOOD SENSITIVENESS OR ALLERGY

"It must have been something I ate!" It probably was. People who complain of indigestion usually find that it can be traced to food. Other signs of food sensitiveness are hives, hay fever or asthma. Allergy specialists have found that milk, eggs and chocolate seem to be the great offenders—cabbage, onions, tomatoes, pork and strawberries are also high on the list. Some people are sensitive to wheat in any form, to potatoes and to seafoods. The doctor finds the troublesome food by starting with a diet of foods that seldom cause trouble, such as lamb, rice, butter, sugar and canned pears. If the symptoms disappear, other foods are added, one at a time, until the harmful food is found.

It takes skill to feed people who are highly sensitive to common foods. Substitutes containing the same food elements must be found. Then, large amounts of these, given every day, may make the person sensitive to the substitutes. Avoid this problem by rotating these foods and giving small amounts at a time. Be careful, too, about giving dishes that are prepared from the offending foods, such as cakes made with wheat flour if the person is sensitive to wheat. A person who is only moderately sensitive to a particular food may eat it occasionally—for instance, if he is sensitive to eggs, an egg twice a week will not make him uncomfortable, but he cannot eat one every day.

MAIN IDEAS OF THIS CHAPTER

A special diet is so important in the treatment of a patient that you have to find ways to get around his food prejudices by supplying needed foods in forms that he will like.

Invalid diets are classified as liquid, soft, light and full.

A special diet is planned for the needs of an individual. It may be special in form, in nutrients or both and is a modification of the normal diet.

Some common conditions that require special diets are infections, constipation, diarrhea, anemia, allergy, overweight and underweight.

ADAPTING SKILLS TO SITUATIONS

Discuss any personal experiences that you may have had with the kinds of diets mentioned in this chapter.

Mrs. Collins, 75 years old, is recovering from a fractured hip. Mrs. Collins is small and thin; she says she always has been troubled with constipation. She calls herself a "small eater" and loves tea. The doctor has put her on a full diet. What will you give Mrs. Collins to eat?

Ask your classmates to discuss with you some of the problems you possibly may meet in carrying out your menu plans.

24

FROM MARKET TO MEALS

Food goes with friendliness and hospitality, especially on such occasions as morning coffee or afternoon tea, a picnic on the shore, dinner by candlelight. To "break bread" with a man means to entertain him and honor him as a friend. The Bible speaks of manna in the wilderness and the miracle of the loaves and the fishes. Modern poets write about the delicious smell of new-baked bread and the spicy fragrance of pickles cooking. All over the world we find that each nation has its special foods—the onion soup of France, Italian ravioli, Scandinavian lutefisk, Mexican tamales, the plum pudding of England. American food is a combination of the dishes introduced by people from many lands and the specialties of the early settlers of many parts of the United States—clam chowder and baked beans in New England, Southern biscuits and fried chicken, Texas barbecue, Wisconsin cheese, crabmeat and red salmon from the Pacific Coast. The recipes of famous cooks are handed down in families, collected in cookbooks and used to prepare specialties at noted inns and restaurants.

FOOD HABITS

Nationality

The United States was settled by people from many different countries who brought their food habits with them. When you know something about these different ways of eating, you can understand why some patients are unhappy about their diets. Let us consider some examples of national food habits, always remembering that these habits, for the majority of the people anyway, are influenced by the kinds of foods that are the most plentiful and the least expensive.

Italians are accustomed to eating green, leafy vegetables because they grow abundantly; they use a great deal of macaroni and spaghetti—both are inexpensive foods. Olive oil and garlic are plentiful and flavorsome; wine is one of Italy's chief products. Goat's milk and cheese are plentiful.

The Chinese people eat more vegetables than meat because China raises very few meat-producing animals. Rice and soybeans are important crops, and now wheat-growing is a rising industry in North China; therefore, the Chinese diet is high in these cereal foods. Few people can afford to buy meat, poultry and eggs because they are scarce and very expensive.

In central Europe the principal crops are rye and barley; root vegetables are grown rather than leafy ones, although they do grow and use a great deal of cabbage. Cottage cheese, fish and pork are the main protein foods. Raw fruits and vegetables are seldom used because they do not grow plentifully in these countries.

The Mexican people use a large amount of whole corn which they grind into meal and use in various ways. Tomatoes, kidney beans and chili peppers are their main vegetables. Meats, when the family can afford them, are chicken or beef. Butter, milk and eggs are luxuries for most of the Mexican people.

Religious Customs

Religious customs affect eating habits too.

In the Catholic religion, abstinence from meat is practiced on designated fast days, such as Fridays and certain church holy days. The religious rules of the Church of Latter Day Saints (or Mormon church) exclude tea, coffee and alcoholic beverages from the diet.

The Orthodox Jewish religion follows the ancient dietary laws defined in the Torah, which impose 3 definite regulations about food. These are:

1. Animals and fowl must be killed and processed by a prescribed method.
2. Pork, as well as all sea creatures that do not have scales and fins, are forbidden.
3. Meat and dairy products must not be eaten at the same meal. There are no restrictions about using fruit, vegetables, cereals or bread (made without milk and animal fat) at any meal. In an Orthodox Jewish home you will find separate sets of dishes, cooking and washing utensils for meat and milk foods. In some Jewish hospitals the food for Orthodox Jewish patients is prepared in a special, or kosher, kitchen.

PLANNING AND PREPARING MEALS

You need up-to-date information about nutrition and preparing food (1) for your own health and (2) for the health of your patient. Diet is an important part of nursing care. Even if you do not always prepare your patient's food yourself, you are responsible for carrying out the doctor's orders. Sometimes it is necessary to consider racial and religous food customs in serving and preparing meals and diets. You cannot guide someone else in planning and preparing your patient's meals unless you yourself know how. Sometimes you may need to use tact in explaining changes in family meal plans and cooking methods; you can manage this if you stress the needs of the patient. Everybody in the family is interested in your patient's recovery.

Making a Plan

It takes imagination and skill to plan combinations of color, taste and nutrients that tempt the appetite and build a healthy body. The artist begins a picture by sketching in the outline. Planning meals is like the artist's sketch. Preparing the food and serving it is like his next step, when he paints in the trees, the sky and the bank of roses. You have enough information now to choose the foods that should be included in the daily meals of well people.

Meal Patterns. Meals follow a pattern in any household or hospital. The same basic pattern can be used to meet the nutritional needs of everyone; you begin your meal plan as a dressmaker begins a dress, by planning for the essentials as she plans for a waist, a skirt and sleeves. She must use the material she has and consider style and effective color combinations. You must think of:

1. The cost of meals
2. The types of meals
3. The attractiveness of meals
4. Foods that go together in flavor
5. Variety in texture of foods
6. Individual preferences or individual requirements (activity, age, illness or body disturbances)

Most people are used to the pattern of 3 meals a day; the hours for serving these meals may vary to fit into family schedules for school, work or leisure time. These meals are usually breakfast, lunch and dinner. If dinner is served at noon, supper is the evening meal, with much the same kind of food as would be served for a noon lunch. It is possible to keep to a familiar pattern, to include the essential foods and to provide variety through their preparation. Below are examples of adequate meals:

BREAKFAST

Fruit or fruit juice
Cereal or bread and butter
Cream, sugar
Eggs or bacon
A beverage—coffee, tea, milk or cocoa

LUNCH (OR SUPPER)

Soup and/or salad
Sandwich or roll or bread and butter
Fruit or other dessert
Beverage

DINNER

Meat, fish, cheese or eggs
Potatoes or rice or macaroni
Vegetable and/or salad
Dessert
Bread and butter
Beverage

The Most for the Least Money

Fortunately, it is possible to have a balanced diet, whether the food budget is small, medium or generous. The secret of economy is to buy wisely and not to waste anything. Therefore, you need to know how to judge the quality of fruits, vegetables and meats and how to interpret the labels on canned or packaged goods. Proper storage and the use of leftovers also help the budget. Here are some guides for planning meals and selecting food with an eye to health and the budget:

Choose ripe, firm fruits (except bananas and pears—they will ripen on standing).

Select crisp, firm vegetables of good color.

Buy foods that are in season. They cost more when they must be shipped in.

Read the labels on canned and packaged goods—labels tell the amount, the quality (grade) and the ingredients used.

Buy staples in quantity if you have storage space and if there is no danger of their spoiling before they can be used.

Buy from markets or stores where the handling and the care of food are hygienic.

Take advantage of lower food prices in reputable cash-and-carry stores. This is not always possible if you must shop by telephone.

Substitute the inexpensive for the higher-priced foods in the same food groups.

Be sure that bargains are really of good quality. You do not save anything if you have to throw away most of your purchase.

Substitute dried or evaporated milk for fresh milk; use top milk instead of cream.

Substitute fortified margarine for butter.

Substitute canned fruit juices and canned and dried fruits for the fresh articles.

Plan a week's menus in advance to save time and money. Sunday's roast can provide meat for meals later in the week; leftover peas and carrots combined are enough for another meal.

Why Do We Cook?

Although many foods can be eaten uncooked, such as the fruits and some of the vegetables that are considered daily essentials in the diet, cooking greatly increases variety in the use of foods. Cooking changes the flavor, the color, and the texture of foods so that the same foods can be served in many ways. Cooked food is also more digestible. (You remember how cooking changes starch so that digestion takes place much faster.) Cooking softens the fibers in meat, fruits and vegetables. It serves another important purpose in destroying micro-organisms and parasites in food. Pork, for instance, must be cooked thoroughly to kill trichinae which might possibly infest it. And finally, we should not underestimate the effect of the sights and the smells of cooking in stimulating our appetites and enhancing the pleasure of eating a meal which we have been awaiting eagerly.

Methods of Cooking

The ABC's of cooking are easy to learn and are important to know in preparing meals, or diets, so that foods will retain their maximum nutritive values.

Foods may be cooked by dry or moist heat. The *dry heat* methods are:

1. *Broiling:* Cooking quickly under direct heat at a high temperature which sears the surfaces. This may be done directly under a flame or in a pan on the top of the stove.
2. *Roasting or baking:* Cooking in an oven for a longer time at lower temperatures.
3. *Frying:* Cooking in fat on top of the stove. Pan-frying is cooking without fat. *Sautéing* means to fry lightly and quickly, turning often.

The *moist heat* methods are:

1. *Simmering:* Cooking in liquid for some time at temperatures below the boiling point.
2. *Braising:* Cooking in a covered pan with a small amount of fluid after searing in fat.
3. *Boiling:* Cooking in water at a temperature of 212° F.
4. *Parboiling:* Partially cooking in liquid preliminary to other cooking processes.

Sometimes it is necessary to remove the fibers or the seeds from food to aid in digestion. This is *puréeing* and is done by putting the food through a sieve. *Dicing* is cutting food into small cubes of the same size.

Cooking a Meal

Modern home economics instructors teach us

the principles of cooking with the complete meal in mind, rather than by concentrating on 1 dish only. Suppose you are one of a small group, and each person has one responsibility at a time, until everyone has learned to plan, cook, serve meals, to use leftovers and to clear away the dishes. This is much more interesting than the old way of making every person in the class practice the same thing at the same time—cooking an egg, for example. It helps you to think of the whole day's meals and of a total meal; it leads to learning ways to use time to the best advantage. A considerable part of the evening dinner can be prepared as a part of the morning work in the kitchen; a casserole dish ready to put into the oven or the makings of a salad or a dessert waiting in the refrigerator make quick work of dinner preparations.

Modern kitchens are designed to save steps; electrical appliances and other appliances and gadgets save time and make cooking easier. Packaged mixes of all kinds are available.

KITCHEN HOUSEKEEPING

Housekeeping rules for health protection apply to the care of the kitchen, too. The kitchen must be clean—no flying dust and no decaying food to tempt disease-carrying insects. People with colds or other infectious conditions should not be in the kitchen or working on the preparation of food; they are a menace to the health of the household. The care and the disposal of garbage, the care of the refrigerator and the care of dishes and cooking utensils all have an effect on health.

Safety in the Kitchen

Every year thousands of people die as a result of home accidents—many of these happen in kitchens. Here are some ways to avoid kitchen accidents:

1. Use safety matches; close the box before lighting a match; keep matches out of the reach of children.
2. Turn the handles of cooking utensils on the stove inward, to prevent upsetting them and to keep children from reaching for them.
3. Use potholders for handling hot utensils.
4. Wipe up spilled grease, water or parings immediately, to prevent slips and falls.
5. If grease catches fire in a frying pan, cover the pan tightly with a lid or throw salt or soda on the grease—*never use water*. If you do, the result will be a virtual explosion of flaming grease in your face.
6. Keep sharp knives in compartments separate from other small utensils; never cut toward your hand with a sharp knife.
7. Turn off gas burners tightly.
8. Keep sharp utensils, electric equipment, ammonia, cleaning fluids and lye out of the reach of children.
9. Keep basement and back stairways clear.

Hospital Kitchens

You can apply these kitchen housekeeping rules to the floor diet kitchens in the hospital. You will not be responsible for washing the dishes used for the main meals for patients, but you may have to wash and put away dishes that you use to prepare nourishment for them. You may also be responsible for the care of the water glasses and the pitchers used on the bedside tables, unless this work is the responsibility of a ward maid.

ATTRACTIVE SERVICE

Eye appeal is the first appeal to anyone's appetite. Can you think of a more appetizing sight than a golden-brown Thanksgiving turkey on a silver or china platter? Attractive service makes the most of food by giving it the best possible setting. Modern equipment for the table is so varied and colorful that you can make any table or any patient's tray alluring without using expensive linen, china or silver; there are many attractive and inexpensive substitutes in cotton, paper and plastics.

Your Patient's Tray

Figure 88 shows a family table; the individual place setting gives you the arrangement you would use in setting your patient's tray.

FIG. 88. Place mats, napkins, silver, china and glass are combined here to create a beautiful and harmonious patten in this table setting (Fostoria Glass Company)

If the household does not own a suitable tray, you can suggest buying one at the 5-and-10-cent store. The type with folding legs is the best to use for the person who must have all of his meals in bed, unless you have an overbed table. It is more comfortable and makes him feel safer about spilling food. Oblong, straight-sided trays are more useful than round ones for serving a full meal.

In the photograph, the fruit-cup glass is placed on its own plate on the dinner plate used for the main course. For tray service, you might bring in the main course after the patient has finished the first course of fruit, juice or soup. You can also serve the dessert after you have removed the main course plate. You can be more certain of keeping hot food hot, and cold food cold, if you serve a meal in courses and the tray will be less crowded.

Always use a tray to carry a glass of water or any kind of drink or nourishment; choose one of an appropriate size—a plate is an acceptable substitute for a tray. Most bed patients need a drinking tube; paper straws are not expensive and can be discarded after use, while glass tubes do break, and glass and plastic tubes are sometimes difficult to clean.

Key Points. These are the key points in table and tray setting:

The mat or the cloth and the napkin are spotless—no traces of this morning's orange juice or yesterday's gravy! These table linens may be made of white or colored linen, cotton or paper materials.

The china, the glass and the silver are sparkling clean.

The dishes and the silver are arranged correctly and conveniently. The silver is placed in the order in which it is to be used, the first pieces farthest from the plate. The knife (blade turned in) and the spoons are at the right, the forks at the left. Cup and pitcher handles are turned to the right.

None of the glasses or the silver used should be associated with medicines.

A flower or a bit of green adds a colorful touch.

Serving Food. Follow these simple rules when you serve food:

Time the preparation of a meal so that the food can be served when it is ready. Some dishes are spoiled if they must stand.

Keep the servings small. The sight of quantities of food may take away the appetite.

Serve hot foods hot and cold foods cold. Cover hot dishes.

Avoid dribbles of food on the edges of dishes.

Fill cups and glasses about three quarters full to avoid spilling the contents.

PREPARING THE PATIENT

A tired patient, or one in pain, will neither take nor digest food well. Plan to carry out a lengthy or an uncomfortable procedure well before or after meal times. Emotional upsets affect the appetite and the digestion. Patients get the best effects from food when they are comfortable, happy and relaxed. As far as possible, have your patient ready for a meal before you bring the tray. Wash his hands; make him comfortable by giving him the bedpan, if necessary. Adjust his pillows and backrest if he is allowed to sit up; a patient with a poor appetite sometimes eats more if you can plan to give him a meal at the times when he is allowed to sit up in bed or in a chair. Do not let him get overtired before the tray arrives.

SOME BASIC FOODS AND THEIR PREPARATION

Beverages

A beverage is any fluid taken into the body to relieve thirst, provide nourishment and soothe or stimulate body processes. Most beverages are composed chiefly of water, but often other ingredients are added. Milk is an important beverage because it has great nutritive value. Many people are accustomed to drinking milk and are fond of it, and as a drink it has many variations. Frequently, eggs are added to milk to make eggnog, or chocolate syrup for chocolate milk. Eggs also add extra nourishment to fruit drinks. Fruit and vegetable juices are popular beverages because they are refreshing; they also add necessary vitamins to the diet. Coffee and tea are popular drinks, especially with meals. Coffee and tea (without cream or sugar) have no food value, but each contains a stimulant—caffeine in coffee and theine in tea. Both of these beverages acquire a bitter taste if they are boiled or allowed to stand for any length of time, since this permits excessive extraction of a substance called tannin.

Here are some key points to remember about beverages:

Serve promptly after preparation.

Serve hot beverages hot, serve cold beverages cold.

Avoid overdilution.

Serve in attractive glasses of an appropriate size.

Garnish attractively to tempt a jaded appetite.

Avoid oversweetening of fruit juices.

Milk. Milk is an indispensable and popular food. Large quantities are consumed in the United States—it has been estimated that over 50 billion quarts are produced and consumed yearly. The recommendations about milk in our daily diet show how important this food is (see p. 203). Although milk contains most of the substances known to be essential for adequate nutrition, it is low in iron, and an anemia could develop on a straight milk diet. The amount of vitamin C is also low, particularly in pasteurized milk, but milk is a good source of vitamin A and calcium. It is also a good medium for carrying vitamin D.

The nutrients in milk are readily absorbed—the protein is a complete one; the fat is in an emulsified form which can be acted upon readily by the digestive juices; the carbohydrate is lactose, which is a sugar peculiarly suited to the young because it is less sweet, less soluble and more stable than some of the other sugars.

Safe milk must be assured for health protection; health regulations and inspection in most communities make sure that dairy herds, milk handlers and conditions for milk production meet safe standards. Today most milk is pasteurized for safety (see p. 56). Pasteurized milk is nutritionally equal to raw milk except for vitamin content; vitamins are usually added before it is marketed.

Many kinds of milk are on the market today in different forms. The information that follows will explain them to you:

Whole milk: Milk with all its components of water, fat, protein, carbohydrate and minerals.

Fat-free (skim) milk: Whole milk with practically all of the fat removed.

Buttermilk: Skim milk which is a by-product of butter-making. Buttermilk can be made artificially (cultured milk) by adding lactic acid bacteria cultures to skim milk.

Irradiated milk: Whole or skim milk to which vitamin D has been added to meet standards of 400 international units (I.U.) per quart.

Cream: The fat in whole milk which has risen to the surface or has been separated out mechanically. It is designated as *light* or *heavy*, according to the fat content. *Half and half* is composed of milk and cream in equal proportions which has a fat content of about 11 per cent.

Homogenized milk: Whole milk which has been processed to break the fat into small droplets distributed throughout the liquid so that the fat does not rise to the surface as cream.

Evaporated milk: Whole milk with approximately 60 per cent of the water removed. (You can make whole milk from equal parts of evaporated milk and water.)

Condensed milk: Whole milk which has been evaporated after the addition of sugar.

Dried milk: Whole milk from which the water has been extracted, leaving a fine powder.

Refrigeration preserves the nutritive content of milk. It should be kept in clean, tightly covered containers to prevent contamination. The *three C's* in the care of milk are *Clean, Covered* and *Cold.*

Milk can be used in the diet in other ways than as a beverage. Some of the common uses are in soups and desserts and in reinforcing other foods such as breads, cereals, casserole dishes, mashed potatoes, etc.

Cheese

Cheese is the curd which has been separated out by coagulating milk. There are over 400 varieties of cheese; the difference in varieties is due to a number of things and depends upon: the kind of milk that is used; the amount and the kinds of seasonings; the amount of moisture retained; the type of bacteria or mold used in ripening; the method of curdling the milk and the temperature and the humidity during the ripening process. There are 3 general types of cheese:

Hard: Time-ripened or cured cheese, such as Cheddar, Swiss, Edam and Gouda. American Cheddar is very popular in this country.

Semihard: Mold-ripened cheese, such as Roquefort, blue, Gorgonzola.

Soft: Unripened cheese, such as cottage and cream cheese.

A type of cheese that is widely used in America is called *process cheese.* It is made from one or more types of natural cheese, ground and blended with an emulsifying agent.

Cheese is high in protein and can be used as an economical substitute for meat in the diet. It also contains important minerals and vitamins and rather large amounts of the essential amino acids. It can be used in meals as a main dish and in sandwiches, salads, sauces, salad dressings, casserole dishes and as a dessert.

Points to remember in storing and using cheese are:

Keep it wrapped.
Keep it in a cool place.
Keep soft cheese in the refrigerator.
Cook cheese at a low temperature—temperatures above its melting point of 160° F. will make it rubbery and stringy.

Eggs

Eggs are such a valuable addition to the diet that they should be used in some form every day, with a possible minimum of 4 eggs weekly. Egg white is a complete protein; egg yolk provides fat, minerals and vitamins—notably vitamin A. They can be used as a substitute for meat and in a wide variety of ways. Since eggs are so digestible they are a "natural" for invalid diets.

Eggs are graded according to appearance (color, size, cleanliness and freedom from cracks) and on internal quality. Candling (concentrating light on the shell) will show the size of the air cell in the larger end of the egg which indicates whether or not some of the fluid has evaporated and how much. A large air cell is an indication that the egg has been stored too long or in a place that is too warm. As an egg ages, the white becomes more liquid, and the water content of the egg yolk increases. A fresh egg will sink to the bottom of a pan of cold water.

Graded in relation to quality. *AA* means the finest quality of fresh eggs; *A*, excellent quality; *B*, acceptable for cooking; *C*, still acceptable for cooking. The size of an egg has no relation to its quality, but it does affect the price. Eggs are marked as jumbo, extra large, large, medium and small. The nutritive value of brown and white eggs is the same. Cold storage eggs (kept by refrigeration) have the same nutritive value as fresh eggs and are more economical. Freezing and drying are other ways of preserving eggs.

Eggs can be used as breakfast or lunch dishes: soft-boiled, coddled, poached, scrambled and in omelets. They can be used as reinforcements in desserts and in combination dishes, in sandwiches and salads.

In cooking an egg it is important to know that the egg white becomes tough and unpalatable if it is cooked at high temperatures (212° F.). A simmering temperature is best for soft-boiling or hard-boiling or poaching eggs.

Cereals

Cereals are the seeds of grains. Cereal foods are the most economical source of energy. The cost of production is low, and they are easily transported; they keep well and can be used in many ways at every meal. The grains most commonly used for food are wheat, rice, corn, barley, oats and rye. Wheat is used most extensively in our country, but rice is used more extensively throughout the world; the natives of China, India and Japan use it as a basic staple food. Corn is used in great quantities throughout the Southern states—their cornbreads and spoon breads have gained renown throughout America. Rye and barley are used by European people in their breads more commonly than these grains are used in the United States; however, the heavy breads which these flours produce are becoming more popular here.

The seed, or kernel, of cereal grains is divided into 4 parts. Unfortunately, the outer layers, *bran* and *aleurone*, are removed in milling, taking with them valuable roughage, vitamins, minerals and proteins. The *endosperm*, the white center, is the part milled for highly refined flour. The *germ*, the heart of the grain, is the best source of protein and valuable B vitamins. Since many of these valuable nutrients are lost in milling, most states have adopted regulations requiring the addition of vitamins and minerals to cereal products. Whole grain cereals are still superior to the enriched products and of better nutritive value.

Breakfast cereals are so numerous that there are ones to fit any taste or fancy. The prepared cereals and those with sugar added are higher priced than the uncooked cereals. Both cooked and prepared cereals are used as breakfast dishes, in breads and in desserts.

Cooking of cereals softens the fibers and makes the starch more digestible. Quick-cooking cereals are popular because it takes less time to prepare them.

Fruits

The seeds of many plants are contained in a fleshy growth, which, with the seeds, makes up the type of food we call fruit. Fruits are not high in fuel value (dried fruits are an exception) but do contain many important vitamins and minerals. The carbohydrate content varies widely in different fruits; percentagewise they have been classified as containing 6, 9, 12, 15 and 18 or more per cent. The many variations in color, texture and flavor of fruits give a pleasing variety to the diet. Their effectiveness in stimulating the appetite and their function as a regulator of body processes add to their dietary importance. Fruits make up part of the Basic 4; 1 citrus fruit and 1 other are recommended for inclusion in the daily diet. Because of its vitamin C content, orange juice is usually in the daily diet of babies and children.

It is interesting to note that although fruits contain acids, most of them do not have acid effects in the body but help to maintain an alkaline balance in body fluids. Cranberries, rhubarb, plums and prunes are exceptions and are used in certain diets for that reason.

Fruits and fruit juices can be used raw or cooked, as appetizers, salads or desserts at any meal. Because they can be canned, dried, preserved or frozen they can be included in the diet the year round.

Things to remember in selecting and preparing fruits are:

Use tree-ripened fruit if possible.

Wash thoroughly to remove dirt or insect spray contamination.

Use peeled or cut fruits as soon as possible after they are prepared. Lemon juice will prevent the discoloration of fresh fruits.

Most fruits are more palatable if served chilled.

Simmering is the best way to cook fruits.

In cooking fruit, sugar added at the beginning will help to retain the shape of fruit. Added at the end of the cooking process, sugar helps to bring out the flavor.

Use frozen fruits as soon as they are thawed—do not refreeze.

Cover citrus fruit juices tightly to prevent loss of flavor.

Vegetables

Vegetables are the edible parts of plants. They are essential in the diet because they contain many important minerals and vitamins (A-C-B-complex). They add great variety to the menu as well as making it colorful and attractive. Vegetables are included as one of the Basic 4 groups (see chart, p. 203), which shows that they supply a substantial portion of our daily diet requirements. Because most vegetables are fibrous they aid digestion and elimination. The cost of vegetables varies greatly, depending upon abundance, distance in shipping, the cost of harvesting and weather conditions. Vegetables of good quality are crisp, ripe, firm and free from blemishes. Wilted or overripe vegetables have less nutritive value.

Canned and frozen vegetables are popular because they are convenient to use; modern preservation technics conserve most of the original nutritive value of the fresh food. Fresh vegetables should be used or properly stored as soon as possible after they are purchased; root vegetables keep best in a cool, dark, dry place; other vegetables should be stored in the vegetable compartment of the refrigerator.

Some vegetables can be served raw, preserving all their food values; it is important to know how to cook vegetables properly, to retain as much of food value as possible; important points to observe are:

Cook vegetables in their skins when possible.

Peel vegetables as thin as possible to retain the many valuable minerals and vitamins that are in the layer just beneath the skin.

Cook vegetables whole or in large pieces if possible to reduce the amount of surface exposed to air.

Cook vegetables in small quantities of water.

Prepare vegetables near to time of cooking—do not soak in water for long periods. If they have been soaking in water, you will retain the water-soluble vitamins by cooking in the same liquid.

Use vegetable cooking water in sauces or gravies since it is rich in vitamins and minerals.

Avoid overcooking and serve hot.

The most common methods of cooking vegetables are boiling, steaming and baking; sautéing and broiling add further variety.

Meats

Meat is the great source of protein in the diet. In this discussion of meats, poultry and fish will be included, although in referring to meats we usually mean the flesh of animals, such as beef, pork, lamb, mutton and veal. Meat has good nutritive value in that it contains, besides protein, fat and many valuable minerals. It is rich in iron, phosphorus, sulfur, potassium and iodine (the last especially in salt water fish). Vitamin A is found in liver, and oils from some fish supply large amounts of vitamin A and D. Meat is a popular food and it has a long-lasting, satisfying quality not duplicated in other foods. The price of meat varies widely, and there are many inexpensive cuts and kinds which can be used. Organ meats such as tongue, liver, brains, heart and sweetbreads can be used as replacement for the more common meats.

In selecting meat we should consider these factors:

1. *Safety of Meat.* (See p. 57 for additional information.) Federal inspection of meat which is handled interstate ensures protection for the consumer. The government seal (a stamp of purple vegetable coloring material) indicates that the meat is free from disease and has been handled by sanitary methods.

2. *Grades of Meat.* The U. S. Government

grades meat as Prime, Choice, Good, Standard, Commercial, Utility, Cutter and Canner. The last 2 are used mostly in manufacturing and are rarely found in the retail markets. U. S. Choice and Good are the highest grades that are generally found in retail markets.

3. *Appearance of Flesh Meats.*

Color—beef, bright cherry red; lamb, reddish pink; pork, white to grayish pink; veal, light pink.

Presence of fat—beef, well marbled with white or creamy fat; lamb, creamy and slightly pinkish; veal, white and brittle

Tissue—elastic and firm, fine grained and velvet to touch.

Pleasant odor

4. *Cuts.* The choice of a tender or of a less tender cut should be determined by the method of cooking, the price and your budget. A less expensive cut from a high-grade carcass is preferable to a best cut from a low-grade animal; the amount of waste in bone, fat and gristle should be considered.

5. *Appearance of Poultry.*

Compact, with rounded, firm breast, meaty thighs

Soft, smooth, dry skin

Pliable breastbone in young fowl

6. *Appearance of Fish.*

Bright skin, adherent scales

Firm body with little slime on skin

Important Points

Important points to observe in the care and the cookery of meat, poultry and fish are listed below:

Remove wrapping and cover lightly with wax paper.

Keep in the refrigerator—no longer than 1 or 2 days. Organ and ground meats spoil more rapidly, so use them immediately.

Handle carefully to avoid bacterial contamination.

Do not refreeze.

Cook tender cuts of meat by dry heat—broiling (oven or pan) and baking. Roast or bake at a temperature of 300° F. Pork requires longer cooking time to ensure the destruction of trichinae.

Cook less tender cuts of meat by moist heat—braising, simmering or stewing. Vinegar, tomato juice or commercial tenderizer help to make meat more tender.

When cooking shell fish: oysters are cooked sufficiently when the edges curl; shrimp should be deveined before they are eaten.

HOSPITAL FOOD SERVICE

The regular meals and the special diets for the patients in a hospital are planned and prepared by the dietary department, which is headed by the chief dietitian. Hot food may be served from heated carts brought into the wards or the floor diet kitchens, where the trays are set up. Each tray is labeled with the patient's name, and the type of his diet and should be checked with the posted diet list. Every hospital has its own system of food service.

Train yourself to check each tray with the diet ordered. Learn to notice whether the napkin, a spoon or a glass is missing before you carry the tray to the patient. See that bedside tables or overbed tables are ready; see that the patients are prepared for their meals. If you have a patient who must be fed, serve the trays to the other patients first. You are responsible for recording the necessary observations on the patients' charts and also for calling the attention of the head nurse to any unusual occurrence, from a poor appetite or the refusal of food, to nausea or vomiting. This is important for the patient because you will need direction about what to do next to provide him with the food that is so essential for his recovery.

MAIN IDEAS OF THIS CHAPTER

Health, fun, skill and imagination enter into the proper use of food.

A knowledge of nutrition is of little value unless you know how to plan meals and to prepare food.

The Basic 4 food groups are a practical guide in planning balanced meals.

In planning meals, you consider the types of meals, the cost, the appearance, the flavor and the texture of foods, as well as the individual requirements and preferences of people.

Knowing how to market, how to store food and how to use leftovers saves money.

Manufacturers now add essential nutrients to many foods.

Modern methods and inventions make meal planning and cooking easy.

The proper cooking of meats and vegetables preserves their food values; you can provide a balanced diet with the less expensive foods properly cooked.

Kitchen housekeeping should protect health by observing the rules for cleanliness and safety.

Attractive table service encourages good nutrition.

A comfortable, relaxed patient is more likely to enjoy and digest his food than one who is tense and tired, or in pain.

The basic rules about food service apply to both the hospital and the home.

ADAPTING SKILLS TO SITUATIONS

Discuss one of your own family recipes with your classmates and point out its nutrition values.

Compare what you ate yesterday with the food listed in the Daily Food Guide, p. 204.

Look in your home refrigerator and list the possibilities for new dishes from the leftovers you find.

Plan a week's menu for a family where there are some differences in individual energy requirements and where there is a person who dislikes some necessary food.

What would you do if one of your hospital patients refused his dinner tray?

Suppose your home patient refused his supper—would you call the doctor immediately?

If a patient refused a meal, would you give him some milk later? Why or why not?

Find out how it feels to be fed. Have someone feed you a meal and notice the good and the bad points about the procedure.

Unit Six:

Fundamentals of Nursing

25

THE PATIENT IN HIS SURROUNDINGS

Although your first experience with patients will be in a hospital, directions for their care also apply to the care of the patient who is sick at home or who needs additional nursing care after discharge from the hospital. The hospital has all the necessary nursing equipment, but in the home the patient must provide it. The local visiting nurse service and the Red Cross Chapter frequently have equipment they lend for home use; some types of equipment can be rented from a surgical supply house. It may be necessary for the patient to purchase special equipment that is essential for his care; however, you can sometimes improvise by using things the patient already owns and has in his home.

THE PATIENT'S IMMEDIATE SURROUNDINGS

Hospitals today give a great deal of thought to providing patients with surroundings that are pleasant as well as practical. Walls that once were a muddy beige may now be a restful pale green or blue; draperies adorn bare windows; attractive furniture has replaced those dull brown or glaring white pieces. The patient has a light that he can control and adjust. He may have a telephone and a radio with earphones; television equipment is also available. In a ward or semiprivate room, cubicle curtains give him privacy. Air-conditioning equipment regulates temperature and ventilation.

These changes are due to the realization that pleasant surroundings have important psychological effects on a patient as well as to the scientific improvement in hospital equipment. Also, the modern emphasis on rehabilitation and self-help has led hospitals to adopt such devices as side rails on corridor walls and steadying handholds on bathtubs and toilets.

You will not find every modern device in many of the smaller institutions. Therefore, it is necessary to know how to make a patient comfortable and how to give him protection if some of these devices are lacking. A safe and comfortable environment is necessary for good nursing wherever you are—in a hospital or in a patient's home.

Ventilation

Ventilation means providing a supply of clean air, with the proper amount of moisture, at a comfortable temperature. The problems of ventilation vary with the climate, the season, the living quarters and individual preferences. Every building has some natural ventilation because air comes in through walls and cracks and other openings. In a house, individual rooms, doors, windows, transoms and fireplaces provide ventilation. Large buildings install mechanical systems to force the air in and out.

In any case, some way must be found to keep the air moving because the comforting and healthful effects of good ventilation are produced by the movement of the air currents against the skin.

Air. Pure air is composed of gases in approximately these percentages: oxygen, 20 per cent; carbon dioxide, 0.04 per cent; and nitrogen, 78 per cent. Of course, we never breathe absolutely pure air because air always contains organisms and particles of dust; we do want clean air, which is air containing a minimum amount of dust and other particles and is free from unpleasant odors. It is hard to provide clean air in crowded cities or in crowded rooms because the amount of dirt and body waste products in any place increases with the number of people in it. This is why we need to protect health in a community with regulations on smoke, dust, garbage and refuse.

Animals, including man, use oxygen to burn food in their bodies; they give off carbon dioxide wastes. Plants do exactly the opposite: they take in and use carbon dioxide and give off oxygen. This is Nature's thrifty way of using supplies. The proportions of the gases in the air keep remarkably even under ordinary conditions. Only when the air in a comparatively small closed space is flooded with a poisonous material (such as carbon monoxide from a kerosene or gasoline stove) and the amount of the outside air coming in is limited, does the oxygen supply run dangerously low. Poor ventilation affects the skin, not the lungs, and is more uncomfortable than it is dangerous. Science has shown us, too, that night air is not poisonous (as people once thought) nor is fresh, outside air dangerous for sick people. On the other hand, overexposure to cold air can be harmful. Medical authorities tell us the belief that a window must be thrown wide open at night, regardless of the temperature outside, is nonsense—in fact, it is not essential to open the window at all.

How to Ventilate a Room

Warm air is lighter than cold air, and outside air is colder than inside air; if you open a window from the top and from the bottom, the warmed used air escapes, and the cooler fresh air comes in. Sometimes it is impossible to open a window from the top, but you can still get a circulation of air by opening it at the bottom and leaving a door or a transom open. If you cannot open the windows in a patient's room, open them in the next room and leave the adjoining door open. An electric fan will keep the air moving in a room. The draft in a fireplace always provides ventilation. Water in a pan, or in a container made to hook over a radiator in a room, will increase the amount of moisture in the air.

Precautions in Ventilation. Always protect your patient's body from contact with strong air currents or drafts, to prevent chilling. Open a window that is not parallel with his bed; if his bed and the door are parallel, use a doorstop to prop the door part way open. If there is no choice of windows, put a screen between the window and the bed. You can improvise a screen with chairs or a clothes rack and blankets.

Inexpensive window ventilators of metal or cloth are available. They let in air, but break the force of the air currents. Place an electric fan so that air currents will not blow directly on the patient.

When a patient is out of bed, you can protect his body from chilling by using extra clothing and blankets and by placing his chair out of the way of drafts.

Air-conditioning equipment now washes and strains fresh air, heats or cools it to a comfortable temperature, brings it to the proper degree of humidity and circulates it.

Temperature

The food-burning process that goes on in the body cells produces heat—more than the body needs to keep its internal temperature normal. The extra heat is given off into the air, some of it through the breath and the excretions, but most of it through the skin. The heat given off rises above the cool air next to the body and is taken up by cooler objects, such as the walls and the furniture and the things we touch; a great deal of heat is used up in the evaporation of the moisture from the body surface. If a large amount of heat remains in the air or if too much is removed, we feel the uncomfortable effects on our bodies. You can prove this by noticing what happens when you take a shower on a hot day and leave the water on your skin; you feel cool as some of the heat from your body is removed in the process of evaporating the extra moisture. But, on a cold day, if you do the same thing, you will feel chilly because the air currents that strike your skin are less warm than your body, and the excess moisture will conduct the heat from your body into the cold air.

Comfort, then, is the right balance between the heat your body produces and the heat it loses. It is the temperature of the air around you that affects your comfort. The balance between the heat you lose and the heat you produce must be right. The room temperature that keeps this balance is between 65° and 70° F.

Hot weather, artificial heat or body activity will increase the amount of heat in a room; cold weather, lack of artificial heat and inactivity will decrease it. Apply these principles to the care of patients, and you can see why you need to be sensitive to the temperature of a room and to adjust it to individual needs.

Moisture

Water conducts heat. If the air is cold and full of moisture, heat is conducted away from the body rapidly; yet on a hot moist day, perspiration evaporates more slowly from the skin because the air already has about all the moisture it can hold. The percentage of moisture, the *humidity*, is higher in hot than in cold air. The body feels most comfortable when the humidity of the air is about 70 per cent. Moist, hot air feels cooler if it is moving.

Odors

Odors come from body discharges, perspiration and destruction of body cells, industrial processes, cooking and decaying food. Odors are most noticeable when they are first smelled or when they become stronger. This explains why people get used to an odor and may not realize that a room is stuffy. Unpleasant odors take away the appetite.

Dust

As you know, dust carries harmful organisms and settles on every surface. Dust-catching litter, such as yesterday's newspaper, falling flower petals or dust fluffs from the bedclothes, accumulates in any room and around every patient. The air in a room carries dust that is scattered about by careless flicks of a dry dust cloth.

Soft cloths, such as cheesecloth, dampened with oil or waxy furniture polish, preserve the finish on polished wood and pick up dust instead of scattering it. Furniture polishes should be applied to a dust cloth and used sparingly; dust collects in excess oil and makes dirty patches on furniture; soapy water will dull and remove the finish on oiled or waxed, painted or varnished surfaces if it is not rinsed off. Wet dust cloths can be used to clean painted surfaces. A dry or slightly dampened dust cloth is best for varnished or shellacked finishes.

Wash used dust cloths in plenty of hot water and dry them. Store oiled dust cloths in a metal container to prevent fire hazards.

Heat or the alcohol in perfumes, medicines and beverages damages the finish on wood surfaces. Protect wood surfaces from liquids or from hot dishes by using trays or heat-proof and moisture-proof pads.

Using Electrical Equipment

Remember that water conducts electricity, so be sure that your hands are dry before you insert a plug in an electric outlet; never turn a light off or on, or touch a radio when you are in the bathtub or standing on a wet floor. Always disconnect equipment by grasping the plug—pulling on the cord loosens it from its plug connection. Always have frayed or worn cords repaired to prevent short circuits and blown fuses. Disconnect equipment or turn off motors as soon as you have finished using electrical apparatus. Motors are lubricated with grease packed inside; some equipment is lubricated with light oil. Motors should not be overheated or allowed to run dry; excess heat or burning odors from a running motor indicate that something is wrong.

Flowers and Plants

In a hospital you need to be sure that flowers or plants are not lost or mixed up. When flowers are delivered, look for the card and take it to the patient with the flowers. Label each patient's flowers if they are removed to a common room at night.

Care of Equipment

Once you know how to take care of wood surfaces, enamelware, glass, rubber goods and linens for the bed or the table, you can apply what you have learned to either housekeeping or nursing equipment. Oil will have the same effect on an enema tube as will grease on a rubber-covered dish drainer. Boiling water poured over a glass measuring graduate will behave like boiling water poured on a drinking glass at the kitchen sink. The scouring powder used on enamel saucepans will be equally effective on enamel bath basins.

The care of different types of equipment is discussed in Chapter 29 in relation to asepsis.

THE PRACTICAL NURSE IN THE HOSPITAL

Your work schedule in the hospital will be different in some ways from the plan you make in a home. You will have more than one patient to take care of and you will need to consider hospital routines. Meal hours, doctors' rounds, patients' appointments for the operating room or the x-ray room and for laboratory procedures must also be considered when you make your work plan. You may be asked temporarily to assist with the emergencies that come up on a busy service. In any situation, remember that your patients are your first responsibility.

In a hospital, much of the housekeeping may be taken care of by other workers; but you are responsible for keeping your patient's immediate surroundings neat and clean, and the head nurse expects you to cooperate with other workers who may help with this part of your work.

THE CARE OF A PATIENT AT HOME

Many practical nurses are employed in hospitals today, but there is also a great need for practical nurses to take care of patients who are sick in their own homes. Modern medicine encourages home care for patients who do not need the special services of a hospital during a long-term illness. Many patients are happier in a home environment. With a shortage of hospital beds, home care makes more beds available for acutely ill patients. The practical nurse who is employed by the patient as a private duty nurse has closer relations with the patient's family, and these interpersonal relations must be handled tactfully. She also is responsible for planning the patient's care, as well as carrying it out—a real challenge to her executive ability.

Make a Plan

As a private duty nurse, you will need to make a work plan that fits in with your patient's needs and the activities of the household. Organize your day and your week to take care of the jobs that must be done every day and those you do less often. Give yourself a margin for emergencies that may come up. It is not necessary to put down every detail in minutes; you can estimate approximately how long it will take to do a number of related jobs. For instance, "7:30 to 8:30—prepare breakfast, get patient ready and serve breakfast," covers a block of time. You always can move the time limits one way or the other if you need to.

Plan to save yourself steps, if your patient is on the second floor, by collecting equipment when you go up or down stairs—a basket is very convenient for this. If you can, arrange to stay on one floor until you finish what you have to do. You can work faster and more efficiently if you collect all the necessary equipment before you begin.

Caring for the Bathroom

If your patient has a private bathroom, you are responsible for keeping it clean. You will see that a family bathroom is clean after you have used it for your patient. You should notice whether or not poisonous drugs are kept in the cabinet where children can get at them. The toilet bowl cleanser is poison and should be kept in a safe place and plainly marked.

Decide on the best place in the bathroom to keep your patient's equipment and keep it out of the way, as much as possible; you may need to encourage children in the household to help to keep the bathroom tidy.

Safety in the Home

Every year, more people are injured in accidents in their own homes than in any other way. They slip on skidding rugs, fall from improvised steps, take medicines in the dark or from unlabeled bottles, tip hot liquids over themselves, go to sleep holding lighted cigarettes or are careless about electrical equipment. Everybody should know the ordinary safety rules. As a nurse, you need to be on the lookout for safety hazards because you will be in houses that are unfamiliar to you; you may also be able to point out dangers of which the members of a household are not aware.

Other Hazards. Remove small rugs from places on slippery floors that you, or other members of the household, cross constantly. These may be in your patient's room, in the room of an elderly member of the family or at the top or the bottom of a stairway. Be careful about dark, unlighted corners and be sure to replace burned-out light bulbs at once. Children can be taught to remove wagons, roller skates, blocks or other toys from places where people may stumble over them.

Possessions

Most of us have definite feelings about our possessions; we value them because they are useful, expensive, beautiful, old or sentimentally dear. Therefore, you can understand why it is important to take the best possible care of other people's things. Your patients will expect you to know the ordinary things about taking care of a house. Many people never have had to keep house; even the experts are continually learning new things and changing their methods to keep up with scientific progress.

Responsibilities

A nurse is always responsible for the care of her patient's room and his bathroom; sometimes you may need to give a certain amount of attention to other parts of the house to relieve your patient's mind if an emergency comes up. Your first obligation is to your patient, but cooperation with the other members of the household is also an obligation; you should try to time your work to interfere as little as possible with other people's activities.

THE PATIENT UNIT

We call the place where the patient's bed is *the patient unit.* It includes the bed and the other furniture and most of the equipment used in his care. This unit may be in a private or a semiprivate room or in a ward. In the patient's home, it is some room in the house which may or may not be his own.

This is the basic equipment for a patient unit:

Furniture: Bed, bedside table and chair, lamp, overbed table

Linen: Sheets, drawsheet, pillow cases, blankets, spread, bath blanket, face towel, bath towel, washcloth, bedpan cover, gown

Toilet equipment: Wash basin, soapdish, toothbrush container, kidney basin, tumbler, comb and brush, toothbrush, orangewood stick, nail brush, bedpan (and urinal for male patient)

Other equipment: Moisture-proof drawsheet, water pitcher and drinking glass, thermometer in container, call bell or button, screen or curtain

Equipment for nursing treatments is kept outside the unit. In the hospital, it is kept in the treatment, tray or utility room. In the home, you can keep it in the bathroom or other suitable place—a dressing tray and thermometer equipment can be kept on the bureau in the patient's room.

The unit should always be complete and ready to use. This saves steps and time and delay that is wearing for the patient.

To Restock the Unit

Check and replace used supplies; check the equipment and inspect it for breaks, cracks or rough places that might injure patient or nurse.

Replace broken or damaged equipment and report the damage to the head nurse so that the equipment can be replaced or repaired. It is customary in many hospitals to keep an inventory of the equipment on each floor as a basis for ordering new or replacing damaged articles.

Cleaning the Patient Unit After Use

For years, cleaning the unit had been the nurse's responsibility. In many hospitals today, auxiliary personnel attached to the nursing or the housekeeping departments are responsible for this procedure, thus giving nurses more time for the care of patients. However, every nurse should know how to clean a unit according to the policy of the hospital and principles of asepsis. In some situations this procedure is still the nurse's responsibility.

Everything in the unit is considered soiled and must be cleaned before it can be used by another patient. This prevents the possibility of transferring infection from one person to another, and it is esthetically satisfying to the patient to know that he is not using someone else's things.

You clean the unit after a patient has been discharged from the hospital, transferred to another room or ward or after a patient dies. It is important to handle pieces of bed linen separately, making certain none of the patient's possessions is discarded with the soiled bedclothes. Remember that the hospital is responsible if a patient's personal possessions are lost. Be sure that you leave the patient's room clean and in order when you have finished taking care of him at home. Choose the cleaning agents suitable for the furniture in the room.

KEY POINTS IN THE PROCEDURE

Avoid touching your uniform with soiled linen or equipment.

Principle: *Microorganisms are transmitted by contact.*

Use a dampened brush to remove dust or lint, thus avoiding the scattering of microorganisms.

Principle: *Microorganisms are found on dust particles.*

Wash furniture with soap and water or detergent and rinse in clean water and dry.

Principle: *Cleansing removes organisms and foreign material.*

Clean the least soiled areas first.

Principle: *Moving from a soiled area to a cleaner area spreads organisms.*

Wash all equipment used by the patient with soap and water or detergent before sterilizing it.

Principle: *Cleansing helps to make sterilization effective.*

26

THE ADMISSION AND DISCHARGE OF THE HOSPITAL PATIENT

ADMITTING THE PATIENT

The Patient's Feelings

The reception which a patient receives when he enters a hospital can affect his progress during his entire illness. People have definite feelings about hospitals; no one looks forward to being ill, and if you consider a patient's personal fears about his condition, his worries about his home and his bodily pain, you may have some idea of how he looks upon entering the hospital.

If this is his first hospital experience, he may be embarrassed because personal services have to be performed for him. Superstitions and ignorance about his body or his limited understanding of the English language may present added difficulties.

The patient is in a similar position when a nurse comes to the home. The family will want a nurse who is competent, considerate and easy to get along with. Their past experience with nurses also will affect their attitude.

Be Friendly. Wherever you meet the patient, the most important thing is to be friendly. The patient must feel at ease with you and trust you if you are going to gain his cooperation and confidence. You will not know very much about his background at this first meeting, but you do not need this information to be courteous and friendly. Introduce yourself at once; learn the patient's name and use it. It makes a patient feel that he is more than a body in a room or a bed number.

Explain. You can sense when a person is worried, frightened or confused. Put the new patient at ease by explaining the arrangement of his room, by making comments on everyday things, by letting him know that you were expecting him. You need to be sensitive to his mood at the time—do not begin by trying to be funny with a frightened person. Feel your way. Explain hospital procedures if this is his first experience; if he has been in a hospital before, let him see that you understand that he is familiar with one.

These guides apply to the family, too. They will feel more confident if they know that you are kind and that they can trust you. Tell them the hours for visiting and the general rules of the hospital (such as bringing food for the patient). Explain that the patient will have 24-hour care and that the hospital will contact them immediately if an emergency should arise. Let them see that you understand their anxiety, and that you see them as individuals whom you are happy to know. Treat them as welcome guests and try to make them comfortable while they are visiting the patient.

The family often feels in the way and helpless when one of its members is ill. Nurses, who have considerable authority over patients and their families, must understand these feelings. The patient and his family will not always say how they feel, for fear that the hospital personnel will treat them badly if they are critical.

When this happens, the patient or his family will wait until they leave to criticize—then the reputation of the hospital suffers in the community.

The Admitting Department

Certain general routines are necessary for the admission of the patient and are usually carried out in a separate department. A member of the clerical staff records such information as age, sex, marital status and whether or not the patient has hospital insurance. An identification band also may be applied at this time. During these preliminary procedures, every effort is made to make the patient feel at home and to alleviate the feeling of tenseness he may be experiencing.

Someone from the department or a member of the auxiliary personnel then brings the patient to his unit. Every hospital has its own admitting procedures, but most follow the general pattern that is described here.

The Patient Arrives

Before the patient arrives, check the unit to be sure that it is equipped completely and in order and open the bed. The patient may walk in, arrive in a wheelchair or on a stretcher. Unless there are orders to the contrary, the patient undresses, puts on a hospital gown and goes to bed in preparation for an examination by a house physician—a routine procedure in most hospitals.

Removing the Patient's Clothes. Give the patient whatever assistance he may need in undressing; sometimes a member of the family can be of assistance, particularly when the patient is a child for he may resist being undressed by a stranger or he may not understand going to bed during the day.

If the patient is a female, push a garment off one shoulder. Push the sleeve down in a roll to the wrist, then slip it off. Unfasten the waistband; push all the lower garments down as far as you can around the hips—then ask the patient to raise her hips (if she is lying down) while you pull the clothes down. Take the upper garments off over the head in the same manner. If the garments must come off over the head, slip the arms from the sleeves, push the clothing up to the hips and ask the patient to raise her hips. Pull the garments up to the shoulders—you can turn the patient's shoulders first to one side and then to the other and slip the garments off over the face; raise the head and remove them. Gather the clothes together into as much of a roll as possible to keep them from dragging over the patient's face. Put on the gown. Cover the patient with a bath blanket and work under it as much as possible to avoid exposing or embarrassing her. If you remove the garments above the waist first and put on her gown, she will not be exposed while you take off her lower garments.

Placing the Patient in Bed. If a patient is weak or tired, remove his shoes and outdoor clothing and put him on the bed immediately—cover him with a bath blanket or with the bedclothes. This prevents more fatigue. He already has exerted an extra effort in making the trip to the hospital.

Find out from the head nurse what the patient is allowed to do for himself; show him the bathroom and put his bathrobe and slippers where he can reach them, if he is allowed bathroom privileges. If necessary, give him instructions about such things as using the urinal instead of the toilet, because a urine specimen is to be saved. Arrange his things and tell him where they are; put special items on his bedside table where he can reach them. Show him how the communication system works and put a signal cord where he can reach it. Be sure that the shades are adjusted; regulate the ventilation and adjust the bed for his comfort. If the patient will be getting in and out of bed without assistance, adjust the bedside footstool for his convenience.

Explain how the bed works as you adjust it—tell him that if it is not comfortable, you can change it. Inform him of the hours for meals and that you will find out what he may have to eat and when. Sometimes a patient goes without a meal because he does not know what to expect, and the nurses have overlooked him. If he is in semiprivate accommodations, introduce him to the other patients.

Toilet Equipment. Every hospital has its own

system for supplying such essential toilet articles as toothbrushes, toothpaste, combs and toilet soap. Usually the supplies are available for purchase in the hospital pharmacy or gift shop if the hospital does not supply them. Many patients have personal preferences and like to provide these articles themselves. Disposable tissues are provided, either at the hospital's or the patient's expense.

Patients usually bring their own bathrobes and slippers with them. However, most hospitals provide these articles if the patients are unable to supply them. For bed patients it is customary to use the gowns provided by the hospital. They can be sent to the hospital laundry and are easy to put on and remove. Explain to the patient that the hospital gown is used for its convenience, comfort and economy. During convalescence or as patients become ambulatory, they may wear their own nightgowns, pajamas or bed jackets, provided they are able to make arrangement for the laundering of these articles outside of the hospital.

Private and ward patients alike should learn as soon as possible that individual equipment is set aside for them during their stay in the hospital—these are *their* things and no one else uses them. Any one of us ought to be able to feel confident that a ward is as safe and clean a place as a private room. The luxuries are lacking in a ward, but the necessities are provided, and no patient should have any reason to feel that equipment used for him is also used indiscriminately for someone else. This is especially important in an open ward where the patients have an opportunity to see so much of what goes on with all kinds of illnesses.

Routine Procedures Included in Admission

The temperature, pulse and respiration tell important facts about the patient's condition. You must decide whether to take a rectal, a mouth or an axillary temperature; you know how to choose the best method. Write down the readings on a slip of paper to be recorded on the patient's chart.

Obtain a specimen of urine and send it to the laboratory. Explain that this is information that the doctor needs in planning the patient's care. If there is anything unusual about the specimen, ask the head nurse to look at it before you send it to the laboratory. Record these observations on the chart.

Of course, many people make very careful preparations for coming to a hospital; they obviously do not need a bath or attention given to personal grooming. Others may not have learned good health habits, or they may have been admitted as a result of an accident or a sudden illness which gave them little or no time to attend to the details of grooming. If the patient's body is not clean, he is given a bath; if possible, this should be done before the house physician comes to examine him.

Essential Information

The following information is essential for the doctor and for the patient's record:

1. Date and hour of admission and his name —his ward number or section.
2. How he was admitted—walking, in a wheelchair, on a stretcher.
3. Temperature, pulse and respiration.
4. Amount of urine voided for specimen—unusual appearance, if any—note that it was sent to the laboratory or that the patient was unable to void.
5. Any symptoms that the patient tells you—headache, nausea, etc.
6. What you notice about him—flushed face, swelling, discomfort, fear, irritability, difficulty in moving.
7. Weight and height.

Care of the Patient's Clothing

A private-room patient has more leeway with his belongings than other patients. Clothing can be hung in the closet of his room; he has a place for his bathrobe and slippers; dresser drawers provide space for personal things.

Ward patients' clothing may be sent to a special room for storage. No matter what the condition of the clothes, they should be placed on hangers and protected from dust. Many hospitals provide garment bags for this purpose. The ward patient has little space for personal belongings at his bedside. If he is using a robe and slippers provided by the hospital they should be set aside for him and not serve as common property in the department. List every item of clothing for every patient. It is important to follow the system that the hospital has established; it protects the patient, the hospital and you.

Care of the Patient's Valuables

Valuables, such as a watch, jewelry and money must be put in a safe place. Usually the items are listed and kept in the hospital safe. When the patient learns that he will not be able to keep these things at his bedside or wear them, he may prefer to send them home with his family. Again, it is important to list them carefully for everyone's protection. The fact that the patient or a member of the family signs the slip verifies the list. Explain why it is best to put valuables in a safe place. Once a wristwatch went through a hospital laundry because the patient forgot to remove it from under her pillow; it was gathered up with the sheet when the bed was changed. Even if the patient wears her watch all the time, she will not be allowed to wear it or any jewelry if she goes to the operating room. Then the problem of keeping it safe until she can wear it again is a difficult one, for a great many people go in and out of a patient's room, including visitors. Take it to the hospital safe and note that this has been done.

Report

Report to the head nurse when you have completed the admission procedures. She is a busy person and does not always know exactly when a new patient reaches her department. She is the one who is responsible for seeing that there are instructions about the patient. She relays the order for his diet to the dietary department and notifies the house physician of the patient's arrival. Report everything you can about the patient; you have been making notes on paper and in your head all the time you were with him. Anything that you can tell her is important for the patient's care.

WHEN THE PATIENT IS DISCHARGED

Many medical authorities believe that the patient improves faster at home if he is happy there and has the care that he needs. Even if there is little hope of physical improvement, he may feel more comfortable and contented at home. Many patients leave hospitals today while they still need considerable medical and nursing care. The modern hospital is trying to assume its responsibility as a community health center; part of its job is to see that everything has been done to assure the patient the kind of care he needs when he goes home. Everybody who can help is brought in to make a plan with the patient and his family—doctors and nurses, the dietary and the social service departments.

Some hospitals have set up a home-care program so that patients can go home and still have medical and nursing care. The hospital provides medical supervision and makes arrangements with the community visiting nurse service for the necessary nursing care. Good health care means doing as much as possible to help the patient who is almost well to *stay well.*

Some families employ a professional or a practical nurse to take care of the patient when he goes home. Sometimes a member of the family can take over. The plan that any patient or his family makes depends on the amount of care that is needed, who is available to give it and the financial circumstances.

Making a Plan

In the hospital, the head nurse is responsible for seeing that the patient or the family has the necessary instruction. She begins to make a plan as soon as she knows that the patient is about to be discharged. You may be asked to assist with some part of it. You should know what such a plan includes so that you can give her any information that you have about the patient's problems. The plan includes the same procedures to be performed when you are leaving a home patient. Some of the things that the person who will be responsible for the home care must know are:

The day and the date for the next visit to or by the doctor or to the clinic for a checkup. Remind him to get advice from the doctor when he needs it.

How and when to give medications. Explain the need for care, caution and accuracy. Teach him to do it exactly as you do.

How to change dressings if the patient has them. Show how and explain why. Tell him where you get the dressings and how to get them sterilized if sterile dressings are used and are unsterile when received.

The amount of rest that the patient must have and the amount of activity that he is allowed.

The diet. Describe it as simply as possible—name the foods that are not allowed, the foods that are musts every day and the amounts allowed. The patient might make out a day's menu and discuss it with you. In the hospital the dietitian usually gives instructions about a special diet.

For a bed patient, give instructions about making the bed, giving the bath, moving and turning the patient, giving the bedpan, adjusting the pillows and keeping good body alignment.

Equipment needed. Find out what he already has at home. Tell the family what they must buy and discuss substitutes that can be used for some equipment. Discuss the need for a hospital bed or the way to use blocks or other means to make a home bed higher; the need for a wheelchair and the possibility of renting equipment from a medical supply house.

Danger signs to watch for. These would vary with the individual and may include an abnormal reaction to insulin or other medications, excessive drainage or bleeding on the dressings or pressure areas from casts, splints, or prolonged bed rest.

Ways that you have learned to get the patient to cooperate with you; the patient's own preferences; things to be firm about and those you can be lenient about without doing harm.

Things the patient can do for himself. He should be encouraged to continue doing them. If the family knows that this is a part of getting well, they are less likely to coddle the patient unnecessarily.

Services offered by the visiting nurse association. Sometimes a visit once or twice a week is enough to take care of special treatments or essential nursing.

As you take care of a patient, you have an opportunity to learn a great deal about his habits, his problems, his interests and his family. This is what helps you to plan his future care.

The Day He Leaves

Before the day comes for the patient to go home, discuss the best time to leave. The family is instructed to bring clothing, pillows or blankets, if they are needed. If he is anxious to go home, as most patients are, he probably can hardly wait to get dressed when the day arrives. If he seems to be eager to be ready, and his condition permits it, he can get dressed and rest on his bed until it is time to leave. These are the things to be done before the patient leaves:

The discharge order must be signed by the doctor. This prevents misunderstandings and protects the patient and the hospital.

The medications he is to take with him are ready.

A wheelchair is ready to take him to the hospital exit. He may walk if he has been an up-patient and his condition warrants it. Otherwise, use a wheelchair to prevent fatigue.

His clothes and valuables are returned to him; he checks the list with the nurse and signs it. As was previously stated, this list, signed when he came in and before he goes home, is a safety measure.

The nurse takes him to the business office to pay his bill, or a member of the family may attend to this detail. If the patient or a member of the family says the bill is paid, check with the business office before you take the patient to the waiting car or taxi. You tactfully can say that every nurse must report when she brings down a patient for discharge. Accompany the patient to the car and help him to get in; this gives him a feeling of security.

The Release

Sometimes a patient leaves the hospital against the doctor's advice. He must then sign a release slip which relieves the doctor and the hospital of responsibility for any harm that may come to him as a result of leaving. Parents or relatives sometimes take the responsibility of removing the patient from the hospital against the doctor's wishes; then they must sign the release slip.

The nurse who assists with discharging the patient brings the chart up to date, records the hour of discharge and how the patient left—walking, in a wheelchair or by ambulance. This rounds out the record of his stay in the hospital. When you leave a patient whom you have been taking care of at home, you are the one who is discharged. You should record the hour that you leave and sign your name.

Every hospital has its own routine for discharging a patient. You will be told what your part in that routine will be. After the patient leaves, his unit is cleaned and prepared for the next patient. You, or a member of the auxiliary personnel, will be responsible for cleaning the unit.

27

ASSISTING THE PHYSICIAN

Judgment is needed when taking care of patients to decide what can be done safely without an order, and the procedures for which the doctor or the head nurse must leave definite orders. Sometimes a professional nurse must perform even the simplest procedures for a patient if he is critically ill or must have special treatments or close scientific observation. You learn that certain symptoms are serious and that others are only signs of discomfort.

In a hospital, the professional nurse interprets the doctor's orders to you; someone is always there to turn to if advice or help is needed. Everything about your patient is reported to your team captain or to the professional nurse to whom you are responsible; you make a record on each patient's chart.

When taking care of a patient in his home, you have more responsibility. There is no one to turn to immediately, so your judgment has to be good, and your patient's record complete and accurate.

THE DOCTOR'S ORDERS

You rely on the doctor's orders, and in turn, the doctor will depend on you to interpret his orders correctly, to make accurate observations about the patient and to record them. The doctor's orders tell you what to do, and nursing procedures show you how to do it. Doctors use abbreviations and symbols that all nurses learn. Many of them are abbreviations of Latin words also used in prescriptions, and a druggist translates them into the language that the patient can understand. It is important for the druggist to see what the doctor has written; this prevents mistakes that might be made in copying or in reading a prescription over the telephone. Abbreviations also are used for other orders about the patient.

The doctor may give verbal directions to explain the written ones. Read his orders before he leaves to be sure that you understand them. Some orders are absolute and positive; others may require judgment on your part. You must be sure you know what the doctor means when he writes "S.S. enema (soapsuds), if necessary." Does he mean if the patient says he is uncomfortable, or if his bowels have not moved you will give it right away, or that you will wait to see whether perhaps the patient will have a bowel movement?

THE PATIENT'S CHART

The chart is the story of the patient—his care and his progress, hour by hour. Hospitals have a variety of forms that go on every chart. These records are filed after the patient goes home and are the written evidence of what was done for him while he was in the hospital. Sometimes a patient is dissatisfied with his medical or hospital treatment and brings suit against the doctor or the hospital for negligence or injury; the patient's chart is important legal evidence in a lawsuit.

The standard hospital chart includes forms for recording the temperature, the pulse and the respiration, the fluid intake and the output, the laboratory and the x-ray reports, the doctors orders, the patient's history and the bedside notes. The charting system used will be explained to you in the individual hospital. You can purchase printed record forms to use for your bedside notes in the patient's home.

How to Chart

Most of the observations recorded on the patient's chart are made by the nurses. It is important to know how to chart plainly and accurately; you must know also what is important to record. You learn the customary expressions to use, but you must say what you mean, and people must be able to read and understand it. Nurses' notes are always printed because individual handwriting is often difficult to read. Practice until you can print clearly and neatly.

For the Record

You record what you learn about the patient and what is done for him and what he tells you about himself. Record favorable changes in the patient's condition—they are as important as the unfavorable ones. There are standard expressions to use; perhaps soon some of them will be improved to give a better picture of the patient as a person. It was a shock to one patient, a nurse who had the doctor's permission to see her chart, to find herself described as a "middle-aged female lying quietly in bed!"

The chart is information for the doctor about his patient. It should be accurate and complete. The notes should not ramble, nor should they be so brief that they really tell nothing. Some hospital patients are ill for months, and their charts become very bulky. Others need little special care; they have baths routinely, eat regular meals, and nothing seems to happen which can be recorded; yet, many observations might be made about the patient as a person. If efforts are being directed toward rehabilitation, there should be something to report.

Personal and Private

The chart is very personal, and many of the recordings are in language that the layman does not understand. This is why the patient and his family are not permitted to read it—they may misunderstand or become apprehensive and worried without reason. Hospital charts are usually kept in a rack near the head nurse's desk or the nurses' station. In the home, the chart should be kept in a drawer of the patient's bureau where it is out of sight, and the family is not tempted to read it.

The Right Words

Charting is an important part of every nursing procedure that you do. In this text, the section on symptoms gives you the descriptive words to use and indicates how to record the observations you make. It is sometimes difficult to describe a patient's moods and attitudes, but you will learn with practice. You have to be careful not to make snap judgments about a patient, or to let your own prejudices influence your observations. You have many guides to use; you will use them more efficiently as you have more experience with sick people. There is always a temptation to judge one patient entirely by another—remember that individuals are different.

Avoid using too many abbreviations; some are permitted because they save time and space—for example, *lab.* for laboratory, *T.P.R.* for temperature, pulse and respiration and $\bar{c}$ for with. A list of the abbreviations commonly used with medications is included in Chapter 30.

THE PHYSICAL EXAMINATION

Health authorities have tried with some success to have people accept the idea of having a regular physical examination. They emphasize its importance in preventing disease, and they urge everyone under 40 years of age to have an annual health examination—twice a year for those over 40. Unfortunately, many do not follow this advice, and, therefore, too many people develop illnesses which might have been avoided by a timely check-up.

The doctor relies on the physical examination and the patient's history for much of his information about the patient. The history tells him about the patient's parents, his past illnesses, his habits and his present complaints. From the physical examination he learns the patient's height and weight and makes general observations. He examines the body from head to toe including the eyes, ears, nose, mouth, throat, neck, chest, breasts, abdomen and extremities. He listens to the heart and lung sounds. A vaginal, rectal or other such internal examinations are performed as indicated. (A vaginal examination is considered essential for women over 35 because of the possibility of cancer.)

Certain laboratory tests, such as urine and blood examinations and a chest x-ray are included routinely as part of the physical examination.

Assisting With the Physical Examination of an Adult

The doctor usually questions the patient first and writes down what is said. In a hospital, an intern may take this history. You should already have told the patient that he is to have an examination and explained the reason for it. You come in when the doctor is ready. Remember your own health examination and do everything you can to make the patient feel comfortable and unembarrassed. You arrange the covering sheets, hand equipment to the doctor and put the specimens in a safe place. If the patient's temperature has not been taken, you do that also. The patient will lie flat on his back with 1 pillow under his head for most of the examination; he sits up while the doctor examines his chest. The doctor may also want him to stand so that he can check his posture and examine his spine. Spread paper towels on the floor on which he can stand.

A physical examination is most satisfactory if the patient is relaxed and cooperative. Explaining the procedure beforehand and assuring privacy for him will contribute to his mental comfort and make him less tense and apprehensive. The patient wears a hospital gown, which is easy to adjust and affords movement without exertion. This will enable the doctor to examine him without exposing him unduly. Equipment should be assembled beforehand:

Hospital gown or pajamas
Sheet or bath blanket
Basin for soiled instruments
Tape measure
Tongue depressors
A tray with:
- Flashlight
- Rubber gloves
- Lubricant

Ophthalmoscope
Otoscope
Blood pressure apparatus
Percussion hammer
Red and blue pencils

Add a rectal and a vaginal speculum if the doctor wants to examine the rectum or the vagina.

When the examination is over, have the patient put on his gown; draw up the bedclothes, remove the bath blanket and make the patient comfortable. He may want another pillow under his head or the back rest raised and his bed adjusted. If specimens were sent to the laboratory, make a note on the chart of the time and the kind of specimen sent.

Assisting With a Physical Examination of an Infant or a Child

The equipment is the same as for an adult. One of the most important aids in this examination is the child's cooperation; if he is too young or too ill to understand how to cooperate, you will have to restrain him for parts of the examination. Figure 89 shows how to restrain an infant or a small child with a blanket; Figure 90 shows how to restrain an infant or a child while the doctor examines the front chest and the abdomen. For examination of the spine and the chest, hold him upright, one of your arms around his legs, the other supporting the lower end of his spine, his head against your shoulder. Restraint frightens the child more than the examination—no one likes interference with his body movements. So do your best to get a child to cooperate without restraint.

Putting a Patient in Different Body Positions

Patients are sometimes put in special positions as a part of their treatment or examination; a number of different positions are used for a physical examination, for nursing treatments, for tests and to obtain specimens. You will put patients in some of these positions and see others used, and you should know how to assist the patient and adjust the necessary drapes.

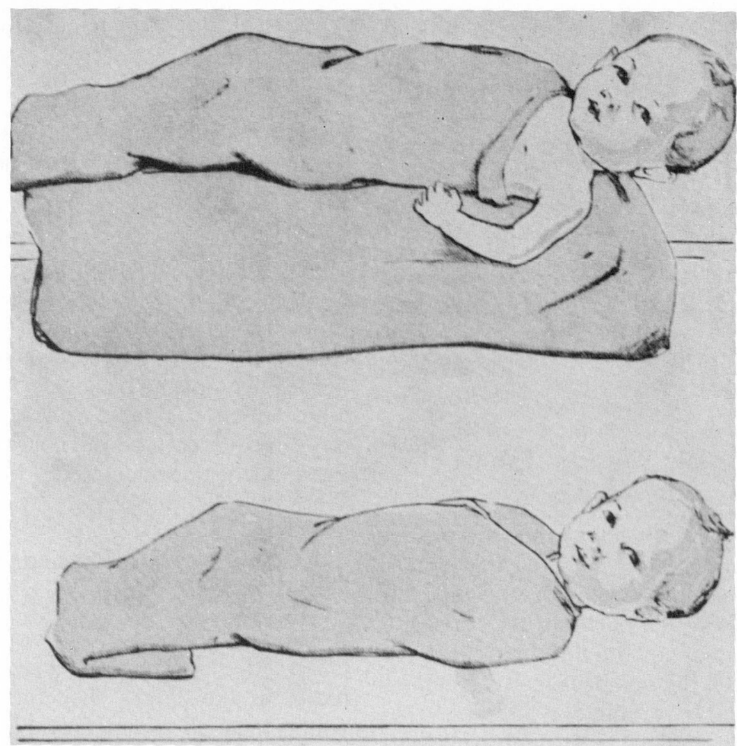

FIG. 89. Method of restraining an infant with a blanket. The 2 steps of the procedure are illustrated.

Horizontal Recumbent Position. (Fig. 91A.) Put the patient on his back, with 1 pillow under his head with the legs extended, the arms above his head, folded on his chest or lying along his body. This is his position during most of a physical examination. Cover him with a bath blanket.

Dorsal Recumbent Position. (Fig. 91B.) Put the patient on his back with the knees flexed and the soles of his feet flat on the bed. Put a sheet or a bath blanket folded once across his chest; put a second sheet crosswise over his thighs and legs; wrap the lower ends of the sheet around the legs and the feet and expose the genital region. This is the position for a vaginal examination. You cannot put a patient with injured legs or knees in this position.

Prone Position. (Fig. 91C.) Put the patient on his abdomen—turn his head sidewise for comfort; put his arms above his head or along his body; cover him with a bath blanket. This position is used to examine a patient's spine and

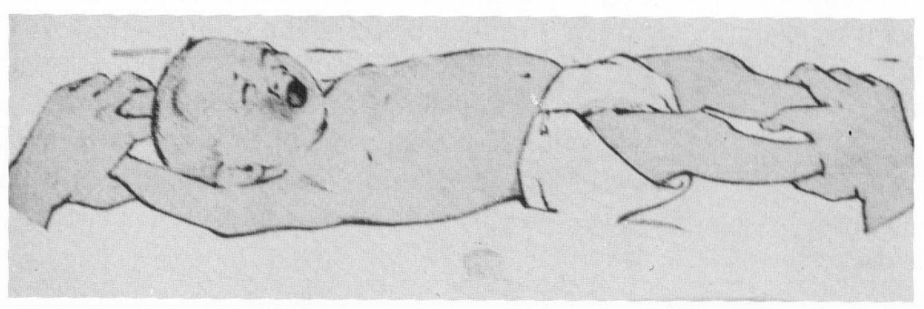

FIG. 90. Method of restraining an infant for an examination of his head, anterior chest and abdomen. (Wolf, L.: Nursing, New York, Appleton-Century)

back or when a patient has had a back injury or an operation. If a patient has an abdominal incision, is unconscious or has difficulty in breathing, he cannot lie in this position.

Sims's Position. (Fig. 91D.) Put the patient on his left side with a pillow under his head; flex his right knee against his abdomen; flex his left knee but not as much; put his left arm behind his body—his right arm in the position most comfortable for him. Cover him with a bath blanket. This is the position for a rectal examination. A patient with leg injuries or arthritis cannot assume this position.

Fowler's Position. (Fig. 92A.) Adjust a back rest to the desired height; raise the bed section under the patient's knees. As a brace against his feet and to keep him from sliding down, a rolled pillow can be placed between the patient's feet and the foot of the bed. This position is used for most patients to help drainage or to make breathing easier. Watch the patient for dizziness or faintness.

Knee-Chest Position. (Fig. 92B.) Put the patient on her knees, with her chest resting on the bed; rest her elbows on the bed or put her arms above her head. The thighs should be straight up and down, the legs flat on the bed. This position is used for rectal and vaginal

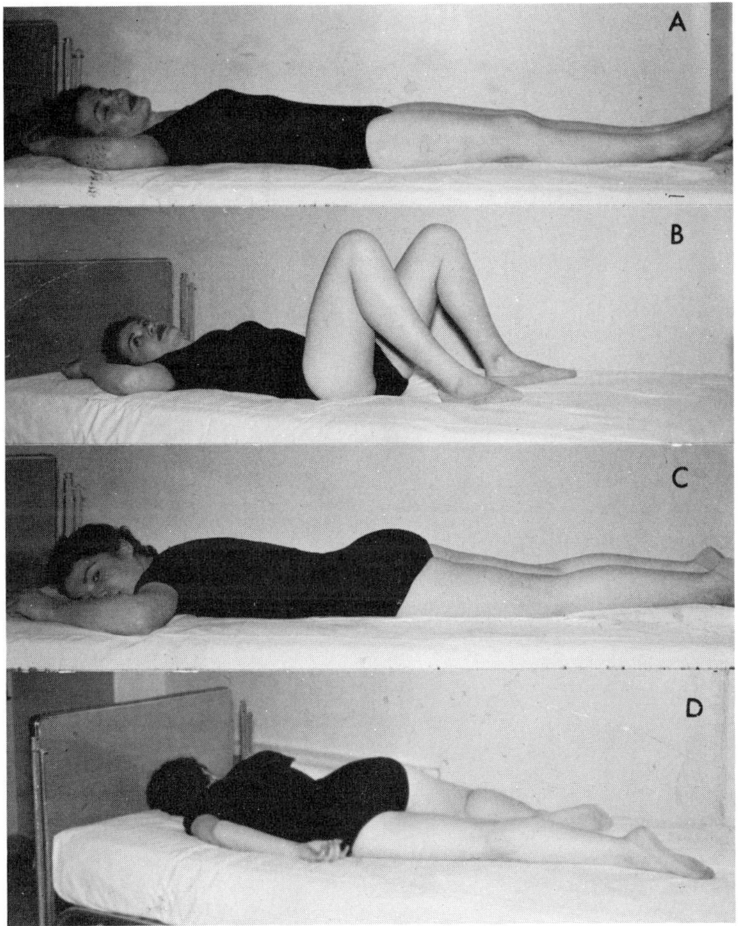

Fig. 91. Body Positions. (A) The horizontal recumbent position. (B) The dorsal recumbent position. (C) The prone position. (D) Sims's position.

examinations and as a treatment to bring the uterus into a normal position. A patient in this position might become dizzy or faint and fall out of bed so do not leave her alone.

Dorsal Lithotomy Position. (Fig. 92C.) The patient is placed in the same position as dorsal recumbent except that the legs are well separated and the thighs and the legs are more acutely flexed. This position is used for examinations of the urinary bladder, vagina, cervix, rectum and perineum. Many times the patient is turned sideways in bed and the buttocks are brought to the extreme edge of the bed. It is a common position used on an examination table where the legs are supported by stirrups on upright rods. The draping is similar to that used for the dorsal recumbent position.

The Gynecologic Examination

Some women are likely to look upon a vaginal, or gynecologic examination with mixed feelings—partly dread and partly embarrassment. A woman may fear the examination because she thinks that it may be painful or that it may show that something is wrong. She also may be embarrassed by a dread of physical exposure or of questions which the doctor may ask. This is when the nurse's matter-of-fact, friendly attitude is very comforting, as is her assurance that she will stay with the patient throughout the examination. An informed patient is a more relaxed one, and relaxation is an aid to the doctor in obtaining the information he wants.

Assisting With a Vaginal Examination. The

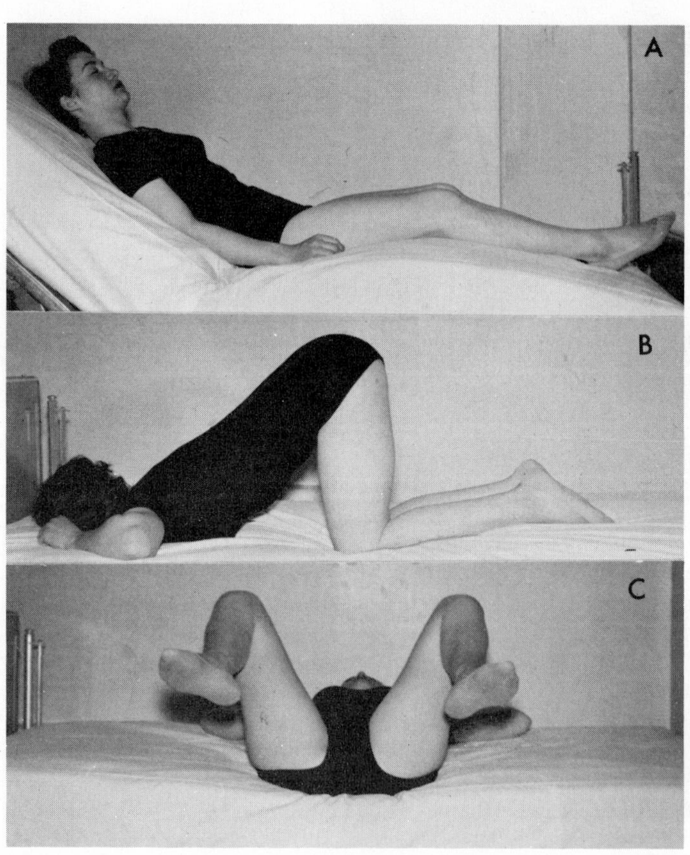

Fig. 92. Body Positions. (A) Fowler's position. (B) The knee-chest position. (C) The dorsal lithotomy position.

purpose of a vaginal examination is to examine the external genitals and the pelvic organs for signs of irritation, growths, displacement or other abnormal conditions and to take vaginal smears.

The patient is given a gown to protect the upper part of her body during the examination. Be sure that she empties her bladder prior to being examined. You assist the doctor by putting the patient in the lithotomy position (see p. 254), adjusting the drape and placing the examining tray conveniently near.

The doctor palpates the pelvic organs by inserting 2 fingers in the vagina, at the same time placing his other hand on the patient's lower abdomen. He inspects the vagina and cervix after inserting the lubricated speculum. If he wants to take smears of vaginal or cervical secretions, he uses applicators and glass slides.

Stay by the patient, helping her to relax. After the examination is over, wipe traces of the lubricating jelly from the perineum and adjust her position; provide her with a sanitary pad if necessary. Label the specimens if any have been taken and send or take them to the laboratory. Make a note of this on the patient's chart, with the time and the kind of specimen. Care for the equipment as indicated in your procedure sheet.

These are the guides to remember in carrying out this procedure:

The lithotomy position, with the knees drawn up, relaxes abdominal muscles.

Mental reassurance also promotes relaxation.

Lubrication of the speculum reduces discomfort during the insertion.

Proper aftercare of the equipment prevents infection.

The Rectal Examination

The purpose of the rectal examination is to inspect the rectum for signs of hemorrhoids, fissures, growths or irritations, or for examination after surgery on the rectum. Rectal examinations are made also periodically during labor.

A rectal examination is usually included in the physical examination of a man over 40 years of age because digital examination of the rectum is an aid in discovering cancer of the prostate gland while it is still in an early stage.

The patient is placed in either the dorsal recumbent position with the knees flexed or in the Sims's position (see p. 253). However, if the patient has a rectal condition which requires examination with special instruments (proctoscopy) the patient is placed in the knee-chest position (see p. 254). This procedure is usually carried out in the operating room or treatment room. An enema, to empty the lower bowel, precedes a proctoscopic examination. The nurse explains the procedure beforehand, shows the patient how to assume the knee-chest position and encourages him to have patience with its awkwardness.

28

HEALTH AND COMFORT MEASURES FOR THE PATIENT

THE PATIENT'S NEEDS

Many of the needs of patients are the normal needs of every human being plus the special needs connected with illness. The essential needs of patients are for:

Cleanliness and comfort	Pleasant and safe surroundings
Proper food	Correct body position and exercise
Sleep and rest	Essential medical treatment
Elimination of body wastes	Restorative encouragement
Emotional and spiritual support	Diversional interests

As you can see, the above needs are physical, mental and emotional; the patient's progress toward recovery, his comfort and his happiness depend upon the extent to which these needs are satisfied. Meeting them involves teamwork between the doctor, the professional nurse, the practical nurse, the aide, the social worker and the technicians—in fact, by anyone who comes in contact with the patient, including the patient's family. If any one team member fails to do his or her part, the patient suffers.

Meeting the Patient's Needs

The doctor prescribes the treatment in an illness, and the nurse carries out his orders. The doctor makes a brief visit to check on the patient's condition and progress, but the nurse is the member of the team on whom the patient must rely for constant care and comfort throughout the 24 hours. Therefore, in addition to her responsibility for nursing care, she must be sensitive to the patient's fears and worries, she must be observant of physical symptoms and aware of the problems an individual patient is facing. Patients say they would like to find help for their worries as well as treatment for a disease or injury—they want someone to be interested in them.* True interest begins with a sympathetic attitude toward a patient's problems.

NURSING PROCEDURES

Practical nursing students usually learn nursing procedures as they are practiced in the hospital where they are having their nursing experience. There may be minor differences in procedures. For instance, the policy in one institution may be to make square corners on the beds—in another the corners may be diagonal. Disposable equipment may be widely used or utensils may be made of different materials. Such differences do not matter. However, there are reasons why certain steps in every nursing procedure must be followed to achieve the desired results. These reasons are the principles, or known facts, which guide you in making a procedure effective. The steps tell you what to do, and the principles tell you why. It is

* Brown, Esther Lucile: Newer Dimensions of Patient Care, Russell Sage Foundation, 1961.

important to know the guiding principles for the key points in every procedure.

Individual procedures vary, but the general directions given here must be followed for each one. To avoid tiresome repetition, they are not listed with the individual procedures but must be included as an important part of each.

GENERAL DIRECTIONS

Wash your hands before carrying out a procedure and after it is completed.

Assemble all the necessary equipment so that the procedure can be carried out as expeditiously and effectively as possible.

Explain the procedure to the patient to allay his fears of pain or discomfort. Patients are likely to be apprehensive about apparatus or machines, especially if appliances have electrical connections. They also may fear sharp instruments or needles, applications of heat or cold, or any apparatus that covers the face. If possible, avoid using the words "hurt" or "painful." Instead, say "you will feel a pin prick" or "you will have to lie in one position, but we will help to make you comfortable." Emphasize the positive aspects—"it won't take long" or "it will make you feel better." A patient will be more cooperative if he knows what to expect. Never tell a patient "there is nothing to it" when you know a procedure has some painful or uncomfortable aspects. Make him as comfortable as possible before beginning the procedure.

Assure the patient of privacy by closing the door or using cubicle curtains or screens.

Care for the equipment and store it as indicated by hospital policies and by the procedure itself (wash, sterilize, store or return to surgical supply department).

Record the treatment, the time it was given and the results, including any unusual patient reactions.

Grouping Nursing Procedures

You carry out many nursing procedures for the patient's health and grooming and to make him comfortable. You often do them in connection with each other, but each procedure is complete in itself. Some procedures are grouped together because they are associated with a time of day or a special kind of treatment—these blocks of nursing care are known to nurses by group names. Here are some examples:

EARLY MORNING CARE—given before breakfast for health and comfort:

Washing face and hands
Brushing teeth
Giving bedpan or urinal
Adjusting bed and bedclothes
Taking temperature, pulse and respiration
Changing patient's position
Adjusting table for the tray

LATER MORNING CARE—given after breakfast for health and comfort:

Giving bath
Making bed with clean linen
Changing patient's position
Giving back rub
Combing hair
Caring for nails
Tidying and dusting unit
Caring for flowers

EVENING CARE—given for health and comfort—prepares the patient for his supper and for the night:

Washing face and hands
Brushing teeth
Giving back rub
Combing and tidying hair
Giving bedpan or urinal
Changing patient's position
Adjusting bed and bedclothes
Adjusting table for the tray

There are many more combinations which you will learn as you go along, but you must learn to do the separate procedures first before you can give complete care to a patient. If you are uncertain about one or more of them, your care of the patient will not give him the most skillful combination of everything that he needs—it will be spotty and uneven. Some procedures are repeated many times during the day, whenever they are necessary. Often you do bits of a procedure, such as changing only the drawsheet instead of the entire bed. This chapter shows how to do the things that build the *whole* around-the-clock care in all types of patient care.

Progressive Patient Care

Progressive patient care is organized to give patients the amount of medical and nursing care which they need with different degrees of illness. It is set up this way to provide:

Intensive care—for the critically ill patient.

Intermediate care—a moderate amount of care.

Self-care—for the patient who is physically able to take care of himself but needs restorative care, such as teaching and rehabilitative activities, or who is having diagnostic tests.

Long-term rehabilitative care—requires hospital services.

Home care—the patient is at home, but the hospital plans and helps with his care.

An *intensive care* unit may be set up in subunits of 1, 2, 3 or 4 beds, equipped with routine and emergency supplies and equipment, such as oxygen tents, suction machines, routine and emergency drugs. An intercom system enables the nurse to communicate with those outside without having to leave the unit. Patients needing intensive care may be cardiacs, patients who are hemorrhaging or patients who have been severely injured in accidents. The average stay of patients in an intensive care unit is 5 days. Patients are admitted directly to the unit; the professional nurse in charge is aided by professional and practical nurses and an aide, or aides.

Intermediate care patients may be able to get out of bed, but they are still in need of some nursing care, although they can take care of themselves to some extent. They also may be the patients with a chronic or terminal illness or fractures, or the hemiplegics who need considerable nursing attention and restorative measures.

With *self-care,* the patient may live in a residence outside of the hospital which is still considered a part of the hospital facilities with a professional nurse in charge. Patients go to the hospital for meals, tests and x-rays, but otherwise lead a relaxed life in pleasant, homelike surroundings. (See Fig. 93.)

Progressive patient care gives nurses more time to give patients the kind of care they need, when they need it. The convalescent patient is

FIG. 93. Patients in the self-care unit eat in the hospital cafeteria. The nurse (*right*) eating with the patients has the opportunity both to observe them and to talk with them. The dietitian, who is standing, helps those on special diets to choose their food and is available to all of the patients. Eating with others has many advantages over eating alone in bed. (Overlook Hospital, Summit, N. J.)

not neglected even though critically ill patients must have most of the nurse's attention.

BEDS AND BEDMAKING

Types of Beds

Rest in bed is usually a part of the patient's treatment—sometimes the all-important part, as it is for patients with heart conditions or tuberculosis. Therefore, the bed must be right for comfort and for good posture. A good bed is made of metal or wood and is durable, lightweight, easy to move and easy to clean. These are the measurements that meet the requirements for comfort: 6 feet 6 inches long; 3 feet wide; and 26 inches from the floor to the springs. Most hospital beds today are the Gatch type, equipped with a spring frame and a crank so that they can be adjusted to different positions.

Hospital beds (Hi-Lo) are now available equipped with an electrical mechanism to lower and raise the bed so that the patient can get in and out of it easily. The patient who is being encouraged to help himself can operate this mechanism. The CircOlectric bed makes it possible to put the quadriplegic patient in an upright position. The rocking bed is mounted on a frame which stands on the floor, instead of on a bedstead. It is sometimes used for patients with circulatory or respiratory difficulties to aid breathing and to improve circulation.

A hospital bed may also have a towel rack at the head and equipment for holding solutions during treatment. Rubber-tired wheels make it easy to move the bed, and brakes keep it from sliding. The springs are woven of strong wire and are easy to clean.

Equipment

The Mattress. The mattress may be of cotton, wool, curled hair, kapok or foam rubber. The ones preferred today are those made with inner springs. The foam rubber type can be used when it is important to prevent pressure. A mattress should be firm enough to allow good body alignment. A bed board can be used to support a sagging mattress. Plastic covers which can be washed easily can be used to protect mattresses from soiling. Brushing or vacuuming is usually considered adequate for cleaning a mattress, unless it has been used by a patient with a virulent infection or a communicable disease. Steam pressure sterilizers, made especially for sterilizing mattresses, are provided in some hospitals. Most home beds are equipped with a quilted washable mattress pad—they also are used in some hospitals to add to the patient's comfort.

The Alternating Pressure Mattress Pad. If a firm mattress places constant pressure on one or more parts of the body, it may cause a bedsore (see p. 267). The alternating pressure mattress pad is made so that sections of it are distended with air or fluid, while other sections stay flat: then the flat sections fill and the distended sections flatten out. This alternating process is continuous and prevents steady pressure on any one point. Patients seem to have little difficulty in adjusting to this mattress.

The Pillows. Pillows are filled with feathers, hair or kapok. Foam rubber pillows may be used for patients who are allergic to these materials. However, foam rubber is not as adjustable as feathers. Pillows are used for comfort and for support in keeping the body in good alignment—different sizes help to do this. Pillows should have moisture-proof coverings to protect them from soiling if they are likely to be contaminated by body secretions or drainage, including contamination from respiratory infections. Pillows should be aired or vacuumed after every use.

Towels and Washcloths. The bath towel is made of terrycloth, which is absorbent and soft. An adequate size is 44 by 22 inches. Face towels are a mixture of linen and cotton, 36 by 18 inches in size. In the home, they may be all linen or some people prefer terrycloth face towels. Washcloths are also made of terrycloth.

Bed Blankets. Blankets are used for warmth. They should contain enough wool to be both light and warm. (They usually contain from 70 to 80 per cent wool and are from 60 by 80 inches to 72 by 90 inches in size.) The mixture of cotton with wool prevents shrinkage and makes the blanket stronger. The number of blankets on the bed depends on the climate, the temperature of the room and the individual patient's preferences.

Bath Blankets. Bath blankets are made of cotton; they are used to protect the patient during the bed bath, or to drape patients for treatments or examinations. They are made of flannel-like material which is warmer and more absorbent than other cotton materials.

Bed Linen. Bed sheets are made of cotton. If the hems are the same width at the top and the bottom, the sheets are more likely to get even wear. A sheet 72 by 108 inches gives enough margin to tuck in and to keep the sheet tight under the patient. This size is large enough to cover the blankets and still cover the patient if a bed cradle is used.

Pillowcases are made of the same material as sheets—the ordinary size is 42 by 36 inches. A pillowcase should be loose enough on the pillow to prevent strain on the seams—the open end should come well over the end of the pillow to protect it.

Protective Sheet and Drawsheet. A moisture-proof sheet, made of rubber or plastic material and covered with a cotton or muslin drawsheet, may be used over the lower bed linen to protect the middle portion of the bed, an area most likely to become soiled. The drawsheet must be wide enough to extend at least 6 inches beyond the edges of the protective sheet on each side—long enough to tuck in firmly. A bed sheet folded crosswise through the middle can be used. These sheets are particularly useful with incontinent or very ill patients since the drawsheet can be changed without disrupting the entire bed.

Bedspreads. Bedspreads are made of a durable cotton that is light in weight and easy to launder. Those in the home are more likely to be heavy and may not be washable. If a more appropriate spread is not available, a sheet can be used in its place.

Purpose in Bedmaking

The main objective in bedmaking is to add to the comfort of the patient. This means clean linen: a tight lower sheet to prevent wrinkles that irritate the skin; and upper bedclothing which does not weigh on the patient's body or restrict his movements, but still covers his shoulders. Adjustments in the procedure may be necessary for the comfort and the convenience of individual patients and to suit temperature conditions and the patient's condition.

Making the bed every day is a routine procedure in patient care which is carried out after breakfast, following the patient's bath or morning care. Exceptions to this rule are made when changing the bed may prove harmful to the patient. For example, a patient may be bleeding, having a special treatment or may be too weak or exhausted to move.

Keep the patient's body in as good alignment as possible while making his bed and at the same time, be certain *you* are practicing good body alignment.

Making a Bed. Each hospital has its own method for making different types of beds, and you will learn the procedure followed by the hospital in which you are working. The details may vary, but the principles to follow are the same. Since you will make a great many beds while you are a student nurse and many more as a graduate, it is important to know how to make them correctly and with the least amount of effort. Good body mechanics are essential.

BODY MECHANICS IN BEDMAKING

Face in the direction of your work and move along with the work as you place bedclothing on the bed to avoid twisting and over-reaching.

***Principle:** Muscles work in groups. Twisting distorts their position and causes strain.*

Separate your feet slightly and flex your knees when tucking bedding under the mattress.

***Principle:** The longest and the strongest muscles are made to do the work when the knees are flexed and the back is in good alignment.*

Open and spread bed linen on the edge of the bed—lifting it to shoulder level puts strain on the back.

***Principle:** Lifting uses more energy to overcome the pull of gravity.*

Work with your hands palms downward when pulling sheets tight, using arm and shoulder muscles. Advance one foot and rock back.

***Principle:** The longest and the strongest mus-*

cles are the most efficient. Firm support and rocking backward and forward add the power of body weight and reduce the effort required of the muscles.

Making an Occupied Bed

The method used to make an occupied bed should be one that disturbs the patient the least and requires minimum exertion for patient and nurse. Opinions vary as to the most efficient ways of reducing efforts, but with any method, you will need to make necessary adjustments for the individual patient. For example, bed cradles and other appliances require special arrangements of the bedclothing. Some patients need extra blankets for additional warmth, and some may have fractures or injuries that necessitate their being turned or moved in a special way.

Equipment. The amount of linen listed here is what you would use to change a bed completely or to make up a bed after cleaning a unit. Hospitals do not usually allow this much clean linen every day; adjustments in using the necessary minimum amount are explained:

1 bed pad	May not be used in some hospitals or may not need to be changed daily.
2 large sheets	One clean sheet may be allowed if the used top sheet is to replace the bottom sheet on the bed and if you have a cotton drawsheet.
1 protective sheet	For making the bed after cleaning the unit.
1 cotton drawsheet	If a folded top sheet is used for this, you will need 2 large sheets.
2 pillow cases	You may use only 1 and change the pillowcase on alternate pillows every day.
2 blankets	The number of blankets depends on the weather, the patient's condition and his preference.
1 bedspread	

SUGGESTED PROCEDURE

Bring clean linen to bedside table or chair.

Guide: *The linen should be placed on a clean, clear space and arranged in the order in which it is to be used.*

Loosen the linen all around the bed.

Guide: *Place one hand under the mattress to prevent tearing the linen.*

Pull mattress up to the head of the bed.

Guide: *Ask the patient to help or get assistance, if necessary.*

Fold back and remove the spread, placing it over the back of the chair.

Guide: *Fold the top down to the bottom and pick it up in the center. If the spread is to be discarded, put it in a laundry bag or a hamper for soiled linen. Never put soiled linen on the floor (which is always contaminated) or allow it to touch your uniform.*

Fold the blanket, remove it and place it over the back of the chair.

Place the bath blanket over the top sheet.

Guide: *If the patient's condition warrants it, ask him to hold the top of the blanket in preparation for the next step; if not, tuck it under his shoulders.*

Remove the top sheet.

Guide: *Fold from head to foot and place it on the back of the chair if it is to be used in remaking the bed.*

Remove pillows and one or both cases.

Guide: *Leave 1 pillow if the patient is uncomfortable without it; put the soiled case or cases with the soiled linen.*

Turn patient toward the other side of the bed.

Roll soiled drawsheet toward the patient—repeat with the protective sheet and bottom sheet.

Guide: *Gather together in folds and push close to patient.*

Pull mattress pad smooth if it is not being changed.

Guide: *Patients with excessive drainages may have to have the pad changed daily. It is rolled toward the patient in the same manner as above.*

Place a clean large sheet or used top sheet on the bed.

Guide: *Center it lengthwise, lower edge even with the mattress surface—if it is long enough after allowing 18 inches at the top, the sheet will also tuck under the bottom.*

Gather the farther half of the sheet into a

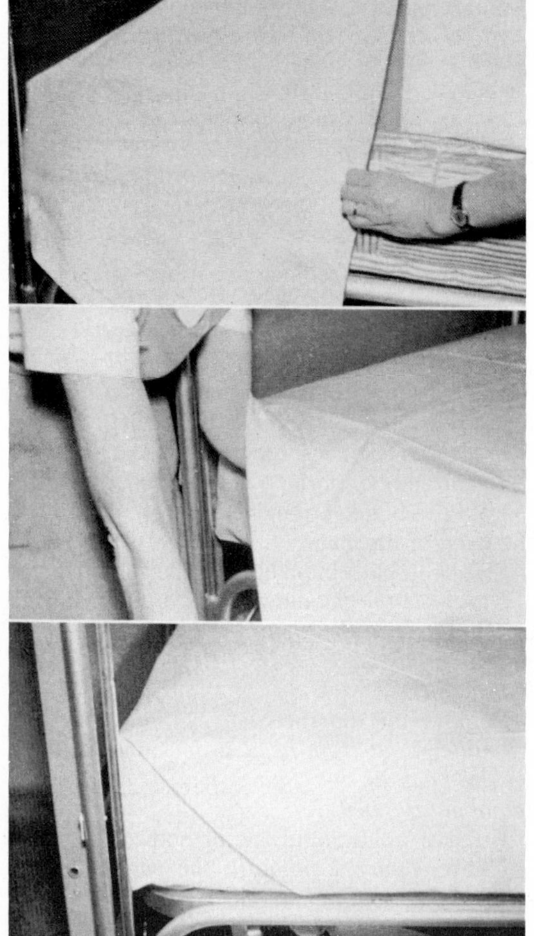

FIG. 94. (*Top*) The first step in making a diagonal corner. (*Center*) The second step in making a diagonal corner. (*Bottom*) The completed corner.

roll and push it against the patient and under the soiled bottom sheet.

Tuck a clean sheet under the mattress at the top.

Guide: *Pull it under and toward the foot as far as you can reach easily.*

Make the corner: Pick up the selvage edge; lay a triangle back on the bed; tuck the hanging part under the mattress; drop the triangle over the side of the bed; and tuck the hanging edge under the mattress.

Guide: *The selvage is straight up and down against the side of the mattress—the palm of one hand is next to the springs.*

Tuck the sheet under, all along the side of the bed.

Guide: *If the sheet covers the lower end of the mattress, make a corner.*

Unroll the rubber sheet toward you and tuck it under the mattress.

Lay the cotton drawsheet, folded through the center crosswise, over the rubber sheet.

Guide: *If a folded large sheet is used, fold it crosswise through the center—push the farther half against the patient with the fold toward the top of the bed—single edges are more likely to wrinkle down.*

Tuck the nearer half of the drawsheet under the mattress.

Turn the patient back toward you—lift his feet over all sheets.

Guide: *Lift the edge of the blanket slightly so that he will not lie on it. Be sure that he cannot roll out of the bed.*

Push the rolled sheets out.

Go to the other side of the bed and pull the sheets through.

Roll and remove the soiled bottom sheet—straighten the rubber sheet—remove the soiled drawsheet.

Guide: *Bunch each soiled sheet as you remove it and put it with the soiled linen.*

Turn the patient on his back.

Guide: *Do not turn him if you want him to lie on his side, or he is unable to lie on his back.*

Adjust the bottom sheet.

Guide: *Tuck it under at the top, make a corner, tuck in the sides—pull all the way down to the side, a diagonal pull—tight and smooth; brace your thigh against the bed and keep your back straight for good posture and efficient body mechanics.*

Pull the rubber sheet tight and tuck it under the mattress—repeat for the drawsheet.

Put the clean pillowcases on one pillow or both.

Guide: *Do this with the pillow resting on a flat surface. Open the case down into corners and grasp it at the outside at the center of the end seam. Turn the case back over your hand and grasp the pillow from the outside and ad-*

just the corners into the case. Turn the case up over the pillow and adjust it evenly; the pillow should not touch your clothing.

Place and adjust the pillow or pillows under the patient's head.

Place the top sheet over the bath blanket.

Guide: *Place it wrong side out. This will be right side out when turned back over the blanket. Allow sufficient length to turn it back.*

Remove the bath blanket. Put the wool blanket over the sheet.

Guide: *The patient can hold the sheet at the top if he is able; pull the bath blanket out. Place the wool blanket shoulder high.*

Make a box pleat in the blanket and the sheet together at the center of the lower end of the bed.

Guide: *This allows for toe room.*

Tuck together under the mattress—make a corner.

Put on the spread; turn the top edge back under the top edge of the blanket.

Guide: *The upper edge extends beyond and above the end of the blanket. The turn-under holds the top covers and protects the blanket.*

Turn the top sheet down over the spread.

Guide: *This protects the spread and the hem is now right side out.*

Making a Closed Bed

You usually make a closed bed when preparing the unit for a new patient, following the same procedure as in making an occupied bed with these exceptions:

Start with an empty bed.

Stay on one side of the bed until it is finished completely.

Fold the top sheet back over the blanket before putting on the spread.

The top of the spread is even with the top edge of the mattress.

The pillows are placed one above the other with the open edges facing away from the door.

Opening a Bed for a Patient

A bed is opened for a new patient, and it may be left this way when the patient is out of bed for a short time.

SUGGESTED PROCEDURE

Turn the spread down from the top and fold it under the top edge of the blanket. Turn the top sheet back over the spread.

Guide: *This protects the blanket, keeps the rough blanket away from the patient's skin and makes it easier for the patient to handle the bedclothes.*

Turn the top bedding down to the foot of the mattress and fold it back on itself.

Guide: *This shows the patient that his bed is ready for him. It is also easier to help him back into the bed when it is open.*

BED COMFORT

Changing Body Positions

You change the position of a patient's body for several reasons: to restore body functions, to prevent deformities, to relieve pressures and strains, to stimulate circulation, to give treatments. If the doctor specifies a certain position or forbids another, you follow his order exactly. You never let a patient sit up or get out of bed until the doctor has left an order permitting the change from one of these positions to the other. You never use fracture boards, splints, body frames or other appliances, unless the doctor orders them. You may use comfort devices, such as pillows, rolls, pads and bed cradles, except in certain conditions. You will learn what these conditions are, and the doctor will point them out to you—arthritis is an example. You must

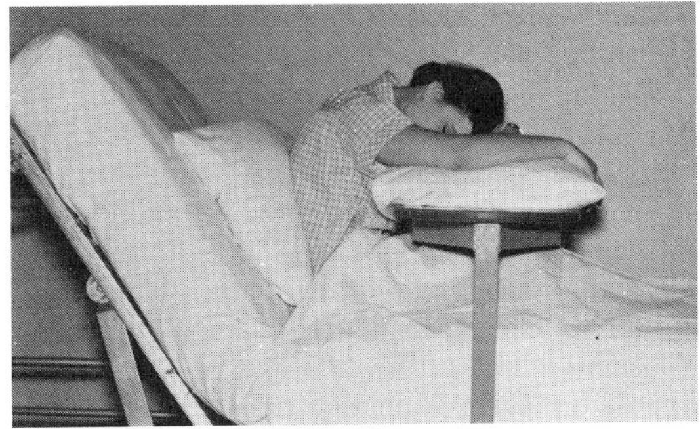

FIG. 95. This is a restful position for a patient who is unable to lie down in bed.

use these devices in such a way as to promote good body alignment and comfort, not to interfere with it.

The points to remember in changing the patient's position are: good body alignment, the safety of the patient, the need to reassure the patient, proper handling of the patient's body to prevent pain or injury, your posture in order to do the procedure effectively without strains on your own body and assistance, if you need it, for heavy or helpless patients.

Explain to the patient why you are changing his position and how you will do it. Tell him that you will not hurt yourself because you know how to lift him. If a patient can help, tell him what to do. Your own posture is an important part of the know-how in lifting or moving the patient. You advance one foot—this gives you a wider base to balance your body. You keep your back straight and bend forward from your hips, so that you use your strong thigh and hip muscles instead of putting a strain on the muscles in your back.

Following is a list of the kinds of equipment that you will need for keeping the body in good alignment in the different positions that patients assume when they are in bed. The specific things you need depend on the position in which you are placing the patient.

EQUIPMENT

Pillows—large and small	Pads—folded towels and sponge rubber
Bed boards for a sagging mattress	Sandbags
Rolls for support—cotton blankets	Bed cradles

Turning a Patient and Maintaining a Side-Lying Position. Sometimes turning the patient is such an important part of his treatment that the doctor specifies how often to do it. This is especially important for elderly patients to prevent lung congestion. In other conditions, it may be impossible to turn the patient (as in the case of fractures with traction appliances), or it may be harmful (with spinal injuries). You may want to turn a patient only to wash or rub his back or change his bed. Many patients are able to help themselves; others need some assistance; you will have to turn the helpless patients—*you* may even need assistance, if the patient is heavy, to keep him from falling out of bed and to prevent pain. When turning a patient on his side, you put him in the *side-lying* position. You proceed in the same way to turn him temporarily on his side (to rub his back, for instance) or to leave him in that position. You may not need pillows for support in the temporary position unless he is very uncomfortable without them (see Fig. 96). The following key points will guide you in placing a patient in the side-lying position:

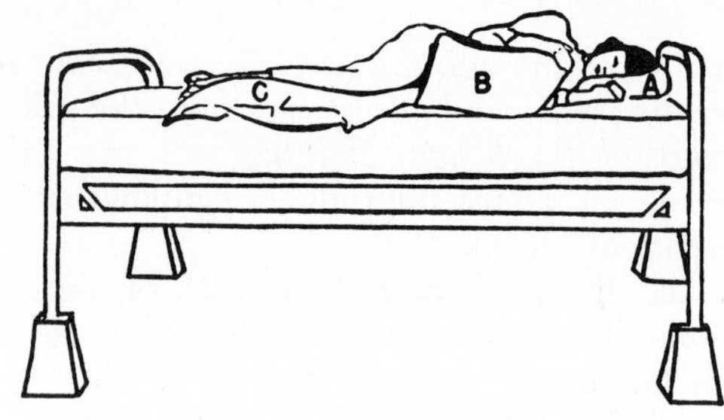

FIG. 96. Side-lying position to add to the patient's comfort. Small pillow (A) supports head and neck in the midline position. A folded pillow (B) provides support for the upper arm, so that it does not fall forward across the chest. The underneath hip and knee are in very slight flexion, and the upper leg is brought forward to rest on pillow (C) to avoid pressure on the leg underneath.

KEY POINTS

Stand on the opposite side of the bed toward which the patient will be facing when he is turned.

Slip one arm under the patient's shoulders, the other under his hips.

Advance one foot, bend forward from your hips—move the patient toward you without lifting.

Roll the patient over on his side, supporting his back and his hips.

Flex the underneath knee and hip slightly to prevent strain on the hip joint.

Bring the upper leg forward to rest on a pillow, thus preventing pressure on the underneath leg.

Put a folded pillow in front of the chest to

keep the upper arm from falling across the chest and to keep the shoulders in line.

Put a folded pillow against the back if it makes the patient feel more secure.

Adjusting the Back Rest and Pillows

If your patient is in a Gatch bed (one that can be adjusted to different positions), it is no problem to raise or lower the back rest. However, to adjust the pillows, his shoulders and back must be lifted. This is also done to adjust the pillows and the improvised back rest for the patient in a home bed. The following are the key points:

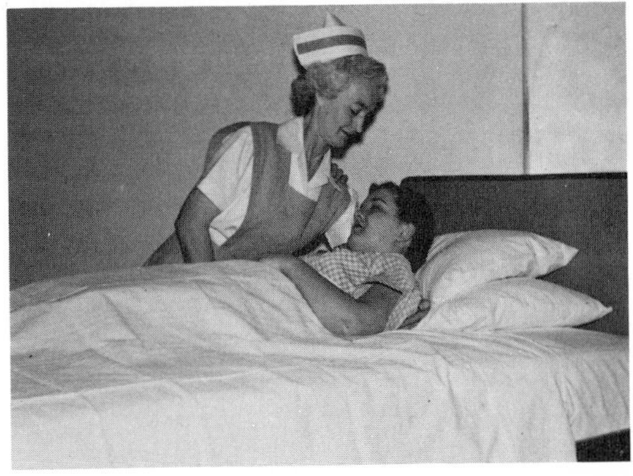

Fig. 97. Helping the patient to sit up.

PROCEDURE

Stand facing the patient with one foot forward and the body bent forward from the hips.

Put one arm under the patient's shoulders—put his nearest arm over *your* shoulder—put your other arm under his and across his back.

Tighten your thigh and hip muscles and bring your body and the patient's upright together.

Continue supporting the patient while you adjust the pillows or back rest with the hand that has been under his back.

Putting a Patient on a Back Rest (Sitting Position)

A patient may be sitting up for a short time to eat his meals or to work on a table or as a change of position; he may need to be in this position continuously to make breathing easier (as in cardiac conditions). Support is needed when the body is resting in a sitting position. Pillows support the back, the neck and the head to keep the spine in its normal curves. Folded pillows support the arms and keep the shoulders up. Pads in the hands support the wrists, keep the fingers bent a little and the thumb out—the position for grasping things. The knees are supported in a comfortable position—the slanting footrest is comfortable for the feet and prevents footdrop.

Figure 98 shows a Gatch bed, but you can use any back rest so long as you keep the body alignment the same. If you have to use a substitute back rest that is not adjustable, use pillows to keep the body in the proper alignment. Some substitute back rests are: a triangular pillow or a canvas back rest. If necessary you could make a triangular back rest from a strong cardboard carton; a covered carton also makes a good footrest. You can use it slanted or straight.

There is more of a tendency for the mattress to slip to the foot of the bed when a back rest is used. This makes it difficult to keep the body

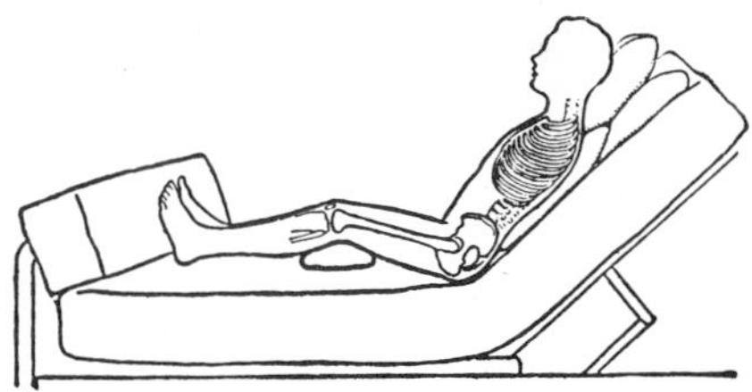

Fig. 98. Patient in a Gatch bed, backrest position, with 3 pillows arranged to support the normal spinal curves. This drawing pictures the body and the skeletal landmarks with a small pillow under the slightly flexed knees and the feet against the slanting footrest, which enables the patient to relax in a position to preserve function. In addition, pillows, not shown in the drawing, are placed one under each arm from elbow to fingertips, and in each hand are small pads to support the wrists. The fingers and the thumb are in moderate flexion.

in good alignment. To avoid this, a pillow or rolled blanket is sometimes placed in the space between the edge of the mattress and the lower end of the bed.

The bed must be flat to move the mattress to the top of the bed in its proper position. If the patient can help, he grasps the bars at the head of the bed; you grasp the mattress at the top and the side. Then pull together. It is easier if someone pulls with you on the opposite side of the mattress.

You put a patient in the sitting position for the first time during an illness only on the doctor's order. He should be observed closely for signs of fatigue and faintness until his body has adjusted to the change.

Good Body Alignment With the Patient on His Back

Many patients must lie on their back for most of the time; some patients may stay in this position through a long illness. It is important to make such a patient as comfortable as possible and to prevent body deformities. Figure 99 shows how to preserve good body alignment when a patient is lying on his back. Look at the 3 pillows—the middle one supports the lumbar part of the spine, the other two support the shoulders and the head. This position gives the breathing and the digestive organs room to work normally. The small knee roll supports the knee at a normal angle; the covered box is slanted to support the feet at right angles to the legs—a normal angle—and prevents footdrop.

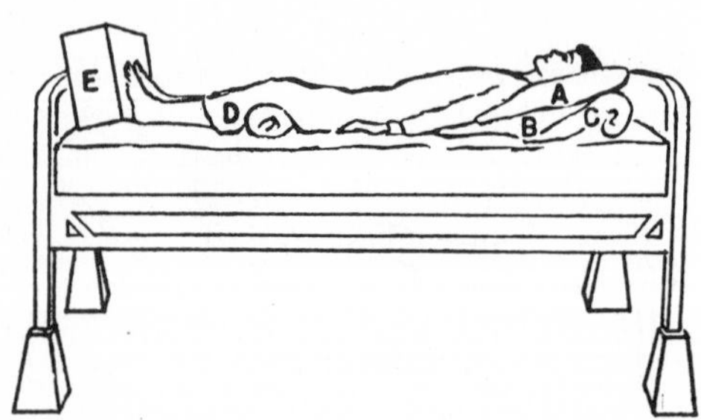

Fig. 99. This bed is elevated on blocks (head and foot) to place the patient on a more convenient level to save the nurse from unnecessary backstrain. Note the position of the patient on the bed and the arrangement of the 3 pillows (**A, B, C**) where the middle pillow (**B**) supports the lumbar spine and pillows **A** and **C** the head and the shoulders. Cotton-roll pillow (**D**) is placed under the knees, and the feet are kept against the pad (**E**) to maintain their position at right angles.

If the patient's body trunk must lie flatter, he will have only one pillow to support his head and neck; the knee roll is lowered; he has a pad under his ankles to prevent pressure on his heels; the box at the foot is more nearly upright.

Moving Specific Parts of the Body

Parts of the body may be elevated to improve the circulation, to relieve congestion or pain or to check hemorrhage. Pillows are used to elevate a leg or an arm; protect a pillow with a rubber pillowcase if necessary. Sandbags also may be used to keep the part in position. You would not elevate any part of the body without an order from the doctor—but if you do it in an emergency, such as a hemorrhage, then call the doctor and report what you have done and why.

Always support an arm or a leg along its entire length when you move it. Move it gently and slowly. Phlebitis, or inflammation of a vein, usually occurs in the leg. Move the leg as little as possible and carefully, to prevent dislodging a blood clot from the inflamed area. If a moving clot should obstruct an artery that supplies a vital organ—the lungs, the heart, the brain—it would cut off the blood supply and may prove fatal to the patient.

Observing Pressures on the Body

Continuous pressure on any part of the body makes a patient uncomfortable; pressure hampers the circulation and may cause pressure sores (also called bedsores or decubitus ulcers). Thin people who must lie in bed for some time feel pressures on the bony parts of the body that are not protected by fat pads. These are the main pressure areas: the shoulder blades, the elbows, the buttocks, the end of the spine, the heels and the back of the head. Tight bedclothes also press on the legs and the feet.

You always should be on the alert for signs of pressure on the body especially when you bathe a patient or rub his back. The condition of an individual patient and the probable length of his illness tell you when you should be using aids to prevent pressure sores. The patient also tells you about painful spots. Report signs of pressure and be suspicious of reddened areas that stay red after rubbing them.

Preventing and Taking Care of a Bedsore

The preventive treatment is most important. Bedsores are caused by pressure on the parts of the body that are not covered by pads of fat or other tissues, and this causes a break in the skin and destruction of the tissues beneath it. The skin is more likely to break down if the area is continually moist or is not clean. Rest in bed affects the circulation and increases the pressure on the bony prominences of the body, such as the spine, the shoulder blades and the elbows. The dangers are increased if a patient must lie in 1 position or if he has a cast or splints or a disease condition that affects the circulation. As soon as a break in the skin occurs, the way is open to infection.

Gentle rubbing of reddened areas, keeping the skin dry, removing wastes from the skin when caring for incontinent patients and changing the patient's position to relieve pressures are good preventive treatment.

If a bedsore does develop, 2 points in the treatment are most important: (1) protecting the broken area by sterile dressings and (2) relieving the pressure on the area as much as possible. The doctor will prescribe the treatment to be used for the ulcer; this may be the application of such ointments as zinc stearate, Peruvian balsam or scarlet-red ointment, or it may be exposure to light rays or to heat from electric light bulbs. It is essential to keep the area *clean* and *dry*. When a patient lies on a sheet over a rubber or synthetic protective material for a long period of time, moisture from perspiration does not evaporate and with continuous pressure, predisposes to bedsores. While the skin can cope with its own flora of microorganisms, the presence of microorganisms from an infected wound or feces can be dangerous, particularly if there is a break in the skin.

An airfoam mattress aids in distributing pressure evenly on every part of the body; smooth, tight undersheets eliminate skin irritation. At the first signs of redness, the best treatment is washing with soap and water and rubbing with skin lotion. The area should be covered with large cotton pads which are changed frequently: air-foam or lamb's wool pads are excellent because air spaces in the wool permit the skin to dry.

Authorities no longer recommend the use of doughnuts, air cushions, or air rings for most patients; instead of relieving pressure, these devices create a circle of pressure and constrict the circulation. Instead, large soft pads placed next to the pressure point to provide a smooth distribution of pressure are recommended. However, an air ring (covered by a pillow case to absorb perspiration) is acceptable as a temporary aid for a short time after rectal or perineal surgery.

Using a Bed Cradle

A bed cradle is a frame used to keep the bedclothes from touching all or part of the patient's body. A wide cradle fits across the bed; a narrow one fits along the bed lengthwise —it can be used over one arm or leg. Bed cradles usually are made of metal, but you can improvise a cradle from a wood crate or a cardboard carton.

A cradle is used for fractures, extensive burns and wounds. Some cradles are equipped with light bulbs fastened under the top of the frame; they are used to supply heat or for special treatments. If you are using an electric heat cradle, make sure that the temperature of the patient's skin is checked frequently to prevent burns. With impeded circulation, the patient may not be aware of excessive heat. Be careful not to get water on the connections when you clean this kind of a cradle; be sure that your hands are dry if you handle it when the current is on. Clean a cradle as you would any metal or enamelware.

A patient using a cradle may feel chilly with so much air space around him. You will make the foot end of his bed first, using extra linen if the cradle is over his feet and legs. This provides covering long enough to protect his shoulders and to tuck in snugly over the cradle.

Adjusting Bedsides

Bedsides, also called side rails or safety sides, are used to prevent restless patients from getting out of bed and to protect others from falling out of bed. Metal bedsides with self-adjusting hooks covered with rubber to protect the bed are easy to handle. Long boards tied to the bed at the top and the bottom can be used.

Bedsides are used for restless or irrational patients or people who are unable to control their movements. If a patient resents bedsides, remember that this is natural. Most people have a fear of being shut in or otherwise treated as if they were irresponsible. Try to make a patient understand that the bedsides are used to protect him. Explain this to the family, too. Failure to provide for the safety of the patient until the need arises may result in injury to the patient. Because courts have held the nurse liable in similar situations, it is always wise to know the policy of the institution in which you are employed. If you are on a home case, make sure that the family is aware of the dangers of patient injury due to insufficient physical guards.

Usually you notice signs of confusion and loss of muscle control before you actually need the bedsides. Report such signs. If you have any reason to think that it is dangerous, never leave a patient alone. Sometimes the patient's condition changes so rapidly that you need this protection for him suddenly. Let the head nurse know immediately if this happens. Never put on the sides or remove them without permission. You can remove one side when you are bathing a patient or giving him other care. Be sure that help is near if the patient is likely to try to get out of bed. If it is necessary to protect the patient from pressure or injury, pad the bedsides. Restless patients may press or throw themselves against the hard metal or wood surfaces.

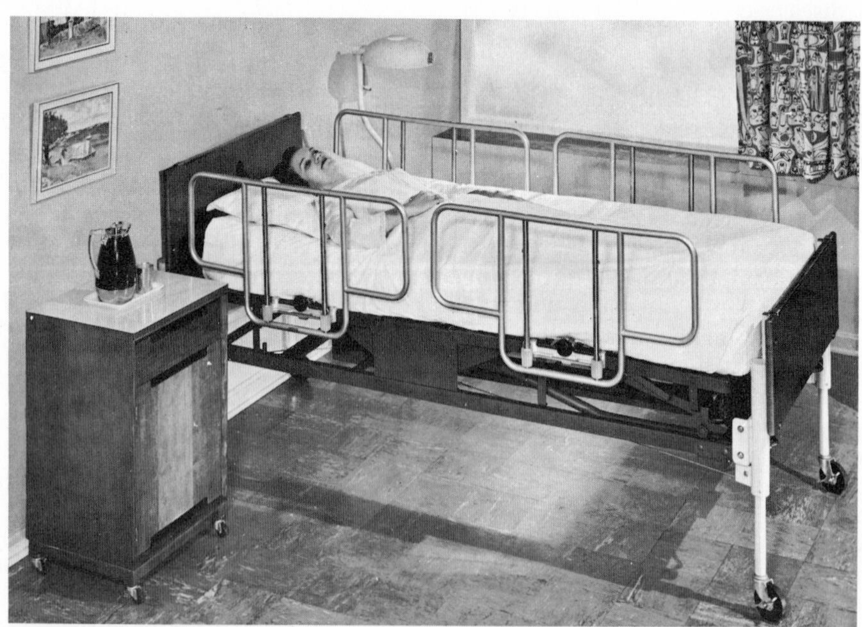

FIG. 100. Metal side attachment for hospital beds used when patients are restless and likely to get out of bed. (Hill-Rom Co. Inc., Batesville, Ind.)

Giving a Body Rub

You will not be expected to give massage since this is the job for an expert with special training. The doctor may want a patient to have *light massage* that you can give; find out specifically just what he wants you to do. The simplest strokes used in massage are described here.

Massage is applying pressure and friction to the body with your hands; it may be given for a stimulating or for a soothing effect. Light pressure is soothing; heavier pressure is stimulating. These are the movements used in light massage:

Stroking: Stroke the large surfaces of the body with the palms of your hands; stroke in the direction of the venous circulation *toward* the heart. You can use your thumb and fingers for the smaller surfaces; keep the strokes and the pressure even. You begin and end light massage with *stroking.*

Kneading: Press on muscle groups or single muscles, picking them up and squeezing them gently. Use the palms of your hands for the large muscles; use your fingers and thumbs for the single muscles. Use this movement for the extremities, the abdomen and the back.

Friction: This is rubbing around the bony prominences of the body—the end of the spine, the shoulder blades, etc.

These are the simplest and most effective movements for the kind of light massage that you can give to stimulate circulation and relax contracted muscles. You would give this kind of body rub only after the doctor orders it. Do not give a rub of this kind if the patient is bleeding or shows signs of phlebitis (inflammation of a vein).

Giving a Back Rub

A back rub is refreshing and relieves tired muscles; it stimulates the circulation, so it is especially helpful over pressure areas to prevent pressure sores. Alcohol hardens and dries the skin—pressure sores are more likely to develop if the skin is moist. Skin lotions containing oil are widely used because of their soothing and softening effect on overly dry skin. You rub the back when you give the morning bath and as a part of the evening care of the patient; you will do it at other times during the day and the night when it is necessary in the patient's treatment or for his comfort. Warm your hands and the skin lotion or alcohol before you begin, to prevent chilling the patient. Be sure that your nails are short enough to rub the back effectively without scratching it. Use long, firm strokes and give extra attention to pressure areas.

EQUIPMENT

Skin lotion or 50 to 70 per cent rubbing alcohol
Bath powder

The following detailed procedure may sound complicated, but with practice, it can be done easily and quickly. Patients find it very comforting.

PROCEDURE

Place the patient comfortably on the side or prone, with the entire back exposed. Apply lotion or alcohol to the entire area of the back, rub dry, dust powder on the hands and apply it to the back if alcohol has been used. Then proceed with the following steps; in each step, repeat the motion 3 times.

Using the first 3 fingers of both hands, rub under the hairline with a circular motion.

Using the first 3 fingers of one hand, rub in the hollow at the back of the neck with a circular motion.

Separating the thumb and the finger of one hand, place on either side of the neck and beginning at the hairline, rub the length of the neck with a circular motion.

Using the first 3 fingers of both hands, continue the circular motion down each side of the spine to the coccyx.

Using the heel of the hand, make a firm, circular motion over the coccyx.

Using the flat of both hands, with the fingers extending toward the front, rub the shoulders with a circular motion.

Continue the circular motion with the flat of the hands down the entire surface of the back and the buttocks.

Separating the first and the second fingers of

one hand, place the hands on either side of the spine and run them lightly up from the coccyx to the hairline and firmly down.

Finish with a dusting of powder.

Your Posture. Pay attention to your posture when you are giving a back rub. This will sound familiar—stand with one foot slightly forward and your knees bent slightly, with the patient as near your side of the bed as possible. This makes your strong arm and shoulder muscles do the work and prevents back strain.

PERSONAL CLEANLINESS

Caring for the Fingernails

The patient's general condition and his health habits affect his nails. Brittle, broken nails may be the result of improper diet or fever. Emotional tensions cause nail-biting. Some types of work make the nails stained and broken, and water, strong soaps and washing powders make the nails and the cuticle dry. Well-cared-for nails are pleasing to look at and are a health protection; conditions like torn cuticle are an invitation to infection. Report reddened areas or breaks in the cuticle; if this area is broken, infection can enter the body. Dirty nails can carry infection through handling food or scratching the skin. It is better to file the nails than to cut them since filing prevents rough edges that catch on the clothing and break.

Essential daily care is cleaning beneath the nails and pushing back the cuticle. The best time to do this is after the patient's hands have been in water. Soap and water loosen dirt and soften the cuticle temporarily. Oil on the nails and the cuticle softens dry, tight cuticle and dry nails. Use an orangewood stick to clean the nails and to push back the cuticle. The stick is blunt and smooth and less likely to injure the nails than the tip of a metal nail file. Cut off hangnails with manicure scissors to keep them from tearing still more.

The convalescent patient may be able to care for her own nails. Arrange the necessary equipment on the overbed or bedside table. You will need:

- A basin ⅓ full of warm water
- Soap
- Towel
- Nail brush
- Orangewood stick

She may have other things she wants to use such as nail polish, cuticle oil, nail file

Never give sharp-pointed or cutting equipment to a patient with unsteady hands or to a depressed patient—she may injure herself.

Caring for the Toenails

In caring for the toenails, you follow the same procedure as for the fingernails, with some exceptions. If the toenails are thick and hard, you may have to cut them first, then smooth them with a file or emery board. Cut them straight across; if you cut the corners down, you may encourage ingrown nails. If the nails tend to grow inward at the corners, a wisp of cotton tucked under the nail prevents pressure on the toe. Toenails need the same care as fingernails. Long toenails catch on the bedclothes and break or they may scratch the skin. Dirty toenails may cause infection by scratching the skin. Do not cut toenails of patients with diabetes or nails of newborn babies. This is not a nursing measure unless specifically ordered.

Notice corns and calluses; you may apply oil to soften them but nothing else. If the patient is distressed by corns, calluses, ingrown nails, or bunions, report these conditions. People sometimes have infected corns or calluses as a result of cutting them with razor blades or using corn removers that contain salicylic acid. You may cover an infected area with a sterile dressing, but the doctor prescribes any other treatment.

Caring for the Patient's Hair

Brushing and dressing the patient's hair is part of her daily care. It keeps the hair in condition and makes the patient feel better; it gives us an opportunity to note scalp disorders or pediculi. Brushing stimulates the scalp circulation and distributes the oil over the hair to give it sheen. Short hair should have the same care as long hair. When a patient is ill for some time, he or she may need the services of a barber to cut the hair. In some hospitals, beauty parlor and barber services are available for patients who need them. You will not have time to do elaborate hair arrangements for hospital patients; you can spend more time on the hair of the patient at home. Try to arrange the hair as becomingly as you can in the time you have since it gives any woman a bit of an uplift to feel that her hair looks well. Ribbons raise both adult and childish spirits. Encourage patients to comb their own hair—it is good exercise for the shoulder joints.

Comb one strand at a time, beginning at the end; wrap the strand firmly around your forefinger, leaving it slack between your hand and the patient's head. This prevents pulling. Braid long hair to prevent tangles and avoid using hairpins or bobby pins that might be uncomfortable or injure the patient's head. Start the braids toward the front so the patient does not have to lie on them and fasten them at the end with rubber bands or ribbons. This is the easiest and least disturbing way of caring for the hair if a patient is very ill or unable to move her head.

Wash the brush and the comb frequently; this helps to keep the hair clean and prevent reinfection of the scalp in infectious conditions. Report such conditions as excess dandruff, falling hair, crusts or sores on the scalp.

Giving a Shampoo. The purpose of a shampoo is to cleanse the hair and the head; it may be necessary after ointments or other medications have been applied to the scalp or as a part of the treatment for pediculosis, or for cleanliness during a long-term illness. A shampoo is never given without the doctor's permission nor should it be given if the patient is weak or exhausted, has a respiratory infection or fever or is not allowed to exert herself. Sometimes a patient is admitted to the hospital with really dirty hair and should have a shampoo but usually it is not necessary during a short stay in the hospital.

The procedure for giving a shampoo is determined by the equipment available in the individual hospital. Some of the larger institutions have beautician services available for patients. Equipment similar to that used in beauty parlors may be provided. It is often necessary to give a shampoo without these aids, using ordinary equipment and methods which are simple and effective.

Precautions to observe in giving a shampoo are:

Protect the patient from drafts and be sure that the room is warm enough.
Use warm water (105° to 110° F.).
Protect the patient's eyes and ears.
Use enough solution to make a thick lather.
Rinse and dry the hair thoroughly.
Protect the bed and the floor.
Assure continuous drainage for the shampoo water.

Usually a solution of a mild soap is used. Find out about the patient's preferences. She may want to provide a soapless shampoo or a special soap preparation for you to use. Of course, you would not attempt to apply hair dye or rinses. Soap and water and soapless shampoos remove the oil from the hair—used too frequently or too lavishly, they may remove too much; oily hair is not affected by them as easily as dry hair.

Giving a Shampoo to an Ambulatory Patient. The patient who is up can have her shampoo in the bathroom, using the lavatory bowl. Choose a chair low enough to let the patient's head rest comfortably on the edge of the bowl. She may prefer to sit facing the bowl, resting her forehead on the edge and holding a folded towel over her eyes. If a spray is used, adjust the temperature of the water before you begin. If the patient feels faint, stop the procedure, wrap her head in a bath towel and get her back to bed at once.

The patient who can be moved on a stretcher can be wheeled to a convenient sink for a shampoo lying on the stretcher.

Giving a Shampoo to a Bed Patient. The most difficult part of this procedure is providing continuous drainage of the shampoo to prevent wetting the patient and the bed.

EQUIPMENT

2 Bath towels
1 Large pitcher of water 105° to 110° F.
1 Small pitcher for pouring
Small container for shampoo solution
1 Hand towel
Safety pins
Nonabsorbent cotton
Moisture-proof sheet
1 Pail
Newspapers to protect the chair or the floor in the home
Moisture-proof pillowcase

SUGGESTED PROCEDURE

Cover the patient with a bath blanket and turn back the bedclothing.

Cover the pillow with a moisture-proof and cotton cases and place it under the patient's head.

Move the patient's head and shoulders to the edge of the bed.

Reason: *It is easier to use the strongest muscles efficiently when working close to the body.*

If it is necessary to improvise a trough, roll the sides of a good-sized moisture-proof sheet over towels toward the center or use a Kelly pad.

Reason: *The flow of water is directed by a confining trough.*

Pin a folded towel around the patient's neck to absorb dripping and keep water from running down the patient's back. Cover her eyes with a folded towel and put cotton in her ears.

Reason: *Wet clothing causes chilling. Soap and detergents may injure delicate structures.*

Put one end of the trough (or Kelly pad) under the patient's head; direct the other end into the pail at the side of the bed—protect the floor with newspaper.

Reason: *The pull of gravity aids in the flow of fluids.*

Wet the hair thoroughly, apply the shampoo and rub it into a good lather and rinse well.

Reason: *Friction loosens particles; soap (or detergents) and water wash away loosened particles.*

Apply shampoo, rub and rinse again. Rinse until the hair squeaks.

Wrap a towel around the patient's head and slip the trough into the pail. Rub the hair dry with a bath towel.

Reason: *Moisture absorbs heat and causes chilling.*

Permanent Waves. A permanent wave helps to make the hair more manageable and attractive—it can be a morale-booster in a long-term illness. It must be given with the doctor's permission and by a competent person. Many women have learned how to give themselves home permanents; however, a nurse is not expected to perform this service for a patient, but she may help if she feels competent to give assistance.

Treating Pediculosis

Pediculi are lice; these tiny insects live on the blood of the person they infest. They are found on the hairy parts of the body. There are over 50 kinds of pediculi, but the ones found on the body are head and body lice.

Body lice are found on the clothing and *crab lice* on the hairy parts of the body, especially the pubes. They cause itching on the back, the neck and the abdomen; be suspicious of scratches on the body in these areas.

Head lice are found on the hair and the scalp. They are tiny, oval-shaped, grayish insects. The eggs—*nits*—look like dandruff but are solid specks, not flakes; they stick tightly to the hair and are hard to destroy.

Pediculi spread disease and harm the body in other ways; they cause itching, and the scratches sometimes become infected. They spread from person to person on clothing, bedding and combs and brushes.

Part of your observation of a patient on admission to the hospital is to notice signs of skin irritation and pediculi. Pediculi are not always a sign of unhygienic living and indifference to cleanliness. The wonder is that more of us do not have them, since we brush against so many people in crowds every day.

If you find pediculi on a patient's head or body, treatment will kill the live ones and destroy the nits. Be tactful and matter-of-fact when you tell the patient what you are going to do—it can always be assumed that the pediculi came from someone else's clothing that the patient had touched. You have an opportunity to impress the patient with the harmful effects of pediculi on the body as you explain why it is fortunate that he is having treatment in time.

If you find pediculi, report your discovery to the head nurse or the doctor; either one will tell you what treatment to use. Every hospital usually has its own method of treating pediculosis. A number of effective preparations are available, some of which will destroy both lice and nits. An old reliable remedy for dissolving nits is a 10 per cent solution of acetic acid or vinegar.

It is usually necessary to repeat treatments of pediculosis several times; treatment may include shaving the pubes and axillae. The treatment includes a bath after it is completed.

Sometimes the patient's clothing is infested with body lice. It may have to be burned if badly infested; otherwise, it can be disinfected by boiling or steam sterilization or by ironing. The method you use depends on the material. Always care for infested clothing at once—pediculi move fast. Wear a protective gown to prevent spreading lice and to protect yourself and others from infestation.

Shaving a Male Patient

Most men feel untidy and know that they look so if they are unable to shave every day. A barber is usually available to shave male patients in the hospital, and at home, the patient's own barber may come in to do it. You will have to decide when it is safe to let a patient shave himself and whether you should stay with him or not. A patient with unsteady hands and poor eyesight should not be allowed to shave himself; a patient who is mentally depressed or upset may harm himself. If it is safe, allow a patient to shave himself because it encourages him to do one more thing for himself as a part of his recovery. You can get the equipment ready for him, make him comfortable and provide a mirror and a good light.

It is possible that you may have to shave a patient if no one else is available to do it. Be sure the razor is sharp—dull blades make shaving a painful process. Always use plenty of lather and shave in the direction of the hairs, holding the skin taut. Be careful not to nick the skin—broken skin provides an avenue for infection.

The procedure described here applies to the use of a straight or safety razor. If an electric razor is used, study the directions carefully and follow them.

EQUIPMENT

Basin of hot water
Shaving brush
Shaving soap or cream
Razor, straight or safety
After-shave lotion
Tissues
Powder
Mirror
Light

SUGGESTED PROCEDURE

Place a light so no shadows fall on the face.

Put a safety razor together tightly—use a sharp blade.

Use plenty of lather to soften hairs.

Shave with the direction of the hairs; hold the razor at an angle of about 250°; use short firm strokes; hold the skin taut.

Wipe the hairs and lather from the razor frequently.

Shave carefully around the nose and lips—these areas are especially sensitive; wash the face to remove soap.

Lotion and powder are soothing, however, some men may not like to use them.

If the skin is nicked, apply an antiseptic and cover with a sterile dressing.

Washing the Patient's Face and Hands

Wash the patient's face and hands before breakfast, with a bath and before dinner. You may do it at other times for comfort; you always see that his hands are washed after he has had a bedpan or a urinal.

If he is able, the patient who can sit up should be encouraged to wash his face and hands himself, with the equipment arranged conveniently on the overbed table. This is a step in rehabilitation.

GENERAL DIRECTIONS

Protect the bedclothing with a towel placed under the patient's chin.

Wring the washcloth sufficiently to prevent dripping.

Do not use soap on the face unless the patient wants it. Never use soap on the eyes and if soap is used on the face, remove it thoroughly by rinsing.

Wash each eye from the nose outward.

Put the hands in the basin of water to wash them and use soap. Use a hand brush if necessary for grimy nails.

General Mouth Care

Many disease organisms enter the body by the mouth; food particles in the crevices between the teeth cause decay and breath odor. Some illnesses cause irritation or dryness or brownish deposits on the tongue and the mucous membranes. Some infections of the gums are communicable. Any mouth condition that interferes with taking food or causes infection in the mouth or another part of the body harms the patient's health. Breath odors or decayed teeth make sensitive people self-conscious.

People who have not learned good health habits need to be taught why good mouth care helps them to keep well. Poor teeth and other mouth conditions prevent people from eating necessary foods and interfere with the appetite. When you tell a patient why you are doing any nursing procedure, two things happen: (1) you reassure him and (2) he learns something. Patients do learn to improve their health habits if a tactful nurse is really interested in helping them. If you want a patient to go on brushing his teeth after he leaves the hospital, you might comment on such things as the improved appearance of his teeth and how much better his appetite is.

Ideally, people should always brush their teeth after eating but since this is sometimes impossible, we settle for brushing night and morning. Rinsing the mouth with water is the next best thing; children especially should be taught to do this. Bacteria in the mouth act on food particles clinging to the teeth to form an acid which destroys tooth enamel.

Some mouth problems are caused by conditions about which you can do nothing. Always report difficulties you observe, so they can be corrected.

Brushing the Patient's Teeth. The purpose of mouth care is to keep the mouth, the teeth and the gums clean and healthy. Many patients can brush their own teeth; be sure that they know *how* to do it. Consider a patient's preferences in dentifrices or mouthwashes. The taste or the odor of a specific brand may be displeasing to him. A dentifrice may be a powder or a paste. A satisfactory mouthwash can be made by dissolving ½ teaspoonful each of salt and sodium bicarbonate in a glass of warm water.

The toothbrush should have short bristles, firm but not so harsh as to injure the gums, and be small enough to reach every tooth. Battery-operated (electric) toothbrushes are now available; studies show that they are more effective and less likely to harm the gums than hand brushes.

Dental authorities differ as to the best method of brushing the teeth. Many of them recommend using *downward* strokes on the upper teeth and *upward* strokes on the lower ones. It is important to brush all tooth surfaces. Dental floss can be used to dislodge particles wedged between the teeth provided care is taken to avoid injuring the gums.

Observations. Observe the condition of a patient's mouth and teeth. Record the effect of brushing. If a patient begins to bleed from the gums, with no previous history of this condition, it may be important to the physician. If the toothbrush bristles hurt his gums, he will not brush his teeth properly. Perhaps he needs special mouth care, substituting cotton applicators for the brush. Swollen, bleeding gums may indicate *Vincent's angina* (trench mouth). This condition is infectious and requires special treatment and special precautions in caring for the patient's equipment. A 2 per cent solution of sodium perborate is often prescribed to be used as a mouthwash frequently, perhaps hourly.

Hospitals provide a toothbrush and a mouthwash solution for patients who do not have their own.

EQUIPMENT

Toothbrush	Small curved basin
Toothpaste, powder or mouthwash	Container, if mouthwash is used
Glass of cool water	Towel

If the patient is able to brush his teeth himself, see that he is sitting up comfortably and that the equipment is placed conveniently.

PROCEDURE

Protect the patient's gown and the bedclothing.

Turn the patient's head to one side if he is lying down.

Caution the patient about swallowing the mouthwash.

Provide sufficient water for rinsing and rinse freely.

See that he brushes his teeth effectively—show him the correct method, if it is necessary to do so.

Wipe his mouth and chin and rinse the toothbrush well.

Caring for the Mouth When a Patient Wears Dentures. People may be sensitive about wearing dentures, so be careful about privacy for these patients when you give them the toothbrushing equipment. If the dentures are left out of the mouth, put them in an opaque container—preferably covered—out of sight. Handle the dentures carefully to avoid breaking them; they are expensive, and the patient is handicapped without them.

Frequently you find a patient who is constantly removing his dentures; you may find them under the pillow or on the bedside table. Look for irritated areas in the mouth; many dentures fit poorly. Poorly fitting dentures are often the reason for poor eating habits and poor nutrition; the afflicted person neither chews his food well nor does he eat the proper foods. This is one of the reasons for older people's dietary problems.

Dentures may be complete or partial. The mouth needs the same care when dentures are worn as it does with one's own teeth. Mouths and dentures that are not clean cause breath odor—toothpaste advertising makes a great point of "denture breath." Specially designed brushes and preparations for soaking dentures to remove deposits are available. Always hold dentures over a basin of water when cleaning them, if they should be dropped on a hard surface they are likely to break.

Most dentists encourage their patients to wear their dentures all the time. If dentures are removed for long periods, the gum line changes and the dentures do not fit. If they must be removed, they should never be stored in cups or glasses that are used for drinking.

Always remove dentures if a patient is unconscious or irrational or having convulsions; remove them if a patient is going to the operating room. The danger is not that the patient may swallow them, although removable bridges have been swallowed, but that they may obstruct the trachea and cut off the patient's air supply.

Special Mouth Care

If a patient is helpless, you will have to care for his teeth; you may have to give special mouth care in some illnesses if brownish material (*sordes*) collects on the tongue and teeth, or if the patient breathes through his mouth. If the patient cannot take fluids by mouth or if fluids are restricted, it may be necessary to give special mouth care as often as every hour. If a patient needs to be encouraged to take food, cleansing the mouth before eating helps to make food more palatable.

Some patients like the aromatic taste of a medicated mouthwash, but water or salt water is just as effective.

If the patient is unable to cooperate by opening his mouth, a tongue blade can be used to hold it open. Sometimes it is necessary to use a mouth gag. Never try to hold open a patient's mouth with your fingers—you may be bitten and the wound can become infected.

PROCEDURE

Turn the patient's head to one side to keep the patient from aspirating the slightest amount of fluid.

Cotton applicators of a suitable size and gauze wrapped around a tongue blade are effective cleansing tools, for all surfaces (mouth and tongue).

Moisten the mucous membrane with water after cleansing.

Apply an emollient cream to the lips to prevent drying and cracking—moisture evaporates rapidly from the thin skin of the lips.

If the patient has an infectious mouth condition, use the same precautions in the care of his equipment, wastes, linen and dishes as for any communicable disease. Explain to the family why you use these precautions and caution them about touching things which the patient handles. People put their hands to their mouths more often than they realize.

The Bedside Table

In the hospital, the bedside table is made of metal, which is easy to keep clean because it can be washed with soap and water. It is durable, and the legs are rubber tipped or have casters so that it can be moved easily and quietly. The top is covered with a composition material that prevents noise when you place things on it. Bedside tables now come with a drawer and an enclosed storage space below, with shelves. Some of them have a ring attached that holds the wash basin.

The drawer provides a place for personal belongings, the comb and the brush and the orangewood stick. Basins, tooth powder, toothbrush and cup and bath blankets are stored on the top shelf of the table; if the patient's bedpan and urinal are kept at the bedside, this equipment and the toilet tissue go on the bottom shelf. In any storage arrangement, always keep the bedpan and the urinal apart from toilet and personal things.

FEEDING THE PATIENT

Even patients who can feed themselves may need some assistance in spreading butter on bread, cutting meat or pouring tea. Always warn a patient about extremely hot foods to prevent his burning his mouth, especially if he is using a drinking tube. Encourage him to help himself—it develops his self-confidence and his sense of progress toward getting well. Occasionally, you will find a patient who wants to prolong being taken care of, or who resists any suggestion that he feed himself. Try to change this attitude by gradually leaving him with more responsibility for handling his food, taking it for granted that he finds it more pleasant to feed himself.

You will have to feed very young or helpless or irrational patients to make sure that they take the necessary food and to keep them from possible injuries or accidents. Use your judgment about how much the patient can help—sometimes he can hold a piece of bread although he cannot manage other food. You will have to decide how much he can be allowed to do without tiring himself or without taking so much time to eat that the food becomes unpalatable.

How to Do It

Clear the bedside table or put the overbed table in place before you bring in the tray. You should sit at the patient's right, unless you are left-handed. Try to make the patient feel that you have time to feed him and that you enjoy doing it.

The Patient's Comfort

The patient's comfort is the first consideration in making mealtimes pleasant and satisfactory. It is impossible for anyone to enjoy eating if he is in an uncomfortable position, too hot or too cold or if he feels hurried through his meal.

POINTS TO OBSERVE

See that the patient is as comfortable as is possible—give him an opportunity before his tray comes to void if he wishes.

Avoid changing dressings or giving treatments immediately before or after mealtimes.

See that bedpans, urinals and dressing carts are out of sight.

Cut the food into small pieces and slowly feed the patient small amounts at a time.

Give different kinds of solid foods and liquids alternately to provide variety.

Let the patient help in every possible way.

Record significant observations on his chart, such as good or poor appetite, nausea, his refusing food, his difficulty in swallowing and his likes and dislikes.

GIVING AND REMOVING A BEDPAN AND A URINAL

The patient eliminates urine and feces as

waste products from the body by voiding and defecating. The utensils used for this purpose if the patient is confined to bed are the *bedpan* and the *urinal.* Females use the bedpan for both; males use the bedpan for defecating and the urinal for voiding. A female urinal may be used for a female patient in certain conditions, such as when she is in a body cast or in some other constricting appliance.

Bedpans are usually made of metal or enamelware. They feel cold on the skin and should be warmed before being placed under the patient. Some of the newer bedpans are made of nylon resin which feel warmer to touch, are less noisy to handle and can be cleaned and sterilized by conventional methods.

The position of the body which the patient must assume often makes it difficult to get on and off the bedpan, and many need assistance. Male nursing personnel usually help male patients who cannot manage by themselves. In any case, it is essential to provide privacy for the patient.

You can help to establish regular defecation habits by giving the patient the bedpan at a definite time every day; keep to the regular time already established by the patient, if possible. Usually the best time is after breakfast, but this varies for individuals. The desire to urinate comes more frequently; it depends on the amount of fluids the patient takes, his specific illness and bladder conditions. A full bladder makes a patient uncomfortable; in a hospital it is customary to *pass bedpans* to the patients before meals, before visiting hours and when they settle down for the night.

It is harmful to keep a patient waiting for a bedpan; it weakens the tone of the sphincter muscles in the urethra and the rectum and distresses the patient physically and emotionally. Most patients feel embarrassed about having anyone do such a personal service for them; explain to a patient that there is no need to feel self-conscious about the natural functions of the body; assure him that he will have privacy and that you can place the bedpan to avoid soiling the bed. If a patient is restless or unable to follow directions, protect the bed with a pad.

The Bedpan Procedure

There is less strain on the patient's back if the head of the bed is elevated slightly before he is placed on the bedpan. Folding back one corner only of the upper bedclothing makes it possible to slip the bedpan under him without exposure. If he needs some assistance, you can help him to raise himself by putting your hand under his buttocks and lifting. If he is unable to help himself, turn him on his side and hold the bedpan against his buttocks as he is rolled back onto it. It is sometimes difficult to do this by yourself.

After giving a patient the bedpan, be sure that the signal bell is within reach and that toilet tissue is conveniently placed. Soap and water for washing his hands should also be available. Always cover a bedpan when taking it to the patient and immediately after it is used.

If a patient is forced to wait when he needs a bedpan or he does not have prompt attention after using it, he may try to walk to the bathroom on his own and fall and injure himself, or he may upset the bedpan and soil the bed. Many patients become emotionally upset in such situations which, of course, is detrimental to their condition.

A child's bedpan is smaller than the standard size; you may be able to use a small bedpan for an adult who is helpless or unable to lie on the larger pan.

A female patient may be allowed to sit up on the bedpan or even to dangle her legs over the edge of the bed if she is having difficulty in voiding. She must have whatever back support is necessary and should not be left alone.

Observation and Recording

The urine and the feces tell many things about the patient's condition, especially in disturbances of the digestive and the urinary systems. You always observe the contents of a bedpan or urinal carefully and note unusual conditions. Be alert about orders to save specimens of urine or feces; save the entire content if you note unusual conditions and show it to

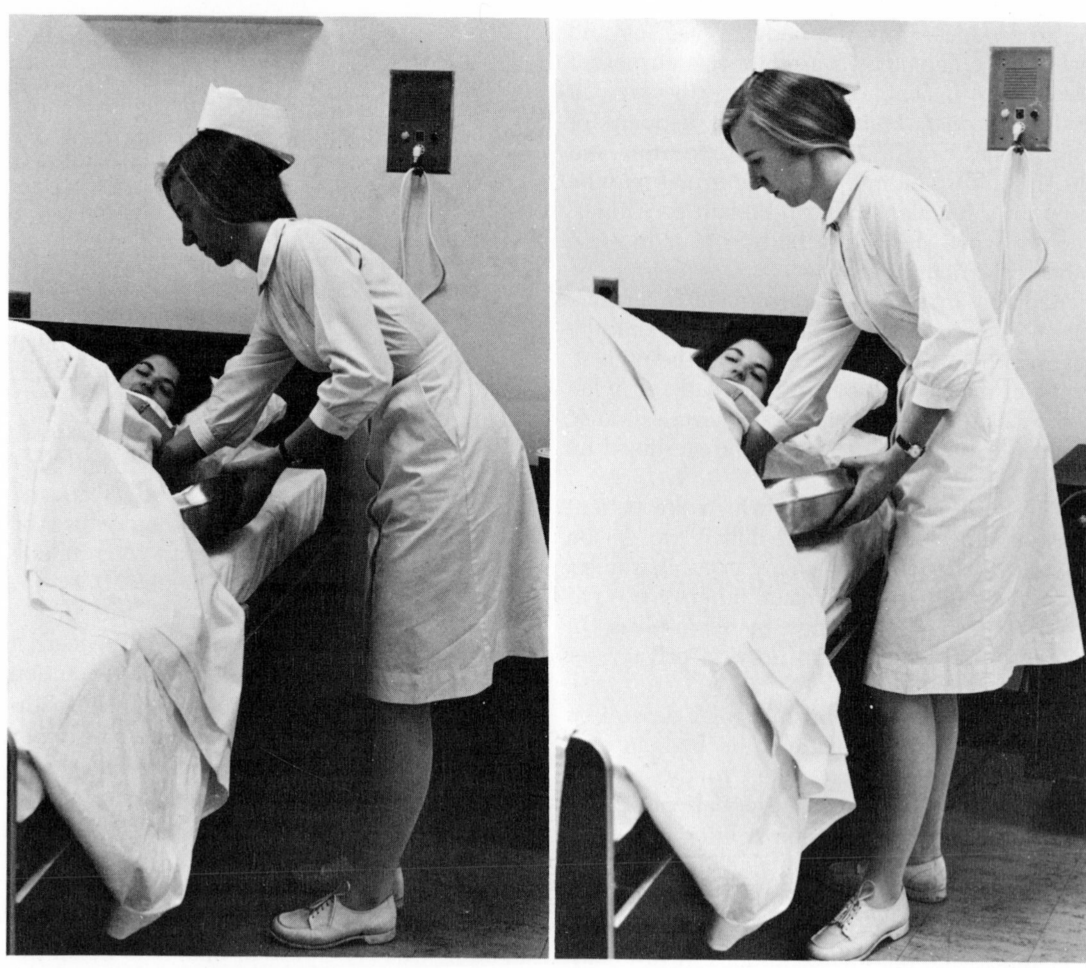

FIG. 101. (*Left*) This nurse is in a poor position for adjusting the bedpan. (*Right*) Here she is standing correctly—see how much closer to the bed she is.

the doctor or head nurse. Record difficulties in voiding or in eliminating feces.

The Urinal Procedure

The urinal is used for a male patient for voiding. Cover the urinal when you bring it to the patient and when you remove it. Help the patient to place the urinal if necessary; provide for washing his hands. After urination, measure urine; rinse the urinal first with cold water, then with hot. If the urinals are kept in the utility room for general use, sterilize each one in the same way as the bedpan every time it is used.

Using a Commode

Some people have great difficulty with urination and bowel movements when using a bedpan. If such a patient is unable to go to the bathroom, the doctor may permit him to get out of bed to use a commode at the bedside. A commode is a straight-back chair or wheelchair, with an open seat and a place beneath to hold a bedpan or other receptacle. Stay with the patient if he is weak and likely to become faint. The directions for using a bedpan also apply to using a commode—wash the patient's hands, note the contents of the commode, clean the commode after use, etc. It is better to keep the commode out of sight, but it may be covered and kept at the bedside.

BATHING THE PATIENT

A complete daily bath is not necessarily essential or even advisable for every patient. For instance, his condition, or the weather, may determine how often a bath is necessary; personal bathing habits have an influence on the frequency of bathing. Until comparatively recently, it was almost universal hospital practice to expect nurses to have all the patients bathed by the middle of the morning at the latest, or by the time the doctors began to make their rounds. Today, we try to be more considerate of the patient's comfort and not so concerned with a deadline for having everything tidy. If a patient has had an uncomfortable sleepless night, a rest after breakfast may be much more appealing than a bath. In some cases, a bath may do the patient more harm than good.

Another long-standing (and disturbing) custom was the practice of washing the patient's hands and face hours before his breakfast was served. This often necessitated waking the patient at a very early hour, rousing him so thoroughly that he was unable to go back to sleep. In some cases, having a good night's sleep may be much more important to the patient than being bathed. Many hospitals have adjusted their routines with the patient's comfort in mind. Modern equipment includes showers and bathtubs equipped with self-help devices for patients who are able to bathe themselves. Daily baths now are considered less of a sacred ritual "to be observed at any cost."

A bath helps elimination by removing the waste products of perspiration from the skin; it stimulates circulation and is refreshing. The main purpose of a bath is to keep the body clean. The 3 kinds of cleansing baths are the shower, the tub and the sponge bath in bed. The patient's condition determines which kind of bath is the safest and the best for him. A sponge bed bath involves the least exertion for the patient and is the safest if he has any difficulty in moving or is irresponsible.

Bathing Routines

Most hospitals establish bathing routines which may seem strange to patients although they are convenient for nurses and other personnel. Explaining the reasons for these routines helps the patient to adjust to them. For instance, the bed patient who is accustomed to taking his bath at ten o'clock at night when he retires needs to realize that in the hospital at that time only 1 night nurse may be available on the service to do everything for everyone. The patient who can take his bath by himself has more leeway in choosing the time he prefers. In any case, the nurse is still responsible for his protection and for giving him whatever assistance he needs. If he is allowed to take a tub bath or a shower, she must be within calling distance and the bathroom door must not be locked.

Giving a Tub Bath

Some patients can safely have a shower or a tub bath on admission to the hospital. Convalescent patients progress to the point where a tub bath is another step toward their normal habits. A patient gains independence and is encouraged by this evidence that he is getting well. In the patient's home, consider the time that is best for the patient and most convenient for the family. Always get permission to give the first tub bath when you have been giving bed baths to a patient. It is better not to give a bath immediately after a meal because a bath draws the blood to the skin and takes it away from the digestive organs.

You must be the judge of how much assistance the patient will need. Some patients may prefer to wait until they are able to carry on alone; others will not feel embarrassed by assistance. In any event, you can do much to spare the patient exertion; you are also responsible for his comfort and safety.

EQUIPMENT

Blanket
Bath mat
Bath towels
Face towel
Washcloth
Soap
Bath powder
Clean gown or pajamas
Clean bed linen as in "Making an Occupied Bed" (Chap. 28)
Bath thermometer

Preparation. Check the temperature of the bathroom. If you use an electric heater, put it at a safe distance from the tub; caution the patient about touching it with wet towels or hands. Place a chair near the tub with a bath blanket opened over it. This is convenient for the patient to sit on while he dries himself or while you do this for him; it prevents fatigue and allows him to keep part of his body covered as he dries himself, to prevent chilling and exposure. Place towels, washcloth and soap where he can reach them easily. Fill the tub about half full of water—less for a child. The temperature varies anywhere from warm to very warm—never hot or over 100° to 110° F. Test the water with a bath thermometer or your elbow. Elderly and thin people usually find a warmer temperature more comfortable.

Place the bath mat in front of the tub. Bring the patient to the bathroom. Help him to remove his dressing gown, gown and slippers and help him into the bathtub, if he needs assistance—otherwise you may leave him.

Safety Precautions. Devices attached to the tub or a rail on the wall make it easier to get in and out of a tub without assistance. A rubber mat in the bottom of the tub prevents slipping. By sitting on a chair beside the tub, the patient can ease over onto the tub's edge and then swing his feet into the tub; by steadying himself on the opposite edge he can gradually lower himself into a sitting position. This procedure is good muscle exercise; however, it may be easier for some patients to get into the tub before running in the water.

Ask him not to lock the door—tell him that you will see that no one comes in, and that you will be near if he needs help. Come back in a few minutes and call through the door to find out whether he is all right or if he wants anything. Do this often enough to be sure that he is safe. Never leave a child or a depressed person alone in a tub or a person who is unsure or unsteady in his movements. Poor eyesight and stiff joints cause accidents—many home accidents happen in the bathroom. If his condition allows it, the patient may luxuriate in his bath for 10 or 15 minutes; you will need to check with him frequently to see that he does not go to sleep or become faint and slip under the water.

Help him out of the tub and dry him, if he needs assistance. Put on his gown, dressing gown and slippers and assist him back to bed.

The Shower Bath

A guide rail on both the inside and the outside of a shower stall is essential. Two rails are better than one—one rail at a level the patient can reach for support when he is sitting down on a stool and the other higher up for support when he is standing. When the shower is attached to the bathtub rather than being in a separate stall, the suggestion of using a stool in the tub is often welcomed by some apprehensive patients. It is safer for most patients to sit down while taking a shower, especially if they are elderly or weak. In fact, any patient who is very weak or unsteady should not be permitted to take a shower unattended. The patient should have the necessary assistance, and the same precautions should be taken for his safety as for a tub bath. Regulate the temperature of the water first and protect the hair of a woman patient with a waterproof covering. Caution the patient about standing on one leg, as the stool is there to sit on while he washes his feet and legs.

Giving a Sponge Bath to a Bed Patient

The bath is given in such a way as to get the desired effect with the least exertion for the patient and without chilling him. Patients do not always look forward to having a bath—some people are shy and embarrassed; others are afraid of being chilled; a patient may dread a bath because it hurts to move or he feels too tired to make an effort. You can reassure a patient by explaining that the door will be closed or the cubicle curtains drawn, that he will be covered with a blanket to keep him from "catching cold," that you will close the window and use comfortably warm water.

Sometimes even a sponge bath would be harmful; for example, if the patient had considerable pain, was bleeding or weak. You will have to decide when a patient can be allowed to help with his bath and when you must spare him every bit of exertion you can. For instance, some patients can turn and move themselves—others must not be allowed to make the slightest effort. Consider the patient's feelings—if he is uncomfortable unless he has 2 pillows under his head, if he wants another blanket over him, if he says the water feels cold—try to make him comfortable while he is having his bath.

The time a bath is most refreshing is in the morning, to make the patient comfortable for the day, or at night before he goes to sleep. If a patient perspires a great deal or feels hot and uncomfortable, a bath at night may help him to sleep. An hour or so after breakfast is the usual time for bathing a patient; in the patient's home you have more leeway to consider the patient's condition and his preferences. You do need to choose a time when other members of the family are not using the bathroom; also consider your other duties, the doctor's visit or special treatments to be given at a definite time.

In the hospital, the time for the bath is governed by a patient's condition and the number of patients for whom you are responsible. You have less leeway in choosing the time for a bath but you can plan to bathe the most uncomfortable patients first or to leave to the last any patient who has been vomiting or has just had a painful treatment or dressing.

You will be able to give the bath itself in about 20 minutes when you become skillful; you have to allow extra time for the other procedures that go with the bath—getting ready for it, making the bed, caring for the equipment, the soiled linen and the unit afterward. Sometimes other workers, such as ward aides, tidy and dust the unit in the hospital. In the home, you will do it. It is not always possible to give every patient a bath every day in a public hospital ward. A common procedure is to give 2 complete baths a week and partial baths on the other days. The very sick patients have a complete bath every day. You make a plan every day according to the number of patients you are assigned and the number of complete or partial baths you are giving. The head nurse or your team captain helps you with this plan; it changes every day because the doctors' orders change, the patient may go to the operating room or the x-ray department or have special tests or treatments.

EQUIPMENT

Check the patient unit for:
Bath basin
Bath blanket
Bath towel
Face towel
Rubbing alcohol or lotion
Bath powder
Clean bedspread, if necessary
Clean linen, as allowed and necessary
Washcloth
Patient's gown or pajamas
Extra bath towel
Soap
Hot water bag for feet, if necessary
Laundry bag or hamper

Preparation

The preparation for the bath is especially important because you should be able to complete the procedure without leaving the unit for forgotten equipment. When the bath is interrupted, the patient may become chilled and uneasy and the bath water becomes cold. The following key points can be used when preparing for a sponge bath:

KEY POINTS

Tell the patient about the bath.

Check the temperature of the room; protect the patient from drafts, close the window if necessary.

Close the door or draw the cubicle curtains and place a straight chair beside the bed at the foot.

Clear the bedside table for bath equipment.

Fill the bath basin ⅔ full of quite warm water—it can be about 120° F. because it will cool slightly while you are getting the patient ready.

Remove the bedspread, fold it and hang it over the back of the chair. If you are discarding the spread, put it in the receptacle for soiled linen.

Place the bath blanket on the bed and draw it down, remove and fold the bed blanket and hang it over the back of the chair.

Remove and fold the top sheet and place it over the back of the chair.

Remove all but 1 pillow. Remove the pa-

FIG. 102. The bed bath for the helpless patient is often refreshing and relaxing. Here the student nurse is skillfully holding and supporting the patient's leg in preparation for placing it in the basin of water. In addition, the student nurse has the patient well draped, the bed protected with the towel, and her equipment placed conveniently and ready for use. (Fuerst, E. V., and Wolff, L.: Fundamentals of Nursing, p. 237, ed. 3, Philadelphia, Lippincott, 1964)

tient's gown; place it with the soiled linen or over the chair if it is to be worn again.

The suggested procedure described assumes that the patient is unable to move without assistance.

SUGGESTED PROCEDURE

Bring the patient to the side of the bed nearest you by segmentally moving the head and the shoulders, the hips, the thighs and the lower legs.

Guide: *Stand facing the bed, opposite the part to be moved each time, with one leg forward and the knees flexed. Slide your forearms under the part, lean forward and rock back, making effective use of the longest and strongest muscles.*

Spread a bath towel under the patient's chin and wash the face.

Guide: *See "Washing the Patient's Face and Hands," p. 273.*

Use soap to wash the ears and the front of the neck. Rinse and dry.

Guide: *Have the wash cloth wet enough to rinse well without dripping.*

Put the towel over the chest and fold the blanket back. Wash, rinse and dry the chest.

Guide: *Expose the areas under the breasts and observe for irritation.*

Allow the towel to remain on the chest and turn the bath blanket back. Wash, rinse and dry the abdomen.

Guide: *Wash well around to the back, over the pubic area and the upper thighs. If necessary, use a cotton-tipped orangewood stick moistened with oil to cleanse a dirty umbilicus.*

Remove the towel and replace the blanket. Uncover the arm nearest you and place a towel under it. Wash, rinse and dry the arm.

Guide: *Support the arm—lift it and wash the axilla.*

Guide: *Always protect the bottom bedding with a towel while washing any part of the body to prevent the linen from becoming wet and chilling the patient.*

Wash the hands and care for the nails. Replace the bath blanket.

Guide: *See "Caring for the Fingernails" p. 270.*

Repeat for the other arm and hand from the same side of the bed.

Wash, rinse and dry the thigh and the leg nearest you.

Guide: *Flex the patient's knee and drape the bath blanket around the thigh to prevent the exposure of the genital area.*

Place the soapdish and the basin of water at the foot. Support the leg on your arm and carefully place the foot in the basin. Wash, rinse and dry and clean the toenails.

Guide: *See "Caring for the Toenails" p. 270.*

Repeat for the other thigh, leg and foot from the same side of the bed.

Change the bath water.

Guide: *Always change the water at this point, but change it more often if it becomes excessively soapy or soiled. Carry the basin close to the body to reduce strain on the arm muscles.*

Turn the patient on his side and bring him close to the edge of the bed.

Guide: *While the patient is on his back, cross his nearest leg over the opposite—place the arm he will be lying on away from his body with the elbow bent and the hand pointed toward the head of the bed. Go to the opposite side and put one hand on the patient's shoulder, the other on his buttocks. Standing with one leg forward and braced against the bed with your knees flexed, rock back, bringing the patient over on his side.*

Go to the other side of the bed and slip your hands under the hips and draw them to the edge of the bed.

Place the towel along the back. Turn the bath blanket back and wash, rinse and dry the back of the neck, the shoulders, the back, the buttocks and the posterior upper thighs.

Guide: *Stand with one foot forward and rock slightly* ***forward*** *with the upward strokes and* ***backward*** *with the downward strokes. Rocking helps to make strokes even and smooth.*

Rub the back with alcohol or lotion and powder the back following an alcohol rub.

Guide: *Do not use powder with the lotion. It will cake and cause irritation of the skin.*

Roll the patient back to the back-lying position.

Guide: *Put one hand on the patient's shoulder and one on his hip. Place one foot forward and pull him over by rocking back. Go to the other side of the bed. Put your hands under his buttocks. Separate your feet and rock back to bring the patient's body in good alignment.*

Wash the genital area if the patient is unable to do so. Otherwise place the necessary equipment within easy reach and leave the unit.

Put a clean gown on the patient, and make the bed and comb his hair.

Guide: *A towel can be used to protect the bed from combings.*

If a male patient is unable to finish his bath unaided, a member of the male nursing personnel can perform this service for him with the least embarrassment. However, if a male nurse or attendant is not available, and the nurse neglects this necessary procedure, she is guilty of poor nursing. No patient should be penalized because of his sex.

The sponge bath provides an opportunity for the nurse to give close scrutiny to the condition of the patient's body. She should record the type of bath given and any significant observations such as skin eruptions or reddened pressure areas.

Giving a Partial Bed Bath

The patient should have a partial bath on the days when he does not have a complete one. It consists of bathing the face and the hands, the axillae, the back, the buttocks and the genital area. Some patients are able to do this for themselves. You draw the cubicle curtains, regulate the room temperature, prevent drafts and prepare the equipment, remove it and make the bed afterward. A patient may need some assistance, especially in washing the back area. Every patient should be encouraged to accomplish as much of the procedure as possible because it is good muscle exercise and helps to make him self-sufficient.

WHEN THE PATIENT GETS UP

Bed Exercises

Bed exercises are sometimes necessary for

the patient to prepare him for getting out of bed and for such activities as walking, getting into a wheelchair or crutch-walking. These exercises strengthen the muscles in arms, shoulders, legs and thighs which have become weakened from lack of use.

The patient sits up in bed and lifts his hips by pushing his hands down into the mattress. For push-up exercises, he lies face downward and extends his elbows stiffly to raise his head and chest up off the bed. The thigh and leg muscles can be strengthened by asking the patient to contract the *quadriceps femoris*, the large muscle on the anterior thigh. This gives him the feeling that he is pushing the popliteal space behind the knee downward into the mattress and pulling the foot forward.

Some of the daily activities of a patient can be turned into useful exercise. These include such things as reaching for objects on the bedside table, pulling the overbed table forward and pushing it away and brushing the hair. Muscles are strengthened by using them, and the patient will many times create his own exercises when he understands their purpose.

The physical therapist sometimes introduces the exercises to the patient, but since they are often repeated several times a day, the nurse must be able to supervise them.

Getting a Patient Out of Bed

Some patients are allowed out of bed for the entire day. Others are up for a certain length of time each day as their condition improves or permits—to change their position, to strengthen muscles and to prevent deformities.

The patient usually views being up and dressed as a hopeful sign. He is encouraged to wear his own clothes if they are available and his condition warrants it. However, some patients show little interest in being dressed. They may dread the fatigue of putting on clothes, or the pain of moving. Others know that dressing means getting well and taking up problems that they do not want to face. Look for the reason when a patient does not want to be up and dressed.

Make It Easy. The doctor will tell you when a patient may be up for the first time, and for how long. Remember that merely being up is tiring after an illness, so do not put on many garments at first. Begin by warming the patient's garments. Choose those suitable for the time of year. Elderly people probably will need warmer garments than younger people.

A woman patient, especially, feels more self-respecting if she can exchange the shapeless hospital gown for one of her own. Perhaps you can put on her gown in the daytime and change to the hospital gown at night. Bed jackets are attractive, useful and gay. Colors that the patient likes build up her morale. Encourage a patient to help dress herself when she is able. This is especially important for a child because it teaches him to be independent and gives him something to do. It carries on habits he had before he came to the hospital or teaches him how to begin to take care of himself. This is part of rehabilitation.

Decide on the best time to get the patient up. He should be rested; the room should be warm enough. Most patients enjoy having a meal out of bed or talking to visitors at that time. Be careful about tiring the patient the first time he gets up. If you need assistance in helping the patient to get up, choose a time when the assistance is available.

Reassurance and Protection. Reassure the patient by explaining how he will be protected —patients worry about falling, or getting tired. Tell him not to worry if he is not as strong as he expected to be. Even 1 day in bed can make wobbly legs and a feeling of needles in the feet. As he uses his muscles again, his strength will come back. This is how you protect him:

Keep him out of drafts and protect him with clothing and blankets.

Spare him extra exertion by using fewer clothes and more blankets; lift or support him as he moves. You will need help in moving the more helpless or the weak or the unusually heavy patient (see pp. 287-289).

Remove loose rugs near the bed; choose a chair that will not slide; keep a footstool steady; use extra care if the floor is slippery.

Check the pulse rate before and after putting the patient into a chair. The change in position affects the circulation and the supply of blood to the brain. He may feel faint and you must watch for signs of fatigue.

EQUIPMENT

A comfortable chair with arms or a wheelchair
Pillows, blankets, footstool—as necessary
Dressing gown, stockings and slippers or shoes
Moisture-proof pillowcase, if necessary

Preparation. Move the chair close to the bed; put a pillow in the seat—cover it with a moisture-proof pillowcase if the patient is likely to soil it; put a pillow lengthwise against the back. Spread a blanket across the seat and leave enough at the lower end to spread beneath the patient's feet if he needs extra warmth.

Transferring a Patient to Another Unit

There are a number of logical reasons for transferring a patient to another unit: the assignment to a certain unit is only temporary; a change in condition necessitates placing the patient in another department; he requires more quiet or he may be disturbing others; the patient needs a less expensive room due to an unexpected prolonged stay; or his condition becomes serious and alarms the other patients.

A patient often needs reassurance about a transfer. He may think his condition is so serious that he is being moved somewhere to die; he may think that other patients do not like him or have complained about him; he may be ashamed of having to move to a less expensive room or to a ward. Tell him why it will be more advantageous for him in his new quarters; give him truthful reasons. It is true that departments are set up to give special care for different types of illness. Tell him that his new nurses will be very efficient and assure him that he will be moved carefully and explain how. He should be moved when he is feeling his best; the time should not interfere with his meals, his treatments or his rest. Explain that the office knows that he has been moved; they will direct his family and friends to his new quarters.

To transfer a patient, place him in the wheelchair or on the stretcher together with his belongings and chart. Be sure that he is protected from drafts in the halls as he travels from one unit to another. As a friendly gesture, see that he is comfortably established in his new unit.

Getting a Patient Into a Wheelchair

A wheelchair is used to move patients who cannot walk or who should be spared fatigue as much as possible. If a wheelchair is available, it can be used instead of a chair when a patient is allowed to get out of bed. Its advantage over an ordinary chair is that it can be moved or the patient can move himself in it; it can be adjusted. There are several types of wheelchairs, and their prices vary. They are made of wood and metal or all metal. The best ones are made of tubular metal—lightweight and easy to manage. Some of them are collapsible, so that they can be stored easily and carried conveniently from place to place. A patient can travel and take this kind of wheelchair with him without difficulty.

Precautions. The first thing you do is check the wheelchair that you are going to use. Look at the tires; they should be intact—broken tires cause bumps and jars as the wheels move. The footrest should stay in position when you adjust it; the rods that hold the back up should stay adjusted at any angle. If everything is in good working order, the wheelchair is safe and comfortable. Hospitals are liable for accidents that harm a patient; it is dangerous to take chances by using a wheelchair that is broken or out of order.

Remove the patient's fears of falling by explaining how you protect him. These are the precautions you take when putting a patient into a wheelchair:

Get someone to help you if the patient is helpless, heavy or unusually nervous.

Bring the chair against the bed and steady it.

Fold back the footrest so that the patient will not step on it and tip the chair.

Block the wheels to keep the chair from moving.

The Procedure. Lock the wheels of the wheelchair and place it by the side of the bed, facing the head. If the wheels cannot be locked, an assistant must steady it. Prepare the chair with a blanket and pillows as described above. Bring the patient to the side of the bed and assist him to sit up. Proceed slowly: a change in his position may make him feel faint.

Supporting his shoulders and his legs, swing the patient around with his legs over the side of

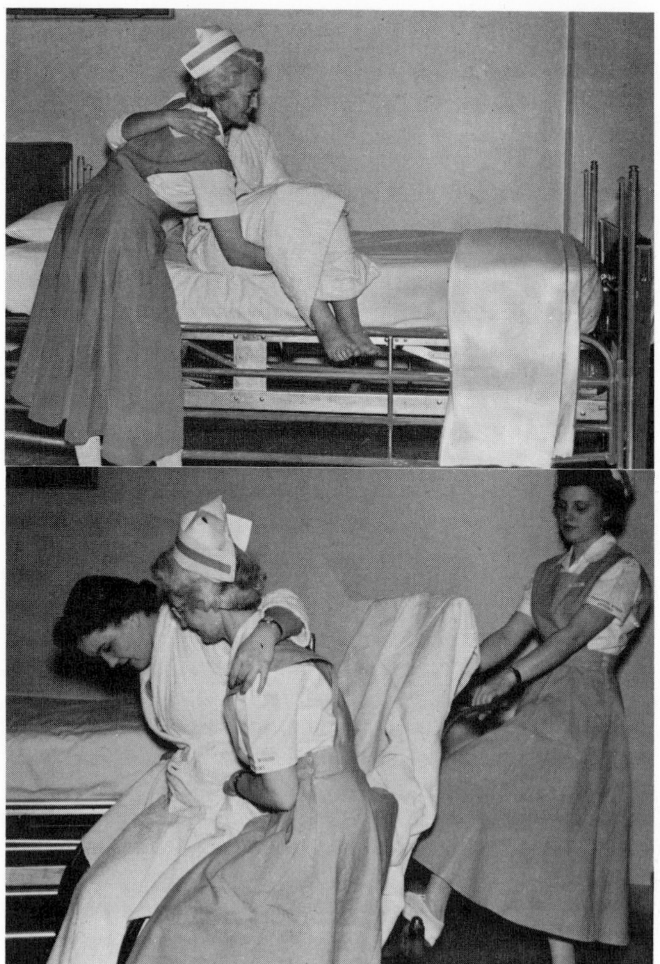

Fig. 103. (*Top*) While an assistant brings a wheelchair forward, the nurse swings the patient's legs over the edge of the bed. (*Bottom*) The nurse helps the patient to lower herself into the wheelchair. Her assistant steadies the chair.

the bed and rest his feet on a chair. This prevents him from sliding off the bed and is more comfortable than if his feet are allowed to dangle. (Dangling is sometimes prescribed as the first step toward ambulation.)

At this point, it is easy to put on the patient's robe, stockings and slippers or shoes. Facing the patient, with his hands on your shoulders, put your hands, thumbs up, under the axillary region. In this position you are able to support him if he falters or falls forward, as he steps onto the footstool and to the floor. Let him rest for a few seconds between steps. Then, turning him with his back to the chair, lower him to the edge of the chair and assist him to move back on the chair seat. Practice good body mechanics—stand with one foot slightly forward and your knees flexed. Prevent strain on your back by using your arm and leg muscles as a lift and lower the patient (see Fig. 103).

Adjust the footstool or wheelchair footrests, the pillows and blanket. If the patient is left alone, be sure that the signal cord is within easy reach and is secured so that it cannot be displaced. This is a good opportunity to turn the mattress. After making the bed, fold back the covers in preparation for the patient's return.

Care of the Wheelchair. Dust the chair to keep it clean; see that its parts are oiled often enough to keep it running smoothly. Check it to see that the adjustable parts are in order and that it is safe. Tell the head nurse about needed repairs; if a damaged chair cannot be removed immediately, put an OUT OF ORDER label on it to prevent injuries to patients.

Putting a Patient on a Stretcher

A stretcher is a 4-wheeled, rubber-tired cart with a moisture-proof mattress. This is what it is used for:

1. To move patients who cannot sit up.
2. To move those with appliances or casts that would not fit into a wheelchair or would be disarranged.
3. To move patients to the operating room or the x-ray department, or to rooms for special tests, treatments or examinations.
4. To transfer patients from one unit to another.

The tires should be intact to prevent jarring the patient; the stretcher covering should be clean; enough blankets should be provided to keep the patient warm. You protect the patient from injury by lifting him correctly and putting him down carefully; by having enough people to lift him; by never leaving him alone when he is on the stretcher.

If the patient is able to help himself, place the stretcher parallel to the bed. Be sure the wheels of the bed are locked. Cover the patient with a blanket and turn back the bedclothes; steady the stretcher and assist the patient to move onto it from the bed. It takes 3 people to move a helpless or unconscious patient to a stretcher (see Fig. 104). An extra person may also be needed in handling a patient with an injured arm or leg. A strap fastened across the patient's body prevents injury from falling. Never move an irresponsible patient without assistance.

Moving and Lifting Helpless Patients

Some patients can help to get themselves in and out of bed; others are partially helpless; still others, such as paralyzed or unconscious patients, are completely helpless and unable to move their bodies or stand on their feet. A change in position helps the patient's muscles as well as his morale.

Body Mechanics. The secret in lifting and moving any weight lies in using good body mechanics. By following these principles, a nurse can move and lift helpless patients with the least amount of strain on the patient or herself. Knowing how to do this safely and efficiently can be very useful in caring for patients at home or in a nursing home, where there is often a scarcity of help. Assistance is usually available in a hospital; however, having to wait for it may mean that the patient is not moved often enough or at the time that is best for him. Of course, the 100-pound nurse must realize that it is physically impossible for her to lift a 250-pound man without help.

Moving Up a Helpless Patient in Bed. It is usually quite easy to slide children or lightweight adults up in bed by yourself but with heavier adults, you need another person to help you. After locking the bed wheels, one person stands on each side of the bed, facing the head. Ask the patient to flex his knees. Each of you puts your nearest arm under the patient's axilla —one person will be responsible for moving the pillow up against the head of the bed as the other supports the patient's head. Advance one foot, flex your knees, and on signal, the patient pushes with his feet as you rock forward, sliding the patient toward the head. The pillow keeps the patient's head from hitting the bed frame as he is moved.

If the patient is unable to push with his feet, you flex his knees, holding them in place if necessary. The pillow is placed against the head of the bed. You stand facing each other on opposite sides of the bed at the patient's hips. Flexing your knees and leaning close to the patient, join hands under his hips and shoulders and on signal rock toward the head of the bed, sliding the patient up. Care must be taken to avoid twisting the patient's head and neck.

The Draw Sheet Method. This is a 2-person method which is easier for all concerned. Lock the bed wheels and slip a wide draw sheet or folded large sheet under the patient, from his head to below the buttocks. Roll the sides of the sheet close to his body—this gives you a firm hold. Stand opposite each other, near the patient's shoulders and chest; face toward the foot of the bed, with the leg nearest the bed behind the other leg. Grasp the sheet near the neck

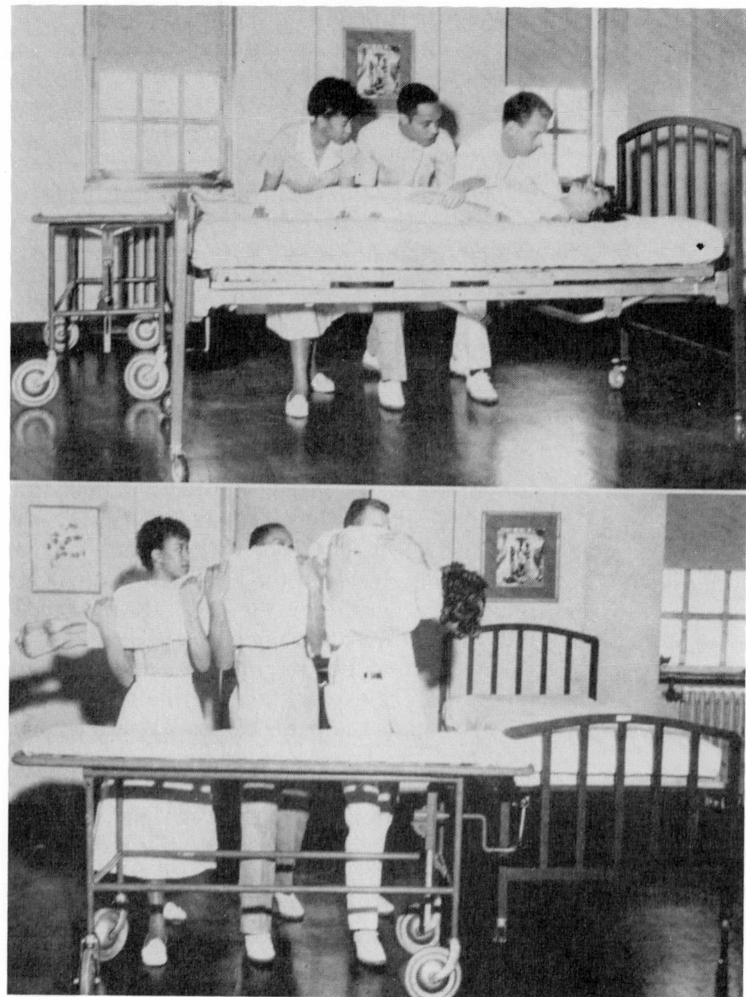

FIG. 104. (*Top*) the 3-man lift. The patient has been brought to the edge of the bed, the stretcher is at a right angle to the foot of the bed and the 3 persons preparing to lift the patient have their arms well under the patient with the greatest support being given to the heaviest part of the patient. Each has a wide base of support and each is leaning over close to the patient in preparation for the lift.

(*Bottom*). On a given signal, the 3 persons rock back and simultaneously lift the patient and logroll her onto their chests. They then pivot and place the patient on the stretcher. As the patient is being lowered onto the stretcher, all 3 carriers maintain a wide base of support and flex their knees.

and near the lumbar region, lean forward and rock backward together. Your combined weight slides the draw sheet and patient up toward the head of the bed.

The 3-Man Lift. This method is used to move a helpless patient while maintaining his horizontal position to do it. The procedure described here is for moving a patient from his bed to a stretcher (see Fig. 104).

SUGGESTED PROCEDURE

Lock the bed wheels.

Place the stretcher at a right angle to the foot of the bed.

Carrier No. 1, the tallest, stands at the patient's head; next tallest is No. 2; the shortest is No. 3.

***Related body mechanic:** The tallest people have the longest arms making it easier to support the patient's head and shoulders.*

No. 2 slides both arms under the patient's buttocks.

***Related body mechanic:** The heaviest part needs the strongest support.*

No. 1 puts one arm under the patient's neck and shoulders with the other arm against the arm of No. 2.

***Related body mechanic:** The touching arms add support.*

No. 3 puts one arm against the arm of No. 2, with the other arm under the patient's ankles.

All 3 lean over the patient and moving on signal, together they rock the patient back and slide him to the edge of the bed.

Related body mechanic: *The lifters' weight and arm and knee power combine to move the patient.*

The lifters slide their arms farther under the patient, advance one foot, flex their knees and logroll the patient onto their chests, then pivot around to the stretcher and lower the patient onto it, bringing their bodies down with him.

Related body mechanic: *Logrolling brings the centers of gravity closer together to stabilize lifting power and reduce strain. The large leg and arm muscles are stronger than the back muscles.*

Moving a Helpless Patient From the Bed to a Chair. This is a useful technic, especially when a helpless patient is too heavy for 1 person to lift alone and no other help is available. It also can be used to slide a patient onto a commode.

SUGGESTED PROCEDURE

Place the chair facing and against the bed, and opposite the patient's buttocks.

Slide your arms under the patient's head and shoulders and advance one foot. Rock backward drawing the upper part of the patient's body to the edge of the bed.

From behind, put your arms well under the patient's axillae, resting his head and shoulders against you.

Related body mechanic: *Distributing the weight makes lifting easier.*

Move around to the back of the chair, drawing the patient into it as you move. Rock back, pulling the patient into the chair.

Related body mechanic: *Brace yourself and the chair by leaning against the chair back.*

Grasping it at the seat, slowly pull the chair back until only his feet and ankles are resting on the bed.

Flex the patient's knees and legs as you lower his feet to the floor keeping your knees flexed.

Related body mechanic: *Leg and thigh muscles are stronger than back muscles.*

Moving a Helpless Patient From a Chair to a Hospital Bed. This procedure is slightly different from the one you follow when the bed and the chair levels are the same. The hospital bed is higher than the chair.

SUGGESTED PROCEDURE

Bring the chair to the side of the bed, with the patient facing the center.

Related body mechanic: *If the chair does not roll, slide it to the bed rather than lifting it. This conserves energy.*

Stand behind the patient, to one side of the chair and place your arms under the patient's axillae drawing him close against you.

Related body mechanic: *Arm and shoulder muscles are long and strong for lifting. Supporting the upper portion of the patient's body on yourself reduces the weight to be moved.*

Standing with the foot nearest the chair drawn back and the other foot forward, rock the patient's trunk strongly upward, lifting the entire body and the buttocks onto the bed.

Related body mechanic: *Rocking adds the weight of the body to muscle power.*

Supporting the thighs by resting against them, slide the chair away with your foot.

Lift the patient's legs onto the bed and roll and slide him into position.

Related body mechanic: *It takes less energy to move an object by rolling or sliding it than it does to lift it.*

THE SPIRITUAL NEEDS OF THE PATIENT

You will take care of people of different faiths and creeds; religion is a vital part of people's lives. You will find the Bible and a prayer book on many bedside tables. People feel a need for reassurance when they are sick; sometimes they talk to you about it. Some of them are lonely, without friends or in a strange city. They may talk to you about their beliefs; be sensitive to the clues that mean that a patient would like to talk to a clergyman or a priest or a rabbi. A patient may think that you have no time for his spiritual needs. Respect his confidences as professional secrets. Let your patients feel that you are sympathetic to this part of their lives, too.

The Religious Adviser

Religious belief is a strong spiritual support in time of trouble. Many people rely on and find comfort in their relationship with a spiritual adviser who helps to resolve their doubts and fears. As a member of the health team, he can often help in interpreting the patient's treatment and help him to accept it. It is true that some procedures violate a patient's religious principles. For example, blood transfusions are forbidden for Jehovah's Witnesses. A nurse must try to understand how much a patient's religious beliefs matter to him and respect his right to have them. On the other hand, she must also respect the rights of patients to adhere to no religious faith at all.

Chaplains and Religious Services

In many of the larger hospitals chaplains of the various faiths are available to visit patients. Some hospitals also have chapels in which religious services are held on Sunday and at other times for the 3 most common faiths. Hospitals maintained by a religious denomination may follow the services of that denomination. Every Catholic hospital has a chapel where patients may attend services; the doors are always open and a patient, depending on his condition, may go in as he wishes, to worship or meditate.

Religious Faiths and Rituals

Every nurse should be familiar with the customs of the 3 most common religious faiths—Protestant, Catholic and Jewish—and should understand their significance. Religious faith teaches us to know and serve God and to love our fellowmen. The forms of these 3 faiths are old and beloved and familiar to those that follow them. They are as much a part of some people's lives as moving and breathing. They feel comfortable with them and cling to them. Yet one individual's attitude toward his religion may be different from that of others of the same faith.

The Protestant Faith. There are many denominations in the Protestant faith. They agree on some things and disagree on others. Their forms of worship are different, but most of them recognize 2 ceremonies—baptism and communion. Therefore members of the different denominations would be expected to consider these ceremonies important. The Protestant minister is a friend and a spiritual adviser to his congregation. He is interested in the members of his church as people and is ready to talk with them about their spiritual difficulties—to give them reassurance and explain their doubts. Again, individual needs differ. A person who has found strength and comfort in talking with his minister is more likely to want to see him when he is ill. Yet you must never upset a patient by ushering in a minister without first finding out whether or not he wants to see him.

The Jewish Faith. The Orthodox Jew follows many ancient and honorable religious customs that are sacred to him. The custom that perhaps matters most and is most difficult to follow when he is sick is related to his food. (See page 224 for the Orthodox Jewish food laws.) It is impossible to serve kosher meat in a non-Jewish hospital, but you can be sure that you do not serve meat and dairy foods together to an Orthodox Jewish patient. You can let the head nurse know that the patient is an Orthodox Jew; she can tell the dietary department. Then you are able to let the patient know that his religious beliefs will be respected. Even though the Jewish patient is not required to observe these dietary regulations when he is ill, he is very reluctant to disobey a sacred religious law.

Circumcision is the surgical removal of the foreskin of the penis; it has a religious significance for the people of the Jewish faith. This operation is dealt with in more detail in Chapter 51.

The Catholic Faith. The Catholic Church holds Baptism, Confession, Holy Communion and Extreme Unction as sacraments of the Church. These ceremonies are a vital part of a sincere Catholic's faith. He will want the spiritual comfort of these sacraments for himself and for those who are dear to him. The priest is confessor, friend and adviser to his parishioners and is given authority to administer these sacraments. It would be a matter of deep sorrow to a Catholic if he or a member of his family were to die without them. As a nurse, you may play a vital role in providing a Catholic patient with these services.

During a long illness a Catholic patient usually wants a priest to hear his confession and to give him communion, from time to time. You should provide as much privacy for the patient and the priest as possible, prepare the table for the communion and place a chair at the patient's bedside. You cover the table with a clean white cloth; place 2 blessed candles and a crucifix upon it; provide a container for holy water, a sprinkler, a small glass of plain water for rinsing the priest's fingers after he has given the Host, a spoon to give the patient water afterward, if he needs it, and 3 small linen cloths—the priest uses 2 of them, and the third is placed under the patient's chin while he receives. You may not be able to provide everything, but you can prepare the covered table, the 3 napkins, a glass of water and a spoon. However, most hospitals provide a sick-call kit for the priest containing the articles necessary to administer the sacraments.

According to the present fasting rule, solid foods and alcoholic beverages may be taken up to 1 hour before a person receives communion. Any true medicine, solid or liquid, nonalcoholic liquids, and water may be taken anytime. It may comfort the patient to have you read the appropriate prayers with him before the priest comes. These prayers are in every Catholic prayer book.

The symbolism of the Catholic Church provides an opportunity for showing religious faith. The crucifix, statues and pictures represent religious facts in the Catholic belief; devotion to them is an expression of love and reverence for the things for which they stand. You can see why these symbols are comforting and significant to the Catholic patient and may be among his most cherished possessions, and such articles should be handled respectfully by the nurse.

Extreme Unction is a sacrament of comfort and consolation; it is not offered solely to prepare a Catholic patient for death. Many Catholics look upon Extreme Unction as a positive sign that death is imminent. Because they are unable to face that knowledge, they may delay in receiving the sacrament. If a priest is not available to explain the real purpose of Extreme Unction you can reassure the patient, explaining that sick people often need its spiritual comfort and reassurance.

If a Catholic patient has been ill for some time, his family will be aware of his spiritual needs. However, you may be responsible for telling them of sudden serious changes in his condition that may mean death is near. Many patients are brought into hospitals unconscious or in a serious condition. Always look for indications that such a patient is a Catholic, if he is unable to tell you. You may find a rosary or a medal on his person or information on an identification card. Always call a priest so that the patient may have Extreme Unction; if the patient is conscious, he also should have an opportunity to confess and receive communion. To prepare for Extreme Unction, loosen the covers at the foot of the bed—the priest will wish to anoint the feet. A table is set up as for communion and if a kit is not available, you provide 6 or 7 cotton pledgets on a plate, an empty plate for the used pledgets, a small container of salt and some holy water.

The last rites of the Church are a vital part of the Catholic faith and comfort both the patient and the members of his family. If a patient dies suddenly, the priest can administer them conditionally within 2 hours after death.

When the death of a newborn child of Catholic parents is imminent, it may be necessary for the nurse to administer Baptism. This procedure is discussed in Chapter 51.

29

NURSING TREATMENTS

APPLYING HEAT TO THE BODY

Applications of heat are used widely to treat disease and to relieve pain. Heat may be used also to make the chilly patient more comfortable or to raise the temperature of the body. Since heat must be fairly intensive to produce the desired effect, there is one great danger in using it—the danger of burns. This is why you never apply heat to relieve pain in any part of the body without an order from the doctor. As an emergency measure, you can apply external heat for chills or cover the patient who is in shock with light blankets to elevate the body temperature.

Heat dilates the blood vessels in the skin and brings more blood to the surface to warm an area. It stimulates the circulation and the sweat glands and as a result helps to remove poisonous wastes from the body. It relaxes tense muscles and stimulates inactive ones. Heat applied to certain parts of the body stimulates the circulation in the internal organs. For example, heat applied to the feet will dilate the blood vessels in the feet and, thereby, relieve congestion in the abdomen and the head. Very hot applications may have the opposite of the desired effect —that is, they may contract the blood vessels in the skin and decrease the blood supply.

Sensitivity to Heat

Precautions to prevent injury from burns are necessary for these reasons:

The nerves in the skin are numbed easily, and the patient may not feel the pain of a burn, especially if he has had repeated applications of heat.

Some parts of the body are especially sensitive to heat—for example, the eyelids, the neck and the inside surface of the arm.

Large applications provide more heat to the skin than small ones.

Infants, old people and people with fair, thin skin have less resistance to heat. Lowered body resistance also makes the body tissues less resistant to heat.

Patients who are unconscious, under anesthesia, or some patients suffering from cerebral hemorrhage cannot tell when heat is intense.

Impaired circulation and some metabolic diseases make people more susceptible to burns. This is true of the patient in shock or the diabetic patient.

An insensitive person does not feel pain as quickly as the high-strung individual and may not realize or feel the pain in time to prevent a burn.

Heat is applied only when ordered by a doctor. This is true regardless of the form of application.

Dry Heat

Heat can be applied to the body as either dry or moist heat and is usually applied for its local effects. The common methods for applying dry heat are exposure to the sun, a hot-water bag, an electric pad, a heat lamp or an electric cradle.

When you apply heat to any patient, think of the reasons why this particular individual may be sensitive to heat. It helps you to determine what degree of heat is safe for him and how long you can safely leave any heat application on the skin. The application must be hot enough to accomplish its purpose but must keep within the safety range. For example: the doctor leaves orders to apply an electric pad to the patient's back continuously; if you find that the skin is becoming red and sensitive, you report this condition and decide whether you should keep the pad at a lower temperature or leave it off altogether for a time.

Preparing and Applying a Hot-Water Bag. A hot-water bag is applied to relieve aches and pains, to increase the circulation or to warm a patient. It must be leakproof to prevent burning the patient and wetting his clothing or his bed. The temperature of the water in a hot-water bag may be anywhere up to 125°F., depending on the area to which it is applied, the age and the condition of the patient. Tell the patient that you have tested the temperature of the water but that some people are more sensitive to heat than others, so he must tell you how it feels to him. The bag always is placed in a cover which can be previously warmed to hasten the transmission of heat.

Never place a hot-water bag directly against the skin of an unconscious patient or a patient in shock. Never allow a patient to lie on a hot-water bag or a heating pad. If possible, place the heating unit on the top of the area to be warmed. When the heat is confined in a small place, the possibilities of burning are increased. If you are going to treat a patient by applying heat to the back, turn the patient onto his side or abdomen. Regulate the temperature of the water in a hot-water bag so that it will be safe for a patient who may shift it to a sensitive area in an effort to obtain relief from pain. Never make it hotter than 125°F. A safe temperature range is:

Infants under 2 years of age: 105° to 115° F.

Children over 2 years of age and adults: 115° to 125° F.

Refill the bag often enough to maintain the desired temperature. Inspect the skin regularly to see whether or not it looks red. When the bag is no longer needed, empty it and hang it upside down to drain and to dry. Prevent losing the stopper by putting it in a safe place or tying it to the bag. When the bag is dry, screw in the stopper, leaving the bag inflated to keep the sides from sticking together. Store the bag in its accustomed place.

A heated iron, or bricks, or sandbags or saltbags heated in the oven can be used as an emergency substitute for a hot-water bag to supply warmth. Obviously, you could not apply a brick to the abdomen as a treatment, but you may be able to use a light saltbag in this way. Emergencies do arise in the home when a hot-water bag is not available or when "Old Faithful," after hanging in the bathroom for years, suddenly springs a leak.

If you are in a patient's home where a thermometer is not available, make the water only as hot as you can bear it on the inside of your wrist.

EQUIPMENT

Hot-water bag and cover (cotton flannel makes an excellent cover)
Pitcher of hot water
Bath thermometer

SUGGESTED PROCEDURE

Inspect the stopper for the washer.

Reason: *Leakage wets clothing and the bed, and it may also burn the patient.*

Test the temperature of the water with a thermometer. Bring it to the temperature desired, not over 125°F.

Reason: *A thermometer is accurate. Hand testing is unreliable.*

Pour the water into the bag, filling it about ⅔ full.

Reason: *The heavier the bag, the more uncomfortable it is on the patient and the more difficult it is to adjust.*

Expel the air: place the bag flat on the table —when the water is seen in the neck, screw in the stopper.

Reason: *Air distends the bag and makes it hard and unadjustable.*

Test for leaks by holding the bag upside down.

Reason: *A missing washer or loosely screwed in stopper causes leaks.*

Dry the bag and apply the warmed cover.

Reason: *A warm cover helps the heat to reach the body more quickly.*

Apply as ordered and record the treatment on the patient's chart.

Applying an Electric Pad. An electric pad is a covered network of wires that give off heat when an electrical current passes through them. Pads with a waterproof covering are best and the only kind safe to use in moist conditions. There also are special plastic pads, filled with tubes containing water which is heated by an electric unit to a set temperature. A key is necessary to alter the temperature setting; therefore, the patient is unable to change it. This type of pad is safe to use over wet dressings. A patient may accidentally turn up the temperature on an ordinary pad and burn himself. Never put pins through a heating pad—if a pin touches the electric wires it may cause an electric shock. If the wires are crushed or bent the pad may overheat and cause burns or even a fire. And always remember that the pad may get too hot—the temperature of the water in a hot water bag goes down, but in the heating pad the temperature is constant. This means that there is a greater danger of burning the patient.

Special precautions are necessary when electric pads are used for children, very old people or for irrational or unconscious patients.

Before you apply the pad, connect it with an electric outlet; turn the heating switch to "high" to see whether the pad heats promptly; turn it off and disconnect from the outlet. Cover it with its washable case or a towel, connect to the outlet at the bedside, adjust to the proper temperature and apply. Inspect frequently to prevent burning the patient.

Giving Lamp Treatments. Lamp treatments usually are given by trained personnel because exposure to light rays must be regulated carefully to prevent injury to the patient. Information about light rays is included here to explain why lamp treatments may be dangerous unless they are given properly.

Lamp treatments apply heat through infrared or ultraviolet light rays. The directions for these treatments vary according to the condition to be treated and the kind of light that is used. Only the surface to be treated is exposed to the light—the adjoining parts are covered with towels or a sheet. It is important to follow directions exactly about adjusting the bulb above the surface of the skin; the height is determined by the purpose of the treatment and the kind of light that is used. The length of the exposure is governed by these same factors.

Infrared rays are used to relax muscles, stimulate the circulation and relieve pain; they have the same effect on the body as other forms of dry heat. *Ultraviolet* rays are not so penetrating as infrared rays—sunlight provides mild ultraviolet light rays. However, prolonged exposure to the sun will burn a sensitive skin. Ultraviolet rays are used to treat skin infections and wounds. Authorities say that these rays stimulate the body cells to make protective substances that increase our resistance to infection. They are used also in treating rickets because they stimulate the body cells to make vitamin D (see p. 211).

Adjusting the bulb at the proper distance from the skin and the exact timing of the exposure are important safeguards for the patient. Ultraviolet light irritates the eyes; they must be protected with moist cotton pads or dark glasses. Skin redness is not a guide in preventing a burn because redness does not appear until several hours after the treatment, nor does the patient feel the heat.

You prepare a patient for a lamp treatment by explaining the reasons for it and by cautioning him about keeping his eyes covered and his body quiet. He should be in as comfortable a position as possible and feel confident that he will be watched carefully.

Moist Heat

Water is a better heat conductor than air; therefore, moist hot applications heat the skin more quickly than applications of dry heat. This is why you wring hot wet compresses or packs as dry as possible—excess water may burn the skin. Prolonged applications of moist heat also soften and weaken the skin. Moist heat is more penetrating than dry heat and is more effective for relieving pain in the deeper tissues. Gauze compresses, woolen or flannel packs (stupes), baths and inhalations are used to apply moist heat.

Applying Hot Moist Compresses and Packs

Hot moist compresses and packs are used to apply heat to an area to stimulate circulation and to promote drainage in infections. Packs are made of wool or flannel and are used on larger body areas than are gauze compresses. (Terrycloth toweling may be substituted for packs if wool or flannel material is not available.) The applications need not be sterile unless there is a break in the skin. Water or a mild antiseptic solution such as 2 percent boric acid or normal saline may be used.

The doctor prescribes the kind of application and how it is to be used; it may be applied for long or short periods at a time, changing the application frequently to keep it hot. The length of time varies from 10 to 30 minutes, changing the application from every 2 to 5 minutes. Thick compresses or packs, covered to keep the heat in, will stay hot longer than thin ones. They are applied as hot as the patient can comfortably tolerate them. He may feel chilly, so take precautions to keep him warm and protected from drafts.

The preparation of the patient is especially important because the sight of hot steaming water is rather frightening; explain that you wring the material very dry so that there is no danger of dropping hot water on his skin, and that it loses heat quickly and will not be nearly as hot as the water by the time it reaches his skin. Apply it gradually so that he can tell you how hot it feels—only the patient knows when an application is too hot for comfort.

EQUIPMENT

Basin containing the prescribed solution	Oiled silk, plastic or aluminum foil
Electric plate	Dry pack
Compresses or packs of suitable size	Applicators
	Petroleum jelly
2 Forceps or wringer	Waste container

KEY POINTS IN THE PROCEDURE

Heat the solution until it steams.

Immerse the compresses or packs in the hot solution.

Principle: *Woolen material absorbs water slowly but holds moisture. Gauze absorbs moisture quickly and dries out quickly.*

Arrange the waterproof cover and the dry pack to place over the moist compress or pack after it is applied.

Principle: *Covering the moist pack or compress keeps air out, and contact with the air cools the pack.*

Apply petroleum jelly to the area with an applicator.

Principle: *Coating on the skin allows heat to penetrate gradually.*

Wring the compress or the pack with forceps or wringer, removing as much of the water as is possible.

Principle: *Hot water burns the skin.*

Shake them lightly.

Principle: *Slight heat loss from contact with the air reduces the possibility of burning.*

Apply to the area lightly at first, gradually pressing against the skin. In a few seconds lift the pack slightly to inspect the degree of redness of the skin.

Principle: *Air is a poor heat conductor. Eliminating air spaces between the compress or the pack and the skin makes it more effective. The degree of redness of the skin shows whether or not the pack is too hot.*

Cover the moist compress or pack with the dry pack and moisture-proof cover.

Principle: *Covering provides insulation against heat loss and evaporation of moisture.*

Change the compress or pack often enough to keep the area heated.

Principle: *Small applications cool more quickly than large ones.*

Continue the treatment for the prescribed time, then remove the dry and moist applications. Dry the skin and cover it.

Principle: *Moisture softens the skin and makes it susceptible to chilling.*

Make the patient comfortable and care for the equipment.

Record the treatment on the patient's chart, noting the patient's reactions.

Turpentine Stupes. Turpentine stupes are packs applied to the abdomen to relieve pain, congestion and distention due to gas in the intestines. The same procedure is followed as for hot moist packs, and the same precautions are observed. The combination of heat and turpentine may burn the skin, and the treatment is discontinued if it becomes very red before the prescribed time period is over.

In applying turpentine stupes, applicators are used to first paint the skin with a mixture of 4 parts of cottonseed or mineral oil to 1 part of turpentine, or for a child, 8 parts of oil to 1 part of turpentine. The mixture is reapplied every third or fourth pack. An abdominal binder is sometimes used to keep the application secure on the abdomen.

When the treatment is given to relieve distention, a rectal tube is inserted in the rectum to aid in expelling gas. Place the end of the tube in a urinal or a kidney basin between the patient's thighs and let it remain in place for half an hour following the treatment.

Applying Hot Compresses to the Eye. The eyelid and the skin around the eye are thin and delicate structures; precautions to prevent burning are especially important. If the eye is discharging, discard each compress when you remove it. Boil all equipment after it is used for an infectious condition. If compresses are applied to both eyes, use separate equipment for each to prevent spreading the infection. Eyesight is very precious, and eye treatments must be given carefully, since they may be the deciding factor between preserving and losing sight.

Soaks. Moist heat also can be applied to the extremities or to an area of the torso by immersing the part in warm water, or a solution, for a prescribed time. This procedure is called a soak. The purpose in giving a soak may be to improve circulation, to increase the blood supply in an infected area, to aid in breaking down infected tissues (suppuration), to apply medication or to cleanse discharging or encrusted wounds. This treatment requires a basin or receptacle large enough to hold sufficient water to cover the part and to accommodate it comfortably. A tub shaped for giving arm or leg soaks is available in most hospitals.

Usually, it is not considered necessary to sterilize the tub, but it should be cleaned thoroughly with soap and water. Tap water is used for soaks unless otherwise specified since it is generally recognized as being free from harmful bacteria.

The temperature of the water usually ranges from 105° to 110° F., although the doctor may prescribe a definite temperature. The usual length of a soak is 15 to 20 minutes. The temperature of the water should be tested frequently and hot water added as needed. When adding hotter water, pour it in near the edge with your hand between the stream and the patient's body, stirring the water as you add it to distribute the heat evenly.

If the soak is given with the patient in bed, protect the bed with a waterproof covering beneath the tub. Place the basin or tub so that the patient's body is in good alignment and in a comfortable position, avoiding pressure on the arm or leg. If necessary, place a folded bath towel over the edge of the tub beneath the body part and a folded pillow beneath the knee or elbow. Depending on the patient's condition, a soak may be given with the patient in bed or sitting in a chair.

The procedure described here applies to an arm or leg soak.

EQUIPMENT

Arm or foot tub
Bath thermometer
Pitcher of hot water or solution
Protective sheet and cover
Bath towels
Bath blanket
Sterile dressings, if necessary

KEY POINTS IN THE PROCEDURE

Adjust the protective sheet and cover it with a bath towel. Prepare the water in the tub (105° to 110° F. unless otherwise specified).

When the tub is removed at the end of the bath, the arm or leg can rest on the towel.

Remove the dressings if there is a wound and lower the part into the water gradually.

Adjust the pad on the edge of the tub and support the knees or elbow with a folded pillow if necessary.

Principle: *Pressure on the blood vessels on the backs of the legs or the arms interferes with the circulation. Unsupported parts cause fatigue and poor alignment.*

Test the temperature at intervals.

Principle: *The proper degree of heat is necessary to make the treatment effective.*

Add hot water as needed to maintain the required temperature, stirring the tub water as it is poured.

Principle: *Stirring the water hastens the diffusion of the hot water in the cooler water and distributes the heat evenly.*

Remove the part from the bath in 15 or 20 minutes (or as ordered). If there is a wound, apply a sterile dressing. Dry the other areas.

In the case of a discharging wound, disinfect the equipment.

Principle: *Contact with infected material spreads infection to others.*

Record the treatment on the chart, noting the patient's reactions.

Hip or Sitz Bath. The purpose of a sitz bath may be to apply heat to the pelvic area or to cleanse a wound. It is also known as a hip bath and consists of placing the patient in a tub containing enough water to reach the umbilicus. A regular bathtub can be used, but a special sitz tub or seat built to accommodate the patient's hips and buttocks may be provided if the baths are ordered frequently. The advantage of a sitz tub is that the patient's legs and feet do not have to be in the water and heat is concentrated on the pelvic area. If the aim of the bath is to apply heat, the temperature of the water should be 110° to 115° F. If it is given for cleansing purposes and to promote healing, the bath temperature should be from 94° to 98° F. The doctor will prescribe the length of the treatment according to its aim. It is usually 15 to 20 minutes.

The effect of heat on a relatively large area of the body may make the patient weak or faint. He should be observed closely and protected from drafts and chilling by covering the upper part of his body with a blanket. The same precautions should be taken after the bath. Usually the patient goes to bed for a time until the circulation has returned to normal.

The height of a sitz tub cannot be adjusted, and a short patient may need a stool under his feet to prevent pressure on the blood vessels in his legs. A folded towel in the lumbar area will help to support his back and keep his body in good alignment during the treatment.

KEY POINTS IN THE PROCEDURE

Fill the tub to the required depth with water of the specified temperature.

Principle: *Higher temperatures produce relaxation of the body parts to relieve pain. Moderate temperatures relieve congestion and aid in cleansing.*

When the patient is in the bath, cover the upper part of his body with a blanket.

Principle: *Exposure to cold and drafts causes chilling.*

Test the temperature of the water often and add hot water as needed to maintain the required temperature.

Principle: *A constant degree of heat is necessary to make the procedure effective.*

Watch for signs of fainting or weakness.

Principle: *The supply of blood to the brain is reduced as heat stimulates the circulation in the pelvic area.*

Assist the patient in getting out of the bath after the specified time.

Principle: *The success of the treatment depends on sufficient exposure to heat.*

Protect the patient from drafts and chilling by covering him adequately in bed. Request ambulatory patients to remain in bed for a short time.

Principle: *It takes a little time for the pelvic circulation to return to normal.*

Record the treatment on the chart, noting the patient's reactions.

Giving a Steam Inhalation. A steam inhalation is a method of administering soothing drugs and warm moist heat to irritated and congested mucous membranes in the nose and throat. The drug is added to heated water which vaporizes and carries the drug to the affected part as the patient breathes in the vapor. Moist heat alone is effective in relieving inflammation and congestion. *Compound benzoin tincture* and *oil of eucalyptus* are drugs that are often used in inhalations for their soothing effects.

Most hospitals are equipped with electrically

FIG. 105. Inhalations from a kettle. A large carton has been used to confine the steam somewhat. It has been lined with turkish towels to absorb the moisture. Clothespins have been used to pin back the towels which cover the tent. A piece of rubber tubing has been used to guide the steam into the tent, care having been taken to anchor it in such a fashion that the steam is not directed to the face.

heated apparatus for giving steam inhalations. In the home, a teakettle with tubing and funnel attached can be used; an electric plate will keep the solution steaming. (Do not use the family teakettle if benzoin is being used. It leaves a sticky deposit that defies cleansers.)

Continuous inhalations sometimes are given following operations on the larynx or trachea. Some kind of an enclosure may be necessary to confine the steam to the patient's breathing area. Blankets draped over screens around the head of the bed will serve if nothing else is available. The front of the tent should be open so that the patient's face can be seen. For a brief or occasional inhalation a fair-sized pitcher can be used. Place a paper bag over the top of the pitcher and cut a hole in the bottom of the bag to go over the patient's nose and mouth. The patient sits up in bed and holds the pitcher in his lap in a basin. He may place a large bath towel over his head and the pitcher to enclose the steam. Hot solution may be added if the inhalation is prolonged beyond 10 minutes.

A tent over the crib is the best method of ensuring a high humidity in the air when giving a steam inhalation to an infant or a child; this is a common treatment for croup.

The hot kettle and the plate should be out of the patient's reach to prevent the possibility of burns; the steam spout should be directed toward the nose of the patient, but at a sufficient distance to prevent burns from direct steam or contact with the spout. The spout should extend into the tent from the side or the back. Precautions are especially important in giving an inhalation to a child, and it is safest to keep the spout at the end of the crib away from the child's face. A child should have particularly close attention during an inhalation.

EQUIPMENT

Inhaler, croupkettle or teakettle
Hot plate, if necessary
Solution ordered
Towel

KEY POINTS IN THE PROCEDURE

Prepare the solution as it was ordered. If benzoin is ordered, use 1 dram to a pint of water.

Attach the inhaler to an electric outlet or put the kettle on an electric hot plate.

Principle: *Heating a liquid produces steam.*

Move the apparatus to the bedside when the steam rises, and place it on a chair or stool near the head of the bed.

Protect the patient's eyes with a folded towel.

Principle: *Concentrated heat may irritate the eyes and forehead.*

Direct the spout toward the patient's nose and mouth.

Principle: *Moist heat soothes irritated mucous membranes and relieves congestion.*

Replenish the solution in the inhaler if necessary.

Principle: *Steam is produced by the evaporation of water. Constant heat causes evaporation.*

At the end of the prescribed period, discontinue the treatment. Dry the patient's face and neck and protect him from the cold air or drafts.

Principle: *Moist heat dilates surface blood vessels. Heat loss from the skin causes chilling. Exposing the patient to a change in the temperature of the room can counteract the beneficial effects of an inhalation.*

Record the treatment on the chart, noting the patient's reactions.

APPLYING COLD TO THE BODY

The first effect of cold on the body is to contract the surface blood vessels. This prevents the escape of heat from the body; it also controls hemorrhage. Cold affects the skin like a local anesthetic because it numbs the nerve endings. Prolonged applications of cold can be as damaging to the tissues as prolonged heat. If the patient complains of numbness in the area and the skin looks white or spotty, the applications should be discontinued. Cold applications as a continuing treatment may be discontinued at intervals to prevent tissue injury.

Cold is applied to sprains or bruises to prevent swelling (edema); it will not reduce edema which is already present in the tissues. As cold decreases the flow of blood in one area of the body, it increases the flow to other areas. This explains why cold or chilling drafts striking the body often cause congestion in the nasal passages. Continued applications or prolonged exposure to cold affects the deeper tissues (frostbite).

Cold applications relieve pain, such as a headache; they make the patient with a fever more comfortable. They slow up bacterial activity in infections and relieve congestion in the parts where they are applied. Cold is applied to the body by using icecaps, ice collars, compresses or cool sponge baths.

Filling and Applying an Icecap or an Ice Collar

The doctor prescribes the application of an icecap to specific parts of the body; you may apply an icecap for headache or in an emergency, such as a nosebleed, without an order from the doctor. Always remember that cold has harmful effects on a weakened or an undernourished person although it may be stimulating to a healthy person.

An icecap is a flat, oval rubber bag with a leakproof, screw-in top. The opening in an icecap is wide so that it can be filled easily. An ice collar is a narrow rubber bag curved to fit the neck. These bags are used for headache; after throat operations or tooth extractions to check and prevent bleeding; to prevent intestinal movement in abdominal inflammation, such as appendicitis; to relieve pain in engorged breasts; to prevent painful swelling in injured tissues; and for some heart conditions. The procedure described here applies to either an icecap or an ice collar.

EQUIPMENT

Icecap or ice collar
Icecap cover—cotton flannel or a towel
Basin of ice
Safety pins for towel

KEY POINTS IN THE PROCEDURE

Inspect the top for a washer and test the bag for leakage.

Reason: *Leaking water will wet the bedclothes and chill the patient.*

Fill an icecap about ¾ full, using small pieces of ice.

Reason: *It is easier to fit it closely to the body if the ice is in small pieces.*

Flatten the icecap on a hard surface, and press on it to expel the air.

Reason: *Air is a poor conductor of heat and interferes with the removal of heat from the body.*

Screw in the top, making sure that the washer is in place.

Reason: *The washer prevents leakage.*

Dry and cover the icecap with an absorbent cover or towel.

Reason: *Moisture condenses on the outside which is uncomfortable for the patient if the icecap is uncovered.*

Adjust the icecap on the part of the body to be treated.

Apply the icecap for ½ to 1 hour as directed. Leave it off for 1 hour before reapplying unless directed otherwise.

Reason: *Prolonged applications of cold slow up circulation which may cause tissue damage.*

Record the treatment on the patient's chart, noting "on" and "off" periods.

Many hospitals provide icecaps that are filled

with a solution and are kept frozen in a refrigerator ready for use. This does away with refilling, since the used icecap can be disinfected and returned to the refrigerator for refreezing.

Applying Cold Moist Compresses

One method of applying moist cold to a part of the body is by means of cold compresses. Cold compresses are often applied to relieve pain and inflammation in eye injuries or after a tooth extraction. Sometimes they are applied to hemorrhoids. They may be made of gauze or of thin pads of cotton covered with gauze, depending on the thickness which is most suitable for the condition to be treated. A folded washcloth can be used as a compress for the forehead, cheek or jaw. Cold compresses are not sterile.

The patient needs to know that the treatment is given to relieve his discomfort and that it will not do him any harm—some patients live in fear of "catching cold."

THE PROCEDURE

Put the compresses in a basin containing pieces of ice and a small amount of water.

Principle: *The amount of water increases as the ice melts.*

Wring the compress thoroughly to prevent dripping; apply the compress to the part to be treated. Change it frequently.

Principle: *The compress absorbs heat from the body. A warm compress will not accomplish the purpose of the treatment.*

Continue the treatment as ordered, usually for 15 to 20 minutes, to be repeated every 2 to 3 hours.

If the patient is able, he can be allowed to apply the compresses himself.

Principle: *Encouraging a patient to help himself is a rehabilitative measure and helps a patient to become more self-reliant.*

Record the treatment on the patient's chart, noting the duration.

Giving an Alcohol or Cold Sponge Bath

An alcohol or cold sponge bath is ordered occasionally to reduce elevated temperature. Usually, this bath is given with tepid rather than cold water, with alcohol sometimes added to the water. The first effect of cold water on the skin is the constriction of the blood vessels and the reduction of heat elimination; some patients are unable to tolerate a cold bath. Alcohol evaporates rapidly from the skin and aids in eliminating heat.

The patient's first reaction to a cold or cool sponge bath is chilliness, which disappears as the body adjusts to the cold temperature. Therefore, the bath must be continued long enough to allow for this adjustment—at least 25 to 30 minutes. Each extremity is sponged for 5 minutes, the back and the buttocks for 5 to 10 minutes more. Moist cloths placed in the axillae and the groin reduce temperature in the large blood vessels which lie close to the surface in these areas. A hot-water bag (warm) at the patient's feet reduces chilliness; an icecap applied to his head helps to prevent congestion and headache. The patient's body temperature shortly after the bath has been completed (½ hour) shows the effect of the treatment. A cold sponge bath is often given for its temporarily soothing effect and may not produce a marked temperature drop. In conditions that cause a dangerously high temperature, such as neurosurgery, an ice mattress (a plastic mattress pad through which ice water flows continuously) can be used.

Contraindications. Some patients react unfavorably to cold baths: cold baths are not advisable for older people with inelastic arteries, arthritic patients, patients with lowered resistance or very young children. The first effect of cold on the body is depressing and may produce undesirable reactions. If the patient has a weak, rapid pulse, bluish lips and nails and chills, the bath should be discontinued and heat applied.

Reassurance. Explain the procedure to the patient. Point out that the room is warm to keep him from catching cold; explain that he will be covered as in any bath. If the patient is nervous and fearful, the bath is not likely to be effective. Explain the procedure to the family, who probably realize that the patient has an elevated temperature and are apprehensive. Give the patient a urinal or a bedpan before the bath.

EQUIPMENT

Basin of water (70° to 85° F.)	Face towel
Basin of chipped ice	2 Washcloths
Bath thermometer	Hot-water bag and cover
Bath blanket	Icecap and cover
Bath towel	

KEY POINTS IN THE PROCEDURE

Add ice to the water to bring it to the required temperature (65° F. to 80° F.).

Principle: *Cool water brings blood to the surface of the skin.*

Add alcohol if prescribed.

Principle: *Alcohol evaporates rapidly from the skin and removes heat.*

Apply a warm hot-water bag to the patient's feet and an icecap to his head.

Principle: *Warmth reduces chilliness, and cold prevents congestion and headache.*

Place moist, cool cloths in the axillae and groin. Wring the cloths just enough to prevent dripping.

Principle: *Large blood vessels are close to the skin in the groin and the axilla. Temperature reduction takes place through the evaporation of water.*

Sponge each limb for at least 5 minutes. Sponge the back and the buttocks for 5 or 10 minutes more.

Principle: *It takes about 25 to 30 minutes for the body to respond to cold applications.*

Take the patient's temperature ½ hour after the procedure is completed.

Record the treatment on the patient's chart, noting his reactions.

THE USE OF IRRITANTS AND COUNTERIRRITANTS

Irritants are chemicals used on the skin to produce a process similar to inflammation, causing dilation of blood vessels and increased circulation. The skin reacts much the same as it does from the local application of heat. When a chemical is used for other than local effects (as in the deep underlying tissues), it is called a counterirritant.

Less use is being made of irritants and counterirritants today because antibiotics and pain relievers are more effective. However, many people, especially older persons, still cling to a faith in proprietary remedies to be rubbed on the skin as a cure for colds or bronchitis.

Applying a Mustard Plaster

The mustard plaster is the most commonly used counterirritant. Prepared adhesive plasters can be purchased in the drugstore, but they can be made easily by mixing dried mustard, flour and tepid water.

The ratio of 1 tablespoon of mustard to 5 tablespoons of flour is usually used for adults. For children, the proportion is from 1:8 up to 1:15. Tepid water is used to mix the mustard and the flour until it reaches the consistency of paste. (Hot water interferes with the enzyme action of the mustard.) The paste is then spread to the thickness of about half an inch on a clean cloth. It should be large enough to cover the area of application. The cloth is folded, and the plaster is kept warm by wrapping it in a piece of flannel or placing it on a warm water bottle until it is applied.

No oil is used on the skin prior to the application of the plaster since it would interfere with the reaction. It is placed on the dry skin and covered with a light cloth. The skin is inspected frequently to prevent burns or blisters. A safe degree of redness usually appears within 5 minutes, at which time the plaster is removed. Fair-haired and red-haired people are more sensitive to burning. If the plaster is allowed to remain until the skin becomes a bright red, the results may be disastrous. It is important to follow the instructions on purchased plasters.

After the plaster is removed, the skin is washed and patted dry to avoid irritation. Petroleum jelly or some other lubricant is applied, and the area is covered with a towel or piece of flannel.

BOWEL TREATMENTS

Enemas

An enema is the injection of fluid into the large intestine (the colon) through the rectum.

To understand the uses of enemas we begin with the digestive system. The digestion of food results in certain waste materials that normally are moved along the intestinal tract by peristaltic waves until they reach the lower colon and are expelled through the rectum (see Chap. 17). In supposedly healthy people, poor health habits, such as failure to eat the right foods, or to drink enough fluids or to get sufficient exercise, may interfere with this process. Also certain types of illnesses interfere with bowel elimination, especially those that require a restricted diet, prolonged bed rest or immobilization of the body in one position for a long period of time. Enemas may then be necessary. Enemas are also essential to empty the intestinal tract before a surgical operation or before x-ray or rectal examinations. They are useful in giving certain types of medicines and in relieving distention caused by gas (flatus) in the intestines.

Kinds of Enema

Enemas are classified according to their purpose:

Purgative or cleansing—to aid in expelling feces

Carminative—to stimulate peristalsis as an aid in expelling gas

Anthelmintic—to destroy intestinal parasites

Emollient—to soothe or protect the mucous membrane

Medicated—to administer medication

Nutritive—to supply food materials

Effective Enemas

Certain factors, such as the size of the rectal tube, the method of giving the enema, the amount and the temperature of the solution have a great deal to do with making an enema effective. Never underestimate the importance of giving an enema correctly.

The Rectal Tube

All enemas are given with a rubber or plastic rectal tube, which is smooth and flexible so that it will not irritate the rectum if it is inserted carefully. Rectal tubes come in different sizes —the larger the size, the more it stimulates the anal sphincter muscles to expel the rectal contents. The sizes used for a cleansing enema range from No. 26, Fr. to No. 32, Fr.; for an enema to be retained, No. 14, Fr. to No. 20, Fr. A retention enema is given when results are not expected immediately. Smaller amounts of solution are given (150 to 200 cc.) so that the patient is able to retain the amount. The size of the rectal tube also affects the rate of the flow of fluid—it will flow faster and with more force through a larger tube.

The Methods and Equipment

In addition to the commercially prepared, disposable enema unit, an enema may be given by 2 other methods. With the *can and tubing method*, the solution flows from a can or bag through a length of tubing which is attached to the rectal tube by a connecting tip. With the *funnel method*, the solution is poured from a pitcher into a funnel attached to the rectal tube.

The height at which the solution is poured affects the force and speed of its flow—the higher the can is held, the greater the force. With the funnel method, the height is limited to the length of the rectal tube; this makes it impossible to introduce the fluid at a pressure that might harm the colon or distend it so rapidly that it would be impossible to give enough to make an enema effective. Therefore, the funnel method is safer; it is always used for a retention enema.

The Solution. The temperature of the solution should be only slightly higher than body temperature to avoid injuring the lining of the intestine. From 105° to 115° F. is usually considered a safe range. This refers to the temperature when the solution is prepared—if it is to be given with a can and tubing, naturally it will be cooler when it reaches the patient than if the funnel and rectal tube are used. Allowance should be made for this when preparing the solution. Disposable enema units are usually stored at room temperature. Patients sometimes complain of chilliness with disposable enemas, so these units should never be stored in a cool place.

It is difficult to determine the amount of solution which is necessary for a cleansing enema, because so much depends on the individual patient's ability to retain fluid and on how easily the impulse to empty the rectum is stimulated. Usually, the amount needed for an adult ranges from 750 to 1,000 cc. It is needlessly distressing for the patient if the nurse insists on giving the maximum amount if satisfactory results can be accomplished with less. On the other hand, larger amounts may be needed and sometimes a patient needs a great deal of encouragement to retain fluid at all—this is especially true of patients who are tense and fearful.

Enema Treatments

The Cleansing Enema. The purpose is to inject enough fluid into the colon to soften the feces, stimulate the peristaltic waves and produce a bowel movement that empties the rectum and the colon. This procedure often is a necessary part of the treatment in illness when body functions are disturbed. Otherwise, a proper diet, sufficient fluids and a certain amount of exercise, together with regular elimination habits should make the need for enemas unnecessary.

Usually, after eating breakfast, a peristaltic wave is set up which moves the feces from the colon into the rectum: the fecal mass stimulates the nerve endings in the rectum and brings the desire to empty it. If this impulse is ignored, it disappears, the feces become dry and hard, and defecation is difficult. The colon and the rectum become distended and lose muscle tone as the feces accumulate. An enema provides an artificial stimulus and helps to remove the feces, but, unless normal stimulation and regular defecation are established, taking an enema can become a habit.

A variety of fluids may be used for a cleansing enema such as soap solution, hypertonic solution, normal saline solution, tap water or cottonseed, mineral or olive oil. Oil is given when it is necessary to soften and to lubricate the feces, and it is given in small amounts because it must be retained for a time to be effective. Sometimes, if an oil solution has not been effective after several hours, it is necessary to follow with an enema of soap or saline solution.

Soap solution, saline or tap water enemas are prepared in larger amounts (500 to 1,500 cc.), enough to stimulate peristalsis and expel the feces. Action may result immediately or it may take longer—usually it occurs in less than 15 minutes.

Soap solution is easily made by dissolving a bland white soap in the water if prepared soap solution is not available. Adding prepackaged soap concentrate to water is a more accurate method. Soap is added because it irritates the mucous membrane of the colon and stimulates peristalsis. Mild soap is used to avoid excessive irritation. Some *proctologists* (rectal disease specialists) forbid the use of soap in enemas before rectal examinations or for patients known to have rectal disease.

The commercially prepared, disposable enema unit contains a hypertonic solution in small amounts—usually 4 ounces (120 cc.). Acting on the principle of osmosis, it draws fluid from the body to create fluid bulk in the colon. The solution is not irritating; it is easily given and usually brings good results in less than 10 minutes. It is especially useful for patients who are unable to retain larger quantities of fluid or have anal incontinence. It helps to prevent anal impaction in patients who must lie in one position or who are unable to sit up. The disposable enema is also widely used in preparing a patient for x-ray or rectal examinations. It comes ready for use and the equipment can be discarded afterwards.

The Carminative Enema. The carminative enema is given to stimulate peristalsis to expel gas from the intestine. The solutions in common use are milk and molasses, turpentine and mixtures of magnesium sulfate, glycerin and water.

Molasses and milk are combined in equal

parts—250 cc. of each. Molasses irritates the mucous membrane and milk makes it stick to increase the irritation, which in turn stimulates peristalsis and the expulsion of gas. The patient should be encouraged to retain a milk and molasses enema as long as possible before expelling it.

Turpentine is sometimes added to soap solution—4 cc. of turpentine to 500 cc. of soap solution—for its irritating effect on the mucous membrane. Turpentine does not dissolve in water, so the mixture must be stirred thoroughly to prevent unmixed particles from causing overirritation.

The combination of magnesium sulfate, glycerin and water is known as the 1-2-3 enema because it contains 30 cc. of magnesium sulfate solution, 60 cc. of glycerin and 90 cc. of water. Together, these ingredients irritate the mucous membrane and distend the colon to stimulate peristalsis and expel the accumulated gas.

The Anthelmintic Enema. Anthelmintic drugs help to destroy intestinal parasites and usually are given orally. They must be given carefully because they are toxic drugs, and this method is unsafe for some patients, such as those with liver damage. In such instances, a solution of an anthelmintic drug may be instilled into the rectum to be retained.

The Emollient Enema. An emollient enema consists of a small amount of olive or cottonseed oil, given to protect or soothe the mucous membrane of the colon. This enema is to be retained.

The Medicated Enema. The medicated enema, or instillation of a drug into the rectum, sometimes is the only way to give a patient a drug. It also may be the best way to make a drug effective quickly—some drugs are absorbed by the mucous membrane very rapidly. This is true of some anesthetics, such as Avertin, and of sedative drugs, such as paraldehyde and chloral hydrate. It is almost impossible to take paraldehyde by mouth because of its offensive taste. The drug is combined with a small amount of oil or saline to reduce its irritating effect on the mucous membrane and to lessen the desire to expel it, since it is given to be retained.

The Nutritive Enema. This method of supplying nutritive materials has been replaced largely by intravenous feeding, which is more efficient. It is impossible to maintain adequate nourishment by rectal feeding since the colon is very selective in what it will absorb. A solution of dextrose is used most often.

Emergency Measures

Occasionally, fluids are given by rectum to tide the patient over an emergency until more effective methods are available, such as giving coffee as a stimulant to a patient in shock.

A quantity of fluid can be given by rectum over a long period of time by a drip method known as *proctoclysis.* Equipment similar to that included in the can method of giving an enema is used and the rate of flow is controlled by a clamp. This procedure is less common since other methods of administering fluids have been perfected.

Explaining the Procedure

Many patients are familiar with the cleansing enema which is given to produce a bowel movement but do not understand the purpose in giving an enema to be retained. In any case, the procedure and the reason for it should be explained as simply as possible. A nurse may have an opportunity to relate the patient's diet and fluids to their effects in preventing constipation. The patient who is having an enema for the first time may be fearful of pain or of soiling the bed. The patient's cooperation has much to do with making an enema effective.

The Patient's Position

The descending colon lies on the left side of the abdomen so it has always been assumed that an enema would be more effective if it were given with the patient lying on his left side. Today, it is thought that it is relatively unimportant, as the fluid runs into the colon as easily from one side as the other. In fact, if for example he is in traction, an enema can be given with the patient lying on his back. So there is no need to be unduly concerned if the patient is unable to lie on his left side. However, an enema should never be given with the patient sitting up because without the help of gravity, it takes a great deal of pressure to force the fluid into the colon; also the patient may be unable to retain it long enough to make the procedure effective.

Inserting the Rectal Tube

The anus has an inside and an outside sphincter muscle which control the opening (see p. 174). The tube should be inserted past both of these muscles—3 or 4 inches would be more than sufficient, since the anal canal is only 1 to 1½ inches long. Attempts to force the tube into the rectum against resistance may harm the tissues. If the tube does not go in easily, let a small amount of solution enter and withdraw the tube slightly, then reinsert it. Resistance may be caused by a kink in the tube, by a spasm of the colon or by feces impacted in the rectum.

It is no longer considered necessary to expel air from the rectal tube and tubing—in fact, air may help to stimulate peristalsis by distending the intestinal wall. The exception to this is in giving an enema to be retained. Then, air may stimulate peristalsis to expel the fluid. However, running a small amount of the fluid through the tubing warms it so that the fluid reaches the patient at the proper temperature from the beginning of administration.

Giving a Cleansing Enema (Can and Tubing Method)

EQUIPMENT

Irrigating can and tubing, glass connecting tip, clamp	Solution as prescribed
Rectal tube No. 28 to No. 32, Fr. (Use a catheter for an infant or a child)	Lubricant
	Protective sheet and cover
	Standard
	Toilet tissue
	Bedpan and cover
	Bath blanket

KEY POINTS IN THE PROCEDURE

Prepare the solution as ordered, 750 to 1,500 cc. for an adult at a temperature of 105° to 110° F.

Principle: *The adult colon holds 750 to 2,000 cc. The solution should be approximately at body temperature when it reaches the colon. It loses heat as it travels through the tubing. Heat stimulates the mucous membrane.*

Lubricate the tip of the rectal tube for 2 to 3 inches.

Principle: *Lubrication prevents friction when the tube is inserted.*

Put the patient on his left or right side. If this is impossible, he can lie on his back.

Principle: *Gravity aids the flow of fluid.*

Slowly insert the rectal tube for 4 to 5 inches.

Principle: *The anal canal is 1 to 1½ inches long, and 4 to 5 inches insures entering of the colon. Slow insertion is less likely to cause spasms of the intestinal wall.*

Raise the can (or funnel) high enough to allow the fluid to flow into the rectum slowly—let the patient indicate when the flow may be too rapid.

Principle: *Gravity aids the flow of fluid. The higher the container is held, the more rapid the flow and the greater the pressure on the colon and the desire to expel the fluid.*

When the patient feels a strong desire to empty the rectum, discontinue the flow of fluid and withdraw the rectal tube gently.

Principle: *Distention of the colon stimulates peristalsis and a desire to expel the rectal contents.*

Put the patient on the bedpan (sitting up, if possible) or assist him to the commode or bathroom toilet.

Principle: *Contracting the abdominal and perineal muscles helps to empty the colon. This is easier in a sitting position.*

Encourage the patient to retain the fluid for a short time.

Principle: *Most patients think the enema should be expelled immediately. Fluid helps to soften the feces and makes expelling it easier.*

Record the treatment on the chart, noting any unusual conditions, characteristics of feces, flatus expelled and the patient's reactions.

Care of Equipment

Autoclaving is considered the safest way to care for enema equipment, unless disposable equipment is used, in which case it is simply discarded. Sterile equipment is not necessary in giving an enema, but it is important to sterilize enema equipment *after* it has been used, to prevent carrying infection to others. In many hospitals this is taken care of by preparing enema sets in the surgical supply room.

When the Patient Is Unable To Retain an Enema

If the patient is unable to contract the anal sphincter muscles or the muscles have lost their power to contract, it will be necessary to give the cleansing enema with the patient on the bedpan. Elevating the head of the bed slightly and placing a pillow in the lumbar region help to prevent back strain. The advantage of using a disposable enema unit for this type of patient is that it is given in a small amount.

When the Patient Is Unable To Expel an Enema

When the muscles do not respond to stimulation and the patient is unable to expel an enema, the solution must be withdrawn. The bedpan is placed on a chair at the bedside, beneath the level of the rectum. When the rectal tube is directed into the pan the force of gravity helps to drain off the fluid. If this is not effective the fluid is siphoned off. The rectal tube is withdrawn and attached to a funnel; then the tube is filled with water and pinched off at the funnel end to prevent the water from escaping. It is reinserted in the rectum and, after allowing a small amount of fluid to flow into the patient, the funnel is lowered into the bedpan. If fluid drains continuously into the pan the siphon is working. If not, more solution is introduced and the procedure repeated until siphonage is established.

Giving an Enema to a Child

An infant or a small child will not be able to retain an enema, so you must provide a pad, a basin or a small bedpan to catch the solution, which is almost sure to be expelled as you give the enema. It may be necessary to restrain the child or to ask someone to assist you.

It is difficult to state the specific amount of solution that should be given because this depends on the age and size of the child. For an infant, the amount of solution should not exceed 300 cc. and might be less. The amount increases with the age of the child but usually is no more than 500 cc. up to the age of 14.

The irrigating can or the funnel should not be more than 18 inches above the mattress; use a No. 10, Fr. to 14, Fr. catheter for an infant; a No. 14, Fr. to 16, Fr. rectal tube for a child.

A rubber-tipped bulb syringe (100 cc.) is easy to manage with infants or small children. The fluid should be injected with the least possible amount of pressure.

The Doctor's Orders

An enema is never given without a doctor's order. The order may be for an enema every day, or it may state "when necessary," which leaves the decision up to the nurse. She is guided somewhat by the patient's feelings—some people are distressed if they do not have a bowel movement every day. In the hospital, the practical nurse consults her supervisor about carrying out a "when necessary" (p.r.n.) order.

Inserting a Rectal Tube To Relieve Flatus

Sometimes a rectal tube is used to aid the patient in expelling flatus (gas) from the intestines. Inserted in the rectum, the tube provides an outlet for accumulated gas and relieves the discomfort of intestinal distention. Insert the tube as for an enema and place the outer end in a urinal or a small basin. A piece of tubing can be attached to the rectal tube and the end placed in a container with sufficient water to cover it; air bubbles in the water will show whether or not gas is being expelled. From 20 to 30 minutes is long enough to leave the tube in the rectum; after that time the sphincter muscles become numbed and the tube ceases to stimulate peristalsis. Note the result on the patient's chart—the length of the insertion, the amount of gas and of feces expelled, if any, and whether or not the patient felt relief.

Inserting a Suppository

A suppository is a small solid substance that melts at body temperature, such as cocoa butter or glycerin, and is inserted into the rectum to stimulate peristalsis and defecation. Some suppositories contain medication to relieve pain and irritation. Since a small amount of absorption takes place in the large colon, some medications for systemic effect can be given by a suppository.

The intake of food and fluids usually stimulates peristalsis; therefore, a suppository is likely to be more effective if it is inserted half an hour before a meal. This allows time for it to soften feces in the rectum and makes defecation easier.

Insert the suppository past the internal anal sphincter (2 inches). Lubricate it to make insertion easier and protect your finger with a rubber glove or finger cot. Explain the purpose of the procedure and tell the patient it may be half an hour or more before it is effective. If the patient is tense, instruct him to breathe through his mouth to help relax the internal sphincter. Some patients may be able to learn how to insert a suppository for themselves.

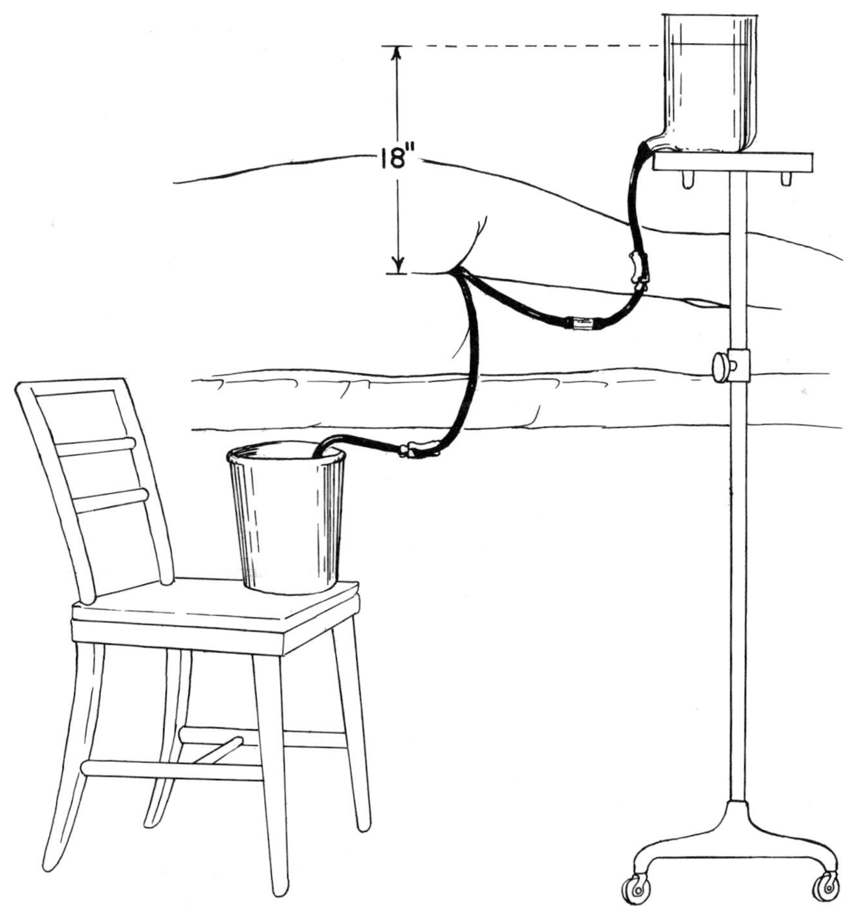

Fig. 106. Position of equipment for colonic irrigation using the 2-tube method. (Fuerst, E. V., and Wolff, L.: Fundamentals of Nursing, ed. 3, p. 391, Philadelphia, Lippincott)

The Colonic Irrigation

A colonic irrigation is a prolonged washing-out of the large intestine. It bathes the intestine with a considerable amount of fluid, some of which the intestine absorbs. Occasionally, colonic irrigation is given to cleanse the colon and as a treatment for such conditions as colitis and uremic poisoning; it is also given to supply heat and fluid to the body.

Obviously, no one should have a colonic irrigation unless his doctor prescribes it, but this treatment led to a widespread form of quackery —the colonic irrigation operators. In many cities the window sign *Colonic Irrigations Given* was an all-too-familiar sight. Americans—a bowel-conscious people—seem to be irresistibly drawn to this type of treatment, without the benefit of a doctor's advice. Like the enema addicts, full of false notions about bowel action, they pin their faith on the benefits of a so-called "good cleaning out." When the doctor prescribes a colonic irrigation, he is also concerned about other aspects of the patient's treatment—the diet, for example. Self-prescribed colonic irrigations may actually do harm by delaying proper treatment.

A colonic irrigation consists of introducing water into the colon and siphoning it off. The kind, the amount and the temperature of the solution are determined by the reason for giving the irrigation. Plain water or normal saline are the solutions most commonly used; the amount varies from 1 to 4 gallons; the temperature of the solution is usually about 105° F., unless a higher or a lower temperature is prescribed. A cleansing enema is given first, if necessary, to empty the lower colon of fecal material.

The colonic irrigation can be given by the *one-tube* or the *two-tube* method.

Method I. A glass Y-tube is attached to the irrigating can tubing; the rectal tube (No. 30, Fr.) is attached to one branch of the Y; a piece of tubing long enough to reach well into the drainage pail is attached to the other branch of the Y; clamps on the inflow and the outflow tubings control the flow.

Method II. *Two* rectal tubes are inserted in the rectum; one is smaller than the other, and the irrigating can tubing is attached to the smaller, or the inflow, tube. A piece of tubing that reaches into the drainage pail is attached to the other rectal tube for the outflow. Two clamps are used, as in Method I.

The procedure for both methods consists of allowing the solution to run into the colon and to drain off alternately. Except for the rectal tubes, the equipment is the same (Fig. 106).

The Colostomy Irrigation

The method of removing fecal material from the bowel after a colostomy has been performed is the colostomy irrigation. This procedure is described in Chapter 38.

CATHETERIZATION

Catheterization is the procedure of inserting a catheter through the urethra into the bladder to remove urine.

The bladder is the reservoir for the urine secreted by the kidneys (see Chap. 18). Usually, when 200 to 250 cc. accumulate, the urge to void occurs. If the bladder cannot be emptied normally, urine accumulates and distends it or dribbles continually from the urethral opening.

Reasons for Catheterization

The practical nurse may do this procedure less often in the hospital than when caring for a patient who is ill at home with a urologic condition or a long-term illness. The urethra and the bladder are delicate structures; injury to the mucous membrane or infection in these organs can have serious effects on the patient. On the other hand, if the bladder becomes overdistended or retains urine for a long period, these conditions may also be harmful. Causes of the retention of urine and ways of encouraging the patient to void will be discussed in Chapter 32. Catheterization is a last resort when these measures have failed or it may be necessary when physical conditions make normal voiding impossible. Some of the reasons for catheterizing a patient are:

To relieve the retention of urine when the patient is temporarily unable to void.

To remove the urine remaining in the bladder when voiding only partly empties it.

To empty the bladder of an incontinent patient at regular intervals—to keep the patient dry and to prevent bedsores.

To obtain a sterile specimen of urine.

To prevent urine from touching stitches in the perineum.

Modern Practices. The need for catheterization following a surgical operation has diminished as the practice of early ambulation for surgical patients has increased. *Position* is a very important aid in emptying the bladder. Women who cannot void lying down often are able to void if they are allowed to sit up. Men find it easier to void when standing. With support in these positions many patients are able to void normally.

Formerly, catheterization was considered necessary to obtain an uncontaminated specimen of urine. Normally, the inside of the bladder is considered sterile. Many doctors now feel that catheterization may carry infectious material from the urethra into the bladder to contaminate the urine specimen. They recommend a method instead which is called "clean catch." This consists of first thoroughly cleansing the urinary meatus with an antiseptic solution, such as aqueous Zephiran, then asking the patient to void 100 to 200 cc., which are discarded. The patient then voids 100 to 200 cc. into a sterile specimen bottle, after which he voids the urine remaining in the bladder. This urine remaining is discarded.

Sometimes tension or sedation preceding surgery interfere with the patient's ability to empty the bladder. A full bladder can hamper a surgeon in carrying out surgical procedures. A urologic difficulty may interfere with voiding. In some instances, it is necessary to insert a retention catheter which is retained in the bladder to provide continuous drainage of the urine (see Fig. 167).

In any catheterization procedure it is not considered safe to remove more than 750 to 1,000 cc. of urine from the bladder at any one time. If the flow of urine seems undiminished after this amount is withdrawn, report it to the head nurse so the doctor can be notified and determine further action. If a patient is admitted to the hospital with a greatly distended bladder, it is usually considered safer to relieve the distention gradually, to prevent bladder damage and possible shock with chills and fever.

Types of Catheters

The catheters most commonly used are made of rubber or plastic. Glass or metal catheters are used occasionally. Silk or rubber woven catheters are frequently used for male patients; these catheters are firm but flexible and are more easily inserted into the male urethra. Every type of catheter has a rounded tip, to prevent injury to the meatus or the urethra. A catheter with a rough surface or one that is limp from repeated sterilization should be discarded. Catheters are graded in the same way as rectal tubes. Sizes No. 14, Fr. and No. 16, Fr. are suitable for the female patient. For the male patient, sizes No. 20, Fr. and No. 22, Fr. are usually used. Sizes No. 8, Fr. and No. 10, Fr. are appropriate for children.

The Retention (In-dwelling) Catheter. The retention catheter provides temporary or permanent drainage of urine. This may be necessary for incontinence in an unconscious patient, for bladder injury or surgery or in other bladder conditions, such as cancer or infection.

The Foley catheter is a commonly used retention catheter. It has a small tube within it that opens into a small balloon below the opening in the tip which provides an outlet for the urine. After the catheter is inserted, the balloon is inflated with sterile water or saline through a small projecting tube near the outer end of the catheter, and the tube is clamped off. The inflated balloon keeps the catheter from slipping out. There are other varieties of the retention catheter which may be used, such as the so-called mushroom type.

Preparing the Female Patient

Explain to the patient that you are going to drain urine from the bladder to make her more comfortable and that you will use a small tube

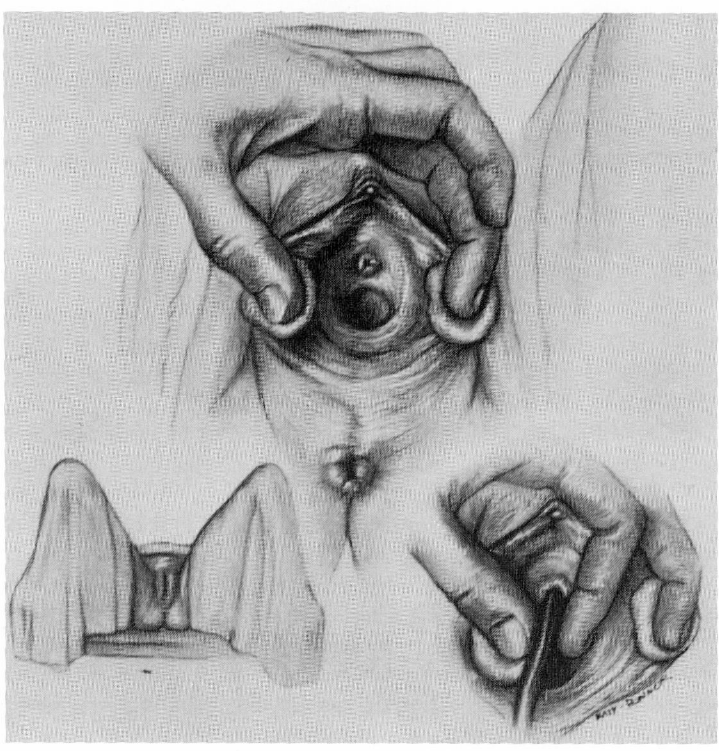

FIG. 107. (*Bottom, left*) Position of the female patient for catheterization. (*Top*) Visualization of the meatus by properly separating the labia minora. (*Bottom, right*) Fingers in position to pinch off the catheter.

that slips in easily because it is oiled. Explain how she can help by relaxing—that she will barely notice when you slip in the little tube if she is not tense. Be sure that the room and the patient are warm enough. Chilliness makes people tense. Ask her to breathe through her mouth to assist relaxation.

Essential Precautions

Catheterization is an aseptic procedure which requires sterile equipment. In the hospital sterile catheterization sets are prepared in the surgical supply room or sterile disposable equipment may be provided. These sets are so wrapped that the catheters lie straight and are easy to handle. In the home, it will be necessary to provide and boil equipment. There is no substitute for a catheter.

The preliminary cleansing of the area is important in preventing the introduction of bacteria into the meatus. Soap-and-water washing is effective—sometimes a mild antiseptic solution is used. Some agencies provide sterile gloves for the nurse as part of the equipment. Gloves are not essential, but sometimes they make it easier to separate the labia and locate the urethral opening. An accessory light is also an aid.

The position of the female patient is the same as for a vaginal examination (see Fig. 107).

EQUIPMENT

Sterile	Unsterile
Rubber catheters No. 14, Fr. and No. 16, F. (2)*	Protective sheet and cover
1 Small basin	Towel
2 Large basins	Extra bath blanket
Sponges or cotton balls	Waste container
Solution	
Lubricant	
Specimen bottle and cover, if required	
Forceps	

* If one catheter becomes contaminated, another one is available.

KEY POINTS IN THE PROCEDURE (FEMALE PATIENT)

Prepare the cleansing solution and squeeze the sterile lubricant onto a sterile sponge before bringing the tray to the bedside.

Principle: *Thorough preparation aids speed and efficiency.*

Place the patient on her back. With a sagging mattress, place a pillow under the patient's hips to elevate the bladder.

Principle: *Gravity aids the flow of urine.*

Adjust the drapes and cover the patient's chest as conditions indicate.

Principle: *Embarrassment and chilliness increase tension. Tension interferes with the insertion of the catheter.*

Arrange the equipment for convenience and to prevent contaminating the catheters.

Principle: *Reaching across sterile equipment may contaminate it.*

Put on gloves (if gloves are worn), otherwise protect the thumb and the finger with cotton balls; separate and press upward on the inner labia.

Cleanse the area according to the prescribed procedure, using and discarding cotton balls until the area is clean.

Principle: *Microorganisms introduced into the bladder will cause infection.*

Continuing to keep the labia separated, lubricate the tip end of the catheter for at least 3 inches.

Principle: *Lubrication reduces friction.*

Pick up the catheter 3 inches from the tip.

Principle: *The sterile tip prevents bladder contamination.*

Insert the catheter for 2 to 3 inches or until urine begins to flow.

Principle: *The female urethra is about 1½ inches long.*

To collect a specimen, pinch off the catheter. Place the end of it in the sterile specimen container and let the urine flow. Place your hand on the pubis to help to keep the catheter in place.

Principle: *Moving the catheter back and forth increases the possibility of contamination.*

When the urine flow begins to diminish, withdraw the catheter slowly by half-inches until only a drip of urine appears.

Principle: *The catheter continues to remove urine as it is withdrawn.*

Make the patient comfortable and clean all the equipment immediately.

Principle: *Secretions and other substances are more easily removed when not coagulated.*

Record the amount of urine obtained, noting its appearance (clear or cloudy), evidences of blood or pus, etc.

Catheterization of the Male Patient

It is more difficult to catheterize a male patient because the urethra in the male is longer and has more curves than that of the female. An enlarged prostate gland constricts or obstructs the male urethra; previous infection in the urethra also causes strictures. Usually the doctor or a male nurse is the one who catheterizes a male patient, but any nurse should be prepared to do it, if necessary. It may seem embarrassing to a male patient, but a matter-of-fact, assured attitude helps to put the patient at ease and to prevent body tensions that might interfere with the procedure.

The main differences between catheterizing a female and a male patient are with the insertion of the catheter because of the differences in shape between the female and male urethra. The male urethra is longer with 2 curves in its passage to the bladder which makes it more difficult to insert a catheter. One of these curves can be straightened out by lifting the penis; the other one is fixed. For this reason, the penis is held upright, at right angles to the patient's body when the catheter is inserted.

The patient lies on his back with his legs spread apart and his knees flexed slightly. The receptacle for the urine is placed between his thighs. With the end of the penis held between the thumb and the forefinger, the meatus is cleansed as in the female patient. Holding the penis upright, exert slight pressure on the organ to widen the opening for the insertion of the catheter, which has been lubricated for 1½ inches. A drop of sterile lubricant on the meatus also aids in the insertion of the catheter.

If slight resistance is felt, usually it can be overcome by twisting the catheter a little. With more pronounced resistance, the pull on the penis can be increased as the catheter is withdrawn slightly, then pushed ahead, with a series of short shoves, until the urine begins to flow.

Instructing the patient to breathe deeply helps to relax the perineal muscles and to overcome resistance to the entry of the catheter.

Care of a Patient Who Has a Retention Catheter. Undoubtedly you will be taking care of patients who have retention catheters inserted to care for urine drainage. It is your responsibility to care for the equipment that is used and to see that the drainage apparatus is working properly. The equipment consists of the drainage tubing attached to the catheter and the container for the urine. You never remove the catheter. If it should come out and the patient is in the hospital, report it to the head nurse. In caring for a patient at home, notify the doctor. If the patient has a long-term illness, the doctor may instruct the nurse as to what she is to do in case this happens. He may allow her to remove and to reinsert a catheter for cleansing. Never reinsert a catheter without first sterilizing it.

In observing this type of drainage apparatus, check the following points:

The catheter should be in place.

The tubing should be long enough to allow the patient to turn freely without displacing it from the drainage container.

The tubing should reach well into the container, but the end of it should be above the level of the urine.

Note whether or not urine drainage is taking place by looking at the glass or plastic connecting tube and the level of drainage in the container.

The tubing should pass over the patient's thigh. If it passes under the thigh and buttocks, pressure may interfere with drainage. The adhesive tab around the tubing should be pinned to the sheet, allowing enough leeway for the patient to turn without pulling on the catheter but not so much that the tubing will become tangled. Catheter or tubing should never be bent as this shuts off the flow of urine.

The tubing should be detached and replaced every 2 or 3 days because salts from the urine collect on the inside and are difficult to remove. A glass container should be washed every day. If a disposable container is used it can be discarded. Measure all urine that is collected. If you are to irrigate the catheter, you will be shown the method to use.

VAGINAL TREATMENTS

Vaginal Irrigation (Douche). This consists of directing a flow of fluid into the vaginal canal and allowing it to flow out by gravity. The purposes of a vaginal irrigation are to cleanse the vaginal canal of discharge and to apply heat to relieve pain and inflammation.

The vaginal canal is a passage about 3 inches long, lined with mucous membrane, that extends from the uterus to the vulva; the inner labia enclose the vaginal opening. The secretions of the mucous membrane protect it from infection; it is not desirable to wash away these secretions by douches unless such treatment is necessary. Strong irritating solutions may also set up inflammation in the vaginal canal. Mild antiseptic solutions, such as boric acid or normal saline, are suitable for vaginal irrigations and safe; sodium bicarbonate solution is sometimes used for an overacid condition; a solution of potassium permanganate may be used for an odorous discharge. Vinegar solution (2 tablespoons to a pint of water) may be used because it resembles normal vaginal secretions.

The doctor specifies the kind of solution to be used. The temperature of the solution for a cleansing vaginal irrigation should be about 105°F. If the doctor prescribes a hotter douche, it may be given at a temperature of from 110° to 115°F. The inside of the vagina can safely stand a considerable degree of heat, but the hotter fluid may burn the more sensitive vulva and the perineum. These parts should be protected with an application of oil if the temperature of the solution is as high as 110°F.

A vaginal irrigation is given with an irrigating can and tubing attached to a douche tip, which is inserted into the vaginal canal. Douche tips are made of glass, hard rubber or plastic. (Plastic douche tips cannot be sterilized by steam or boiling; a disinfectant must be used. This is an argument in favor of using disposable tips.) They must be inspected before they are used to be sure that they are in good condition; a cracked, rough or broken tip would injure the vaginal tissues. The vaginal canal curves up and back when the patient is lying down; the tip is inserted to follow this direction. The flow of the fluid into the vagina should be gentle, to prevent forcing infection into the uterus. The cervix projects down into the vagina in such a way that a pocket is formed between the cervix and the rear wall of the vaginal canal. The douche tip is rotated during the irrigation to be sure that the solution washes out discharge collected in this pocket and reaches every part of the vagina.

Infectious Conditions. If the patient has a gonorrheal or a syphilitic infection, special precautions are necessary, to protect both the patient and the nurse. The patient should be instructed to keep her hands away from the perineal area, to prevent carrying infection to her eyes. The nurse wears gloves and may also wear goggles to prevent possible splashing of infected material into her eyes. If gloves are not available, a thorough hand washing will protect her—soap and hot water kill the organisms. The equipment must be sterilized after use.

The can, the tubing and the douche pan for an unsterile vaginal irrigation are *clean*, and the douche tip is *sterile*. In some hospitals, the complete equipment for a vaginal irrigation is done up as a sterile package in the central supply room; in the patient's home, you can boil the tip in a pan, pour off the water and take the pan and the tip to the bedside.

EQUIPMENT

Irrigating can, tubing and clamp	Standard
Douche tip and container	Bath thermometer
Douche pan and cover	Protective pad and cover
Solution as prescribed	Perineal pad
	Tissues

KEY POINTS IN THE PROCEDURE

Have the patient void before beginning the treatment.

***Reason:** A full bladder interferes with the insertion of the douche nozzle.*

Prepare the prescribed solution (about 1,500 cc.) at the required temperature (100° to 110° F.) according to the purpose of the treatment.

***Reason:** Heat relieves inflammation but solution at high temperatures will burn the mucous membranes and the skin around the meatus when flowing back.*

Put the patient on her back with only one pillow under her head and place her on the douche pan.

***Reason:** Gravity aids the flow of solution to reach the farthest part of the vagina.*

Place the irrigating can slightly above the level of the patient's hips to insure a continuous but gentle flow of the solution.

***Reason:** The higher the can, the more forceful the flow. Force can drive infectious material into the cervical opening.*

Separate the labia, using sponges, and insert the nozzle directing it downward and backward.

***Reason:** In the dorsal recumbent position, the direction of the vaginal canal is down and back.*

Rotate the nozzle gently during the treatment.

***Reason:** Rotation of the nozzle directs the fluid over all parts of the vagina.*

Clamp the tubing and withdraw the tip from the vagina. Detach the tip from the tubing and place it in the waste basin.

***Reason:** Microorganisms cause infection. Harmful organisms are transferred to individuals and to clean objects by contact.*

If the patient is able, have her sit up on the pan for a few minutes, to drain the fluid from the vagina. Then place a pad over the vulva.

***Reason:** Draining fluid soils the bed and makes the patient uncomfortable.*

Disinfect the douche tip and the waste basin before returning the equipment to the surgical room.

***Reason:** Disinfection kills harmful microorganisms and prevents the spread of infection.*

Record the treatment on the patient's chart.

Inserting A Vaginal Suppository

Vaginal suppositories are used to apply medication to the vaginal canal. The medication is incorporated in a round cocoa butter base; like the rectal suppository, it melts after it has been inserted. The suppository can be inserted with the patient lying on her back or on her side. Use a jelly lubricant for the suppository and insert it full length into the vagina; wear a rubber glove or finger cots on the right-hand thumb and finger. Record the kind of suppository used and the patient's reaction.

THE VITAL SIGNS

Body temperature, the pulse, the respiration (TPR) and the blood pressure often show changes going on in the body that affect a patient's condition. They have long been called the vital signs. Although modern medicine now has many other methods for detecting body changes, these signs are still important. If you are uncertain about having observed them correctly, ask your supervisor to check your observations. Unusual changes should also be called to her attention—for example, a marked increase in the pulse rate or a sudden rise in temperature.

The temperature, the pulse and the respiration are usually observed together. It has been the practice in hospitals to require this observation morning and evening as a routine procedure for every patient. In some hospitals today, these routine observations are omitted for certain patients, such as those in self-care units, the long-term ill patients or those under psychiatric observation, unless the doctor asks that they be made. In some illnesses it is important to make frequent observations of these symptoms, such as every 4 hours in the immediate postoperative period; observations may be made more often if the nature of an illness makes it necessary. An elevated temperature in the afternoon is a typical symptom in tuberculosis. In some illnesses it may be necessary to check the pulse frequently, in other the respiration is the most significant symptom. Changes in one of these symptoms may affect the others, which is one of the reasons for observing them at the same time.

The Nurse's Responsibility

When routine TPR's are omitted, the nurse must be aware of changes in the patient's condition which indicate that these signs should be checked. The temperature of the convalescent patient who appears flushed and restless and refuses his breakfast may indicate that he is developing an infection—his temperature, pulse and respiration should be taken.

THE PULSE

Every beat of the heart sends a wave of blood which causes vibrations through the arteries. Just as you can hear the slap of waves against the side of a boat, you can *feel* the vibrations of a wave of blood in the arteries. This vibration is the *pulse*. You can feel it through the nerves in your fingertips if you place your fingers over one of the large arteries that lie close to the skin, especially if the artery runs across a bone and has very little soft tissue around it. You can feel the pulse most plainly over these arteries:

Temporal—just in front of the ear
Mandibular—on the lower jawbone
Carotid—on each side of the front of the neck
Femoral—in the groin
Radial—in the wrist at the base of the thumb

The radial artery is the one most commonly used to count the pulse, because it is convenient, being located in the wrist at the base of the thumb, as noted above. In taking a pulse, use your first 3 fingers—your thumb has a strong pulse of its own which may be stronger than the patient's pulse.

Anything that interferes with the action of the heart or the blood vessels or with the amount of the blood affects the pulse. Heart disease and heart disorders, activities, emotional tension, infection, hardening of the arteries or hemorrhage will bring characteristic changes in the pulse. The observations that you make about the pulse furnish significant information about the patient's condition; they are concerned with the rate, the force and the rhythm of the pulse beat.

The Rate

The pulse tells how often the heart beats; the pulse rate varies with the age, the size and the weight of an individual. The normal rate for an adult man is from 60 to 65 beats per minute—it is slightly faster in a woman. The pulse of a newborn infant varies from 120 to 140 beats per minute; rates for children are in between the adult and the infant rates, according to the size and the age of the child.

Activity affects the pulse rate; the heart does not work as hard when a person is sleeping as when he is sitting or standing; if he runs or takes violent exercise or does heavy physical work, the heart beats faster, and the pulse rate increases. Excitement, anger and fear increase the rate; some drugs increase it—caffeine, for example. The pulse rate is more rapid in fever and when the thyroid gland is overactive. It increases in proportion to the temperature—the pulse rate goes up about 10 beats for every 1° rise in body temperature. Many of these conditions cause a rapid rate *temporarily,* but an abnormally rapid rate may be a sign of heart disease, heart failure, hemorrhage or other serious disturbance. If the pulse rate is consistently above normal, the condition is called *tachycardia;* the first treatment is rest.

Sometimes the pulse rate is continuously slow—below 60 beats per minute. This condition is called *bradycardia*; it may occur in convalescence from a long, feverish illness. It is a serious sign in cerebral hemorrhage because it shows increased pressure on the brain. It is also a sign of complete heart block. Some drugs, such as digitalis, are given to decrease the heart rate.

The Volume

The volume of the pulse varies with the volume of blood in the arteries, the strength of the heart contractions and the elasticity of the blood vessels. In hemorrhage, when a considerable amount of blood has been lost, every pulse beat may be *weak* or *thready.* When every beat is strong, we describe the pulse as *strong.* A normal pulse can be felt with a moderate pressure of the finger—a stronger pressure obliterates the beats. If a pulse is difficult to obliterate it is called *full* or *bounding.* The pulse may have both strong and weak beats within the minute—then the force is *irregular.*

The Rhythm

The rhythm of the pulse is the spacing of the beats. With normal or *regular* rhythm the intervals between the beats are the same. When the pulse occasionally skips a beat, this irregularity is described as an *intermittent* pulse. A pulse may be regular in rhythm but irregular in force, that is, every other beat is weak; in fact, these beats may be so weak that they are not felt in the pulse at all. This is very serious because the heart is actually beating twice as fast as the pulse rate indicates. If a patient is having treatment with digitalis—which decreases an overrapid heart rate—it may seem that the treatment is satisfactory, when the real truth is that the patient is having too much digitalis, which is actually increasing the heart rate alarmingly and harming the heart itself.

The pulse may be irregular in both force and rhythm—a sign of some forms of heart disease or an overactive thyroid gland.

What the Pulse Tells

Accuracy in recognizing and reporting the qualities of the pulse are highly important. The pulse is an indicator of the condition of the heart and the circulation; in health and illness the pulse shows how well the heart is standing up under the strains that are put upon it. No irregularity is too slight to report; the doctor notes these signs and proceeds to make further investigations to find the cause of the difficulty because the pulse is only a *symptom,* not a disease.

Taking the Pulse

The patient should be in a comfortable position when you take his pulse—sitting or lying down, with his arm supported. You will not get a reliable estimate of his pulse immediately after exercise, excitement, pain or emotional tension. His pulse rate is more rapid when he is upright than when he is lying down. Just the fact that his pulse is being taken may affect the rate in a nervous, apprehensive person. He should be at ease and quiet. As you take the pulse you also have an opportunity to notice other things about a patient without seeming to observe him closely.

The radial artery has been mentioned as the most convenient to use in taking the pulse. If the radial arteries are not accessible because of injuries, casts, splints, dressings, etc., you can use others, such as the temporal artery. Also, the carotid artery is large and not far from the heart, so the pulsations are stronger and can be felt when they are imperceptible at the radial artery. This is also true of the femoral artery as this artery is close to the aorta and receives a large quantity of blood. Use the same artery every time you count the pulse because individual arteries differ in size. The only equipment you need for taking a pulse is a watch with a second hand—add a pencil and paper if you are taking the pulse of all the patients in a department or a ward.

KEY POINTS IN THE PROCEDURE

Rest the patient's arm and hand at his side, palm upward.

Reason: *An uncomfortable position can increase the pulse rate.*

The radial artery is on the inside of the wrist.

Press the 1st, the 2nd and the 3rd fingers gently on the artery and against the radius until you feel the contraction and expansion of the artery with each heartbeat.

Reason: *The radial artery lies along the radius close to the skin surface. Excessive pressure will obliterate the pulse. You may be counting your own pulse if you use your thumb which has a strong pulse of its own.*

Using a watch with a second hand, count the pulse beats for a half-minute and multiply by 2. Count for a full minute if the pulse is abnormal in any way. Repeat if necessary.

Reason: *Irregularities can be detected in ½ a minute—counting for a full minute makes allowance for irregular spacing between beats and is more accurate.*

Record the pulse rate, noting irregularities that have been observed.

Reason: *Pulse irregularities are significant symptoms.*

TAKING THE RESPIRATION

Respiration is the process that brings oxygen into the body and removes carbon dioxide wastes. This exchange takes place in the lungs.

A review of the respiratory and circulatory systems will refresh your memory about the organs involved in the respiratory process. The lungs breathe in air, which contains oxygen, and breathe out carbon dioxide wastes. Breathed-in air travels to the lungs where it gives up its oxygen to the blood. The arteries deliver the oxygen to the body cells, and the veins return the carbon dioxide wastes to the lungs which are then expelled in breathing. Respiration is a constant interchange of oxygen and carbon dioxide wastes. Oxygen keeps body cells alive; accumulated carbon dioxide wastes kill them. Therefore, it is vitally important to observe respirations closely in order to detect signs of interference with the breathing process.

Respiration Control

Respiration is controlled and regulated by the respiratory center in the brain and by the proportion of carbon dioxide in the blood. Injury to the respiratory center or to the nerves that connect it with the lungs will affect respiration; too little or too much carbon dioxide in the blood affects it. The body apparatus that accomplishes breathing is the chest muscles and the diaphragm; injuries to these parts of the body will affect breathing.

Normally, respiration is automatic; you breathe without thinking about it. You can control the action of your breathing apparatus to some extent, to take deeper or shallower breaths or even to hold your breath for a limited time; when the limit is reached, the automatic control takes over, and your chest muscles relax in spite of your efforts.

Rate and Depth of Respiration

The rate of respiration for a normal adult is from 14 to 18 per minute—women have a more rapid rate than men. For the newborn infant, the rate is about 40; for children, it varies from 25 to 30 per minute. Excitement, exercise, pain and fever increase the rate; rapid respiration is characteristic in the diseases that affect the lungs, such as pneumonia. Heart disease, hemorrhage and nephritis increase the rate; some drugs increase it. Rapid respirations indicate that the body is making an increased effort to maintain the right balance of oxygen and carbon dioxide. The body also tries to adjust the balance by taking deeper breaths.

If a patient takes in and breathes out small amounts of air, the respirations are described as *shallow*. Pressure on the respiratory center in the brain decreases the rate of respirations—cerebral hemorrhage has this effect. Some drugs, such as opium preparations, depress the respiratory center. The poisons that accumulate in the body in uremia and diabetic coma slow the respirations. Respirations *below* 8 or *above* 40 per minute are serious symptoms.

Sounds of Respiration

Snoring or *stertorous* breathing occurs when the air is passing through the secretions in the air passages. These bubbling noises or rattles are characteristic before death when the air passages fill with mucus. Obstructions near the glottis cause a hissing, crowing sound.

Difficult Breathing (Dyspnea)

When a person is making a definite effort to get more oxygen and get rid of carbon dioxide, his breathing is *difficult*: the term for difficult breathing is *dyspnea*. This may be a temporary condition—a runner breathes in gasps at the end of a race; you run upstairs and pant "to get your breath" at the top. Normal exertion may make breathing difficult for fat people. In some diseases, breathing difficulty is more or less constant, as in the acute stage of pneumonia, in emphysema or some types of heart disease. When the difficulty is so marked that the patient can breathe only in an upright position, it is called *orthopnea*.

Obstructions of the air passages, either by secretions (croup) or by a foreign object, interfere with breathing. Asthma causes difficult breathing because the bronchial tube muscles contract; fluid in the abdomen interferes with the action of the diaphragm. Normally, the proportion of respirations to the heartbeats is 1 to 4. Respirations usually increase if the pulse rate increases, but not always in a definite proportion—usually the pulse rate goes up faster than the respiration rate. However, the respiration rate goes up faster in respiratory diseases.

Signs of Breathing Difficulties. The characteristic signs of breathing difficulties are heaving of the chest and the abdomen, a distressed expression and cyanosis (bluish tinge) in the skin—especially in the lips. In severe conditions, cyanosis spreads to the nails and the extremities and eventually is apparent over the entire body.

Cheyne-Stokes Respirations

Cheyne-Stokes respirations are periodic: that is, the patient breathes deeply and rapidly for about 30 seconds, stops breathing for from 10 to 30 seconds, then repeats the cycle. The respirations begin as being slow and shallow and gradually grow faster and deeper, then taper off until they stop entirely. Cheyne-Stokes respirations are a serious symptom and usually precede death in cerebral hemorrhage, uremia or heart disease.

KEY POINTS IN THE PROCEDURE

Count the respirations with your fingertips on the patient's pulse.

Reason: *The patient thinks you are counting his pulse—if he knows you are counting his respirations, he may not breathe naturally.*

Count the respirations by watching the rise and fall of the patient's chest.

Reason: *Taking in and expelling air make one respiration.*

Count for a half-minute and multiply by 2 to get the rate per minute. Count for a full minute if the respirations are abnormal.

Reason: The timing between abnormal respirations may be uneven.

Record the procedure on the patient's chart, noting the respiration rate and anything that is unusual such as noisy or Cheyne-Stokes breathing, cyanosis, etc.

TAKING THE BLOOD PRESSURE

Measuring blood pressure is important for patients who have unusually high or unusually low blood pressure, for postoperative patients after anesthesia, or following serious injury or shock. The blood pressure gives significant information about changes that may be taking place in the patient's body in certain types of illness.

Because the heart *forces* the blood into the circulation, there is always a certain amount of pressure in the arteries. Two things determine the degree of pressure: the rate of the heartbeats and the ease with which the blood flows into the smallest branches of the arteries. If the normal elasticity of the arteries and the arterioles is maintained, and the heart contraction exerts normal force, the blood pressure will be within the normal limits. However, if the heart rate or force is increased due to exertion or illness, the blood pressure will increase. If the quantity of blood within the circulatory system is reduced (as in hemorrhage) with the other factors remaining normal, the blood pressure will fall. By contrast, if the blood-volume is normal and the rate and the force of the heartbeat are normal, but the elasticity of the arteries is reduced, the blood pressure will rise (typical of aging).

Measuring the level of the pressure is called taking the blood pressure. The pressure is at its height with each heartbeat when the heart is contracted—this is called the *systolic* pressure. The pressure diminishes as the heart relaxes and is at its lowest when the heart is relaxed before it begins to contract again—this is the *diastolic* pressure.

Normal Blood Pressure

Normally, the difference between these 2 pressures is a number which is a third of the highest, or systolic, pressure. Both pressure readings give information; for example, a wide difference between the 2 pressures is a symptom of some kinds of heart disease. Normal systolic pressure for a man at the age of 20 is about 120, diastolic pressure about 80. Blood pressure increases gradually with age; at 60, the systolic pressure can be expected to reach 140, as a result of the effects of aging on the heart and the arteries. This pressure might be alarming in a person of 20. Any pressure that is very much higher than the normal for the person's age is a sign of difficulty in the circulatory system (hypertension).

Measuring Blood Pressure

Blood pressure is measured with an instrument called the *sphygmomanometer*—usually called the blood pressure apparatus. One type of apparatus is a cloth-covered broad rubber bag, or cuff, with 2 rubber tubes extending from it. One tube is connected to a rubber bulb air pump; this bulb has a valve which can be opened and closed. The other tube is connected to a glass tube of mercury, the manometer, which is closed at the top and marked for the blood pressure readings. The manometer is fastened firmly to a standard or to a case. You obtain the blood pressure reading by listening to the heartbeats with a stethoscope, which you place over the artery on the inside bend of the elbow. The stethoscope magnifies sounds in the arteries. With another type of apparatus, a dial is attached to the arm wrap instead of the mercury manometer. This method is considered less accurate, but it is more convenient for use outside of the hospital.

When you take a blood pressure, you must do 2 things at the same time: *listen* to the heartbeat through the stethoscope and *watch* the manometer. You listen for the first sound to appear and listen for its disappearance; you note the manometer figures at these points—they are the 2 pressure readings.

Take the blood pressure when the patient is resting and quiet; physical exertion or emotional distress will affect the level of blood pressure. Prepare the patient by explaining that the

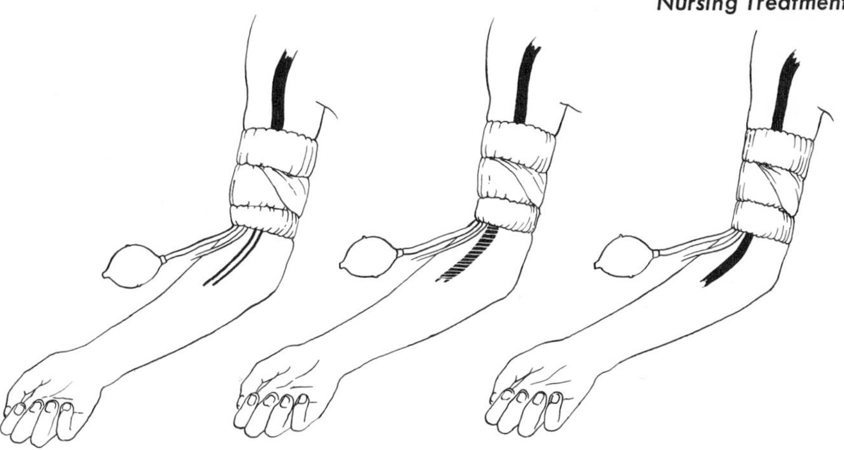

FIG. 108. When the cuff has been inflated sufficiently, it will occlude the flow of blood into the forearm (*left*). No sound will be heard through the stethoscope at this time. When pressure in the cuff is released sufficiently for blood to begin flowing through the brachial artery (*center*) the first sound is recorded as the *systolic* pressure. As the pressure in the cuff continues to be released, the last distinct sound heard through the stethoscope is the *diastolic* pressure. At this time, blood flows through the brachial artery freely (*right*).

cuff on the arm may feel tight for a second or two—otherwise the procedure will not bother him, and he only needs to keep his arm quiet for a few minutes. Tell him that taking the blood pressure is one method of obtaining information about any adult patient. Be sure that there are no leaks in the rubber bag or the valve.

KEY POINTS IN THE PROCEDURE

Make the patient comfortable, lying down with his arm supported by the bed and his palm turned upward to expose the brachial artery on the inside of the elbow.

Principle: *A more normal reading is obtained when a person is lying down. The stethoscope is placed over the brachial artery.*

Sit to take blood pressure, so you can read the height of the mercury column on the manometer at eye level.

Principle: *An accurate reading is insured at eye level.*

Apply the cuff just far enough above the elbow to leave the space over the brachial artery free—wrap it firmly around the arm and tuck in the end under the last turn of the cuff.

Principle: *Smooth and even wrapping insures even pressure on the arm to obtain an accurate reading.*

Find the pulse in the artery and place the stethoscope over the spot where you can feel the strongest pulsations.

Principle: *The beat is easier to hear with the stethoscope directly over the artery.*

Pump the manometer bulb until the mercury rises to about 20 mm. above a possible systolic pressure—this allows leeway in releasing air.

Principle: *As pressure on the cuff increases it shuts off the flow of blood in the brachial artery.*

Manipulate the valve on the manometer bulb to gradually release air from the cuff—note the level on the mercury column at which you first hear a heartbeat. This is the systolic pressure.

Principle: *As pressure in the cuff is reduced, the heart is able to force blood into the brachial artery. The point at which the heartbeat can be heard measures that force.*

Continue releasing small amounts of air from the cuff—the point on the column of mercury when the heartbeat cannot be heard is the diastolic pressure reading.

Principle: *Diastolic pressure is the point at which the only pressure on the blood is exerted by the walls of the arteries, with the heart at rest.*

Release the remaining air from the cuff.

Record the blood pressure reading on the patient's chart by writing the systolic pressure above the diastolic pressure. For example:

$$\text{B.P.}\frac{(\text{systolic})}{(\text{diastolic})}$$

BODY TEMPERATURE

Body temperature is the measure of the heat in the body—the balance between heat produced and heat lost. The body generates heat when it burns food—it loses heat through the skin, the lungs and the body discharges. When heat is produced and lost in the proper balance, the body temperature is normal—98.6° F. If the temperature goes much higher or lower, it means that the balance is upset. The signs of an elevated temperature are easy to recognize: a flushed, hot skin, unusually bright eyes, restlessness and thirst. A lifeless manner and pale, cold and clammy skin are signs of a subnormal temperature.

Changes in Body Temperature

Weather, clothes, activity, food and emotions affect the body temperature. Water affects it—the body uses water to regulate heat. Normally, if the body loses water it loses heat with it: perspiration cools the body because, as it evaporates, heat is lost. In hemorrhage, the body loses both water and heat; if heat is lost rapidly, the body feels cold. If too little heat is generated in the body, even a normal heat loss upsets the temperature balance. This happens when a patient takes almost no food but continues to lose heat in body discharge and perspiration.

The temperature rises above normal in infections or if no fluid is taken into the body; if the body processes slow down or fail, the temperature may fall below the normal balance.

Body Temperature Regulation

The heat-regulating centers in the brain control body temperature through the temperature of the blood when it reaches the brain. Heat is a product of metabolism. Muscle and gland activities generate most of the heat in the body. When you are cold, exercising your muscles warms you; if you get angry or excited, the adrenal glands become very active, and you feel warm—probably this is the reason for using the expression "hot under the collar." The process of digestion increases the body temperature. Drugs, cold and shock depress the nervous system, and decrease heat production.

Normal Body Temperature

Temperature is measured on the Fahrenheit (F) or on the Centigrade (C) scale. If you have been using a Fahrenheit thermometer and are asked to use one with Centigrade markings it is easy to convert the reading to Fahrenheit.* Average normal temperatures for adults are:

Mouth	98.6° F. (37° C.)
Rectal	99.5° F. (37.5° C.)
Axillary	98° F. (36.7° C.)

Normal varies with individuals. A difference of 0.5 to 1 degree either way is within normal limits. Body temperature is usually lowest in the morning and highest in the late afternoon and evening. The normal temperature for newborn infants and children is usually higher than the normal adult temperature. Other influences on body temperature have already been mentioned.

Elevated Body Temperature. An elevation above normal body temperature is called *pyrexia* (fever). It often accompanies illness and may be a sign that the body is fighting infection and attempting to destroy bacteria.

The body temperature rises when heat production increases in the body or when heat loss is decreased. Both of these processes may be going on at the same time. Extremely high temperatures can have fatal effects; patients

* To change Centigrade to Fahrenheit, multiply by 9/5 and add 32. To change Fahrenheit to Centigrade, subtract 32 and multiply by 5/9.

with a temperature of 108° F. seldom survive. Fever temperatures range from low fever of 100° F., to 103° F. to 105° F., which is high fever. A temperature that alternates between fever and normal, or subnormal, is called an *intermittent* temperature. A temperature that rises to several degrees above normal, then drops a little but never reaches normal is a *remittent* temperature. A *continued* temperature stays elevated. A sudden drop from fever temperature to normal is called a *crisis*. If a fever temperature gradually returns to normal it is called *lysis*.

Lowered Body Temperature. A temperature below normal is called *hypothermia*. Such temperatures usually precede death. Survival is rare when it falls below approximately 93.2° F. (34° C.). In some instances, body temperature slightly below normal is helpful because it slows body metabolism and decreases the body's need for oxygen.

The Clinical Thermometer

Body temperature is measured by a *clinical thermometer*, marked in Fahrenheit or Centigrade measurements. The clinical thermometer is a hollow glass tube, or stem, with a bulb filled with mercury on one end of it; the other end is sealed. Heat expands mercury, which makes it rise into the stem which is marked in degrees and two-tenths degrees. The markings range from 93° F. (33.9° C.) or 94° F. (34.4° C.) to about 108° F. (42.2° C.), which cover the average range of temperatures possible for a living person.

The thermometer tip is placed where it will be surrounded by body tissues in as closed a space as possible. The usual places are the mouth, the rectum and the axilla. Every hospital establishes its own routine about taking temperatures and the method to be used; for instance, a hospital may require temperatures to be taken by rectum whenever possible. The main thing is to use the method that will give the most accurate reading in the light of the patient's condition.

There are 2 types of thermometer tips: thin and slender, or rounded and bulb-shaped. The bulbous-tipped thermometer is used for taking rectal temperatures because it is safer for insertion; the slender-tipped or mouth thermom-

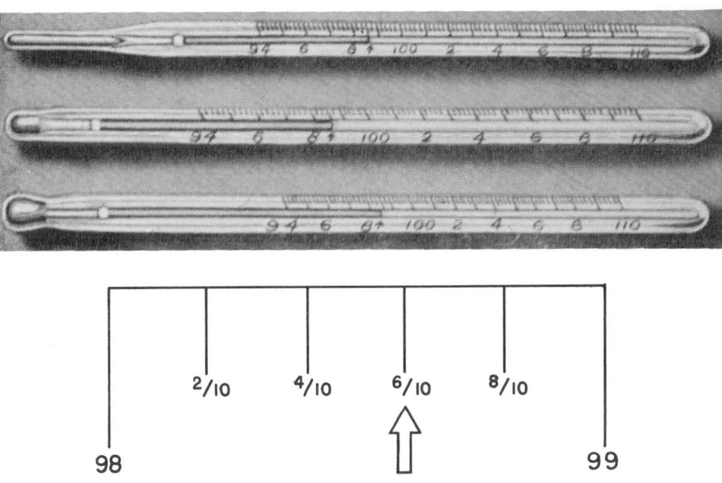

Fig. 109. (*Top*) Clinical thermometer used for measuring body temperature. The 2 upper thermometers are used to record mouth temperatures. The thermometer at the bottom is used for rectal temperatures. Note that the column of mercury is at 98.6° F. in all 3 thermometers. (Becton, Dickinson & Co., Rutherford, N. J.) (*Bottom*) Sketch of 1 degree magnified.

eter is used in taking oral temperatures. Some mouth thermometers also have a bulbous tip. Thermometers used for taking the temperature by mouth should not be used interchangeably with thermometers used for taking rectal temperatures and vice versa.

The Oral or Mouth Temperature

The oral method is never used if a patient is unconscious, delirious or otherwise irresponsible, or an infant, because of the danger of injury from a broken thermometer. This method is also contraindicated in surgery or injury of the nose or mouth, or in conditions when the patient must breathe through his mouth. If a patient has had a hot or a cold drink, wait 15 minutes before taking a mouth temperature; the temporary effects of heat or cold will have disappeared from the tissues in that time.

The Rectal Temperature

The rectal temperature is the most accurate, since the thermometer is placed in an enclosed cavity and is not affected by the temperature of the patient's environment. If there is any question about the accuracy of an oral temperature, it can be checked rectally. Some hospitals make it a policy to check oral temperatures by the rectal method when they are above a certain level. This method is used for unconscious or irrational patients, for infants and young children. To prevent injury, the nurse holds the thermometer in place. The method is contraindicated in such conditions as diarrhea, rectal disease or rectal surgery.

The Axillary Temperature

Taking the temperature by axilla is the method of last resort when conditions make it impossible to use any other method. The axillary temperature is the least accurate because the skin surfaces in the axillary space may not come together to form a closed cavity around the thermometer tip. It is often necessary for the nurse to hold the thermometer in place while the temperature registers. An axillary temperature should never be taken immediately after washing the axilla because the temperature of the water and the friction used in washing and drying the skin alters skin temperature.

Taking the Temperature

A patient who is ill at home must have his own thermometer; hospitals either provide individual thermometers for the patients or supply a number of thermometers in each nursing division. Individual thermometers usually are kept in the patient's unit and are cleansed after use, wiped dry and kept in a safe container. If a common supply is used, provision must also be made for sterilizing each thermometer after use, before it is used for another patient. This means that each thermometer must be cleansed after it is used, then placed in a disinfectant solution long enough to destroy harmful organisms. Every hospital has its own method for thermometer care, but the principles are the same no matter what solution is used; it is most important to follow the directions for the time that the thermometers must remain in the solution, because the time varies according to the effectiveness of the solution.

EQUIPMENT

Thermometer
Thermometer container
Container with soap or detergent solution (cleansing solution)
Jar of tissue wipes
Waste container
Lubricant for rectal temperature

KEY POINTS IN THE PROCEDURE

The Oral Method. If the thermometer is kept in a chemical solution, dry it with a wipe. Wipe up from the bulb with a twisting motion.

Principle: *Chemicals irritate mucous membranes and may have an unpleasant taste. Twisting insures contact with all of the surface. Wiping from the cleaner to the less clean area prevents spreading organisms.*

Hold the thermometer firmly by the thumb and forefinger. With quick snaps of the wrist, shake the mercury down to the lowest marking on the thermometer.

Principle: *The constriction above the mer-*

cury tip keeps the mercury column at the previous reading until it is shaken down.

Check the drop in the mercury column by holding the thermometer at eye level, turning it slowly until you can see where the mercury stops.

Principle: *Holding at eye level gives the true level of the mercury column. Moving an object brings it in focus.*

Place the mercury tip under the patient's tongue, telling him to close his lips but not to bite down.

Principle: *Enclosing the tip on the superficial blood vessels under the tongue insures a reliable temperature registration.*

Leave the thermometer in place for 3 to 4 minutes (unless otherwise directed).

Principle: *It takes a certain amount of time for the mercury to register the temperature of the tissues.*

Remove the thermometer and wipe it toward the bulb.

Principle: *Mucus on the thermometer obscures the column of mercury and the markings. Movement is from the cleaner to the less clean surface. Friction loosens materials.*

Read the thermometer and shake it down as before.

Follow the hospital procedure for disinfecting and storing the thermometer.

Principle: *Disinfection of contaminated articles keeps organisms from spreading.*

Record the temperature on the patient's chart.

KEY POINTS IN THE PROCEDURE

The Rectal Method. Wipe and shake down the thermometer as in taking an oral temperature.

Lubricate the bulb and the area up to 1 inch above it with lubricant placed on a wipe.

Principle: *Lubrication reduces friction and makes it easier to insert the thermometer without injuring the tissues. Applying the lubricant with a wipe prevents contamination of the supply of lubrication.*

Turn the patient on his side—fold back the bed clothes and separate the buttocks so that the anal opening is easily seen. Insert the thermometer for about 1½ inches. Hold it in place if the patient is irrational or a child.

Leave the thermometer in the rectum for 2 minutes.

Principle: *It takes a definite amount of time to register the temperature of the tissues.*

Remove and wipe the thermometer as with the mouth thermometer.

Principle: *Fecal matter on the thermometer obscures the mercury and the markings. Friction is an aid in cleansing.*

Read the thermometer. Shake it down.

Follow the hospital procedure for disinfecting and storing the thermometer.

Record the temperature on the patient's chart.

KEY POINTS IN THE PROCEDURE

The Axillary Method. Wipe and shake down the thermometer as in taking an oral temperature.

Place the thermometer in the axilla and point the bulb toward the patient's head. Bring his arm down against his body as tightly as possible, with his forearm resting across his chest.

Principle: *Close contact of the thermometer with the superficial blood vessels in the axilla insures a more accurate registration of temperature.*

Keep the thermometer in place for 10 minutes.

Principle: *It takes longer to get an accurate temperature reading when the thermometer is less tightly enclosed.*

Remove, read and shake down the thermometer. Disinfect and store it according to the hospital procedure.

Record the temperature on the patient's chart.

Cleansing and Disinfecting Clinical Thermometers

It is impossible to use heat as a thermometer disinfectant because heat expands mercury; a temperature high enough to destroy organisms will expand the mercury right out of the thermometer tube. Many sad stories are told of the student nurse who boiled the thermometers; therefore, clinical thermometers must be disinfected by a chemical solution. The procedure is the same for each type of thermometer, with one exception—attention must be given to removing the lubricant from a rectal thermometer. Lubricants form a film on the thermometer which prevents the disinfectant from reaching organisms on the surface. Detergents are more effective than soap and water in removing oily substances.

KEY POINTS IN THE PROCEDURE

Wipe the thermometer with a soft tissue, using a clean tissue each time.

Principle: *Body material on a surface prevents a disinfectant from reaching organisms. Soft tissues contact a surface more closely than harsh ones.*

Wipe from the top downward, with a twisting motion.

Principle: *Spreading organisms from the more contaminated area to a cleaner area is poor asepsis.*

Using a wipe and friction, cleanse the thermometer with soap or detergent solution.

Principle: *Soap or detergent solutions help to loosen material from a surface.*

Rinse the thermometer under cold running water.

Principle: *Rinsing removes organisms, loosened material and soap solution. Soap interferes with the disinfectant action of some chemicals (Zephiran is one of them).*

Dry the thermometer.

Principle: *Water left on the thermometer reduces the strength of the disinfectant solution.*

Place the thermometer in the disinfectant called for in hospital procedure for the designated time.

Principle: *To be effective, chemical solutions must be used at a definite strength and for a definite length of time.*

After disinfection, rinse the thermometer with water.

Principle: *Traces of chemical solutions can irritate mucous membranes (the mouth and rectum) and may have an unpleasant taste.*

Store the thermometer according to hospital procedure.

Principle: *A thermometer is used in unsterile body cavities—it is not necessary to keep it sterile after disinfection.*

The Graphic Chart

The temperature, the pulse and the respiration are recorded on the graphic chart; it shows the relationship between these 3 symptoms. The readings throughout the patient's illness are recorded in continuous lines that show the peaks and the levels of each—one below the other across a page. Each reading is recorded as a dot in the proper space, with lines connecting the dots. Every hospital has its own printed graphic form and method for recording the temperature, the pulse and the respiration, with space for recording other information, such as the blood pressure and the total intake and output of fluids.

ASEPTIC PROCEDURES

As a result of Pasteur's discoveries so many years ago, we know that disease and infection are caused by living things so small that they can be seen only through a microscope (and some of them not even then). When they enter the body, if the individual's resistance is low, these harmful organisms attack and destroy tissues and produce poisons.

Scientists have learned a great deal about the habits of harmful organisms since Pasteur's day —we know now that the germs of disease are in the air and on objects all around us; they are in the normal body discharges and in the material from discharging wounds; they spread by direct and indirect contacts. We also know where *specific* organisms are likely to be found. This knowledge of the ways of organisms helps to prevent and control disease because it indicates the kinds of precautions necessary to keep a particular organism from spreading.

Medical Asepsis

Medical asepsis is the prevention of the transfer of disease-causing organisms from one person or place to another. Preventive measures should be so much a part of nursing care that a nurse includes them as a matter of course in the care of every patient. Some of them are health practices that people use in everyday living to prevent the spread of disease, such as providing individual towels, washcloths and toothbrushes for the members of a family. In public facilities disposable towels and drinking cups are available. In the home the mother washes her hands before preparing food and teaches her children to wash their hands before meals and after using the toilet.

Preventive Measures. There are a number of ways of protecting yourself and others from infection: good health practices; immunization against some communicable diseases; avoiding contacts with persons who have communicable diseases; special procedures to prevent contacts with infectious organisms.

In an infection, the harmful organisms multiply and many of them leave the body in discharges from the parts where they are active. One way to keep organisms from spreading is to destroy them when they leave the body; another preventive measure is to keep live organisms from entering the bodies of other persons. This means that protective procedures must be centered on the following list of entrances and exits.

ENTRANCES

The respiratory system
The gastro-intestinal system
The urinary and the reproductive systems
Breaks in the skin and mucous membrane

EXITS

Sputum, droplets from sneezing, coughing and breath
Feces, saliva and vomitus
Urine and mucus discharges
Exudates from surface wounds

Additional precautions are necessary during illness to protect both the nurse and the patient from harmful organisms present in body and wound discharges. The nurse protects herself, first, by good nutrition and adequate rest to build up her resistance to infection; secondly, she protects both the patient and herself by the way she handles contaminated materials.

She washes her hands after every contact with a patient and with equipment used in caring for him: before handling food (the patient's or her own) and after using a handkerchief or using the toilet. She cleans the area beneath her fingernails frequently.

When handling soiled linen she holds it away from her uniform and puts it in the soiled linen hamper or laundry bag immediately.

She wraps dressings soiled with drainage or discharges so they can be handled safely.

She uses a dampened dust cloth to avoid spreading dust particles and is careful not to shake the bed linen.

She disinfects contaminated equipment before returning it to its place.

She provides disposable wipes and instructs the patient to cover his mouth and nose and turn his head aside when coughing or sneezing.

She sees that the patient's hands are washed after using the bedpan and toilet tissue.

Staphylococcal Infections and How They Grew

The discovery of antibiotics led doctors and nurses to relax some of the common precautions used in preventing infections. No doubt this was partly because of the feeling that if an infection did occur an antibiotic would control it. Unfortunately, some organisms are made of stout stuff and develop a resistance to antibiotics. The staphylococcus is an example—staphylococcal infections are a serious problem in our hospitals today. This has led to renewed attention to every precaution that can be taken to prevent infection by the health team. However, the members of the nursing team are largely responsible for controlling this problem since they have the opportunity to practice good aseptic technic and teach meticulous cleanliness to auxiliary personnel, patients and visitors.

General Sterilization Guides. There are many factors which influence the method of sterilization or disinfection used for specific articles. The following are general guides.

Rubber Goods and Glassware: Boil for 5 minutes in order to sterilize.

Enamelware or Metalware Utensils: Boil for 10 minutes.

Instruments: Boil for 10 minutes or put into a 5 per cent solution of phenol for 20 minutes and rinse with 70 per cent alcohol. Alcohol neutralizes the acid, which would burn tissues if it were left on instruments. Never sterilize tubular or lock instruments in phenol because it is difficult to rinse them thoroughly. Chemical disinfectants are used for instruments that boiling might harm.

Dressings and Linen: Must be sterilized in the autoclave.

Special Equipment: Always ask about the sterilization of special equipment; heat softens wax catheters, and some chemical solutions roughen the surface; boiling dulls sharp instruments. The specialist often gives instructions about handling and sterilizing his delicate instruments.

Plastic Materials: The sterilization method depends on the type of plastic.

Soap and water, sunlight and fresh air are good disinfectants. Fresh air and summer sunlight will destroy the organisms in 6 hours' exposure. Boiling for 10 minutes makes contaminated articles safe to use. Neither of these methods is safe for spore-forming organisms; they need to be exposed to steam under pressure or to a boiling period of 30 minutes. The organisms that cause tetanus and gas gangrene are spore-forming; this means that they go into a resting stage but burst into action when conditions are favorable. These organisms are not easily killed by heat.

Surgical Asepsis

Surgical asepsis is accomplished by making and keeping objects sterile—first, by sterilizing them to destroy all bacteria and secondly, by avoiding any contact with unsterile objects. When a sterile object is touched by an unsterile object it becomes contaminated and is no longer sterile. Surgical asepsis is essential in surgical operations and in deliveries and in many nursing procedures, such as giving hypodermic injections and catheterizations. We call this method surgical aseptic technic. It prevents bringing organisms to a patient.

Sterilization and Disinfection. Sterilization and disinfection are necessary in carrying out surgical asepsis, but they are also necessary in preventing spread of harmful bacteria from one patient to another. Sometimes we know that a patient harbors specific organisms, but we know that others may be present also, others about which we know nothing. Therefore, we sterilize equipment used for a patient before we use it for another. For instance, when a patient is discharged, we sterilize the wash basin, mouth care utensils and the bedpan he used while in the hospital. Thus we know that any remaining organisms have been destroyed, and the next patient can safely use the equipment.

Methods of Sterilization

Sterilization is exposing articles to heat or to chemical disinfectants long enough to kill harmful organisms. Some germs are harder to destroy than others; boiling for 10 minutes destroys most organisms; exposure for 15 minutes to steam under 18 pounds of pressure at a temperature of 257° F. will kill even the toughest ones. (Pressure steam sterilizers are known as autoclaves.) Chemical disinfectants powerful enough to destroy germs cannot be used for some articles; for example, phenol (carbolic acid) would destroy organisms on a rectal tube but also would destroy the tube. Moist heat destroys the sharp cutting edges of some instruments; they are better sterilized by dry heat or chemicals. Dry heat (hot-air sterilization) involves the use of equipment similar to the ordinary baking oven. For most articles, sterilization occurs in this method when a temperature of 320° F. is maintained for 1 hour or preferably 2 hours. The method you use must be effective and practical for the article to be sterilized.

Equipment for nursing treatments is sterilized in various ways; in some hospitals, the treatment trays are prepared and sterilized in a central supply room; some articles are sterilized before and after they are used by boiling in a steam sterilizer in each department or floor. You can sterilize articles in the home by boiling them on the kitchen stove. When you boil articles to sterilize them, the water must completely cover them and must boil for the required time; if possible, use a covered container.

Sterile Supplies

The supplies used for surgical and other sterile procedures must be free of all organisms, both pathogenic and nonpathogenic. Anything that comes into contact with an open wound or break in the skin, is introduced into a sterile body cavity or punctures the skin must be sterile. In most hospitals today sterile supplies are prepared in a central supply unit. Gauze sponges and compresses, pads, cotton balls, applicators and towels are sterilized, packaged in cloth, paper or plastic wraps, secured with adhesive masking tape and labeled. Some institutions prepare certain types of supplies in covered glass enamel or metal containers. It is more difficult to keep supplies sterile in containers because once the container is opened the contents are exposed to air contamination. Packaged supplies can be put up in "one use" amounts. If many people are using supplies from a container, the chances for contamination are increased.

More About Surgical Supplies

Surgical supplies are made up to suit the purpose for which they are to be used. They may differ slightly in form, from hospital to hospital, but the same basic supplies will be used in every hospital and will be prepared for sterile or unsterile use. The materials and forms are chosen for their effectiveness and suitability—sometimes less expensive materials are more suitable and also more economical for the patient.

Gauze Dressings. Gauze with a firm mesh is used for sponges and compresses because it is more absorbent than the looser meshes which are suitable as covering for cotton pads. Gauze dressings are always folded with the raw edges on the inside, to prevent loose threads and fringes from brushing off into a wound to cause irritation.

Cotton. Cotton comes in different grades; some are finer and more absorbent than others. A good grade of absorbent cotton is used to make tipped applicators and cotton balls; the cheaper grades are used for pads. *Cellucotton* is composed partly of cellulose fibers; it can be used for pads for incontinent patients and is cheaper and more absorbent than cotton and an economical choice when many pads are used.

Applicators. Applicators are long fine wooden sticks or tooth-picks tipped with cotton. They are used to apply medications or to cleanse areas that are too small to be reached by a sponge. A wisp of cotton is twisted on the end of the stick so that all the sharp edges are covered; the cotton must be thinned out at the edges so that it can be twisted securely around the stick to anchor the cotton firmly; otherwise the tip may slip off and be lost in a cavity when the applicator is used.

Bandages. Bandages come in different sizes and qualities. The firmer gauze is best because it covers dressings more adequately and stays in place. Muslin bandages are heavier and are sometimes used to hold splints in place. The woven elastic bandage is often used as a supporting bandage. It can be washed and re-used.

Adhesive Tape. Adhesive tape is used to hold dressings or splints in place or as support for parts of the body, such as the chest or the ankle. It comes in various widths, wrapped on metal spools. Some of the newer products have a plastic backing and one firm offers an "ouchless" type which can be removed painlessly because skin hairs do not stick to it.

Ready-Made Supplies

Sterile supplies in different sizes can be purchased at drug stores. The Band-Aid and the Steripad are examples of dressings done up in cellophane wrappers and ready for use; they are more expensive if used in quantity but are the best choice for an occasional dressing because they are convenient and can be purchased in small amounts.

The extensive use of sterile disposable equipment, such as plastic tubing, gloves and syringes, has made it possible for nurses to give less time to caring for equipment and more time to nursing. The surgical supply unit has also helped to make this possible. However, in the smaller institutions such as nursing homes and in patients' homes, the nurse must assume the responsibility of caring for equipment.

HOW TO CLEAN EQUIPMENT

Glassware

Wash glassware in soap or detergent solutions. Special small brushes are available to clean the inside of syringes. Take a syringe apart as soon as possible after using it to keep the inner plunger from sticking to the outside barrel. Soaking prevents material from drying on the surface. The best method of sterilization for glass is steam under pressure, but boiling is acceptable and is the only method available in the home. Boiling times for different types of equipment are discussed on pages 325-326.

Monelmetal and Enamelware

Clean monelmetal and enamelware with soap or detergent solution and remove stubborn spots with an abrasive. Sterilize under steam pressure if possible, but boiling is satisfactory. Pay special attention to cleaning bedpans and urinals. Equipment for flushing bedpans after use is provided in many hospitals. Do not confuse a *bedpan flusher* with a *bedpan sterilizer*—another type of equipment that may be provided. The sterilizer flushes the contents of a bedpan and then releases live steam into it for a minute or two, to destroy organisms that may be present. Some authorities question the effectiveness of this method, since so short an exposure to steam is not sufficient to destroy some organisms. Bedpans should be handled in the same manner as other similar ware.

Instruments

Instruments are made of stainless steel, nickel-plated steel or chromium. Scrub instruments with a brush and soap or detergent solution to remove material from grooves and crevices. Dry them well to prevent rust. Instruments should be sterilized under steam pressure except for those with a cutting edge, which are sterilized with dry heat or sometimes with a chemical disinfectant.

Needles

The most satisfactory type of needle is made of stainless steel, which is strong and resists rust. Needles are cleaned by forcing cold water through them to rinse out particles; alcohol or ether help to remove oily substances. Those with a hook on the point or a roughened surface should be discarded. Needles can be sterilized with dry heat, steam under pressure or by boiling.

Rubber and Plastic Goods

These articles should be washed with soap or detergent solution, forcing the solution through catheters or tubing to clean the inside. They should be rinsed as soon as possible after being used. Tubing which has contained blood is usually discarded because it is very difficult to be sure all traces of blood have been removed. Rubber goods are best sterilized under steam pressure although dry heat or boiling may be used.

Rubber gloves are powdered before they are sterilized so that they will slip on easily; a packet of sterile powder is provided to powder the hands. Dry heat and boiling may be used for certain types. In some hospitals plastic disposable gloves are provided. Gloves may be sterile or unsterile, depending upon the purpose for which they are used. In any case, they should be airtight (unperforated).

Linens

Normal laundry processes are usually considered adequate for cleaning linens. In hospitals, linen from patients with infectious diseases is placed in specially marked bags to be washed with special precautions. Similar precautions should be taken when caring for a patient with an infectious condition in the home.

HANDLING STERILE SUPPLIES AND EQUIPMENT

Remember these 2 points in handling sterile equipment: (1) never touch sterile articles with unsterile ones and (2) discard an article if you should happen to contaminate it. Every movement in aseptic procedures is a link in the chain of asepsis—if you break one link by contaminating something, the chain is broken, and you open the door to infection.

The Transfer Forceps

You can handle sterile equipment with a forceps which is sterile on the end that touches the sterile articles. A long forceps with a flat broad tip—a sponge forceps—is often used to handle sterile materials, in removing sterile dressings from containers, or sterile instruments and basins from the sterilizer, to set up trays, etc. The forceps is kept in a tall wide-mouthed jar of antiseptic solution, such as alcohol, which is a sterilizing agent and keeps the forceps sterile. The container and the forceps are sterilized; the container is filled with enough solution to cover at least two-thirds of the forceps, and the forceps is placed in the solution, ready for use.

Follow these directions in using transfer forceps:

Never put more than one forceps in a container because it is difficult to remove one of them without touching the sterile part against the unsterile handle of the remaining forceps.

Keep the prongs of the forceps together and avoid touching the rim of the container.

Always keep the tip of the forceps pointed downward to prevent the solution from flowing down over the unsterile handle and then back onto the sterile part.

Avoid touching the rim or outside of a container with a sterile article when removing it.

The Sterile Tray

A sterile tray can be prepared by covering a tray with a sterile towel and placing the sterile equipment on it with the sterile handling forceps. In removing supplies from sterile jars, put the covers down *inside up*, to keep them sterile; avoid touching the outside unsterile part of the jar with the sterile forceps or with the sterile article you are removing. If you spill liquid on the sterile towel covering the tray, it is no longer sterile because the wet spot furnishes a point for organisms to penetrate from the unsterile tray beneath.

ASEPTIC PROCEDURES IN COMMUNICABLE DISEASE

Certain diseases are easily communicated from one person to another by direct contact with the organisms of the disease which are present in body discharges or in droplets in the air from coughs and sneezes. Methods of communication and control were described in the preceding discussion of medical and surgical asepsis.

The purpose of the procedures discussed here is to prevent communicable disease organisms from spreading. This is done: (1) by keeping the patient and everything that is in direct or indirect contact with him away from other people; (2) by destroying the organisms that leave his body; and (3) by protective measures for the person who is taking care of him. Therefore, the patient is isolated; the linen, dishes, silver and other articles that have been in contact with him are disinfected; his body discharges are disinfected before they are disposed of, if they contain disease organisms. Tissues used by the patient as handkerchiefs can be burned or wrapped in a bundle with a clean outside covering for garbage or waste disposal.

Concurrent Disinfection

The practice of disinfecting all contaminated articles and body discharges and disposing of contaminated materials during the daily care of the patient is called *concurrent disinfection.* It is very important in controlling the spread of communicable disease because it reduces the number of organisms in the patient's surroundings; this protects the patient from reinfection and leaves fewer organisms to spread to others.

Isolation Technic

The patient may be isolated in his own unit or in a special hospital unit; the actual facilities for carrying out isolation technics may not be the same in every hospital, but the guiding principles in carrying out the procedures are the same, whatever the method. In the home, the patient is isolated in his room. If the room has its own adjoining bathroom, the care of the patient is much simpler because less isolation equipment is needed. The bathroom provides running water for hand washing and a toilet for the disposal of excreta.

The first thing a nurse does in setting up isolation procedures is to explain them to the patient and to the patient's family. You explain how easily disease germs can be spread unless certain precautions are used and why visitors are not allowed to touch the patient or anything around him. Explain that children are not allowed to visit a patient with a communicable disease because they are extremely susceptible to these diseases. Explain the reason for wearing a gown, the care of the dishes and the linen, so that the members of the family will co-operate with you intelligently when you need assistance.

It is important to remember that isolation can be frightening, for the patient may fear he has some dreaded disease and people are afraid to come near him. He may be lonely in a room by himself, missing the companionship of other patients and the normal contacts with hospital personnel, such as the maid who sweeps the floor and the aides who bring his tray.

Setting Up an Isolation Unit

If an adjoining bathroom is not available, you will bring all the equipment that the patient uses into his room and keep it there instead of in the family bathroom. This includes the basins, the toothbrush, the bedpan and the urinal. You will also need to provide hand-washing equipment for yourself. Keep all the articles that the patient handles on his bedside table, to prevent spreading infectious contacts over the entire room. Remove rugs and articles that might be hard to disinfect without ruining them.

The floor is always considered contaminated, as are the bed, the bedside table and the wall near the patient. If you must provide hand-washing facilities, set up a table near the door and away from the immediate surroundings of the patient. Provide a hook or a hat rack for your gown in or near the contaminated area; the gown hangs contaminated side out. On the clean table, place a pitcher of water, a wash basin, soap and a soap dish, hand lotion and paper towels. Put a wastebasket lined with newspaper beside the table—you will use this for dry waste, such as discarded paper towels.

Put a newspaper on the floor near the table; on it assemble a covered receptacle for liquid waste. This might be a leak-proof garbage can or an old-fashioned slop jar. If you need to disinfect excreta, put the disinfectant into the jar: also provide a long-handled brush and a stick in a container of soap solution and a pitcher of soap solution.

Lavatory and Toilet Facilities. If you are using the bathroom lavatory basin, the inside is considered contaminated—you keep the outside clean. Keep the seat and the outside of the toilet bowl clean. Before you empty excreta or water used for the patient into the bowl raise the seat while your hands are clean or lift it using a paper towel, if your hands are contaminated. Handle the flush lever in the same way.

Washing Your Hands

Bacteria are always present on the hands but washing with soap and water or a detergent for one-half to 1 minute is usually sufficient to remove them. The hands should be washed for 2 to 3 minutes if they have touched pus, blood, mucus or other body secretions: attention should always be given to cleaning beneath the nails. If a brush is used, care should be taken not to injure the skin—breaks in the skin lead to infection. Washing the hands under running water is the best method, with the water controlled by faucets operated by the elbow, knee or foot. If hand-controlled faucets are provided, hospital policy decides whether they are to be considered clean or contaminated. If clean, a paper towel is used when *opening* them; if contaminated, a paper towel is used to *close* them.

Liquid soap in a dispenser operated by a foot lever is easier to use than a bar of soap. If bar soap is used, do not put it down until you have finished washing your hands. You can "park" the soap on the back of the brush as you use it. Rinse the soap when you finish and return it to its container. Keep your hands down to prevent soiled water from running back on your arms and wash well above your wrists; rinse and dry your hands thoroughly and use a hand cream or lotion to prevent chapping and roughness which may lead to breaks in the skin. One more thing—if you touch the inside of the sink or basin you have contaminated your hands and must again time yourself for washing.

Handwashing is always important, but it is doubly so in a hospital because there are so many opportunities for infection and we are responsible for helping and protecting patients. Added infections only increase their problems. Studies have shown that sometimes patients do acquire infections after they enter a hospital—

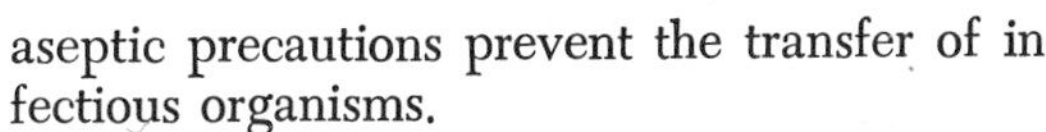

aseptic precautions prevent the transfer of infectious organisms.

Putting On and Removing the Gown

You wear a gown to keep your clothing clean while you are caring for the patient. The *inside* of the gown is clean; the outside is contaminated. The gown must be long enough to cover your uniform completely; it must open down the back and must be full enough to overlap at the back; a tie around the waist keeps the gown in place. A smock or a coverall apron opening down the back can be used for a protective gown. The neck is clean because you never touch that part of the gown with contaminated hands. Roll your sleeves above your elbows before you put the gown on.

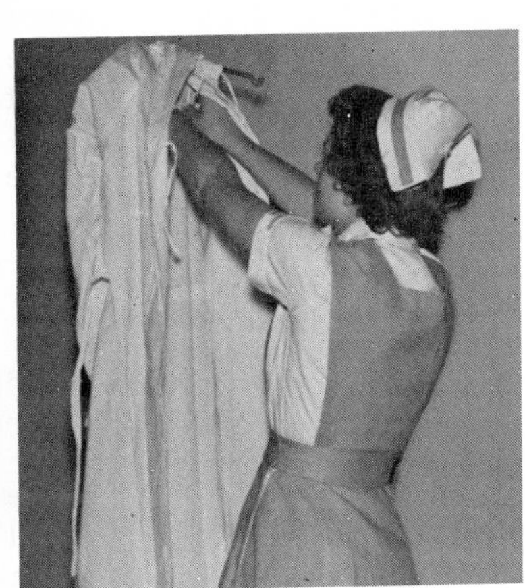

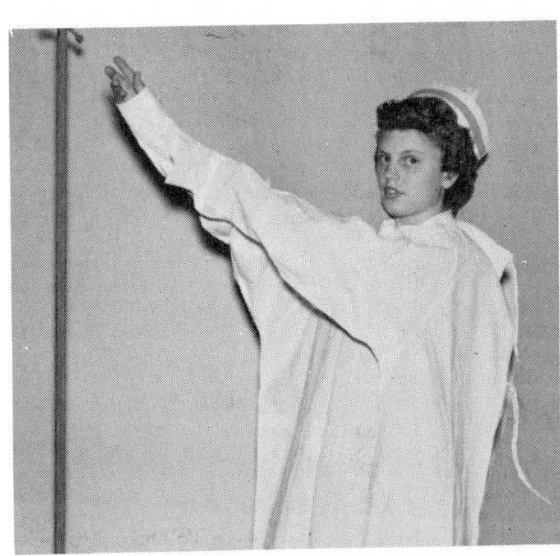

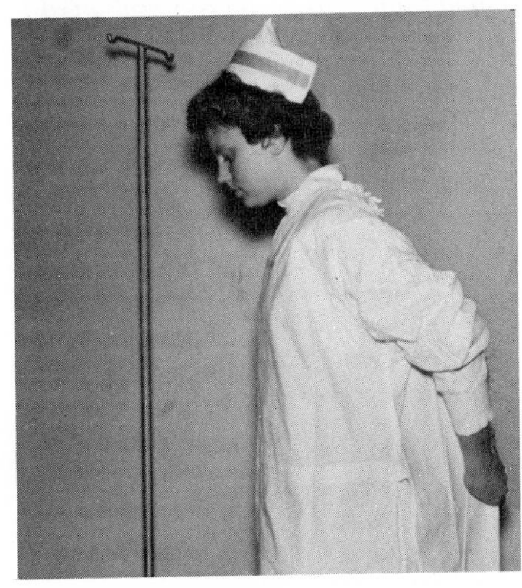

Fig. 110. (*Top, left*) Removing the gown from the hook. The nurse grasps the gown at the inside of the neckband.

(*Top, right*) The nurse keeps 1 hand *inside* 1 sleeve as she adjusts the other.

(*Bottom*) The nurse draws the back edges together and away from her body before folding the back over and fastening the ties.

Everyone coming into close contact with an isolated patient must wear a gown. With the re-use technic, the nurse's gown hangs in the unit with the *contaminated side out.* With the throw-away technic, the gown is discarded after it is used by folding it *inside out* and placing it in the receptacle provided for contaminated linen. A supply of clean gowns is ready outside to put on before entering the unit. After removing the gown, the wearer washes her hands.

The following procedure describes the re-use technic:

SUGGESTED PROCEDURE

Slip your hands inside the shoulders of the gown and lift it from the hook.

***Principle:** Clean hands touch the clean inside of the gown.*

Slip your arms into the sleeves and keep one hand inside on the sleeve as you adjust the other.

***Principle:** A clean hand touches the clean inside of one sleeve.*

Without touching the front of the gown, fasten it at the neck, keeping the sleeves away from your hair.

***Principle:** Clean hands touch the clean neck.*

Bring the back edges of the gown together at the waistline, drawing them away from your body and folding them over. Tie the belt.

***Principle:** Clean hands are now contaminated by touching the contaminated part of the gown.*

REMOVING THE GOWN

Untie the strings at the waistline.

***Principle:** Contaminated hands touch the contaminated strings.*

Wash your hands—unfasten the neck strings.

***Principle:** Clean hands touch the clean neck.*

Wriggle your arms and shoulders out of the gown, drawing hands up through the sleeves.

***Principle:** Clean hands touch the clean inside of the gown.*

With hands inside the shoulder of the gown, bring the shoulder seams together and grasp the gown and hang it on the hook. Wash your hands.

***Principle:** Clean hands are contaminated by touching the contaminated outside of the gown.*

Masks

Some communicable diseases are transmitted through the respiratory tract. The individual hospital establishes a policy about wearing masks. In some hospitals, everyone in contact with the patient, including visitors, wears a mask; in others the patient also wears one. In other situations, only the patient wears a mask.

The principal reason for wearing a mask is to keep organisms from entering and leaving the respiratory tract. In caring for the patient with a severe upper respiratory infection, the masks protect those who are attending the patient. In the operating room or in the nursery, masks protect the patient from possible infection by nursing or other personnel. It is generally agreed that the best mask is one made of several layers of closely woven gauze, which launders well and keeps its shape. Those made of paper and plastic are less satisfactory because it is difficult for filtered air to enter or expired air to leave through the mask, so it enters and escapes around the edges without being filtered at all.

Once a mask is removed from the nose and mouth, it should be discarded. The mask which dangles like a necklace beneath a nurse's chin when not in use is a menace rather than a protection. Also, to be effective, it should be changed often.

Disposing of Excreta

In some communities, sewage disposal technics destroy organisms. In diseases where the organisms are excreted in the urine or feces, special precautions are needed to destroy these organisms if the sewage disposal system is inadequate. The usual method is to treat the urine and the feces with chlorinated lime for 8 to 12 hours before disposing of it in the toilet.

Care of Linen

Modern processes in a hospital laundry are generally effective for destroying most communicable disease organisms. Linens contaminated by spore-forming organisms, such as those causing tetanus or anthrax, are an exception and should be sterilized first by steam pressure before they are handled by laundry workers. Exposure to sunlight for 6 to 8 hours is an effective way to destroy some organisms and is suitable for articles that might be damaged by the usual laundering methods.

Care of Dishes

Mechanical dishwashers are an ideal solution to the problem of disinfecting dishes used by a patient with a communicable disease. If a mechanical dishwasher is not available, dishes should be rinsed and boiled. Disposable dishes and tray-setting materials may be used which leaves only the silverware to be disinfected by boiling. If boiling is the method used, dishes must be rinsed first to avoid coagulating food particles. By far the best method is the use of disposable dishes and "barrier" trays. It is safe, saves time and disposes of the unappetizing sight of a used tray lying around until the nurse has time to care for it.

Disposing of Other Body Discharges

Discharges from the patient's eyes, nose and mouth require the use of paper wipes that are disposed of as soon as they are used by dropping them into a paper bag pinned to the patient's bed. The closed bag can then be placed on a clean newspaper outside of the contaminated area to be wrapped up by the nurse for disposal after she removes her gown and leaves the unit.

Terminal Disinfection

Terminal disinfection means the care of a patient's unit and belongings after the infectious period has terminated. The process is the same whether the patient remains in the hospital, has been discharged or has expired. Sometimes the Sanitary Code of the city or community prescribes the methods to be used. The methods should be sufficiently thorough to destroy the particular organisms causing the disease. Airing, sunlight and washing with soap and water are usually enough to make the unit safe for the next patient. Medical science has given us so much information about organisms that cause disease that it should be possible to select the best and most appropriate methods of disinfection in each instance. Some organisms are harder to destroy than others and ordinary methods are not effective.

Modified Isolation Precautions

Precautions should always be taken to prevent spreading infection from a patient with such conditions as a cold, cough or draining sinus. Disposable wipes should be provided with provision for disposing of them safely; equipment he handles should be isolated or disinfected, and his hands should be washed frequently. He should be instructed to cover his nose and mouth with a wipe and turn his head away when he coughs or sneezes. He should be told not to exchange magazines or newspapers with the man in the next bed—the reasons for all these prohibitions should be explained. Most people are anxious to avoid giving the infection to someone else.

The Final Responsibility

As a nurse, you are responsible for your patient's protection. He must trust your ability and integrity to see that no harm comes to him. You are the only one who may know that a sponge or an instrument has been contaminated. It is up to you to recognize a break in the chain of asepsis and to correct it. This may not be easy. You may fear criticism for clumsiness or for delaying a procedure while you replace contaminated equipment. If you do not understand the principles of asepsis, the cautions about contamination sometimes seem exaggerated, but the practice of asepsis is a combination of knowledge and conscientious regard for the welfare of your patients.

30

PHARMACOLOGY AND THE ADMINISTRATION OF DRUGS

INTRODUCTION TO PHARMACOLOGY AND DRUGS

Pharmacology is the study of drugs and their actions. A drug is a substance, other than food, used in preventing disease, in aiding the doctor to diagnose a disease, in treating disease, and in restoring or maintaining normal functions in the body tissues. Drugs act to speed up or to slow down body functions; the amount or the *dosage*, influences the drug's effect on the body. Drugs, or medicines, are prescribed as part of the patient's treatment; the doctor regulates the dosage to produce the desired effect.

Drug Standards Are Necessary

Standards for the strength and purity of drugs are essential to protect the public from the dangers of misuse or adulteration. The *Pharmacopeia of the United States of America* (usually called the U.S.P.) is a book that defines standards for the approval of drugs used in medical practice. The first U.S.P. was published in 1820, and it is revised every 5 years by a committee of outstanding physicians, pharmacologists and pharmacists.

Another publication that defines standards is the *National Formulary* (N.F.) which provides a supplementary list of drugs and is prepared and kept up-to-date by the American Pharmaceutical Association. The Food, Drug and Cosmetic Act designates the U.S.P. and the N.F. as the approved standards for listing the official drugs.

The Council on Drugs of the American Medical Association has been publishing a yearly up-to-date list for physicians on the actions and uses of commercial drug products and their dangers. This information helps to protect the public and physicians against false claims and misleading advertising about drugs and their effectiveness. This is not an official publication, but it is widely used and provides much valuable information about the newer drugs.

The Food, Drug and Cosmetic Act designates the Federal Drug Administration as the agency empowered to enforce drug standards (see p. 56).

Names of Drugs

The rapid increase in the number of drugs and the variety of names for the same drug is confusing. The *official*, or *generic*, name of a drug is the one under which it is listed in the U.S.P. or the N.F. It also may be known by one or more trade names. For example, meprobamate is the official name of a drug which is also marketed under the trade names of Miltown and Equanil. By registering a trade name for a drug, the manufacturing company obtains the sole right to use that name. At present, there is some concern about the higher cost of some trade name drugs as compared with the cost of the same drug purchased under its official or generic name. Authorities would like to make it a legal requirement to include the generic name of a drug on the prescription label. In some hospitals, pharmacists are already including the generic name and the trade name on the label.

Sources of Drugs

The main sources of drugs are:

Minerals (iron, salt)
Animals (insulin, liver)
Plants (opium, digitalis)
Chemical substances made in the laboratory (synthetics)

A synthetic drug has the same composition as the drug in its natural form and can be made in the laboratory less expensively than by using the natural source. However, every drug cannot be made in this way.

Forms of Drugs

The form of a drug, its properties and the effect desired determine the method for giving it. Combinations of drugs are sometimes given because together they produce desirable effects that would not be possible if one of them were given alone.

Drugs are prepared in forms suitable for the various methods of administration. These forms are liquids, solids and semisolids.

Liquids.

Solutions: Drugs dissolved in water.

Syrups: Drugs dissolved in sugar and water.

Mixtures: Drugs mixed with a liquid but not dissolved in it.

Milks: White drug substances mixed with water.

Emulsions: Drugs mixed with oils and water.

Elixirs: Drugs dissolved in a sweetened, flavored solution containing alcohol.

Tinctures: Drugs dissolved in alcohol or alcohol and water.

Fluid extracts: Drugs that have been boiled and evaporated to a concentrated strength and dissolved in alcohol.

Liniments: Drugs mixed with oil, soap or alcohol (for external use only).

Lotions: Drugs mixed with water for external application.

Solids and Semisolids.

Capsules: Drugs enclosed in various-sized gelatin containers. Hard capsules are used for liquids or powders, soft ones for oils.

Powders: Drugs in powder form. May be put in papers.

Pills: Drugs molded with some adhesive substance into a round or oval shape, and sometimes coated with another substance to disguise the taste or to delay their action.

Tablets: A solid dosage form of varying weight, size and shape, which may be molded or compressed; contains a medicinal substance in pure or diluted form: *buccal* (to be held between the cheek and the gum, permitting direct absorption of the medicinal substance contained therein); *hypodermic* (to be dissolved in water, containing a medicinal substance for hypodermic injection); *sublingual* (to be held beneath the tongue for direct absorption); and *triturate* (contains a medicinal substance diluted with a mixture of lactose and powdered sucrose, in varying proportions, with a moistening agent).

Troches or Lozenges: Drugs mixed with sugar and mucilage into hard disks. Dissolved in the mouth to treat the throat.

Ointments: Drugs mixed with oil or fat, such as mineral oil, olive oil, lanolin, etc.

Pastes: Ointments with various powders added, to make them more adhesive.

Suppositories: Drugs mixed with a firm substance (cocoa butter, glycerin) and molded to a cone-shape for insertion into a body cavity (rectum, vagina, urethra) where they dissolve.

Ampules and Vials. *Ampules* are sealed glass containers that usually contain one dose of a powdered or a liquid drug; powders must be dissolved in sterile water or normal saline solution before they can be given. *Vials* are rubber-stoppered glass containers that contain several doses of a drug. *Disposable syringes* containing single doses of a drug for hypodermic injection are now widely used. Another type of "disposable" (Tubex) contains one dose of a drug in a cartridge unit with a sterile needle attached which fits into a metal frame. Cartridge and needle are discarded after they are used.

The Action of Drugs

In ancient times, the use of drugs was largely a matter of guesswork—if a drug was effective nobody knew exactly why. A combination of drugs was often given to the hapless patient, hoping that something in the mixture would produce the desired results. Scientific research has changed this procedure by greatly increasing our knowledge of how drugs act in the body. It has also increased the number of drugs considerably, which has led to regulations to control their use, thus protecting the public from false claims for drugs that are worthless or harmful.

How Action Takes Place. It is known now that drugs bring about chemical changes in body cells by (1) local action—at the point at which they are applied (ointments, sprays) and by (2) systemic action—which occurs after they are absorbed in the circulation. The various forms of systemic action are:

Stimulation: An increase in the activity of certain body cells, as in the effects of caffeine on the central nervous system.

Depression: A decrease in cell activity, as in the action of sedatives such as Nembutal.

Therapeutic Effect: The action of a drug in illness or on diseased tissues (thyroid extract in toxic goiter).

Selective Action: More pronounced effects on some tissues than on others (morphine on the respiratory centers of the brain).

Side-Effects: A drug given to produce a specific effect may have other effects as well (atropine decreases respiratory secretions and also dilates the pupil of the eye).

Cumulative Action: A drug may be absorbed more rapidly than it is excreted; it accumulates in the body and may have toxic effects (digitalis).

Synergistic Action: Drugs may work together, each in its own way, with one intensifying the effect of the other (epinephrine intensifies the effect of procaine as a local anesthetic).

Idiosyncrasy: Effects of a drug that are abnormal or the opposite of its usual effects (excitement instead of sleep after a dose of morphine).

Tolerance: Increasingly larger amounts of a drug are required to produce the desired effect (opiates).

Habituation: Mental dependence on a drug habitually taken but no longer physically necessary (a little white pill always taken at bedtime).

Addiction: Certain drugs taken over a long period of time become so psychologically and physically necessary that their withdrawal causes both mental and physical suffering (morphine, heroin). Drug tolerance usually accompanies addiction.

Hypersensitivity: An allergic reaction caused by a drug. A patient who is sensitized may develop only a skin rash or hives, or he may go into anaphylactic shock and die. Tests for sensitization should precede the administration of drugs known to cause severe allergic reactions, such as penicillin, serums and vaccines.

Drugs and the Individual Patient

It is not unnatural to be apprehensive about medicines. A patient may fear that a hypodermic will hurt, a medicine will have an offensive taste or a capsule will stick in his throat. He may think he is being made a subject for experimentation, that nothing will help him, or he may simply be tired of swallowing things every 2 or 3 hours. Encourage him to talk about his feelings, and let him know you sympathize with him. Patients often conceal their real feelings because they are afraid of offending a nurse. Also, most patients want to know why a medicine is being given. If a patient is worried, it is reassuring to be told that something is being done. You can help to give him this reassurance when you give a medicine—"I've brought you something for your cough" or "to relieve your pain" or "to help you sleep."

It is important to know about the possible actions of drugs to be able to observe and report their effects intelligently. This knowledge is applied every time a medication is given in order to observe its effects on an individual patient. This is not as difficult as it seems because the science of pharmacology has given us detailed information about the action of a vast number of drugs. This helps you to recognize both favorable and unfavorable effects. It also reminds you that drugs affect people as individuals. In other words, you are concerned about the effect of digitalis on John Gray instead of simply giving digitalis to a "heart" patient.

Drug Dosage

The dose is the amount of a drug given as treatment. Drug dosage is regulated and described in this way:

Minimal Dose: The smallest amount necessary for a therapeutic effect.

Maximal Dose: The largest amount that can be given safely.

Toxic Dose: An amount that causes unfavorable symptoms or poisoning.

Lethal Dose: An amount that will cause death.

In prescribing the dosage of any drug the doctor always considers certain individual differences that are known to affect drug dosage, such as:

Age: Children are more sensitive to drugs than adults; the effects of drugs on elderly people may be different from the effects on younger adults due to body deterioration or loss of body function.

Sex: Some drugs given to the mother may be harmful to the unborn fetus or to the nursing infant. However, authorities are not in agreement that sex is important in prescribing the dosage of drugs.

Weight: Drug dosage is often prescribed in relation to a patient's weight, especially when concentration of the drug in the blood is desirable. This usually requires larger doses for the heavier person.

The Patient's Condition: The nature of a disease and its severity may make a difference in the dosage. It takes more of a drug to quiet a highly disturbed patient or to control severe pain.

Disposition: A highly nervous person requires less of a stimulant and more of a depressant drug. The opposite is true of a less excitable or more stoical patient.

The Method Used: The speed with which a drug enters the circulation may affect the dosage. This, in turn depends on how the drug is given. The intravenous method is quicker than the subcutaneous—both are more rapid than the oral method. Less of a drug may be required if absorption is rapid; with some drugs, the method makes no difference.

Distribution: Some drugs are distributed evenly throughout the body and reach every cell; others appear only in certain body fluids or tissues. For example, one antibiotic may enter the spinal fluid, but another may never reach it.

Elimination: Normally, a drug remains in the body long enough to do its work and is eliminated by the excretory organs (in the urine, feces, breath, perspiration). Some drugs leave the body in their original form; others have been made inactive by chemical changes that have taken place in their structure. If these processes are slow, it may prolong the effect of the drug for too long a time; if they proceed too rapidly, the drug may be excreted before it has a chance to do its work effectively. Chemical changes also may form substances that are harmful if the body is unable to dispose of them rapidly enough.

Methods of Giving Drugs

The method chosen depends on the nature of the drug and the effect that is wanted. This may be *local* (at the point where the drug is applied) or *systemic* (absorbed into the circulation and carried to body cells).

For local effects:

Application to the Skin: Antiseptics and soothing drugs are applied directly to the skin (iodine on a cut or scratch, lotion on an itchy rash).

Application to Mucous Membranes: Drug preparations are applied to mucous membranes of the eye, mouth, nose, throat or genitourinary tract by swabbing, spraying, instillation or irrigation; they are applied to the vagina and rectum in the form of suppositories. Drug-saturated packs can be inserted in body cavities.

For systemic effects there are a number of methods for introducing drugs into the circulation. Again, the choice depends on the nature and the amount of the drug to be given, the speed of its action and the patient's condition:

Oral: The patient swallows the drug. This is convenient and economical, but the method has its drawbacks. Some drugs have an unpleasant taste or odor; others injure the teeth. Patients who are nauseated or vomiting cannot take drugs by mouth; some irritate the lining of the stomach causing nausea and vomiting. Digestive enzymes destroy the effectiveness of certain drugs.

Sublingual: The drug is placed under the patient's tongue, where it dissolves and is absorbed. The patient must be able to understand instructions: keep the drug under the tongue; do not swallow it; do not take a drink until it is absorbed.

Few drugs are given this way—nitroglycerine in tablet form is one of them.

Rectal: This method consists of the injection of a liquid drug preparation into the rectum. It is used if a patient is vomiting, if the taste of a drug is offensive or if the action of the digestive enzymes interferes with a drug's effectiveness. It also can be used for an unconscious patient. The drawbacks in using this method are that the patient may not be able to retain the drug, or if part of it is expelled, there is no way of knowing the amount retained. Drug preparations administered by rectum are usually given in small amounts and are preceded by a cleansing enema to empty the rectum and make absorption easier. As was stated in Chapter 29, medicated rectal suppositories are occasionally used also for their systemic effect.

Inhalation: Drugs that can be vaporized may be given through the respiratory tract. So much absorbing surface is available in the lungs and the bronchi that the drug is quickly absorbed and is immediately effective. This is highly important in an emergency such as administration of oxygen.

Drugs may be injected into body fluids or tissues through a needle. They must be soluble, absorbable and sterile and must not irritate or injure the tissues. Injection has the advantage of rapid action, but this can be dangerous if there should be an error made in dosage. Repeated insertions of a needle may also make the tissues tender and sore; there is always the possibility of infection when the skin is pierced. Injections are given in a number of ways:

Intradermal Injection: A small amount of a drug is injected just beneath the outer layer of the skin, where it is absorbed slowly. The doctor uses this method in making allergy tests.

Subcutaneous Injection: A small amount of a drug is injected into the subcutaneous tissues (hypodermically). This method is used to give drugs that are soluble and nonirritating, often using disposable syringes and needles (a simpler and more accurate procedure for this method).

Occasionally, substantial amounts of a therapeutic solution are injected into subcutaneous tissues (hypodermoclysis). The fluid is injected slowly, through long needles, into loose connective tissue—usually under the breasts. Intravenous infusion has largely replaced this method.

Intramuscular Injection: A drug is injected into the muscle which lies beneath the subcutaneous tissue. This method is used in giving irritating drugs because deep muscle tissue has fewer nerve fibers; also, absorption of the drug is faster because muscle tissue has a great many blood vessels. The injection is most commonly given in the gluteal or deltoid muscles.

Intravenous Injection: A drug is injected directly into a vein. It is used to get a rapid effect or when it is impossible to inject a drug into other tissues. If a large quantity of solution is given it is called an *infusion.* The procedure requires technical skill and is usually done by a doctor. However, in some hospitals, professional nurses now perform this procedure under a doctor's direction. Intravenous injections and infusions are commonly given for dehydration, excessive loss of blood, to dilute poisons in the blood and other body fluids and to provide electrolytes, drugs and foods. (See Chap. 33.)

How Drugs Are Prescribed

A prescription is a written formula for preparing and giving a drug preparation. Physicians, dentists and veterinarians are the only persons licensed to write prescriptions. *The nurse may give a drug preparation only on an order from a doctor.* In the hospital the doctor writes his orders in an order book or on an order form attached to the patient's chart. Sometimes orders are given verbally in an emergency or over the telephone. The nurse sees that such an order is written in the proper place and signed by the doctor later. *This is important*—a written order is protection for the doctor, the patient and the nurse. It is a permanent record which cannot be disputed and always is available for reference. The nurse is responsible for carrying out an order as it is written—she is not permitted to make the slightest change. If she has any reason to question an order or does not understand it, she must consult the head nurse or the doctor about it before she proceeds.

Prescription Drugs. Some drug preparations can be purchased without a prescription, but Federal law now requires one for any drug that is not considered safe to use without a doctor's supervision, such as narcotics. Such a prescription cannot be refilled without written or telephoned authorization by the doctor.

Preparing Prescribed Medicines

The pharmacist is the only person qualified

and licensed to make up drug preparations. In a hospital, the prescription is sent to the hospital pharmacy; otherwise, it is prepared by a local pharmacist. Every hospital has its own procedure for handling orders for prescribed drugs.

The Doctor's Orders. The doctor uses standard abbreviations in writing orders, prescriptions and labels to be used for drugs. Some of the most common are listed as follows:

ABBREVIATIONS	MEANING
aa.	of each
a.c.	before meals
ad lib.	as desired
alt. hor.	every other hour
A.M.	morning
b.i.d.	twice a day
c̄	with
cc.	cubic centimeter
ʒ	dram
Gm.	gram
gr.	grain
gt., or gtts.	drop, or drops
H	hypodermic
h	hour
h.s.	at bedtime
i.m.	intramuscularly
i.v.	intravenously
L.	liter
m., or min.	minum, or minums
ml.	milliliter
℥	ounce
p.c.	after meals
per	by
P.M.	afternoon
p.o.	by mouth
p.r.n.*	when required
pt., or O.	pint
q.	every
q.d.	every day
q.h.	every hour
q. (2,3, etc.) h.	every (two, three, etc.) hours
q.i.d.	4 times a day
℞	take
s̄	without
Sig or S	write on label
s.c.	subcutaneously
s.o.s.*	if necessary
s̄s̄	one half
stat.	at once
t.i.d.	3 times a day

* Note the difference between these abbreviations: *s.o.s.* (if necessary) means for *one* dose only; *p.r.n.* (when needed, as often as necessary) means the nurse is expected to use her judgment about repeating the dose. For instance, the doctor may leave a p.r.n. order for a cathartic: if the patient has an adequate bowel movement a cathartic is not necessary on that day; 2 days later it may be needed.

The Parts of a Prescription. The doctor's prescription has several parts:

The Patient's Full Name: This avoids the danger of confusion with another patient having the same surname.

The Date and the Time of Day: This tells when the order begins. If it is for a specified number of days it also tells when the order is to be discontinued. An order for a narcotic is usually legally valid for 24 to 48 hours only. This means that the order must be rewritten if the drug is to be continued beyond that time.

The Name (or Names) and the Amount of the Drug in the Preparation: The use of the generic name is preferred to the trade name.

The Dosage: This may be stated in either the metric system (gram, cc.) or in the apothecaries system (grain, dram, ounce), depending on the system used in the individual hospital. Equivalents for fluid and weight measures are given on p. 340.

The Time and the Frequency of Dose: The hospital nursing service usually determines the time schedule for drug routines. For instance, for drugs to be given every 4 hours, one hospital may choose the even-numbered hours, another may choose the odd. The doctor may give other less definite directions, such as once or twice a day, before or after meals, at bedtime. Hospital policy sets the definite hour.

The Method To Be Used: Usually it is understood that the oral method is to be used if no other method is specified. Otherwise, the doctor specifies the method, especially if the drug can be given in more than one way.

The Physician's Signature: This is essential for legal reasons or if there is some question about the order. An unsigned order may mean that the doctor had not finished writing it.

THE ADMINISTRATION OF MEDICINES

In most hospitals, a special unit in each patient area is provided for storing and measuring medicines. It is equipped with cupboards, a sink, running water and work space and is usually located in the nurses' station. Wherever it is, it should not be accessible to the public. It must provide a locked compartment to store narcotic drugs. Medicines should be placed on the shelves in an orderly fashion. Every drug should be plainly labeled. If a label is illegible, send the container to the pharmacy for relabeling—never label or relabel a drug yourself. Some drug preparations must be stored in the refrigerator to preserve their effectiveness.

The Medicine Card

Most hospitals use a card system for giving medications. A card is made out for each medication, with the patient's name, the drug, the dosage and the time for giving the medicine. These cards are kept in a file and taken out for use when the medications are measured and given. Sometimes different-colored cards are used—each color represents a different time of day. For example, red cards might be used for all the medicines to be given before meals; yellow cards for those to be given after meals, and so on.

As each medication is measured, it is placed with its card on a tray to be carried to the patient; this identifies the medicine from the time it is measured until the patient takes it.

Measuring Systems

Drugs are measured by both dry and liquid measures; 2 systems are used for measuring drugs—the *metric system* and the *apothecaries' system*. In addition, there is the system of *household measures* that you use in cooking; household measures are not accurate for measuring medicines but can be used if other measuring equipment is not available in preparing solutions to be used externally. The measures given in the tables are those that you will use in measuring medicines, solutions used in nursing treatments and the fluids taken in and excreted by the patient. All hospitals may not use the same system; you may be asked to measure urine in *cc.'s* or in *ounces*. Therefore, you need to understand both systems and to know the household measure equivalents if you have to use household equipment. The units of measure are listed:

METRIC SYSTEM		APOTHECARIES' SYSTEM		HOUSEHOLD MEASURES	
gram	Gm.	grain	gr.	drop	
cubic centimeter	cc.	minim	m.	teaspoon	tsp.
liter	L.	dram	dr., ʒ	tablespoon	tbsp.
		ounce	oz., ℥	measuring cup	c.
		pound	lb.		
		pint	pt.		
		quart	qt.		

The following tables show these systems in their equivalent relationships:

DRY MEASURES

METRIC SYSTEM	APOTHECARIES' SYSTEM	HOUSEHOLD MEASURES
1 Gm.	15 gr.	¼ tsp.
4 Gm.	1 dr.	1 tsp.
30 Gm.	1 oz.	8 tsp. or 2 tbsp.

LIQUID MEASURES

METRIC SYSTEM	APOTHECARIES' SYSTEM	HOUSEHOLD MEASURES
1 cc.	15 m.	15 drops
4 cc.	1 fl.dr.	1 tsp.
30 cc.	1 fl.oz.	8 tsp. or 2 tbsp.
500 cc.	1 pt.	2 measuring cups
1,000 cc.	1 qt.	4 measuring cups

MEASURING EQUIPMENT

Minim glasses	Medicine droppers
Graduates measuring from 5 to 30 cc.	Glass rod
Medicine glasses	Small paper containers or
Drinking glasses	Teaspoons

Measuring Medicines

Routines may vary slightly from hospital to hospital, but the safety rules are the same everywhere. If you are tempted to deviate from these rules, remember that they have been set up to protect the patient and to protect you from mistakes which could have serious results.

Give your undivided attention to the job at hand when you measure and give medicines.

Fig. 111. Safeguards in the preparation of medicine dosage. The check-list, when followed for each medication, will assure correct identification of the prescribed drug. (Veterans Administration Training Guide)

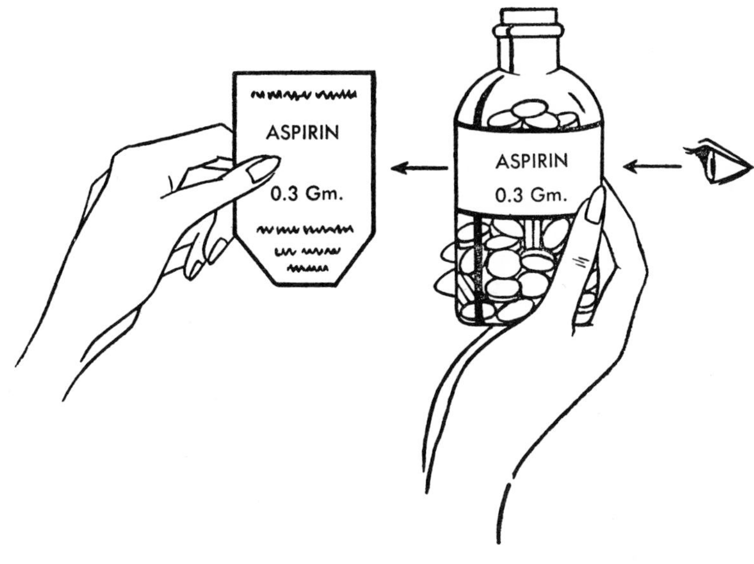

Preparation for Patient

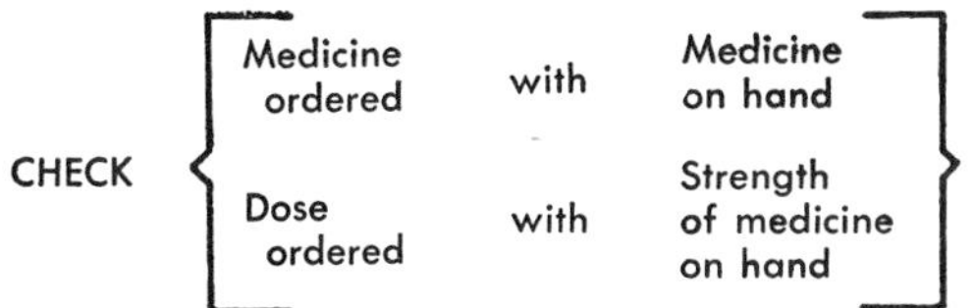

Selecting the RIGHT medicine

Read the order, check it with the medicine card and the label on the medicine—they should check exactly.

Read the medicine label 3 times: (1) when you take it from the shelf; (2) before you remove the medicine from the container; and (3) before you put back the container (see Fig. 111).

Measure the dose with appropriate equipment. Hold the measure at eye level when measuring liquids, with your thumbnail on the line of the desired amount. Pour liquid medicines from the unlabeled side of the bottle, to avoid soiling the label (see Fig. 112).

Never give a medicine from an unlabeled container.

Shake the required number of tablets or capsules into the container you are using. Small paper cups are usually provided for this purpose. Never handle medicines with your fingers.

Assemble each medicine, with its card, on the medicine tray as you prepare it.

Administering Medicines

Be sure that you are giving the correct medicine to the right patient. Check the name on the medicine card with the patient's identification band if he has one. Otherwise, address him by his name: "It's time for your medicine, Mr. Winter." If you are not sure of his identity ask him his name. Saying a name helps to associate it with the name on the medicine card (see Fig. 113).

Stay with the patient until he has swallowed the medicine. If left alone with a medicine, patients have been known to dispose of it in various ways, such as pouring it in their plants on the bedside table.

Never leave the medicine tray within the reach of patients. If you must leave the room or the ward, take the tray with you.

Chart medicines as soon as you have given

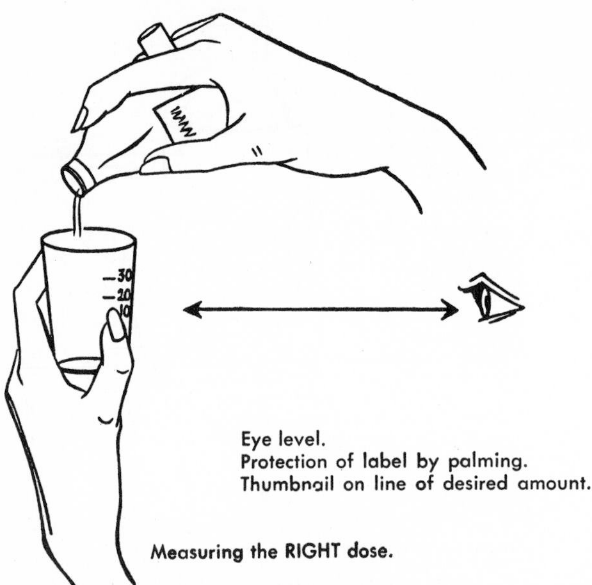

FIG. 112. Basic steps in the preparation of liquid medication. (Veterans Administration Training Guide)

them. Never chart a medicine before you give it. Record the time, the name of the drug, the dosage and the method of giving it. Record and *report immediately* any unusual reaction, such as vomiting the medicine, an unfavorable change in the patient's condition, his refusing to take the medicine or inability to take it all. If you find that you have forgotten to give a medicine you must report it promptly.

Discard an unused dose of medicine—never return it to the stock container.

Never give a medicine that someone else has prepared. If a mistake occurs, you will be held responsible.

Listen when a patient questions a medicine; if he has been getting a red pill and is offered a white one instead, it is not surprising if he suspects a mistake. Recheck the order, the label and the medicine card.

Wash equipment that is not disposable in hot, soapy water.

Administering Drugs by Mouth. More medicines are given by mouth than in any other way. Liquid medications may be given full

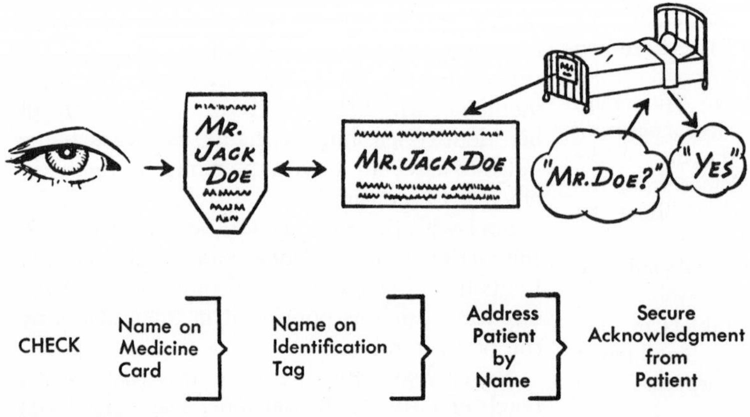

FIG. 113. Safeguards for the correct administration of medications. (Veterans Administration Training Guide)

strength or may be diluted with water after they are measured. Small amounts, measured in minims, must be diluted or most of the medicine will be left in the glass. Preparations given to soothe the throat are given undiluted. Adequate water is provided to aid in swallowing tablets and capsules and to act as a "chaser" after other medicines (except when a patient is on restricted fluids). For your convenience, directions are given below:

Liquids: As measured, or diluted with water after measuring.

Powders: Dissolved in water, unless ordered otherwise—sometimes given in capsules if the amount is not too large.

Pills: Given as they are, unless the order directs that they should be crushed and dissolved in water.

Capsules: Given as they are.

Some types of medications are given in a specific way:

Cough Medicines: Given undiluted, to get the maximum soothing effect on the throat membranes.

Unpleasant-Tasting Medicines: Holding a piece of ice in the mouth before taking the medicine numbs the taste buds. Orange or lemon juice, or the fruit, helps to remove the taste of oil.

Castor Oil: Add orange or lemon juice to the oil—add ½ teaspoon of sodium bicarbonate—mix and give, or beat orange or lemon juice into the oil and give; usually it is a good idea to give a piece of orange after the oil also.

Acid and Iron Preparations: Give through a straw or a drinking tube—these medicines discolor and injure the teeth.

Administering Drugs by Injection. *Injection* is a method of introducing drugs into the tissues through a needle. This is done in slightly different ways, but the principles discussed here apply to every form of injection. Drugs given by injection must be in liquid form. This means that if a drug comes as a tablet, it must be dissolved in sterile water or normal saline solution.

An injection is momentarily painful when the needle pierces the skin; therefore, the needle should be sharp and free from burrs that make its insertion difficult. An injection is less painful if the needle is inserted and withdrawn quickly. The needle should be of the smallest gauge that is appropriate to use for each type of injection. Injecting the solution slowly distributes it more evenly in the tissues and prevents painful pressure. Rubbing the area after the needle is withdrawn speeds up absorption of the drug.

Sterile Equipment. Sterile equipment is a "must" in giving injections, to prevent introducing harmful organisms into the tissues or the blood stream. Sterilization under steam pressure is the most reliable method; in many hospitals all equipment for giving injections is prepared in this way in the surgical supply room, or sterile disposable equipment may be provided.

Cleansing the Skin. It is impossible to sterilize the skin but it should be as *clean* as possible. A cleansing agent or antiseptic applied to the area of injection helps to reduce the possibility of infection. A sterile cotton ball or a sponge is moistened with the prescribed solution, then it is applied at the point of the injection and moved firmly over the rest of the skin area in a widening circle. Haphazard wiping drags contaminated material back over the point of injection. Some antiseptic preparations commonly used are 70 per cent alcohol, pHisoHex and Zephiran. Soap and water cleansing is also indicated if the injection is in an area which is soiled by drainage or discharges.

The Subcutaneous Injection. A hypodermic injection is the introduction of a drug into subcutaneous tissues with a needle and a syringe. This method is used (1) to obtain rapid action of a drug, (2) when the patient cannot take medications by mouth and (3) when the digestive juices would change the action of a drug. Drugs to relieve pain (morphine, codeine), stimulants (caffeine) and insulin are examples of medicines that are given by hypodermic injection. The drug may be in a vial, an ampule or in the form of a tablet. A tablet must be dissolved in a liquid before it can be given; normal saline or distilled water are considered the most desirable solutions to use, but tap water is also considered safe (in an emergency) if it has been boiled.

The solution and the equipment must be

sterile, and the skin area where the injection is given must be cleansed with an antiseptic; these precautions are necessary to protect the patient from infection. Hospitals set up trays for giving hypodermics; every hospital has its own method. The important principles for giving a hypodermic injection safely and effectively are the same in every method; you will follow these principles in any situation, whether you are using hospital equipment or set up your own hypodermic tray in the home.

You may be using sterile normal saline or distilled water from a flask on the hospital tray, or you may be using tap water that you boil in a spoon. The syringe and needle may be sterilized in the autoclave, in an antiseptic solution or over the gas flame of the kitchen stove. If you are giving a drug which comes in tablet form, you must have a tablet which is the *exact dosage* ordered.

Syringes. A subcutaneous injection is given with a 2-cc. glass syringe; there are special syringes for giving tuberculin and insulin. Some syringes, Luer or Luer-Lok, have a metal tip to ensure proper fastening of the needle. There are newer types—the so-called disposable syringes: in one type the entire unit is thrown away after one use; in another, the medication is contained in a disposable cartridge-needle unit which is clamped in a nondisposable syringe. The disposable syringe, of course, necessitates less time for sterilization, decreases the chances of cross infection and reduces the "breakage" problem (see Fig. 115).

A syringe has 2 parts: the *barrel* and the *plunger*. Some syringes have metal guards to keep the plunger from falling out when the syringe is held upside down. The barrel and the plunger are ground with great precision to fit together smoothly and without leakage; the same number is stamped on the barrel and the plunger, so that the parts of an individual syringe can be matched to each other. Syringes should have good care and handling; they are

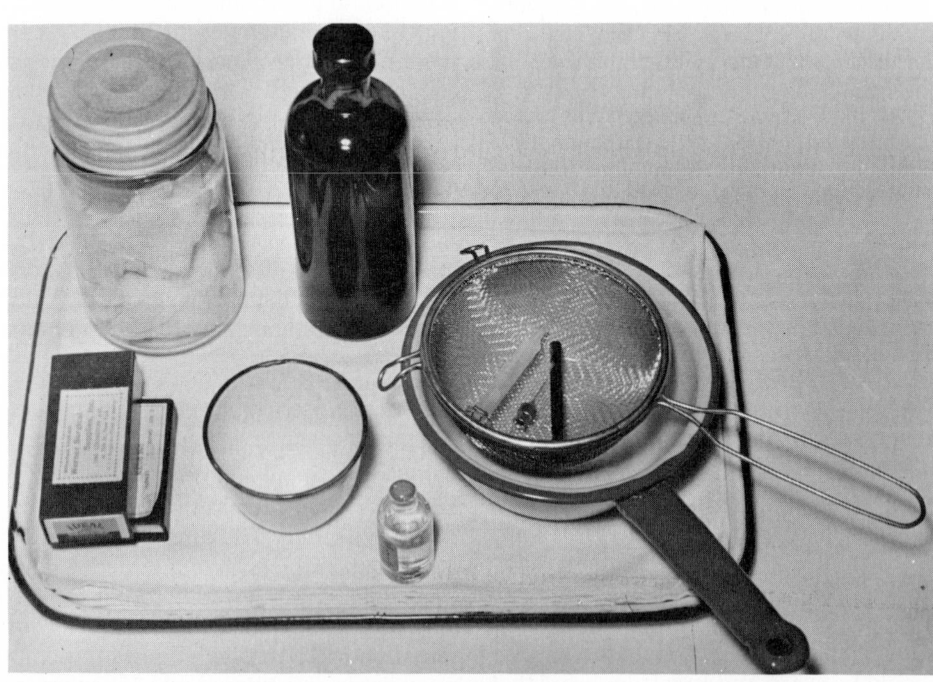

Fig. 114. Equipment for a hypodermic tray assembled for use in a home. Note the strainer for convenient handling of the syringe.

expensive and are useless when out of order. A syringe that is stuck or *frozen* or one with mismatched parts may cause serious delay in giving a medication. Syringes should be cleaned thoroughly and matched properly after they are used.

Two kinds of markings for measuring medications are stamped on the barrel of the syringe. One set of markings measures 2 cc.—the other measures 30 minims. The cc.'s are also marked in *tenths*—the minims are marked from 1 to 30. You will never give more than 2 cc. in a hypodermic injection with this type of syringe. Insulin syringes are marked in units on 2 sides of the barrel. One set of markings is used for U-40 insulin, the other for U-80 insulin.

Needle. The hypodermic needle is hollow—the part that is attached to the syringe is called the *hub*; the slender pointed shaft is the *cannula*; the wire that is threaded through the needle is the *stylet*. The stylet keeps the needle open and ready for use. The needle has a sharp point and a beveled edge, so that it can be inserted easily and with a minimum amount of discomfort to the patient. Always inspect a hypodermic needle to be sure that the point

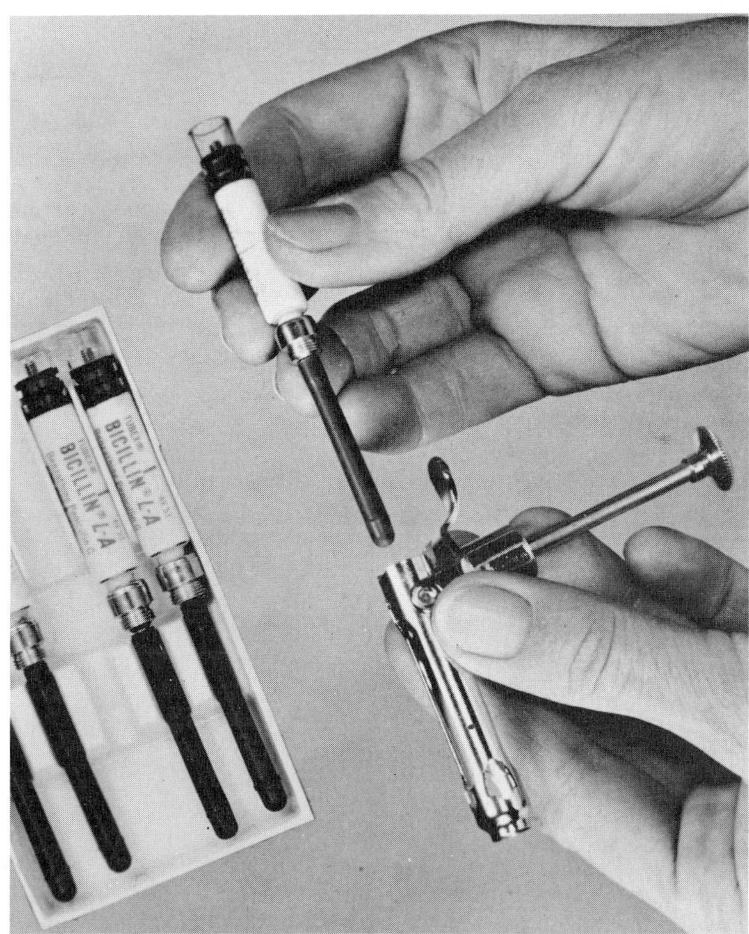

FIG. 115. One type of disposable injection unit is the Tubex closed injection system. The prefilled disposable sterile cartridge-needle unit containing the medication is being placed in the reusable syringe. (Wyeth Laboratories)

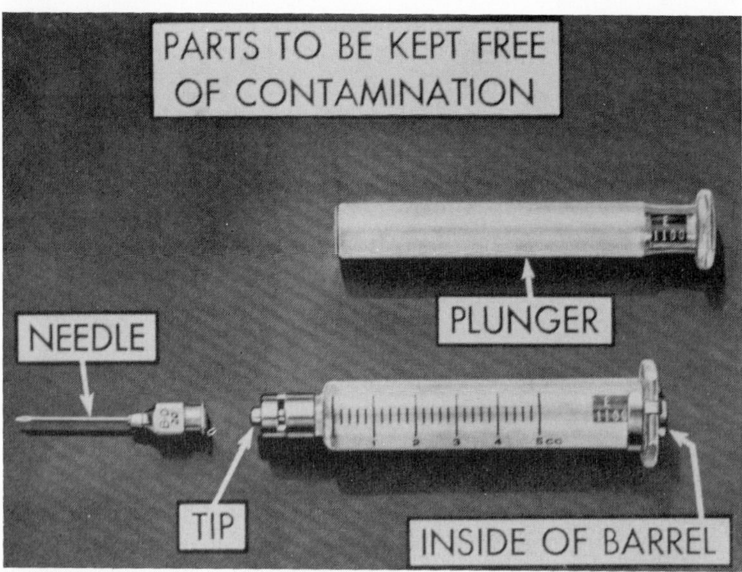

FIG. 116. This illustration shows the parts of the syringe and the reading which must not be touched while they are being assembled for use. (Becton, Dickinson & Co.)

is perfect—a burr or a hook on the point will injure the tissues and cause pain.

Handling the Sterile Syringe. Never touch the shaft of the plunger, the inside of the barrel, the tip or the shaft of the needle with your fingers when you are handling a sterile syringe; never handle the hypodermic tablet with your fingers—shake it into the cover of the bottle,

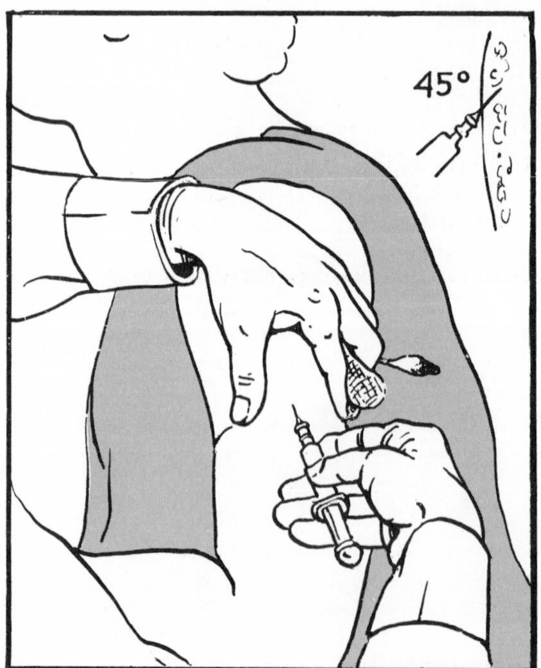

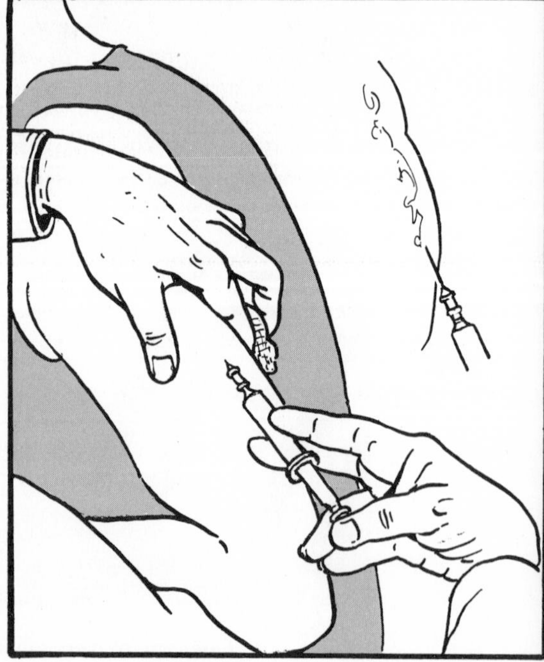

FIG. 117. (*Left*) Subcutaneous injection. Needle introduced at an angle of 45° to skin. (*Right*) Injection of the fluid.

then into the spoon when you dissolve it. Secure the needle to the syringe by a *twist* to anchor it, or the pressure may force the needle off, the medication will be lost and the needle contaminated.

Area for Injection. A hypodermic is given in an area where the bones and the blood vessels are not near the surface; the areas commonly used are the upper part of the arms and the thighs. For the occasional hypodermic, the arm is the most convenient site. If a patient is having hypodermic injections regularly, you choose a different location each time; for example, use the right arm, then the left arm; the right thigh, then the left thigh. Try to find a spot in each area that has not been used for a previous injection.

The skin is cleansed with alcohol (70 per cent), or some other antiseptic such as pHiso-Hex or Zephiran Chloride (1 to 1,000), to prepare the area for the injection. This is a precaution against introducing harmful organisms into the body through pierced skin.

An undernourished or emaciated person has less subcutaneous tissue than a stouter person. The solution is usually injected at a 45° angle, but it may be necessary to vary this angle slightly—in a very fat person the needle may not even reach the subcutaneous tissue.

The following procedure describes the method for giving and for sterilizing the equipment for a subcutaneous injection.

EQUIPMENT

2 cc. syringe
Hypodermic needle—¾ inch, 24 or 25 gauge
Prescribed medication
Antiseptic solution
Sterile sponges or cotton balls in container
Small basin
Strainer
Tablespoon—kitchen variety
Waste container

PROCEDURE

Check the medicine card with the drug order and the drug label.

Reason: *Repeated checking prevents mistakes.*

Take the syringe apart; remove the stylet from the needle; boil the syringe and the needle in the strainer for 5 minutes.

Reason: *Boiling destroys bacteria.*

With the thumb and the forefinger of the right hand, pick up the plunger by the flat top; grasp the middle of the barrel in the left hand; insert the plunger and push it completely down.

Reason: *Sterile parts remain sterile if untouched by unsterile surfaces.*

Boil a spoonful of water for 1 minute. Draw up a little more than 1 cc. into the syringe and discard the remainder.

Shake the tablet into the bottle cap, and then empty it into the spoon.

Reason: *Handling a drug with the fingers increases the possibility of infection.*

Expel the water in the syringe over the tablet in the spoon. Draw the solution into the syringe and expel it again.

Reason: *Solid drugs must be dissolved before they can be injected and absorbed.*

Draw the solution into the syringe; pick up the needle by the hub and attach it to the syringe with a slight twist.

Reason: *Fixing the needle firmly helps to prevent separation from the syringe.*

Expel the air from the syringe and the needle by pushing gently on the plunger until a drop appears on the needle tip.

Reason: *Injection of air into the tissues can be harmful. Loss of a minute amount does not affect the dosage appreciably, but the effectiveness of a drug depends on accurate dosage.*

Protect the needle with a sterile dry cotton ball or a sterile sponge and bring the syringe and needle to the patient on a tray.

Reason: *Exposure to air or contact with unsterile surfaces will contaminate the needle.*

Cleanse the area for the injection with a sterile cotton ball and antiseptic solution; wipe firmly from the center in circles outward.

Reason: *Rubbing helps to remove contaminated material from the skin.*

With the left hand, pinch up the area around the site of the injection to form a cushion.

Reason: *Insertion into a tissue pad prevents the needle from penetrating to bone or muscle tissue.*

Insert the needle quickly at a 40° to 50°

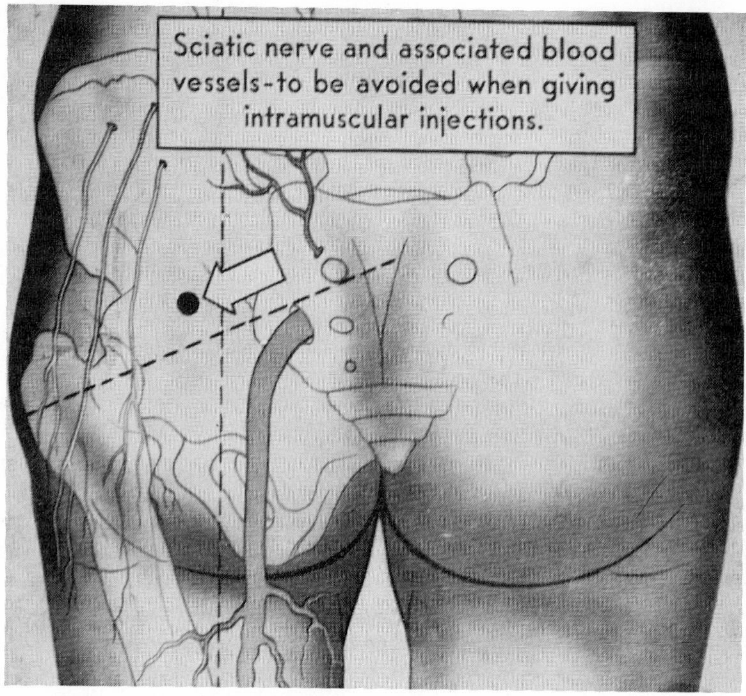

FIG. 118. The buttock has been divided into quadrants by one line extending from the greater trochanter, bisected by a second line from the crest of the ilium. Injection should be made near but not at the inner angle of the upper, outer quadrant. If injection is made too close to the crest of the ilium, the needle may strike bone; if it is made too close to the center point, there is danger of striking the sciatic nerve. The loose tissue of the lower quadrants always should be avoided. (Becton, Dickinson & Co.)

angle depending on the plumpness of the tissue cushion (see p. 346).

Reason: *Well-nourished individuals have more subcutaneous tissue than thin or emaciated people.*

After the needle is inserted, release the hold on the tissue; pull back on the plunger slightly to see if the needle is in a blood vessel.

Reason: *Drugs injected into a blood vessel are absorbed rapidly—with some drugs this may be dangerous.*

If the blood is not evident, inject the solution slowly.

Reason: *Rapid injection of fluid causes pressure on the nerves and pain.*

Withdraw the needle quickly.

Reason: *Slow withdrawal pulls the tissues, which is uncomfortable.*

Rub the area gently with the sponge.

Reason: *Rubbing helps to distribute the drug in the tissues and aids absorption.*

GIVING AN INTRAMUSCULAR INJECTION. Until fairly recently, intramuscular injections were given only by the doctor. Today, so many of the newer drugs are given in this way that intramuscular injections are now a recognized part of the professional nurse's responsibilities. The trained practical nurse also may give intramuscular injections, provided that she has had both instruction and supervised practice.

An intramuscular injection is given in much the same way as a subcutaneous injection, except that a longer needle is used, and the drug is injected into the muscles instead of into the tissues directly beneath the skin. This method is used when a drug is irritating to the tissues and when rapid absorption is desired. Also larger doses can be given.

Dangers in the Method. Intramuscular injections are more difficult and dangerous to give than subcutaneous injections, for these reasons:

1. The needle must penetrate thick muscles —if the drug is injected into subcutaneous tissues, it is not absorbed quickly and may cause pain and serious irritation.

2. The possibility of striking bones, large nerves and blood vessels is greater when a longer, larger needle is used.

Intramuscular injections are usually given in the thick gluteal muscles of the buttocks, although small injections may be given in the front of the thigh in the vastus lateralis muscle (part of the quadriceps femoris) or in the outer part of the upper arm in the deltoid muscle. The spot in the buttock can be located by drawing 2 imaginary intersecting lines to divide the buttock into 4 equal parts—the needle is inserted toward the *outside* and *above* the point where the lines cross each other (see Fig. 118).

Another safe area on the buttock for an intramuscular injection is found by locating an imaginary line from the posterosuperior iliac spine to the greater trochanter of the femur. The injection is made lateral and slightly superior to the midpoint of the line (see Fig. 119).

Important Points in Giving an Intramuscular Injection. 1. A 5-cc. or 10-cc. syringe may be needed to give the larger amounts of some intramuscular injections. The needle should always be at least 1½ inches long and 20 to 22 gauge.

2. The injection is prepared in the same way as the subcutaneous injection; the skin preparation is the same.

3. The flesh at the site of the injection is stretched and flattened and held in this position until the needle has been inserted.

4. The syringe is held perpendicular to the skin, and the needle inserted straight down into the muscle; the needle is then withdrawn slightly, and a pull is made on the plunger of the syringe to see whether or not the needle is in a blood vessel—if blood is sucked back into the syringe, the needle must be withdrawn and inserted in another spot. A drug that can be injected into the muscles without doing harm may cause a serious reaction if it is injected directly into the circulation.

5. Following the injection, the site is massaged thoroughly to promote the absorption of some drugs.

The following procedure describes the method of giving an intramuscular injection in the gluteal muscles of the buttocks.

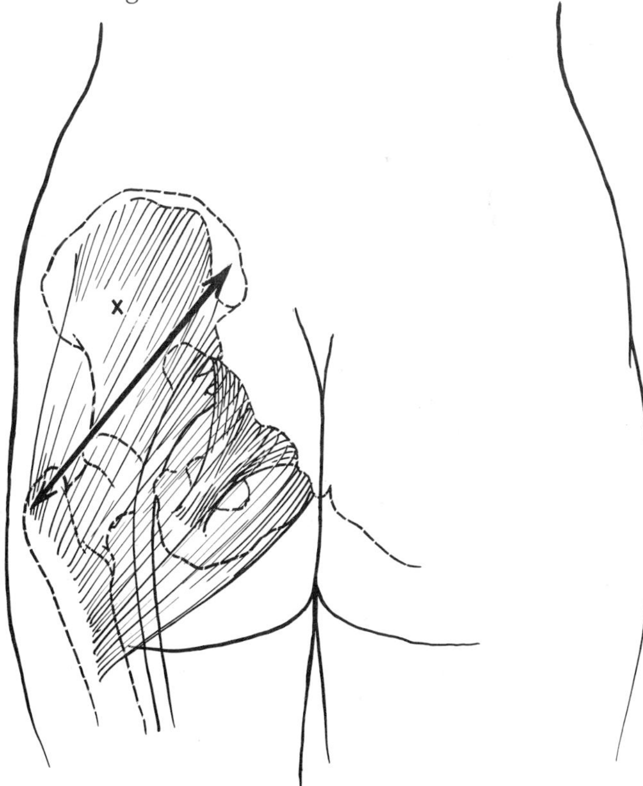

FIG. 119. "X" indicates a second safe area for an intramuscular injection in the buttock. Note that the needle is inserted lateral and slightly superior to the midpoint of the imaginary line running from the posterosuperior iliac spine to the greater trochanter of the femur. (Fuerst, E. V. and Wolff, L.: Fundamentals of Nursing, ed. 3, p. 459, Philadelphia, Lippincott)

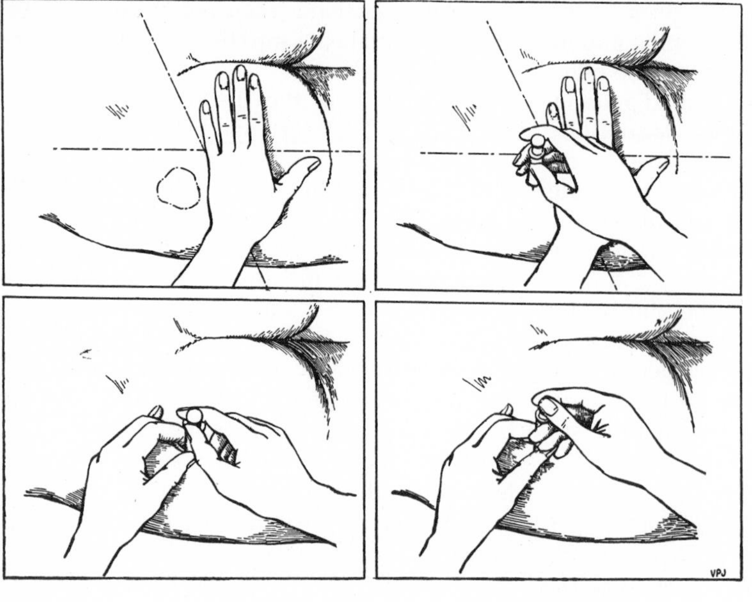

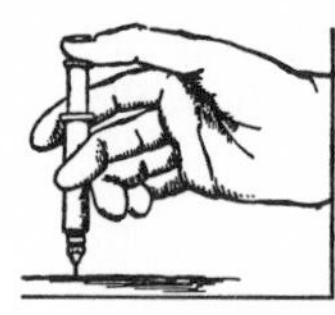

Fig. 120. (*Top, left*) The left hand is exerting pressure on the buttock, thus flattening and fixing the tissue. (*Top, right*) The needle has been thrust into the buttock. Note that a portion of the needle extends above the skin surface. (*Bottom, left*) The operator is withdrawing the plunger in order to be sure the needle tip has not entered a blood vessel. (*Bottom, right*) The solution is being slowly injected. (Inset) Close-up of injection.

PROCEDURE

Place the patient in the prone position with the arms at the sides and the feet over the edge of the mattress, with the toes pointed inward. If this position is not possible for a patient, place him on his side.

Reason: *The prone position relaxes muscles —injection into tense muscles is painful.*

Locate the spot for the injection in the inner angle of the upper outer quadrant.

Reason: *This point is beyond the sciatic nerve and the large blood vessels.*

Cleanse the area.

Reason: *The needle can introduce bacteria from the skin into the tissues.*

With the thumb and the first 2 fingers, spread the tissues beyond the site of the injection.

Reason: *Pressure flattens the subcutaneous tissues so the needle can penetrate to the muscle.*

Swiftly thrust the needle straight into the tissues.

Reason: *Slow motion is more painful. Force drives the needle for its entire length to enter the muscle.*

Pull back slowly on the plunger to see if the needle is in a blood vessel. If blood appears, withdraw the needle slightly and test again.

Reason: *Muscle tissue contains many blood vessels. Drugs entering a blood vessel are absorbed rapidly, which might be dangerous.*

If blood is not evident, inject the solution slowly.

Reason: *Slow injection reduces painful pressure on the tissues.*

Withdraw the needle quickly.

Reason: *Rapid withdrawal of the needle is less painful.*

Rub the area of injection.

Reason: *Rubbing helps to distribute the solution in the tissues and hastens the absorption of the drug.*

If a patient must have intramuscular injections frequently, the sites should be rotated, and a notation of the site used each time should be made on the patient's chart.

Withdrawing a Drug From an Ampule. A drug put up in a glass ampule usually is for a single dose and must be withdrawn with a sterile hypodermic syringe and needle. The stem of the ampule may be constructed to break off easily or it may be necessary first to scratch the glass with a metal file. By grasping the stem with a sterile cotton ball as it is broken off, the fingers are protected and the open ampule is not contaminated. The drug is then drawn up into the syringe (see Fig. 121).

Withdrawing a Drug From a Vial. A vial is a small rubber-capped bottle which may hold either a single dose of a drug or a number of doses. The rubber cap on the vial usually is covered with a metal cap which is easily removed when the drug is to be given. Although the rubber cap was sterilized when the drug was prepared, it is common practice to cleanse the cap with an antiseptic before inserting the needle into the vial. In withdrawing the solution, it helps to first inject an equal amount of air into the vial; the increased pressure moves the solution up into the syringe (see Fig. 122).

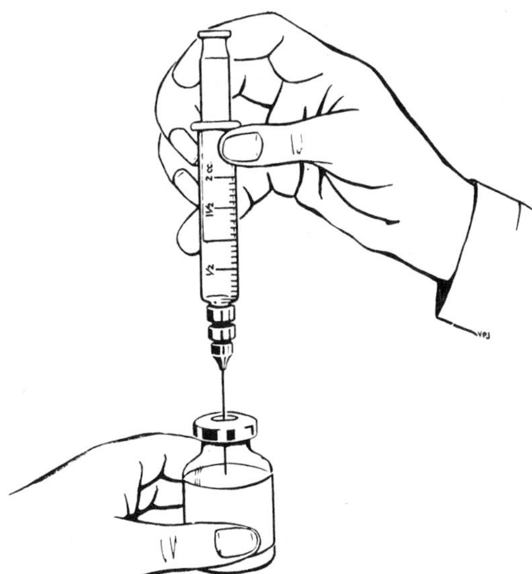

FIG. 122. One cubic centimeter of air is being injected into the rubber-stoppered vial. Note that the forefinger is exerting pressure against the plunger, thus preventing its forceful expulsion in case there is excessive pressure within the vial.

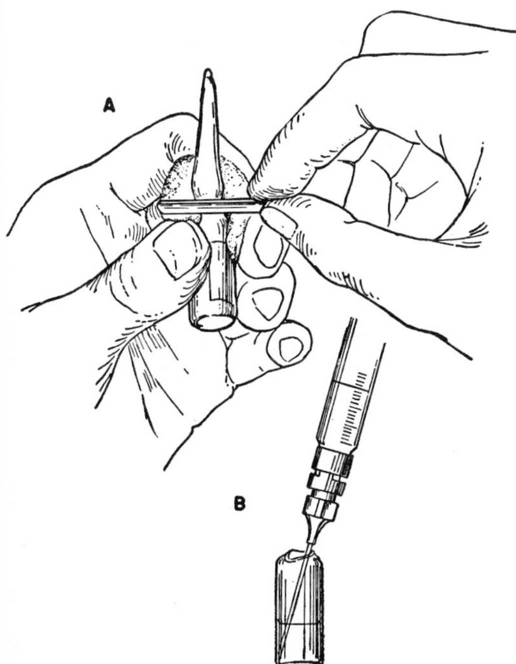

FIG. 121. (A) The fingers are protected by cotton when the stem of the closed glass ampul is scored with a file and then broken off. (B) When the stem of the glass ampul is removed, the drug is drawn up into the syringe easily because air displaces the fluid. The sterile needle should not touch the rim of the ampul.

If a vial contains several doses of a drug, the above procedure is followed, but only the amount of the prescribed dose is withdrawn.

The Injection of Insulin. Insulin, a drug used to control diabetes, must be given subcutaneously; it cannot be given by mouth because the digestive enzymes destroy it. The doctor prescribes the dosage according to the needs of the individual patient and adjusts it if necessary.

Insulin is measured in *units*; it is put up in different strengths—the ones commonly used

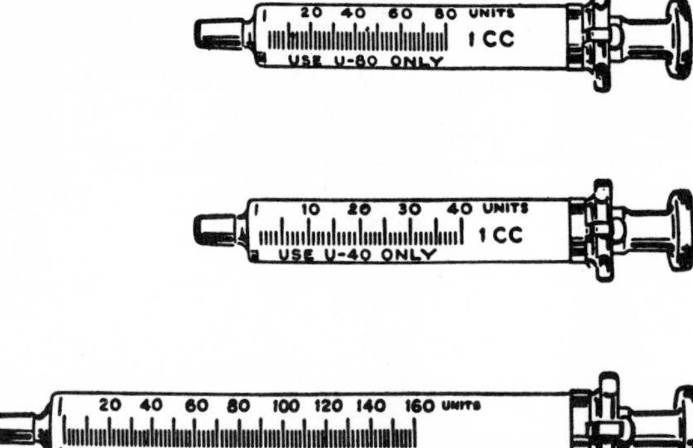

FIG. 123 (*Top*) Insulin syringe used for the administration of U-80 insulin. It will allow the dosage up to 1 cc. or 80 units. (*Center*) U-40 insulin is given with this syringe. It will allow the administration of up to 1 cc. or 40 units. (*Bottom*) This syringe is used when the patient is receiving more than 80 units of U-80 insulin. A total of up to 2 cc. or 160 units may be given with this syringe.

are 20, 40 and 80 units in 1 cc. It comes in small bottles, or vials, with sealed tops; the kind and the strength are marked on the label.

You use a special syringe, with a clear glass barrel and a colored plunger. The barrel is marked either in units or with 1 cc. divided into 10 equal parts—each division holding *one tenth* of 1 cc.; some syringes have both markings. Figure 123 shows how to measure insulin units using different strengths of insulin.

It is very important to use the proper syringe when giving insulin. If you were to use the U-80 syringe when giving U-40 insulin and did not check your dosage carefully, you could easily make the mistake of giving twice the dosage. Many diabetics are taught to carry out this procedure for themselves.

The administration of insulin in the treatment of diabetes mellitus will be discussed in Chapter 42.

Observation of the Patient During an Intravenous Infusion. Intravenous infusion is a widely used method of treatment in hospitals today to restore the fluid and electrolyte balance in body fluids. You will not be responsible for giving an infusion, but you should know what to observe since you may be taking care of a patient who is having this treatment.

A needle is inserted in a vein—usually in the antecubital space in front of the elbow. To this is attached a length of tubing connected to a glass container of the prescribed solution. A clamp on the tubing regulates the flow of fluid and a dripmeter measures the number of drops per minute. A glance will tell you whether or not the solution is running properly; inspection of the needle will tell you if it is in place. Swelling around the needle indicates that the needle has come out of the vein, and the fluid is running into the tissues. If this occurs, close the clamp to shut off the flow and report it immediately. Nausea, vomiting, rapid breathing or increase in the pulse rate are signs of an unfavorable reaction and must be reported promptly, first shutting off the flow of solution.

An infusion often necessitates keeping the arm in one position for several hours, so every effort should be made to make the patient as comfortable as possible. When the infusion is completed, the needle is withdrawn from the vein and pressure is applied over the puncture for a short time to prevent the oozing of blood.

ANTISEPTICS AND DISINFECTANTS

An *antiseptic* is a chemical agent that slows the growth and the development of microorganisms but does not necessarily kill them. We are likely to think of antiseptics as agents that are applied directly to body tissues, especially to the skin. Many of these antiseptics have been mentioned under drugs that affect the skin. They include soaps and detergents, such as green soap preparations and pHisoHex, Zephiran, etc.

A *disinfectant* is a chemical agent that kills harmful microorganisms. A germicide and a bactericide are two other substances that destroy bacteria, and it has become common practice to use these terms synonymously with disinfectant. It is only on rare occasions that any of the three are effective against bacterial spores.

Commonly Used Antiseptics and Disinfectants

Phenol (Carbolic Acid). Phenol as an antiseptic has largely been replaced by less irritating and more efficient drugs. Solutions strong enough to kill bacteria may also destroy tissues; taken internally, phenol burns the mouth, throat and stomach and in concentrated solutions may cause death. Very weak solutions are sometimes used to relieve itching, as when they are added to calamine lotion. Five per cent phenol solution is sometimes used to disinfect toilets or excreta. Alcohol neutralizes phenol and can be used as a rinse for articles disinfected in phenol or to remove it from the skin or mucous membrane.

Amphyl and *O-Syl* are phenol compounds used to disinfect utensils, furniture and floors.

Cresols. The cresols, derived from phenol, are more effective in killing germs, are cheaper and are more widely used. They are poisonous but not so much so as phenol. Many cresols are mixed with green soap and other preparations and are sold under trade names, such as Lysol, Creolin, Cresolin, Sanatol, etc. As a disinfectant, a 2 to 5 per cent solution is used to disinfect excreta, bedpans and toilets.

Resorcinol. Resorcinol has much the same antiseptic effects as phenol but is less irritating and less toxic. It is used as an ointment or as a paste in treating various skin diseases.

Hexylresorcinol. Known as "ST 37," this drug is used as a urinary antiseptic and in treating worm conditions. It occasionally causes allergic reactions.

Hexachlorophene (pHisoHex, Gamophen, Surgi-Cen). This preparation is a mixture of phenol and chlorine. It is an ingredient used in cleansing creams, soaps and in some deodorants for an antiseptic effect on the skin. It is most effective with repeated applications, as an aid to mechanical cleansing of the skin. It should not be used with alcohol.

Thymol. Thymol is a distant relative of cresol which is effective against hookworm. It is an acceptable antiseptic in mouthwashes and gargles because it has a pleasant taste and odor.

Dyes. A number of dyes are used for their antiseptic effects on the skin and mucous membranes and on wounds. These dyes include gentian violet, methyl violet, crystal violet, brilliant green and fuchsin. Acriflavine is another dye with an antiseptic action.

Mercury Preparations. Mercury bichloride is seldom used today as a disinfectant because other agents are more effective and have fewer undesirable side-effects. It is still used occasionally to disinfect objects that would be damaged by heat.

Ammoniated mercury ointment is used as an antiseptic in some skin diseases, and ammoniated mercury ophthalmic ointment is used as an antiseptic on the eyelids.

Mercurochrome is a mildly effective, nonirritating antiseptic which is no longer widely used. It was used to disinfect the skin and in some types of infections as an antiseptic irrigation. It is available in either a 2 per cent solution (Tincture of Mercurochrome), or as a 2 per cent water solution (aqueous solution). The alcohol solution is the most effective. Chlorinated soda solution will remove the red stains of mercurochrome from linens.

Merthiolate and Metaphen are mercurial preparations that are used respectively as a skin antiseptic and as a skin disinfectant. A solution of Metaphen is sometimes used to disinfect instruments that cannot be boiled.

Silver Compounds. These preparations have antiseptic, caustic, or astringent effects on tissues, depending on the strength of the preparation used. Silver nitrate is used in a 1 per cent solution in the eyes of the newborn infant immediately after delivery to prevent gonorrheal conjunctivitis. Silver nitrate solutions in strengths of 1 to 1,000 or stronger are used for bladder irrigations. Lunar caustic is silver nitrate molded into a pencil which is used as a mild caustic on wounds and ulcers. It should be handled with forceps—silver preparations turn tissues black. Protargol (strong) and Argyrol (mild) are used as antiseptics on the mucous membranes of the bladder, the conjunctiva and the nose and the throat.

Iodine. Iodine ranks high as an effective disinfectant. Its chief use is disinfection of small wounds and preoperative disinfection of the skin. Alcohol removes the brown stains of iodine from the skin; boiling water removes them from cloth. Iodine can be used in an emergency to disinfect water contaminated with amoebas. One drop in a quart of water will kill amoebas and bacteria in 15 minutes and will not give the water an unpleasant taste. Iodine preparations are iodine tincture and iodine solution in various strengths, combined with water or alcohol.

Chlorine. The most extensive use of chlorine is to purify water. It is the most effective disinfectant for a community water supply—one part of chlorine to a million parts of water destroys bacteria in a few minutes. It does have a disagreeable odor in full strength and this odor and an objectionable taste are sometimes perceptible in a community water supply. Chlorine is an effective bleach (Chlorox) and deodorant. People who dislike the odor of chlorine sometimes feel that as a deodorant it only replaces one offensive odor with a worse one. Diluted sodium hypochlorite solution (Dakin's solution) was used extensively to cleanse wounds in World War I but is seldom used now because of its effects on blood clotting and its irritation of the skin. It is sometimes used to disinfect floors.

Chloramine-T is used for wound irrigations and for dressings. Halazone tablets are available for sterilizing small quantities of drinking water. One to 2 tablets in a quart of water will kill all pathogenic bacteria in 60 minutes.

Combined-Action Drugs. Some preparations act both as cleansers and as antiseptics. Zephiran and Diaparene are such drugs. They are ineffective if used with soap; if soap has been used on an area first, it must be rinsed off well before these preparations are applied. The same thing is true of diapers that have been washed with soap. One tablet of Diaparene dissolved in 2 quarts of water is sufficient for disinfecting 6 diapers if they are left in the disinfectant solution for 3 minutes.

Alcohols. Alcohols have long been used as skin disinfectants, especially before the needle punctures the skin in giving injections and when taking blood samples. Ethyl alcohol is most effective in 50 to 70 per cent solutions. Isopropyl alcohol is slightly more antiseptic than ethyl alcohol when it is used at full strength (99 per cent). It is used as a rubbing compound when diluted to 70 per cent with water and in this strength it is sometimes used also to disinfect mouth thermometers.

Formaldehyde (Formalin). Formalin solution is a penetrating disinfectant once widely used to fumigate rooms. In combination with air it gives off an irritating gas which will kill all organisms, including spores and viruses, in 6 to 12 hours. Solutions used to sterilize instruments that would be injured by heat sterilization, such as the Bard-Parker solution, are combinations of formalin and alcohol with an anti-rust agent. Formalin also hardens tissues and is used to preserve laboratory specimens. It irritates mucous membranes and tissues, and its odor is unpleasant.

Boric Acid. Boric acid is a mild antiseptic that is often used when other drugs would be irritating, as in solutions for eye or bladder irrigations or wet dressings. It is used for skin conditions in the form of dusting powders or ointments.

Ethylene Oxide. This gas has been found to be effective in sterilizing plastic parts of machines or instruments that cannot be sterilized by heat or by chemicals. It is flammable and explosive unless it is mixed with an inert gas such as carbon dioxide, or unless it is used in specially constructed cabinets or autoclaves. It is on the market as Carboxide and seems to be highly effective in killing all organisms, including spores. It is the only chemical that has been legally approved for use in hospitals, but the need for special equipment for its use makes it a costly disinfectant.

DRUGS THAT AFFECT THE SKIN AND MUCOUS MEMBRANES

Drugs are used to treat pain or discomfort caused by itching, to treat infections and to soften the skin. The skin does not absorb drugs readily because a substance (keratin) in the outer layer sheds moisture just as a "weather-proof" raincoat does. Absorption is better if the skin is softened by soaking in water or by perspiration, or if the drug is applied to an area where the skin is thinner. Substances combined with alcohol or natural fats are absorbed more readily.

Emollients

Emollients are preparations which are used to soothe irritated skin or mucous membranes or are used as carriers for medicinal substances. Some of the common emollients are:

Oils: Used to lubricate the skin, such as olive, flaxseed or cottonseed oil.

Glycerin: Used in combination with water or rose water to soothe irritated lips and skin.

Petrolatum (Petrolatum Jelly): Used as an ointment base.

Liquid Petrolatum: Used for medicines applied locally.

Cold Cream: A combination of water and oil with other ingredients. There is a nonallergic type available for those allergic to the perfumed cold cream.

Cocoa Butter: A solid oil, used mainly for suppositories.

White Ointment and Yellow Ointment: Mostly petrolatum with white or yellow wax added to make it stiffer.

Zinc Oxide Ointment: Vitamin A and vitamin D in a petrolatum-lanolin base.

Lanolin: A combination of the purified fat in sheeps' wool and water, with petrolatum added. Lanolin never becomes rancid.

Lotions and Solutions

Aluminum Acetate Solution (Burow's Solution): Used diluted with 10 to 40 parts of water. Aluminum subacetate solution, diluted in the same way, is used as a wet dressing.

Calamine Lotion: A combination of drugs used for poison ivy rash, prickly heat rash and insect bites.

Powders

Powders are dusted on the skin to absorb small amounts of moisture; in very moist areas they cake and are not beneficial. Those containing antiseptic drugs also have a mild antiseptic action. Some commonly used powders are:

Purified Talc: A native magnesium silicate used to absorb moisture and soothe the skin.

Zinc Stearate: A fluffy white powder with a slightly slippery feel used for its antiseptic effect.

Thymol Iodide (Aristol): A powder containing a mixture of iodine derivatives of thymol used for its drying and antiseptic action.

Antiseptics

It is impossible to sterilize the skin—antiseptics strong enough to destroy bacteria will injure it. Strong antiseptics cause irritation which makes it easier for bacteria to enter. Soap-and-water washing, using mild friction, followed by the application of a mild antiseptic does help to remove loose skin flakes and bacteria, lessening the danger of infection.

Infectious skin lesions sometimes do occur, caused mostly by staphylococci and streptococci which enter through broken skin. Certain drugs are helpful in combating such infections:

Antibiotics: Cacitracin is used in an ointment or powder. Tyrothricin is effective in wet dressings. Neomycin is applied to the lesion—sometimes it irritates the skin. Vioform and Xeroform are also helpful. Antibiotics are also given orally or by injection in treating such infections as boils or carbuncles.

Ammoniated Mercury Ointment and Furacin (Ointment and Solution): Effective preparations when applied to an infected area. Furacin sometimes causes allergic reaction.

Antifungal Drugs

Iso-Par: An ointment used for fungal infections of the hands and feet and for eczemas of the ear. It is applied at bedtime and again in the morning.

Asterol: Especially effective for athlete's foot, ringworm of the scalp and for fungus infections around the nails. It is not suitable for treating young children who may carry the drug to their mouths with their fingers and so develop harmful side effects.

Propion Gel: A jelly used to treat vulvovaginal infections (moniliasis).

Gentian Violet: A dye with antiseptic properties, but it does stain clothing.

Whitfield's Ointment: A preparation containing a salicylic acid which is used in treating athlete's foot.

Grifulvin and Fulvicin: Comparatively new preparations for the treatment of fungus infections which can be taken orally at the same time ointments are being used.

Pediculicides

Pediculicides are preparations used to kill lice (pediculi):

Gexane and Kwell (Lotion or Ointment): Applied to the scalp will kill lice but will not kill nits. A 10 per cent solution of acetic acid or vinegar is effective in removing nits, with a shampoo and bath 24 hours after this application.

Bornate: Also effective, but since it is irritating to the skin, it must be removed after 10 minutes with a shampoo.

Scabicides

Scabicides are drugs used in treating scabies or itch caused by the itch mite. The itch mite burrows under the skin and also attaches itself to clothing, especially in the seams. Therefore, to prevent reinfection after the application of scabicides, particular attention is given to sterilizing clothing and bed linen. The newer drugs are more effective—1 application may be sufficient. More than 2 applications are almost sure to cause skin irritation.

Gexane and Kwell: Effective scabicides.

Benylate and Albacide: Preparations to be applied to the skin after it has been scrubbed with soap and water. After the first application has dried, a second one is applied to the worst areas. In 24 hours, the patient is given a warm bath, clean clothing and clean bed linen.

Precautions which are necessary in using pediculicides and scabicides are: (1) to avoid causing skin irritation by too frequent applications and (2) to keep the preparations away from the eyes.

Stimulants and Irritants

Some drugs stimulate healing in skin lesions and wounds by their mildly irritating action. Tars obtained from wool or coal, such as juniper tar, cade oil, coal tar, have this effect. Some of them are used in treating psoriasis. Compound Benzoin Tincture is often used for bedsores, ulcers, cracked lips or anal fissures.

Other drugs, the *kerolytics,* are used to soften scales and loosen the outer layers of the skin. Salicylic acid and Resorcinol are used for corns, warts, fungous infections and chronic dermatitis. These preparations are available as plasters, ointments or combined with collodion.

Antipruritics

Drugs used to relieve itching are called antipruritics. Progress in understanding skin disorders has given us new remedies for itching. Hydrocortisone (lotion or ointment) is an effective remedy, and other remedies that can be taken internally are small doses of barbiturates, preparations or ergotamine (Gynergen) and the antihistamine drugs (Caladryl).

Lotions, pastes or ointments are effective also. Dressings wet with potassium permanganate (1 to 4000), boric acid or normal saline solution are soothing, as are calamine lotion, starch baths, etc.

Protectives

Protective drugs are soothing because they form a thin film over the skin. They should be nonabsorbable, nondrying and should not soften the skin. Two effective protectives are preparations of collodion and adhesive plaster. Nonabsorbable powders are sometimes used as protectives, but they are not very satisfactory because they have to be scraped off moist surfaces and will not adhere to dry surfaces.

Some water-soluble protectives (solution or ointment) are used for their soothing and deodorizing effect and for stimulation of healing in ulcers, burns or wounds. Chloresium is such a drug.

Deodorants and Nonperspirants

Bromidrosis is the technical name for "BO" (body odor), a condition that afflicts many people who are troubled by excessive underarm or foot perspiration. It is caused by overactivity of the sweat glands in these areas and is treated by applying certain drug preparations to the skin. Many preparations are available as deodorants and nonperspirants. The deodorants are composed of combinations of benzoic acid, zinc oxide and boric acid. The nonperspirants contain aluminum chloride. Potassium permanganate (1 to 1,000 solution) or 2 per cent formaldehyde solution also may be used as a footbath.

Medicated soaps (Dial, Neutrogena, etc.) are advertised for their antiseptic qualities but it must be remembered that soaps are most valuable for their cleansing properties.

THE ANTIBIOTICS

An antibiotic is a substance, produced by microorganisms, that destroys other microorganisms or prevents their growth. Sir Alexander Fleming, an English scientist, made this discovery in 1928 when he noticed that a Penicillium mold on some staphylococcus organisms was inhibiting their growth. He extracted the effective substance from the mold and named it *penicillin*. Further study and experiments in using penicillin to fight disease yielded spectacular results, but they were mostly temporary because the supply of the drug was insufficient for prolonged treatment or large doses. In 1941, wartime needs for an antibiotic became so pressing that the United States began to manufacture penicillin on a large scale. Since then, many other antibiotics have been made available for the treatment of infections and are widely used.

The Action of Antibiotics

Antibiotics interfere with the nourishment of microorganisms, which inhibits their growth and weakens them so that the normal body defenses are able to destroy them. Antibiotics may also destroy bacteria outright. A microorganism may not be susceptible to the action of an antibiotic or it may develop resistance. Resistance is the power of a microorganism to "hold out" against an antibiotic—to remain unaffected by it.

Antibiotics may sensitize a patient if they are used indiscriminately for every minor ailment. Medical authorities discourage this use of antibiotics which may create a hypersensitivity and, therefore, makes it dangerous to use a drug when it is really needed for a severe infection.

Antibiotics Today

At the present time, the *penicillins, streptomycin, erythromycin* and the *tetracyclines* are the most effective and most widely used antibiotics. In some infections any one of several antibiotics will be effective—in others, only one will be of any value. Sometimes it takes a combination of antibiotics to control an infection. If there is a choice between several which are equally effective, usually the one given most often is the one which is the least expensive and the least toxic.

Penicillin. Penicillin is made from the common bluish grey mold (Penicillium) which we often find on fruit or bread. It interferes with the growth of those bacteria that are susceptible to it and kills many of them, provided there is a sufficiently high concentration of the drug in the body. Penicillin is excreted rapidly in the urine and is remarkably free from toxic effects.

ITS ACTION. Penicillin is most effective against the gram-positive organisms, such as streptococci, staphylococci and pneumococci. It is also active against some gram-negative organisms, such as gonococci and meningococci and against the *treponema* which causes syphilis. However, some of the gonococci and staphylococci have become resistant to it. It is not effective against the tubercle bacillus or in viral infections or typhoid fever.

METHODS OF GIVING PENICILLIN. This drug can be given in a variety of ways. The commonly used methods are:

Intramuscular (IM): This is the method most often used to give the slower acting penicillins most widely used at the present time.

Intravenous (IV): Penicillin is given intravenously in severe infections when quick action is needed.

Oral (O): This is the easiest method of giving penicillin and is usually effective for all but the most severe infections.

Side-Effects. Penicillin has almost no toxic effects even in large doses, except for the person who is sensitive to it. Then it causes an allergic reaction, which may be comparatively mild causing hives or a rash or, in severe cases, it may cause anaphylactic shock, which is now occurring more frequently. Patients with a history of allergy or of previous reaction to a drug should have a sensitivity test before receiving penicillin. Sometimes a patient is sensitive to one type of penicillin but not to another.

The usual treatment for a mild allergic reaction is an *antihistamine*. In severe reactions, epinephrine, aminophylline or oxygen may be given. Penicillinase (neutrapen), an enzyme that makes penicillin inactive, is sometimes recommended.

Types of Penicillin. Penicillin preparations are available in powder, liquid or tablet form. The dosage is measured in units, grams or milligrams. It varies with individual needs and with the type of penicillin—rapid acting or slow acting. For instance: 200,000 units of rapid-acting penicillin, given 3 to 8 times a day, may be increased to a million units every 3 hours in a severe infection; 300,000 to 400,000 units of slowly-absorbed penicillin may be given once a day or twice in 24 hours; and 600,000 to 1,200,000 units of long-acting penicillin may be given as a single dose and not repeated from several days to a month.

Penicillin Preparations. Many penicillin preparations are available, some of them in several forms suitable for every type of administration and others in fewer forms. The following table does not include every penicillin preparation, but it does include examples of those most commonly used and the variety of forms in which they are available. The commonly known names capitalized are the trade names. In some cases a penicillin preparation is best known by its generic name—not capitalized. You must remember that these are only a few of the preparations, and that scientific researchers are constantly searching for and finding new ones.

PREPARATION	COMMONLY KNOWN NAMES	METHOD OF ADMINISTRATION*
Potassium Penicillin G	benzyl penicillin potassium	IM, IV
Procaine Penicillin G	Crysticillin, Druacillin, Wycillin, Lentopen	IM
Penicillin G Tablets	potassium or sodium	O
Benzathine Penicillin G	Bicillin, Permapen dibenzyl penicillin	O, IM
Penicillin O	Cer-O-Cillin, Depo-Cer-O-Cillin	O, IM
Penicillin V	V-Cillin-K, Pen-Vee K, V-Cillin, Pen-Vee, Compocillin	O
Phenethicillin	penicillin 152, Alpen, Chemipen, Darcil, Maxipen	O
Methicillin	Staphcillin, Dimocillin, Syncillin	IM, IV
Oxacillin	penicillin P-12, Prostaphlin, Resistopen	O
Penicillin Ointment†		

* IM: Intramuscular.
IV: Intravenous.
O: Oral.

† Rarely used—often causes allergic reactions.

The Streptomycins. Streptomycin is an antibiotic obtained from a fungus. *Dehydrostreptomycin* is obtained from streptomycin. The main use of streptomycin is in the treatment of tuberculosis to inhibit the growth of the tubercle bacillus; it is also effective for infections of the urinary tract and for infections resistant to penicillin. Tuberculosis requires prolonged treatment and during this time the tuberculosis organisms may become resistant to streptomycin. PAS (para-aminosalicylic acid) is given at the same time to delay this effect. (See p. 520). Penicillin is also given with streptomycin for certain other infections, such as subacute endocarditis.

SIDE-EFFECTS. Streptomycin may cause toxic effects in the kidney and liver. Some individuals are allergic to this drug and develop rashes, hives, nausea and vomiting. Deafness, dizziness and vertigo are not uncommon as a result of damage to the 8th cranial nerve. This is most likely to happen with *dihydrostreptomycin.*

PREPARATIONS. The commercial preparations of *streptomycin sulfate* are available in the form of powders and solutions. They are most effective when given intramuscularly because the intestinal tract does not absorb them readily. The dosage is determined by the intensity of the infection and by the susceptibility of the organism to the drug.

Erythromycin (Ilotycin). Erythromycin has much the same action as penicillin but is not as effective. It is used against organisms that are resistant to penicillin or when a patient is allergic to penicillin. It is available in tablets, sterile solutions for injection and in oral solutions. The usual dosage ranges from 1 to 2 Gm. a day.

SIDE-EFFECTS. Erythromycin has few toxic side-effects, although in large doses it may cause nausea, vomiting and diarrhea. Patients rarely become hypersensitive to it.

Chloramphenicol (Chloromycetin). Chloramphenicol is a synthetic preparation which is effective against many gram-positive and gram-negative bacteria and against certain large viruses; it is *the* antibiotic effective against typhoid fever. It is also effective against organisms resistant to penicillin.

SIDE-EFFECTS. Chloromycetin may cause nausea, vomiting and diarrhea. However, its most serious toxic effect is on the bone marrow, causing plastic anemia. For this reason frequent blood examinations are made to detect signs of harmful effects.

PREPARATIONS.

Chloramphenicol (Chloromycetin): capsules, solutions, ointments, 1 to 4 Gm. daily

Chloramphenicol Palmitate: oral

The Tetracyclines. The tetracyclines are called broad-spectrum antibiotics which means that they are effective against a wide variety of organisms, such as cocci and bacilli and certain viruses. These drugs are easily absorbed in the gastrointestinal tract and are usually given by mouth, but are also available in solutions for intramuscular or intravenous injection. They are not effective against true viruses, such as those causing the common cold, polio, etc.

SIDE-EFFECTS. Compared with other antibiotics, the tetracyclines have few toxic side-effects. Those which do occur are chiefly in the gastrointestinal tract, such as nausea, vomiting and diarrhea. Giving the drug in milk, or in sodium or calcium carbonate reduces these effects. Symptoms of gastric irritation or vaginitis should be reported because they are signs of developing infections due to the suppression of helpful bacteria.

PREPARATIONS.

Aureomycin Hydrochloride, Oxytetracycline Hydrochloride, Panmycin, Sumycin, Tetrex and *Declomycin Hydrochloride:* Oral, 25 to 500 mg. every 6 hours.

Antibiotics With Special Usefulness

The antibiotics discussed in detail on previous pages are those which are most effective and most widely used. Other antibiotics are more limited in their usefulness but are very valuable in special conditions, such as in treating infections resistant to the commonly used antibiotics (such as penicillin). Among these less frequently used antibiotics are:

Seromycin: Used with other drugs in treating tuberculosis.

Kanamycin (Kantrex): Active against many forms of staphylococci.

Neomycin Sulfate: Used in serious infections which do not respond to the safer antibiotics, but only as a last resort because it has dangerous effects on the kidneys and the 8th cranial nerve.

Novobiocin: Used for certain staphylococcal infections or when a patient is allergic to other antibiotics. Patients easily become sensitized to it and develop skin rashes and urticaria (hives).

Matromycin: Used when commonly used antibiotics are not effective.

Cyclamycin, Spontin, Vancocin: Especially effective against staphylococcal infections.

Viomycin Sulfate (Vinactane, Viocin): Used in tuberculosis infections resistant to other drugs.

Fumagillin (Fumidil): Used for intestinal amebic infections.

A Last Word

As with other drugs, you may not find that every antibiotic used to treat infections is listed here, and new ones are appearing all the time. The U.S.P. and manuals on drugs will help to keep you up to date. What you should know about antibiotics in general is that:

1. Certain antibiotics are widely used because they are effective against many organisms.
2. Other antibiotics may be used because they are effective against organisms that are resistant to the commonly used antibiotics.
3. Certain antibiotics are used because an individual is sensitive to the commonly used ones.
4. The dosage prescribed depends on the severity of the illness and the resistance of the organism to the drug.
5. The side-effects of antibiotics vary; some have very few or mild side-effects; others may have side-effects that are serious and can cause permanent damage in the body. It is important to know the possible side-effects of an antibiotic and to be alert in observing and reporting them.

DRUGS THAT AFFECT THE CENTRAL NERVOUS SYSTEM

The nervous system affects many body processes. When its functions are disturbed, certain drugs will increase or decrease the activity of the nerve centers in the brain or in the nerve pathways. *Stimulants* help to speed up certain mental and physical processes; *depressants* slow them down.

STIMULANTS

Many drugs have a stimulating effect on the central nervous system, but only a few of them are especially valuable for that purpose. The most valuable are: (1) drugs that stimulate the respiratory centers in the brain; and (2) drugs that alleviate depression and make people more mentally alert and counteract the toxic effects of depressant drugs, such as overdoses of barbiturates.

Caffeine. Caffeine is obtained commercially from tea leaves, but it is also found in the coffee bean and so is present in the beverages we call tea and coffee. Actually, tea leaves contain more caffeine than coffee beans, but in this country we are likely to make our coffee stronger than we do our tea—naturally, this increases the amount of caffeine we consume since we are a nation of coffee drinkers.

The main value of caffeine is as a stimulant to the respiratory center of the brain, but it also acts as a mild stimulant to the thinking centers, to make a person more alert and less aware of fatigue.

Side-Effects. The side-effects of caffeine are restlessness, irritability, insomnia, heart palpitation and some increase in the output of urine. Signs of mild caffeine poisoning often appear in people who work at night. Night nurses who habitually depend on large amounts of coffee to keep them alert when they are sleepy or physically exhausted may develop these symptoms. People who are used to drinking moderate amounts of tea or coffee every day develop a tolerance for caffeine.

Preparations. The most widely used preparations of caffeine are:

Citrated Caffeine: Powder, tablet, oral, 0.3 Gm. (5 gr.)

Ergotamine With Caffeine (Cafergot): Tablets, oral, 1 to 2 tablets

Caffeine Sodium Benzoate: Liquid in ampul, oral, IM, 0.5 Gm. (7½ gr.)

Amphetamine. Amphetamine is a synthetic

drug which increases energy and alertness, overcomes sleepiness and increases muscle strength. It also stimulates the respiratory center and depresses appetite.

Amphetamine is used to relieve depression in patients with mental disease or for mild depression after childbirth, during the menopause or in old age. Some drug preparations marketed as appetite-reducers contain amphetamine. However, this effect is only temporary—appetite returns as soon as the person stops taking the drug. Amphetamine is also used to combat persistent drowsiness and sleepiness or to counteract poisoning from depressant drugs.

SIDE-EFFECTS. It is dangerous to take amphetamine regularly as "pep pills" because it can obscure signs of fatigue which may be symptoms of an underlying condition that should be corrected. It is dangerous for people with cardiovascular disease or hypertension or for those who are overly anxious or excited. It is also a habit-forming drug. It may cause mouth dryness, insomnia and irritability.

PREPARATIONS.

Amphetamine Sulfate (Benzedrine): Tablets, capsules, solution, oral, inj.

Amphetamine Phosphate (Raphetamine): Tablets, liquid, capsules, oral

Phenmetrazine Hydrochloride (Preludin): Tablets, oral, 25 mg.

Dextro Amphetamine Sulfate (Dexedrine): Tablets, liquid, capsules, oral

Two of the newer preparations having fewer toxic side effects are Pipradol Hydrochloride (Meratran Hydrochloride) and Methylphenidate Hydrochloride (Ritalin Hydrochloride). They are used to relieve depression and to restore a sense of worthwhileness to elderly people who feel life does not matter any more. They are also effective in counteracting the effects of oversedation. Other mood elevators known by the trade names of Marsalid, Marplan, Niamid, Tofranil and Nardil are used also to relieve depression. Picrotoxin, Coramine and Metrazol are especially useful to counteract the depressant effects of overdoses of barbiturates. Strychnine, once widely used as a stimulant, is rarely used today for medical purposes. Occasionally, instances of strychnine poisoning do occur.

DEPRESSANTS

Drugs that depress the activities of the central nervous system are (1) *analgesics* to relieve pain, (2) *hypnotics* and *sedatives* to bring rest and sleep and (3) *general anesthetics* to cause loss of consciousness. In addition to discussing these depressants, we will consider also some of the drugs known as "selective depressants" which are used for the symptomatic treatment of various conditions.

Analgesics

The analgesic drugs relieve pain but do not cause unconsciousness. The patient may go to sleep because he is more comfortable, but the drug does not induce sleep.

Narcotic Analgesics. Opium is the hardened dried juice of a poppy which is grown mostly in China, India, Iran and Asia Minor. It was first used in its crude form by physicians in Greece and Arabia; later, it was found that the effective component of opium was the alkaloid morphine. This led to the discovery of other useful opium alkaloids; those most widely used are morphine, codeine and papaverine. Morphine and codeine mainly affect the central nervous system; papaverine affects smooth muscles.

All drugs produced from opium or opium derivatives or having habit-forming effects are subject to the narcotic regulations of the Harrison Narcotic Act.

MORPHINE. The most important function of morphine is its ability to relieve severe pain and so bring rest and sleep. It also relieves fear and anxiety and promotes a feeling of well-being. It is helpful in checking peristalsis in such conditions as diarrhea, peritonitis or stomach and bowel surgery. It relieves apprehension before an anesthetic, and it keeps a patient quiet after pulmonary hemorrhage.

Side-Effects. Morphine depresses respiration—severe morphine poisoning may cause respiratory failure and death. It contracts the pupil of the eye, it may cause nausea and vomiting and in toxic amounts it lowers blood pressure and slows the heart rate. Because it slows peristalsis, it may cause constipation. Allergic reactions to morphine occur fairly frequently.

Morphine is not recommended to relieve pain when a milder drug will do as well. This is especially true of pain in a prolonged illness since habit-formation is almost sure to occur. Exceptions are such painful conditions as inoperable or terminal cancer when recovery is impossible, and morphine is the patient's only source of comfort and relief. Morphine is more effective if it is given before pain becomes extreme. Nurses sometimes withhold a dose of morphine as long as possible for fear of encouraging addiction. There is little or no danger of habit formation when morphine is given for a short time to relieve severe pain which in itself can be damaging.

Symptoms of addiction (withdrawal symptoms) appear when the addict is deprived of the drug (see Chap. 6). He becomes irritable and jittery, has no appetite and loses weight, is unable to sleep, perspires freely and complains of muscle pains. These symptoms disappear when he is given the drug. Morphine and heroin are the most potent addicting forms of opium. Codeine is addicting to a degree but less so than morphine. Addicts often use other drugs as well, such as barbiturates and alcohol.

Poisoning. Opium or morphine poisoning is usually the result of medical overdosage or a suicide attempt. The usual dosage is ⅙ to ¼ gr.; 1 grain is a toxic dose, and 4 gr. is a fatal dose. The significant early symptoms of poisoning are *slow respirations* (less than 12 per minute), *deep sleep* and *constricted pupils.* Emergency treatment begins with respiratory stimulants such as nikethamide, caffeine and sodium benzoate, amphetamine or ephedrine. If breathing decreases dangerously, artificial respiration followed by intratracheal oxygen are used. The stomach is emptied if the drug has been taken by mouth and strong black coffee as hot as it is safe to give may be given by tube, mouth or rectum.

SYNTHETIC SUBSTITUTES FOR MORPHINE. Some synthetic drugs are now available which are effective pain relievers and have fewer unfavorable side-effects than morphine. Some of these drugs are meperidine hydrochloride (Demerol) and Methadone Hydrochloride.

DEMEROL. Used instead of morphine to relieve pain which is not severe, Demerol acts quickly, but its effect is not prolonged. It is often used before anesthesia. It is less likely than morphine to cause nausea and vomiting, and normal doses have few ill effects on respiration or heart action. Demerol is often given to obstetric patients in combination with other drugs.

Side-Effects. Demerol may cause dizziness, nausea and vomiting, headache and fainting, and in toxic amounts may cause dilated pupils, mental confusion, convulsions, respiratory depression and death. It is definitely habit-forming, perhaps even more so than morphine.

METHADONE HYDROCHLORINE. Methadone is much like morphine in that it is an effective pain reliever and has similar lasting effects. It is slightly more effective than morphine in relieving chronic pain and is effective for cough.

Side-Effects. Like morphine, it may cause nausea and vomiting, itching, constipation and respiratory depression. It is also habit-forming.

OTHER SUBSTITUTES FOR MORPHINE. Other preparations used as morphine substitutes are Nisentil, Levo-Dromoran Tartrate and Prinadol. Some of the drugs which are used effectively in combating narcotic poisoning are Nalline Hydrochloride and Lorfan Tartrate.

CODEINE. Codeine is a derivative of morphine, but its action is milder. It is especially effective in relieving a dry cough, but it also relieves minor irritations and mild pain. It is less depressing than morphine and less habit-forming; it is also less constipating. Codeine is a common ingredient of cough mixtures, such as terpin hydrate and codeine elixir.

PAPAVERINE. Papaverine is not a pain reliever, but is useful in relaxing muscle spasm and is less depressing than morphine.

DILAUDID. Dilaudid is prepared from morphine and has about 5 times the analgesic effect of morphine, but the effect does not last as long. The effect is prolonged if the drug is given by suppository. It causes very little drowsiness, nausea or vomiting but does depress respiration. Dilaudid is an addictive drug.

OPIUM TINCTURE. Opium Tincture (Laudanum) and camphorated opium tincture (Paregoric) are liquids used to check peristalsis.

These preparations are always given by mouth. Brown's Mixture is a compound of opium and glycerin which is used as a cough mixture.

PREPARATIONS. Opium preparations and average doses are:

Morphine: Tablet, hypodermic, 0.01 Gm. (1/6 gr.)

Codeine: Tablet, hypodermic, oral, 0.03 Gm. (½ gr.)

Dilaudid: Tablet, hypodermic, oral, rectal (suppository), 0.002 Gm. (1/30 gr.)

Metopon: Tablet, oral, 0.003 Gm. (1/20 gr.)

Paregoric: Liquid, oral 4 cc. (1 fluid dram)

Brown's Mixture: Liquid, oral, 4 cc. (1 fluid dram)

Non-narcotic Analgesics. There are certain drugs such as Darvon, that relieve pain but are not prepared from opium and are not habit-forming, that may be used alone or combined with other drugs such as aspirin; Zactirin is such a drug.

Colchicine is a drug that is used to relieve acute attacks of pain in gout. It is also helpful in preventing such attacks.

Signs of toxic side-effects from colchicine are nausea and vomiting, abdominal pain and diarrhea. Scanty urine and blood in the urine are signs of kidney damage. In severe poisoning, death may result from impaired heart action and respiratory failure. Some new drugs are being tested for their effects in gout (see Chap. 35).

Antipyretics. Some non-narcotic drugs have the ability to both reduce fever and relieve pain. These drug preparations, products of salicylic acid or of coal tar, are not habit-forming and are comparatively inexpensive.

THE SALICYLATES. The salicylates are derived from salicylic acid and are most effective in relieving pain in the joints and muscles and in reducing fever by increasing the elimination of heat from the body. Normal doses of salicylates do not affect respiration or harm the heart. Salicylates do not cause sleep and are not habit-forming. They are readily absorbed from the stomach and duodenum and are excreted rapidly by the kidneys. They give the urine a brownish-green color. They will reduce the misery of a cold or influenza, but they will not "cure" it. They are specifically effective for headache, neuralgia, rheumatoid arthritis, rheumatic fever and dysmenorrhea. The most widely used preparations of salicylic acid are aspirin and sodium salicylate.

Acetylsalicylic Acid (Aspirin). Aspirin is a bitter drug available in tablets (plain or enteric-coated) or capsules. The usual dose for adults is 0.6 Gm. (10 gr.) every 3 or 4 hours as necessary. Candy-coated tablets of 65 mg. (1 gr.) are available for children. They should be kept out of a child's reach since they may be mistaken for candy.

Sodium Salicylate. Sodium salicylate is a powder that tastes salty-sweet and is available in 300 mg. and 600 mg. (5 and 10 gr.) plain or enteric-coated tablets. Like aspirin, it should be given with large amounts of water. It is absorbed more rapidly than aspirin, but it has similar effects. The usual dose is 0.6 Gm. (10 gr.) as often as is necessary. It is also available in ampules for intravenous injection when it is desirable to give large amounts of the drug.

Methyl Salicylate (Wintergreen Oil). This preparation is very irritating and cannot be used internally (except as flavoring). It is no longer considered valuable as a remedy for pain in joints or muscles when applied externally—in fact, it has poisoned children when applied over a large area of the skin.

Phenyl Salicylate. This is mainly used to coat tablets (enteric coating) to keep irritating drugs from dissolving in the stomach.

Salicylic Acid. This is too irritating to be taken orally, but it is often used in ointments and other preparations. So-called "corn removers" contain salicylic acid.

SIDE-EFFECTS. The salicylates have remarkably few toxic side-effects, but if they are used extensively for every minor discomfort they can cause mild poisoning, with such symptoms as dizziness, ringing in the ears, hearing and vision disturbances, nausea and vomiting and diarrhea. They may also cause skin eruptions and other allergic symptoms. Extreme reactions result in respiratory depression with labored breathing, coma and an unsteady pulse and blood pressure. Children are especially susceptible to overdosage, and since aspirin is likely to be considered a harmless drug, it is often left where children have easy access to it.

Salicylates should never be given to children indiscriminately.

The Coal Tar Analgesics. This group of drugs is derived from coal tar products; they are used to relieve pain and reduce fever, mainly headache and muscle aches. Headache remedies often contain one or more of these drugs.

SIDE-EFFECTS. The prolonged use of these drugs, as in taking a proprietary headache remedy, may cause poisoning. The symptoms are nausea and vomiting, sweating, skin eruption, cyanosis, slow respirations and slow, weak pulse. Some people seem to be susceptible to these drugs while others show no ill effects from them. Some of them may damage the blood and bone marrow. Symptoms of fever, malaise, sore throat and ulcerated mucous membranes should be reported at once.

PREPARATIONS. The most widely used preparations in this group with their average dosage are:

Acetophenetidin (Phenacetin): Oral, 0.3 Gm. (5 gr.)

Antipyrine (Phenazone, Felsol): Oral, 0.3 Gm. (5 gr.)

Acetaminophen (Apamide): Oral, 0.3 Gm. (5 gr.)

Acetanilid: Oral, 0.3 Gm. (5 gr.)

Acetylsalicylic Acid, Acetophenetidin and Caffeine Capsules: Oral

PHENYLBUTAZONE (BUTAZOLIDIN). This is a synthetic preparation which is chemically related to the antipyrines. It is a highly potent drug in relieving pain in rheumatoid arthritis, bursitis, etc. Because of the high incidence of its toxic effects, it is usually not recommended unless other drugs are ineffective. It may be used in acute attacks of gout and to reduce the accumulation of uric acid in the blood.

Side-Effects. The serious side-effects include edema, hepatitis, hypertension and a deficiency in white blood cells. Patients having this drug are closely observed and have frequent blood examinations for signs of toxic effect. Other side-effects include nausea, skin rash and dizziness.

Hypnotics and Sedatives

Sleeplessness is not always caused by pain; a hospital patient may be disturbed by unfamiliar noises, lack of privacy, personal worries or minor discomforts, such as cold feet, backache, too much or too little fresh air; he may even be hungry or thirsty. A nurse can correct many of these irritations without drugs, but sometimes drugs are necessary to assure adequate rest and sleep. A *hypnotic* is given at bedtime and produces sleep rather quickly. A *sedative* is given in divided doses throughout the day and has a soothing, quieting effect so the patient naturally sleeps better at night. The tranquilizing drugs have effects similar to sedatives (see p. 369).

The Barbiturates. The ideal hypnotic acts quickly, brings a natural sleep without "hangovers," is not habit-forming and does not have harmful effects on the body. The search for this kind of drug has given us hundreds of barbiturates, but for one reason or another only a few of them approximate these requirements. These drugs are widely used and, in many states, can be obtained only through a doctor's prescription. Formerly, anyone could purchase barbiturates over the counter anywhere, and they were—and still are—often used indiscriminately—sometimes for suicide attempts.

Barbiturates produce sleep; they quiet restless and nervous patients; they relieve tension in patients with such emotionally-upsetting conditions as colitis or gastric ulcer; they prevent and control convulsive seizures, such as epilepsy. Barbiturates are used before anesthesia and for obstetric sedation. In psychiatry, they lessen a patient's resistance to treatment and enable him to be more cooperative.

Barbiturates are easily absorbed and can be given orally or by injection. Preparations are available for many types of action—ultrashort, short, intermediate and long acting.

SIDE-EFFECTS. The patient may have "hangover" reactions—he may be depressed and listless or emotionally disturbed. Sometimes a barbiturate causes a skin rash or urticaria (hives) or can even precipitate an asthmatic attack. It may cause restlessness and unpleasant dreams or delirium. Elderly patients, especially, are likely to become confused and need careful watching if they must get up to go to the bathroom at night or look after themselves in other ways. Severe poisoning causes a deep sleep or stupor—the patient becomes comatosed, with slow or rapid and shallow breathing and a weak, rapid pulse. This may lead to death from respiratory failure.

Slow poisoning from barbiturates may also occur with such symptoms as mental confusion and depression, loss of memory and incoherent speech, weight loss, gastrointestinal upsets and anemia. The person's judgment is impaired to the extent that it is unsafe for him to drive a car or work with machines. Poor motor co-ordination makes him liable to injury from falls; he may fall asleep while smoking or may turn on the gas burner and forget to light it. Also, a person may become addicted to barbiturates if he takes them every day in fairly large doses for a long period of time. Many opium addicts are also barbiturate addicts who take these drugs when they cannot get opiates—a habit that some authorities consider even more undesirable than opium addiction.

Preparation	Usual Adult Dose	Usual Method of Administration	Length of Action
Barbital, N.F. (Veronal); Barbitone Sodium B.P.*	300 mg. (5 gr.)	Orally	Long acting
Phenobarbital, U.S.P. (Luminal); Phenobarbitone, B.P.*	30-100 mg. (½ to 1½ gr.)	Orally	Long acting
Mephobarbital, U.S.P. (Mebaral)	400-600 mg. (6 to 10 gr.)	Orally	Long acting
Metharbital (Gemonil)	100 mg. (1½ gr.)	Orally	Long acting
Amobarbital, U.S.P. (Amytal)*	100 mg. (1½ gr.)	Orally	Intermediate
Aprobarbital, N.F. (Alurate)	60-120 mg. (1 to 2 gr.)	Orally	Intermediate
Probarbital Sodium (Ipral Sodium)	120-250 mg. (2 to 4 gr.)	Orally	Intermediate
Butethal (Neonal)	100 mg. (1½ gr.)	Orally	Intermediate
Butabarbital Sodium, N.F. (Butisol Sodium)	8-60 mg. (⅛ to 1 gr.)	Orally	Intermediate
Pentobarbital Sodium, U.S.P. (Nembutal Sodium); Pentobarbitone Sodium, B.P.	100 mg. (1½ gr.)	Orally; rectally	Short acting
Secobarbital Sodium, U.S.P. (Seconal Sodium); Quinalbarbitone Sodium, B.P.	100-200 mg. (1½ to 3 gr.)	Orally; rectally	Short acting
Cyclobarbital Calcium, N.F. (Phanodorn); Cyclobarbitone, B.P.	200 mg. (3 gr.)	Orally	Short acting
Butallylonal (Pernoston)	200 mg. (3 gr.)	Orally	Short acting
Hexobarbital Sodium, N.F. (Evipal Sodium)	2-4 ml. 10%	Intravenously	Ultrashort acting
Thiopental Sodium, U.S.P. (Pentothal Sodium); Thiopentone Sodium, B.P.	2-3 ml. 2.5% in 10 to 15 sec. repeated in 30 sec. as required	Intravenously	Ultrashort acting

From Krug, E. E.: Pharmacology in Nursing, St. Louis, Mosby, 1963.
* Sodium salts are available.

Overdosage is fairly common, due either to suicidal intentions or because a dose does not seem to be effective, and the person takes more tablets when he is partially drowsy and does not know what he is doing.

Preparations. Phenobarbital (Luminal) does not take effect quickly, but its action lasts for 6 hours or more. It is useful in such nervous conditions as chorea (St. Vitus Dance), stomach and intestinal upsets, menopausal disturbances and to relieve tension before or after an operation. It is one of the least toxic drugs that can be given for epilepsy, but in doses large enough to control convulsions it is more depressing than the anticonvulsant drug, Dilantin (see p. 369). Phenobarbital is often given for a prolonged period after brain operations.

Phenobarbital Sodium Injection has the same uses as Luminal but is in injection form. A nurse must be careful to note this difference in these 2 preparations.

The table on page 365 lists some of the commonly used barbiturates.

Other Hypnotics. Some hypnotics that once were widely used have been replaced by the barbiturates. Others that are used less extensively than they formerly were are still recommended because they have the advantages of quick action and a wide margin of safety.

Paraldehyde. Paraldehyde is a hypnotic that depresses the central nervous system to bring almost natural sleep in 10 to 15 minutes after it is given, in spite of pain. It is especially effective in preventing possible convulsive seizures or for extreme nervous excitability in such conditions as tetanus, strychnine poisoning, delirium tremens or maniacal behavior. It is sometimes given rectally to children before an anesthetic. The usual adult oral dose is 8 ml. (2 fluid drams), which should be given in fruit juice or in a flavored syrup or very cold wine to hide its disagreeable odor and taste and to mitigate its irritating effect on the throat and stomach. Paraldehyde can also be given by rectum and intramuscularly in a sterile solution.

Side-Effects. The disadvantages of paraldehyde are its unpleasant taste and odor and its irritating effect on the stomach unless it is well diluted. Paraldehyde is partially excreted by the lungs and consequently the breath reeks of the drug; it is seldom given to patients who are up and about. It is an exceptionally safe drug and if mild poisoning does occur, the effects can usually be "slept off" like alcohol poisoning. The symptoms of poisoning are like those of chloral hydrate poisoning. It is possible to become addicted to paraldehyde.

Chloral Hydrate. Chloral hydrate is a sedative which has a hypnotic effect in insomnia when it is not caused by pain. (Chloral hydrate is not a pain-reliever.) It is one of the best hypnotics; it acts quickly (in 10 to 15 minutes) and brings nearly natural sleep for 5 or more hours. It has a wide safety range and is inexpensive. Its disadvantages are its unpleasant taste and its irritating effect on the stomach. However, it can be given in capsule form and as a suppository. The usual dose is 500 mg., given 3 times a day.

Side-Effects. Taken orally, chloral hydrate may cause nausea and vomiting. Symptoms of poisoning are those of depression, profound sleep, stupor, coma, fall in blood pressure, slow respiration, weak, slow pulse and cyanosis. Long range effects are kidney and liver damage. It is never given to patients with heart disease or to those with disturbed kidney or liver functions. Habitual users of the drug may show signs of nervous and gastrointestinal disturbances, skin irritations and weakness.

The Bromides. The bromides (especially sodium bromide) once widely used for their sedative effects have largely been replaced by more effective drugs. They are still found in some headache remedies. They have a slowly depressing effect on the nervous system.

The Anesthetics

Anesthetics are drugs that cause lack of sensation. General anesthetics do this by dulling sensations and producing unconsciousness. They also promote muscle relaxation. Local anesthetics cause lack of sensation in the area or nerves where they are applied or injected, without loss of consciousness.

Anesthetics to relieve pain and bring unconsciousness during a surgical operation were unknown 125 years ago. Up to that time doctors could only perform such operations as could be done quickly because the only available aids in relieving pain were alcohol and opium and these were woefully inadequate. This meant that surgeons had to work fast—the speediest surgeon was considered the best.

The successful use of anesthesia for surgery began in 1846 when a dentist, William Morton, anesthetized a patient with ether at the Massachusetts General Hospital in Boston. The successful use of chloroform and nitrous oxide as anesthetics followed later. Many more anesthetics are available today and medical science has found ways to make anesthetics more effective and less disturbing for the patient.

General Anesthetics. *Ether:* Ether is a clear colorless liquid and because it evaporates when exposed to the air, it is kept in a sealed metal container. It is also highly flammable and mixtures of air or oxygen and ether are explosive. Ether will dissolve fats and oils and is effective in removing adhesive plaster. Ether is most frequently given in combination with oxygen and nitrous oxide gas. It is an excellent muscle relaxant in surgical procedures and is a comparatively safe anesthetic. The recovery period following its use may be unpleasant because of nausea and vomiting. Ether is slightly irritating to the kidneys and may reduce the amount of urine, causing albumin to appear for several hours after anesthesia. It is not used for patients who have acidosis or severe kidney disorders, nor when a cautery or open flame is employed during surgery.

Chloroform: Chloroform is also a clear, colorless liquid with a sweetish odor. It is not explosive and is not irritating to mucous membranes. In spite of these advantages, chloroform is seldom used in this country because of the damaging effects it may have on the heart. It is said to be 5 times as dangerous as ether.

Ethyl Chloride: Ethyl chloride is a flammable, powerful, quick-acting anesthetic which is seldom used for anything but a minor surgical procedure, such as opening an abscess. It is a liquid and produces temporary insensibility to pain by freezing the tissues when it is sprayed on the area to be incised. Inhaled in concentrated amounts, it has a dangerous effect on the heart and may stop it entirely. Ethyl chloride is put up in small sealed glass tubes or metal cylinders.

Nitrous Oxide: Nitrous oxide is a gas with a slight odor, sometimes called "laughing gas" because it often makes patients mildly intoxicated when they first inhale it, and they laugh and talk before they lose consciousness. Combined with oxygen, it is an effective anesthetic for minor surgical procedures or as a preliminary to other anesthetics. Combined with oxygen and ether, it is an anesthetic for major surgery. Nitrous oxide alone depresses the nervous system, but it is one of the safest anesthetics when combined with sufficient oxygen to maintain normal respirations. Like the other anesthetic gases, nitrous oxide is compressed in steel cylinders and is administered by a qualified anesthetist or anesthesiologist.

Halothane: Halothane (Fluothane) is a nonflammable general anesthetic, more potent than ether. It acts quickly, is not irritating to mucous membranes and rarely causes nausea and vomiting. The patient loses consciousness quickly and recovers rapidly. It may cause hypotension and rapid, shallow breathing which can be controlled by giving adequate amounts of oxygen with it. This is made possible by a special inhalator.

Ethylene: Ethylene is a colorless gas with a slight odor. Mixed with a certain proportion of oxygen it is highly flammable and explosive unless the proper precautions are taken when it is used. Ethylene depresses the nervous system to produce anesthesia smoothly and quickly. It does not irritate mucous membranes, increase saliva or depress respiration, and the patient wakes up speedily with few, if any, undesirable aftereffects. Ethylene alone will not produce deep anesthesia; it is often used in obstetrics to alleviate labor pains. Its greatest disadvantage is its high explosiveness unless proper precautions are taken.

Cyclopropane: Cyclopropane is also a flammable gas when mixed with air or oxygen. It is a powerful anesthetic but is remarkably safe. It is not irritating and in normal amounts does not depress respiration. It is widely used in all types of surgery and is especially helpful in chest operations and in obstetrics. Cyclopropane may cause some nausea and vomiting or disturbance of the heartbeat.

BASAL ANESTHETICS: A basal anesthetic is a drug given to produce unconsciousness preceding the complete anesthesia necessary for a major surgical operation. These drugs are usually given rectally or intravenously and do away with the dread patients often have of "going to sleep" or being smothered by a face mask. These drugs act very quickly and help to reduce the amount of the general anesthetic necessary for the operation.

Avertin: This is a nervous system depressant which is given rectally. It makes the patient drowsy and produces sleep in approximately 15 minutes after its administration. Avertin is often given to the patient in his room before he goes to the operating room, and its effects carry over into the postoperative period. It is a powerful respiratory depressant and often causes a drop in blood pressure. The patient who has had Avertin must be watched for breathing difficulties both before and after surgery. He may not recover consciousness for some time and never should be left alone. Avertin is rarely given to elderly patients, never to chronic alcoholics or to people with kidney or liver damage.

Pentothal Sodium: This drug is a form of barbiturate which is widely used before other anesthetics. It is given intravenously and acts with great speed—the slang expression "out like a light" is a good description of the effect of this drug on the patient. Combined with other drugs, it is useful for minor and major surgical procedures. Its rapid action is both an advantage and a danger; while it brings almost immediate unconsciousness, it can also cause dangerous respiratory depression or spasm of the larynx. Other short acting barbiturates with similar effects are Evipal, Surital and Brevital.

LOCAL ANESTHETICS: Local anesthetics are drugs that act by blocking nerve impulses along nerve fibers. They may be injected into the tissues to deaden the nerves in an area (infiltration anesthesia), swabbed on the mucous membranes (surface anesthesia), injected into the spinal canal (spinal anesthesia) or injected into a main nerve trunk (block anesthesia).

Local anesthetics are dangerous drugs if they are injected directly into a blood vessel; therefore, they are not given in highly concentrated amounts. Epinephrine or similar drugs which constrict blood vessels when added to the anesthetic keep it from being absorbed too rapidly.

Cocaine: Cocaine is used to anesthetize the mucous membranes of the nose, throat and eye. It is dangerous if it is absorbed rapidly and for this reason it is not injected into the tissues, but it is applied with swabs instead. If it is absorbed rapidly it causes dizziness, headache, fainting, palpitations and sometimes convulsions and collapse. Respiratory failure causes death. A nurse must be extremely careful in preparing solutions and equipment for local anesthesia; to inject cocaine instead of novocain may be fatal.

Procaine: Procaine (Novocain) is less powerful as a local anesthetic but is also much less toxic. It is used more than any other local anesthetic for infiltration and nerve block anesthesia. It seldom causes unfavorable reactions. Epinephrine used with it prolongs its effect.

Other local anesthetics with effects similar to procaine are: Nesacaine, which is quicker-acting than procaine; Surfacaine, which relieves itching or pain caused by fissures and ulcerations and is used in ointments and in suppositories; Pontocaine, used as an eye anesthetic or on mucous membranes of the nose and throat; Butacaine, Nupercaine, Cyclaine (relatively new), Xylocaine, Piperocaine and Anesthesin relieve pain in ulcers and open wounds; Butesin Picrate is used for the pain in burns. Eugenol is a clove oil preparation that dentists use for painful dental conditions.

Selective Depressants

THE ANTICONVULSANT DRUGS. Convulsive seizures are signs of brain disorders associated with changes in the electrical activity of the brain. Anticonvulsant drugs are nervous system depressants which help to prevent or to control the different types of seizures which vary from mild to severe forms. The safest and the most effective drugs in use today are phenobarbital, Dilantin and Tridione.

Other anticonvulsant drugs are Phenurone,

Mesantoin and Paradione, used for their specific effect on certain types of seizures. Still others now under investigation are Celontin, Mysoline and Milontin.

Phenobarbital. Phenobarbital is effective for almost all types of seizures and is one of the safest anticonvulsant drugs. However, it has one disadvantage: often it must be given in such large doses that it causes sleepiness and sluggishness.

Dilantin. Dilantin controls grand mal seizures (epilepsy) but does not cause drowsiness nor mental deterioration (see p. 364). It can be taken orally; the usual dose is 100 mg. 3 times a day which may be increased if necessary. Side-effects may be nervousness, dizziness, loss of muscle coordination and blurred vision. Sometimes the patient has hallucinations and tremor, with nausea and vomiting. Dilantin is sometimes combined with other drugs, such as phenobarbital (Hydantal).

Tridione. Tridione is especially effective in treating mild epileptic seizures (petit mal) in children. It must be given under careful supervision because it may have serious side-effects. Nausea and vomiting, skin eruptions, blurred vision and sensitivity to light are signs of trouble. The patient has periodic blood examinations because some patients taking this drug have developed aplastic anemia.

ALCOHOL. Although alcohol is not considered to be a selective depressant, it is mentioned here as a drug which affects the nervous system. Alcoholism as a national health problem was discussed in Chapter 6.

ETHYL ALCOHOL: Once considered a stimulant to the nervous system, ethyl alcohol is now known to be a depressant. It has a variety of medicinal uses which are described under the various conditions for which it is used. Its chief uses are (1) as an *antiseptic* to disinfect and harden the skin, (2) as a *solvent* for other drugs and (3) as a *dilator* for surface blood vessels in impaired circulation.

Side-Effects. Alcohol dilates skin blood vessels and causes heat loss—an intoxicated person is more likely to freeze to death than a sober one. Excessive consumption of alcohol eventually causes stomach disturbances and poor nutrition. Alcohol adds nothing to food but calories. In excess it can cause kidney and liver damage, arteriosclerosis, tremors and muscular weakness. Its prolonged use may result in the delusions of delirium tremens, with visions of snakes or other horrors, or in insanity.

METHYL ALCOHOL (Wood Alcohol). Taken internally, methyl alcohol is a destructive poison, which causes nausea and vomiting, abdominal pain, headache and blurred vision which may lead to blindness. Fatal doses lead to convulsions, coma and death.

The Tranquilizers. The tranquilizing drugs (*ataractics*) have been an aid to troubled patients in every type of illness. They calm the anxious and apprehensive; they relax the tense; they bring rest and sleep. Troubled people, sick or well, are unable to function at their best—indeed, extreme anxiety is in itself an illness.

The tranquilizers are especially effective in behavior disorders and in mental disease. They have spectacular effects on violent behavior in mental illness although they cannot cure it. Unlike sedatives, they do not cause stupor and coma—the patient may go to sleep because he feels calmer and more relaxed but he can be awakened easily.

RESERPINE. Reserpine (Serpasil) is derived from the roots of a group of plants called *Rauwolfia*, which grow in India and various tropical regions. In these countries the powdered roots of the plant have long been used to treat mental illness. Reserpine calms and quiets without causing drowsiness, mental confusion or insensibility. It gives people a feeling of well-being and makes them less sensitive to small irritations. It is most effective when it is used to treat mentally ill patients who are overactive, excited and destructive. It does not relieve pain, nor does it help the depressed and withdrawn patient. It may actually harm him.

Reserpine acts slowly and improvement may not be noticeable for several weeks after the patient has begun to take the drug, but it has lasting effects even after it has been discontinued. Some patients continue to take small doses of the drug indefinitely. Reserpine is very valuable in making the disturbed patient receptive to psychotherapy, which otherwise he might resist. It is useful in treating some types of hypertension (see Chap. 36). It can be given orally, intramuscularly or intravenously.

Side-Effects. Reserpine seems to have few toxic side-effects but increased dosage may cause nasal stuffiness, diarrhea and a gain in weight. Other undersirable effects that sometimes appear are nosebleeds, insomnia, anxiety and fatigue, with skin eruptions and stomach irritation.

Other Rauwolfia preparations, similar to Serpasil in action, are Harmonyl and Moderil.

CHLORPROMAZINE. This drug is widely used to relieve tension, anxiety and overactive behavior in psychotic and psychoneurotic patients. With the aid of Chlorpromazine (Thorazine), many patients whose behavior made it necessary to confine them to mental institutions are now able to live at home. The drug does not cure mental disease, but it changes the patient's behavior to make it more acceptable. The dosage varies according to the needs of the individual patient.

Side-Effects. Chlorpromazine causes drowsiness and sleep which may be a desired effect in some instances. Other side-effects may be mouth dryness, nausea and vomiting, sensitivity to light and dermatitis. Toxic effects, such as trembling, drooling, muscular rigidity, jaundice, sore throat and anemia are warnings to discontinue the drug immediately.

Other newer drugs resembling Chlorpromazine in their action are being used; time will tell how comparatively effective and safe they are. These drugs are marketed under the trade names of Compazine, Trilafon, Pacatal and Phenergan, etc.

MEPROBAMATE. Meprobamate (Miltown, Equanil) is a calming drug which relieves anxiety and tension (thus relieving insomnia) decreases irritability and promotes a feeling of well-being and relaxation. It is not as potent as reserpine or chlorpromazine.

Side-Effects. The most common unfavorable reactions are skin rash and urticaria, with itching. Sometimes chills and fever develop, with edema, double vision and diarrhea; large doses may cause coma and a marked fall in blood pressure. If a patient becomes mentally and physically dependent on the drug, it is habit-forming.

Tranquilizers are not a substitute for an understanding nurse but rather are aids in helping a nurse to find the reasons for disturbed behavior.

DRUGS THAT AFFECT THE AUTONOMIC NERVOUS SYSTEM

As you have learned, we do not consciously control the activities of the autonomic nervous system—its responses take place automatically. However, certain drugs do affect these responses. Some of these drugs are prepared from natural hormones (see Chap. 20). Two important hormones are epinephrine and norepinephrine—hormones produced by the adrenal glands.

Epinephrine

Epinephrine (Adrenalin) constricts blood vessels when applied to the mucous membrane or wounds or when injected into the tissues. It has no effect on the unbroken skin. Digestive enzymes destroy it; therefore, it is never given by mouth. It speeds up the heart rate, raises blood pressure, constricts surface blood vessels and relaxes smooth muscles in the respiratory tract—it is the most valuable drug that can be used to relieve acute attacks of bronchial asthma. It is especially valuable in treating allergic reactions, such as anaphylactic shock, serum reactions, hay fever and urticaria. It is a powerful heart stimulant but must be used with great care so that it does not interfere seriously with the heartbeat. As a last resort, when the heart has stopped beating, injection of adrenalin directly into the heart muscle or into nearby veins has been known to restore heart action and bring the patient "back to life."

One thing important to remember about giving adrenalin is that it is a powerful drug and is usually given in small doses. The usual injection dose is 3 to 8 minims.

Side-Effects. Nervous patients and those with hypertension or exophthalmic goiter who take this drug may become more nervous and develop tremor, anxiety, headache, difficulty in breathing and stomach pain. More dangerous symptoms resulting from large doses or intravenous administration are dilatation of the heart, edema of the lungs and cerebral accident. Adrenalin is unsafe for patients with heart disease, hyperthyroidism or those who are nervously unstable.

Norepinephrine

Norepinephrine (levarterenol) constricts blood vessels in most of the vascular beds of the body. Levarterenol bitartrate is used to maintain blood pressure in hypotensive states resulting from such conditions as hemorrhage, trauma and myocardial infarction.

Side-Effects. Excessive amounts of levarterenol may raise blood pressure in elderly people to dangerous levels and cause cerebral accidents. Like epinephrine, it can interfere with the heartbeat and must be used with caution.

DRUGS THAT AFFECT THE MUSCULOSKELETAL SYSTEM

Certain drugs are useful in relieving muscle spasm, as in back strain or in cerebral palsy; to relax muscles during anesthesia in surgical operations; or in the manipulation of bones and joints in reducing fractures. Some of these drugs are potent ones which can be dangerous and must be used with great care; they may cause respiratory paralysis and heart failure.

Curare

Preparations of curare, a drug used by the South American Indians as an arrow poison, are seldom used today because they have been replaced by safer and more effective drugs. Some preparations which are now available are Tubadil, Metubine and Mecostrin Chloride. Other drugs now considered more effective than curare are Soma, Succinylcholine Chloride (Anectine) and Syncurine. New ones affecting the musculoskeletal system are Paraflex, Robaxin, Quiactin, etc.

Side-Effects. The side-effects of these drugs are similar. In different degrees, they tend to depress respiration and to speed up heart action. In toxic amounts, they may be fatal.

Quinine

Quinine is a muscle relaxant which is effective in relieving cramps in the leg muscles which sometimes trouble people at night.

DRUGS USED IN TREATING DISTURBANCES OF THE HEART

Drugs are used for their effect on the action of the heart itself or for their effect in dilating or constricting the blood vessels. Failure of any part of heart action or circulation interferes with the body's supply of oxygen and nutrients and with the removal of waste products. The heart muscle is responsible for pumping the blood through the circulatory system—it literally pumps 9 to 10 *tons* of blood through 60,000 to 100,000 *miles* of blood vessels every day.* It also must maintain its own circulatory system—the coronary circulation. One common form of heart disease is circulation failure; when the heart loses its efficiency as a pump, the circulation fails. Disease or degenerating changes in the heart itself or in the blood vessels impair its efficiency.

Heart Stimulants

Certain drugs will make the heartbeat faster; others slow it down but strengthen its force. Sometimes the heart is forced to beat faster than it should to make up for the weakness of its beat, and is in danger of exhaustion from overwork. Cardiac stimulants which strengthen heart action are:

Atropine: To strengthen the heartbeat

Caffeine: A quick stimulant to make the heartbeat strongly and rapidly

Epinephrine: A powerful emergency stimulant to the circulation

Digitalis. Digitalis is a drug which is ob-

* Soehren, Irene: New Treatment for coronary disease, Today's Health, Feb., 1957.

tained from the leaves of the purple foxglove. It makes the heart beat slower and more strongly, giving it time to rest between beats. This improves circulation to reduce edema in the lungs and abdomen, thus making breathing easier. Digitalis does not cure heart disease, but it helps to prevent heart failure.

The amount of digitalis prescribed for an individual patient is regulated by the dose that gives him the optimum benefits it is possible for him to obtain from the drug. This is usually determined by giving the total amount necessary to produce the desired effect—the *digitalizing dose*—in divided doses, over a period of 2 to 4 days. This dose, slightly reduced, is the amount he will receive every day thereafter—his *maintenance dose*. This will vary according to the needs of the individual patient. Many patients who need digitalis must take it for the rest of their lives.

Signs of Overdose. A patient who is receiving digitalis needs close medical and nursing observation. Accuracy is especially important in giving this drug because it is very powerful, and even a minute difference in amount can be dangerous. It is important to observe the pulse closely—it should be counted before giving each dose. If it is lower than 60 beats a minute or if there is a change in the rhythm, withhold the dose and report these conditions to the head nurse. Other symptoms of disturbance include nausea and vomiting, headache, diarrhea and sometimes drowsiness and blurred vision. A record of the patient's intake and output of fluids is kept and he is watched for signs of edema and breathing difficulty.

Preparations. Some preparations of digitalis that are used are:

Digitalis Tincture: Oral, 0.1 ml.
Digitoxin (Crystodigin, Purodigin): Oral, 0.1 mg.
Gitalin (Gitaligin): Oral, 0.5 mg.
Digoxin (Lanoxin): Oral, 0.5 mg.

Heart Depressants

Heart depressants make the heart less active and decrease the heart rate. Heart disease affects the rhythm of the heartbeat—the heart quivers without rest between beats. This affects the circulation and may lead to congestive heart failure. Some drugs steady the heart rate by increasing the rest period, which changes a rapid irregular pulse to one that is slow and regular. Quinidine is such a drug. The difference between Digitalis and quinidine is that Digitalis stimulates more power in the heart muscle, while quinidine restrains erratic heart muscle activity to slower and more regular action.

Quinidine and procainamide (Pronestyl Hydrochloride) have essentially the same effects, except that procainamide is much less toxic and its effects last longer.

Preparations.

Quinidine Sulfate: Oral, 0.2 to 0.4 Gm.
Procainamide Hydrochloride (Pronestyl Hydrochloride): Oral, 0.25 Gm.

The Effect of Drugs on the Blood Vessels

Some drugs affect the circulatory system by constricting or dilating the blood vessels. The vasodilators raise blood pressure; the vasoconstrictors lower it. They produce their effects indirectly, by their action on the nervous system, or directly, by action on the muscle cells in the blood vessels.

Vasoconstrictors. The vasoconstrictors are used to control superficial hemorrhage, to raise blood pressure and to relieve nasal congestion. The most important ones are epinephrine (Adrenalin), levarterenol bitartrate (Levophed Bitartrate), ergotamine tartrate and phenylephrine hydrochloride.

Blood vessel constricting drugs are most widely used to shrink mucous membranes and relieve nasal congestion in mild infections of the upper respiratory tract. A number of preparations are available—Neosynephrine, Privine, Vonedrine and Benzedrex—to mention a few of them. They are comparatively safe, but taking large doses, too often, is unwise.

Epinephrine. The most important use of epinephrine is as a local application to constrict small blood vessels to stop bleeding from the eye, nose or ear or to reduce swelling in the mucous membrane of the nose. It will not stop hemorrhage from a large blood vessel, and it must be applied directly to the area to stop superficial bleeding. It is used also with local anesthetics to prolong their action, to check bleeding and to make them safer. It relieves hives, itching and edema in allergic reactions.

LEVARTERENOL (LEVOPHED). Levarterenol is used to raise blood pressure after surgery, hemorrhage or in shock. It is given intravenously in a solution of dextrose and saline.

EPHEDRINE. In small doses, ephedrine stimulates the heart and raises blood pressure. Large doses depress heart action. Local applications reduce swelling in the turbinates.

PHENYLEPHRINE HYDROCHLORIDE. This drug relieves congestion in mucous membranes and is used to treat some types of shock. It raises blood pressure and stabilizes it and is used sometimes to treat allergic reaction.

ERGOTAMINE TARTRATE (GYNERGEN). Ergotamine tartrate is especially valuable in treating migraine headache; it is more effective if it is taken when the first signs of an attack appear. This drug accumulates in the body so it must be taken cautiously. Symptoms of trouble are numbness and tingling in the fingers and toes, muscle pains and weakness, gangrene and blindness.

Vasodilators. Drugs that dilate the blood vessels are used to treat peripheral (toward the surface) blood vessel disease, coronary artery disease and hypertension. Some of them (the *nitrites*) have been used for many years, especially in an acute attack of angina pectoris or to prevent an attack, by relieving angina pain caused by spasm of the coronary blood vessels.

NITROGLYCERIN. Nitroglycerin acts quickly —in 2 or 3 minutes; when a tablet is placed under the tongue it is rapidly absorbed by the mucous membranes. Its effects last for about 30 minutes. The usual dose is 0.4 mg. (1/150 gr.) which can be repeated several times a day.

AMYL NITRITE. Amyl nitrite comes in glass ampules (pearls) covered with a thin material so that it can be crushed easily and the drug inhaled. It has a strong and rather disagreeable odor, and 2 or 3 inhalations are a safe limit—more may cause overdosage.

Other nitrite preparations are available; some of them, such as Peritrate Tetranitrate, have longer-lasting effects—up to 6 hours or more.

Side-Effects of the Nitrites. The patient may feel dizzy and faint from a sudden lowering of blood pressure and may have headache. Large doses of these drugs exaggerate these symptoms and also make the face and neck flushed and the pulse weak and rapid. In nitrite poisoning, the patient's head should be lowered and he is treated for shock; administer oxygen if he is cyanotic. People who are subject to attacks of angina usually carry these drugs with them to use in an emergency, so the nurse should know what to do for a person who takes an overdose.

PAPAVERINE. Papaverine is particularly effective in relaxing spasm in the coronary, peripheral and pulmonary arteries. The average dosage ranges from 30 to 60 mg. when given intramuscularly.

AMINOPHYLLINE. Aminophylline has some effect in dilating blood vessels and is thought to be effective in preventing attacks of angina pectoris. It is sometimes used in coronary occlusion.

ALCOHOL (ETHYL). Alcohol dilates the blood vessels in the skin and is used for this effect in some diseases of the peripheral vessels, such as Raynaud's disease. For cardiac patients, alcohol is usually given in the form of whisky, with soda, for its mildly sedative effects in producing rest and relaxation.

Drugs That Reduce Blood Pressure

RAUWOLFIA DRUGS. The tranquilizing action of these drugs has been discussed (see p. 369). and they also are effective in treating the less extreme forms of hypertension. They relieve dizziness and headache, lower blood pressure and slow the pulse rate. They are sometimes given with other drugs. The most common side-effect is a stuffy nose, but they may also cause drowsiness, nightmares and depression. Some preparations commonly used are:

Rauwolfia (Raudixin): Oral, 200 to 400 mg. daily
Reserpine (Serpasil and others): Oral, 0.25 to 1 mg. daily

APRESOLINE. Apresoline reduces blood pressure and helps to control hypertension. Treatment begins with small doses, 10 mg. taken after meals and at bedtime; the dosage is adjusted to obtain the desired effect. It often causes unpleasant side-effects that are not necessarily serious, such as headache, heart palpitation, depression, nausea and vomiting. More serious symptoms include chills, fever, pain in the heart region and edema of the legs and feet.

CHLOROTHIAZIDE (DIURIL). Although chlorothiazide is used primarily as a diuretic, it is also effective in lowering blood pressure in hypertension when used alone or with other drugs. It has few unpleasant side-effects. Other preparations are Hydrodiuril, Ademol Renese and Naturetin.

GUANETHIDINE (ISMELIN). This is a powerful drug used to reduce blood pressure; its effect is more noticeable when the patient is sitting or standing up. Patients may feel weak and dizzy when they move about. It is especially important to safeguard elderly patients who may get up to go to the bathroom during the night. Other side-effects are diarrhea, fainting and a slow pulse.

DRUGS THAT AFFECT THE BLOOD

We have discussed the effects of drugs on the circulation of blood. Drugs also are used to treat disturbances of the blood itself, such as anemia or leukemia, and to influence blood clotting. Blood is composed of plasma, red cells, white cells and platelets. Red cells are made up mainly of a substance called hemoglobin, which contains iron. Hemoglobin has the all-important job of carrying oxygen to every cell in the body. (See Chap. 15.)

Normally, an adequate diet provides the essentials to form blood (iron, vitamin C and parts of the vitamin B complex, vitamin B_{12}, animal protein). Some disease conditions need treatment that will get results more rapidly, and certain drugs help to do this.

Iron

Iron is not only an essential part of hemoglobin but is also distributed throughout the body cells and is stored in the blood-forming organs. Actually, the body needs only small amounts of iron from the diet because it salvages iron from the worn-out blood cells and uses it again. Adolescents (especially girls) and women during pregnancy and the menopause need more iron than at other times; in fact, women up to and through the menopause need 4 times as much iron as men. Iron deficiency causes anemia and is usually due to a massive hemorrhage or to prolonged slow bleeding from a tumor or hemorrhoids or to profuse menstrual bleeding.

Iron Preparations. The market is flooded with iron preparations but only a few justify the claims made for them. Among the most effective are:

Ferrous Sulfate (Feosol): Prepared in enteric-coated tablets of 3 and 5 gr. and is given after meals.

Ferrous Sulfate Syrup: The usual dose is 8 ml. 3 times a day.

Ferrous Gluconate (Fergon): Tablets of 5 gr. each, usual dose is 1 tablet, 3 times a day. It is less likely to cause stomach distress than ferrous sulfate.

Ferrocholinate (Chel-Iron, Ferrolip): One of the newer iron preparations that is considered less toxic than some of the older products. The normal dose is 330 to 660 mg., 3 times a day.

Ferric Ammonium Citrate: One of the most soluble iron preparations. The usual dose is 500 mg., 3 times a day.

Iron is usually given by mouth, but preparations such as Imferon and Astrafer that can be given by injection are also available if the oral method is not feasible.

SIDE-EFFECTS. Iron taken over a prolonged period may cause loss of appetite, nausea and vomiting, headaches, stomach pain, diarrhea or constipation. Large doses can cause poisoning, especially if taken by children.

Many iron preparations are irritating to the stomach, which is the reason why they are given after meals or with food. Solutions should be taken through a straw because they stain the teeth.

Vitamin B_{12} (Cyanocobalamin, Rubramin, Redisol, Normocytin). It is 40 years now since 2 medical scientists, Minot and Murphy, discovered a substance in liver, vitamin B_{12}, that would cure pernicious anemia, which at that time was a fatal disease. Vitamin B_{12} is necessary for the manufacture of red blood cells, but for some reason, certain people cannot absorb this vitamin from their diet and develop pernicious anemia if it is not supplied in some other way. It is thought that these people lack a substance in the stomach (the intrinsic factor) that makes it possible to absorb vitamin B_{12}. Therefore, the treatment is to give injections of vitamin B_{12} which will arrest the disease. Since the discovery of vitamin B_{12}, the patient is no longer forced to consume large quantities of liver.

The patient with a marked vitamin B_{12} deficiency feels tired, weak and breathless; his tongue and mouth are sore; he has difficulty in coordinating his movements; his skin takes on a pale yellowish tinge; and he develops tingling and numbness in his extremities. The dosage is measured in micrograms; the amount depends on the seriousness of the patient's need for it. Usually it is given intramuscularly to hasten the effects. Hydrochloric acid frequently is given with the vitamin B_{12} since most patients with pernicious anemia have a deficiency of this acid in the stomach. Vitamin B_{12} has no undesirable side-effects.

WHOLE BLOOD, BLOOD PLASMA, BLOOD PROTEINS

A transfusion of *whole blood* increases the number of red blood cells quickly, restores the volume of blood and so raises blood pressure. It may save a patient's life when his survival depends on quick action. The blood must be of a type compatible with the patient's blood type.

Blood plasma is that fluid part of the blood which has been separated from the blood cells. It restores blood volume in shock, in severe hemorrhage and in severe burns. It can be used as a liquid, or it can be dehydrated, concentrated and stored for a long time without losing its effect; by adding sterile distilled water it is ready to use, without considering blood groups. Plasma is obtained by processing the blood of qualified blood donors to remove blood cells.

Blood proteins are other constituents of blood plasma that can be separated from blood plasma for use. For example, albumin has the same effects as plasma in treating shock and can be administered in smaller amounts. Thrombin and fibrinogen together in a solution form fibrin, which can be applied locally to stimulate blood clotting, or it can be given intravenously. Other preparations are normal human serum albumin (used in treating shock) and antihemolytic human plasma (a temporary aid to the hemophiliac).

Blood Coagulants

Drugs that promote blood clotting are called *hemostatics*. When blood plasma lacks the elements that make blood clot, certain drug preparations can be used to supply this deficiency. Some of them are:

Absorbable Gelatin Sponge (Gelfoam): This is a form of gelatin that is used to stop capillary bleeding and can be left in a surgical wound where it will be absorbed completely.

Fibrin Foam: A dry preparation of human fibrin that can be applied to a bleeding surface to stop hemorrhage. It is used in kidney, liver or brain surgery.

Tolonium Chloride (Blutene Chloride): A dye that lessens a tendency to excessive bleeding from the uterus. Used for profuse menstruation for which no cause can be found.

Oxidized Cellulose (Oxycel, Hemo-Pak): A treated cotton or gauze pack that is absorbable and can be applied to check hemorrhage.

Thrombin: A preparation from plasma which is used to check surface bleeding.

Vitamin K: A vitamin that is necessary to make prothrombin, which is the substance that starts the formation of a blood clot. Vitamin K is found in many foods, but sometimes the intestine is unable to absorb it. It may be given to patients who have a prothrombin deficiency, as in jaundice, or to the newborn. Many preparations are available; among them are Vitamin K_1, Synkayvite, Menadione, Hykinone, Mephyton and Konakion. They are in forms that can be given by mouth, by injection or intravenously. The dosage is measured in milligrams and varies from 0.5 to 20 mg. or more, according to the needs of the individual patient.

Anticoagulants

Drugs to prevent abnormal clotting of blood are highly important, since clots in major blood vessels are one of the chief causes of death in this country (coronary occlusion and cerebral accidents). Some drugs that prevent blood clotting or make it less likely to occur are:

Sodium Citrate: Used to prevent the coagulation of blood to be used in transfusions.

Heparin: This drug is especially useful in preventing postoperative thrombosis and embolism. If a patient is receiving heparin, the nurse should watch for bleeding from the wound or blood in the urine and if they occur, should report them at once. Heparin is given by injection or intravenously.

Dicumarol: Dicumarol is given to prevent venous thrombosis and pulmonary embolism and thrombophlebitis (inflammation of a vein). It is available in tablets and capsules and the usual beginning dose is 200 to 300 mg. daily, given by mouth. Later doses vary according to the patient's needs. This drug has few side reactions, but overdosage can cause hemorrhage. Nosebleed, bleeding into the skin or blood in the urine should be reported. Other anticoagulants with similar action are Coumadin, Indon and Dipaxin.

DRUGS THAT AFFECT THE URINARY SYSTEM

The urinary system consists of the kidneys, the ureters, the bladder and the urethra. The kidneys are the chief organs for excreting waste substances from the body. Excess water and other substances the body does not need are excreted in the urine. When kidney function is impaired, there are drugs which help to alleviate the problem.

Diuretics

Diuretics are drugs used to increase the elimination of water and salts from the body by increasing the flow of urine. One way of doing this is to give the patient increased amounts of fluid. Taking in more fluid seems to stimulate an increase in fluid loss. Therefore, water is also a diuretic, although it is not a drug. When the flow of urine is inadequate, water and salts accumulate in the tissues and cause edema. An increased flow of urine reduces edema.

Caffeine, theobromine and theophylline have a limited diuretic effect. The mercurial diuretics, such as Thiomerin, Cumertilin, Mercuhydrin, Neohydrin and Mersalyl are among the most effective in reducing edema, especially edema caused by cirrhosis of the liver, kidney nephrosis or cardiac edema. These drugs are given orally or intramuscularly every 3 or 4 days, preferably in the morning so that most of the urine elimination will take place during the day. A patient may void as much as 8 or 9 quarts of urine during the day the initial dose is given.

Side-Effects. Signs of unfavorable reactions are inflammation of the gums, increase in saliva, diarrhea, albumin and blood in the urine, flushing and skin reactions. Prolonged use of these drugs may cause kidney damage. Urine specimens are examined periodically for blood cells, albumin and casts.

Cardrase and Diamox may be used to prevent edema in cardiac patients and to increase the output of urine.

Chlorothiazide preparations are effective in relieving edema associated with congestive heart failure and hypertension and cirrhosis of the liver. Diuril and Lyovac Diuril are the commonly used prepartions. The usual dose is from 500 mg. to 1 Gm. every day. The side-effects include allergic reactions, nausea, stomach discomfort, dizziness and muscle cramps. Some of the newer drugs related to this group are longer-lasting, less toxic, can be taken orally and are relatively inexpensive (Renese, Ademol and Naturetin).

Antidiuretics

In some conditions, such as diabetes insipidus, the patient excretes an excessive amount of urine. This condition is caused by the lack of a pituitary hormone. (This should not be confused with diabetes mellitus, which is caused by lack of insulin.) Pituitary extract, injected hypodermically or applied to the nasal membranes, is given to supply this deficiency.

Drugs That Affect the Bladder

Bladder difficulties are often caused by a frequent desire to empty the bladder or by an inability to empty it. Either way, the trouble is caused by muscle tone. Drugs that improve muscle tone in the bladder are neostigmine and bethanechol chloride (Urecholine Chloride). Hyoscyamus tincture is given to relax bladder muscle.

Urinary Antiseptics

Urinary antiseptics are used to combat infection in the urine and urinary tract. This type of infection is often caused by colon bacilli but it may also be caused by forms of staphylococci or streptococci. These organisms are carried easily to the urethral opening from the rectum if the proper precautions are not observed in carrying out nursing procedures involving these parts.

A number of the sulfonamides and antibiotics destroy or inhibit the growth of infectious organisms in the urine and urinary passages. The one selected is chosen for its specific effect on the organism causing the infection. This is determined by microscopic examination or laboratory culture of a urine specimen.

Some of the sulfonamides commonly used are Gantrisin, Sulamyd and Kynex. The usual dosage is 0.5 Gm., daily.

Of the antibiotics, penicillin is the least effective in urinary infections because so many of the organisms causing the infection are resistant to it. Streptomycin, erythromycin, novobiocin and kanamycin are effective. Chloramphenicol, bacitracin and neomycin are effective but must be used cautiously because they have certain damaging effects on the bone marrow and the kidneys. Methenamine (Mandelamine) is effective in cystitis, pyelitis and pyelonephritis. Furacin is one of the more expensive drugs, but the dosage required is small. Pyridium is given to soothe the mucous membrane of the bladder and urethra and to relieve frequency of urination. It also helps to relieve discomfort caused by a retention catheter.

DRUGS USED IN TREATING GASTROINTESTINAL DISEASES AND DISORDERS

Drugs affect the gastrointestinal tract through their action on muscles and glandular tissues, to stimulate peristalsis, to correct enzyme deficiencies and excess acidity and to relieve vomiting.

Drugs That Affect the Mouth

Good oral hygiene to keep the mouth and teeth clean is more effective than drugs, although some drugs are mildly helpful.

Mouthwashes and Gargles. Drugs used for this purpose do not have a very powerful germ-killing effect because they cannot be used in strong enough concentrations without harming the tissues. They are useful as disinfectants and in removing mucus from the mouth and throat. A 1 per cent *sodium bicarbonate solution* (½ teaspoon in a glass of water) is a useful mouth wash for removing mucus. A 0.9 per cent solution of *sodium chloride* (common salt) is as satisfactory a gargle as any mixture.

Sodium perborate in a 2 per cent solution is a useful mouthwash and is effective in treating Vincent's infection and pyorrhea. It is an ingredient of many tooth powders. Most hospitals use a mouthwash prepared in their own pharmacy, with directions about whether it is to be used full strength or diluted.

Dentifrices, Tooth Powders or Abrasives. The usual ingredients in a dentifrice are an abrasive, a foaming agent and flavoring materials. A safe dentifrice is one that will not harm the teeth or gums. Some dentifrices claim they contain a special ingredient that prevents tooth decay. (The Council of Dental Therapeutics investigates and reports on such claims.) Stannous fluoride is recognized as having some beneficial effects of this kind. The American Dental Association and the American Medical Association have recommended the fluoridation of drinking water as a method of reducing dental decay; but the decision to fluoridate its water supply is made by a city or community, and some cities have voted against fluoridation (see Chap. 5). A 2 per cent solution of sodium fluoride applied to children's teeth has been found effective in preventing dental caries. Other ways of giving fluorides in milk, table salt and fluoride tablets are being investigated.

Drugs That Affect Stomach Conditions

Certain drugs are used to control the excessive production of stomach acids, to aid digestion, to relieve gas distention, and to cause, to prevent or to control vomiting.

Antacids. Antacids are used in treating peptic ulcer to reduce and to control stomach acidity and give the ulcer a chance to heal. Two widely used and readily absorbed antacids are sodium bicarbonate (ordinary baking soda) and sodium citrate, an ingredient of proprietary drugs for relieving stomach distress. The dosage depends on the needs of the individual patient. Many people have completely mistaken notions about stomach acid, not realizing that a certain amount is necessary for the digestion of food. The habit of taking sodium bicarbonate to avoid "acid stomach" can interfere seriously with the electrolyte balance in the blood and cause alkalosis (an excess of alkali in the blood). In the eyes of the public, advertisers have made "acid" an unfavorable term—a public enemy to be fought.

Other antacids are often preferred because they are not readily absorbed and are not apt to cause alkalosis. Some of the most commonly used ones are:

Aluminum Hydroxide Gel (Amphojel, Creamalin, Alkajel): In tablet or liquid form and is given orally in doses of 4 to 8 ml. every 2 to 4 hours. It is usually diluted in a small amount of water or followed by a drink of liquid to make sure the medicine is washed down from the throat into the stomach.

Magnesium Oxide (Light Magnesia and Heavy Magnesia): A powder insoluble in water. The usual dose is 250 mg. It is slow-acting but has a lasting effect. It has also a laxative effect which sometimes causes diarrhea.

Sippy Powders (No. 1 and No. 2): A mixture of antacids that are given alternately with a milk and cream diet.

Milk of Magnesia: A liquid mixture, sometimes combined with other magnesium salts as Maalox; the usual dosage is 8 ml. which is given with a small amount of water or followed by a small amount of water or milk.

Digestants. Digestants aid digestion in the gastrointestinal tract and supply digestant deficiencies.

Hydrochloric acid aids in the digestion of protein; it kills bacteria and helps to maintain electrolyte balance. Some people, elderly ones especially, are deficient in hydrochloric acid because too little is secreted by the stomach. This deficiency is associated with gastric carcinoma, pernicious anemia, gastritis and other conditions. Dilute hydrochloric acid is given to remedy the deficiency. The usual dose is 4 ml., given in half a glass of water (through a tube because it injures tooth enamel). Eating food or using an alkaline mouth wash after taking it will help to kill its sharp, sour taste.

Acidulin: Another preparation containing hydrochloric acid which comes in capsules and is usually given before meals.

Pepsin: A stomach enzyme that aids protein digestion but is seldom used today because hydrochloric acid is considered more effective.

Bile Salts: A constituent of bile which is essential in the digestion of fats. They are used in the treatment of liver disorders to aid digestion and to increase bile drainage. Some commonly used preparations are Ox Bile Extract, Zanchol and Decholin.

Carminatives. Carminatives are mildly irritating drugs that help to expel gas from the stomach and intestines. They are chiefly home remedies, such as peppermint water either alone or combined with brandy or whisky in hot water.

Emetics. Emetics are given to make a patient vomit to rid the stomach of its contents, usually as first aid in emergencies when quick action is necessary (see Chap. 48). The drug apomorphine, given by injection, causes vomiting quickly but is a depressing drug when given in large doses. Gastric lavage (washing out the stomach) is the most effective way of emptying the stomach.

Antiemetics. Antiemetics are given to relieve nausea and vomiting. These symptoms may be the result of a number of things—emotional distress, motion sickness, the effects of drugs, gastrointestinal disease or reaction to x-ray or other treatments. They are sometimes relieved by simple remedies, such as a cup of tea, carbonated drinks (ginger ale, cola), sodium bicarbonate in warm water (to wash out the stomach), or gastric lavage. Quieting drugs (barbiturates) and the antihistamines (chlorpromazine) are also effective.

Drugs Used for X-ray Procedures

Barium sulfate is used in x-ray examinations of the gastrointestinal tract, to detect peptic ulcer, cancer and other conditions (see Chap. 38). Iodine compounds (Iodekon, Priodax, Telepaque) are useful in examinations of the gall bladder and the bile passages.

Drugs That Affect Intestinal Action

Cathartics. Far too many people have very hazy notions about intestinal activities. To miss even one daily bowel movement is considered a catastrophe; they believe that poisons are piling up so rapidly they must get rid of them at all costs and they rush for a pill. First cousin to this notion is the firm belief that a regular daily movement is not enough—that a "good cleaning out" every so often is necessary for something they call "the system." The advertising claims for cathartics bolster these ideas. Healthy people should not need cathartics.

On the other hand, many people do suffer from true constipation, much of which could be prevented by proper diet and eating habits, attention to the impulse to defecate and sufficient exercise. People who must lie in bed in one position, who are having drugs such as morphine or codeine or have impaired muscle tone which affects the colon are likely to be constipated. Constipation is also often associated with mental disorders, anemia or sick headaches. The doctor determines when a cathartic is necessary and prescribes a suitable one.

Some legitimate uses of cathartics are:

To keep the intestinal contents soft to avoid intestinal irritation (colostomy, rectal conditions)
To eliminate poisons caused by food or drugs
To reduce edema
To empty the intestines before x-ray examinations
To get rid of intestinal parasites
To obtain a stool specimen to be examined for parasites

Elderly people who have been taking cathartics for constipation for most of their adult lives may be exceptions. For one thing, it is not always possible to prescribe roughage in the diet of a person who is unable to chew it. Elderly people, like everyone else, are not likely to take kindly to the idea of changing lifetime habits. A mild cathartic taken regularly as prescribed by the doctor is not likely to be harmful.

The Action of Cathartics. Cathartics act in several ways:

To stimulate peristalsis by increasing the bulk or water content of the feces
To moisten the stool
To irritate the lining of the intestine

AGAR, METAMUCIL. Dry agar, obtained from seaweed, and Metamucil, a preparation of psyllium seed, swell when moistened and give bulk to the feces. Both are given with a sufficient amount of water. Agar can also be sprinkled in such foods as mashed potatoes, cereal or soup; it may be combined with liquid petrolatum (Petrogalar). In spite of advertising claims, Petrogalar is an ineffective bulk producer because it contains very little agar. Other preparations used to produce bulk are Methocel, Carmethose, Cellothyl and Konsyl.

SALINE CATHARTICS. Saline cathartics are the most effective ones to reduce edema, to obtain a stool specimen, to empty the intestines in cases of food or drug poisoning or worms. They are used also to remove feces. Saline cathartics produce watery stools. Those preparations most frequently used are:

Milk of Magnesia: A mild cathartic and is often used for children. The usual adult dose is 15 ml. (½ fluid ounce). Milk of magnesia is also an antacid.

Magnesium Sulfate (Epsom Salt): A crystalline

or powdery substance with a salty, bitter taste and must be dissolved in water. The usual dose is 15 Gm. (½ ounce). It should be given with fruit juice which helps to disguise the taste.

Seidlitz Powders: Seidlitz powders are put up separately, one in a blue and one in a white paper. The contents of each paper is dissolved separately in ⅓ of a glass of water and the two are combined *at the bedside* immediately before swallowing. Since the mixture is effervescent and flavored, it is easy to take.

Magnesium Citrate: A mild cathartic which is easy to take because it is carbonated. The usual dose is ½ to 1 bottle (6 to 12 ounces).

MINERAL OIL. Liquid petrolatum, or mineral oil, is a petroleum product that is simply a lubricant to soften feces. It is given to prevent straining with a bowel movement after rectal operations or for chronic constipation in inactive persons, such as elderly people. Mineral oil is said to interfere with the use of vitamin A in the body, and some doctors will not prescribe it. It should be given between meals or at bedtime to avoid delaying the passage of food from the stomach. The dosage ranges from 15 to 30 ml.; only standard official preparations should be used.

Other preparations such as Colace or Doxinate, moisten the feces so that soft stools are formed.

IRRITATING CATHARTICS. *Castor Oil (Oleum Ricini):* Castor oil irritates the small intestine to expel its contents rapidly to completely empty the bowel. It often produces a number of semiliquid stools in 2 to 6 hours after it is taken. This means that there are likely to be no more bowel movements for a day or two—an aftereffect that sometimes worries patients. Castor oil is excreted into the milk of a nursing mother and may affect the baby's bowel elimination. Castor oil is unpleasant to take, but the taste can be disguised in various ways—for example, by giving it with fruit juices. Most hospitals determine the method to use. It is not prescribed as frequently today as formerly.

Cascara Sagrada: Cascara is obtained from the bark of a shrub and acts mainly on the large intestine. Like similar drugs obtained from plants, it is likely to cause cramps and acts in 6 to 12 hours. The fluid extract is flavored and easy to take; the adult dose is 2 to 12 ml. given orally.

Compound Licorice Powder: This is a combination of senna and other ingredients which resembles cascara in its action but is more powerful; the usual oral dosage is 4 Gm. mixed with water. Other senna preparations are senna syrup and senna fluid extract.

Phenolphthalein: This is a synthetic substance which produces mild bowel irritation and does not cause griping. It is incorporated in tablets not unpleasant to take and is sold in proprietary preparations that resemble candy. They should be kept out of children's reach since they might take a fatal overdose of the drug.

Dulcolax: Dulcolax stimulates peristalsis in the colon and is effective for constipation and for cleansing the bowel before an operation and x-ray or rectal examinations. The average oral dose is 10 to 15 mg. in the evening or before breakfast.

S. S. B. and C. Pills and Hinkle's Pills: These pills are a combination of aloin and other cathartics. The usual dosage is 1 pill given orally.

Antidiarrheics. Certain drugs act on the intestine to soothe the mucous membrane, to form a protective coating over it, to shrink swollen and inflamed tissues and to fight infection. The particular remedy used in treating diarrhea depends on what is causing it.

Kaolin and Kaopectate: Preparations of charcoal take up poisonous substances or gas from the intestines. Kaolin dosage varies from 15 to 60 Gm. every 3 or 4 hours until the symptoms are relieved. Kaopectate is effective when given in fairly large doses of 15 to 30 ml., several times a day. The use of these preparations is questioned by some authorities on the ground that nutrients cling to them and are also removed.

Bismuth: Preparations have a soothing effect on irritated intestinal mucous membrane. In powder or tablets, the usual dose is 1 to 4 Gm., 4 times a day.

Azulfidine: Used in treating ulcerative colitis, in 1 Gm. doses every 4 hours around the clock, later reduced to 1 Gm., 4 times a day when the patient is up and around.

Sulfadiazine: Used in treating dysentery in doses beginning with 2 to 4 Gm., followed by divided doses of 1 Gm. every 4 to 6 hours.

Tannic Acid: Protects the mucous membrane and checks secretions. The usual dose is 1 Gm. given in a capsule.

Antibiotics: Streptomycin, chloramphenicol and combinations with penicillin are sometimes used.

Camphorated Opium Tincture (Paregoric) and

Opium Tincture (Laudanum): Sedative preparations for relieving diarrhea. The dose for paregoric is 4 to 8 ml. (1 to 2 fluid drams) and for laudanum is 0.3 to 1 ml. (5 to 15 minims). Codeine and morphine are also effective but are not used for chronic conditions because they are habit-forming. Belladonna tincture helps to relieve intestinal spasms, given in 10-drop doses.

In addition to drugs to check diarrhea, patients also need replacement of the fluids, electrolytes, vitamins and food lost by the overactivity of the intestines.

DRUGS THAT AFFECT THE RESPIRATORY SYSTEM

Respiration, or breathing, is an essential life process for supplying the body with oxygen and for eliminating the waste product, carbon dioxide. The respiratory system involves the nose, pharynx, larynx, trachea, bronchi, lungs, the chest muscles and the diaphragm, the respiratory center in the brain and the blood. Some drugs stimulate the respiratory system; others depress it.

The chief respiratory stimulants are carbon dioxide, caffeine, atropine, Coramine and Metrazol. They act on the respiratory center in the brain and have been mentioned already on pages 360-361, under "Drugs Affecting the Nervous System." They are useful in a variety of respiratory diseases and disorders.

Carbon Dioxide: Carbon dioxide is a gas that increases the capacity of the lungs to take in oxygen and to expel carbon dioxide waste—it deepens breathing. It is used to relieve asphyxia (suffocation) in carbon monoxide poisoning, in preventing postoperative pneumonia and with anesthesia to deepen breathing. It relieves postoperative hiccough—ordinary occasional hiccoughs can be relieved by breathing and rebreathing into a paper bag held tightly over the mouth and nose. Otherwise, carbon dioxide is given by using a face mask attached to a tank of the gas. Overdosage causes difficult breathing (dyspnea), greatly increased movements of the chest and abdomen and increased systolic blood pressure.

Caffeine: Caffeine stimulates the respiratory center. Some authorities believe that other stimulants now available are more effective.

Atropine: Atropine is often given with morphine to counteract the depressing effect of morphine on the respiratory center and to check mucus secretions and prevent spasm of the larynx.

Coramine: Coramine stimulates the respiratory center, increases the rate and depth of respirations and constricts surface blood vessels.

Metrazol: Metrazol stimulates the respiratory center and is especially effective in counteracting barbiturate poisoning.

Respiratory Depressants

Respiratory depression may occur as an undesirable side-effect from the opiates and barbiturates, or from an overconcentration of carbon dioxide in the blood. Strangely enough, carbon dioxide stimulates respiration, but too much of it has the opposite effect.

Drugs To Relieve Cough (Antitussives)

A cough that helps to rid the respiratory passages of irritating substances is helpful and is referred to as *productive*; a *nonproductive* cough is annoying and exhausting.

Narcotic Drugs: Morphine, Levo-Dromoran and dihydromorphinone are potent cough depressants, but they also depress respiration and are habit-forming drugs. Codeine and Hycodan are less effective but have fewer side-effects. Methadone is also effective but is habit-forming.

Non-narcotic Cough Relievers: Other drugs that relieve cough are Nectadon, Toclase and Romilar Hydrobromide. These drugs seem to be as effective as codeine and have few undesirable side-effects.

Cough Syrups: These preparations relieve coughs by forming a protective coating on the mucous membrane of the throat. The most common ones are tolu, acacia, citric acid and glycyrrhiza syrups. A plain syrup, honey or hard candy are home remedies often used for a cough. (Liquids or food should not be given immediately after a cough syrup.) Aromatic substances such as menthol or oil of pine are sometimes added to the water in a steam inhalation for their soothing effect.

Sprays: Nasal sprays containing ephedrine, epinephrine, amphetamine, etc., relieve congestion in nasal mucous membranes. They should be used sparingly as the doctor directs because overspraying may force the infection into the sinuses or middle ear and do more harm than good.

Antiseptics

Antiseptics powerful enough to kill bacteria in nasal or throat infections would injure the mucous membrane. Therefore antibiotics used as sprays, and sulfonamides, such as sulfadiazine, taken internally are used instead.

Expectorants

Certain drugs *increase* the secretion of mucus in the bronchi and help to expel sputum. Among these drugs are ammonium chloride and potassium iodide, 0.3 Gm. (5 gr.), given in a syrup 4 times a day with a full glass of water. The water is important because it helps to increase the flow of mucus to protect the mucous membrane from irritation. These drugs may cause skin eruption, frontal sinus pain or coryza if they are used for a long period of time. Ipecac syrup is a preparation that is also used, especially for children, for bronchitis accompanying croup. The adult dose varies from 1 to 8 ml. The dosage is 5 minims for infants 1 year old, increased slightly for each year of age.

Expectorants used to *decrease* secretions have a healing effect on the irritated lining of the bronchi. Terpin hydrate, an elixir, alone or combined with codeine is such a preparation. The usual dose is 4 ml. (1 fluid dram).

Cold Remedies

Many cold remedies contain atropine, which checks secretion in some types of bronchitis. Authorities are cautious about recommending the wholesale use of these antihistamine drugs, such as Benadryl and Pyribenzamine. These drugs seem to be useful in relieving the sneezing and continuous nasal discharge that accompany cold infections, that is, if they are taken when the first signs of a cold appear. The Council on Drugs of the American Medical Association cautions people about using these drugs indiscriminately because they may cause drowsiness to the extent that the user may fall asleep when driving or manipulating machinery. Prolonged use also may harm the nervous system and the blood-forming tissues.

DRUGS THAT AFFECT THE REPRODUCTIVE SYSTEM

The female reproductive system consists of the ovaries, the fallopian tubes, the uterus and the vagina. The male reproductive organs are the testes, the seminal vesicles, the prostate gland, the bulbourethral glands and the penis. In both male and female the endocrine glands control the reproductive organs to a great extent, through the hormones they secrete. The pituitary gland is especially influential; the ovaries and the testes (the sex glands or *gonads*) are also endocrine glands that secrete hormones that influence secondary sex characteristics. This function and the reproductive function of the sex glands diminishes in middle life and finally ceases. As was stated in Chapter 19, this is the period of the climacteric which in women is accompanied by the cessation of menstruation (menopause).

As hormone production diminishes it often causes a number of unpleasant symptoms which can be relieved by *hormone extracts.* Hormone extracts are used also to supply deficiencies in hormone production that result in retarded sexual development, or to stimulate or to depress the activities of the reproductive organs.

Drugs That Affect the Uterus

The uterus is a muscular organ with great power to expand or contract. The drugs that affect the uterus are those that increase or decrease this power and the sex hormones.

Oxytocics. The drugs used to *increase* uterine contractions are called *oxytocics.* The commonly used ones are preparations of ergot and extracts from pituitary gland hormones. Ergot is a dried portion of a fungus that grows on grain—especially on rye. Preparations of ergot are used to promote the contraction of the uterus to its normal size after childbirth and to constrict the smaller blood vessels to prevent postpartum hemorrhage. Some preparations are:

Ergotrate: Given subcutaneously or intramuscularly immediately after delivery; the usual dose is 0.2 mg., which may be repeated every 4 hours for 6 doses after delivery. Tablets for oral administration are also available.

Methergine: Resembles ergotrate in its action, but it is more powerful, has more prolonged effects and is less likely to raise blood pressure. The usual dose is 0.2 mg. given by injection or by mouth.

SIDE-EFFECTS: Possible side-effects of these drugs are nausea and vomiting, dizziness, headache and diarrhea and abdominal cramps. These are most likely to occur after large doses of the drug, such as in attempted abortion. Severe poisoning may cause gangrene, brain degeneration and blindness.

Posterior Pituitary Hormone Extracts. These preparations are given during childbirth to increase uterine contractions at the time of delivery; they may be given during a long labor when normal contractions fail to expel the fetus. They are also used to contract the uterus and reduce hemorrhage after the placenta is expressed. *Obstetrical* Pituitrin and Pitocin are commonly used preparations available in ampules. The first is given subcutaneously, the second intramuscularly. The usual dosage varies from 0.3 to 1 ml. They are rarely used in the first stage of labor. Patients receiving these drugs *during labor* must be watched closely, with frequent checks of blood pressure and fetal heart tones. Prolonged contractions of the uterus diminish the blood and the oxygen supply of the fetus.

Drugs To Decrease Uterine Contractions. Sometimes it is desirable to relax the muscles to quiet down uterine contractions, as when premature labor threatens or when contractions are rapid and irregular. Large doses of the barbiturates or opiates (morphine, Demerol) are effective. Phenergan relieves fear and enhances the action of morphine when they are given together.

Lutrexin is sometimes used to relax spasmodic tightening of the muscles in dysmenorrhea. Magnesium sulfate given by mouth acts as a cathartic but given intramuscularly or intravenously it depresses muscle activity. It is given to ward off convulsive seizures in eclampsia.

Hormone Extracts That Affect the Sex Glands (Ovaries and Testes)

Certain hormone extracts affect the development and the functions of the female and the male sex glands. Three hormones made by the anterior lobe of the *pituitary gland* (FSH, LH, LTH) are thought to have a definite effect on the functions of the ovary. Two of these hormones also affect the male sex glands. Completely satisfactory preparations of these hormones have not yet been developed; consequently, there are no *officially* approved preparations listed, although some have been used with some success in treating amenorrhea and sterility.

Placental Hormones. During pregnancy the placenta secretes hormones that affect the development of the corpus luteum in the female and the testes in the male, to promote the development of the accessory sex organs. The preparations Follutein and Entromone are used in treating undescended testicles.

Ovarian Hormones. The ovaries themselves secrete 2 important hormones that affect the activity of the sex glands. One of them, the *follicular hormone*, is made up of substances called *estrogens*, that are especially effective in relieving the discomfort of the menopausal disturbances that occur when the ovaries stop functioning. They are also used to relieve engorged breasts when it is desirable to suppress lactation. They have a limited effect in easing discomfort in inoperable breast cancer.

ESTROGEN PREPARATIONS. These preparations are usually given intramuscularly, in doses that vary from a fraction of a milligram to 5 mg. or more, and are given once or twice a week for as long as necessary. Available natural estrogen preparations are: Theelin, Diogyn B, Ovocyclin, Progynon, Estinyl, Depo-Estradiol and Premarin.

The synthetic estrogen preparations are equally effective and are less expensive. Also, they can be given orally. Among those used are diethylstilbestrol, Synestrol, hexestrol and Benzestrol.

Side-Effects. The side-effects of estrogens usually include nausea and vomiting, diarrhea and a skin rash. When these symptoms appear, they are likely to be mild and disappear with an adjustment in the dosage, with the use of another estrogen or with a change in the method of administration. Many doctors believe that estrogens should never be given to women who have had cancer of any part of the reproductive system or have such a family history. The reason is that estrogens are known to cause cancer in animals that have an inherited sensitivity to certain types of cancer.

Progesterone. Progesterone, the *luteal hormone*, is secreted by the corpus luteum which influences the conditions of pregnancy. It prepares the lining of the uterus for the implantation of the ovum and nourishment of the embryo, suppresses ovulation during pregnancy, and reduces the irritability of the uterine muscle. Sometimes it is used for uterine bleeding for which no cause can be found or for menstrual irregularity. It is used also in treating repeated miscarriages (abortion) or to promote fertility.

Preparations. Various preparations of this hormone are available, such as Progestin, Proluton, Lutocyclol, Provera, Norlutin and Delalutin. They seem to have few serious side-effects; some patients complain of headache, dizziness and allergic reactions. Most of these preparations are available in tablet form and can be taken orally. The dosage varies from 5 to 25 mg. or more, taken daily.

The Androgens (Male Sex Hormones). The androgens are essential for the development of male sex characteristics, and for maintaining normal conditions in the sex organs. Androgen preparations are given to supply a hormone that is missing. Both men and women produce male and female hormones but their effect on men is opposite to the effect on women and vice versa. They are used in treating male reproductive organ deficiencies, disturbances during the male climacteric and in women, for dysmenorrhea and to suppress lactation. Androgens are also used for temporary relief in advanced inoperable breast cancer.

Preparations. Testosterone can be given by injection or by mouth. The dosage varies from 10 to 60 mg. several times a week as needed.

Other preparations of testosterone or similar to it are Oreton, Delatestryl, Neodrol and Halotestin.

Side-Effects. Undesirable effects on a woman are the development of such masculine characteristics as a deep voice, excessive body hair and shrunken breasts. General and more serious effects may be edema, caused by an accumulation of salts and water in the body, which may lead to heart failure in either sex. Androgens are never given to patients with prostatic cancer.

DRUGS USED TO TREAT EYE CONDITIONS

Drugs that affect the eye are used to treat eye infections and irritations, to dilate or to contract the pupil, to prevent or to relieve pain or to reduce pressure in the eye. Some of these drugs produce their effects through their action on the autonomic nervous system by relaxing and contracting smooth muscle; others act directly on the tissues.

Pupil Dilators

Atropine is used to dilate the pupil of the eye to examine the interior of the eye, to determine the needed strength of lenses for glasses (refraction), or to rest inflamed or irritated eyes. It is a powerful drug which is used in small amounts to avoid such toxic effects as excessive mouth dryness, fever and rapid heart action, which may extend to acute glaucoma and blindness. Atropine is used in 0.5, 1 and 3 per cent solutions.

The effects of atropine on the eye may last for a week or more; the patient should be told that objects will appear blurred and out of focus for a time until the effects of the drug disappear.

Scopolamine (hyoscine) resembles atropine in its effect on the eye. Homatropine is an atropine preparation that has shorter-lasting effects (24 hours). Cyclogyl acts rapidly but its action is brief; it is especially useful for an eye examination or refraction. Eupthalmine dilates the pupil for a few hours only.

Epinephrine (Adrenalin) is used in dilute solutions to treat eye allergies. A concentrated preparation (Epitrate) is used to treat certain types of glaucoma. Neo-Synephrine is used for eye examinations.

Eye Anesthetics

Local anesthetics (injected or applied locally) are used to prevent pain in eye examinations or eye operations. They should not be used repeatedly for painful or irritated eyes because they will injure the cornea. Cocaine and Opthaine are some commonly used preparations.

Antibiotics

Eye infections can be treated with whatever antibiotics are effective against the microorganism causing the infection. Some of the antibiotics used in solutions and ointments are tetracycline, streptomycin, bacitracin, neomycin, gantrisin and others. Antiseptics are generally conceded to be of little use in eye treatments except as cleansers.

Antiseptic solutions are used for eye irrigations. Among those used are silver nitrate, metaphen and merthiolate solutions.

Drugs in Glaucoma

Glaucoma is caused by an abnormally high production of the fluid in the eye (aqueous humor) making pressure on the eyeball. Some drugs used to reduce the production of this fluid are dichlorphenamide, echothiopate iodide, D.F.P., Neptazane, Diamox, Cardrase, and Daranide. Some of them are given orally; others are used as eye drops.

For Contact Lenses

A solution of benzalkonium chloride is used in cleaning and inserting contact lenses.

DRUGS USED IN TREATING ALLERGIC REACTIONS AND MOTION SICKNESS

In allergic reactions an excessive amount of a substance which is stored in the body (*histamine*) is released into the tissues to cause itching, swelling and other irritations. In severe reactions it causes breathing difficulties (asthma). The antihistamine drugs help to counteract and prevent these unpleasant effects.

The Antihistamines

The antihistamines are most effective in relieving the discomfort of the sneezing, dripping victim of hay fever or other pollen-caused irritations. These drugs will not cure an allergy, but they do bring temporary relief and comfort.

The most common unpleasant side-effect is drowsiness, which may progress to deep sleep. Other side-effects may be mouth and throat dryness, uncertain muscular coordination and muscular weakness.

Preparations. Some of the most commonly used antihistamine preparations are:

Antazoline: Nose drops, spray, oral, 50 to 100 mg., 3 times a day (or more)

Pyribenzamine: Oral, spray or nose drops, 50 mg., 3 times a day

Benadryl: Oral, spray, 25 to 50 mg., 3 or 4 times a day (causes drowsiness)

Coricidin: Oral, 2 to 8 mg. (enteric-coated tablet with prolonged effect)

Antihistamines in Motion Sickness. Many of the antihistamines are effective in preventing and relieving motion sickness. They are also used to control nausea and vomiting and dizziness in ear conditions, such as fenestration surgery (a delicate operation for deafness) and Meniere's disease. Among those used are:

Marezine Hydrochloride: Oral, rectal, 50 mg. ½ hour before a trip (repeated 3 times a day if necessary)

Dramamine: Oral, rectal, intramuscular, 50 mg., 30 minutes before departure, up to 100 mg., every 4 hours for nausea and vomiting

Drugs Used in Treating Asthma

Certain drugs relieve bronchial spasms and edema in asthmatic attacks. Ephedrine, epinephrine, aminophylline, the nitrites and belladonna have been discussed previously under their specific therapeutic uses.

Drugs used to treat lung infections (PAS, INH, streptomycin, etc.) are discussed in Chapter 39.

OXYGEN THERAPY

Oxygen is used to reinforce the oxygen supply in the blood in such conditions as (1) pneumonia, (2) carbon monoxide gas poisoning, (3) severe asthma, (4) heart failure, (5) respiratory failure in nervous system injuries and (6) severe abdominal distention caused by bowel paralysis.

The body's supply of oxygen normally is obtained from the air—air is 20 per cent oxygen. In some types of illness, the body is unable to take in enough oxygen or cannot use it effectively. This is true in respiratory diseases, heart diseases, asphyxia, shock, etc. The tissue cells must have a constant supply of oxygen to live, since oxygen is not stored in the body. If the lungs are not taking in enough air to provide this supply, oxygen can be given to increase the amount. The signs of oxygen shortage are rapid and shallow respirations, rapid pulse, cyanosis and restlessness.

Oxygen makes the patient more comfortable; he breathes easier; his pulse rate drops and he takes food more readily. The cooperation of the patient is highly important in oxygen therapy. He is likely to be apprehensive and worried about the treatment and especially fearful of apparatus that covers his nose and mouth.

Face Mask. The advantages of using a face mask are several: it is not irritating, it provides the best concentration of oxygen, it does not interfere with nursing care, it does not give the patient a feeling of being "shut in" as a tent may do. The main disadvantage is that oxygen must be discontinued when the patient eats or drinks if the mask covers both the mouth and the nose.

The mask should fit properly to prevent loss of oxygen; pressure on the face should be relieved by thin pads if necessary. The mask should be removed at regular intervals and washed and dried. The patient's face should also receive this attention.

Nasal Catheter. The nasal catheter has many of the advantages of the face mask in allowing the patient freer motion than the tent. However, it may become irritating to the nose and the nostrils may become dry, or an irrational patient may pull the catheter out. It is not possible to determine the concentration of oxygen as easily when a catheter is used. The catheter should be changed at least every 8 hours, and more often if necessary, and if possible, it should be alternated from one nostril to the other. Another device, the nasal cannula, has 2 short tubes, one for each nostril, instead of the single catheter. The catheter should be washed and sterilized before it is reinserted.

Oxygen Tent. The oxygen tent is made from rubberized fabric or transparent plastic material. The latter has distinct advantages because it gives the patient less of a shut-in feeling and he is clearly visible to the nurses. One type of tent covers the entire bed; the one most frequently used covers only the upper third of the bed. The tent provides a cool, humidified atmosphere and the patient's movements are restricted to the extent that he must not be allowed to displace the tucked-in edges of the tent. These edges must be tucked in closely to preserve oxygen concentration. The tent is the most expensive method of giving oxygen.

Regulation. In oxygen therapy, it is important to maintain the prescribed liter flow, understand how to operate the regulator and keep the patient as comfortable as possible. When oxygen therapy is discontinued, it should be done gradually, allowing the patient to be without it for short periods at a time. He should be watched closely. If he shows signs of difficulty with breathing, becomes pale or cyanotic, if his pulse rate goes up or he complains of pain in his chest or of fatigue, oxygen should be resumed at once even though the allotted time is not up.

An explanation of the treatment, reassurance about his breathing and the relief that oxygen will give him are essential in oxygen therapy.

Equipment. Oxygen is stored in tanks or cylinders and is furnished by oxygen firms. Many hospitals are equipped with an oxygen piping system. Oxygen equipment is available for use in private homes. In some hospitals, an oxygen therapy technician is responsible for oxygen apparatus; he sets it up, keeps it in working order, inspects it while it is in use and cleans and stores it. Otherwise, the nurse is responsible. Practical nurses are assisting professional nurses in the care of patients who are having oxygen therapy and are wholly responsible for oxygen therapy in the home. They should know how oxygen is administered and how the apparatus works.

Precautions. Everyone should know the precautions that must be taken when oxygen is used—the patient, his visitors and other patients in the same unit. Oxygen *by itself* cannot burn; but if oxygen comes in contact with anything that is burning, even so small as a spark, the result is a fire of almost explosive violence.

1. Explain the dangers of lighting matches, smoking cigarettes or pipes. Be sure the patient has no matches or cigarettes in his bedside table.
2. Warning signs should be posted on the patient's door or bed: (OXYGEN—NO SMOKING).
3. Electrical devices, such as heating pads, electric blankets or the ordinary signal light must not be used. Some hospitals provide a special kind of signal light which has a grounding device.
4. Oil must not be used on the oxygen regulator because oil can ignite by itself if it is exposed to oxygen. The nurse should be sure there are no traces of oil on her hands before she adjusts oxygen apparatus.
5. Woolen blankets should never be used; nylon or rayon clothing never permitted. Static electricity from these materials may cause an explosion. For this reason many hospitals require nurses to wear cotton uniforms.

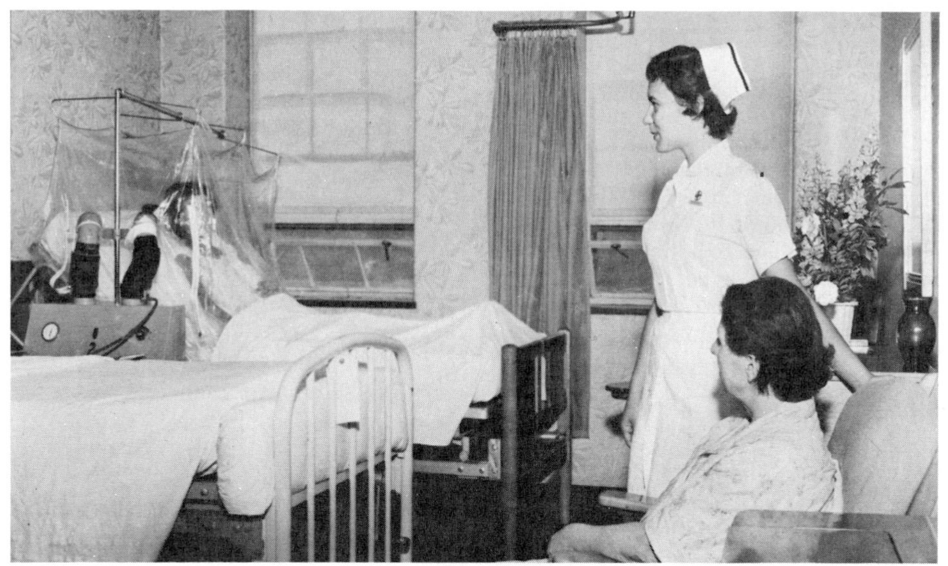

FIG. 124. Helping the patient and his visitors to understand the precautions necessary when oxygen is in use is essential. Very often patients in the same unit need cautious explanations of their restrictions in order not to make them apprehensive. The nurse's manner of interpreting matters of patient care or agency regulations can be a very effective public relations device. (Fuerst, E. V., and Wolff, L.: Fundamentals of Nursing, ed. 3, p. 485, Philadelphia, Lippincott, 1964)

FIG. 125. The regulation apparatus which is attached to the top of the oxygen supply tank gives an easily readable record of both the amount of oxygen in the tank and the rate at which it is being dispensed. By passing the oxygen through the humidifier, patient discomfort is alleviated. Many hospitals use the humidifier as a routine measure. (Linde Company, Division of Union Carbide Corporation)

Methods of Administration. Oxygen can be administered by face mask, nasal catheter, cannula or oxygen tent. The method chosen depends on the patient's condition, the facilities available for giving oxygen, the concentration needed and the method preferred by the patient and the doctor. Any method requires an oxygen cylinder and a reducing gauge. Oxygen is given in different concentrations, measured by the flow of liters per minute. Concentration may vary from 50 to 100 per cent. In giving oxygen to premature babies it is extremely important to give it in low concentrations and only when absolutely necessary. High concentrations of oxygen can damage the retina in the eye of a premature baby.

EQUIPMENT

Oxygen cylinder or piping system
Regulator—reduces high pressure of oxygen coming from cylinder and controls oxygen flow
Gauges (2)—Oxygen contents gauge (attached to regulator) shows how much oxygen is in cylinder. Liter-flow gauge (attached to regulator) shows flow of liters per minute.

PROCEDURE FOR PREPARING EQUIPMENT FOR USE

Remove the protective cap from cylinder.

With the outlet pointing away from you, open the cylinder valve a *very little* and close it *quickly*. This blows away any dust that may be in the valve opening.

Insert the regulator inlet into the valve opening and tighten the nut with the wrench.

Loosen the flow-adjusting handle on the regulator. This must be done before opening the valve on top of the cylinder.

Open the cylinder valve very slowly until the needle on the nearest gauge stops moving.

Tighten the flow-adjusting handle (turn to right, clockwise) until prescribed flow of liters per minute is registered on the liter-flow gauge.

Loosen the flow-adjusting handle (turn left, counterclockwise) until needle on the liter-flow gauge returns to zero. Now you are ready to connect the oxygen equipment to the face mask, catheter or oxygen tent.

When the oxygen is to be discontinued for 30 minutes or more, or an empty cylinder must be replaced with a full one, follow this procedure:

Close the cylinder valve.

When needles on both gauges have returned to zero, loosen the flow-adjusting handle until it moves freely.

Disconnect the regulator from the cylinder by unscrewing inlet nut with the wrench.

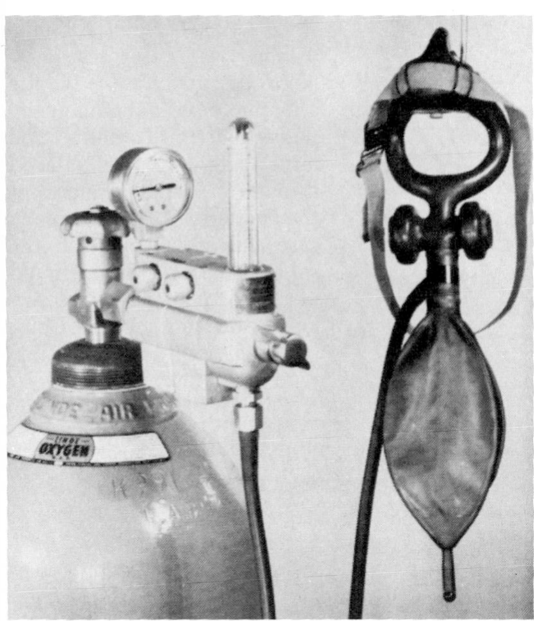

FIG. 126. Open-type face mask for the administration of oxygen. (Linde Company, Division of Union Carbide Corporation)

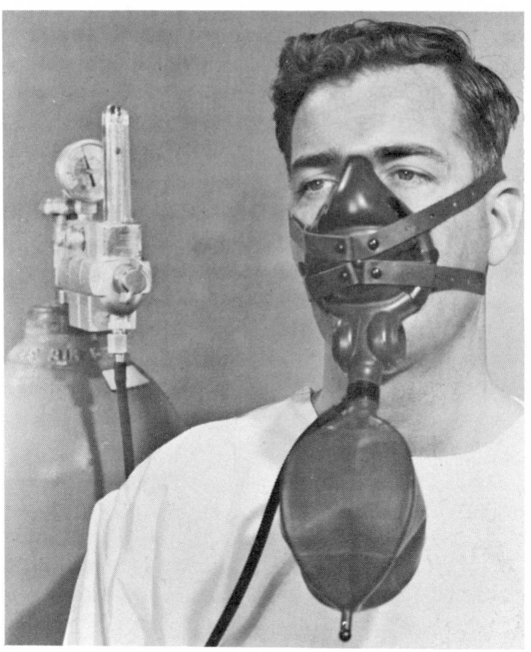

FIG. 127. Closed type face mask, including the rebreathing bag, for the administration of oxygen. (Linde Company, Division of Union Carbide Corporation)

GIVING OXYGEN WITH A FACE MASK

EQUIPMENT

Face mask—There are 2 kinds, one which covers the nose and one which covers both mouth and nose. The mask is attached to a breathing bag and tubing. Part of the exhaled air stays in the breathing bag and is rebreathed.

PROCEDURE

Attach the end of the rubber tubing to the outlet of the regulator (below the liter-flow gauge).

Turn the regulator handle until the needle on the liter-flow gauge registers a flow of 10 to 12 liters per minute.

Apply the mask to the patient's face, asking him to exhale as it is applied.

When first deep and rapid breathing subsides, adjust the oxygen flow so that the breathing bag almost but not quite collapses when the patient inhales. This allows a flow of from 6 to 8 liters per minute.

GIVING OXYGEN WITH A CATHETER

EQUIPMENT

Rubber catheter (size No. 8, Fr. to 10, Fr. for children, No. 12, Fr. to 14, Fr. for adults)
Rubber tubing (5 feet)
Connector to attach catheter to tubing
Lubricant
Humidifier
Adapter

PROCEDURE

Attach catheter to one end of the rubber tubing with the adapter. Attach the other end of the tubing to the humidifier.

Attach the humidifier to the oxygen regulator.

Measure on the catheter the distance from the tip of the nose to the lobe of the ear and mark it with adhesive tape.

At the taped mark, hold the catheter be-

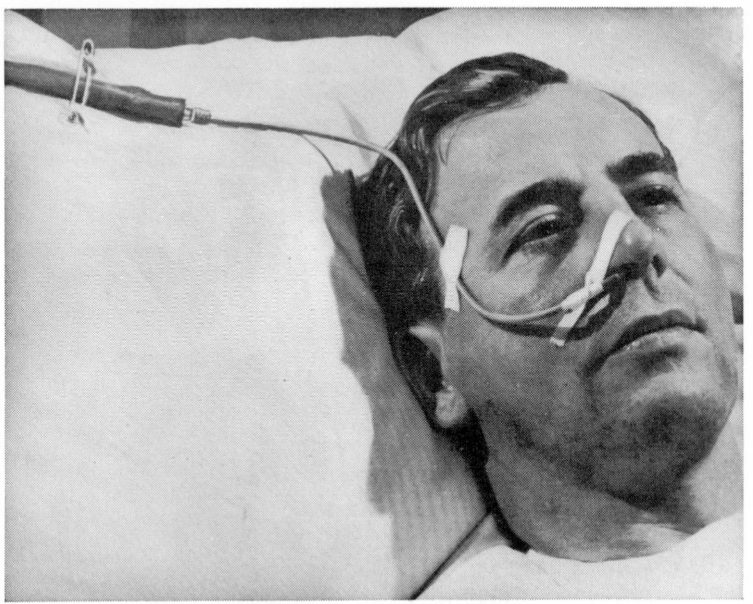

Fig. 128. Oxygen administration via nasal catheter. Note the placement of the adhesive tape to maintain the position of the catheter. The large safety pin is placed through a small amount of the material of the pillowcase on either side of the rubber tubing. Care should be taken to prevent puncturing the tubing. (Linde Company, Division of Union Carbide Corporation)

tween the thumb and the forefinger to determine natural "droop" of the catheter.

Adjust the flow of oxygen to about 3 liters per minute.

Lubricate the catheter lightly while oxygen

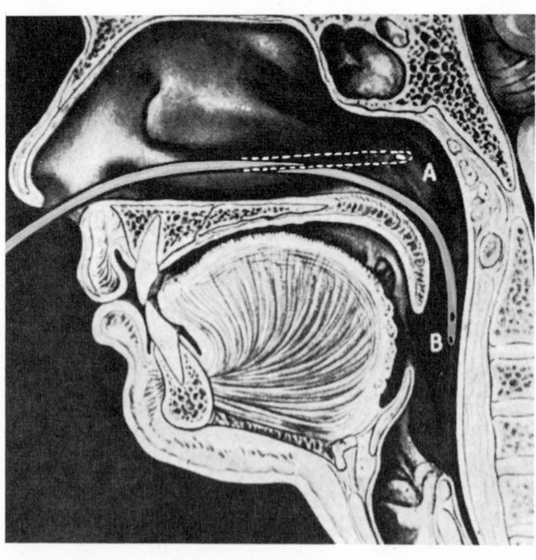

Fig. 129. Position of catheter in: (A) nasopharynx, (B) oropharynx. (Barach, A. L.: Physiologic Therapy in Respiratory Diseases, p. 320, Philadelphia, Lippincott)

is flowing; hold the tip in a glass of water to be sure that the holes are open.

Grasp the catheter at the taped mark between the thumb and the forefinger and slowly rotate it until the tip hangs at its lowest level.

With the oxygen flowing, elevate the tip of the nose and insert the catheter slowly in the nostril to the mark.

To make sure that the catheter is placed correctly, insert it slightly beyond the mark until the patient has swallowed a gulp of oxygen; then draw it back until he no longer swallows (about ¼ inch).

Tape the catheter over the end of the nose and on the forehead with strips of adhesive. It may be taped to the cheek and brought over toward the ear and taped to the side of the face if the patient prefers.

Increase the oxygen flow up to 4 to 6 liters per minute, or as the doctor orders.

Pin the tubing to the pillow or back of the mattress, leaving enough slack so that the patient can move his head without displacing the catheter.

Be sure that the patient is comfortable and his call bell is within reach before you leave him.

Check the humidifier at regular intervals

and add water when necessary. Turn off the oxygen before adding water and fill the humidifier quickly so that the patient will be without oxygen for the least possible time.

Giving Oxygen in a Tent

EQUIPMENT

Motor-driven or motorless tent
Canopy to cover the patient (rubberized fabric or plastic film)
Cabinet connected to a supply of oxygen

PROCEDURE

Check the tent outside of the patient's room to make sure that the unit is complete; fill the cabinet with chunks of ice (size of a grapefruit). The newer models have a self-contained refrigeration unit. No ice is necessary.

Bring the tent to the bedside and explain what you do as you go along (you have already talked to the patient about the treatment). Put a wrap around the patient's shoulders.

Turn on the flow of oxygen; adjust the canopy over the patient, keeping it from touching his face. Tuck the canopy in as far as possible under the mattress at the head and the sides of the bed. Make a wide double cuff with a sheet or bath blanket and tuck the remaining edge of the canopy into it and tuck the ends of the sheet under the mattress.

Raise the oxygen flow to 15 liters per minute and keep it there for about 15 minutes. Then analyze the atmosphere within the tent to be sure that the patient is getting the right concentration of oxygen. Usually 50 per cent is prescribed.

Put a drain bucket in place and open the water drain, if necessary.

Check the thermometer in the tent to be sure that the temperature is not too cold for the patient. If he is cold, give him an extra wrap and turn the temperature control to medium or warm.

After analyzing the oxygen content in the tent, if the concentration of oxygen is as prescribed, reduce the liter flow to between 6 to 10 liters per minute.

Be sure the patient has his call bell before you leave him.

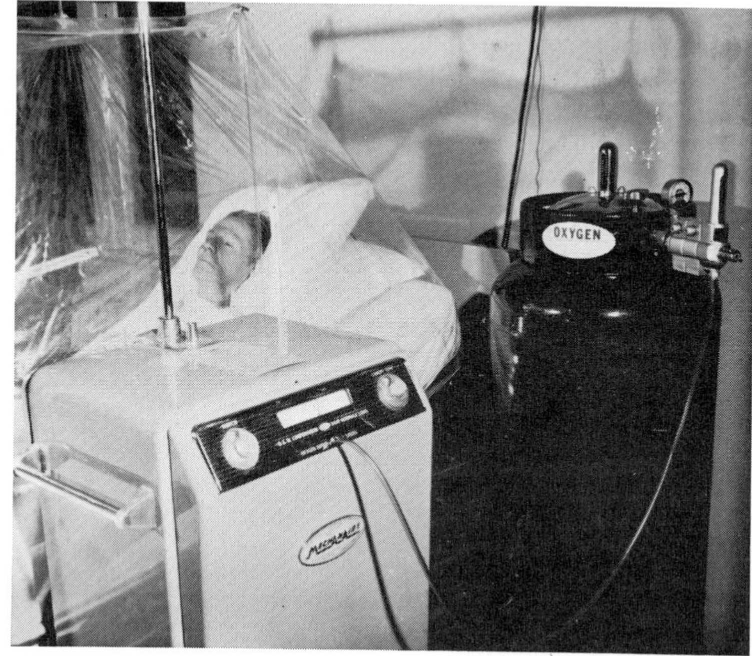

Fig. 130. Use of the oxygen tent with the automatic humidification and refrigeration apparatus in the care of the bedfast patient. The clear plastic canopy enables the nurse to make frequent visual checks of the patient and also helps to prevent the "closed-in" feeling of which the patient sometimes complains. (Linde Company, Division of Union Carbide Corporation)

The air within the tent should be analyzed regularly (every 3 or 4 hours) and after the canopy has been opened for treatments or examinations. When the tent is no longer needed, it should be washed with soap and water and aired before storing it. Handle the canopy carefully—do not fold it. Tears in plastic material can be mended with cellophane tape. Use adhesive tape to mend rubberized material.

DRUGS TO DESTROY PARASITES

Anthelmintics (meaning against worms) are drugs used to expel worms (*helminths*) from the body. Worms may infect the intestinal tract, muscle tissue, the blood and other parts of the body. The successful treatment of worms depends on the recognition of the type of worm that is present, then selecting the most effective drug and observing the results.

Aspidium (Male Fern)

Aspidium, a green liquid with an unpleasant taste, paralyzes worms so that they then can be expelled with the aid of a cathartic. It is effective for pork and fish tapeworms. The patients' dinner and supper are omitted and he is given a saline cathartic in the evening. The next day he is given the drug on an empty stomach, in divided doses an hour apart. It is usually given in enteric-coated capsules. Two hours after the last dose he has another saline cathartic, and this is followed in 2 hours by a soapsuds enema. As soon as the cathartic is effective, he can resume eating.

Every bit of stool must be saved—this is very important to see if the head of the worm has come through. If not, the worm will grow again, and the treatment will have to be repeated.

Aspidium is toxic if much of it is absorbed by the intestine, which is an additional reason for giving cathartics and enemas to remove it. This drug is not used for children.

Quinacrine (Atabrine)

One dose of quinacrine usually eliminates a beef tapeworm; this drug is effective also for pork and fish tapeworm. It is preceded by a saline cathartic and no food. It may cause gastric irritation—usually sodium bicarbonate is given with it to prevent nausea and vomiting. Quinacrine is effective also in treating malaria, another parasitic infection.

Piperazine Preparations

These drugs are effective in destroying roundworms and pinworms. They are more effective on the mature worms than on the newly-hatched; therefore, a course of treatment of a week or more may need to be repeated a week after the first one. Some of the preparations used are Piperat, Antepar, Perin, Hetrazan. The advantages of these drugs are that it is not necessary to go without food or take cathartics while they are being given.

Hexylresorcinol

This drug paralyzes roundworm, pinworm, hookworm and dwarf tapeworm. Often, a single dose is effective; if necessary, the procedure can be repeated in 3 or 4 days. A saline cathartic is given before and after and no food is allowed during the treatment.

The following is a brief summary of the preparations used in treating the various types of worms:

Tapeworms: Aspidium, quinacrine, hexylresorcinol

Roundworms and Whipworms: Dithiazanine, piperazine salts, diethylcarbamazine

Pinworms: Hexylresorcinol, dithiazanine, gentian violet—pinworms deposit their eggs around the anus so this region should be kept clean

Hookworms: Tetrachloroethylene, hexylresorcinol

Amebiasis

Amebiasis is caused by intestinal parasites called *amebae*. They destroy tissues outside of the intestine, in the parts of the body where they choose to locate, such as in the liver or spleen, and also in the intestine itself. Drugs used to treat amebiasis in the intestine are

Carbarson, Milibis, Balarsen, Diodoquin, Vioform and others. The antibiotic Fumidil is also effective.

For amebiasis outside of the intestine, Emetine is the most effective in controlling amebic dysentery. It is used extensively in treating amebic hepatitis and liver abscess. Undesirable side-effects are degenerative changes in the liver, kidney, heart and muscles. Aralen is another effective drug in treating amebic hepatitis and amebic abscess.

SERUMS AND VACCINES AS DRUGS

The part played by serum and vaccines in preventing or treating disease has been emphasized in the discussion of immunity (see Chap. 52). Specific serums and vaccines are mentioned also in connection with specific disease conditions in which they are used.

Serums

There are two kinds of serums—immune and antitoxic. Immune serums are obtained from normal blood or from the blood of people who have recovered from a disease. They are used to prevent the disease in others. Examples are the human serums used to prevent measles, infectious hepatitis, whooping cough and poliomyelitis. Examples of these serums are immune serum globulin, human gamma globulin and pertussis human serum.

Antitoxins (Antitoxic Serums)

Antitoxic serums are produced in the bodies of animals. They are given to neutralize the poisons produced in the bodies of people by certain diseases. These serums are the diphtheria, tetanus and gas gangrene antitoxins.

Vaccines

Vaccines are preparations of disease organisms (which have been killed) that produce immunity to infectious disease. It may take several weeks for immunity to develop; sometimes, if an effective human serum is available, a dose of the serum is given first to insure immediate protection from a disease. This might be done when there is danger of immediate infection, as when many cases of an infectious disease appear in a community and individuals run the risk of being exposed to it.

Vaccines are available to prevent or to treat mumps, whooping cough, typhoid, yellow fever, smallpox, rabies, tuberculosis, influenza and poliomyelitis. Polio vaccine (the Salk vaccine) has practically eliminated poliomyelitis in this country (see Chap. 43); however, there is some doubt about the effectiveness of the influenza vaccines now being used.

Toxoids

Certain infectious conditions produce poisons (toxins) in the body. *Toxoids* are toxins with the poisonous effects modified to make them nontoxic but still capable of building up immunity to a disease. Toxoids are effective in building up immunity to diphtheria and tetanus. They are used separately or in various combinations with whooping cough vaccine—a combination of the three (*triple toxoid*) is the choice for immunizing children.

Immunity Tests

Tests can be done to determine whether or not a person is susceptible to certain disease organisms. A small amount of the toxin produced by a disease is injected intracutaneously on the forearm. If his body has not produced enough antitoxin to protect him from the disease, a reddened area appears around the point of the injection—a positive reaction. *Schick test toxin* is available to test diphtheria susceptibility.

A positive reaction to a test with *old tuberculin* will show whether or not a person has had tuberculosis at some time, but it does not necessarily mean that the person has active tuberculosis at the time of the test.

ENZYMES AS DRUGS

Enzymes are substances that speed up chemical reactions in the body without being changed themselves during the process. Used as drugs, they help to promote the absorption of fluids or drugs, to reduce thick, purulent discharges to thin fluids and to dissolve blood clots. They also destroy certain toxins or allergens. Some enzyme preparations in current use are Alidase, Wydase, Trypsin (Tryptar), Varidase and Chymar. Penicillinase (neutrapen) is effective in treating a penicillin reaction by "pulling the teeth" of the allergen that is causing the trouble.

VITAMINS, MINERALS AND HORMONES AS DRUGS

The body does not always have enough of every substance necessary to keep it healthy; therefore, these deficiencies must be supplied. Also, these substances are sometimes given in large amounts to produce a desired effect in disease. In this sense they are considered drugs. The uses of specific vitamins, minerals and hormones in treating body disturbances are discussed under the individual body systems affected. Information about their general effects is presented here.

Vitamins

People depend on food to supply the body with the vitamins needed to maintain body processes. A balanced diet provides the essential vitamins. An inadequate diet causes vitamin deficiencies that can be replenished by giving vitamin preparations. Elderly people with poor eating habits often resist attempts to change these habits, so it is simpler to add the necessary vitamins to their food. Additional vitamins may be needed in pregnancy, in infections or by rapidly growing children and young people.

Vitamins and Health. The discovery that vitamins are essential for health opened the market to a flood of proprietary vitamin preparations. The trouble is that many of these preparations contain either more or less of an individual vitamin (or vitamins) than is needed to meet normal requirements or to remedy a deficiency.

The sale of proprietary vitamin preparations, especially the multivitamins, has become a multimillion dollar business in this country; even normally healthy people have been led to believe that taking vitamins will make them healthier. The truth is that the body absorbs only enough of any vitamin to meet its daily vitamin needs and some vitamins are not stored in the body. This wholesale consumption of vitamin preparations puts vitamins in the class of drugs.

The U.S.P. and the World Health Organization have established official standards for stating the vitamin content of vitamin preparations in milligrams, except for vitamins A and D, which is stated in units.

Vitamins as Drugs. The place of vitamins in nutrition has been discussed in Chapter 22. Some uses of vitamins in treating body disorders or diseases are:

Vitamin A: Used for night blindness, softening of the cornea, hardening of the cells in the outer skin. Vitamin A is often combined with vitamin D in preparations such as Oleovitamin and Oleovitamin A and D capsules, Cod Liver Oil and Halibut Oil.

Vitamin D: Used for prevention of rickets, to promote bone healing in fractures (especially in older people), for tuberculosis of the skin, for psoriasis and to prevent cataract. Preparations used are Calciferol, vitamin D_2, vitamin D_3, Viosterol and Hykaterol. People who live in a climate with very little sunshine need vitamin D supplements.

Vitamin B Complex (Thiamine, Riboflavin, Nicotinic Acid, etc): Thiamine (Thiamine Hydrochloride, Aneurine Hydrochloride, Dried Yeast Tablets) is used to prevent beriberi and to treat polyneuritis. Riboflavin (Lactoflavin) and Hyflavin are used to prevent deficiencies and are combined with niacin to treat pellagra.

Nicotinic Acid (Niacin): Used with riboflavin and thiamine to treat pellagra. Some preparations are Nicotinic Acid (Niacin) and Nicotinamide.

Vitamin B_6 (Beadox): Used to treat nausea and vomiting in pregnancy and for irradiation sickness.

Biotin: Used to counteract the effects of large amounts of egg white in the diet which cause fever, malaise and dermatitis.

Vitamin C (Ascorbic Acid): Used to prevent scurvy. Heat destroys vitamin C and it should be added to a baby's formula *after* the formula is heated.

Vitamin preparations may be given orally, intramuscularly or intravenously. They have few, if any, toxic effects. They are given for conditions caused by vitamin deficiencies or to prevent these conditions. The dosage is determined by individual needs.

Minerals

About 70 per cent of the body is water, since water fills the cells and the spaces between the cells and makes up the main part of the blood stream. Substances derived from minerals (the electrolytes) are essential to maintain the proper proportions of fluid in and around the cells and in the blood stream—the fluid balance in the body. (See Chap. 33.)

Dehydration. Vomiting, diarrhea and profuse sweating not only deplete the body's water supply but they also cause an electrolyte loss. These losses result in dehydration. This condition cannot be corrected simply by drinking large quantities of water—the mineral loss also must be replaced. For instance, unless the excessive loss of salt is replaced, it can cause muscular pains and spasms and may cause convulsions.

The necessary minerals are supplied by giving preparations of sodium, potassium and calcium. Certain minerals are essential in treating disease; sodium is needed in Addison's disease or in loss of gastric secretions. Potassium must be supplied in some metabolic diseases and in kidney diseases. Extra calcium is most likely to be needed during pregnancy, for nursing mothers and for parathyroid deficiency. Calcium is also necessary for bone growth and to regulate muscle and nerve activities.

Sodium Chloride Solution (Sodium Chloride Tablets): Has a higher concentration of salt than does the blood (hypertonic) and is given to supply a sodium deficiency. If quick action is needed the solution is given intravenously.

Potassium Chloride (Solution or Tablets): Prepared for oral or intravenous use. When given intravenously, it is important to control the amount very carefully; an excessive amount of potassium can stop the heart.

Calcium Chloride: Available in capsule or liquid form. When given intravenously, care must be taken to prevent the needle from slipping out of the vein—calcium is very irritating when it is injected into the tissues.

Calcium Lactate: Given orally, dissolved in hot water. It does not dissolve readily in cold water.

Calcium Gluconate: Can be taken orally or by injection.

Hormones

Hormones have been discussed in preceding chapters as substances secreted into the blood stream by the endocrine glands. They affect many tissues and organs and help to regulate body processes—for example, body growth and growth and development of the sex organs. Hormone extracts are given when an endocrine gland does not produce enough hormone to meet body needs or for their effects in certain disease conditions. The uses of individual hormone extracts are discussed with other drugs used in treating disorders of the various body systems.

Important Hormones and Their Effects on the Body

Anterior Pituitary Hormones

Somatotropin: Influences body growth and development. Its use is still experimental.

LH or ICSH: Influences the development of the corpus luteum and ovulation in women; in men, it influences sperm production and development of the sex organs.

Luteotropic Hormone: Necessary for the production of progesterone and influential in mammary gland secretion.

Thyrotropic Hormone: Necessary for the development and function of the thyroid gland.

ACTH: Stimulates the adrenal cortex and has many of the same uses as cortisone. Preparations are Corticotropin Gel, Acthar.

Posterior Pituitary Hormones

Vasopressin (Pitressin): Stimulates muscle in superficial blood vessels and in the gastrointestinal tract.

Oxytoxin: Stimulates uterine muscle.

ADH (antidiuretic hormone): Reduces the amount of urine in diabetes insipidus.

THYROID HORMONES

Thyroid and "T3": Used to treat cretinism and myxedema—conditions caused by thyroid deficiency. An adequate amount of iodine in the body is necessary for the effectiveness of these hormones. Preparations are thyroid, Synthroid Sodium and Cytomel.

ANTITHYROID DRUGS. Some drugs are used to check overactivity of the thyroid hormones. They are the iodides and are given to hyperthyroid patients before the surgical removal of the thyroid gland (thyroidectomy). Preparations are Lugol's Solution, sodium iodide, potassium iodide solution. Muracil, Tapazole and Methiocil have similar effects.

PARATHYROID HORMONE

Parathyroid Injection: Usually given with calcium salts to relieve the twitching muscle spasms or convulsions in tetany (a disease caused by calcium deficiency).

ADRENAL HORMONES

Epinephrine: Used to check capillary bleeding, to relieve spasms in bronchial asthma, to relieve symptoms in allergic reactions and as a heart stimulant. Preparations are solutions of epinephrine and of adrenalin. These solutions do not keep well—sediment and brownish discoloration indicate that the solution should be discarded.

Cortisone and Hydrocortisone: Used in Addison's disease, in allergic reactions and in rheumatoid arthritis. Preparations are Cortone, Cortril, Cortef, Sterane, Medrol and Meticortren.

Insulin. Insulin is a pancreatic hormone that controls carbohydrate metabolism. Its main use is in treating diabetes mellitus which is discussed under "Diabetes," Chapter 42. It is used also to produce insulin shock in shock therapy treatment for the mentally ill patient.

DRUGS USED IN TREATING CANCER

So far, no drug has been found that will cure cancer—only early surgery and x-ray will do that and then only if all of a cancerous growth is removed before the cancer cells have been carried to another part of the body (metastasis). However, antimalignant (antineoplastic) drugs help to retard the progress of malignant disease that has spread to another part of the body and help to make the patient more comfortable, sometimes for months and even years. These drugs are used specifically to treat malignant tumors and cancerous conditions of the blood (leukemia), the bone marrow and the spleen. They are used only when there is no hope of recovery because they affect healthy cells as well as malignant ones; they also are harmful to bone marrow and lower the patient's resistance to infection.

Some of the drugs that are known to be palliative in metastatic cancer are listed here. Experimental work is constantly going on in the search for a drug that will cure cancer. Thousands of drugs are being tested every year under the direction of the National Cancer Institute of the U. S. Public Health Service, in cooperation with hospitals, research centers, industry and government. Every year a number of drugs are approved for testing with patients, but so far, none of the drugs tested has given indisputable scientific proof that it cures cancer.

Nitrogen Mustards

Nitrogen mustard preparations help to make a patient more comfortable by relieving pain and itching, improving appetite and strength and reducing an enlarged spleen. Their effects may last anywhere from a few weeks to several months. One of them, Mustargen, is used in treating some chronic leukemias, lymphatic sarcoma and Hodgkin's disease (a disease of the lymphatic system). It is most effective after the disease has become generalized and before it has reached the terminal stages. It is usually given intravenously and the dosage is calculated very carefully in relation to body weight, since too much may cause thrombosis, phlebitis or a decrease in blood cells. It is also very irritating if it gets on the skin or mucous membranes.

Other preparations have similar effects, although some of them have fewer side-effects or are more effective in one condition than another. Some of these preparations are Leukeran, Cytoxan, Myleran and TEM.

Aminopterin is used to treat acute leukemia in children. Other drugs especially effective for children are Purinethol and Methotrexate. In inoperable cancer of the rectum, sigmoid and colon or for advanced breast cancer, 5-Fluoracil (5-FU) is effective.

Some hormone preparations, such as ACTH, prednisone and some of the androgens and estrogens that inhibit cancer growth are discussed more fully elsewhere.

Radioactive Isotopes

These are radioactive substances that give off rays that penetrate tissues and arrest the growth of cancer cells. They affect the cells of the ovaries and the testes particularly, as well as the lymphocytes and the bone marrow, and they act on cells in the intestinal tract to reduce accumulations of fluid. Patients undergoing this treatment are likely to be troubled with nausea and vomiting and diarrhea.

Precautions are necessary in handling isotopes, as their rays damage normal tissues, such as the skin, and cause radiation burns. (See Chap. 37.) The rays of some isotopes are more penetrating than others; some can be taken orally, others are given intravenously. Among the various isotopes that are used are sodium radio-phosphate (P^{32}), radiogold (Au^{198}) and sodium radio-iodide (I^{131}).

KEEPING UP WITH DRUGS

Since new drugs are constantly being tested for approval by the Federal Drug Administration and appearing on the market, you will not find every drug used in treating patients listed in this book. Some drugs already listed may be replaced by newer drugs that are more effective; others may be removed from the approved list because their continued use has been shown to have dangerous effects on health. For example, a drug approved for use in treating profuse menstruation was the suspected cause of heightened blood coagulation in a number of patients; taken as a "birth control pill," it was reported as causing thrombophlebitis and even death.

31

REHABILITATION

The National Society for Crippled Children and Adults reported recently that there are nearly 22 million disabled people in the United States—an increase of over 2 million in a single year. This means that 1 in every 9 Americans must contend with some sort of handicap that requires special attention. This rapid increase in the number of disabled people is partly due to modern medicine which saves afflicted babies and prolongs life to the ages when people are more likely to develop disabling conditions, such as strokes, heart ailments and arthritis. Accidents are another great cause of disability.

DEFINITION OF REHABILITATION

The modern definition of rehabilitation is the restoration of a disabled person's former abilities or, if complete restoration is not possible, helping him to make the most of the capabilities he has. Until recently, we were accustomed to thinking of rehabilitation as attention to overcoming some very marked physical disability such as the loss of an arm or a leg. Highly trained, skillful people have worked with the big disability problems—the polio victims, the amputees, the spastics. In past years, a vast number of people with disabilities such as those caused by heart conditions, strokes or arthritis were condemned to a life of semi-invalidism or complete invalidism because they were considered incapable of anything else.

Changing Attitudes

Attitudes toward rehabilitation have changed markedly in the last few years. Federal funds have been made available and the individual states have established rehabilitation programs. Public consideration of the handicapped now includes ramps in public places for people in wheelchairs or with crutches. Mechanical devices, such as special typewriters, electrically operated wheelchairs and ingenious prostheses are available. It is estimated that more than 100,000 people have been re-established as wage earners, with total wages amounting to over $200 million a year. This amounts to an average return for each person of $10 a year in income tax for every dollar spent on his rehabilitation. People once considered unemployable are now holding jobs successfully. Above all, those who will not be able to work again are being helped to make the fullest use of their remaining abilities.

RESTORATIVE NURSING CARE

Rehabilitation from an illness begins with the treatment to halt destructive processes and repair body damage. It also includes preventing further injury and restoring normal functions. This is restorative nursing—every nurse's responsibility in rehabilitation. It includes the whole person, but unfortunately we do not always do as well as we might, even with his body. Sometimes we actually do nothing to prevent handicaps that are blossoming under our very eyes. Poorly placed pillows encourage poor posture, unnatural positions let muscles contract. We let a patient strain his eyes under poor reading light or forget to pull down a shade. We frighten a patient with apparatus which we do not explain. We are too busy to help the patient feed himself. This all amounts to tearing down instead of building up—adding more damage to bodies, to self-confidence and to self-respect.

What You Can Do

The practical nurse probably has more opportunity than anybody else to carry on the kind of rehabilitation we are discussing. She is with the patient when he is beginning to be active again; she is his closest companion in a long illness. She has more opportunities than the specialists, who come for the special things—they go, and she stays. She is the one who helps the patient to hold what he has gained, keeps him from slipping back and helps him to move ahead.

The Patient's Attitude

A patient is likely to meet the problem of a disability in much the same spirit as he has faced other problems. He may be resentful, despairing or disbelieving. He may face a disability with the determination to do everything possible to overcome it. The nurse needs to be sensitive to the kind of person he is; she must be prepared to offer encouragement and assistance, with respect for the patient as an adult capable of making decisions. It is a mistake to treat people with body disabilities as if they were also mentally disabled, which is quite different from being mentally depressed. It may take a great deal of patience and perseverance to interest the patient in making an effort to improve his condition and to convince him that it is not hopeless. He and his family must also understand the extent of his disability and how it is possible to regain some—perhaps all—normal functions. Even in such illnesses as arteriosclerosis (hardening of the arteries), which grow progressively worse, the patient should be encouraged to help himself as long as possible.

The Doctor Prescribes

The doctor will tell you how much the patient can be permitted to do—his activities may be very limited or he may be able to do much more than he seems inclined to do. He discovers it is comfortable to lie back and have everything done for him. Perhaps he finds it very pleasant to be the center of attention and

FIG. 131. Although confined to a wheelchair, this young lady has learned to live with her disability and efficiently carries on her work as a secretary.

does everything he can to prolong this desirable state of affairs. This may be a fixed habit with him or only an escape from responsibility that he dreads taking up again. You will have to hold some patients back and gently push others forward. As always, it comes back to the individual patient—you must think of *his* illness, *his* temperament, *his* interests in order to help him.

Choosing the Activity

First, you must know how much physical strength an activity takes and how much concentration is necessary. Then you find out what the patient's interests are and suggest things he can choose. If an older person is childish and unable to concentrate on one thing very long, he will do best at the kinds of things you would give to a child. A young child, for instance, would use building blocks; a grandmother might be able to put one block of a quilt together. The difference is that you are using an activity the grandmother would think suitable. She would not think it appropriate to play with blocks! The child, of course, would not know how to use a needle. However, it is not always so simple—the grandmother may have arthritis and be unable to hold a needle—but you get the general idea.

The Patient's Interests

The key to selecting activities that keep a patient interested or amused lies in his interests. With a woman who likes to sew, do not take it for granted that she is interested in reading too, if she has never read much. People like to use their minds in different ways—to direct their hands or their thoughts or both. The more things a person knows how to do, and the more things he is interested in, the easier it will be to find something to divert and occupy him.

The wife and mother who loves to cook may resent illness most because it keeps her out of her kitchen. It may not be easy to sell her the idea of playing solitaire—perhaps she *would* like to take this time to copy those recipes lying loose in a kitchen drawer.

The Patient's Limitations

Of course, it all comes back to the patient's physical condition and the things he is able to do and can do safely. Often you can persuade a patient that this is the time to relax and do something silly and amusing; perhaps this is his opportunity to learn something he never has had time for. Many of us have secret longings to do things that seem to serve no practical purpose and feel guilty about taking time for them—such as crossword puzzles or mystery stories. Some people get the most satisfaction out of making something useful.

Planning Ahead

Determine the patient's needs and plan accordingly. A patient may need only some diversion to pass the time until he is able to get back to normal life. If he is left with some handicap, a long-range plan is needed to build up physical strength, to retrain muscles, to learn how to carry on his work with the handicap or to learn new ways of looking after himself and making a living. There are many examples of people who have made outstanding successes of their lives in spite of serious handicaps. Clarence Day wrote *Life with Father* after he became a chronic arthritic. Marjorie Lawrence continued her singing career in a wheelchair. Betsey Barton lost both legs but learned to go around by herself and wrote 2 successful books. Franklin Delano Roosevelt was elected President of the United States 4 times in spite of a crippling deformity after an attack of polio.

It takes a determined spirit to overcome serious handicaps, and people need help. One brilliant career woman, whose legs seemed to be hopelessly paralyzed, reached the point where she could travel in a taxi to the rehabilitation center for her treatments. She was a determined and courageous person, but often said that she never could have done it without the steadfast encouragement and help of her trained practical nurse. This patient had had many special services, but her nurse was the one who was there in the low moments to encourage perseverance when progress seemed at a standstill and the future looked hopeless.

The Cardiac Patient. Let us look at a few suggested activities for patients. For example, the cardiac patient's activities depend on the kind of heart condition that he has. Physical activities may be permitted; they may be limited; they may be forbidden. Perhaps he can use his hands to play solitaire or to work on a hobby, such as stamp collecting, wood carving, working with plastics or fly-tying. Sometimes a hobby will bring in money—an additional satisfaction. If activities are forbidden, you will concentrate on making him as contented as possible.

The Diabetic Patient. You always have to think of possible dangers to the patient's body. A diabetic is susceptible to infection. Never give him things that might injure his skin, such as sharp tools or rough materials. His eyesight may be poor, so he must have good light to work in. His muscles are weak, so pay attention to his posture and do not let him get tired.

When the Nervous System Is Affected. Anything that affects the nervous system is likely to interfere with muscle coordination and fine movements. If the patient's mental ability is impaired, he will be unable to do complicated things. If the brain deteriorates, the activities must become more simple. Avoid the activities that require small, fine movements—they are impossible for such a patient and only discourage him when he finds that he cannot carry them out. Some conditions grow progressively worse; others improve. Begin with large movements. A patient might be able to grasp a washcloth to wash his face yet be unable to feed himself. You can work up the finer movements gradually, as the condition improves.

After Polio. Aside from the special training required to re-educate paralyzed muscles and

FIG. 132. This man, who is a bilateral arm amputee, is feeding himself by using mechanical prosthesis. (Liberty Mutual Insurance Co., Boston, Mass.)

to learn to use braces, polio patients need encouragement. They can use their hands and minds in spite of paralyzed legs. They may need new interests, to take the place of those that are physically impossible, or help to see how they still can participate in their former interests to some extent. A youngster who cannot play football still can watch a football game; perhaps he can keep an eye on sweaters and hold wristwatches and valuables for the players. He should be encouraged to be as nearly like people of his own age as possible.

After Surgical Operations. Choose activities that prevent handicaps and improve physical limitations. If Mrs. Gray has had her breast removed, the breast muscles will contract, if they are allowed to, and prevent her from raising her arm. The doctor will tell you how much she can do safely, and when. Help her to stretch the muscles by encouraging her to powder her nose and comb her hair. When Mark comes out of his cast, think what it will mean to him to get his leg back to normal—Mark is a truck driver. Listen carefully to the directions that the doctor or the head nurse gives you and use every opportunity that you have to help Mark. Often he does not understand why he needs to be careful or to persist with certain exercises himself. As his nurse, you know that the bone that bridges the break needs protection until time hardens it; the cast protected it, but now the cast is off.

When Eyes Fail. The patient who is going blind is bewildered and lost. He needs to develop his sense of touch as a substitute for his eyes. Help him to experiment with finding his way around his room and around the house. He still can hear; point out that he can learn to recognize footsteps and also that he can talk with people as well as ever. Help him with his food; tell him where things are on the plate, at 12 o'clock, at 3 o'clock, etc. Always try to put the same kinds of things in the same places. You can learn to help him to help himself to the extent that people will forget that he is blind.

FIG. 133. The voiceless. Many people who have lost the use of their vocal cords can learn to talk again with the help of an electronic artificial larynx, developed by Bell Telephone Laboratories. Held against the throat, this small 7 ounce device replaces the vibrations of normal vocal cords in producing speech. Two models, one simulating a man's voice and the other a woman's, are available at cost on the doctor's recommendation. (The Bell System)

The Deaf Person. The deaf person is lonely. Companionship depends so much on hearing that the deaf person feels out of things. He sees lips move and does not know what they say. He dreads bothering people to repeat their words. A hearing aid is the answer for certain types of deafness. If a hearing aid will not help, many people can learn lip reading. Of course, the deaf person can read and do things with his hands that the blind person has to give up.

Color and Materials. Color is important. Some colors are soothing; others have an irritating effect. Find out what colors the patient likes and those that he cannot bear. Some people hate the feeling of woolly things; some materials have an odor that people dislike. The plastics are new, useful and gay.

Reading Aloud. When you read aloud, choose the parts of the newspapers, the magazine article or the book that the patient likes. If he likes the sports page, read that. Before you read anything, learn *how* to read. Pronounce the words distinctly—do not gallop but do not crawl, either. Put some expression into your reading; be interested yourself. Practice now, while you are a student, and get your classmates to criticize your performance.

The Family Can Help. Take the patient's family into your confidence. Explain why one activity is good for mother, or grandfather, or Johnny, and why another might be discourag-

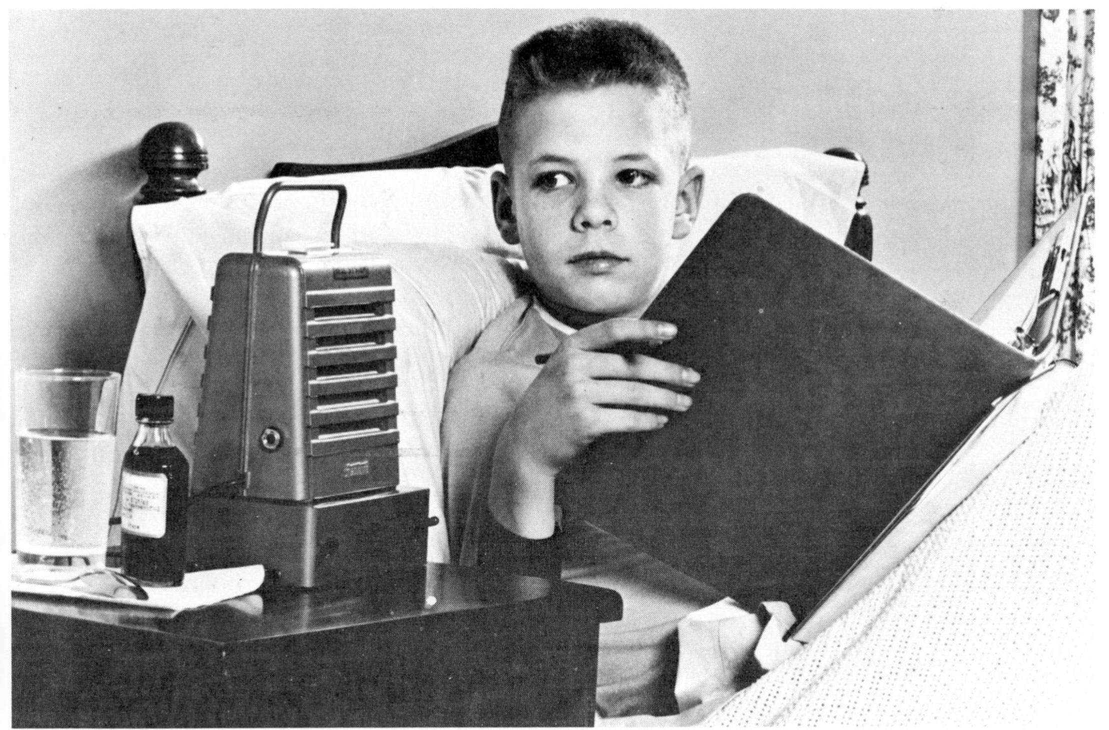

Fig. 134. The bedfast. Over 5,000 shut-in students go to school from home or hospital with the help of Bell System School-to-Home Telephone Service—and keep up with their classes almost as if they were present in person. Speakerphones which don't have to be held or lifted help other invalids keep in touch with their worlds. Some ingenious installations have been devised for wheelchairs and beds by local telephone men. (The Bell System)

ing or harmful. "Isn't she doing too much?" they will say. Or "Poor Grandpa—I can't bear to see him fumbling with his washcloth. Wouldn't it be better to wash his face yourself?" Without meaning to, the family may make the patient more dependent instead of less so. Explain that pity emphasizes a handicap and makes people feel "different."

Watch the Results. Watch the effect of an activity. Begin it when the patient is rested; stop before he gets tired. Notice whether he seems bored. Use an activity to fill up the empty places in the day. Encourage the patient to show his work and talk about it.

It all amounts to this: your job really is to feel with your patient what it means to him to be a human being, to be able to enjoy himself, to work again, to accept a handicap and learn to be independent in spite of it. You watch out for things that may cause deformities—sheets tight over the toes, lack of support under the knees, pillows that are too high, harmful body positions. You help patients to adjust appliances, to use crutches correctly, to protect themselves from accidents. And, most important of all, you build up their self-confidence by encouraging them to help themselves.

REHABILITATIVE AIDS

The Bell Telephone System has developed

Fig. 135. The blind. Special "Seeing Aid" equipment has been designed so that blind operators can serve regular telephone switchboards. Its basic principle is a sensitive probe which causes a buzz in the operator's earphone when it passes over a lighted lamp. By moving the probe up and down a central row of lamps, she learns what level the call is coming in on and which side. Then she uses the probe to find the proper hole and goes on to complete the call. (The Bell System)

many valuable aids for the handicapped. Special equipment makes it possible for a blind person to operate a telephone switchboard. A device that can be incorporated in a telephone receiver helps the hard of hearing. Shut-in students can keep up with their school work from home or hospital with speakerphones that do not have to be held or lifted. For the voiceless, an electronic artificial larynx substitutes for the vibrations of normal vocal cords. Information about these aids is available from local offices of the Bell Telephone System. (See Figs. 133, 134, 135, 136.)

In Chapter 26 we spoke of the nurse's responsibility in making a plan for the patient's care when he is discharged from the hospital. The physician will many times make a referral to a public health agency such as the Visiting Nurse Association to continue the patient's care including supervision of the rehabilitative measures that have been initiated during the patient's hospitalization. The nurse must make a summary of these activities and see that the physician is aware of them so that the public health nurse going into the home can continue the plan of care.

Other health agencies will provide special services, many of which are free. For example, the local Cancer Society may lend a wheelchair when the family is unable to provide it. In some cases, the National Foundation will arrange for physical therapy treatments for the polio victim who is retraining muscles. The nurse must explore available community resources when help is needed and instruct the patient or his family accordingly. Many people are unaware of these special services.

Look and Listen

Many patients are not in the hospital long enough to start activities that help to provide interest and keep them occupied during convalescence or a long-term illness. However, if you are alert you can learn a great deal about a patient while you are giving him nursing care. He will talk to you, perhaps will ask questions or discuss his worries with you. This

Fig. 136. The hard of hearing. Some people with impaired hearing find it hard to use an ordinary telephone. For them, there is a special handset. It looks like any other, but it has a convenient fingertip control in the center which steps up the volume of incoming voices to the best listening level. It can be used with any model telephone. (The Bell System)

gives you an opportunity to make helpful suggestions for activities that will occupy his time and may even be useful as well as interesting. At the same time you can emphasize the importance of following orders that are part of his treatment, such as diet regulations, medicines, exercises, etc. The opportunities for restorative nursing in a nursing home are almost unlimited, for we now know that many more of these patients can be encouraged to do things for themselves that once were considered impossible for them to accomplish. People who are helping themselves are likely to be happy people.

Unit Seven:

Conditions of Illness

32. *The Signs and the Symptoms of Illness*
33. *The Surgical Patient*
34. *The Patient With a Skin Disorder*
35. *The Patient With a Disorder or Injury of the Musculoskeletal System*
36. *The Patient With Cardiovascular Disease and Blood Disorders*
37. *The Patient With Cancer*
38. *The Patient With a Disorder of the Digestive System*
39. *The Patient With a Disorder of the Respiratory System*
40. *The Patient With a Disorder of the Urinary System*
41. *The Patient With a Disorder of the Reproductive System*
42. *The Patient With a Disorder of the Endocrine System*
43. *The Patient With a Disturbance of the Nervous System*
44. *The Patient With a Psychiatric Problem*
45. *The Patient With a Disorder of the Eye or the Ear*
46. *The Patient With a Disorder of the Nose, the Throat or the Mouth*
47. *The Patient With an Allergy*
48. *Care In Emergencies*

32

THE SIGNS AND THE SYMPTOMS OF ILLNESS

The responsibility of the practical nurse is increasing, so she must know enough about illness and disease to be a safe bedside nurse. She must have sufficient information about disease conditions to prepare her to give the necessary nursing care intelligently. Since the practical nurse now takes care of acutely ill as well as chronic and convalescent patients, her knowledge has been increased and broadened. It is always easier to increase your knowledge if you have a good foundation to build upon. Being able to perform nursing technics alone is not enough. A nurse must have the ability to make careful, complete observations, be able to recognize symptoms and, as her experience increases, to understand the significance of certain symptoms in relation to an individual patient and his illness.

WHAT IS ILLNESS?

Illness and *disease* are the opposites of health and normality. Illness is a disturbance of the normal functions of the body and the mind as a result of a condition that is not normal. Disease is a change in the tissues of the body, or in the operation of body systems or in mental adjustments. Infection is a form of change in body tissues brought about by disease organisms. It is not to be confused with pathology, which is the study of *disease processes* in the body. Changes in body tissue that cannot be seen with the naked eye can be studied under the microscope. (See Chap. 7.)

DISEASE CLASSIFICATION

There are various classifications of disease, none of which is really satisfactory because categories continually overlap. Also, the ultimate cause of many diseases is still unknown. For example, diseases may be classified: (1) according to their cause; (2) according to the system of the body that is affected; and (3) according to the way in which they are acquired.

Some common classifications of disease and causes of illnesses are:

Hereditary Diseases: If one or both parents passes on to the embryo a trait through genes that impairs some body function, the resulting disease is called hereditary. Hemophilia (prolonged blood coagulation time) is inherited. Hemophilia is transmitted by the female but appears only in the male. The mother is the "carrier" and is free of symptoms.

Congenital Diseases: Congenital diseases are also present at birth, but unlike hereditary diseases, they are not transmitted through the genes. They are due to the effects on the fetus of some unfavorable condition which interferes with its normal development. Syphilis in the mother can be transmitted through the placenta; German measles, contracted by the mother during pregnancy, or drugs (thalidomide is a recent example) may cause body abnormalities or defects. Examples of abnormal fetal development are cleft palate, congenital heart disease and clubbed feet (deformities of the bones in the feet).

Infectious Diseases: The most common of all causes of disease is invasion of the body by microorganisms, such as bacteria, viruses and animal parasites. (See Chap. 7.)

Deficiency Diseases: These are disorders of nutrition as a result of a deficiency of one or more vitamins in the diet. For example, lack of vitamin C causes scurvy. Deficiency in several vitamins, or general malnutrition, is more common in this country than a single vitamin deficiency. One possible exception to this is the lack of iron-rich foods which cause certain anemias.

Metabolic Diseases: These are conditions like obesity which is due to the body's failure to burn fat fast enough to keep it from accumulating in the body; or diabetes mellitus, which is due to the body's not producing sufficient insulin to burn the sugar.

Neoplastic Diseases: This term is used to describe new growth of abnormal tissue, or tumors, which may be benign or malignant. A benign tumor is a growth of cells similar to the tissue in which it appears and is covered by a capsule. Once removed, it usually does not recur. It may be disfiguring, but it is not dangerous unless it crowds other structures or robs surrounding tissues of their blood supply. A malignant tumor (any form of cancer) is a wild and disorderly growth of cells that are unlike the tissues where they are located. This cell growth weakens bones, causes breaks in blood vessels and robs normal tissues of nutrients; the cells also tend to spread to other parts of the body—this process is metastasis.

Traumatic Injuries: This type of illness is the result of physical or mental injuries or shocks. It includes physical injuries, such as those incurred in automobile accidents or falls, or mental suffering from a personal loss.

Occupational Diseases: Certain occupational groups suffer from conditions peculiar to their jobs. For example, divers and airplane pilots contract diseases caused by oxygen deprivation.

Predisposition to Disease

Besides direct causes of disease, there are indirect causes as well. These are called predisposing factors, and their effect is to make a person more vulnerable to the direct causes. For instance, a person who is continuously worried, does not get a normal amount of sleep and is generally "run down" will probably be more susceptible to the direct action of disease organisms.

Some people seem to have a higher natural resistance to disease than others. For instance, they never seem to catch cold even though they live with people who have many colds. Race, sex or age predispose to certain illnesses. Measles, for instance, is a childhood disease. The climate accounts for certain diseases, such as those found in tropical countries. Medical progress has changed the occurrence of disease. We rarely see a case of smallpox today, and surely in the near future we rarely will see a child with poliomyelitis.

The Course of Disease

Diseases progress in short or more lengthy stages. An *acute* disease comes on suddenly and runs its course in days. A *subacute* condition may go on for weeks or even months. The course of a *chronic* disease may be prolonged for years or for a lifetime. Complications may occur at any stage, involving other parts of the body.

OBSERVING THE PATIENT

Because the nurse is with the patient continuously, her observations are invaluable as a guide to the doctor in determining the patient's treatment and judging its effects. The doctor depends on you to include everything that is important. Your notes about every patient should create a picture of the person as an individual during his illness. When Dr. Harvey Cushing, the famous surgeon, was a medical student, he illuminated his notes by little sketches of every patient that he observed. *We* have to depend on words to describe the patient's appearance.

Your observations are tied in with the nursing procedures that you assist with or carry out yourself, and this chapter tells you what and how to observe. You also observe and record things that the patient tells you about his feelings and you observe his behavior. (The important points in making observations about the behavior of mental patients apply here.) Record what you see and report what the patient says in his own words, as nearly as possible, without putting your own interpretation on them.

Trained Observation. Show a picture to 3 people; then ask each one to write down what he saw—all 3 descriptions will be different. Some people are naturally more observant than others, but almost everyone can train himself to be a better observer. One way to improve the powers of observation is to know what to observe. On a field trip, for instance, you must know what to look for and why the information is important. Such information also helps you in giving nursing care to each patient. As an example: You observed that Mrs. Dean ate very little supper; you also have weighed Mrs. Dean and you know she is on a high calorie diet. Put all this information together, and it tells you to give her milk or cocoa or other nourishment before she goes to bed.

Signs of Illness

The patient is able to give only part of the information about himself because he reports only the things that seem important to *him*. The nurse must be aware of signs she can see, hear, smell and feel which are her responsibility to observe and report. It is the doctor's responsibility to decide what the symptoms mean and to prescribe the necessary treatment, but he depends on the nurse to observe them accurately. The nurse, in turn, must understand the significance of certain symptoms in order to give intelligent nursing care. Before taking up these observations in detail, it will help to consider the general categories to be included in observations of patients, such as:

1. The condition of the patient's body
2. His movements
3. The amount of rest he gets
4. The food he eats
5. Pain
6. His body processes
7. His behavior
8. His emotional and mental reactions
9. Treatments and their effects.

Symptoms

Symptoms are the *signs* of disease. *Subjective symptoms* are sensations that only the patient knows about and can report—pain, itching, nausea, fear, worry. *Objective symptoms* are those signs that can be noted by an observer, such as a doctor or a nurse would note—a rash, swelling, pallor, pulse and temperature changes, hysteria or weeping. Symptoms may be *local*, that is, limited to the affected part (swelling); or *general*, affecting most or all of the body (fever). In any case, it is clear that a nurse must first know what is normal, before she can recognize the deviations that she should record and report.

WHAT TO LOOK FOR

1. *Nutrition:* Is the patient overweight or underweight? Are these signs of malnutrition characteristic of his disease? Is his face puffy?

2. *Physical Comfort* as shown by his position: Does he seem to be comfortable? Why is he uncomfortable?

3. *Mental State:* Is he wide awake, dull, in coma or stupor? Does he talk sensibly? Does he understand English? Is he depressed, overexcited? Can he hear and see well? Does he know where he is? Indications of mental disturbance are very significant. Precautions may be necessary to prevent injury, and specific treatment may be needed.

4. *Facial Expression:* Does he look anxious and worried? Is he expressionless, stupid? Is his mouth open? Is he pale or flushed? Pallor is characteristic in anemia and nephritis, in hemorrhage and in patients with edema.

5. *Skin:* Is it dry and parched? Is it moist, cold or clammy? Is it hot? Are there scratches, bruises, wounds, rashes, sores, reddened areas? Is it grayish, bluish or yellowish in color?

6. *Posture:* Is he able to lie, sit and walk comfortably? Is he comfortable only in certain positions? In some heart conditions the patient is unable to breathe lying down. Arthritis and paralysis affect joints and muscles.

7. *Movements:* Can he control his movements? Does he have tremors, muscle spasms? Are his movements jerky? In a convulsion, it is important to notice the way it began, the length of it, the parts of the body involved, and in

what order; movements of the eyes; stupor or coma; involuntary urination or defecation; symptoms after the seizure.

8. *Pain:* Location, how it began, how long it lasts, severity, kind of pain (describe it in the patient's own words as nearly as possible). The patient can understand terms such as *knifelike, steady, dull, crampy, spasms.* Some patients will try to conceal pain; others will exaggerate their symptoms. Still others complain of pain when no cause for it can be found.

Pain is so much a part of illness and is so often misunderstood that we need to discuss it more fully, perhaps, than other symptoms. It is a combination of physical and emotional suffering which varies greatly in intensity with individuals. The sensitivity of parts of the body to pain varies greatly. For instance, very little pain is connected with cutting compact bone or subcutaneous fat, yet arteries and veins react painfully to a needle puncture. Puncturing muscles is only slightly painful but introducing solutions causes severe pain. A sensitive or highly emotional person might feel great pain from a slight wound; a calmer person might not complain of pain from an operation or serious injury. Pain may be *local,* that is, affecting one part of the body, or it may be *general,* affecting more than one part. Pain is sometimes felt in one part of the body while the cause of it is located in another—this is *referred* pain. For example, the area between the shoulder blades is a common site for the pain associated with gallbladder disease.

Listen to the Patient. A nurse cannot arbitrarily assume that she knows more about the patient's pain than he does. After all, he is experiencing it and should be encouraged to express his feelings in his own way without being accused of complaining. What is more important is that his complaints may call attention to a serious condition that might otherwise be overlooked. The first thing a good nurse does to make a patient comfortable is to *listen* to him, which in itself is a form of reassurance. She is responsible for giving any medications ordered by the doctor to relieve pain. She uses these medications promptly whenever they are necessary for the patient's comfort, because she knows that pain is relieved more easily before it becomes too severe. She does not give a patient the impression that he should "stand" pain as long as possible and that she is giving a medication reluctantly. She knows that delay in relieving pain increases the patient's discomfort and, if prolonged, severe pain can cause shock.

Attitudes

You learn how a patient feels *about* himself and his treatment by observing his actions and listening to what he says. Is he cooperative, unreasonable, fearful, worried, cheerful? Does he talk about his problems? What clues does he give to his physical and mental condition? Again, you can report what you see him do, but he is the only one who can give you his reason for doing it. He may not give the real reason, but the reason that he gives may be a clue to his behavior and is valuable information for the doctor. This is why it is important to report this kind of information in the patient's own words.

Often the most effective and revealing way to describe certain symptoms is to tell what the patient does or does not do. For example, recording "unable to turn today without help" says more about the patient's condition than the mere statement "appears to be weak." Or the notation: "tries repeatedly to get out of bed," is a great improvement on "behaves irrationally." A nurse avoids making pronouncements about a patient's condition. She reports what she sees and what the patient says and does. In short, she collects the evidence and the doctor makes the judgments.

Sleep

How many hours does he sleep? Is his sleep unbroken? Is he restless? Does he dream? Is he worried about not sleeping? Does he take naps in the daytime? Is he drowsy most of the time? Does he sleep more than he thinks he does?

Food

What kinds of food does he like? What kind of diet is he having? Does he enjoy his food?

Is his appetite poor? Is he abnormally hungry or thirsty? How much does he eat at every meal? Does he have between-meals feedings? Is he gaining or losing weight? What is the condition of his mouth and teeth? Does he wear dentures? Does he have difficulty in swallowing? Difficulties in taking food may be signs of disorders of the digestive system, such as stomach ulcers or obstructions in the food passages; poor teeth or badly fitting dentures; mouth infections; food habits; mental disorders, such as fear of being poisoned; constipation.

SIGNS OF TROUBLE

Some symptoms that are commonly associated with specific diseases are fully discussed under the disease itself. Because they may also occur in other illnesses we mention them briefly here.

Cough usually indicates irritation somewhere along the respiratory tract. It is present in most respiratory diseases and in some heart conditions. A cough may be helpful or harmful. In some diseases it aids greatly in draining an infected area. In the absence of pulmonary secretions it serves no useful purpose and may even be harmful.

Dyspnea (difficult breathing) and *orthopnea* (inability to breathe except when upright) usually indicate some difficulty in obtaining or utilizing oxygen. These symptoms are frequently seen in cardiac and respiratory conditions.

Cyanosis (blueness of the skin due to a lack of oxygen in the blood) often occurs in the 2 conditions mentioned above; with diminishing bright red color in the blood, the patient's skin has a bluish pallor especially noticeable in the lips or the fingernails.

Edema (swelling) is the result of an abnormal amount of water in the tissues; there are several reasons for it. (1) The pressure on the capillaries increases if the return flow to the veins is obstructed in some way and increased pressure forces more fluid into the tissues. (2) Normally, the plasma proteins are retained in the blood vessels and help to maintain the osmotic pressure which keeps fluid in the blood vessels. If these proteins are reduced by disease, the fluid escapes into the tissues. (3) A high intake of salt tends to keep water in the tissues because the body attempts to retain fluid to dilute the salt. (4) Obstruction of the lymph vessels prevents them from carrying off tissue fluid. (5) Injury to blood vessels so that they lose plasma proteins will cause edema.

Edema frequently occurs in loose tissues, such as the eyelids and the genitalia, because they favor it while tightly constructed tissues resist edema formation. Edema is also more likely to occur in areas where the return flow of blood is slowest—in the fingers and the ankles, for example. Since edema fluid is toxic, the patient's fluid intake is not always radically restricted because fluids are needed to dilute these toxins.

Emesis (vomiting) has many causes. Sometimes it follows mental or emotional disturbance and has no physical cause. It may be due to disturbance or obstruction of the alimentary tract, varying in form according to the location of the difficulty; the vomited material also tells much about this. Fermented, undigested food indicates it has been returned from the stomach; bile-stained fluid is returned from the upper small intestine; fecal vomitus is returned from the colon. Blood in the vomitus indicates hemorrhage and is always regarded as a serious symptom.

Hemorrhage, or abnormal loss of blood into the tissues may also indicate certain conditions. In the emesis or the sputum, blood may be a sign of disease of the digestive or the respiratory systems. Bright red or blackish, tarlike blood in the stool indicates digestive tract disturbance (Chap. 38). Hemorrhage from accidental or surgical wounds can be fatal in a short space of time if it is not controlled. Bleeding into the tissues in varying amounts may be associated with diseases of the digestive and the urinary systems (see Chap. 38, 40).

Diarrhea, or the passage of liquid, unformed, watery stools may be caused by physical or emotional difficulties. It is sometimes a protective mechanism that the body uses to get rid of irritating or toxic materials. If diarrhea is the result of a deep-seated emotional problem, a nurse can help the psychiatrist or the physician in guiding the patient to a better understanding of and an adjustment to the problems of daily living.

Fever is an elevation of body temperature above normal and is another sign of the body's attempt to fight disease. It may develop suddenly or gradually. Associated with rise in temperature are 2 other symptoms of body changes: *increase in pulse and in respiratory rates*, which rise proportionately as the body temperature goes up.

Inflammation is the body's attempt to cope with damage to body cells as the result of an injury causing a break in the skin (a wound), or to fight infection. The following symptoms usually are found in some degree where there is injury or infection: (1) pain, (2) redness, (3) swelling, (4) heat, (5) loss of function and eventually (6) the formation of pus. This, for example, is what happens when a splinter gets into your finger and the body sets up a resistance:

Symptom	*Cause*
Redness	Increase in circulation to the part
Swelling	Fluid and leukocytes leave blood stream to enter tissues
Pain	Pressure of fluid on nerve endings
Heat	Increased circulation
Loss of function	The body's attempt to keep finger at rest.

The Process of Inflammation. Inflammation may be subacute or chronic. In acute inflammation an excess of fluid and cells is usually present in or issuing from the tissues (*exudate*). Exudates may be *clear* (serum) such as the discharge from a nasal cold; *fibrinous*, which causes adhesions to form as the tissues are repaired; *bloody*, as a result of small hemorrhages in the area; and *purulent*, due to bacteria. The formation of pus is called *suppuration*. In this process the poisons of the bacteria kill off white blood cells and destroy tissue. The death of tissue is called *necrosis*.

The destroyed tissue may be cast off (*slough*), leaving behind it an area which needs to be filled in with new tissue. Sometimes a local unhealed area (of epithelial tissue) is called an *ulcer*. A blind channel from a twisting wound which does not heal is called a *sinus*; a wound which has a small persistent opening that does not heal and connects with an internal hollow organ is called a *fistula*.

Repair or Regeneration of Tissue. After suppuration, sloughing, or surgical removal of dead material, the area must be refilled with new tissue. The repair process proceeds in two ways: *healing by first intention* and *healing by second intention*. A simple wound, with clean-cut sharp edges (incised) heals by first intention with a minimum of repair tissue. An irregular, jagged wound (lacerated) with much tissue damage requires extra tissue to fill in empty spaces and so heals by second intention.

The body attempts the repair of wound areas by replacement with new cells of the same type, or by repairing the defect with connective tissue; the body forms new connective tissue from blood vessels and connective tissue already available in the area. The cells of the capillaries produce small buds that grow into the area and unite to form hollow arches that permit the passage of blood. The new connective tissue is formed by the cells surrounding the buds and is laid down between these arches. Eventually, the blood vessels as such disappear and leave behind a white tissue which is the *scar* (cicatrix). Scar tissue can be damaging, as it sometimes fastens loops of the intestine together (adhesions) or causes fixation or loss of movement in joints (ankylosis).

A *local* inflammation may spread throughout the body and become a *general* infection. Some infections start in the blood stream and rapidly become general infections.

TREATMENT OF ILLNESS

Certain procedures are a part of the nursing care of practically every patient. Among them are:

Personal hygiene measures to promote health and keep the patient comfortable.

Maintaining fluid balance and recording fluid intake and output. The elimination of toxic materials is primarily the function of the kidneys.

Fluids are increased to dilute these toxins and encourage elimination (see Chap. 18).

Providing a diet adequate and appropriate to the patient's needs; these may indicate a diet modified, restricted or supplemented as a part of his treatment (see Chap. 23).

Drug therapy is a common form of treatment. With the multiplicity of drugs available and in use today, we seldom find a patient who is not getting some form of medicine.

Applications of heat or cold are frequently used in the form of hot-water bags, icecaps, compresses or baths. Heat and cold are also considered in providing suitable bedcoverings and regulating ventilation.

Preventive measures, such as handwashing, are essential to prevent spreading disease from one patient to another and to protect the nurse from infection.

Measures to insure adequate rest apply to physical and mental rest. They may apply to complete or partial bed rest, to regulation of activity to some degree or to the amount of sleep a patient gets. Procedures include soothing back rubs, sedatives and providing as quiet an environment as possible.

A Bird's-eye View

You now have a bird's-eye view of what you, as a practical nurse, will be expected to know. The procedures mentioned here will be discussed in detail with the illnesses in which they are especially significant, and under nursing procedures. Gradually, you will become familiar with them.

RESTORATIVE NURSING

Restorative nursing is an aspect of rehabilitation (which has been fully discussed in Chap. 31). It can easily be overlooked because it is not concerned with the spectacular achievement of rehabilitation, such as teaching the use of an artificial arm or leg. It has to do with helping a patient to continue carrying out the simple, every-day activities he took for granted before his illness, such as washing and feeding himself, getting around unaided, etc. Because it is quicker, nurses often do things for patients that they should be encouraged to do for themselves. We emphasize this point here because it is important that you see it as a vital part of nursing care from the very beginning of your experience. Everything the patient does to help himself is a step away from dependence on others and a step forward toward a normal life.

OBSERVATION OF THE URINE

Urinalysis

Urinalysis is included in a health examination and is a part of the examination of every patient at the beginning of an illness. One of the first things that is done for a patient on admission to a hospital is to collect a specimen of urine and to send it to the laboratory. Except for simple tests, it takes special knowledge to analyze a specimen of urine. In the hospital, technicians trained to do all sorts of laboratory tests do the urine examinations.

The urine may be examined from time to time during an illness; in some illnesses it is examined every day. About four-fifths of the excess water, some carbon dioxide, most of the solid wastes of the body and poisons that appear in the blood are removed from the body in the urine. For example, diphtheria organisms produce poisons in the body that are harmful to the kidneys; a urine examination is made every day to see whether the kidneys of a patient with diphtheria are affected. In disturbances of the urinary system, the urine tells a great deal about the condition of the kidneys and the bladder.

The Amount. Urine is secreted by the kidneys and carried through the ureters to the bladder reservoir, which expels it from the body through the urethra. The amount voided in 24 hours averages from 500 to 3,000 cc.; the total output is influenced by the amount of fluid taken into the body and the amount removed by the lungs, the skin and the intestinal tract. In hot weather, or when a patient perspires freely, the amount is less than in cold weather; it is less in illnesses when perspiration is absent or fluid is retained in the body tissues. To keep a normal balance of fluid in the body, from 6 to 8 glasses of fluids are required every day. If this amount is supplied and other conditions are normal, between 1,000 and 1,500 cc. would be a normal output of urine. The normal output for an adult naturally will be more than for a child.

A great increase in the amount of urine is called *polyuria*—an output of over 3,000 cc. a day. It may be the result of drinking a large amount of water; diabetes mellitus and insipidus, and nephritis (at some stages) also cause polyuria. A marked decrease in the amount is called *oliguria*. It may be due to the amount of fluid taken into the body or to other causes that will be discussed shortly.

Color. Freshly voided normal urine is transparent and light amber in color. The kinds and the amounts of wastes in the urine make it lighter or darker. Blood in the urine colors it. If the amount of blood is large, the urine will be red. Practically always, some red blood cells are present in the urine during a flare-up of chronic nephritis, and give the urine a smoky appearance. Some medications will discolor the urine, each of these medicines having a distinctive coloring effect; for example, Pyridium gives a bright orange-red urine, which may frighten a patient not forewarned of this effect.

Odor. Normal, freshly voided urine has a characteristic aromatic odor. When the urine stands, certain changes take place that give it an ammonia odor. These changes affect the urine so that some tests will not be reliable indications of urine conditions. Sometimes preservatives are added to a urine specimen to keep it in good condition to be examined. If this is necessary, the doctor will tell you what preservatives to use. Ideally, a urine specimen that is not examined right away should be kept in a refrigerator. In diabetes mellitus the urine has a sweetish odor; some drugs and some foods affect the odor.

Retention. Usually, when the bladder contains about 200 to 250 cc. of urine, a person feels the distention and has a desire to void. Failure of the bladder to expel the urine is called *retention*. If the amount of urine increases, the bladder muscles stretch, with the danger of weakening them or making them less sensitive. One cause of retention is an obstruction of the bladder outlet or of the urethra—this may be due to swelling in the tissues or to masses of fecal material in the rectum pressing on the urethra. Fear or pain may cause tension in the muscles that control the urethral opening so that they will not relax to expel the urine. Another common cause of retention is the position of the bladder when the patient is lying down.

A number of things may help to relieve retention. The sound of running water, putting the patient's hands in warm water or pouring warm water over the genitalia of the female patient often help to stimulate the muscles to function. If the doctor can allow the patient to sit up, either in bed, on the edge of the bed or on a commode, she may be able to void.

Incontinence. Incontinence is the opposite of retention. Loss of muscle tone, injuries or paralysis destroy the ability of the urethral muscles to constrict and so to keep the urine outlet closed; the urine dribbles away constantly. If the nerve pathways to the control center in the brain are injured, the patient either does not feel the impulse to urinate or is unable to control the outlet muscles and voids involuntarily.

Suppression. In some illness conditions, the kidneys fail to secrete urine. This brings about suppression of urine, or the condition called *anuria*. This condition occurs if both kidneys are injured or destroyed by disease, if a poison stops their work or if the ureters are blocked. Remarkably enough, when one kidney is destroyed or removed, if the other is normal, it is able to take over the work of both. Other signs of suppression that may appear with the failure to void urine are headache, dizziness, puffiness beneath the eyes, spots before the eyes, nausea and dim vision. Suppression is dangerous because poisonous wastes accumulate in the body.

The treatment for suppression is to stimulate the skin and the bowels to eliminate wastes more freely; to rest and to relieve the kidneys by diet (low salt); to force fluids in order to dilute the wastes; to give medications that stimulate the kidneys to be more active.

THE URINE SPECIMEN

You know now what to observe about urine and why observations about the amount, the color and the odor of urine are important. You also know what normal conditions are. Nursing procedures in relation to urine are observing, measuring the amount and recording it, and collecting urine specimens. The contents of every bedpan and every urinal are important for giving information that will help the doctor in treating the patient. This means that you must know when the urine is to be measured and when a specimen is required; and that you do not dispose of the urine until it has been measured. Prevent the patient from unknowingly destroying a specimen and encourage him to void by explaining that the doctor needs the information that a urine test will give. Tell the patient who has bathroom privileges to use the bedpan or the urinal instead of the toilet. You can control this situation more easily in the home, but precautions are necessary in a hospital where you are responsible for several patients. Always save an unusual specimen and show it to the doctor or the head nurse.

Measure the urine in a graduated container marked in *ounces* or *cc's*. You can get a large kitchen measuring cup at the 10-cent store if you need a measure in the home. Note the number of ounces or cubic centimeters voided each time and record your observations on the patient's chart. The doctor may or may not want you to measure the urine as the patient convalesces. Always measure the urine until the doctor says that it is no longer necessary.

Collecting A Single Specimen of Urine

The amount and the content of a urine specimen vary with the time of day, the food taken in and the amount of rest. The doctor may ask for specimens at different times in the day. Usually, it is customary to collect a routine specimen when the patient wakes up in the morning. A specimen of urine is usually collected as soon as the patient is admitted to the hospital. It may be a hospital rule to collect a specimen of urine from every patient on a specified day of the week. It is important to note on the specimen label if the patient is menstruating at that time. Because of the bacteria normally present on the labia, the perineum and around the anus of the female patient, it is easier to contaminate a voided urine specimen. To avoid this possibility, and the necessity of collecting another one (with the extra cost to the patient), soap and water cleansing of the genitals immediately preceding the collection of the specimen is advocated.

EQUIPMENT

Covered 6-ounce specimen bottle (wide-mouthed bottle is best)
Label
Bedpan or urinal

SUGGESTED PROCEDURE

Instruct the patient to void. Remove the bedpan or urinal after the patient has voided.

Guide: *If the patient feels that her bowels may move, ask her to urinate first. Remove the bedpan with the specimen and give her another bedpan.*

Pour about 120 cc. of the urine into the specimen bottle and cover the bottle.

Guide: *It is important to have enough urine to do the required tests.*

Label the bottle with the date, the patient's name, room and department identification, and the doctor's name. Take or send the specimen to the laboratory.

Guide: *Note on the label whether other than routine tests are to be done.*

In the home, the doctor takes the urine specimen away with him. Be sure that the bottle is corked *tightly* or has a nonleak screw top; label the bottle with the date and the patient's name. A tag or a piece of paper secured around the bottle with a rubber band is better than a pasted-on label that may come off.

Collecting an Accumulated Specimen of Urine

An accumulated specimen of urine gives more detailed information than a single specimen because it shows what wastes the kidneys are eliminating and the amount of each. The urine may be collected for 24 hours or for some part of that period; this depends on the specific information desired. The fractional specimen is often collected from a patient with diabetes mellitus because it helps to determine the diet and the amount of insulin needed. You can start to collect the specimen at any time, but you begin by asking the patient to void and discarding that single specimen. However, you note the *time*, as the beginning of the 24-hour period.

EQUIPMENT

Large, clean bottle with cover or stopper
Measuring graduate
Bedpan or urinal

SUGGESTED PROCEDURE

Give the bedpan or urinal to the patient and ask him or her to void. Discard the urine, and record the time on the patient's chart.

Guide: *Collection begins with an empty bladder.*

Measure each specimen of urine voided and pour into the bottle; record each amount on the chart.

Guide: *Continue for 24 hours from the time the urine was discarded. Caution the patient as before in relation to bowel movements.*

At the exact hour, 24 hours after beginning the collection, ask the patient to void. Pour the specimen into the bottle.

Guide: *The last voiding completes the 24-hour total; collection ends with an empty bladder.*

Label the bottle as for a single specimen and add the *time* collection began and ended, along with the *total amount* of urine. Cork the bottle and take it to the laboratory.

You will need more bottles if the urine is to be collected for separate parts of the 24-hour period. You begin the collection at the time that you discard the first specimen. If the periods run this way: 6 A.M. to 12 NOON, 12 to 6 P.M., 6 P.M. to MIDNIGHT, 12 to 6 A.M., you ask the patient to void and discard the specimen at 6 A.M.; at noon you complete that fraction of the 24-hour period by asking the patient to void and saving the specimen. The next period then begins properly with the bladder empty.

The common tests made on a single specimen are for: acid or alkaline reaction, specific gravity, sugar and albumin. Sugar in the urine is a symptom of diabetes mellitus and is described in Chapter 42 in connection with that disease. You may need to make this test for a diabetic patient at home.

If ordinary tests show albumin in the urine, it is a sign of kidney inflammation. Albumin is protein (like egg white), and heat coagulates it. If the urine becomes cloudy or thickened when it is boiled, it indicates albumin. A quantity of albumin will form a solid mass.

Some tests are done to find out how efficiently the kidneys are working. A dye (phenolphthalein) which is excreted only by the kidneys is injected into the patient's veins or muscles. He then is asked to void at intervals, and the amount of the dye in each specimen is estimated by laboratory analysis.

OBSERVATION OF THE FECES

The feces are mostly refuse left from the food we eat. In the process of digestion, the food taken into the body is reduced to a semiliquid mass; the nutrient elements are extracted and absorbed; the waste passes on through the intestines until it finally reaches the rectum and is expelled. The residue of a meal leaves the body in 24 to 48 hours afterward. This waste is called the *feces*; the amount of the feces expelled at any one time is called the *stool*—commonly known as a *bowel movement*. The process of expelling the feces is called *defecation*; the common expression is to say that the *bowels move*. This term is used because *bowels* is another word for *intestines*.

The feces are an important source of information about conditions of the digestive system. They tell about digestion, inflammation in the intestinal tract and obstruction of it, the presence of parasites, etc.

The peristaltic waves move the material along until it reaches the rectum. By this time, the wastes, or the feces, are a soft mass; when it enters the rectum it presses on the nerve endings in the wall and creates a desire to *defecate*. Most people feel this stimulus after breakfast. A daily bowel movement is the rule, but some people have several; others may have one only every 2 or 3 days. The rate of digestion and the movement of waste material differs in individuals. The appearance of the feces tells much about the movement of it. Because the food mass loses water as it moves along, liquid feces indicate a rapid movement; while hard feces show a slower rate or that the feces have been in the rectum for some time. Observation of the feces includes a number of things, which are discussed below.

Consistency. Normal feces are soft, formed stools. Liquid feces show irritation of the intestinal tract; this may be due to a chronic inflammation or to a temporary irritation. Hard, dry-looking stools indicate constipation. The size of the mass shows the amount of roughage or waste material in the diet and the time that it has accumulated. The feces are always considered in relation to the diet.

Color. Normal feces are a greenish brown; this color comes from bile. Clay-colored stools show that the normal amount of bile is lacking—a mark of gallbladder disturbances. Light-colored stools are sometimes due to undigested fat. A dark, tarlike stool is a sign of hemorrhage, either in the stomach or high up in the intestines. Bright red blood in the stool indicates hemorrhage lower down in the intestinal tract—perhaps in the rectum—and the blood will be free and not mixed with the stool. The digestive system tries to digest everything that appears in the food passage, including blood. Digested blood is dark and makes the stool tarry. Some foods and medications affect the color of the stool.

Odor. The odor of the feces is characteristic, but unusual odors should be noted. Some medications affect the odor; protein decay in accumulated feces also affects it.

Pus in the stool may be due to intestinal infection or the rupture of an abscess into the intestinal tract. *Mucus* indicates irritation of the lining of the intestinal tract. In dysentery, which is an acute inflammation, the stool may be entirely mucus and blood. *Blood*, of course, indicates hemorrhage and is always a danger signal which should be reported at once.

There may be times when a patient will be admitted to the hospital with a history of having swallowed a foreign object. This is especially true in the pediatric department where we find children who have swallowed buttons, safety pins, marbles or other objects. You will be expected to save each fecal specimen, break it down from the solid mass, and examine it carefully to see if the object has been passed. If you place a small amount of warm water in the bedpan and use wooden tongue blades to stir the mass, it will facilitate the examination of the stool. Any stool that is unusual should be reported to the head nurse or to the doctor. If there is any question in your mind, save the bedpan for inspection by your superior.

Collecting a Specimen of Feces

EQUIPMENT

Clean bedpan and cover—2, if the patient wishes to void
Paper container and cover
Wooden tongue blades
Paper bag for used tongue blades

SUGGESTED PROCEDURE

Give the bedpan to the patient and ask him to defecate.

Guide: *Give another bedpan or urinal first if patient wishes to urinate.*

Remove the bedpan. Put a portion of the feces in the container and cover it.

Guide: *Use the tongue blade to transfer the specimen.*

Label the container in the same manner as for a urine specimen.

Guide: *Note any special examination requested.*

Take the container immediately to the laboratory. Sometimes the bedpan and the entire contents are taken to the laboratory.

Guide: *Stools should be examined when fresh. Examinations for parasites, eggs and organisms must be made when the stool is warm.*

When an infant's stool specimen is to be examined, take the diaper to the laboratory wrapped in a paper towel or bag and label it. Small-sized paper food containers are excellent for stool specimens. A small glass jar with a leak-proof top can be used; place the jar in a container of fairly warm water if it is necessary to keep the specimen warm.

OTHER SYMPTOMS

Cough

A cough is the contraction of the muscles in the pharynx as a result of irritation. If material is expectorated after the cough, we say that the cough is *productive*. A cough may be loose or dry. A cough may be only occasional or it may come in spasms that are frequent or prolonged. Note the color of the patient's face when he coughs—a bluish tinge indicates an obstruction in the air passages.

Sputum

Sputum is material expectorated from the mouth. It may be coughed up from the bronchi or the lungs, or may be a discharge from infection of the nasal or the throat cavities. Discharge from infected sinuses also drains into the throat at the back of the nose. The amount expectorated varies and should be noted; usually this is estimated as "small," "medium" or "large." It can be estimated more accurately by filling an identical container with water to the same level as the sputum, then measuring the water. Sputum is characteristic of such conditions as tuberculosis, pneumonia and lung injuries.

Consistency and Color. Sputum may be thin, watery, thick or purulent. Expectorated mucus is colorless. Pus gives sputum a yellow color, or it may be gray or black. In pneumonia, it has a rusty color and is thick and tenacious; it may be streaked with bright red blood. In lung abscess and cancer of the lungs, the sputum may be green. Sometimes sputum has no odor or it may have an unpleasant odor —in lung abscess the odor is very noticeable. Precautions relating to the care of sputum in infectious conditions are discussed with tuberculosis in Chapter 39.

The purpose in examining a specimen of sputum is to see whether or not specific disease organisms are present. It is important to instruct the patient, if you are collecting a specimen because the patient is coughing. Usually the specimen is collected in the morning. You ask the patient to cough deeply to bring up material from the bronchi and the lungs. Otherwise, the specimen may be only saliva and nasal and throat secretions.

Collecting a Specimen of Sputum

EQUIPMENT

Waterproof waxed cardboard container
Tissues—wax-backed tissues are best for an expectorating patient

SUGGESTED PROCEDURE

Have the patient rinse his mouth.

Guide: *This is done in order to remove food particles.*

Instruct the patient about the procedure.

Guide: *Have him cough deeply. Tell him to be careful not to soil the outside of the container. Wipe his lips with tissues.*

Cover the specimen, label it and send or take it to the laboratory.

Guide: *This is done in the same manner as for urine or feces specimens.*

Symptoms are related to the systems of the body; in connection with the digestive system, one symptom that appears is belching air through the mouth. It may be due to a habit of swallowing air, which is caused by emotional disturbances, or it may be caused by the fermentation of food in the intestinal tract. Other symptoms are *nausea* and *vomiting*, both of which can be caused by disorders of the intestinal system, by disease in some other part of the body or by emotional tensions. In any case, these symptoms indicate that something is upsetting the nervous control of the stomach.

Vomiting

Vomiting is the act of expelling material from the stomach; it is the result of muscle contractions so strong that they force the contents of the stomach out through the esophagus and the mouth. Severe and prolonged vomiting has a serious effect on nutrition. There is a difference between merely spitting up, or the *regurgitation* of food, and vomiting. A baby often spits up a small amount of milk after he is fed.

Nervous people sometimes bring up food after eating; children do it as a trick to get attention. A senile or a partially paralyzed patient may fail to swallow his food and hold it in his mouth in a ball, which he finally spits out. It is necessary to encourage this type of patient to swallow after he chews each mouthful.

Vomiting for emotional reasons is not usually accompanied by nausea; however, nausea may occur if emotional tension is interfering with digestion. If the amount of food lost by vomiting is small, the patient's nutrition is not affected. Persistent vomiting is serious because the body is deprived of essential foods and fluids. Rectal and intravenous feedings are sometimes needed to replace these losses.

Observe and report any of these symptoms carefully—they give the doctor important information. Vomiting may be due to inflammation of the mucous membrane that lines the stomach—alcohol, salicylates and poisons sometimes cause this kind of irritation. Irritation may be due to disease in other body organs—uremia in acute nephritis is an example. Vomiting is one symptom of acute appendicitis. Always remember that the patient who vomits should not have anything by mouth until the doctor has given instructions.

Note the type of vomiting. For example, in brain disturbances and in some obstructions of the intestines, vomited material is ejected with great force—this is called *projectile vomiting.*

Vomitus. Vomiting is not an illness in itself but is a symptom of illness. Vomitus is stomach contents; its appearance and odor tell something about the cause of the vomiting. Notice whether it is undigested food; is odorless or has a sour smell; or is liquid. Does it contain mucus or pus? Vomitus containing bile is a yellowish or greenish color. If it is material that has been forced back into the stomach from the intestine, it has a fecal odor—typical of intestinal obstruction. Vomitus the color of coffee grounds—often described as *coffee-ground vomitus*—contains digested blood and of course is a sign of hemorrhage and a danger signal. Bright red blood sometimes appears. This may be a sign of stomach ulcer. Distinguish between the expectoration of discharges from the nose and the throat and vomiting.

Specimens. Always save for inspection vomitus that is unusual in any way. It may be legal evidence in suspected poisoning; the doctor's trained eyes will get information from the specimen that is more reliable than a word description. Note the amount of vomitus, if possible; it can be measured. The doctor may want the entire specimen sent to the laboratory for examination or may send only a specimen of the vomited material. As with other specimens, a single specimen should be in a moisture-proof, covered container and properly labeled.

Care of the Patient. Assist the lying-down patient who is vomiting by lifting his head slightly and placing a curved basin under his chin. Always turn his head to the side to aid in draining material from the mouth and to prevent it from entering the air passages. If the patient is sitting up, hold the basin for him and support his head with your other hand on his forehead. A towel under the basin protects the bed. If vomiting is frequent, protect the pillow with a moisture-proof covering under the pillow case. Remove soiled linen and wash the face and the hands, if necessary, to remove all traces of offensive and nauseating odors. Rinsing the patient's mouth helps to eliminate a disagreeable aftertaste. Wash the emesis basin.

Test Meal

Digestive system disturbances do not always cause vomiting. The doctor may want an analysis of the stomach contents because other symptoms indicate trouble in the digestive system. One method of securing a specimen of the stomach contents is by the test meal. A test meal is given to stimulate the secretion of gastric juice in the stomach; then small amounts of the stomach contents are withdrawn at intervals and analyzed. The stomach contents are withdrawn in the morning because it is known what the normal amount of gastric juice should be at that time. Then the test meal is given when the stomach is empty.

Preparing and Serving a Test Meal. The doctor orders the type of test meal that he considers suitable for giving him the information he wants. It may be bread or toast (without crusts) given with water or tea (without cream and sugar). After the stomach is emptied, the patient eats the test meal.

Removing Stomach Contents. Prepare the patient by explaining that the test meal will give the doctor information about his stomach and digestion. Explain that the procedure need not even be uncomfortable if he obeys directions. Explain that the tube has nothing to do with the breathing apparatus; the doctor will guide the tube; the patient will be asked to swallow, then to breathe through his mouth to keep from closing his lips and teeth on the tube and obstructing it. Tell him what the food will be, to remove fears about disagreeable tastes; explain that it is important to eat it all to get the best results from the test.

In assisting with this procedure, you can put the towel under the patient's chin, wipe his mouth, encourage him in following directions, hold the container for the stomach contents. You can remove and care for the equipment when the procedure is finished, label the specimens and see that they get to the laboratory.

Information Through X-Rays

The doctor also obtains information about a patient by photographing parts of the patient's body or examining them under the fluoroscope or x-ray screen. Many patients come into the hospital for a series of x-ray examinations of the stomach and the intestines. (This is sometimes referred to as a GI, or gastro-intestinal, series.) Hard bone tissues contain mineral salts that the x-rays do not penetrate easily, so the shape of bones will show on the film. The stomach and the intestines are soft tissues—in order to see their shape, it is necessary to give the patient another kind of test meal containing a substance that x-rays will not penetrate (barium).

Barium by Mouth or Rectum. Barium salts are heavy and are used most commonly. The patient drinks a preparation of barium (in buttermilk or chocolate milk or a similar drink) for examinations of the stomach and the duodenum; the preparation is given by rectum if the colon is to be examined. The area to be examined is under the fluoroscope as the patient drinks the fluid, and the outlines of the stomach and its outlet and the intestinal tract are observed. X-ray pictures are taken at definite intervals afterward, to photograph the outlines of the stomach and the intestines and to note the progress of the material through the digestive tract.

Preparation for X-Ray Examination and After-care. The entire alimentary tract is prepared for the examination by emptying it as thoroughly as possible. This is done by the use of cathartics and enemas. The patient is not allowed to have food preceding the examination or for some time afterward. The doctor leaves definite orders about the time when food may be given; this is usually some time after the first follow-up x-ray picture has been taken. It is important to be alert about patients who are having a series of stomach and intestinal or other x-ray investigations. The orders about giving anything by mouth are very explicit and must be observed exactly. Food or water at the wrong time could make the entire examination worthless. When the examination series is completed, cathartics or enemas usually are ordered to remove all traces of barium from the intestines.

Assisting With X-Ray Examinations. Be sure the area around the rectum is clean before the patient goes for the examination. You may be asked to take him to the x-ray department—he will go on a stretcher or in a wheelchair, depending on his condition at the time. Stay with him until someone in the x-ray department takes over; he has had no food and may become faint or fall from the stretcher or wheelchair if left alone. If you are required to stay during the examination, you help the patient out of and into the wheelchair or assist in moving him to and from the x-ray table and the stretcher.

SPECIMENS OF SPINAL FLUID

The brain and the spinal cord are covered by 3 membranes—the cerebrospinal fluid is enclosed between the 2 innermost ones. This fluid really surrounds the entire central nervous system; examination of it helps the doctor to identify disease conditions. The pressure of the spinal fluid is also an indication of the kind of difficulty the patient is having. Swelling of the brain tissues, meningitis and cerebral hemorrhage raise the pressure above normal; a block in the circulation of the spinal fluid between the lumbar part of the spine and the brain lowers the pressure. An instrument similar to the one used to measure blood pressure—a manometer—is used to measure spinal fluid pressure.

Reasons for Obtaining a Specimen. The organisms of the diseases that affect the nervous system are present in the spinal fluid—as, for example, in meningitis. Syphilis in the advanced stages causes deterioration of the brain (paresis); it also causes loss of control of the action of the legs (locomotor ataxia). Some of the patients in mental hospitals have paresis. A positive Wassermann reaction of the spinal fluid is a definite proof of the presence of syphilis.

Obtaining Specimens

A specimen of the spinal fluid is obtained for any test by inserting a special needle in the space between the 3rd and 4th lumbar vertebrae. This particular spot is chosen because the spinal cord does not extend this far down, and there is no danger of injuring it. The pressure is measured by the manometer, which is attached to the needle; specimens of the fluid are collected in sterile test tubes and examined in the laboratory.

EQUIPMENT

Labeled sterile test tubes
Manometer and sterile manometer tubing
Sterile lumbar puncture needles
Sterile rubber gloves
Sterile sponges
Sterile towels
Sterile anesthetic solution
Sterile syringe—for withdrawing fluid
Sterile hypodermic syringe for injecting the anesthetic solution into the skin
Sterile hypodermic needle
Sterile medicine glass—for the anesthetic solution
Antiseptic solution—to cleanse the skin
Adhesive tape

Notice that sterile equipment is used in this procedure. The two main reasons for this are to prevent introducing any organism into the spinal fluid specimen and to protect the patient from infectious organisms that might enter his body from the punctured skin or by means of the other equipment used in the procedure. Use the technic required for handling any sterile equipment.

Assisting to Obtain a Specimen

If it is necessary for you to assist with this procedure, you can bring the equipment to the bedside. In the patient's home, it would be impossible to get all the equipment ready yourself—the doctor would have to provide most of it. He might ask you to boil the syringes and the needles and a medicine glass for him; you might or might not be able to provide sterile sponges, an antiseptic solution to cleanse the skin and adhesive tape.

Explain to the patient that the doctor is collecting some spinal fluid to get information that will help him (the patient). Tell him that the doctor will use a needle but will make the small spot where he is working numb; explain that lying on his side makes the procedure easier and quicker.

Put the patient in the proper position (on his side), with the lower part of his back at the edge of the bed, his knees well drawn up toward his chin and his back arched outward; this position increases the space between the vertebrae and makes it easier to introduce the needle.

During the procedure, you can reassure the patient and encourage him to cooperate. You may remove the stoppers from the test tubes, hold the tubes for the doctor, hold the stoppers to keep them sterile and restopper each tube. You can apply strips of adhesive tape to hold the dressing in place over the puncture wound.

When the procedure is over, replace the bedclothes and make the patient comfortable. Keep him in bed, with his head low, for several hours. Explain to him that this prevents severe headache. Headache is likely to occur if the position interferes with the return of the lowered spinal fluid pressure to normal. Remove and care for the equipment and see that the specimens are labeled properly and taken to the laboratory.

BLOOD SPECIMENS

Specimens of blood are taken to get information about the different kinds of cells and to look for disease organisms. In some body disturbances, one or another of the different kinds of blood cells will increase in number or change in shape. Thus, the number and the shape of the red cells give information about anemia; the number of the leukocytes tells about infection. The organism that causes syphilis is found in the blood; this is also true of malaria.

A specimen of the patient's blood is obtained by inserting a needle into a vein and drawing out the required amount of blood with a syringe. If only a few drops are needed, they are obtained by puncturing the patient's finger and smearing the blood directly on a glass slide. Blood usually is taken from a vein on the inside surface of the forearm, near the elbow. The veins are near the surface and easy to see or feel, although other areas where the veins stand out prominently may be chosen. The patient lies on his back with his arm resting comfortably on the bed. The tourniquet is applied around the upper arm, tightened and secured by a slip knot. The tourniquet prevents the blood from flowing back, and the vein enlarges and stands out. The patient can also force more blood into the vein by opening and closing his fist several times. The area over the vein is cleansed with alcohol before inserting the needle to remove infectious organisms from the skin. The protective sheet is placed under the arm to prevent soiling the bed; when the required amount of blood has been collected the tourniquet is released. A sponge is laid over the needle where it enters the skin, the needle is withdrawn, and the patient bends his elbow to put pressure on the vein and check bleeding.

A blood specimen is obtained from an infant or a young child by puncturing the jugular vein in the neck. The mummy type of restraint is used. The nurse holds the child with his head over the edge of the treatment table and steadies his head.

The doctor or the laboratory technician usually collects a blood specimen, although the professional nurse may sometimes do this procedure. The equipment is provided by the laboratory.

The specimen is labeled and taken to the laboratory. In caring for the equipment after use, it is important to rinse the syringe with cold water and to force cold water through the needles. Then the needles and the syringe must be sterilized. Be careful as you handle this equipment if you have uncovered scratches or cuts on your hands. Remember that harmful organisms enter the body through cuts and scratches. Syphilis organisms, when present, are found in the blood; other organisms also can cause infection.

33

THE SURGICAL PATIENT

PREOPERATIVE NURSING CARE

In the beginning of her experience with patients, it is impossible for the student to have detailed information about each disease and the specific nursing care entailed. However, it is reassuring if she has a good basic knowledge of how certain types of patients may look and behave, what their common problems may be and how she can best take care of them. More information about the surgical patient and the nursing care needed in specific illnesses will be given in the chapters which are devoted to such illnesses.

PREPARING A PATIENT FOR A SURGICAL OPERATION

In the hospital, you will be asked to assist the professional nurse in the care of preoperative patients because you know how to do many of the procedures in this preparation. It is very important to carry out preoperative orders exactly—they effect the success of the operation. These orders concern the physical preparation, but, as you carry them out, remember the patient's feelings and his need for reassurance.

No patient looks forward to an operation—he is more likely to dread or even fear the ordeal. An adult knows that he is expected to conceal his feelings; he has been taught that it is a sign of weakness to admit that he is afraid. Therefore, it is up to the nurse to explain what is about to happen and to provide an opportunity for the patient's questions, to let him express his doubts and fears without losing face. Agreeing with him that it is natural to feel apprehensive is vastly more reassuring than saying there is nothing to worry about, no matter how true that may be. Remember that a patient may hesitate to ask questions because he wants you to think well of him. After all, he is in your care, and he might expect to fare better if he does the things he thinks will please you.

The Patient's Feelings. If you ever have had an operation, you should be able to put yourself in the patient's place and sense his feelings. To begin with, his previous experiences will effect him now: if he has had an operation before, he is thinking of all the things that happened then—perhaps he had nausea, pain, a draining wound, a long illness. He may be fearful of having cancer or of being disabled. If this is his first experience, he may have all sorts of vague fears. People are likely to imagine large sharp knives and torturing instruments as being a part of an operation. Some people dread losing consciousness or being "sick from the ether." Most people fear pain after the operation. Others are afraid that they will die. The mother worries about her children's care while she is in the hospital; the father, about his family's support. Every person meets this ordeal of an operation very much as he or she is accustomed to meeting any difficult situation. The more you know about an individual patient, the better; it will help you to sense the kind of reassurance that he needs.

Explain the preparations for the operation

to the patient as you go along—how they help him and help the doctor. Observe and report to the head nurse anything unusual that happens: failure to expel an enema or to void urine, an elevation of temperature, a weak pulse or decreased respirations.

Admission

Sometimes a patient has been in the hospital for some time before an operation, either to improve his physical condition or to make the necessary tests. Many patients are admitted the day before, and although the doctor has essential information about his patient, he usually wants a final check on some points. It is important to send a urine specimen to the laboratory promptly; other specimens may be requested as well. Every patient who is of age and in his right mind must sign a permit giving his consent to an operation. The written consent of a relative or guardian must be obtained for an operation upon a minor or an unconscious or irresponsible person.

Skin Preparation

One of the most important procedures in the preparation of the patient for a surgical procedure is the cleansing of the skin. Because the skin is normally oily and contains a large quantity of bacteria, care must be taken to cleanse it properly to remove as much of this material as possible to prevent contamination of the wound.

Preparation will begin on the evening before the scheduled day of operation, except in the case of emergency. Cleansing agents, either soap and water solution or one of the many proprietary skin detergents such as pHisoHex will be used. As you have been shown previously, mild friction is one of the most efficient ways to remove foreign material. This is followed by carefully shaving the area, because microorganisms stick to hair. The hair growth on many parts of the body is very fine and can be seen only in a brightly illuminated room. Therefore, make sure that your lighting facilities are adequate.

Be careful not to cut the skin with the razor and thereby open up a potential source of infection.

Prepare an area in excess of the actual operation field. This allows for the proper draping of the patient without contamination caused by touching an unprepared area.

Unless you have been expressly directed as to the area to be prepared follow the diagram on page 427 (Fig. 137).

Intestinal Preparation

The orders of individual doctors vary, and the preparation of the patient will be in keeping with the kind of operation to be performed, the type of anesthetic he will have and his general condition. Usually the patient is given an enema to empty the colon; this makes the operation easier for the surgeon and prevents distress for the patient afterward. In intestinal surgery the tract should be as empty of feces as possible. Be sure that the patient has expelled all of an enema, since when he is relaxed under an anesthetic, he may expel the remainder on the operating table.

Usually no food is given on the morning of the operation and probably a very small amount the night before. Again, this depends on the

---

FIG. 137 (*Facing page*). Areas to be prepared for operation. The shaded areas are those to be shaved. (A) Preparation for amputation of breast. Note that the area to be prepared includes the front and the back of the trunk and extends from the neck to the umbilicus. The axilla and the upper portion of the arm also are included. (B) Area of preparation for operation on the thorax. (C) Area of preparation for operation upon the abdomen (laparotomy) and for hernia. The preparation should extend from the nipple line to well below the crest of the ilium. For herniorrhaphy the upper limit of preparation may be the area of the umbilicus. (D) Area to be prepared for nephrectomy. Note that the preparation should be on both the anterior and the posterior sides of the trunk. (E) Area to be prepared for operations on the perineum. These areas should be shaved completely for all gynecologic operations, operations around the anus and for such combined operations as an abdominoperineal resection of the rectum.

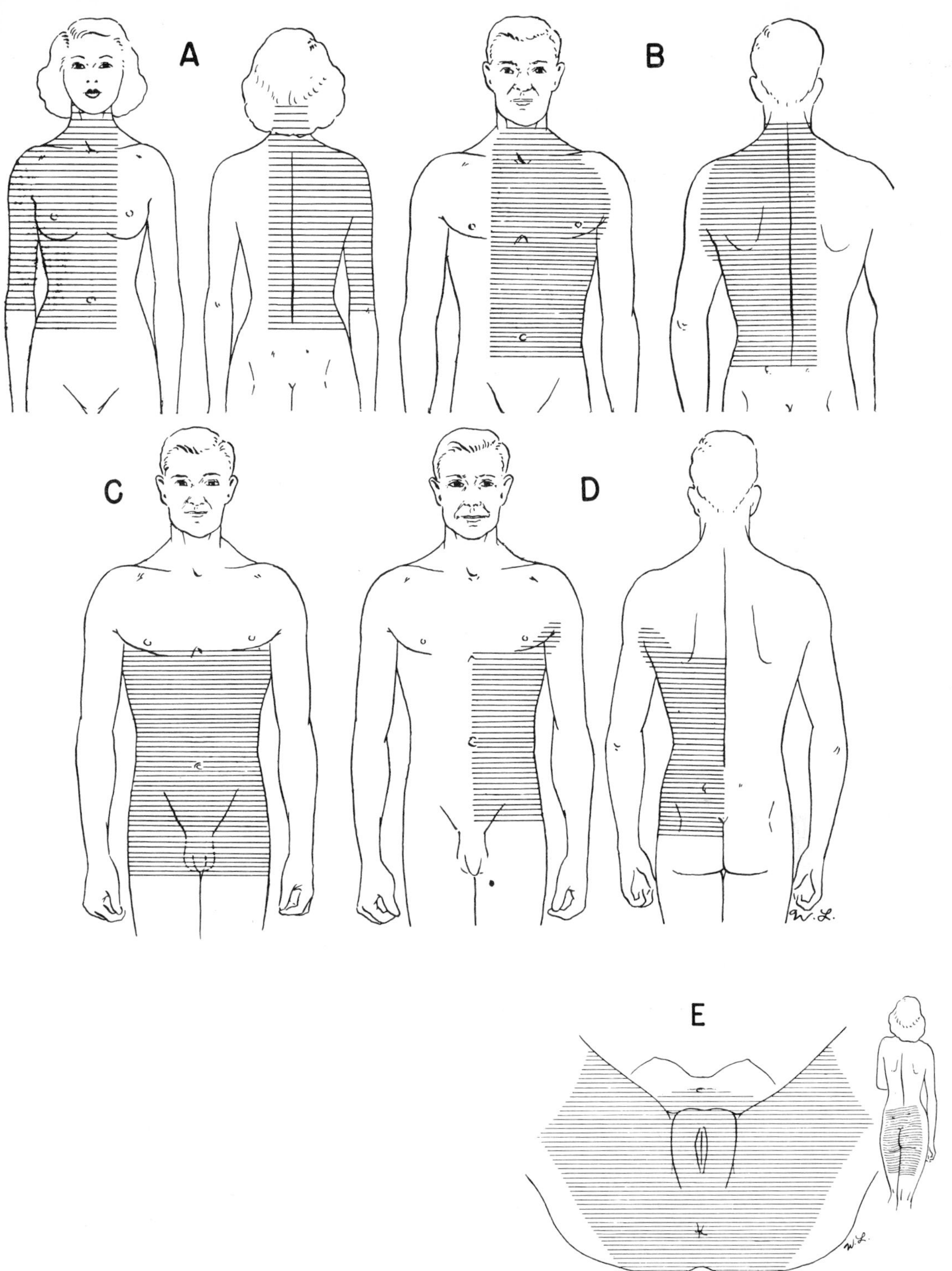

FIGURE 137. (*Caption on facing page.*)

type of operation and the time of day that the patient goes to the operating room. A patient is less likely to be nauseated or to vomit if his stomach is empty; a general anesthetic tends to aggravate nausea, and vomiting interferes with the anesthetic. Undigested food brought up into the throat in vomiting may choke the patient.

Preoperative Medication

The doctor usually orders a medication the night before an operation, to ensure a good night's rest for the patient; this may be any one of the barbiturates, such as *phenobarbital.* An exceptionally high-strung and jittery patient is sometimes given a tranquilizer, such as *meprobamate*, for several days before surgery. A narcotic such as *morphine* or *Demerol* is given for its relaxing effect an hour before the patient is scheduled to go to the operating room. Allaying the patient's anxiety makes it easier for him to take the anesthetic. If he is to have a general anesthetic, *atropine* may be combined with the narcotic to reduce respiratory secretions. If this is done, the patient should be informed that the medicine will make his mouth dry.

You may be asked to assist the anesthetist in giving a rectal or other anesthetic to the patient before he leaves his room. Frequently, such anesthetics are given some time before the patient goes to the operating room. You can put the patient in position, reassure him and make him comfortable afterward.

Effect of Quiet. On the day of the operation, the patient should be quiet and free from excitement or emotional upset. Members of the family or friends who are weepy or emotional should be tactfully barred from remaining in his room. Usually the patient has had a medication to quiet and relax him; you can explain that the effect is lost if he is allowed to talk with people. It is understandable that he would wish to see some members of his family briefly before he goes to the operating room, and that the family would have the same feeling about seeing him. You will need to explain why it is best to make this contact brief—always assuming that his family will want to do what is best for him. However, he should not be denied the comfort of having his wife or some member of his family sitting quietly nearby, if this is what he wants.

The Helpless Bystander. For their own and for the patient's sakes, it is important that members of the family are made to feel that they have a right to be concerned about the patient and even that they may be helpful. It is very easy to give the impression that outsiders are only in the way during the preparations for surgery; a nurse should take time to explain what is going on. Then, after the patient has gone to the operating room, the anxious husband or wife or other relative can only wait. Sitting in the patient's room or pacing up and down in the sunparlor, the time can seem endless. How easy it is for a thoughtful nurse to stop long enough for a few reassuring words, perhaps to suggest that there is time for a visit to the coffee shop before the patient returns. This is an anxious time at best, and it is callous and inhuman to permit needless additional worry.

Personal Preparation

1. See that the patient's body and gown are clean before he goes to the operating room. It is most embarrassing to the operating room personnel to find that they must stop to remove the evidences of feces before a waiting surgeon. The patient is given a bedpan or a urinal before going to the operating room; a full bladder interferes with surgical procedures in an abdominal operation, or, like the rectum, may empty itself on the operating table when the patient relaxes under anesthesia.

The gown should be untied and left open in the back. This is done for many reasons. The preoperative medication, the patient's anxieties and the temperature of the operating room all have a tendency to make the patient perspire more than usual, thus necessitating a change of gowns while he is in the operating room and the recovery room. Also, a gown open in the back makes surgical painting of the operative area easier; all areas of the body are easily accessible without having the patient roll back and forth on the operating table.

For example, consider the following positions: receiving spinal anesthesia; placing the legs in a dorsal position for gynecologic surgery; rolling on one's side in Sims's position for rectal or gynecologic surgery and abdominal or chest surgery.

2. Remove any jewelry that the patient may be wearing. At this point, you can see the reason for removing and safely storing the patient's valuables and jewelry on admission. What to do with a wrist watch or a valuable ring may present a problem. Sometimes a ring fits so loosely on a finger that it may slip off; a clasp comes unfastened and a watch falls on the floor and breaks. If the patient does not wish to remove a wedding band, it must be bound to the finger with tape, or tied with roller gauze and fastened securely around the patient's wrist. In this way, the band cannot become dislodged during the operation.

3. Remove all dentures, complete or partial. Put them in a container—preferably in a drawer or in the bathroom, out of sight. People are likely to be sensitive about wearing dentures; some member of the family might be in the room before the patient is awake, and dentures are not particularly attractive ornaments. If you put dentures in a folded sponge, be sure to attach a label, or someone may unknowingly pick it up and let the dentures fall out and break.

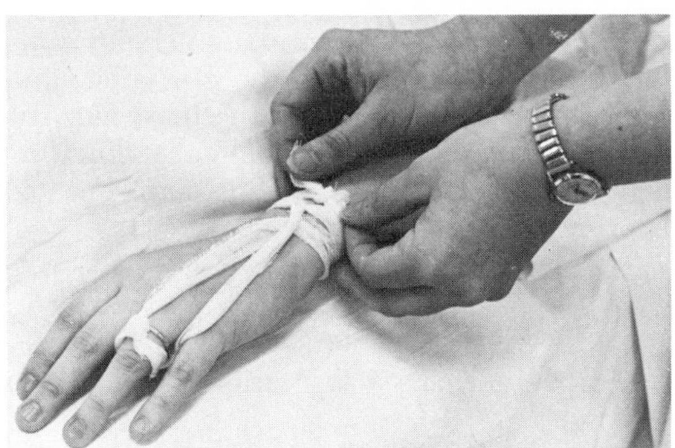

FIG. 138. To prevent loss during surgery, the nurse has secured this patient's wedding band to her hand by slipping the gauze under the band and looping it around the finger and ring as shown. It is important not to tie it tightly enough to impair circulation.

4. A patient should always wear a hospital gown to the operating room. In some hospitals he will also wear ether stockings (cotton leggings which keep the patient warm and protected from exposure). The patient's head must also be covered. Most hospitals provide a turban or cap for this purpose, to protect and confine the hair. Remove all pins, combs or ornaments—sharp instruments left in the hair may damage anesthesia equipment. If the hair is long, braid it and tie the ends with roller gauze.

5. See that a woman patient is without make-up or nail polish. The surgeon and the anesthetist watch the natural color of the skin and the nails for signs of lack of oxygen.

Organization of Preoperative Care

The preceding afternoon:

1. Check the chart and note the doctor's preoperative orders (enema, catheterization, medicine, etc.).
2. See that the operation permit is signed.
3. Prepare the operative area (if ordered).
4. See that all specimens have been collected.
5. Note and attend to change in diet (as ordered).
6. In the evening, give the sedative if ordered.
7. Withhold fluids as directed.

The morning of the operation:

1. Record T.P.R. and B.P. Report any marked deviation from normal to the head nurse right away, so that she can report it to the doctor.
2. Help the patient with bath and cleanliness measures as necessary.
3. Remove prostheses and dentures if present.
4. Remove jewelry and valuables and put them in a safe or give them to the family. Be sure that the wedding band is included with these, unless the patient does not wish to remove it and it is securely bound to the hand.
5. Help the patient put on the gown, the leggings and the head covering.
6. Have the patient void (if the patient is

unable to void, tell the head nurse and report this fact on the chart).

7. Check to be sure that the charting is completed, with reports and the operation permit attached to it.

Transporting the Patient

The patient goes to the operating room on a stretcher. This should be made as comfortable and warm as possible, since there is a possibility that the corridors and the elevators leading to the operating room will be drafty and colder than the patient's room. His chart goes with him, with all information completed to date. The chart should be given to the anesthetist or a nurse in the operating room; *it is never left with the patient;* neither is it left in the room where the family could have access to it or misplace it. Always be certain that the patient is properly identified before taking him to the operating room. Identification bracelets or bed tags help to prevent errors and assure that the right person is going to surgery. Let the patient know that you will be glad to see him when he comes back. If the patient is to go to the recovery room instead of returning directly to his own room, he should be told about it. Upon their arrival in the operating room, the nurse should remain with the patient until he is relieved by either an operating room nurse or an anesthetist.

The Patient in the Operating Room. It is most helpful if the patient can meet the anesthetist beforehand and have a short visit with him. Some anesthetists make it a point to visit a patient before the day of the operation. This gives the patient an opportunity to ask questions and to receive explanations which will do away with many of his anxieties. Most people have listened to detailed descriptions of the surgical experiences of their families and relatives and have heard enough about upsetting incidents to make them uneasy. If the patient can be spared any contact with strange noises and unusual sights from other operating rooms, he will be less apprehensive—this is particularly true of children. Friendly voices and a lack of rush or hurry will also be encouraging. Too much technical conversation on the part of the operating room personnel is likely to mystify and frighten a patient. The hospitals which have anesthesia induction rooms with standard hospital room furnishings have gone far in maintaining the patient's feeling of security.

ANESTHESIA

The Anesthesiologist. Modern surgery is often so highly technical and delicate that the surgeon must be able to depend on the skill of the anesthetists to keep him informed about the patient's condition throughout the operation. Today the preferred anesthetist is a physician, trained in *anesthesiology,* the science of anesthesia. If an anesthesiologist is not available, a nurse specially trained in anesthesia takes his place.

Anesthetics. Anesthetics have been divided into 2 main classes: (1) general anesthetics which suspend the sensations of the whole body and (2) local, regional or spinal anesthetics which bring about the insensitivity of parts of the body without general unconsciousness. General anesthetics can be administered by inhalation, intravenously or rectally. The most common anesthetics given by inhalation are ether, nitrous oxide, cyclopropane and ethyl chloride. Other anesthetics act directly on the nerve trunks and their branches. Sometimes the anesthetic solution is injected into the spinal canal, directly into a controlling nerve, or into the tissues in the area of the operation. Procaine is used most widely in this way. The basal anesthetics, such as Pentothal Sodium, act very quickly and are usually supplemented later by others, such as ether.

Stages of Inhalation Anesthesia

General anesthesia is decribed as having 4 stages:

1. *Stage of Beginning Anesthesia.* First, the patient feels drowsy and warm, with a heavy "drugged" sensation. He is still conscious but cannot lift his arms or his legs. He can still hear, even to an exaggerated point, but he cannot speak. At this time most patients remember a feeling of anxiety lest the operation

begin before they have completely lost consciousness.

2. *Stage of Excitement.* Many times the patient will begin to struggle (possibly because he wants to show that he is not yet unconscious). There should be no preparatory work on the operative site at this time, since it only aggravates the patient's excitement. The pupils become dilated but will still contract with light. The pulse rate becomes rapid, the respirations irregular.

3. *Stage of Surgical Anesthesia.* The patient becomes unconscious. The pupils are small but will respond to light. Respiration is regular. The pulse is normal and of good volume. The skin is warm and pink. This stage may be continued for hours if the proper administration of anesthesia is maintained and the patient's condition remains good.

4. *Stage of Danger.* This condition may occur in deep anesthesia or in shock. The respirations become shallow; the pupils are dilated and do not contract in response to light; cyanosis develops. The anesthetic is discontinued, and stimulants are given to prevent collapse and death. Asphyxia (suffocation) may occur, due to the aspiration of vomitus, saliva or blood, or because the tongue falls back in the mouth and obstructs the airway.

POSTOPERATIVE NURSING CARE

The Recovery Room

Many hospitals now have a room, or a suite of rooms, set aside for the care of patients immediately after surgery. This *recovery room,* as it is called, ideally should be on the same floor as the operating rooms so that doctors and nurses are quickly available if a postop-

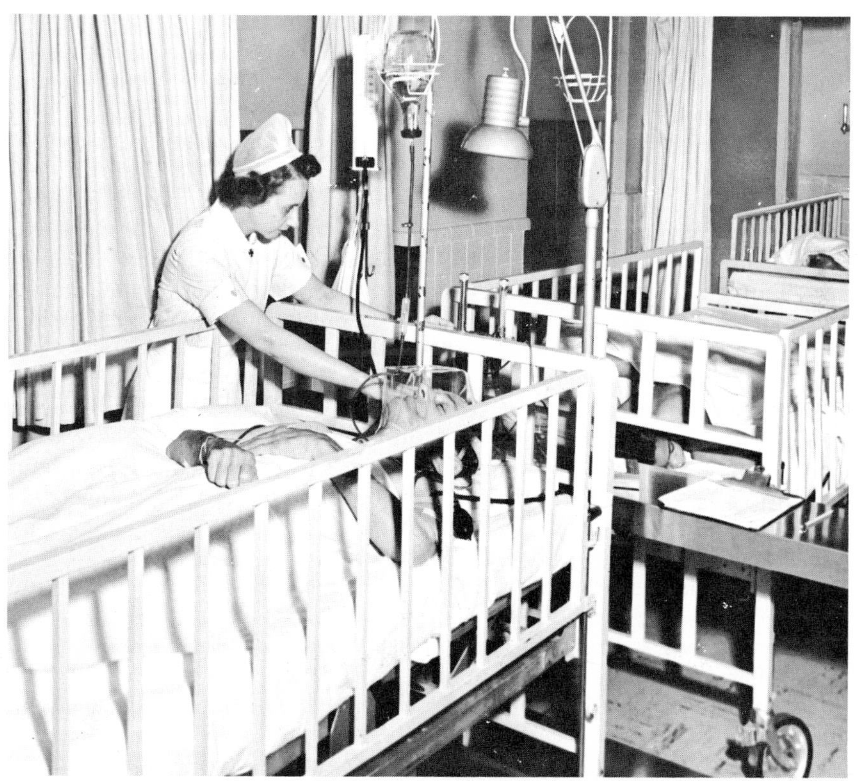

Fig. 139. Recovery room. (Brunner, L. S., *et al.*: Textbook of Medical-Surgical Nursing, p. 273, Philadelphia, Lippincott, 1964)

erative patient needs emergency attention. Concentrating postoperative patients in a limited area makes it possible for one nurse to give close attention to 2 or 3 patients at the same time, which she would not be able to do if they were scattered through a ward or in separate private or semiprivate rooms.

Equipment. Another advantage of the recovery room is that it has every type of equipment at hand and ready for use. This includes:

1. Breathing aids: oxygen, tracheostomy sets, laryngoscopes, suction equipment and bronchial instruments
2. Circulatory aids: blood pressure apparatus (sphygmomanometer), stethoscope, intravenous and cut-down trays, universal donor blood, plasma, intravenous solutions, cardiac arrest equipment, tourniquets, syringes and needles, cardiac drugs and respiratory stimulants
3. Narcotics, sedatives and emergency drugs
4. Surgical dressing carriage and linen supply

The patient unit has a recovery bed, equipped with side rails for the patient's protection, intravenous poles, wheel brakes and a chart rack. The bed can be moved easily and can be adjusted to elevate the head or the foot. The unit has a bedside stand which holds tissue, emesis basin, tongue depressors, face cloth and towel. Each unit has its own outlet for piped-in oxygen and for suction.

The recovery room staff consist of registered professional nurses and licensed practical nurses. Professional and practical nurse students commonly have a period of experience in the recovery room. In a large hospital, the recovery room may give 24-hour service; smaller hospitals usually limit it to shorter periods—for example, from 8:00 to 4:00, 5 days a week. The patient is kept in the unit until he has "reacted" from the anesthetic—this means until he is conscious, is breathing without difficulty and has a stable blood pressure.

The Trip to the Recovery Room. When moving patients every effort is made to avoid unnecessary strain or possible injury, and to accomplish the transfer as quickly as possible with the least amount of exposure. A perspiring patient should leave the operating room in a warm, dry gown, covered with warm, dry blankets. These precautions guard against lung complications and shock. The anesthesiologist goes to the recovery room with the patient, to make certain that the patient's condition is satisfactory before leaving his care. The doctor reports the patient's condition to the nurse in charge and leaves postoperative orders and any special directions about what to watch for.

Postoperative Care in a Ward or a Room. Suppose that you find yourself taking care of postoperative patients in a ward or in a private room. After the patient goes to the operating room you make the recovery bed and place the equipment for postanesthesia care on the bedside table. Provide all the necessary equipment and see that it is in good working order. This will prevent a loss of time when the patient arrives, and then you will be able to give your full attention to the patient. Remember that all postoperative patients must be protected from falling out of bed. The need for this precaution is especially apparent when the patient is recovering from general anesthesia but is also true for patients who have remained conscious during surgery. Preoperative medications can also cause dizziness and confusion. No patient should be left alone until he has fully regained consciousness. Check the doctor's orders and carry them out immediately—such as giving oxygen, connecting draining tubes, giving special medications and using suction.

The Recovery Bed. No matter where the recovery bed is, it serves the same purpose: to provide protection and warmth after an operation or treatment. Every hospital has its own adaption of the recovery bed, but in making it they all are guided by the same principles:

1. Light blankets provide warmth, but too many blankets cause excessive perspiration and loss of body fluids.
2. The upper bed clothing is arranged so that it can be turned back easily to receive the patient.
3. A pillow placed upright at the head of the bed protects the patient's head from injury.
4. A waterproof sheet is necessary to protect the head of the mattress from soiling.

5. Hot-water bags, if placed in the bed, must be removed before the patient is put into the bed. They could burn an unconscious patient without his knowledge (see Fig. 140).

IMMEDIATE POSTOPERATIVE NURSING CARE

A patient may return from the operating room in excellent condition, or his condition may be serious. It all depends on his condition before the operation, the kind of operation and the length of time it took. You will not be expected to carry the entire responsibility for a patient who is recovering from anesthesia. You should be able to take care of his immediate needs under the supervision of the professional nurse, who should check with you frequently regarding the patient's condition while he is recovering from an anesthetic. You should know what to look out for and be able to recognize dangerous symptoms if they appear. Remember that every anesthetic has some depressing effects; the patient who returns from the operating room awake may need as careful watching as the one who is unconscious.

Danger Signs

Never leave an unconscious patient alone; be on the lookout for 3 serious complications that can appear: hemorrhage, shock, and lowered oxygen supply (hypoxia).

Hemorrhage. Hemorrhage or excessive blood loss at the time of surgery indicates the need for blood transfusions. Secondary hemorrhage sometimes occurs after the patient returns from surgery; consequently, the wound dressing should be inspected frequently. In some cases, bleeding can be stopped by exerting pressure on the wound or by compression on the arteries. (This is described in more detail in Chap. 48.) However, concealed bleeding must be recognized by observing the patient's symptoms. These are the signs to watch for:

1. Restlessness and anxiety
2. Thirst
3. Cold, moist and pale skin
4. Increased pulse rate (rapid and thready)
5. Drop in body temperature
6. Deep, rapid, gasping respirations (air hunger)
7. Drop in blood pressure
8. Ringing in the ears and spots before the eyes
9. Pallor of the lips and conjunctiva

As you can see, prompt action may be necessary—continued bleeding can cause death.

Shock. *Traumatic* shock occurs after severe hemorrhage but may also be the result of pain, fear, burns, infection, injury and other factors. The blood supply in the peripheral blood vessels is reduced, and the circulation of blood becomes insufficient to carry out its normal functions. The symptoms of shock are similar to those of hemorrhage, including a cold, moist

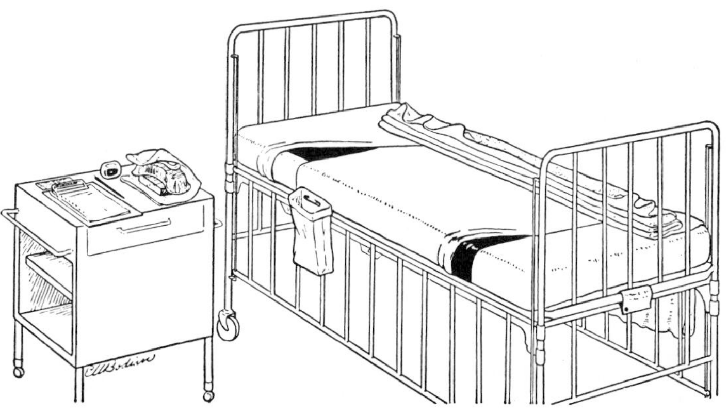

Fig. 140. The recovery bed.

and pale skin, a rapid and thready pulse, rapid grasping respirations (air hunger) and a drop in blood pressure. Preventive treatment is most important, but some factors that cause shock cannot be controlled. Then general supportive procedures and the restoration of the blood volume must be established speedily. The supportive measures are:

1. Elevate the lower part of the body so that the patient's feet are higher than his head (unless the patient has had brain surgery or spinal anesthesia, in which case he should be kept flat).
2. Supply heat sufficient to keep the body at a normal temperature.
3. Give oxygen and drugs as ordered by the doctor to elevate the blood pressure.
4. Control hemorrhage.
5. Restore fluid balance by administering blood, plasma or other parenteral fluids. The term *parenteral* refers to injection by any method other than the gastrointestinal tract.

Shock is discussed more fully in Chapter 48.

Hypoxia. Anesthetics and preoperative medications sometimes depress respirations and interfere with the oxygenation of the blood, causing a condition known as *hypoxia*. Mucus blocking the tracheal or the bronchial passages lowers the amount of oxygen entering the lungs, and the patient suffers from difficult breathing and cyanosis. Oxygen and suction equipment should always be on hand for emergency use to meet these problems.

Additional Nursing Responsibilities

It may be some time before the patient becomes conscious and still longer before he has fully recovered from the anesthetic. He may recover consciousness quietly, or he may be restless and groan as he begins to feel pain. When he opens his eyes, speak reassuringly to him. The nurse's responsibilities during this recovery period are to:

1. Carry out orders for drugs or oxygen to be given immediately.
2. Attach drainage apparatus as ordered (for bottle drainage from cholecystostomy, catheters, chest tubes, etc.).
3. Attach gastric or Miller-Abbott tube to Wangensteen suction drainage.
4. Take vital signs, which include temperature, pulse, respiration and blood pressure as follows: pulse and respiration every 15 minutes for the first 2 hours; every one-half hour for the next 2 hours. Watch respirations for depth as well as rate. Take a pulse a full minute if there is any doubt. Temperatures should be either rectal or axillary (depending on the surgery involved), since the patient has not fully recovered from the effect of anesthesia and is therefore irresponsible. *Never* leave an irresponsible or unconscious patient during this procedure. Take blood pressure as ordered. *Report* a temperature over 100 or under 97; respirations over 30 and under 16; a systolic blood pressure under 90.
5. Inspect dressings and note signs of hemorrhage and any unusual amount of drainage. If necessary, reinforce but *do not change* dressings.
6. Assist the patient when he vomits. Turn his head to the side, to empty his mouth and throat of fluid that might be drawn into the air passages and interfere with his breathing. Hold the curved emesis basin below the jaw to catch the vomited material and note the amount and the color. Wipe the patient's chin and, if he is fully conscious, allow him to rinse his mouth to remove the taste which may continue to make him nauseated.

   If extensive retching or vomiting takes place, check the dressings to be certain that they are still in place and be sure that drainages and suction equipment continue to function properly.
7. If the patient is having a parenteral injection such as a transfusion or intravenous infusion of fluid, check its rate of flow (about 60 to 80 drops per minute is usual) and make sure that the needle is in the vein. Clamp off the tubing before the container becomes completely empty, to prevent air from entering the vein.
8. Observe, note and report at once any unusual or alarming symptoms. Be certain that the time is also recorded. A nurse is responsible for keeping intelligent and accurate records.

Postoperative Discomforts

By the time the patient has returned from the recovery room to his ward or room, he is awake and fully aware of a number of discomforts.

Pain. Pain is the first postoperative discomfort that the patient will encounter. The competent nurse is wise enough to know the value of sufficient medication to ease pain throughout the first 24 hours. If the patient receives medication early and it is spaced properly, he will be kept relatively comfortable. The first hypodermic injection of an opiate can be given before he recovers completely from the anesthetic; it will allow him several hours more of restful sleep. Many times he will also be spared the early postoperative nausea and vomiting. Nausea and vomiting may continue at intervals during the first 24 hours. However, if vomiting persists, fluids will be restricted.

Thirst. Thirst is present, usually due to a decrease of fluids preoperatively, the loss of fluids during surgery and anesthetic recovery, and the dryness following the use of atropine which inhibits mucous secretion. Most patients receive fluids intravenously during surgery and immediately postoperatively. This helps to prevent thirst. Rinsing the mouth helps to decrease thirst. Most physicians allow sips of water or ice chips in small amounts.

Distention. Temporary paralysis of the intestinal movement of peristalsis allows gas to accumulate in the intestines which causes distention. Normal peristalsis is halted temporarily by the handling of the intestines during a surgical operation, the lack of solid food and the restricted body movements. Accumulated gas (flatus) causes sharp pains which often are more distressing than the pain related to the incision. Early ambulation, which permits the patient to get out of bed soon after an operation, helps the patient to expel the flatus; small amounts of solid food also help. If discomfort increases and nursing measures do not bring relief, the doctor usually orders one or more of the following:

1. Application of heat to the abdomen by a hot-water bottle (temperature 115 to 120° F.), or an electric heating pad (thermostat set on "low").

2. Insertion of a rectal tube (see p. 306). This dilates the anal sphincter and provides an outlet for the accumulated gas. Usually, the tube is inserted for a short time, 20 minutes or so, and then withdrawn, cleaned and reinserted perhaps an hour later. If the rectal tube is left in continuously, the patient will become uncomfortable. It is desirable to place the free end of the rectal tube in a urinal or a small specimen bottle in order to catch any feces which might be expelled accidentally with the flatus. If the rectal tube is to be inserted for a shorter period of time, an ABD pad can be wrapped and taped around the free end of the tube rather than placing it in a receptacle. These procedures give assurance to the patient and may save him from embarrassment.

3. Intramuscular injections of neostigmine (Prostigmin), a drug which stimulates peristalsis; 1 cc. of a 1:1,000 or 1:2,000 solution.

If intestinal paralysis persists, a serious condition may develop which is known as *paralytic ileus,* which is the reason for the presence of one tube which you may see in a patient's nose. This is known as the Levin tube, which passes through the nose into the stomach and sometimes into the small intestine; fluids and accumulated gas can be removed by attaching suction to the outer end. The symptoms of this condition are, as you would expect, distention and vomiting.

In the same way, the stomach may become distended with fluids which accumulate instead of passing on into the intestines as they normally would. The symptoms of this condition (*acute gastric dilatation*) are a distended abdomen and the regurgitation of small amounts of fluid (not the same as vomiting). If the condition gets progressively worse, shock may develop. The Levin tube is used for relief. Some surgeons order suction of the gastrointestinal tract as routine preventive treatment.

Urinary Retention. Simple nursing measures to help patients to void are discussed later. However, the situation for the patient who has had abdominal or pelvic surgery is made more difficult if the operation has been disturbing to the bladder region, causing a temporary numbness. The patient may be tense because he is afraid to try to void lest it be painful. Women especially find it difficult to void lying down, and many doctors will allow the patient to sit up on the bedpan or sit on the edge of the bed.

If everything else fails after 8 to 12 hours, catheterization will bring relief. Measures to encourage normal voiding are preferable because they carry no risk of bladder infection. However, some urologists feel that the possibility of damage from an overdistended bladder is greater than the risk of infection by catheterization. In any case, do not give the patient the impression that catheterization is a dangerous or "hush-hush" procedure used only when a patient is *in extremis*. Pain and distention in the bladder region and frequent small voidings are signs of bladder distention. A large fluid intake without a correspondingly ample fluid output are also symptoms. A record of postoperative intake and output is kept routinely for several days, or for longer periods of time if the patient's condition indicates a need for such a record.

In some conditions the surgeon inserts a retention catheter into the bladder at the time of operation, which can be connected to drainage tubing or clamped off to be released at intervals. The care of the patient who has a retention catheter is discussed on page 312.

Constipation. Disruption of the normal diet and the daily elimination schedule may cause constipation. However, usually in 3 or 4 days, the patient is back to his regular bowel habits. He is eating normally again and able to move about more freely. Then peristaltic action will be resumed. If constipation persists, a soapsuds enema (S.S. enema) or oil retention enema will take care of the situation. The commercially prepared enema equipment which is used only once, such as the Fleet enema, is often employed for this purpose.

Restlessness and Sleeplessness. The patient may be restless and have difficulty in sleeping as a result of operative pain, headache, thirst, apprehension, retention of urine, uncomfortable dressings or casts, or even the strange surroundings of a hospital. Every attempt should be made to relieve these symptoms by the ordinary nursing measures. Medications to promote sleep and relieve pain also play an important part but should be given judiciously. Pain from a surgical wound is most severe during the first 48 hours after the operation, and medicine to relieve it should be given as soon as it is needed. Narcotics commonly prescribed for postoperative pain are Demerol or morphine. Look for unexpected reactions—morphine makes some people nauseated. It also depresses respiration and may cause shock if the blood pressure is low or fluctuating. Both narcotics and sedatives may have a confusing effect on older people.

POSSIBLE POSTOPERATIVE COMPLICATIONS

Much can be done to keep these complications from developing. Attention to preventive measures, advances in medical science and early ambulation have all gone a long way toward eliminating the hazards that once accompanied an operation.

Pneumonia and Atelectasis

The patient who must be operated upon and has an existing respiratory difficulty, such as bronchitis, or the more elderly patient, will be more prone to develop respiratory complications, such as hypostatic pneumonia. This type of pneumonia shows the same symptoms as are discussed in Chapter 39 and is treated in the same way with antibiotics.

Atelectasis. Atelectasis, the collapse of a portion of the lung due to a plug of mucus closing one of the bronchi, will cause acute and severe symptoms. The patient becomes somewhat cyanotic and develops very rapid respirations in an attempt to get oxygen. Removal of the mucus plug (by coughing, forceful pounding of the chest, or aspiration) will relieve this difficulty. Deep breathing is a preventive measure. The nurse can instruct surgical patients (unless contraindicated) to take 10 deep breaths every hour. She should demonstrate this breathing technic, to make certain that the patient understands and cooperates.

Another important part of the treatment is a frequent change of position as far as is compatible with the patient's limitations—a patient with a fractured arm could not turn on the injured side.

Thrombophlebitis

If a patient constantly lies in one position, without moving his legs, pressure on the legs from a tight strap or hard underknee roll can interfere with the venous circulation. The blood flows more slowly, inflammation may develop, and clots might form and stick to the walls of the veins. This is *thrombophlebitis*, or the inflammation of a vein in connection with a blood clot. The symptoms include redness of the area, tenderness, swelling and fever. This condition is caused by too little motion, yet the treatment requires keeping the leg quiet and elevated on pillows to reduce the inflammation and swelling. The patient is given an anticoagulant, such as *heparin* or *Dicumarol*, to prevent further clots from forming. Pillows under the knees and the use of the knee gatch are now taboo in postoperative procedures because they cause pressure.

EMBOLUS. Sometimes a clot becomes dislodged from the wall of the vein and travels with the blood stream. If it becomes stuck in a blood vessel and obstructs the circulation of blood to some vital organ, like the lung or the heart, it may cause death. Such a clot is called an *embolus*. Two things to avoid in the treatment of thrombophlebitis are massaging or exercising the affected leg, because of the danger of loosening a clot from the blood vessel wall.

Wound Infection. An otherwise unexplainable temperature elevation 2 or 3 days after an operation, and a redness and swelling occurring around the incision are usually signs of a wound infection. In spite of the use of antibiotics, staphylococcal organisms persist widely, which demands an increased vigilance on the part of nurses to prevent the infection from spreading. The treatment consists of the injection of antibiotics, rest and an adequate diet to build up resistance. If necessary, the wound is drained.

Evisceration. This is not a common occurrence, but it does happen occasionally when the edges of the wound separate and allow the abdominal organs to protrude. Evisceration may be due to poor nutrition, defective suturing, excessive coughing or hiccoughs. The patient will describe his sensations as though "something *gave*." The most a nurse can do is to cover the protruding organs with sterile sponges wet with normal saline and lose no time in reporting it.

Early Ambulation

Advantages. Attitudes toward the postoperative activities of patients have changed radically since the days when the removal of an appendix kept the patient in bed for a week to 10 days. Today, that patient is encouraged to be out of bed and walking in 24 to 48 hours. *Early ambulation* is an important aspect of postoperative treatment. It has many advantages, but its primary purpose is to prevent complications. Physically, it improves and stimulates the circulation, improves breathing and prevents lung congestion and it helps to overcome constipation and urinary retention. It makes people eat better and sleep better. Psychologically, it encourages people to help themselves and gives tangible evidence to a patient that he is making a quick comeback and that things are going well.

The Patient's Reaction. Make it clear to the patient that ambulation is *not* sitting up out of bed; ambulation is taking frequent short walks and sitting for short periods, alternated with rests in bed. Of course, the patient will need help and reassurance. He is understandably apprehensive about getting out of bed and walking the day after his operation—it looks to him like a dangerous and impossible performance. He may be far from enthusiastic about making a somewhat painful journey down the corridor several times, and on that first day the tactful nurse will refrain from asking him how he feels! Gratitude for his progress will have to come later. It requires a considerable sensitivity and the power of persuasion to get a patient to do something that is painful, no matter how good it is for him.

In any event, care should be taken not to tire the patient and to keep his first attempts within the bounds set by his age and the type of operation he has had.

PARENTERAL REPLACEMENT THERAPY

Indications. The importance of maintaining fluid and electrolyte balance in the body was mentioned in Chapter 11. Any disease or injury to the tissues, such as pneumonia or severe burns, which interferes with the normal metabolism of cells may disturb this balance. As far as the surgical patient is concerned, during, after and many times prior to a surgical procedure there is inevitably a loss of fluids and electrolytes through bleeding, vomiting, excess perspiration and drainage. When the loss is severe, and the patient is unable to replace it by taking fluids orally, the fluids and the electrolytes are restored by injection. This process is known as *parenteral replacement therapy,* and the various methods of injecting large quantities of fluid into the body are referred to as *infusion.*

Methods. There are 4 available routes for the injection of parenteral fluids, namely, the intravenous (into the vein); the intramuscular (into the muscles); the subcutaneous (into the tissues directly beneath the skin); and the intramedullary (into the bone marrow cavity). However, the most commonly used is the intravenous route, referred to as the intravenous infusion (IV). This procedure was described on page 338. The solution drips slowly into the blood stream through a vein, usually at the rate of 60 to 80 drops a minute or as ordered by the physician. Some of the commonly used solutions are isotonic saline (0.9% sodium chloride solution), electrolyte solutions containing many of the electrolytes found in the intracellular and tissue fluids, glucose in water solutions (5% to 10% solutions), blood plasma and whole blood.

Fluids and Electrolytes

Electrolytes were described in Chapter 11 as elements such as sodium, potassium, magnesium and calcium which ionize (acquire an electrical charge) when dissolved in water. It was also stated that in order for the body to function normally, electrolytes must be present in precisely the right quantities in the fluids both inside and outside the cells.

Dr. W. D. Snively, in his book *Sea Within,* likens our body fluids to the salty sea water which for millions of years served as a source of food, an outlet for waste and a medium for chemical exchange in the original simple, single forms of life. When these single cells first evolved to form many-celled creatures, they enclosed sea water in their bodies as body fluid. Our tissue fluid, which composes about 70 per cent of our bodily weight, bears a striking resemblance to sea water (although over the years, sea water has become considerably saltier than it was originally, when it nourished the first forms of life, and it is certainly saltier now than the body fluid). Whatever its beginnings, we know that the intricate balance between the components of our body fluid is essential in maintaining homeostasis, the harmonious functioning of all body activities.

The cell membrane plays a vital role in maintaining this balance. The fluid surrounding the cell contains many dissolved elements needed by the cell to survive as well as some that are not needed. By a process known as *selective permeability,* the cell membrane has the ability to allow those elements that are needed to enter, but not the others. The size of the openings in the membrane is considered as being influential in keeping out many elements. For instance, some of the larger and more complex protein molecules are unable to slip through the tiny pores.

The concentration of the fluid inside and outside the cell must be equal. (Concentration means the ratio of dissolved materials—the *solute*—to the volume of the dissolving substance—the *solvent.* The solute and the solvent form the *solution.* Water is the most important solvent in the body.) The water in solutions of different concentrations on opposite sides of a membrane has the tendency to move across the membrane to dilute the solution that is more concentrated. If we find in the body that more salt molecules are present in the tissue fluid than are in the fluid within the cell, some of the water molecules will leave the cell to dilute the surrounding fluid. The reverse is also true. If the concentration of salt molecules is greater in the intracellular fluid, the water molecules will leave the surrounding fluid and enter the cell. This process is known as *osmosis.*

The principle of osmosis must be kept in mind when injecting solutions into the blood stream to replenish lost body fluids and electrolytes. The concentration of salt in the blood cells is 0.9 per cent. The concentration of the salt in the fluid to be injected must also be 0.9 per cent, which would make it *isotonic* with the blood. If it has a lower concentration of salt, such as 0.4 per cent, the injected fluid would be hypotonic to the blood, causing the blood cells to take in so much water that their membranes would rupture and burst, a situation called *hemolysis.* A higher concentration of salt (for example, 11 per cent) would make the injected fluid hypertonic to the blood, and the blood cells would give up so much water that they would shrivel, a condition known as *crenation.* Either crenation or hemolysis can be fatal. Remember the rule that *water goes where the salt is.* Death can be caused by making an error and administering distilled, sterile water instead of 0.9 per cent sodium chloride solution which has the same appearance. In

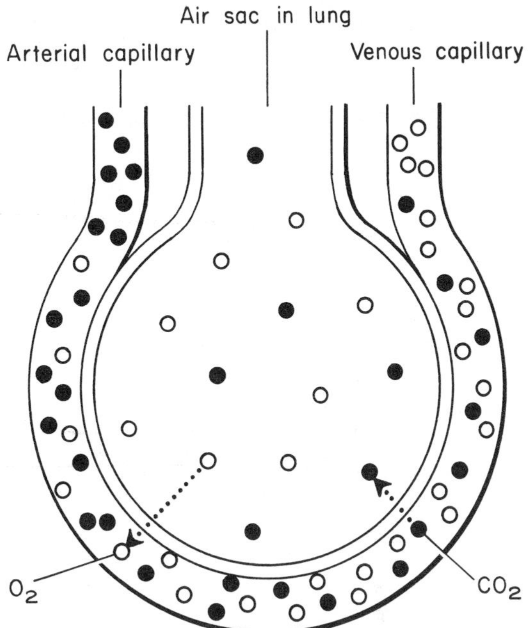

Fig. 142. Diffusion of gases in an air sac of the lung. In the diagram circles represent oxygen and dots represent carbon dioxide. The diagram shows diffusion of carbon dioxide and oxygen by changes in the number of dots and circles on the arterial and venous sides of the capillaries. (Chaffee, E. E., and Greisheimer, E. M.: Basic Physiology and Anatomy, p. 25, Philadelphia, Lippincott, 1964)

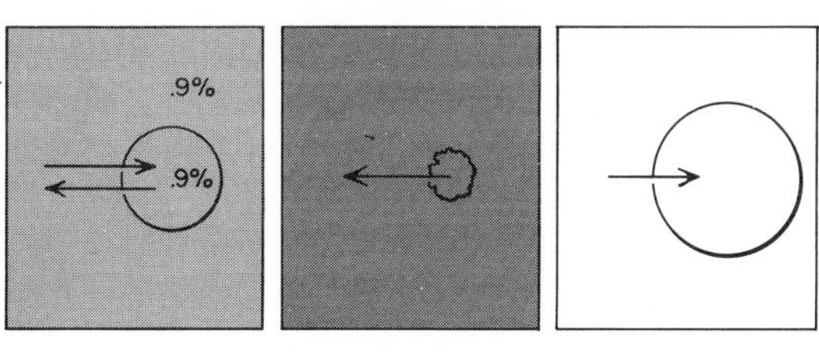

Fig. 141. Osmosis. (A) There is no change in the size of the red blood cell since the salt solution in the surrounding medium is the same as that within the cell. (B) The cell shrinks as water leaves to dilute the hypertonic solution. (C) The cell swells as water enters it to dilute the higher concentration of salt in the cell, since the injected fluid is hypotonic to the blood.

some hospitals, the intravenous fluid bottles are stored separately from the distilled, sterile water to avoid this accident. The principle of osmosis is illustrated in Figure 141.

A cell membrane also permits *diffusion* of a gas or a liquid. Molecules are constantly moving, and it is believed that they are continuously bumping into each other and bouncing away. There is a tendency for them to scatter to an area where there is less pressure. This is the process involved when oxygen from the outside air in the tiny air sacs in the lungs diffuses into the blood where it is less concentrated, and carbon dioxide diffuses in the opposite direction from the blood to the atmosphere. Molecules diffuse easily through membranes which are permeable to them.

For instance, simple waste products produced by a cell during metabolism will diffuse easily through the membrane into the less-concentrated tissue fluid. However, protein molecules, which are the main constituent of protoplasm, are too large to pass through normal membranes. The cell protoplasm must be made from combinations of diffusable amino acids, the building blocks of proteins. The diffusion of glucose (which is high in the blood after meals) into the tissue fluid and then into the tissue cells is another example. The process of diffusion is illustrated diagrammatically in Figure 142. Diffusion, osmosis and selective permeability are only a few of the mechanisms which keep the body and the electrolytes in a state of harmony.

Observing the Patient

Every patient receiving parenteral replacement therapy should be observed closely for an abnormal reaction whether he is the postoperative patient, the patient who has retained fluid in the tissues as a result of malfunctioning kidneys or the one who has experienced severe blood loss from an accident. The reaction may occur during the procedure or may be delayed as long as 24 to 48 hours after the infusion has been discontinued. Reactions due to faulty technic and equipment are becoming less frequent as a result of better methods of preparing solutions, improved sterilization and the use of disposable equipment. However, they may also occur from patient sensitivity. (See Chap. 47.)

During the infusion, the most common symptoms of an abnormal reaction are nausea, vomiting, chills and an increase in the pulse rate. Should they occur, the infusion should be stopped, and a report made to the physician. Nausea and vomiting also are seen frequently in a delayed reaction and should be reported.

Signs that the desired effects are being obtained are noted as well. For example, if the infusion is being administered to counteract the effects of hemorrhage, the nurse should observe the blood pressure, the rate and the volume of the pulse and the respirations to see if they begin to return to normal and note whether other signs of hemorrhage are disappearing.

34

THE PATIENT WITH A SKIN DISORDER

Dermatology is the term applied to the study of diseases of the skin. A *dermatologist* is a doctor who specializes in this field.

Dermatitis

Dermatitis literally means an inflammation of the skin. However, the term is used in connection with specific conditions. *X-ray* or *radiation dermatitis* may occur after heavy exposure to x-rays. *Dermatitis venenata* is caused by direct contact with certain plants, such as poison ivy, poison oak or nettles. Some drugs cause dermatitis. The general treatment for dermatitis is to remove the irritant and to use such local remedies as the doctor may prescribe. These may be wet compresses of boric acid solution, Burow's solution, or calamine lotion. In order to relieve the itching, these compresses are applied to the affected area.

Urticaria

Urticaria (hives) is characterized by the sudden appearance of edematous, raised pinkish areas that itch and smart. Sometimes they disappear as quickly as they come, but they may remain as long as several days. In most instances, urticaria is an allergic reaction to a foreign protein substance. It may be face powder, an insect bite, a serum, or a food protein. Occasionally, it seems to be caused by emotional pressures. Edema is only a temporary annoyance, but it can be dangerous if it involves extensive and vital areas. If it should develop into *angioneurotic edema,* with the lips and the tissues around the eyes swelling tremendously, or involve the larynx, causing it to interfere seriously with breathing, it might cause death. Mild cases can be treated with soothing lotions, such as calamine lotion; antihistamines are also effective; and in some severe cases Adrenalin may be used.

Pruritus

Pruritus (itching) is usually a symptom of some skin disease but may appear with general disease conditions such as liver ailments, cancer, diabetes mellitus or thyroid disturbances. It may also occur in elderly people. Pruritis presents real nursing problems, because the patient is almost irresistibly compelled to scratch, which leads to breaks in the skin and possible infection. It is best to be practical and realize that telling the patient not to scratch probably will be futile. Try to get his mind on something else, avoid overheating, keep irritating materials away from his skin, keep his nails short, and if necessary, give him cotton gloves to wear at night. Soothing baths or local skin applications often give relief.

Acne Vulgaris

Acne vulgaris is a chronic skin disorder marked by blackheads, pimples, cysts, nodules and scarring. It usually appears on the face, the back, the chest and the upper arms. Often it is associated with puberty and adolescence; it seems to be affected by general health, diet and hormonal balance. Rich foods, lack of sleep and emotional pressures are known to aggravate acne, but no one of these things alone causes it. It is believed that hormonal imbalance during adolescence is partly responsible. Acne is not only disfiguring, but it also may leave permanent scars on the victim's face and personality, for it comes at a time when a young person is agonizingly conscious of how he looks and of what people think of him.

Treatment usually consists of practicing good personal hygiene (diet, cleanliness, good elimination, sunshine and outdoor exercise). The patient should be under medical supervision to prevent the use of "quack" remedies which are inefficient and often harmful. Ultraviolet light treatments sometimes help and, when all else fails, x-ray therapy is often beneficial. Scalp treatment should be carried out if it is necessary—dandruff might aggravate acne.

Scabies

Scabies (7-year itch) is caused by itch mites that burrow under the outer layer of the skin. A month or more after they enter the body, the skin begins to itch, especially when it is warmly covered. Red spots with a row of blackish dots from ⅛ to ½ inch long appear with tiny blisters and depressions, especially between the fingers. The parasites get into bed clothing and personal garments, so special precautions are necessary to keep scabies from spreading. Ironing or boiling clothing kills the parasites. The usual treatment recommended is a bath to open up infected spots, followed by the application of a prescribed ointment, such as benzyl benzoate, to the entire body. The infected person puts on clean clothing and uses clean bed linens and does not remove the ointment for 24 hours.

Athlete's Foot

Athlete's foot is a fungus infection that attacks the skin between the toes; watery blisters become moist, weepy spots that burn and itch. The organism lurks on the floors of public baths and showers and grows lustily in any damp place. Get a physician's advice about the treatment of athlete's foot. Many manufactured remedies are available, such as Whitfield's ointment or Desenex powder and ointment. The greatest preventive measure is to dry thoroughly between the toes after a bath or a shower and especially after swimming. Athlete's foot may recur if the skin is not kept dry and clean, since the fungus may continue to

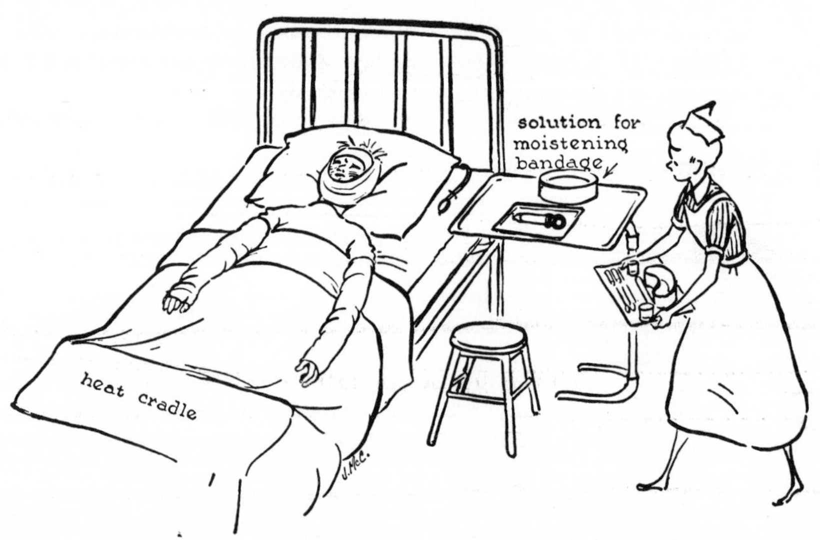

FIG. 143. Patient with a skin disorder.

live in the shoes. Keep shoes thoroughly ventilated and expose them to sunlight and fresh air as often as possible.

Warts

Warts are small brownish or yellowish lumps with a rough surface that appear on the skin singly or in bunches. They are caused by a virus and may remain for years or may disappear of their own accord. They are not painful, with the exception of the *plantar* type, which appears on the soles of the feet and grows inward under pressure from the weight of the body. Warts are destroyed by treatment with short, high-frequency electric sparks (electrodesiccation).

Vitiligo

Vitiligo is a condition in which areas of the skin do not produce the pigment (melanin) that gives the skin its normal color. As a result, the pigment-deficient areas appear as light-colored patches. No really effective remedy has been found for this condition, although the use of drugs called *psoralens,* followed by exposure to sunlight or ultraviolet light, has been found to be temporarily beneficial. The treatment is prolonged and time-consuming and must be done under the close supervision of a physician. The use of cosmetics designed to cover birthmarks is a practical solution to the problem of vitiligo.

Dandruff (Seborrheic Dermatitis)

This condition is common enough—how often we see the tell-tale greasy scales on coat collars and shoulders! Other signs are an oily scalp, which is itchy and irritated. A very severe case of dandruff may cause premature hair loss. Persistent treatment will improve this condition, and good health practices will keep it under control; some cases respond to treatment better than others. Chronically overactive sebaceous glands seem to be influenced by a number of things: endocrine imbalance, heredity and diet.

The treatment consists of frequent shampoos as advised by the doctor (not the hairdresser). He may recommend tincture of green soap, pHisoHex, or some other cleansing solution. Sometimes medicated ointments are prescribed to alternate with shampoos, along with scalp massage and brushing. A low fat diet, exercise and rest are also important aspects of therapy.

Eczema

There are many kinds of *eczema,* all of which are more or less chronic and look and behave alike. Eczema appears as small blisters on a reddened and itchy skin; sometimes these vesicles burst and ooze, after which crusts form in the affected area. Perpetual irritation and scratching make the skin leathery and thick. Eczema usually appears in the folds of the elbows and the knees and on the face and the neck; it may spread to other areas. Sometimes it is so severe that the victim must stay at home. It may disappear completely for months, sometimes for years. Unfortunately, it may recur at any time.

Eczema has a definite relation to heredity and allergy and also to emotional stress. In one type of eczema, the patient's family history usually shows allergy in some of its members—this may be in the form of hay fever, asthma or eczema. As a person grows older, emotional factors seem to aggravate eczema. The treatment consists of applying soothing ointments, such as hydrocortisone, wet dressings or starch baths for inflamed skin and sedatives or tranquilizers to relieve tension and itching. Remember that emotional tension unknown to you may be affecting the patient, and you must try to relieve that tension. Be on the alert to protect him from allergens to which he is sensitive. Reassure him about his condition—tell him that eczema can improve and even disappear and that worrying about it is the least helpful thing he can do.

Psoriasis

Psoriasis is a chronic disease that affects young adults and people in early middle age. Men suffer from it more often than women.

The cause of psoriasis is unknown, although it is sometimes attributed to heredity or a metabolic disorder. It is characterized by red patches covered with silvery scales which have a tendency to shed. These patches usually appear on the extensor surfaces of the elbows and the knees, on the scalp and on the lower back.

Treatment of psoriasis is not very satisfactory. Ointments containing ammoniated mercury or salicylic acid are used; a low fat diet may be tried. Ultraviolet light and x-ray therapy may also help.

Impetigo Contagiosa

Impetigo contagiosa is an infection which is seen at all ages but most frequently in babies and children. It is caused by streptococcal and staphylococcal organisms whose natural homes are on hands, clothing and objects. Redness appears, and vesicles break open to leave a sticky yellow crust, usually on the face and the hands. Impetigo is highly contagious, and the utmost care should be taken to isolate the patient and his equipment in order to prevent the spread of infection. It can be very serious in a nursery for newborns where, given a chance, it will spread like wildfire.

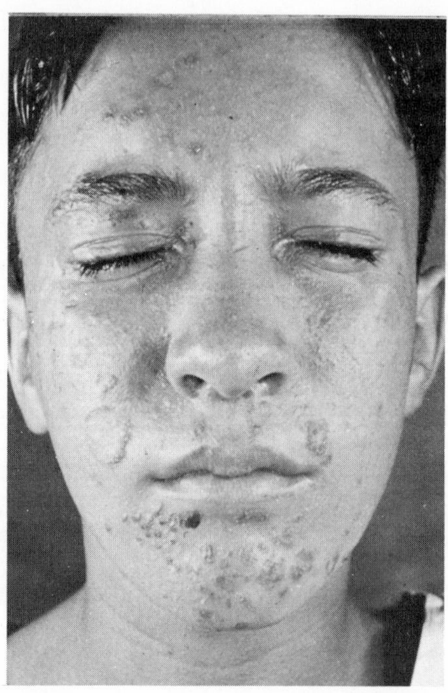

Fig. 144. Impetigo contagiosa. Note crusts that form over lesions. (Medichrome–Clay-Adams, Inc., New York City)

In treating impetigo, the crusts are removed with soap and water, or with mineral oil, then any one of a number of ointments can be applied: neomycin, ammoniated mercury, gentian violet, to name a few. Severe cases may require antibiotics.

Herpes Simplex (Cold Sore)

The cold sore is caused by a virus. There is a theory that this virus lurks in the body and pounces in the presence of a cold or a fever, or that a cold sore may develop as the result of an emotional upset or at the beginning of the menstrual period. It appears as a group of small blisters, usually on the mouth, which burn and are painful. It usually does not last long and does not require treatment. If this lesion appears inside the mouth, it is called a *canker sore*..

Herpes Zoster (Shingles)

Herpes zoster is caused by a virus that affects the nerves. Groups of vesicles appear along the course of a sensory nerve, usually on the face or the trunk of the body. The blisters are preceded by fever and malaise, followed by neuralgic pains that may be quite severe, especially in elderly persons. Sometimes this neuralgia persists for weeks after the eruption has disappeared, which usually occurs within 3 to 5 days. Treatment is designed to keep the patient comfortable with analgesics and to soothe the painful lesions with calamine lotion.

Furuncle, Carbuncle, Furunculosis

A *furuncle* (*boil*), is an acute infection of a hair follicle. A *carbuncle* is composed of several boils in a cluster. *Furunculosis* is a condition of many and recurrent boils.

These conditions are caused by staphylococcal infection; when boils keep recurring it usually means that the patient has poor general health, an inadequate diet and a lowered resistance.

A furuncle is a whitish, tender, painful spot in the middle of a reddened area, which after a few days discharges pus and finally a *core.* A carbuncle is a large swollen area, frequently occurring on the back of the neck. It is very painful and has pus draining from several openings. Furunculosis, characterized by many boils, may be accompanied by fever and weakness.

Boils usually are caused by bacteria that enter the skin through areas that have been broken by rubbing or scratching—sometimes by pinching or squeezing a pimple. It is dangerous to pick or squeeze a boil since this may spread the infection to the surrounding tissues and possibly to the blood stream. Hot wet dressings or soaks are used to *localize,* or center the infection at one point. Antibiotics, such as penicillin or tetracycline, help to control the infection. It is sometimes necessary to incise a boil to get a drainage of pus. If the patient has frequently recurring boils, it is safe to assume that the condition of his general health needs investigating. An *autogenous vaccine* (a vaccine made from the organisms causing the boil) is sometimes given if boils persist.

The Problem of Disfigurement

Skin troubles make people uncomfortable and irritable, but perhaps one of their most damaging effects is on appearance. Since advertisers seize upon any twist to emphasize a lovely skin and place such a premium on youth and beauty, the person with a disfiguring skin condition is made doubly conscious of his appearance. It is no wonder that the patient's personality is affected, especially if job opportunities are closed to him or his social life is restricted. A patient may have a skin condition in addition to the illness for which he is being treated—this very fact may affect his behavior, and a nurse should take this into account when caring for such a patient. It is especially important that the patient feel that you are not repelled by any disfiguring condition that he may have.

Plastic Surgery

Plastic surgery may be done for its *cosmetic effects* or to *repair defects* that are congenital or the result of accident or injury. Improvement in plastic surgery opened up a whole new world of hope for the wounded of World War II. It is now possible to replace parts of the body with plastic prostheses so natural looking that no one can detect them. It is also possible to remove tissue from massive breasts, to improve posture and thereby to lessen self-consciousness.

Skin Grafts. Skin grafts are a means of covering areas where skin has been lost through wounds, burns or infections. They are transplants of skin from another part of the patient's body or of skin from another person. It is a painstaking procedure which may be prolonged for many months, depending upon the size and the number of areas to be covered and the success of each operation. Every surgeon has his own preferred method of caring for the plastic surgery area; it usually includes scrupulous attention to aseptic technic and protection of the grafts.

A nurse sometimes worries about what she should say to a patient who has had plastic surgery. If there does not seem to be improvement, how can she keep from letting her patient know this? Should she let the patient have a mirror if this was a facial repair? How can she encourage patience during repeated trips to the hospital?

In the first place, most plastic surgery looks rather hopeless immediately after the operation, when swelling and black-and-blue spots predominate. The nurse can explain this and warn the patient against expecting too much too soon. The doctor has told the patient what improvement to expect, but sometimes the nurse can give further reassurance. After the first day or two, a mirror may help him to get used to his changed appearance and see it as an improvement over his previous condition, even though it might be less than he expected.

35

THE PATIENT WITH A DISEASE OR INJURY OF THE MUSCULOSKELETAL SYSTEM

Disturbances of the muscles and the bones often require a combination of medical and surgical treatment. The branch of surgery that treats bone and joint diseases and injuries and the correction of deformities is called *orthopedics*. The surgeon who specializes in this field is an *orthopedist*.

COMMON DISORDERS

Bones give structure to the body—anything that interferes with their firmness puts health off balance. Soft, displaced, broken or infected bones weaken the body framework, interfere with movement, limit body activity and may deform the body permanently. Here are some of the common disorders that can happen to bones, muscles and joints.

Rickets

Rickets is a nutritional disease that comes from a lack of vitamin D in the diet. It affects the hardening process in bones and is brought about through the faulty absorption from the gastrointestinal tract of calcium or phosphorus needed for bone structure. The bones stay soft and are distorted out of shape until they finally harden in this deformed state. *Bowlegs* is a good example of the effect of rickets on the bones. Children with rickets are slow in learning to walk and in cutting teeth; they are pale and irritable and inactive. We have been much concerned about the hundreds of children in Europe and Asia who develop rickets because they were starved and lived in dark places without sunshine during the war. We also have reason to be concerned about the large numbers of undernourished children in this country who develop rickets. Rickets is prevented and treated by regular doses of cod-liver oil and exposure to sunshine, both of which provide vitamin D. Any extensive calcium deficiency can cause a ricketslike condition of the bones.

Sprains

Sprains are injuries to the ligaments around a joint which cause the ligaments to be stretched and torn. Sprains are painful but seldom serious; they cause swelling and interfere with movement. Rupture of the nearby blood vessels makes the skin black and blue. The usual treatment is to elevate the injured part and to provide a firm support for it, such as an elastic bandage.

Dislocations

When a ligament gives way so completely that a bone is displaced from its socket, the joint is said to be dislocated. This causes pain, an abnormal position of the bone and inability to manipulate the joint. Following an x-ray picture, the doctor is able to put the bone back into position. This is usually done under anesthesia by stretching the ligaments and manipulating the joint. He then applies a splint or Ace bandage to immobilize the parts until they heal. It may take several weeks to allow the joint capsule and the surrounding ligaments to return to normal position.

The Patient With a Fracture

Any break in a bone is called a *fracture*. Since bones can break in a number of ways, we have the following classifications:

Greenstick: The bone bends and splits but does not break completely. This is common in children and occurs at an age when bones are still soft and pliable.

Complete: The fracture goes all the way through the bone, transversely or in a spiral direction.

Comminuted: A fracture in the bone in several places.

Impacted: One portion of the bone is driven into another portion of it.

Compound: The bone breaks through the skin, causing an open wound and exposing the patient to infection. This is a more serious condition since it is necessary to consider both the fracture and the danger of wound infection.

Complicated fracture: This is a fracture in which there is also injury to nerves, blood vessels and joints.

Spontaneous (pathologic) fracture: One which occurs without force or injury sufficient to break a normal bone. This may occur in such conditions as certain types of malnutrition, porous bones (osteoporosis), cancer and as a side-effect of cortisone and ACTH therapy.

Causes of Fractures. Accidents are the chief causes of broken bones. These may occur by striking hard surfaces, falls in sports activities, automobile accidents and accidents with machinery. Up to the age of 45, more men than women have fractures; after this time, more women are affected. Elderly people in particular are susceptible to home hazards, such as slippery floors and bathtubs, loose rugs and dark stairways or corners. They often are unable to refrain from climbing on chairs or stepladders—precarious undertakings for people with brittle bones and impaired coordination. However, it is often very difficult to persuade them that it is sensible to give up some of these activities; it seems to be both a dreaded admission of advancing age and a threat to their independence, and they want none of it.

Symptoms. The most pronounced symptom of a broken bone is the pain which becomes more severe with movement of the part and with pressure over the fracture. Pain is accompanied by loss of function and deformity (an unnatural position of the part). Other symptoms are swelling over the part and discoloration due to bleeding in the tissues. First aid for fractures is described in Chapter 48.

Treatment. The next step after first aid has been given for a fractured bone is to take an x-ray picture of the injured area (Fig. 145) in order to find the extent of the fracture and the position of the fragments of the broken bone. The doctor then takes steps to restore the bone so that it can resume its original function. The method he chooses will depend on the place and the extent of the break and the condition and the age of the patient. His object is to bring the fragments back into place (*reduction*) and to hold them in that position (*immobilization*) until the break is healed. One method of immobilizing a fracture is by applying a plaster cast.

The Patient in a Cast

The nurse's chief concern in observing a patient in a cast is to watch for signs of *pressure*. Undue pressure of any kind can cause the most serious kind of damage to nerves and blood vessels and death to the tissues. Signs of pressure are:

1. *Edema:* Swelling at the edges of the cast and in the parts beyond, such as the fingers or the toes
2. *Blanched or cyanotic skin color:* Fingers and toes must be inspected frequently to note any signs of circulatory impairment
3. *Temperature of fingers or toes colder than*

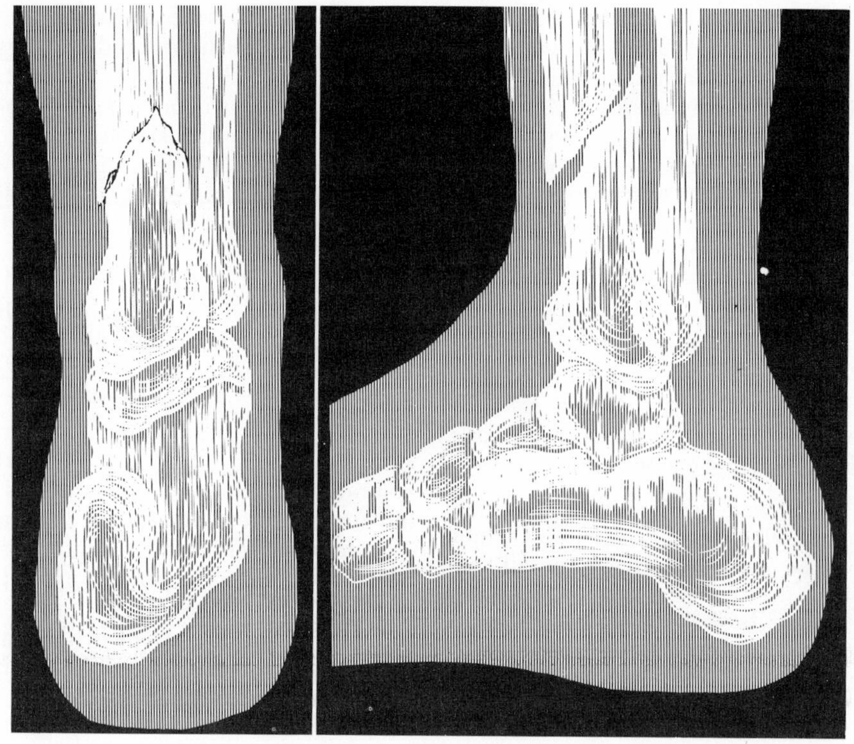

FIG. 145. Reproduction of an x-ray picture of a leg showing back and side views of a broken shin bone (fracture of the tibia). Note the position of the fragments. The unbroken fibula acts as a splint.

on the unaffected side: Compression of nerves and blood vessels can do a great amount of damage. A loss of oxygen to the tissues over an extended period of time results in tissue death

4. *Odor:* A pressure sore may develop without the patient's knowledge. The only indication of this would be the odor emitted by decaying tissue.

Since a cast is not the most comfortable thing in the world, a patient may have many complaints to make about his general discomfort. However, it is well to listen and report repeated complaints about the same thing —that pain in his back may be from a pressure sore.

A patient in a *spica* (body cast) needs special attention in addition to the items already mentioned. He must be turned frequently, and this procedure causes apprehension at first, because he is helpless and naturally afraid of falling. Specific attention must be given to elimination and the area near the buttocks. In hot weather, this patient is very likely to be uncomfortable and to complain of itching and burning. Smith and Gips in *Care of the Adult Patient* suggest slipping a corset stay wrapped in cotton and dipped in alcohol under the cast to soothe the itchy spot. The patient should be encouraged to exercise as much of his body as possible to promote good circulation. Make it as easy as possible for him to do things for himself, even though it takes more time to arrange the necessary equipment. When a patient is made to feel adequate rather than helpless, it helps his morale. It is less boring to be able to stretch and exercise when doing things for himself than it is to exercise mechanically.

The patient with an arm cast who is up

and about should support his arm in a sling. If the cast is on the leg, the patient can get about in a wheelchair which can be adjusted for leg support.

The Patient in Traction

Traction means *pulling*; it is used in fractures to keep the bone fragments in a good position to heal properly. The strength of the pull on the bones, by means of weights, must be enough to counteract the over-all pull of the muscles. For an adult, 8 to 10 pounds is usually sufficient. Traction is applied by:

1. Adhesive straps applied to the skin and attached to weights and pulleys
2. Direct application to the skeletal system by
   A. Driving a Steinmann pin or a Kirshner wire through the end of a bone (this is common practice in leg fractures)
   B. Crutchfield or Vince tongs attached to the skull (this is used for fractured cervical vertebrae).

A Balkan frame can be attached to the bed, or one of the new steel fracture beds equipped with the apparatus needed for traction may be provided. *Russell traction* allows the patient to move a little in bed. A *Thomas splint* is used for both emergency and continuous traction.

Nursing Care

Some doctors order the leg supported with pillows; others believe that pillows create pressure behind the knee, which may cause thrombosis. If pillows are used, they should be covered with oiled silk to eliminate friction and should support only the entire thigh and calf, *not* the heel. In order to prevent *footdrop* (contraction of the foot into an abnormal position), keep the foot in a normal position with a footboard. This gives the patient something to push against and keeps the covers from pressing on his toes. Encourage him to exercise by pushing against this board and tell him to point his toes "in" while he is on his back. Every effort should be made to prevent the deformity of footdrop. Watch the pulleys and the ropes because ropes sometimes slip out of their grooves. If the footpiece is touching the pulleys at the bottom of the bed, report it at once. Be sure that the weights are swinging free. *Never remove the weights without an order.* Note the color and test the feeling of the hand or the foot. Watch the patient's elbows for irritation and apply lanolin. Also observe the buttocks for redness and signs of irritation.

Body Alignment. Keep the patient's body in good position. See that he does not slump,

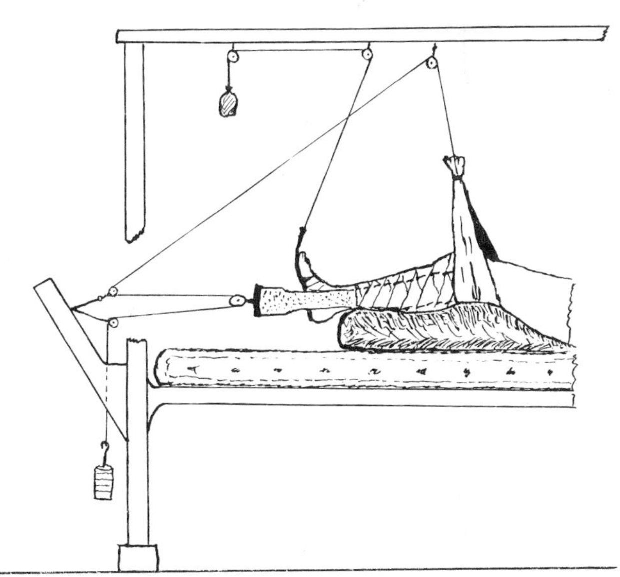

FIG. 146. The Russell method of treating a fracture of the shaft of the femur. A small spring scale sometimes is inserted between the pulley and the traction block so that the amount of traction may be estimated accurately. (Brunner, L. S., *et al.*: Textbook of Medical-Surgical Nursing, p. 1008, Philadelphia, Lippincott, 1964)

with his chin resting on his chest. Make sure that parts of his body are in line and prevent the affected extremity from rotating outward.

If the break is such that a walking cast can be applied, the patient will be able to get around out of bed with the help of a cane. Otherwise, the patient must use crutches when he is allowed to get up following a leg fracture.

The doctor determines the amount of movement allowed. One nursing problem is getting enough movement in the elderly patient to counteract the danger of *hypostatic pneumonia* (congestion in the lungs). A method to prevent this is by deep breathing exercises, which can be carried out by blowing up balloons or by blowing bubbles into a glass of water by using a straw. However, any movement that interferes with the traction pull must be avoided.

Complications

In addition to the ones already mentioned, there can also arise the problem of *nonunion of the bone ends.* This may be due to: 1) poor physical condition, including nutrition; 2) poor circulation; or 3) age.

The speed with which bones generate new growth varies with individuals. One 85-year-old was able to walk again after fracturing first one hip and then the other within a 5-year period. Yet a younger person might show little evidence of new bone growth at the end of 10 weeks. An attempted remedy for nonunion is to insert a piece of new bone (bone graft); if this fails, braces may enable the patient to carry on most of his normal activities.

Constipation can be a problem accompanying recovery from a fracture because of the patient's age, inactivity or eating habits.

Wound infection, in compound fractures, interferes with healing and may cripple the patient permanently if the bone itself becomes infected. It will prolong the patient's illness and necessitate wound dressings.

Confusion, especially in the elderly, is not uncommon. The patient may try to get out of bed, disarrange apparatus and tear off the bed coverings—usually at night. Side rails provide safety.

Bursitis

Bursae are sacs filled with synovial fluid that act as pads on bony prominences in joints. *Bursitis* is inflammation of a bursa. In diseases of the bursae the amount of fluid in the sac increases and distends it. Eventually, the wall of the bursa hardens and becomes calcified. One type of bursitis is the result of long-continued irritation or friction in a joint. It is comparatively painless and does not cause disability. The usual treatment for bursitis includes heat and rest of the affected part. Chronic inflammation of a bursa may result in calcification, which causes pain and tenderness in the joint and interferes with its motion. X-ray treatments often relieve this condition; if these are not effective, the bursa must be excised.

Tenosynovitis

Tenosynovitis is the inflammation of a tendon. It may be caused by a gonococcal infection, which particularly affects the wrist or the ankle. The infected tendons swell and cause pain and disability and can be treated by heat and antibiotics. Tenosynovitis may also develop from an infected wound or from infection in nearby tissues. Sometimes it comes from a bloodstream infection. The treatment indicated here is surgery and antibiotics. Noninfectious tenosynovitis is caused by strains or blows or by the prolonged use of a particular set of tendons. Examples of overuse are extensive piano playing or typing. The symptoms are pain and tenderness, especially when there is motion. (Incidentally, this is not the same thing as "writer's cramp.") The treatment is resting the sore part and applying heat, and changing to another activity which does not involve the affected tendons.

Ganglion

A *ganglion* is a "bump" caused by a distended synovial sac, which appears under the skin near a joint, usually at the wrist. Strains or bruises, especially if they are repeated, may cause a ganglion. Usually it is painless, and sometimes the sac ruptures and the bump disappears. It can be ruptured by a sharp blow. Our greatgrandmothers' remedy for a ganglion was a brisk rap with the Bible. It can be removed by surgery, but often it returns.

Gout

In the process of protein digestion substances called *purines* are produced. If the body is unable to metabolize these substances, uric acid accumulates in the bloodstream and forms crystal deposits (tophi) in the joints. This condition is called *gout*. It usually appears in the big toe, the instep, the ankle or in the knee, but it may appear in any joint. It attacks periodically, causing swelling and excrutiating pain, and eventually gout limits motion in the affected joint.

Symptoms. An attack of gout begins with agonizing pain, swelling and redness. It lasts from 3 to 14 days, when it disappears as suddenly as it came. It may return anytime from a month to a year later; in the meanwhile the joint gives no trouble. The slightest touch or weight is unbearable during an attack. As time goes on, repeated attacks damage the joint permanently as they come closer and closer together. The list of things that may set off an attack is a long one: alcohol, allergy, an emotional upset, surgery, injury, infection, nitrogenous or fatty foods, a reducing diet, antibiotics, liver extract, vitamin B, a mercurial diuretic.

Treatment and Nursing Care. Gout cannot be cured, but the attacks can be controlled and prevented. However, the patient must stick to the routines set up for him and must see his doctor regularly to be advised about changes that will be necessary as the course of the disease changes.

Diet comes first and foremost in the treatment, especially in preventing pain. The diet is not restricted rigidly unless gout is severe, except for restrictions in high-purine foods; these are taboo for all gout patients. Most gout attacks are brought on by emotional crises or by changes in the patient's surroundings, although individuals react differently to such things as food and alcohol. The high-purine foods to be avoided include liver, kidneys, sardines, bacon, goose, mackerel, salmon, turkey and leguminous vegetables, such as peas and beans. The patient may have such low-purine or nonpurine foods as breads, cereals, spaghetti, fruits, eggs, milk and nonleguminous vegetables.

A bed cradle to protect the affected joint is a necessity. Protection from bumps and jars of the affected part or of the bed is so important that a sign warning everybody to be careful about this may be necessary. Gentle application of warm or cold compresses is sometimes ordered, and elevating the affected joint may make the patient more comfortable. Begin exercise as soon as the pain and the redness are gone, to prevent the joint from stiffening.

Colchicine is a drug that works wonders in relieving gout. If it is given early enough, it relieves the pain in 12 to 24 hours, and the other symptoms also disappear. The side-effects are nausea, vomiting and diarrhea. ACTH and phenylbutazone are also effective.

Bone Tumors

There are 2 kinds of bone tumors: those that start in a bone and those that travel to a bone from somewhere else in the body. The symptoms of a bone tumor are pain and swelling. The treatment consists of surgical removal of the tumor, which may be extensive, including the removal of a limb. X-ray therapy is also used but not always successfully. The nursing care is centered on making the patient as comfortable as possible.

Osteomyelitis

Osteomyelitis is infection of a bone. It may develop as the result of a compound fracture, which exposes the bone to outside infection. Most often, it is caused by organisms such as the staphylococcus or the streptococcus which are carried by the blood to the bone from infection somewhere else in the body. The first signs of trouble are fever and pain, often accompanied by nausea and headache, with an increase in the white blood cells and tenderness and swelling in the affected area. Then pus forms in the shaft of the bone, gets under the covering (periosteum) and separates it from the bone. Fragments of dead bone loosen and have to be removed.

Treatment. The treatment consists of:

1. Surgical drainage to remove the pus. The surgeon may drill a number of small holes in the bone.
2. Antibiotics, placed directly in the wound, and a catheter inserted for irrigation purposes and to provide for drainage.
3. Rest and good nutrition to build up the body's defenses.

Nursing Care. Osteomyelitis is extremely painful, and the affected part is sensitive to the slightest movement. Avoid moving it any more than is absolutely necessary; when it must be moved, support it, splint it with a pillow and lift and move it as you move the rest of the body. Sandbags, a cast or a brace help to immobilize the limb. Again, extreme care should be taken to avoid jarring the bed.

The prescribed diet is high in proteins, carbohydrates and fats to build up the patient's resistance, and he is encouraged to take fluids freely.

Swelling, redness or pain in some other region may be signs that the infection is spreading to another bone and should be reported. Pathologic fractures may also occur and may not be recognized because the pain of the fracture is eclipsed by the greater pain in the infected area. A growth of new bone may lengthen the infected bone; bone destruction may shorten it. Careless aseptic technic in changing dressings could introduce outside organisms into the wound. Osteomyelitis tends to become chronic, and the wound may drain for years. The patient may develop muscle spasms because he is inactive; he often becomes thin and weak, and eventually it may be necessary to amputate his limb. Antibiotics have greatly increased the chances for recovery from bone infection.

THE PATIENT WITH AN AMPUTATION

Once amputation was the only remedy for a compound fracture, because otherwise the patient died after developing wound infection. Modern treatment makes amputation unnecessary in most cases unless the blood supply to the limb is permanently cut off as the result of a severe injury or gangrene. Cancer or an extensive infection may also make amputation necessary. It may be desirable to remove a useless or deformed limb to replace it with a useful prosthesis (artificial limb).

Surgical Treatment

With surgery, dead or damaged tissue is removed, leaving a firm, smooth stump which is freely movable and long enough to direct the movements of a prosthesis. The flaps of skin that cover the stump are sutured together to bring the scar where it will not be directly over the end of the bone. From the standpoint of fitting a prosthesis later, it is easier to restore a natural walk if the amputation is in the middle third of the lower leg; preserving the elbow makes it easier to use a prosthetic hand. Saving the knee is a help in walking or climbing stairs. Sometimes an amputation must be done when the patient's condition is critical and a general anesthetic would be dangerous. Then refrigeration anesthesia may be used by keeping the temperature of the limb at 45° to 74° F. The limb becomes numb but is not actually frozen.

Preparing the Patient

In an emergency, an immediate amputation may mean the difference between life and death; if the patient is very weak or is unconscious, there is no opportunity to prepare him for the shock of losing a limb. It is a shattering experience for a healthy person to emerge from an anesthetic to find that one of his legs is gone. For some people amputation is a last resort after a long and debilitating illness, and there is time to help the patient to get mentally used to the prospect and to accept it. In either case the patient with an amputation faces many problems, physical and psychological. A man in the prime of life faces the possibility of losing his job, of giving up the ball games with Junior and the vacation trips with his family. It can be tragic for the teenager, cut off from active sports, dancing or driving a car. The older person wonders how he can contend with more problems in getting around when he already has difficulty. These are the things the patient actually thinks about. Many of them are the little things of everyday life, done so easily and without a thought, such as might trouble a mother who runs up and down stairs and goes back and forth in her kitchen dozens of times a day. To some people an amputation is humiliating —evidence that one is no longer a whole person.

How a Nurse Can Help. A nurse—*you*—can help by letting the patient talk about his fears, listening for clues to what he is really thinking. She can explain the possibilities in the use of crutches and with a prosthesis, if he can be fitted with one. Perhaps she knows someone who is using a prosthesis who would talk to the patient about it. Films of active amputees are available from the Veterans Administration. As you seem to have no doubts about his ability to handle this handicap the patient is reassured. If his condition permits, he can do exercises to strengthen his muscles preparatory to using crutches.

Nursing Care

Two primary dangers following an amputation are hemorrhage and infection. A tourniquet always should be within reach in case of hemorrhage. This means watching the dressing for signs of bleeding, and using aseptic technic in changing dressings. Usually, the stump is elevated on a protected pillow for the first 24 hours after surgery but no longer, for fear of causing hip contractures. For the same reason his mattress should be firm. Skin traction is applied to the stump as soon as the patient returns from the operating room; it can be manipulated to allow the patient to move and turn and to be out of bed in a wheelchair.

Exercises. The patient begins to get ready to walk almost as soon as he recovers from the anesthetic. The physical therapist begins exercises to maintain muscle tone and directs the nurse in helping the patient to prevent contractures. Usually, the patient is helped to sit up on the edge of the bed by the 2nd or the 3rd postoperative day and soon progresses to a wheelchair. He should go back to bed and lie down at intervals; prolonged sitting may also cause contractures.

Care of the Stump. Elastic bandages are sewed together and applied to the stump in order to shrink it as soon as the incision is healed. It shrinks rapidly at first, but usually some shrinkage is evident for a year or more. Two sets of bandages are needed, because the bandage is changed at least twice a day—more often if the patient perspires freely. The patient and some member of his family are taught how to apply the bandage and how to dry it flat to prevent it from stretching. A device made of leather or canvas called a "shrinker" is sometimes used instead of a bandage; it should have the same attention to cleanliness, changing, etc., as is given to the bandage. Watch for skin irritation in any case.

Massage and exercise are physical therapy procedures that are usually started about a week after the operation. If a bed cradle and electric bulbs are used, see that the temperature is no higher than 96° F. This is especially important if the patient is a diabetic or has a vascular disease, because these patients burn easily. The physical therapist may show you how to help the patient carry out some simple exercises.

Phantom Limb. The *phantom limb* is an annoying complication that often afflicts patients after an amputation. The patient will tell you that it feels as if the amputated limb were still there, and he feels pain in it. Sometimes a patient hesitates to mention this for fear everybody will think he is crazy. If he seems to be disturbed and uneasy for no apparent reason, encourage him to tell you what is bothering him. Then you can explain that this often happens after an amputation and is caused by the nerves in the stump and that it will gradually disappear. If the pain persists it may interfere with fitting a prosthesis. The doctor can inject the nerves with alcohol, which will eliminate the painful sensations temporarily.

Crutch-Walking

The first step toward walking after a leg amputation is learning to use crutches. The patient may begin by using parallel bars, which support him and give him confidence in moving on his own. He should be proficient in using his crutches before he leaves the hospital. He may have a temporary prosthesis, but the permanent one will not be fitted until the stump is well shrunken, which may be months after the amputation.

We see people on crutches every day, but we notice them more if they are awkward or seem to make hard work of getting around. When a person uses crutches correctly, his movements are so graceful and efficient that we admire his skill. A patient has to be taught how to use crutches and must learn this technic thoroughly. He must know how to stand, balance his body and walk in good posture—as skillfully and as easily as possible.

The patient's attitude toward using crutches is influenced by how long he is going to need them. He is not likely to be sensitive about temporary crutches; he may feel depressed and hopeless about using them for the rest of his life. He may not mind using them for a long time if there is hope of discarding them eventually. Of course, he may want to discard them too soon because they are a sign of disability. Older people are afraid of falling; a child is overconfident because he does not understand the risks. A timid person is afraid to try; a determined person will persist in trying. A previous experience with crutches is likely to make a difference. It all adds up to this: the individual patient may look forward to having crutches or he may dread it.

The first steps in using crutches come *before* the patient tries to use them to stand or to walk. Reconditioning exercises prepare his body for action; he dangles his legs over the edge of the bed, sits in a chair and learns to stand by the side of the bed. As he does this he is learning good posture—head and chest up, abdomen in. If his disability allows, he may be encouraged to press his feet down on a footstool to get the feeling of standing again; or, arms extended, be shown how to press his palms down on the bed to exercise his arm muscles.

Now for the crutches: they must be right for him. If they are too long, they cause pressure in his axilla—if they are too short, he slumps. Crutches are measured for length in several ways; for one method, the patient lies straight in bed and is measured from the front axillary fold to a point 6 inches out from the side of the foot. The placement of the hand bar is just as important; it should be at a height that allows the patient to extend his arm almost entirely when he leans on his palms. If he can use a pair of adjustable crutches until he learns to walk, he will have the correct measurements before his crutches are ordered. Even if the crutches are the correct length, individual arm lengths are different—just as a dress pattern may be the right length but the sleeves too long or too short. Shortening the crutches more than an inch usually means the position of the hand bar must be changed.

A crutch tip should be made of a good rubber that will wear well; it should fit snugly and not move when the weight is placed on the crutch. A large vacuum tip now available is almost a necessity for the severely disabled person who must place his crutches wide apart to give him a firm base. This tip sometimes gives a patient more confidence, even if the ordinary tip is perfectly safe for him.

It should not be necessary to pad the top of the crutch; if the crutches fit and are used properly, there is no pressure under the arm. A patient may tend to lean on his crutches if the tops are padded. Once he learns how to use his crutches, rubber pads can be used to protect his clothing; sponge rubber covered with some soft material or rubber pads made to fit the crutch are inexpensive. Properly fitted crutches are comfortable to use.

The patient should wear a shoe that fits well, with a low, broad heel and a straight inner border. If he has a disability, such a shoe is a *must*. An old pair of good, comfortable shoes is excellent. Bedroom slippers give no support and may damage the foot seriously.

High, narrow heels are dangerous. A woman who has nothing but high heels should get a pair of shoes with broad, medium-high heels; a sudden change from high to flat heels will cause pain in the shortened heel cords.

The patient's first practice with his crutches is in *standing*. He is shown how to stand properly, how to place his crutches and how to rest his weight on his palms. He holds the crutches in front of his body and leans forward slightly from his ankles; if he leans the upper part of his body forward, his body alignment will be poor. The crutches should be held widely enough apart to give him a good base of support and room to step; if they are too far apart, they may slip sidewise. When he learns how to use his crutches, he can make the base narrower to walk in narrower spaces.

It is important to tell the patient the reason why pressure on the axilla may paralyze the elbow, the wrist and the hand muscles. A controlling nerve is very close to the surface in the axilla; if this nerve is injured, he might need treatment for a long time before he could use his crutches again.

In his next lesson, the patient learns how to shift his weight, according to how much weight he is allowed to put on the disabled leg. He practices first without lifting his foot from the floor—then he bends his hip and knee and lifts one foot, supporting his weight on the other foot and his crutches. He must follow the doctor's orders exactly to prevent injuring the disabled leg.

Slippery floors, loose rugs, loose electric cords and small objects scattered about the floor are hazardous—for the beginner they are downright dangerous. He should learn to walk on a smooth, level surface; later he can learn to walk on an incline or a rougher surface and climb stairs. He should practice on shallow stairs with wide steps and a hand rail.

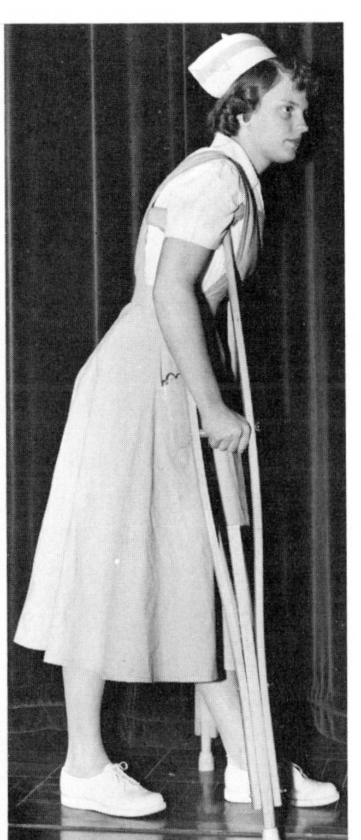

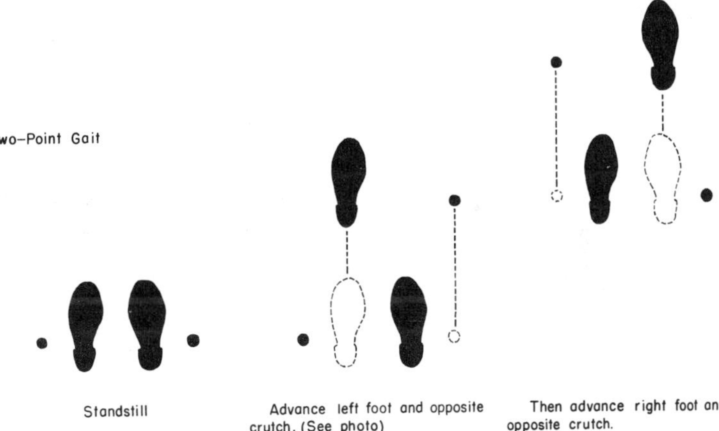

Fig. 147. Two-point gait.

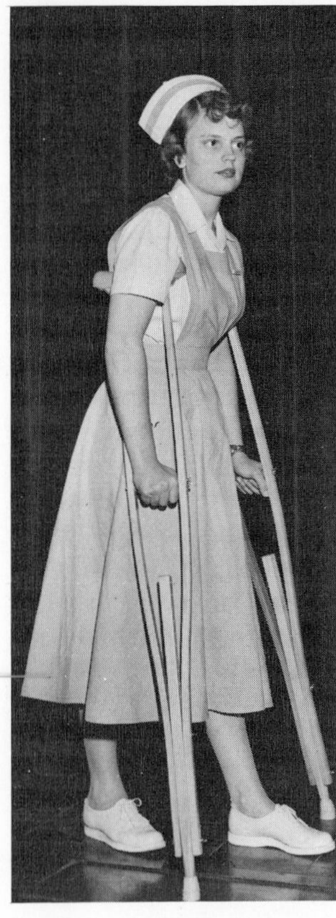

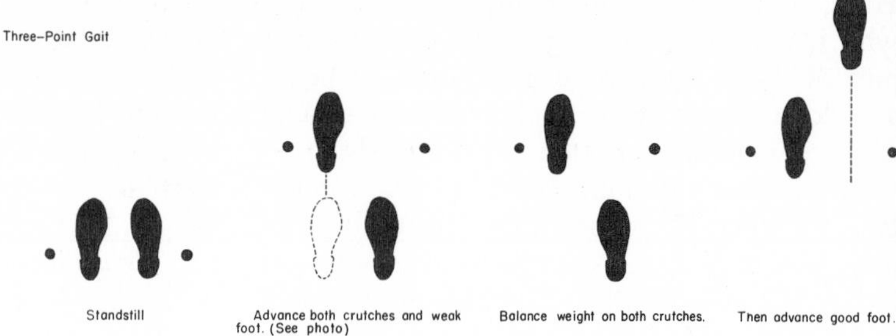

FIG. 148. Three-point gait.

Technic of Crutch-Walking

The patient's strength and disability determine the method of crutch-walking best for him. He should use and improve as many muscles and joints as possible. There are 4 types of crutch-walking:

1. TWO-POINT: The patient puts his weight on one leg and the *opposite* crutch, brings the other crutch and leg forward together and shifts his weight to them; then he brings the other leg and crutch forward. This gait is faster and less boring for the patient; as his muscle power improves he can change to it.

2. THREE-POINT CRUTCH-WALKING WITH BOTH CRUTCHES AND ONE FOOT ADVANCED AT THE SAME TIME: The weak leg and *both* crutches are advanced together, the weight is balanced on them and the *good* leg is advanced. Equal-length steps are important, and there is equal timing without a pause before advancing the good leg. This method is used when one leg is disabled but the other is strong enough to bear all the patient's weight.

3. FOUR-POINT: One crutch is placed forward, and the *opposite* foot is advanced; the second crutch is brought forward, and the opposite foot follows. Rhythm and short equal steps are important; counting helps to develop rhythm: ONE—right crutch forward; TWO—advance left foot; THREE—left crutch forward; FOUR—advance right foot. This is the easiest gait and the safest—the patient always has 3 points of support. He must be able to bring each leg forward and clear the floor with each foot. Polio paralytics, patients with fractures of both legs or an arthritic can use this gait.

4. SWINGING OR TRIPOD-WALKING: The patient stands on his good leg, puts both of his crutches the same distance in advance, rests his weight on the palms of his hands and swings himself forward slightly ahead of his crutches; he rests his weight again on his good

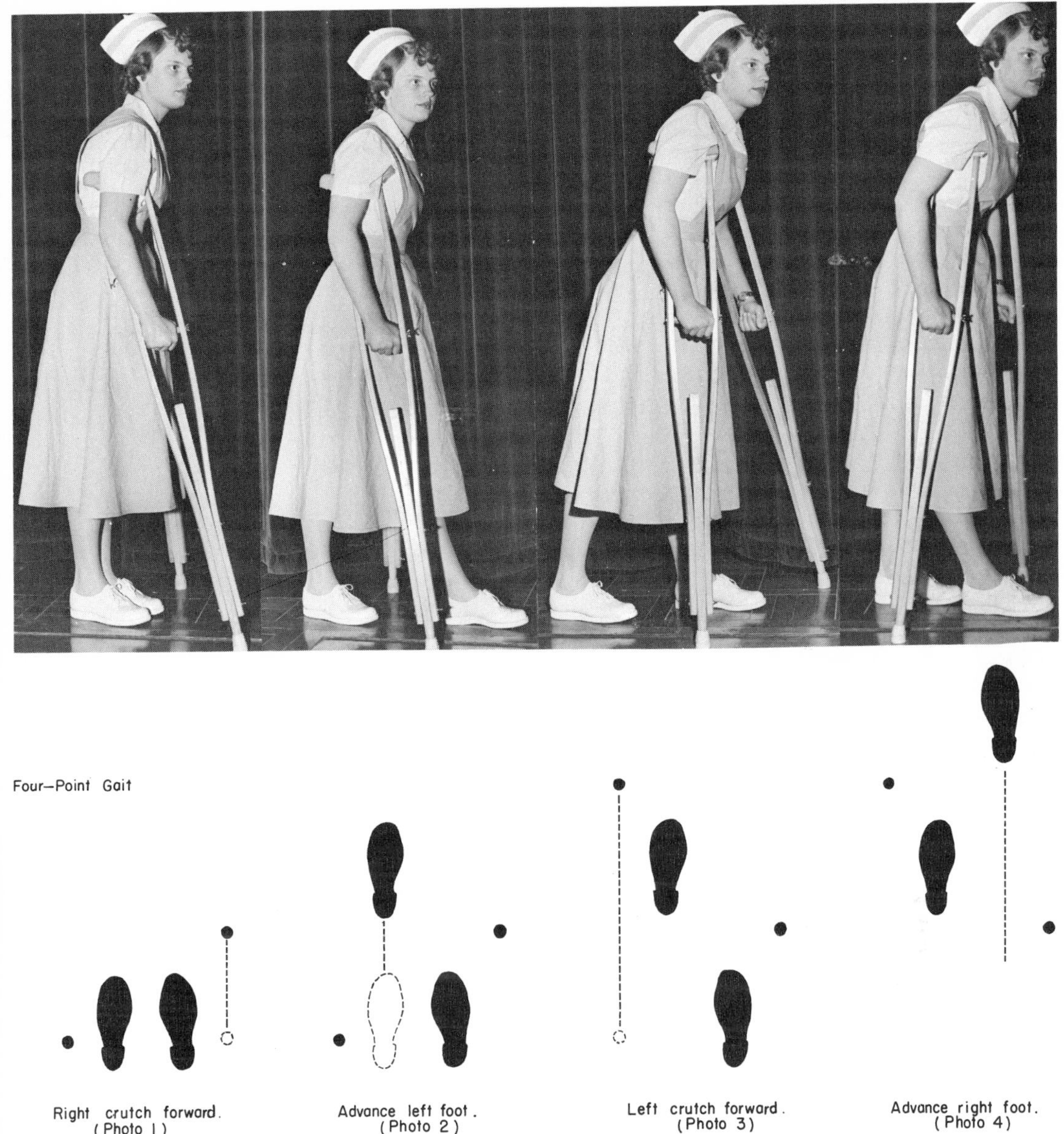

Fig. 149. Four-point gait.

leg and gets his balance for another step. This is a fast gait, and the patient should not attempt it until he has learned balance. The patient who is allowed to put his weight on one leg and must hold the other up should bend his *knee* (not his hip). This gives him better balance. This is the best method for an amputee, a recent fracture or a patient with little power in his legs. Bending the knee is tiring—the patient should rest frequently, with this leg elevated.

When the patient is able to progress to using only one crutch, he places it on the *strong* leg side. Later he may use a cane; it should

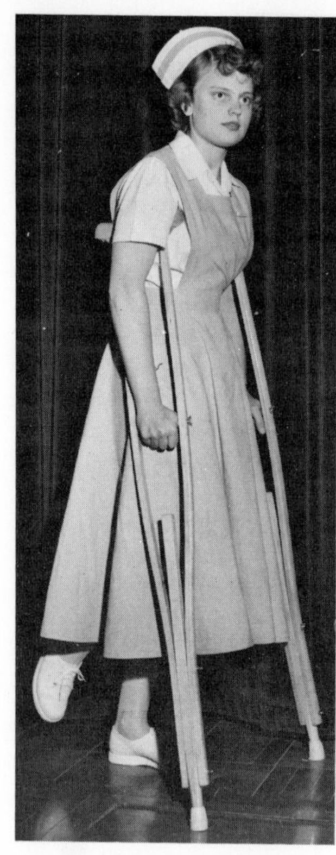

Swing or Tripod Gait

Disabled leg

Standstill

Put both crutches same distance in advance with weight on good leg. (See photo)

Then swing forward with weight on good leg again.

FIG. 150. Swing or tripod gait.

have a curved handle, not too well-polished in order to provide a secure grip, and a good, well-fitted rubber tip. It should be long enough to allow the patient to bear his weight on his palm with his arm almost completely extended. The Canadian crutch is shorter and has no axillary bar: in one type, the uprights end halfway between the elbow and the wrist; in the other, they end halfway between the elbow and the shoulder. A soft leather or canvas band fastened to the upper part of the uprights passes around the arm. These crutches are lightweight and easy to keep out of the way when they are not in use.

The patient should have a place to rest his crutches when he is not using them—where he can reach them and no one will fall over them. A hook is one solution. A patient who can walk safely can go to the bathroom if he has a strong handhold by which to lower himself. A child's crutches should be replaced as he outgrows them.

To sum up your part in helping a patient with crutch-walking: understand how he feels about using crutches; encourage him to persist and tell him what to expect; assist him until he has confidence and skill; watch his gait and help him to correct mistakes; set a definite accomplishment every day that he will be able to reach; stop when he is successful and before he gets tired; be sure that his crutches are right for him and in good condition.

The Prosthesis

Skirts and trousers hide a leg prosthesis which has a shoe that is exactly the same as its mate on the well foot. An arm prosthesis is more conspicuous, since the hand end of it cannot be covered and still be useful. Besides, it is difficult to make an artificial or "dress" hand look real. A practical prosthetic hand is fashioned with a mechanical hook consisting of metal prongs placed opposite each other which take the place of fingers. The amputee works the prosthesis by means of a harness which extends around the opposite shoulder; a wire connects the harness to the hand. The amputee thrusts his shoulder forward to open the prongs and relaxes it to close them. The shoulder movements are barely noticeable, but the patient learns how to make them very effective.

A limb-maker makes and fits the prosthesis and shows the patient how to adjust it and take care of it. The prosthesis may be made of metal, wood or plastic and has a socket at the upper end into which the stump fits. It must be fitted with great care, or it will irritate the skin. A poorly fitted leg prosthesis will affect walking until the patient begins to find excuses for using his crutches instead of the prosthesis (like people with poorly fitted dentures who go without them at every opportunity). If a canvas band is used to keep the prosthesis in place, it should be washed frequently. The joints of the apparatus should be oiled at intervals. Watch for loosening of the parts, cracks, signs of wear in the leather and for irritation, swelling or tenderness of the stump. The stump should be bathed, dried and powdered twice a day. Stump socks should be washed every day and discarded when they become worn—a darn or seam may cause a pressure sore.

Practice Makes Perfect. The leg amputee develops correct walking habits by maintaining good posture in everything he does. For example, he should take pains not to get into the habit of standing with his feet too far apart or of raising the shoulder and the hip on the affected side. Often he is unconscious of these faults until his attention is called to them, because his immediate concern is with keeping his balance and getting around. Some people become more proficient than others in using crutches or a prosthesis. Elderly people are hampered by the physical limitations that usually develop as a part of aging. A patient may be hampered by some physical defect that limits his activities. Every patient should be encouraged to surmount his limitations to the best of his ability. Smith and Gips in *Care of the Adult Patient* quote Al Capp, the famous cartoonist, who lost a leg when he was 9 years old. His advice to the amputee is to forget that he is different—other people soon forget it—and concentrate on making the most of his one-legged life.

Aid for the Amputee. Assistance for the amputee is available from the American Rehabilitation Committee, the Division of Vocational Rehabilitation in your state and often from local voluntary agencies. Their services include medical and financial aid, counseling and job placement.

ARTHRITIS

This disease is as old as time itself. It is one of a group of rheumatic diseases that cause more disability in the United States than any other ailment. Rheumatic diseases afflict between 10 and 11 million people and totally disable some 200,000 of them.

A Joint Disease. *Arthritis* is inflammation of a joint. You will remember that a joint is the place where 2 or more bones meet and are held together by ligaments and tendons. A joint is enclosed in a capsule lined with a synovial membrane which secretes a lubricating fluid (synovial fluid).

Causes of Arthritis. Some causes of arthritis are:

Infection—caused by an organism such as the tubercle bacillus or the streptococcus
Direct injury
Tissue degeneration
Disturbances of metabolism

Nobody knows *exactly* what causes arthritis, but everything on the above list seems to play a part in its development. Eventually, it may be found that arthritis is the result of a combination of causes, rather than being any one thing.

Infectious Arthritis. Infectious arthritis is caused by an organism that gets into a joint and causes pain and swelling as the result of an increase in the synovial fluid. A culture of the fluid will tell what the offending organism is. The antibiotics that are most effective against this organism are then given; sometimes they are injected directly into the joint. Antibiotics have practically eliminated infectious arthritis.

Traumatic Arthritis. This condition is the result of a blow on a joint, a sudden twist or a repeated series of small blows. An example of the latter is arthritis in the feet of ballet dancers.

Rheumatoid Arthritis

Rheumatoid arthritis is one of the 2 chief causes of arthritic disability. It occurs all over the world, although some people believe that it is less common in hot climates. The figures on rheumatoid arthritis are startling—it afflicts 4 million people in the United States, half of them under 45 years of age. This is rather appalling when we realize what this means to people in the best years of their life. It affects 3 times as many women as men.

How Rheumatoid Arthritis Develops

Nobody knows exactly what causes rheumatoid arthritis. Whatever the cause, inflammation makes the joints swell, destroys cartilage and forms a tough tissue that interferes with joint motion. If this tissue becomes calcified, the joint is obliterated, and movement becomes impossible (ankylosis). The process may go on for years before ankylosis occurs. In some patients nodules appear under the skin and over pressure points, such as the spine or the elbows; these are usually painless unless pressure is put on them.

In general, rheumatoid arthritis begins gradually. The patient notices painful twinges and stiffness in one or more joints when he gets up in the morning. As time goes on some joints, particularly the fingers, become swollen, red and sore. Gradually, other joints are affected. Sometimes these symptoms disappear for a time, only to return later. The patient does not feel well; he tires easily, has fever and loses weight. He becomes more than usually sensitive to changes in temperature and is anemic.

Body Changes. The muscles around the affected joints become wasted. The finger joints next to the hand swell; fingers and toes feel cold and moist and look bluish. The joint ligaments relax, and the joints become distorted and may even become dislocated. All of these symptoms develop gradually, and although they may disappear suddenly, they almost always return. This process may go on for years, but every new flare-up of the disease causes more joint damage. Without treatment, and sometimes in spite of it, the joint is destroyed in 10 to 15 per cent of the victims.

As calcification increases, the joint becomes immovable and stiff. The pain is less, but the discomfort from lost motion remains. The purpose of the treatment is to lessen the inflammation before the joint is permanently damaged.

General Treatment. Arthritis cannot be cured, but early treatment will do much to lessen joint damage. This includes measures to build up body resistance, such as rest and a good diet. Consistent exercise helps to prevent immobile joints and wasted muscles. Deep breathing also helps to strengthen body tone.

Drug Therapy. Drugs will not cure rheumatoid arthritis, but they do help to reduce pain and sometimes slow down inflammation. Narcotics are avoided because this is a long-drawn-out disease. Salicylates are used to relieve joint pain. *Aspirin* (acetylsalicylic acid) is the first choice as a pain reliever, and it seems to reduce inflammation.

Exercise. Exercise is important to keep the joint functioning, to maintain muscle tone and to prevent contractures and deformities. Exercise is planned to alternate with rest. Gentle stretching is beneficial, especially if the patient does it himself rather than being "stretched" by someone else. Deep breathing should be practiced several times a day, with frequent changes of position. Braces or splints help to prevent deformities in painful joints. Excessive strain on a joint, caused by poor posture, can be relieved with a corrective corset.

Surgery is sometimes used as a last resort, to manipulate a joint, transplant tendons or even to build a new joint (arthroplasty). If a joint is very painful, and if there is no hope of making it useful again, the surgeon may ankylose, or solidify, it. Joint motion is lost, but the pain is also gone.

Hope for These Arthritics. Some patients can avoid being crippled by paying strict attention to diet, rest, exercise, medication and physiotherapy. They still have to contend with constant pain. Many of them become discouraged and turn to anything that promises a cure. Quacks are quick to take advantage of the fact that rheumatoid arthritis often does disappear for a time, and claim that these let-ups are the result of taking their remedies. Desperate arthritics spend millions of dollars every year on products advertised as vibrating pillows, copper rings and radioactive earth.

Some ointments, such as oil of wintergreen, which contain salicylates, are absorbed from the skin and are helpful. A course of mineral waters or mud baths does little more than provide a change of scene and perhaps give a psychological boost. They are so expensive that the patient is convinced that they must be good for him. Warm climates improve circulation, but they do not cure arthritis, although the patient may be happier in Florida, Arizona or California.

Rheumatoid Arthritis of the Spine

Sometimes called *rheumatoid spondylitis*, this disease is an inflammation of the joints of the spinal column, accompanied by increasing stiffening and pain. It mainly afflicts young men; it almost always appears before the age of 50. Rheumatoid arthritis of the spine begins gradually with aches and pains which alternately disappear and reappear in the lower part of the back (sacro-iliac area). As the inflammation moves upward it interferes with chest expansion. The stiffening spine eliminates the lumbar curve and causes a humpback curvature in the chest area. Stiffening of the neck makes it impossible to turn the head, and the patient has pain and muscle spasm.

Treatment. Salicylates are given to relieve the pain; moist heat helps to relax muscle spasm. Steroids are not helpful, except in acute attacks. Phenylbutazone is sometimes given. Exercises are important to keep the spine as movable as possible and to aid chest expansion. During an acute attack, the patient remains in bed, and attention is centered on relieving his pain and keeping him as comfortable as possible.

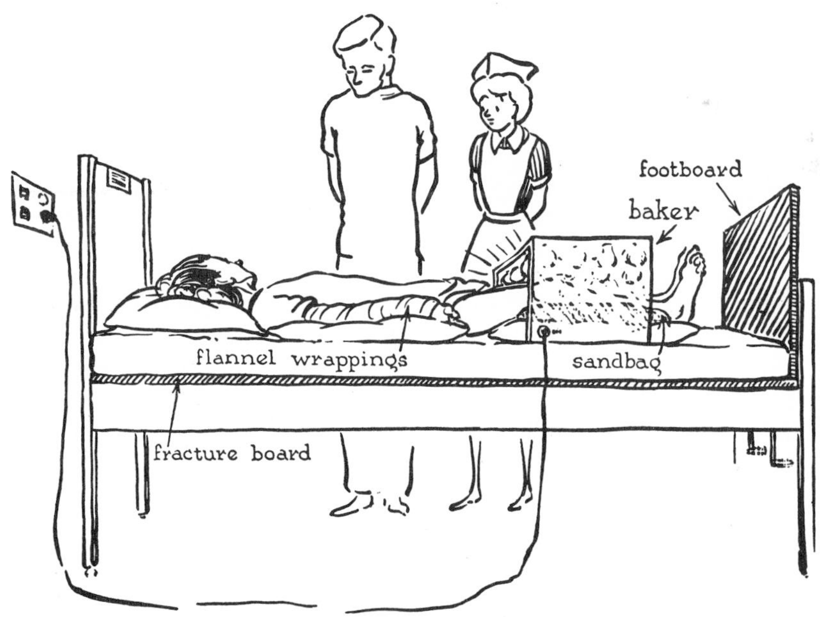

Fig. 151. Patient with arthritis.

Aspirin can be given safely in fairly large amounts, although large doses sometimes cause nausea and vomiting, ringing in the ears and deafness. It may affect kidney function; usually, the fluid intake is stepped up for patients who are having large doses of aspirin, to prevent renal calculi (kidney stones).

Phenylbutazone (Butazolidin) helps in about 50 per cent of these patients. A 10-day to 2-week trial period will show whether or not it is effective. Some patients have uncomfortable side-effects, such as nausea, visual disturbances, dizziness, abdominal pain, fever and a skin rash. Edema may appear if the patient has a cardiac difficulty. Periodic blood counts will tell whether or not he is anemic.

Antimalarial drugs (Atabrine, Chloroquine, Plaquenil) are sometimes used to control inflammation. Occasionally, nausea or a skin rash appear as side-effects.

SOLUBLE GOLD SALTS. Recent studies have shown that gold salts definitely are effective in treating rheumatoid arthritis. In some patients, gold salts cause a mild skin rash. More serious side-effects are jaundice, hematuria, hepatitis, change in urinary output and severe intestinal upsets.

Steroids. These hormones relieve pain and stiffness quickly but when used over a long period, their side-effects cause more disability than would have occurred without them.

The *cortisones* are synthetic reproductions of the adrenal cortical hormone *hydrocortisone.* This hormone strengthens the body's ability to stand strain and regulates metabolism and fluid balance. The preparations commonly used are prednisone (Meticortin, Deltra, Deltasone), prednisolone (Delta-Cortef, Meticortelone, Hydeltra, Sterane) and cortisone (Cortogen, Cortone).

Corticotropin (ACTH, Acthar) has the same effect as cortisone. It cannot be given orally, because it is destroyed in the intestinal tract.

SIDE-EFFECTS OF THE CORTISONES. Cortisones often cause toxic effects, because they are given over such long periods of time. They reduce inflammation, and consequently infection may go untreated because the patient has none of the symptoms. Therefore, it is important to report even a slight elevation of temperature or a minor discomfort, as they may be signs of really serious trouble. The patient who is taking cortisones may gain weight and develop edema. A daily weight check and a continuous weight record should be kept.

The steroids increase the amount of glucose in the bloodstream which might lead to overproduction of insulin with symptoms of insulin shock. They can also cause peptic ulcers—symptoms of stomach distress should be reported. Sometimes skin disturbances appear, menstruation may cease, and the patient may be mentally depressed. The symptoms disappear when the patient stops taking the drug. After a course of steroid treatment patients seem to be able to carry on without these remedies.

Physiotherapy. Physiotherapy is excellent for improving the condition of an arthritic patient. The warmth of infrared heat and diathermy on inflamed joints relaxes muscles and relieves pain. Heat also increases the flow of blood to the affected part. Massage is helpful if the joint is not acutely inflamed.

Osteoarthritis

Osteoarthritis, a degenerative joint disease, progresses slowly in a series of destructive changes. Unlike rheumatoid arthritis, it never lets up and is not accompanied by fever. It may begin in the middle 30's, but it usually afflicts middle-aged and elderly people, both men and women. Osteoarthritis in the joints of fingers and toes is common in women during the climacteric. Obese people are more likely to develop this disease because of the effect of the extra weight on their joints. As the disease progresses and the tissues harden around the joints, the cartilage that covers the ends of the bones becomes thin and uneven and loses its movement. The result of this process is pain and limited movement in the affected joint, although it does not become fixed or ankylosed. There is some evidence that heredity and possibly altered metabolism play a part in the development of osteoarthritis.

Symptoms. Osteoarthritis develops slowly; its victims first notice joint stiffness in the morning. This is more marked when the weather is damp or after they have been unusually active. Any joint may be involved—the spine, the hips and the knees are most commonly affected. At first, the patient is merely uncomfortable, but eventually movement is painful. The joints are not swollen, and the muscles remain firm. Warmth, rest and aspirin make the patient comfortable as long as he does not exercise the affected parts. As time goes on, motion becomes more and more limited.

Treatment. Rest of the affected joints is important. Exercises in moderation are helpful, being careful to avoid strain. Heat is comforting, and aspirin relieves the pain. Weight loss is recommended for obese individuals. Belts, braces, crutches and canes give support and relieve strain on the affected joints. Sometimes traction is used to give relief.

Rheumatic fever also affects joints, but since its most serious effects are upon the heart it is discussed under heart disease in Chapter 36.

Long-Term Management of the Arthritic

A patient with osteoarthritis should be told how arthritis progresses and should understand the importance of preventing deformities. He needs to know the effects of fatigue and how to avoid it by spaced rest periods. He should know that much depends on his own efforts—that if he persists faithfully in his treatment, much can be done to prevent crippling deformities. Many things can be done to make things easier for him. He should have a flat, firm bed, the same height as the seat of his wheelchair, to make it easier for him to move from one to the other. Any chair that he sits in should be 3 or 4 inches higher than an ordinary chair, to prevent overbending at the hips. Pillows tend to force him into a hunched position, which is tiring. In their anxiety not to be a trouble to anyone, some arthritic patients need to be cautioned about overexerting themselves.

The arthritic has a far from cheery future to look forward to, with his activities becoming more limited, constant pain and eventually a more or less housebound life. The extent of his activity will depend on how far the disease has progressed but a thoughtful nurse will try to find ways to make his life more bearable. His family usually needs encouragement as well. Sometimes it helps them just to be able to talk to somebody about their feelings. A member of the family who may be tied down to the care of a more-or-less helpless arthritic is bound to feel depressed at times, as she watches him grow progressively worse.

36

THE PATIENT WITH CARDIOVASCULAR DISEASE AND BLOOD DISORDERS

Cardiovascular Disease

Cardiovascular diseases as presented in this chapter includes those conditions which interfere with the heart as a pump, those which disturb the blood flow in the blood vessels supplying it, and the peripheral vascular diseases which disturb the blood flow in the vessels in some localized area such as an extremity. These conditions are the leading cause of death in this country in people over the age of 25—the number of deaths from cardiovascular disease in the older age groups increases every year. It not only kills but it disables more people after 65 than any other disease and ranks second as a cause of disability in younger people. In spite of the statistics, the outlook is not hopeless; there are reasons for the increase in the number of deaths that the figures do not show. For one thing, people are now living longer, and elderly people are more likely to develop cardiovascular disease. As the body processes are weakened, the heart and the blood vessels may be the first to give out. We also know that in the past many deaths were really caused by heart and vascular diseases but were not included in the statistics because they were attributed to other causes. However, death after 80 from a worn-out heart is not the same as death at 50 from an obstruction in a coronary artery. Many individuals die from heart disease before other body processes fail.

HEART DISEASE

To most people heart disease, the most common of the cardiovascular diseases, has a sinister sound, which they fear means the end of everything, the end of a normal life or complete invalidism. A person's attitude toward heart disease can have a tremendous effect on his chances for recovery. Some people are so frightened that they are almost afraid to move and give up every activity, when all they need do is to be more careful. Others disregard orders about diet, rest or smoking and take the point of view that life is not worth living if they must give up so much, even though some habits are harmful.

People should know that it is now possible to live normally and happily with heart disease for many years. Advances in treatment have been spectacular, not only in heart surgery but in new drugs that make the cardiac patient more comfortable. The cardiac patient should be encouraged to talk about his fears and worries so that he can learn enough about his condition to understand his treatment, without being frightened by it. As a nurse, you need to "know enough to know" when you should turn a problem question over to the head nurse or the doctor to handle. The main thing is to relieve the patient's worries, and you are likely to be one person with whom he will discuss them. You should know what a patient can or cannot be allowed to do—everyone cannot do the same things. Some people cannot be helped, such as the old people whose hearts are failing, or young people whose hearts have been seriously damaged by rheumatic fever. These people need more care and reassurance as they gradually become more dependent and more uncomfortable. You may know that there is little or no hope for a patient's recovery, but this knowledge should never make you indifferent about his care.

The Heart. Understanding heart disease begins with a good general understanding of how a normal heart works. The following is a brief review of the structure and the function of the heart.

The heart is a strong, muscular organ which keeps the blood circulating throughout the body. It is divided into right and left sides, each of which has 2 chambers. The upper chambers are the right and left auricles (atria); the lower chambers the right and left ventricles. The right auricle (atrium) receives the blood returned from the veins of the body and passes it on to the right ventricle below, which pumps it to the lungs to pick up oxygen and get rid of carbon dioxide. The blood then returns to the heart, enters the left auricle, and passes down into the left ventricle. From here it is pumped into the large artery leading out of the heart, the aorta, and into all its branches distributed throughout the body. The blood leaves its oxygen and food materials in the body tissues and picks up carbon dioxide, collects in the veins and returns to the heart, starting the process all over again. The heart muscle contracts to provide the force necessary to pump the blood, and it works continuously

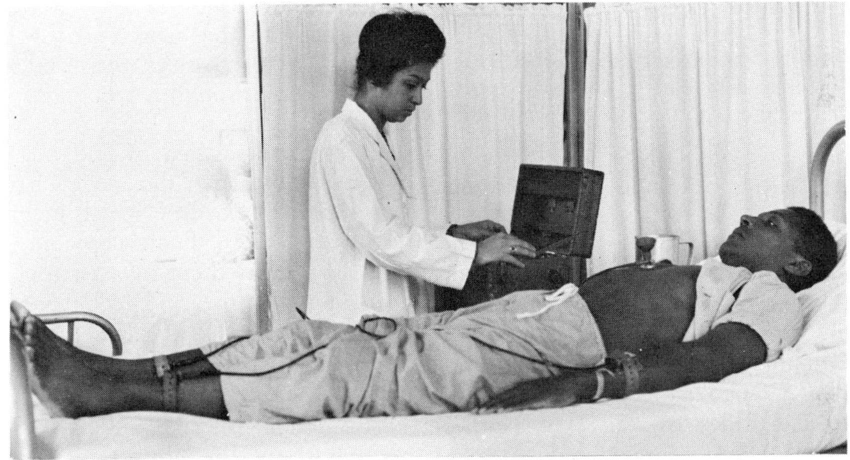

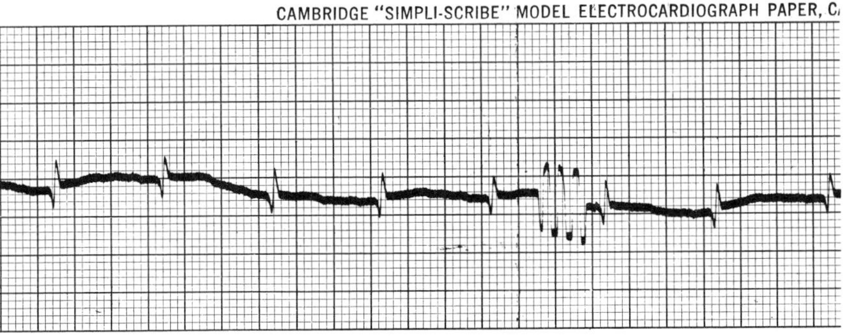

FIG. 152. (*Top*) Technician taking an EKG. Leads have been placed on the arms, the legs and the chest. (*Bottom*) A sample of the graphic record obtained by electrocardiography. (Smith, D. W., and Gips, C. D.: Care of the Adult Patient, p. 680, Philadelphia, Lippincott, 1963)

—the only rest it has is the slight pause between the contractions or heartbeats. The heart adjusts its action according to the needs of the body—it can send out more blood more quickly when the body needs it, as when running to catch a bus. We cannot consciously control heart action to speed it up or slow it down; this is done by the nervous system.

Signs and Symptoms. Some forms of heart disease can be cured, while others can be controlled and made bearable by treatment. Certain symptoms can be expected to appear in almost every form of heart disease. In general, signs of heart difficulty of some kind are:

Changes in the rate, the quality and the rhythm of the pulse

Rise or fall in blood pressure

Edema, especially in the feet and the ankles (faulty heart action causes the collection of fluids in the tissues)

A gain in weight from excess fluid in the tissues

Difficulty in breathing, cough, cyanosis, due to lack of oxygen in the blood and circulatory difficulties

Tests. Tests help to determine the particular form of heart disease in each case.

Electrocardiogram (EKG). An *electrocardiogram* is a record on a graphic sheet made by the action of the electric currents generated by the heart muscle; it gives the doctor information about heart action and heart damage. A technician takes this test by placing lead electrodes on the skin (chest, wrists and ankles) and connecting them to a machine, the *electrocardiograph,* which measures and records these currents. The test may be done at the patient's bedside or in a room set aside for this purpose. The patient should be told that the test is painless. The graphic sheet is placed on the patient's chart; it usually is returned with both a detailed statement and a brief summary of what the test shows. The patient does not usually require any special treatment either before or after the test. (See Fig. 152.)

Angiocardiogram. An *angiocardiogram* is the record of a test to show abnormal conditions in the heart and the large blood vessels. A radiopaque dye (Diodrast or Urokon) is injected into a vein, and x-ray pictures are taken to record the course of the dye from the heart to the lungs and back again and out through the aorta. It is used only as a last resort to get necessary information, because it is uncomfortable and sometimes dangerous.

The patient's breakfast is omitted on the morning of the test, and he is given a sedative an hour before the test is scheduled. The test is given in the x-ray room. The patient may have an allergic reaction to the dye and must be watched for signs of a delayed reaction after he returns to his room. The dye is irritating if it gets on the skin, and sometimes the point of injection becomes swollen and painful.

Cardiac Catheterization. The purpose of this test is to get information about congenital defects in the heart. A long, flexible catheter is passed into the heart and the large blood vessels. The pressure is measured as the catheter passes through each part, and blood samples are taken in each one. These blood samples are analyzed to find out how much oxygen and carbon dioxide each contains. It is a delicate procedure which includes cutting down on a vein, fluoroscopy and x-ray pictures. It is carried out by a team of physicians, professional nurses and technicians and takes from 1 to 3 hours. Cardiac catheterization is comparatively painless but somewhat uncomfortable.

The patient may be understandably apprehensive about the procedure—it will help to tell him that it is really not painful, although he may be a little uncomfortable. If he is told that the test is always done by a team that routinely does these tests he is less likely to be alarmed when he sees the number of people required to carry out the procedure.

Cardiac catheterization usually has no complications, but it is not entirely without danger. The patient's pulse is checked every 15 minutes for an hour after the test and frequently after that for several hours. A rapid or irregular pulse is reported immediately. Some doctors keep the patient in bed for the rest of the day; sometimes he is allowed to go back to his normal activities.

Coronary Artery Disease

From your reveiw of the anatomy of the heart you will remember that the heart itself gets its blood supply through the coronary arteries. If deposits of fat and calcium collect within the walls of these arteries they cause atherosclerosis (see p. 475). One of these fatty substances, *cholesterol,* is thought to be the chief offender. Cholesterol is taken into the body in food fats—animal fats are especially high in cholesterol. Studies are being made to determine the relationship of diet and smoking to high levels of cholesterol in the blood.

People over 50 are the most common victims of coronary artery disease, but it may occur also in younger people. During the early middle years more men than women are affected; after the menopause the number is about the same for both sexes. There seems to be a tendency in some families to develop the disease. However, it is believed that coronary artery disease develops over many years, and precautions to prevent it should begin early in life. More attention is given now to discovering the disease early, before an attack has occurred and before atherosclerosis has severely damaged the heart.

Angina Pectoris

Angina pectoris, usually referred to as angina, is a sudden and severe pain in the chest. Angina occurs when extra exertion calls for an increase in the blood supply to the heart which the narrowed arteries are unable to provide. Consequently, the heart muscle suffers. In addition, if a fragment from fat and calcium deposits in the arteries lodges in one of the coronary arteries, the blood supply to the heart is shut off completely.

Angina is most severe over the heart, although it may spread to the shoulder and the arm on the left side or to the jaw. The patient is pale, feels faint and has trouble getting his breath. The pain is over in less than 5 minutes but is intense while it lasts. This is a warning that the heart is not getting enough blood, and the victim who ignores this warning is risking serious illness or sudden death if he does not put himself under a doctor's care. He may have recurrent attacks of angina, but treatment lessens the danger of a fatal attack.

Treatment and Prevention. The patient who is under a doctor's care knows what to do for an angina attack. He has been instructed always to carry nitroglycerin tablets with him and to dissolve a tablet under his tongue as soon as the attack begins. Nitroglycerin brings quick relief by dilating the coronary arteries. Patients use this drug safely for many years with no ill effects. Amyl nitrite is equally effective in relieving angina. It comes in am-

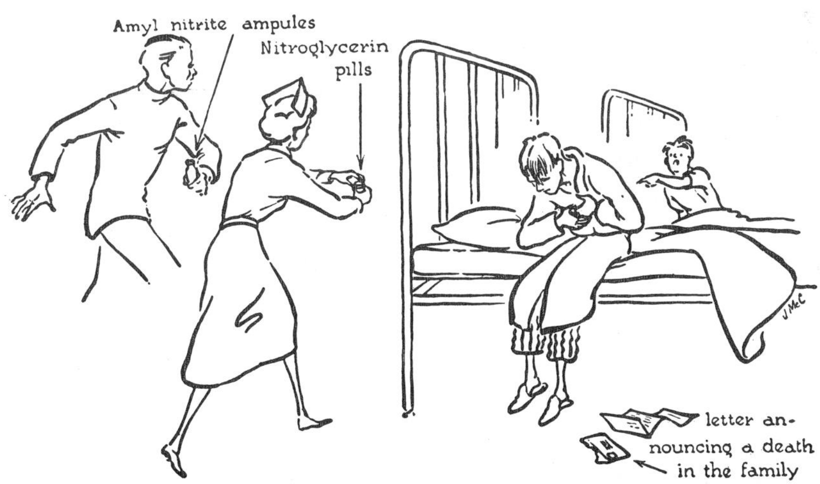

FIG. 153. Patient with coronary artery disease—angina pectoris.

pules that are broken in a handkerchief and inhaled.

Aminophylline and peritrate are drugs that may be given to prevent attacks of angina. These drugs also dilate the coronary arteries; however, they do not help everyone.

When a patient knows that certain things bring on an attack he can learn to be more careful. If the attacks become more frequent and more severe, he may have to curb all of his activities. The patient who has angina never knows when he may have an attack; he may live for years or dies suddenly. The best he can do is to follow the rules for his treatment, learn what he can and cannot do and live accordingly.

Myocardial Infarction

Myocardial infarction is the correct name for what is commonly called a "coronary" heart attack. It is caused by the obstruction of a coronary artery, and if it does not cause sudden death it damages the heart. Atherosclerosis is usually the cause.

Symptoms. The attack begins suddenly with a sharp severe pain in the chest, sometimes radiating to the left arm and shoulder. It is like angina but lasts longer and is more severe; exertion may have nothing to do with bringing it on. Also, unlike angina, it does not go away with rest, and nitroglycerin or amyl nitrite does not help.

First Aid. Everyone should know what to do for the victim of a coronary heart attack. Much harm has been done by well-meaning but misguided ministrations in this emergency. If chest pains persist in a person suspected of having a heart attack, insist on keeping him quiet and call a doctor. This means *complete rest; do not* take off his shoes or try to undress him or get him into bed, *no matter where he is when this happens.* Cover him with a blanket or coat; something under his head will help him to breathe more easily. If he shows signs of shock, keep him flat. Do not allow him to sit up or move around before the doctor has seen him, no matter how much better he says he feels. Even if this is not a coronary attack, it is better to be safe than sorry.

Treatment and Nursing Care. Tests will help to determine the nature of this attack. First, an electrocardiogram will be taken; tests will also be done for the presence of an enzyme in the blood that always appears in greater amounts after a coronary occlusion. Tests of the sedimentation rate of the red blood cells almost always show that it is higher after a myocardial infarction. Some of the important points in nursing care are the following:

Rest comes first. The injured heart must have time to repair its injuries. The damaged spot in the heart takes from 3 to 6 weeks to heal. Without healing, the heart may rupture, and the patient might die.

The amount of activity the patient is permitted will depend on the severity of the attack. He may not be allowed any activity—not even to wash his face or feed himself. Some patients are permitted to do these things for themselves and may be up in a chair for a short time each day. Some may be allowed to use a commode at the bedside or go to the bathroom once a day for a bowel movement. Many doctors want a patient to exercise his feet and legs gently to prevent thrombophlebitis.

Prevent exertion, such as straining with a bowel movement, or reaching for things on the bedside table or picking them up from the floor. After giving him his bath, let him rest for a little while before making his bed. The patient with breathing difficulties is sometimes more comfortable in an upright position with a back rest built up by pillows and supporting pillows for the arms and knees (Fig. 154).

See that his family or visitors do not stay too long or talk too much, especially about things that might upset him.

Do not upset him yourself by brushing off his questions with "Just you don't worry, now" or "We'll take care of everything." Do not make predictions about how long it will take him to get well either, or try to answer involved technical questions. Refer him to the doctor for information you are not qualified to give.

Watch his pulse, measure his intake and output, note any sign of pain or difficulty in breathing or fatigue. His blood pressure is taken regularly. Demerol may be prescribed for pain, since pain interferes with rest. Anticoagulants, such as heparin, are given to lessen the danger of the formation of blood clots.

The Patient's Future. The prospect for survival after a coronary attack is not hopeless—

about 70 per cent of these patients live for 5 years or more. Many of them live longer. If the patient follows orders about his treatment, is careful to avoid violent physical exertions and rests for about 3 months, he may be able to return to his job at the end of that time provided that his work is not too strenuous.

Rehabilitation. As with all rehabilitation, the purpose is to help the patient to lead as normal, useful and satisfying a life as is possible for him. He will have much the same problems as any patient will have who has had a physically damaging illness. If he looks and feels well it may be difficult for him and others to realize that there are certain things he should not do. On the other hand, he may be unduly fearful and afraid to do anything. Every patient needs specific directions about what he can or cannot do. Telling a patient to be careful is not enough unless he knows what "being careful" means in his particular case.

Functional Heart Disease

Although nothing may be organically wrong with the heart, anxiety can bring on many of the symptoms of heart disease, such as pain over the heart, shortness of breath and exhaustion. If a thorough examination shows no physical abnormality, tranquilizers or sedatives may be prescribed to lessen the patient's anxiety. Every effort should be made to find out what is causing these symptoms and to help the patient to realize that his heart is normal.

Congestive Heart Failure

Congestive heart failure means that the heart is failing and is unable to do its work. Heart failure affects individuals in different ways and to different degrees—one person may suffer from it and go about his business as usual, showing no signs of heart failure. Another person may be seriously ill. The heart will try to keep up with the demands made upon it; treatment will help it to make a satisfactory adjustment. Abnormal conditions in the heart may make continued treatment necessary or signs of heart failure will appear again.

When the heart is failing we say it is *decompensated.* After treatment, when it is able to carry its normal load, we say that the heart is *compensated.*

Causes. Congestive heart failure is the result of strain on the heart which may be caused by heart disease, blood vessel disease, con-

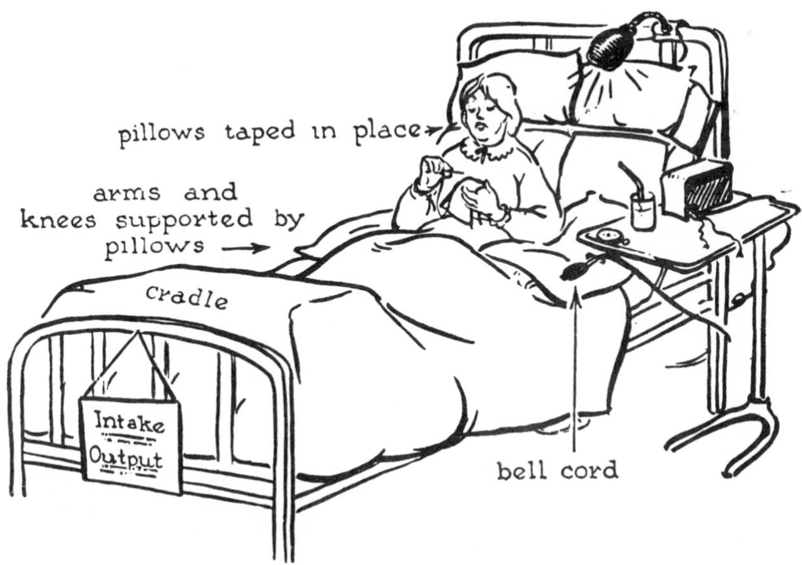

Fig. 154. Cardiac patient.

genital defects or other diseases, such as hyperthyroidism which speeds up heart action. Damage to the heart valves from rheumatic fever is another cause of heart failure. Older people are subject to heart failure because the blood vessels lose their elasticity (arteriosclerosis).

Symptoms. The first sign of a failing heart that the patient may notice is that his work makes him unduly tired. He has to rest part of the way up the stairs, or he may need two pillows at night when he has always slept on one. He may also develop a persistent cough, and his ankles might swell during the day. Although this swelling disappears overnight, it comes back as soon as he is on his feet again. When he gets on the scales he finds that he has gained weight, which is actually due to an accumulation of fluid in his tissues. When he presses on a swollen part his finger leaves an indentation which lasts for a time (pitting).

Tests. The usual tests for detecting heart disease are taken, such as the electrocardiogram, x-ray examination and cardiac catheterization. A test for measuring the speed of the circulation may also be made, and arterial and venous blood pressure are measured. Arterial pressure is determined by "taking the blood pressure," the familiar procedure described in Chapter 27. Measuring the *venous* pressure is a more complicated procedure which is done by the physician. It involves his making a venipuncture in the patient's arm and then measuring the resistance of the venous blood to the injection of sterile normal saline. The venous pressure is always increased in congestive heart failure.

Treatment and Nursing Care. In heart failure, the heart is laboring under difficulties, and the treatment and the nursing care are designed to make its work easier. Some important aspects of therapy are:

Rest, including sedation if it is needed

Digitalis to slow the heart rate

Diuretics, such as Mercuhydrin or Diuril, which are administered to help the body to rid itself of excess fluid and salts

Oxygen, if the blood is not getting enough from the lungs

Use of a footboard alternately with the gatch knee rest, which allows the patient to move his legs and promotes circulation

Massage and a foam rubber pad for the patient's buttocks, since he usually sits up much of the time

Restriction of salt in his diet

Recording the patient's weight at the same time every day (the patient wears the same amount of clothing for each weighing)

Measuring intake and output.

The amount of digitalis administered is larger at first than it will be later. The dosage is gradually decreased until the amount needed to stabilize the heartbeat is found. If the amount is too large the patient will have undesirable side-effects. When the heart rate is slowed down sufficiently, we say that the patient is *digitalized.* Sometimes a patient has to continue taking digitalis for the rest of his life.

Rheumatic Fever

Rheumatic fever is the cause of 90 per cent of organic heart disease in people under the age of 50. It often leaves the victim with heart damage which leads to chronic rheumatic heart disease. Although young adults may contract rheumatic fever, it usually is found in children between the ages of 5 and 15 years. For this reason, it will be discussed in Chapter 52 (Care of the Sick Child).

Chronic Rheumatic Heart Disease

The most common cause of *chronic rheumatic heart disease* is a narrowing of the mitral valve between the left auricle and left ventricle of the heart. This is called *mitral stenosis.* Blood collects in the chambers of the heart and enlarges them, causing congestion in the lungs. The left side of the heart is the first to be affected. The condition progresses to the right side and leads to heart failure.

Symptoms. The first signs of this trouble are a difficulty in breathing, a cough and sometimes cyanosis and the expectoration of blood. If the condition grows worse, the patient's feet and ankles swell, his liver enlarges, and his abdominal cavity fills with fluid—unmistakable signs of heart failure. There may also be a lowering of the systolic blood pressure.

Treatment and Nursing Care. Heart surgery provides relief for many of these patients. However, it is not always necessary, and an operation is performed only when the patient has such serious changes in his heart and lungs that nothing else will help him. The nursing care includes watching for symptoms of heart failure, giving the care required for heart failure and encouraging the patient to persevere with his treatment. He must know what his limitations are and behave accordingly.

Bacterial Endocarditis

The heart is covered and lined with membranes. The membrane that lines the chambers and the valves of the heart is the endocardium. Infection of this membrane causes inflammation, a condition known as *bacterial endocarditis.* This is a serious disease which was once nearly always fatal. Although antibiotics have changed this gloomy picture, bacterial endocarditis is still a common health problem. However, modern treatment helps to control it and to keep it from disabling the patient.

People with damaged heart valves are more susceptible to infection, especially those who have had rheumatic fever or have congenital heart defects. The extraction of an infected tooth, childbirth or an upper respiratory infection may release disease organisms into the bloodstream which attack damaged heart valves. The streptococcus is a frequent offender.

Symptoms. One of the first signs of bacterial endocarditis is a low-grade fever, which gradually increases. The patient has chills and perspires, he loses his appetite and loses weight. His face has a brownish tinge, and tiny reddish-purple spots (petechiae) appear on his skin and mucous membranes. Usually, he is anemic. As the disease progresses the signs of congestive heart failure appear. Blood cultures will show what organism is causing the trouble.

Treatment and Nursing Care. Large doses of antibiotics to which the causative organism is sensitive are given. The nursing care consists of conserving the patient's energy while he is a bed patient and making him as comfortable as possible. He should be observed closely for fluctuation in body temperature, the rate and the quality of the pulse and symptoms of complications. For example, hematuria (blood in the urine) or pain and impaired circulation in an extremity might be the result of a blood clot (embolus) which originated in the diseased valve.

Heart Block

Heart block means that the contractions of the heart are weakened and do not have enough force to send the blood from the auricles into the ventricles. This is a disturbance of the nerve impulses from the auricles to the ventricles. If the contractions are only weakened, heart block is *partial*; if they cease altogether, it is *complete.*

Heart block is not a disease in itself but it is associated with many kinds of heart disease, especially disease of the coronary arteries or rheumatic heart disease. The toxic effects of digitalis may cause heart block. In complete heart block, the patient dies unless the contractions are started again. Epinephrine is given immediately; in a prolonged attack it is injected directly into the heart. At the beginning of an attack the patient becomes unconscious and may have convulsions.

The *electric pacemaker* is a machine which is used to stimulate heart contractions by means of wires connected to electrodes which are applied to the chest. Sometimes the electrodes are inserted into the heart. Patients who experience frequent difficulty with heart contractions may use this device all the time. A portable pacemaker about the size of a small transistor radio is now available. The patient wears it underneath his clothing. Still smaller models can be implanted surgically underneath the patient's skin. For some patients, the pacemaker can be discontinued gradually, but others cannot live without it.

Cardiac Arrest

Cardiac arrest means that the heart has stopped beating. Electric shock, coronary heart disease or general anesthetics may cause cardiac arrest. Treatment is useless unless it is given at once, and it should be started by the staff or people who are nearest to the victim. Two things are vital: to keep the patient breathing and to restore the heartbeat. The procedure takes 2 people—one to give closed-chest cardiac massage and the other to administer artificial respiration. If a doctor is present, he usually takes care of the cardiac massage, but anyone who has been instructed properly may do it. Policemen, firemen and members of first aid or rescue squads may be trained in these technics.

Closed-Chest Cardiac Massage. The patient should be lying on a flat, firm surface (never on a mattress). His airway should be unobstructed. The operator kneels beside the patient, places his hands on the center of the chest, one on top of the other and at right angles to each other. He presses downward, depressing the sternum 1 to 1½ inches, and releases the pressure briefly. He repeats this process—press, release, press, release—about 60 times a minute, until the patient responds or until a doctor pronounces the patient dead. These procedures can save a life if they are started *immediately*—if necessary, it is imperative to start them without waiting for a doctor to arrive. Mouth-to-mouth resuscitation, which is given at the same time, is described in Chapter 48. (See Fig. 155.)

Open-Chest Cardiac Massage. In some cases of cardiac arrest, the doctor may perform open-

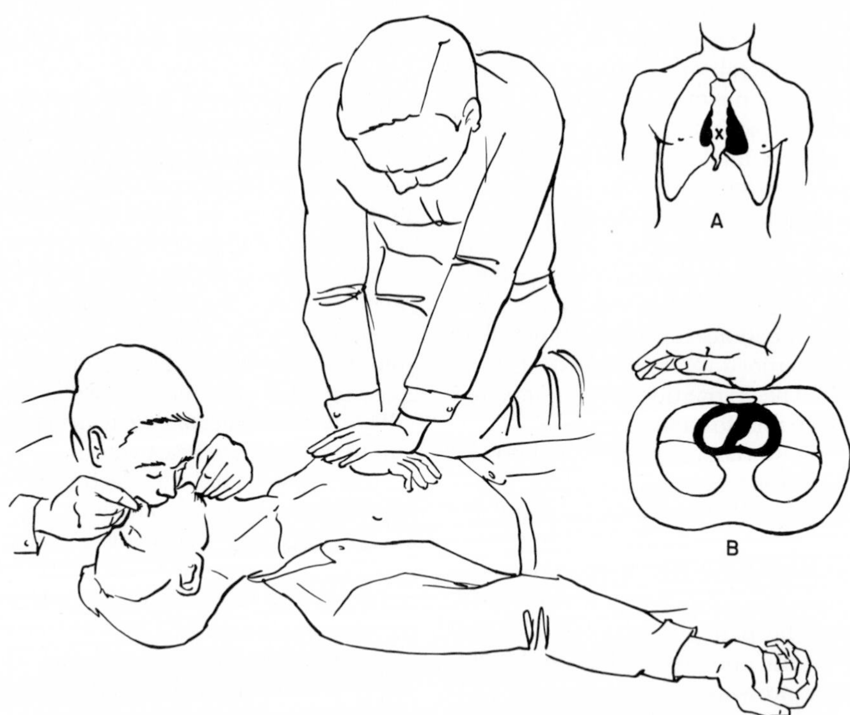

Fig. 155. Technic of closed-chest cardiac massage. One rescuer gives mouth-to-mouth resuscitation. The other massages the heart by pressing downward on the patient's chest approximately 60 times a minute. Insert (A) indicates the area where pressure should be applied. Insert (B) shows manual pressure on the chest, compressing the heart and forcing blood out of it. (American Heart Association, Inc., New York City; adapted from Kouwenhoven, W. B., et al.: Heart activation in cardiac arrest, Modern Concepts of Cardiovascular Diseases 30[2]:642)

chest cardiac massage by making a surgical incision in the anterior chest wall and exposing the heart. He grasps the heart in the palm of his hand and cardiac pumping, avoiding finger pressure, is carried out rapidly (80 to 100 times per minute). This is sometimes effective in restoring the heartbeat.

Open Heart Surgery

You may wonder how it is possible to operate on a structure as delicate and vital as the heart. Open heart surgery is accomplished by means of a device equipped with pumps and oxygenators that keeps the blood circulating and supplied with oxygen. This machine takes over the work of the heart temporarily, which allows the surgeon to open the heart and repair defects in the valves or in the chambers. The machine can do this safely for about an hour, without harming the body. Most heart surgery takes less than half of that time.

Preparation of the Patient

When the patient decides to have open heart surgery on his doctor's advice, he knows he is taking a risk, but he chooses to take that risk rather than to be condemned to partial or complete invalidism. If the patient is a child, the parents must make this decision.

Usually, the patient comes into the hospital for 2 weeks before the operation. This allows time to prepare him physically and emotionally for this experience and provides an opportunity to show him that he can have confidence in the people who are caring for him. It gives him a chance to express his own feelings, to ask questions and reveal his fears and to be prepared for his postoperative care. He will be assured that he will have whatever is necessary for pain, and that everything will be done to make him as comfortable as possible. The nurse explains to the patient that if his chest feels tight at first, this feeling soon disappears. Rest is important during the preparation time because the patient will have a number of tests taken which will tire him. Also, he will practice deep breathing. His family will need reassurance and information so that they will be able to cooperate in every possible way.

Professional nurses are responsible for the immediate postoperative nursing care following heart surgery. It involves knowing how to use complicated equipment as well as expert nursing knowledge and skills.

Some patients become depressed 4 or 5 days after heart surgery. This may be only the letdown after a dreaded ordeal, but sometimes a patient thinks of committing suicide. Tranquilizers may be given to help the patient through this feeling of depression. If the patient becomes disoriented, bedrails will be needed. The patient may be conscious of such a vast improvement in what he is able to do that he has to be kept from overexerting himself. He should return to his normal activities gradually over a period of approximately 3 months. Other patients go to the opposite extreme and are afraid to do anything. Despite the surgery, some patients may never be fully active, and a comparatively few do not improve at all.

Rehabilitation of the Patient With Heart Disease

Rehabilitation following a coronary attack has already been mentioned, but diseases and disorders of the heart afflict so many people in so many ways that the resultant disabilities also differ widely. Many people with heart disease look perfectly normal, yet they must limit their activities even though they appear to be strong and healthy. The cardiac patient may continue to be a patient for the rest of his life, although he may feel able to do vigorous work which his heart cannot accommodate.

Rest may be a necessary part of his treatment to protect his heart from further damage, but unless he has specific instructions about what is meant by rest in his case these orders may be useless. Some patients can carry on all ordinary physical activities without harm; others can do the ordinary things but must never do anything strenuous; still others must definitely restrict even ordinary activities. Some cardiac patients must have complete rest in bed or in a wheelchair. Tests will determine just how much the patient's heart can tolerate. The amount of activity he can be allowed is considered also in relation to his job and his recreation.

Some things make it easier for an impaired heart to function. Heat and humidity affect the efficiency of the heart; air-conditioning helps to conserve its efforts. Since obesity puts a strain on the heart, diet restrictions may be ordered to keep weight down. Climbing stairs and running make the heart work harder, so these should be avoided.

The Housewife. Often the busy housewife finds it most difficult to make the necessary adjustments. It seems laborious to sit down to iron or to prepare vegetables or to cook; she is tormented by specks of dust when she is supposed to be resting. Rearrangement of equipment in her kitchen will save steps. The housewife with a cardiac difficulty has to make up her mind as to whether she wants to stay well or wear herself out with unnecessary work, trying to live up to standards that are unnecessarily high.

The Wage-Earner. At one time, heart disease meant the end of work. Today the cardiac may go on working happily and efficiently in the light of his capabilities. He may be able to continue working, but perhaps not in the same job or perhaps working only part-time. He may be able to do some of his work sitting down. Work Classification Units in many parts of the country help to determine the kind of work possible for an individual with a heart difficulty. These units work with patients, doctors and employers to fit people into work they can stand without harm, which helps them mentally, physically and financially. Some cardiacs are willing and able to work, and work might be a financial necessity for them—their employment at a suitable job should be encouraged. Information about cardiac disease helps to make employers more willing to employ these people in such a position.

Hypertension

Hypertension is high blood pressure. Although not considered as a heart disease, hypertension can lead to serious conditions, such as congestive heart failure and cerebrovascular accident, often referred to as CVA. A consistently high blood pressure leads to heart damage. As people grow older blood pressure tends to rise, although the reasons for this are not completely clear. One thing is certain: the condition of the heart and the blood vessels has the greatest effect on blood pressure. The range in normal adult blood pressure can vary from 100/60 to 130/80.

Who Develops High Blood Pressure? Hypertension runs in families; heredity plays a part in its development. People who use a great deal of salt on their food are prone to develop hypertension, as well as obese people and those who "bottle up" their feelings and tensions.

Position, exercise and emotional tensions affect blood pressure. It is higher when a person is sitting or standing up than it is when he is lying down. It is lowest when he is asleep. Some types of illness affect the blood pressure —it is lower in anemia and may be elevated in an acute infection.

Symptoms. High blood pressure affects people differently. Some people complain of fatigue, dizziness and headache—others show none of these symptoms. Sometimes the first sign of high blood pressure is heart, kidney, brain or eye damage, which causes hemorrhage or coronary artery occlusion.

Treatment and Nursing Care. Hypertension cannot be cured, but treatment will help to lower the blood pressure. The treatment includes:

Reducing weight and avoiding overweight

Reducing the amount of extra salt in the diet—some people pour excessive salt on all their food

Building up good health habits for sleep, rest and relaxation

Avoiding emotional upsets, such as angry outbursts or violent enthusiasms

Drugs with a tranquilizing effect (which were discussed in Chapter 30)

Reassuring the patient is an important part of his care. It may be a great shock to him to learn that he has high blood pressure. He may think that his active life is over and death is just around the corner. He can be told that many patients with blood pressure problems live for many years by following orders in caring for themselves. If a patient has been having treatment for high blood pressure for a long time, he may have been taking his blood pressure at home. Therefore, he may be justifiably resentful if not allowed to know what his blood pressure is when a nurse takes it in the hospital. Should this situation occur, the doctor should be consulted. The patient's family must learn how important his diet is and how rest and peace of mind help to keep his blood pressure within a safe range.

PERIPHERAL VASCULAR DISEASE

Arteriosclerosis and Atherosclerosis

Arteriosclerosis means hardening of the arteries and the loss of their elasticity. *Atherosclerosis* means the deposit of fat and calcium inside the arteries. Usually these conditions accompany aging. Since these two conditions are almost always found together, when most people say "arteriosclerosis" they are referring to both disorders. Arteriosclerosis and atherosclerosis can affect different parts of the body and help to cause different forms of heart disease. Often they develop over a long period of time and do not appear until after the age of 50. Diabetics or people who have been in the habit of eating a great amount of fatty foods may develop these conditions earlier. Also, these conditions seem to run in families.

Symptoms. The signs of these conditions often appear in the extremities, especially in the feet and the legs. The patient notices that the affected part is pale or bluish, feels cold and numb or tingles. He has cramps in his legs at night, and sometimes experiences pain. His skin is dry, and his nails are brittle. Breaks in the skin do not heal easily and may develop into ulcers and gangrene.

Treatment and Nursing Care. Two main objects of his care are to make the patient comfortable and to prevent infection. This includes:

Keeping the affected parts warm, with care to avoid burns

Elevating the head of the bed on bed blocks to keep the affected parts lower than the body

Preventing pressure that constricts the blood vessels, such as crossing the legs or sitting or standing for long periods of time

Preventing cuts and scratches and bruises and providing cleanliness when caring for them if they do occur

As much exercise as his condition will allow

Preventing exposure to cold

Encouragement to stop smoking

Drugs to relax the blood vessels, such as Priscoline or Regitine

If gangrene develops, an amputation may be necessary; therefore, extreme caution should be taken to ensure cleanliness and prevent injuries.

Thrombophlebitis

Thrombophlebitis is the inflammation of a vein, in which one or more clots form. It is caused by pressure or by prolonged inactivity, such as might occur after surgery or in any illness when the patient remains in one position for long periods of time. Since early ambulation in illness has become an accepted routine, there is less chance for this difficulty to occur. The legs are most likely to be affected.

Elderly patients or people with heart disease are prone to develop thrombophlebitis. Prolonged sitting may cause it—people are cautioned about sitting for hours at a time while looking at TV. Older people especially should know that it is important to change position frequently.

Symptoms. The symptoms of thrombophlebitis include pain in the affected leg, redness and swelling, fever and the symptoms that usually go with fever, such as fatigue and loss of appetite.

Treatment and Nursing Care. Opinions differ about the treatment for thrombophlebitis: some doctors want the leg elevated, with complete rest; others recommend exercises to promote circulation. If exercise is ordered, wriggling the toes, bending the knees and turning the ankle back and forth are simple exercises that the patient can do himself. If he is not able to do them, the nurse helps him. Exercises cannot be left up to the patient by simply

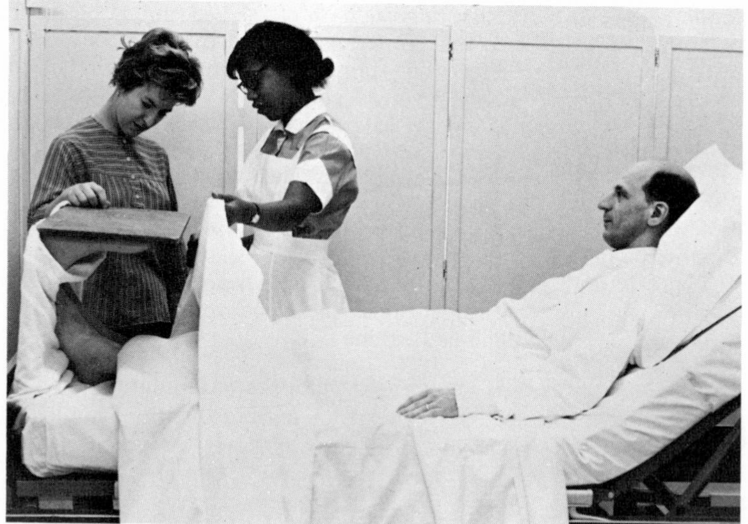

Fig. 156. The nurse is explaining to a member of the family how a padded board at the foot of the bed prevents pressure on the affected limb of a patient with thrombophlebitis. This is more satisfactory than a bed cradle because there is less danger of the patient striking it with his foot or leg and dislodging a blood clot.

telling him he is expected to do them. He needs definite instructions such as, "Bend your knee 5 times" as you show him how to do it. Remind him that it is time to do his exercises and encourage him as you watch him do them. Left to himself, he may feel too tired to make the effort or consider that it is nonsense.

Sometimes warm wet packs are ordered for pain and inflammation. If hot-water bags are used they should be placed beside the leg to avoid pressure. Pressure from pillows and bed clothes, and continuous use of the knee gatch or prolonged sitting should be avoided. Be careful never to rub or massage the leg—this might loosen a clot and release it into the bloodstream.

Anticoagulants are often ordered to prevent more clots from forming. Analgesics may be necessary for pain.

The patient may have to stay in bed for several weeks; he progresses gradually from complete bed rest to the time he is allowed to walk again. An elastic stocking or an elastic bandage helps to support the veins and promote circulation.

Embolism

Pulmonary embolism is an often tragic complication of thrombophlebitis. You will remember that an embolus is a blood clot that may be carried in the circulation to some vital spot, such as the heart or the lungs, and can lodge in a blood vessel. If the obstruction occurs in a large pulmonary blood vessel it may cause sudden death. The obstruction of a small vessel may not be so damaging; the patient is liable to complain of chest pain and breathing difficulty, and he coughs and becomes cyanotic. The immediate treatment is oxygen and complete rest. He may also be given anticoagulants, such as heparin and Dicumarol.

Embolism and Thrombosis in a Limb. An embolus may completely obstruct a blood vessel in an arm or a leg and cause thrombosis. The effects are serious, because if it happens in a large blood vessel it shuts off the main blood supply below the obstruction, and the tissues die. The affected area becomes white, cold and unbearably painful, and the pulse disappears—soon the limb is numb, and the patient is unable to move it. Immediate treatment is imperative or the limb may have to be amputated. The first thing to do after calling for help is to keep the patient warm. Let the limb hang down to help the circulation, keep it at complete rest and wrap it in cotton for warmth. The doctor may order heparin, to prevent more clots from forming, and Demerol to relieve pain. Surgery may be necessary to remove the obstruction.

You may never have seen an embolism, but

when one occurs it happens suddenly and quick action is needed to save the limb.

Buerger's Disease

Buerger's disease is the result of inflammation which causes obstruction of the veins and the arteries of the extremities, especially in the legs. It is more common among men than women, and heavy smokers especially are affected.

Usually the first sign of the disease that the patient notices is cramps in the muscles in the calves of his legs. Cramps are brought on by exercise but disappear when the patient rests. When the feet and the legs hang down they become a mottled purplish red; when they are raised they become abnormally pale. Ulcers may develop which could result in gangrene. As the disease progresses, pain continues even when the patient is resting.

Treatment. The patient must be careful to avoid the things that make this condition worse, especially chilling of his hands and feet. Tobacco in any form is forbidden because it constricts the blood vessels. The patient may exercise mildly if it is not painful. The Buerger-Allen exercises consist of alternately raising, lowering and resting the legs. The smooth, seesaw motion of the electrically operated oscillating bed is beneficial. If heat is used, it must be regulated thermostatically and never above body temperature. Drugs, such as Priscoline and Dibenzyline, may be given for blood vessel spasm. Sometimes a sympathectomy is performed, an operation which eliminates the constriction of the blood vessels by the sympathetic nerves. If ulcers become infected, gangrene may develop and make an amputation necessary. As you would expect, antibiotics and analgesics may be necessary for infection and pain.

Raynaud's Disease

Raynaud's disease is a condition caused by the spasmodic constriction of the arteries that supply the extremities. It affects the fingers and the toes particularly, often only the fingers. Nobody knows exactly what causes Raynaud's disease, but it seems to be related to exposure to cold and to emotional tensions. It affects more women than men, especially young adults.

Symptoms. The symptoms of the disease are distressing. The patient's hands are blanched and cold, perspire and feel numb and prickly. Later they become blue—especially the fingernails—and are painful. As heat brings the blood back, the hands become red and warm. In the early stages of the disease, these symptoms disappear after an attack, and the hands seem to be normal again. Later, as it grows worse, cyanosis remains between attacks, and ulcers which are slow to heal may develop on the fingertips. The skin looks tight and shiny, and the nails become deformed.

Treatment. The most important treatment for Raynaud's disease concerns the avoidance of chilling at all times. This means always wearing warm clothing out of doors in the winter, such as wool gloves, socks and overshoes. One victim carried a small electric heating unit in her muff and was never without a light wrap indoors the year round. An electric blanket at night provides steady warmth. Emotional upsets and tensions of any kind should be avoided. Smoking is definitely contraindicated. Drugs to relieve spasm of the arteries, such as Priscoline and Dibenamine, and papaverine to dilate the blood vessels provide considerable relief. A sympathectomy may be done. This is a most distressing and difficult disease to cope with, since even the slightest chilling may cause trouble.

Varicose Veins

Varicose veins are enlarged and twisted veins filled with blood that does not move on because the valves in the veins do not close properly. This allows the blood to trickle back and collect in the veins instead of moving forward toward the heart. Varicose veins usually occur in the legs, but they also appear in the rectum (*hemorrhoids*) and sometimes in the esophagus. They seem to be hereditary and may appear with pregnancy and with abdominal tumors. Standing for long periods of time, constriction of the legs by round gar-

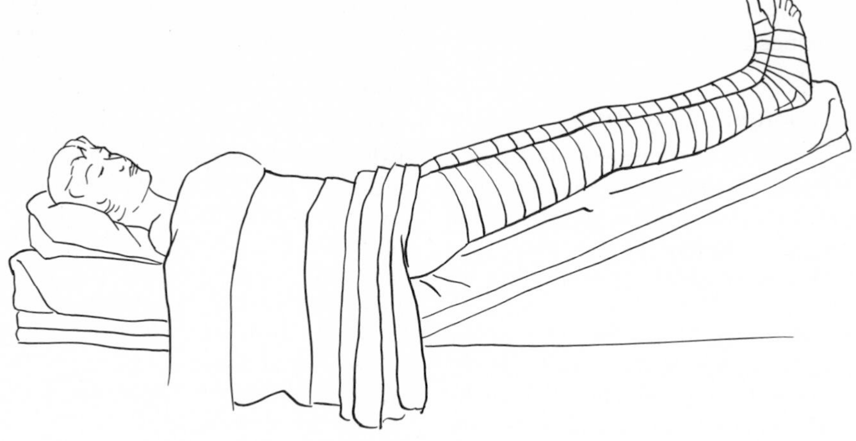

FIG. 157. Postoperative positioning in surgery for varicose veins. The feet and the legs are elevated to aid venous return. Elastic bandages from the feet to the groin were applied in the operating room. (Smith, D. W., and Gips, C. D.: Care of the Adult Patient, p. 820, Philadelphia, Lippincott, 1963)

ters and obesity may cause varicose veins or make existing ones worse.

Symptoms. The veins appear as bluish streaks or swollen, knotty bunches under the skin. The patient's legs are swollen and achy; they feel heavy, and he tires easily. Sometimes a vein breaks down and causes an ulcer.

Treatment and Nursing Care. Small varicose veins are sometimes treated by injecting a solution to plug the vein. However, the usual treatment for varicose veins is surgery; the offending vein is tied off and removed. Elastic bandages are supplied to the leg postoperatively, and the foot of the bed is elevated to encourage the return of venous blood. The patient may experience considerable pain and stiffness in his leg as first, and analgesics may be ordered. Early ambulation to promote circulation is important after this operation; often the nurse is instructed to get the patient out of bed to walk as soon as he recovers from the anesthesia. The patient may be alarmed by this procedure so soon after his operation while his legs are so stiff and sore, and he will need reassurance and an explanation of the need for moving around.

Usually the patient is allowed to go home in 2 or 3 days, with instructions to elevate the leg while he is sitting, to walk but not to stand still for any length of time and not to wear anything tight around his legs. If he is obese, he may be put on a reducing diet. Before he leaves the hospital, he learns how to apply the elastic bandage.

BLOOD DISORDERS

Anemia

Anemia is a condition in which there is a reduction in the number of red blood cells and a deficiency in hemoglobin in the blood. It may be caused by losing red blood cells in hemorrhage; by the destruction of red blood cells in certain types of infection; or by the interference with the production of red blood cells, such as is caused by injury to the bone marrow. Anemia is also caused by cancer, rheumatoid arthritis and many other diseases.

Symptoms. There are several types of anemia, but the symptoms are essentially the same for all types: pallor, fatigue, faintness and loss of appetite. The pulse is rapid because the heart is rushing the reduced number of blood cells to the tissues and trying to circulate them faster. The anemic person is likely to feel chilly most of the time.

Iron-Deficiency Anemia. Young people are prone to develop this type of anemia—it may begin with dieting or hurrying meals. When anemia actually results, a poor appetite follows. This deficiency can be remedied easily by taking extra iron and by including foods which are high in iron in the diet (see Chap. 23). Under certain stress conditions the body needs more iron, for example, during adolescence or pregnancy.

Pernicious Anemia. The patient with *pernicious anemia* lacks a substance in the gastric juice, the *intrinsic factor*, which is necessary to enable the body to absorb vitamin B_{12} from food. Diet cannot help this patient; he must have vitamin B_{12} supplied to him because he cannot use it as it comes in food. A pernicious anemia patient has to take vitamin B_{12} (cyanocobalamin) the rest of his life, but an injection every 2 or 3 weeks enables him to live normally. The symptoms of pernicious anemia include digestive disturbances, sore mouth, diarrhea, and numbness and tingling in the extremities which are signs of nerve damage. The patient is often irritable or depressed.

Sickle Cell Anemia. *Sickle cell anemia* is a disease in which the red blood cells are destroyed more rapidly than usual, and there is present an abnormal type of hemoglobin. This is a hereditary condition which is found chiefly among Negroes. The symptoms are similar to those of other types of anemia, and leg ulcer, fever and pain sometimes occur. Transfusions can be given, and although the patient seems to improve for a time, sickle cell anemia shortens life expectancy.

Aplastic anemia. *Aplastic anemia* is caused by interference with the work of the bone marrow in producing red blood cells, white blood cells and blood platelets. It appears as a toxic side effect of such drugs as streptomycin and nitrogen mustard. Nobody knows exactly what causes aplastic anemia because sometimes it appears without an apparent cause. A patient becomes very weak and tired and short of breath on the least exertion; he has a tendency to bleed and is extremely susceptible to infection. Extra precautions are taken to protect the patient from infection and antibiotics are given to prevent it. The patient will have many transfusions. If the bone marrow is so damaged that it is unable to produce the needed blood cells, the patient will die. Specimens of the bone marrow are examined to determine its activity. Aplastic anemia is very serious, and the patient is extremely ill.

Anemia from Blood Loss. Hemorrhage or continued slow bleeding will cause anemia. If the loss of blood is chronic, as for example, from an ulcer, the treatment begins by determining and treating the cause of the bleeding. The usual treatment is to replace the lost blood by transfusions, and sometimes to administer iron supplements.

Agranulocytosis

In *agranulocytosis* the production of white blood cells is decreased. One cause of this condition is the toxic effects of drugs, especially barbiturates, tranquilizers and sulfonamides. The signs of this disease are chills and fever, headache, and ulcers on the mucous membranes in the mouth, the nose and the throat and in the rectum or the vagina. It is frequently the result of self-medication with "sleeping pills," taken for a long time without advice from a doctor. The treatment begins by removing the drug that is causing the trouble. Since the patient's white cells are low, he is more than normally susceptible to infection, and extreme care is taken to protect him from exposure to it.

Leukemia

Leukemia is a fatal disease in which the white blood cells (leukocytes) increase in an abnormal abundance. We usually think of an increase in white blood cells as a sign that the body is fighting disease, but this is not true in leukemia. The increase is so abnormal that it reduces the number of other cells in the blood, including blood platelets and erythrocytes, which are essential to prevent bleeding and anemia.

Statistics show that every year 1 in every 14,000 Americans dies of leukemia. It affects both children and adults. Next to accidents, leukemia is the second most frequent cause of death among school-age children. Some authorities think that leukemia may be caused by infection, but there is a growing belief today that the cause of leukemia is linked in some way with cancer. Leukemia is sometimes called cancer of the blood or blood-forming organs (the bone marrow, lymph nodes and the spleen). Scientists are hopeful that they are on the right track when they are researching evidence that cancer may be caused by a virus, and they believe that this virus, or a similar one, may also cause leukemia. However, we still lack definite proof that this theory is correct. So far, no cure for leukemia has been found—only ways of delaying death.

The increase in the number of cases of leukemia is attributed to several factors: it may be that because people live longer there is a greater chance for the disease to develop. Also, it has been discovered that people whose work exposes them to considerable radiation run a greater risk of developing leukemia, and the increasing danger of excessive exposure to radiation may be a factor in leukemia incidence.

The Course of Leukemia. Leukemia may be acute or chronic and may occur at any age. *Acute leukemia* is more common in people under 25 years of age; after the age of 40, *chronic leukemia* is more common. With treatment, people with acute leukemia may live for a year or longer. Chronic leukemia victims may live for 2 or 3 years after the disease begins or, as sometimes happens, it may be 8 or 10 years before death finally occurs. Advances in treatment not only prolong life but also make the victim happier and more comfortable. With longer time to live, the patient can always hope that ways will be found to prevent and cure this now fatal disease.

Acute Leukemia. SYMPTOMS. Acute leukemia symptoms appear suddenly, often with an acute respiratory infection. Unless the patient is admitted to a hospital for treatment where a blood count will be part of the admission routine, the unusual increase in the white blood cells may not be detected. The blood count will also show that not only are the white blood cells numerous, but many of them are not fully developed. Other symptoms are:

Anemia, which is usually severe. The patient is pale, weak and tired.

A tendency to bleed, externally or internally. Bleeding often occurs from the nose or the mouth, the gastrointestinal tract or the vagina. Even the slight prick from a hypodermic needle may cause excessive bleeding.

Fever, especially as the disease grows worse.

Sometimes the symptoms disappear temporarily, perhaps for several months, but usually they grow steadily worse.

TREATMENT. Treatment is given to relieve the symptoms. It consists of:

Blood transfusions to give the patient more red blood cells, hemoglobin and platelets.

Drugs: Aminopterin and A-Methopterin are given to slow down the rapid production of leukocytes. These drugs must be used cautiously because they can interfere with the production of all blood cells and have toxic side-effects, such as nausea and vomiting and diarrhea. Frequent blood counts are made when the patient is having one of these drugs. Antibiotics are given for secondary infections.

However, in spite of treatment, the time comes when nothing seems to help him, and he grows steadily worse—his life then is a matter of only a few weeks.

Chronic Leukemia. Often the first signs of chronic leukemia are swollen lymph nodes in the neck, the axilla or the groin or a swelling in the upper left side of the abdomen which makes the victim's abdomen feel heavy. This swelling is caused by the enlargement of the spleen. The patient has all the symptoms of anemia plus difficulty in breathing if the spleen is enlarged. Treatment will help this patient to live perhaps 5 years or longer. Eventually, he becomes very weak, bleeds easily and has fever. He is susceptible to secondary infections, such as pneumonia, and treatment no longer helps him.

TREATMENT. As in acute leukemia, the treatment includes transfusions and antibiotics. In addition it includes:

X-ray therapy

Drugs, such as 6-mercaptopurine, to slow down the production of leukocytes, and chlorambucil, a derivative of nitrogen mustard which is poisonous to all growing cells and must be used cautiously. Busulfan, a similar drug, depresses the bone marrow and it, too, is used with caution lest it cause anemia. Radioactive phosphorus is also used. The general purpose in prescribing these drugs is to slow down the processes that cause the disease and those that aid its development.

Nursing Care. Improvement in the patient with leukemia after treatment is often spectacular. In 2 weeks he may be ready to leave the hospital. It is hard to believe that he is the same person who required almost constant attention and alert observation. During the treatment period the nurse must:

Watch for signs of bleeding—in the bedpan, the urinal, the emesis basin.

Watch for a weak and rapid pulse or a drop in blood pressure.

Note the patient's color and purple spots on his skin.

Watch for signs of toxic effects of drugs, such as nausea and vomiting, diarrhea, or stomach distress.

Turn the patient frequently to avoid decubitus ulcers.

Put side rails on the bed if the patient is confused or disoriented.

Give mouth care often and gently, using cotton sponges—never use a toothbrush; it may injure the gums and cause bleeding.

Protect the patient from infection by hand washing and by guarding him from contact with people who have respiratory infections.

Watch for chills, fever, difficult breathing, pain in the lumbar region, restlessness, urticaria.

Above all, this patient needs an *understanding* nurse, a nurse who, although she knows his improvement can be only temporary, will rejoice with him in his transient recovery and encourage him. It is generally agreed that the leukemia patient should be encouraged to return to his normal life insofar as this is possible. Activity will not harm him, and complete rest will not halt the progress of the disease. A determination to live is all-important, for there is always the possibility that a cure may be found. If he is a young person, he may have important decisions to make, such as getting married or planning his career. The circumstances in every individual case will determine whether or not he should know that he has a fatal disease (see Chap. 37). He will make regular visits to his doctor and no doubt will return to the hospital many times for treatment which brings temporary improvement, although each time it is of a shorter duration.

The leukemia patient's final illness is a very difficult time for his family, who must stand helplessly by as he grows steadily worse and finally slips into unconsciousness. The death of a child or young person is especially difficult to accept. To the family life means hope, and they need the reassurance that everyone is doing everything that can possibly be done in the way of treatment and comfort.

Hodgkin's Disease

The cause of *Hodgkin's disease* is not known—it may be due to infection or to a malignant tumor in lymphatic tissue. Whatever the cause, it begins with a painless enlargement of the lymph nodes in the neck (cervical) and in the groin (inguinal). It affects more men than women, usually young adults, and is almost always fatal. People with Hodgkin's disease may live 10 years or more, but usually they die within 4 or 5 years. It is diagnosed by examining tissue from an affected lymph node under the microscope.

Symptoms. The disease begins with the enlargement of one or more lymph nodes. This is painless at first, but as the nodes become larger they may press on the surrounding tissues and cause pain. The patient loses a great amount of weight, has a poor appetite and feels weak and tired. Often he has chills and fever and complains of itching. He may develop anemia and a tendency to bleed. Treatment seems to help for a time—sometimes months or even years—but eventually nothing seems to help, and he dies from respiratory obstruction, from lack of nutrition or from infection.

Treatment and Nursing Care. The patient may be treated by x-ray therapy; *nitrogen mustard* may be used intravenously; *chloram-*

bucil may be given. Antibiotics are given for infection. Nitrogen mustard usually causes nausea and vomiting, which the sight of food usually aggravates. Treatment seems to help at first, and it may be repeated a number of times; but gradually it loses its effect, and the patient dies.

The nursing care is similar to the care for leukemia.

Purpura

Purpura is the term used to describe small hemorrhages in the skin, the mucous membranes or the tissues under the skin. Sometimes they appear as tiny red spots (*petechiae*) or they may extend over larger areas. These hemorrhages are caused by lack of platelets in the blood or by damage to the blood vessels. They are signs that the patient has a tendency to bleed, and he may bleed from the nose, the mouth or the intestinal tract. The treatment may include ACTH and cortisone, transfusions of *whole* blood or removal of the spleen. Some patients recover without treatment.

In the nursing care of a patient with purpura it is important to watch for signs of internal bleeding, such as unusual pallor, rapid pulse and restlessness. Care includes protecting the patient from bruises that might be caused by falls or bumping into objects.

Hemophilia

Hemophilia is an inherited condition in which the blood is slow to coagulate, due to the lack of prothombin in the blood plasma, a substance that makes blood clot. Unchecked bleeding may be severe; in hemophiliacs, even a pinprick may cause prolonged oozing of blood. The most minor surgical procedure is often risky and is usually preceded by a transfusion. Prothrombin and pressure on the bleeding can be applied, and antihemolytic human plasma can be administered as a temporary measure to curb the bleeding. Hemophilia can shorten life, and many children with this disease die young. Women are not susceptible to the condition of hemophilia, although a mother may inherit the trait and pass it on to a son who then develops hemophilia. The trait is never passed on by the father.

37

THE PATIENT WITH CANCER

A National Health Problem

Cancer is next to heart disease as a cause of death in the United States. It affects all areas of the body, and takes hundreds of thousands of lives every year. Most of the people who have cancer are 40 years of age or over, but it attacks people of all ages. Often it can be cured if it is discovered in time. In a health checkup, the doctor may recognize signs of cancer; people themselves can recognize certain suspicious signs.

The American Cancer Society and its divisions are especially concerned with cancer education, aimed at detecting cancer and treating it before it is too late. Untreated cancer grows worse and is always fatal. This national organization also supports cancer research; many of its divisions provide home care for needy cancer patients by giving funds to local visiting nurse associations. Then these associations can employ additional full-time or part-time nurses to make home visits. The Society has developed a large army of volunteer workers; these lay people make dressings, take patients to and from hospitals and clinics, keep up loan closets for sickroom equipment and provide recreational activities for home patients. Cancer detection and treatment centers have been established in many places, but medical authorities say that in order to do the job, every doctor's office must become a detection center. The National Cancer Institute of the National Institutes of Health is also engaged in cancer research.

Mistaken Beliefs About Cancer. Cancer is not contagious. Not a single example ever has been found of one person's contracting cancer from another. There is no positive proof that it is hereditary. It is believed that people may inherit *tendencies* toward cancer. This means that if parents have had cancer, their children should be sensibly watchful for suspicious signs in themselves. There is no proof that eating very highly seasoned food or drinking alcoholic beverages causes cancer of the stomach. Medicines, serums or diets will not cure cancer. Quack doctors and patent medicines are responsible for many cancer deaths because they help delay proper treatment until therapy is of little or no value. Unfortunately, the symptoms of cancer may not appear until the disease has progressed beyond its earliest stages; this is unfortunate because, if cancer is discovered early enough and treated, the patient has a good chance for recovery.

CANCER AND HOW IT SPREADS

Cancer is a wild, disorderly growth of body cells that undermines and spreads through normal tissues. It can be identified without doubt by examining a specimen of suspected tissue under the microscope. Not all growths or tumors are cancers. The *benign* growths are noncancerous, but the *malignant* ones are cancers. Two common forms of malignant growths are *carcinoma* and *sarcoma.* Malignant tumors usually are not confined within a capsule and can spread to nearby tissues; they also spread by *metastasis* to other parts of the body through the blood and the lymph. There is no way to tell whether or not this has happened until symptoms of a growth appear or an x-ray film reveals it. Some types of cancer grow more rapidly than others. Cancer spreads through the body in 5 ways:

1. By extending directly into nearby tissue
2. By spreading along lymphatic vessels
3. By traveling through lymphatic vessels to nearby lymph nodes
4. By traveling through blood vessels to other parts of the body, especially to the lungs, the bones and the liver
5. By invading a body cavity, especially the abdomen and the chest, and spreading within it

Cause of Cancer

Medical science has not been able to pinpoint any one cause for cancer; authorities now are inclined to believe that it develops from a combination of causes rather than from any one thing. For example, studies of the occurrence of lung cancer show beyond a doubt that it develops with much greater frequency in cigarette smokers than it does in nonsmokers. Yet researchers have not been able to prove that any one substance in cigarette smoke causes cancer. Among the suspected causes of cancer are:

Long-continued irritation, such as exposure to strong sunlight; lip irritation from a pipe; friction on a mole from a belt, the suspenders or a brassière strap; cervical irritation

Exposure to specific agents, especially in industry, such as coal soot, oil, friction, aniline dyes or other chemicals, luminous paint, asphalt. Work with radioactive materials may present new hazards of which we are not yet aware. Also, exposure to substances in cigarette smoke and car exhaust fumes may be a cause.

Benign tumors that have a tendency to become malignant, such as growths in the mouth and the rectum, pigmented moles, ovarian cysts, x-ray or radium irritations of the skin

These predisposing causes do not always result in cancer; some people develop cancer even though they never have been exposed to any of the above conditions. There is reliable evidence that there are other predisposing causes *within* the body—this makes it seem likely that several factors working together cause cancer.

Symptoms

No one can know whether or not he has cancer without seeing a doctor. This is one of the reasons that a regular health checkup is so important. There are 7 danger signals that people can recognize; anyone should consult a doctor at once if one or more of these symptoms appears. According to the American Cancer Society they are:

1. Any sore that does not heal
2. A lump or a thickening in the breast or elsewhere
3. Unusual bleeding or discharge
4. Any change in a wart or a mole
5. Persistent indigestion or difficulty in swallowing
6. Persistent hoarseness or cough
7. Any change in normal bowel habits

Usually, pain does not appear until the later stages of cancer; unfortunately, people do not always pay attention to slightly uncomfortable sensations that are warnings. Pricking, tingling, tightness or soreness are not normal feelings; if they last for any length of time, they should be investigated. Weakness and loss of weight always are danger signals—these symptoms may indicate cancer.

Cancer in the Body. Cancer develops in many places in the body. Statistics show that more women than men die of cancer; the reasons for this difference are: (1) there are more women than men in the population; (2) the average life span of women in the population is longer than that of men; (3) cancer of the breast and the female reproductive organs is very common. Thousands of women die of breast cancer every year; cancer of the reproductive organs is the next most frequent cause of cancer deaths in women. A periodic and complete physical examination is very important. Women over 30 years of age should be examined once a year. Those with cystic disease or a family history of cancer should be examined twice a year.

Cancer in men occurs most frequently in the following order: in the stomach, the prostate gland, the intestines, the bronchus and the lungs, in the rectum and the anus. Most cancer of the esophagus occurs in men. Cancer of the stomach affects twice as many men as women.

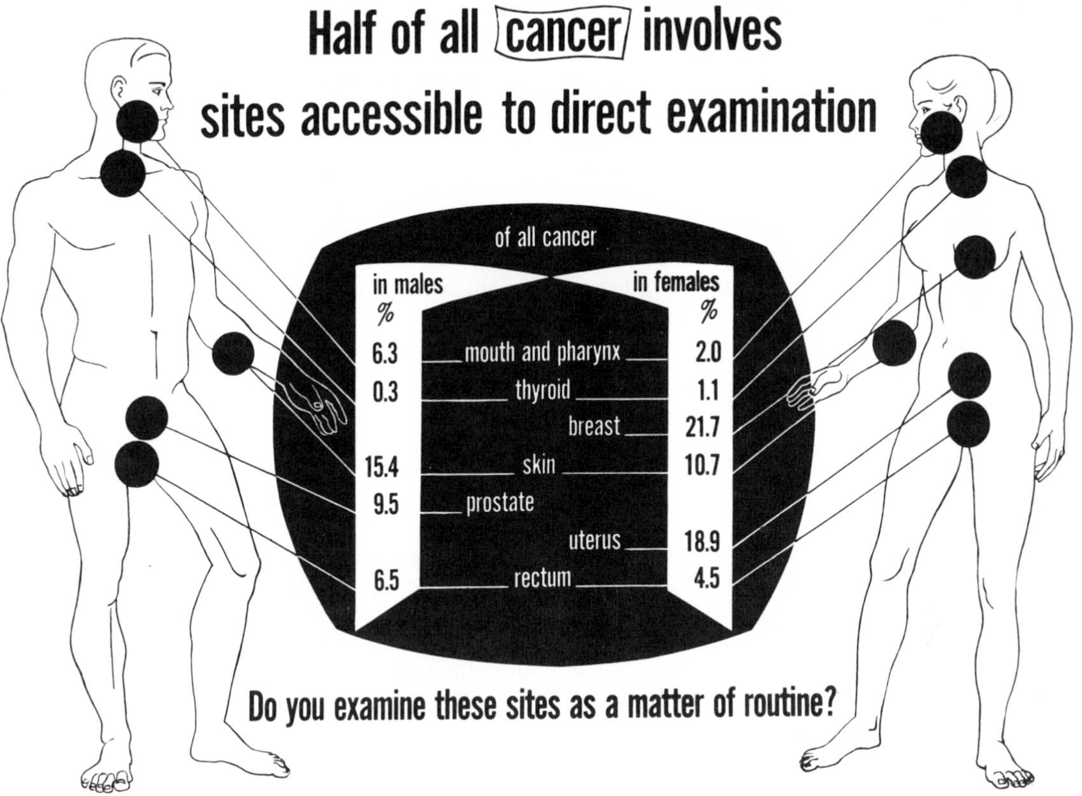

FIG. 158. One of the diagrams distributed by the U.S. Department of Health, Education and Welfare for the purpose of early detection of cancer.

More men than women have cancer of the rectum. Leukemia is believed to be cancer of the blood or blood-forming organs (the bone marrow, the lymph nodes and the spleen). Hodgkin's disease is primarily considered as being a malignant tumor of lymphatic tissue. (Chapter 36 has a further discussion of leukemia and Hodgkin's disease.) Cancer occurs more rarely in the kidneys, the bladder, the testis and the bones.

How Cancer Is Discovered

A physical examination may reveal a suspicious growth in the breast, the uterus or the prostate. The patient may report pain or loss of weight. Growths on internal organs can be spotted through roentgenograms, rectal and bladder examinations. Cytologic or Papanicolaou tests will detect cancer cells in body secretions that have been shed from malignant growths. A definite diagnosis of cancer can be made by examining a "frozen section" of tissue taken from the tumor; this microscopic examination for cancer cells is called a *biopsy*.

TREATMENT

Surgical Treatment

Complete removal of all malignant tissues before they have metastasized to other body tissues is the best treatment for cancer. This sometimes involves extensive surgery, including the removal of the tumor and a wide area of the tissue surrounding it, in an attempt to include all the malignant cells that may have spread. Typical of such surgery is the removal of not only the breast, in some cases of carcinoma of the breast, but also a large area of the overlying skin, the underlying muscles, the axillary lymph channels and the lymph nodes which drain the area. This surgical procedure is known as a radical mastectomy and is discussed in Chapter 41.

Surgery is also used frequently to prevent cancer. For example, certain lesions, such as small tumors in the colon, which sometimes become cancerous, are removed. This is called *prophylactic* or preventive surgery. In addition, some of the glands in the body which are known to influence the development of cancer can be removed. This situation is true in women who have had cancer of the breast and have not yet reached the menopause; the surgeon may remove the ovaries, hoping to increase the patient's chance for a cure.

Radiation

Treating cancer by radiation involves exposing tissues to radioactive substances which destroy malignant cells. Generally, radiation is used in medicine for diagnosis, therapy and research.

Radiation affects tissues by altering the chemical structure and the behavior of atoms in the cells, a process known as ionization (see Chap. 11). Experimental evidence shows that atoms contain positively charged, negatively charged and neutral particles which vary in number and determine the "weight" of the atom. The atoms of most elements remain intact and stable because of the neutralizing effect of the charges upon each other, i.e., the negative charges balance the positive charges. However, some of the heavier atoms, such as those in radium, have more positive and neutral charges and consequently, become unstable with a tendency to disintegrate (fall apart). In their attempt to remain intact, they give off *rays*, a process called *radioactivity*. We call these elements *isotopes*. In addition to the natural radioactive elements such as radium, there are isotopes such as iodine and gold which are produced artificially by mechanical bombarding—smashing the atoms in special machines and changing their weights.

Because of their ability to penetrate and destroy tissues, these rays are widely used as a means of diagnosing and treating cancer and other illnesses. The photograph (x-ray plate) produced by the x-ray machine with which most of us are familiar is extremely important in diagnosis. The rays which penetrate the tissues and are responsible for the picture are produced by bombarding radioactive elements in the x-ray machine. Extreme precautions are taken to protect both the patient and the personnel administering radiation therapy, since healthy cells are destroyed as well as diseased cells, and there are many hazards involved in exposing normal tissues to the rays. Little need be said about the warnings and the cautions issued by the Atomic Energy Commission should we become involved in an atomic warfare, which is based on radioactive elements and the atomic bomb. We are still studying the many people who were involved at Hiroshima and Nagasaki in World War II to determine the effect of radiation exposure.

Radiation of Cancer. Radiation therapy is indicated in many cases of cancer and may be used as either a therapeutic or as a palliative treatment, i.e., one which gives relief but does not cure. Many patients are fearful of this treatment and should be told what to expect. The patient can be told that he may have a temporary systemic reaction with nausea and vomiting, loss of appetite and a general feeling of weakness. Normally, some degree of injury to the tissues is to be expected—this injury should not be designated as a burn, since burning could imply careless treatment to the patient. The care of the skin in the treated area is important. It should be kept dry, and neither soap nor water should be used. Itching may be relieved by powders or ointments prescribed by the doctor.

Chemotherapy

Some drugs are used to halt the progress of cancer—no drug has been found that will cure cancer. Drugs such as aminopterin and amethopterin are sometimes given, which restrain the formation of folic acid in the body and thereby halt the growth of body cells. Nitrogen mustards, which attack cells that are growing rapidly, are used in the treatment of blood and lymph cancers. Some hormones slow malignant growths—the male hormone (testosterone) is used in treating cancer of the breast in women; the female hormone (estrogen) is given in treating prostatic cancer in men. Adrenal hormones (ACTH and cortisone) are sometimes given for temporary relief.

NURSING CARE OF THE CANCER PATIENT

The Nurse's Attitude

In her professional life, a nurse is likely to take care of a great many patients who have cancer, and the kind of care that she gives these patients will be affected by her own attitudes toward this disease. Her feelings about cancer probably will be colored by her previous knowledge and experience. It may not be easy to discard false notions about cancer. She must accept the sad fact that too often cancer is fatal; perhaps she will have to disguise her unhappy knowledge of its effects. It may be difficult to carry out dispassionately some of the nursing procedures that become necessary, such as the care of a colostomy, a bladder drainage or a tracheostomy. A patient is so dependent upon a nurse for understanding and support that he never must be made to feel that she is disturbed or revolted by any aspect of his care.

The Patient's Attitude

Patients react to illness in very different ways; cancer patients are confronted with a knowledge that they find hard to face. While other illnesses may be disabling, they often promise hope of living; unfortunately, this is not so with cancer, in far too many instances. A nurse is bound to be faced with the patient's questions about his illness: "Do I have cancer?" or "Will I get well?" are questions uppermost in the patient's mind even if he is afraid to ask them. So much information is available to the public today that it would be unusual, in most instances at least, if the patient did not recognize some indications of his disease. Yet some patients seem to prefer not to know; perhaps they feel that, unknowing, they still can hope for the best. Others want the truth and face it realistically. The decision to tell or not to tell a patient that he has cancer has to be made by the doctor and the patient's family. Whatever the decision, the nurse accepts it and behaves accordingly.

The Nurse's Role. Cancer patients who have gone to a doctor in time have a good chance of being cured; you will take care of them after surgery or radiation therapy. You will also take care of cancer patients during a terminal illness—the patients in whom cancer was discovered too late. Remember that a terminal illness is difficult for the patient's family; your sympathetic care of the patient will help them through a trying time. Your role is a difficult one; to be sympathetic but not emotional; to be cheerful but not aggressively so; to be patient and kind; to understand the patient's fears and depression and to sense ways of comforting him. Sometimes spiritual consolation can be a great source of strength; contact with the hospital chaplain or with a clergyman of the patient's own religious faith may be most welcome.

For those who will get well, the hope of a satisfactory return to a normal life is the best reassurance they can have. Your cheerful encouragement of any patient to help himself restores his shaken confidence in his ability to look after himself. Some patients are afraid to try anything active.

Common Nursing Problems

Many of the nursing problems that are a trial to one cancer patient affect *all* cancer patients. These problems are no different than those of other patients, but cancer patients are apt to have more of them at the same time and to have them more severely. For example, pain not only may be accompanied by nausea and incontinence, but also by bleeding and infection.

Skin Care. Some cancer patients must be in bed for months. They lose weight and become emaciated. The skin over bony prominences should be kept clean and dry, to prevent pressure sores or decubiti. Rub it with skin lotion frequently; use pads to relieve pressure. After radiation treatments for cancer of the pelvis or the abdomen, the skin over the sacrum needs special attention. Keep incontinent patients dry; absorbent pads will help. Any patient in bed should be turned frequently to relieve pressures and to prevent lung congestion. Care of the skin was discussed in Chapter 34.

Colostomy. Surgery involving the large intestine may necessitate a *colostomy*, a permanent opening into the intestine through the abdomen, to provide for the drainage of feces (see Chap. 38). After surgery, these patients will have dressings, often continuing through convalescence. Change soiled dressings promptly to prevent skin irritation and unpleasant odors. Room deodorizers are available.

Diet. Cancer depletes the body proteins and affects nutrition generally. The diet should be high in body-building foods and vitamins. For colostomy patients, the amounts of fruits and vegetables should be regulated to prevent diarrhea; vitamin concentrates may be prescribed to make up deficiencies. Colostomy patients work up to a normal diet and soon learn how much food they can eat.

A cheerful, unworried patient is more likely to have a good appetite. See that his dressings are clean and that fresh air is circulating through the room at mealtime. If his appetite is poor, tempt it with small servings of food and an attractive tray. Sound the hopeful note with convalescent patients by emphasizing the normal diet they are permitted to have. Encourage every patient, if he is able, to feed himself; ask him to tell you what foods he likes.

Control of Pain. Terminal cancer patients usually have considerable pain. Follow the doctor's orders about giving morphine or other pain-relieving drugs when the patient needs them. Nurses sometimes are reluctant to give habit-forming drugs, but prolonged pain in terminal cases can do more harm than the drug. Sedatives are sufficient to keep some patients comfortable; everything you yourself do to make a patient comfortable will help to make any medication more effective.

Secondary Infection. In cancerous growths, if the cells are deprived of food and oxygen, they die or become necrotic. As this dead tissue falls away, it may leave a raw open area or *ulcer*, which may bleed if the cancerous growth involves blood vessels. This open surface provides an excellent entrance for bacteria. The odor attributed to cancer is caused by this infection. Good nursing care in keeping the wound clean by irrigations and frequently changing dressings is very important. As infection decreases, the patient's general condition may also improve.

38

THE PATIENT WITH A DISORDER OF THE DIGESTIVE SYSTEM

Disease and disorders of the digestive tract may affect the mouth, the throat, the stomach, the intestines or the rectum. Too often, people disregard the early signs of trouble—loss of appetite, indigestion, constipation, or diarrhea—until more serious symptoms appear, such as nausea and vomiting (with signs of blood), bloody stools and abdominal pain. On the other hand, large numbers of people consult a doctor about gastrointestinal disorders which are the result of emotional distress rather than physical difficulties. The digestive tract is very sensitive to strong emotions such as fear, anger or anxiety. Almost everyone has felt this effect in some way: for example, as a student you may not be able to eat on the morning of an examination.

The Nurse's Role

The problems of these patients are inevitably involved with nutrition and are concerned with food. They also arise from anxieties and worries, real or imagined. A great part of the nurse's job is using patience and ingenuity in dealing with these problems, to offer the kind of reassurance and support that the physically upset, overwrought and apprehensive patient needs. Gastrointestinal conditions may be treated medically or surgically or by a combination of both methods. For the nurse, this means that she should be sufficiently familiar with test procedures and various types of apparatus to be able to give intelligent nursing care.

Diagnostic Tests

The *special* tests commonly used in diagnosing gastrointestinal difficulties include laboratory examinations of vomitus, stomach contents and feces, examination of various parts of the digestive tract and x-ray studies. The nurse's part in these procedures is to collect specimens, assist the doctor with examinations, to prepare the patient and to reassure him during procedures that are often tedious and uncomfortable.

Gastric Analysis. One way of obtaining information about stomach difficulties is by analyzing the stomach contents in order to find out how much free hydrochloric acid is present—too much may point to peptic ulcer; too little could be a sign of cancer or pernicious anemia. This analysis can be done by examining a specimen of vomitus or of the stomach contents which has been aspirated by a syringe attached to a nasogastric tube inserted into the stomach. Another method of analysis is the oral administration of a dye, *azuresin*. Azuresin will color the urine blue if it is acted upon by hydrochloric acid, indicating the presence of this acid in the gastric juice.

PROCEDURE. The usual procedure followed in gastric analysis is:

1. No food or fluids are given for 8 hours before the test. This order means that nothing is allowed by mouth after midnight for an 8 A.M. test.
2. Insert the nasogastric tube.
3. Withdraw the specimen. Clamp the tube

after this withdrawal to prevent air from entering the stomach.

4. Withdraw the other specimens at the prescribed intervals (if ordered).

5. Label the specimens according to the order in which they were obtained.

6. Withdraw the tube, give the mouth care and serve the patient his breakfast.

Sometimes histamine is given subcutaneously after the first specimen has been collected in order to stimulate gastric secretions. Since some people are sensitive to histamine, these patients should be watched closely for signs of shock. Pallor, sweating, and a weak and rapid pulse are danger signals. Some doctors leave an order to give epinephrine immediately if shock occurs.

Stool Specimens. Laboratory examination of stool specimens is a method for discovering disease organisms, parasites and eggs, and occult (otherwise invisible) blood. The procedure for collecting a stool specimen is discussed in Chapter 32.

X-Ray and Fluoroscopic Examinations. The development of x-ray photography (roentgenography) and of the fluoroscopic screen (fluoroscopy) have made it possible to photograph or view conditions anywhere within the gastrointestinal tract. This is done by means of a radiopaque substance, usually barium sulfate, which is given orally or rectally, depending upon which area is to be investigated. The progress of this substance through the gastrointestinal tract is noted on films at suitable intervals and on the fluoroscopic screen. The doctor observes how long it takes the barium to pass through and notes any abnormalities in the shape of the organs or the passages that might indicate ulcers or tumors.

The Nurse's Responsibility. This series of pictures is often called a *G.I. series.* The nurse prepares the patient, looks after him during the series and after it has been completed. Her responsibilities are:

To see that the patient has no food or fluid for the 8 hours preceding x-ray pictures of the upper gastrointestinal tract

To give the laxative and the enema (or enemas) prescribed in preparation for x-ray studies of the large intestine—this varies from hospital to hospital

To check with the x-ray department, to make sure that the series has been completed before giving the patient something to eat

To note bowel movements and whether or not barium is passed—sometimes a cathartic is necessary to eliminate it. A hard mass of retained barium might cause a bowel obstruction

The Patient's Point of View: A "G.I. series" is something of an ordeal. The patient goes without food from midnight until the following afternoon, is compelled to drink a mixture that tastes like chalk (although some hospitals flavor it), and must assume various unaccustomed positions on the x-ray table. It is a long and often exhausting procedure, and the patient will be grateful for food, rest and quiet when it is completed.

Endoscopy. Certain hollow instruments, or *scopes*, make it possible to look at different parts of the gastrointestinal tract by means of tiny electric bulbs within the instrument. According to the part which is being examined, the most common of these procedures are called *esophagoscopy* (esophagus), *gastroscopy* (stomach) and *proctoscopy* (rectum and anus). The nurse carries out the prescribed preparations for these procedures but the examination itself is usually performed in an operating or examining room. The patient may be apprehensive and tense beforehand and in need of reassurance. Because this type of examination is often uncomfortable and may be painful, a sedative may be ordered for the patient both before and after the examination.

Suction Drainage (Gastrointestinal Decompression)

The patient with a small rubber or plastic tube extending from his nostril is a fairly common sight on hospital wards. The inner end of this tube may terminate in the patient's stomach (Levin tube) or, if the tube is longer (Miller-Abbot, Cantor or Harris tubes), it may extend into the intestine. The outer end may have a clamp attached, or a glass connection may link it to longer tubing attached to one or more bottles at the bedside (Wangensteen apparatus). Suction operates by creating a vacuum by means of an electric machine, a built-in wall attachment, or through the specific arrangement of the tubes and the bottles. Suction can also be created by drawing on the end of the tube with a syringe.

Suction is used to get periodic or continuous drainage in gastrointestinal conditions:

1. To get a specimen of stomach or intestinal contents for examination
2. To treat intestinal obstruction
3. To prevent and treat distention after surgery by removing gas and toxic fluid materials from the stomach or the intestines
4. To empty the stomach prior to emergency surgery or after swallowing poisons

Nursing Care. Special points to observe in the care of a patient with suction drainage are:

Measure and record fluid intake and output, *including drainage,* because it is important to keep a careful check on the patient's fluid balance.

Give soothing mouth rinses and apply a lubricant to the patient's lips and nostril, and K-Y jelly to the catheter where it touches the nostril. Because he must breathe through it, the patient's mouth becomes dry and parched. If he is able, let him brush his teeth himself but tell him to rinse his mouth well and not to swallow.

Check to see that the drainage is flowing into the bottle and that the nasal catheter is in place. Check the level of the fluid in the drainage bottle; it should be emptied when it reaches a designated mark.

You may not be responsible for irrigating the nasal catheter, but you should know that in order to keep the tube open, small amounts of water or saline solution are injected through it from time to time.

Nausea and Loss of Appetite

Distaste for food (*anorexia*), *nausea* and *vomiting* are almost always associated with gastrointestinal disturbances. They may be signs of physical difficulties, but frequently they are related to emotional problems and may reflect a person's attempt to avoid facing difficult situations.

Nausea and loss of appetite may be accompanied by vomiting and abdominal pain; if prolonged, they may lead to loss of weight and emaciation from poor nutrition. Naturally, these disturbances have a profound effect on a person's eating habits. The sufferer develops abnormal notions about food that are hard to dispel, and it often takes a long time to get at the root of his difficulties and help him to overcome them. It is useless to try to force such a patient to eat by ridiculing his fears or by hinting at the consequences unless he changes his ways. It is also important to avoid seeming to watch his every mouthful or making him feel that he is being constantly watched, lectured and spied upon. It is more helpful to try to promote a relaxed attitude toward his problems by encouraging him to express *his* feelings for a change. Present new kinds of food for him to try; serve all his food in small, attractive portions. The nurse should do everything possible to prevent emotional upset before mealtime.

Diarrhea, Constipation and Disorders of Food Ingestion

People sometimes have a wrong conception of true diarrhea—doctors define it as frequent, loose watery stools and consider the *consistency* of the stools as more important than their frequency. It may be normal for some people to have 2 to 3 bowel movements a day; large amounts of fresh fruit and vegetables increase the number of stools. If the bowel contents move unusually rapidly through the intestinal tract, they retain more water; stools are soft or liquid.

Conversely, constipation is characterized by hard, dry and infrequent stools. It may be the result of a lack of roughage in the diet or of ignoring the impulse to empty the rectum and thereby allowing the feces to become dry and hard. Some medicines have a constipating effect; morphine is an example.

Heartburn and Belching. Sometimes the stomach regurgitates part of its contents into the esophagus, where it burns and stings the linings. Although this is called *heartburn,* the heart has nothing to do with causing it. It usually happens after hearty eating or in connection with emotional stress. The doctor may recommend an antacid, such as sodium bicarbonate or aluminum gel, and advise eating smaller meals more slowly. Another annoyance is *belching,* which is the result of swallowing great gulps of air—a habit some people unwittingly fall into when they are upset. Making people aware of this practice will often help them to overcome it.

Overeating. The opposite extreme from refusing to eat is eating too much, a habit that is easy to acquire and to find excuses for. Obesity, aside from being a health problem (for example, in diabetes and heart disease), is also a social liability. It may be the result of lack of exercise, an unbalanced diet or emotional tensions. If weight reduction is a major problem, it should be carried out under the direction of a physician.

Irritable Colon

This condition is also known as *mucous* or *spastic colitis.* The large intestine becomes greatly overactive, causing cramps and diarrhea which, if they continue, can cause a loss of weight and dehydration. Emotional upsets can trigger an attack and the treatment begins with an effort to get the patient to realize that his attacks are related to his emotions. His diet during attacks is regulated to avoid irritating and gas-forming foods such as raw vegetables or baked beans. It is important for the patient to realize that no particular food causes his attacks, or he may build up false notions about his diet which will interfere with his nutrition.

Opinions differ about what constitutes the most suitable diet for these patients. Some doctors prescribe milk; others limit it. Some impose no diet restrictions and encourage the patient to work up gradually to a tolerance for all foods. (See diet suggestions in Chapter 23). Kaopectate or bismuth and paregoric may be given to check diarrhea. Belladonna, sedatives and tranquilizers may be prescribed to quiet bowel activity.

Ulcerative Colitis

In *ulcerative colitis* the lining of the intestine becomes inflamed and ulcerated. As in colitis, it is difficult to determine the exact cause of this condition, but there is evidence that it occurs most frequently in people who have emotional problems. It is most likely to affect young adults or the middle-aged, both men and women. Typical symptoms are diarrhea, with blood and mucus in the stools, abdominal cramps, fecal incontinence, loss of appetite and weight, and nausea and vomiting. Ulcerative colitis may come on gradually or in a sudden attack. In its severest form it may cause death from hemorrhage or peritonitis. People with ulcerative colitis are more likely to develop cancer and should have periodic examinations of the digestive tract.

Treatment. The treatment in most instances centers around resting the bowel and obtaining good nutrition through a bland, nonirritating diet. Vitamin supplements are often given because the restricted diet may not contain some of the essential nutrients. The patient must rest in bed while the illness is acute. The treatment may include drugs that slow down peristalsis (atropine, tincture of belladonna) or soothe irritation (kaolin, pectin), and sedatives or tranquilizers. Penicillin or streptomycin may be given. ACTH and cortisone often provide amazing relief, but they must be used cautiously, because they are known to have potentially damaging side-effects.

A Nursing Challenge. The patient with ulcerative colitis will challenge the ability of any nurse. He is weak and miserable and often frightened by his condition, since he has a serious illness that could be fatal. He has many problems to contend with—emotional tensions, dietary restrictions, incontinence and perhaps an ileostomy if the colon has to be removed. Procedures that are necessary in his care may precipitate emotional crises. It takes infinite patience and understanding to handle the daily problems that arise.

Incontinence is a major difficulty. If possible, a bedpan should be handy to forestall soiling the bed. The patient should have the necessary help to keep the rectal area clean and to wash his hands. The area around the rectum may become sore; a soothing ointment, such as petrolatum, may be applied. If the patient is incontinent, disposable pads can be used to absorb the fecal discharge. It is important to maintain an adequate fluid intake and to record it faithfully. The patient should be encouraged to take an interest in his surroundings and to see his family and friends as his condition permits. A fresh point of view often helps to build up his morale.

There also exists the very real threat of a perforation of the intestine, causing hemorrhage and peritonitis, a condition which requires drastic surgery to remove the colon and open the ileum onto the abdomen. This operation may also be performed as a last desperate measure to bring relief after all other treatment has failed.

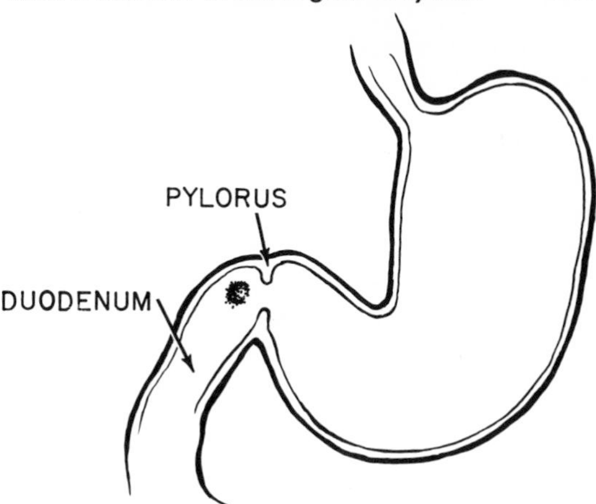

Fig. 159. A peptic ulcer in the duodenum. (Smith, D. W., and Gips, C. D.: Care of the Adult Patient, p. 866, Philadelphia, Lippincott, 1963)

Peptic Ulcer

Peptic ulcers usually occur in the duodenum, but they may appear in the stomach or at the lower end of the esophagus (Fig. 159). The action of acid gastric juice and pepsin on the lining of these organs causes peptic ulcer. The reason why some people have ulcers and others do not seems to be related to the emotional pressures of individuals, which stimulate an excessive secretion of gastric juice which in turn creates an oversupply of hydrochloric acid in the stomach. People with an abnormally low supply of hydrochloric acid do not have ulcers. People tend to think that ulcers are a disease of executives when really they affect people of all classes all over the world. The increase in the number of ulcer victims is, rightly or wrongly, often attributed to the pace and the pressures of modern living.

Symptoms. The symptoms are:

1. Burning sensation in the stomach, usually occurring from 1 to several hours after eating. Milk, or other protein foods, relieve the pain. Sometimes the victim becomes nauseated and is relieved by vomiting.

2. Tenseness and irritability: the recurrent pain causes sleeplessness and inability to work.

Gastric analysis, gastroscopy and x-ray pictures help to diagnose peptic ulcer and to differentiate it from a cancerous lesion.

Medical and Dietary Treatment. The main purposes in ulcer treatment are to eliminate the irritation of the ulcerous lesion and to reduce the amount of acidic secretions. The acids are neutralized by protein foods, such as milk, cream, eggs and custard. The *Sippy diet,* given while the illness is acute, consists of 30 to 90 cc. of milk and cream taken every hour. The cream is given because it stays in the stomach longer and thereby prolongs relief from distress, since ulcer pains appear when the stomach is empty. As the patient improves, his diet is gradually expanded to include soft foods, such as custard, gelatin or soft-cooked eggs (see Chap. 23). The patient progresses from the hourly feedings to 3 to 4 meals a day, as his condition permits. There is a tendency among some doctors today to allow a more liberal diet in treating peptic ulcer, encouraging the patient to stay away from troubling foods but to try to get back to as normal a diet as is possible.

Antacids, such as Amphojel, Gelusil or Maalox may be given as acid neutralizers. Sippy powders, Number 1 and 2, made up of sodium bicarbonate, with magnesium oxide and bismuth subcarbonate, are also used. These preparations are given between the hourly feedings or between regular meals.

Tincture of belladonna and atropine, drugs given to decrease acid secretion, are being replaced to some extent by the newer drugs Banthine and Pro-Banthine. All these drugs have similar side-effects, including dryness of the mouth, dilation of the pupils and blurred vision, although the newer drugs produce them to a slightly lesser degree.

Rest is an important part of ulcer treatment, although it does not necessarily imply rest in bed. Relaxation is even more important, and for this purpose doctors like to begin ulcer treatment in the hospital, where the patient is away from disturbing outside influences that aggravate his condition. Once the course of treatment is firmly established, the patient may be able to maintain his routines at home. However, the ulcer patient who thinks that he is cured must remember that an ulcer has a tendency to recur and that it behooves him to follow orders.

Surgical Treatment. *Gastrectomy* is a surgical operation to remove an ulcer when other treatment fails. The lower one half to two thirds of the stomach are removed (*subtotal gastrectomy*), and the portion that is left is joined to the jejunum (*gastroenterostomy*). (Gastrectomy for the treatment of cancer of the stomach is discussed on p. 497.) *Vagotomy* is the division of the vagus nerves, which reduces the stimulation to secrete hydrochloric acid and gastric motility.

Nursing Care. The patient returns from the operating room with a Levin tube in his stomach, where it usually remains for 2 or 3 days. Suction is attached and operated according to the doctor's orders, to keep the field of operation clean and to eliminate pressure from accumulated fluids. The drainage is noted carefully. It may be tinged with bright red blood at first; if the amount of red increases or persists it should be reported. Normal drainage should go from dark or brownish red to greenish yellow, the normal color of gastric secretions mixed with bile.

The patient will not be allowed anything by mouth for the 1st day. On the 2nd day he may be given a small amount of water (30 cc.), which is increased to 60 cc. and then to 90 cc. in the next 2 days. He gradually progresses to liquid, soft and solid food which is given frequently in small amounts.

Complications. *Hemorrhage* is one of the most serious and most frequent complications of peptic ulcer. It occurs when the ulcer eats through a blood vessel and may be so slight that the bleeding is not noticed if the blood vessel is small. Vomiting of blood, or tarry stools are evidence of more extensive hemorrhage; if the bleeding is massive, all the signs of shock appear: pallor, weak and rapid pulse, faintness and collapse. The treatment is rest, enforced by sedatives, transfusion and intravenous fluids. If bleeding continues, surgery is necessary to tie off the bleeding blood vessel. Above all, the patient must be kept absolutely quiet and should be assured that everything possible is being done to control the bleeding and replace the lost blood.

Perforation occurs when an ulcer penetrates the wall of the stomach or the intestine, allowing the contents to escape into the abdomen and cause peritonitis. The symptoms of perforation are startling—a sudden viciously sharp pain in the abdomen that makes the patient blanch and drenches him with perspiration. His abdomen literally becomes as hard as a board and is tender and painful. He breathes rapidly, with his knees drawn up in an attempt to relieve the pain: later, his face is flushed and he becomes feverish. This condition demands immediate emergency surgery to close the perforation, since the patient will die if treatment is delayed. One important thing to remember is that a perforation can occur without warning and may not be preceded by marked signs of digestive disturbance.

Nursing Care. The patient will have a Levin tube inserted to which suction is attached. He will have nothing by mouth for at least 24 hours and will be given fluids intravenously. Massive doses of antibiotics will be given to counteract abdominal infection. Continued distention, without passing flatus or feces, is a sign of serious interference with peristalsis causing intestinal paralysis (*paralytic ileus*).

Intestinal Obstruction

Intestinal obstruction occurs when intestinal paralysis or a tumor interferes with normal peristalsis to block the movement of gas and bowel contents through the intestinal tract. Sometimes a loop of intestine pushes through the abdominal wall and gets pinched off; this is a *strangulated hernia* and is another cause of obstruction. The blockage may be partial or complete; complete obstruction necessitates surgery.

Cancer is a common cause of this condition—a tumor within the intestine becomes larger and larger until it finally blocks the passage. If the obstruction is high in the gastrointestinal tract, vomiting occurs. Since the stomach contents are unable to pass the obstruction, this is Nature's way of emptying the stomach of accumulated digestive fluids. As these materials continue to accumulate, the vomitus becomes thick, dark and foul-smelling, because the number of bacteria normally present in the digestive tract increases. Vomiting may not appear if the obstruction is farther down. The patient becomes dehydrated, and is unable to take fluids by mouth. Surgery may consist of temporary relief through a colostomy. When the patient's condition is improved, the portion of the bowel containing the tumor may be removed and the ends of the bowel sewed together. Then the temporary colostomy is closed. This is not possible if the malignant process is too extensive. Suction is used to relieve distention; intravenous fluids are given, and antibiotics may also be prescribed.

Peritonitis

Peritonitis is inflammation of the *peritoneum*, the membrane that lines the abdominal cavity and covers the abdominal organs. In the upper abdomen it is usually the result of a perforation of the intestine, which permits intestinal contents to escape into the abdomen. Since the intestinal tract is normally filled with bacteria, the result of a perforation may be inflammation and infection of the peritoneum. The most common causes of perforation are appendicitis, ulcer or a malignant growth. *Pelvic* peritonitis may be the result of an infected fallopian tube. Peritonitis may be generalized, extending throughout the peritoneum, or it may be localized as an abscess.

Symptoms. Peritonitis often develops suddenly, with severe abdominal pain, nausea and vomiting and a gradual rise in temperature, with a weak, rapid pulse and low blood pressure. The patient's respirations are shallow, because breathing hurts the abdomen; he tries to avoid moving his abdomen and draws his knees up to prevent pressure from the bedclothes and to relieve the pain. The abdomen is tense and boardlike and becomes very distended; flatus and the intestinal contents are stationary in the intestinal tract, and paralytic ileus may develop. If the infection does not respond to treatment, the patient grows weaker; his pulse is thready, his breathing becomes more shallow, his temperature falls, and death follows.

Treatment. Surgery is generally necessary to close the perforation and promote drainage. Surgery is not necessary if the perforation closes by itself, as sometimes happens. Postoperative treatment centers on replacing fluids and electrolytes, and fighting infection by administering massive doses of antibiotics and analgesics, such as Demerol, to relieve pain and provide rest. The head of the bed is elevated to promote drainage. The patient must be watched closely, with the nurse observing the pulse and temperature, vomiting, the amount of drainage through the gastrointestinal tube, the amount of intake and output of fluids, abdominal distention, and whether gas and feces are passing through the rectum.

Special attention is given to mouth care because the patient has no fluids by mouth; fever and the gastrointestinal tube make his mouth dry and parched. Side rails on the bed may be necessary to prevent him from harming himself if he becomes disoriented. Above all, everybody concerned with his care must proceed gently. The least movement or jarring of the bed intensifies his pain. Lifting and moving are agony for him, and he suffers intensely from even the slightest pressure on his acutely sensitive abdomen.

Fortunately, the number of people who develop peritonitis is less today, and recoveries are more frequent. This is largely due to improvements in surgery and to the use of antibiotics.

CANCER IN THE GASTRO-INTESTINAL TRACT

Cancer occurs within the gastrointestinal

tract in the mouth, the esophagus, the stomach, the large intestine, and the rectum; cancer is rarely seen in the small intestine. The general symptoms are the same as for cancer in any other part of the body: fatigue, loss of weight, weakness and anemia. Unfortunately, pain does not appear in the early stages. Cancer of the mouth, the esophagus, the stomach and the rectum affects more men than women; however, more women have cancer of the colon.

Symptoms. The specific symptoms of cancer of the gastrointestinal tract are:

1. Digestive disturbances, such as loss of appetite, indigestion, changes in bowel habits
2. Interference with the passage of food, fluids and flatus
3. Bleeding, colored either bright red or dark brown (coffee grounds), appearing in vomitus or in tarry stools

Cancer of the gastrointestinal tract is detected by the appropriate tests and examinations, including biopsy, the microscopic examination of a piece of the suspected tissue.

Cancer of the Mouth

The chances for a complete cure are excellent if the malignant tissue is removed in the early stages of cancer of the mouth. If the surgery is extensive, edema may interfere with breathing and swallowing, so that tracheostomy or nasogastric feedings are necessary.

Nursing Care. Suction is used to remove secretions from the mouth. The head of the bed is elevated to make breathing easier. The patient is instructed to cough and to breathe deeply, as the nurse supports his head by placing her hands on either side. This exercise is important to prevent pneumonia and lung collapse. Danger signals are blood on the dressings, coughing up bright red blood, a rapid pulse, a fall in blood pressure, or respiratory difficulty. If the patient becomes cyanotic it may be necessary to perform a tracheostomy—equipment for this procedure should be ready at the bedside. Cancer of the mouth is treated also by radiation, which may be carried out by placing radium in the malignant tissue or by deep x-ray therapy.

Mouth care is important, for comfort and the prevention of odors. Liquids are given through a nasogastric tube until the patient is able to swallow, which may be possible only after a long time if the surgery was extensive. As soon as the patient is able, he is encouraged to give himself his feedings.

The special problems of this patient are many; the thoughtful nurse can do many things to help him to adjust to them. For example, she can provide a pad for him to write on, so that he can express his wishes. Many hospitals provide a "Magic Slate" for these patients. By lifting a plastic cover, the writing on the slate is erased, and it is ready for reuse. The nurse can provide the patient with an adequate supply of disposable tissues to take care of drooling. She can take special pains with his personal grooming. Above all, she must never do anything to make the patient think that he is repulsive. The time may come when he asks for a mirror. This operation is often followed by plastic surgery to correct facial defects; the wisdom of letting the patient see the result of a disfiguring operation before it is corrected may be debatable, and this is a decision which the doctor should make.

This patient may have to return to the hospital many times for plastic surgery, and therefore it is especially important to give him the kind of reassuring care that allows him to come back with confidence.

Cancer of the Esophagus

Cancer of the esophagus is very distressing for the patient, because he is unable to swallow or, if he does attempt it, his food is regurgitated. This creates a disagreeable taste in his mouth and mouth odor. Often he has to have parenteral fluids. Surgery is the only effective method of treating his disease and his only hope of eating normally once again. Otherwise, he faces slow starvation or being fed through a tube in his stomach for the rest of his life (gastrostomy).

Treatment. There have been rapid advances in the treatment of cancer of the esophagus in recent years, which are mostly the results of modern developments in chest surgery. In this procedure, 1 or 2 catheters are positioned in the chest for postoperative connection to drainage bottles. This arrangement permits the withdrawal of accumulated fluids. Surgery consists of removing all the malignant tissue, which may cure the disease if the treatment is early enough. Even if the complete removal of the tissue is impossible because the disease has spread, often surgery can be performed which will make it possible for the patient to eat normally.

Nursing Care. After surgery, the patient is fed intravenously for several days. The nurse watches for signs of bleeding in the drainage from the nasogastric tube. A small amount of blood may be evident immediately after the operation, but after this disappears the drainage should soon be the yellow-green color of normal gastric secretions. If the patient has had chest surgery special attention should be given to promote deep breathing and coughing. Oxygen is administered, and care is given to the chest drainage area. The patient, tubes and all, is often allowed to sit up in a chair the next day and walk a little, to encourage deep breathing and to improve circulation. After several days, the patient progresses from taking small amounts of water to soft foods and a normal diet.

Gastrostomy. *Gastrostomy* is a comparatively simple operation in itself; it is not performed as often as it once was now that the treatment of esophageal diseases and difficulties has improved. A temporary or permanent gastrostomy may still be necessary to treat conditions that cause esophageal obstructions. The operation consists of making a small incision in the upper abdomen and inserting a catheter into the stomach. The catheter is sutured into place. The tube is clamped between feedings. Special attention is given to the care of the skin around the tubes because gastric contents are very irritating. For this purpose, ointments may be applied (petrolatum, zinc oxide). Tube feeding technic is discussed under cancer of the larynx (Chap. 46). The principles and the technics which apply to the nasogastric tube also apply to the gastrostomy tube.

After sufficient healing has taken place, the tube is removed after feedings and reinserted each time. A permanent plastic button in the opening (stoma) has a removable plug which keeps the stoma closed when the tube is removed. As soon as he is able, the patient it taught to feed himself and learns how to insert and remove the tube. Sterile technic is not necessary.

Cancer of the Stomach

The treatment of cancer of the stomach often requires surgery for complete removal of the stomach and joining the esophagus to the jejunum. If the tumor is small, only part of the stomach may need to be removed.

Gastrectomy. Removal of the entire stomach is called *total gastrectomy*; removal of part of it is called *subtotal gastrectomy*. In either case, the spleen is removed also, because metastasis to the spleen is a common occurrence in cancer of the stomach. The nursing care for subtotal gastrectomy is essentially the same as for peptic ulcer. For total gastrectomy there are these differences:

1. The chest cavity has to be opened, which requires procedures similar to those following chest surgery.

2. Drainage from the nasogastric tube is very small, because this drainage normally comes from the stomach secretions.

Cancer of the Colon

Cancer of the colon requires surgical treatment with the hope of removing the cancerous tissue. The cut ends are sutured together, thus re-establishing normal function in the gastrointestinal tract. Sometimes the tumor is too extensive or the patient's condition will not permit this procedure, in which case the obstruction is relieved by a temporary or a permanent colostomy (see page 498).

Cancer of the Rectum

If the cancerous growth is in the upper part of the rectum, it can be removed without removing the rectal sphincter, so that ultimately the bowel will continue to function normally. If the tumor involves the rectal opening, a dual operation is necessary—through the abdomen from above (including a colostomy) and through the perineum from below. The danger of shock following this extensive surgery is very great.

Nursing Care. This patient requires an almost incredible amount of nursing care. It includes caring for a colostomy, the administration of parenteral fluids (including blood transfusion), the use of suction, caring for bladder drainage (a Foley catheter is usually inserted in the bladder), and irrigating and caring for drainage from the perineal wound. The patient must be turned frequently to prevent respiratory complications and thrombophlebitis; it is difficult for him to find a comfortable position. If his condition permits, he gets out of bed in 3 or 4 days after the operation. He will need much assistance to accomplish this. Despite a long and trying convalescence, a patient can recover if all of the malignancy has been removed and he learns to accept the inconvenience of a colostomy.

The Patient With a Colostomy or Ileostomy

Many of the diseases or conditions that affect the intestinal tract require surgical treatment which includes a *colostomy* (an opening into the colon) or an *ileostomy* (an opening into the ileum). The purpose in this operation is to provide an artificial outlet for feces when irritation or obstruction of the intestinal tract makes it necessary to divert fecal material from the normal rectal outlet. An incision is made in the abdomen, a loop of intestine is brought through the incision and opened to allow the drainage of feces. One difference between a colostomy and an ileostomy is that ileostomy drainage is more liquid and more irritating to the skin.

A colostomy or an ileostomy may be only temporary, if treatment to eliminate or relieve the condition that made it necessary is successful. If this is the case, an operation to close the intestinal and abdominal openings is performed, and the feces are allowed to resume the normal outlet through the rectum. If treatment necessitates the removal of the colon or the rectum, the colostomy will have to be permanent.

The Patient's Reactions. The patient who learns that he is to have a colostomy must face a radical readjustment, especially if the colostomy is to be permanent. The doctor is not always able to assure the patient before his operation that this will be only a temporary arrangement. One never knows exactly what a patient is thinking or how many fears he is keeping to himself. Naturally, he wonders how much of his life will be disrupted, perhaps imagining it as beset by offensive odors, discharges and soiled dressings. He may be worried about the effect on his marital relationships, about his care and the possibility of becoming repulsive to his family and friends. He dreads the thought of being "different" and may think that bulky dressings or an awkward appliance will affect his appearance.

The Effect on His Family. The implications of a colostomy can have a very disturbing effect on the patient's family, who will worry about many of the same things that bother him—they may be especially concerned about the care that he will need and how it will affect their home life. Also, they may be afraid that they will find a colostomy revolting and worry about concealing their feelings from the patient.

Helping the Patient. The patient should be encouraged to talk about his worries and to ask questions about the things that trouble him. This provides an opportunity to unburden his mind and to get correct information that will give him reassurance about his future. He must be shown that a colostomy does not necessarily mean that he is condemned to a useless, unhappy life. However, this point of view will not be achieved in a day. The patient will need time to come to terms with this revolutionary change in his life—to feel that it will be possible to learn to live with it. Therefore, he may not be ready mentally or physically to accept detailed instruction about the care of a colostomy before his operation. One thing that helps to prepare a patient for a hopeful outcome is to have him talk with someone who has a colostomy and is living a normal, active life. "Ileostomy clubs" throughout the country arrange for this type of contact which also is an opportunity to benefit from the experience of others in caring for a colostomy.

After the Operation—The Colostomy. The colostomy opening, or *stoma,* is separate from the incision through which the operation was performed. When the patient returns from the operating room, the stoma is covered by gauze dressings or by a plastic disposable bag or pouch which is held in place by double-faced adhesive. This bag fits tightly, to catch the drainage—the end is held firmly by elastic bands to make it leak-proof (Fig. 160). These bands are removed to empty it, and the contents are allowed to drain into an emesis basin. The bag is replaced by a clean one whenever this is necessary. Later, when the stoma has shrunk, the bag is replaced by a permanent appliance. If dressings are used, a combination of gauze fluffs and cellulose pads held in place by Montgomery straps (tapes) is applied to absorb the drainage. The adhesive ends of the straps are placed on the skin (which has been painted with compound benzoin tincture) well away from the stoma, while the other ends remain free with the sticky sides covered. Tapes passed through eyelets on the free ends are tied over the dressings to secure them. This prevents irritating the skin by not having to remove adhesive every time the dressing is changed.

The constant discharge of liquid feces at first after the operation makes it necessary to change the dressings or empty the bag frequently. This also helps to reduce odor and to prevent irritation of the skin around the stoma. Clean, rather than sterile, technic is adequate in changing the dressings, because the opening is contaminated by the bacteria that are always present in feces. It is important to avoid contaminating anything else by the soiled dressings.

The essential equipment for this procedure often is kept by the bedside. It consists of:

- Dressings or plastic pouches
- Montgomery straps
- Newspapers or bags for soiled dressings
- A skin lubricant
- Basin for soap and water

Changing the Dressings. Remove the soiled dressings or pouch to the newspaper; wash the skin around the opening with mild soap and warm water. Use only water if the skin is

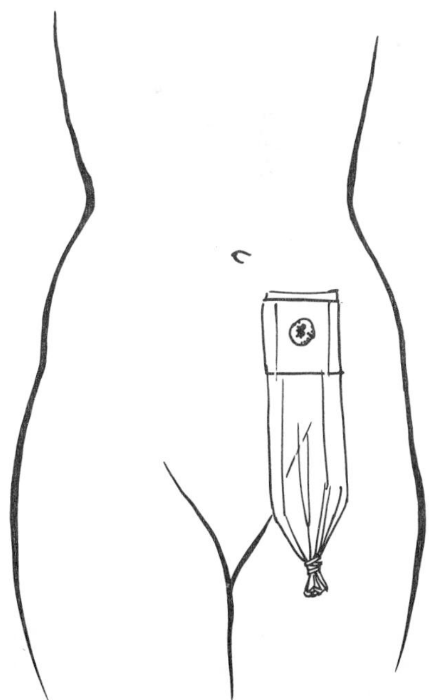

FIG. 160. A plastic drainage bag. The bag is held snugly around the stoma by adhesive. The bag can be emptied from the bottom by removing the elastic bands. (Smith, D. W., and Gips, C. D.: Care of the Adult Patient, p. 903, Philadelphia, Lippincott, 1963)

irritated. If necessary, apply whatever lubricant is ordered—petrolatum gauze, aluminum paste or Amphojel. Remove the lubricant from the skin often enough to inspect it for irritation. Put on the dressings or pouch; if a pouch is used fit it snugly to prevent leakage around the edges. The skin must be dry, or the adhesive will not stick. The ambulatory patient will need an elastic belt to support the pouch.

THE IMPORTANCE OF CLEANLINESS. Cleanliness is of the utmost importance. The patient is likely to feel soiled enough without having to be conscious of a soiled gown or bedclothing and saturated dressings. Be careful to change everything that becomes soiled, trying to do this before mealtime approaches in order to avoid affecting the patient's appetite. Be gentle but professional about everything you must do for the patient. Let him see that you take these procedures for granted as part of his nursing care and that they are not distasteful to you. Patients are often embarrassed and distressed for the nurse's sake because she must carry out unpleasant procedures.

TEACHING THE PATIENT. Before the patient can learn how to change his dressing himself, he must be ready to accept the idea of doing it. It may be some time before he can even bear to look at the colostomy opening or shows any interest in how you change the dressing. Eventually, he must learn to do this himself, and the nurse has to decide when he is ready to be taught. As he gradually learns that he is accepted and that nobody is avoiding him, he takes things more calmly and begins to take an interest in what is being done for him. A nurse can always help to stimulate his interest by casual but encouraging comments about his progress, such as: "Having more to eat makes the drainage more like a regular bowel movement. It looks as if you might be ready for your permanent colostomy arrangement before too long."

When the patient begins to show signs of being interested in his dressing, you can explain each step of the procedure, telling him why it is done. Let him watch you several times, then let him help by holding the equipment and handing you supplies. Encourage him to try doing the dressing himself after a while, assuring him that you will stand by to advise and help him. Do this enough times to be sure that he is ready to try doing it on his own. This does not mean that after he takes over you will abandon him. You must make it a point to watch him periodically to see if he remembers how to do the procedure correctly and to check on the drainage and on the condition of the skin around the stoma.

The Colostomy Irrigation. The irrigation may be given with the patient in bed but it is better to give it in the bathroom as soon as he is allowed up, since he can sit on the toilet and the drainage can go into the toilet bowl. While he is still in the hospital he should learn to perform the irrigation himself. At first, he may be appalled at the prospect of having to accept this as a procedure that he must carry out every day for the rest of his life. It may take a little time before he is convinced that, compared with the embarrassment and the inconvenience of fecal leakage and soiled dressings, it is well worth the effort. With a controlled low-residue diet and regular evacuation well established, some patients do not need an irrigation every day. However, this depends on the individual patient's needs.

The patient may be afraid to attempt the procedure on his own; he should have enough practice to give him self-confidence before he leaves the hospital, with sufficient supervision to ensure a correct performance.

The procedure* for a colostomy irrigation consists of alternately injecting warm tap water (or other prescribed solution) into the bowel and allowing the fluid and feces to return through an outlet into the toilet bowl. This procedure is repeated until the return flow is clear of fecal material.

EQUIPMENT

A No. 16 or a No. 18, French catheter
Irrigating set with tubing and adaptor and clamp
Lubricant
Toilet tissue
Newspaper or bag for soiled dressings
Solution as ordered

* Adapted from The New York Hospital booklet of instruction for patients with a colostomy.

Provision for hanging up the irrigating can
Colostomy irrigator (can be obtained from a surgical supply house–several makes are available)

SUGGESTED PROCEDURE

The solution is injected by inserting the catheter into the stoma, attaching the catheter to the irrigating can tubing and allowing the solution to run into the bowels.

***Guide:** Lubricate the catheter.*

The amount of solution will vary–500 cc. or more may be given until the patient complains of a full feeling or cramps.

***Guide:** Control the rate of flow by raising or lowering the can.*

The feces and the fluid drain into the toilet through the irrigator outlet which hangs down between the patient's legs.

***Guide:** More solution is given when the return flow stops.*

Continue the irrigation until the return flow is clear.

***Guide:** The total amount for this irrigation may be anywhere from 1 to several quarts.*

Stimulate peristalsis by using warm solution; by using sufficient fluid to distend the bowel; by massaging the abdomen and by exercise (instruct the patient to stand up a few times).

***Guide:** Peristalsis moves the feces through the intestines.*

When the return flow is clear, the inflow tubing and the outlet into the toilet bowl are closed off, and the catheter is withdrawn.

***Guide:** Prevent soiling by leaving the catheter in place until the last of the fluid has been expelled.*

When the catheter is removed, the area around the stoma is washed with soap and water and dried to prevent irritation, and the stoma is covered with a clean dressing.

If the Patient Is Confined to Bed. The procedure for an irrigation if the patient is not allowed out of bed is the same as for the ambulatory patient, with these exceptions:

The patient lies on his side near the edge of the bed.

The outlet tube for the drainage must be long enough to reach into a pail at the bedside.

OTHER DISORDERS

Hemorrhoids

Hemorrhoids are swollen (varicose) veins of the anus or the rectum. *External hemorrhoids* protrude as lumps around the anus. They are painful, especially if the patient is constipated and is in the habit of straining to produce a bowel movement. They may alternately appear and disappear. Usually, external hemorrhoids do not bleed but may become so large as to be painful and itchy. *Internal hemorrhoids* develop inside of the anal sphincter; they may bleed but are less likely to be painful if they do not protrude. Signs of bleeding may be no more than a drop on toilet paper, or bleeding may be so extensive and continuous as to cause anemia. Internal hemorrhoids almost always protrude with defecation, but at first they can be pushed back with the finger; later as the masses grow larger, this is no longer possible and they discharge blood and mucus. Bleeding is one of the signs of cancer, and this symptom should never be ignored. The proctoscope makes it possible to inspect the inside of the rectum.

CAUSES. The pressure of the uterus on the rectum during pregnancy, intra-abdominal tumors, constipation or infection from feces are the chief causes of hemorrhoids.

Treatment. Sometimes hemorrhoids disappear without treatment. Often they can be relieved by warm sitz baths or anesthetic ointments, such as Nupercaine. Correction of constipation may both prevent and eliminate hemorrhoids. If surgery is necessary, the veins are either tied off and excised or a cautery is used. Sometimes a solution is injected to shrink the tissues.

PREOPERATIVE PREPARATION. A cleansing enema is given on the night before and the morning of the operation. The rectal area is cleansed and shaved, in addition to other prescribed routines.

POSTOPERATIVE CARE. When the patient returns from the operating room he may be placed on his abdomen to prevent pressure on the operative area. He is given an analgesic for pain, preferably as soon as he awakens, or when the local anesthetic wears off. Demerol may be ordered, to be repeated at stated intervals. He will be allowed a liquid diet for his first meal after the operation, then a full diet for the following meals. He is allowed to sit up—this will be painful, and a rubber ring under his buttocks will help to relieve the pressure on the operative area. The next day the doctor may permit him to get out of bed and may order daily sitz baths to relieve pain and soreness. He must have assistance with getting in and out of the tub and should never be left alone, since the effort he must make might make him faint. He stays in the bath for 20 minutes, with the temperature of the water at 110° F.

The First Bowel Movement. The patient is naturally apprehensive about the first bowel movement after the operation. The nurse tells him what is being done to make it easier: that he will be given mineral oil twice a day to soften the stool, so it will pass more easily, and that he will have some pain but probably much less than he imagines. When he feels that his bowels are going to move, she tells him she will be just outside the bathroom door to be sure that he is all right, and reminds him not to use toilet paper. The anal area must be cleansed with moist cotton balls and dried carefully. This is a good time to give the sitz bath because some pain is inevitable after the first bowel movement.

Never underestimate the patient's pain and discomfort after rectal surgery. It may seem to be a very minor operation, but the effects on the patient can be very distressing.

Anal Abscess and Anal Fistula

Infection of the tissues around the rectal area causes *anal abscess*. This condition is very painful, and the patient may have fever and chills. It is treated by opening the abscess and draining it, or it may rupture spontaneously. Often an unfortunate result of an anal abscess is the formation of an *anal fistula*, which is a small tunnel in the tissues which discharges pus through one or more openings onto the skin. Surgery is necessary to open up the fistulous tract; then it is packed with gauze to keep the edges of the wound apart. This allows the tissues to fill in and eliminate the fistula.

Nursing Care. In general, the nursing care for an anal fistula is similar to the care given to any patient after rectal surgery, with these differences:

1. The fistula wound is packed with gauze which is changed every day.
2. The drainage from the abscess is profuse, purulent and foul smelling. The gauze dressing on the wound and cellucotton pads need to be changed frequently.

Anal Fissure. An anal fissure is an ulcer in the skin of the anal wall which causes severe pain with defecation and sometimes slight bleeding. The patient may dread the pain so much that he delays defecation to the extent that he becomes constipated.

Sitz baths and local anesthetic ointments are the treatments commonly used for anal fissure; mineral oil may help to soften the feces. The only cure for this condition is surgery to remove the ulcer.

Appendicitis

The appendix is a slender blind tube about 3 inches long which opens out of the tip of the cecum. Nobody seems to know why it is there, and people get along perfectly well without it. However, it may become obstructed by a hard mass of feces, which is followed by inflammation, infection and gangrene, which may lead to perforation. A ruptured appendix is serious, because intestinal contents can escape into the abdomen and cause peritonitis or an abscess (Fig. 161).

Symptoms. An acute attack of appendicitis usually begins with progressively severe generalized pain in the abdomen, which later localizes as pain and tenderness in the lower right quarter, at a point midway between the umbilicus and the crest of the ilium (McBurney's point). Usually, the pain is accompanied by fever, nausea and vomiting and an increase in white blood cells—a sign of the body's resistance to infection. An attack of appendicitis may subside and recur later (recurrent appendicitis).

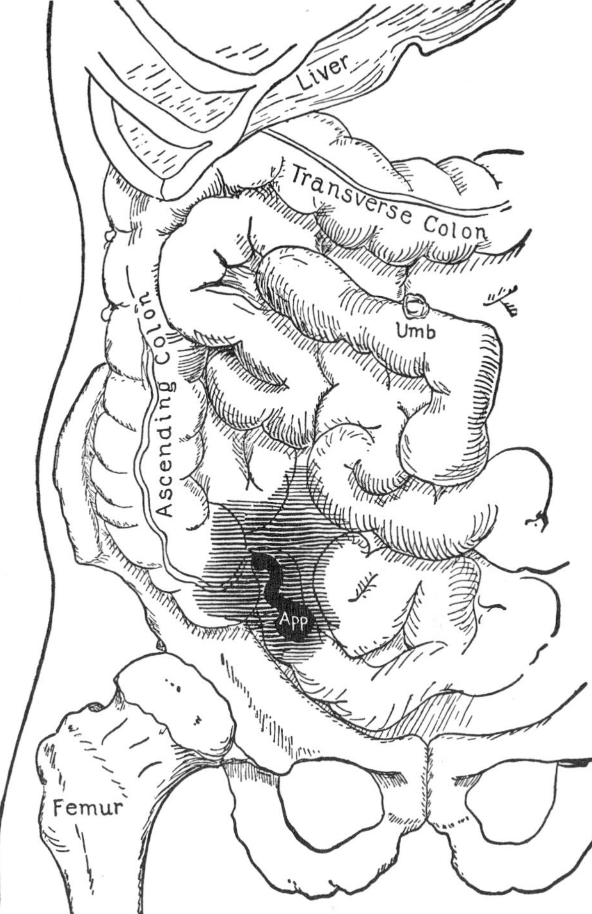

FIG. 161. Acute appendicitis, gangrene of the appendix, perforation and spreading peritonitis. In this case, the appendix was not removed, and the inflammation spread to the surrounding loops of bowel. An abscess will form in the shaded area, or the inflammation may spread through the entire peritoneal cavity. (Brunner, L. S., et al.: Textbook of Medical-Surgical Nursing, p. 617, Philadelphia, Lippincott, 1964)

Treatment. Prompt surgical treatment is necessary to remove the appendix if possible before it ruptures. In most instances, the patient recovers rapidly; he is permitted fluids and food and allowed out of bed the day after the operation and may go back to work in 2 or 3 weeks, with cautions to avoid heavy lifting and to "take it easy" for a while. If the appendix has ruptured, treatment for peritonitis is necessary (see p. 495). This is a serious complication which can cause death. However, modern treatment, with suction devices, intravenous fluids and antibiotics has greatly reduced this danger.

To Prevent Complications. Abdominal pain, nausea and vomiting are more or less common occurrences. It is easy for the victim to mistake them for a temporary intestinal upset, probably due to "something I ate," for which he takes a cathartic or an enema as a remedy. Everyone should know what to do and more especially what *not* to do for severe abdominal pain:

Do *not* take an enema or a cathartic. They increase peristalsis, and the result may be a perforated appendix and peritonitis.

Take nothing by mouth—even water may make matters worse. Call a doctor for any attack of severe pain or for pain that persists.

Abdominal Hernia

Abdominal hernia is a protrusion of the intestine through the abdominal wall; the layman's name for this condition is *rupture.* The abdominal wall is weak in spots, and it is at these points that a hernia develops. Often it is possible to push the intestines back by lying down and pressing on the abdomen, thus *reducing* the hernia. Another method of control often used by the hernia victim is to wear an appliance called a *truss,* which places continual pressure on the spot. If it is impossible to reduce the hernia by these methods and the condition is allowed to go on, the intestine becomes constricted, and the blood supply is cut off. This is a *strangulated hernia,* a serious condition which requires emergency surgery to save the patient's life.

Causes of Hernia. Congenital defects are responsible for a large number of hernias; therefore, a hernia may appear in infants. Hernias may occur also in young adults from such strains as heavy lifting, pregnancy, or coughing or sneezing. Later in life obesity and muscle weakness may cause hernia. The most common types of hernia are the incisional, the inguinal, the umbilical and the femoral.

A hernia can be repaired by surgery. If it has gone unrepaired for many years, a repair may not hold, since the tissues are weakened and do not heal as easily. Hernia repair is likely to be neglected, since hernia is not a painful condition, and the victim puts up with the discomfort. A hernia may interfere with getting a job, especially in strenuous types of work.

The operation for the repair of hernia is called *herniorrhaphy.* It consists of closing the defect in the abdominal wall. Usually, the nursing care is not complicated; the patient is allowed out of bed the day after the operation and can have food and fluids. He may be allowed to stand up to void if voiding is a difficulty immediately following the operation. In a male, the scrotum becomes swollen and painful, and an ice cap and a suspensory support may be ordered for relief. Every precaution is taken to avoid sneezing or coughing, and the patient is instructed, if he should sneeze or cough, to press his hand firmly over the area of the incision. He is encouraged to move about but cautioned to avoid movements that cause strain, such as lifting. Adjust the bed to its lowest position or provide a footstool to avoid strain when he gets in or out of bed.

Under normal conditions, the patient is out of the hospital in a week, with cautions to avoid strenuous activity. His return to work depends on such things as the nature and the extent of the hernia, his age and his weight. It also depends on the type of work that he does—if it is very strenuous he may have to change to a lighter type of work. When a patient realizes that he must change his type of work, he may be worried or upset and may even need assistance in finding a job. This should be called to the attention of the head nurse, who can take the proper steps to direct him to such assistance, which may be available through the social service department of the hospital.

DISORDERS OF THE LIVER

The liver is not only the largest organ in the body but it is also the busiest. The body could not function without the liver. Some of the many activities of this vital organ are listed on page 175.

Jaundice

Jaundice is a symptom of liver difficulty. It is the result of an abnormal concentration of bile salts in the bloodstream, which causes a yellow discoloration of the tissues. When something interferes with the work of the liver or obstructs the flow of bile into the intestines, *bilirubin* accumulates in the bloodstream. Signs of jaundice are a yellowish color in the whites of the eyes and in the skin. A blood test (icterus index) will show how much bilirubin is in the bloodstream. A shortage of bile in the intestines interferes with fat digestion, and the stools are pale and fatty and have a disagreeable odor. The bile salts that have escaped into the tissues make the skin itchy; the urine is dark and discolored. Lack of vitamin K causes a tendency to bleed.

Treatment and Nursing Care. The *treatment* of jaundice begins with finding out the cause of the condition and then doing whatever is necessary to correct it. This includes a number of tests:

Examination of the feces and urine for bilirubin

Liver function tests, which include injecting a dye into the blood stream (bromsulphalein) to estimate the amount of liver damage

Glucose tolerance tests to see how well the liver is doing its work (see Chap. 42).

Sometimes a surgeon performs a biopsy of the liver. Since this procedure involves cutting into the liver, it is important to watch for signs of bile on the dressing and for abdominal pain. These signs indicate that bile may be spilling into the abdominal cavity.

The nursing care includes measures to relieve itching. Starch baths or calamine lotion may be prescribed; tepid sponges also are comforting. If calamine lotion and cotton are placed at his bedside, the patient can apply it to itchy spots himself and prevent scratching. Things to remember are:

1. Watch for signs of bleeding in the stool and the urine or when the patient brushes his teeth. Look for black-and-blue marks on the skin. After the needle is withdrawn at the end of an intravenous procedure, exert pressure on the puncture for a longer time than is normal. This prevents a hematoma from oozing blood which would make it impossible to use the vein again. This is important, because people with liver conditions need frequent blood tests.

2. Explain to the patient that jaundice is not unusual with his ailment. Tell him that he can have dark glasses to hide his yellowed eyes. Prepare visitors for his changed appearance so that they will not show alarm or make unfortunate comments. Patients are sometimes embarrassed by having anyone see them in this condition.

Cirrhosis

Cirrhosis is a condition which destroys the liver itself and thereby interferes with liver functions. In the effort to repair itself, the liver may become so enlarged that the blood vessels going into and out of it are obstructed. This can cause such disturbances as indigestion, vomiting blood, blood in the stool, constipation, fluid in the abdomen and an enlarged spleen. It may also cause enlarged veins to form in the esophagus, an extremely dangerous condition. These disturbances show that the liver is not working properly and are signs of interference with blood clotting, with metabolism and with the elimination of waste products.

Causes. Alcoholism is blamed for more than half of the cases of cirrhosis in this country. Drinking leads to poor eating habits, and good nutrition is essential to keep the liver working properly. Yet doctors are puzzled to find that the alcoholics who do have good eating habits also have cirrhosis; most of them agree that nobody knows the exact cause. Cirrhosis is more prevalent among men than women. It occurs most often between the ages of 45 to 65. A great many of the people affected are of Irish or Italian stock. Whatever the cause, liver disease is increasing. It may be that the stepped-up use of such drugs as the Aureomycins and the sulfonamides is partly responsible. These drugs are excreted by the liver, and the added burden may be more than it can carry.

Symptoms. Cirrhosis may develop so gradually that the patient may not realize that anything is wrong nor have any signs of the disease. He may not be aware of a low-grade fever or notice a loss of weight because the weight loss is offset by an increase in abdominal fluid. As the disease advances the fever increases, the patient has abdominal pain, his pulse becomes rapid, and breathing becomes difficult because of his enlarged abdomen. He tends to bleed easily: blood appears in vomitus or as nosebleed, and veins become dilated. He is jaundiced, and his skin is dry; he feels weak and mentally dull and confused. Some of these symptoms are signs of 2 dangerous complications:

Hemorrhage: because his tendency to bleed is increased.

Infection: his body defenses are reduced, and he is more susceptible to outside infections. A nurse should always come to this patient with clean hands, no matter what she does for him, and should prevent visitors with colds or other infectious conditions from seeing him.

Treatment and Nursing Care. All treatment for cirrhosis of the liver is aimed toward helping the body to repair itself. It does this by:

Adequate bed rest: Since body comfort aids

rest, frequent care must be given to the patient's mouth and skin, since he is annoyed by itching. Soothing baths may be ordered.

Transfusions to combat anemia

A diet high in vitamins and carbohydrates and low in sodium. If these essential nutrients are not supplied, the body burns up its store of protein, thus increasing the accumulation of ammonia (a waste product) in the blood. Since the liver must transform ammonia into urea for elimination by the kidneys, this accumulation puts an extra burden on the diseased organ. Alcohol, tobacco and very fatty foods (pork, bacon, gravies, pastries) are forbidden. Small liquid or semisolid meals given frequently will be more appealing to a poor appetite.

Diuretics to reduce edema and fluid in the abdomen (ascites). Aldactone, a recent drug, may be given with other diuretics such as prednisone, Thiormerin, Diuril, or Mercuhydrin. *Paracentesis* (aspiration of fluid with a syringe and a needle) may be necessary to relieve ascites.

The patient should be told that his treatment may take a long time, so he knows what to expect and does not become discouraged if his progress seems to be slow. With careful attention to diet and the omission of alcohol, the cirrhosis patient may live for many years. Unfortunately, many patients do not take proper care of themselves, and liver damage becomes so extensive that they are beyond help. *Uncontrolled* cirrhosis may result in *hepatic coma.* Drugs to counteract the destructive processes can be given and may help temporarily, but death is inevitable in a very short time.

Viral Hepatitis

Viral hepatitis is a liver infection that has become very common since World War II. This increase is attributed to the wider use of intravenous procedures and to the difficulty in recognizing carriers of the disease. It may also be that people are becoming more susceptible to hepatitis or do not develop an immunity to it. It affects primarily children or young adults, and more "white" people than nonwhites. It occurs most frequently in the fall and the early winter.

Causes and Types of Hepatitis. Two different viruses cause hepatitis. *Virus B* is found in the bloodstream (*serum hepatitis*); *virus A* is found in the bloodstream and also in the gastrointestinal tract (*infectious viral hepatitis*). These viruses are tough—they can survive the extreme temperatures that kill most organisms. They are at home in blood bank bottles, and no way has been found to make whole blood or blood plasma safe from them.

Serum hepatitis is transmitted by contaminated fluids given intravenously, by infected needles or by unsterilized dental equipment. Viral hepatitis (virus A) is transmitted in the same way and also by an infected food or water supply, infected food handlers, and the rectal thermometers, the bedpans or the feces of a person with the disease. Both types are infectious and affect the patient in much the same way: he loses his appetite and is nauseated and feels sick all over. His head aches, and he has chills and fever. His stools are light-colored, and his urine is dark; he may become jaundiced. Laboratory tests will tell which type of hepatitis he has.

Prevention. *Gamma globulin* is partially successful as protection against virus A but is useless as protection against virus B and is of no use at all once the patient has hepatitis. Blood banks can be helpful by using every possible precaution to avoid collecting blood from persons who have had hepatitis or from healthy carriers. (A healthy carrier is a person who is harboring the virus but has no symptoms of the disease.) It is almost impossible to identify a healthy carrier who does not know that he is one.

Treatment and Nursing Care. The only treatment that has any effect on hepatitis is centered around building up the patient's resistance. No drug is known to affect the virus directly. Much depends on good nursing care. A comfortable position is important for rest, and the nurse can explain to visitors the need for rest. The patient needs a nutritious diet but is likely to be revolted by the very thought of food. His food should be served in small quantities and as attractively as possible. He needs plenty of fluid, especially if he has jaundice, in which case he should try to take about 3,000 cc. every day. The nurse's strict attention to hand-washing before doing anything for the patient will help to protect him from other infections.

PRECAUTIONS. With virus B, contact with the patient's blood is a source of infection. Needles and syringes used for this patient are not safe to use until they have been autoclaved at 20 pounds pressure for 20 minutes or have been immersed in briskly boiling water for 30 minutes. Using disposable equipment is safer and quicker.

Since virus A is in the intestinal tract, it is necessary to place the patient in isolation. The nurse should wear rubber gloves when giving an enema.

CONVALESCENCE. The patient must avoid overexertion when he begins to feel better. Too much activity too soon is very likely to bring on a recurrence of his symptoms. This may be a boring time for him, especially if he was a very active person before he became ill. The news that his convalescence may take a year will not be received with enthusiasm. However, he has to be told what the situation is—that he must follow instructions or he will have a relapse. He should also be warned that he must never donate blood. During his stay in the hospital there are many opportunities for him to ask questions and plan with his family for his convalescence. As he gradually recovers he will feel stronger and not as depressed and can discuss the restrictions he must accept.

Toxic Hepatitis. Toxic hepatitis is the result of the action of certain chemicals on the liver, such as fumes from cleaning solutions and insecticides. The treatment is the same as for viral hepatitis.

Cancer of the Liver

Cancer rarely begins in the liver, but it is often the result of metastasis from a cancerous growth elsewhere in the body. A cancer that does begin in the liver can be removed by a surgical operation to remove part of the liver. This procedure may prolong the patient's life for 5 years—he would not live that long without the operation. If cancer is the result of metastasis, an operation is out of the question; the patient probably has only a few months to live.

Massive Liver Necrosis (Acute Yellow Atrophy)

This is a disease which, for some unknown reason, affects middle-aged women. It is a destructive condition which seems to be precipitated by the hepatitis virus, by poisons or by a drug. The symptoms are the same as in hepatitis, and in spite of treatment the patient grows steadily worse, with the presence of coma, hemorrhages and convulsions. A characteristic symptom is the evil-smelling, fishy odor on the victim's breath.

Liver Abscess

Liver abscesses are caused either by the spread of infection from some part of the intestinal tract, perhaps from the appendix or from the gallbladder, or by amebae in the intestines. The symptoms of a liver abscess are chills, a temperature that shoots up and down, extreme loss of weight, nausea and vomiting, and abdominal distention. Jaundice frequently appears. Pain over the liver is a later symptom. If the abscess bursts, it scatters infection through the abdominal or chest cavity. Antibiotics are given, and the results depend upon how successful they are in combating the infection. Sometimes drainage is attempted by puncturing the liver with a trochar and establishing drainage. The nursing care includes precautions in caring for equipment and drainage, to prevent spreading the infection.

Liver Injuries

Frequently, the liver is injured in automobile accidents. Extensive damage is likely to be fatal, and the patient may die from hemorrhage before he reaches the hospital. Sometimes surgery is done for liver injuries to control the bleeding or to remove a portion of the damaged liver. One great danger accompanying liver surgery is the occurrence of shock. Nursing care for this patient will include assistance with treatment for shock, preventing infection and observing the color of the wound drainage for indications of bile. More than 75 per cent of the patients with a rupture of the liver die.

THE GALLBLADDER

The Liver-Gallbladder-Bile Combine

The gallbladder lies on the undersurface of the liver; it is the storage reservoir for the bile which the liver manufactures continually. A small amount of bile is always retained in the gallbladder, ready for release at the next meal. Fat digestion cannot take place without bile.

As was described in Chapter 17, the flow of bile in the biliary apparatus proceeds through the hepatic duct from the liver into the cystic duct leading to the gallbladder for storage. Upon hormonal stimulation, the gallbladder contracts, releasing the bile back through the cystic duct which, with the hepatic duct, enters the duodenum as the common bile duct.

Two Common Diseases

Two common forms of gallbladder disease are the inflammation of the gallbladder (*cholecystitis*) and gallstones (*cholelithiasis*). These conditions often occur together, and each makes the other worse. Infection causes stones; stones block the duct which leads out of the gallbladder and imprison bacteria in its wall, which in turn causes infection. Stones may injure the wall, which also leads to infection. The most likely victims of gallbladder disease are obese women over 45; frequent pregnancies also seem to make women more susceptible. People from the Orient seldom have cholecystitis or cholelithiasis, but the reason for this is unknown.

Cholecystitis. The symptoms of cholecystitis are:

Indigestion, due to the lack of bile. The patient complains of feeling "full" after eating. Fatty foods make this condition worse.

Light-colored stools, because bile pigment is missing

Fever and malaise

Jaundice, caused by stones obstructing the bile passages or by a spasm of the common bile duct. Bile backs up in the gallbladder; the liver stops manufacturing bile, and the bilirubin it would normally use in this process goes into the blood stream.

Gallstone colic, a sharp pain over the gallbladder, which sometimes extends to the back or to the right shoulder. The pain usually comes on suddenly a few hours after a heavy meal, when the gallbladder is trying to contract to send bile into the intestine to help digest the food. If this effort forces a stone into the cystic duct the pain is excruciating. Usually, the patient vomits, which causes further distress instead of relief. If gallstones are very small, a person may be only slightly uncomfortable at times, or they may never give him any trouble.

Tests. An x-ray picture will show stones and their location in the gallbladder. The patient is given a fat-free supper the night before the roentgenogram is taken, and a dye (Priodax, Telepaque, Cholografin) is given by mouth or intravenously. The liver excretes this dye into the bile, which then goes to the gallbladder. The patient has nothing to eat for the next 12 hours, to give time for the dye to concentrate in the gallbladder. The x-ray picture will show the outline of the gallbladder, and the stones, if they are present. Then the patient is given a fatty meal, and another picture is taken which will show how well the gallbladder is contracting. This test may not be used if the patient is jaundiced, for fear of further damage to the liver by subjecting it to the additional strain of a test.

A blood coagulation test helps to determine liver damage. If the coagulation time is dangerously slow, vitamin K can be given; this is important to lessen the danger of hemorrhage if an operation is to be done. Tests for bile pigment in the blood are the *van den Bergh* and the *icterus index.*

Treatment. The diet is restricted to nonfatty foods (see Chap. 23). Such foods as cheese, cream, greasy fried foods, fatty meats and gas-forming vegetables are forbidden. The patient may have lean meat (never fried), plain, mashed or baked potato, or rice. Alcoholic beverages are forbidden. Immediately after an attack he is given liquids only.

Heat to the abdomen and a plain enema help

to relieve pain in a mild attack. If the attack is severe, Demerol is usually given, since morphine may increase the spasm. Pro-Banthine may be given for the spasm. Usually the most effective treatment after an acute attack of cholecystitis is to remove the gallbladder (*cholecystectomy*).

Nursing Care. The postoperative treatment and the nursing care for a cholecystectomy are essentially the same as for any major surgical operation, with an additional provision to care for bile drainage from the wound. The patient who has had his gallbladder removed may feel that his pain was of minor importance compared with the discomfort of the many tubes attached to him—a nasogastric tube, an intravenous infusion, and tubes for wound drainage and perhaps a Foley catheter. In spite of all this, the patient is expected to turn and cough, to prevent pneumonia from congested lungs. The nurse helps the patient through this trying time by placing her hands firmly on either side of the incision, making a "splint" when the patient coughs. The nurse can assure him that most of the tubes probably will be removed soon; she can hold the tubes up when the patient turns, and she can tuck a pillow against his back for support.

By the 2nd day after the operation, if recovery is proceeding normally, the patient will be out of bed for a short time and will be taking fluids by mouth. He also will be voiding. If he has gas pains, he may be able to expel flatus; in 2 or 3 days he may be given a Fleet enema. The wound drainage tube is removed after approximately 1 week. The nurse notes the amount of bile on the dressings; if the amount does not diminish in a few days, it may be an indication that the bile is not going through to the intestine properly.

THE PATIENT'S DIET. Most doctors will put the patient on a low-fat diet for several months after a cholecystectomy. However, later these patients in most instances have no trouble in digesting fats. The patient may want to talk over what he sees as problems after he has been told that he must keep on with a low-fat diet for some time.

Complications of Cholecystitis. Sometimes the infected gallbladder fills with pus and may rupture, causing peritonitis. Chronic gallbladder disease may damage the liver. Pneumonia may develop. One reason for deep breathing and coughing is to prevent pneumonia.

Cancer of the Gallbladder. Often cancer of the gallbladder is not treated early enough because it is not easily detected in the early stages. In the advanced stage treatment comes too late. Surgery may be tried in the *early* advanced stage. More women than men develop cancer of the gallbladder.

The Pancreas

Pancreatitis. The pancreas, a gland immediately behind the stomach, secretes pancreatic juice which aids digestion. The pancreas also contains the islets of Langerhans, groups of cells which secrete insulin. Bile is not supposed to enter the pancreas, but sometimes it does, producing *pancreatitis*, a process that destroys pancreatic tissue and leads to hemorrhages, edema and severe pain. Pancreatitis is also caused by infection. This condition can now be treated without surgery. Demerol is given to relieve pain; nitroglycerin may be administered to relieve muscle spasms. Banthine may also be used to reduce pancreatic activity in producing pancreatic juice. The prescribed diet is low in fat and high in protein and carbohydrates.

If the islets of Langerhans are affected, treatment for diabetes is necessary. Rest and freedom from emotional strain and upsets are important. Because the pain is so intense, narcotics are given frequently and may lead to drug addiction if acute pancreatitis becomes chronic.

Cancer of the Pancreas. Jaundice is sometimes the first symptom of cancer of the pancreas. The only hope of cure is to remove the cancerous growth. Before the operation, attention is concentrated on building up the patient's resistance. He may need to gain weight, but his appetite is poor—an obstacle which takes patience to overcome. He needs rest, yet he must have so many things done for him that rest is hard to attain. By the time the cancer has extended to the tail or the body of the pancreas, an operation is useless.

39

THE PATIENT WITH A DISORDER OF THE RESPIRATORY SYSTEM

Allergic Rhinitis (Hay Fever)

Hay fever is the name most commonly given to an inflammation of the mucous membranes of the nose, *allergic rhinitis,* which is caused by an allergic reaction to some protein substance (see Allergy, Chap. 47). It may be due to pollens from weeds, flowers or grasses at certain seasons of the year, or a reaction to dusts, feathers or scales from the skin of animals. Contact with these foreign substances causes edema, itching and a watery discharge from the eyes and the nose. People with an allergic background (a family history of allergy) are more susceptible to hay fever, as are people who have asthma or eczema. The number of people with a hereditary tendency is fairly high, including about 10 per cent of the population. All ages are affected, and it may appear suddenly at any age and may disappear as suddenly.

Symptoms. It is a most disagreeable and inconvenient disease. The victim's nose itches, he sneezes endlessly and is tormented by a profuse, watery discharge from his nose and eyes. It is aggravated on windy days and worse in the morning and the evening. It takes painstaking detective work to track down the cause, and detailed questioning and many skin tests are needed to find the offending substance. Sometimes several substances are the offenders.

Treatment. The first step in the treatment of allergic rhinitis is to avoid the substance that is causing the allergy. This may mean eliminating an offending food from the diet, avoiding cats or curtailing drives in the country. Air-conditioning also helps. Antihistamines relieve the symptoms; desensitization (Chap. 47) may do away with them entirely. Sometimes cortisone and ACTH are given for severe attacks. An untreated allergy of this kind may lead to asthma or sinusitis.

The Common Cold

The *common cold* is classed as a minor respiratory infection, yet it is one of the minor respiratory diseases that causes more than half of all illness every year, results in the loss of many work days and restricts many activities. Think what this means in absence from school and work, to say nothing of parties missed and trips postponed or only half-enjoyed. The average loss per person in a year from respiratory disease is estimated as 4 days—more than half of these losses were caused by minor respiratory infections such as the common cold.

Colds are caused by one or more filtrable viruses. If the body's resistance is lowered by fatigue, chilling or gases that continually irritate the nasal membranes (smog), the virus moves in. The usual symptoms of a cold are sneezing, a scratchy throat and headache. These conditions are followed by a sore throat, nasal discharge, a cough and sometimes a slight fever. This unpleasantness usually lasts for 4 or 5 days but may last longer.

Treatment. The most important treatment

for a cold is bed rest, which has the added advantage of taking the afflicted person out of circulation and keeping him from infecting others. (Of all people, a nurse with a cold should stay at home.) Rest is especially important where babies or elderly, weakened people are concerned, to prevent the development of more serious complications. The administration of plenty of fluids aids recovery; strict attention to washing the hands and using disposable tissues to prevent spreading the infection are essential. Aspirin relieves discomfort. Nose drops should be used with discretion, because many of them have harmful effects on the body. Antibiotics have no effect against the virus that causes a cold.

Influenza

Influenza (commonly called "flu") is an acute respiratory disease caused by one of several different strains of a virus: Types A, B and C. Influenza breaks out in epidemics, which occur periodically and are usually caused by Types A and B—Type C is almost never seen. In 1957, a virus similar to Type A was the cause of an epidemic that was almost world-wide. In 1918, at the close of World War I, an influenza epidemic took many lives in this country as well as abroad. Most patients recover, but others die as the result of complications, such as heart disease or the harmful effects on pregnant women. Influenza also frequently causes death among elderly people.

Symptoms. Influenza attacks suddenly: the patient becomes very ill, suffering from muscular pains, fever, headache and chills. Also, he may sneeze, cough, have a nasal discharge and complain of sore throat. Fever is high (100° to 103°) and lasts for 2 to 3 days, but the other symptoms, especially the cough, last longer. In its severest form, influenza may cause the patient to collapse.

Treatment and Nursing Care. The influenza victim is given quantities of fluids, including fruit juices, and milk-and-egg drinks for their nutritional value. As soon as he feels better he may have a regular diet. Aspirin is given to relieve headache and muscular pains. Codeine may be given to relieve a cough. The patient is isolated to prevent spreading the infection while it is acute. He is watched for signs of secondary infection, such as pain in the chest, purulent or rust-colored sputum, or a rise in temperature and an increase in the pulse rate.

Polyvalent vaccine can be given as a protection against influenza. However, vaccination only protects people for about 6 months, so it is not possible to give it much in advance of an epidemic, and there is very little time to develop a special vaccine after an epidemic strikes. Moreover, some authorities doubt the effectiveness of influenza vaccines. An effort is made to give this protection to health workers and military personnel and to people who are very susceptible, such as the elderly and people with chronic disease. During an epidemic people are urged to stay away from crowds—sometimes all public gatherings are suspended, such as group meetings or movies and shows.

Chest Injuries

Accidents, such as a blow, a fall or an automobile accident which fracture ribs, are the most common cause of chest injuries. Fractured ribs may injure adjoining parts of the body, by puncturing a lung or tearing blood vessels. If there is none of these further complications, fractured ribs can be treated by immobilizing the chest with an Ace bandage or by strapping it with adhesive, which is applied firmly to lessen the pain which breathing causes.

Compression of the chest as the result of an explosion may rupture a lung and cause death from hemorrhage or suffocation. Wounds that penetrate the chest are very serious and may require chest drainage or surgery.

Bronchitis

Bronchitis is an inflammation of the bronchial tubes—it may be acute or chronic.

Acute Bronchitis. Acute bronchitis often follows a respiratory infection, especially during the winter months. A dry cough is an early symptom; later, the cough produces mucus and pus. Other symptoms are fever and malaise.

TREATMENT AND NURSING CARE. Rest in bed,

a nutritious diet and plenty of fluids are the usual prescribed treatment. Humidifiers help to moisten the air—dry air aggravates bronchitis. Antibiotics help to control the infection, and precautions are taken to prevent it from spreading. Salicylates are sometimes given. As in any respiratory disease, the patient is instructed to cover his mouth when coughing, and the sputum cup is kept covered and emptied and the contents disposed of in a way that will not endanger others. Every hospital has its own method of disposing of infectious wastes.

Chronic Bronchitis. Chronic bronchitis is a more serious condition which often develops so gradually that the victim disregards its most significant symptom, a chronic cough. Consequently, the disease is firmly established before he decides that he needs treatment. Repeated attacks of acute bronchitis may lead to a chronic condition, or it may develop after an acute respiratory infection, such as influenza or pneumonia. Cigarette smoking is undoubtedly one of the most common causes of bronchial irritation; air pollution may also be responsible. People who are exposed to irritating dusts or chemicals seem to be more likely to develop bronchitis. It affects all ages but is most common after 40, probably because people wait that long before coming for treatment, even though they should have had it earlier.

SYMPTOMS. Chronic bronchitis begins with a dry cough which is most severe when the patient gets up in the morning. As time goes on, he coughs up mucus and pus, and sometimes streaks of blood appear. Shortness of breath becomes apparent with exertion; as the disease progresses it persists even when the patient is quiet. The patient's history of a cough and of his living habits helps the doctor in making a diagnosis. He is also aided by x-ray pictures of the chest, fluoroscopic examinations and sputum tests.

TREATMENT AND NURSING CARE. Treatment is a long, drawn-out process; there are no drugs that will work a miracle. However, treatment will reduce the symptoms and prevent complications. Untreated, the disease may progress until the bronchioles of the lungs are permanently damaged, or it may lead to asthma or emphysema. It is important to build up the patient's general health and to use precautions to avoid exposure to respiratory infections. He should have plenty of rest and be free from emotional pressures. He may have to change his job if his work exposes him to dust or bad weather. If he is a cigarette smoker, he has to face the fact that the habit is definitely harmful for him. Antibiotics will help to clear up additional respiratory infections, but such infections will aggravate his condition.

Bronchial Asthma

Asthma is a bronchial spasm, accompanied by swelling of the membrane which lines the bronchi and by a thick, mucus secretion. The spasm imprisons the air that is in the alveoli and shuts out fresh air. An asthma attack is a frightening experience for the patient as he struggles to get air into his lungs. He becomes pale, sometimes cyanotic, in a severe attack; he perspires and wheezes. As the attack subsides, he coughs up thick, white mucus. It can be equally frightening to a nurse who never has seen an attack of asthma before.

Causes. Allergy, infection and emotional tensions are the chief causes of asthma. A person may develop asthma from a combination of all 3 of these factors, which makes it difficult to trace the cause of any one attack. Attacks may occur only occasionally, or they may be frequent. Frequent attacks of asthma may lead to emphysema. People who have hay fever or bronchitis are especially susceptible; it can occur at any age and at any time. Asthmatic children have fewer symptoms as they grow older, but the symptoms of adults grow worse with age.

Treatment. The most important aspect of treatment during an asthmatic attack is to relieve the breathing difficulties. Doses of Adrenalin are given to dilate the bronchi. Adrenalin is a powerful and dangerous drug that brings immediate relief; it also has distressing side-effects if the dose is not measured exactly. Aminophylline, given intravenously, has a similar effect, as does ephedrine to a lesser degree. Long-term treatment of asthma consists of treating the allergy and other difficulties.

Bronchiectasis

Bronchiectasis is an abnormal dilatation of one or several bronchi. Saclike cavities may form and fill with pus. The main cause of this disease is infection, frequently following influenza or pneumonia or chronic sinusitis. Often it begins in young adulthood and progresses slowly over a long period of time.

Symptoms. The characteristic symptom of bronchiectasis is a cough, which produces greenish-yellow sputum with a foul odor. The cough is most severe when the patient gets up or goes to bed. As the disease progresses, the amount of sputum increases. Sometimes he coughs up blood. He loses weight, and has chronic fatigue and a poor appetite. Bronchiectasis will show on an x-ray picture of the bronchial tree after a radiopaque substance (Lipiodol) has been instilled into the bronchi.

Treatment and Nursing Care. Drainage of the purulent material is part of the treatment. This is accomplished by *postural drainage,* a position with the head lower than the chest. The patient is encouraged to cough and to breathe deeply. Antibiotics are given to control the infection; good nutrition and rest are important. Special mouth care is needed, because the sputum leaves an offensive taste and breath odor. Attention to the patient's comfort helps to promote rest. Prompt attention to such conditions as bronchial asthma and bronchitis help to prevent bronchiectasis. Advising young people against smoking and encouraging smokers to give it up are part of prevention. If only a small part of the lung is affected, surgery to remove the diseased area will cure bronchiectasis. Nothing will bring damaged bronchi back to normal.

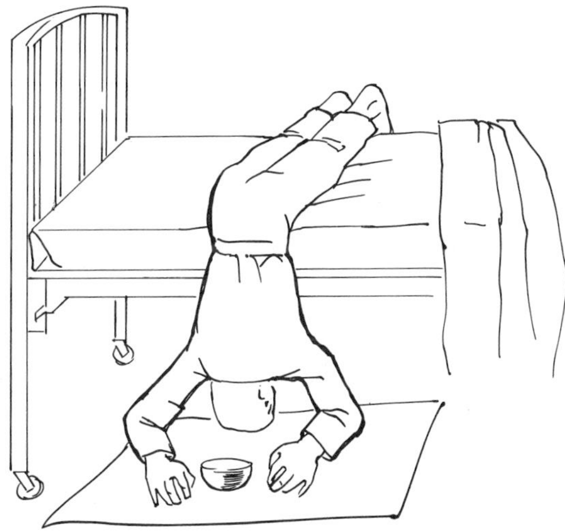

FIG. 162. This is one position that is commonly used for postural drainage. Note that the patient's sputum cup is handy, and that a towel has been placed on the floor, so that the patient's hands do not touch the floor. (Smith, D. W., and Gips, C. D.: Care of the Adult Patient, p. 591, Philadelphia, Lippincott, 1963)

Emphysema

Emphysema is overdistention of the alveoli of the lungs which causes loss of elasticity and destroys alveolar tissue. To review the structure of the lungs briefly: the branches of the bronchi, the bronchioles, end in millions of tiny air sacs called alveoli. It is in the alveoli that the exchange of carbon dioxide and oxygen takes place. When the alveoli puff up with air that the patient is unable to breathe out, the lungs become distended and the muscles suffer from lack of oxygen. This condition becomes worse as more and more air is imprisoned in the alveoli, and the heart works harder and harder to push the blood through the body, trying to get oxygen to the muscles and other body tissues. The result may be congestive heart failure.

Causes. Authorities believe that chronic bronchitis is the direct cause of emphysema. It may also follow chronic bronchial asthma and bronchiectasis. Evidence seems to be clear that the increase in the number of cases of emphysema in the last 10 years is also due to air pollution and cigarette smoking. A recent report* states that "cigarette smoking is the most important of the causes of chronic bronchitis in the United States." It also states that "the smoking of cigarettes is associated with an increased risk of dying from pulmonary emphysema." It is estimated that this disease now

* Smoking and Health. Report of the Advisory Committee to the Surgeon General of the U. S. Public Health Service.

affects more than 7 million people in this country; nearly 10,000 people die of emphysema every year. Men over 40 are the group most frequently afflicted.

Symptoms. The first symptom of emphysema is difficulty in breathing after exertion, which often progresses to difficulty at all times. Other symptoms are wheezing and a chronic cough, with the expectoration of mucus and pus. The victim is pale and drawn and is afraid of choking. He does not dare to lie down and sits up leaning forward and contracting the muscles of his neck with every breath. In the advanced stages, as carbon dioxide accumulates in his blood, he becomes listless and drowsy.

Treatment. Until recently, emphysema was considered to be a hopeless disease for which there was no help. However, modern treatment is proving that patients can be helped with intensive treatment. Preventive treatment is most important to correct the conditions that cause emphysema. This means, for one thing, alerting the public to the danger signs, such as morning cough or smoker's cough.

The treatment includes:

Drugs such as Adrenalin, aminophylline or ephedrine, which dilate the bronchial tubes and relieve breathlessness

Expectorants and postural drainage to remove secretions

Antibiotics to control infections

Administration of oxygen with caution (it may be dangerous if there is a high concentration of carbon dioxide in the blood)

Breathing exercises to use the diaphragm more effectively and to relieve the chest muscles

Blowing exercises to improve breathing (blowing out a candle or blowing into a bottle half-full of water).

The emphysema patient must be faithful in carrying out his breathing exercises, because his life depends on staying active at all costs. He must limit his activities to whatever his heart and breathing power will stand. He can choose to be an invalid or to lead a fairly active life.

Pneumonia

Pneumonia is an acute infection of the lung in which the air sacs fill with fluid and affect breathing. There are 2 general types of pneumonia—*bacterial* pneumonia, which is caused by bacteria such as the pneumococcus or the streptococcus, or *hypostatic* pneumonia, which develops when a person lies in one position for prolonged periods and the lung tissues fill with fluid. Fluids may also get into the lungs of an unconscious patient through the epiglottis, which does not close completely when the patient does not swallow. The nurse must be careful when a patient is recovering from anesthesia, to drain or suction out fluids that accumulate in the mouth and the throat, to prevent them from getting into the lungs. Breathing exercises and changing a patient's position frequently help to prevent hypostatic pneumonia.

Pneumonia is also caused by a *virus*, which for some reason does not respond to the usual treatment. It is seldom fatal but leaves the patient feeling weak and ill for a long period of time after the attack.

Symptoms. Pneumonia affects the lobes of the lung (*lobar pneumonia*) or it affects the bronchi (*bronchial pneumonia*). It is most prevalent in the winter; infection spreads through droplets in the air. The pneumococcus is often found in the throats of well people where it does no damage unless their resistance is lowered.

Bacterial pneumonia starts suddenly with:

A severe sharp pain in the chest and a chill, followed by fever which may go up to 105 or 106°

A painful cough, with rust-colored sputum and pain on breathing

A rapid pulse and sometimes cyanosis. The patient feels very ill.

Treatment and Nursing Care. Blood cultures are taken, and the sputum is analyzed to find out what organism is causing the infection. An x-ray picture of the chest will show what part of the lung is affected and how much. Antibiotics have revolutionized the treatment of pneumonia. In 2 days the fever usually disappears, and the other symptoms improve dramatically. In some unfortunate instances, the organisms causing the disease are not affected by antibiotics. The antibiotics that are commonly used in the treatment of bacterial pneumonia are:

Penicillin, for pneumococcal and streptococcal pneumonia. It seldom has unpleasant side-effects unless the patient has had penicillin before or is sensitive to it, in which case he may have an allergic reaction which causes hives and fever.

Streptomycin is effective against some of the organisms that cause pneumonia. It is more toxic than penicillin and may produce such side-effects as nausea, abdominal pain, skin rash and fever. Sometimes it causes damage to a nerve in the brain—signs of this effect are dizziness, ringing in the ears and deafness, which should be reported immediately.

Tetracycline may be used when a patient is sensitive to penicillin or does not respond to penicillin. It may also be used when the organism causing the disease cannot be identified. It has few side-effects unless the patient is allergic to it.

Chloromycetin is effective in atypical pneumonias or in cases when penicillin has no effect.

Erythromycin has effects similar to chloromycetin.

The usual treatment to build up body resistance is given, along with rest and administering large amounts of fluid, including fluids with nutritious value. Codeine may be given for the cough. If breathing is markedly difficult, oxygen is administered usually by placing the patient in an oxygen tent. Sedatives may be necessary to promote rest. If the abdomen is distended, Prostigmin may be given to stimu-

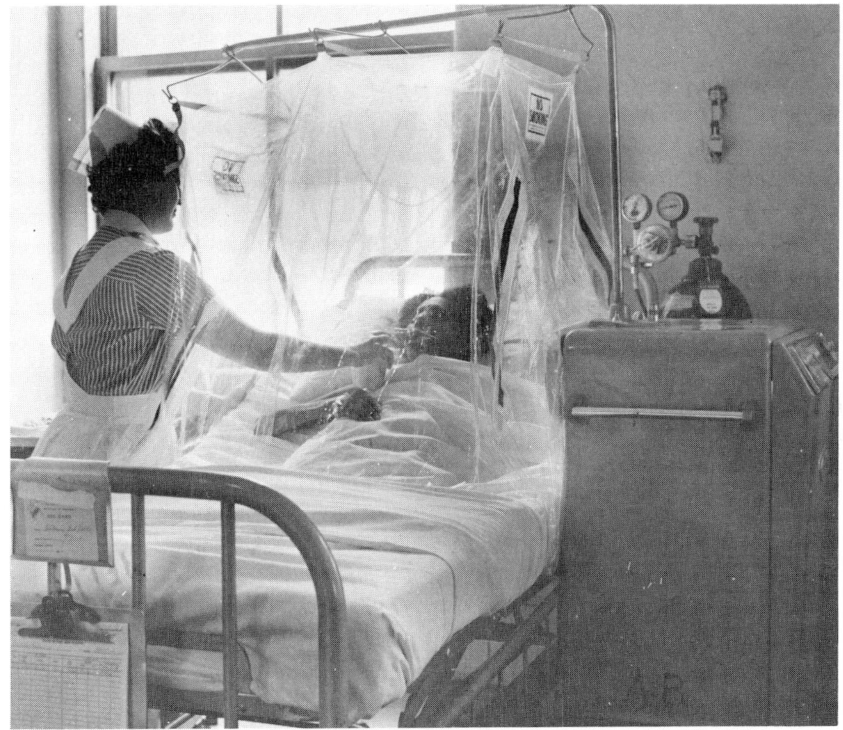

FIG. 163. Fluids are offered frequently to the patient who is acutely ill with pneumonia. The intake and output record is at the bottom of the bed. The head of the bed is elevated to facilitate breathing. The patient's thermometer (on the wall above the oxygen tank) is kept for her use alone. When the nurse opens the zipper in the tent, she is careful to dilute the oxygen content inside the tent as little as possible. (Smith, D. W., and Gips, C. D.: Care of the Adult Patient, p. 562, Philadelphia, Lippincott, 1963)

late peristalsis. Points to observe in nursing care are:

The patient's position, adjusting it to aid in breathing and to calm his fear of choking. A pillow placed lengthwise under his back helps to expand the chest. A blanket around his shoulders makes him more comfortable during chills.

Take the temperature, pulse and respiration every 4 hours. A rapid increase in the pulse rate and increasingly labored respirations are signs that the disease is advancing.

Measure intake and output.

Change his bed linen when necessary if he perspires profusely.

Give mouth care frequently.

Encourage him to cough and bring up the excessive secretions.

Put side rails on the bed if he becomes delirious.

Observe isolation technic during the acute stage of illness.

Give small amounts of liquid foods frequently.

Keep the patient quiet. Instruct him not to talk or exert himself in any way.

With antibiotics, the patient usually improves rapidly—in 48 to 72 hours he is markedly better. However, he is still weak, and remains in bed for several days after his temperature is normal. Then gradually he is allowed more activity and convalesces slowly while his resistance is built up. An x-ray picture is taken to make sure that the infection in the lungs has cleared up completely. Complications from pneumonia seldom occur today, since antibiotics control the disease before it has time to spread and affect other parts of the body. Complications which were seen frequently in the past were empyema, endocarditis or arthritis. If the infection spreads, it also may cause inflammation of the middle ear (otitis media), sinusitis or bronchitis.

Colds and influenza lower resistance and make people more susceptible to pneumonia, especially in alcoholics or older people who are less active. A nurse who is taking care of elderly people should remember this fact and stay at home until she recovers from a cold.

Empyema

Empyema is a collection of pus in the pleural cavity. It is caused by infection and may follow tuberculosis, lung abscess or pneumonia. Before antibiotics were developed, empyema was a frequent complication of pneumonia. Now antibiotics subdue the infection in the lung before it spreads to the pleura.

Symptoms. The symptoms of empyema are chest pain, fever, difficulty in breathing and a generally toxic feeling. If empyema is suspected, more decisive information can be obtained by a chest roentgenogram and by aspirating a specimen of the chest fluid (thoracentesis).

Treatment and Nursing Care. The treatment starts with antibiotics to combat the infection and with measures to remove the pus collected in the pleural cavity. This may be done by closed or open drainage—open drainage is sometimes necessary if the pus is thick and heavy. Then soft rubber drainage tubes are inserted in the wound, and large, absorbent dressings and pads are applied. Usually, the drainage is profuse at first, and it will be necessary to change the dressings frequently. As soon as drainage begins, the patient's temperature falls to normal or near-normal, and his condition improves.

Lung Abscess

A *lung abscess* is a localized area of infection in the lung, which breaks down and forms pus. It can be caused by a foreign body in the lung or by aspirating respiratory secretions, or it may follow pneumonia. One precaution we take to prevent aspirating secretions is to turn an unconscious patient's head to the side to allow these secretions to drain out through the mouth.

The *symptoms* of a lung abscess are chills and fever, with a loss in weight and a cough which produces purulent sputum with a foul odor. It is treated by establishing drainage, which may require surgery to open the chest wall.

Pleurisy

Pleurisy is an inflammation of the pleura, the double membrane that covers the lungs. If only a small amount of fluid accompanies the infection it is called *dry pleurisy*. On the other hand, the amount of fluid may be so great that a large amount collects in the space between the 2 layers of membrane which creates enough pressure to collapse the lung and affect the heart. This is called *wet pleurisy* or *pleurisy with effusion*.

Dry pleurisy usually occurs as a complication of pneumonia by infection spreading from the lungs. Wet pleurisy may be the result of tuberculosis, lung cancer, heart and kidney diseases and general infections. The pleura becomes thickened, and the 2 membrane surfaces rub together, causing sharp pain with every breath. Later, as fluid forms, the pain diminishes, and a dry cough takes its place, accompanied by shortness of breath and exhaustion after the least effort.

Treatment and Nursing Care. The treatment of pleurisy is very much like the treatment for pneumonia: bed rest and the restriction of activity. The patient is encouraged to cough; since this is painful, a tight chest binder and a heating pad over the area help to make him more comfortable. Sometimes *thoracentesis* (chest tap) is necessary to remove excess fluid. Usually, pleurisy heals with the improvement in the condition that caused it.

Cancer of the Lung

Lung cancer has increased markedly during the last 20 years. It appears in most instances after the age of 40, or at least it is not discovered until then. It affects 6 times more men than women. Several reasons are given for the increase in deaths from lung cancer. One of these is the increasing pollution of the air. Also, the report of the Surgeon General's Advisory Committee* finds that in the majority of lung cancer deaths the victims were cigarette smokers, and cigarette smoking is on the increase. There are more older people in the population today, which may account partly for the high incidence of lung cancer, since it is not a disease primarily of young people.

Symptoms. It is hard to detect lung cancer in the early stage because the symptoms do not appear until the disease is well advanced. Lung cancer is a malignant tumor which usually appears in the bronchi and shows no symptoms until it enlarges. The first indication of trouble that the patient has may be that he begins to cough up mucus and blood-streaked sputum. Even then he may think that he is smoking too much and simply resolves to cut down a little. Later, he begins to feel tired, loses weight and experiences chest pains and difficulty in breathing. When he finally consults his doctor, bronchoscopy and a sputum examination help to confirm the diagnosis of lung cancer.

Treatment. The only possible cure for lung cancer is surgery to remove the malignant tissue. Even this is not likely to be effective unless it is performed in the early stages of the disease. The operations that are performed are *lobectomy* (removal of a lobe of a lung) or *pneumonectomy* (removal of a portion of the lung tissue), depending upon the size of the tumor and its location in the lung. Radiation therapy sometimes helps to arrest the spread of the disease temporarily and to make the patient more comfortable. Chemotherapy may also be helpful. The mortality rate from lung cancer is high. Metastasis to the other lung or to the esophagus may have occurred by the time the disease is discovered. The patient slowly wastes away, constantly beset by a cough, pain and trouble in breathing.

The final days for a patient with terminal lung cancer are most difficult for the patient's family, as he is in such evident physical distress. The nurse is most helpful who gives compassionate attention to the patient's comfort and shows the utmost regard for the feelings of his family by relieving their minds of the small worries. She should explain any new procedure that has been introduced and show concern for their comfort by suggesting rest or a cup of coffee in the coffee shop.

* Smoking and Health, U.S. Department of Health, Education and Welfare.

TUBERCULOSIS

In the early 1950s, people were rejoicing about the discovery of isoniazid, a drug that promised an end to tuberculosis. However, tuberculosis is still the most common infectious disease in this country. Large cities are reporting an increase in the number of cases; in some instances, this increase is quite alarming. This may be the result of a "letting up" on the war against tuberculosis. Public health officials tell us that we know how to control this disease if we will only use our knowledge. Also, we must renew our efforts to find and treat every case. An official of the National Tuberculosis Association attributes the recent rise in the number of cases to a general relaxation of control measures by federal, state and local governments and to reductions in funds formerly appropriated for tuberculosis control.

Who Gets Tuberculosis? Although the death rate from tuberculosis has gone down dramatically in the last 50 years (in 1900 it was the first cause of death, today it is 13th), it is still the cause of much disability in this country. In many of the underdeveloped countries it is a major health problem. It is more common among poor people and is prevalent among Negroes and Indians. Crowded and unsanitary living conditions and poor nutrition account for the high tuberculosis rate in the slums of large cities. Some occupations, such as mining and stonecutting, expose workers to silica dust, which makes them more liable to tuberculosis infection. Children, young people and the elderly are particularly susceptible. The illness and death rates vary across the country—they are highest in the Southwest and in the East Central States.

What Causes Tuberculosis? Tuberculosis, also known by the abbreviated form of TB, is caused by the tubercle bacillus which was discovered by Robert Koch in 1882, who later learned how to prepare tuberculin. In this country, Edward Trudeau, a physician who had TB when it was considered to be a hopeless disease, went to the Adirondacks for a rest and mountain air. He improved so much that he later established a sanatorium at Saranac Lake which became famous for its fresh air treatment for tuberculosis victims. About 10 years after this development, Roentgen brought x-rays into use and added a valuable tool for locating tuberculous lesions in the lungs. The National Tuberculosis Association was organized and centered its interest on the study of tuberculosis and its treatment. The sale of its Christmas Seals helped to finance a program of information about tuberculosis and methods for its control.

THE TUBERCLE BACILLUS. The *tubercle bacillus* is enclosed in a waxy coating, making it difficult to destroy. Many people have tubercle bacilli in their bodies but do not have active tuberculosis. The disease develops only if the body's resistance is lowered by poor nutrition or lack of rest, when the organisms multiply and become active. It is possible to arrest the disease to the point where it is not infectious and remains inactive. There are several types of the tubercle bacillus; the 2 types we are most concerned with are the *human,* and the *bovine* which affects cattle and can be transmitted to people. Bovine tuberculosis is well under control now through the testing of milk-producing cattle and the pasteurization of milk. The human type is spread mainly by contact with people who have tuberculosis in an active form.

The bacillus lives in dried particles of sputum but can be destroyed by a few hours of exposure to direct sunlight. Ordinary disinfectants have little effect on it, because they are unable to penetrate its waxy coating. Pasteurization for 30 minutes at 62° C. will kill it; boiling for 5 minutes will also destroy it. The organisms are found in the sputum, the urine and the feces and in milk from tuberculous cows.

How Tuberculosis Spreads. Tuberculosis spreads by inhaling infected droplets released into the air by a person who has an active infection. It also spreads by kissing an infected person, or by contact with contaminated utensils or equipment used by them. Isolation measures are used for a patient with an active infection. When the tubercle bacilli are no longer present in the sputum, the urine or the feces, isolation technic is unnecessary.

Where Tuberculosis Attacks. The tubercle bacillus most frequently attacks the lungs, but sometimes the blood carries the TB organism to other parts of the body, such as the kidneys or the bones. Organisms in the lungs may start a small infection which is not enough to produce any symptoms. It heals over, and the person never knows that this minor infection was there. However, it will show up in a chest roentgenogram as a small scar and is a sign that at some time there were active tuberculosis organisms in the body.

Detecting Tuberculosis

Tuberculin Tests. Tuberculin tests will show whether or not TB organisms have ever been active in the body. A *positive* reaction to the test does not mean that a person *has* tuberculosis—it means that at sometime he *had* a tuberculosis infection.

MANTOUX TEST. A minute amount of tuberculin (PPD) is injected into the skin of the forearm. If the person has ever had any tuberculosis infection, the area around the point of injection becomes reddened and hard. Everyone having a tuberculin test in a health examination needs to have this test explained, especially if the reaction is positive, or he may think that he has active tuberculosis. A positive reaction should be followed by a chest roentgenogram to be sure that this was an old infection and to determine its extent.

PATCH TEST (VOLLMER). A patch containing tuberculin is placed on the skin. The patch is removed in 48 hours; if the skin is reddened the test is positive. A similar test is the *scratch test* (Von Pirquet), in which the surface of the skin is scratched, and tuberculin is applied to the spot.

The Chest Roentgenogram. The x-ray picture of the chest is our most helpful aid in detecting tuberculosis. Used with or without a preliminary tuberculin test, programs for chest roentgenograms of community groups have been most successful in finding cases of tuberculosis, many of whom were people who were apparently well. A chest roentgenogram has one great advantage: people can receive treatment while the disease is in its early stages. Such a program also reveals the more advanced cases. In addition to the advantages of early treatment, by finding cases of tuberculosis we prevent people from spreading the disease. Authorities say that every person who has a positive tuberculin test should also have a chest roentgenogram. (Since we hear much about the dangers from radiation, some people are fearful of having an x-ray picture of any kind—these people need reassurance.)

Symptoms

The symptoms of tuberculosis appear so gradually that sometimes the disease has a good start before they are noticed. They are often mistaken for signs of ordinary fatigue, with some loss in weight and perhaps a cough so slight that the patient ignores it. Then other significant symptoms appear, such as a slight rise in temperature in the afternoon and the evening and night sweats. The patient begins to cough up thick and sometimes blood-streaked sputum and may cough up blood. As the disease advances, the patient becomes weaker and emaciated and may have chest pains, causing difficulty in breathing.

If a Tuberculosis Infection Becomes Overly Active. If the body resistance is low and a person is exposed to repeated contacts with tuberculosis, the spot of infection grows larger and breaks down into cheesy material. Later, this may slough away and leave a cavity in the lung, or it may enter a bronchus and cause tuberculous bronchopneumonia. Sometimes the bloodstream carries this material to other parts of the body to start up many small infections, a phenomenon called *miliary tuberculosis.*

Treatment

Chemotherapy now makes tuberculosis inactive if it is detected early and the patient follows directions for his treatment. Some people refuse to believe that they have the disease and disregard such orders. Since many tuberculous patients come from poor living conditions, the treatment begins with providing better ones. A patient may be financially unable to improve his living conditions or health habits. He may not be able to afford the proper food, and in many cases, he has not learned proper health practices. The various states have established institutions for the free care of tuberculous patients who cannot afford to pay for this care.

Education in new aspects of self-care is of very little use to the patient who cannot practice them. Also, it is easier to teach good health habits in a place where they are routine for everyone.

It is no longer considered necessary to send tuberculosis patients to the mountains or to hot climates. It is almost imperative that a patient with tuberculosis in the advanced stages be in a hospital because of the care he needs and the danger of infecting others. Convalescent patients can be cared for at home where they are usually happier and more contented during the long convalescence. Home care is never wise if there are children in the family, because children are very susceptible to the disease; sometimes it is impossible to give the patient a room of his own at home or to carry out his routine for rest.

Rest. Rest is still the most important "first" in treating tuberculosis. Effective as drugs are, they cannot do the job without the patient having his rest. He may need complete bed rest, or he may be allowed bathroom privileges and may sit up for prescribed lengths of time every day. Complete bed rest which lasts for weeks is not considered as necessary for many patients as it once was. Patients do well if they are allowed to increase their activity as they improve with treatment. However, a definite amount of rest is still important, because the lungs are less active when the patient is resting and so have a chance to heal. Inactivity is especially hard to tolerate if the patient always has been active in his work and recreation; the patient who likes to read is better adapted. Some patients cannot rest because they are worried and tense, and rest periods do them no good. The solution to this problem is to attempt to discover why they are worried and try to correct the situation if it is possible.

Most young people are naturally active when they are well and rebel at having to rest when they begin to feel so much better and consider themselves cured.

Chemotherapy. Drugs have done miraculous things for tuberculosis patients. They speed recovery and help to arrest the disease in the more advanced stages. Drugs do not *cure* tuberculosis—they do slow the growth of tubercle bacilli and give the body a chance to build up resistance. They have 2 drawbacks—some of them have toxic effects, and the continued use of a combination of drugs may make the tubercle bacillus resistant to them.

Streptomycin was the first drug to be used effectively in the treatment of tuberculosis. It has some unpleasant side-effects, such as nausea and vomiting, fever, dizziness, deafness and sometimes a rash.

Isoniazid (*INH*) has fewer toxic effects, although it may cause voiding difficulty and constipation and sometimes neuritis and muscle twitching. Isoniazid and streptomycin are the two main drugs used in treating tuberculosis.

Para-aminosalicylic acid (*PAS*) is often combined with one of the above drugs to make them more effective and less likely to build up the organism's resistance to them. A number of other drugs occasionally used are Viomycin Sulfate, tetracycline and kanamycin sulfate.

These drugs must be taken for a long period of time without interruption in order to produce results, so long, in fact, that the patient may begin to wonder if they are necessary. Explaining that his body resistance was well below normal to start with gives him a reason that he can understand for the treatment.

Hemorrhage. *Hemorrhage* may appear as a complication of tuberculosis, especially in the advanced stages. The signs are streaks of blood in the sputum, but a massive hemorrhage may happen suddenly. It is not likely to cause immediate death, but a severe hemorrhage may speed up the advance of the disease and cause anemia. The patient must be kept quiet; usually, a mild sedative is given, and he is disturbed as little as possible for routine personal care. Transfusions or other fluids are given to replace the blood loss.

Surgical Treatment. Surgery is sometimes needed in advanced tuberculosis or if medical treatment is not effective. This may be an operation to remove part of the affected lung (partial pneumonectomy). Another procedure to collapse and rest the lung is *pneumothorax,* which involves introducing a measured amount of air between the layers of the pleura. Sometimes some of the ribs on the affected side are removed by *thoracoplasty,* an operation to collapse the diseased part of the lung permanently.

Tuberculosis of Bones and Joints. The bloodstream may carry tubercule bacilli to the bones and the joints. This is more common in children, where it affects the spine (Pott's disease), the hips and the knees. In the spine, the vertebrae collapse, which causes a pronounced spinal curvature (*kyphosis*) or humpback. These patients have the same treatment as does any tuberculosis patient, with the addition of devices to prevent motion in the joints, such as casts or traction. Sometimes surgery is done to immobilize the joints.

Tuberculosis in Other Organs. Infection may spread to the fallopian tubes, the ovaries and the uterus. It may be necessary to remove the diseased organ surgically. Infection may also appear in the gastrointestinal tract, the kidneys or the meninges.

Skin. Tuberculous lesions (lupus vulgaris) may appear on the skin as yellowish or red spots, most commonly on the face.

Diet and Environment. The diet is planned to maintain the patient's normal weight (Chap. 23). It is no longer considered essential for the patient to gain weight beyond a normal level. He does not burn calories rapidly unless the disease is acute and he has fever. It is important to provide him with plenty of protein and with vitamin A and vitamin C, since the use of these vitamins is interfered with in tuberculosis. *Cold* air is not necessary but *fresh* air is. Pleasant surroundings help the patient's morale; since he is likely to be in the same environment for a long period of time, everything that makes him comfortable and contented will help to speed his recovery. If he can be at home, with his own things around him, so much the better.

Nursing Care

The nursing care of the tuberculosis patient is centered on building up his resistance, preventing the spread of the infection to others and helping him to adjust to his treatment. Therefore, it will include:

Attention to his diet, to make sure that he is eating enough of the foods he needs

Making him comfortable before his rest periods, and watching to see that he does not overexert himself or stay up too long if his "up" periods are limited

Seeing that his medications are given on time if you are responsible for their administration

Carrying out isolation technic if the infection is

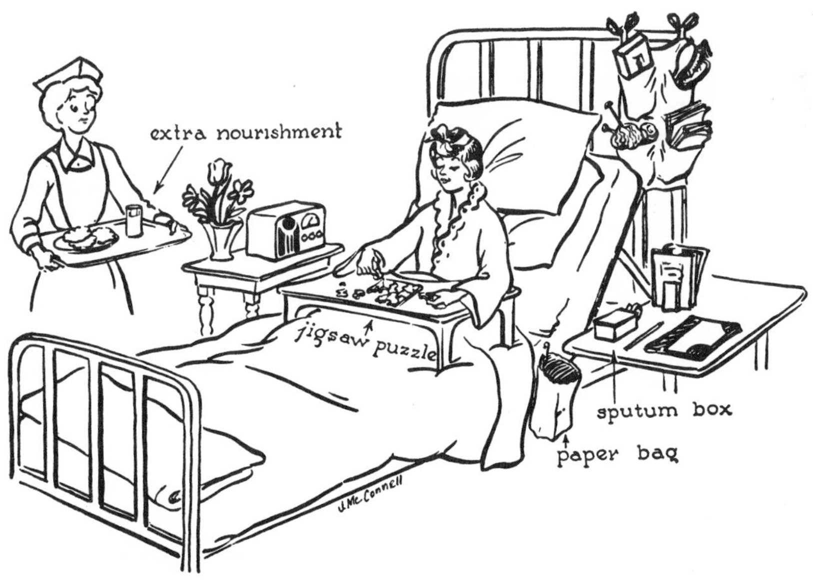

Fig. 164. Convalescent tuberculosis patient.

active. Keep the sputum cup covered and dispose of the sputum safely according to the method used in any individual institution. (It is always safe to wrap it securely and burn it.)

Teaching the patient to keep the sputum cup covered and to wash his hands frequently

Teaching the patient to cover his mouth with a disposable tissue when he coughs. If the patient is too ill to do this, wear a face mask yourself. Change the mask frequently—if it becomes moist it can give organisms a home instead of keeping them away. A mask should not be left dangling around a nurse's neck but should be discarded when it is not in use.

What Do You Say? A nurse can make many small adjustments to suit the needs and the temperament of an individual patient. Some patients are impatient of restraints; others need gentle urging to begin to do things for themselves. Some patients are optimistic and hopeful, but others are easily discouraged and fearful. Encourage good health habits: "You've been so good about eating and resting the doctor says you can begin staying up longer." Comment on signs of improvement: "I hear you got along just fine without your sleeping pill last night," or "Your weight is almost back to normal today." Try different ways of making him comfortable: "Let's try tucking this pillow in against your back." Young people find it more difficult to adjust to a long, quiet convalescence. They want to be active. If you have had children yourself you probably have a better idea of what to say to them. You can try to find out what their interests are and suggest ways to maintain them. If Joe can't play ball he can watch the game on television. He can try to keep up with his school work by studying a bit every day—this goes for Joan, too. If Joan is an average adolescent, she probably would enjoy keeping up on the latest in teen fashions and topics. A little personal concern shown by a nurse can do wonders to break up an otherwise boring day for a patient.

Rehabilitation

Rehabilitation begins as soon as the disease is discovered. The first step to be taken by the patient is accepting the fact that he has tuberculosis, and that he can recover from it if he follows orders. If he refuses to do this (and some patients do) he is throwing away his chances for a satisfactory life, as well as shortening his life expectancy. He is also spreading TB to unsuspecting people. A tuberculosis patient must also face the fact that he may not be able to return to his former job or may be able to work only part-time. He must avoid dust hazards and heavy physical labor, and he must have a certain amount of rest.

It is possible to arrest TB, and many such patients are living and working satisfactorily. The Altro Workshops in New York City were started to give employment to patients recovering from a tuberculosis infection, in work that is safe and suitable. Altro makes uniforms and the employees spend 8 hours in the shop every working day, even though some of them may only be able to work for part of that time. It is considered helpful for their recovery to spend the time away from home and to be with other people.

One Last Word

Contrary to what you may have heard, tuberculosis is by no means obsolete. It is dangerous to think that we can relax our efforts to detect and treat tuberculosis and to educate the public about this disease. As a citizen, each one of us has a responsibility for supporting any program to protect the health of all citizens in the community—especially the health of groups which are known to be susceptible to tuberculosis, such as children and young people and the elderly.

40

THE PATIENT WITH A DISORDER OF THE URINARY SYSTEM

A review of the urinary system will remind you that it is composed of the *kidneys*, which secrete urine; the *ureters*, that carry urine from the kidneys to the bladder; the *bladder*, which is the urine reservoir; the *urethra*, which is the outlet tube from the bladder through which urine is voided. This is the system of the body that removes from the blood the waste products which are left after the body burns food and eliminates them in the urine. The kidneys process the blood, collect the wastes and pass them on through the ureters into the bladder. The bladder outlet into the urethra is closed tightly until about 200 to 250 cc. has collected, at which time the nervous system signals that the bladder needs emptying. Interference with the operation of this system causes disease and illness.

Urinalysis

Urinalysis gives much information about the condition of the kidneys and how well they are working. It tells whether disease is interfering with the function of the different parts of the kidneys (*renal tubules, nephrons, glomeruli*); it shows whether disease organisms are at work in the kidney and whether food materials which should go to the body cells are escaping into the urine. The methods of collecting urine specimens are discussed in Chapter 32.

Tests

Urea Clearance Test. This test shows how efficiently the nephrons are filtering urea from the blood. A fasting blood specimen is taken, and the patient voids. He drinks several glasses of water, and after 1 hour he voids again. A comparison of the amount of urea in each specimen shows whether or not the kidneys are removing urea from the blood at a normal speed.

Blood Chemistry. This test is an analysis of a specimen of blood to find out how efficiently the nephrons in the kidney are removing the waste products BUN (blood urea nitrogen) or NPN (nonprotein nitrogen) from the blood. If the amounts found in the blood are higher than normal, they indicate kidney damage or disease. The normal amount for BUN is 12 to 25 mg. per 100 cc. of blood, and for NPN it is 15 to 35 mg. per 100 cc. of blood.

Phenolsulfonphthalein Test (PSP). When this red dye is injected into a vein it is excreted by the kidneys. For the test, the patient drinks a measured amount of water; in 20 minutes he voids, and the urine is discarded. The doctor injects the dye (1 cc.), and 15 minutes later the patient is asked to void, and again in 30 minutes, in 1 hour and in 2 hours. The entire specimen is saved each time and labeled with the time it was voided: the first specimen is also labeled with the time that the dye was given. The specimens are sent to the laboratory to be analyzed. The percentage of dye in each indicates how normally the kidneys are performing. The dye will come through more slowly in kidney disease.

It is obvious that when a patient is having

one of these tests, the test would be ruined by discarding a specimen of urine or by giving a patient a drink of water at the wrong time.

Intravenous Pyelogram. This is a series of x-ray pictures taken after a radiopaque dye has been given intravenously; they show the outlines of the kidneys, the ureters and the bladder. The patient has nothing by mouth for 12 hours before the test, but he is given a cathartic the night before and an enema the morning of the test. When the test is over, the patient takes fluids to compensate for the fluid that he was not allowed to have before the test was given.

Cystogram. A *cystogram* is an x-ray picture of the bladder and the urethra, made by injecting a dye directly into the bladder through a catheter. It will show the outline of the bladder. A picture can be taken to show the outline of the urethra while the patient is voiding.

Cystoscopy. A *cystoscopic examination* is a viewing of the inside of the bladder through a tubular instrument, the *cystoscope*, which has a mirror and an electric light on the end of it. The cystoscope is passed into the bladder through the urethra. This examination will detect bladder inflammation or a tumor in the bladder which may be the cause of the appearance of blood in the urine. The openings of the ureters into the bladder are also visible; fine opaque wax catheters can be threaded into these openings to collect separate specimens of urine from each kidney, which helps to determine which kidney is diseased. The patient should have at least 400 cc. of water before the examination, and an enema if roentgenograms are to be taken. Usually he also has a sedative, since the procedure is uncomfortable and may be painful. Sometimes a local or general anesthetic is necessary.

The urine specimens are examined in the laboratory. Voiding may be uncomfortable for a day or two after the examination—sometimes sitz baths are ordered for comfort. The urine has a reddish tinge at first; if this lasts more than 24 hours or increases, it should be reported. Chills and fever are signs of infection that should also be reported. The patient is encouraged to drink fluids.

Urinary Obstructions

Obstructions in the urinary system may be caused by a stone, a growth, a spasm of the ureter or a kink in the ureter. An enlarged prostate gland in older men may interfere with the passage of urine. Urinary obstructions can damage the kidneys eventually. They may become enlarged with dammed-up urine (hydronephrosis), and waste products accumulate in the blood, causing uremia. An obstruction in the urethra causes an accumulation of urine in the bladder, where it becomes stagnant and provides a favorable place for infection to develop. Bacteria also reach the urethra through the bloodstream and from the outside. The first step in treating urinary obstructions is to establish urine drainage and later to remove the cause of the obstruction.

Stones. The urine is full of salts which, if they do not dissolve, form stones. Stones form primarily in the kidneys and descend through the urinary passages. No one knows exactly why stones form, although some authorities believe that infection helps to cause them. Sometimes people who have a tendency to form stones are allowed only a limited amount of milk, since milk is high in the mineral calcium. Patients with a long-term illness that keeps them in bed in a more-or-less fixed position, for example paraplegics, seem to have a tendency to develop stones. Bed exercises and plenty of fluids help to prevent this condition, provided, of course, that these are allowed.

Symptoms. The signs of stones are *blood* or *pus* in the urine from irritation or infection; *retention* of urine, if the bladder opening into the urethra is blocked; *pain* in the region of the obstruction; and *colic*, which is an excruciating pain that comes in waves as the ureter tries to force an obstructing stone to move on. This pain is violent and unbearable—only a strong sedative will relieve it. If the stone is very small, the spasm may move it along, and the patient passes it. Urine containing gravel or small stones should be saved for laboratory examination. If colicky attacks recur, surgery is usually necessary to remove the obstruction.

Urethral Strictures. Fibrous bands may form anywhere along the urethra to narrow it and interfere with the passage of urine. Stagnant urine in the bladder leads to infection. With a urethral stricture, the patient has difficulty in voiding. He has a desire to void frequently, but voiding is accompanied by an intense burning sensation. A urethral stricture can be stretched by inserting metal instruments (*sounds*) of graduated sizes into the urethra, beginning with the largest size that will go past the stricture and gradually increasing to larger ones. Strictures have a tendency to tighten up again; the patient will have to return to the hospital periodically to have this *dilatation* process repeated. Sometimes surgery is necessary to cut the constricting bands.

Pyelonephritis

Pyelonephritis, or inflammation of the kidney, is the most common form of kidney disease. It is usually caused by infection by organisms from somewhere in the body. These organisms reach the kidney through the bloodstream, causing inflammation, edema and sometimes many small abscesses. Early treatment of acute pyelonephritis is important to prevent permanent kidney damage.

Symptoms. The patient is very ill, with pain, pus in the urine, chills and fever, nausea and vomiting. If the bladder also is infected, he will have a desire to urinate frequently, although burning will accompany voiding.

Treatment and Nursing Care. Bed rest, plenty of fluids, attention to mouth and skin care, nourishment and change of position are important. Antibiotics are given for the infection. Every effort is made to prevent this condition from becoming chronic, by eliminating the infection and building up good health habits.

Chronic pyelonephritis may develop if the infection recurs or an obstruction interferes with the passage of urine. The kidney becomes permanently damaged, and nothing will replace kidney tissues. The patient may develop hypertension or uremia. The treatment consists of continued efforts to prevent more damage. Sometimes, if hypertension develops, the kidney may be removed by surgery, provided that the other kidney is functioning normally.

Cystitis

Cystitis is inflammation of the urinary bladder. Normally, the inside of the bladder is sterile, but bacteria may enter it from infected kidneys and lymphatics, and also from the urethra. One reason for using sterile technic in catheterization is to prevent the introduction of bacteria into the bladder. Cystitis is usually the result of infection somewhere else in the urinary tract or in the reproductive system. Diabetes that is not well controlled may make a person more susceptible to bladder infection.

Symptoms and Treatment. The patient with cystitis has a desire to urinate frequently, although the bladder does not need emptying, and very small amounts are voided each time. Urination is accompanied by a painful, burning sensation; sometimes there is blood in the urine. Antibiotics are given, with forced fluids, and sometimes a drug (potassium citrate or sodium bicarbonate) to alkalize the urine if it is markedly acid. Warm sitz baths help to make the patient more comfortable. Cystitis is common when the prostate is enlarged.

Nephritis (Bright's Disease)

Nephritis is a disease in which the kidneys are damaged and partly destroyed by inflammation in the *glomeruli.* Often the signs of *acute* nephritis appear about 2 or 3 weeks after an upper respiratory infection, or after scarlet fever or chicken pox. The patient himself may not notice the symptoms at first—it may be his family that senses something is wrong as they become aware of his pale, puffy face and swollen tissues. He is getting up many times in the night to void, his head aches, and he is noticeably irritable. Without treatment, uremia and congestive heart failure may be the next and fatal development.

Treatment. No single drug or special treatment will cure acute nephritis. The patient must stay in bed, sometimes for several weeks. He is given plenty of fluids; and in cases of edema and congestive heart failure, salt is restricted. He receives antibiotics to counteract any infection he may have. With treatment, almost all patients recover from acute nephritis;

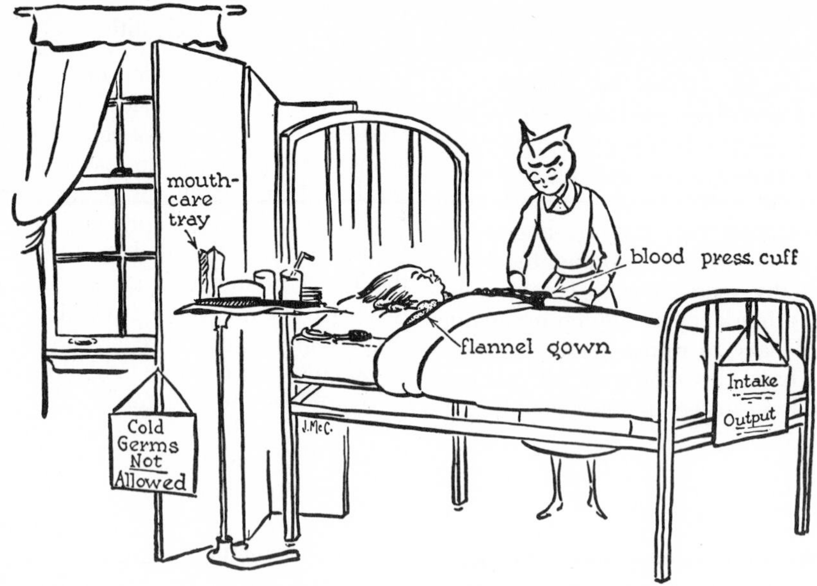

FIG. 165. Patient with nephritis.

they are not considered as being well until the urine has been free of albumin and red blood cells for 6 months.

Chronic Nephritis

Chronic nephritis is another story—it damages the kidney permanently by destroying nephrons and interfering with kidney functions. The symptoms are much the same as in acute nephritis, with marked edema all over the body. The disease flares up at intervals, but the patient usually feels very well between attacks. However, if uremia develops, the patient may die very quickly.

Complications and Treatment. Chronic nephritis can have serious complications—pulmonary edema, increased blood pressure, cerebral hemorrhage and congestive heart failure. In the advanced stages of the disease, vision may become blurred, followed by blindness. Nosebleeds and gastrointestinal bleeding are not unusual in the terminally ill patient. However, a patient may live for years if he protects his health and builds up his resistance to infection. He cannot afford to risk catching cold, for it may lead to uremia. When signs of a flare-up of the disease appear, he must go to bed, lower his salt intake and regulate the amount of protein in his diet. He must avoid exposure to infection of any kind. He will have transfusions if he needs them for anemia, and sedatives if he needs them for headache and insomnia. With this treatment, the symptoms usually subside in about 3 weeks, and the patient gradually returns to his normal routines.

Nephrosis

Nephrosis is a destructive process that goes on in the renal tubules and usually occurs only in children. It interferes wtih the blood flow to the kidneys and may lead to the supression (stoppage) of urine and uremia. The treatment is centered on keeping the patient alive until the kidneys repair themselves and function normally again. The patient is put on a low-sodium diet, diuretics are given for edema, and ACTH or adrenocortical steroids may also be given. His weight is watched to see if he is retaining fluid in his tissues. If there is no improvement in kidney function, and if death from uremia is imminent, *dialysis* (see p. 527) may be used in the hope that complete rest for the kidneys will have a healing effect and enable them to function again.

The Artificial Kidney (Dialysis). The artificial kidney is an apparatus which takes over the work of the kidney temporarily when (1) a damaged kidney is not filtering wastes from the blood and excreting them in the urine and when (2) the kidneys cease all operations as a result of acute kidney disease, shock or lethal doses of poison. This procedure is used only as a last resort, when everything else has failed to restore kidney function. However, this apparatus is being perfected and will be put into greater use in the future.

Uremia

Uremia is failure of the kidneys to remove wastes from the blood and the body cells and to excrete them in the urine. This may be the result of kidney disease or of urinary tract disturbances, or of an injury that decreases the blood supply of the kidneys.

Symptoms. Uremia may develop suddenly, but it usually comes on so gradually that the patient is not aware of it. He may pay little attention to his mild headaches, occasional intestinal upsets and a tired feeling. His family is more likely to be aware of his growing irritability than he is.

Gradually, these symptoms become more pronounced—the headaches are more persistent, he feels nauseated and vomits, and he is thirsty and air-hungry. These are signs of *acidosis*, which means there is an accumulation of waste products in the body. Although he may be restless, the patient is more likely to become comatose and may have convulsions. If he does not respond to treatment, inevitably the signs of heart failure will appear.

Treatment and Nursing Care. Everything is done to treat the primary cause of uremia and to treat the symptoms as they appear. Sedatives are given for restlessness; transfusions for anemia; digitalis for heart difficulty; fluids are restricted because the kidneys are not excreting urine; alkaline solutions are given for acidosis; the patient is put on a diet high in fat and carbohydrates and low in protein and potassium. If the condition which is causing uremia cannot be improved, the patient will die a lingering death.

Tumors

Tumors of the Kidney. Tumors of the kidney are almost always malignant, and frequently they are the result of metastasis from a cancerous growth somewhere else in the body. The tumor is usually well developed before signs of it appear. The first sign may be blood in the urine. Other symptoms are fever, loss of weight and malaise; pain may appear later. Surgical removal of the kidney (nephrectomy) may be done if the other kidney is healthy.

Tumors of the Bladder. Tumors may be imbedded in the bladder wall or may be like small warts on the inside surface. The tumors may or may not be malignant. Superficial tumors can be removed by an electric cautery (resectoscope) which can be inserted into the bladder through the urethra. Patients with this type of tumor return at 6-month intervals for a check-up by cystoscopic examination to see if the tumor has recurred or if new ones have developed. Larger tumors are removed through an incision made in the bladder.

Kidney Transplants

Organ transplants are a comparatively new development that is causing something of a sensation in the medical world. In this new field of surgery, doctors take an organ, such as a *kidney*, from a well human being and transplant it to the body of another to replace a diseased organ. The chief difficulty with transplants is that the body does not like foreign materials, and its natural response is to reject them. This seems to be less of a problem if the transplant is from the body of an identical twin.

Medical authorities pioneering in this field make it plain that a kidney transplant should be attempted only when experts think that it has a chance to succeed and when everything else has been tried to save the dying patient. Even then, they emphasize that this is not a procedure for general surgeons but should be attempted only by doctors who have had special training and study. Enough kidney transplants have been successful to encourage medical scientists to go on with research in this kind of surgery.

The Patient With Urinary Incontinence

Two muscles, called the *sphincter muscles*, control the voiding of urine. The *internal* sphincter controls the opening of the bladder into the urethra; the *external* sphincter controls the opening at the outer end of the urethra. When sufficient urine collects in the bladder, it stimulates nerve endings which cause a desire to void. An unconscious or a senile patient does not feel this stimulation, and the sphincters relax involuntarily. Disturbances or damage to the urinary system or interference with the spinal nerves deprive the sphincters of their control over voiding. For example, a paraplegic who has lost sensation in the lower part of his body has no control over voiding.

Establishing a Routine. Often it is possible to control incontinence by establishing a voiding routine. This project will take patience and some experimenting, but it can be successful. Start by keeping a chart, noting when the patient's bladder empties—it may follow a pattern, such as every 3 hours, every 2 hours or at other more or less regular intervals. See that he is given the bedpan or goes to the bathroom just before these times. This sets up a routine for emptying his bladder and keeps him dry. If he wants to go for a ride and would like to increase an interval between voidings, fluids can be limited at that time. The amount must be compensated for at other times because fluids might be an important part of his treatment.

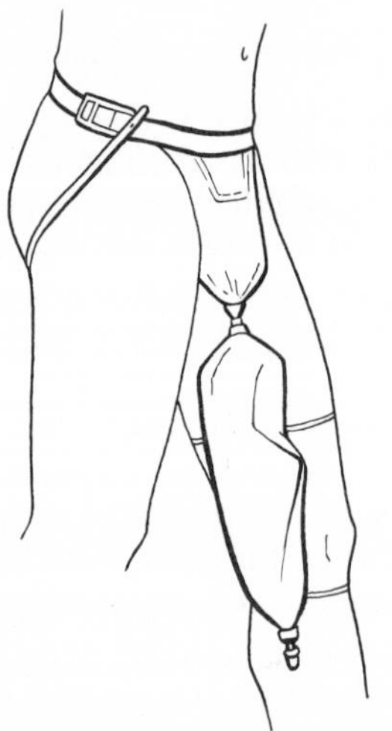

Fig. 166. A rubber leg urinal placed over the penis and held in place with a belt. (Smith, D. W., and Gips, C. D.: Care of the Adult Patient, p. 1188, Philadelphia, Lippincott, 1963)

Appliances. Appliances for collecting urine are available for the male patient. Such an appliance consists of a rubber bag that slips over the penis and is attached to a belt. The patient wears the appliance under his clothes. The bag has an outlet at the lower end which can be opened to empty it.

The problem of urinary incontinence is greater for a woman, since no similar appliance is available for collecting urine for a female. She can wear a perineal pad; perhaps a better solution is the plastic protective pants, with absorbent material and a liner inside. The liner is made of nonabsorbent nylon and is placed next to the skin; it dries very rapidly after the urine passes through it, so it protects the skin and prevents irritation. In any case, it is important to wash the buttocks and the genitals frequently with soap and water and to dry them well. An antiseptic such as *Diaprene* (ointment or liquid) may be applied to the skin to prevent irritation. Cleanliness and prompt attention to removing soiled pads help to eliminate urine odor. Any appliance or protective device should be washed thoroughly inside and out with soap and water at least once a day.

When the Patient Goes Home. Many patients go home from the hospital with the problem of incontinence. This then becomes a family problem as well, since they may dread the odors and the wet pads and the interminable laundry work that they fear they must cope with. The nurse has an opportunity to give the family some practical help in dealing with this problem. She can show them how to keep the patient dry without changing the entire bed every time, by using absorbent pads covered by a liner next to the patient. The pads can be changed easily, and the liner helps to prevent

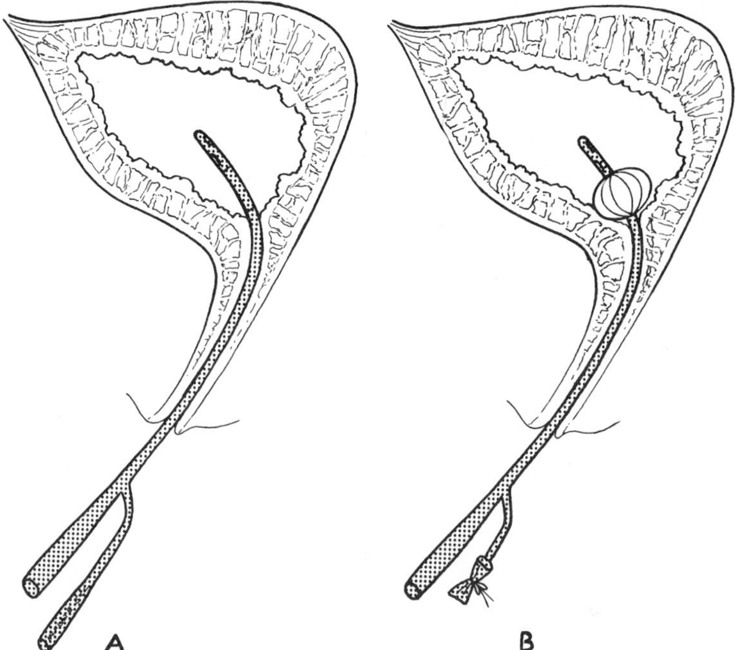

FIG. 167. Foley catheter. (A) The catheter is inserted into the bladder. (B) The inflation of the bag prevents the catheter from leaving the bladder. The inner tube that leads to the balloon is tied. (Smith, D. W., and Gips, C. D.: Care of the Adult Patient, p. 1181, Philadelphia, Lippincott, 1963)

irritation. If the patient has established a routine for voiding, she can be sure that they understand how important it is to keep to that routine. She should emphasize the importance of fluids, diet and cleanliness.

The Patient With a Catheter. After surgery the patient usually has a catheter inserted for urine drainage. The Foley catheter is frequently used, although there are several catheters of this type. The Foley catheter has a collapsed bag attached, which can be inflated like a small balloon after the catheter is inserted. This holds the catheter in place (Fig. 167). A length of tubing is connected to the catheter, and the urine drains into a bottle at the patient's bedside. If a catheter comes out, the nurse inserts a clean one. Usually an in-dwelling catheter is changed every week if it is needed for some time.

The Problems of Urologic Patients

There are many urologic diseases and conditions, but most of these patients have many of the same problems. The most common ones are: edema, a dry, itchy skin, headache, nausea and vomiting, infection, frequent urination with pain and burning, urine drainage—especially after surgery—boredom with enforced bed rest and inactivity, and irritability.

The *treatment* and the *nursing care* of urologic patients can be expected to include: diuretics and antibiotics, attention to skin and mouth care, measured intake and output of fluids and observation of urine, a modified diet, such as low-sodium or high-fat and carbohydrate, bed exercises for the bed patient. A male patient may be embarrassed by having a woman carry out some of the procedures that are necessary. If a male nurse is available, so much the better. However, a male patient should never be exposed to the risk of incompetent treatment at the hands of an inexperienced orderly just because he (the patient) is a man. To a nurse, the patient's welfare comes first. This helps her to carry out any procedure as calmly and matter-of-factly as if she were giving the patient a drink of water.

41

THE PATIENT WITH A DISORDER OF THE REPRODUCTIVE SYSTEM

THE FEMALE PATIENT

A review of the reproductive system reminds us that the female reproductive organs are the *ovaries*, the *fallopian tubes*, the *uterus*, the *vagina*, the *external genitals* and the *breasts*. Diseases and disorders of this system are often allied with urinary system difficulties. The branch of medicine that is concerned with genitourinary conditions is *gynecology*. The specialist in this field is the *gynecologist*. These disorders usually occur during adult life, but occasionally during early adolescence menstrual difficulties require the attention of a gynecologist.

Disturbances of Menstruation

The most common menstrual disorders are amenorrhea, menorrhagia, metrorrhagia, dysmenorrhea and premenstrual tension.

Amenorrhea is absence of or abnormal stopping of menses. If the menses have not been established by the 15th year, treatment is necessary to ensure normal sex development. The difficulty may be a hormonal problem, but in any case it should have the careful and wise attention of a specialist. Amenorrhea may be due also to nutritional or emotional causes or to malformations of the female organs. The menses are normally absent in pregnancy and after menopause.

Menorrhagia is bleeding in excess amount and duration at the menstrual time. If this irregularity occurs in the young girl it may adjust itself but should be observed. If it occurs during the menopause (see p. 188 for a review of this normal process), it may be significant as an indication of cancer. For excessive bleeding which is unexplained by organic causes, endocrine therapy may be helpful. Curettage, which is scraping out the lining of the uterus, may be effective. Dilatation (stretching the cervical opening) and curettage (sometimes termed a "D & C") may be performed on the young unmarried girl as a therapeutic treatment (see p. 531).

Metrorrhagia is bleeding between the menstrual periods. This is abnormal and should have the attention of a physician, since it may indicate cancer, retained placental tissue in the postpartum patient, etc.

Dysmenorrhea is painful menstruation. Normal menstruation should not be a painful process. However, many times, through lack of information, a young girl has been led to expect menstruation to be difficult and painful, an affliction imposed upon her that she has to bear. Consequently, the slight cramps and backaches which may normally accompany the menses may be magnified consciously or otherwise to create a painful situation. Re-education and proper mental hygiene should eliminate these misconceptions. Increased functional causes of menstrual pain may stem from constipation, insufficient exercise, poor posture and fatigue and can be remedied easily. If the pain is intense and consistent, a medical examination is indicated, followed by the appropriate treatment for any abnormal organic conditions which exist.

Premenstrual tension is associated with symptoms common to many women. Complaints of abdominal distention, headache, generalized edema and occasional vomiting are typical, as are irritability and moodiness or depression. Recent information relates these symptoms to a disturbance of salt balance. Some relief has been brought about by a salt-free diet for a week or so during the premenstrual cycle and by medications which increase the excretion of sodium ions. Menstrual headache in some instances is very severe and has been treated with ergot preparations.

Vulvitis

Inflammation of the vulva may be the result of improper cleansing or of irritating vaginal discharge; more often it is caused by a gonorrheal infection. Infection in this area usually involves the Bartholin glands and may result in an abscess. Pain during urination or defecation and swelling are usually associated with vulvitis or Bartholin gland infection. If treatment with antibiotics is not wholly effective, usually the gland is excised.

Gynecologic Testing

The Emotional Side. Women are likely to be emotionally upset by a gynecologic disorder for various reasons. Perhaps a woman may be afraid that it will interfere with having children; that it will disturb marital relations; or that it may mean cancer. Whatever the cause, a nurse should remember that a gynecologic disorder is likely to be emotionally disturbing, and she should listen to what the patient says for a clue to her feelings. Often the nurse can tell the doctor about a particular worry that only he can relieve. When the doctor discusses the situation with both husband and wife, it gives them an opportunity to ask questions about matters that they do not understand and prevents needless worries. The first consideration in the treatment of gynecologic conditions during the child-bearing years is to preserve the ability to have children, if this is possible without endangering the patient. For women past the child-bearing years, it is equally important to correct difficulties for the sake of the patient's health and comfort.

The Gynecologic Examination. Many women dread the ordeal of the gynecologic examination. They may worry about exposure or embarrassing questions and shrink from knowing what they fear will be "the worst." The patient will be relieved if the nurse assures her that she will be fully covered during the examination and that her nurse will be with her during the entire procedure (a nurse *always* is). The patient should be encouraged to tell the doctor everything about her difficulty—she should feel that nothing is too unimportant to mention. If she has a vaginal discharge, she may be distressed because she is not allowed to have a douche before the examination. Explain that the doctor will want to see the extent of the discharge and perhaps will want to have a smear of the discharge examined in the laboratory.

Test for Cancer (Papanicolaou Test). A malignant growth in the reproductive organs drops its cells into the uterine and vaginal secretions. By examining a smear from these secretions microscopically, it is possible to detect these cells before the actual symptoms of cancer appear. This examination is known as the *Papanicolaou test.* Through this early detection no time will be lost in starting treatment to prevent a malignant growth from advancing. *Cancer of the cervix* is one of the most common forms of cancer in women. If the test is positive, and the cervix looks suspicious, a biopsy of the suspected tissue can be done.

Dilatation of the Cervix and Curettage of the Uterus. In addition to serving as a therapeutic measure, dilatation of the cervix and curettage of the uterus are also done to find the cause of abnormal vaginal bleeding. The uterine scrapings are examined in the laboratory for evidence of malignant or nonmalignant growths. Sometimes a "D & C" is done just before the menstrual period in an effort to find the cause of sterility.

Nursing Care. The preoperative preparation is as for any patient about to receive general anesthesia, perhaps with the addition of a cleansing douche. Postoperatively, the patient usually makes an uneventful recovery. She will wear a perineal pad and require perineal care as long as a vaginal discharge persists. Any minor discomfort is usually relieved by aspirin. She is out of bed the next day and goes home in a day or two, unless she has lost much blood prior to the operation. Sometimes the vagina is packed with gauze at the time of the operation, which may make voiding difficult; but usually the pack is removed the next day.

Ectopic Pregnancy

An *ectopic* (extra-uterine) pregnancy occurs when a fertilized ovum does not reach the uterus but becomes implanted in the fallopian tube or, very rarely, in the abdominal cavity. The growing ovum distends the tube until eventually it bursts, rupturing many blood vessels. Usually the patient has all the signs of pregnancy, but the first indication of its being an ectopic pregnancy is a sudden, sharp pain in the abdomen, followed by hemorrhage and shock when the tube ruptures. Surgery is necessary at once to tie off the ruptured blood vessels and remove the ruptured tube (*salpingectomy*). The patient is treated for shock and is given blood transfusions to replace the blood loss. Nausea, vomiting and abdominal pain may be signs of peritonitis due to the bleeding into the abdominal cavity.

This may be an emotionally upsetting experience for the patient—she has lost her baby and may fear that she cannot have another, or she may feel that in some way it was her fault. She can be assured that there is no medical evidence whatsoever that a mother can do anything to cause an ectopic pregnancy. She also may be comforted to feel that she still has one tube left and therefore can become pregnant again. Certainly, this is not the time to tell her that the woman who has had one ectopic pregnancy is likely to have another, even though this happens to be true.

Vaginitis

Vaginitis is an inflammation of the vagina. Normally, the secretions in the vagina protect it from infection. However, two organisms often do cause vaginal infection—*Trichomonas vaginalis* and *Monilia albicans.* The outstanding symptom of vaginitis is a whitish vaginal discharge called *leukorrhea.* The discharge is odorous and profuse, making the perineum and the urethra burn and itch. It may be frothy or thick and whitish. The usual treatment consists of a vaginal jelly or a suppository, douches with vinegar, soda bicarbonate or tincture of green soap solutions, the application of a sulfonamide cream. Diabetics whose urine is not sugar-free are frequent victims of this infection. Sometimes the husband is also infected and needs treatment.

Vaginitis is hard to cure; early, persistent treatment is the only way to prevent the disease from becoming chronic. It can be extremely irritating; it persists for a long time (6 weeks or more), and even then the infection can return. The patient feels that she is never clean and that she must be offensive to others. Changing the pad frequently and administering perineal care when necessary will help to prevent odor and irritation; however, the patient grows very tired of this routine. The patient must have 3 negative vaginal smears before the doctor will pronounce her cured.

Cervicitis

Inflammation of the cervix, *cervicitis,* is caused by any one of a number of organisms, notably the *staphylococcus* or the *streptococcus.* Small lacerations in the cervix during childbirth make such infections more likely. Formerly, gonorrhea was a major cause of cervicitis and sometimes still is. Cancer also causes cervicitis. The main symptoms are leukorrhea and sometimes bleeding. Pain with sexual intercourse may be a symptom. Unless cervicitis is treated promptly, it may be difficult to cure. Periodic vaginal examinations help to discover cervicitis.

The chief treatment is douches and antibiotics. Sometimes the cervical opening is cauterized. After this treatment, a watery discharge appears which later becomes odorous; douches may be ordered for this condition. It takes about 6 to 8 weeks for the area to heal after cauterization.

Pelvic Inflammatory Disease (P.I.D.)

Infection of the pelvic organs causes inflammation of the ovaries (*oophoritis*) and of the fallopian tubes (*salpingitis*); if pus forms in the tubes, the condition is called *pyosalpinx*. Infection may enter through the vagina, the peritoneum, the lymphatics or the bloodstream. The *tubercle bacillus* often enters the pelvic organs through the bloodstream. Once the *gonococcus* was the chief cause of pelvic infection, but penicillin is now effective in killing that organism.

Symptoms and Treatment. A vile-smelling, infectious vaginal discharge is a common symptom of P.I.D. The patient may also complain of backache and pelvic pain, with fever, nausea and vomiting. Antibiotics are given, and the patient is usually placed in Fowler's position to encourage pelvic drainage. Sitz baths may be ordered to relieve the pain; douches may or may not be ordered. Precautions should be taken to wrap soiled pads well for safe disposal as soon as they are removed; always wash the hands thoroughly after handling the pads. If the infection is gonorrheal, the patient will be placed on isolation precautions, and the nurse will wear gloves when changing the pads and giving perineal care. If the discharge is profuse, the patient should have perineal care after removing the pad and after using the bed pan.

If P.I.D. is not treated, it may become a chronic condition and cause sterility. The husband is also examined, since he may be infected and need treatment. If he is not infected, sexual intercourse is forbidden as long as the wife has any trace of infection. Sometimes an abscess forms, and the surgeon institutes drainage through an incision in the abdomen. Dressings soiled with discharge from this wound should be handled with the same precautions as the perineal pads.

Ovarian Tumors

Ovarian tumors, or *cysts*, may form from fluid retained in the ovary. They usually do not cause any trouble. However, cysts may enlarge and press on other abdominal organs and cause pain if they rupture or twist. Cancer of the ovaries may spread dangerously, unknown to the patient, and enlarge enormously to cause pressure on the bladder and the liver. If cancer develops in the ovaries, the uterus, the tubes and the ovaries are removed surgically (*panhysterectomy*—hysterectomy referring to the removal of the uterus).

Benign Uterine Tumors. The *fibroid tumor* is the most common type of tumor of the uterus. These tumors are all sizes and usually grow slowly; many times the patient is not aware of the tumor at all. The usual symptom to appear is vaginal bleeding, with a feeling of heaviness and pressure in the pelvic region. This type of tumor is called a *myoma* and it may prevent or interfere with pregnancy. Such a tumor may also become so large that it presses on the urethra and the bowel, causing the retention of urine and constipation. The treatment depends somewhat on the patient's age—often a nonmalignant tumor can be removed from the uterus without removing the uterus itself. This is important for a woman during her childbearing years. If it is necessary to remove the uterus, a *hysterectomy* is performed. A nonmalignant tumor usually tends to shrink after the menopause. Bleeding after this time is seldom caused by a myoma.

Cancer of the Uterus

Cancer of the cervix, the neck of the uterus, is the second greatest cause of cancer in women (breast cancer is first). It would be impossible to emphasize too strongly the importance of the Papanicolaou test for women over 40 years of age, because it is possible to cure cancer of the cervix if it is discovered early, before it has a chance to spread. *Bleeding* is the first symptom of cancer of the cervix, but bleeding does not occur in the early stages when a positive Papanicolaou smear would indicate cancer. Bleeding usually appears first as spotting, then a watery discharge appears that turns to a darker, more bloody one, with an unpleasant odor. If the cancer is confined to the cervix and has not spread, a *hysterectomy* is the usual treatment. If this is impossible and the cancer is in the advanced stage, radium or x-ray therapy is used.

Some doctors warn of the dangers involved in using female hormone drugs over long periods of time because of the possibility that they might cause cancer—for example, birth control pills which contain estrogen.

Cancer of the Fundus of the Uterus. The *fundus*, the body of the uterus, is not attacked as frequently by cancer as the cervix; however, malignant growths do occur in the fundus. They are most likely to appear during and after the menopause. Vaginal bleeding is the first symptom, which may begin as a watery, bloodtinged discharge. If it occurs before the menopause, it may be mistaken for a menstrual irregularity. A diagnostic curettage, to get scrapings from the uterus, is done if a Papanicolaou smear looks suspicious. If the condition is due to malignancy, a *hysterectomy* is performed, followed by radium and x-ray therapy in the pelvic cavity. Cancer of the fundus of the uterus is most likely to occur in women in their 50's or older, when diabetes or hypertension may be complicating factors, making surgery a greater risk for them.

TREATMENT AND NURSING CARE. In addition to the usual preparation for abdominal or perineal surgery, the patient may have a vaginal irrigation. She may be catheterized, since it is more than usually important that the bladder be empty, to lessen the danger of damaging it while removing the uterus. Abdominal distention may make the patient uncomfortable for a day or two following the operation; a rectal tube or a carminative enema may be necessary. Exercise is important to prevent *thrombophlebitis*, which is a frequent complication. The patient should be turned frequently and encouraged to move her legs at least every hour. She is assisted out of bed, and she takes a few steps on her first postoperative day. She may have trouble voiding at first; often a Foley catheter is inserted in the bladder at the time of the operation in anticipation of this difficulty. The patient with a *vaginal hysterectomy* (removal of the uterus through the vagina) wears a perineal pad and has frequent perineal care.

The Patient's Point of View. Uterine disturbances can be very upsetting for a woman. Fear of cancer, sterility or the disturbance of marital relations are worries that any patient may have. She may feel that she is not up to making some of the adjustments that will be necessary. A nurse who is sensitive to these worries can learn what they are by listening to the patient's questions and comments and can help to give her some of the reassurance she needs. Some questions must be referred to the head nurse or doctor for an answer, but at least the nurse should feel responsible for referring them.

The Advanced Malignancy. The patient with a malignant condition in the advanced stages slowly wastes away; she is unable to eat or to control body functions, perhaps drifting into a coma and uremia. Treatment must be centered on faithful attention to her physical comfort with sedatives for pain. Even in the most hopeless situation, someone may be still hoping for a miracle and so will be doubly sensitive to any indication of indifference or neglect. This is a painful period for the patient's family—they need the reassurance that the approach of death does not lessen attention to the patient's care and comfort.

Pelvic Perfusion. This comparatively new treatment for pelvic malignancy circulates cancer-destroying drugs, such as nitrogen mustard, through the pelvic bloodstream about 2 hours by means of a pump oxygenator. These drugs have toxic effects on the bone marrow and the spleen, and the patient must be watched for signs of infection or bleeding after the treatment. Pelvic perfusion seems to make some patients more comfortable, but it is still too new to know how effective it can be.

Vaginal Fistulas

A *fistula* often is a complication of cancer in the pelvis. A fistula is an opening between 2 organs that normally do not open into each other. It is the result of an ulcerating process, such as cancer, irradiation or childbirth injury. A fistula may develop between the ureter and the vagina (ureterovaginal), between the bladder and the vagina (vesicovaginal), or between the bladder and the rectum (rectovaginal). It is a most troublesome condition. If the fistula is between the ureter or the bladder and the vagina, urine will leak into the vagina. If it is between the rectum and the vagina, it causes fecal incontinence. A long-standing fistula is difficult to repair successfully, because the tissues are eroded. Efforts are made to assist the healing process by building up the patient's resistance and by keeping the patient as clean as possible with perineal irrigations. Heat-lamp treatments to the perineum are sometimes used. The patient with an unrepairable fistula is distressed by the odor and the constant drainage. Sitz baths and deodorizing douches are aids to cleanliness.

Cystocele and Rectocele

Due to the improvement in obstetric care, cystocele and rectocele are not seen as frequently as they once were. *Childbirth tears* that have not been repaired, *frequent childbearing* or *multiple births* may relax the pelvic floor, allowing the bladder to sag downward and protrude into the vagina (*cystocele*), or into the rectum (*rectocele*). The uterus may sag (*prolapse*) into the vagina or even outside it.

These conditions are the cause of nagging discomforts: pelvic pain, backache, fatigue and a sagging weight in the pelvis. They may interfere with emptying the bladder or with bowel movements or cause a dribbling of urine if the patient coughs or strains. A protruding organ becomes irritated and sometimes infected.

Treatment and Nursing Care. The surgical repair of a cystocele is called *anterior colporrhaphy;* the repair of a rectocele is called *posterior colporrhaphy.* Repair of the *perineum* is called *perineorrhaphy.* Preoperative orders for these procedures are likely to include a cleansing douche. Postoperatively, the patient will have sterile perineal care. With rectocele repair the diet will be liquid for several days, to avoid defecation until some healing has taken place. With a *cystocele,* a Foley catheter is inserted to keep the bladder from becoming overdistended. Sometimes a patient is afraid to try to urinate after the catheter is removed and needs assurance that it is safe to void naturally.

The Displaced Uterus

A displaced uterus is usually a congenital condition, but it may be the result of childbearing. Backward displacement is called *retroversion* or *retroflexion.* Forward displacement is called *anteversion* or *anteflexion.* These terms mean that the uterus is *turned* or *bent* backward or forward. A displaced uterus may cause backache, dysmenorrhea or sterility.

Uterine displacement can be corrected by surgery to suture the uterus back in place. If a complicating condition makes surgery inadvisable, a *pessary* will help to reduce the prolapse. A pessary is a device made of hard rubber or plastic which is inserted into the vagina to hold the uterus in place. If it is inserted correctly, it usually causes no discomfort. The patient is instructed to return to the doctor at the time he designates—this is usually in a week and about every 2 months after that. The pessary can be left in place for 6 weeks at a time. Usually, the patient takes douches several times a week, and she is instructed to make every effort to keep the pessary clean. Assuming the knee-chest position for a short time once or twice a day helps to keep the pessary in place.

THE PATIENT WITH BREAST DISEASE

The breast is part of the reproductive system; it functions in relation to menstruation and fertilization and is affected by the hormones produced by the reproductive organs. The breast is a glandular organ filled with blood and lymph vessels, and after pregnancy it manufactures milk from certain substances in the blood. This process is called *lactation.* Milk is carried to the nipple by numerous ducts distributed throughout the fatty tissue. Progesterone, an ovarian hormone, and prolactin, a pituitary hormone, stimulate lactation. Estrogen, another ovarian hormone, suppresses lactation.

Cystic disease is the most common breast disorder. Breast tissue cells mass together, shut off the ducts, and form cysts. These masses may form fibrous tumors, *fibromas* (lumps), in the breast.

Cancer is next as a cause of breast disorders. More than 60,000 women develop breast cancer every year; as a cause of cancer in women it comes first. Over half of these women are cured, but the number would be higher if more cases were discovered and treated earlier. Breast cancer tends to appear in women who have a family history of this disease; it is not as common in women who have nursed babies.

Breast Changes. Breast changes may be evident before pain appears. Women are urged to consult a doctor if they notice a lump or any other changes in the breast. Prompt action may mean the difference between life and death. More than half of the women who consulted a doctor immediately after finding a lump in the breast were alive 5 years later; less than a third of those who delayed this visit lived that long.

Symptoms of Breast Disease

Lumps in the breast are always a suspicious symptom. They may be harmless; again, they may not. Beginning cancer is not likely to be painful. A discharge that oozes from the nipple without squeezing is a suspicious sign. Sometimes a malignant growth makes a dimple in the skin or retracts the nipple, or breast tissue becomes fixed to the chest muscles. Lumps in the axilla are indications that cancer has spread to this area. The American Cancer Society has prepared a booklet, *Breast Self-Examination,* which describes the technic for self-examination of the breast. A woman who has a phobia about cancer and shrinks from self-examination is better off if she consults her doctor regularly and leaves the breast examination to him. Every woman over 30 should have her breasts examined by a physician once a year. A woman who is subject to cystic disease or one who has a family history of cancer should be examined every 6 months. In this way she runs less risk of undetected cancer. If a lump appears, it can be removed, and a biopsy done to rule out or detect malignancy.

Breast Surgery

The doctor will excise a benign tumor; if the tumor is malignant, he will amputate the breast, together with the overlying skin, the axillary channels and the lymph nodes which drain the area. This is called a *radical mastectomy.* When only the breast is removed the operation is called *simple mastectomy.*

The Patient's Point of View. The patient who is going to have a breast operation is understandably apprehensive. Will she lose her breast? Will she hear the dread word "cancer"? Will she be repulsive? These questions and many more may be going through her mind. She knows none of the answers nor will she know until it is all over. She can only hope. She thinks of Mrs. Gates who had a breast operation and in 6 months was dead. She may wish wildly that she never had gone to the doctor; how does he *know* an operation is necessary?

Be patient with her questions and worries. Show that you are willing to listen; encourage her to talk about the things that trouble her. Assure her that she was sensible to consult her doctor—thousands of women are doing this regularly.

Radical Mastectomy. If the pathologist's report following a biopsy shows that the growth is malignant, the surgeon will do a radical mastectomy. This operation involves removing an extensive amount of skin, and it may be necessary to take a skin graft from the thigh to close the wound. The patient's arm is bandaged against her body to avoid pull on the graft, with her elbow bent at a right angle and the arm supported by a pillow. If there is no skin graft, the arm is free.

Treatment and Nursing Care. Change the patient's position often; exercise her arm and her legs even though she will not be able to turn on the affected side. In a day or two, if her condition permits, she will get out of bed and walk with assistance. Encourage her to keep her shoulders level and relaxed—patients tend to hunch the affected side. It may be difficult when the arm is first unbandaged from her side to get her to move it away from her body. It is important to keep the muscles from becoming permanently contracted.

EXERCISES. Exercises to bring back the normal use of the arm are started as soon as the arm is freed, if the skin graft permits. Steady, persistent exercise every day is necessary to stretch the muscles gradually. The exercises should be done for a *short time* 3 or 4 times a day to avoid fatigue. Meanwhile, the patient should be encouraged to use her other arm to do things for herself, such as washing her face and brushing her hair. She will not be able to cut her meat or butter her bread, but she can feed herself. The American Cancer Society publishes a booklet, *Help Yourself to Recovery,* telling how to do postmastectomy exercises at home. Some exercises can be combined with ordinary daily activities, such as sliding a towel back and forth over the back and reaching with the arms when making a bed. The patient has a good start in learning how to exercise the muscles before she goes home. Some hospitals have postmastectomy classes for patients to exercise together (see Fig. 168).

The Prosthetic Breast. A *prosthesis* answers the problem of disfigurement. It can be fitted to duplicate the remaining breast so there will be no change in the patient's appearance. Until the doctor decides that she is ready for the prosthesis, she can purchase a padded brassière (many of them are available), or she can pad her own brassière with cotton temporarily. Surgical supply houses and corsetières that carry prostheses usually have an experienced fitter. Ordinarily, the doctor will recommend the place where this can be done. One of the most adaptable types of a prosthetic breast is made of foam rubber which is light and washable.

Complications. Infection in the wound area is always a possible development. Edema in the arm usually follows a radical mastectomy; normally, this is temporary, but if it persists it may be a sign of infection. Edema does not disappear as rapidly in obese patients. In the case of infection, antibiotics will be given. Signs of infection in the arm or the hand should be reported immediately.

Metastatic Cancer. Metastases in another part of the body are always a threat with cancer. Any local pain should send the patient to her doctor without delay. Periodic check-ups are routine for any patient who has had a malignant growth removed. X-ray therapy is usually employed as treatment following the removal of a malignant growth. If the patient is not yet past the menopause, a second operation may be performed to remove the ovaries and so to remove the source of the hormone estrogen, which is thought to stimulate tumor growth. The production of estrogen ceases with the menopause. In cases where metastasis has taken place, hormonal therapy may be used in the hope that it will make the patient more comfortable and give her a few more years to live—and sometimes it does. However, the side-effects of hormonal therapy may be nausea and vomiting, uterine bleeding and edema.

Breast Abscess

Most breast abscesses occur during the period when the mother is nursing her baby after childbirth. The disease organisms enter the breast through cracks in the nipples. The staphylococcus is the most common offender. Antibiotics are given, and the patient is placed on isolation precautions; sometimes the abscess is incised and drained. Moist dressings may be ordered to promote drainage and to relieve pain and discomfort. Every precaution is taken to prevent the spread of infection, since the staphylococcus spreads rapidly and is hard to eradicate.

THE MALE PATIENT

The male patient with a disease of the reproductive system is treated by the *urologist,* since his condition often is genitourinary in nature. Treatment usually involves many of the same procedures that are used in caring for the urologic patient. In reviewing some organs of the male reproductive system, we see that they are the *testes,* which produce the male

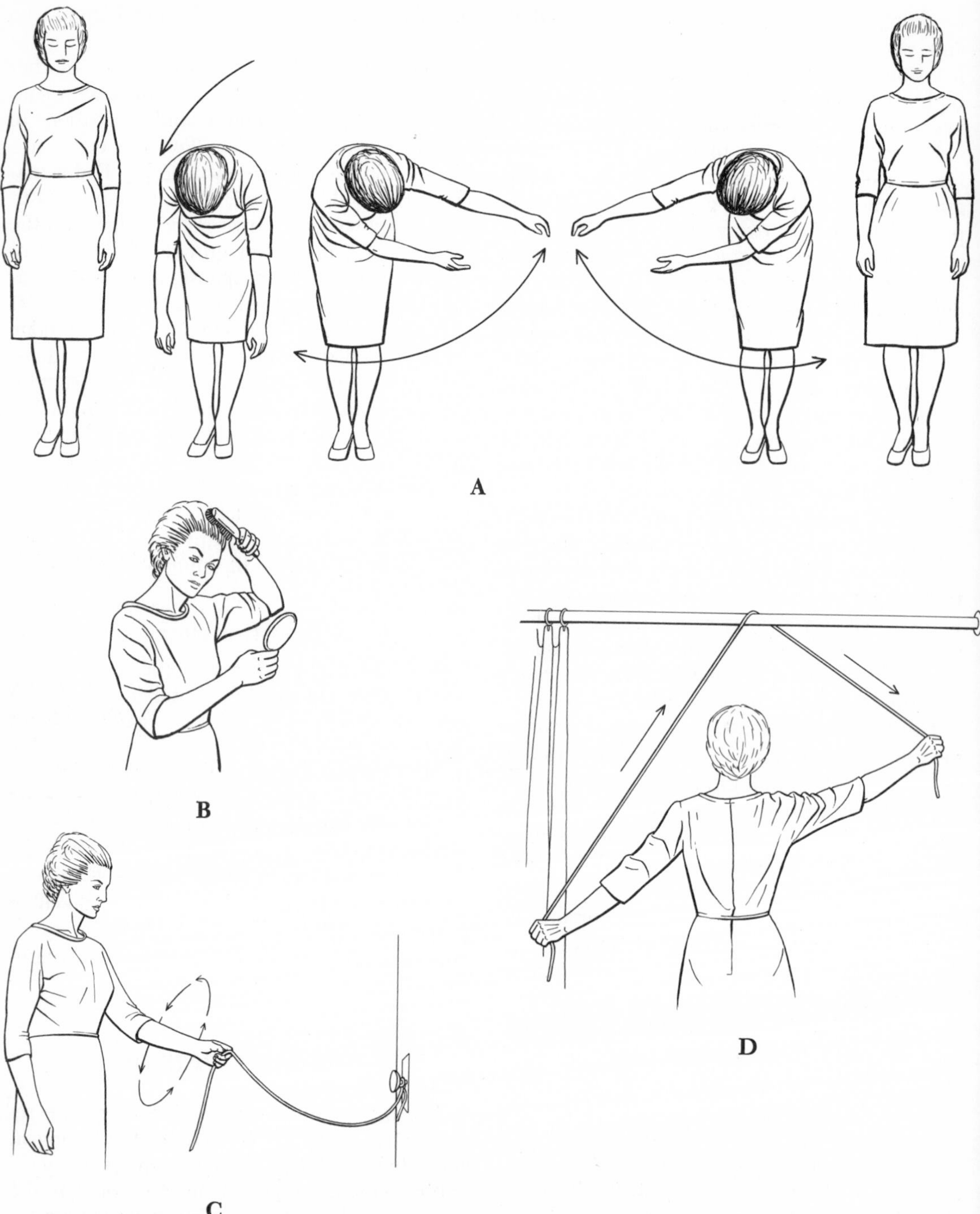

Fig. 168. Exercises for the postmastectomy patient. (A) Pendulum-swinging exercise. (B) Hair-brushing exercise. (C) Rope-turning exercise. (D) Rope-sliding exercise. (E) Wall-climbing exercise. (Smith, D. W., and Gips, C. D.: Care of the Adult Patient, p. 1114, Philadelphia, Lippincott, 1963)

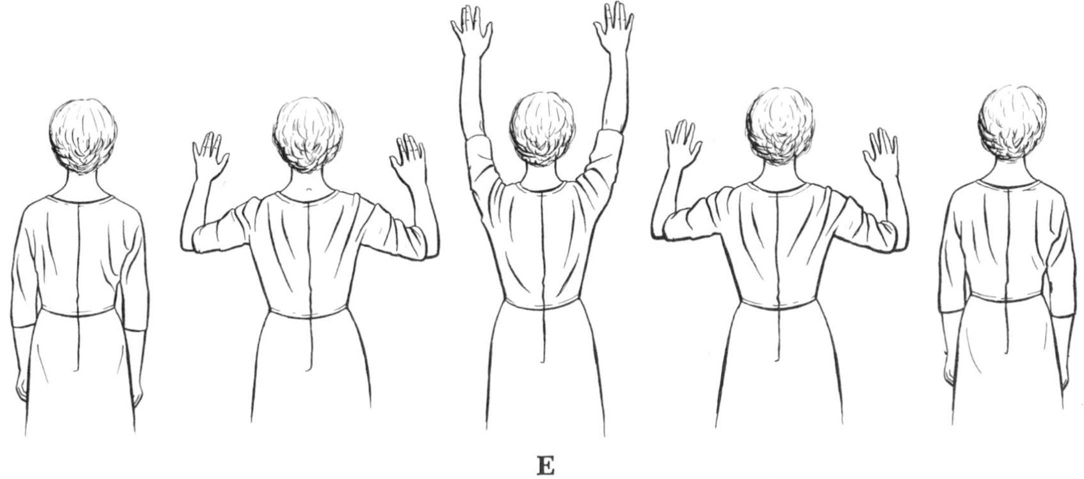

E

Fig. 168 E—(*Caption on facing page.*)

sperm cells (the spermatozoa), the male *hormones,* and the *semen,* the fluid that carries the cells; the *epididymis,* the *seminal ducts,* and the *ejaculatory ducts,* which are the passageways for the semen; the *prostate gland,* which adds a secretion to the semen; and the *penis,* in which the urethra provides the outlet for the semen. The male urethra is the passageway for both urine and semen. The tissues in the penis stiffen and fill with blood to hold the penis erect during sexual intercourse.

Spermatozoa are produced in large numbers and are extremely active. They are able to wiggle their way through the vagina into the uterus and on up into the fallopian tube to impregnate the ovum. Conception takes place only if an ovum is present in the tube. The ovaries usually produce only one ovum each month.

Disorders of the Male Reproductive System. One of the main psychological difficulties for a male patient with a disorder of the reproductive system may be his embarrassment because the nurse taking care of him is a woman. He may also be worried about impotence or cancer, and naturally he feels hesitant to mention these fears, thus making it difficult to relieve his worries by discussing them or asking questions. He should have an opportunity to talk with the doctor alone if he seems unduly worried or disturbed. Men at any age may be apprehensive about the loss of sexual powers.

Prostatic Difficulties

We have already seen that an enlarged prostate can cause urinary difficulties (Chap. 40). As a man grows older, the prostate gland tends to enlarge and may constrict the urethra. This does not necessarily indicate cancer nor does it always mean that surgery is necessary. In 100 men, 65 of them will have some prostatic enlargement by the time they are 65 years old.

Symptoms. The first symptom to appear may be difficulty in urination. The patient does not empty his bladder completely when he voids, and he finds that he must get up several times during the night. He may also find it increasingly difficult to start to void and may notice traces of blood in his urine. This may lead to infection and cystitis. The doctor can find out the effects of prostatic enlargement on the urinary system by examining a catheterized specimen of urine and by cystoscopy; a blood chemistry test will also indicate how well the kidneys are functioning.

Treatment and Nursing Care. The usual treatment for *nonmalignant* prostatic enlargement is the surgical removal of the prostate. Before the operation the patient may have a catheter inserted for continuous drainage of urine, to prevent an accumulation of stagnant urine in the bladder. The patient is given plenty of fluids, with proper diet and rest to build up his resistance. The prostrate is removed, either through the urethra, using a cystoscope that carries a cutting device which slices the prostate away bit by bit, or by dissecting it out through an incision over the bladder (suprapubic). This operation may be done in 2 stages. First, a cystostomy (an incision into the bladder) is done to relieve retention of urine; secondly, the prostate is removed. After the 1-stage suprapubic operation, the patient returns with 2 in-dwelling catheters in place: one in the urethra and the other in the suprapubic wound. The wound catheter is attached to an irrigation apparatus, and the urethral catheter is attached to a bottle for drainage. This arrangement provides for irrigating the bladder and for urine drainage. The wound catheter is usually removed in 5 or 6 days; the urethral catheter stays in for about 10 days. Some urine will dribble onto the dressings after the wound catheter is removed, so attention must be given to keeping the skin clean and dry. It takes a while for the wound to heal, perhaps a month or more.

The prostate may also be removed through an incision in the perineum. In this case, catheter drainage is through the perineal incision only. Since the patient will find sitting up painful, a foam rubber pad should be provided. Sitz baths are usually ordered. Care to avoid contaminating the wound will be necessary after a bowel movement. Cleansing should not be left to the patient simply because a male nurse or orderly is not available. These patients are elderly and often lonely people, who become confused by the tubing arrangements and procedures; they feel unwanted and without hope of ever being well again. They need to be noticed and encouraged often to let them know that someone cares about their recovery.

Cancer of the Prostate. *Cancer of the prostate* does not usually occur until after 50 years of age. Of the men who have prostatic difficulty after that age, 25 per cent have cancer. The symptoms may not appear for years, but when they do appear as the result of metastases to the nerves, they are in the form of pains in the back and sciatica. A rectal examination will show a hard mass which did not cause pain until metastases had spread, which is one of the reasons why it is hard to discover cancer of the prostate early enough.

A biopsy of the tumor will determine the diagnosis as cancer. A *radical prostatectomy*, removing the prostate gland, the seminal vesicles and part of the urethra, will sometimes cure cancer of the prostate if metastases have not developed. With metastasis, the most that can be done is to make the patient as comfortable as possible. The administration of female hormones (estrogens) and radiation therapy may help, but the relief is temporary. As the disease advances, sedatives are given, and sometimes bladder drainage is necessary.

Other Disturbances

Undescended Testicle. A small percentage of male babies are born with testicles that have not descended to their normal place in the scrotum. Sometimes the testicles descend without treatment; but if this does not happen before puberty, they should be brought into place, since this condition may cause sterility. After puberty, an operation for 2 undescended testicles will not be effective in preventing sterility.

Orchitis. *Orchitis*, inflammation of the testes, may be the result of an infection or of an injury. *Mumps* after puberty may cause orchitis which results in sterility; gamma globulin may help to make mumps less severe. The symptoms of orchitis are pain and swelling in the scrotum and sometimes urethral irritation. A 4-tail bandage is used to support the testes, and an ice cap is applied. Heat is *never* used, because even a few degrees of heat may damage spermatozoa.

Hydrocele. A *hydrocele* is an accumulation of fluid in the space between the membrane covering the testicle and the testicle itself. It may be due to infection (orchitis) or to an injury. The scrotum enlarges but does not cause pain, unless the hydrocele is a sudden development, in which case there may be both pain and swelling. It is treated by aspirating the fluid or by injecting a substance that disposes of the sac in which the fluid collects. Sometimes the sac is removed surgically. The treatment includes providing support for the scrotum and keeping the dressings changed to prevent skin irritation.

Epididymitis. *Epididymitis* is an inflammation of the tube that carries the sperm cells away from the testes. It is usually due to gonorrheal, staphylococcic, streptococcic or colon bacillus infection, and it often follows an infection of the urinary tract or prostatitis. The symptoms are redness, pain and swelling in the scrotum, which are sometimes accompanied by chills, fever, nausea and vomiting. The treatment includes giving antibiotics for the infection and applying support and an ice cap to the scrotum. If an abscess forms, it usually is incised and drained surgically. Repeated or chronic infection will destroy the production of sperm.

Varicocele. A *varicocele* is caused by dilatation of the veins in the scrotum. It may be caused by an abdominal tumor which obstructs the spermatic vein. The symptoms of varicocele are swelling and a nagging pain in the scrotum. It is treated by removing the cause of the obstruction and sometimes by removing a mass of dilated veins. A snug suspensory is applied for support.

VENEREAL DISEASE INFECTION

Venereal disease considered as a national health problem is discussed in Chapter 6. We are concerned here with the effects of venereal disease on the reproductive organs and with its treatment. Venereal disease has certain moral aspects, since it often is contacted through illicit sexual intercourse. These aspects should never influence the nurse's attitude toward the patient—her only concern is with helping the patient to recover from an infectious illness. In fact, the patient may be the innocent victim of infection in the husband or wife. The treatment is all-important for the patient's health and the protection of others. Beware of adopting a self-righteous, disapproving attitude and be your normal friendly, matter-of-fact self.

Gonorrhea

Gonorrhea is the result of infection with the gonococcus organism and is the most common venereal disease. It affects more than 200,000 people in the United States every year. It attacks the genital tract in men and women and can spread to other parts of the body. It is contracted through sexual intercourse—it would be rare indeed to find an instance of gonorrhea contracted from a toilet seat or the bottom of a bathtub!

Symptoms. The symptoms may appear anywhere from 3 days to 2 weeks after intercourse with an infected person. Usually, the first symptom is pain and a burning sensation upon urination, followed by a yellowish discharge which contains pus. Without treatment, the disease progresses to infect the uterus and the fallopian tubes in women and the epididymis in men. In women, the tubes are filled with pus (salpingitis); strictures form and cause sterility. In men, prostatitis or an infection of the seminal vesicles and sterility may develop. In women, douches, sexual intercourse and menstruation may spread the infection to the ovary and cause an abscess. This infection is also the cause of urinary difficulties in both men and women. If the organisms enter the bloodstream, they can cause arthritis and heart disease. Before antibiotics were known, many patients with gonorrhea became arthritics.

Treatment. One dose of 1,200,000 U. of penicillin cures 95 per cent of the cases of gonorrhea in the early stage. If people delay treatment, the disease may spread to other parts of the body, and they may continue to infect others. While the infection is active, soap and water should be used freely in washing the hands; toilet equipment should be isolated, and the toilet seat used by the patient should be scrubbed after each use. Precautions to avoid touching the eyes are especially important, because the eye is particularly susceptible to gonorrheal infection. With an advanced infection, the patient is on bed care and may require sitz baths and douches. The nurse wears gloves in giving these treatments, or the patient may be on isolation precautions.

Syphilis

Syphilis is a destructive disease that may result in many lesions throughout the body. It *kills* over 4,000 Americans every year and infects 5 times that many. The increase in syphilis has been great in the last 10 years. Furthermore, only about 10 per cent of the cases are reported. Syphilis is caused by a spirochete (*Treponema pallidum*), which thrives in moisture and lives for a very short time outside the human body. It is hardly possible to contract syphilis from a toilet seat or a drinking glass unless the contact is immediate and direct. Syphilis is almost always contracted by sexual intercourse. Persons with untreated syphilis can infect others for about 3 years after the infection starts; after this time they are seldom infectious. Syphilitic infection can be detected by a blood test such as the Kahn, Wassermann, Massini or Kolmar tests, or by a smear taken from a syphilitic lesion.

Transmission. Contact with a syphilitic lesion by kissing or by sexual intercourse transmits the spirochetes to mucous membranes, which they enter through cracks where they immediately multiply. From there, they enter the bloodstream and in about 3 weeks the first syphilitic lesion appears, the *primary lesion* or *chancre.*

Stages of Syphilis. The primary lesion may appear on the penis, inside the vagina, on the nipple or in a crack at the side of the mouth. It contains millions of spirochetes, but in 3 to 8 weeks this lesion will disappear. Sometimes enlarged lymph nodes also appear. The patient has no other symptoms. This is the *primary stage* of syphilis. About 6 weeks after the initial infection, the *secondary stage* begins. Usually, the first sign is a skin rash which appears suddenly but soon disappears as quickly as it came. Wartlike spots may develop on the mucous membranes or around the anus. These spots are extremely infectious. Patches of the patient's hair may come out, and he may also have fever, headache or sore throat; however, he may have none of these symptoms and feel normal and well.

In the third, or *tertiary stage*, all the symptoms disappear. Half of the patients who reach this stage without having had treatment will have no more trouble; but for the other half, there is a different story. The disease may stay dormant anywhere from 1 to 20 to 30 years, and then trouble begins.

A serology test will now be positive. The lymph nodes may enlarge, and neuritis may appear. If the infection reaches the joints, arthritis develops. Again, very likely all the symptoms will disappear in a few weeks, but they will continue to reappear and disappear at intervals. This gives the patient a false sense of security, and he still may go untreated. By this time the spirochetes have penetrated to all the body tissues, and syphilis may develop in any organ.

Effects of Syphilis. Untreated syphilis in a pregnant woman may cause a miscarriage; the baby may be born with congenital syphilis, or it may be deformed. Syphilitic lesions may affect the blood vessels or the heart valves. In the nervous system, they may cause meningitis. A common disturbance is *paresis*, which affects the patient's personality—he becomes unable to concentrate or use judgment, is careless about his clothes, is irritable and, in the advanced stages, may become exuberant or depressed. His speech is slurred, and he may lose his sight and eventually become paralyzed and be a complete invalid.

Another manifestation of syphilis at this stage is *tabes dorsalis* (locomotor ataxia), a condition in which there is a loss of function in the legs. It is accompanied by a sharp burning pain in the legs; they feel numb, then cold or warm. The patient feels as if he cannot tell where his legs are, and as if he cannot manage them. He must watch them in order to walk, and his gait is jerky. He is unable to walk at all in the dark. Another complication is loss of function in a joint; the knee and the spine are affected most frequently.

Treatment. One injection of 2,400,000 to 4,800,000 U. of long-lasting penicillin will eliminate spirochetes in 85 to 90 per cent of the cases of syphilis. This is not considered as a cure, and the patient must return to the doctor at 2-week intervals at first, then monthly for 6 months and then every 3 or 4 months for the next 6 years. If the patient is allergic to penicillin, he can be treated by *tetracycline* or by *carbomycin.*

FERTILITY AND INFERTILITY

There are a number of causes for barren marriages. About 12 per cent of all marriages in this country are barren; although most of these couples want children, conception does not take place. Sterility in the man seems to be the cause in about one third of these marriages. It may be due to undescended testicles, orchitis after mumps, irradiation of the testes, obesity, infection or emotional tensions. Sterility in women may be due to the same systemic causes as in men. In addition, she may have a displaced uterus, obstructed fallopian tubes, or a cervical or a vaginal infection. Although 1 cc. of semen contains literally millions of sperm cells, the number of *normal* and *active* spermatozoa may be comparatively small, which lessens the chances of fertilization.

If conception has not taken place after several years of marriage, a doctor should be consulted. He will check on the general health of husband and wife; will make tests of the semen and of the vaginal and cervical secretions. He may inflate the fallopian tubes with carbon dioxide. Sometimes a light curettage of the uterus is done to determine whether the lining of the uterus is undergoing the normal changes necessary to receive a fertilized ovum.

What Every Woman Should Know

Many women, even the married ones, have hazy ideas about conception and childbirth. They are confused about the functions of the urethral, the vaginal and the rectal openings. Often a patient reveals these misconceptions by the questions she asks, which gives the nurse an opportunity to give her correct information. She may reveal other areas of ignorance. Does she know that infection and hemorrhage may be the dangerous consequences of a criminal abortion? Does she know that tensions can cause frigidity? Does she know that the normal vagina does not need douches for cleanliness; in fact, that they may irritate it and lead to infection and should not be used unless the doctor orders them? Above all, she should know that, after 35, every woman should have a gynecologic examination at least once every year.

42

THE PATIENT WITH A DISORDER OF THE ENDOCRINE SYSTEM

The *endocrine* glands (ductless glands) are groups of cells that produce chemical substances called *hormones* (see Chap. 20). They secrete the hormones directly into the bloodstream, where they play a part in metabolism and influence the growth and the activity of cells and body systems. Normally, they produce, store and release hormones as they are needed. It is known that many of the endocrine glands are sensitive to stimulation from each other, but even the authorities in this field do not wholly understand this relationship. Endocrine disorders are usually caused by the overproduction or underproduction of hormones, which sets up unfavorable reactions in the body. Diabetes mellitus, which occurs when the pancreas gland fails to produce the hormone insulin, is one example of hormone underproduction.

THE PITUITARY GLAND

The pituitary gland is a tiny gland, but it has tremendous influence in the body and affects the operations of every other gland. For this reason it is sometimes called the master gland. It lies in the sphenoid bone at the base of the brain and has 2 parts—the anterior and the posterior lobes. It secretes at least 9 hormones, but only the most important ones will be mentioned here.

The Anterior Lobe

To give some idea of the important activities of the pituitary gland, consider that the anterior lobe alone produces a growth hormone; the milk-producing hormones; ACTH; 2 hormones that stimulate the thyroid gland; 2 hormones that regulate ovarian function. In men, one of these hormones stimulates the testes to produce the hormone testosterone (Fig. 82).

Giantism and Acromegaly. Disturbances of the anterior lobe of the pituitary gland may cause overproduction of the growth hormone somatropin. If this occurs in childhood, it causes prolonged growth of bones, or *giantism*. In an adult an excess of this hormone causes an overgrowth of other tissues (*acromegaly*). The victim's features coarsen, forming a massive lower jaw, thick lips, a bulbous nose and bulging forehead; his hands and feet seem to be enormous. In women, facial hair also appears, and their voices deepen. Headaches develop, and the patient may become partially blind. The spleen, the heart and the liver may enlarge; the muscles weaken; and pain and stiffness may appear in the joints. Impotence or amenorrhea may develop.

TREATMENT. Acromegaly is treated by irradiation of the pituitary gland; sometimes estrogens are given. Treatment can stop the progress of the disease, but it cannot undo the damage that has already been done.

Simmonds' Disease. This rare disease occurs when the pituitary gland is destroyed by a tumor, by surgery or by postpartum emboli. The genitalia become atrophied; the patient ages prematurely and becomes wasted. This disease can be treated by irradiation if a tumor is causing the difficulty. Hormones of the glands that depend on the pituitary for stimulation may also be given.

The Posterior Lobe

The posterior lobe of the pituitary secretes hormones that increase blood pressure (vasopressin), stimulate uterine contractions (oxytoxin), and increase the reabsorption of water by the kidneys (ADH).

Diabetes Insipidus. *Diabetes insipidus* is a rare disease caused by underproduction of the hormone ADH, which regulates the passage of water through the kidneys. As a result, the elimination of urine is so copius that the patient has no peace. He may void as much as 15 to 20 quarts in 24 hours; he is constantly thirsty and restricting fluids has no effect. This condition makes him weak in spite of an abnormally large appetite and upsets his living patterns in general. The treatment consists of giving pituitary extract to control the output of urine and to reduce it to a normal amount.

THE THYROID GLAND

The thyroid gland has 2 lobes that lie in front and on either side of the trachea. It secretes the hormone thyroxin, which regulates metabolism. If it secretes too much thyroxin, the tissues burn oxygen rapidly; if it secretes too little, the reverse is true. The thyroid gland must have iodine to produce thyroxin; a pituitary hormone also contributes to the production of thyroxin.

Hyperthyroidism

Hyperthyroidism is also called *Graves' disease* and exophthalmic goiter. It is a condition in which the metabolic rate is increased by overproduction of thyroxin. The exact cause of this overactivity is not known, but it seems to develop as a result of physical or emotional strain or of the changes that take place during adolescence or pregnancy. It occurs most frequently in women.

Symptoms. Hyperthyroidism makes the patient highly excitable and overactive. She is unable to keep quiet, twists and turns and moves her head and arms constantly. She may have tremors that make it impossible for her to feed herself. Her pulse is rapid; she may have heart palpitations that cause heart damage if she does not have treatment. She feels hot; she eats voraciously but loses weight because her body burns calories at such a fast rate. Another common symptom is bulging eyes (exophthalmos), and frequently the neck is swollen due to the enlarged thyroid gland. Pressure from the gland may make it difficult for the patient to swallow or may cause hoarseness.

Tests

Basal Metabolic Rate (B.M.R.). This test was described in a previous chapter as a means of measuring the basal metabolic rate, which is the rate at which the patient uses oxygen when she is resting. The test is given after the patient has been without food for 8 to 10 hours. She lies quietly in bed and breathes into a tube connected to a measuring machine. Variations from 20 below normal to 20 above normal are considered to be within a normal range; 20 per cent or more above normal is a sign of hyperthyroidism. It is important to assure the patient that the test is not dangerous nor will it disturb her in any way, except that she must wait for her breakfast and stay as quiet as possible until after the test. Precautions to prevent worry or excitement or activity are necessary because they can raise the metabolic rate temporarily and give an incorrect record.

Radioactive Iodine Uptake Test. This is also a test to determine how active the thyroid gland is. The patient is given a small amount of radioactive material (sodium iodide^{131}) in distilled water. Twenty-four hours later, a scintillator (an instrument that measures radioactivity) is held over the thyroid gland to measure the amount of iodine that the gland has removed from the bloodstream. A normally active thyroid will remove 15 to 20 per cent in that time—in hyperthyroidism it may remove as much as 90 per cent. Some radioactive iodine is also excreted in the urine; the urine is saved during this period so that this amount of iodine also can be measured.

PROTEIN-BOUND IODINE (PBI). The amount of protein-bound iodine (a component of the thyroid hormone) in the blood is measured by this test. The concentration above or below normal indicates either hyperthyroidism or hypothyroidism, respectively.

Sometimes the amount of cholesterol in the blood is lowered in hyperthyroidism, but a test for this is not always reliable.

Treatment and Nursing Care. The treatment for hyperthyroidism may be medical or surgical. Medical treatment consists of antithyroid drugs to block the secretion of the thyroid hormone. Propylthiouracil may be given either as a medical treatment or as a preparation for surgery. Medically, it is given daily, generally over a long period which may extend to a year or more. Some of the toxic effects that may appear are fever, skin rash and enlarged lymph nodes, with an increase in the white blood cells. The patient also has a weekly blood count taken.

Radioactive iodine may be given as a single dose. *Lugol's solution* (iodine and potassium iodide in water) is often given for a limited time (10 days to 2 weeks) before surgical removal of the thyroid.

Thyroidectomy

Thyroidectomy is the surgical removal of the thyroid gland. Before the operation the patient has a course of treatment with antithyroid drugs, a high-caloric and high-vitamin diet; her weight is checked every day. Her pulse is observed frequently, since the hyperthyroid patient's heart may be affected. In every possible way, the patient is protected from excitement or worry by keeping her in a quiet environment, controlling visitors and moving unhurriedly when caring for her. Many of these patients are exceedingly apprehensive; such a patient may not be told beforehand just when the operation is to be done. Then on the morning of the operation, the doctor may order the administration of Avertin by rectum or Pentothal Sodium intravenously to put the patient to sleep before the operating room stretcher appears.

FIG. 169. In making the thyroidectomy patient comfortable in a chair, the nurse sees that the head and neck are well supported with pillows. The overbed table enables the patient to reach frequently needed articles without turning her head. It is also convenient to use this table when inhalations are given to relieve excessive mucus secretions.

Postoperative Care. The patient is placed in semi-Fowler's position with the head elevated and supported by pillows. She will be given morphine for pain. Occasionally, a patient is placed in an oxygen tent to make breathing easier. The patient should be told why this is being done, so that she will not be frightened. Her pulse and blood pressure are checked frequently, and the dressings are inspected for signs of excessive bleeding. She may have sips of water as soon as nausea ceases. Noisy breathing or cyanosis must be reported immediately—a tracheostomy may be necessary. A tracheostomy set should *always* be at hand for a thyroidectomy patient. Observe signs of hoarseness, which may indicate injury to the laryngeal nerves. Suction may be used or inhalations given, to relieve an excessive secretion of mucus.

Usually, the patient is allowed out of bed the day after the operation, first dangling her feet, then supported as she takes a few steps.

Her head and neck should be supported when she sits in a chair. An overbed table makes it convenient for her to reach things without turning her head. The average patient is usually discharged from the hospital on the 5th postoperative day. She must have B.M.R. tests at periodic intervals. An occasional patient may be disturbed by muscle spasms, if the parathyroid glands have been removed. Parathyroid hormone and calcium are remedies for this condition. A thyroidectomy usually prevents the recurrence of hyperthyroidism, since only enough of the gland is left to maintain normal function.

Simple Goiter (Colloid)

Sometimes, although the thyroid gland may become enlarged, it does not cause toxic symptoms. Usually, the enlargement is caused by a deficiency of iodine in the diet. The thyroid gland must have iodine to produce the thyroid hormone; if a sufficient supply is not available, the gland enlarges in a greater effort to produce the hormone. In some localities the soil and the drinking water are deficient in iodine—this is especially pronounced in the Alps and other mountain areas. The Pacific Northwest, the Great Lakes region, Ohio and Minnesota are deficient areas in the United States.

Colloid goiter affects more women than men and may appear during pregnancy, adolescence or during an infection. Except for its appearance, a colloid goiter usually does not have a harmful effect on health, unless it becomes so large that it interferes with swallowing or breathing. It is treated by giving iodine for a period of 2 or 3 weeks, repeating the treatment 3 or 4 times during the year if the diet is deficient in iodine. Surgery may be necessary if the gland causes excessive pressure on the trachea. It is not difficult to reinforce the body's supply of iodine, because it needs such a very small amount. Salt manufacturers have added iodine to table salt, and in many instances this provides enough to prevent colloid goiter.

Tumors of the Thyroid

A thyroid tumor may be cancerous, in which case it is removed surgically or treated by irradiation with radioactive isotopes. It usually appears as a small nodule on the gland; it most often appears in older persons, but not always. A biopsy will tell whether or not such a growth is malignant.

Hypothyroidism

Hypothyroidism (*myxedema*) occurs when a deficiency of the thyroid hormone slows down metabolic processes. This may be due to the removal of the thyroid gland or to a decrease in its activity for some reason. It is more likely to affect women than men. Symptoms of myxedema are a slowing up of physical and mental activity, accompanied by forgetfulness and chronic headache. The victim's expression becomes masklike, her skin is dry, her hair coarsens and tends to fall out, her voice is hoarse and low, and she gains weight. She may become chronically constipated and anemic; her heart may be affected. Her basal metabolic rate will be below normal.

Treatment. Thyroid extract is given to supply the hormone deficiency. The results are dramatic—in a week the patient seems to have a new lease on life. She is more alert mentally and physically, and her appearance becomes normal again. This rapid change is not without danger; for example, her heart may show signs of strain from so much increased activity. Anyone with a thyroid deficiency is more than usually susceptible to respiratory depression from sedatives or hypnotics. Some people have to take thyroid extract all their lives, but with well-regulated treatment they stay normally well and healthy. Such a patient must see her doctor for periodic check-ups.

THE PARATHYROID GLANDS

The parathyroids are tiny bean-shaped glands (4, 6 or 8 in number) located on either side of the under part of the thyroid gland. They secrete the parathyroid hormone which, aided by vitamin D, regulates the amount of calcium and phosphorus in the blood and helps the bones to use these minerals.

Hyperparathyroidism

Hyperparathyroidism occurs when there is an excess of the parathyroid hormone, which causes a calcium loss in bones. This leads to skeletal tenderness, and the bones tend to break easily, even without pressure or injury (pathologic fractures). The patient's muscles become weak, and she is tired, nauseated and constipated. She may develop kidney stones and uremia.

Treatment and Nursing Care. Hyperparathyroidism requires surgery to remove some of the gland. If, after the operation, muscle spasm appears, the patient is given calcium lactate to restore the calcium-phosphorus balance in the blood. The prescribed diet is high in fat and carbohydrate. This patient needs special care to prevent bumps and pressures that might cause a fracture.

Hypoparathyroidism

This condition, as you might guess, is a deficiency in the parathyroid hormone. It is caused by lowered production of the hormone, with a consequent reduction of the amount of calcium and phosphorus available to the body in the blood. This causes tremors and muscle spasm (tetany), with loss of hair, coarsening of the skin and brittle nails.

The treatment is to give either parathyroid hormone extract or a preparation that is similar to vitamin D (A.T. 10 or Hytakerol). Calcium preparations are never given intramuscularly, because they would injure the tissues.

THE ADRENAL GLANDS

The adrenals (suprarenals) are 2 small 3-cornered glands, one on the top of each kidney. Each has 2 parts. The medulla secretes the hormones epinephrine (norepinephrine). The cortex, or outer covering, secretes several hormones called cortisones. The cortex is stimulated by the nervous system and the pituitary hormone, ACTH. Epinephrine is secreted instantly to increase the flow of blood to the brain, the heart and the muscles and other vital organs when quick action is needed. The cortisones influence many vital functions, such as helping to regulate metabolism to supply quick energy, aiding in the control of electrolyte balance and controlling the development of sex characteristics.

Addison's Disease

Destruction or degeneration of the adrenal cortex causes a condition called *Addison's disease*. It is comparatively rare and can be the result of tuberculosis, cancer, or a massive infection. It decreases the production of adrenal hormones, with the result that the salt and water balance in the body is upset, and the level of sugar in the blood is lowered (hypoglycemia). The patient becomes dehydrated and anemic and loses weight. His skin has a dark, bronzed appearance and his hair becomes thin. He may develop tremors and be disoriented, finally going into coma and convulsions. Strain or stress of any kind may send him into adrenal shock, with abnormally lowered blood pressure, nausea and vomiting, diarrhea, headache and restlessness.

Treatment. The treatment consists of supplying the needed hormones by giving cortisone, hydrocortisone, prednisone or prednisolone. The patient must cooperate by seeing his doctor regularly and avoiding strain or excitement of any kind, such as overwork, infection or exposure to cold. By protecting his health, the patient with Addison's disease can get on very well. His outlook was gloomy indeed before hormones became available. However, he should always carry a card which says: "Addison's disease. If ill, call Dr. (name and telephone number of his physician)." Instructions for dosage of cortisone as prescribed by his doctor should be included, in case his doctor cannot be reached. Time means everything to a patient in adrenal shock.

This patient's diet is usually high in protein and salt and low in fluid—sometimes 5 or 6 small meals a day are given instead of the regulation 3 meals, or he may be given between-meal snacks of milk and crackers. He should be watched for dizziness or lowered blood pressure and be protected from falling.

Tumors of the Adrenal Medulla

A tumor on the medulla of the adrenal gland increases the secretion of the hormones epinephrine and norepinephrine. This, in turn, causes hypertension, tremor, headache, nausea and vomiting, dizziness and increased urination (polyuria). The treatment for this condition is surgical removal of the tumor, a dangerous operation because it may cause sudden and extreme changes in blood pressure.

Hyperfunction of the Adrenal Cortex (Cushing's Syndrome)

This disease is the opposite of Addison's disease and is not common. It is caused by the overproduction of the adrenal cortex hormone or of ACTH by the pituitary gland. Fat accumulates in spots, particularly on the face, giving a "moon face" appearance. As the disease progresses, the patient becomes weaker, his bones soften and he may have backache. He also develops edema and has a reduced urinary output. The treatment involves surgical removal of the adrenal gland, or x-ray therapy. Adrenal cortical hormones will be given as indicated. After surgery the patient will be treated as though he had Addison's disease.

THE PANCREAS

The pancreas lies against the posterior abdominal wall behind the greater curvature of the stomach. It was stated in Chapter 17 that the pancreas produces 2 secretions: the pancreatic juice which drains into the duodenum and is important in digestion in the gastrointestinal tract; and insulin, which is produced by the islets of Langerhans and is poured into the bloodstream to regulate glucose metabolism. Without insulin, glucose can neither be stored in the body nor used by the cells. This condition causes a disease which affects a large number of people. It is called *diabetes mellitus*, or more commonly, diabetes. (This is not to be confused with diabetes insipidus.)

Diabetes Mellitus

At the present time, there are more than 1½ million known diabetics in the United States, and it is estimated that 1½ million more have diabetes and do not know it. The yearly increase (50,000) in the number of known diabetics may be due to the increase in the number of diabetic detection centers and clinics, and also to the fact that because people live longer, diabetes has more time to develop. These figures are not as depressing as they sound. The discovery of the hormone *insulin* in 1921, by Sir Frederick Banting and his colleague Dr. Charles Best, revolutionized the treatment of diabetes. Today most diabetics can control the disease and lead normal, or nearly normal, lives if they follow orders.

Who Gets Diabetes? There is a heredity factor in diabetes. Studies show that the person with diabetes almost always reports that some relative has had it. If both parents have diabetes, eventually their children will develop it if they live long enough. If one parent has it and the other has the gene, their children have a 50-50 chance of escaping it. For instance, in a family of 4 children, 2 of them might develop diabetes. If both parents have the gene but are not diabetics, the children's chances of escaping the disease are increased by 25 per cent—that is, only 1 child is likely to develop it. Obesity may hasten the development of diabetes, but it does not cause it. For some unknown reason diabetes is highly prevalent among Jewish people, while it is found less frequently among Orientals, who develop a less severe form.

What is Diabetes? As was stated above, diabetes mellitus is a condition which results from the inability of the body cells to use glucose due to a deficiency in the production of the hormone insulin by the islets of Langerhans in the pancreas. The body gets its supply of energy from glucose, a product of carbohydrate digestion. Normally, the liver stores glucose in the form of glycogen and releases it when the body needs it—that is, when the amount of glucose in the circulating blood falls below a normal level. A glucose deficiency is called hypoglycemia. This deficiency can be corrected by giving the patient insulin, which enables the cells to use glucose. If the cells are unable to use insulin, glucose accumulates in the blood (hyperglycemia) and spills over into the urine (glycosuria).

Symptoms. Diabetes mellitus usually comes on more quickly in children than in adults, and it is more than likely to be severe, causing a loss of weight, sugar in the urine, copious urination, and a high level of glucose in the blood. In adults, diabetes often develops so gradually that it may not be noticed for months or even years, until it is discovered through a routine urine examination in connection with some other disorder. The most common and noticeable early symptoms are loss of weight and strength, copious urination, excessive thirst and appetite, and itchy, dry skin. In cases where diabetes has gone untreated for a long time, additional symptoms are the presence of boils and carbuncles, arteriosclerosis and gangrene of the feet, cataract, neuritis and coma.

Tests for Diabetes

Sugar in the urine does not necessarily mean that a patient has diabetes, nor does every diabetic excrete sugar in the urine. However, if sugar is consistently present in the urine, and if the patient's blood sugar level is above normal, there is a good probability that he has the disease. Tests of the blood and of the urine are routine for suspected diabetics.

Glucose Tolerance Test. The blood sugar level in the nondiabetic who has fasted goes up after eating sugar, but in about 2 hours it is back to normal again. This is not so with the diabetic. His blood sugar level is above normal with fasting and may not return to even that level for more than 2 hours after eating sugar. A glucose tolerance test will show whether or not sugar is accumulating in the blood. This is the procedure:

Specimens for examination of both blood and urine are taken before breakfast.

The patient drinks glucose in water (the amount is determined by his weight).

Blood and urine specimens are taken at prescribed intervals, such as a half-hour, 1 hour, 2 hours and 3 hours after the last swallow of glucose. Time the collection of specimens from then.

The laboratory technician takes the blood specimens, and the nurse collects the urine specimens and labels the bottles with the time when each was collected. The patient may have tap water to drink while the test is going on, but he is not permitted any food.

Urine Tests for Sugar. Normal urine is free from sugar or acetone, but both may be present in the urine of the diabetic. Excess sugar in the blood spills over into the urine; acetone appears as a by-product of faulty metabolism. Tests for sugar in the urine are easy to do and are not expensive, even on a large scale such as in a community diabetes detection program. The most commonly used tests are discussed here.

Benedict's Test

1. Add 8 drops of urine to 5 cc. of Benedict's solution in a test tube and mix.
2. Slanting it away from your face, hold the test tube directly over a flame and boil the contents for 5 minutes.
3. Let it cool, then compare the color of the mixture with the color chart available for that purpose. Color indications are:

Clear blue	No sugar
Pale green	Trace of sugar
Yellow	Up to 0.5% sugar
Orange	0.5% to 1.5% sugar
Brick red	1.5% sugar and over

This is the cheapest test to do. Enough Benedict's solution to last for a month (4 ounces) will cost less than a dollar.

Tes-Tape. Dip a strip of fresh Tes-Tape into urine. It will turn green or blue if sugar is present. Avoid touching the testing end and do not use it if it has been previously exposed to light and air.

Clinitest. Add 5 drops of urine to 10 drops of water in a test tube and drop in the Clinitest tablet. Compare the result with the color chart.

Clinistix. Dip the test end in urine and read against the color chart.

The last 3 tests above have a decided advantage over Benedict's test because they are so convenient to carry around and to use. They are especially useful when traveling, and most drugstores carry the necessary supplies.

Test for Acetone. Acetest tablets and acetone test powder are used most commonly to test for acetone in the urine. Place 2 drops of urine on the tablet or on a small heap of the powder. If the tablet or the powder turns purple, the test is positive.

(In using these test materials it is important to keep the containers tightly covered. Otherwise, they absorb moisture from the air and are useless.)

The test for acetone is especially important if the patient is vomiting, if he has a fever, or if sugar is present in the urine. Acetone and sugar may show up in the urine at one time of the day and be absent at another. Therefore, it is best to test freshly secreted urine rather than urine that has been in the bladder for some time. This means having the patient void, to empty his bladder, half an hour before you collect the specimen to be tested.

Test for Carbon Dioxide Combining Power. This test measures the amount of carbon dioxide in the blood. A lower-than-normal amount indicates an excess of ketones in the body.

The Treatment of Diabetes Mellitus

Diet. One of the most important factors in controlling diabetes is the patient's diet. If he takes in more carbohydrates that his body can use or store, the diabetic will develop *ketosis* and *acidosis*. With too little food he will be undernourished, and if he is taking insulin, he will be threatened with insulin shock. Therefore, he must have the right kind of food as well as the right amount of food to prevent these complications from developing. The doctor calculates the diet for the individual diabetic in relation to his age, sex, activity, health, cultural background and his usual dietary habits. Diabetics, like everyone else, must have the essential amounts of vitamins, minerals and calories, but the amounts will vary with each patient. Mr. Noble, a retired businessman, will not have the same requirements as Mr. Mason, a professional baseball player.

A diabetic must accept the fact that he will have to observe dietary rules all his life. At first this may seem to be an impossible prospect, but once he understands that in other ways his life can be normal if he follows the doctors orders, the diabetic can accept his disability and learn to live with it. The diet of the diabetic is discussed in more detail at the end of this chapter.

Insulin. With luck, a diabetic fifty years ago might expect to live 5 or 10 years at the most after he discovered that he had diabetes. Insulin has changed that picture. Today insulin is not only available for diabetics but it is also available in many different forms, to meet the needs of individual patients. However, all forms of insulin must be given hypodermically, because the digestive juices destroy its effectiveness if it is taken by mouth. The table below lists the different forms of insulin, with their effects.

Forms of Insulin. *Crystalline insulin* is merely a slightly different form of *regular insulin* and has the same effects. Both of them are quick-acting and are given 15 to 30 minutes before a meal so that they will reach the bloodstream at about the same time that the glucose does. Long-acting insulins are usually given 30 minutes before a meal. Quick-acting insulins usually have to be repeated during the day because their effects do not last as long as those of the other forms of insulin. Researchers found that by adding other substances to insulin the effects could be prolonged. Protamine zinc insulin (PZI) and neutral protamine Hagedorn (NPH) are examples of these combinations. These compounds have made it possible for many diabetics to get along with 1 insulin injection a day, since their effects last 20 hours

Forms of Insulin

	Regular	Crystalline	Globin	NPH	Protamine Zinc	Lente
Onset	½–1 hour	1 hour	1–2 hours	1–2 hours	4–8 hours	1–2 hours
Peak Action	2–4 hours	2–4 hours	8 hours	8–20 hours	12–24 hours	8–20 hours
Duration	6–8 hours	6–8 hours	18–24 hours	20–48 hours	Over 30 hours	20–28 hours

or longer. *Lente insulin* is both quick-acting and long-lasting.

Insulin is a liquid that comes in units of varying strengths—U 40, U 80, and so on—which are marked on the bottle. Syringes for giving insulin are marked in units for measuring the dose of insulin. However, these unit scales are different for U 40 and U 80 insulin. Sometimes both scales are marked on one syringe, but it is simpler, and there is less chance of making a mistake, if separate syringes are used with each type of dosage. For example, a U 40 syringe should be used to give only U 40 insulin. The doctor specifies the type of insulin and the number of units to be given.

To preserve its effectiveness, insulin is kept in the refrigerator, but it should not be frozen. The diabetic who must travel can keep his supply of insulin cool in a thermos or an insulated bag.

Oral Medications (Hypoglycemic Agents). Insulin itself is not effective when given by mouth, but several products that can be given orally stimulate the pancreas to secrete more insulin. These agents are not insulin, but they are effective in the milder forms of diabetes; they are useless in treating severe conditions. The agents most commonly used are tolbutamide (Orinase), chlorpropamide (Diabinese) and phenformin (DBI).

Orinase is the most widely used. It acts quickly, within an hour after it is given, and the effects last almost 24 hours. Orinase and Diabinese have few side-effects which are more common with DBI: the patient may have headache, gastrointestinal disturbances and skin irritation, and a lowered white blood count. DBI is the least widely used of these agents.

Insulin Shock. The dose of insulin is calculated to control an individual's diabetic condition. The purpose of giving insulin is to keep the patient's sugar level in the blood at normal. Too much insulin in relation to the amount of glucose will reduce this level to below normal and will cause a reaction which is called *insulin shock.* The patient feels weak, cold and suddenly exhausted; he is hungry and nervous, and he trembles and perspires. With the longer-acting insulins he may experience headache and drowsiness, nausea and vomiting. Without treatment, other symptoms develop, such as dizziness, confusion and loss of speech. The patient is unable to coordinate his movements; he sees double, and if he is still untreated, he may have convulsions and become unconscious. Without treatment, his brain may become permanently damaged, and he may die, although this rarely happens. This condition may develop so rapidly that the patient is having convulsions or becomes unconscious before anybody knows that something is wrong. The nurse should be quick to recognize the early symptoms of insulin shock.

Treatment. The administration of carbohydrates is the treatment for an insulin reaction. For a conscious patient this is sugar in some form, such as orange juice, candy, honey, sweetened warm tea or coffee. The unconscious patient is given dextrose intravenously. An insulin reaction requires emergency treatment, which is followed by the adjustment of the patient's carbohydrate intake and his insulin dosage to regulate his disturbed metabolism. This is not easy in the first 24 hours following the reaction, and the patient needs close observation to notice unfavorable symptoms that may reappear.

What the Patient Should Know. Infection or severe emotional strain may upset well-regulated treatment after it has been established. Sometimes the patient does not understand how important it is to obey orders, or he becomes careless about his diet and then attempts to adjust his insulin dosage himself. Every diabetic should know that he should report loss of appetite, hunger or any gastrointestinal upset that is severe enough to keep him from eating or to cause diarrhea or vomiting. He should know that sugar-free urine is a sign that his treatment is progressing favorably, but when sugar is evident in his urine it is an unfavorable sign which should be reported at once to his doctor.

Acidosis. To make up for the loss of sugar as a source of energy, the body uses more fats and proteins, which are broken down into substances called *ketones* and sent to the muscles to provide energy. If an excess amount of these ketone bodies accumulate in the body (ketosis), it upsets the alkali-acid balance in body fluids and causes a condition called *acidosis.* In this process, a volatile substance called acetone is produced; it has a characteristic sweetish odor which can be detected on the breath. Any condition that interferes with the storage of glycogen in the liver and increases the body's need to burn fat for energy, such as lack of insulin, vomiting, surgery, or anesthesia, may increase the production of ketone bodies.

Ketosis and Diabetic Coma. The signs of ketosis are weakness, drowsiness, vomiting, thirst, abdominal pain and dehydration, with flushed cheeks and a dry skin and mouth. The patient's breath may have the sweetish odor mentioned above; his breathing may become slow, deep and labored; his pulse may be rapid and weak, and his blood pressure low. This may lead to coma. Sometimes the comatose patient who is admitted to the hospital does not know that he has diabetes. Others have a diabetic condition that is hard to control, and it gets out of hand even when the patient follows rules faithfully.

TREATMENT. While waiting for the examination of blood and urine specimens to be completed, blankets are applied to the unconscious patient to keep him warm, and his pulse and respiration are checked frequently. If he has dentures, they are removed. As soon as the examinations show that he is a diabetic, insulin is given. Insulin, by lowering the production of ketones, makes more carbohydrate available to the tissues and builds up the glycogen supply in the liver. Regular insulin is given because it acts rapidly. Intravenous fluids help to relieve dehydration.

Sometimes insulin is given and the urine is tested every half-hour. Blood specimens are tested for sugar frequently, and a record is kept of the patient's fluid intake and output. In extreme cases, a stimulant may be necessary, such as epinephrine or caffeine. When the patient's metabolism is in balance again, he continues with the indicated routine.

Circulatory Disturbances. For some unknown reason, arteriosclerosis is more common in diabetics than in nondiabetics. Other complications are numbness, itching and pains in the legs. Diabetics burn easily, because they may not feel intense heat. Poor circulation leads to

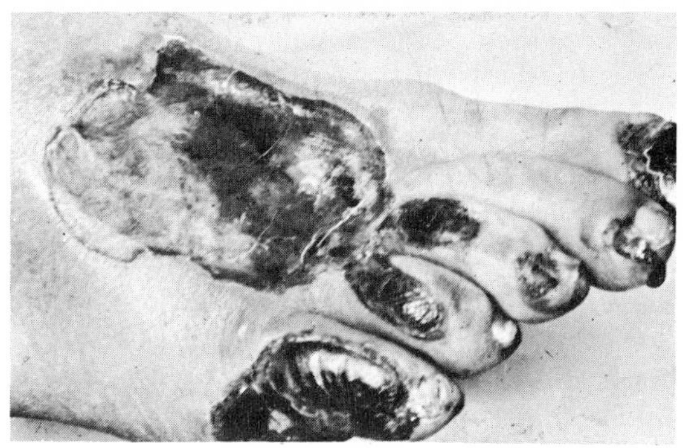

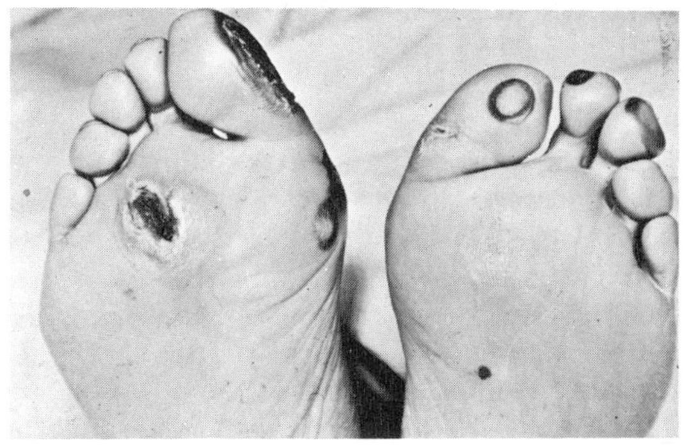

FIG. 170. Gangrene of the feet in diabetes mellitus. (Dr. John R. Williams, North Carolina Med. J.)

infection, obstruction of the arteries, ulcers and gangrene and eventually to amputation. In diabetics, wounds are slow to heal, and surgery is always a risk.

Care of the Feet. Painstaking care of the feet is so important to the diabetic that the detailed treatment* is given here, as directions that both the nurse and the diabetic can follow easily.

Soak in warm, soapy water for 5 minutes every day.

Dry thoroughly, especially between the toes.

Massage gently with cold cream or pure lanolin.

Exercise daily to improve circulation: sit on the edge of the bed, point toes upward, then downward. Do this 10 times. Make a circle with each foot 10 times.

* Adapted from Smith, D. W., and Gips, C. D.: Care of the Adult Patient, ed. 1, p. 1041, Philadelphia, Lippincott, 1963.

Make sure that shoes fit well. Wear new shoes only for a short period each day for a few days.

Never wear circular garters.

Avoid sitting with crossed knees.

Cut nails straight across with sharp scissors. See a chiropodist for treatment of corns and calluses. Self-treatment in any form is dangerous and absolutely forbidden.

Never pick at sores or rough spots on the skin.

Do not walk around barefooted.

Do not use adhesive tape on the skin.

Put lamb's wool between overlapping toes.

For cold toes, use warm socks and extra blankets at night. Heating pads and hot water bags are dangerous.

See a doctor for a cut, no matter how small it is. If first-aid treatment is necessary, cleanse the area gently with 70 per cent alcohol (no harsh antiseptics) and apply a dry sterile dressing. It is still essential to see a doctor as soon as possible.

Get the answers to your questions from the doctor or the nurse. It is not enough to give the diabetic a list of the things he must do unless the reasons for these precautions are explained carefully. Some of them may seem to be trivial, and he may hesitate to bother the doctor with things that to him seem to be so trifling.

Infections. Infections aggravate diabetes, and diabetics are susceptible to tuberculous infections and to carbuncles and furuncles. The common cold is another menace. If the diabetic has a stomach upset, he should go to bed, drink a glass of water every hour, take his insulin, test his urine, and call the doctor.

Vision Problems. Inflammation of the retina (retinitis) occurs 10 times more frequently in diabetics than in nondiabetics, and it may damage the retina permanently. Cataracts may develop and often do. A cataract may be removed surgically if retinal damage is not too great. The blind or almost-blind diabetic fears losing his independence, but there are devices that can be used to help him to continue to give himself insulin and test his urine. For example, special syringes are available (Tru-Set or Cornwall) with the plunger fixed at the correct dose. Furniture can be placed where he is less likely to bump into it—a bump may cause a break in the skin.

The Outlook for the Diabetic. Diabetes cannot be cured, but it can be controlled, and sometimes it improves slightly. The diabetic can be reassured by knowing that the outlook for a satisfactory life is hopeful if he obeys orders. He can hold a job; prejudice against hiring diabetics is much less than it used to be. Diabetics have proved that they can compete successfully with nondiabetics in the working world. He can eat almost anywhere if he has learned how to estimate portions and knows the foods he is allowed to have. He can take his equipment with him when he travels and can use it handily by using a cup and a small metal heating device that he can plug into any electrical outlet to sterilize the syringe and the needle. It boils water in 2 minutes.

The Diet of the Diabetic

Diet is a vital part of the treatment of diabetes, but the patient does not have to worry about planning his diet while he is in the hospital. When the patient goes home, the picture changes, for then he (or she) or some member of the family must be able to calculate the diet. This means that the patient must have instructions before he leaves the hospital. The American Diabetes Association offers *Meal Planning With Exchange Lists* to help the diabetic to plan his diet. It gives 6 lists of food of equal value, showing possible food exchanges. Thus, if a patient does not want an egg, he can substitute an ounce of chicken without upsetting the calculated balance in his diet. The *ADA Forecast*, a magazine for diabetics, gives recipes for preparing food. Directions for portions or servings of food give cup or spoon measurements.

Meals. The dietary allowance is usually divided between 3 meals and includes snacks. The patient cannot have more than his food allowance, and he must eat all of it. Otherwise, he will upset the balance between his diet and his insulin dosage. The doctor may want him to spread the amount of carbohydrate in his diet throughout his meals in different proportions, such as one fifth of the total carbohydrate allowed for breakfast, two fifths for his noon meal, one fifth for his evening meal and one fifth at bedtime.

Diabetic Foods. Sugarless products are on the market in increasing numbers, but some doctors feel that a diabetic patient should learn to adjust his diet while using regular foods, since these special products are more expensive and have no special nutritional advantages. Patients are usually allowed to use saccharin or sucaryl in tea or coffee or to add them to foods. If they are added to foods during cooking they have a bitter taste. No-Cal sugar-free beverages are available, as are cookies and candies made with artificial sweeteners. Patients should be cautioned to steer clear of products that do not spell out their sugar, fat and protein content on the label. "Dietetic" alone is not enough. A diabetic has a lot to learn when he first takes over the routines that he must follow. The public health nurse can make follow-up visits after he goes home, to see how he is getting along and to help him and his family with any problems that may come up.

Identification

Every diabetic should carry an identification card, such as the one that is available from the American Diabetes Association (Fig. 171). It tells people what to do in an emergency, such as in an insulin reaction, and may prevent a diabetic's being carried off to jail or being thought of or possibly ignored as a common drunk.

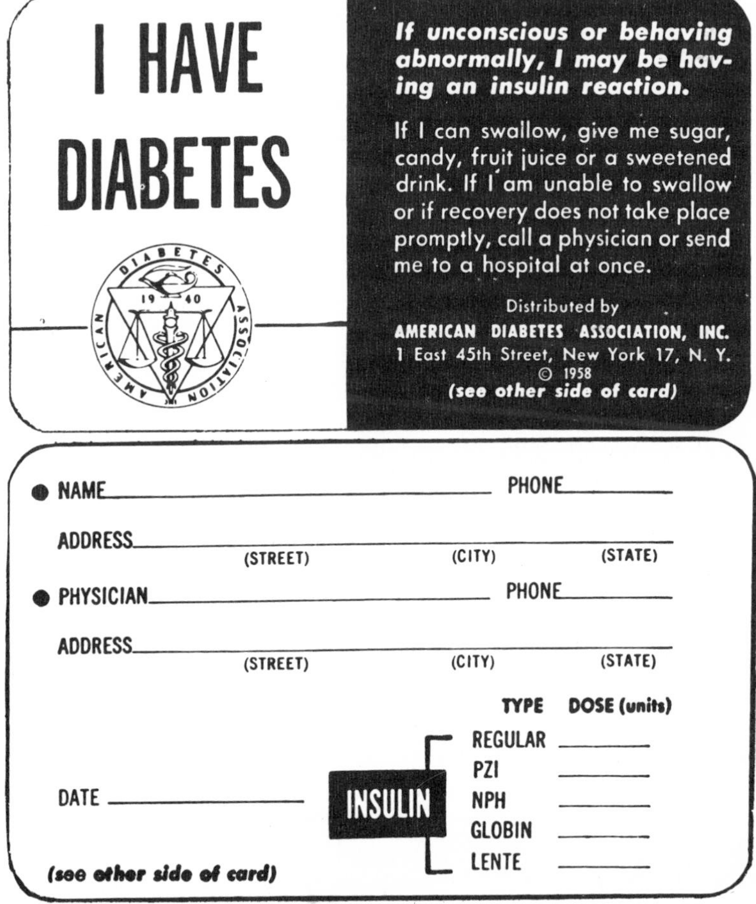

Fig. 171. Identification card for diabetics. (American Diabetes Association, 1 East 45th Street, New York 17, New York)

43

THE PATIENT WITH A DISTURBANCE OF THE NERVOUS SYSTEM

The nervous system controls every mental and physical adjustment that must be made to meet any situation. It controls reasoning and thinking, body movements and body processes. The central and the peripheral nervous systems, which consist of the brain, the spinal cord, and the cranial and the spinal nerves, control voluntary actions. The autonomic nervous system consists of a specialized group of peripheral fibers which regulate involuntary processes, such as heart action.

The Nurse's Responsibility. Anything interfering with the operation of the nervous system causes a neurologic disorder. It may be a minor one, or it may be severe. Although you may not be solely responsible for the care of the acutely ill patient, you are likely to have some responsibility for his care. Since you will be associated with some who are partially or wholly disabled by neurologic disorders or disease, either at home, in the hospital or in a nursing home, it is important to know the causes of these difficulties and the reasons for a patient's behavior as a result of disease or injury. You must understand why it is important to help him to help himself. Modern nursing is not satisfied with merely keeping a patient clean and fed—it hopes to help him to be as useful and contented as possible, to feel wanted and worthwhile. Neurologic patients need help and understanding. It may be your good fortune to be able to meet this need.

THE BRAIN

The lobes of the brain contain the centers that control our actions, sensations and thought processes: memory, reasoning and the emotions, as well as movements, hearing, taste, smell, vision and speech. Some of these centers are illustrated in Figure 57. (The speech center is located in the left side of the brain in right-handed people, and in the right side of the brain in left-handed people.) Groups of nerves (tracts) carry impulses from the brain to the rest of the body and from the body to the brain. The *left* side of the brain controls movements on the *right* side of the body and vice versa; therefore, injury to the left side of the brain causes paralysis on the right side of the body. Injured outer nerves may gradually repair themselves, but the nerves within the brain and spinal cord that have been destroyed do not have this power. The extent of any damage to these nerves determines how much of his normal function the patient can recover.

The Neurologic Examination

The neurologic examination includes a number of special tests to estimate the damage to the nervous system. The doctor will test movements, muscle strength, vision, hearing, taste and smell, sensations of pain, heat and cold. He will test the patient's ability to reason, his knowledge of where he is and what is going on around him; he might ask who the governor of the state is, a question that almost anyone normally could answer.

The patient's state of consciousness will affect his responses to tests. The variations from normal consciousness are:

Coma: The patient responds only to the most painful stimulus.

Stupor: The patient can be partially aroused momentarily with great difficulty.

Delirium: The patient is disoriented, restless and has no real idea of where he is or what he is doing.

Confusion: The patient seems to know vaguely where he is and has difficulty in remembering.

Patients with neurologic disease often have little control over their emotions—they may be deeply depressed one minute and wildly happy the next, for no apparent reason.

Special Tests

Lumbar Puncture. The brain and the spinal cord are enveloped in the *cerebrospinal fluid,* which acts as a cushion to protect them and to maintain an even pressure within the parts of the brain. A *lumbar puncture* is the insertion of a needle into the spinal canal, usually between the 3rd and the 4th lumbar vertebrae, which is done for several reasons: (1) to obtain a specimen of the spinal fluid for laboratory examination; (2) to inject a drug (spinal anesthetic); (3) to measure the pressure of the spinal fluid; (4) to withdraw spinal fluid to relieve excess pressure; (5) to inject a radiopaque dye before taking roentgenograms of the brain and the spinal canal.

Many neurologic disorders cause changes in the spinal fluid that help the doctor to locate the cause of the patient's trouble. Disease organisms, such as the tubercle bacillus or the spirochete of syphilis, may be present. Pus may indicate an inflammation of the membranes surrounding the brain and the spinal cord; increased pressure may be a sign of cerebral hemorrhage; lowered pressure may indicate an obstruction to the flow of spinal fluid.

Nursing Care. This procedure is only slightly uncomfortable because of the position which the patient must take. If the patient knows what to expect, he is likely to be cooperative, in which case everything will proceed smoothly and quickly.

The patient may have a headache after a spinal puncture. Some doctors keep the patient

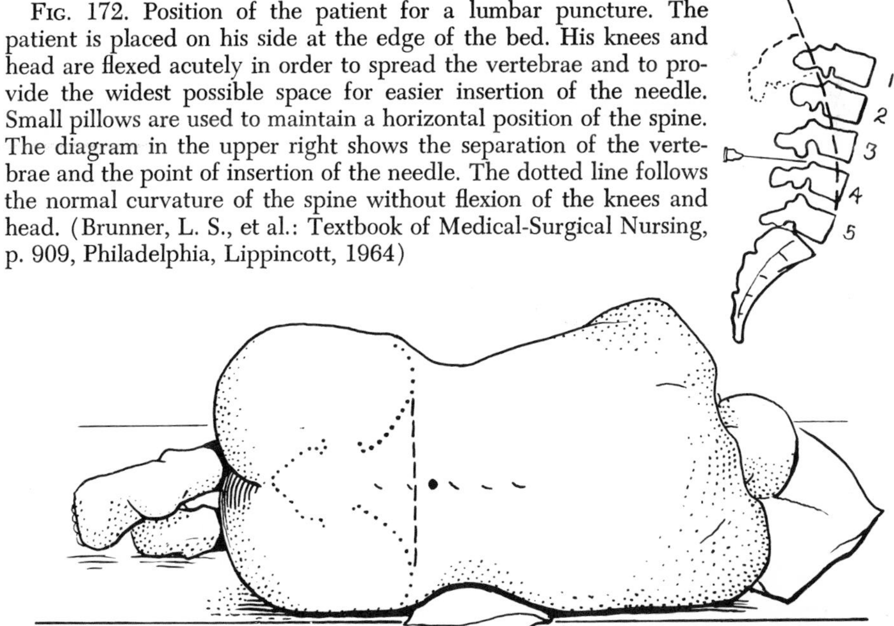

Fig. 172. Position of the patient for a lumbar puncture. The patient is placed on his side at the edge of the bed. His knees and head are flexed acutely in order to spread the vertebrae and to provide the widest possible space for easier insertion of the needle. Small pillows are used to maintain a horizontal position of the spine. The diagram in the upper right shows the separation of the vertebrae and the point of insertion of the needle. The dotted line follows the normal curvature of the spine without flexion of the knees and head. (Brunner, L. S., et al.: Textbook of Medical-Surgical Nursing, p. 909, Philadelphia, Lippincott, 1964)

flat in bed for several hours, but others allow the patient to be up and about as usual.

Cisternal Puncture. The procedure for a cisternal puncture is the same as for a lumbar puncture with the exception that the puncture is made between the lower part of the occipital bone in the skull and the first vertebrae. It is not done as frequently as the lumbar puncture.

Pneumoencephalography. This procedure is done to discover lesions or growths of the brain. It consists of a lumbar puncture to withdraw spinal fluid, followed by the injection of filtered air which rises through the spinal canal to the ventricles of the brain. X-ray pitcures are then taken to show any abnormal condition, such as a tumor. The patient has regular preoperative preparation for this procedure: an enema and a sedative the night before; a sedative before the procedure the next morning and nothing by mouth for 6 hours prior to the procedure.

Nursing Care. Usually pneumoencephalography is followed by a severe headache. Nausea and vomiting may occur and sometimes shock, convulsions or breathing difficulties. The patient lies flat in bed and should be bathed and fed. He should avoid turning his head, since this increases his discomfort. An ice cap applied to his head, and codeine or aspirin may be ordered to relieve pain. Usually, his blood pressure is taken every 15 or 30 minutes for a time immediately after the procedure. The patient may be allowed up in a day or two but should be assisted to sit up gradually before he stands and walks.

Ventriculography. *Ventriculography* is similar to encephalography, except that the air is injected through holes drilled in the skull. This procedure is only used when it is impossible to do pneumoencephalography. The preoperative preparation is the same, with the addition of shaving the area on the skull where the holes are to be made. The after-care is the same.

Cerebral Angiography. A radiopaque substance is injected into the carotid artery, and x-ray pictures are taken of the blood vessels in the brain, to discover a tumor or abnormal conditions in the blood vessels. Usually, an ice cap is applied to the neck after this procedure, to reduce edema and oozing from the puncture in the carotid artery. Sometimes the patient shows signs of muscular weakness in the face or in the extremities, or he may have respiratory difficulties. A tracheostomy set is kept at hand.

Myelography. When a *myelography* is taken, a lumbar puncture is made, and a radiopaque substance is injected into the spinal canal; then x-ray pictures can be taken to discover tumors or a ruptured intervertebral disk. The dye is drained off after the roentgenograms have been taken, to avoid irritation of the meninges. The patient is kept in bed for a few hours after this test and observed for signs of irritation, such as a stiff neck or pain when he bends his head forward.

Electroencephalography. This test records the electrical impulses generated by the brain and is used frequently in the diagnosis of epilepsy. The *electroencephalograph* is the machine that makes the graph (encephalogram) of these impulses by its connection with electrodes placed on the patient's scalp. The procedure is painless and has no after-effects—it takes about one half to 2 hours to do the test. The use of electrical equipment may frighten the patient unless its use is explained beforehand and he is assured that there is no danger of an electric shock.

PARAPLEGIA

Paraplegia is the paralysis of both lower extremities due to a spinal cord injury. It may result from a trauma: a gunshot or other wound, or an automobile accident; or it may be caused by a disease, such as poliomyelitis or multiple sclerosis. It may occur suddenly, or it may develop gradually. It will cause disability depending on the injury to the spine and its severity. The disability is greatest when the cervical vertebrae are injured—the victim then usually has paralysis of all 4 extremities (*quadriplegia*). A lumbar vertebrae injury affects only the lower part of the body. At the highest cervical level, the injury will affect the chest muscles and the diaphragm and will cause death from respiratory failure. Lower in the cervical region, an injury affects the chest muscles, but diaphragmatic breathing is still possible. If the spinal cord is only partially damaged, some function may still be possible, but if the cord is severed, function below the level of the injury cannot be restored.

Improvements in Treatment. Most of the paraplegics are young people with injuries resulting from accidents or diseases such as *poliomyelitis* or *multiple sclerosis,* diseases which affect young people more than older persons. Many paraplegics are veterans of World War II, but the number of disabled civilians is far greater than those crippled because of the war. However, since World War II, tremendous strides have been made in the rehabilitation of paraplegics. In the first place, many more lives were saved during the war by improved treatment for shock and by antibiotics. Also, rehabilitative technics have improved, and the importance of physical medicine is now widely recognized.

Available Treatment. The Veterans Administration provides treatment for disabled veterans, but civilians have not fared as well. The necessary large-scale treatment is expensive, and there are not enough trained people to carry it out. A single patient may need the services of many specialists: a psychiatrist, a neurologist, a physiotherapist, or an occupational therapist. For the most part, these services are available in special institutions and in large medical centers and are not provided by many community hospitals or clinics. However, state health departments have extended their efforts toward establishing centers for rehabilitation, and much progress has been made.

Treatment of Spinal Cord Injuries

Treatment begins with taking care when moving the victim immediately after the injury has occurred, to prevent making it worse. The patient with a spinal injury should be kept flat on a firm surface; he should be moved by rolling and never lifted by the head, the shoulders, or the feet, since this will bend the spine. He may need treatment for shock and hemorrhage. After an x-ray picture has been taken to determine the extent of the injury, the proper treatment is prescribed. Surgery may be necessary to remove a part of a vertebra pressing on the spinal cord, or traction by a head halter or Crutchfield tongs may be applied. (Crutchfield tongs are inserted through small holes made on either side of the patient's head and traction is applied to the head by ropes and weights.)

Complications. A spinal cord injury may have some or all of the following damaging effects in varying degrees:

Loss of sensation—varying from tickling, burning and numbness to partial or complete paralysis of any one or more parts of the body

Loss of movement—varying from muscle weakness to partial or complete paralysis

Loss of mental functions—varying from confusion to coma and often involving loss of speech, sight or hearing.

Nursing Care. Once you know the possible effects of a spinal cord injury, you can determine the kind of nursing care that will be necessary. The following directions apply to the patient who is powerless to help himself or to control his body functions:

1. His position must be changed frequently to prevent pressure sores and pneumonia. The Stryker or the Foster frame or the CircOlectric bed may be used to turn helpless patients (Fig. 173). Cleanliness, massage and change of position help to prevent pressure sores. A footboard helps to prevent footdrop.

2. He will have to be fed; in some instances the only way a patient can be given food or fluids is intravenously or by tube. He needs a high protein diet to keep his body tissues healthy, and a high fluid intake to prevent urinary tract infections.

3. He will have urinary incontinence; usually, a retention catheter is inserted into the bladder to drain the urine. If disposable pads are used, special attention must be given to keeping the skin clean and dry, in order to prevent pressure sores.

4. The patient will have fecal incontinence and may have fecal impaction. A daily enema may be ordered to prevent these conditions.

5. Passive exercises to preserve any remaining muscle function and to restore all possible function will be needed. Paralyzed muscles that are limp at first may later develop spasms; exercises sometimes help to relieve them. Breath-

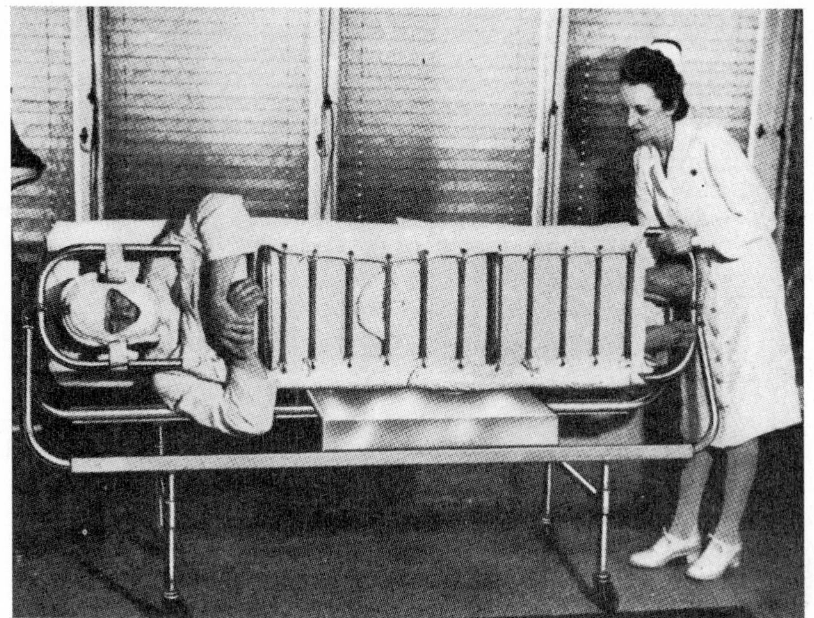

A

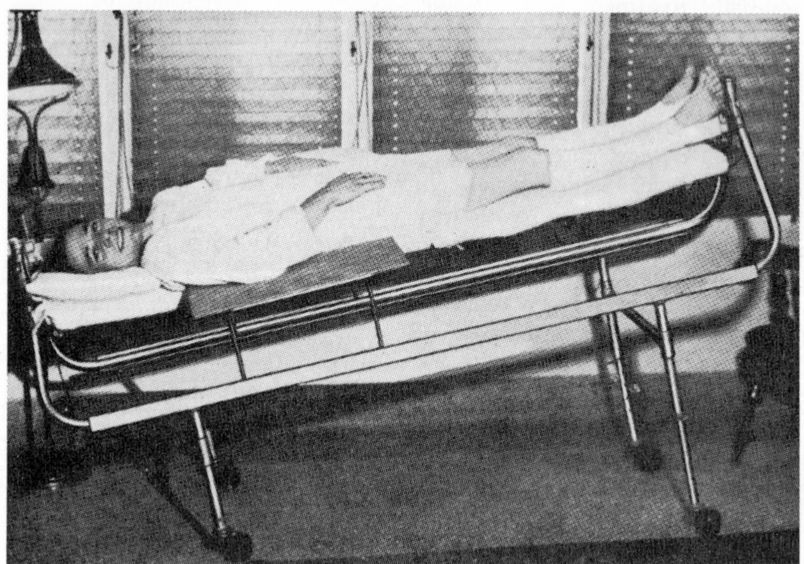

B

Fig. 173. The patient in a Stryker frame. (A) Turning the patient may be accomplished by one nurse with no lifting and with a minimum of discomfort to the patient. The patient is held firmly between the 2 frames which are fastened to the turning device by wing nuts at each end. The upper frame is removed after turning is completed. Rubber fasteners keep the canvas continuously and evenly taut, add comfort, and allow for variations in contour. (B) The patient on the posterior

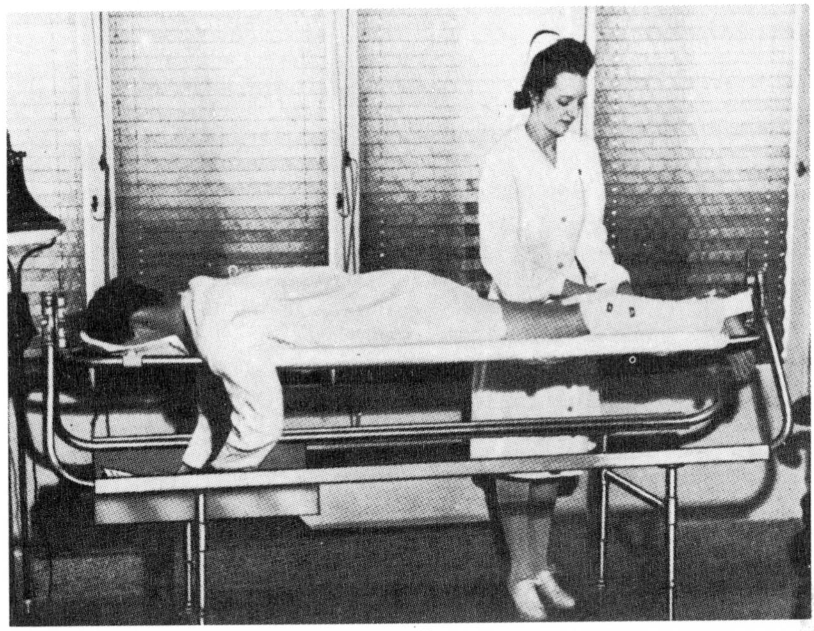

C

ing exercises, if they are possible, will help to prevent pneumonia.

Psychological Effects Upon the Patient. The shock to the patient who is able to realize what has happened to him can be terrific. Gradually, as he becomes stronger, he visualizes his future, perhaps as a life of inactivity and helplessness. It is not always possible to give the patient the encouragement that he hopes for—a quadriplegic, for example, may be completely helpless for the rest of his life. It is mistaken kindness to foster false hopes of complete recovery, but the patient should be encouraged to make every effort to improve his condition. Fortunately for the paraplegic, improvement can be expected, but he has a long, hard road to travel before he can accomplish even the simplest task, which even then will be possible only through his own will power and perseverance. Without these efforts no amount of assistance will do the job. Often, he will be discouraged, and a nurse helps most by letting the patient express his frustration and discouragement, and acknowledging these feelings, rather than constantly reminding him that he should be glad he is alive. At this point, the patient probably feels that he would rather be dead. Just to be able to let go and say how he really feels may be a great relief for him from always trying to keep up a brave front. Knowing that no one blames him for being discouraged may renew his courage to go on.

Fig. 173—(*Cont.*)

frame. The foot end of the cart is elevated for leg traction in pelvic and intertrochanteric fractures and the traction straps fastened to hooks in the turning disk. For head traction in fractures of the cervical spine, the Crutchfield tongs are attached to the disk; this allows continuous traction before, during, and after turning. The center section is dropped for bedpan service. (C) The patient on the anterior frame. This permits more adequate nursing care in conditions affecting the back. It facilitates the medical and postoperative treatment of spinal cord injuries, back wounds, burns, and many other conditions. The patient can feed himself in this position, thus saving nursing time.

PROBLEMS THAT THE PATIENT FACES

His Family. The patient may feel that he must always appear brave and cheerful before his family, an effort which he may find too great for him. Instead of welcoming their visits he begins to dread them. The family should know his probable limitations and just how much to expect of him in the way of rehabilitative efforts. They should know that the smallest amount of progress often represents untiring effort and perseverance, and they should rejoice with the patient in his slightest accomplishment. The nurse's interest and pride in his progress is reassurance that everything is being done to restore him to as nearly normal a life as is possible.

Helplessness. The paraplegic or the quadriplegic is continually frustrated by his inability to do things for himself and by having to wait for help. He sees every muscle spasm as a sign of some new and hateful difficulty. If he is left alone, he fears that people think that he is no longer worth bothering about. It may be a long time before he shows any interest in what is going on around him, laughs at a joke, or looks forward to anything. Meanwhile, he may be asking himself many questions for which he has no answers—how will he pay his bills, earn a living, or be taken care of when he leaves the hospital?

He is humiliated by his incontinence and by the fear of distressing others with odors or embarrassing accidents. If he is impotent (many paraplegics are) he feels ashamed. Marital relations may be inadvisable or impossible. He may be confined to his bed or to a wheelchair. He may live in the perpetual fear of falling or of being caught in a fire.

The Payoff. Gradually, the patient's efforts begin to pay off—he moves his fingers, his hands and his arms. Physical therapy brings back strength to his arms and shoulders, and ways are found for using that strength; ingenious devices help him to do things for himself and sometimes to develop a skill. One problem for the paraplegic is to keep his mind, which is not paralyzed, from getting too far ahead of his body, which moves at a far slower speed, and expecting too much too soon. Once the patient understands this, he is less likely to be discouraged by his slow progress.

Rehabilitation

The rehabilitation of any patient with paralysis is centered on preventing his disabilities from increasing and on strengthening and making the most of whatever powers he may have. It begins immediately with preventing such disabilities as decubitus ulcers or foot drop, and with exercises to develop muscle strength and movement. It is true that the degree of the patient's success does depend on the nature and the extent of nerve damage, but we now know that success, through the use of modern physiotherapy and the patient's own perseverance, often is much greater than was once thought to be possible. In spite of paralysis, many patients become able to move about and to look after themselves to some degree. (See Chapter 31 for more details on rehabilitation.)

Help for Incontinence. Bowel and bladder incontinence is one of the major problems encountered by the paraplegic. However, it is possible for many patients to establish regular habits if everyone concerned will take the time and the effort necessary to make these habits automatic. Help in controlling bowel movements includes:

Providing a large amount of liquids and bulk foods in the diet, such as fresh fruit and vegetables, and avoiding those foods which have been found to produce loose stools.

Establishing a regular time for giving the patient the bedpan or taking him to the toilet each day. If possible, get him to the bathroom, because moving helps to stimulate a bowel movement and also gives the patient the satisfaction of feeling less helpless.

If the patient must have enemas at first, they should be given at the same time every day. Later, a suppository at this time may be all that is necessary to stimulate a bowel movement, until finally the patient needs neither of these aids.

This patient will not be able to retain the enema solution. One device which has been effective in helping the paralyzed patient to retain an enema is to pass the enema tube through a hole which has been made in a hard rubber ball, and to press the ball against the anus while administering the solution.

Bladder incontinence is more difficult to control, but with patience and perseverance this is possible for many patients. At first, the patient has an in-dwelling catheter to prevent retention of urine and to provide a constant urine drainage into a disposable plastic bag. The catheter is irrigated at intervals to keep it open, for which sterile normal saline, distilled water, or perhaps Renacidin solution is used. Later, the catheter is clamped off, and the clamp is released every 1 to 2 hours to accustom the bladder to holding and emptying urine as it does when it functions normally. The length of time between releases is gradually lengthened to 3 to 4 hours, until finally the catheter is removed, and the patient is encouraged to void every hour. At first, an hour is usually as long as he can retain urine, but this period can be lengthened gradually to 2, then to 3 or 4 hours. During the night, the male patient wears a rubber sheath over the penis which is attached to tubing and a disposable plastic drainage bag. Women must wear absorbent pads and rubber pants.

Be prepared for accidents during the training period by protecting the bed with a waterproof sheet and pads. Make light of such accidents and assure the patient that bladder control takes time, that accidents are to be expected and are by no means a sign that he has failed. Applying pressure over the pubis often helps the patient to urinate at the scheduled time. A careful record is kept of the fluid intake and output to be sure that they balance and that urine is not being retained.

Complete bowel and bladder control is not possible for every patient, but many do accomplish it. Bladder control is especially important because a permanent catheter in the bladder greatly increases the danger of bladder infection, which is a dreaded complication for paraplegic patients. Male patients with a catheter can attach the tube to a rubber urinal strapped to the leg, which can be concealed by their clothing. Women are not so fortunate, since they must rely on pads and rubber pants to catch the drainage. This sometimes drives women to make greater efforts toward control.

The Paraplegic at Home. With care and thoughtful planning, adjustments can be made in the home that make it possible for the paraplegic to be more independent. A toilet stool can be built up to the level of the wheelchair seat so that the patient can go to the toilet without help. The bed height can be adjusted similarly; with the aid of an overhead bar the patient can transfer himself to and from the bed and the wheelchair. A ramp enables the paraplegic to wheel his chair out-of-doors. The kitchen equipment can be arranged so that it is accessible and convenient for the paraplegic housewife (Fig. 174).

Most Likely to Succeed. Any degree of rehabilitation is worth all the time and the effort that it takes to accomplish it. Anything that makes the patient more independent of others and more self-sufficient, perhaps even to the extent of holding a job, is worthwhile. Encouragement and perseverance are the keys to success. In a paraplegic ward, some patients will have greater disabilities than others, which tends to be discouraging. On the other hand, a paraplegic may be more willing to accept his disability when he sees other people with greater ones. Remember that, in general, paraplegics are more than usually sensitive to any action that looks like favoritism. Because a patient tries harder or seems to accomplish more, you must avoid seeming to be partial to him. Progress is so discouragingly slow at times that a patient may think that you are critical of him for not progressing faster.

Intelligence, education and the "stick-to-itiveness" of the patient count most in helping the paraplegic to get and hold a job. The person whose former work was physical labor is not as fortunate because his physical power is impaired. The interest and the services of professional and other persons, the patient's own determination, and the use of mechanical and other devices are still the greatest help that the paraplegic patient can have.

GENERAL NURSING CARE FOR NEUROLOGIC PATIENTS

Many of the nursing measures that the para-

Fig. 174. These women have learned to continue their activities as homemakers from their wheelchairs. (*Top*) This woman can roll her wheelchair close to the stove because under the adjacent counter there is space for her chair. The supplies frequently used in cooking are kept handy on the shelf. (*Bottom*) This woman uses a board placed across her wheelchair to carry supplies. The open shelves keep utensils within easy reach. (Institute of Physical Medicine and Rehabilitation, New York University Medical Center, New York City)

plegic patient needs will also be necessary in caring for patients with other types of neurologic diseases or disorders which are accompanied by some degree of paralysis. Instructions about such care of these patients will not be repeated in each case in detail, since you can apply what you have learned about the care of the paraplegic; additional instruction which is needed for special conditions is included where it applies.

Multiple Sclerosis

Multiple sclerosis is a disease that destroys areas in the covering of many nerves in the body. It leaves scars in the white matter of the brain and the spinal cord which affect the connections between the brain and certain muscles and organs of sense. Several parts of the body may be affected—for example, a person might become a paraplegic and might also be blind. This disease usually causes a slow paralysis and a slowly developing disturbance of speech and vision. It begins with a few symptoms which gradually increase and become more serious. Sometimes, the symptoms disappear in the beginning of the disease, and the patient may seem to be absolutely well for years. However, each time the symptoms reappear they are more severe and of longer duration.

Symptoms. Nobody knows what causes multiple sclerosis. Often it is difficult for the doctor to diagnose this disease until certain symptoms appear together which demonstrate a widespread disturbance of the nervous system. Some common symptoms are:

Weakness and clumsy movements
Tremor when using the hand
Blurred or double vision or blindness
Slurred speech
Paraplegia
Bowel and bladder incontinence or retention

Treatment and Nursing Care. Multiple sclerosis cannot be cured, but attempts are being made continually to find a cure or to discover ways to slow the progress of the disease by various drugs and diets. Authorities agree that it is important to build up the patient's general health by providing him with plenty of rest and a good all-around diet, and avoiding excitement and exposure to infection. A patient may live 20 years or more after he is known to have the disease; however, he gradually becomes disabled in some way, with other disabilities developing. Paralysis may appear, and eye disturbances may progress to total blindness. The patient may have sudden emotional upsets, becoming either depressed or exuberant. His body becomes wasted, making him susceptible to decubitus ulcers. He is also susceptible to infection, especially pneumonia; if he is confined to his bed, his position must be changed frequently, and he should practice deep breathing. Paralysis and weakness can cause body deformities; therefore, attention should be given to maintain good body alignment.

The Patient at Home. Unless it is physically necessary, the patient does not need to stay in bed; instead, he should be encouraged to live as nearly normal a life as possible. The multiple sclerosis victim can live at home as long as he does not require physical care that he cannot carry out himself or which cannot be provided. Sometimes work can be found that he is able to do at home until the advancing disease makes this impossible. He should be encouraged and helped to learn to make the most of each day as it comes.

Epilepsy

Epilepsy is probably as old as the human race—Hippocrates described this disease as early as 400 B.C. As recently as 100 years ago it was believed that it was caused by good or evil spirits. Although modern treatment has done away with many of the superstitious beliefs about epilepsy, there are still many people who think of it as a mysterious, dreadful and shameful disease. We know now that it is a disease that can be treated and controlled, and that many people who have epilepsy are otherwise perfectly healthy and normal.

The Epileptic Attack. Epilepsy is a condition that causes a loss of consciousness for a short time, which is usually accompanied by convulsive movements of the body. An epileptic attack is called a *seizure.* Scientists have found that the electric waves given off by the brain of some persons follow a different pattern from that of most healthy persons; people with these "different" brain waves seem to be susceptible to epilepsy. Head injuries or brain infections, body disturbances and emotional upsets can also cause seizures. This irregular brain wave pattern seems to run in families, although not every member of the family may have seizures. There are about 800,000 epileptics in the United States. In most cases, the disease shows up in childhood and early adulthood.

The patient usually has a warning or *aura* before an attack. He may see a flash of bright light, smell a peculiar odor, or hear a queer sound. If this happens long enough before an attack to give the patient time to lie down, he can avoid falling and hurting himself when he becomes unconscious. There are several types of seizure:

Grand Mal ("Big Sickness"). In this type of seizure, the patient cries out and falls down unconscious, with his body muscles contracted in a rigid spasm. Spasm of his larynx and chest muscles temporarily interferes with his breathing, and he may be cyanotic for a few moments, then breathing resumes. This is followed by jerky movements caused by violent alternate contraction and relaxation of the muscles all over his body. Saliva froth appears on his lips and he may bite his tongue. He perspires freely and may void involuntarily during the convulsion. After the seizure, he usually does not remember anything about the attack but may have a headache; he feels exhausted and often sleeps for some time.

Petit Mal ("Little Sickness"). This involves only a momentary loss of consciousness, sometimes with a slight twitching of the head or the eyes that is hardly noticeable. Petit mal is most common among children.

Psychomotor Attacks. These attacks are temporary mental disturbances during which the patient does not know what he is doing and does not remember anything about it afterward. The patient behaves erratically for no apparent reason, and he usually behaves the same way during each attack. During an attack, one woman who was in charge of the linen room began removing all the linen piles from the shelves that she had just finished arranging. It is useless to try to stop this behavior, because the person has no idea of what he is doing and pays no attention to anyone. Such actions do no harm unless the person becomes aggressive when he has an attack. For example, if he always began to brandish a knife, the patient would be considered as being

Fig. 175. Patient with convulsions.

dangerous. Some patients have this type of epileptic attack instead of grand mal seizures.

JACKSONIAN SEIZURES. These convulsions are caused by a brain tumor or a lesion in the brain, and they affect the side of the body opposite the side on which the brain is afflicted. The seizure starts with jerky movements of one part of the body, which spread to include every part on that side.

Care During a Convulsion. One convulsion is not proof of epilepsy. Drugs can cause convulsions, and high fever in children is a frequent cause. In any case, it is important to protect the patient from injury. If he has fallen, do not attempt to restrain him or move him, but protect him from striking against harmful objects. Insert a soft pad between his teeth to keep him from biting his tongue; a padded wooden tongue depressor is ideal but a folded handkerchief will do. Be careful not to injure his teeth. The attack is usually over quickly; it lasts about 3 minutes. Try to discourage curious onlookers from gathering around to gape at the patient as he recovers.

Treatment of Epilepsy. Seizures that are caused by a lesion in the brain sometimes can be cured by removing the cause if this is possible. Otherwise, there is no positive cure for the attacks. Sometimes, they may disappear of their own accord, especially in the young, but in most cases continuous treatment is necessary to control seizures. Drugs, called anticonvulsants, increase the patient's resistance to seizures and sometimes do eliminate them. The most effective drugs are:

Dilantin Sodium to be taken as ordered (often required daily). It is especially effective for grand mal attacks. Its possible toxic effects are tremor, nausea and vomiting, skin rash, and occasionally weight loss and fatigue.

Phenobarbital controls seizures, but doses large enough to be effective also cause drowsiness.

Tridione is particularly effective for petit mal seizures, but it is a dangerous drug that can cause aplastic anemia. The person who takes this drug must have frequent blood examinations.

Mesantoin is similar to Dilantin in its action and is used to control grand mal and psychomotor attacks. Its side-effects include drowsiness, fatigue, skin rash and possibly aplastic anemia.

Other drugs being used are Diamox, Milontin and Celontin. People taking anticonvulsants should know that they are not cures for epilepsy but that they will control the seizures if taken regularly. They should also understand that it is dangerous to take these drugs without a doctor's supervision.

The Problems of an Epileptic. Superstitious attitudes toward epilepsy increase the problems of an epileptic. Most patients are capable of living normal lives if the seizures are controlled medically. False notions about these people interfere with their employment. Like everyone else, they need a chance to live normal lives; comparatively few epileptics need to work in sheltered workshops. Epilepsy, like many other difficulties, is a handicap that can be overcome by regular treatment just as a person's need for glasses for nearsightedness is controlled and accepted.

Headache

Headache is associated with many diseases and difficulties. It is not a disease in itself but it often appears with such conditions as eye strain, sinusitis, brain tumor or emotional tensions. Many of us have an occasional headache that disappears after taking an aspirin tablet. This should not be confused with a persistent pain that drives the victim to take headache remedies every day. Such headaches are caused by some more serious condition which needs the attention of a doctor.

Migraine. *Migraine headache* is thought to be the result of constriction, followed by dilatation, of the cerebral arteries. No single cause of it has been determined, but emotional strain seems to bring on an attack. It appears to run in families.

A migraine attack usually begins with fatigue and irritability. Before the actual pain begins the patient may have visual disturbances, such as the presence of spots or a sort of "ric-rac" pattern before the eyes. Pain usually begins on one side but may spread over the entire head during the attack. The pain is intense—a throbbing, bursting feeling—which is aggravated by light. The patient may be nauseated and vomit. Sometimes the attack lasts for several days, in which case the patient can only lie quiet in a darkened room until the pain subsides. *Ergotamine tartrate* brings relief if it is taken immediately, when the signs of an attack first appear; sometimes it will prevent an attack from developing. Nausea and vomiting and muscle cramps are possible side-effects of this drug. People who are subject to migraine should avoid emotional upsets, since these can trigger an attack.

Myasthenia Gravis

Myasthenia gravis is a disease that greatly weakens the muscles. This weakness is especially noticeable after exercising the affected muscles. It usually attacks young adults and the middle-aged, but it is not a common disease. The cause of myasthenia gravis is not known; however, it seems to be related to the conduction of nerve impulses to the muscles.

Symptoms. Myasthenia gravis comes on gradually; usually the patient notices that certain muscles seem to be very weak immediately after using them, but muscle power comes back after a rest. The muscles of the face may be affected, especially those used in chewing, swallowing, coughing and speaking as well as the eye muscles. The patient looks sleepy, and his face is expressionless, as his eyelids droop and his facial muscles become flabby and weak. If the muscles of respiration are affected, he finds it difficult to breathe. Also, he may develop pneumonia, if he is unable to expectorate the respiratory secretions.

Treatment. Neostigmine relieves the symptoms quickly, but it will not cure the disease. Myasthenia gravis may persist for years, or it may become fatal rapidly. In the mild form, the patient can be active as long as he avoids activities that are very tiring. In the severe form, he will have to have everything done for him—he may need tube feeding if he cannot swallow, and suction may be necessary to remove respiratory secretions.

Cerebral Vascular Accidents (CVA)

The brain receives its supply of food and oxygen from the blood. A sudden interruption of the blood supply to some vital center in the brain is known as a *cerebral vascular accident* (usually abbreviated to CVA). It is also known as apoplexy ("shock" is the term often used in New England). It may cause complete or partial paralysis or death. More than 250,000 people die in the United States every year as a result of CVA, which makes partial or total invalids of a million more victims.

Causes. The direct causes of CVA's are:

Cerebral hemorrhage: an artery in the brain bursts, due to a rise in blood pressure or to arteriosclerosis.

Cerebral thrombosis: a blood clot blocks an artery that supplies some vital center in the brain, usually as a result of arteriosclerosis.

Cerebral embolism: a blood clot breaks off from a thrombus somewhere else in the body and is carried to the brain, where it gets stuck in a blood vessel and shuts off the blood supply to some part of the brain. A thrombus may form anywhere in the body as a result of infection, or it may be the result of an obstruction in the coronary arteries (coronary thrombosis).

Symptoms. With a cerebral hemorrhage, the CVA happens suddenly with very little, if any, warning; sometimes the patient feels dizzy or has a strange sensation in his head just before he collapses. He becomes unconscious, his face is red, and he breathes noisily and with difficulty. His pulse is slow, but full and bounding. His blood pressure is elevated, and he may be in a deep coma which becomes deeper and deeper until he dies, or he may gradually regain consciousness and eventually recover. Patients who are comatose for a long period of time are less likely to recover. The extent of the damage to the brain determines a patient's chances for recovery; if it was slight, he will recover more rapidly and completely. Some elderly people have a series of "little strokes," caused by thrombi in small blood vessels in the brain, which only cause dizziness or a slight temporary paralysis. If this happens frequently, it may lead to eventual mental deterioration or senility.

Degrees of Consciousness. A patient may be in a *semicoma*, which means that he may not move but may groan and be aware of painful sensations. When he is in a *stupor*, a patient is restless and picking at the bedclothes or trying to get out of bed; side rails will be necessary to protect him from injury. In *somnolence*, a person is delirious and restless, or very still, falling into sleep again after he is aroused. He may answer questions, but he is confused. In any case, always remember that although the patient may not be able to speak, this does not always mean that he cannot hear, so be very careful never to discuss his condition with other people as he lies helpless before you.

Brain Damage. The most common result of a CVA is *hemiplegia*—paralysis of one side of the body. You will remember that the nerves from one side of the brain cross over to the opposite side of the body; if the *left* side of the brain is injured, the *right* side of the body will be paralyzed. A form of brain damage that affects the speech center is *aphasia*, which is the loss of the ability to use or understand spoken or written language. This means that the patient has trouble in reading, writing or speaking. He cannot name an object correctly, or if he is able to speak he does not say what he thinks that he is saying. Many patients recover some speech, but others never do.

Treatment and Nursing Care. Heparin, an anticoagulant, is sometimes given to prolong the clotting time of blood and to prevent blood clots from forming. Dicumarol or Coumadin may be given for the same purpose. Any of these drugs must be used with great care because of the danger of hemorrhage.

Some attempts have been made recently to remove surgically blood clots collected on the brain in the hope that the brain would recover with the pressure removed. It is too soon to recommend this procedure as being generally effective; so far it has not been widely successful.

The general care of the patient who has had a CVA includes many of the procedures described for the care of the paraplegic, with the addition of procedures needed in the care of the unconscious patient, such as special mouth care, tube feeding and suction. Note every sign of improvement, no matter how slight; also note the lack of it. The patient should be turned often, at least every 2 hours, keeping his body in good alignment and supporting it by pillows. As the patient recovers, the doctor specifies the amount of activity that he wants the patient to have. If a physical therapist is available, he assumes the initial responsibility for these activities. The exercises may be passive at first, but the patient should be encouraged to do them himself as soon as possible. Exercise prevents muscle contractures and keeps the muscles strong and ready to be used when the patient needs them to get around.

The Patient's Point of View. It is difficult for a well person to realize the despair and the discouragement of a person who suddenly finds that he is unable to do even the simplest things for himself. As his mind clears, he begins to realize that neither he nor anyone else knows to what extent he will recover. However, one never can tell just how much can be accomplished by perseverance. Although some indication of his limitations should be apparent after 6 months, the patient should not give up his exercises or allow his muscles to become flabby and his joints to become stiff. We have come a long way from the old attitude that nothing could be done for these patients beyond keeping them clean, dry and fed, or perhaps propping them up in a wheelchair to sit staring into space.

The Case of Mrs. Wright. We never know how much can be accomplished by a patient who really tries. Mrs. Wright is a happy example of what determination and perseverance can achieve. After a CVA she was hospitalized for several weeks, during which time exercises were begun. After she came home she persevered, with her husband's help, in doing these exercises faithfully and progressed to getting out of bed and to walking. Today, 5 years later, she is running her house again. She gets around with the aid of a cane, is able to dress and undress with very little assistance and plans and participates in social activities at home and elsewhere. Her husband, who has since retired from business, helps her in many ways, and together they have worked out plans to make it possible for her to continue as a housewife. For example, when they are alone they have most meals at a small table beneath a kitchen window looking out on the garden, which saves countless steps between the kitchen and the dining room. They have installed a portable dishwasher; cooking equipment has been made easily accessible. A divan in the den provides a place for rest periods during the day. Their persistent and combined efforts have rescued Mrs. Wright from the life of a semi-invalid.

Parkinson's Disease

Parkinson's disease, also known as *paralysis agitans* and *shaking palsy,* is a disease of the nervous system that grows progressively worse. The patient's muscles stiffen, his movements are slowed, and his muscles develop fine rhythmic tremors that go on constantly, even when the muscles are not being used. It also affects automatic movements such as blinking, eating, walking and maintaining the posture. However, Parkinson's disease does not affect thinking ability.

The Causes. It is estimated that probably 1½ million people in the United States have Parkinson's disease. The cause is unknown. It affects more men than women, and usually it appears in the 50's or the 60's. People with arteriosclerosis or syphilis sometimes have the symptoms of Parkinson's disease. Following the Spanish influenza epidemics in the early 1920's, many people were left with Parkinsonian symptoms.

Symptoms. The symptoms appear gradually and become worse so slowly that it may be years before the patient becomes alarmed and consults a doctor. The tremors are regular, but they are so fine that they are scarcely noticeable. Sometimes these tremors affect only one side of the body, from which they spread to the other side; this may happen immediately or after as long a period of time as 15 years. The tremors disappear when the patient is asleep, except in the final stages of the disease. They may start in the fingers, then extend to the arm and finally spread to the entire body. Severe tremor is constant—about 2 to 5 shakes in a second, with the thumb beating against the fingers in a sort of "pill-rolling" movement. All of the patient's body muscles become rigid; he keeps flexing his limbs slightly; and all his movements are slowed. The disease affects his spine and the neck, and he sits or stands in a stooped position. His arms no longer swing when he walks, and he is unable to shift his position quickly in order to keep his balance. Therefore, he shuffles along when he walks, in order to keep from falling. Movement in the small muscles that control changes in his facial expression is affected—he cannot blink his eyes or smile, and his face has a masklike look. He stands tense and stiff, bending his body forward.

Treatment and Nursing Care. Parkinson's disease progresses very slowly; it does not shorten life or affect the mind. Continued efforts are being made to find new and more effective treatment.* Many drugs now in use do decrease muscular spasms, tremor and sluggishness. Among the drugs most commonly used are Artane, Benadryl and Dexedrine. A single patient may be taking a number of drugs at the same time, each for a different symptom. Some attempts have been made to use surgery, but as a remedy this is still in the experimental stage, and it is too soon to tell how effective it is.

Physical therapy helps to keep the patient active, able to feed and dress himself, and to get in and out of bed or a chair. The patient can be taught how to do leg and finger exercises, how to keep his balance and how to keep his neck muscles from contracting. Exercises do not help the tremor, but they are valuable in preventing rigidity.

What the Family Can Do. The patient's family should have some instruction on how to be helpful. They should encourage the patient to do everything he possibly can for himself. They should be patient with his slow speech and movements. The family should protect him from strain, fatigue and anxiety, all of which tend to aggravate his symptoms.

Meningitis

Meningitis is an inflammation of all or part of the membranes that cover the brain and the spinal cord. Infection can travel to the meninges

* The Parkinson's Disease Foundation and the National Parkinson Foundation, both of which are located in New York City, are devoted to research and to the service of patients with Parkinson's disease.

from nearby structures, such as the sinuses or the middle ear, or it may be carried by the bloodstream. The infection may be caused by viruses, fungi, or bacteria such as the pneumococcus, the streptococcus, the staphylococcus, the meningococcus, the tubercle or the influenza bacillus. Meningitis is a serious disease to which children are particularly susceptible.

Symptoms. Meningitis usually attacks suddenly, accompanied by a high fever, a painful and stiff neck, headache, nausea and vomiting. The patient may be in a stupor or a coma, and he may have convulsions.

Treatment and Nursing Care. After a lumbar puncture has been done to determine the causative organism, the appropriate antibiotics, such as sulfadiazine or streptomycin, will be administered. The patient is very ill: cooling sponges may be ordered for his high fever, and he will be given plenty of intravenous fluids and nourishing liquids. Tube feedings may be necessary. Side boards should be in place for the patient's protection. Meningitis is a communicable disease, and isolation precautions should be carried out.

Antibiotics are highly effective in treating meningitis in adults, but if the infection is exceedingly virulent, the patient may die. Sometimes the nerves of sight and of hearing are damaged as a result of a meningitis attack.

Encephalitis

Encephalitis, sometimes called *sleeping sickness,* is an infection of the central nervous system which is caused by viruses, bacteria or chemical poisoning. It destroys nerve cells and may be a consequence of vaccination or a viral infection somewhere else in the body, such as measles or smallpox. Encephalitis seems to be more prevalent after influenza epidemics. The disease is transmitted by mosquitoes and by ticks. The insect bites an infected person, then bites a healthy person, thereby passing on the infection.

Symptoms. *Viral encephalitis* attacks suddenly, causing violent headache, fever, nausea and vomiting and drowsiness. The patient may show muscular weakness, and he may have tremors, convulsions, or sight disturbances. Some types of viral encephalitis are more lethal than others; the death rate has varied from 5 per cent to 70 per cent, depending on the cause of the infection.

Treatment and Nursing Care. No drug specifically effective for treating encephalitis has yet been found. The treatment consists of reducing the fever with cooling sponges and maintaining a quiet environment with subdued lighting. Tube feedings are necessary for the comatose patient; hot moist packs may be ordered to relieve muscle spasm. Side boards should be in place.

Many patients who recover from encephalitis are left with mental changes or convulsive disorders, or with Parkinsonian symptoms which become increasingly disabling.

Brain Injuries

Severe blows on the head can affect the brain, which is protected from injury from minor blows by the thick bones of the skull. A blow on the head may cause hemorrhage and edema of the brain, creating intracranial pressure which may result in brain damage.

Concussion. A blow on the head may shake the brain violently to cause a *concussion.* It may also cause unconsciousness, which lasts for varying lengths of time, depending upon the individual case. As the patient becomes conscious, he may be nauseated and vomit. He might complain of headache or dizziness, and sometimes he becomes restless and irritable. Some patients seem to recover from a blow on the head with no apparent ill effects, although symptoms of concussion may appear later. Patients with head injuries should be observed closely for at least 24 hours. If slow internal bleeding is taking place, the patient becomes drowsy, then comatose, but these symptoms may not appear for some time after the injury. Prolonged unconsciousness is a sign of extensive internal bleeding, and a surgical operation may be necessary to tie off the bleeding vessel and to remove the blood clot.

Depressed Skull Fracture. A severe blow on the head may break the bone and force the broken edges to press in on the brain. The symptoms of a *depressed skull fracture* vary according to the location of the brain injury. For example, if the fragment is pressing on the area of the brain that controls speech, the patient will be unable to talk until the pressure is relieved. Many skull fractures are minor, being no more than cracks in the bone, which heal without trouble. However, any fracture at the base of the skull may injure the nerves entering the spinal cord or interfere with the circulation of the spinal fluid.

TREATMENT. *Every patient* who has had a blow on his head needs watching until it is certain that the injury has not damaged his brain. As you can see, the symptoms of damage do not always appear immediately. The patient who is conscious should be watched for headache, dizziness, blindness, deafness or signs of bloody drainage from his ears, nose or mouth. A patient released after receiving first aid treatment following a head injury should be told to consult a doctor immediately if he has a dizzy spell, suddenly feels drowsy or begins to see double.

Brain Tumors

Even a benign brain tumor can be fatal, because the pressure it makes as it enlarges causes brain damage. Only a small percentage of brain tumors are malignant and the result of metastasis from some other part of the body. Brain tumors occur in all age groups.

Symptoms. Increased intracranial pressure, causing headache, sudden projectile vomiting and eye signs, will appear. The area of the brain affected by the pressure determines other signs; for example, if the motor area is affected, numbness or twitching in the arm may appear. A tumor on the frontal lobe of the brain causes changes in the person's personality and affects his memory or his ability to reason. Greatly increased intracranial pressure near the brain stem which is not relieved will cause severe respiratory difficulties, and death results from respiratory failure. With all brain tumors, the symptoms get progressively worse.

Treatment. The only cure for a brain tumor is surgical removal. The success of the operation depends upon the location of the tumor and whether it can be removed without damaging the brain. Sometimes it is impossible to remove a tumor without causing brain damage or ending the patient's life. The operation is called a *craniotomy* (making an incision through the skull) or a *craniectomy* (removing part of the skull). Brain surgery is successful in about 40 per cent of the patients.

Nursing Care. A patient may have come into the hospital before the operation with only slight symptoms of a brain disturbance, or he may be unconscious or in a coma. If he has only slight symptoms, he is almost certain to be apprehensive and perhaps frightened by the very thought of an operation on his brain. Your interested and competent preoperative care will help him to feel that he is in good hands, ready and able to give him whatever help he needs.

His family will be anxious too; they are probably trying to conceal their feelings from the patient, but they are uncertain about what to say to him. The operation will be a long one; most brain operations take from 3 to 6 hours. Anything you can do to make the waiting period more bearable for the family will be helpful. Just taking time to say a few words to them at intervals will let them know that they are not forgotten.

Following the operation, the patient requires expert observation and nursing care during the immediate postoperative period. During his convalescence he will need encouragement and understanding of his difficulties—for example, it may take time to regain control of his bodily movements. He may spill food and drop things and become dizzy when he walks. Assurance that these difficulties are to be expected and are a part of getting well will lessen his discouragement with what seems to him to be slow progress.

Brain Abscesses. A *brain abscess* is usually caused by the spread of an infection in the middle ear. Fortunately, antibiotics have practically eliminated this possibility. It may also be the result of an infection carried to the brain in the bloodstream. The symptoms of brain abscess are the same as for a brain tumor, with the additional appearance of fever followed by drowsiness or stupor and sometimes convulsions. Surgical treatment is necessary to drain the abscess. The patient may be left with some brain damage, or he may be completely cured.

Aneurysms. An aneurysm is a "ballooning-out" at one spot in the wall of a blood vessel. In most instances, an aneurysm in cranial vessels develops slowly, and the symptoms do not appear until it becomes greatly enlarged. Blood may leak slowly from a puncture in the wall of the aneurysm, or it may burst and cause severe hemorrhage and pressure on the brain. If possible, the aneurysm should be removed surgically before it breaks. About 45 out of 100 patients survive an aneurysm of the brain, and of those who live, about one third suffer some brain damage.

Pressure on the Spinal Cord

Pressure on the spinal cord can either lessen sensation or remove it altogether. It can cause muscular weakness, paralysis or muscle spasms. Those parts of the body which are below the area of pressure will be affected. For example, pressure in the cervical region could paralyze the body from the neck down, while pressure in the lumbar region might affect the nerves that control movements in the lower extremities but would not affect nerves above that point.

Causes of Pressure. Pressure on the spinal cord may be due to an injury which fractures a vertebra and pushes the broken bone into or against the cord or severs it completely. When the cord is severed, it causes permanent paralysis below the level of the injury because the spinal nerves cannot repair or replace themselves. The disk of cartilage located between 2 vertebrae may become weakened and press against the spinal nerves (*herniated disk*). Tumors, caused by metastasis from a malignant growth somewhere else in the body, may cause pressure on the spinal cord.

Treatment and Nursing Care. Spinal cord injuries are treated surgically by removing the cause of the pressure, if possible. The surgeon removes a portion of the vertebra to expose the spinal cord and takes out the bone fragment, the herniated disk, the tumor or the clot which is pressing on the cord. This operation is called a *laminectomy*. Sometimes the weakened vertebra is strengthened by grafting a piece of bone, taken from the tibia or somewhere else, onto the vertebra and the sacrum. This is called a *spinal fusion*. When the graft heals, the spine will be stiff in that area.

Another form of treatment for a herniated disk consists of providing rigid support beneath the spine with a bed board, or a Stryker frame which allows the patient to be turned without twisting his body. Traction can be used to relieve muscle spasms, and antispasmodic drugs such as Artane may be given. Exercises are started as soon as possible. Ambulatory patients may wear a lumbosacral corset or brace to keep the body in good alignment. If none of these measures helps, surgery will be necessary.

Postoperative Care of a Laminectomy Patient. Rest for the back is most important. This does not mean that the patient must lie in one position without moving. He can be taught to help the nurse turn him by making his body as rigid as possible, and keeping his arms straight at his sides. The nurse *rolls* him over in one motion, keeping his body in line. A turning sheet can also be used in this procedure. The patient should never be lifted but should be rolled onto a brace or the bedpan. He should be taught that during convalescence, he should never reach or stretch for objects on his bedside table or elsewhere.

Frequently, the patient is allowed out of bed in 5 or 6 days following a laminectomy, usually wearing a brace or a corset to give support to his back. In applying a brace, a thin cotton shirt goes on first to protect the skin. Be sure to remove all wrinkles. Then, with the patient on his side, the middle of the brace is placed over his spine and, with assistance, he rolls onto it. After the brace is fastened, he is helped to the edge of the bed, so that his legs will fall over the side when he sits up; then he is assisted to sit up slowly.

After a *spinal fusion*, the patient must remain in bed longer. Sometimes, turning this patient is not permitted without special equipment, such as a brace or a halter or a Stryker frame. Never attempt to move a patient after a spinal injury or operation unless you have been given permission and have been taught how to do it in each instance. The patient who is para-

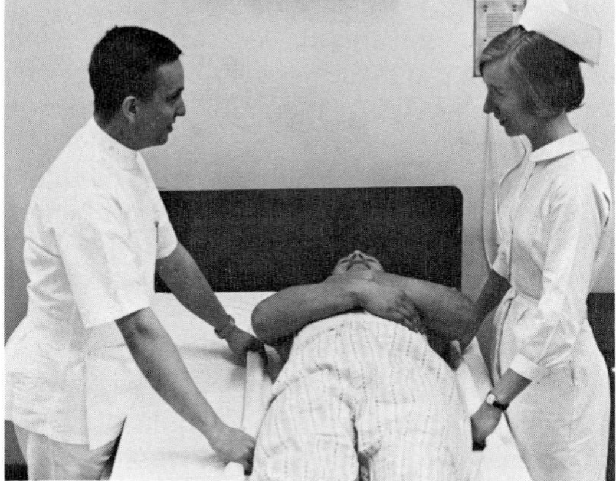

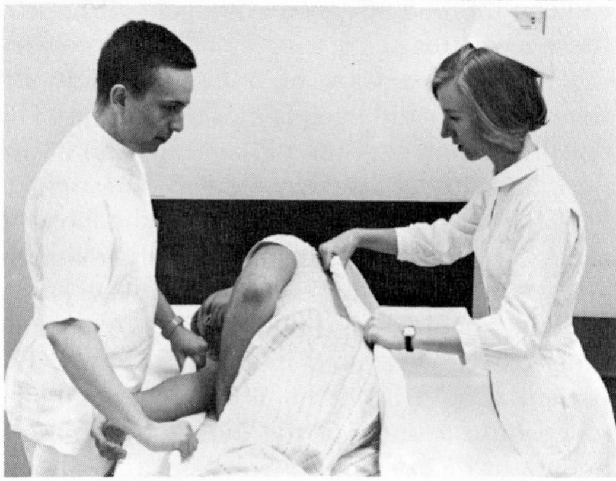

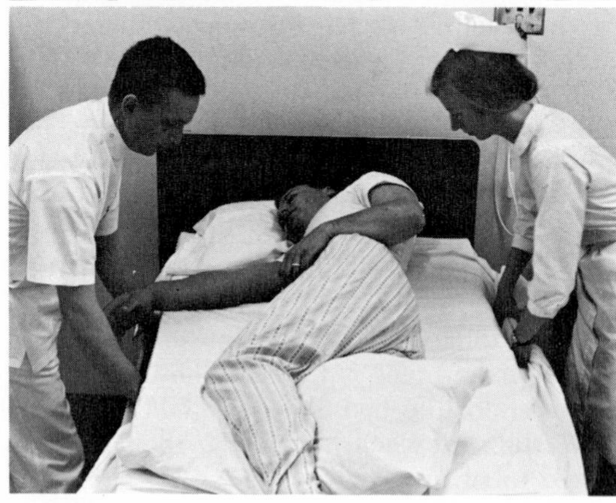

FIG. 176. Turning the patient who has had a laminectomy. Two nurses are required. This procedure is known as logrolling, because the patient is turned as a whole. A turning sheet or a drawsheet is kept under the patient to facilitate the rolling. (*Top*) The pillow is removed from beneath the patient's head. Each nurse grasps a side of the drawsheet and the patient is moved to the side of the bed. His arms are folded across his chest. (*Center*) The patient has been rolled like a log by pulling the sheet upward on his left side. (*Bottom*) The turning sheet is straightened and anchored. The patient is made comfortable, with his body put in good alignment by the use of pillows.

lyzed also needs the same kind of care as a paraplegic.

After a *laminectomy*, the patient will gradually be allowed to do light work, but he must always be careful to avoid heavy lifting, and he should use caution when doing lifting of any kind for at least a year after the operation. A nurse has many opportunities to emphasize the importance of sticking to this rule, pointing out to the patient during his convalescence that even one instance of disregarding this safeguard may cause him harm.

Trigeminal Neuralgia (Tic Douloureaux)

Sometimes, in older people, the 3-branched facial (*trigeminal*) nerve becomes very painful. Nobody knows why this happens, but the pain is excruciating and comes in spasms that last from 2 to 15 seconds. The pain may be touched off by the slightest touch to various parts of the face, or by a breeze, strains of music, a change in temperature, a mouthful of food, depending upon where the trigger zone is. The patient lives in constant dread of an attack of searing pain.

Some drugs—*Bartine*, for instance—may help temporarily, but surgery is the most satisfactory treatment. Partial removal of the nerve roots eliminates the pain permanently, although it sometimes leaves burning, tickling sensations for a time. Injecting alcohol into the nerve to paralyze it brings relief for about 6 months, after which the injection must be repeated. If the patient is elderly and surgery is not desirable, this treatment can be used.

After surgery, the patient may have some eye irritation or experience difficulty in eating until he gets used to a certain amount of numbness. Usually these seem like minor problems compared with the agony of the previous attacks of pain.

Poliomyelitis

Poliomyelitis, otherwise known as *infantile paralysis* or *polio*, has long been a much-dreaded disease for 2 reasons: it attacks primarily young people, and it often has crippling effects. People who have children in the age group that tends to contract poliomyelitis are especially afraid of this disease. One reason for this is that, before the development of polio vaccines, when polio struck it affected whole communities, and parents lived in terror lest their children be the next victims.

SOME FACTS. Polio affects more children than adults, but adults can contract it too. Most people believe that polio always cripples its victims. On the contrary, in the past thousands of people had polio but never knew it—this may even apply to you. Polio seemed to break out in different parts of the country each year, and sometimes it became epidemic.

About half of the people who contract polio recover without paralysis. Twenty-five per cent of its victims experience only a mild paralysis which does not affect their lives seriously. This means that about 25 per cent of the polio victims are left with severe handicaps. However, these people have a chance to carry on some activities with the aid of mechanical devices and rehabilitation procedures.

Causes. Polio is caused by a virus that attacks the nerve cells. It affects the motor nerves that run from the brain or the spinal cord to the muscles. The virus usually enters the body through the mouth or the nose and travels along the nerve fibers to the nerve cells connected with a group of muscles. It may damage the cells only temporarily. It may destroy some of them. A muscle becomes paralyzed if enough of the nerve cells are destroyed.

There are 3 types of paralytic polio:

1. *Spinal*, causing damage to the nerve cells in the spinal cord that control body movements, including breathing.

2. *Bulbar*, damaging nerve centers in the base of the brain and the cranial nerves. These nerves control breathing, swallowing and circulation.

3. *Bulbospinal*, involving both of the above, is the most serious and is likely to require help for respiration.

HOW DOES IT SPREAD? Nobody yet knows how polio spreads. The virus has been found in many places—in pools, streams, water, tanks, swimming pools, food and garbage. It is present in the nose and throat secretions and in the feces of perfectly well people. In spite of this information, there is no proof that a person who contracts polio after swimming in polluted water has picked up the virus there. Why some people are susceptible and others are not is still a mystery. People who become chilled or overtired seem to be more susceptible. Climate does not seem to make any difference in susceptibility. In the United States, the disease is more prevalent during the summer months.

The Fight Against Polio. The National Foundation is the organization which has long been the leader in the fight against polio. Through the "March of Dimes" it has helped to finance research, provide funds to purchase equipment, to train personnel and to provide care for polio victims. March of Dimes funds have paid out almost 4 million dollars for medical care alone. The Foundation also succeeded, by persistent effort, in interesting other organizations as well as the public in the search for the cause and the prevention of this disease.

TODAY'S SUCCESS STORY. The first big step toward success in conquering polio was the discovery of the virus that causes it. This achievement was followed by the perfection of a vaccine, given by injection (*Salk vaccine*), to prevent the disease; later Dr. Albert Sabin developed the oral vaccine. The results of the first tests of the effectiveness of the vaccine were so promising that scientists felt that the time had come to test its effectiveness on a nation-wide scale. Accordingly, in 1954 the National Foundation, with the cooperation of many other organizations, sponsored the first mass immunizations with the Salk vaccine of the age groups known to be most susceptible to polio. Since then, over a million people have been inoculated or acted as controls. Thousands of parents and other volunteer and professional workers share the credit for this accomplishment.

The results of this mass immunization program have been spectacular. In 1952, two years before mass immunizations began, there were *58,000* reported cases of poliomyelitis in this country—in the first 15 weeks of 1964 there was *not even one* reported case.* To realize what this means, we have only to think of the thousands of children and young adults who have been rescued from disfigurement, handicaps and death—the reward for years of effort to solve a major disease problem.

The polio triumph does not mean that we can relax our efforts to prevent the disease. Each new generation must be immunized, and each person's present immunity must be kept active by the required "booster" doses of vaccine. Education programs informing the public about polio and immunization must be continued, enlisting public support for the immunization programs.

Symptoms. After exposure to polio, it takes 7 to 18 days for the infection to develop. The victim complains of a sore throat and a headache. He may feel nauseated and vomit, and he has a slightly elevated temperature. At first he is sleepy, then he is restless; he is always irritable. The disease may stop here, with a mild attack. On the other hand, the patient may suddenly become ill again in a day or so and complain of stiffness in the back or the neck and pains in the muscles of the arms and the legs. Tenderness and rigidity may appear. These symptoms may be the forerunners of paralysis. No matter how mild or severe the symptoms are, this is the acute infectious stage of polio. The patient should be isolated, and strict precautions should be taken by the people who must be in contact with him.

PARALYSIS. The second stage of polio, paralysis, appears about the 2nd or the 3rd day. Paralysis will affect the muscles controlled by the damaged parts of the nervous system. It may be slight or extensive—this depends on how far the polio virus has spread through the nervous system. Usually, groups of muscles in the legs are affected, especially in the backs of the legs. In the upper part of the body, often the shoulder girdle is affected; sometimes the diaphragm is paralyzed. The paralysis immediately goes as far as it ever will; it does not increase during convalescence.

Treatment and Nursing Care. Hot moist packs are used for the relief of muscle pain and spasms. Antibiotics may be given as a preventive measure although they do not affect the course of the disease. The patient is observed closely during the first few days of acute illness for any further progression of the disease, particularly respiratory difficulties. Emergency equipment such as a tracheostomy set, suction apparatus and a respirator should be ready for immediate use.

Positioning the patient is extremely important. Weak muscles should be supported and the body kept in good alignment. The patient with polio often has difficulty with elimination, due to the flaccid state of internal muscles; frequent enemas and an indwelling catheter may be necessary. If muscles used in swallowing are affected, he must be tube fed.

As soon as the active infection has subsided, the physical therapist begins to exercise and massage the affected parts to keep the muscles from contracting. Water baths and special apparatus also are used in the rehabilitative treatment.

Doctors prescribe treatment according to the needs of the individual patient. During the convalescent state, braces and supports are sometimes ordered. Some patients must be taught crutch walking (see p. 454). The polio victim needs encouragement to persevere in the exercises that he must do himself—every member of the health team can play an important part in his rehabilitation.

* Basil O'Connor, President of the National Foundation, in an address to the Conference of National Organizations, Los Angeles, California, May 1964.

44

THE PATIENT WITH A PSYCHIATRIC PROBLEM

The principles of psychiatric nursing apply in some degree to the care of any patient—in fact, this is where you will have the most opportunity to apply these principles, since as a student, any experience you have with psychiatric patients may be brief. Many patients with other illnesses also have psychiatric problems, and often these problems interfere with their recovery. A psychiatric problem does not necessarily mean that a patient is mentally ill to the extent that he needs care in a mental hospital. However, it may mean that his feelings and behavior are having a serious effect on his progress. If his attempts to handle his problems result in erratic or dangerous behavior, he is mentally ill.

Changing Attitudes. Not long ago, a patient was sent to a mental hospital only when he was a danger to the community and when the community was no longer a safe place for him. Certainly, a patient who is potentially dangerous to himself and to others must be protected, and responsibility must be taken for him. However, to assume that a mental patient must reach this stage before he can be treated is as old-fashioned as to think that mental illness is a disgrace to be hidden away and denied.

Mental illness gradually is becoming recognized to be like any other illness; patients are sent to hospitals voluntarily for treatment, just as they might go to a general hospital for an appendectomy. Early hospitalization tends to shorten the illness; by removing the emotional stress often found in the home, the hospital provides a more suitable environment for the patient.

A patient with beginning psychiatric difficulties may go to an out-patient clinic for treatment. Some psychiatric hospitals have established a service whereby a patient may spend his nights at the hospital and carry on with his regular job in the daytime. This plan assures him of the treatment he needs and removes him from a home environment which may be disturbing.

Changing attitudes toward mental illness and the discovery of the tranquilizing drugs have made community hospitals willing to take care of mentally ill patients. These drugs are so effective in quieting agitated or disturbed patients that barred windows and restraining jackets are no longer necessary, and the fears of hospital personnel have largely been eliminated. More and more general hospitals are providing space for the in-patient care of psychiatric patients.

Emergency Services. A recently developed service to the mentally disturbed exists now in many of our larger cities in connection with individual hospitals and medical centers. This is the *emergency psychiatric clinic*, a part of the hospital's emergency ward of which a psychiatrist is in charge around the clock. Here disturbed people who find everything is too much for them may come for help. They find a sympathetic listener with whom they can discuss their troubles. They can come back for help as often as they need it. Treatment may include antidepression drugs or a stay in the hospital's psychiatric ward, or periodic return visits to the clinic. They pay if they can; if not, the services of the psychiatrist are still available. One hospital reports that three fifths of the patients who come to this service can be taken care of adequately without being hospitalized, which is a great relief for the overcrowded mental hospitals.

The *Home Treatment Service* is another type of emergency service for disturbed people which sends a psychiatrist to the patient at home. It has the advantage of seeing the patient in his home environment. Modern psychiatry recognizes the importance of working with the family of the mentally disturbed person, since his troubles often stem from his family environment. Home treatment also solves the problem of the patient who refuses to go to a psychiatrist, and it often seems to accomplish more than hospitalization, which many disturbed people fight and fear.

Admission to a Mental Hospital

The terms of admission to a mental hospital vary from state to state and even within a state. Generally speaking, one of 4 methods is followed: (1) voluntary admission, (2) admission on the certification of 2 physicians, (3) temporary care certificates, (4) court commitments. The people who go into the hospital by voluntary admission often go to a private hospital and pay for their care and treatment. However, there are many state hospitals that admit patients voluntarily, sometimes for special treatment. For instance, if a patient has paresis (see page 542), in some states he may go voluntarily to the state hospital for treatment; when the treatment is completed, he may return to his home.

No matter how unlikely the chances of recovery seem to be, no patient in a mental hospital is neglected or condemned as hopeless. Science is constantly finding new ways of treating patients.

The Patient's Security. The mentally disturbed patient needs security in his environment. Security means protecting the patient from himself, from other patients and from the outside world. It is the hospital's responsibility to provide this protection, which is particularly important in relation to visits from relatives and friends. Often, with the kindest intentions, they will distress the patient by reminding him of things better left undiscussed. For the patient's sake, relatives and other visitors should be permitted to see him only with his consent. He may be uncommunicative, so that his consent cannot be obtained, but if he objects to any visitors, they should not be allowed to see him. The doctor must decide when exceptions should be made.

Minor and Major Mental Illnesses. Mental illnesses may vary considerably in the degree to which a patient is affected. Some of the minor abnormalities which do not completely incapacitate a patient are classified as *psychoneuroses,* of which all the symptoms seem to be connected with anxiety. Psychoneuroses should be recognized as real illnesses because the patient suffers keenly from them. Many times the psychoneurotic patient remains in society without displaying marked personality changes. The person suffering from hysteria, compulsions, unreasonable fears and hypochondriasis (a condition of extreme worry and concern about health) is frequently not in a mental hospital.

Marked deviations from normal behavior and seriously irregular conduct usually signify a *psychosis.* The psychotic person is unable to "see into himself" (possess insight), and he has poor contact with reality. Frequently, he is disoriented (does not identify the time, the place, or the people around him). His behavior is strange, and his thinking is disturbed. Psychoses can result from a physical cause, such as syphilis, brain tumors or infection, or they may be functional disorders (maladjusted, warped personalities which show no sign of tissue changes or disease). *Schizophrenia* and *manic depressive* psychoses are 2 major disorders of the latter type.

Toxic psychoses include alcoholism and drug addiction. Also, a large group of people become mentally ill during the *involutional* period (those series of changes which take place during the menopause). This illness is sometimes spoken of as "agitated depression," which is a good description of the symptoms. *Paranoia* is another psychosis; it is characterized by a system of well-organized delusions or false beliefs about persecution and grandeur. It can be a serious social problem, since paranoiacs may become quite dangerous.

Some illnesses are on the borderline of psychiatry. A *psychopathic personality* is involved with the law more frequently than with psychiatric treatment, although neither has a good answer for his problem. The psychopath usually has normal or superior intelligence, and he seems to be in trouble frequently. Many times his illness takes the form of sexual perversions. *Mental defectives* might also be included in this borderline classification. (A more thorough listing of mental illnesses is included at the end of this chapter.)

APPROACH TO PATIENTS

The Patient's Good Will. The significance of the correct approach to patients cannot be overemphasized. This is the foundation on which all the nurse's work will rest. Her success or failure will, in a large measure, depend on her ability to understand how important the correct approach is and to adjust her own behavior accordingly. To be successful with mental patients, it is essential to have their good will. This does not mean bribing patients with favors, such as special privileges. The nurse must be kind but firm. A patient may appear to be out of contact, yet he may remember an unkindness, which he will hold against the nurse and have no respect for her. This is bad for both the patient and the nurse. A calm, matter-of-fact attitude—friendly but not familiar—is important at all times. A nurse should *never* discuss her personal affairs with patients or have financial dealings with them.

The Rights of the Mental Patient. A nurse must realize that, although the patient may be psychotic, he is not necessarily demented; his opinions, wishes and desires are as important to him as normal desires are to a well person. Even when a patient's expressions seem bizarre and out of harmony with reality, they still have meaning and significance *for him.* A nurse should never laugh at a patient's beliefs—this tends to destroy his confidence in the people who should be his protectors, and such an action has a demoralizing effect on other patients as well. She must be tolerant and kind to patients at all times, even in the face of abuse. An irritable or impatient attitude will only provoke the patient and lead to difficulties. A patient's request should be granted whenever possible. In many instances, the patient is a person who, in his previous, everyday life, has been attending to his own needs and affairs and may even have been in a position to direct others. To go from this state of mind to utter dependence on others requires a considerable adjustment on his part. Everything possible should be done to help the patient to maintain his dignity as an individual during these trying circumstances.

Even though he is not capable of being responsible for himself, a mental patient has certain rights which may not be violated. For instance, he may not be denied the privilege of seeing friends and relatives, except in rare instances on the order of the doctor. He also may receive all mail addressed to him and has a right to send out mail. However, since the patient is not responsible, this must be supervised carefully, to prevent him from violating postal regulations by sending out obscene material, writing threatening letters, and so on. All communications should be reviewed by the doctor in charge, or by his appointed representative.

A Middle Road. When it is necessary to refuse patients' requests or to control them, the nurse should explain that she is obeying hospital rules, rather than have the patient feel that *she* is trying to rule him. She must never punish the patient in any manner whatsoever or threaten him with punishment. His behavior and ideas must never be ridiculed. Neither should the nurse encourage and foster his peculiar patterns of thought and behavior. To agree with a patient's false beliefs is to reinforce them. It is equally useless to argue with him because it focuses attention on undesirable attitudes. It is better for the nurse to tell the patient that she cannot agree with him and then change the subject. The nurse must try to exercise self-control and always be cheerful.

This is not so difficult when she realizes that nothing could be more worthwhile than helping mentally ill people to get well, or at least to live more happily.

The Nurse-Patient Relationship

Interest in the Patient. To understand patients well, it is necessary to understand what they consider to be pleasures. The nurse must understand their ambitions and disappointments. She must be actively interested in learning about them, but she must avoid morbid curiosity. She will be a little more tolerant, a little more attentive to requests, if she sees each patient clearly in relation to his surroundings.

The nurse should talk to the patient in a normal tone of voice and should not show fear. She should never "talk down" to him—this only makes him feel inferior or aggravates the inferiority feelings that he already has. If she is unable to find something acceptable to talk about, she should be a good listener. She should never make idle promises that she may not be able to keep. These are the qualities that a nurse must have to establish a good relationship with the mental patient:

She must be polite and tactful, qualities which go hand in hand.

She must be skillful in handling situations.

She must be friendly to all patients. A nurse can show a warm feeling that reaches out to the patient and includes politeness, confidence and institutional hospitality.

She must be truthful but neither brutally so nor evasive. She demonstrates this by an earnest manner and sincerity.

She must be even-tempered and uncritical. Sometimes this is difficult, but she remembers that the patient is ill.

She must have poise—it gives her confidence in herself and lets the patient have confidence in her.

She must be an interested listener, always a desirable quality.

On the other hand, some of the things that are likely to create an unsatisfactory relationship are:

A superior attitude
Overrating what the patient says
Intimate friendships with patients
Hurried contacts

Adapting the Approach to the Situation. The approach to the patient is influenced by the type of mental illness that he has:

1. The Excited Patient: a quiet atmosphere is important in dealing with a restless person; the quieter the better. Use a calm voice. Avoid long discussions and forcing issues.

2. The Retarded Patient: this type should be encouraged to talk. Encourage him to assist about the ward in any way that is possible.

3. The Preoccupied Patient: this patient may become annoyed because some pleasant fantasy is interrupted. By suggestion, divert his attention to some desirable action.

4. The Hypochondriacal Type: the less you ask this patient about his condition, the better. Physical complaints must not be disregarded entirely, but they should not be emphasized.

Observing and Recording

Admission Observations of the Patient. The patient's physical condition is checked when he is admitted to the mental hospital, as it would be in a general hospital. The nurse makes the same kind of observations, but she also makes very careful, detailed observations and notes about his *behavior*. She notices:

1. Appearance—as to dress and facial expression
2. Sociability—degree of
3. General behavior—co-operativeness; responsiveness
4. Emotional reactions
5. Speech—normal or defective
6. Conversation—whether it appears normal in amount of content. Complaints of patients are noted in detail.

Ward Observations. The purpose of the ward observations and notes is to record, from time to time, the condition of the patient. They are mainly descriptions of the patient's conduct and behavior. They are made without the patient's knowledge by observing him carefully on the ward. The following outline can be used as a guide:

Appearance. Is the patient neat, clean and tidy, or dirty and untidy?

Sociability. Does the patient associate freely with other patients? Or does he keep to himself?

Behavior. Is the patient orderly or disorderly, still or restless, quiet or noisy, friendly or indifferent, interested or disinterested, destructive or violent? How does he spend his time? Is he bedridden? Is his conduct always the same, or does it change at times? Does he obey simple commands? Does he pay attention to what is said to him?

Emotional Reaction. Is the patient irritable, angry, excited? Does he have sudden impulsive actions, unprovoked outbreaks of excitement, temper tantrums, assaultive tendencies? Is he depressed, distressed, perplexed, uneasy, fearful? Does he appear happy? Are his emotions relatively constant?

Speech. Does his speech seem natural or is it flighty, rapid and disconnected or slow and retarded? Does his speech indicate that he understands what is said to him or what is wanted of him? Are his answers relevant and coherent? Are there any particular speech defects, such as stuttering, lisping or stammering? Does he talk voluntarily, or only when questioned? Does his conversation pass from one subject to another without order or apparent connection? Do his replies answer the questions asked? Does he repeat set words or phrases, or make new words? Is his language obscene?

Body Complaints. Does the patient complain of pains in the stomach, pains and weakness in the legs, suffocation, difficult breathing, nausea, heart trouble, headache or dizziness?

Physical Condition. Note the general physical condition and anything unusual. Physically ill patients will have orders for medication and treatment in addition to other records.

Sleep. Is the patient's sleep normal or does it appear disturbed? Does he talk or cry out during sleep?

Appetite. Note the patient's attitude toward food. Does he eat willingly or must he be urged and coaxed? Is he spoon-fed or tube-fed? Note any peculiar habits in relation to food or eating.

Excretions. Observe whether or not the normal functions occur; chart menstruation in female patients of reproductive age.

Other Observations. Any unusual occurrences, such as injuries or altercations between patients, should be recorded, with the names of witnesses. Overnight visits and long visits outside of the hospital should be recorded.

IMPORTANT POINTS ABOUT OBSERVING AND RECORDING

1. Some people are naturally observant, but observation can be cultivated.
2. Be alert with all the senses—report with absolute accuracy. It is better to turn in no report than a misleading one.
3. Nothing is too small or unimportant to mention; it may be just the small point or incident which throws light on the patient's behavior.
4. Tell only what you see or hear, without mentioning your own conclusion about it.
5. Do *not* say that the patient has delusions or hallucinations or is confused, excited or incoherent. *Examples* of the patient's talk and descriptions of his actions and expressions give the information which the people who read the notes will use to judge mental and emotional disturbances.
6. Do not ask the patient leading questions; generally it is better to ask no questions unless the doctor tells you to.
7. It is important to report whether the patient seems to be absorbed in himself or takes no notice of his surroundings, or whether he seems to know what is going on.
8. Record in detail any attempt at self-injury or any accident involving a patient.
9. Choose your words carefully when writing notes.
10. Keep charts locked out of sight of the patients or their visitors.

The Suicidal Patient

From a nursing standpoint, suicide is probably the greatest single problem to handle in caring for mentally ill people. Any mental patient presents a potential risk, but certain types of patients are more likely to commit suicide than others. Any attempt at suicide should be considered serious—*the nurse must report every attempt, however minor it seems.* Conversations which express the uselessness of life, the desire to die, and similar comments should be noted on the chart and reported. The approach to this problem is to win the patient's confidence and to keep up a constantly hopeful attitude about his recovery. The method for preventing suicide is that of giving constant, continuous and effective supervision.

Attempts at Suicide

Patients often attempt suicide by means of forbidden or restricted articles or materials. Nurses should watch patients very closely while they are working in occupational therapy shops to prevent them from secreting tools, bits of metal and glass or similar objects. Poisonous medications should be kept under lock and key. Any injury to patients through forbidden articles shows a slip in supervision somewhere. However, there are other ways of committing suicide, such as diving to the floor from a window ledge, or ramming the head into a wall. A mental hospital probably has barred windows, but there is no such protection in a general hospital or a home—newspapers carry accounts every day of people falling or jumping from windows. In most instances, the more desperate and self-destructive type of patient chooses this method, but suicide should have been anticipated in such cases and thereby prevented.

Frequently, patients will plan their suicidal attempts to take advantage of a change in shifts of nurses. The early morning hours are a crucial time for depressed patients because they dread to face another day. Deeply depressed patients may be too unalert to carry out a suicidal attempt or even to try. However, as they begin to recover and their will power returns, they become alert and may attempt suicide. The depressed patient who is recovering seems so much brighter that he may not be watched as closely. The greatest danger to depressed patients is in the early stages of illness and during convalescence. Some of the reasons for suicidal tendencies are:

A feeling on the part of the patient that his illness is a disgrace

Ideas of guilt and unworthiness and imaginary disease

Lingering or malignant disease

An overwhelming sense of failure

Loss of a motivating goal in life—"Nothing to live for"

Impulsive acts to seek attention

SUICIDE METHODS RESORTED TO BY PATIENTS

1. Cutting arteries with glass or sharp instruments
2. Hanging by sheets, blankets, belts, ties, etc.
3. Standing on high places and falling on the head
4. Banging the head on the floor, the furniture, etc.
5. Turning chairs over to break the neck
6. Drinking poison from dressing trays, cleaning solutions or sterilizing solutions
7. Biting and swallowing thermometers, glass, needles, nails, etc.
8. Bribing privileged patients to obtain destructive articles
9. Drowning in the bathtub

TYPES OF PATIENTS NEEDING CLOSE OBSERVATION

1. New patients
2. Patients who have agitated depressions
3. Depressed patients—going into and coming out of illness especially
4. Patients suffering with insomnia
5. Acute alcoholic patients
6. Patients with ideas of persecution; of being disgraced; of having an incurable disease; and those responding to voices
7. Patients in confused states
8. Patients with sudden impulses—changes in mood
9. Patients undergoing special treatments
10. Hypochondriacal patients—particularly when they have a fixed idea about one organ or system
11. Patients who have made previous suicidal attempts
12. Patients who talk about suicide and express the wish to die

PREVENTIVE MEASURES

1. Know where each patient is and what his condition is at all times.
2. Provide a sense of security for the patient.
3. Remove the utensils essential for his plans:
   a. Sharp instruments should be kept locked in the head nurse's office and accounted for by each shift.
   b. Bottles or glassware of any sort should not be left on wards where there are suicidal patients.
   c. All glass and silverware should be collected and counted after each meal.
   d. Lock all doors carefully, including such outlets as laundry-chutes, dumb-waiter shafts, etc.
4. Provide an impersonal, understanding service which encourages the patient's confidence.
5. When possible, inject doubt into the patient's strange and bizarre ideas, his fears, etc., but do not ridicule the patient or argue with him.
6. Actively suicidal patients should be "specialed" (be given a special nurse who takes care of one patient exclusively) during the full 24 hours of the day.

TECHNIC OF "SPECIALING" SUICIDAL PATIENTS

This type of specialing is very different from that in a general hospital.

A patient specialed in a mental hospital is never left alone for one second.

1. Watch carefully every movement of the patient.
2. The nurse should remove from her person and from the patient any article that could be used for self-destruction.
3. Permit no strings, belts or ties on the patient's clothing.
4. Do not permit the patient to use scissors, needles, etc., even while the nurse is standing at his side. (Except by written order of the physician.)
5. Do not leave the patient alone when reporting off duty; wait with the patient until relief arrives.
6. Occupy the patient with suitable games where possible. Encourage the patient to read, but do not read to him. Help the patient to gain a motive for living by interesting him in accomplishing something.
7. Anticipate the patient's behavior by being aware of changes in his mood. Occasionally, patients will pretend improvement to gain an opportunity for suicide.

Suicide Prevention Centers. An attempt to help disturbed people outside of mental hospitals who contemplate suicide is the establishment of suicide prevention centers in some of our larger cities. The person who calls the center to say that he is going to commit suicide can talk to a psychiatrist who listens to his story and discusses his situation with him, and tries to persuade him to change his mind or at least to delay acting. Some centers may try to rush a psychiatrist to him to prevent him from carrying out his suicidal threat.

Absence Without Permission

Know the Patient. Every precaution should be taken to prevent patients from running away from the hospital. Many patients are in the hospital against their will and will use any ruse to get out. Others may be perfectly content to remain in the hospital for treatment, yet wish to take leave for a particular reason. Those of the latter type frequently will return to the hospital of their own accord. The best way to prevent absence without permission is to know the patient thoroughly. People tend to follow certain patterns of behavior, and if a patient runs away or attempts to run away once, he is apt to do it again if the opportunity presents itself. Therefore, the history of the patient is revealing and should be studied for this as well as for other reasons. Every hospital has certain routine procedures or regulations to control this aspect of patient care.

Visiting Privileges. The present tendency is to allow patients rather liberal privileges. It is believed that, while the patient is still in the hospital and can have guidance, trial visits to his home or to relatives help to direct his readjustment to society. They give the patient renewed hope and a pleasant change from hospital routine. In this way, the patient gradually regains his place in the world and his sense of security and responsibility; the transition upon discharge is not so great. Naturally, chances are taken. If a patient shows symptoms at home that did not appear when he was given permission to visit, very often the relatives may bring him back. In other instances, his condition may not have been appreciated by the relatives, and he may be gone from them before they realize his intention. The hospital's responsibility in this varies, but it usually is not a responsibility which falls on the nurse.

Visitors to Patients

The Family and Friends. Learning to receive patients' visitors in an appropriate manner, understanding what to do and what not to do, is most important. If a nurse is so unfortunate or tactless as to offend a patient's visitors, she may work ever so hard for the patient's welfare and receive only criticism for her efforts. If, on the other hand, she can gain the relatives' good will and cooperation, it will help her to handle many of the problems of the patient. Visitors take up much of the time of hospital personnel, but it is time well spent. The relatives and other visitors of patients are often greatly distressed by the patient's illness. Frequently, they are unable to appreciate his condition. Often they have the idea that mental hospitals are places where people are mistreated; with this prejudice, they are apt to exaggerate little things which otherwise would go unnoticed. Therefore, the nurse must show by word and deed that every possible consideration is being given to the patient. By thoughtful attention to the visitors who come to the hospital, she is establishing the reputation of the hospital in the community. In other words, every nurse is a representative of the hospital; if she has proper pride in her work and loyalty to her institution, she will do the things which will bring credit upon it and her.

When Visitors Come. To avoid overwhelming surprise, the patient should be prepared for the visit by being told in advance. He should be clean and neat, with hair combed, and nails, teeth and clothing clean. He should be fully dressed, if possible. Under no circumstances should the nurse give out information about his condition. All requests of this nature should be referred to the physician or the supervisor in charge.

Points to Observe in Supervised Visits

1. See that no letters are exchanged.
2. See that the patient does not sign any papers.
3. Watch to prevent the patient's receiving sharp instruments, such as scissors, razor blades, crochet hooks.
4. See that packages are opened in the presence of the nurse.
5. Permit no smoking in the building by either patients or visitors, unless the regulations provide for this.
6. Watch the patient for suicidal attempts or efforts to leave without permission.
7. Terminate the visit if the patient becomes disturbed.
8. Record the patient's reaction to the visit.

Points to Observe in Patients After Visits Which Are Not Supervised

1. If the patient is suspected, search for letters, matches, cigarettes.
2. Inspect any package that the patient brings back to the ward.

Observation of All Patients After Visits

1. Report and chart any unusual behavior during or after visits.
2. Report any articles taken from the patient.

Preventing Injuries

Although, generally speaking, mental patients are not so dangerous as many people believe, in any hospital there are certain patients who are dangerous. The nurse's duty is to prevent injuries to herself, other employees and other patients. Also, some patients are prone to attempt self-mutilation, such as scratching, biting or beating themselves. It is difficult for persons unaccustomed to the behavior of mental patients to realize the kinds of things that they will do.

Violent Patients. Proper supervision will do much to prevent injuries. If certain patients tend to antagonize others, they should not be permitted to have close contact. If a patient is violently assaultive, the nurse should not attempt to handle him without sufficient help. Under no circumstances is a nurse to retaliate for any injury she receives. She must always remember that the patients are not responsible for their actions—that she is there as a leader, their protector, as it were, and not to enforce discipline. Patients are to be *helped* with their difficulties, not *punished*. It is sometimes difficult for the nurse to maintain her dignity and poise under trying circumstances, but if she cannot do this, she is not the proper person to be entrusted with the care of these sick people. Vigilance will do much to prevent assaults; prevention is the keynote to success. Any intensive program of occupational therapy, recreation and other physical activities will be helpful in releasing tensions that otherwise may lead to assaultive attacks.

Using Restraint

Early Attitudes. The restraint of mental patients was an almost universal practice in the 15th, the 16th and the 17th centuries. During this dark period of medicine and nursing, we find that patients were chained in dungeons, living in their own filth, without benefit of heat or sunlight or normal human contact. However, it is interesting to note that not all early cultures followed cruel customs. For example, in the 8th century in Arabia, patients were placed beside running brooks for the soothing effect which this had upon them.

The great pioneer in changing this state of affairs was a French physician, Philippe Pinel. He was convinced that such barbaric methods were not necessary but were degrading and harmful. He freed the patients under his care, some of whom had been chained for years (1792). This humane treatment spread in England under the influence of William Tuke, founder of the York Retreat. The idea also was advocated by the early psychiatrists in America.

Present Practice. However, restraint has been more prevalent than is generally believed. The latitude in this respect is wide. At present, there are hospitals in America where restraint does not exist—where no mechanical devices for restraining a patient, even to a partial degree, can be found. In other hospitals, wristlets, camisoles (straight-jackets) and other restraining devices are being used. Such conditions need not exist and should not be tolerated. In a rare instance, for the protection of surgical dressings, a temporary restrain may be indicated. Restraint will tend to excite a patient, and his struggles to free himself may lead to exhaustion.

Substitutes for Restraint. The substitutes for restraint are therapeutic treatments, such as the continuous bath, the wet pack or seclusion. The last should be used with care, and no patient should be secluded without the written order of the physician. The patient should be observed carefully while in seclusion and, when his condition permits, he should be released. The room temperature should be comfortable; there should be fresh air. Patients should be given water to drink frequently while in seclusion. They should have exercise and frequent attention for toileting. The number of hours out of every 24-hour period that a patient spends in seclusion should be noted. The patient is secluded alone—never with another patient. There are hospitals in which the most acute cases are cared for with neither restraint nor seclusion. Where insufficient facilities and personnel make seclusion necessary, it should be carried out with every conscientious consideration for the patient.

Restraint. If it becomes necessary to restrain a patient to keep him from removing a dressing or interfering with a surgical treatment, certain precautions should be taken:

1. When restraining the arms and the legs, be very careful not to make the apparatus tight enough to impede the circulation. Stockinet or soft bandage should be used under the restraint to prevent injury.
2. Do not fasten the arms and the legs in an uncomfortable position. Remove the restraint every hour and allow the patient to exercise.
3. If it can be avoided, do not apply a restraint over the chest.
4. Never restrain only one side of the body. Even if it is unnecessary to restrain both hands

or both feet, restrain the hand on one side and the foot on the opposite side, too.

5. Frequently feel the pulse of the patient who is struggling against restraint and watch his general condition carefully. Death might result from exhaustion, from the extra work thrown on the heart.

6. Remove any patient in restraint every 2 hours for an alcohol or bathing-solution rub and powder. This reduces fatigue.

Special Therapies

Occupational Therapy. Occupational therapy is probably the nurse's best tool for handling the convalescent patient, whether a child or an adult. If the nurse is able to interest the patient in some project that must take shape and grow from day to day, this mutual interest will bring satisfaction to both. It entertains and also shortens the period of convalescence. It brings strength to the patient and gradually prepares him for the activities that temporarily have been laid aside.

Occupational therapy is particularly valuable for the mental patient. Often the patient will refuse to accept a nurse as such because he will not recognize himself as a patient. He may consistently refuse all treatment, and yet some household craft which he does not associate so directly with the hospital will appeal to him. Patients may already have some interest, such as knitting, and they will gladly seize upon an opportunity to show that they are perfectly able to carry on. The nurse who understands this particular craft may help the patient with materials, design, etc. Once the nurse has introduced the wedge of occupational therapy, she may be able to gain the confidence of the patient.

The value of occupational therapy has been recognized for centuries. The great philosopher and physician, Galen (A.D. 172), wrote: "Occupation is nature's best physician and essential to human happiness." However, it was not until World War I that occupational therapy won the right to be classed along with other therapies as an important method of treatment. Today it occupies a major place in the curative program for mental patients.

Recreational Therapy. Recreational therapy activities are used in 2 ways: (1) for the underactive patient, to stimulate and draw him out; (2) for the overactive patient, to direct his activity into useful channels. The underactive patient is withdrawn from his environment; by encouraging him to participate actively in games or other activities, the environment is interwoven with his behavior. When a patient is interested in games, his thoughts do not dwell to such a great extent on his own difficulties. Furthermore, we sometimes substitute worthwhile activities for less desirable habits. The normal person likes to do things with other people. If patients can continue the activities to which they are normally accustomed, the hospital seems more like home and less like an institution.

The benefits of recreational therapy are not only mental but also physical. Circulation is increased; digestion and sleep are improved; the body is able to throw off certain poisons; muscle tone is improved; the patient feels better generally. Recreation also encourages group effort and brings about co-operation. That these activities are beneficial has been demonstrated both through observations and by scientific study.

Nurses working with mental patients should be encouraged to play with them, to get them outside of the wards at every possible opportunity, and to realize that in doing this they are helping the patient as much as they would by giving medication.

Hydrotherapy. The value of the external application of water to the human body has long been recognized. It was practiced by the early Romans. As mentioned previously, the Arabians, during the period of Avicenna, treated their sick both by the application of water and by having the patients sit beside soothing brooks for the beneficial effect. This was not developed as a scientific method of treatment in the United States until the beginning of the 20th century, when Dr. Rebekah Wright advanced the theory and the practice of hydrotherapy, particularly for the mentally ill.

Usually, it will be found that a large mental hospital has a separate hydrotherapy department. Also, many wards, particularly in the admission and the disturbed services, are provided with continuous baths. Wet packs, both hot and cold, may be given to the patient on the wards or in the home. The effects of hydrotherapy on mental patients may be stimulating, sedative or tonic.

Individual and Group Psychotherapy. Psychotherapy is the process of helping a mentally disturbed person by talking with him and letting him talk, and by helping him with and sharing in his activities. Group psychotherapy takes in more than one patient and provides the same opportunity for everyone's participation in introducing and discussing individual problems. Thus the patient comes to know other people, becomes concerned with someone besides himself and is drawn out of his little private world to become a part of the world around him. This type of therapy, directed by trained people, is helping many patients toward recovery from mental illness.

Psychotherapy depends on the personal relationship between the patient and the physician. The aim of psychotherapy is to relieve the patient of his symptoms and to eventually free him of the disabling conflicts which caused the symptoms. The treatment encourages the patient to tell his story and to discuss his problems with an impartial adviser. Hypnosis and psychoanalysis are among the methods used to achieve this end.

Shock Therapy. Several types of shock therapy have been used in the treatment of mental illnesses. The treatment produces a convulsion which in some unexplained way effects a change in the brain, and the patient improves. The drug *metrazol* can be given intravenously to cause a convulsion. The great disadvantage of this therapy is the patient's fear before the treatment and the brief period of intense anxiety and distress between the moment of administration of the drug and the loss of consciousness.

Electroconvulsive therapy (also referred to as E.C.T. and electroshock therapy) causes a convulsion by sending an electric current through the brain. It has been used in the treatment of a very wide range of mental illnesses, but present opinion tends to restrict its use to a rather limited group of patients. When successful, this treatment can radically change nursing problems in connection with the patient's behavior.

Lobotomy. Lobotomy is an operation which severs certain association tracts in the frontal lobes of the brain. Ordinarily, it is done only after the patient has failed to respond to other types of treatment. There is no doubt that it lowers tension greatly and makes the patient less difficult to care for.

Drug Therapy. The tranquilizing drugs have made a revolutionary change in the treatment of mental illness. These drugs arrest or greatly alleviate many mental disorders to the point where hospitalization is not necessary. The rate of patients' discharge from mental hospitals is also greatly increased by their use. Tranquilizing drugs seem to decrease anxiety and disturbed behavior very quickly, and they make the patient more receptive to psychotherapy (see Chap. 30).

CARING FOR PATIENTS ACCORDING TO BEHAVIOR GROUPS

Generally speaking, from a nursing viewpoint, mental patients are classified in groups according to behavior or symptoms. Several of the outstanding groups will be discussed from the standpoint of their nursing care.

Overactive Patients

Activity is a characteristic of all forms of life, and therefore it is normal for people. However, certain people are by nature more animated and more forceful than others. Just as the degree of activity varies between normal people, so the behavior of mentally disturbed people varies among patients, from the person who is slightly agitated to the one who is in an extreme state of frenzy. Naturally, the nursing care for these 2 types of patients is not the same. Also, marked changes may occur in the same person from time to time, and the nursing care of the individual patient will have to be adjusted to meet them.

The Hypomanic Patient. The person who is

only slightly more active than would be considered to be normal falls into the so-called *hypomanic* group. These patients can be more difficult to care for than the more acutely disturbed patients. Very often they are witty, breezy and enterprising; because of their keen memory and quick repartee, they are not recognized as being the sick people they really are. This type of patient is also apt to be interfering, domineering and irritable, going quickly from one mood to another. He rarely accepts hospitalization willingly; as a rule, he makes many unreasonable demands. He is continuously busy, and the chief problem in his nursing care is how to use this activity.

The nurse should:

1. Be firm but kind.
2. Avoid familiarity.
3. Avoid arguments.
4. Keep the patient from irritating others.
5. Keep the patient occupied—if unable to permit him to participate in occupational activities off the ward, let him have writing material for use in the ward.

This type of patient usually is fond of writing, particularly letters to important people, recording his history or promoting schemes. This keeps him harmlessly occupied.

Along with this there usually will be an active program of treatment, such as sedative hydrotherapy. Care should be taken to supply extra nourishment to an overactive patient because of the energy he expends, which consumes extra calories. His appetite is usually good, unless he is extremely overactive.

The More Disturbed Patient. Proceeding to the more disturbed patient, his management and nursing care include physical protection of himself and others, whereas, in the less disturbed or hypomanic type, the patient is more apt to be a nuisance than a real danger. In theory, active patients should be allowed a wide scope to work off this surplus energy. In actual practice, this is not always possible because of limited space and personnel. Therefore, seclusion may be used as a last resort. It should be used only for a stated period on written order from the physician. Under no circumstances should disturbed patients be placed in a mechanical restraint. This aggravates their condition, and they may die of exhaustion in attempting to free themselves.

Useful Activities. Every attempt should be made to direct the activities of the overly active patient toward useful ends. Even the most excited cases will sometimes tear rags for rugs. These patients are destructive, and for that reason should have a plain room. This does not mean that the environment is to be stripped of everything but bare walls and floors. Patients should be provided with every comfort which it is possible for them to have under the circumstances. They should be bathed frequently, and their toilet habits cared for. Every measure to keep them clothed should be tried, but, if nudity is inevitable, they should not be exposed in this condition to other patients. When taken from their rooms, they should be covered by a robe, a sheet or a blanket.

Nursing Care. An abundance of fluids should be given, along with an adequate diet. When patients are too disturbed to take proper nourishment, they should be tube-fed or spoon-fed. Care of the mouth and the skin is important. The patient may have injuries, such as abrasions of the skin, which may become infected if not given attention. In general, hydrotherapy is the best treatment for the disturbed patient; it provides an opportunity for a much-needed rest. Warm milk at night may help to produce sleep—insomnia is one of the problems of these patients. They should be kept away from excitement and stimuli. When possible, disturbed patients should be taken for walks or to play outdoor games. Outdoor activities should never be attempted without adequate help. In fact, it is important in giving any treatment to a disturbed patient to have adequate assistance at hand before attempting it.

Precautions for handling disturbed patients:

1. Know your patient.
2. Do not allow the patient to get behind you.
3. Approach a fighting patient from the rear.
4. Use a mattress as a protecting shield if the patient is threatening and has a weapon. In this manner, several nurses can approach safely to disarm him.
5. Never get between 2 disturbed patients to separate them.

6. Take the utmost care not to injure a patient, even so slightly as to inflict a scratch or a bruise.

7. Anticipate what you are going to do.

8. Avoid becoming excited.

Suicide is not so likely to be a problem here except with the so-called agitated type of patient. These patients are constantly in motion, pacing up and down, wringing their hands, picking at their fingernails, pulling their hair or otherwise engaging in the small-type pattern of activities. They are resistive but rarely assaultive.

Underactive Patients

Underactive patients are of 2 main types: (1) those who are withdrawn from reality and apparently unemotional, and (2) those who are depressed, and whose thinking and physical activities are sluggish.

The Withdrawn, Unemotional Patient. As a rule, the patients in this group appear to be quite happy and content if they are left alone to think at leisure and enjoy their own fantasies. If they are permitted to do this, they will deteriorate to the point of merely existing like vegetables. Therefore, the aim of their nursing care is to hold these patients to reality. Stimulate them to respond to things about them; to take an interest in life. They are rarely suicidal and not usually assaultive; however, these 2 possibilities are to be kept in mind. When either occurs, it is apt to be sudden and without warning—the opposite of the threatening overactive patient.

Matters of the utmost concern to the normal person become completely unimportant to the patient who is no longer interested in the world or in keeping his place in it. He does not care about food, nor does he attend to his toilet habits, and he frequently soils himself. He is not interested in conversation with the people about him, although he may talk to imaginary people who are more real to him.

The nursing care varies widely from patient to patient and even with the same patient. However, the nurse should care for the *physical needs* of the withdrawn patient by:

1. Regularly bathing and otherwise keeping the patient clean—that is, keeping his nails cut, his hair combed, etc. A lack of tidiness tends to hasten his disorganization.

2. Seeing that he receives an adequate diet, spoon-feeding him if necessary. If the patient does not eat, the physician should be notified.

3. Having an exercise routine, preferably out-of-doors

4. Checking on physical functions, defecation, emptying of the bladder, and regularity of menstruation in women patients

5. Weighing the patient at stated intervals

The Inactive Depressed Patient. The inactive patient who is depressed has some of the problems mentioned above, and others that are different. In this case, the main nursing objective is to prevent suicide. This patient requires much more constant observation than the patients previously referred to. As mentioned in relation to suicide, the period when the patient begins to improve but still has periods of returning depression is most dangerous (see page 582). The nursing care is essentially the same for all stuporous patients. The depressed always lose weight because they eat too little, and the body does not use food properly. Therefore, feeding is important, including nourishment between meals and at night.

Because all body processes are slowed up, constipation is a symptom to watch for. These patients should also be observed for symptoms of physical disease, for they rarely complain of pain.

Provide a cheerful, sunny room. Do not put depressed patients with groups of exuberant patients in an effort to cheer them up; this usually has the opposite effect and tends to make them more conscious of their own unhappiness.

Do not force them into activities too rapidly, although occupational therapy is of great value. When it does begin, it should be simple and for brief periods. These patients tire quickly. As convalescence continues, reading, games and amusements are helpful. Indecision is a frequent symptom; the patient should not be asked to make decisions until he is well on the road to recovery. Continuous baths help to relieve tension and to produce sleep.

The Regressive Patient

Regression is a return to infantile or childish behavior, such as eating with the hands instead of using a spoon or a fork, urinating on the floor, soiling the clothing instead of using the toilet, masturbating or making homosexual advances to other patients. For some patients, this behavior is an attempt to recapture pleasurable childhood sensations; sometimes it is reviving methods that "worked" in childhood to get what they wanted. Regressive behavior is still another way the patient takes to escape from problems he finds too hard for him to handle. He disclaims all responsibility for himself by forgetting how to do the ordinary things that he once did automatically and considered acceptable.

It takes infinite patience to begin all over again to teach adult patients toilet habits and how to use a knife, a fork and a spoon. It takes a great many people to provide enough service to have someone take care of such patients—teaching them proper eating habits at every meal, or taking them to the toilet at regular intervals (24 hours daily) to prevent them from soiling clothing or bedclothes. It takes planning and persistence in the face of the present personnel shortages in our mental hospitals to give this type of care, but we now know it is important and are gradually working toward it.

Psychological Nursing. The most important duty of the nurse in relation to the patient's mental state is to get him to focus on reality, to interest him in practical affairs and to help him to keep in contact with his surroundings. To do this:

Encourage self-respect.

Do not try to show him that he is behaving foolishly; his behavior is more real to him than that of the people about him.

Do not scold the patient if he soils himself, etc. Often these patients are extremely sensitive, in spite of seeming oblivious to everything.

Be patient and kind during all contacts with him.

Occupation is most valuable. Useful work stimulates pride and gives the patient something to hold on to. Avoid stereotyped activities which can be performed without thought on the part of the patient.

Initiate games and participate in them along with the patients.

Use every opportunity to bring the patient into stimulating contact with others.

Strive to gain the confidence of the patient.

Be on the alert for outbursts of violence and suicidal attempts.

If the patient becomes inactive to the point of being stuporous, care for him in bed; also bathe him daily, with particular attention to the skin. Change his position frequently and give special care to proper feeding and elimination.

Patients in Continued Treatment Services

All mental institutions of the state hospital type have many patients who are classified as being in the continued treatment group. In the main, they are the patients who have passed the acute stages of illness without improvement and are tending to deteriorate. Treatment is continued although there is little hope of recovery. They show a variety of symptoms, ranging from the actively disturbed to the emotionally dull or the bewildered senile cases. Many of them are untidy. Some who have been able to respond fairly well to life within the hospital cannot adjust to the outside world. Occasionally a patient from this group recovers, but, generally speaking, the problem is to establish a routine for the best possible hospital existence—many of them will remain patients for the rest of their lives.

Nursing Care. The program of nursing care should be approached from 3 angles: physical care, habit training, and occupation. Many of these patients will be unable to care for their physical needs, so soiling is one of the greatest problems. Therefore, at regular intervals they should be taken to the toilet. This does not mean that they should be herded into a toilet room and rapidly put through a process with unproductive results. Patients, although deteriorated, should be treated with *respect* and *consideration.* This requires time and personnel, but efforts have proved again and again that it is worthwhile. The entire atmosphere can be changed in this one way alone, besides the fact that odors disappear and linen is saved.

Keeping Up Morale. Patients should be bathed regularly, and suitable clothing should be provided. Even the most deteriorated patients often will respond in the most unexpected fashion to a treatment at the beauty parlor and a pretty, bright dress. Disregard of personal appearance hastens disorganization; therefore attention should be given to keeping these patients presentable at all times. Feeding is also a problem. Many eat too much and too rapidly; others take insufficient food. They should have a normal, well-balanced diet, with attention given to their eating habits. Many times patients are given all of their food on tin plates with only a spoon or even their fingers with which to eat. When so little is expected, certainly little will be achieved. Never take it for granted that a patient cannot use a knife or a fork, but try again and again. Success often rewards persistence.

The value of recreation and occupation to this group is incalculable. Certain projects have been tried which included whole wards of untidy patients; by arranging simple activities such as walks, games and crafts, they were kept busy all day, and untidiness disappeared. Such activities also tend to lessen combativeness and destructiveness; tensions are worked off in a healthy manner.

Grooming in general has been mentioned, but the nurse should pay daily attention to the care of the fingernails and the toenails, combing the hair and brushing the teeth. Patients should be encouraged to do these things for themselves, but the nurse is responsible for seeing that they are done properly; she does them herself if the patient cannot do them adequately.

The Senile Patient

The senile patient may present the same problems mentioned above, but certain problems are associated definitely with the care of elderly people, such as the prevention of fractures due to falling. Such patients frequently have a tendency to seize either the nurse or the furniture when they are lifted or moved; therefore, it is essential to be extremely careful in handling them. Small rugs that may cause them to slip should be removed. Old people get up frequently during the night; for this reason, their beds should not be too high and, if possible, should be placed against the wall.

Old people should not be moved from their accustomed place. This also applies to their possessions. Change confuses them. The same principle should apply in the assignment of personnel. Insofar as possible, senile patients should have the same nurses regularly. Even when they seem to be entirely out of contact, they often are soothed by a familiar voice or touch. Due to physical handicaps, the senile patient rarely is able to do much in the form of occupational therapy; it is a waste of time to attempt to teach him the new crafts. However, occasionally an older patient can do very well at some work which he or she has learned and practiced years ago—knitting, for example. Even if she does it poorly, encourage her to keep on.

In general, the care and the management of the senile patient centers around these points:

Temperament and Behavior. The reactions of the senile patient are often unpredictable; these patients are subject to sudden changes in mood, varying from interest and co-operation to apathy or rebellion.

Diet for Aged Patients. It is necessary to provide a diet that includes the essential food elements for a person with limited activities and at the same time get around the difficulties that elderly people have with chewing, elimination, etc. Frequent light meals and night nourishment are desirable.

Bathing. Bathing is important for skin care and cleanliness—senile patients cannot be trusted to bathe themselves adequately and may not be able to do so. The nurse can use the bath procedure as a golden opportunity to make observations about the patient and can be sure that this procedure is done safely and without chilling the patient.

Clothing. Elderly patients need warmer clothing than other people; their garments should be comfortable and not irritating to the skin and should be easy to get into, durable and easy to keep clean.

Physical Care. Adequate daily bowel and bladder elimination must be assured—elderly people are forgetful, and the senile patient cannot be held responsible for reporting anything accurately. Cathartics or enemas may be necessary. Care must be taken to ensure an adequate amount of fluids for these patients.

Prevention of Injuries. Elderly people should never be hurried—they move with difficulty and fall easily. The senile patient frequently does not understand directions. They are also likely to stay in one position for long periods of time and may soil their clothing with urine or feces without being aware of their incontinence or being disturbed by it. Careful and frequent observations will prevent skin irritation. If any type of injury does occur, it should have prompt attention and should be reported at once to the proper authorities.

Occupation and Exercise. Most elderly patients have poor eyesight, so special attention must be given to helping them with daily routines and to providing diversions that do not involve using their eyes. They may be feeble, with impaired muscle control, and tire easily; they are inclined to make as little effort as possible. They are easily confused and can take part only in simple activities that do not require concentration or extensive movements.

Convalescent Patients

In spite of the fact that they are on the way to recovery, convalescent patients present many nursing problems; in some instances, these patients are more difficult to care for than they were during the acute stages of mental illness.

When the Patient Goes Home. It is in the interest of the patient and the hospital to get him ready for discharge as soon as possible. Yet, there are certain responsibilities in this respect which the hospital cannot ignore. The community must have reasonable security, and patients must be safe in the community. No one can be absolutely certain about whether or not a patient will have a relapse, yet everything possible must be done to help his adjustment when he is discharged to prevent a relapse. If it is probable that he is going to have a relapse, his re-education and guidance in the hospital should make it easier to accept when it happens.

The care and treatment of the convalescent patient should be planned for certain definite purposes. We should think of convalescence as beginning early and encourage the patient to do as many normal things as he can. The keynote, then, is *normal activities leading to normal adjustment.* The nurse must be prepared for irritability in these patients and also for periods when the patient cannot go forward, but she should not be discouraged. This is when the nurse must endure, persist, and be ready to give reassurance to the patient. A hopeless attitude on her part will be reflected most surely in the behavior of the patient.

The Patient's Feelings. People often fail to realize how long it takes to recover from mental illness. Often no symptoms are evident, yet this must not be taken to mean that the patient is entirely well. Another important factor is that, while the physician and others who have had the care of the patient are always pleased and happy over his convalescence, to the patient it may be a period of intense suffering. This may be because he realizes what he has been through and sees the problems he faces, coupled with the insecurity that the future holds now that he has been a mental patient. Often this is so thwarting that he is unable to bring himself to face it and therefore continues to seek refuge in the hospital.

Back to Independence. Therefore, while the nurse must be sympathetic, she should not be oversolicitous and so allow the patient to become too dependent on her as a nurse or on the institution. From the moment he is admitted to the hospital, the patient should be encouraged to help himself in every way he can; as soon as possible, he should be permitted to resume the direction of his own affairs in accordance with his ability. However, patients should not be permitted to assume burdens that they are unable to carry.

Routines governing this period of the illness vary, but, in general, they proceed somewhat along these lines:

Participation in minor activities on the ward
Participation in activities in the occupational therapy departments
Participation in recreation under supervision, such as dances and entertainments
Extended privileges, such as home visits
Ground parole

Outside parole
Discharge

The Doctor's Responsibility. The psychiatrist is the doctor with special training in the treatment of mental disorders. However, every doctor has to consider the mental difficulties of his patients, as well as the physical ones. These difficulties may arise from a patient's everyday problems or from conditions around him that affect many other people, too—floods, hurricanes, plane and train disasters, fires or wars. In a war, doctors are responsible for the selection of men for the armed services. They must decide on a man's physical fitness to serve; they also must decide on his ability to stand the emotional strains of training and combat. They must treat the mental disorders that develop as a result of training or war experiences. They must deal with the civilian casualties after bombing attacks.

THE MENTAL ILLNESS PROBLEM

Approximately one half of the hospital beds in the United States are occupied by mental patients. The number of draft board rejections in World War II showed that far too many people were suffering from personality disorders. The monthly army discharge rate for psychiatric disorders was 30,000. Many of these men were in combat but were unable to stand the radical change to military life. Few of them needed hospital care. Many combat soldiers were treated successfully near the battle front; others are now in the mental hospitals of the Veterans Administration.

It costs about one billion dollars every year to care for mentally ill patients. Possibly 1 out of 12 children in our schools is destined eventually to require treatment in mental hospitals. The awakened interest in the treatment of mental illness has come from the tremendous need to reduce the social and economic waste that it creates. The program starts with prevention. Parents and teachers are informed about child training and learn how to recognize the symptoms of mental distress. Personnel departments in industry help with the adjustment problems of the workers. However, we need more psychiatrists, more professional and practical nurses, and better laws to provide the right kind of protection and care for the mentally ill.

What Is Being Done. The American Psychiatric Association sets up standards for the care of mental patients and encourages psychiatric training for doctors and nurses. The National Mental Health Act of 1946 authorized the U.S. Public Health Service to set up a National Institute of Mental Health as a training and research center. Funds are available to train psychiatrists. Money is not provided for routine care of mental patients but is to be spent on detecting mental difficulties and preventing them.

The National Association for Mental Health has been working since 1909 to prevent mental illness, to improve the treatment of mental patients and to educate the public about mental disorders. On a nationwide basis, state mental health organizations are working to improve and expand care facilities, but these efforts must be doubled to give psychiatric services to the millions who need them.

Where the Practical Nurse Comes In. The care of the psychiatric patient provides a challenging opportunity for the practical nurse to use her abilities to the utmost. Working closely with the patient day by day she is his stability—she is always there, will always listen, is always kind, does not condemn or punish but believes in him and gives him hope. It is a rewarding experience to have had a part in his recovery. Special postgraduate training in the care of psychiatric patients is available, but the number of these courses is as yet limited.

Every nurse should know the facts about mental illness because she can use this information to help her understand the emotional problems of any patient. Unco-operative behavior mildly resembles the symptoms shown by the patient who is definitely mentally ill. Mr. Johnson, in the general hospital, may refuse to take his medicine, but Mr. Roth, in the mental hospital, may hurl the medicine glass across the room. Every person has what is *to him* a good reason for what he does, and it is important to remember this to know what some of the possible reasons for such actions might be, and how to meet the problem. You will have endless opportunities in any hospital to use your knowledge of mental health and mental illness.

A BRIEF CLASSIFICATION OF MENTAL ILLNESS*

I. Organic Mental Illnesses, Caused by or Associated With Damage of Brain Tissue

A. Acute Brain Disorders

1. Associated with either brain or bodily infection (i.e., meningitis, brain abscess, or pneumonia, typhoid fever, etc.)
2. Associated with either drug or poison intoxication
3. Associated with alcoholic intoxication (i.e., delirium tremens, or "D.T.'s," and acute alcoholic hallucinosis)
4. Associated with head injury, including surgery
5. Associated with circulatory disturbance (i.e., high blood pressure, "stroke," etc.)
6. Associated with seizures (convulsive disturbance)
7. Associated with glandular disorders (i.e., diabetes, vitamin deficiency, etc.)
8. Associated with brain tumors

B. Chronic Brain Disorders

1. Associated with birth injury, illness, or defect
2. Associated with syphilis
3. Associated with intoxication (i.e., chronic drug addiction, chronic alcoholism, etc.)
4. Associated with circulatory disturbance (i.e., hardening of the arteries of the brain)
5. Associated with convulsive disorder (i.e., "idiopathic" epilepsy, or seizures without known cause from injury or illness)
6. Associated with illnesses of unknown or uncertain cause (i.e., Huntington's chorea, multiple sclerosis, and illnesses of a familial or hereditary nature)

II. Mental Deficiency: a defect in intelligence existing since birth, without demonstrated organic brain disease, or known cause before birth. The degree of intelligence defect is mild (vocational impairment), moderate (requiring special training and guidance), or severe (requiring custodial or complete protective care)

III. Illness of Psychogenic Origin, or Without Clearly Defined Physical Cause or Changes in the Brain

A. Psychotic Disorders

1. Involutional psychotic reaction (depression occurring at middle age—change of life—in both men and women, without previous history of depressive reaction)
2. Manic depressive reactions (marked by severe mood changes from elation to overactivity to depression, with a tendency to occur again. Three types: manic—overactivity, both motor and verbal; depressed—underactivity, both motor and verbal; manic depressive reaction, other—mixed overactivity and underactivity)
3. Psychotic depressive reaction (differs from the manic depressive reaction by the absence of a previous history of mood swings, and the frequent presence of environmental reasons for reaction)
4. Schizophrenic reactions
   a. Simple type (characterized by gradual withdrawal from human relationships, and by an indifference in attitude)
   b. Hebephrenic type (characterized by childishness, silly behavior and mannerisms and by inappropriate moods)
   c. Catatonic type (characterized by either marked resistiveness and negativism or excessive excitement)
   d. Paranoid type (characterized by unrealistic thinking and daydreaming, with delusions of persecution and/or grandeur, and often hallucinations. Also characterized by unpredictable behavior and a fairly constant attitude of hostility and aggression)
5. Schizophrenic reaction, acute and chronic undifferentiated types (characterized by mixed symptoms of other types of schizophrenia—cannot be specifically classified in any of the other types)
6. Schizophrenic reaction, childhood type (characteristically appearing before puberty, and consisting mainly of autism, or absorption in phantasy)
7. Paranoid reactions
   a. Paranoia (sometimes called "true paranoia." Characterized by a slowly developing delusional system, often

* Adapted from the American Psychiatric Association Mental Hospital Service Diagnostic and Statistical Manual on Mental Disorders, 1952, pp. 12-43.

logically developed after a false interpretation of an actual occurrence; without hallucinations, and with the remainder of the personality remaining relatively the same)

b. Paranoid state (characterized by paranoid delusions, but lacking the logical system seen in paranoia; does not show the bizarre behavior and deterioration of the schizophrenic reactions)

B. Psychophysiologic Autonomic and Visceral Disorders ("Psychosomatic Disorders")
1. Skin reaction (dermatitis, pruritus, etc., in which emotional factors play a causative role)
2. Musculoskeletal reaction (some tension headaches, backaches, muscle cramps, etc., in which emotional factors play a causative role)
3. Respiratory reaction (hiccoughs, sighing respirations, etc., in which emotional factors play a causative role)
4. Cardiovascular reaction (high blood pressure, migraine headaches, etc., in which emotional factors play a causative role)
5. Gastro-intestinal reaction (mucous colitis, constipation, "heartburn," etc., in which emotional factors play a causative role)
6. Genito-urinary reaction (including some types of menstrual disturbances, etc., in which emotional factors play a causative role)
7. Endocrine (glandular) reaction (glandular disturbances in which emotional factors play a causative role)
8. Nervous system reaction (fatigue, and some convulsive disorders in which emotional factors play a causative role)

C. Psychoneurotic Disorders
1. Anxiety reaction (anxiety, or feeling of tension is spread, and not restricted to specific persons or objects)
2. Dissociative reaction (personality disorganization, sometimes resulting in running or "freezing"–i.e., amnesia–loss of memory–or somnambulism–"sleep walking")
3. Conversion reaction (anxiety is "converted" into functional symptoms in organs or parts of the body, as blindness, deafness, or paralysis)
4. Phobic reaction (anxiety is displaced by a specific fear, as, for example, fear of syphilis, dirt, high places, etc. Patient attempts to control this anxiety by avoiding the phobic object or situation)
5. Obsessive compulsive reaction (anxiety is associated with the persistence of unwanted ideas and repeated impulses to perform acts which may seem unreasonable, but must be carried out)
6. Depressive reaction (anxiety is somewhat relieved by depression and self-depreciation. Often associated with a feeling of guilt for past failures or deeds)

D. Personality Disorders
1. Inadequate personality (patient shows poor judgment, lack of physical and emotional energy, and lack of social presence)
2. Schizoid personality (including avoidance of close relations with others, inability to express direct hostility or even aggression, and daydreaming. Later demonstrates seclusiveness and eccentricity)
3. Cyclothymic personality (characterized by an "outgoing" personality, personal warmth, friendliness and surface generosity. There are frequently alternating moods of happiness and sadness)
4. Paranoid personality (characterized by suspiciousness, envy, extreme jealousy and stubbornness)
5. Emotionally unstable personality (reacts with unusual excitement when confronted by minor stress)
6. Passive-aggressive personality (three types: passive-dependent type–helplessness, tendency to cling to others; passive-aggressive type–pouting, stubbornness, and inefficiency; and aggressive–irritability, temper tantrums and destructive behavior)
7. Compulsive personality (characterized by chronic, excessive, or obsessive concern with standards of conscience, or conformity. May be overinhibited, overconscientious, or may work too hard)
8. Antisocial reaction (always in trouble, does not profit from experience or punishment, and maintaining no real loyalties to any person, group or code. Frequently lack sense of responsibility, lack of judgment, and the ability to rationalize their behavior so that it appears justified)
9. Dissocial reaction (manifest disregard for the usual codes of living)
10. Sexual deviation (diagnosis will specify the type of abnormal behavior, such as

homosexuality, fetishism and sexual sadism)

E. Transient Situational Personality Disorders
   1. Gross stress reaction (diagnosis is justified only in situations in which the individual has been exposed to severe physical demands or extreme emotional stress, such as in combat, or other catastrophe as fire, earthquake, tornado, etc.)
   2. Adult situational reaction (superficial maladjustment to a difficult situation or new experience, with no evidence of serious underlying personality defects)
   3. Adjustment reaction of infancy (undue apathy, undue excitability, feeding and sleeping difficulties)
   4. Adjustment reaction of childhood (habit disturbance, conduct disturbance, neurotic traits manifested when faced with immediate situation or internal emotional conflict)
   5. Adjustment reaction of adolescence (temporary reactions of the adolescent as the result of his beginning intellectual and emotional strivings)
   6. Adjustment reaction of late life (an expression of the problems of physiologic, situational, and environmental readjustment, for example, retiring from work, breaking up of families through death, etc.)

45

THE PATIENT WITH A DISORDER OF THE EYE OR THE EAR

THE PATIENT WITH AN EYE DISORDER

The eye is such an important organ that the care of it should begin at birth and continue through old age. Industry has realized the value of safeguards for eyesight. The need for adequate and well-placed lighting is generally accepted.

Many people are confused about the meaning of the titles of those professionals who are concerned with eye difficulties. The science which studies eye diseases and difficulties is called *ophthalmology*. The *ophthalmologist* and the *oculist* are medical doctors who have had special training in this field, which includes a knowledge of refraction and the ability to prescribe glasses. The *optician* fills these prescriptions by making the lenses and adjusting the glasses properly. The *optometrist* has special training in testing vision and he can prescribe glasses to correct errors in refraction. Since poor vision may be a symptom of a more serious eye difficulty, perhaps one that glasses will not correct, anyone with eye trouble should consult an ophthalmologist or an oculist at once. The eye examiner will perform refraction tests, and he will ask the patient to read a special chart. He may also use an *ophthalmoscope*, an instrument used to examine the interior of the eye, or a *tonometer*, which measures the pressure within the eyeball.

Refraction Test. Refraction is the function which the lens performs in order to focus light rays on the retina; in this way, we can see objects clearly at different distances. To do this, the lens is constantly adjusting the curvature in its shape, a function called accommodation. Drops of the drug atropine, or homatropine (which acts for a shorter time) instilled into the eye will temporarily paralyze the iris, the muscles of the eye which control the opening to the lens. This keeps the iris wide open so that the ophthalmologist can see how correctly the lens focuses the light rays. Then he can correct a refractive error with the strength and the type of artificial lens necessary. He will try different lenses over the eye until he finds the one which will correct the error, so that he can prescribe the correction. The optician then grinds a lens to this prescription.

Types of Lenses. As people grow older, the lens loses some of its elasticity and does not adjust completely for near vision. This condition is called *presbyopia*—one can see evidences of presbyopia in people who hold their newspapers at arms' length. These people probably need *bifocals* (two lenses in one), which are ground to correct defects in both far vision and near vision. Trifocal lenses are also used; these add still another correction, making things sharper in the 27-inch to 50-inch range of vision. The *contact lens* is a type of lens which fits directly over the eyeball instead of in glasses.

Contact Lenses and Glasses. Most contact lenses are made of plastic. They are lightweight and paper thin, and they fit over the eyeball where they *float* on the eyeball fluid.

They are kept in place by capillary attraction and the upper eyelid. Contact lenses have a special appeal for people who dislike the looks of conventional glasses; people who are engaged in active sports; or for people who make their living in the entertainment world where their appearance matters considerably to them. Contact lenses are not suitable for everyone—the shape of the eyeball may prohibit their use, and they are not recommended in conditions such as glaucoma (see p. 600), corneal infection or iritis. Also, they are more expensive than conventional glasses, and getting used to them sometimes requires time and patience. Usually, the patient becomes accustomed to them gradually by wearing them for short periods of time at first. It is important to keep them clean and avoid scratching them so that there is no interference with vision. They should be washed with soap and water or a solution of benzalkonium chloride, dried carefully and handled gently.

Glasses have become so ornamental and glamorous, with a variety of attractive frames available, that most people scarcely mind wearing them. The wearer can choose a shape and colored frame to suit his or her face and personality, and also to fit different occasions. There are glasses for study as well as those for business, with more elaborate types for social use.

People are sometimes concerned about wearing sunglasses. Sunglasses are not harmful if the lenses are carefully ground and do not distort vision. People who wear glasses all the time should have dark glasses ground to their prescription, or else wear clip-on dark lenses over their conventional glasses.

Questions have also been asked concerning the use of eyedrops which are advertised as effective in soothing or resting the eyes. Generally, these preparations are harmless unless they are used for irritation caused by a condition requiring medical attention, such as eye infection or glaucoma.

Everyday Care. Sound advice for daily eye care is the following:

Always work in a good light.

Rest the eyes at intervals when doing fine, intricate work.

Include sufficient vitamin A in a nutritious diet.

Get enough sleep.

Avoid touching or rubbing the eyes.

Never use eye cups (they help to spread infection).

Be careful about excessive exposure to sun lamps or strong sunlight—these can burn the eyelids and may harm the eyes.

Instillation of Eyedrops. Eyedrops are instilled for various reasons—to contract or dilate the pupil of the eye, to treat an infection or to produce local effects, such as anesthesia. The solution ordered by the physician will depend on the purpose of the instillation. It is often the nurse's responsibility not only to carry out the procedure herself but also to instruct others.

The lids and the lashes are wiped clean, and the patient lies down or sits with his head tilted backward. He keeps a tissue in readiness in case there is a slight overflow. The nurse rests the hand in which she is holding the dropper against the patient's forehead and, with the other hand, depresses the lower lid (Fig. 177). The patient is asked to look up, and the prescribed number of drops is allowed to fall into the center of the everted lower lid. Then the patient is instructed to close his eyelids gently and to move the eye to distribute the solution.

Extreme caution should be heeded to prevent the drops from falling on the sensitive cornea. It is also important to remember that any unused solution cannot be returned to the stock bottle, so an effort should be made to avoid being wasteful when drawing the solution into the dropper.

Common Eye Disorders

Errors in Refraction. Refractive errors are a common type of eye disorder which can be inherited. *Myopia* (nearsightedness) is caused by an elongation of the eyeball, while *hyperopia* (farsightedness) is the result of a shorter than normal eyeball (see Chap. 21). An irregularly shaped cornea or lens produces *astigmatism* (distorted vision), causing objects to look wider or taller and blurred. *Presbyopia* was mentioned previously in this chapter as a condition of old age in which the lens loses its ability to change focus readily. People with presbyopia are sometimes reluctant to admit that they need glasses, and they are a great hazard to themselves as well as to others. Holding objects at a distance, squinting and headaches are some of the signs that may indicate refractive errors and the need for corrective lenses.

Strabismus. *Strabismus* (squint) is the condition commonly called "cross-eye." In looking at an object, one eye appears to be looking somewhere else and is turned either inward or outward. Strabismus frequently occurs in children. It can be caused by an injury, disease, or eye defects. The initial treatment usually consists of eye exercises; if this is not successful, properly fitted glasses may be effective. If both these measures fail, a surgical operation may be necessary to straighten the eyes.

Conjunctivitis. *Conjunctivitis* is an inflammation of the conjunctiva, the membrane lining the eyelids and covering the front of the eyeball (except for the cornea). It causes pain, redness and irritation and sometimes a discharge. A common name for conjunctivitis is *pink eye*. It may be caused by an infection, in which case it is treated with the appropriate antibiotic. Proper washing of the nurse's hands and the disinfection of the patient's linen are essential to prevent the spread of infection. Early medical care is important in order to prevent eye damage. Allergy may also cause conjunctivitis, in which case the treatment consists of avoiding the offending allergen, giving antihistamines, and desensitization (see Chap. 47). Boric acid or saline solution irrigations are given at frequent intervals to remove the discharge from the eye.

Stye (Hordoleum). A *stye* is an infection on

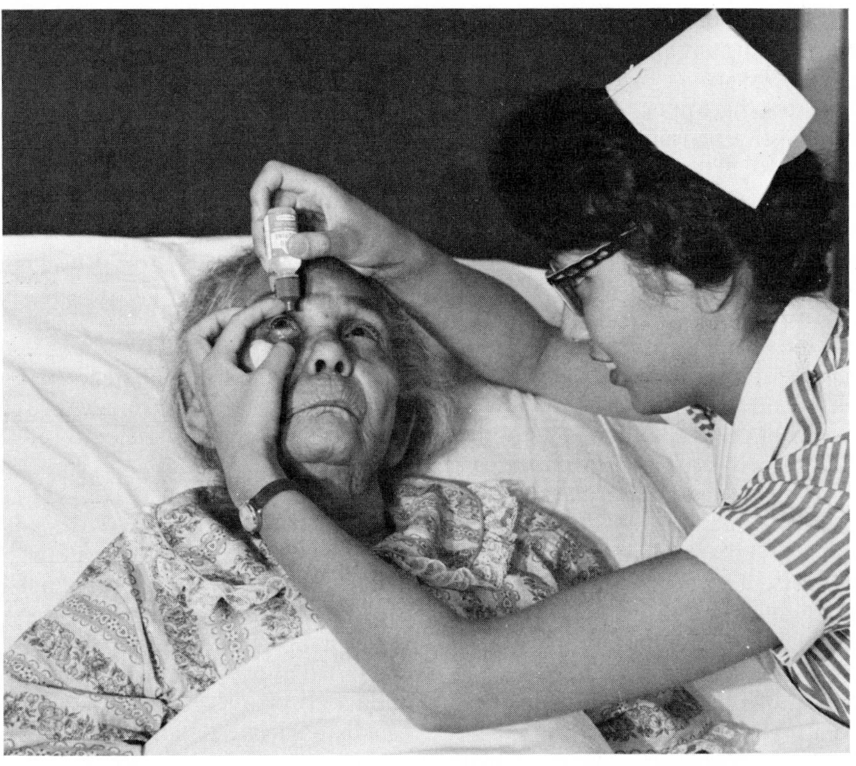

Fig. 177. The nurse rests her hand against the patient's forehead, thus steadying her hand and controlling the movement of the bottle. The drop is placed inside the lower lid. (Smith, D. W., and Gips, C. D.: Care of the Adult Patient, p. 1339, Philadelphia, Lippincott, 1963)

the edge of the eyelid which starts in a hair follicle or a sebaceous gland. Styes are red, swollen, painful and usually rupture, discharging pus. This drainage relieves the pain, and then the wound heals itself. Hot, wet compresses applied to the area will help to localize the infection, which is often caused by the staphylococcus. Antibiotics are usually given, and in some cases the swelling must be incised and drained. The infection is easily spread by unnecessary picking or squeezing. People with poor health and lowered resistance to infection may have a succession of styes. A better diet and rest, with relief from worry and tension, will help to improve the patient's resistance to infection.

Ectropion, Entropion and Ptosis. *Ectropion* is the turning-out of the eyelid. This condition is often seen in older people. It is usually accompanied by tears because the lachrymal fluid cannot be excreted in the normal fashion.

Entropion is the turning-in of the eyelid, usually caused by a spasm.

Ptosis is a drooping upper eyelid. It can be caused by injury or a neurologic disorder, or it may be congenital. The usual treatment for these 3 conditions is surgery.

Trachoma. *Trachoma* is a highly communicable disease of the eyelids which is caused by a virus. The eyes become red and swollen, and small granulations appear on the conjunctiva. A scar forms on the eyelid, causing the lid to turn in. The eyelashes then scratch the cornea, infecting it. Trachoma may eventually lead to ulceration and blindness. Antibiotic treatment which is started early may control the disease. Trachoma is rarely seen in this country but is a serious health problem in some parts of the world where sanitation methods are poor.

Corneal Ulcers. The cornea is transparent, thus allowing light to enter the eye. If anything causes the cornea to thicken or become scarred, vision will be affected, and blindness may result. Inflammation of the cornea (*keratitis*), resulting from injury or infection, may destroy corneal tissue and cause ulcers. The main treatment for corneal ulcers is rest, with the administration of antibiotics and atropine drops to dilate the pupil. The symptoms of corneal ulcer are pain, tearing and a marked inability to tolerate light (*photophobia*). The eye appears bloodshot. The treatment consists of eye irrigations with antibiotic solutions and warm compresses, along with tetracaine (Pontocaine) to relieve pain. Frequently, fever therapy is used, or small doses of x-ray are given. The patient should wear dark glasses to relieve the photophobia. Fluorescein, a green dye, may be instilled into the eye in order to outline the ulcer. One of the important reasons that we are cautioned against rubbing or poking our eyes, or removing foreign bodies without caution, is the danger of injuring the cornea. First aid to remove foreign bodies from the eyes is outlined in Chapter 48.

CORNEAL TRANSPLANTATION. If the cornea is so scarred that vision is affected seriously, it is sometimes possible to restore sight by transplanting a normal cornea in place of the affected one. Anyone who wants to help a blind person to see again can make provisions for donating his eyes for corneal transplants after his death. Each state has an agency for the blind which will provide information about the procedure to follow. Immediately after the donor's death, his eyes are removed and placed in the nearest eye bank. The National Eye Bank for Sight Restoration is located in New York, N. Y. After a corneal transplantation, the patient must remain flat in bed for about 1 week, without moving his head. Any sudden movement, such as coughing, sneezing or vomiting, before the corneal graft has healed sufficiently, could tear it away from the eye. It is extremely necessary to preserve these grafts, since the supply of corneas for transplantation is limited.

Glaucoma. Glaucoma is a condition of increased pressure or tension within the eye. The cause for *primary glaucoma* is not known, except that it usually occurs in people over 40 years of age and seems to accompany conditions such as emotional disturbances, endocrine imbalance or allergies. *Secondary glaucoma* is usually associated with some other disturbance in the eye. The tonometer is the instrument used to measure pressure within the eye. If this pressure is not relieved, blindness results. The symptoms are the impairment of side vision, blurred vision, pain in the eye, and the appearance of rainbowlike halos around lights or objects.

Glaucoma is a serious health problem. The Prevention of Blindness Society estimates that glaucoma has blinded almost 50,000 people, and partially blinded 150,000 others. Early and continued treatment is highly important to preserve vision. A medical survey conducted in one state showed recommendations that a test for glaucoma be done in every routine physical examination.

Treatment. Many new drugs, such as Humorsol, Phospholine-iodine and Epitrate, have been introduced in the treatment of glaucoma. Other miotic drugs used to contract the pupil are pilocarpine, eserine and Carcholin. If drugs do not control the tension, then surgery is necessary. The successful control of glaucoma depends on the patient's perseverance in following the doctor's orders, which usually consist of avoiding worry and tension, following good health practices, avoiding tight collars and belts (in order to keep circulation active), staying out of dark rooms as much as possible and limiting any activities which strain or fatigue the eyes.

Cataract. A *cataract* is opacity of the lens of the eye. Since light entering the eye must pass through the lens in order to reach the retina, vision is impaired when the lens loses its transparency. This condition develops slowly, but eventually all sight will be lost in the affected eye. If cataracts develop in both eyes, the patient will become totally blind. A cataract usually occurs after middle age, but younger people may also be affected. Occasionally, a baby is born with a cataract, a condition called congenital cataract. Cataracts are also common among patients with certain diseases, such as diabetes.

Treatment. The only remedy for cataracts is surgery to remove the lens. The patient does not usually have any pain after this operation, but if he does experience severe pain, it may be due to a serious complication such as hemorrhaging and must be reported immediately. After the operation, the affected eye (or sometimes both eyes) are covered with eye patches, which may cause the patient to become confused, especially if he is elderly and worried about the outcome of the operation. A pleasant "voice in the dark" will be most reassuring to him. Six or 8 weeks after the operation, the patient will be fitted with glasses or a contact lens strong enough to take the place of the lens that was removed. After 6 months, the patient will be fitted with his permanent glasses or contact lenses. Because the power of accommodation is lost when the lens is removed, the patient will always have to wear corrective lenses, usually bifocals.

A cataract operation restores sight to many elderly patients and can be performed safely at any age. As a result, many a grandmother has been able to retain her independence and interest and keep up her contacts with others.

Detached Retina. A *detached retina* is a separation of the 2 layers of the retina, which deprives the layer receiving sight images of its blood supply. Separation of these layers usually follows a hole or a tear in the retina, the result of a blow or an injury, or degenerative changes. Whatever the cause, vision in the affected area is lost.

The symptoms may occur suddenly or gradually. If a large area of the central part of the retina is affected, the loss of vision is greater than if the outer edges are destroyed. The patient sees flashes of light, his vision is blurred, and he will see moving spots or experience gaps in his vision. There will be no pain, but the patient is likely to become bewildered and apprehensive. The usual treatment is surgery in order to put the separated layers back into place. After the operation, the patient must lie quietly, keeping his head still. Any sudden motion may loosen the retina again. The postoperative orders will vary with the individual operation and the ophthalmologist. The patient may be allowed out of bed the day after the operation, or on the other hand, he may have to stay in bed for 2 weeks. Surgical treatment of detached retinas has greatly improved, and patients today have a more favorable outlook for recovery.

Sympathetic Ophthalmia and Enucleation. Several weeks after a disease or an injury affects one eye, inflammation may develop in the other eye, a condition known as *sympathetic ophthalmia.* Nobody knows why this occurs, but it often follows a penetrating injury to the eyeball. To prevent the loss of sight in the unaffected eye, it is frequently necessary to remove a severely injured eye at once. The surgical removal of an eye is called an *enucleation.* The patient and his family may hesitate to consent to this operation, in the hope that the injured eye will recover. They will find it hard to believe that the injury could cause trouble in the untouched eye.

THE PROSTHETIC EYE. Enucleation may also be done for cosmetic reasons when sight has been destroyed either by disease or injury. After the eye is removed, a metal or plastic ball (implant) is buried in the empty eye capsule. The ball is moved by the eye muscles attached to the capsule. After healing is complete, a glass or plastic "shell" is fitted over the buried ball. This shell, which is tinted to match the good eye, is the prosthesis familiarly known as a *glass eye.* Artificial eyes are so cleverly made today that they often are undetected. An artificial eye is usually fitted 8 weeks after an enucleation. The patient must learn how to insert and remove the eye and how to care for it. It is usually removed for the night. When the patient practices inserting and removing the eye, he should lean over a soft or padded surface to prevent breaking the eye if it should drop.

To insert a prosthetic eye: wet the eye and lift the upper eyelid; slip the eye under the lid by holding the eye with one hand and pulling down on the lower lid, slipping it over the edge of the eye. To remove a prosthetic eye: pull down on the lower lid and press inward under the eye. The eye will then slip out.

The doctor will instruct the patient about the care of the eye socket, if it is felt that this should be done. Rinsing with tap water is usually considered as adequate care for the artificial eye.

Before an Eye Operation. The patient who comes into the hospital for an eye operation often cannot see very well, or perhaps not at all. You can help him to get his bearings and give him a sense of location. By doing this, he will not feel as completely lost when he returns from the operating room with his eyes covered. While he is ambulatory, encourage him to find his way around the room and to the bathroom. Remember to tell him that both eyes may be covered for a short time after the operation and be sure that he can locate his call bell. His preoperative preparation might include an enema and a sedative to ensure a good night's sleep. Elderly patients sometimes become disoriented after taking sedations and may need special attention.

Eye operations on adults are usually performed under local anesthesia. The patient who is awake can be questioned by the surgeon, and there is less danger of nausea and vomiting afterward; the surgeon is anxious to avoid this strain after such delicate procedures.

POSTOPERATIVE CARE. The postoperative treatment is centered on preventing strain and hemorrhage. Special precautions are taken to keep the patient's head from moving or turning suddenly. He must be lifted gently from the operating table directly onto his bed while someone holds his head firm and steady. He may have a small pillow on either side of his head; sandbags are not considered safe because they are too hard. Although the patient is awake, he may be drowsy and disoriented, especially since his eyes are covered. *He should not be left alone.* If he complains of nausea, it should be reported at once and he should be given nothing by mouth. The patient will have to be fed as long as his eyes are covered, and his head must be retained in one position. The doctor will decide how long this is to be. He may be allowed to get up in a day or two, or perhaps a week. After he begins to move around, he must be very careful not to stoop, to lift anything heavy, to cough or to laugh heartily. When he goes home the doctor will tell him how much he is allowed to do.

What is Blindness?

Sight difficulties are correctable for so many people that the need to wear glasses is considered as a minor inconvenience. Unfortunately, there are some people whose vision cannot be improved with the use of glasses or by any other means. The lives of these people are profoundly affected by the loss of sight, which afflicts so many older people.

If an eye test showed a visual acuity of

20/200, it would mean that the person being tested could see only the test letters at 20 feet. A person with normal vision would see these test letters at 200 feet. Blindness is visual acuity of 20/200 or less. The patient is considered partially sighted with a reading between 20/70 and 20/200, even with the aid of glasses.

The Partially Sighted. As was stated in Chapter 6, the needs of the partially sighted person are not the same as those of the blind. The partially sighted need a different kind of assistance. It is more difficult for these people to get assistance from agencies, since most of these organizations are set up to help the blind. Special lenses and magnifying glasses may help his vision, and his opthalmologist will tell him how much he can use his eyes without harming them.

The kind of work he can do depends on his ability to see. He should not be doing work which would endanger him or others. In most states, the law governing automobile drivers includes a vision test. Many drivers are not aware of defective vision until they are denied a renewal of their driver's licenses unless they correct their defective vision.

The Blind. Blind people do not "live in darkness." Many of them can see light or "see" a grayness resembling a fog. Many people believe that the blind develop hearing and touch to a very sensitive degree, but tests have shown that this is not true. Probably what happens is that the blind learn to use these other senses more effectively *because* they cannot see. For instance, a blind person cannot see a person's angry expression, but he learns to detect anger in other people's voices. Assistance for the blind from the federal government and various organizations was discussed in Chapter 6.

Where the Nurse Comes In. Unfortunately, we are inclined to pity the blind and to do everything for them, when many times they would be far better off if we encouraged them to be more self-reliant. To make it easier for the blind person to feed himself, place his food on the plate in the same "clock positions" every meal. Always remember to tell him about changes—if a chair has been moved, or if he is having eggs instead of cereal for breakfast. Encourage him to shave himself and comb his hair and attend to the details of grooming himself. Be sure to keep his toilet articles in the same place and never disturb them without telling him. Guide him in his activities such as going out of doors or getting seated in a chair. When walking with a blind person always let *him* take your arm, instead of propelling him along in your grasp. Be sure, too, to warn him of steps going up or down.

One of the hardest things for a person recently blinded to get used to is that he cannot read as he did previously. This handicap can be remedied if he learns to read in Braille. Braille is a system of raised dots which correspond to the letters of the alphabet and punctuation marks; the blind person discerns these characters with his fingertips (Fig. 10). It takes patience to learn Braille, but it is well worth the effort, since there are many books available in Braille. You can direct the blind person to agencies for the blind in his local area, so that he can find out how to get these books and where to find a teacher of the Braille system. Talking books, which are recordings on long-playing records of books and magazines, can be purchased or taken out on loan, and special typewriters that type in Braille are available. (Learning to type is no more of a problem to the blind person than it is to her sighted sister, since both use the touch system.)

Traveling Aids. Another problem for the blind person is getting around outside of his home and in his community. He is bound to encounter traffic, which today is difficult enough for those who can see. He probably cannot afford to employ a companion to guide him, and there may be no one in his family who is free or willing to undertake this service. One answer for this person would be the use of a Seeing Eye Dog; another would be a cane.

The Seeing Eye, Inc., Morristown, N. J., was the first center in the United States to train dogs to guide the blind. State agencies have additional information about similar centers. The guide dog is taught to recognize danger spots, such as curbs, obstacles or holes. The dog wears a harness, fitted with a U-shaped handle which the blind person grasps; dog and master can then communicate with each other through the movements of the harness.

A Seeing Eye Dog is recognized almost anywhere and has special privileges. He is allowed to enter restaurants, subways, hotels and other public places which might be off-limits to other pets. If his master is not moving, he will lie quietly nearby.

A blind person who wants a Seeing Eye Dog must live at these training centers for a period of time in order to learn how to use and take care of his particular dog. Sometimes, after a short trial period, dog and master find that they are temperamentally unsuited to each other. Then the trainer will exchange the dog for another, with no hard feelings! Some people are not able to use a dog, nor do they want to if they dislike dogs in general or are allergic to them. Dog and master become devoted and inseparable companions.

The blind are taught to use their specially constructed cane to locate curbs and other obstructions in their progress. The cane is usually painted white as an indication to everyone that the user is blind.

MISTAKEN KINDNESS. We are apt to overestimate a blind person's need for assistance. More often than not, the blind person knows where he is going and how to get there, and he is perfectly capable of managing his own affairs. A blind person who seems to be bewildered or uncertain may be glad to accept a courteous offer of aid. Giving him directions or quietly offering him your seat on the bus is unobtrusive assistance that is not embarrassing.

Perhaps it is the little things that count most in helping a blind person. Speak to him by name—he cannot see that you are addressing him. Tell him what you have in your hand and what it looks like; tell him when you enter or plan to leave a room. If you want to shake his hand, you must grasp it yourself, since he does not know that you are extending your hand.

THE PATIENT WITH AN EAR DISORDER

The ear has 3 parts—the outer, the middle and the inner. The outer ear collects sound waves and transmits them to the ear drum (tympanum), a membrane between the outer and the middle ear. Vibrations from the ear drum are carried across the middle ear by 3 tiny bones (malleus, incus, stapes) to the inner ear, which contains the organs of hearing.

Impaired Hearing

This is a common difficulty that may occur at any age. Many a child has been scolded for poor marks in school or branded as dull when the real trouble was a hearing defect. As people grow older, hearing difficulties are likely to appear. Injuries to the hearing center in the brain, to the auditory nerve or to the eardrum can cause deafness; closed ear passages or poor conduction of sounds will affect hearing.

Hearing loss may vary from slight to moderate or to complete deafness. Hearing may be impaired by disease, injury, exposure to excessive noise, or a person may be born deaf (congenital deafness). There are 2 kinds of deafness. *Conductive deafness* is an interference with the conduction of sound waves to the organs of hearing. An accumulation of ear wax in the auditory canal or disease or injury of the vibrating bones may cause conductive deafness. *Perceptive deafness* (sometimes called nerve deafness) is a disturbance of the organs of hearing. A hearing aid is most helpful to people with conductive deafness because it helps to conduct sound. A person who is losing his hearing because of impairment of the hearing organs has little chance of escaping deafness if the cause of the difficulty is not discovered before these organs are damaged.

Hearing Tests. Hearing tests will tell how well a person can hear and what type of deafness he has. Determining at what distance from his ear a person can hear a watch tick is a simple test. The *audiometry* test is much more accurate and reliable and is done with a measuring machine called an *audiometer.*

Hearing tests are a part of the modern school health program. The audiometer tests several children at a time, by using individual earphones. Children who show defective hearing are tested again individually.

The Patient With a Hearing Loss. A person

with a marked hearing loss cannot hear sounds that warn him of danger, such as the horn of an approaching car or the hiss of escaping steam. He loses the thread of a conversation and may ask questions or make comments that have no relation to the discussion. This becomes embarrassing, and finally he lapses into a silence that makes him seem to be disinterested or inattentive. Because he is unable to hear his own voice he may talk very loudly or in a monotonous undertone. People are less tolerant of deafness than eye defects and become impatient when they are asked to repeat their words. Some people with impaired hearing stubbornly refuse to admit that they do not hear well and they deny themselves the help of a hearing aid because they feel that there is something degrading about an honest admission of deafness, as if it were something of which to be ashamed.

Helping the Hard-of-Hearing. The branch of medicine concerned with diseases and disorders of the ear is called *otology*; the doctor in this specialty is known as an *otologist*. He tests hearing, examines the ear for signs of disease and determines the treatment. Hearing loss which is due to advancing age cannot be restored, but there are ways of helping a person to make up for it. He can learn *lip reading*—it is sometimes called speech reading because it includes watching facial expressions as well as lips. He can have the doctor look for and remove accumulations of ear wax. Others can help him by speaking slowly and distinctly in a moderately loud tone and by not allowing their voices to drop at the end of a sentence. Always try to include a patient who is hard-of-hearing in conversations as much as possible. We do not always realize how "left out" a deaf person feels. People with normal hearing often miss parts of an ordinary conversation because words are mumbled and voices are low; a deaf person is in complete silence.

HEARING AIDS. Hearing aids have renewed life for many deaf people. A hearing aid will not restore hearing loss to a normal level, but it will improve hearing. The doctor will determine whether or not a hearing aid will help, and which type of aid will be of the most benefit to an individual patient. No hearing aid will help deafness as effectively as glasses help sight. It takes time and patience to get used to wearing it and to learn to adjust it.

Up-to-date hearing aids, like the midget radios, are operated on dry cells and transistors encased in a light-weight container. This device amplifies sounds and transmits them to a tiny receiver inserted in the ear. The wearer can regulate the volume and the intensity of sounds. One difficulty encountered when getting used to a hearing aid is that distracting sounds are amplified, as well as the ones the patient wants to hear. However, the difficulties can be overcome if the patient perseveres and wears the aid all the time, not just occasionally. The ear piece should be washed every day with mild soap and water and dried well; a pipe cleaner will help in cleaning the cannula.

If a person who is hard-of-hearing asks your advice about getting a hearing aid, tell him to consult an ear specialist. Do not make overenthusiastic statements about what it will do for him just because a hearing aid has done wonders for your Aunt Ethel. If his doctor is prescribing a hearing aid for him, tell him not to be discouraged if it seems to be difficult to adjust to it, but that he should keep on trying.

Preventing Hearing Loss. The prompt treatment of infectious diseases, such as upper respiratory infections which can spread to the ear, helps to prevent deafness. Also, avoid prolonged exposure to loud noise. Antibiotics and soundproof buildings have reduced these hazards. The American Hearing Society and its branches provide information about employment and social clubs that is helpful to the deaf and the hard-of-hearing.

Conditions That Affect the Middle Ear

Otosclerosis. *Otosclerosis* is a bony fixation of the stapes—one of the small bones in the middle ear which helps to transmit sound to the inner ear. This condition interferes with the vibration of the stapes and is usually slow in developing. No one knows exactly what causes otosclerosis, but it seems to have something to do with heredity, since it usually runs in families.

The patient may not notice that he is growing deaf until he begins to have difficulty in hearing ordinary conversation, especially when people speak in low tones, although if they speak loudly he can hear them. Another symptom is *ringing* in his ears (*tinnitus*), which is accentuated at night when everything around him is quiet. Although this condition cannot be cured, a conductive hearing aid may help.

STAPES MOBILIZATION. Surgery to restore vibration to the stapes (an operation known as stapes mobilization) may or may not be effective; therefore, it is usually left to the patient to decide whether or not he wants to take that chance. The operation is done under local anesthesia and frees the stapes so that it can vibrate.

The patient is usually allowed to be up out of bed following surgery and may be discharged in 2 days. He may feel dizzy and need assistance in walking, so precautions must be taken to prevent falls. He is told not to blow his nose violently for fear of spreading infection to the operative region through the eustachian tube, and he is warned not to get water in his ear. In about 2 weeks he can resume his normal activities. If this operation is not successful, a *fenestration* operation may be considered.

Fenestration Operation. Fenestration involves making a new window from the middle to the inner ear to let the vibrations through. This "window" is about as large as the head of a pin! The operation is more disturbing than the stapes operation, and the patient often experiences severe dizziness and nausea. He is cautioned to move slowly and to keep his head flat. Chewing is painful, so he is given soft foods and fluids. He may lie on his back or on the operative side—lying on the other side might allow drainage from the operative area to run into the inner ear. Usually, such patients remain in the hospital for 10 days to 2 weeks.

The patient's hearing may not be noticeably improved for a month to 6 weeks after the operation. He must avoid blowing his nose violently and be careful not to get water in his ears. Hearing tests will show how successful the operation has been.

Ear Infections

The ear is especially susceptible to upper respiratory infections because they spread to the ear through the eustachian tube from the nose and the throat. Children are the most vulnerable to these infections, but they also affect adults as the result of childhood infections. Before antibiotics became available, long, drawn-out ear infections did a great amount of damage and even caused death before they subsided. Antibiotics changed this picture, but now we are faced with a new worry because some microorganisms are becoming resistant to antibiotics.

Otitis Media. *Otitis media* is an inflammation of the middle ear. There are 2 types: in *serous* otitis media, fluid forms in the middle ear as a result of obstruction of the eustachian tube—a condition which may be caused by such things as infection, allergy or growths, or by sudden changes in altitude. The symptoms are crackling sensations and fullness in the ear, with some hearing loss. If this condition is not treated promptly, the pressure of the fluid may rupture the eardrum. It is treated by puncturing the eardrum and aspirating the fluid, followed by treatment for the cause of the difficulty.

Acute *purulent* otitis media is caused by an infection spreading through the eustachian tube in upper respiratory infections. Pus forms and collects in the middle ear to create pressure on the eardrum. The symptoms are fever, earache and impaired hearing. The eardrum is red and bulging and may rupture. Prompt treatment to puncture the eardrum prevents a rupture; a rupture heals slowly and leaves a scar which may interfere with the vibrations of the drum and damage hearing.

The puncture (*myringotomy*) releases the pressure and relieves the pain, and it heals quickly. The discharge from the ear is bloody at first and becomes purulent later. The ear should not be plugged tightly with cotton since this interferes with drainage; a small piece of cotton can be placed in the outer ear to absorb the drainage. This should be changed frequently. The appropriate antibiotics are given to fight the infection. Further treatment consists of rest, an adequate diet and the prevention of chilling.

Inflammation of the mastoid cells (*mastoiditis*) is a possible complication of acute otitis media, or meningitis may occur if the infection spreads to the meninges of the spine. Other complications include nausea and vomiting, dizziness, injury to the facial nerve causing facial paralysis, or a brain abscess: all this may start with a simple earache. If acute otitis media is neglected or is not treated properly, it may become chronic, inflicting the patient with a discharging ear, a noticeable hearing loss, and the danger of the infection's spreading to the mastoid cells or to the brain.

Mastoiditis. Due to antibiotics, mastoiditis is rarely seen today. In acute mastoiditis the patient has fever, chills, headache and experiences tenderness over the mastoid process. The treatment includes the administration of antibiotics and a mastoidectomy to remove the infected mastoid cells and to secure drainage. Usually, the patient's hearing is not affected.

Chronic mastoiditis often requires much more drastic treatment, which involves removing the eardrum and the 3 little bones in the middle ear, as well as removing the mastoid cells. An extensive operation causes a marked loss of hearing. Some of the newer surgical procedures reconstruct the middle ear to preserve vital parts, with less impairment of hearing.

External Ear Disorders

Most external ear disorders are more annoying than serious. If treated properly, they disappear. Unfortunately, many people attempt to treat difficulties themselves, or they turn to someone who is not qualified to give either advice or treatment. The good intentions of zealous amateurs often do more harm than good.

Impacted Earwax. Impacted earwax in the auditory canal is one example of a condition which needs a doctor's attention. It is not unusual for a patient to complain that his ear feels stuffed up and he cannot hear, so he will ask the nurse to wash it out or dig it out with a hairpin. There are several reasons why an otologist should prescribe the treatment:

Impacted earwax may not be the cause of the trouble. Children are noted for putting things in their ears. If the object happens to be a pea, an ear irrigation will make it swell.

If the patient has a perforated eardrum, an irrigation might force the wax and the solution into the middle ear and cause infection.

Poking at the wax with a finger, a hairpin or an applicator may injure the canal and cause infection, or it may push the wax further in. Sometimes the doctor advises a patient to put a few drops of warm olive oil in the ear occasionally, to soften the hardened wax so that it will come out by itself.

Furuncles. *Furuncles* (boils) are infections in the auditory canal; they often are the result of picking at the ear to remove wax. They are intensely painful, and codeine may be necessary to relieve the pain. Heat may be applied, and antibiotics are given.

Fungus Infections. These infections in the auditory canal occur in warm, damp climates, especially when the auditory canal has not been completely dried. Dead skin cells collect in the canal as a sort of mold. They can be treated with ear drops composed of copper sulfate, alcohol and glycerin. They resist treatment and often it is necessary to continue it for a number of weeks.

Insects. Sometimes insects enter the auditory canal. If they remain they cause agonizing distress by their fluttering and buzzing. If a flashlight is held to the ear, the light may draw the insect out; sometimes a few drops of mineral oil or alcohol may kill it and it will float out if the patient's head is turned to one side. If none of these expedients works, the patient should see a doctor at once. It is dangerous to try to remove an insect with forceps; it is a delicate procedure to remove an insect from the ear which requires great skill.

Disorders of the Inner Ear

Almost every disorder of the inner ear makes treatment difficult. In the first place, neither surgery nor hearing aids help inner ear deafness (perceptive). Also, many drugs used to treat other conditions in the body may be injurious to the inner ear. Streptomycin, for instance may injure the auditory nerve. Diseases such as measles, as well as the aging process, may also cause inner ear damage. Often, safe treatment consists merely in preventing further injury, and training the patient in speech reading.

Meniere's Syndrome. Meniere's syndrome (also known as *Meniere's disease*) is a disturbance of the semicircular canals in the inner ear, a body mechanism that is important in maintaining body balance. There are many theories about how disease upsets this mechanism, but authorities have not been able to agree on any one cause.

The symptoms are devastating and alarming. The patient has sudden attacks of severe dizziness, accompanied by nausea, vomiting and a ringing sensation in the ears, and eventually his hearing deteriorates. The attacks are violent; they may last only a few minutes or several weeks. The patient lives in constant fear of an attack, and he may have to give up his work because of his condition.

In Meniere's disease the normal amount of fluid in the spaces between the semicircular canals increases. The patient may be put on a low-sodium diet to reduce the amount of fluid; he may be given sedatives to quiet his apprehension. Drugs, such as Dramamine and Bonamine, may be given to relieve dizziness and nausea. Nicotinic acid also may be given to relieve spasm of the auditory artery. Sometimes, when only one ear is affected, an operation to cut the auditory nerve is performed, which of course results in complete deafness in the affected ear.

When caring for these patients, every possible precaution is taken to avoid precipitating an attack from jarring the bed or making sudden movements. Everything must be done slowly and explained to the patient beforehand. If the dizziness is severe, the patient is in danger of falling. He should have side rails on his bed, and assistance when he is up. If he is nauseated, he may be more willing to take food and fluids if they are given in small amounts. These attacks are so devastating that the patient is understandably apprehensive. He needs the reassurance that relief is possible if he keeps quiet and follows orders.

46

THE PATIENT WITH A DISORDER OF THE NOSE, THE THROAT, OR THE MOUTH

THE NOSE

Deviated Septum. The nasal septum was described in Chapter 16 as a partition made of bone and cartilage, which divides the nose into right and left cavities.

The septum rarely is absolutely straight, but unless the deviation is marked it usually gives no trouble. An unusually crooked septum can interfere with drainage in one nostril. An injury that causes a deformity in the septum should have the attention of a doctor; if it is not corrected, it can cause sinusitis. The operation to correct such a deformity is called a *submucous resection.* Following the operation, which is done under local anesthesia, the patient's nostrils are packed with gauze, which is removed in 24 to 48 hours. A *mustache* dressing—a gauze pad held in place with strips of adhesive—is applied beneath the nostrils to catch the drainage.

Nosebleed (Epistaxis). The irritation or injury of a small mass of capillaries on the nasal septum may cause bleeding. It can also be caused by hypertension, in which case the bleeding is more likely to be severe and not as easily controlled. It may also develop in connection with certain blood conditions or with rheumatic fever. Nosebleed is a fairly common occurrence but if it is severe it can be frightening and may be dangerous. First aid for nosebleed is simple: with the patient sitting down, apply pressure by holding the nose firmly between the thumb and the forefinger. The patient is less likely to faint in this position, and elevating his head lessens the flow of blood to the nose. Cold compresses on the bridge of the nose sometimes help. If the bleeding persists or is profuse, call a doctor. He may insert cotton pledgets saturated with epinephrine solution in the nostril. If this is not effective, he may pack the nasal cavity with gauze to create pressure on the bleeding area or he may cauterize it.

Nasal Polyps. Polyps are tumors that look like small bunches of tiny grapes. Nasal polyps obstruct breathing and sinus drainage. They are removed easily under local anesthesia, but unfortunately they have a tendency to return, and the operation has to be repeated. A biopsy of the tissue should be done to determine if the growth is malignant.

Plastic Surgery of the Nose. Plastic surgery of the nose (*rhinoplasty*) may be done to correct deformities resulting from injury, or for cosmetic reasons.

Nasal Spray. Sometimes a nasal spray is used to apply medications. Usually this is done with a hand atomizer, and the patient may be allowed to do it himself. He sits up, and, holding up the end of the nostril, he inserts the atomizer tip just inside, pointing it backward.

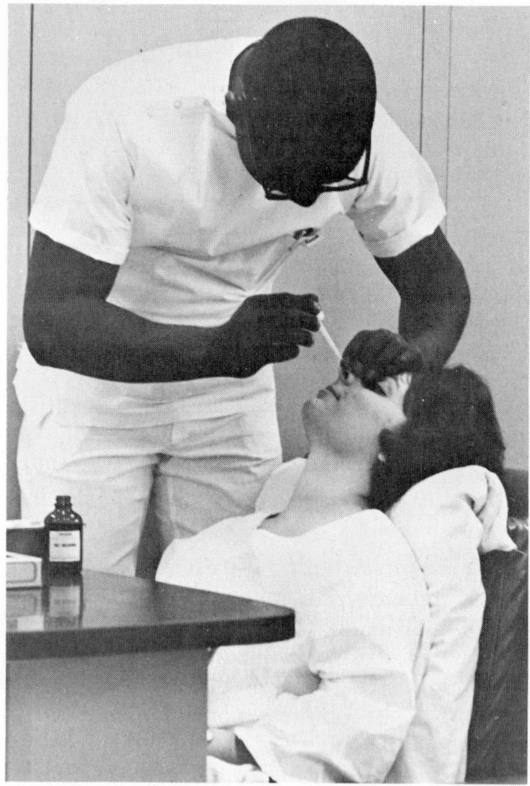

FIG. 178. When instilling nose drops, the patient's head is tilted back to allow the solution to flow into the nostrils and is maintained in this position for a few minutes afterward to prevent the solution from draining out. The patient is instructed to expectorate any solution that may drain down into his throat.

At the same time, he closes the opposite nostril by pressing it with his finger. The force of the spray should be just enough to spread the solution over the nasal membrane. Too much force may force the solution into the sinuses or the eustachian tubes.

Nose Drops. Some people use nose drugs far too often. As a result, the medications lose their effect and eventually cause a swelling of the turbinates, the condition they are supposed to prevent. Many of these preparations are sold over the counter without a prescription, and their prolonged use can be damaging. People with hypertension should never use nose drops.

A medicine dropper, paper wipes and the prescribed solution comprise the necessary equipment for administering nose drops. The following points should be kept in mind when carrying out this procedure:

1. A sitting or lying position, with the head tilted back, allows the solution to flow into the nostrils. Having him lie across the bed with his head lowered over the edge prevents the solution from running down the patient's throat.
2. A piece of soft rubber tubing placed over the tip of the dropper prevents injury to the nasal membrane and is necessary if the patient is an infant or is irrational.
3. Keeping the head tilted back for a few minutes afterward prevents the solution from draining out and preserves the effect of the medication.

Sinusitis

Sinusitis is the inflammation of one or more of the sinuses located in the skull. A maxillary sinus (*antrum*) is the one most frequently affected by an infection spreading from the nasal passages. If the patient's resistance is low, he is more susceptible to sinus infection. Although a sinus infection may not be deadly, it is most uncomfortable, and it is especially annoying to people who live in climates where respiratory infections tend to occur. The presence of an allergy, frequent colds, or a nasal obstruction of any kind make people more susceptible to repeated attacks of sinusitis. If it is neglected, sinusitis becomes chronic and damages the mucous membranes, making treatment less effective. Of all the possible complications of sinusitis, infection of the middle ear or the brain are the most serious. Sinusitis may also lead to bronchiectasis or asthma. Early treatment is important to prevent these complications.

Acute sinusitis begins with the presence of pain and pressure, usually over the maxillary or the frontal sinuses, and pain is felt in the cheek or the upper teeth if the maxillary sinuses are affected. Frontal sinus pain occurs over the eyes. The patient has a low-grade fever, fatigue and a poor appetite. A purulent nasal discharge appears, accompanied by a postnasal drip which irritates the throat. Sinus congestion will show up in an x-ray picture. The treatment usually prescribed includes bed rest, forced fluids, and salicylates to relieve the pain. Nose drops containing neosynephrine and ephedrine are often used to shrink the swollen turbinates and to encourage drainage. Antibiotics to fight the infection may be given.

If drainage is obstructed in an acute sinus infection, the sinus is irrigated with warm saline solution, which is a comparatively painless procedure. However, it may become necessary to puncture the bony wall between the nose and the sinus cavity, which is quite painful for the patient; he may become frightened, feel dizzy, or faint. The doctor always performs these procedures.

Chronic sinusitis is characterized by repeated flare-ups of the infection in spite of treatment. In most cases, the methods of therapy include measures to build up the patient's resistance, and treatment for the cause of the infection. A relatively simple operation to make a new sinus opening may be necessary. Many people suffer needlessly and are under the impression that nothing can be done for sinusitis, thereby allowing it to become chronic.

Nasal Irrigation. Sometimes a purulent discharge forms crusts in the nose, and a nasal irrigation is used to remove them. The irrigating solution flows into one nostril and out through the other. The important point to observe in giving a nasal irrigation is to use the correct amount of pressure—too much pressure may force the fluid into the sinuses and the eustachian tubes, thus spreading the infection.

THE THROAT

The throat (pharynx) is the muscular tube which communicates with the nasal cavity (nasopharynx); the oral cavity (oropharynx); and the laryngeal cavity (laryngopharynx).

Common Disorders

The tonsils (in the oral pharynx) and the adenoids (in the nasopharynx) are bodies composed of lymphoid tissue which often become infected. *Acute tonsillitis* is an infection that may be caused by a microorganism such as the streptococcus, which gets into the body through contaminated food or by inhalation. The tonsils become enlarged and fill with pus which drains into the mouth. The patient feels miserable for about a week, after which the attack usually subsides. The treatment consists of bed rest, hot saline throat irrigations and gargles if the pain is severe and the inflammation is acute. Forced fluids are given throughout the day, and a soft or liquid diet is prescribed, since the patient finds it painful to swallow. Drugs, such as aspirin or codeine, are given to relieve the pain and the cough. Barbiturates may be administered at bedtime to ensure rest. The same communicable disease precautions are observed as in respiratory infections.

Chronic Tonsillitis. Tonsillitis becomes chronic when the patient has frequent attacks, with a sore throat, fever, and the presence of painful nodes in the neck and enlarged, inflamed tonsils. Chronic tonsillitis may lead to rheumatic fever and nephritis.

Peritonsillar Abscess. Sometimes a tonsil infection extends to the tissues around the tonsil and forms an abscess, which may block the throat or even close it completely. If this condition does not improve, it may be necessary to incise the abscess and drain it. A patient with a peritonsillar abscess suffers much pain until the abscess breaks or is incised.

Laryngitis. The larynx (voice box) lies below the pharynx and contains the vocal cords. *Laryngitis* is an inflammation and a swelling of the larynx. It often accompanies respiratory infections, and it may be the result of overuse of the voice or excessive smoking. The patient has a cough, is hoarse and may lose his voice. Talking and smoking are prohibited, and steam inhalations are given to soothe the mucous membranes of the throat. If laryngitis is a complication of another infection, antibiotics may be given.

Chronic laryngitis may be a complication of chronic sinusitis or chronic bronchitis, or it may be the result of repeated attacks of acute laryngitis. Continued irritation of the throat by public speaking, smoking or irritating gases are common causes. The recommended treatment is to abandon the activities that are causing the trouble and to get rid of any infection that may be contributing to it.

Cancer of the Larynx

Cancer of the larynx is most likely to occur in people over 45; it affects men most frequently. It seems to develop in people who have chronic laryngitis, who strain their voices or are heavy smokers. It is also believed that hereditary tendencies have something to do with its occurrence. The symptoms are chronic hoarseness and sometimes the inability to speak above a whisper. If it is detected early, surgery is often successful in effecting a complete cure. The operation consists of either removing the part of the vocal cord which is involved in the tumor (*thyrotomy*) or of removing the entire larynx (*laryngectomy*).

When the larynx is removed, air must enter and leave through the trachea. Provision is made for this by inserting a tube in the trachea through an opening in the lower part of the neck (*tracheostomy*). Before a laryngectomy, the patient not only faces the knowledge that he must breathe through a hole in his neck, but also that there exists the possibility that the tumor is malignant. He may fear that he will choke and perhaps die, or that if he lives, he will never speak again. The nurse can reassure this patient that breathing through the tube will be easier than he thinks, and that the tube does not interfere with swallowing. She can emphasize the fact that, although he will lose his natural voice, voice training (esophageal speech) will make it possible for him to carry on ordinary conversation.

Reconstruction of the esophagus is necessary, so the patient should be told that for a time he will be fed through a tube in his nose, but that this arrangement is not permanent. However, he should know that the tracheostomy tube *will* be permanent, but that he will be taught how to take care of it himself.

Nursing Care. Immediately after a laryngectomy, the patient requires expert care. The respiratory passages become irritated, and the secretion of mucus increases, which must be removed frequently by suction. A suction machine is constantly beside the bed of a laryngectomy patient, and he is never left alone. Remember that he may be terrified of choking or of not being able to breathe. However, the practical nurse will not be asked to assume this responsibility for immediate postoperative care.

The patient probably will be allowed out of bed the next day, and he soon will be taught how to suction the tube and take care of it himself. Everybody concerned with his care should know how to perform this procedure. When the airway becomes obstructed, the patient becomes cyanotic very quickly, and he may die within a few minutes if the obstruction is not removed. In this emergency, call for help and suction the tracheostomy opening. The doctor should be consulted in all cases to see if the tracheostomy tube can be removed as an emergency measure, or he may have previously instructed the head nurse on this matter. The patient's call light should always be within easy reach and should be answered with all possible speed, since he may be in trouble.

Care of the Tube. The tracheostomy tube has 3 parts: an outer tube, an inner tube and an obdurator. The obdurator is inserted in the outer tube, with its lower end protruding from the tube, which is then inserted into the tracheal opening. When the outer tube is in place, the obdurator is withdrawn and replaced by the inner tube, which is locked in position. Tapes are attached to each side of the outer tube and tied behind the neck to hold it firmly in position. A gauze sponge that has been split halfway is placed under the tube to catch the leakage from secretions (Fig. 179). Folded gauze can be placed over the tube to conceal it, but this should never be thick enough to interfere with the passage of air.

The inner tube is removed and cleaned at intervals under cold running water. If this is not sufficient to remove the secretions, a pipe cleaner or a small test tube brush might be helpful. At first, the doctor removes the entire tube when it needs to be changed; later, the patient may be allowed to do this himself. An extra set in the patient's size is always kept at his bedside. By the time the patient is ready to go home, suctioning usually is no longer necessary, but if it is he must have a suction machine

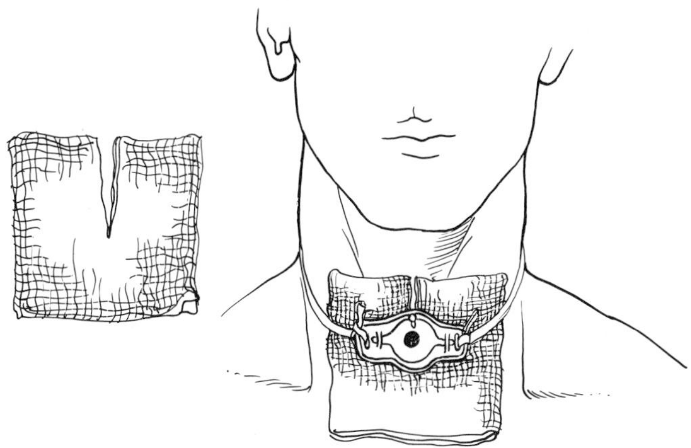

FIG. 179. Gauze squares, slit halfway down, are placed around the tube to catch secretions. These dressings are changed by the nurse as often as it is necessary. Note the tapes that hold the outer tube in place. The tapes are tied in a knot at the back of the patient's neck. (Smith, D. W., and Gips, C. D.: Care of the Adult Patient, p. 1389, Philadelphia, Lippincott, 1963)

at home. At this point he is bathing and dressing himself and is taking care of the tracheostomy tube. As soon as possible, training in esophageal speech should be started. The technic of esophageal speech consists of swallowing air and using the air to make speech sounds while regurgitating it. It takes patience and constant practice to learn how to do this, but patients sometimes learn the technic in 2 or 3 weeks. Some patients use an artificial larynx,

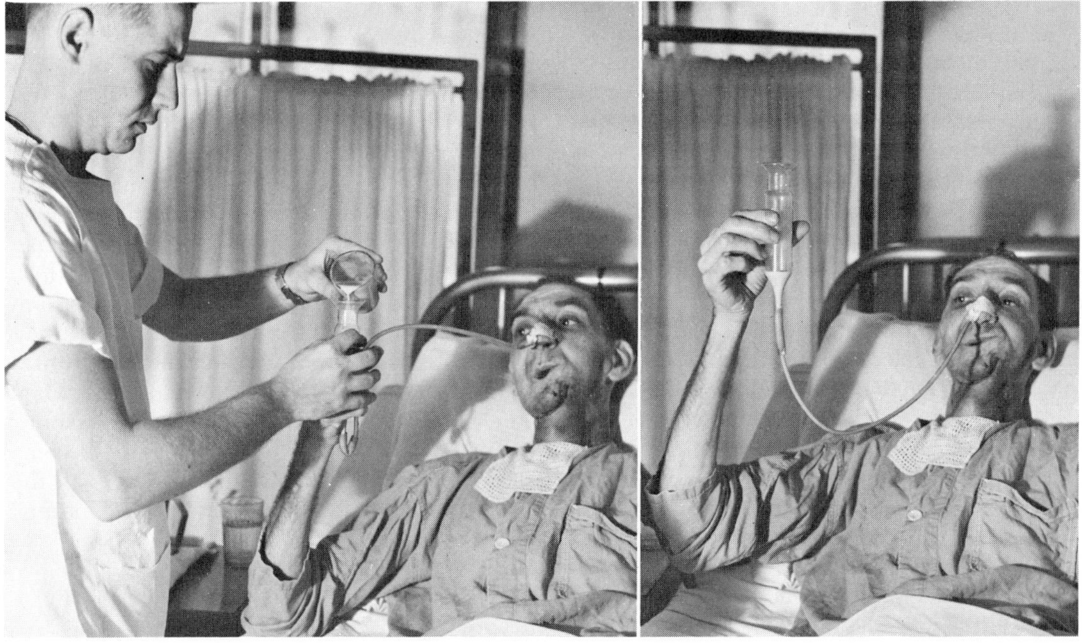

FIG. 180. (*Left*) The nurse is pouring the tube feeding into an Asepto syringe, which is being used as a funnel. The tube is kinked while the syringe is being filled. Note the mesh square that the patient is wearing over his tube. Facial deformity has resulted from the extensive surgery that was necessary to treat his condition. (*Right*) The feeding is permitted to flow through the tube by gravity. Before the syringe is empty, more of the feeding will be added. The patient is encouraged to help with the procedure. (Smith, D. W., and Gips, C. D.: Care of the Adult Patient, p. 1391, Philadelphia, Lippincott, 1963)

an electronic device which the patient holds against his throat (Fig. 133). Anyone who has a tracheostomy must always be careful not to get water in the opening. He must never swim and must use caution when taking showers.

Nasogastric Tube Feedings. The patient is fed through a nasogastric tube for about a week after a laryngectomy. The amount, the type and the frequency of the feedings are prescribed by the doctor. They are warmed to body temperature, and they flow into the body by gravity through a funnel or an Asepto syringe (Fig. 180). Oral medications may also be crushed, mixed with water and administered through the tube. However, it is important to rinse the tube with water following the medication to be sure that the patient receives the entire amount.

THE MOUTH

Mouth disorders may not seem to be dangerous, but they are uncomfortable and often painful. They may also interfere with nutrition or lead to other undesirable or more serious conditions.

Vincent's Angina. Vincent's angina (*trench mouth*) is a mouth infection which is highly communicable and can be spread from person to person, although some people are not susceptible to it. Small ulcers appear on the mucous membrane of the mouth and are sometimes accompanied by fever and the enlargement of the lymph nodes beneath the jaw. Sometimes trench mouth is associated with dental caries or abscessed teeth. Two organisms are its immediate cause (*Bacillus fusiformis* and *Barrelia vincentii*). The gums swell and ooze blood, and the tissues become necrotic. Without treatment, the infection may destroy parts of the bone. The most effective treatment is hourly mouth washes with a sodium perborate solution. Penicillin is also effective.

Stomatitis (Foot-and-Mouth Disease). *Stomatitis* is a contagious virus disease of animals with cloven hooves. It is transmitted to humans by contact with the infected animals and by their milk. The symptoms are fever and an eruption of blisters in the mouth and the throat. These blisters break and leave ulcers. The treatment is a mouthwash of potassium permanganate and the application of silver nitrate to the ulcers. Communicable disease technic is observed.

Canker Sores. *Canker sores* are small, white, painful ulcers that appear on the inside of the mouth. No one knows exactly what causes them, but there is some reason to believe that they are caused by the same virus that causes cold sores. No effective treatment has been found, and they usually disappear in a few days.

Peridontal Conditions. *Peridontal disease* affects the bones and the tissues around the teeth. It may be the result of poor oral hygiene, inadequate dental care or poor nutrition. Teeth become loosened when crooked teeth do not meet evenly (malocclusion), or an accumulation of tartar on the teeth may eventually cause them to loosen. Good dental care is a preventive measure.

Dentures. Many people put off having infected teeth removed because they dread replacing them with dentures which they fear will be unsightly or uncomfortable. Meanwhile, they are exposing themselves to infection in some other part of the body, such as arthritis or heart disease. So much more is known today about the dangers of infected teeth, and so much improvement has been made in the appearance of dentures that people are losing some of their dread of wearing them. Dentures are bound to be slightly uncomfortable when they are first fitted, but the dentist can remove sources of irritation. The only way to become accustomed to dentures is to wear them all the time. This also helps to preserve the normal shape of the face.

Congenital Deformities

Harelip and *cleft palate* are deformities commonly found together at birth. These congenital deformities are the result of faulty development of the embryo, in which the upper lip or the palate (or both) are not closed completely. This leaves a cleft which may be no more than a notch in the upper lip or may extend up into the nostril on one or both sides. Usually, an operation to close a large cleft in the lip is done as soon as possible after the child is born. If the closure is delayed until he is older, his physical condition may deteriorate because the deformity interferes with feeding.

After the operation the child is fed with a medicine dropper for 5 or 6 days to allow time for the wound to heal. The stitches in the lip can be cleansed with a cotton applicator which has been moistened with hydrogen peroxide to remove traces of milk or serum and to promote healing with the least possible scar.

A *cleft palate* may be a cleft occurring only in the soft palate, only in the hard palate, or in both. Usually, the operation to close the cleft is not done until the child is 1 or 2 years old. The bony parts and the tissues are brought together and sutured. The nursing care includes care of the mouth to keep it as clean as possible—it is impossible to make the mouth aseptic. Swabbing the inside of the mouth with a mild antiseptic, such as Dobell's solution, after each feeding, helps to keep it clean.

Following these operations the child is placed on his side to prevent asphyxiation by inhaling blood or mucus. He may have difficulty in breathing at first if his nostrils have been made smaller. Depressing his lower lip with a strip of adhesive aids breathing by mouth until he adjusts to the change. Restraining his arms with padded splints which keep his elbows straight will prevent him from touching the stitches. The splints should be removed every 4 hours and the arms massaged. After his recovery, the child is taught to speak properly; this training requires skill and patience, but it is most important for the child's future.

47

THE PATIENT WITH AN ALLERGY

Allergy is the extreme sensitivity to one or more substances. When a foreign protein substance touches or enters the body, the body produces antibodies for protection against it. Later contacts with this protein may set off a reaction with the antibodies that will cause unpleasant symptoms. This is called an *allergic reaction*, and we say that the person is sensitive or *allergic* to the foreign substance, which is called an *allergen* or an *antigen*. Allergic reactions may cause only minor discomforts, but they often can cause excessive irritation, and in certain severe instances death can result. Allergy occurs at any age.

Causes of Allergy

It is not clearly known why certain proteins cause unpleasant symptoms. Since the antihistamine drugs bring relief, it is thought that the protein-antibody reaction may liberate an excessive amount of histamine in the body.

Scientists also believe that a general tendency toward allergic reactions may be inherited. This does not mean that a specific allergy is inherited; Mrs. Grant may be allergic to eggs, but her son, Richard, may be allergic to cats. Estimates tell us that about 10 per cent of the population has allergic tendencies, including 1 child in every 10. There are many substances to which people are sensitive, but these people may not be equally sensitive to the same substance. For example, Kathy reacts to poison ivy only after the leaves touch her skin, but Sheila breaks out after she walks by a patch of poison ivy. Also, an individual's sensitivity to one substance may disappear while another takes its place, or an allergy may disappear entirely.

Drug Allergy

Drug allergy is common, especially for such drugs as penicillin, quinine and Thiouracil. Some people are allergic to aspirin. It takes only a small amount of the drug to which a patient is sensitive to cause an allergic reaction; this is quite a different matter from an overdose of a drug. A patient with an allergy is frequently given a small dose of a new drug first, in order to test his sensitivity to it. An allergic reaction may appear either immediately or several days later. Pay attention if a patient tells you that he is allergic to something. If he says he cannot take aspirin, do not force him to take it, even though it has been ordered. Instead, report the incident to the head nurse.

Kinds of Allergic Reactions

Allergic reactions most often affect the skin, the respiratory passages and the gastrointestinal tract; they cause a rash (erythema), edema and contractions of the smooth muscles. Some examples of these reactions are:

Asthma: Spasms of the smooth muscles of the bronchi and edema create difficulty in breathing, which causes a cough, an accumulation of mucus and wheezing. The patient may become cyanotic in a severe attack.

Allergic rhinitis (hay fever): The patient suffers

from edema; his eyes and nose are inflamed and watery, and they itch.

Urticaria (hives): Reddened areas occur which itch and burn around swollen patches on the skin. They may appear suddenly and disappear after a few hours, or they may last for days.

Eczema: The skin is covered with tiny blisters that itch and ooze secretions, which usually appear in the folds of the neck, the elbows and the knees. In chronic eczema, the skin becomes scaly and thickened.

Poison ivy: This is a contact allergy. The oils of the plant get on the skin and cause itching, redness and blisters.

Gastrointestinal allergy: The patient experiences nausea, vomiting, diarrhea, and abdominal pain and tenderness.

Angioneurotic edema: Edema occurs in one part of the body, such as the lips and the eyelids. If the swelling presses on a vital organ, such as the larynx, it could have a dangerous effect on breathing.

Frequently, an allergic reaction is caused by the direct contact of the allergen with the affected area. It may be caused by substances breathed in from the air, such as pollens or dust, or the allergen may be a substance found in foods which the patient has eaten.

Anaphylactic Shock. This is a sudden and severe allergic reaction: the patient's blood pressure falls sharply, his pulse is rapid and weak, he perspires, he turns pale and feels faint, and he may become unconscious. Symptoms of shock may appear quickly in severe asthma, urticaria or vomiting and diarrhea when the patient has had a large dose of the substance causing his allergy, or after a small dose of an allergen to which he is sensitive. This is what happens: the amount of circulating blood is decreased, therefore, the heart cannot get enough to the tissues, and the patient may die because of the insufficient blood supply to the heart and the brain.

The usual first aid treatment for shock is given; the doctor will hasten to give treatment to restore the volume of the circulating blood and to restore a normal blood pressure. The treatment may be: epinephrine, plasma, levarterenol or Aramine, together with corticosteroids and antihistamines. Oxygen may be given to make up for the decrease of oxygen in the blood.

Finding the Cause

It is not always easy to find out what is causing an allergy. In some cases the condition seems to have no relation to the substances tested or to anything in the air or in the victim's food. A person might be sensitive to a certain substance only when he is tired or upset. Sometimes he is only occasionally sensitive to it. The doctor should question the patient closely about his family history and any new substance with which he has been in contact.

Skin Tests. In a skin test, a small amount of the antigen suspected of causing the trouble is injected under the skin. The doctor looks at the injected area 20 minutes later; if it is red, with a raised area (wheal) in the center, the reaction is called a positive one. Sometimes, in spite of a positive skin test, an allergen does not cause an allergic reaction. For instance, Jimmy's skin test reaction to cat dander is positive, yet he manhandles the family cat with no sign of a runny nose or itching. On the other hand, Brian's skin test for eggs was negative, yet every time he eats an egg he has nausea and diarrhea. The patient should be observed closely during a skin test, because occasionally a test will cause a severe reaction. This condition is unusual, since the amount of allergen used is very small; however, it can happen if the patient is highly sensitive to the allergen.

Treatment. The first step in the treatment of an allergy is to avoid the offending allergen. Some allergens are inhaled, such as pollens, dust and animal dander; others are taken into the body in the form of foods, such as seafood, eggs and chocolate. Allergens can be skin contacts, such as cosmetics, hair or shoe dyes, and wool or nylon. It is not always easy to avoid an allergen. For instance, while it is no problem to stop eating shrimp, it is more difficult to eliminate white flour from the diet. Foam rubber can be substituted for feather pillows, and cosmetics made especially for allergy sufferers are available. Some people are able to go to a pollen-free area during the heavy pollen season. When people must stay where they are, desensitization methods and antihistamines are often effective.

Desensitization. Desensitization consists of giving minute doses of the allergen, which are gradually increased. This procedure helps the patient to develop a tolerance for the allergen and reduces his symptoms. Sometimes this treatment does away with the allergy entirely, and the injections are given once a week as long as the season lasts. If the allergy is not a seasonal one, the injections must be continued throughout the year. This treatment is expensive, but it helps a great many people to find relief. Some of the newer preparations act more slowly and gradually so that fewer injections are required.

Antihistamines. Antihistamines help to relieve the symptoms. However, they do not reduce the patient's sensitivity to an allergen, and if they are discontinued, the symptoms will return. They are most useful in seasonal or drug allergies. Because some of them make the patient feel drowsy or dizzy, antihistamines should never be taken during the day if the patient drives a car or does work involving concentration and alertness. Some of the antihistamines have a prolonged action and need not be taken as often. Among those most commonly used are: Benadryl, Chlor-Trimeton, Pyribenzamine, Decapryn and Phenergan. The antihistamines were also discussed in Chapter 30.

48

CARE IN EMERGENCIES

THE PROBLEM OF ACCIDENTS

Every year, thousands of people lose their lives in accidents—on the highway, at work, during recreation, or in the home. In the 1 to 34 age group, accidents are the first cause of death; in the 35-44 age group, accidents are second only to heart and circulatory diseases. The fatalities are approximately 100,000 per year. The injury total every year is numbered in the millions. Over 4,000,000 injuries happen in the home. The chances are greater than ever that any person may be at the scene of an accident at some time and should be able to act promptly and intelligently.

It is impossible to expect people to go to a doctor for such things as minor cuts or burns; nor is it necessary. However, it is important to teach people how to distinguish between a serious and a minor injury; to know when medical attention is needed; to give the proper first-aid treatment for any injury. Quick and intelligent action in emergencies may save a life.

The American Red Cross has long seen the need for first-aid training; courses are offered in most communities to give the public this instruction. The dangers of atomic warfare call for the special instruction of civilians in first-aid technics to use in case of atomic bomb attack. Every citizen should enroll in the Red Cross and the civilian defense courses as a means of civilian protection.

Unquestionably, many accidents could be prevented. First-aid instruction should go hand in hand with information about accident prevention. State and local governments provide public protection by means of highway regulations, fire laws and industrial safety requirements. The National Safety Council and the state safety councils carry on a determined campaign for safety; through lectures and films they demonstrate to civic groups how accidents can be prevented. Accident costs amount to staggering sums every year. These costs include medical expense, wage losses, property damage, etc., and are in the billions.

Why Accidents Happen. Accidents often happen to children because they are curious, impulsive and do not have the judgment necessary to protect themselves. The child's surroundings should be made as safe as possible for him —he can be taught to prevent accident hazards by picking up his toys and other objects from the floor, and by learning how to go up and down steps and how to handle objects safely.

Elderly people are often physically handicapped by failing eysight, deafness or crippling conditions which prevent them from moving quickly in the face of danger; pride makes older people reluctant to give up activities that are no longer safe for them. People become so wrapped up in personal problems or so intent on saving time that they forget about traffic signals; fatigue at the end of the day affects judgment both outside and inside the home.

Holiday and week-end travel greatly increases traffic hazards.

Accident-Prone People. Authorities say that some people are *naturals* for accidents—that many mishaps are not accidental but are due to the victim's personality: studies show that some people have one accident after another. The accident-prone individual shows characteristic personality problems that make life dangerous for him. He may be a reckless, rash, impulsive person who loves excitement and rebels against authority. He may have guilty feelings which, without realizing it, he is trying to atone for by punishing himself. Some people expose themselves to accidents through an unconscious wish to avoid responsibility or to be taken care of. The accident-prone person should not be in an occupation that is dangerous to him or where his actions might endanger other people.

Emergencies and Nursing Care. When you are on duty in a patient's home, emergencies are bound to arise—people naturally turn to a nurse when an accident happens, if Tommy scratches his knee, grandma burns her finger or the cook cuts her thumb. Accidents can happen to your patient, too, such as a hot-water bag burn, a fall or a mistake in giving medicine. When an emergency occurs, you must be able to meet it. This chapter is not a substitute for a complete course in first aid, but it does tell you how you can deal with common emergencies. Chapter 54 has important information on the *legal responsibility* of a nurse during an emergency situation.

To begin with, first-aid principles tell you what to do and what *not* to do when accidents happen. In your eagerness to do something, you may do the wrong thing; sometimes the less you do the more helpful you are so far as the victim is concerned. The victim is not the only person you may have to deal with—someone among the bystanders or a member of the family may initiate hasty action, faint or become hysterical. In a serious emergency, if you are confident, matter-of-fact and calm, you reassure the patient and everyone else. You must make up your mind quickly about what you are going to do, and your attitude and your knowledge of first-aid principles will give you command of the situation.

FIRST AID

Principles of First-Aid Care

A few guiding rules will help you in any emergency; your reactions when an accident happens should be almost automatic if you know the principles of first aid. These rules apply to any kind of emergency, to major or minor accidents.

1. *Size up the situation.* Is it serious enough to send for a doctor? A pailful of hot water upset over a child, gushing blood, a dangling arm or an unconscious victim are signs that a doctor is needed. You can deal with excited or hysterical bystanders by giving them something to do—ask one of them to call the doctor at once. This leaves you free to give your whole attention to the patient.

2. *Examine the patient.* In minor accidents this is comparatively easy—Tommy holds up the scratched knee, and a glance tells you what has happened; even so, you must be sure that he has no other injuries. Get the victim to tell you how the accident happened and look for bumps or scratches on other parts of his body if this seems necessary.

3. *Make the victim comfortable.* Be careful not to add to his injury by moving him too much; in most emergencies, it is best to have the victim lying down and comfortable, but moving a limb may displace a fractured bone still further. Keep the patient warm; keep the crowd away.

4. *Give the necessary first-aid treatment.* This may be the only treatment that the victim needs, but in serious conditions you give emergency treatment only until the doctor arrives.

5. *Provide for safe follow-up care.* If an accident happens in public, instruct the victim to see his doctor if a doctor has not been called at the time of the accident. In the home, report an accident to your patient to the doctor later, even though it is a minor one. Record it on the chart. Observe the after-effects of an accident and report disturbing symptoms, such as evidence of infection, pain or interference with motion.

6. *Report the treatment.* Medical aid is always available for emergencies in the hospital; you will always report any accident to the head nurse, no matter how trivial it seems. Hospitals have a legal responsibility for patients' safety; a prompt report and a detailed

account of the accident must appear on the patient's record. In the home, make this report to the doctor immediately or later, depending on how severe the accident is. In any case, every injury requiring emergency treatment *must be reported and noted on the chart.*

Asphyxiation

Definition. In first aid, asphyxiation refers to the inability of the victim to breathe. This may be due to several causes, but the result is the same: anoxia (lack of sufficient oxygen to sustain life) and an excessive amount of carbon dioxide in the tissues.

Physical Causes

Choking or strangling on a foreign object
Electric shock
Drowning
Inhalation of poisonous gases
Compression of the chest by outside force
Overdosage of respiratory depressant drugs

Treatment. The initial treatment is to ascertain the cause of the asphyxia. If a foreign body has obstructed the air passages, it must be removed to allow atmospheric oxygen to reach the lungs. If an electric current has interrupted the central nervous system response so that breathing has stopped, remove the victim from the cause of the shock by turning off the current or by moving him with a nonconducting instrument (a wooden pole). Inhalation of poisonous gases (illuminating gas is one of the most common) requires that the gas be turned off and that the patient be removed immediately to a gas-free atmosphere so that proper exchange of oxygen in the lung tissues may be restored. If the victim's chest is compressed by an outside force (for example, when trapped by a landslide), you must make every effort to remove the compression in order to permit proper expansion of the chest. If the compression is by fracture of the bony cage of the ribs, never use artificial respiration by the application and removal of pressure—*puncture of the lung may result.* Instead, employ the mouth-to-mouth breathing technic. The sedative, hypnotic, opium and coal-tar derivative drugs given in an overdose depress the respiratory center of the brain; each has its own method of treatment.

Whatever the cause of asphyxiation, the main principle of first aid is: (1) to establish an open (patent) airway and (2) to restore the normal mechanism of breathing.

Artificial Respiration

The most effective methods of artificial respiration are the *back pressure-arm lift* method, and the *mouth-to-mouth* or the *mouth-to-nose* methods. All of these are illustrated in Figure 181 (below) and Figure 182, p. 622.

Back Pressure-Arm Lift Method. Place the patient on a smooth surface (the ground is best) in a face-down position. Turn the head to one side. Place both arms up so that the elbows are above the ear level. Make sure that

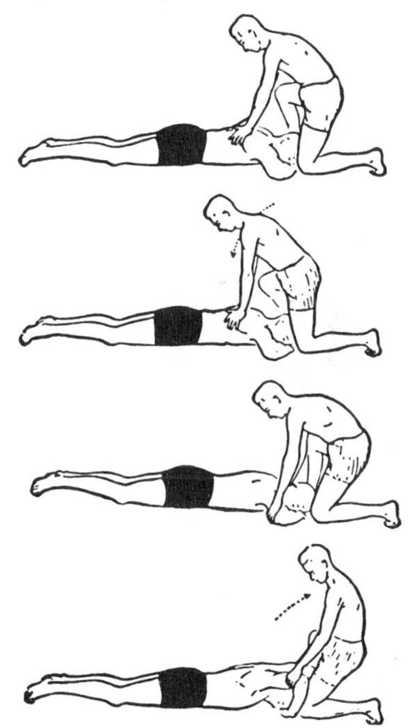

Fig. 181. The back pressure-arm lift method of giving manual artificial respiration (after Holger Nielson). (Gordon, A. S., *et al.*: A critical survey of manual artificial respiration, J.A.M.A., 147: 1444-1453)

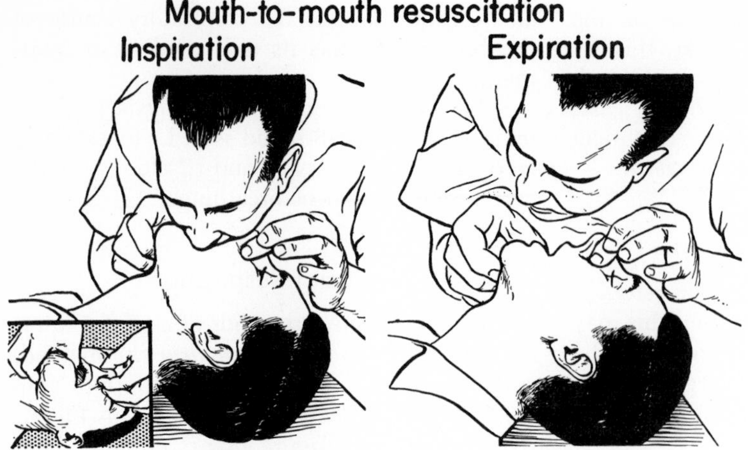

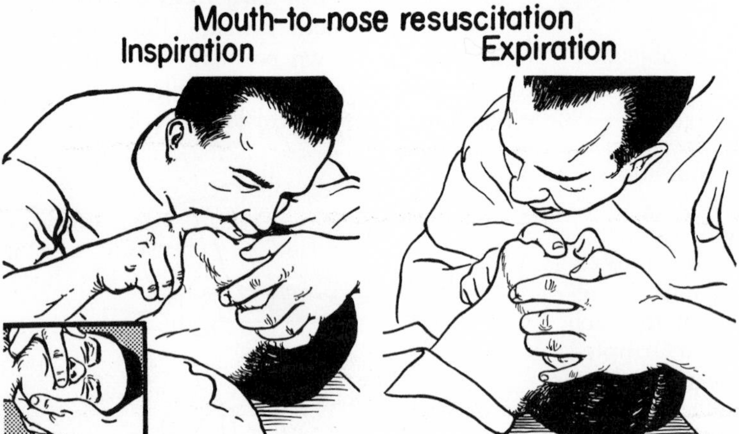

FIG. 182. Technics for mouth-to-mouth and mouth-to-nose resuscitation. (Gordon, Archer S., *et al.*: Mouth-to-mouth versus manual artificial respiration for children and adults, J.A.M.A., 167: 326, 1958)

the tongue is not obstructing the air passage. The person giving the resuscitation kneels at the head of the victim with both hands flat on the back of the chest. To a count of 1-2 (representing 1 cycle of breathing) and a rate of about 12 times per minute follow this pattern:

Rock forward to allow the weight of your body to exert pressure on the victim's chest (causing the expulsion of air).

Rock backward drawing the victim's elbows upward and toward you. This results in inspiration.

Mouth-to-Mouth Method. Place your hand in a cupped position under the victim's chin with the thumb and the forefinger pinching the nose closed. Place your other hand on the abdomen with a steady moderate pressure. Take a deep breath, exhale this air into the victim's mouth. Remove your mouth from the mouth of the victim and allow this air to be expired. Repeat about 18 to 20 times per minute. You must be sure that the airway is open. If the victim shows any resistance to the passage of air, clear the mouth with your finger or by turning the head so that fluid or other material may drain clear.

A mouth-to-nose method may also be used. The victim's mouth is held closed and his chin up while you place your mouth over his nose and blow in. This inflates the lungs if there is no obstruction. When your mouth is withdrawn, the victim should expel air through the nose.

Hemorrhage

The blood is distributed throughout the body by the arteries, which branch again and again until they form the capillaries. From the capillaries, the blood returns to the heart through the veins. When any blood vessel is cut or torn, blood escapes. The amount of bleeding depends on the number and the size of the injured blood vessels. A severe injury to one large blood vessel may cause a serious hemorrhage, but an injury to many small vessels may cause damage which is equally serious. When a severe hemorrhage occurs, the body loses the red blood cells which are necessary to carry oxygen to the cells, and it loses fluid, upsetting the body's fluid balance. Therefore, the most important first-aid treatment in this case is to stop the hemorrhage. The second step is to treat shock, which always accompanies severe bleeding, by keeping the patient quiet and warm. A stimulant can be given after the bleeding is controlled; but until then, a stimulant may only increase the hemorrhage.

Control by Pressure. Bleeding can be controlled by applying pressure to the bleeding area or by shutting off the main arteries that supply blood to it. Normally, the blood flows through all the channels that are open; if some channels are shut off too long, the blood may never flow into them again. When an area no longer has a blood supply to carry food materials and oxygen to the cells, the tissues die. A bandage which is too tight or a tourniquet which is left on too long may cause gangrene, (death of the tissues).

The first thing to do in a case where bleeding is serious or superficial is to apply pressure: pressure at the right spot will control bleeding in most external injuries. Fold a clean dressing to make a pad, and apply it to the bleeding area; you can use a clean handkerchief or cloth if you do not have a sterile dressing. Press the dressing firmly on the bleeding area; then apply a firm bandage to hold the dressing in place. Be sure that the circulation is not shut off entirely.

Pressure Points. You can frequently tell by the flow whether the bleeding comes from an artery or a vein: blood from an *artery* comes in *spurts*, but blood comes from a *vein* in a *steady flow*. Pressure on a large artery supplying blood to the injured part will control bleeding; the artery must lie close to a bone so that there is a firm surface to press against. The 6 main *pressure points* to use to stop bleeding from the various parts of the body, and the arteries they control, are:

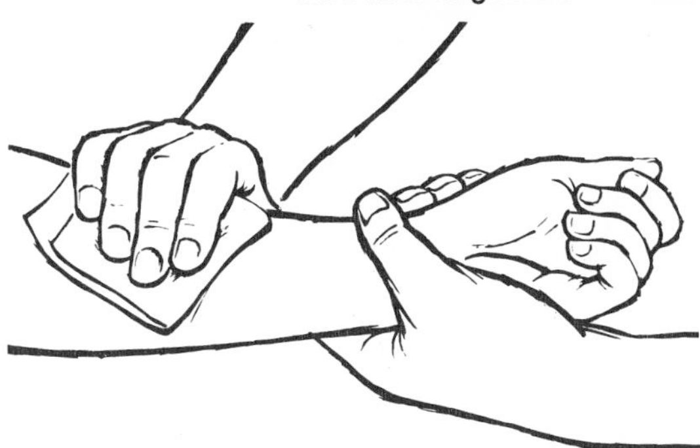

FIG. 183. Direct pressure over wound. You can do this best by placing the cleanest material available (sterile gauze is best) against the bleeding point and applying firm pressure with your hand until a bandage can be applied. (American Red Cross: First Aid Textbook, ed. 4, New York, Doubleday, 1957)

The head and the neck

1. The *carotid artery* in the neck, located beside the windpipe (trachea). Press *back* against the spine—pressure on the trachea will shut off breathing.
2. The *temporal artery*, in front of the ear
3. The *facial artery*, on the jawbone about an inch forward from the angle of the jaw

The shoulder and the arm

4. The *subclavian artery*, just behind the inner end of the collar bone, or clavicle, exerting pressure down against the first rib
5. The *brachial artery*, on the upper arm next to the body, halfway between the elbow and the shoulder

The lower limbs

6. The *femoral artery*, midway in the groin where the artery passes over the pelvic bone

Bleeding is usually not very extensive in a minor wound, but it is important to cover any wound with a clean dressing to prevent infection. You can apply an antiseptic, such as iodine or alcohol, before applying the dressing.

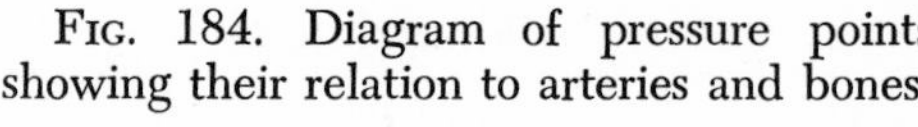

Fig. 184. Diagram of pressure points showing their relation to arteries and bones.

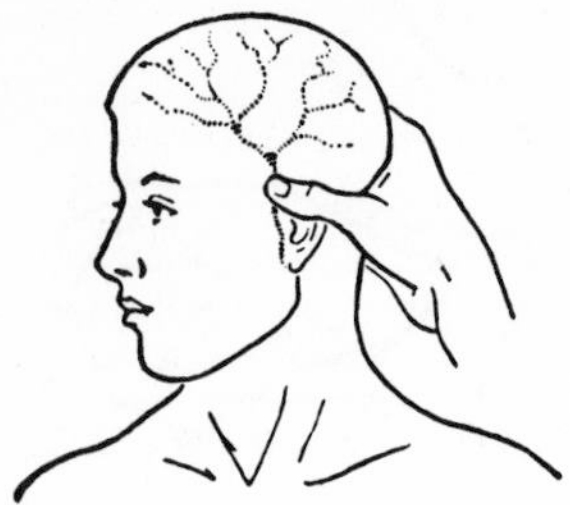

Pressure for face bleeding.

Pressure for scalp bleeding.

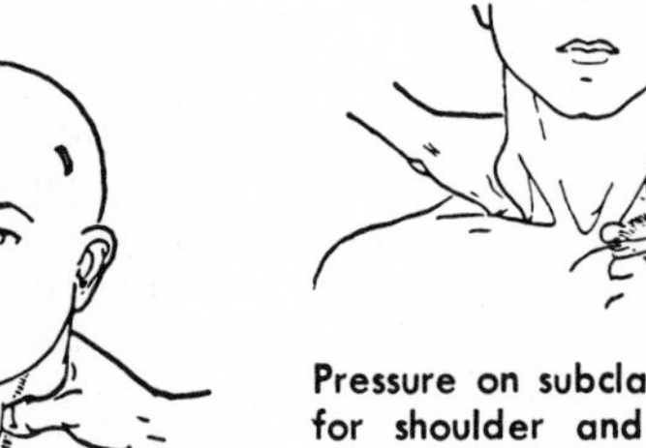

Pressure on subclavian artery for shoulder and high arm wounds.

Pressure for neck wounds.

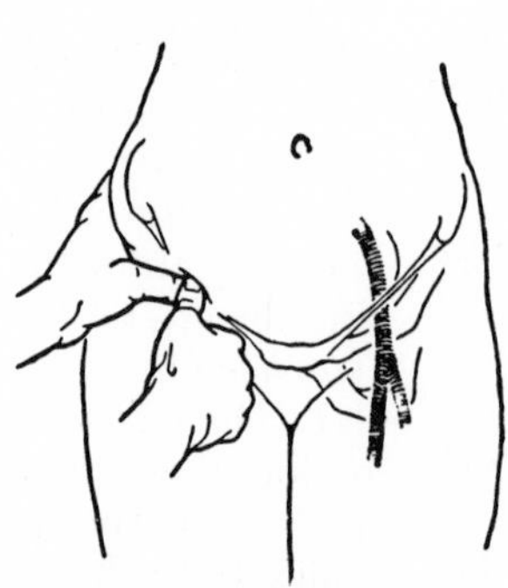

Pressure to stop bleeding in arm.

Pressure point for femoral artery.

Apply the medication with a cotton applicator; always let iodine dry before you apply the dressing, to prevent burning the tissues. Mercurochrome is less painful than iodine, but it is not so effective an antiseptic. Never apply ointments or oils to a wound.

Apply a sterile dressing and secure it firmly with a bandage or strips of adhesive; if the dressing slips or slides over the surrounding skin, the dressing becomes unsterile.

A Band-Aid makes an adequate dressing for small cuts or scratches; Band-Aids come in different sizes and should be in every home medicine cabinet. Be sure never to touch with your fingers the part of a sterile dressing that covers the wound; put the dressing exactly where you want it because you cannot move it afterward without unsterilizing it. Be sure that the bandage or the adhesive is firm but not tight enough to cut off the circulation.

Applying a Tourniquet. *A tourniquet should be used only in case of an extensive hemorrhage which is endangering a life, and in a case which does not respond to the direct pressure method of control. This is only when a large artery has been injured or when a complete or partial amputation of a limb has occurred.*

A tourniquet must be made of materials present at the site of the accident. This can be anything that will make a flat band about 2 inches wide, or rubber tubing if it is available; a strip of inner tube makes an excellent tourniquet. You can use a stocking, a belt or a large handkerchief folded into a cravat—never use cord or wire because it would injure the flesh. Place a compact folded piece of material over the pressure point of the artery controlling the blood flow to the injury. Wrap the tourniquet around this pad, tie a half knot, place a stick or similar object over it, tie a square knot over the stick, then twist the stick to tighten the tourniquet. Fasten in position. *Do not loosen the tourniquet without the permission of a doctor! Tag the patient with a note stating its location and the time of application. Transport the victim to medical aid immediately!*

A tourniquet must be tight enough to cut off the flow of blood in the artery; if it is too loose, it will only prevent the blood from flowing back through the veins and increase the bleeding. A tourniquet is never used to apply pressure to the carotid artery, since it would strangle the patient.

Never cover a tourniquet with anything. If forgotten, it will cause gangrene by damaging the circulation permanently. Apply a sterile dressing to the wound and bandage it. Gauze helps in preserving the blood clot, and the bandage exerts pressure. Never wipe blood clots from a wound—the clot acts as a plug for ruptured blood vessels. Keep the bleeding part quiet and elevate it if possible.

Nosebleed. Nosebleed was treated in Chapter 46, but it is repeated here as an aspect of first-aid treatment.

Nosebleed may be due to an injury or it may occur suddenly if a patient has high blood pressure; it may come on spontaneously, particularly with children. Always keep the patient upright—bending over increases the flow of blood. Loosen anything tight around the neck. Apply cold wet compresses over the nose; press the nostril on the bleeding side against the bridge of the nose. This usually stops the bleeding and gives an opportunity for the clot to form. Keep up the pressure for at least 5 minutes. If this treatment is not effective in 15 minutes, call the doctor; pack a strip of sterile gauze gently into the nostril—pack *back*, not *up*. It is not safe to pack small pieces of cotton into the nose—they become soaked wisps that are hard to find and remove.

Watch the patient with severe nosebleed for signs of fainting or shock. Keep him upright for an hour or two after the bleeding stops and caution him about blowing his nose. Record the nosebleed and report it to the doctor; estimate the amount of bleeding; note the patient's reaction.

Shock

Shock was discussed in Chapter 33 as a postoperative complication. Here we are considering it as a complication following an injury, but the cause and the symptoms are the same as shock occurring after surgery. The skin is cold, pale and moist; the pulse, rapid and thready; the respirations, difficult and gasping. There is also a drop in blood pressure. Shock is usually caused by severe blood loss, externally or internally. Anything that causes or increases hemorrhage should be avoided, especially rough handling or moving the patient.

Every victim should have preventive and precautionary treatment for shock, since these signs do not always appear immediately after injury. Keep the patient lying down to facilitate the flow of blood to the head and the chest; the head and the chest may be elevated if breathing is difficult. Elevate the lower part of the body unless there is a head injury, breathing difficulty, fractures of the lower extremity, or abdominal pain.

Apply sufficient covering to retain body heat; a blanket placed beneath the body if the patient is lying on the ground or the floor is helpful. If it is necessary to use hot-water bags or heating pads in extremely cold weather, be sure that these objects are not in contact with the skin since the victim may not be conscious of a burn.

Blood, plasma, or other parenteral fluids are usually given when the patient is under medical care. If this is delayed, sips of water may be given except when the patient is unconscious, nauseated or has an abdominal wound. *Do not give alcoholic drinks.* Control hemorrhage when possible; keep the patient quiet and maintain his morale with words of reassurance.

Fainting

Fainting is caused by an insufficient supply of blood in the brain. People faint when they are hungry, tired or in close, crowded rooms; emotional shock or the sight of blood may cause fainting. It also occurs after losing a great deal of blood or with severe pain. Standing for a long time may cause fainting.

It is not uncommon to have someone faint at the scene of an accident or while watching an operation. A fainting person may fall and injure himself if he does not recognize the symptoms and behave accordingly.

The signs of fainting are dizziness, blackness before the eyes, pallor and perspiration. The victims loses consciousness, his pulse is weak, and his breathing is shallow. When someone complains of these feelings, bend his head forward between his knees to put his head lower than his heart and bring more blood to the head. Keep him lying down with his head lowered or his limbs elevated; loosen tight clothing. Do not allow him to get up until you are sure he has recovered, then get him to rise gradually, first to a sitting position, before he attempts to walk.

Most people seem to feel that everything will be all right if a person who is recovering consciousness can be made to sit up and move around. Nothing could be worse, and such treatment may be dangerous. Unconsciousness may be due to conditions more serious than fainting, such as skull fracture, concussion, shock or cerebral hemorrhage.

Fractures

When a person has been the victim of a fall or an automotive accident, you must consider the possibility of fractures. Because the bones which are well-padded with flesh may have an obscured fracture site, the cardinal rule of first aid to the victim is *do not move.* Call a doctor, or have someone else do so for you. Question the victim (if conscious). Observe him for obviously deformed limbs. Cover him with a blanket until adequate help can be obtained. Caution the victim against moving if you are suspicious of a fracture. Splint an arm or a leg with the material available. For an arm, rolled newspapers or magazines can be tied in place to maintain the position of the limb. For a leg, a folded blanket reinforced with cardboard or magazines to form a firm support may be eased under the entire length of the leg from the hip to the foot and held in an encasing position with ties of any material available.

Never attempt to replace the ends of bones in a fracture where the skin is broken. Cover the area with a clean cloth and control excessive bleeding by direct pressure on the applicable pressure point.

Frostbite

Frostbite is the freezing of tissues by exposure to extreme cold without sufficient protection of the exposed area. The body is more susceptible in a high wind because warmth is removed from the body more rapidly. Usually the frozen area is small—occurring on the nose, the cheeks, the ears, the fingers and the toes, but it may be larger. The affected area becomes a grayish white color because ice forms in the tissues. Frozen hands or feet are painful, but frostbite in other areas is not usually painful; the victim may not know that his cheeks or ears are frozen until someone notices the color of the frostbitten spot.

A person who is tired or not well is more susceptible to frostbite. Warm clothing provides protection for the body; if a part becomes cold, rubbing helps to stimulate the circulation; physical activity is a good preventive measure.

Never rub the frozen part—rubbing bruises the frozen tissues and may cause gangrene. The victim of mild frostbite can be placed in a warm room, but he should not be near a stove, a radiator or an open fire. Thaw the frozen part gradually in warm water or simply by exposure to air if the victim is in a *cool* room. Heat may cause blisters and is painful. Give the victim a warm drink; coffee is excellent.

After *prolonged* exposure to cold, the victim should be placed in a cool room until the circulation is restored. After chilling and long exposure in water, the temperature of the affected part should be raised gradually, but the victim of long exposure should have immediate medical attention.

The Effects of Excessive Heat

Excessive heat may cause sunstroke, heat exhaustion or heat cramps. The persons most likely to be affected are the very old and the very young, obese individuals, alcoholics, or people with some general disease.

Sweating keeps the body temperature normal during exposure to excessive heat, but a person loses much salt from the body in perspiration. This salt loss is the main cause of heat exhaustion, and it plays an important part in sunstroke. People working in excessive heat need to take from 12 to 15 glasses of water a day and need additional salt—at least a 5-grain salt tablet with every glass of water. The tablets should be dissolved or they may cause nausea and pain.

Loose, thin clothing helps to keep the body cool; moving air helps evaporation of perspiration. Fruit juices, fruit and easily digested food reduce heat production in the body. Reduce muscular exertion, and work in the coolest parts of the day during hot weather if possible. Stay out of the sun and keep your head covered. Too many iced or alcoholic drinks upset the heat regulation in the body.

Sunstroke. Sunstroke and heat stroke are essentially the same, although one is caused by the sun's rays, and the other by indoor heat. The symptoms of sunstroke include dizziness, pain in the head, nausea, a feeling of oppression, and a dry mouth and skin; these symptoms are followed by unconsciousness. Sunstroke kills about 25 per cent of the severe cases. The skin is dry and hot; the face, flushed. The pulse is full and rapid. The temperature often ranges from 107° to 110°. Occasionally, convulsions occur.

Get the victim into the shade and in a cool place; remove the clothing. Put the patient on his back and elevate the head and the shoulders slightly. Apply cold to the head; cool the body by wrapping it in a sheet and pouring on cold water—do this gradually. After several minutes of this treatment, observe the patient and note the effects of the treatment on the skin; go on with the treatment if the skin becomes hot again. Rub the limbs toward the heart, over the wet sheet, to stimulate the circulation. Call the doctor; give cool drinks when the patient becomes conscious; do not give a stimulant.

An ice-water tub bath is also an effective way to cool the body; do not prolong the bath more than 20 minutes. Brisk rubbing is important with any method, and the cold on the head must be continuous.

Heat Exhaustion. Exposure to the sun or to intense indoor heat causes *heat exhaustion*, or *heat prostration*. Alcoholics and people in poor physical health are especially susceptible. The symptoms are dizziness, muscular weakness, nausea and a blundering, staggering gait. Often the victim vomits, and he may have involuntary bowel movements. He is pale, perspires profusely, and his body is clammy and may become cold; his pulse is weak, and his breathing shallow. He may faint before he lies down. Severe cases may die without recovering consciousness.

Get the victim into circulating air. Have him lie down and cover him. Give him one half-teaspoonful of salt in one third of a glass of water until he has had a tablespoonful of salt—strangely enough, this seldom makes the victim nauseated. Give warm tea or coffee; call the doctor if the symptoms persist.

Heat cramps affect the muscles in the abdomen or the limbs. They are most painful and may be accompanied by heat exhaustion symptoms. Treat as for heat exhaustion with drinks of salt solution at frequent intervals.

Giving First Aid for a Superficial Burn

Burns are usually caused by steam or hot liquids, by contact with hot surfaces or by electricity: electric burns occur when the current passes through the body, or through electrical flashes. Strong chemicals also burn the tissues.

There are 3 degrees of burns:

1. *First degree*—the skin is reddened only, and the burn is superficial.

2. *Second degree*—the skin is blistered.

3. *Third degree*—the tissues are charred or cooked.

A superficial burn reddens the skin but does not destroy the tissues, although the outer layer of the skin may peel off afterward. Any burn is painful because exposed nerve endings come in contact with the air. The chief dangers from severe burns are shock and infection.

Preventing Burns. Handles of saucepans on the stove should be turned inward so that children cannot reach them. Children should be taught not to touch hot radiators or stoves. Matches should be kept in a safe place. Electric or gas heaters should be placed where there is no danger of elderly people falling over or brushing against them. Be sure that the cords attached to electrical appliances are placed where no one will trip over them. Keep children away from fireplaces and bonfires. Avoid overexposure to the sun by gradually increasing the time of exposure until the skin has a protective coat of tan, although some skins never build up this protection to any extent.

Treatment. In the case of slight burns apply a burn ointment or petrolatum to the burned area and cover it with a clean dressing; apply a roller bandage to hold the dressing in place. If ointment is not available, wet the cloth in a warm solution of baking soda (3 teaspoonfuls of soda to a pint of water) and apply as above. You can also use a similar solution of Epsom salts.

Severe burns must have medical attention. At home, you can cut away the clothing but do not attempt to remove cloth that sticks to the tissues; outside of the home, do not remove the clothing—cover the patient, keep him lying down and get him to the hospital as soon as possible. For the victim at home, you apply wet dressings of soda or Epsom salts solution to the burned areas and keep the patient warm until the doctor comes. Give the patient small amounts of water frequently because fluids seep out of the tissues in the burned areas.

Do not use boric acid solution for burns; never apply ointments of any kind to severe burns, because the doctor may prefer another type of treatment, and ointments are difficult to remove. Never use absorbent cotton on burns; it will stick to the tissues, and removing it causes more injury. Blisters should be opened only by the doctor.

Chemical burns should be flooded with large quantities of water to wash the chemical away and prevent deeper tissue damage. If a chemical gets into the eye, have the patient lie down, and pour cupfuls of water into the inner eye, with the head turned to allow the water to run off. Follow this with a few drops of castor oil, olive oil or mineral oil.

Sunburn is usually a first- or a second-degree burn; severe sunburn may make the victim really ill and cause blistering and fever. Oils and calamine lotion are soothing for sunburn.

Poisoning

Any substance that affects health or threatens life when it is absorbed into the body or when in contact with body surfaces is a poison. All drugs are potential poisons, but many do not have poisonous effects because they are given in small doses. Poisoning is all too often the result of misreading the label on a drug, taking a drug from an unlabeled bottle, or taking a drug from a medicine cupboard in the dark.

Poisonous substances are all around us in household cleaning agents, insecticides, antifreeze, furniture polish, kerosene, nail polish and many other things. Accidental poisoning happens frequently, especially with children who consume colored tablets of barbiturates, aspirin or other drugs, thinking that they are candy. Sometimes poisons are taken deliberately, with the intention of committing suicide. In this case the barbiturates are often used, or the person inhales carbon monoxide gas from an automobile exhaust.

Food poisoning (ptomaine) is almost always caused by eating food which has been contaminated by bacteria. The normal action of the bacteria on the food causes decomposition which, in turn, causes the formation of toxins (poisonous substances). Other causes include the accidental eating of certain fruits, berries or vegetable materials (for example, toadstools) which contain substances poisonous to humans.

The symptoms of food poisoning include abdominal pain, nausea and/or vomiting, and diarrhea. The onset is acute (within a few hours after taking the contaminated food). The symptoms usually disappear in 1 or 2 days after the toxins have been excreted.

A more severe form of food poisoning is called *botulism.* This is caused by a specific organism, *Clostridium botulinum.* Over 45 per cent of the cases result in death. Home-preserved foods are a common cause and are most dangerous to use unless they have been sterilized at 248° F. to kill possible contamination.

The symptoms of botulinus poisoning are weakness, headache, muscular weakness, paralysis of the eye and the throat muscles and, finally, respiratory paralysis. Specific antitoxins are effective if given early; artificial respiration is essential until the antitoxin takes effect.

The First Principles of Emergency Treatment for Poisoning

1. Always remember that the first thing to do in case of poisoning is to call the doctor.

2. Identify the poison. Question the victim, if possible, as to the possible source. Save *all* vomitus, urine and stools, the remains of the food or the drugs which may have been responsible.

3. Remove the poison from the stomach by inducing vomiting (except in the case of a strong acid or alkali, or if the patient is unconscious). This can be done by giving an emetic made of 1 tablespoonful of mustard in a glass of warm water, or of 2 tablespoonfuls of salt in a glass of warm water. Give this to the victim orally, followed with copious amounts of warm water until vomiting has apparently cleared the stomach of the poisonous substance.

4. Give an antidote. An antidote is a substance which inactivates the poison or keeps it from being absorbed. Common household substances that are available are milk, egg white, strong tea, coffee, or starch.

5. Give supportive treatment. Keep the patient warm by applying external heat to the body. Use artificial respiration or oxygen if the respirations are affected.

To Remove a Foreign Body From the Eye

The important function of the eye is *sight*; the structures of the eye are delicate and easily damaged by either injury or infection. The purpose of first aid is to preserve the sight, by preventing further damage and securing the necessary medical attention for the victim.

Foreign bodies may be particles of dust or soot or an eyelash lodged on the lining of the eyelid, or they may be particles that become embedded in the eyeball. Never attempt to remove an embedded foreign body. Anything that lodges in the eye irritates it, especially when the eyelid is closed; a foreign body has a scratchy effect and makes tears flow. Follow these instructions to prevent serious damage:

Instruct the victim not to rub the eye—rubbing may drive a foreign body in deeper.

Never use an instrument, a toothpick or a match to remove a foreign body.

Never attempt to remove a foreign body if there is the slightest possibility that it is embedded in the eyeball.

This is what you may do to remove a foreign body that is not embedded:

1. Pull down the lower eyelid to see whether the body is on the eyelid membrane; if so, you may be able to lift it off by touching it gently with the corner of a clean handkerchief or with a cotton-tipped applicator moistened in water —always moisten cotton before touching it to the eye.

2. Grasp the lashes of the upper eyelid with your forefinger and thumb; ask the patient to look upward, pull the lid forward and downward over the lower eyelid. Usually this dislodges the foreign body, and the tears wash it away.

3. Flush the eye with a weak solution of salt water. You can do this with a sterile medicine dropper or a small bulb syringe.

4. Put a few drops of mineral oil, castor oil or olive oil in the eye.

If none of these measures is successful, the patient must see a doctor as soon as possible; the longer a foreign body remains in the eye, the greater the danger of injuring the tissues.

POISONS: SYMPTOMS AND TREATMENT

Poison	Symptoms	Emergency Treatment	Supporting Treatment
Acids	Severe burning in mouth, throat, stomach Profuse vomiting and diarrhea Dyspnea, cyanosis, collapse	Milk of magnesia or lime water followed by milk, demulcents, etc. External acid burns—Baking or washing soda with large amounts water	Stimulants and external heat for collapse Sodium bicarbonate intravenously or by rectum for acidosis
Acid, Carbolic (Phenol)	Burning pain, whitening of lips and mouth, dizziness, dyspnea, greenish urine, weak pulse, contracted pupils, collapse	Weak alcohol solutions locally Magnesium sulfate. Soapy water, egg white, lime water or milk	Stimulants—caffeine, atropine External heat, forced fluids, give artificial respiration
Alcohol (grain)	Excitement, followed by general depression	Evacuate stomach	Cold applications to head, heat to extremities. Coffee, caffeine or strychnine if necessary
Alcohol (wood)	Excitement, nausea and vomiting, blindness, dizziness, headache, dilated pupils, delirium	Evacuate stomach	Treat as above Also CO_2 inhalations and artificial respiration
Alkalis	Mucous membranes of mouth soapy, swollen and white. Severe abdominal pain. Vomiting of blood and mucus. Collapse	Dilute acids: Vinegar, tartaric acid, lemon juice Tea, milk, oil	Stimulants Artificial heat Opium preparations if necessary
Alkaloids { Atropine, Cocaine, Morphine, Strychnine }	Symptoms vary	Tannic acid, strong tea, or potassium permanganate by lavage	Support circulation and respiration, and promote elimination
Anesthetics { Chloroform, Ether, N_2O }	Slow shallow breathing Cyanosis, weak pulse, dilated fixed pupil, collapse	When inhaled: oxygen + 5% carbon dioxide When swallowed: lavage stomach with sodium bicarbonate solution	Stop anesthetic Place head low. Give artificial respiration, fresh air, oxygen, stimulants, artificial heat. Dilate anal sphincter. Give epinephrine
Arsenic (Rat poisons, etc.)	Burning pain in esophagus and stomach. Abdominal pain. Nausea and vomiting. Garlic breath Diarrhea, rice-water stools. Thirst. Scanty urine. Collapse	Evacuate stomach Give iron hydroxide with magnesia Sodium thiosulfate Milk, water, olive oil Dimercaprol (BAL)	Stimulants — caffeine, atropine, strychnine External heat

Atropine (Belladonna, Stramonium, Hyoscyamus)	Dry mouth. Thirst Flushed skin. Dilated fixed pupils Rapid pulse and respiration Delirium and collapse	Tannic acid or potassium permanganate lavage	Sedatives for excitement stage Ice bag to head. Artificial respiration if necessary Catheterize. Treat collapse
Chloral (and other hypnotics)	Slow respirations, weak pulse, low temperature, low B.P. Muscular relaxation. Collapse	Evacuate stomach Give tea or coffee Ephedrine sulfate 50 mg. intravenously	Caffeine, strychnine, atropine Artificial respiration, oxygen, external warmth
Cocaine	Excitement and restlessness. Pulse and respirations rapid. Pupils dilated. Skin moist. Delirium. Collapse	If swallowed: lavage with tannic acid, tea or potassium permanganate	Horizontal position. Fresh air and O_2 Treat collapse
Copper Compounds	Metallic taste Nausea and vomiting Abdominal cramps	Potassium ferrocyanide Albumin or milk Lavage stomach and give demulcents	External heat. Stimulants Opium for abdominal pain
Digitalis	Nausea and vomiting Diarrhea Slow pulse—below 60—or a sudden acceleration Headache	Stop drug Lavage with tannic acid or tea Give magnesium sulfate	Artificial respiration Treat collapse Keep patient quiet. Give morphine
Food Poisoning	Abdominal pain Nausea and vomiting Diarrhea. Collapse	Lavage stomach with tea or tannic acid or water Give castor oil	Stimulants. Rest. Warmth Opium for pain
Gas (Carbon Monoxide)	Drowsiness, giddiness, ringing in ears, dyspnea, loss of consciousness. Flushed cheeks, cherry-colored mucous membranes. Violent heart action. Coma	Fresh air. Oxygen with 5% carbon dioxide	Artificial respiration alternating with O_2 inhalations Heat. Coffee enema. Stimulants
Iodine	Nausea and vomiting (blue vomitus if starch is given) Diarrhea, cyanosis, collapse	Starch or flour in water Lavage. Give demulcents	Stimulants. External heat Sodium thiosulfate intravenously if iodism is severe
Lead	Chronic or cumulative: Anorexia, Lead colic Nausea, Constipation Metallic taste, Anemia "Lead line" on gums, Palsies	Magnesium or sodium sulfate Evacuate stomach if recent dose has been taken	Stimulants, opium, external heat for acute condition Viosterol and calcium salts for chronic condition

POISONS: SYMPTOMS AND TREATMENT (*Continued*)

Poison	Symptoms	Emergency Treatment	Supporting Treatment
Mercury	Metallic taste. Stomatitis. Burning throat. Abdominal pain. Nausea and vomiting. Diarrhea—bloody stools. Scanty urine. Convulsions. Collapse	Albumin (whites of 2 to 6 eggs). Milk or flour Lavage with tannic acid Give sodium thiosulfate Dimercaprol (BAL)	Stop drug Heat stimulants. Treat collapse Opium or morphine Treat for nephritis
Opium Laudanum Paregoric Morphine Codeine, etc.	Sleep. Stupor Slow respirations (3 to 4 a minute) Pinpoint pupils Cyanosis. Slow pulse Coma	Lavage with potassium permanganate 1–2,000, or tannic acid	Keep patient awake and active Atropine 1/100 gr. q.1 h. (by order) Oxygen and 5% CO_2 inhalations Catheterize. Give coffee and stimulants
Phosphorus	Abdominal pain. Nausea and vomiting. Stools and vomitus phosphorescent. Necrosis of jaw. Jaundice. Collapse. Coma	Lavage with copper sulfate, hydrogen peroxide, or potassium permanganate solution *Do not give fats or oils*	External heat. Oxygen Opium
Poison Ivy Poison Oak Poison Sumac	Itching swollen areas on skin, which rapidly form vesicles	Scrub skin with strong yellow soap and water Apply alcoholic solution of lead acetate	Sedatives if necessary Soothing lotions, e.g., sodium bicarbonate, calamine lotion, etc.
Silver Compounds	Burning sensation Nausea and vomiting Abdominal pain Argyria	Sodium chloride solution (common salt) Lavage stomach, then give demulcents	Treat as for other metallic poisons
Strychnine	Stiffness of muscles of face, neck, jaw. Twitching. Convulsions. Asphyxia	Tannic acid, tea, potassium permanganate solution, charcoal Lavage stomach before convulsions occur	Rest and quiet. Dark room Artificial respiration. Oxygen and 5% CO_2 Catheterize Ether or chloroform for convulsions Paraldehyde, chloral, bromides
Zinc	Metallic taste Nausea and vomiting Abdominal pain	Lavage stomach Give sodium bicarbonate, milk, lime water, albumin	Treat collapse Morphine

To Remove a Foreign Body From the Nose, the Throat or the Ear

Children sometimes put small objects in their noses; unless the object is clearly visible and at the edge of the nostril, do not attempt to remove it with a finger; a pea or a bean or a kernel of corn in the nose is likely to swell—you can put a few drops of olive or mineral oil in the nostril, which helps to prevent the swelling. You may be able to grasp a small object with a forceps; be careful not to poke the object still farther up the nose; have the victim blow the nose gently with *both* nostrils open.

Objects often become lodged in the throat; children put coins or buttons in their mouths; bits of food or bones lodge in the throat or the esophagus. Do not attempt to remove the foreign body with your fingers unless it is an object that you can dislodge easily. If you are unable to see the foreign body, but the patient is able to breath all right, send for the doctor. You can tell by the patient's color whether or not his air supply is sufficient. If the patient is blue and distressed, hold him upside down and slap his back sharply; this may dislodge the object. By having an adult bend over, his trunk and head are upside down. Sometimes artificial respiration is necessary even though the obstruction has been removed.

If a foreign body lodges in the ear, do not attempt to remove it but call the doctor. Always consult the doctor if a foreign body has been swallowed.

BANDAGES

A bandage is a piece of material used to hold dressings or splints in place, to give support, or to apply pressure. The different materials used for bandages are described in the discussion of dressings, but the methods for applying bandages will be discussed here. Here is a list of rules to use when applying bandages.

1. Apply firmly but not so tightly that the circulation is cut off: after an injury the bandaged part may swell, so watch for evidence of tightness and loosen the bandage if necessary.
2. Always tie a square knot because a square knot will not slip.
3. If possible, leave the tips of the toes and the fingers exposed so that you can tell by their color if the bandage is cutting off the circulation.

The Roller Bandage

Roller bandages of gauze or muslin come in different widths suitable for bandaging the various parts of the body. Appropriate widths are:

Fingers and toes	1-inch
Hand and foot	2- or 3-inch
Head	2-inch
Limbs	2- to 6-inch
Trunk	4- to 6-inch

A roller bandage can be applied neatly and snugly on the extremities because it can be made to fit. Each turn of a roller bandage should be exactly as tight as the one before it; if you make the turns tighter and tighter as you progress, the bandage will constrict the part. If you let the turns grow looser, the bandage will slip and may come off. If you purposely apply the entire bandage loosely to allow for swelling, it can be anchored with strips of adhesive tape. You can use a strip of adhesive tape to fasten the end of the bandage, or you can split the end for 4 or 5 inches, tie a single knot and carry the ends around in opposite directions and tie a square knot.

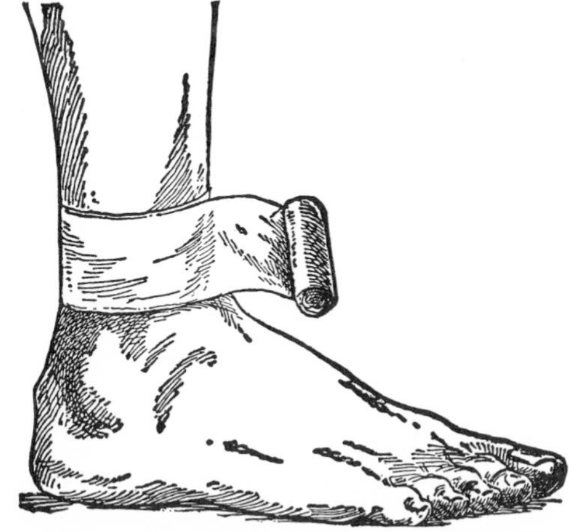

FIG. 185. Circular turns of a bandage.

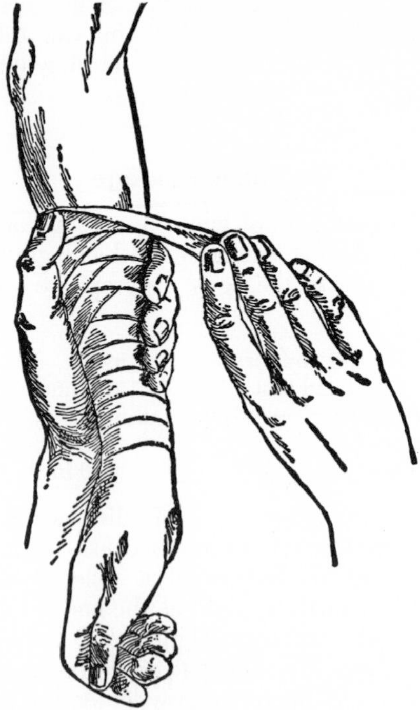

FIG. 186. Spiral reverse bandage.

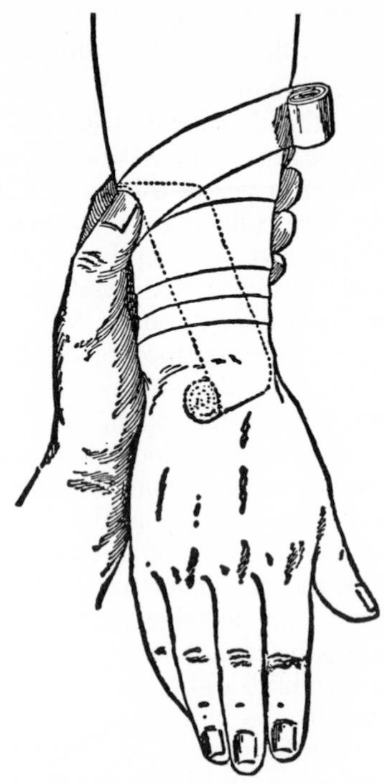

FIG. 187. Spiral bandage.

Circular Bandage

The circular bandage makes 2 or more turns around the part, each layer covering the one below it. When applying any roller bandage begin with 2 circular turns to anchor the loose end firmly (Fig. 185).

Spiral Bandage

The spiral bandage winds like a coil either upward or downward. Anchor the bandage with 2 circular turns, then cover the part with spiral turns slanted evenly, each turn overlapping the one beneath for half its width. Finish with 2 circular turns and fasten (Fig. 186).

Spiral Reverse Bandage

This is a modification of the spiral bandage used to fit a tapering part. Start with a spiral until you reach a point where the layer will not lie flat on the one below it; then reverse the turn, slanting the bandage back on itself. Make as many of these reverse turns as necessary to keep the bandage flat, reversing at the same point each time (Fig. 187).

Figure-8 Bandage

The figure-8 bandage makes slanting turns, alternately ascending and descending around the part and crossing in the middle. This bandage is used for joints, such as the ankle, the shoulder, the knee or the elbow (Fig. 188).

Spica Bandage

The spica bandage is a prolonged figure-8 bandage entirely covering the part, each turn overlapping the one beneath (Figs. 189, 190). The spica is useful for wounds in or near the groin.

Spiral Bandage for Finger

With the back of the hand facing up, make 2 circular turns around the base of the injured finger, then make spiral turns until the area is

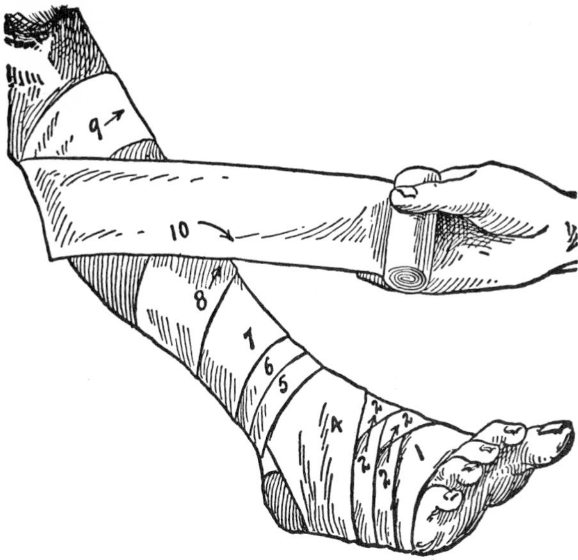

FIG. 188. Figure-8 bandage.

covered. If the injury is at the base of the finger, make 2 turns around the finger, carry the bandage across the back of the hand to the wrist, make 2 turns around the wrist, then carry the bandage back around the finger; repeat as many times as necessary to cover the area and anchor the bandage. To cover the end of the finger, make recurrent loops of bandage over the end in this way: hold a spiral turn at the base of the finger, on the back; bring the bandage up over the end of the finger and down over the front until the finger is covered suffi-

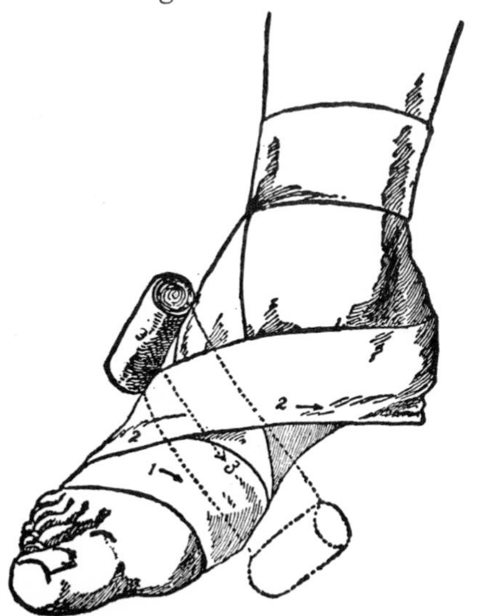

FIG. 189. Spica bandage of the foot (*first step*).

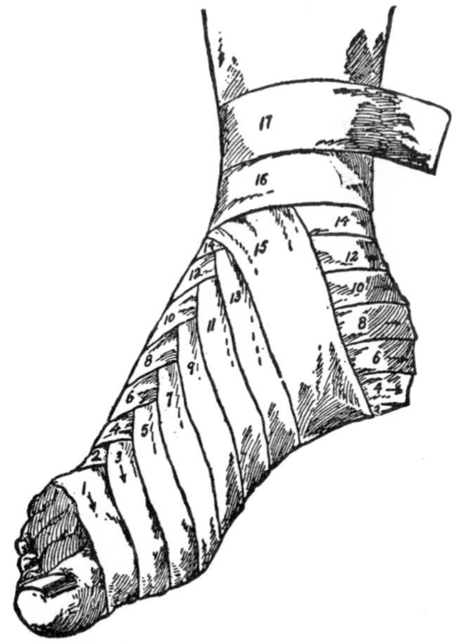

FIG. 190. Spica bandage of the foot (*completed*).

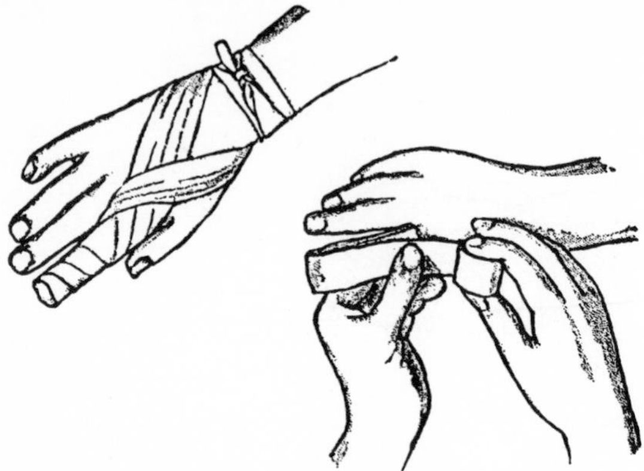

Fig. 191. Spiral bandage to cover the end of a finger. (American National Red Cross: First Aid Textbook, ed. 4, New York, Doubleday, 1957)

ciently—overlap each loop slightly and hold the loops at the base—then continue the spiral, binding down the recurrent loops and finishing with anchorage around the wrist (Fig. 191).

The Handkerchief or Triangular Bandage. This bandage is useful because it can be made from a square of cloth and can be fastened without adhesive tape or pins, if necessary. The 36- or 40-inch square is an adequate size. Cut diagonally through the center to make 2 triangular bandages. The triangle can be folded several times to make a strip, or a *cravat* bandage (Fig. 192).

Arm Sling. The triangular bandage is used to make a sling to support an arm. To apply a sling, use this procedure: put one end of the triangle over the shoulder on the *uninjured* side, with the point of the triangle pointing toward the injured arm and placed under it. Bring the other end of the triangle over the shoulder on the *injured* side and tie the 2 ends of the triangle together at the side of the neck. Then bring the point of the triangle forward and pin it to the sling. You can adjust the sling by adjusting the knot or by pinning a tuck in the front of the sling above the hand; the hand should be elevated 4 or 5 inches above the elbow level (Fig. 193).

Binders

Straight Binder. Straight binders are made of 2 thicknesses of muslin stitched together on the edges. A straight binder can be used to keep dressings in place on the wider areas, such as the abdomen, the breast or the back; it should be at least 12 inches wide and 36 inches long, or even larger for some people. To apply a straight binder, follow this procedure: gather half the length of the binder into folds and slip it under the patient; pull it through and adjust it evenly. Lap one end over the other (fold the upper lap under, if necessary); pin with safety pins from the bottom upward, spacing the pins

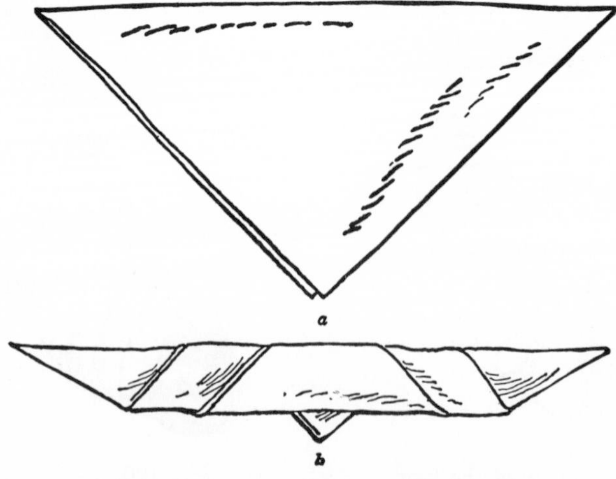

Fig. 192. (*a*) Handkerchief; (*b*) cravat.

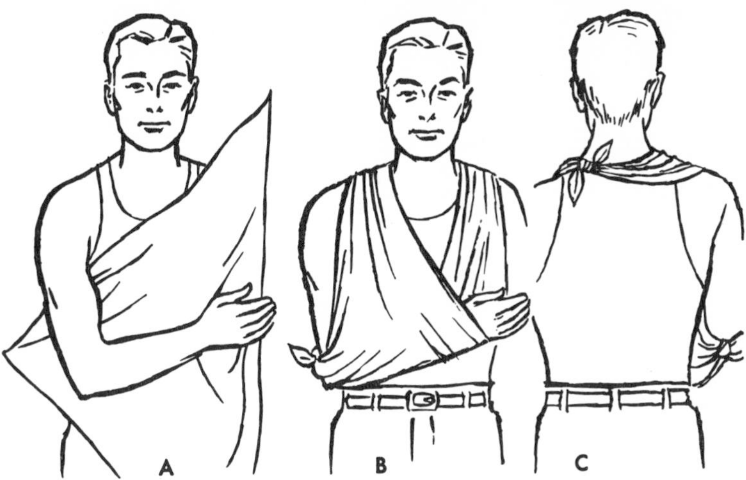

FIG. 193. Triangular bandage used as an arm sling. (A) Step one. (B) Step two. (C) Step three. (American National Red Cross: First Aid Textbook, ed. 4, New York, Doubleday, 1957)

about 2 inches apart, keeping the end of the binder in a vertical straight line. Adjust fullness at the sides by pinning in pleats from the top downward until the binder fits. Put the fingers of one hand between the patient and the binder as you insert the pins to prevent pricking the patient's skin.

Perineal straps can be attached to a straight binder by pinning 2 strips, 2 inches wide, to the bottom of the binder at the back; the other ends of the straps are drawn between the legs and pinned to the bottom of the binder in the front. You can attach shoulder straps to a chest or a breast binder in a similar manner.

T Binder. A T binder gets its name from its shape—it is made of 2 strips of muslin, 3 or 4 inches wide, which are fastened together. This binder is used to hold rectal or perineal dressings in place. The perineal strap is split through the middle to make a T binder for a male patient. Put the band around the patient's waist, bring the perineal strap through between the legs and pin through the band and the strap at the midline.

Many-Tailed Binder. The many-tailed, or scultetus, binder is made by sewing 3- or 4-inch overlapping strips of cloth together. The 48-inch long strips overlap each other by half their width and are stitched together for about 10 inches, leaving strips 19 inches long hang loose at each end of the binder. To apply the binder, begin with the bottom strips, slanting one strip across the abdomen and pinning it to its opposite. Continue alternating opposite strips until you reach the last one—bring this around the waist and fasten. You can pin the strips at the crossing point before you fasten the final strip, to make the binder firm for support. This binder can be used to exert pressure on the upper abdomen by applying it from the top downward.

Adhesive Tape Straps. Strips of adhesive tape of various widths are often used in place of bandages and binders to hold dressings in place or to give support. Adhesive tape is commonly used for a sprained ankle or fractured ribs. The skin should be shaved before applying massive dressings of adhesive tape, because hairs stick to the tape and make its removal a painful process. Ether or benzine, applied to the skin at the edge of the applied strip, helps to remove adhesive tape painlessly. Keep moistening the skin close to the adhesive as you peel the tape off gently. Never use these liquids near an open flame, because they are highly flammable.

Plaster Bandages. Plaster-of-Paris bandages are made of crinoline impregnated with dry plaster-of-Paris; they are used for casts and splints. The bandage is applied wet and as it dries it hardens. There is danger in applying a cast too tightly because it has no "give" once it hardens. Always watch for signs of interference with the circulation, such as swelling and bluish skin. Also watch for skin irritation beneath the edges of a cast or for pressure.

Unit Eight:

Maternal and Child Care

49

PRENATAL CARE

SOME FACTS

Mothers and babies have a better outlook today than they have had at any time in history. Increased interest in better health for everybody has naturally led to interest in special groups, and mothers and babies make up a large segment of the population. When authorities began to collect figures, they were appalled. Far too many mothers and babies died in childbirth; many babies died soon afterward; many mothers had impaired health; many children were handicapped by a poor start.

Why has this situation improved? In the last 3 decades the maternal mortality rate has declined dramatically. In 1935 there were 12,544 registered maternal deaths in the U.S. This is a rate of 58.2 per 10,000 live births, as compared with 1,550 deaths and a rate of 3.7 in 1959. The rate continues to drop. The main reasons for this important advance are: prenatal care (which is a true example of *preventive medicine*), scientific progress, increased medical and nursing interest and education, improved hospital facilities, and maternal and child care programs. The United States Children's Bureau and state and local groups have worked steadily to improve mother and baby care. Mothers are learning how to prepare for their babies. Clinics provide care before the baby is born. Health insurance plans provide hospital care. Hospitalization for childbirth is now the rule rather than the exception; 95 per cent of the live births in this country take place in hospitals.

It is expected that in 1970 there will be 5½ million babies born, as compared with 4½ million in 1960. Serious planning must be done to provide good care for this population explosion. Preparation for parenthood before conception, health supervision during pregnancy, labor and delivery and during the postpartum period: this is the modern concept of complete maternity care.

Obstetrics (from the Latin *obsto*, meaning to stand by or to protect) is the branch of medicine concerned with the management of childbirth. The doctor who practices this specialty is called an *obstetrician.* In the past, women relatives or a midwife attended a woman in labor; recent figures tell us that today a physician is in attendance for 97 per cent of the births in this country. The early midwives were untrained and relied solely on experience for their knowledge. Here and in other countries, the need has been recognized for trained midwives to supplement the work of the obstetrician in isolated areas where doctors are few and far between.

A new trend in larger communities is for midwives to attend patients in the course of normal labor and delivery, thus freeing the doctor to care for patients who present obstetric problems. There is an increasing number of schools for midwives in the United States. The ultimate hope and aim of all workers in the field of obstetrics is to assist a healthy mother to produce a healthy baby with a minimum of danger and discomfort to both.

PREGNANCY

Pregnancy is defined as the condition of

being "with child." To understand pregnancy we must know how it begins, how the baby grows in the uterus and how pregnancy affects the mother. The anatomy and the physiology of the reproductive systems may be reviewed in Chapter 19.

Growth Underway. The mature ovum and sperm both contain 23 chromosomes; their union (*fertilization*) produces the total of 46 chromosomes, which is characteristic of all human cells. Fertilization usually occurs when the ovum is in the outer third of the fallopian tube. After fertilization, the ovum travels down from the fallopian tube into the uterus, where it will have room to grow and be nourished. The lining of the uterus has been preparing for this while the ovum was ripening in the ovary.

Before the fertilized ovum (called a *zygote*) reaches the uterus, it already has begun to divide rapidly. The zygote forms 2 cells; 2 cells form 4 cells; and so on. After about 3 days the mass of cells, now called the *morula*, reaches the uterus where it starts to implant itself in the uterine lining (endometrium). Some of the cells secrete an enzyme which permits the zygote to burrow into the endometrium.

The cells continue to divide to form a hollow ball which has an inner and an outer layer of cells. Some of the outer cells send out projections (*chorionic villi*) which are the "roots" through which the developing baby receives its oxygen and nourishment from the mother. These villi eventually join with an area of uterine tissue to form the *placenta*, a vascular and glandular organ which supplies the developing baby with food and oxygen and also produces hormones. Certain cells in the inner layer of the morula continue to divide, and they begin to differentiate themselves into 3 distinct types, which ultimately will form the body structure of the fetus. Other cells making up this cavity eventually form a fluid-filled sac (the *amnion*) in which the embryo floats. (The developing baby is called an *embryo* during the first 2 months.)

As was described in Chapter 15, the baby in the uterus is attached to the placenta by the *umbilical cord*, which contains 2 arteries and 1 large vein twisted about each other. These blood vessels are contained in a white gelatinous substance called *Wharton's jelly*. There is no direct connection between the bloodstreams of the mother and the baby, but the exchange of substances takes place across the placenta through the process of osmosis—in this way, the mother supplies food and carries off wastes for the baby. The umbilical vein carries food and oxygen to the baby, while the umbilical arteries carry away the wastes. It is obvious that the baby depends on its mother for the right food materials necessary for its growth, and her elimination systems must be in good working order to get rid of the baby's wastes.

How Sex Is Determined. There is no way that a mother can influence the sex of her child; it is determined by the sperm from the father at the time of fertilization. A female ovum carries only one type of chromosome to determine one type of sex; it is called X. A male sperm cell may carry either one of the two sex chromosomes, X or Y. If the ovum is fertilized by a sperm cell carrying a Y chromosome, the baby will be a boy (XY); if the sperm cell carries an X chromosome, the baby will be a girl (XX).

At the present time there is no way to "order" a boy or a girl; however, odds seem to be a little in favor of the boys, since there are about 106 boys born for every 100 girls.

Old Wives' Tales. There are many queer notions that surround pregnancy. The one that comes to mind most often is the belief that the mother can *mark* her baby or influence its mind if she sees something unpleasant or ugly. This is impossible, since there is no direct connection between the nervous systems of the mother and the baby. Nor can the mother tie knots in the umbilical cord by stretching her arms to hang curtains; the child may turn in the uterus and cause a knot, but the mother has nothing to do with it. Also, a hopeful mother's special interest in art and music cannot have any effect on her unborn infant; although he may display interest in these areas, probably it will be the result of environmental direction rather than prenatal influence.

Development of the Baby

The fertilized ovum is called the embryo in the early stages of its growth when the cells are arranging themselves into the layers from which the tissues and the organs of the baby's body will develop. After the 8th week of development the embryo is called the *fetus.*

The expected date for delivery of the child is estimated by counting back 3 months from the first day of the last menstrual period of the mother, and adding 7 days.

A full-term pregnancy, including the devel-

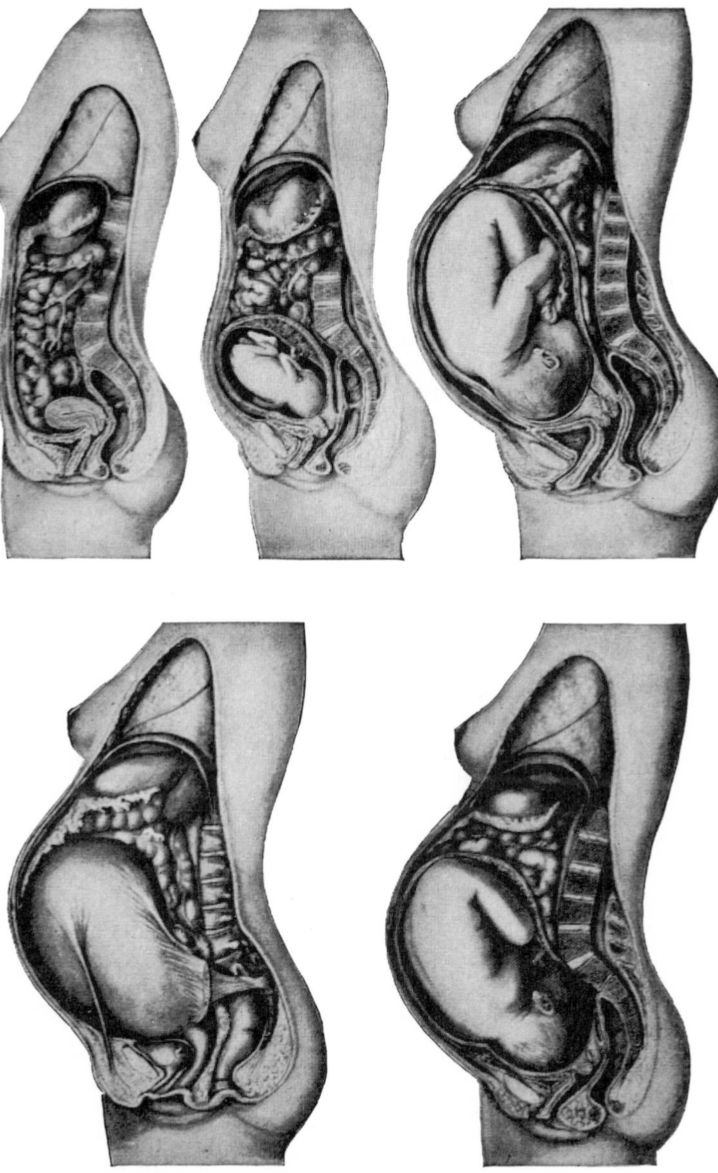

FIG. 194. Charts showing the mother's body at various stages of the baby's growth within the uterus. (E. Schuchardt, Maternity Center Association)

opment of the fetus from embryo to birth, usually takes 280 days, which are divided into 10 months of 28 days each, or 10 lunar months. Fetal growth and development normally follow a definite pattern during each month of pregnancy. This is how that growth progresses:

END OF 1ST LUNAR MONTH. The eyes, the ears and the nose begin to develop, although the embryo is only about the size of a grain of tapioca.

END OF 2ND LUNAR MONTH. The head takes shape—it is abnormally large, because the brain is developing. Arms and legs resemble small buds.

END OF 3RD LUNAR MONTH. The fetus is about 3 inches long, weighs about 1 ounce, and fills the uterus. Fingers and toes, having soft nails, appear.

END OF 4TH LUNAR MONTH. The fetus has grown to about 6 inches and weighs from 2 to 4 ounces. Downy hair (*lanugo*) appears on the back and the shoulders, and the sex can be distinguished.

END OF THE 5TH LUNAR MONTH. The fetus is now about 10 to 12 inches long and weighs about 10 ounces. Downy hair appears over the body, and some hair has developed on the head. Fetal heart sounds can usually be heard with the stethoscope, and the mother feels the baby move.

END OF 6TH LUNAR MONTH. The fetus is about 12 inches long and weighs about a pound. Eyebrows and eyelashes appear; the skin is wrinkled. It is extremely rare that a fetus born at this stage of pregnancy survives.

END OF 7TH LUNAR MONTH. The fetus is now about 14 inches long and weighs about 2 pounds. The skin is covered with a cheesy material (*vernix caseosa*); a greenish, sticky substance (*meconium*) forms in the intestines. The fetus moves freely in the uterus; if it is born now it can breathe and cry and has about 1 chance in 10 of living.

END OF 8TH LUNAR MONTH. The fetus is about 16 inches in length and weighs 3 to 4 pounds. A baby born at 8 months has a good chance to live.

END OF 9TH LUNAR MONTH. The baby is about 18 inches long and weighs 5 to 6 pounds. Fat deposits underneath the skin have smoothed out the wrinkles. If born now the baby has an excellent chance of surviving.

END OF 10TH LUNAR MONTH. The baby now is about 20 inches long, weighs about 7 pounds and is fully developed. The skin is smooth and covered with vernix caseosa; head hair is developed and dark in color. The baby is equipped to enter the world and live. His heredity and his mother's nutrition will have some influence on his weight at birth; a baby weighing 10 pounds or over is usually difficult to deliver. A baby weighing less than 5 pounds 8 ounces at birth is considered as being premature; generally speaking, the smaller the baby is, the more difficult it is for him to survive.

Although the bones of the baby's skull are hardened, they are not yet tightly knit together, leaving soft spots called *fontanels* on the top, the sides and the back of the head. This makes the head less rigid and permits minor changes in shape, which is an advantage during labor and birth.

Signs and Symptoms of Pregnancy

The signs and symptoms of pregnancy are customarily divided into 3 groups: *presumptive*, so called because while pregnancy may be presumed, these symptoms may indicate other common conditions; *probable*, because although more definite than the presumptive symptoms, they are not absolute; and *positive*, because these symptoms, as evidence of pregnancy, are indisputable.

Presumptive Signs. The presumptive signs include absence of menstruation, morning sickness, frequent urination, and tenderness and fullness of the breasts.

ABSENCE OF MENSTRUATION. If menstruation does not take place at the regular time, it commonly is a sign that the uterine lining is feeding a fertilized ovum. If menstrual periods frequently are irregular, this sign alone is not reliable.

MORNING SICKNESS. Nausea and vomiting, especially in the morning, bother about 50 per cent of women in the first 3 months of pregnancy. This morning sickness usually disappears after the mother's body adjusts to the changes that occur when the new life begins to grow. Occasionally, nausea and vomiting are so constant that they threaten the general health of both mother and baby, because the mother is unable to retain the food so vital to both of them.

Frequent Urination. In the first 3 months, as the uterus enlarges and presses on the bladder, there is a frequent desire to urinate. This disappears later as the uterus rises into the abdominal cavity. Late in pregnancy, as the baby's head sinks into the pelvis, pressure on the bladder again causes the frequent desire to urinate.

Breast Changes. Enlarging breasts are a suspicious sign, especially in a first pregnancy.

Other Presumptive Signs. Other indications by which a pregnancy may be presumed are drowsiness and a tendency to fatigue easily; increased pigmentation, both of the nipples and of the *linea negra* (the dark line extending from the umbilicus to the pubis). There is also sometimes said to be a "mask of pregnancy," caused by the presence of dark brown discolorations on the face. The appearance of "quickening," known to the lay person as *feeling life*, and *Chadwick's sign*, which is the darkening in color of the vaginal mucous membrane, are also other presumptive signs of pregnancy.

Probable Signs. Probable signs are designated as enlargement of the abdomen, changes in the uterus, alterations in the cervix and positive pregnancy tests.

There are specific changes in the shape, the size and the consistency of the uterus which are important indications. The enlargement and the changes in shape should correspond to the gradual increase in the size of the fetus and the amount of amniotic fluid. Softness of the uterus at certain stages is also important to the experienced examiner. After the 6th month the fetal outline should be able to be felt or palpated; however, rare uterine tumors may so duplicate the fetal outline that this sign is not considered as being positive.

The cervix usually softens about the time the 2nd menstrual period is missed.

Tests for Pregnancy. It has been possible to develop tests for pregnancy because a hormone is present in the urine of pregnant women which, if injected into certain animals, will produce definite reactions. It is important to have a specimen of urine which has been collected in a clean, dry bottle, and to use it as soon as possible or else refrigerate it until it is used, since heat and delay make the tests less accurate.

Aschheim-Zondek Test is a test in which a small amount of urine is injected into immature mice, and after 96 hours the abdominal cavities of the mice are opened. If there is evidence of change in the ovaries, the test is considered to be positive.

Friedman's Test is similar to the Aschheim-Zondek, except that rabbits are used instead of mice, and the urine is injected directly into the vein. If the ovaries show ruptured follicles after 48 hours, the test is positive. The *Frank-Berman* test uses immature rats, and results are obtained in 24 hours.

Other Tests. Some years ago it was found that the urine of pregnant women injected into the South American toad gave an accurate test of pregnancy. If the toad excretes spermatozoa within 2 hours after the injection, the test is considered as being positive. A similar test using the North American green male frog has also proved to be accurate.

A test is being used with increasing frequency which consists of adding certain chemicals to the urine. This test gives results in about 30 minutes and is reported to be almost 100 per cent accurate.

Positive Signs. The positive signs of pregnancy are the fetal heart sounds, fetal movements felt by an examiner and a roentgenogram showing the fetal skeleton.

PRENATAL CARE

Prenatal refers to the period between conception and the birth of the baby, while *antepartal* refers to the period between conception and the onset of labor. Theoretically, "antepartal" would be the correct term for the discussion in this chapter. The two are often used interchangeably in obstetric literature, but since prenatal still seems to have wider usage, it will be retained here.

Good prenatal care has as its goal the maximum physical and mental fitness of the mother with the reward of an uneventful delivery and a healthy mother and baby. You have learned that the maternal and infant mortality rates have been reduced tremendously in the last decades—certainly one of the first contributing factors in this reduction is the preventive aspects of prenatal care.

Because the public has been made so aware of the value of prenatal care, today a woman goes to a doctor, privately or through a clinic, as soon as she assumes that she is pregnant. Indeed, in recent years emphasis has been placed on *premarital* and *prepregnancy* examinations to encourage positive maternal and child health.

Prenatal care begins with choosing a doctor. Parents should know that a competent obstetrician is one who is trained and experienced in his specialty, and a man who stands well with other doctors and has good hospital connections. Strangers in a city can get a list of obstetricians from the local medical society. The doctor's hospital connections determine the choice of a hospital; naturally, he wants his patients to go to a hospital familiar with his methods. He cannot take patients to a hospital where he is not a member of the medical staff. Most reputable hospitals are those approved by the Joint Commission on Accreditation of Hospitals.

Consulting a Doctor. Any one of the signs of pregnancy is reason for consulting a doctor. When one realizes what an important part the mother plays in the baby's development and future life, it is easy to understand why she needs the best advice and care from the time the baby begins its life within her body until it enters the outside world.

The doctor begins his care of the mother by taking a complete history of both the mother and the father, to learn about their past illnesses and family tendencies to diseases (such as diabetes, which may affect pregnancy). He is interested in learning whether a multiple pregnancy has occurred in either family and is particularly interested in any difficulties experienced by the mother during previous pregnancies or deliveries.

He makes a complete physical examination of the mother, which includes: examination of the gums, the teeth, the thyroid gland and the breasts; blood tests to discover anemia or syphilis; a urine examination to determine the condition of the kidneys, which affects the ability to eliminate wastes from the body; taking the blood pressure and the weight. All of these are important gauges of the possible complications of pregnancy. The doctor examines the pelvic organs and takes measurements to determine whether or not the bony passageway is wide enough to permit the baby to be born, which is especially important in a first pregnancy.

A blood typing should be done and Rh factor information secured (see Chap. 15). If the mother is Rh negative, the husband's blood should be examined to discover whether he is negative or positive. If he is negative also, there should be nothing to worry about. However, if the husband is Rh positive, the mother's blood should then be tested for antibodies; this test is repeated around the 30th week of pregnancy. If antibodies are present, further tests are done regularly so that the doctor can anticipate what treatment, if any, the baby might need immediately after it is born.

The doctor advises the expectant mother about her diet and other health habits. He tells her what to observe about herself between visits and what she must report immediately. Excessive vaginal discharge or loss of fluid is not normal; bleeding should be reported at once. Swelling of the hands or of the feet and the legs, blurring of vision or spots before the eyes, headaches and a decrease in the amount of urine voided are all danger signs.

Usually, the doctor sees the expectant mother every 3rd or 4th week for the first 7 months, every 2nd week about the 8th month and once a week during the last month. If it seems to be necessary, he will see her more often. He will ask for a specimen of urine each time, check her blood pressure and weight and examine the abdomen. Any other procedure will be determined by the individual patient's condition. A special treatment given to one pregnant woman may not be necessary for another.

The father should be encouraged to go with the mother on her first visit to the doctor. It might help both parents if he went occasionally, because then both of them will hear what the doctor has to say. Parenthood is a partnership in which both partners have an equal interest. Also, the mother will be helped to carry out her program if the father understands it too.

Most women adjust to the strain of pregnancy very well. Pregnancy is a normal process for which a woman's body is built. If the mother follows common-sense health rules, she ought to feel well, happy and relaxed. To keep herself this way, she must have the right food, enough rest, some exercise and some recreation.

Food for the Baby

The baby needs the same things that the mother does, and if her diet is well balanced, he will get these food essentials. She will need to increase some foods to take care of the baby's needs in addition to those of her own. If she fails to provide these nutrients, some of them (such as calcium) will be taken from her body tissues.

The Baby's Weight. At one time, people believed that women would have large babies if they overate. Studies show that heavy eating does not influence the size of the baby; this is controlled by heredity or by the length of pregnancy. (Overdue babies are likely to be large; premature babies are usually underweight.) However, overeating does put an extra strain on the mother's body.

The Mother's Diet. In recent years, much attention has been given to the diet of the pregnant mother. Quality rather than quantity is stressed, because it is known that she supplies the building materials for her baby as well as those needed for maintaining her own physiologic fitness. These are the foods required daily: 1 quart of milk; proteins supplied from meat, eggs and fish; whole grain or enriched bread or cereals; green, yellow and leafy vegetables; fruit (which should include citrus fruit); and butter or margerine to which vitamins A and D have been added. She should also have 6 to 8 glasses of fluid daily and extra vitamins as needed to correct any known vitamin deficiencies. If she is anemic, she may also need an extra amount of iron daily.

Changes in the mother's body during the early part of pregnancy may interfere with her appetite; therefore, special attention must be given to supplying her with proteins and vitamins. Rich foods, highly spiced foods, fried foods and hot breads are not desirable. In the latter months, several small meals taken daily rather than 3 large ones will probably help the mother to feel better.

Obstetricians advise that a gain of approximately 20 pounds above normal weight is to be expected. The weight should increase gradually from the 6th week after conception to the end of the full term of the pregnancy. This is the usual weight loss after the baby is born; therefore, it is not regarded as being permanent.

Excessive weight gain may also add strain to the muscles of the back and the legs. Serious complications tend to occur in patients who have had an excessive weight gain.

A certain amount of weight gain is normal. This table shows approximately how this gain is distributed:

The baby	7 lb.
The placenta	1½ lb.
Fluid around the baby	2 lb.
Increase in weight of the uterus	2½ lb.
Increase in weight of blood	3 lb.
Increase in weight of the breasts	2 lb.

General Health Practices

Elimination. The mother who usually has a bowel movement every day should continue to do so. However, a movement every day is not essential if this is not her normal habit and if she is not constipated. Her diet and regular habits should be such as to encourage good elimination. If she has trouble with constipation, she should not take laxatives or an enema without consulting her doctor. If a laxative is prescribed, it is usually a mild one, such as milk of magnesia.

Care of the Skin. The glands of the skin are more active than usual, so a daily warm bath is important. The mother must be careful about slipping or falling in the tub or the shower. There is no proof that a tub bath is harmful at any time during pregnancy.

Teeth. The modern mother who eats a balanced diet and sees her dentist regularly does not need to worry about tooth damage during pregnancy. It is important to have necessary dental work done and to remove sources of infection in the mouth.

Breasts. Good breast care during pregnancy prepares for nursing the baby. The breasts and the nipples should be washed every day with soap and water. Early in pregnancy the breasts begin to secrete a colorless liquid called *colostrum*, which may form crusts on the nipples. These crusts can be removed with cold cream. The mother should wear a brassière with wide straps that supports the breasts without causing pressure on the nipples.

Rest. Rest has been defined as "the ability to relax." The pregnant woman tires more easily, and she should have enough rest to prevent fatigue. (Authorities feel that it is better to *prevent* fatigue than to have to recover from overfatigue.) The mother knows how much rest she ordinarily requires, and she should plan to have more if she needs it. Going to bed earlier, getting up later, or taking an afternoon nap may help. Many women who are employed are able to work all through their pregnancy by planning extra rest. Short daytime periods of rest will be beneficial if the mother really relaxes, even if this involves only sitting in a comfortable chair. Women are able to carry on normal household activities without harm if they avoid heavy work and get additional rest.

Later in pregnancy, postural discomforts may make it difficult for the mother to sleep. Simple measures, such as additional pillows at the back, or a pillow supporting the weight of the abdomen while the mother lies on her side, will usually relieve these minor problems.

Exercise. Exercise improves the circulation, the appetite and the digestion; it also aids elimination and makes the mother sleep better. Doctors feel that the customary exercises of the mother may be continued, but strenuous exercise of any kind should be avoided. Mother can swim or play golf in the early months of her pregnancy; later, exercise will have to be limited as she becomes less agile and begins to tire more easily. Walking in the sunshine is a pleasant way to get both fresh air and exercise. A busy housewife will not need to be as concerned about getting enough exercise as her less active sister, but she still needs diversion to relieve normal tensions and to encourage relaxation. Heavy lifting is forbidden at any time. She should be especially careful at the times when her menstrual period would normally occur.

Posture. Because the weight of the pregnant uterus is "all in front," the mother tends to lean or tilt backward in order to maintain her balance, just as we all would do if, for instance, we carried a heavy bag of groceries. This customary posture of pregnancy is beneficial to those who ordinarily have poor posture. However, the change in body alignment causes a strain on back and leg muscles. This factor, plus the natural softening of the pelvic joints, causes many of the pains of the back, the legs and the feet which are common in late pregnancy. Rib strains and swelling of the ankles and the feet also occur frequently. A special maternity corset which helps to lift the abdomen up and in, while holding the back flat, will help some women by providing the necessary body support.

Clothing. Maternity clothing today can be most attractive and fashionable, as well as comfortable and nonconstricting. Dresses which hang loosely from the shoulder are made in becoming styles and beautiful materials. Other 2-piece fashions have expandable waistbands and a stretch section in the front of the skirt. Even amateur sewers can make maternity dresses in their own favorite colors and fashion which is an aid to the budget; these clothes do not require the usual fitting expertness and can be very successful. A becoming hair style and pretty clothes are good morale boosters at this time.

The support given by an appropriate girdle and a well-fitting brassière cannot be overemphasized. Garters should be attached to the girdle, or a special maternity garter belt should be used; round garters constrict the blood supply and add to the development of varicose veins. High heels contribute to the imbalance of the body—a fashionable style from the many available walking shoes will prevent the mother from falling.

Travel. Most women who drive continue to do so during pregnancy, at least until the last months when driving becomes too uncomfortable. (Baby, mother and steering wheel cannot occupy the same space at the same time.)

Long trips are exhausting for anyone, but since American families are so much on the move, it frequently becomes necessary for the pregnant mother to travel also. Travel by air or train is recommended for long, tiring trips. If the mother is to travel by car, she should plan to stop every 50 miles to stretch, relax and walk around: this prevents circulatory problems such as phlebitis. The Armed Forces have specific regulations concerning travel for the pregnant wives of men in the service.

It is a good idea for the expectant mother to consult her obstetrician about her travel plans, since there are special conditions and special times in pregnancy which make traveling unwise.

Stimulants. A moderate amount of coffee or tea taken in a day is harmless. Moderate smoking is allowed, although there are studies which indicate that there is a causal relationship between smoking and premature births. An occasional cocktail will do no harm. Some pregnant women have food cravings, such as a longing for highly seasoned foods or pickles. There is no reason why mothers should not have the foods they crave, if these foods do not upset them or increase their weight too much.

Employment. Many employed women continue to work during pregnancy; this is permissible within limits, if the expectant mother likes her work, and if her health or the baby's health is not endangered. The Women's Bureau of the United States Department of Labor, and the Children's Bureau of the United States Department of Health, Education, and Welfare have recommended standards for maternity care and the employment of mothers. In part, these recommendations specify an 8-hour day, with rest periods morning and afternoon; a 40-hour week; at least 6 weeks' leave before delivery and 2 months' leave after delivery. They rule out work involving heavy lifting, operating dangerous machines, continuous standing, or working with toxic substances.

Marital Relations. Sexual intercourse is not harmful up to the last 6 weeks of pregnancy; it should not be risked after that period because of the danger of infection. Pregnancy diminishes sexual desire in some women, and a mutual understanding of this physiologic fact by both husband and wife may eliminate the possibility of misundertsandings. Some physicians feel that sexual relations are undesirable during the first 3 months of pregnancy, and also at the times during the month when menstruation would normally occur. There is an increased danger of a spontaneous abortion (loss of the embryo or fetus) taking place at these times.

Minor Discomforts of Pregnancy

Although many women who are pregnant have "never felt better," there are others who do not enjoy such optimum health. Even in normal pregnancies many common complaints appear: these are the so-called minor discomforts of pregnancy. These disorders are not minor in the sense that they do not cause true discomfort but rather because they are not serious and usually terminate during or with the pregnancy.

Some of these discomforts are so common that they are classed as the symptoms of pregnancy, which have been discussed—frequent urination, caused by the pressure of the uterus on the bladder, during the early and the late months of pregnancy; and the occasional painful tenderness and tingling breast sensations which are temporary.

Morning Sickness. Morning sickness is the most common symptom and discomfort of early pregnancy. For many years it was thought that this mild nausea and vomiting was usually an emotional reaction, an unconscious response to the many changes which pregnancy and a new baby bring. However, it is now thought that there is a general reduction in stimuli to the smooth muscles accompanied by diminished gastric motility. The symptoms may be caused by physiologic changes normal to pregnancy.

Although it is called "morning" sickness, the nausea and the vomiting may occur at any time of the day, but only in a small percentage of women does it persist throughout the day. Fre-

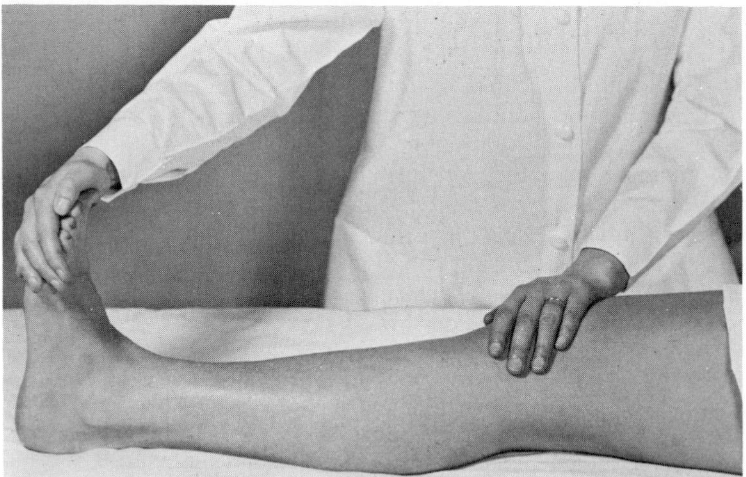

FIG. 195. The nurse is helping the patient during a leg cramp, forcing the toes upward while putting pressure on the knee to straighten the leg. (Fitzpatrick, E., and Eastman, N. J.: Zabriskie's Obstetrics for Nurses, ed. 10, p. 171, Philadelphia, Lippincott, 1960)

quent small meals, as well as dry carbohydrate foods taken before rising, often prove to be helpful, but what helps one person may not help another. There are also medications safe to use during pregnancy which control nausea and vomiting. This discomfort is usually limited to the first 3 months of pregnancy.

Constipation. Constipation and flatulence are not unusual in pregnancy. They are thought to be due to impaired intestinal peristalsis. These disagreeable problems are usually controlled by the diet and the mild laxatives which are prescribed by the doctor.

Shortness of Breath. Dyspnea (difficult breathing) or shortness of breath is caused by the pressure of the baby on the diaphragm. It is usually troublesome only in the latter weeks of pregnancy, and it is relieved spontaneously as the baby settles into the pelvis (*lightening*) or by delivery. It is naturally aggravated when the mother tries to lie down; she will rest and sleep much more comfortably if she is supported and elevated by pillows at her back.

Leg Cramps. Cramping pains in the calf of the leg are astonishingly painful. The general belief is that these are caused by accumulating an excessive amount of phosphorus in the body. Calcium lactate or calcium gluconate, taken before meals, or vitamin B will provide relief and prevent their recurrence. Immediate relief from cramps may be obtained by forcing the toes upward and by creating pressure on the knee to straighten the leg (Fig. 195).

Edema. Fluids may collect in the body toward the end of pregnancy, especially in the feet and the legs; elevating the legs will usually give some relief. Less salt in the diet is recommended, since salt tends to hold fluids in the body. If edema is apparent all over the body, it may be a symptom of toxemia, and the doctor should be notified at once. (See p. 655.)

Vaginal Discharge. In addition to the natural increase in secretions from the vaginal and the cervical glands during pregnancy, certain infectious organisms (Trichomonas vaginalis is one) or an eroded cervix may be the cause of vaginal discharge. The doctor may prescribe medicated vaginal douches except during the last month of pregnancy, when douches are never given.

Gingivitis. Spongy, swollen and sometimes bleeding gums may appear, due to a deficiency in ascorbic acid in the diet. The condition improves when large amounts of ascorbic acid are given. An astringent mouthwash makes the mouth feel better.

Other Discomforts. Faintness or dizziness, nosebleed and heartburn are other comparatively minor difficulties that cause discomfort during pregnancy. Backache due to postural changes and softening of the pelvic joints is another. Treatment of these disturbances is the same during pregnancy as at any other time.

Varicose Veins. Varicose veins may develop in the later months of pregnancy; they usually appear in the legs but may also develop in the groin or in the vulva. The tendency to develop varicosities is familial, and the increased intra-abdominal pressure from the enlarged uterus, as well as any prolonged standing, hastens their development. The patient should not wear round garters or tight clothing that will interfere with circulation; she should avoid being on her feet for any considerable length of time. Elevating her legs against the wall when she goes to bed will help to drain the blood back from her legs; sometimes an Ace bandage is applied before she gets up in the morning or she can wear nylon elastic stockings to make her more comfortable. New support-type stockings are attractively sheer.

Hemorrhoids. The hemorrhoidal veins in the rectum sometimes become congested (varicosed) and may be very painful. This condition is usually a result of constipation and straining to evacuate the bowels, as well as the uterine pressure interfering with the flow of venous blood. Regular bowel habits will help to prevent hemorrhoids; if this condition develops, cold saline compresses or Sitz baths will bring relief from pain. Sometimes the doctor prescribes suppositories or an analgesic ointment.

PREPARING FOR PARENTHOOD

The idea of family-centered care can achieve its fulfillment in the preparation for parenthood. Contemporary social influences have permitted the recognition that an understanding and affectionate husband contributes tremendously to the success of making pregnancy a shared foundation in the building of family life.

Pregnancy should provide a happy experience for the prospective parents; their happiness and affection for each other should enable them to share with joy the responsibilities they will assume. But pregnancy may arouse a new set of emotions, especially in the wife. If she wants a baby, she is overjoyed at first. Then she begins to think of the months ahead, the ordeal of having the baby, and the responsibility that she faces later. She may think that perhaps the baby will interfere with her life with her husband. Baby sitters are expensive; and besides, could she trust her baby to strangers? She feels guilty because she does not seem to be filled with mother love; she longs only to eat a good breakfast without losing it immediately. There is nothing abnormal about these emotions—undoubtedly, she felt low at times before she was pregnant. When prospective parents share the experience of pregnancy, the husband understands what is happening: he can reassure his wife. On the other hand, on days when the coming responsibilities may look overwhelming to the husband, the understanding wife will provide the reassurance that he may need in their joint adventure.

When Pregnancy Brings Problems. Some parents may look upon pregnancy as a disaster, as a discussion of these thumbnail sketches will illustrate:

Mrs. Crane is dismayed to find that she is pregnant. Her husband has just told her that he wants a divorce, and she already has a child.

Mrs. Heath is 37 years old—she was married at 35 and is overjoyed to find that she is pregnant. But Mr. Heath is worried. He has been told that it is dangerous for a woman to have her first baby at that age.

The Martins are worried about money. They already have 4 children, and Mr. Martin has just gone into a new business.

Mrs. Norris had to stay in bed for 3 months before David was born; he was born prematurely, and she had to leave him in the hospital for 6 weeks. Both Mr. and Mrs. Norris are afraid that this will happen again; they still cannot believe that 3-year old David is really a healthy little boy.

The young Careys planned to wait until they had their own home before they had a baby. They now live in a small apartment which is crowded for two.

Problems such as these can have tragic results, and they involve some of the major social problems of our day. However, education on family living, marriage and sex hygiene will hopefully have strong positive effects on the attitudes and the actions of the families of the future. Emphasis on education is not new in preparation for parenthood. The Maternity Center Association in New York City has been conducting mothers' classes since the early

1920's, and in 1938 it added classes for fathers, too. Classes for expectant families are now available in many communities.

MOTHERS' CLASSES. In these classes, mothers learn about the process of pregnancy. They learn how to take care of themselves and what to prepare for the baby; how to bathe a baby and make a formula. The importance of keeping a happy home both before and after the baby comes is explained. Mothers ask questions and get advice. (When agencies have many applicants for these classes, they try to group people with similar backgrounds.) This kind of teaching reinforces the doctor's instructions; mothers are urged to keep in close touch with their doctor.

FATHERS' CLASSES. Fathers learn how to help their wives; how to choose a doctor and a hospital; how to enjoy planning for the baby. They learn how the baby grows month by month; they learn the signs of labor and how the baby is born. They practice changing, bathing and feeding a baby. These classes are intended to make a father feel that he is much more than a helpless outsider, who can only stand by and worry about his wife.

Natural Childbirth

Within the past 2 decades, Dr. Grantley Dick Read, an English obstetrician, has become widely known for his teachings on "natural childbirth." Dr. Read felt that the fears of the unknown processes of labor made the mother tense. This fear-caused tension made the mother resist the muscular forces of normal labor, which prolonged the labor, causing pain.

His program of educating the expectant mother to "childbirth without fear" led to a conclusion of *painless childbirth*; he delivered many of his patients without medication during labor and without anesthesia during delivery.

Dr. Read found many followers in this country. Natural childbirth classes are taught in clinics, physicians' offices and hospitals across the nation.

Information is presented in a general attitude to eliminate fear. The anatomy and the physiology of childbearing is presented; the parents learn the process and the progress of labor and delivery, and how to cooperate with the natural process. The expectant mother is taught exercises which help to develop general muscle tone but particularly strengthen and control the muscles used in labor and delivery. Special emphasis is placed on breathing technics, which will help the mother to relax as well as to cooperate with the muscular activities involved in labor and delivery.

Many doctors feel that this type of education accomplishes many good aims. It is recognized that fear aggravates pain in any situation; therefore, to prevent or eliminate fear through education is ideal. The patients are more relaxed and cooperative; labor time is often shortened. However, many doctors regret and deplore the trend away from the medical advances which have added so much to the safety and the comfort of obstetric patients. Many doctors think that the emphasis has been distorted: the patient feels that she "does not do well" and is left discouraged, if after all her diligent and enthusiastic preparations she "fails" and requires medications to relieve the sometimes dismaying discomforts of labor. However, many patients realize that what is natural is not necessarily painless; that the measure of the success should be the patient's willingness and ability to cooperate with the normal physiologic processes of childbirth, and not merely her ability to endure the process without medication or anesthesia.

The "natural childbirth" philosophy has at present reached a happy middle-of-the-road approach. The value of the classes to educate the expectant parents is clearly accepted, and improving the tone of muscles used in labor is of benefit before, during and after delivery. Relaxing technics help the expectant mother to rest between the intervals of the hard work of labor. Nonetheless, the valued use of medications and methods of anesthesia which benefit both mother and infant are also clearly accepted. The members of the medical and nursing team recognize the contribution that they must make—the individualized care, and the attention and the support of the patient by each doctor and nurse adds greatly to the relaxation, peace of mind and sense of accomplishment of the mother.

The Home Nursery

Further preparations for parenthood involve the fun and the expense of getting "baby things"—clothes and equipment. New materials and products make *baby shopping* a pleasure. Such things as the stretch materials permit a much longer use of baby garments—babies grow rapidly! The soft washable terry cloth, and the durable but light-weight plastics used in baby equipment make mother's work easier.

The mother usually has the baby's things all ready for him when she takes him home from the hospital. The father also can help to get ready for the baby. He may build a bath cabinet or paint a chest for the baby's clothes. He can help to get the room ready. In the following discussion we will mention the equipment and the clothes that the baby will need. It is not intended to be a luxury list, but it will provide everything that the mother needs to take care of the baby safely and easily.

The Baby's Clothes (Layette). The baby's clothes should be comfortable and designed to keep him clean, safe and happy. They should be easy to wash, have no cumbersome frills and be easy to put on and take off. They should be soft, light, porous, warm and durable. They should also allow for his growth and let him move freely. The baby's first clothes must necessarily suit the time of the year and the mother's pocketbook.

DIAPERS. Diaper services are available in many cities; they provide a week's supply of sterilized, packaged diapers, with a container for the soiled ones which they will collect and launder. There are many types of diapers available, some of which are especially sized for the smaller baby, and some which stretch to fit all sizes. Varieties of diapers come prefolded, have snap attachments so that pins are not required or are made of pretty printed material. Disposable diapers are available which are particularly convenient for visiting or for travel. If parents are not planning to use a diaper service, a minimum of 4 dozen diapers is necessary.

SHIRTS. Four to 6 soft knit shirts which open in the front or are styled to stretch easily over the baby's head should be ample.

GOWNS. Five or 6 gowns, having open fronts and drawstrings in the cuffs and in the bottom hem, should be sufficient. If made of cotton knit or batiste, they can double for dresses while the baby is small.

SWEATERS. A soft knit sweater made of washable yarn is needed to provide extra warmth when the baby is out of doors. The color choice is practically unending.

RECEIVING BLANKETS. Several light-weight cotton flannel squares will be needed to wrap the baby when he is taken from his crib; these are also practical as crib covers while the baby is small.

BUNTING. A square of soft warm material, having one corner gathered into a hood for the baby's head, furnishes protection out of doors in cold weather; it can also be used as a crib blanket. There are also small sacks of soft warm materials made with hoods or bonnets which are handy for small babies.

WATERPROOF PANTS. Most protective pants today are made of different types of plastic. Some are gaily colored, and others are covered with cloth attractively ruffled for little girls. These are a great help to the mother. If the skin of some infants is too sensitive, these pants may cause soreness or rashes, in which case other soft padding may be used under the baby as a soaker.

BIBS. It is convenient to have at least 4 bibs. These bibs, made of plastic or terry cloth (sometimes a combination of both), save both mother's and baby's clothes.

Nursery Equipment. BED. A bassinet is handy for the small infant because it makes transportation easy. However, after 2 or 3 months, the baby will have grown enough to need a crib. Cribs should have the bars made close enough together so that the baby cannot get his head wedged between them. There are also durable types of cribs with sides made of screening.

Mattresses for cribs should be flat and firm. Almost all mattresses are covered by waterproof material, but the use of a waterproof sheeting which can be washed frequently will prevent the mattress from being stained or smelling of urine. Lightweight plastic bags such as those used to cover dry cleaned garments should *never* be used near the baby, since he can easily become entangled in this loose plastic and suffocate.

Ordinary pillowcases make acceptable sheets for a bassinet. Four sheets are sufficient for the crib; the knit variety is easy to put on and stays neat. Blankets should be light in weight and suitable for the season. Babies do not need pillows, especially small babies who cannot move their head.

CHEST. A small chest of drawers provides a convenient, clean place for the baby's things, which should be kept apart from household linen and supplies.

BATHTUB. A lightweight plastic tub which is easy to clean and to store is safe for bathing the baby; it should be placed on a sturdy table at a convenient height. A bathinette can also be used; it folds away or serves as a dressing table when not being used for bathing.

DIAPER CONTAINER. A covered pail, preferably operated by a foot pedal, is satisfactory as a diaper container. If a diaper service is used, it will provide this necessary item.

BATH TRAY. This tray is very useful and will keep in one place the supplies used each day. The tray can be purchased complete with supplies, or the mother can organize her own favorite brands on a container; an attractive low cake pan does very well. Included on the tray should be such items as cotton balls and swabs, soap, lotion or oil, and safety pins. (If the safety pins are stuck into a cake of soap, you will find them all in one place and much easier to use.)

RECTAL THERMOMETER. The mother should be able to take the baby's temperature if and when the need arises. If she does not know how, the pediatrician or his office nurse will be glad to teach her.

FEEDING EQUIPMENT. Even those mothers who breast feed their babies need nursing bottles and extra nipples for giving the baby water, fruit juice, or an occasional supplemental formula. Nursing bottles are available in 4- and 8-ounce sizes; the smaller size is convenient for small amounts of juice. Different manufacturers offer different-shaped bottles, as well as different forms of nipples. Glass bottles are easy to clean and sterilize; plastic bottles do not break, but they bend and get out of shape from continuously warming the formula. The mother will need at least 8 bottles for the bottle-fed baby.

There are several manufacturers of disposable milk containers. One popular product consists of a plastic sack which holds the formula and fits into a more rigid container which is easy for the mother to hold. Preprepared formulas in throw-away containers are also available.

STERILIZER. A sterilizer which sterilizes the formula after it is poured into the bottles saves much effort. Sterilizers usually come complete with rack and bottles. You can improvise this arrangement by using a deep pan large enough to hold a rack or a trivet to hold 6 or 8 bottles.

BOTTLE WARMER. Small electric bottle warmers are inexpensive and very convenient. They are particularly nice if you feed the baby in his bedroom at night. There are models which attach to the cigaret lighter in a car; these are ideal for traveling. However, many mothers simply heat the bottle in a pan of water.

PREGNANCY COMPLICATIONS

Although pregnancy is considered to be a normal physiologic process, there are certain major complications which may very seriously affect the baby or the mother. Some of the common major disturbances are the following:

Hyperemesis gravidarum
Toxemias
Hemorrhagic complications
Blood groups and the Rh factor
Coincidental diseases and pregnancy

Hyperemesis Gravidarum

This disturbance is usually connected with morning sickness, in the early months of pregnancy when the processes of digestion and elimination are slowed. If vomiting persists to the point where there is an excessive loss of weight, dehydration and acetone in the urine, it is called *pernicious vomiting* or *hyperemesis gravidarum*. The cause of this is unknown: the disseminations of toxins into the mother's bloodstream, the endocrine and the metabolic changes of normal gestation, and diminished gastrointestinal motility are all considered as being basic factors. Some doctors feel that it is due in a large measure to a neurosis.

If the condition becomes severe, hospitalization is required. The patient is given intravenous fluids, glucose and vitamins. Sedatives are prescribed for the general rest of the patient, which is usually badly needed. Visitors are restricted. After 24 hours, dry foods in small quantities are tried. If no vomiting occurs, the diet is gradually increased.

Fortunately, fewer patients are being hospitalized for this serious complication. Drugs that control vomiting have been found to be both safe and effective (Dramamine, Compazine, Tigan), and they relieve the possibility of the development of hyperemesis in a high percentage of patients.

Toxemia

In April, 1952, the American Committee on Maternal Welfare established the following definition of toxemia:

> The toxemias of pregnancy are disorders encountered during gestation or early in the puerperium, which are characterized by one or more of the following signs: hypertension, edema, albuminuria and, in severe cases, convulsions and coma.

Toxemia is one of the 3 major causes of maternal deaths (totaling approximately 1,000 each year in the United States) and causes at least 30,000 stillbirths and deaths in newborns yearly, primarily through prematurity. Toxemia is common, occurring in at least 1 out of every 20 pregnancies. It develops most frequently in the last 2 or 3 months of pregnancy, and it is likely to occur in young women who are in their first pregnancy.

Two classifications of toxemia are *preeclampsia* and *eclampsia.* In preeclampsia, the patient who previously has shown normal progress in pregnancy develops one or more of the symptoms. In eclampsia the patient also has convulsions.

Although the symptoms of preeclampsia most often allow the doctor to intercept it early and prevent further symptoms, it sometimes develops explosively between visits—perhaps the day after an examination. Because of this, each expectant mother should know that she should report any of the following symptoms to her doctor immediately:

Sudden gain in weight
Edema of the fingers, the face, the legs or the feet
Spots before the eyes or blurring of vision
Severe unremitting headache
Persistent vomiting
Decrease in the urinary output

Most patients with preeclampsia respond to treatment. Very few develop eclampsia. Because eclampsia is largely a preventable condition, the preventive aspect of obstetric nursing —the importance of keen, accurate observation and reporting—must be recognized by the responsible obstetric nurse.

When the patient develops eclampsia, her preeclamptic symptoms become more exaggerated and severe, and she develops convulsions. The convulsions may occur before labor begins, during labor, or after the baby is born. After a convulsion the patient may become conscious in a few minutes, or she may remain in a coma for several hours or days. Convulsions may recur in either instance. Even if the patients are awake after convulsions, they are sometimes confused, and they may present serious nursing problems.

Eclampsia is one of the most severe complications of pregnancy. The fetal mortality from eclampsia is almost 25 per cent, and the maternal mortality ranges from 5 to 15 per cent. As the condition progresses, the urinary output lessens and albumin in the urine may increase. The pulse rate becomes very rapid, and the systolic blood pressure may hover around 200. Convulsions continue, and the coma deepens. The slushy respirations of edema of the lungs can be heard, and the prognosis is poor.

As can be seen from statistics, most patients with eclampsia survive. However, 30 to 50 per cent show symptoms of toxemia in further pregnancies. Some patients are maimed by chronic hypertension. Since the cause of eclampsia is unknown, the best treatment is prevention. The aim in the treatment is to control preeclampsia and to prevent the development of eclampsia with its convulsions which bring severe problems to both the mother and the baby. Sedatives may be prescribed to encourage rest and to limit activity. A diet which is low in salt is of prime importance. The sodium ion from salt is retained in the tissues and causes the retention of fluid which shows in the weight gain and the edema of the mother. Table salt is not used at all, and foods which are high in salt content, such as canned soups, are eliminated from the diet to reduce the edema. A diuretic (to increase urinary output) and antihypertensive medications (to reduce blood pressure) are usually ordered to control the symptoms.

If the symptoms continue and the edema, the hypertension and the albuminuria remain pronounced, the patient is hospitalized. The same treatment is continued, and complete bed rest is prescribed. Closer observations to help safeguard the mother and the baby are facilitated: the patient is weighed daily; the intake and the output of fluids are recorded; urine is tested daily for albumin; the blood pressure is taken at close intervals; and the fetal heart sounds are watched closely.

In severe preeclampsia, heavier sedation is given to prevent convulsions. The patient is kept drowsy and sleepy. The room should be darkened, quiet and comfortable. Needless visits to the room and other stimuli—loud noises and bright lights—are controlled. Magnesium sulfate (I.M.) is regarded as a drug specifically used for toxemia, since it is a vasodilator, a diuretic and also a central nervous system depressant which prevents convulsions. The tranquilizing and hypotensive drugs are also effective. Preeclampsia and eclampsia develop only in pregnancy; therefore, it would seem to be logical that terminating the pregnancy would be the cure. However, cesarean sections are seldom performed for this complication of pregnancy, since experience has shown that this results in such a high mortality rate for the mother. The best therapy seems to be the conservative: to control the symptoms as much as possible and either allow labor to start normally or to initiate it when the safety of the mother and the baby permits.

Abortion

If a fetus is discharged from the uterus before it is capable of carrying on its own life, the lay person usually refers to it as a miscarriage. Medically, the term *abortion* is used to describe this termination of pregnancy before the fetus is viable, that is, before he is able to survive outside the uterus. Generally speaking, this is considered to be before the 20th week of pregnancy.

Nurses will do well to realize that the public generally associates criminal activities with the word "abortion." It has a sordid connotation for the average person. If the patient does not understand that "abortion" is the common medical term, that "miscarriage" is seldom if ever used, she may feel that the nurses and other staff think she has induced the loss of her pregnancy. She may feel very guilty when she has no reason to do so. This is another example where a few seconds of the nurses' time spent in explanation may alleviate a great deal of misunderstanding.

There are a number of common terms used to describe various causes or phases of abortion:

A *threatened abortion* is one in which the mother, early in pregnancy, has bleeding or spotting. She may also have mild cramps. The pregnancy may be saved.

An *inevitable abortion* is one in which the loss of the pregnancy cannot be prevented. Bleeding is heavier, and the cervix is dilated.

An *incomplete abortion* is one in which part of the products of pregnancy are retained and not discarded from the uterus. This usually causes intensive bleeding and usually is treated by dilatation and curettage (scraping the uterus).

Missed abortions are those in which the fetus has died but has not been expelled from the uterus. The dead fetus is usually expelled spontaneously within a few weeks.

Habitual abortion is a problem condition in which a mother spontaneously loses several successive pregnancies. This mother, quite naturally, is usually very upset and depressed.

A *therapeutic abortion* is the termination of a

pregnancy by a physician. In the United States it is legally permitted only in instances where the mother's life is in danger. There are other countries where therapeutic abortions are legally permitted, but in some countries, they are forbidden under any circumstances. Certain religions declare therapeutic abortions to be contrary to the natural law; Catholic hospitals do not permit them to be performed.

A *criminal abortion* is the intervention in pregnancy without medical or legal justification.

Authorities estimate that approximately 1 out of every 10 pregnancies ends in a *spontaneous abortion* (one in which the process starts of its own accord through natural causes). The cause of this problem, so tragic and distressing to the parents, is presently being investigated. There is evidence supporting the theory that this is nature's method of eliminating pregnancies which would have produced abnormal babies. Some of the babies are unable to survive with their deformities. Diseases and infections sometimes lead to abortions. Hormonal problems and disorders of the reproductive tract may also be contributing factors.

The treatment in threatened abortions depends on the severity of the symptoms. If the bleeding is slight, the patient is put to bed for 48 to 72 hours; if the bleeding disappears, she may undertake limited activities. Sexual relations should not be resumed for 2 weeks. If uterine contractions occur, the prognosis is more guarded. Incomplete abortions with heavy bleeding are treated by curettage or surgical removal of the retained tissues from the uterus. If evidence of infection is present (fever, odorous discharge), strict precautions to prevent the spread to others must be carried out. If the abortion is complete, the same care is given that would routinely be given a patient following delivery. The patient is observed closely for signs of hemorrhage; her blood pressure is checked to see that it remains stable; pallor is observed; her pulse is watched for the weak rapidity which is a sign of shock. The nurse can clearly understand the alarm, the stress and the fright of the patient in these circumstances, and she should make all possible efforts to reassure and comfort her. However, if the abortion has occurred, and the patient has been treated to the degree necessary for her safety, the presence of her husband is usually of more comfort than the presence of the nurse. Losing a baby, as well as having one, is a family affair.

Placenta Previa

When the placenta lies low enough in the uterus to cover the internal opening of the cervix either partially or totally, the condition is called *placenta previa. Marginal placenta* is the attachment of the placenta next to the cervix but not covering it. Painless vaginal bleeding during the later months of pregnancy is the primary symptom of this complication. The treatment is usually delivery by cesarean section for complete or partial placenta previa. When possible, bleeding from marginal placenta is treated by the rupture of the membranes, which allows the presenting part to exert pressure on the placenta against the lower uterine segment, thereby slowing or stopping the hemorrhage by compression.

The dangers of placenta previa are bleeding, shock and infection. Since the open blood vessels are low and close to the cervix, infection may develop from microorganisms in the vaginal canal. Rectal and vaginal examinations are done only in the operating or delivery rooms with personnel ready to proceed with emergency surgery if necessary. Since bleeding may be profuse, the use of blood transfusions proves to be a life-saving measure. Again, the constant observation by the knowledgeable obstetric nurse may prevent the development of shock.

By modern surgical methods as well as the use of blood transfusions, the maternal mortality from placenta previa has dropped tremendously; however, it is still regarded as a serious complication. Because the separation of the placenta from the uterine wall reduces or eliminates the infant's oxygen supply, the prognosis for the baby is considered fair to poor.

Abruptio Placenta

Abruptio placenta is a grave complication of later pregnancy in which the placenta separates abruptly from its attachment to the uterine wall. The bleeding may be visible, or it may be concealed because it is higher and contained within the uterus. In most cases, the patient has severe pain. The uterus becomes extremely firm and tender. Shock is often present and may seem to be out of proportion, since the bleeding is not obvious.

Of prime importance in cases of abruptio placenta is the treatment of shock; blood loss must be replaced before proceeding with cesarean section, which is almost invariably necessary. Occasionally, it is necessary to perform a hysterectomy to control the bleeding.

The treatment of abruptio placenta has been developed to the point where it is no longer fatal to most mothers. However, the outlook for the baby's survival depends on the severity of the separation and the degree to which his oxygen supply has been affected.

Ectopic Pregnancy

The word *ectopic* means "outside" or "out of place"; therefore, an *ectopic pregnancy* is one which is attached outside the uterus. Ectopic pregnancies occur most frequently in the fallopian tubes. The symptoms begin with spotting or bleeding 2 or 3 weeks after a missed menstrual period. Often there is accompanying pain which may be quite severe. A tubal pregnancy always requires surgical removal. Very rarely, an abdominal or ovarian pregnancy is encountered.

Hydatidiform Mole

Hydatidiform mole is a condition in which certain products of conception degenerate and form grapelike clusters of vesicles. This is at first a normal pregnancy, but usually with the formation of the mole there is no fetus present. The uterus enlarges more rapidly than usual; the mother has episodes of spotting and bleeding, and frequently she is very nauseated and feels miserable. When the diagnosis becomes certain, the uterus is usually emptied by careful dilatation of the cervix and removal of the hydatidiform mole. The patient receives extensive follow-up examinations, because although the mole itself is benign, it may be the forerunner of a malignant development.

50

CARE DURING LABOR, DELIVERY AND THE PUERPERIUM

The Bible tells us that "A woman when she is in travail hath sorrow, because her hour is come" (John 16:21), but for many expectant mothers labor is a welcome process. They recognize various safeguards of modern medicine as well as its provisions for comfort and accept labor as a natural function—the healthful termination of pregnancy.

A woman who is having her first pregnancy is called a *primigravada.* If she has had one previous pregnancy which resulted in a viable child (one which was *capable* of living outside of the uterus), she is called a *primipara,* regardless of whether the child was living at birth. A woman who has had 2 or more such pregnancies is called a *multipara.*

LABOR

Signs of Approaching Labor

During pregnancy the muscles of the uterus have been getting ready for their work. They have been tightening and relaxing at intervals, a process known as *contraction.* The contractions during pregnancy are usually painless, and frequently the mother is unaware of their occurring. As labor approaches, they may become uncomfortable; these contractions are called *false labor.*

Another indication of approaching labor is the settling of the baby lower into the pelvis. This dropping of the baby is called *lightening,* and it is usually more apparent in a first pregnancy. The mother may suddenly discover that it is much easier to breathe.

Uterine Contractions. True labor is characterized by rhythmic contractions of the uterine muscles. This helps to open the soft cervix and to push the baby through to the outside. The contractions occur at fairly regular intervals between 5 to 15 minutes apart, and they usually last 30 seconds or longer. The intervals between them gradually decrease, and the *show* appears. This is a pinkish or bloody mucous discharge which indicates normal changes in the cervix.

The baby lies in a membranous sac surrounded by amniotic fluid. This is called the *bag of waters.* These membranes may rupture any time during the labor. Contrary to old wives' tales, the rupturing of the membranes prior to the onset of labor, or early during the labor, does not necessarily indicate a long or difficult labor. In fact, the doctor sometimes ruptures these membranes artificially in order to begin the labor process.

Stages of Labor

The First Stage of Labor. Labor is nature's provision for enabling the baby to be born. He must be pushed out of his protected life in the uterus, down the bony passage of the pelvis, through the cervix, through the birth canal and out into the world. The bag of waters must break, and the cervix must open before the baby can be born. The muscles of the uterus contract to supply the pressure which stretches or dilates the cervix in the first stage of labor. For a primigravada this phase usually takes from 8 to 16 hours. The uterine contractions are involuntary, and the mother can do nothing to hurry or to control them.

Some mothers grow discouraged during this first stage of labor, as it may seem long and tedious. The process is slow in order to keep the tissues from tearing as the muscles alternately contract and relax. Labors are shorter for most multiparas, because the tissues are less resistant and stretch more easily.

The Second Stage of Labor. When the cervix is fully stretched, the second stage of labor begins. The abdominal muscles and the diaphragm join the uterine muscles to push the baby out. This is where the mother is able to help—she takes a deep breath and holds it, and then pushes with each contraction. She begins to feel the baby moving down a little farther each time, then slipping back a little as the muscles relax between contractions. If she relaxes too, she can work better when the next contraction comes. It is hard work, but it is deeply satisfying because she is accomplishing it herself, going through with a job that no one else can do. In most cases this stage takes from 1½ to 2 hours for a first baby; second and later babies take anywhere from 5 minutes to 1½ hours. The second stage of labor ends when the baby is born.

Very often during the second stage of labor, the doctor makes an incision in the perineum, which is called an *episiotomy*. This allows the infant to be delivered more easily by enlarging the vaginal opening. It helps to preserve the structure and the strength of the perineal muscles and prevents the occurrence of a jagged laceration, which would be difficult to repair.

The Third Stage of Labor. The third stage begins immediately following the birth of the baby and ends when the placenta and the membranes are expelled. This may take anywhere from 1 minute to 1 hour. The placenta is attached to the uterine wall; but after the baby is born, the uterine muscles contract and expel it. The doctor or the nurse keeps a hand firmly over the empty uterus until it feels firm and hard; this means that the muscles and the blood vessels are contracted and that there is less danger of hemorrhage.

In the Labor Room

Hospital procedures for the admission of patients in labor do not vary greatly, since the information needed and the care of the mother are essentially the same everywhere. The nurse asks the expected date of delivery, because if the baby is premature, special precautions are taken, and special equipment is readied. She also asks how close the contractions are and how long they last, and if the patient has noticed any bleeding. Then she can determine the approximate progress of the patient in labor. If the patient is to have a general anesthetic, the anesthetist will want to know when she last ate.

The mother is given an enema to empty the rectum of fecal material. (The doctor makes rectal examinations throughout labor.) The enema also stimulates uterine contractions. The pubic hair is shaved off, and the area around the vaginal opening is washed with sterile soap and water. A urine specimen is sent to the laboratory. The doctor examines the mother's heart, lungs and abdomen and listens to the baby's heart to see if all is normal. He takes the mother's blood pressure because of the ever-present hazard of toxemia. He makes a rectal examination to see how far labor has progressed. A vaginal examination is not done unless it is absolutely necessary, because of the danger of infecting the birth canal.

The Nurse in the Labor Room. You may be asked to stay with the patient during labor. Your job will be to keep her comfortable and to observe her closely for any symptoms of complications which will affect either her or the baby. The waiting period for the mother should be made as pleasant as possible. Many hospitals feel that having a baby is a family affair, and they encourage the father to be with the mother as much as possible during the early part of labor. However, the nurse in the labor room has specific duties to perform for specific purposes. She listens to fetal heart tones at regular and frequent intervals. (The

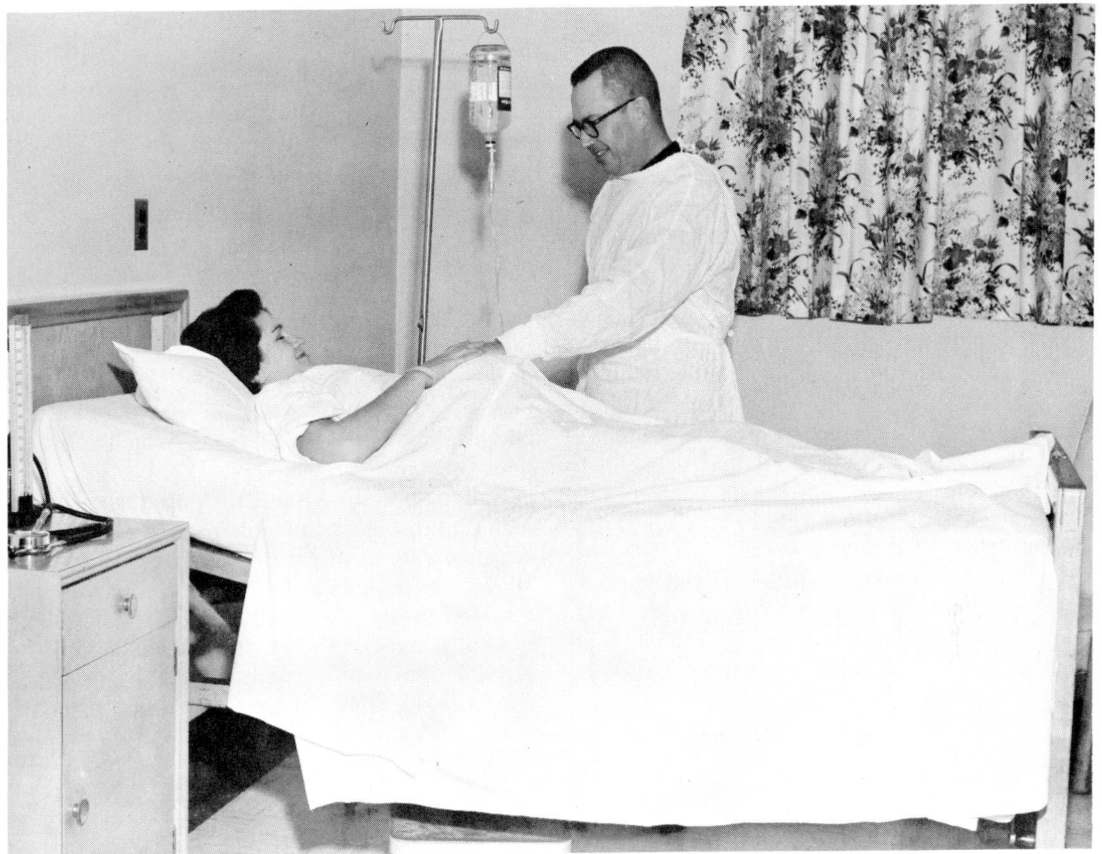

FIG. 196. Expectant parents share experiences of labor together. (Fitzpatrick, E., Eastman, N. J., and Reeder, S.: Maternity Nursing, ed. 11, Fig. 12:5, Philadelphia, Lippincott, 1966)

normal range of the fetal heart beat is 120 to 160 per minute.) Irregularities, rates beyond the normal, or sudden changes may be important indications of fetal distress and must be reported immediately.

Uterine contractions are observed because they are often an indication of the progress of the patient in labor. They can be felt by placing your hand on the patient's abdomen. As the uterus contracts, the abdomen becomes hard and rigid; the uterus then relaxes, which can be felt by the softening of the muscle fibers. When contractions begin, they are usually mild, short and far apart. As the labor progresses, they become longer, more intense and closer together. The frequency of contractions is calculated from the beginning of one until the beginning of the next. As the patient approaches the end of the first stage of labor, she usually complains of the discomfort; the contractions often occur about every 2 or 3 minutes, last 45 to 60 seconds and are forceful and intense.

Another method to check the progress of labor is the rectal examination, usually done by the professional nurse or the doctor. The purpose of a rectal examination is to determine the size of the opening in the cervix—its dilatation. By pushing the thin anterior rectal wall (rectovaginal septum) against the cervix, the amount of dilatation can be felt (Fig. 197). The practical nurse can assist by seeing that the patient is draped properly.

Dilatation is measured in centimeters; the

cervix is considered to be completely dilated at 10 centimeters. The patient is usually in active labor at 4 centimeters and is uncomfortable. Medications are most often given at this time, depending on the doctor's orders.

The mother has to depend mostly on the nurse for comfort; do everything that you are instructed to do and a little more. Stay with her and encourage her. Sponge her face and hands occasionally; rub her back; give her a drink of water from time to time, if it is permitted. These are the comforting things that make a hot, tired person feel better. Change her gown if it gets damp; see that the air in the room is fresh. Labor is exactly what the word says—hard work. Do all that you can to help her relax and rest between contractions. You may have an opportunity to give the father a comforting word, too.

One of the important duties of the nurse is to be sure that the patient has an empty bladder. A full bladder prevents the baby's head from descending into the pelvis and thereby slows the progress of labor.

Some of the untoward symptoms during labor are: sharp unremitting pain; prolonged contractions or the failure of the uterus to relax; marked changes in the mother's pulse rate or blood pressure; change in the fetal heart tone; and bleeding. These symptoms should be reported promptly and recorded.

Water or clear fluids, such as tea with sugar, are usually allowed during the very early stages of labor. Solid or liquid foods may cause vomiting and other problems, particularly if the patient is going to have a general anesthetic. In a prolonged labor, intravenous glucose solutions may be given to maintain an adequate caloric and fluid intake. This lessens exhaustion and dehydration.

Relief of Pain. Almost all patients in labor, including the advocates of "natural childbirth," are given some medication during labor. This allows the patient to be more comfortable and relaxed during the hard work of labor. The type of drug may vary with the locale and the physician, as well as with the condition of the patient. However, there are drugs that are

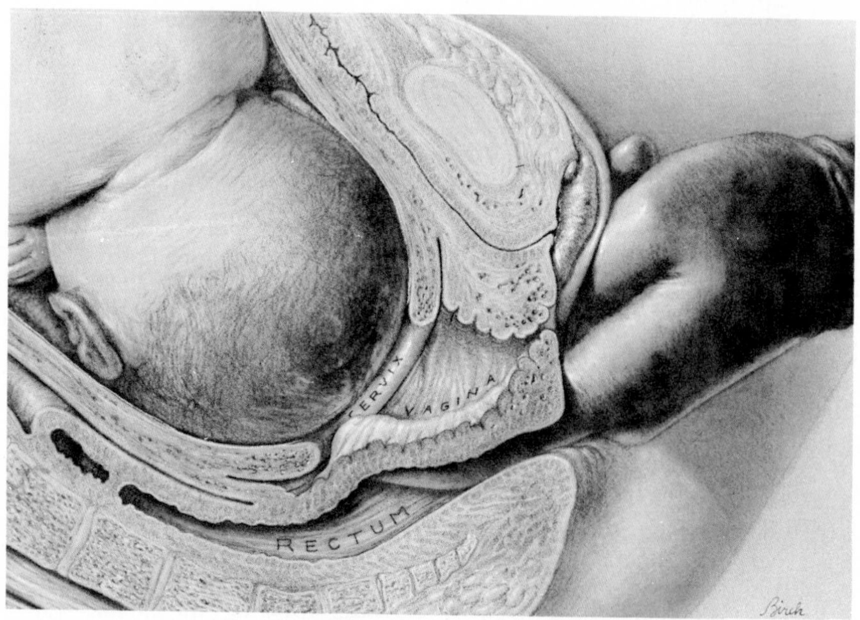

Fig. 197. Rectal examination, showing how the examining finger palpates the cervix and the infant's head through the rectovaginal septum. (Fitzpatrick, E., and Eastman, N. J.: Zabriskie's Obstetrics for Nurses, ed. 10, p. 245, Philadelphia, Lippincott, 1960)

given more commonly than others, for specific reasons. Drugs that relieve pain are called analgesics; and those most frequently administered for labor are Demerol and Nisentil. Often these are given in combination with scopolamine, a drug used for its amnesic effects. (It causes the patient to forget her period of labor.) Scopolamine also dries body secretions which facilitates safer anesthesia. Atropine is sometimes given instead of scopolamine because it also reduces secretions, but it does not cause amnesia.

A third type of drug that may be given is one that enhances the effects of the analgesic, thereby making it impossible to reduce the amount of analgesic given. One such drug is Phenergan. This type of drug is valuable because almost all analgesics have some sedative effect on the baby as well as on the mother. A lesser amount of analgesic reduces the possibility of respiratory depression in the baby. These drugs are also frequently antiemetics; that is, they prevent the nausea which is considered to be a reflex at a certain stage of labor.

Most patients receive some form of anesthesia during delivery. This is usually given during the second stage of labor and may be of different types. A general anesthetic is commonly used (see Chap. 30). A patient receiving this type of anesthesia is asleep when her baby is born.

Other anesthetics are given by injection, either into the spinal canal or into the tissues. These anesthetics affect the nerve supply to an area or a region of the body. Although the patient is awake during delivery, she has no sensation or feeling in the part anesthetized. Pontocaine, procaine and nupercaine are agents commonly used for this type of anesthesia.

Each type of anesthesia has distinct advantages. The doctor chooses the type according to the patient's needs and wants, as well as according to facilities available.

Complications of Labor and Delivery

One of the first duties of the nurse is to observe the patient in labor for any possible complications. Since the lives of 2 persons are at stake, this is a grave responsibility. Some of these complications will be discussed here.

Precipitate Labor and Delivery. A precipitate labor is one which is very short and in which the contractions are usually severe. A precipitate delivery is such a rapid delivery that the mother is usually unable to be taken to the delivery room or in other ways prepared for delivery. Many times the doctor is not present. Of course, the nurse's concern is for the welfare of the patient and the baby; she must care for their needs as best she can, while preserving and applying as many of the principles of asepsis as is possible in the situation. Other problems in precipitate delivery arise from the possible trauma to both the mother and the baby from the unusual force of the labor.

Uterine Inertia. Uterine inertia is sometimes described as a *tired uterus.* The strong contractions which are necessary to force the baby out of the uterus are not present. Perhaps the contractions are strong to begin with and grow weaker, maybe ceasing altogether, or they may be weak from the onset. Sometimes after the mother has been provided an interval of a few hours sleep, more vigorous labor begins.

Abnormal Fetal Presentations. Normally, the baby is born head first, face down, but sometimes the fetus has assumed other positions. Occasionally, the face is uppermost, or a hand or foot or the buttocks present first. This complication is known as an abnormal presentation.

Multiple Pregnancy. A multiple pregnancy is one in which more than one fetus is developing in the uterus at the same time. Twin pregnancy is the most common type, although triplets, quadruplets, quintuplets and even sextuplets do occur. If twins are suspected, an x-ray picture will show whether or not there is more than one fetus.

Cephalopelvic Disproportion. A condition in which the bones of the mother's pelvis are too small to allow the baby to pass through is known as cephalopelvic disproportion. One of the advantages of prenatal care is to discover the mother's small pelvis before labor begins. If the size of the baby and the size of the mother's pelvis are borderline, frequently the doctor will give the patient a *trial labor* before resorting to surgical delivery.

Prolapsed Cord. A prolapsed cord may occur if the membranes rupture and the baby's head is not low in the pelvis. The umbilical cord drops through the cervical outlet. This is a serious complication, because as the baby's head descends it may press the cord against the hard structures in the mother's pelvis, cutting off the circulation to the fetus. A prolapsed cord also may lead to infection.

Ruptured Uterus. A ruptured uterus is one of the most serious complications of labor. Fortunately, it is rare. In this condition the uterus splits from the strain placed upon its muscular wall. The most common cause today is a previous cesarean section, but severe labor contractions, disproportion and the injudicious use of drugs to stimulate uterine contraction can contribute to its occurrence.

Other Complications. Other complications are hemorrhagic conditions, toxemia, severe chronic disease in the mother, and fetal distress. The treatments of these complications depend on the condition of the mother and/or the baby, how serious the complication is, and to what stage of labor the mother has progressed. One of the common treatments for severe complications is cesarean section.

Cesarean Section. A cesarean section is a surgical procedure to deliver the baby through an incision in the abdomen and the uterus. The preparation of the patient is the same as for any surgical procedure. When the need is foreseen, surgery is scheduled to take place shortly before the due date. The factor of safety for both mother and baby has improved tremendously in recent years. Most doctors do not recommend more than 3 or 4 cesarean sections, because they weaken the uterine wall.

CARE DURING THE PUERPERIUM

The period after delivery until the genital organs and tract have returned to normal is called the *pueperium* or *postpartum*; it usually lasts about 6 weeks. During this period, the uterus returns to normal size and function, and the menstrual cycle is re-established. The length of the hospital stay for the patient with a normal delivery varies according to the policy of the physician and the hospital. The average stay is 5 or 6 days.

Immediate Postpartum Care

Immediately following delivery, the mother experiences a feeling of being very tired which is close to exhaustion, just as she would after any extremely vigorous physical activity or hard work. At the same time she is relieved and excited. She is interested in seeing and holding her baby and having a brief visit with her husband, after which she often sleeps to get a much needed rest.

While the mother is still in the delivery room, she may appear to be chilled. This is a very common and brief reaction. There is no accepted explanation, but the chill appears to be reflex in nature. An extra cotton blanket which has been closely tucked around the mother relieves this mild reaction.

The mother is observed closely for several hours after delivery for any symptoms of hemorrhage. The uterus must be checked at frequent intervals—every 15 minutes during the first hour—to see that it remains firm and contracted. If the uterus becomes soft and relaxed, the nurse cups her hand around the fundus and massages it gently until it regains its firmness. The perineal pad is checked for the amount of bleeding. The pulse and the blood pressure are noted as well. It is important to keep the mother in the delivery room long enough to be sure that her condition is satisfactory. All information about the delivery and other procedures should be recorded on her chart before she is taken to her room. This includes items such as the sex and the condition of the baby at birth, the time of birth, the time at which the placenta was expelled, the care of the breasts and the condition of the fundus.

The father should not be forgotten in this interim. He goes through a severe emotional strain that is very frustrating because there is nothing he can do. Probably this is why some fathers feel the need to "celebrate" after the baby is born.

General Postpartum Care

The general care of the postpartum patient is similar to that of other patients. The nurse observes the general comfort of the mother—her appetite, her activity and how well she sleeps and rests. She also notes her temperature, pulse and respiration, which in most instances are within the normal limits. In addition, there are the special needs of the patient which must be met and observations which must be made.

Lochia. The *lochia* is the normal discharge from the vagina after the baby is born. It consists of blood and the broken-down lining of the uterus; it lasts about 3 to 4 weeks. At first it is bright red, consisting mostly of blood, and is called *lochia rubra.* As the bleeding slows, the discharge gradually changes to a pinkish serous color and is called the *lochia serosa.* By the 10th day, the lochia is yellow or white in color, has decreased greatly in amount and is called the *lochia alba.* If the lochia still contains blood after 10 days, the mother should notify her physician.

Fundus. The height and the firmness of the uterine fundus are checked several times daily. The fundus should be firm and directly below the umbilicus. Excessive bleeding or clots should be reported at once.

After-Pains. For the first few days after delivery, the mother often has painful cramps as the uterine muscles contract; these are called *after-pains.* These pains are not so troublesome

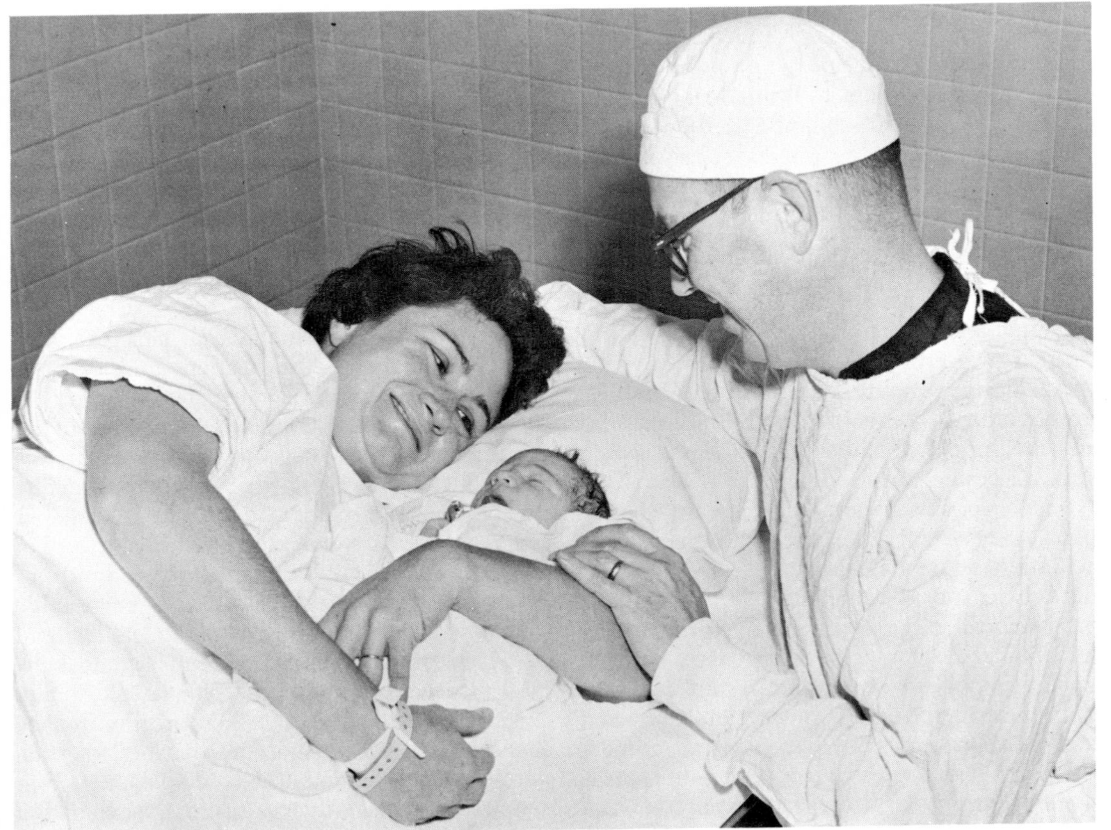

FIG. 198. Parents and baby are having their first visit after delivery. (Fitzpatrick, E., Eastman, N. J., and Reeder, S.: Maternity Nursing, ed. 11, Fig. 14:11, Philadelphia, Lippincott, 1966)

after a first baby, because at that time the uterine muscles have a better tone than they do after several pregnancies. Breast-feeding stimulates uterine contractions, and therefore often brings on after-pains.

Breast Care. The breasts contain a thin watery fluid called colostrum until about the 3rd day after delivery when the milk begins to flow. The breasts often become full and hard (engorged), and sometimes painful. The baby relieves this condition when he nurses. A good supporting brassière or binder helps to support engorged breasts. The mother who does not wish to nurse her baby is given medications to prevent milk production.

Breast care differs in various hopsitals, but the trend is toward procedures as simple as possible, to prevent infection. The nursing mother cleans her nipples before each feeding. The non-nursing mother washes her breasts and nipples at the time of her daily bath. They should be bathed with a clean washcloth and towel before any other part of the body is washed.

Authorities seem to agree that most mothers can nurse their babies, barring such complications as retracted nipples, infections or breast malformations. The first requirement for breast-feeding is a good supply of milk. If the mother is happy, wants to nurse the baby and is not worried or overtired, her chances for having a good milk supply are excellent. The mother's mental attitude seems to affect both the quality and the supply of milk; her emotional upsets may affect the baby's digestion.

Some women are unwilling to nurse their babies because it interferes with their social activities, or they believe that nursing makes the breasts sag. If a mother must work outside her home, nursing may be inconvenient or even impossible. A mother should realize that she gives her baby a much better start in life if she nurses him. There is much emotional satisfaction to be derived by her, too, from nursing her baby.

Expression of Milk. *Expression of milk* (artificial emptying of the breasts) is sometimes necessary. The baby may be too weak to nurse, or it may have a deformity such as a cleft palate or a harelip. Sometimes the mother may produce more milk than her baby needs and can supply another baby. The electric breast pump is the best method to use for expressing milk, because the suction is controlled. Milk may also be expressed by the hands or by a hand pump. The milk is collected in a sterile bottle and kept in the refrigerator.

Bathing. The mother receives a daily bath or shower. It is important that the nurse give the first bed bath after delivery. This gives the nurse the opportunity to teach the mother several details of the self-care for which she will later be responsible. Some doctors do not permit tub baths for several weeks after delivery, but many permit and encourage the mother to shower after her first postpartum day. For this reason, she must be taught the procedures for breast and perineal self-care.

Perineal Care. Care of the perineum, the area between the vaginal orifice and the rectum, is important to maintain comfort and cleanliness to prevent odor and infection. If the mother has had an episiotomy, the healing of the stitches is promoted by keeping this area clean and dry.

Perineal care is no longer the elaborate procedure it used to be. Technics will vary from hospital to hospital, but in one respect they are always the same: cleansing is done from the pubic area back to the rectal area to avoid contamination by fecal material. This care must always be given after the patient voids or has a bowel movement. The nurse does the procedure if the patient is in bed. However, if the patient is allowed to go to the bathroom, she is taught how to give herself perineal care. She first washes her hands and then places a paper bag, a box of small cleansing tissues and a fresh perineal pad (with the clean side up, or preferably, wrapped) on a stool or a table which is adjacent to or near the toilet. The pad she is wearing is removed from front to back and placed in the paper bag for later disposal. After voiding, she cleanses herself from front to back with tissues, using fresh tissues for each stroke and discarding them in the toilet. It is important that undue pressure be avoided if the stitches of the episiotomy have not yet been removed. If she has had a bowel movement, the anal region is wiped in the same way (from front to back). The mother is taught how to handle the clean perineal pad so that the inner surface is not contaminated by her fingers, and to fasten it to the tab of the sanitary belt in the pubic area first so that it will not slip forward. The toilet should be flushed *after* she stands, to prevent any of the flushing spray from touching the perineum.

DIFFICULTY IN VOIDING AND DEFECATING. The new mother may have difficulty voiding after delivery because of the loss of muscle tone in the bladder, or because of perineal soreness or edema. The usual nursing measures should be tried, and many physicians permit the mother to go to the bathroom if she is unable to use the bedpan. A distended bladder causes the uterus to rise in the abdominal cavity and prevents it from contracting, thereby contributing to postpartum hemorrhage. Therefore, it is an important nursing responsibility to see that the mother is able to void. Occasionally, it becomes necessary to catheterize the patient if her bladder is distended and she cannot empty it. The decision to catheterize the patient should depend on the fullness of the bladder, not on the number of hours since delivery. The postpartum patient often voids more frequently than the average patient, because the extra body fluids from pregnancy are being eliminated.

The mother may be constipated for the first week or two following delivery. Diet and activity help to regulate this condition. Many physicians routinely order mild laxatives following delivery until good bowel function is re-established. If necessary, the mother will be given an enema. If hemorrhoids have bothered her during pregnancy, they may still cause discomfort; rectal suppositories or ice packs are prescribed for this condition.

Early Ambulation. The mother may lie in any position in which she feels comfortable. She is encouraged to lie on her abdomen for at least 2 hours every day, to bring the uterus forward. In most modern hospitals she is up the day following delivery. Although this practice seems to have come about mainly through a shortage of nurses and hospital beds, it has worked out well. The following are some of the advantages of early ambulation for new mothers: muscle tone is restored more quickly to the relaxed pelvic and abdominal muscles; the flow of lochia increases, thereby facilitating the return of the uterus to normal; improved circulation aids healing; and the danger of thrombosis and embolism is decreased.

Diet and Weight Loss. The mother should have a normal, nutritious, well-balanced diet. If she is nursing, extra quantities of milk and other liquids may be added.

The mother loses from 8 to 12 pounds during and after delivery. This can be accounted for by the loss of the fetus, the placenta and the amniotic fluid. She loses about 5 to 8 more pounds in the ensuing 5 or 6 weeks, due to the loss of body fluids accumulated during pregnancy. If her weight gain was not excessive, she usually returns to her normal weight in about 6 weeks.

Postpartum Examination and Instruction. The doctor checks the patient closely before discharging her from the hospital, which may be 4 or 5 days after delivery. He instructs her in the home care of her episiotomy as well as in breast care. The mother is given information about her diet, elimination, rest and exercise. She is instructed to let the doctor know if her milk supply decreases and to get in touch with him immediately if she has an increase in vaginal bleeding. She is told to return to him for a follow-up examination at the end of 6 weeks, and she is usually advised not to have sexual intercourse or take vaginal douches before that time.

As was mentioned before, the uterus should have returned to its normal size and position at the end of 6 weeks; this process is called *involution.* Sad as it may seem to new mothers, a slim silhouette takes a while to achieve. Not only must the uterus shrink itself from approximately 2 pounds to 2 ounces, but the skin and the muscles of the abdomen are greatly stretched. If the muscles were in good condition before pregnancy, they soon begin to regain tone. The stretch marks, called *striae*, fade to faint silver lines. Exercises provide a good method to get back into shape; the doctor will usually prescribe these and tell the mother when she may begin.

Menstruation begins again in 6 to 8 weeks if the mother does not nurse her baby. If she does nurse, menstruation is delayed for 4 or 5 months. Although ovulation does not occur in most mothers during the nursing period, prolonging this period is no guarantee that pregnancy will not take place; many nursing mothers do become pregnant.

Postpartum Complications

Some of the complications that may occur during the postpartum period should be mentioned, so that you may know about the nursing care that they require.

Infection. *Puerperal infection* is a condition as old as the race, and it was the main cause of maternal deaths before asepsis was known. It used to be called *childbed fever.* Bacteria which lurk in the lower genital tract and the rectum are capable of causing infection if conditions are favorable, such as the presence of injured tissues or retained pieces of placenta, and lowered resistance. Other common organisms causing puerperal infection are the staphylococcus and the streptococcus. Since these microorganisms can be carried by hospital personnel, those who work in the labor area wear special clothing. Members of the staff who work in the delivery rooms wear caps, masks and gowns.

Because of the many venous sinuses left open by the removal of the placenta from the uterine wall, the infection may spread through the bloodstream, causing septicemia. Fever is the outstanding symptom of infection; it may or may not be accompanied by a chill. Headache, malaise and a foul-smelling lochia are other symptoms of infection.

The infected mother is isolated; many times she is removed from the postpartum floor. The baby is not brought to the mother for feeding. Antibiotics are administered and all technics to prevent the organisms from spreading to other patients are adhered to strictly.

Hemorrhage. Postpartum hemorrhage is a serious complication which can occur any time up to 4 weeks following delivery. Most cases occur within 24 hours after the birth of the baby; late hemorrhage is rare. Hemorrhage is usually caused by the retention of a fragment of placental tissue, which prevents the blood vessels from contracting; by tears in the reproductive tract as a result of delivery; or by the poor tone of the uterine muscle, causing the consequent lack of contraction, and the delayed constriction of uterine blood vessels.

If the fundus is boggy and relaxed, massage and the administration of an oxytoxic (pituitary extract or ergotrate) which causes the muscles to contract aids in establishing tone. If the cause of the bleeding appears to be a tear or retained placental tissue, the patient will have to be prepared for a sterile vaginal examination and treatment. If the blood loss is extensive, she may require a transfusion.

Thrombophlebitis. Thrombophlebitis is a condition in which there is a clot in a blood vessel with resultant inflammation. In the new mother, thrombophlebitis usually occurs in the femoral vessels in the leg. (It used to be called "milk leg.") Early ambulation has greatly lessened the occurrence of thrombophlebitis in mothers, but the symptoms of this complication and the necessary nursing care are fully explained in Chapter 33, The Surgical Patient. In the case of a woman who has just been delivered, the anticoagulants (heparin and Dicumarol) usually administered to dissolve a clot, may or may not be given because of the danger of increasing the possibility of uterine hemorrhage. After the acute stage has passed, it is often necessary for the mother to wear an elastic stocking for a period of time.

Mastitis. Mastitis is an infection of the breast which occurs when microorganisms enter through cracked or macerated nipples. One sign of mastitis is a rise in temperature about the 10th day; the breast becomes red and hot, and the infected area feels hard. The baby is not allowed to nurse. An icecap is applied to the breast, and antibiotics are given. An abscess may form if the treatment is delayed, and an incision and drainage may be necessary.

Recently, a type of mastitis has been reported as a result of infection from an epidemic strain of staphylococcus which is resistant to antibiotics. In this type, the organisms enter through the normal milk ducts in the breast rather than through nipple lesions.

Mental Disturbances. Mental problems occur in some postpartum patients. Pregnancy, labor and delivery are too much to bear for these women, and they feel unable to cope with their problems any longer. The mother who is affected in this way becomes irritable and unable to sleep, she has no appetite and exhibits great anxiety. She may be depressed and dislike both her baby and her husband. This is the time to let the doctor know about these symptoms, so that early treatment may prevent a more serious mental illness from developing. If her condition is entirely the result of the imbalance in her body functions caused by pregnancy, she will recover as soon as her physical condition is normal again. Many patients have *postpartum blues*, which appears to be a normal hormonal reaction on the 4th or the 5th day.

51

CARE OF THE NEWBORN

THE BABY

Initial Care

As soon as the baby is born, the physician removes secretions from the baby's respiratory tract, either manually or with a small soft bulb syringe or catheter; the baby takes his first breath and makes his first sound. His skin has a bluish tinge at first, but as soon as the oxygen from his crying enters the circulating blood in quantity, he turns pink and rosy. Sometimes, if the mother has been medicated recently or had a long anesthetic, the baby does not breathe at once and has to be stimulated. The doctor clamps and cuts the umbilical cord; he puts a prophylactic solution (usually 1% silver nitrate solution) in the baby's eyes to prevent possible gonorrheal infection (ophthalmia neonatorum). Then the doctor hands the baby over to the nurse, who has a warm blanket and bed ready.

Normal Characteristics. Many new parents are accustomed to the pictures of infants commonly seen in magazines and are dismayed by the appearance of their newborn, by his odd-shaped head, his wrinkled skin and perhaps his jaundiced color. Many times the nurse can reassure the parents about the normal physical characteristics of the newborn, putting their fears to rest.

The average newborn (also called a *neonate* for the next 4 weeks) weighs about 7 lbs. and is about 20 inches long. (This does not mean that a baby weighing 5½ lbs., who is 19 inches long, is abnormal—he is just not "average.") A newborn is far from being a miniature adult in proportion. His head is too large for his body and may even be long and narrow—almost pointed. This strange shape of the head is called *molding*; it is a result of shaping to accommodate passage through the birth canal. The contours of the head soon go back to normal.

The newborn does not seem to have a neck, and his jaw is receding; his chest is smaller than his large abdomen; his legs are bowed and drawn up on his body. The skin over his body is covered with a thick cheesylike material called *vernix caseosa*; also over the skin of his body is very fine hair called lanugo. If he has hair on his head, it is usually very fine and in a thick patch. This original hair often falls out to be replaced by some of an entirely different color.

The baby's bones are soft, his muscles weak. He has soft spots on his head (*fontanels*), because his skull bones do not meet. His eyes at birth are usually blue—they change to their permanent color later. After the first 24 hours or so, his hearing seems to be acute. He can move his arms and legs very vigorously, has strong sucking power and cries loudly.

Baptism. If the baby's condition is poor, it should be baptized at once if such action is required by the parents' religion—this is of the utmost importance to Roman Catholic parents. The form of baptism is important to ensure validity. Water is poured on the baby's face or forehead, at the same time that the person performing the ceremony repeats the words: "I baptize thee in the name of the Father and of the Son and of the Holy Ghost." If there is any doubt about the baby's being alive the baptism is given conditionally: "If thou art alive, I baptize thee in the name of the Father and of the Son and of the Holy Ghost." Whenever it has been necessary for the nurse to baptize an infant, a record of the procedure is inserted on the mother's chart on the nursing records. There should be 2 witnesses whenever possible, and their names should be recorded. Anyone can baptize; they do not have to be a Roman Catholic.

Identification and the Chart. Before he leaves the delivery room, the baby is given an identification mark of some kind—a name band on his ankle or wrist, or a necklace of beads which spells his parents' surname; hospitals use different methods. At the time of delivery, the baby's footprints are taken, and a record of them is attached to his chart. This chart contains information which includes the sex of the baby, the hour of birth, the type of delivery, his condition, the care of the eyes, and the Rh status of the mother. The chart is made out before the baby leaves the delivery room.

Cord. A sterile dressing may be applied to the cord stump and kept in place with a binder, although many hospitals no longer use either the cord dressing or the binder. The cord stump usually dries up and separates by the end of the 1st week.

Protection For the Baby. In the nursery, every baby is in his own crib, which has a firm mattress and lined sides. The technics used by the nursery personnel are devised to isolate the baby from any direct contact with other babies. In some nurseries the doctors and the nurses wear gowns and masks, but in many nurseries they do not.

A hospital nursery can be a hazardous place for a baby if an infection is present. Epidemics of skin infection (impetigo) and, recently, staphylococcal infections have broken out in nurseries; a fatal type of diarrhea has also occurred. From the sheltered protection of the uterus, the baby comes into a world filled with germs to which he is very susceptible. This is why visitors are not allowed in nurseries. Hospital nurseries provide a large glass window to let the father and fond relatives look at the baby without coming close to him.

The baby is weighed and measured; his temperature is taken rectally. Methods of caring for the newborn baby's skin vary widely, all the way from leaving the cheesy vernix caseosa on the skin to using medicated oils or washing with pHisoHex and water. Then the baby is dressed, wrapped in a blanket and placed in his crib. His head is placed lower than the rest of his body to faciltiate mucous drainage. He is placed where he can be observed closely by the nurses; any unusual symptom such as cyanosis, convulsions, tremors or shrill crying is reported immediately to the doctor.

Rooming-In. Rooming-in is a plan used in some hospitals when the baby stays in his crib in his mother's room. In this plan the mother feeds and cares for the baby, getting used to handling him. The father also has the satisfaction of getting acquainted with his child; he can look at and hold the baby when he comes to visit his wife.

Rooming-in is completely undesirable unless it is supervised closely by a competent nursing staff; no hospital should try this plan until it has worked out carefully the way to handle it well. Some hospitals have built or redesigned areas in their maternity unit especially for this plan. It is usually set up so that the supervision and care of 2 to 4 mothers and babies is assigned to one nurse. It is not meant to be a plan to make less work for everybody but the mother. In fact, a great many mothers would rather leave the baby in the nursery. Much as a mother may love her baby, she may feel that she will have full responsibility for him soon enough when she leaves the hospital.

The Birth Certificate. A certificate of the baby's birth must be made out and signed by the doctor who made the delivery. This must be filed with the health department for the area where the baby was born. The health department sends the mother a photostatic copy as proof that the birth has been recorded. A birth certificate is an important document which is required many times throughout one's lifetime —when entering school, obtaining a marriage license or a passport, and supplying proof of Social Security rights.

Observing the Newborn

The routine daily care of the newborn involves meeting the needs of any infant for food, cleanliness and comfort, but it also involves close scrutiny and observation for any symptoms of difficulties or abnormalities. While in the uterus, the mother's physiology supplied the baby's wants, but now he must function as an individual organism; the nurse must observe his abilities to do so.

Body Temperature. The baby's rectal temperature is normally between 98° to 99° F. It tends to be slightly subnormal. However, the part of the neonate's nervous system which acts as a temperature control is still immature, so that his temperature may be elevated if he is too warm, or if he does not get enough liquids.

Eyes, Nose and Ears. No special care is required for the baby's eyes, nose or ears; there is no need to insert probes or applicators into these areas. Any redness, swelling, or discharge should be reported and recorded on the chart, and the physician will prescribe the necessary treatment. There may be some reaction in the eyes from the medication used for prophylaxis against gonorrheal infection.

Skin. The skin of the newborn baby, no matter what its racial stock, is usually reddish and is often wrinkled, although it should become smooth and of a normal color within 2 weeks. It is very sensitive and may break out in a rash if irritated. A rash or irritated area should be reported. Many neonates have some jaundice for a few days, but this also usually disappears by the 2nd week.

Stools. During the first days of the baby's life, his stools are dark green and tarry-looking. This is *meconium*, a waste product which is formed in the baby's intestines in the latter months of pregnancy. Then the stool changes to a normal lighter color. The stools of breast-fed babies are bright yellow, smooth and pasty looking; a baby fed a formula of cow's milk has a darker stool. The stools smell like sour milk. Mucus, blood or curds in the stool are signs of disturbance to be reported at once.

Urination. Analysis of the amniotic fluid shows that the fetus has kidney function and voids within the uterus. He often voids immediately after birth, but care should be taken to be certain that he voids within 24 hours after delivery. At first the urine is clear, and then it becomes concentrated. After the first 2 or 3 days, the infant voids from 12 to 18 times daily.

Sleep. Except for the time he is being fed, the newborn baby sleeps almost all the time, but not heavily. He will wake and cry when he is hungry or uncomfortable. Most authorities recommend that the baby sleep on his side, the sides being changed frequently, but some advise not to place him on his stomach until he can raise his head. Sleeping on the back is discouraged for two reasons: there is the possibility of his choking from regurgitation, and the soft skull bones may become flattened from the constant pressure exerted at one point.

Taking Food. The normal newborn baby knows instinctively how to suck and swallow. If he takes too much food or takes it too fast, he may regurgitate it (this is simply an overflow and should not be thought of as vomiting). Food may stick in his esophagus and cause hiccups, which sips of water will stop. A healthy baby is eager for his food; if he refuses to nurse or to take his bottle, spits up or vomits or has an unusual amount of discomfort from gas, the doctor should be notified. Perhaps a change in formula will relieve these digestive woes.

Responses. The newborn baby cries and tightens his muscles in response to sudden loud sounds, changes in position, the feel of something cold touching his skin, or interference with his movements. He relaxes if he is held and rocked while his skin is patted lightly.

Crying. A newborn baby cries a lot, especially if he is hungry or if his diapers are wet. Crying is the only way a baby can ask for help. It has been noticed that the baby who gets more care cries less.

Hunger cries are healthy, demanding cries, and he may put his fingers into his mouth, which is an additional sign that he is hungry. After he is fed, he is quiet unless he has swallowed air from his bottle and needs to "bubble." He also may have colic if his food is not right or his elimination is not good.

A baby will cry if he is wet. The sensitive skin around his genitals and buttocks may be irritated from his urine or stools. Improperly washed or rinsed diapers may also cause irritation.

A baby cries if his bedding is too tight to allow him freedom of motion. He should be able to move his arms and legs to improve circulation and strengthen muscles.

Bathing the Baby. The hospital routine for

giving baths to babies varies. Some institutions order oil rubs, some use medicated lotions, and others use soap and water. Most doctors do not allow a tub bath for a normal baby until the navel has healed; this occurs by the end of the 2nd week.

Today mothers leave the hospital so soon after the baby is born that you may not have an opportunity to give him a tub bath in the hospital. However, many hospitals provide demonstration baths for the new mothers. The important guide lines which apply to any bath procedure apply also to the baby bath:

Have all the equipment ready and conveniently placed before you start.

Be sure that the room is warm enough and that the baby is protected from drafts.

Check the temperature of the water carefully. It should be just warm.

Support the baby's head and body with a firm grip when you put him in the tub (Fig. 199).

Use a soft wash cloth and towel; rinse all the soap off; dry the creases well.

Observe his body carefully for signs of skin irritation or abnormalities.

If his clothes do not open down the front or the back, put them on over his feet. A baby resists even a temporary interference with his breathing or movements.

Clean and care for the equipment and replace used supplies.

Circumcision. In male babies, the foreskin (prepuce) covers the glans penis or extends beyond it (see Chap. 19). The opening may be very small, a condition known as *phimosis.* A secretion called *smegma* collects beneath the foreskin, and drops of urine also may remain to cause irritation. Because of the problem it presents to cleanliness, most male infants today are circumcised—that is, part or all of the foreskin is removed. If circumcision is not performed, the foreskin must be stretched and retracted over the glans penis for cleaning. This may be difficult and must be done with great care and gentleness. The foreskin must be replaced immediately, because if it is tight it causes edema and pain.

If the baby is circumcised, he must be kept clean and watched closely for bleeding. A sterile petrolatum dressing is applied after each voiding for 24 to 48 hours to keep the diapers from sticking. Circumcision is usually done shortly before the infant leaves the hospital; therefore, the mother should be instructed in the care required.

INFANT FEEDING

Breast Feeding

The most inexpensive, easiest and simplest way to feed a baby is by nursing at the breast. There are no formulas to make or bottles to sterilize; the mother's milk is safe from harmful organisms and is always ready. Some authorities say that there are substances in the mother's milk which protect the baby from disease; breast-fed babies are more likely to be well and to stay healthy. Breast-feeding is also a satisfying emotional experience for both the mother and the baby.

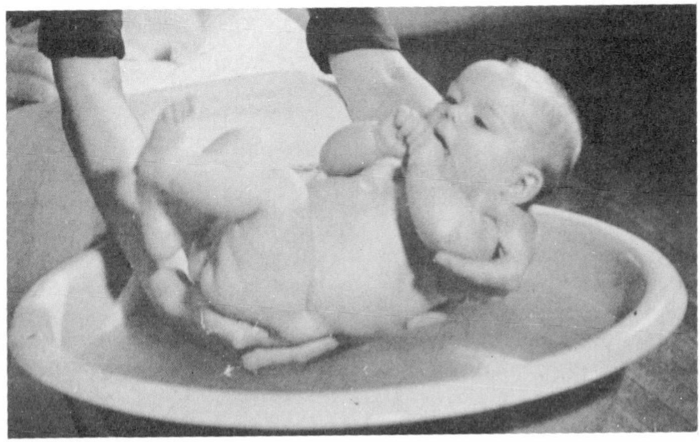

Fig. 199. Putting the baby in the tub (Zabriskie, L.: Mother and Baby Care in Pictures, ed. 4, p. 141, Philadelphia, Lippincott)

If the mother does not want to nurse her baby, her feelings should be respected. Many mothers have definite reasons for not wanting to breast-feed their baby, and research has provided satisfactory formulas for replacing breast milk. Breast-feeding is not desirable when the mother has a chronic disease or mastitis, if the nipples are inverted, or if the baby has certain abnormalities.

Putting the Baby to Breast. If the mother is interested in nursing the baby, she should be encouraged and assisted in every way she can. It is important to put the baby to breast regularly to stimulate milk secretion, even before the milk appears on the 3rd or the 4th day. A thin watery secretion called colostrum is present in the breasts before the milk is produced. Stay with the mother the first time the baby goes to breast to show her what to do. She puts the whole nipple in the baby's mouth, and while he is sucking, she holds the breast tissue away from his nose so that he is able to breathe. When she wants to withdraw the nipple, she presses on the baby's cheeks or pushes back on his chin to break the suction.

Anything that makes the mother nervous or puts a strain on her body will interfere with her pleasure in nursing the baby; if the baby is uncomfortable, he may refuse to nurse as long as he should. The mother is often most comfortable when sitting up, with her back and arm supported. If she is out of bed, an armchair is best, with a pillow under her arm. Give her a footstool if she needs it; be sure that she is warm enough and protected from drafts. Wash both her hands and yours before you put the baby to breast. Some authorities say it is not necessary to cleanse the nipples before or after feedings, but others recommend it.

Comparison of Human and Cow's Milk. Authorities tell us that today more babies are given formulas than are breast-fed. The formulas are prepared to be as similar to breast milk as possible. The following comparison* of human milk and cow's milk shows why some adaptations are necessary.

	Human	Cow's
Carbohydrate	7.0%	4.0–5.0%
Protein	1.15	3.5
Fat	3.5–4.0	3.5–4.0
Salts	0.2	0.75

The difference in the protein and the carbohydrate content indicates why formula milk is diluted and has a form of carbohydrate added.

Bottle Feeding

The basis of a formula is milk. Generally, one third of evaporated milk, two thirds of water and 1 ounce of carbohydrate for every 20

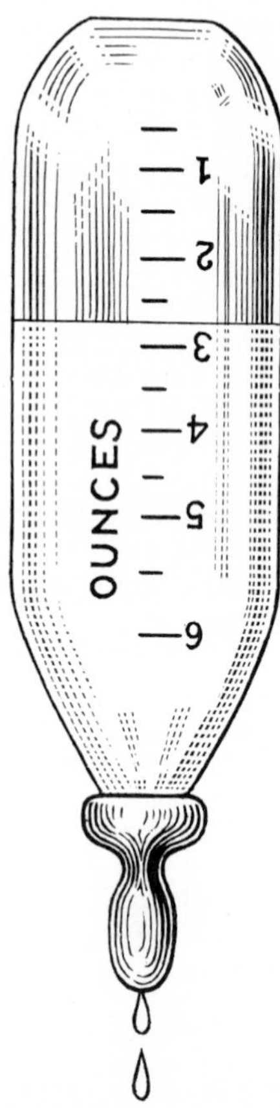

Fig. 200. Testing the size of the opening in a nipple. Milk should drop, as indicated, and not flow in a stream. (Fitzpatrick, E., and Eastman, N. J.: Zabriskie's Obstetrics for Nurses, ed. 10, p. 344, Philadelphia, Lippincott, 1960)

* Elsie Fitzpatrick and Nicholson Eastman: Zabriskie's Obstetrics for Nurses, ed. 10, p. 341, Philadelphia, Lippincott, 1960.

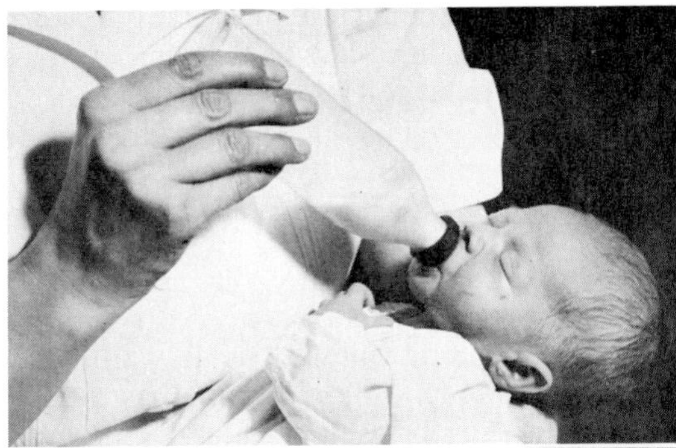

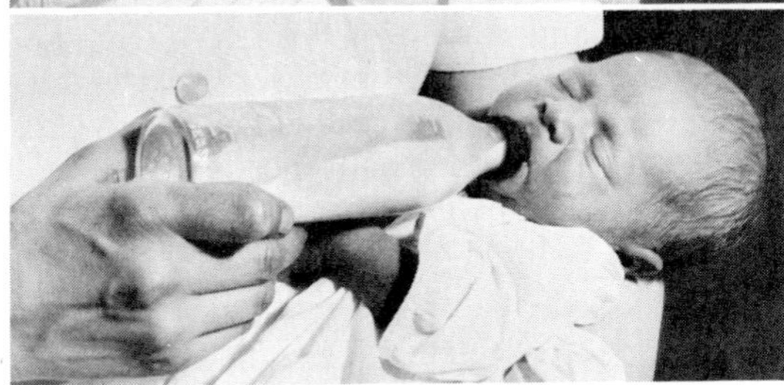

FIG. 201. (*Top*) The right way to hold a bottle. The baby's head should be turned slightly to one side, and the bottle held so that the baby will grasp the nipple squarely. To prevent the baby from swallowing air, the neck of the bottle should be filled with milk at all times. (*Bottom*) The wrong way to hold a bottle. If the bottle is held flat, air enters the nipple, and the baby may suffer as a result of swallowing air. (Fitzpatrick, E., and Eastman, N. J.: Zabriskie's Obstetrics for Nurses, ed. 10, p. 345, Philadelphia, Lippincott, 1960)

FIG. 202. "Bubbling" the baby. While in the hospital, the mother should be taught to "bubble" her baby. Holding the baby upright against the shoulder during and immediately after nursing, gently pat his back to bring up air. Cuddly babies are sometimes difficult to put in this position. (Fitzpatrick, E., and Eastman, N. J.: Zabriskie's Obstetrics for Nurses, ed. 10, p. 347, Philadelphia, Lippincott, 1960)

ounces of the mixture is satisfactory. The baby takes this formula until he is 3 or 4 months old, when he can take whole milk. Most babies increase the amount they take from 12 to 15 ounces the 1st week to 20 ounces by the end of the 2nd week and increase the amount rapidly thereafter.

The same type of special care that is observed when a baby is breast-fed is also observed when a baby is bottle-fed. The mother's hands are cleansed before she is handed the baby. The rate of flow from the bottle's nipple should be checked, to make certain that it flows at a constant drip (Fig. 200). Nipples are made with either a "cross" cut in them, or with holes. If the openings are not the correct size, the holes can be enlarged by putting a red-hot needle through them.

While the baby is eating, the bottle should be tilted so that milk is in the neck of the bottle at all times to keep the baby from swallowing air. The baby should be bubbled (burped) at intervals during the feeding (Figs. 201 and 202).

The physician may prefer that the baby have a formula other than the one prepared from evaporated milk. There are many baby milk products available, each one having certain advantages for particular situations. There are even nonmilk formulas available for infants who are allergic to milk. The doctor orders these according to the infant's need. Most babies are on schedules of approximately 4 hour intervals. Smaller babies may eat every 3 hours. After the 3rd week, the baby skips one of his evening or night feedings, usually the one at 2:00 A.M.

Demand Feeding. Demand feeding refers to the widespread practice of permitting the infant to set his own schedule to meet his needs, rather than feeding him by the clock. Because babies cry for reasons other than food, the reason for his crying must first be ascertained. The majority of babies soon set a fairly regular schedule for themselves, with which they are seemingly happy and content. As one pediatrician stated, "Adults can go to the refrigerator or the cookie jar when they want a snack; babies can't." Babies can be on a demand schedule whether they are breast-fed or bottle-fed. Although in most hospitals it is not possible to feed all babies on a demand schedule, in hospitals where rooming-in is allowed, demand feeding is the rule.

Preparing the Formula. Because bacteria thrive in milk, great care is exercised in the preparation of the infant's formula. There are two generally accepted methods of preparing formulas. In the first method, the bottles, the nipples and the utensils used in the preparation of the formula are sterilized. The contents of the formula are mixed in sterile containers and poured into the bottles. In the second method, called *terminal sterilization*, the contents are mixed in clean utensils, poured into clean bottles and placed in a large pan or sterilizer to boil for 25 minutes. Thus the milk, the bottles and the nipples are all sterilized at the same time.

Supplementary Foods. When the baby is 2 or 3 weeks old he is given vitamin concentrates. Babies begin to take solid food, starting with cereal, much earlier than they used to, sometimes soon after he goes home from the hospital. Some authorities believe that the time to begin such feeding is when the baby shows that he is ready for it; that is, if he will open his mouth when the spoon touches it, depress his tongue and swallow. Many doctors say that he may have any of the mushy foods when he can manage them.

DISORDERS OF THE NEWBORN BABY

The first months of a baby's life are the most precarious. Before he is born he exists without making any efforts himself; he is warm and protected. As soon as he is born he has to take on the work of breathing, eating, digesting, eliminating and stabilizing his body temperature. More than half of the babies who die during their 1st year die in the 1st month. It is easy to see why a newborn baby needs the best of care. Some of these disturbances appear as soon as he is born, when his body begins to function.

Cyanosis

The first thing that a normal baby does when he is born is to cry, which establishes breathing. If he does not breathe properly, he turns blue (cyanotic). Respiratory difficulties may be due to a prolapsed cord (a condition in which the cord becomes compressed between the baby's head and the mother's pelvis), a congenital heart defect, medications or even the anesthetic that the mother has been given, faulty respiratory apparatus, or a birth injury to the brain.

The newborn infant *must* have oxygen. Treatment is initiated promptly for babies who do not breathe as soon as they are born. First, it must be determined whether the air passages are clear of obstruction, such as amniotic fluid and mucus. Soft catheters and mechanical suction machines are used to remove this material. The baby's head is lowered to facilitate postural drainage. His back is rubbed gently or his buttocks patted softly to stimulate him.

If the infant fails to respond, some form of artificial respiration is instituted. In almost every delivery room today there are modern mechanical infant resuscitators which are both convenient and effective. These supply a controlled administration of oxygen at an optimum pressure. If these are not available, other methods are used. A gentle squeezing of the chest, followed by a release, may be tried. Another method is to alternate compressing and extending the infant's body by stretching his legs and then bending them back and curving his body. Probably the oldest method used is mouth-to-mouth breathing.

Atelectasis

One of the causes for cyanosis in the newborn is atelectasis. Before birth the lungs are not used because the mother supplies the fetus with oxygen. When the baby takes his first breath, expansion of the lungs begins. When atelectasis is present, large areas of the lung tissue remain unexpanded, reducing the infant's oxygen supply. The prognosis depends on the extent of the atelectasis.

Hyaline Membrane Disease

Hyaline membrane disease is a condition in which the alveoli of the lungs become filled with a sticky protein substance which prevents aeration. The cause is not known. It is seen most often in premature infants and those born by cesarean section. The primary symptom is respiratory distress. The treatment is the administration of oxygen in an atmosphere of high humidity. If the condition does not tend to reverse itself within a short time, it is usually fatal. A recently reported treatment is the administration of epsom salts enemas; it is said to be successful in a high percentage of babies.

Birth Injuries

Injuries at birth may occur, such as fractures, or nerve injuries causing facial or arm paralysis. Intracranial injury may be a result of birth injury, or asphyxia, and it is a very serious complication in the newborn. Intracranial injury occurs most frequently after a prolonged labor, a difficult delivery, or a very rapid precipitate delivery. The symptoms are convulsions, respiratory difficulties accompanied by cyanosis, shrill crying, and muscle weakness and lack of tone. The prognosis varies with the extent of the brain injury, but complete cures are not widely expected.

Congenital Deformities

Congenital deformities are abnormalities already existing at birth and are due to the defective development of some part of the fetus. Some of the common congenital deformities are defects of the heart, cleft palate and harelip, and spina bifida.

Congenital Heart Disease. Congenital heart disease causes more infant deaths in the 1st year of life than any other congenital defect. The imperfection can be in any of the heart structures or in the vessels. The common symptoms are cyanosis, respiratory difficulties, and fatigue after exertion such as eating. Oxygen usually relieves temporary difficulties. Progress in heart research and surgery promises a permanent cure in many patients.

Cleft Palate and Harelip. Cleft palate is a defect of the palate in the form of a gap in the roof of the mouth. Sometimes it is associated with a harelip, which is 1 or 2 clefts in the upper lip.

Spina Bifida. Spina bifida occurs as a result of incomplete fusion of the spine. The spinal cord or membranes are exposed as a membrane-covered mass on the back. It may be accompanied by the paralysis of the lower extremities and/or the enlargement of the head (hydrocephalus) due to an accumulation of cerebrospinal fluid within the cranium. The mass must be protected from infection by sterile dressings. Surgery has been helpful in correcting this condition in a limited number of instances.

Other Abnormalities. Intestinal tract abnormalities, such as imperforate anus, intestinal obstruction or esophageal difficulties, may also occur.

Jaundice

A common form of jaundice is evident in many newborn babies and is caused by the normal destruction of the newborn's excess supply of red blood cells. Because the new atmosphere in which he lives supplies more oxygen than his previous world of the uterus, he does not need as many red blood cells, so they are eliminated from the body. The breakdown of these cells in the liver produces the pigment which gives the jaundiced appearance to the skin. This type of *physiologic jaundice* (icterus neonatorum), generally disappears after the first 2 weeks.

Hemolytic Jaundice. Hemolytic jaundice is a serious condition which is caused by the destruction of the baby's red blood cells by antibodies from the mother's blood as a result of Rh incompatibility. This phenomenon was described in Chapter 15. The condition is characterized by jaundice, an enlargement of the spleen and the liver and often by skin hemorrhages.

To treat babies severely affected by hemolytic jaundice, which is also called *erythroblastosis fetalis*, an *exchange transfusion* is performed. Immediately after birth, the baby's blood is removed a few cubic centimeters at a time and replaced by blood from a donor. A close check is kept on the baby's blood for several weeks or months to see that anemia and the need for further transfusions does not develop.

An *ABO* incompatibility can also cause hemolytic disease in the newborn, but the symptims are less severe, and the majority of cases do not need treatment. It occurs when the mother's blood group is Type O and the father's Type A or B. The infant will develop Type A or B blood.

Mongoloid Idiocy

Mongolism is a condition recognizable at birth. The face and the head of the mongoloid baby are flat, the eyes slant upward, the corners of the mouth slant downward, the tongue is large and protrudes from the mouth. The muscles of mongolians are flabby and lack tone. It has been discovered that the children who suffer from mongolism have an extra chromosome—47 instead of the usual 46. Authorities believe that there are 2 types: one occurs as a result of an imperfect cell division in the egg cell, and the other is a hereditary form.

Some mongoloid children may have a fair intelligence, but usually the IQ is between 20 and 40. Many of these babies die before they reach their teens, because they seem to be particularly susceptible to infection.

Infections

Infections which may commonly occur in the newborn are thrush, diarrhea and impetigo contagiosa.

Thrush. Thrush is a yeast infection which forms milklike spots in the mouth. The infected infant is isolated and treated with antibiotics, or gentian violet solution is applied to the affected area.

Diarrhea. The cause of diarrhea may lie in the baby's formula, or it may be due to bacteria. Any evidence of severe diarrhea requires the strict isolation of the baby, and, in the hospital, a separate nursing staff which has nothing to do with other babies. Diarrhea causes such concern because the infant can lose body fluids so rapidly that it can easily become a fatal disease.

Impetigo Contagiosa. Impetigo contagiosa is an infection of the skin which is usually caused by the staphylococcus or the streptococcus. This condition was discussed in Chapter 34. Since it is highly contagious, the infected infant is isolated; pHisoHex baths are given, and antibiotics are administered. Sometimes it is necessary to close a nursery to control the spread of impetigo.

Coincidental Diseases of Pregnancy That May Affect the Baby

Unfortunately, pregnancy does not provide immunity to disease. Sometimes the diseases which are present in the mother during pregnancy have an adverse effect on the fetus.

Syphilis. One of the common conditions of pregnancy which can affect the baby's physical development is syphilis. In most states, the law requires that each pregnant woman have a test for syphilis during her pregnancy. If the blood test proves to be positive, prompt treatment with penicillin early in pregnancy will prevent harmful effects on the baby. A mother with untreated syphilis can transmit the disease to her baby, since syphilis organisms are carried in the blood stream. The infant may be stillborn or may be deformed.

Gonorrhea. Gonorrhea is an infection which does not usually affect the pregnancy itself. However, if the organism causing gonorrhea gets into the eyes of the infant during delivery, it may cause blindness (ophthalmia neonatorum). It is for this reason that most states require the installation of silver nitrate or penicillin in the eyes of the newborn as a prophylactic measure.

Rubella (*German Measles*). Studies have shown that the virus of German measles (rubella, 3-day measles) may be very dangerous in pregnancy. Although the virus has no permanent ill-effects on the mother, it causes such defects in the infant as cataract, deafness, congenital heart defects and disease, and mental retardation. Statistics on the percentage of such defects are so variable that it is unwise to quote them, but the definite relationship between the defects and the disease is established.

Diabetes Mellitus. Because of the extreme alterations in metabolism during pregnancy, diabetes mellitus is a disease difficult to control. The infant death rate is higher for babies of diabetic mothers. However, modern prenatal care has increased the chance of infant survival to 90 per cent, compared with 60 per cent 15 years ago. The babies are often unusually large and may have respiratory difficulties as well as other problems. The mother requires close prenatal supervision.

THE PREMATURE BABY

The premature baby today has more than a fighting chance to live. This happy state of affairs is due partly to the production of advanced mechanical devices, but more than anything else it has come to pass through improved medical and nursing care. However, prematurity is still responsible for the deaths of about 50 per cent of the babies who die in their 1st month. Any baby weighing less than 5½ pounds is considered to be premature, regardless of its time of gestation. Of course, the more premature the baby is, the fewer chances he has to live. There is much difference in a baby weighing 5½ lbs. and one weighing 2 lbs.

The smaller he is, the frailer the premature infant looks. He is thin, has sharp features and weak muscles; his breathing is irregular and weak; his temperature is frequently subnormal. Because he has accumulated so little fat, his blood vessels shine through his almost transparent skin.

Care of the Baby

The premature baby must be handled as little as possible. Usually, he is not bathed immediately. Because he cannot regulate his own body temperature, he must be kept warm. His bed is warmed, and his temperature is taken twice a day or oftener. Oxygen is supplied if necessary.

Because prematures are susceptible to infections, their contacts are limited as much as possible. Usually, only certain personnel are assigned to work in the premature nursery.

Incubator Care. If the baby weighs 3 pounds or less, has breathing difficulties or a very unstable temperature, he is placed in an incubator. The incubator is transparent so that the baby can be seen at all times. It maintains an even temperature and humidity for the premature's environment. Oxygen is given to relieve respiratory difficulties, but it is given in a concentration which is as low as possible. It was discovered that the use of concentrated oxygen was causing blindness in prematures. Babies in incubators are always covered by the incubator hoods; the nurses care for them through openings in the sides.

Feeding. The feeding of prematures varies. In some instances, where small babies are concerned, no feeding is given for 36 hours, since it is believed that digestion adds to the burden of a premature's body functions. In other situations, a small amount of glucose solution is given, just as it is to the larger infant. After approximately 3 days, the baby is given milk. In parts of the country where breast-milk banks

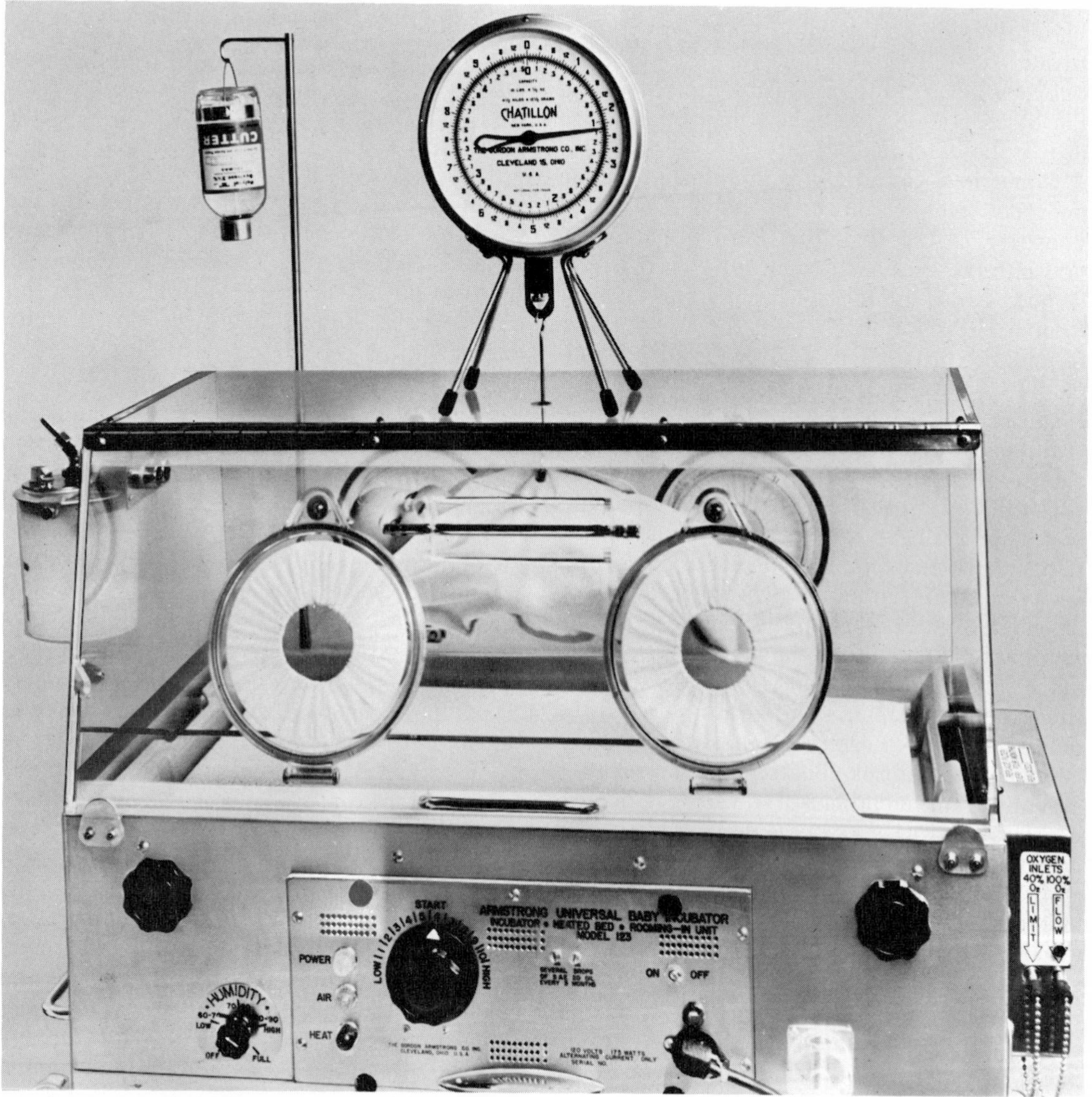

FIG. 203. The Armstrong Universal baby incubator. (The Gordon Armstrong Company, Inc., Cleveland, Ohio)

are available, breast milk seems to be the feeding of choice. In other areas, formulas are prescribed, but always in small amounts so as not to distend the small stomach or to add to respiratory distress. If the baby is not strong enough to suck, he is fed by gavage, whereby a tube is inserted into the stomach through the nose or the mouth.

52

CARE OF THE SICK CHILD

WHEN THE CHILD GOES TO THE HOSPITAL

For many children, hospitalization presents a traumatic and disturbing experience. If it is difficult for some small children to be left with a sitter in their home, how much more terrifying it is to be left alone in a completely different environment with total strangers, and in many instances limited to one room or even confined to a bed.

In the past decade, *patient-centered* pediatric care has evolved from *disease-centered* care, and the need has been recognized to reach the further goals of *family-centered* patient care. Many hospitals are making great efforts to meet this emotional need of the child to remain secure as a part of the family unit.

Even before the child is 1 year old, he becomes frightened of strangers and aware that his mother is absent. From this age through 4 and 5 years of age, he exhibits severe anxiety if he is separated from his home and family. Six- and 7-year-olds continue to show this when they are ill. As a general rule, older children are able to understand the need for hospitalization and the separation from the family circle, but even teen-agers are visibly upset if no family arrives for visiting hours.

Twelve-year-old Arthur is a good example. Yesterday Arthur behaved like a demon during visiting hours. It could have been because he felt unloved and neglected when no one came to see him. He was making up for those feelings by trying to get attention, by shouting rude remarks and throwing things at the other children. You could help Arthur by paying extra attention to him before his rudeness starts; perhaps by remarking to other visitors about his artistic ability. In this manner, he would be drawn into the general feeling in the ward and become a part of it.

Many articles have been written, as well as various workshops and conferences held, to help promote family-centered pediatric nursing. In the larger pediatric centers, the value of parent-child rooms and unrestricted visiting is largely accepted. In other areas, there is a resistance to these changes as well as to other innovations; there are those who feel that the child's family "interferes with his nursing care."

The American Academy of Pediatrics has published a booklet: *The Care of Children in Hospitals*, which encourages the practice of mothers staying to care for their children. It states that: "In hospitals where visiting hours have been replaced by freedom to visit at any hour, parents and children are relieved of much anxiety." It also states that, "In the case of the very ill child or one for whom the separation is especially difficult, arrangements should be made for the mother to stay in the hospital."*

Phases of Adjustment. Robertson† has pointed out that most children, particularly those up to ages of 3 or 4 years, go through 3 phases of adjustment to hospitalization: "(1) protest, (2) despair and (3) denial," and that each phase extends into the next.

The first phase is the *protest* phase in which the child's need for his mother is conscious and

* The Care of Children in Hospitals: The American Academy of Pediatrics, Evanston, Ill., 1960.

† Robertson, J., Young Children in Hospitals, New York, Basic Books, Inc., 1958.

sorrowful. He cries constantly. He rejects all hospital staff because he is so distressed and so afraid—he wants only his mother.

In the second stage, *despair*, the child becomes very inactive and sad. His usual comfort measures, such as thumb-sucking and clutching his blanket, come into prominence. He still watches constantly for his mother, but he is quiet and withdrawn.

The third phase of *denial*, says Robertson, is often accepted by the hospital personnel as adjustment to them, whereas the child is really saving himself from anxiety by rejecting his mother. In truth, his needs for her are more intense than ever.

Children who have experienced separation from their parents show regression in their behavior when they return home. They do not want their mother out of their sight for a second. The loss of this anxiety and the re-establishment of trust takes varying lengths of time, depending on such things as the length of the hospital stay and the understanding of the parents. However, it is important, because as you have learned previously, healthy personality development is significantly related to growth within the mother-child relationship. The nurse must realize how much the child depends on his mother to meet many of his needs.

Parents Are People, Too. As the emphasis in nursing care has changed from the "disease" to the "patient," and from there to the "patient within the family," the role of the nurse has become more difficult. When parents were kept out of the hospital, the nurse gave complete care to the child. However, "the modern nurse must accept the role of mother supplement, not mother substitute, and gain at least some of her job satisfaction from *supporting the mother* in her care of the child."* The nurse shares

* Erickson, Florence, Therapeutic Relationship of the Nurse to the Parents of a Sick Child, Ross Laboratories, 1965.

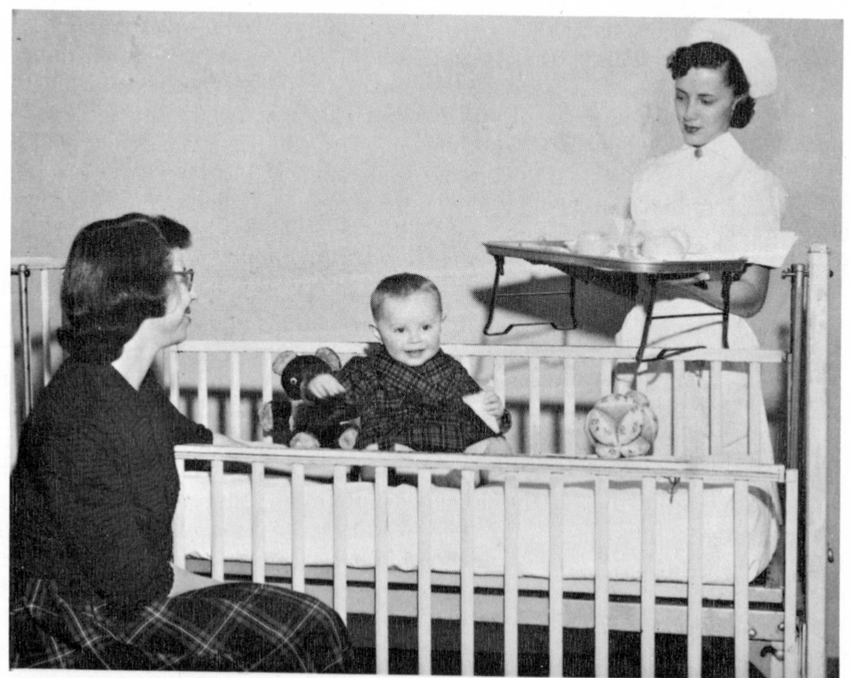

Fig. 204. A nurse who recognizes a child's need for his mother minimizes the discomforts that are associated with hospitalization. (Blake, F. G., and Wright, F. H.: Essentials of Pediatric Nursing, ed. 7, p. 37, Philadelphia, Lippincott, 1963)

the child's care with the mother. This requires an understanding of the effect of the child's illness on the parents.

Let us look at Danny's parents for an example. Certainly, they are worried because Danny is sick. Even though they are adults, the hospital frightens them. Everything they do or do not know about illness has its effect on them. Intelligence, education, nationality, race, religion and previous experiences in hospitals all determine parents' attitudes. Danny's parents are apprehensive about leaving him with strangers. Danny cries and clings to them as they are leaving. The nurse, who calls Danny's parents in an hour to tell that he is sleeping quietly, is more than thoughtful: she is understanding, as well. She is building bridges for a better nurse-parent relationship, which will ultimately reflect in better care for Danny.

Today's pediatric nurse must accept the reactions of parents to their child's illness and have an understanding of the reasons for parents' behavior. Parents may be so fearful and feel so responsible that they hate to leave their child's side. Unhappily, some nurses may then expect the mother to give total care; this is a great misunderstanding of the roles of the nurse and the mother. On the other hand, the parents may feel so inadequate and helpless in meeting the needs of their child that they do not want to be in the room with him; unfortunately, many nurses have only contempt for this latter parent who is in such great need of support.

Studies show us that fewer nursing rounds are made when the parents are with the child. Reasons for this event need further investigation; nevertheless, its effects are poor. Overlooking this opportunity for communication leads to the loss of helpful information which both the nurse and the parents could use. Reasons for the parents' anxiety are often revealed in casual conversation with the nurse. Clues from the mother may help to overcome Tommy's shyness about going to the bathroom, and a little friendly caution and explanation from the nurse about bringing certain foods to Tommy may prevent misunderstanding later. The mother may be longing for the nurse to visit; she may have questions about Tommy's treatment; she may need advice, or she may simply want to talk with someone after being cooped up in the same small room for a long time. (Perhaps this is why mothers visit with each other, a habit which is highly frowned upon by busy pediatric personnel.)

Build a Bridge. Your firm conviction that you *share* the care of the child with his parents is an important one. Anything you can do to help his parents to understand him is a bridge to his future help and happiness. Parents must have hope. It is difficult to reassure the ignorant, frightened mother, whose fears are worse because there are so many things that she does not understand. The intelligent mother is comforted when the treatments and the procedures are explained to her, because she realizes all the important care that you are giving to her child, along with the reasons behind this care.

A general acceptance of the role of the mother and the role of the nurse in their relationships with the sick child will improve the quality of nursing care. Welcoming the assistance of the parents, rather than merely tolerating their presence, will give nurses increased time to care for those who need intensive observation, and to care for the seriously ill child.

The Child's Adjustment to Disability. Children have many of the same illnesses as adults. Although there are some differences in treatments, the greatest differences lie in the effects of the treatment. Consider heart disease. A person past middle age does not find it difficult to be quiet, but a child may have to give up running, jumping, and his favorite sports—activities that are most natural at his age. The older person has completed his schooling and has enjoyed many of life's experiences; the child is just beginning his. The child in his psychological development wants to belong and to imitate his "group." He objects to being different from others his age, whereas the older person has grown into his individual self and can take the differences in his stride.

Rehabilitation. Children do not escape serious diseases and crippling illnesses. More and more attention is being given to finding ways to help disabled children to lead satisfactory lives. Rehabilitation to conduct as nearly a normal life as possible is the goal of all medical and nursing care. Newspapers frequently carry pictures and stories of children in bed receiving their high-school diplomas. Young people in wheelchairs and on crutches learn a trade; some even become practicing physicians. The radio and television help with educational information. Many organizations are trying to give children a better start in life. (See Chap. 31.)

Communicable Childhood Diseases

The diseases that are most common to children are the communicable diseases, those which are transferred from one person to another. Although in some communities, hospitals and hospital departments or wards are set apart to care for patients with communicable diseases, many children having common communicable diseases are cared for at home.

It is impossible to keep people from being exposed to contagious diseases. Methods of the spread of disease and the development of immunity to infectious diseases are discussed in Chapter 7. You already know that science has discovered methods of preventing people from developing some diseases; other discoveries make it possible to provide temporary protection. Early immunization is important to protect children when they are small. An immunization against diphtheria, pertussis (whooping cough) and tetanus is usually started at the age of 1 to 3 months. Smallpox vaccine is often given after the 1st year of life (see Chart).

The period between the time the child is exposed and the time required for the disease to develop is called the *incubation period. Isolation* is the practice of separating a person who has a communicable disease from contact with others. *Quarantine* prohibits anyone from entering or leaving the place where the person with the disease is kept. Except where smallpox is concerned (and sometimes diphtheria), quarantine is not often used. If a child has a communicable disease, he should be isolated until the communicable period is passed.

Chickenpox. Chickenpox (*varicella*) is caused by a virus. It begins with a slight fever which the patient may not even notice. Then a rash appears on the face or the trunk and

Recommended Schedule for Active Immunization and Tuberculin Testing of Normal Infants and Children*[1]

2– 3 months	DTP–Type 1 OPV or Trivalent OPV[2]
3– 4 months	DTP–Type 3 OPV or Trivalent OPV
4– 5 months	DTP–Type 2 OPV or Trivalent OPV
9–11 months	Tuberculin test
12 months	Measles vaccine
15–18 months	DTP–Trivalent OPV–Smallpox[3]
2 years	Tuberculin test
3 years	DTP–Tuberculin test
4 years	Tuberculin test
6 years	TD–Smallpox vaccine–Tuberculin test[4]
	Trivalent OPV
8 years	Tuberculin[4]
10 years	Tuberculin[4]
12 years	TD–Smallpox vaccine–Tuberlin test[4, 5]
14 years	Tuberculin[4]
16 years	Tuberculin[4]

* Abbreviations:

DTP (Diphtheria and Tetanus Toxoids and Pertussis vaccine combined).

OPV (Oral Poliovaccine—if trivalent OPV used —interval should be 6 weeks or longer).

TD (Tetanus and Diphtheria toxoids, adult type).

[1] See separate disease sections for more detailed discussion of recommendations, contraindications, and precautions. [American Academy of Pediatrics: 1966 Red Book, Evanston, Ill.]

[2] Immunization may be started at any age. The immune response is limited in a proportion of young infants and the recommended booster doses are designed to insure or maintain immunity. Protection of infants against pertussis should start early. The best protection of newborn infants against pertussis is avoidance of household contacts by adequate immunization of older siblings. This schedule is intended as a flexible guide which may be modified within certain limits to fit individual situations.

[3] Initial smallpox vaccine may be given at any time between 12 and 24 months of age.

[4] Frequency of repeated tuberculin tests dependent on risk of exposure of children under care and the prevalence of tuberculosis in the population group.

[5] After age 12 follow procedures recommended for adults: i.e., smallpox vaccine every five years and tetanus toxoid booster every ten years.

spreads to the extremities; spots appear which develop into blisters surrounded by a red ring. The blisters are filled with a clear fluid which gradually dries up, leaving a flat crust. The crust falls off in 1 to 3 weeks. The child is usually isolated for 10 to 12 days or until all the crusts have fallen off.

The chickenpox virus is located in the nose, the throat, the blisters and probably in the crusts. Chickenpox takes from 14 to 16 days from the time of exposure to develop. It seldom has serious complications; the most likely one to occur is infection from scratching the blisters. This disease sometimes is confused with a mild case of smallpox because the eruptions are somewhat alike. Smallpox usually begins with more violent symptoms; also, the eruptions appear mostly on the face, the legs and the arms—they are deeper in the skin and have a pearly appearance.

Nursing care for chickenpox includes isolation, a normal diet and the routine comfort care. You will need some ingenuity to keep the child from scratching and to keep him amused until the isolation period is over.

Mumps. Mumps (*epidemic parotitis*) is another virus disease. It affects the salivary glands, especially the parotid. Children under 2 years of age seldom have mumps, and adults rarely have this disease. A closer contact is required to transmit mumps than other contagious diseases. The incubation period lasts from 2 to 3 weeks, averaging about 18 days.

In most cases, the first sign of mumps is a swelling in the parotid gland; occasionally, mumps may begin with a slight fever, headache and malaise before the swelling appears. Sometimes only one of the parotid glands is affected, but both may be affected at the same time, or one after the other. The gland becomes swollen and tender and is very painful. It hurts the victim to open his mouth, but otherwise he may not feel sick. After 2 or 3 days, the swelling begins to go down, and usually it disappears by the 10th day. As a rule, isolation for 2 weeks is long enough.

Children seldom suffer complications with mumps, but grown men and women may. In men, mumps can cause an inflammation of the testes; in women the ovaries, the breasts or the external genitals are affected. Convalescent serum will prevent or lessen the severity of mumps, if the serum is given a few days after the person has been exposed. However, we presently have no proved method which will provide permanent immunity.

Nursing care includes isolation technics, heat applications to the swollen glands to relieve pain, and a diet which does not require chewing. Acid foods taken during the painful stage seem to increase the pain. It is difficult to keep a child in bed until the isolation period is over; modern treatment tends to let him get up if there are no complications.

Measles. Measles (*rubeola*) is caused by a virus which locates itself in the nose, the mouth, the throat and the eyes, and in their discharges. It is highly communicable and may not be recognized early because the symptoms often resemble cold symptoms. The incubation period lasts from 10 to 11 days. Measles begins with a slight temperature rise, and a runny nose and eyes. About the 2nd or 3rd day, bluish-white pinpoint spots with a red rim appear in the mouth; these are called *Koplik's spots.* Small dark red pimples appear on the head and spread gradually over the body. These pimples grow larger and group together, giving a *blotchy* appearance, which is an important difference between measles and scarlet fever. In scarlet fever, the skin appears red all over.

The respiratory symptoms grow worse. The patient sneezes frequently, his eyes are sore, and the discharge becomes purulent. Light hurts his eyes (photophobia). His throat is sore. The rash is greatest about the 4th day, and it may last up to 10 days. During the 2nd week, the skin begins to flake off, and it continues to do so for 5 to 10 days.

Complications are frequent with measles. The infection may spread to the middle ear. Pneumonia is a common development. Encephalitis occurs occasionally and may cause death. The prognosis in a measles case depends on the age and the condition of the child; it affects the very young child most dangerously.

Isolation should be practiced until the discharges from the nose and the eyes disappear and the temperature is normal, which usually occurs 5 days from the time the rash appears.

Recently, medical scientists have found a measles vaccine which confers active immunity, which is being used much more widely. In addition to the measles vaccine, gamma globulin will afford a temporary immunity if it is given a few days after exposure; the attack will be mild if it is given later, but before the symptoms appear. Gamma globulin has no effect if it is administered after the disease develops.

German Measles. German measles (*rubella*) also is caused by a virus, but the disease is mild and lasts only a short time. The symptoms are like measles but are not nearly as severe, and spots never appear on the mucous membrane of the mouth. Sometimes the rash which appears on the face is the first noticeable sign of a rubella infection. The rash spreads quickly and disappears just as rapidly; sometimes it is gone from the face and the neck by the time it reaches the arms and the legs. The rash is usually completely gone in 2 to 4 days. Complications rarely develop; however, two possible ones are serious. One is encephalitis, and the other is fetal malformations which occur when a mother contracts German measles in the early months of her pregnancy.

Isolation usually is very brief or not carried out at all, since the infectious stage is so short; probably there is little danger of passing on the infection after the rash disappears. We presently have no means of developing immunity to German measles, although pregnant mothers are given gamma globulin when exposed to this disease.

Whooping Cough. Whooping cough (*pertussis*) is caused by a bacillus. Infants do not receive immunity to whooping cough from their mothers; therefore, very young infants are susceptible to it. Whooping cough rarely occurs after the age of 10 years. The incubation period is from 7 to 14 days. The symptoms begin with bronchitis and a slight elevation in temperature. The cough steadily grows worse, eventually leading to paroxysms of coughing. The first stage lasts about a week; the severe coughing stage, from 2 to 3 weeks. It takes about 2 or 3 more weeks for the cough to disappear, but whooping cough can last for several months if complications appear, the most serious of which is bronchopneumonia.

Isolation is practiced through the whooping period. (As the child has paroxysms of coughing, he struggles for breath; this indrawn gasping breath has a crowing sound or whoop.) Small infants may not be able to breathe, and they may suffer periods of anoxia. Often the paroxysm is followed by vomiting, so that maintaining nutrition becomes a problem. Since nausea does not accompany the vomiting, the child should be fed again.

Prevention of whooping cough is available through a vaccine which is given as early as 1 month of age. This does not provide permanent immunity, and boosters of the vaccine should be given at intervals.

The child who has whooping cough is given antibiotics and medications to relieve the coughing. The infant must be supervised closely because of his respiratory difficulties and nutritional problems.

Diphtheria. Diphtheria is another communicable disease caused by a bacillus. It begins with a sore throat, fever, and often generalized aching and malaise. Inflammation of the throat (the disease may also appear in the nose, the larynx or the trachea) is followed by the formation of a dirty-gray membrane which is closely adherent and cannot be removed without causing bleeding. The diphtheria bacilli produce a toxin or poison which may weaken the cardiac muscle. The patient is very ill and must be observed closely. The mortality rate from diphtheria lies between 5 and 10 per cent.

Diphtheria can be prevented by the injection of a toxin which produces a long-lasting immunity. It is usually given with the immunization injections for whooping cough and tetanus. Boosters are administered at intervals.

Patients with diphtheria are isolated until cultures from the infected part no longer yield the bacillus. They are treated with antibiotics and diphtheria antitoxin. The patient is kept in bed until the fever disappears. If the heart has been affected, the bed rest is prolonged until recovery is complete.

People who have no symptoms of diphtheria themselves may be carriers of the bacillus (see page 506). Carriers are treated with antibiotics.

Scarlet Fever. Scarlet fever is another contagious disease affecting children. It is caused by a hemolytic streptococcus. Although many persons have sore throats caused by the streptococcus, not all exhibit the rash reaction. The incubation period is from 1 to 7 days. The patient has a sore throat, fever and feels very ill. Scarlet fever (also called *scarlatina*) gives the appearance of a generalized flush or redness but is really a rash of small red pinpoints very close together. Flaking of the skin (desquamation) follows the rash.

The complications most commonly seen are ear infections and nephritis. Arthritis, cardiac problems and pneumonia may also occur. The patient is kept in bed until the symptoms disappear. Antibiotics to which the streptococcus is susceptible are administered. Generally, scarlet fever tends to be a milder disease than it formerly was, and the prognosis is for the complete recovery of the patient.

Rheumatic Fever

Rheumatic fever (not a reportable disease) is both a killer and a crippler. It is the 5th leading cause of death among children. As was stated in Chapter 36, it is the cause of 90 per cent of the heart disease in people under the age of 50. Probably more than a million people in the United States have had some form of rheumatic fever. Usually, it occurs in children between the ages of 5 and 15 years, but during World War II, 40,000 armed service personnel had rheumatic fever. One attack does not guarantee immunity; on the contrary, it increases susceptibility to further attacks.

What It Is. Rheumatic fever belongs to a group of diseases called *collagen diseases*; that is, diseases which affect the connective tissues throughout the body. Its specific cause is still being debated, but several facts are known. Rheumatic fever usually follows streptococcal infections, such as scarlet fever or a sore throat caused by streptococci. Authorities believe that rheumatic fever results from continued infections, in which the patient becomes sensitive to the organism or develops a type of allergic response. The disease occurs in those climates where respiratory infections are most common; it also occurs more in certain families than in others, so that susceptibility appears to be inherited.

Symptoms. The symptoms of rheumatic fever vary in degree from mild to explosively severe. Children may complain of symptoms which are not always recognized as indicating this disease. A loss of weight and appetite, and fatigue and irritability may be signs. Aches, pains, and tenderness in the extremities are suspicious signs which parents might ignore as "growing pains." However, there are more definite symptoms. Rheumatic fever may begin suddenly, especially after a cold or a sore throat. The patient complains of aches and pains in the arms and the legs. The fever varies. Then the joints of the shoulders, the elbows, the wrists or the knees swell and become excruciatingly painful. The pain travels from one joint to another; it may affect several joints at the same time. This pain usually lasts from a few days to a week in each joint, and it subsides gradually. Fortunately, the arthritis of rheumatic fever does not leave joint deformities; the joints usually are completely normal after the attack.

Jerky, uncontrolled movements of the face, the neck, the arm and the leg muscles (*chorea* or *St. Vitus Dance*), are symptoms of rheumatic fever. Small nodules formed under the skin over the elbows, the ankles, the legs, the knuckles and at back of the head are almost certain signs. Frequent nosebleeds may also be an indication of the disease.

Another common and serious symptom of rheumatic fever is the involvement of the heart tissues; this is called *rheumatic carditis*. The nodules develop in the heart; lesions appear on the valves, sometimes interfering with their efficiency and increasing the workload of the also affected myocardium. The symptoms of rheumatic carditis vary from mild disease to cardiac failure.

There is no specific laboratory test which is diagnostic of rheumatic fever. An increase in the sedimentation rate of the blood cells indicates an inflammatory process within the body. Electrocardiograms are valuable in diagnosing rheumatic carditis.

Treatment and Nursing Care. The course of the disease depends primarily on whether or not the heart is involved. It usually lasts from 1 to 4 months, but once the child has had rheumatic fever, he is likely to have recurrences. The keynote in the treatment of rheumatic fever is the prevention of permanent heart damage. Complete bed rest is ordered. Aspirin or other salicylates are given for 2 purposes: they relieve pain, and since they are also effective anti-inflammatory medications, they assist in preventing heart damage. Cortisone therapy is also used to limit the inflammatory processes. Antibiotics are administered to combat the hemolytic streptococci. Bed rest or limited activity is continued until the disease process is inactive.

It is fairly easy to keep a child inactive when the disease is acute. He is very sick; therefore, he feels like being quiet and staying in bed. However, your contact with the rheumatic fever patient may come when he is convalescing, at which point regulated activity becomes more difficult to maintain. Considerable effort is required to keep a child quiet but amused over an extended period of time. The child's cooperation is important; if he can understand that living in bed now will give him the best chance for doing what he likes later in life, he may be able to endure periods of restlessness with greater ease.

The outcome of rheumatic fever, like its progress and the treatment, depends on the involvement of the heart. Neither chorea nor arthritis is likely to leave after-effects. The carditis may be fatal, or it may result in a complete recovery—even heart murmurs may disappear. Most children recover and lead perfectly normal lives.

Because the patient who once has rheumatic fever is susceptible to recurrent attacks, many medical authorities recommend that these patients be kept on a small daily dose of a sulfa drug or penicillin. They can also be given monthly injections of long-acting penicillin. This is continued for 5 years after the first attack, and it prevents reinfection by the hemolytic streptococci.

Heart Disease and Restriction of Activity. How does heart disease affect a child's life? The following classifications of people with heart disease, prepared by the American Heart Association, show what they can do safely:

Patients who can take part in any activity—children can go to school and do anything that the other children do.

Patients who are allowed ordinary activities, but not strenuous ones—children can go to school but must not take part in competitive sports, such as races, football, basketball, or tennis.

Patients who must be moderate about ordinary activities and must avoid strenuous ones—children can go to school but should be given extra time for such things as climbing stairs.

Patients who definitely must limit even ordinary activities—children must learn not to run and never should be allowed to become overtired; they should also have definite rest periods.

Patients who should have complete rest—children may be allowed to sit up in a chair; they may have to stay in bed.

One heart specialist states that we should help children with heart disease to be as much like other children as possible. He emphasizes the need for continuous medical supervision, but he thinks that every child should learn to live within the limits of his disability, instead of being conscious of it.

Rehabilitation. Providing opportunities for education, better living conditions and good medical supervision is important to help children disabled by rheumatic fever to become useful citizens. Some localities have programs underway to do these things. The federal government has given money to help states set up programs for the care of children with rheumatic fever. Individual communities are making efforts to provide medical and hospital services. As with many other health programs, a great effort is being made in the research and the care of heart disease.

Cerebral Palsy

Cause. Cerebral palsy is a comprehensive term used to describe conditions in which a person has difficulty controlling voluntary muscle activity. This is sometimes the result of an infectious disease which causes brain damage after birth. However, many cases seem to be the result of brain injury incurred during delivery or from anoxia immediately following birth.

Symptoms. The most frequent symptom is spasticity or stiffness and rigidity of the muscles of the extremities. Movements are not destroyed completely, but the child cannot control them. Motions are jerky, and the muscles are tense. Any part of the body may be involved—one portion or all. A generalized involvement results in a very helpless child.

If the disability is severe, it may be recognized shortly after birth; more often it is recognized at the time the child should be developing normal muscular skills, such as sitting or walking. For instance, if the legs are involved, the muscle rigidity becomes more noticeable when the child begins to walk. The muscles that draw the feet and the knees toward each other are stronger than those that draw them apart, so the child walks cross-legged—his legs move like scissors.

Mental retardation or behavioral problems may accompany cerebral palsy. However, intelligence also may be normal or above normal. Because the child may have speech difficulties or difficulties communicating in any way, an adequate assessment of his intelligence is often difficult.

Treatment. We presently have no methods for repairing a brain injury. The problems of each child must be appraised and understood; his therapy must be based on his abilities.

The family's acceptance of their child and their willingness to assist in his development may be the greatest factor in his development. The parents should be helped to understand that much can be done for the spastic child. He needs highly individualized care to give him the same opportunities which are open to normal children. The Crippled Children's Service is a community agency that makes this care possible if the parents are unable to pay for it themselves.

One of the primary objectives in the treatment of cerebral palsy is the prevention of muscle contractures. Splints and sometimes surgery are used; muscle relaxants assist in muscle re-education. The spastic child progresses slowly. Attempts to force or hurry the child only make him tense and less able to move.

Psychological Problems. Cerebral palsy is a handicap which creates many psychological problems for the child. The intelligent child is bound to feel frustrated, because it is difficult or impossible for him to make his body respond. He feels insecure; he may be unattractive in appearance. He is incapable of doing many of the things that other children do. He may have speech difficulties; eye defects interfere with reading; lack of coordination makes writing a problem.

Adolescence can be difficult enough for normal children; the spastic child feels his handicap keenly at a time when he wants to be independent, to establish boy-girl relationships or to join in social activities. Parents and teachers must assume attitudes which will help to make other children accept him as a person. He needs to be with people his own age, to make friends, play games and go to parties. His ambitions may go far beyond anything he ever will be able to do. It is important to begin early in childhood to guide cerebral palsy children to the things they can learn to do satisfactorily. The child must learn to face reality and to make the most of his life in spite of his handicap.

Unit Nine:

The Graduate Practical Nurse

53

CAREER OPPORTUNITIES IN PRACTICAL NURSING

The Scope of the Field

There is a constant demand for the practical nurse today in hospitals, nursing homes, visiting nurse services, doctors' offices, private duty nursing, industry and many other areas. She is also being called on more and more to work on committees with professional nurses, to speak to health and civic groups and to participate in the recruitment of students for the practical nursing schools.

The practical nurse has become a valuable member of the health team, and her opportunities for employment are virtually unlimited. Although graduation from an approved practical nursing school is always an asset when applying for a position, employers recognize by evidence presented by a *licensed* practical nurse that she has passed a state examination in which she has been required to demonstrate her competence to practice. (The licensing law, called the Nurse Practice Act, will be discussed in the next chapter.)

In a Hospital. By far the greatest number of practical nurses find positions in hospitals as staff nurses who give bedside care on the various nursing services. If a vacancy exists, consideration may be given to an applicant's preference for a specific service, such as pediatrics or obstetrics. The practical nurse works under the supervision of professional nurses as a member of the nursing team.

When she accepts a position she is entering into an agreement, so she should be fully informed about and understand the personnel policies of the institution. Personnel policies are concerned with such matters as the number of hours in the work week, the tour of duty (morning, afternoon, night), vacation and illness allowances, the salary and the possibility of salary increases, living accommodations and hospitalization coverage. Every hospital establishes its own policies, which vary somewhat from one to another. Salaries vary with the size of the institution, its type and location; they are usually higher in large cities and in certain parts of the country. Most hospitals today provide a cafeteria service where employees may purchase meals at a nominal cost, or they are permitted to bring their own lunches. Some institutions have living quarters available at a moderate price; but for the most part, nurses today live outside of the hospital in their own homes or elsewhere. Many hospitals require employees to carry hospitalization coverage; some provide it for their employees.

In a Nursing Home. There are many openings for positions on the nursing staff of nursing homes. A well-run nursing home establishes policies for employment similar to those of hospitals by stating its requirements for employees. The applicant should inquire about the amount of professional nurse supervision that is provided and the extent of her responsibilities in the care of patients. Patients in a nursing home offer a real challenge to the ability of a practical nurse to encourage and aid in developing the activity and the independence of these patients in spite of their disabilities.

With a Visiting Nurse Service. Many visiting nurse services throughout the country employ practical nurses on the nursing staff. The first requirements for such a position are graduation from an approved school and state licensure. In addition, an applicant is selected on the basis of her nursing ability, her ability to get along with people, and her personal maturity (which may have nothing to do with her age). She makes scheduled home visits to the patients assigned to her care, under the direction of her supervisor who is a professional nurse with special public health preparation. The practical nurse keeps records and makes reports of her visits, and she participates in conferences of the nursing staff. She wears the uniform adopted by the agency for its practical nurse staff members.

In a Doctor's Office. A practical nurse may be employed in a doctor's office, to assist with physical examinations, dressings and other procedures. Her duties may also include answering the telephone, making appointments with patients and serving as a receptionist.

Private Duty. The private practitioner of nursing takes care of individual patients in a home, an institution, or wherever a patient may desire to take her, as in a case when the patient is traveling. This is known as private duty nursing. The nurse is usually paid by the patient or his family, although in the hospital, she is directly responsible to the physician and the hospital administration for the performance of her duties. Private duty gives the practical nurse an opportunity to practice her basic bedside and teaching skills and to meet the total needs of her patient. Since it often includes the care of patients during a long-term illness, or of patients who are wholly or partially disabled, private duty nursing offers steady employment for long periods, and may be especially desirable to the older nurse who finds hospital staff duty on an active service too strenuous.

Other Opportunities

Some positions are available for practical nurses with special qualifications and ability to meet the demands of a specialized job.

Assistant Instructor in a Practical Nursing School. Some practical nursing schools employ a practical nurse to assist with the supervision of practical nurse students. The qualifications for such a position include a good educational background, proficiency in carrying out nursing procedures, and the ability to get along with people. Previous experience in teaching is a valuable asset. It is not uncommon to find an occasional licensed practical nurse who was formerly a teacher.

As an instructor, her duties are to assist with the supervision of students as they practice nursing procedures in the classroom and carry out these procedures with patients in the hospital.

Head Nurse Responsibilities. In some institutions a practical nurse may be given head nurse responsibilities in one unit of a service assigned to patients whose main requirement is custodial care. She works under and is responsible to the department supervisor, a professional nurse who provides guidance and assistance.

In the Operating Room. Many hospitals now employ practical nurses on the operating room staff. The nurse is prepared for this position by on-the-job training in the employing hospital or by a postgraduate course taken in operating room technics.

Postgraduate Courses. Approved postgraduate courses in the nursing specialties, such as pediatric and obstetric nursing, medical and surgical nursing, and operating room technics, are available to the licensed practical nurse in a number of centers. Information about approved courses can be obtained by writing to the National Association for Practical Nurse Education and Service, 535 Fifth Avenue, New York, N. Y. 10017.

The Peace Corps. To practical nurses who can qualify, the Peace Corps offers an opportunity to volunteer for services that are desperately needed in many parts of the world. An interested person can write to the Peace Corps, Washington, D. C., for detailed information.

Placement Services. Many nurses, both registered and practical, get positions through placement services or registries. Nonprofit services usually require a flat fee on a yearly basis.

A commercial registry is operated for profit and may charge a fee every time it places an applicant. However, some registries of this type have been known to be interested in only the fee when placing private duty nurses, disregarding the needs of the patient and the standards of the nurse as well as those of the employer. A good registry operates under policies established to serve the best interests of nurses and patients. Nonprofit registries are usually operated by the official district association of professional nurses, but they may also be operated by similar associations of practical nurses, or by individuals. Some local branches of the State Employment Service provide placement services for practical nurses.

When using a placement service, the nurse notifies the registrar when she is available for work. She also notifies the agency when she is no longer with a patient as a private duty nurse or when she leaves a position, and she indicates when she will be available again. This helps the registry to give better service to the community. At the present time, the demand for practical nurses is so much greater than the supply that many are directly employed as soon as they graduate by the hospital in which they have had their experience as students.

A practical nurse may also obtain employment on the recommendation of a doctor or through personal contacts with the relatives and the friends of former patients. Many find positions by placing personal applications in a hospital, nursing home or agency.

Employment

The Personal Interview. The routine procedure for employment usually includes a personal interview with the prospective employer. When you go for the interview you want to make a favorable impression. This means that you will give careful attention to your appearance and grooming. Leave your tightest skirts, slacks, shorts and toeless sandals at home. These garments all have their proper place in your life, but that place is not in a business interview. Whatever the prevailing style of hair-do, be sure that your hair is clean. Avoid extremes in make-up and nail polish. Employers are likely to take a dim view of glamor girls on the nursing staff. And surely, there is no need to mention *gum.*

Take your license with you and be prepared to furnish the names of people for references, should you be asked for them. Most employers prefer to get references this way, rather than accepting any letters you may present. Naturally, you will not lounge in your chair or indulge in long-winded recitals of the nice things former employers have said about you—your references should reveal this. If you are asked why you left a previous position, tell the truth, since the reasons can be checked.

The Written Application. When you are applying for a position and a personal interview is not immediately possible, your application should include the kind of information that you would be asked to give in an interview. You state the name of your practical nursing school and the year of graduation, whether you are licensed and in what state or states, your age, your marital status, and what previous positions you have held and for how long. You should also mention any special preparation that you may have had in a postgraduate course. Use conservative stationery, and be sure to write legibly in ink—if you can type, so much the better. It is businesslike to include the names and the addresses of 2 or 3 persons to whom the prospective employer may write for references.

Resigning From a Position. When resigning from a position, it is honorable to give your employer advance notice of your intentions. This enables him to find someone to replace you by the time you leave. The advance notice required varies with the position and is established in personnel policies. Customarily, if you leave before the designated time or leave without notice, you will be paid up to the time of your departure. If an employer asks an employee to leave because she is no longer needed, or because her work is unsatisfactory, she may be asked to leave at the end of the time required for a notice. If she is discharged without notice, it is customary to pay an employee for the time required for giving notice.

Keeping Abreast of New Knowledge. As a

student you were learning new things every day with your instructors to guide you, and you had a library to keep you informed and up to date on new developments in nursing and health care. As a graduate practical nurse you are on your own and must turn to other sources of information. These sources are all around you. Books and magazine articles will help to keep you informed about scientific discoveries which are improving the treatment of disease. Radio and TV programs discuss health problems. Workshops, conferences and conventions will be available, through which you can learn how to improve your care of patients. Many hospitals maintain in-service education programs for employee groups to keep them informed about new developments in hospital and nursing procedures. The nurse who does not take advantage of these opportunities to improve her knowledge is in danger of finding herself bringing up the rear in the march of progress.

The State Practical Nurse Association. Every licensed practical nurse has an obligation to support and participate in the activities of her state practical nurse association. She can join through the local division where she lives. The activities of these associations were discussed in Chapter 1. The state practical nurse associations have done and are presently doing a great number of things for their members. Everyone knows that a group working together can get things done which one person never could accomplish alone. A representative of the local division may be given an opportunity to tell your student group about the activities of the association in your area and how you can join. Your instructors will also have this information. *The National Association for Practical Nurse Education and Service (NAPNES), The National Federation of Licensed Practical Nurses (NFLPN)* and *The National League for Nursing (NLN)* are the national organizations with a special interest in the education and the activities of practical nurses. Practical nurses are eligible for membership in these organizations.

The NLN is an organization with its membership open to both individuals and agencies. In addition to professional nurses, practical nurses and those in the para-medical professions, interested laymen may join. Agency membership includes organizations and groups involved in nursing service, and schools or departments which provide educational programs in nursing. Other organizations may join as allied agency members. Membership in the NLN gives the practical nurse a broad view of current areas of nursing education and service, by bringing her into contact with many people interested in community health problems. The test service offered to student practical nurses by the NLN was discussed in Chapter 1. It has also recently established a program of accreditation for schools of practical nursing.

Alumnae Associations. Many schools have an alumnae association with written bylaws stating its objectives and its means of carrying them out. Among their many activities are student recruitment programs, the establishment of scholarship and loan funds, and fund raising events to purchase needed educational equipment for the school. Most schools today also have some form of student government. This group should work closely with the alumnae association and the faculty. Together they can do much to maintain high standards of nursing practice.

Your Personal Plans. Your work life is affected by your personal life. Plan recreation for yourself. Sir William Osler said: "No man is really happy or safe without a hobby . . . anything will do so long as he straddles a hobby and rides it hard." This is good advice because your personal satisfaction is reflected in your work.

Make a plan for financial security. Annuities and retirement plans can be budgeted through your best earning years. Apply for your Social Security account number. Invest in a health examination once a year; it is cheaper than being sick or disabled. Get hospitalization and medical care insurance with a reliable group plan—just in case! Widen your interests; do not wrap yourself up in your work so completely that you feel life is over when you reach the retirement age. All this is insurance for a safer and happier life when you are older, but it begins to pay dividends in peace of mind long before that time comes.

54

THE LEGAL ASPECTS OF PRACTICAL NURSING

The Licensing Law

The legal aspects of practical nursing begin with the licensing law, which gives the practical nurse the legal right to practice nursing; also, it defines her responsibilities. This was discussed previously in Chapter 1, where it was mentioned that every state, as well as the District of Columbia, Puerto Rico, Guam, Samoa and the Virgin Islands, has a law for licensing practical nurses. It was also pointed out that in some states the law is *mandatory*, making it illegal for a practical nurse to practice nursing for pay without a license, while in other states, the law is *permissive*, making it illegal to use the title *Licensed Practical Nurse (L.P.N.)* or *Licensed Vocational Nurse (L.V.N.)* without a license. A mandatory law protects the practice of nursing, but a permissive law protects only the title. Some states have changed the licensing laws from permissive to mandatory; others are working toward such a change.

The practical nurse licensing laws vary in other respects from state to state in their requirements for licensure. It is hoped that eventually more uniform requirements can be established in order that a license issued in one state will be recognized in all other states. This is not true at the present time, but the situation is improving.

The Licensing Examination. *The graduate nurse's first responsibility* is to pass the licensing examination upon her successful completion of an approved practical nursing course and to obtain a license to work as a practical nurse.

Your school must send your application and a transcript of your records, and you must send the required fee to the State Board of Nursing, which is the authority responsible for giving the examination. Licensing examinations are given twice a year—the applicant will be notified of the time and the place. After passing the examination, she receives her license. If an applicant fails, she is given a chance to repeat the examination a limited number of times within a specified period, as stated in the law. After receiving her license, the practical nurse is responsible for renewing it according to the regulations, and for keeping the board informed about any changes in her address.

The Nurse Practice Act. The licensing law is called the Nurse Practice Act. It defines the title and the regulations governing the practice of practical nursing. In some states one nurse practice act covers the regulations for both professional and practical nurses and is administered under one board. In other states practical nursing is regulated by a separate act under a separate board. In many of the states with a single board the law demands that a specified number of practical nurses serve as board members; this gives practical nurses a voice in affairs concerning them. The state practical nurse association makes recommendations for these appointments.

Provisions in a Nurse Practice Act. The

law defines the regulations for practical nursing, which include:

A definition of practical nursing.

The requirements for an approved school of practical nursing (length of the course, the curriculum, admission requirements).

Requirements for licensure (age, graduation from an approved course, the licensing examination).

Conditions under which a license may be suspended or voided.

The State Board of Nursing. The authority for administering the nurse practice act is the State Board of Nursing (sometimes known by other titles, such as the Board of Nurse Examiners). As stated previously, in some states practical nursing may be under a separate board. The board is responsible for approving schools of practical nursing, visiting the schools, administering the licensing examinations, issuing and renewing practical nurse licenses; it also has the authority to suspend or revoke a license. The board is subject to the conditions defined in the law, but it usually has some leeway in its interpretation of these conditions.

Cause for Revoking or Suspending a License. The law defines the conditions under which a license may be revoked. These conditions include unbecoming conduct, such as habitual drunkenness; serious crimes, such as robbery or murder; serious negligence in caring for patients, or practices which might endanger patients, such as drug addiction.

Legal Responsibilities in Nursing Service

In the course of her activities, the practical nurse encounters many situations which involve legal responsibilities. She will be held responsible for maintaining the standards of nursing care which are set up for practical nursing. She may be found negligent: if she performs nursing procedures that she has not been taught; or if she fails to meet established standards for the safe care of patients, or for preventing injury to hospital employees and visitors (for which she may consequently be sued for damages).

Negligence. One of the most common causes of lawsuits instigated by patients is negligence. Negligence is defined as harm done to a patient as a result of neglecting the ordinary precautions expected of a responsible person.

Some common types of situations which might cause injury to a person and involve legal liability are: (1) burns—from hot-water bags, heating pads, contact with steam pipes or with scalding water; from chemicals by either improper mixture or application; (2) sponges overlooked in surgical wounds; (3) falls on slippery floors; (4) falls from an unprotected bed or crib by an unconscious patient (children and adults must be protected by siderails or other means, according to age and physical and mental condition); (5) injury from the wrong medicine or from the wrong dosage; and (6) injury from visibly defective or improperly tested equipment.

A damage suit may be instituted against a nurse for any injury caused by her failure to observe hospital regulations established to protect the patient or to care for his belongings. The patient is likely to have certain property which must be protected from loss, theft or damage, and proper safeguards must be observed in the care of money, jewelry, dentures, spectacles and clothing. When the nurse or the hospital takes over the care of property, she and/or the hospital will be held responsible for it.

Lack of sleep or overwork will not be accepted as legal reasons for carelessness about safety measures or mistakes in medicines.

Personal Liability. Although a practical nurse works under the direction of professional nurses and physicians, she is personally liable for harm to a patient which is a result of her own acts. In a hospital, her employer may also be legally liable for her acts of negligence.

Legal actions involving negligent acts by a person engaged in a professional field are generally known as *malpractice suits.* Many people doing this type of work protect themselves from possible legal suits by carrying *malpractice insurance.* Malpractice insurance for nurses generally covers only nursing acts. Other legal actions involving negligence are not necessarily covered by this insurance.

Criminal Liability. A crime involves the deliberate commission or omission of an act forbidden or required by law. As a citizen, a nurse knows that acts such as murder and robbery are illegal. There are other laws which she, as a nurse, must be equally careful not to violate. For example, the federal law requires that records be kept on dispensing narcotics. This law specifies that narcotics must be given under the direction and the supervision of a physician, a dentist, or a veterinarian, and that all unused portions be returned to the physician, the dentist or the veterinarian. In a hospital all narcotics are kept under lock and key, and every tablet must be accounted for (see Chap. 30). As another example, it is a crime to assist in a *criminal* abortion; only under certain circumstances may an abortion be performed legally by a physician.

Intentional Invasion of a Patient's Rights. A nurse may be held liable for damages arising from intentional acts which invade the personal rights protected by law. Civil suits may ask damages from assault and battery, false imprisonment, restraint of movement, slander and libel.

When a patient enters the hospital, presumably he gives his consent to being treated. He may withhold his consent to certain acts. Surgery, the giving of certain medications, or treatments, and restraining a patient for his own protection, involve a violation of his rights if his consent is withheld. Consent may be given verbally, but in some cases (especially surgery) there *must* be a written permission. The practical nurse has an obligation to follow the policies of her hospital or employer in this matter; in cases where there is any doubt, she should notify her superior.

Every person has the right of protection of his privacy, which is the right to withhold himself and his property from the public eye. For example, stories or photographs of a patient must not be given out without his written consent. Physical freedom is another personal right, unless it has been removed legally following the conviction for a crime or the declaration of mental incompetence. Therefore, if a nurse should confine a patient against his will, she could be liable to a suit for false imprisonment.

A patient's rights may be invaded in ways other than physical damage. If untrue and damaging statements are made about a person, the one who made such verbal statements may be sued for *slander*; if the statements were in writing, the suit would be for *libel*.

Legal Responsibility in an Emergency. In some states a person who is involved in an automobile accident is required by law to give aid to a person injured in that accident. This is on a par with the law which makes a hit-and-run driver liable to prosecution for leaving the scene of an accident. Other than areas where this law applies, no person is legally obligated to render aid during an emergency. However, when one voluntarily does so, he should act as a reasonably prudent person would.

In a true emergency situation, which involves saving a life, a medical act can be performed without being considered a violation of medical practice, whether it is performed by a professional nurse, a practical nurse or a layman. However, it must be remembered that substantial proof must be presented in court which will attest that it was in fact an emergency situation. It must also be remembered that in such legal cases, the nurse, who has had more training and experience than the layman, will be considered as being more capable of evaluating an emergency situation and will be held *more* responsible for the consequences of her actions.

Legal Advice. A nurse should never attempt to advise a patient on his legal rights; he should be encouraged to confer with his family and to consult his attorney. The laws governing the personal and property rights of an individual are many and complex. Professional advice is essential to ensure proper protection.

Gifts. Sometimes an ill person will wish to transfer his personal property to his family or friends, if he has not already made a will. If this is done because he expects to die, the gift is known as a gift *causa mortis*; in the event that the donor does not die, the gift may be revoked. There are many technicalities in the law in regard to gifts, which cover the intention to give, the delivery of the property and its acceptance.

Wills. A nurse should never attempt to help

a patient draw up a will. The law has very formal requirements which a will must meet to make it valid. The law generally requires 2 or more witnesses to the signing of a will; the number varies in the different states. Because of this variance, it is better to have at least 3 witnesses. Certain formalities govern the signing of a will; generally, the will must be declared to be a last will and must be signed in the presence of witnesses, who then must sign in the presence of each other. They must witness the signature of the patient making the will, as well as the affixing of the names, or the marks, of the other witnesses.

A nurse may be called upon to witness a will in the performance of her duties. After the death of a patient, the nurse, as well as the other witnesses, may be called upon to testify to the mental competence of the testator or to other conditions prevailing at the time of the execution of the will. This will enable the court to determine whether or not all legal requirements were met in drawing up the document.

The Importance of the Written Record. We cannot emphasize too strongly the importance of keeping exact records of all treatments, medications and everything that is done for or happens to the patient, as well as a record of the patient's behavior. The patient's chart is the written evidence of his treatment during his stay in the hospital, or of occurrences in the home.

The Nurse's Legal Rights. In employment, a nurse has a right to legal protection by contract (oral or written) which states the terms of her employment in relation to her duties and salary. If either party fails to live up to the terms, the contract can be terminated. If the terms of the contract are not defined clearly for both parties and the contract is broken, either party has the legal right to get a court of law decision as to which party is in the right.

BIBLIOGRAPHY

Nursing History

Bullough, B., and Bullough, V.: The Emergence of Modern Nursing, New York, Macmillan, 1964.

Cope, Z.: Florence Nightingale and the Doctors, Philadelphia, Lippincott, 1958.

Dietz, L. D.: History and Modern Nursing, Philadelphia, Davis, 1963.

Dolan, J.: Goodnow's History of Nursing, ed. 11, Philadelphia, Saunders, 1963.

Griffin, G. J., and Griffin, H. J. K.: Jensen's History and Trends of Professional Nursing, St. Louis, Mosby, 1965.

Jamieson, E. M., Sewell, M. F., and Suhrie, E. B.: Trends in Nursing History, ed. 6, Philadelphia, Saunders, 1966.

Pelley, T.: Nursing: Its History, Trends, Philosophy, Ethics and Ethos, Philadelphia, Saunders, 1964.

Seymer, L. R.: Selected Writings of Florence Nightingale, New York, Macmillan, 1954.

Stewart, I. M., and Austin, A. L.: A History of Nursing From Ancient to Modern Times, ed. 5, New York, Putnam, 1962.

Woodham-Smith, C.: Florence Nightingale, New York, McGraw-Hill, 1951.

Yost, E.: American Women of Nursing, ed. 2, Philadelphia, Lippincott, 1965.

Study Aids, Reviews and Dictionaries

Blakiston's Illustrated Pocket Medical Dictionary, ed. 2, New York, Blakiston-McGraw, 1960.

Cape, B. F.: Bailliere's Nurses' Dictionary, ed. 16, Baltimore, Williams & Wilkins, 1964.

Cardew, E. C.: Study Guide for Clinical Nursing, ed. 2, Philadelphia, Lippincott, 1961.

Edmondson, F. W.: Medical Terminology, New York, Putnam, 1965.

Hansen, H. F.: Pocket Encyclopedic Guide to Nursing, New York, Blakiston-McGraw, 1960.

Houghton, M.: Bailliere's Pocket Book of Ward Information, ed. 10, Baltimore, Williams & Wilkins, 1961.

Keane, C. B.: Saunders Review of Practical Nursing, Philadelphia, Saunders, 1966.

Mosby's Comprehensive Review Book, ed. 6, St. Louis, Mosby, 1965.

Mosby's Review of Practical Nursing, ed. 3, St. Louis, Mosby, 1961.

Olson, L. M.: A Nurse's Handbook, ed. 10, Philadelphia, Saunders, 1960.

Olson, L. M., and Dorland, W. A. N.: A Reference Handbook and Dictionary of Nursing, Philadelphia, Saunders, 1960.

Roper, N.: Oakes' Dictionary for Nurses, ed. 11, Baltimore, Williams & Wilkins, 1961.

Spaney, E., and Jennings, L. A.: The Art of Studying: A Guide for Nursing Students, Philadelphia, Lippincott, 1958.

Speelman, A.: Examination Review for Practical Nurses, New York, Putnam, 1962.

Stedman, T. L.: Medical Dictionary, ed. 20, Baltimore, Williams & Wilkins, 1961.

Sutton, A. L.: Workbook for Practical Nurses, ed. 2, Philadelphia, Saunders, 1964.

Taber, C. W.: Taber's Cyclopedic Medical Dictionary, ed. 10, Philadelphia, Davis, 1965.

Taylor, N. B., and Taylor, A. E.: The Putnam Medical Dictionary, New York, Putnam, 1961.

von Gremp, Z., and Broadwell, L.: Practical Nursing Study Guide and Review, ed. 2, Philadelphia, Lippincott, 1965.

Young, H., and Lee, E.: Lippincott's Quick Reference Book for Nurses, ed. 8, Philadelphia, Lippincott, 1962.

Mental and Physical Health, Personal Development and Human Relationships

Anderson, C. L., and Langton, C. V.: Health Principles and Practice, ed. 4, St. Louis, Mosby, 1964.

Bird, B.: Talking With Patients, Philadelphia, Lippincott, 1955.

Branch, C. H. H. (ed.): Aspects of Anxiety, Philadelphia, Lippincott, 1965.

Burton, G.: Personal, Impersonal and Interpersonal Relations: A Guide for Nurses, ed. 2, New York, Springer, 1964.

Bush, C. H.: Personal and Vocational Relationships for Practical Nurses, ed. 2, Philadelphia, Saunders, 1966.

Crisp, K. B.: Health for You, ed. 3, Philadelphia, Lippincott, 1954.

Crow, L. D., and Crow, A. C.: Human Relations in Practical Nursing, New York, Macmillan, 1964.

———: Understanding Interrelations in Nursing, ed. 3, New York, Macmillan, 1961.

Cruze, W. W.: Psychology in Nursing, ed. 2, New York, Blakiston-McGraw, 1960.

Dennis, L. B.: Psychology of Human Behavior for Nurses, ed. 2, Philadelphia, Saunders, 1962.

Hasler, D.: The Practical Nurse and Today's Family, New York, Macmillan, 1964.

Hayes, E. J., Hayes, P. J., and Kelly, D. E.: Moral Principles of Nursing, New York, Macmillan, 1964.

Hayes, W. J., and Gazaway, R.: Human Relations in Nursing, ed. 3, Philadelphia, Saunders, 1964.

Jacobson, E.: Anxiety and Tension Control: A Physician's Approach, Philadelphia, Lippincott, 1964.

Kempf, F. C., and Useem, R. H.: Psychology: Dynamics of Behavior in Nursing, Philadelphia, Saunders, 1964.

Liebman, S.: Understanding Your Patient, Philadelphia, Lippincott, 1957.

Lockerby, F. K.: Communication for Nurses, ed. 2, St. Louis, Mosby, 1963.

Madigan, M. E.: Psychology, Principles and Applications, ed. 4, St. Louis, Mosby, 1966.

McGhie, A.: Psychology as Applied to Nursing, ed. 3, Baltimore, Williams & Wilkins, 1963.

Milton, O.: Behavior Disorders: Perspectives and Trends, Philadelphia, Lippincott, 1965.

Ross, C. F.: Personal and Vocational Relationships in Practical Nursing, ed. 2, Philadelphia, Lippincott, 1965.

Saul, L. J.: Emotional Maturity, ed. 2, Philadelphia, Lippincott, 1960.

Scheinfeld, A.: Your Heredity and Environment, Philadelphia, Lippincott, 1965.

Skipper, J. K., and Leonard, R. C.: Social Interaction and Patient Care, Philadelphia, Lippincott, 1965.

Smeltzer, C. H.: Psychology for Student Nurses, New York, Macmillan, 1962.

Stevens, D. G.: Principles of Ethics, ed. 5, Philadelphia, Lippincott, 1959.

Turner, C. E.: Personal and Community Health, ed. 12, St. Louis, Mosby, 1963.

Voeks, V.: On becoming an Educated Person, ed. 2, Philadelphia, Saunders, 1964.

Family Living

Babcock, D. E.: Introduction to Growth, Development and Family Life, Philadelphia, Davis, 1962.

Bernard, J., and Thompson, L.: Sociology, ed. 7, St. Louis, Mosby, 1966.

Cavan, R. S.: The American Family, ed. 3, New York, Crowell, 1963.

Chapman, A. H.: Management of Emotional Problems of Children and Adolescents, Philadelphia, Lippincott, 1965.

Cumming, E., and Henry, W. E.: Growing Old, New York, Basic Books, 1961.

Davis, M.: Get the Most Out of Your Best Years, New York, Dial Press, 1960.

Duvall, E. M.: Family Development, ed. 2, Philadelphia, Lippincott, 1962.

Duvall, E. M., and Hill, R.: Being Married, Boston, Heath, 1960.

Hess, R., and Handel, G.: Family Worlds: A Psychosocial Approach to Family Life, Chicago, University of Chicago Press, 1959.

Liebman, S.: Emotional Forces in the Family, Philadelphia, Lippincott, 1959.

Milne, A. A.: Now We Are Six, rev. ed., New York, Dutton, 1961.

Rainwater, L., *et al.*: Workingman's Wife, New York, Oceana, 1959.

Shuey, R. M., Woods, E. L., and Young, E. M.: Learning About Children, rev. ed., Philadelphia, Lippincott, 1964.

Sutherland, R. L., Woodward, J. L., and Maxwell, M. A.: Introductory Sociology, ed. 6, Philadelphia, Lippincott, 1961.

Todd, V. E., and Heffernan, H.: The Years Before School, New York, Macmillan, 1964.

Toman, W.: Family Constellation, New York, Springer, 1961.

Williams, J.: Family Health, ed. 3, Philadelphia, Lippincott, 1959.

Zimmerman, C. C., and Cervantes, L. F.: Successful American Families, New York, Pageant Press, 1960.

Nutrition in Health and Disease

Beck, M. E.: Nutrition and Dietetics for Nurses, Baltimore, Williams & Wilkins, 1962.

Bien, R. V.: Nutrition and Meal Preparation for the Practical Nurse, ed. 2, Albany, Delmar, 1960.

Church, C. F., and Church, H. N.: Bowes-Church's Food Values of Portions Commonly Used, ed. 9, Philadelphia, Lippincott, 1963.

Cooper, L. F., *et al.*: Nutrition In Health and Disease, ed. 14, Philadelphia, Lippincott, 1963.

Field, H. E.: Foods in Health and Disease, New York, Macmillan, 1964.

Garb, S.: Essentials of Therapeutic Nutrition, New York, Springer, 1958.

Harris, C. F.: Handbook of Dietetics for Nurses, ed. 2, Baltimore, Williams & Wilkins, 1963.

Howe, P. S.: Nutrition for Practical Nurses, ed. 3, Philadelphia, Saunders, 1963.

Krause, M. V.: Food, Nutrition and Diet Therapy, ed. 4, Philadelphia, Saunders, 1966.

McDermott, I. E., Trilling, M. B., and Nicholas, F. W.: Food for Better Living, ed. 3, Philadelphia, Lippincott, 1960.

McHenry, E. W.: Basic Nutrition, ed. 2, Philadelphia, Lippincott, 1963.

———: Foods Without Fads, Philadelphia, Lippincott, 1960.

Mitchell, K., and Bernard, M. C.: Food in Health and Disease, ed. 6, Philadelphia, Davis, 1958.

Mowry, L.: Basic Nutrition and Diet Therapy for Nurses, ed. 3, St. Louis, Mosby, 1966.

Peyton, A. B.: Basic Nutrition, ed. 2, Philadelphia, Lippincott, 1962.

Proudfit, F. T., and Robinson, C. H.: Normal Therapeutic Nutrition, ed. 12, New York, Macmillan, 1961.

Robinson, C. H.: Basic Nutrition and Diet Therapy, New York, Macmillan, 1965.

Sense, E.: Clinical Studies in Nutrition, Philadelphia, Lippincott, 1960.

Shackelton, A. D.: Practical Nurse Nutrition Education, ed. 2, Philadelphia, Saunders, 1966.

Shearman, C. W.: Diets are for People: A Textbook of Diet Therapy, New York, Appleton, 1963.

Wayler, T. S., and Klein, R. S.: Applied Nutrition, New York, Macmillan, 1965.

Willis, N. H.: Basic Infant Nutrition, Philadelphia, Lippincott, 1964.

Wilmot, J. S., and Batjer, M. Q.: Food for the Family, ed. 6, Philadelphia, Lippincott, 1966.

Biological Sciences

Anthony, C. P.: Structure and Function of the Body, ed. 2, St. Louis, Mosby, 1964.

———: Textbook of Anatomy and Physiology, ed. 6, St. Louis, Mosby, 1963.

Best, C. H., and Taylor, N. B.: The Physiological Basis of Medical Practice, ed. 7, Baltimore, Williams & Wilkins, 1961.

Boyd, W.: A Textbook of Pathology, ed. 7, Philadelphia, Lea & Febiger, 1961.

Brooks, S. M.: Integrated Basic Science, ed, 2, St. Louis, Mosby, 1966.

Chaffee, E. E., and Greisheimer, E. M.: Basic Physiology and Anatomy, Philadelphia, Lippincott, 1964.

DeCoursey, R. M.: The Human Organism, ed. 2, New York, Blakiston-McGraw, 1961.

Elliott, H. C.: Textbook of Neuroanatomy, Philadelphia, Lippincott, 1963.

Ferris, E. B., and Skelley, E. G.: Body Structure and Function, Albany, Delmar, 1964.

———: Bacteriology for the Practical Nurse, Albany, Delmar, 1959.

Frobisher, M., Sommermeyer, L., and Blaustein, E. H.: Microbiology for Nurses, ed. 11, Philadelphia, Saunders, 1964.

Goss, C. M.: Gray's Anatomy, ed. 27, Philadelphia, Lea and Febiger, 1959.

Greisheimer, E. M.: Physiology and Anatomy, ed. 8, Philadelphia, Lippincott, 1963.

Grollman, S. G.: The Human Body, Its Structure and Physiology, New York, Macmillan, 1964.

Guyton, A. C.: Textbook of Medical Physiology, ed. 2, Philadelphia, Saunders, 1961.

Ham, A. W.: Histology, ed. 5, Philadelphia, Lippincott, 1965.

Hopps, H. C.: Principles of Pathology, ed. 2, New York, Appleton, 1965.

Jacob, S. W., and Francone, C. A.: Structure and Function in Man, Philadelphia, Saunders, 1965.

Kimber, D. C., *et al.*: Anatomy and Physiology, ed. 14, New York, Macmillan, 1961.

King, B. G., and Showers, M. J.: Human Anatomy and Physiology, ed. 5, Philadelphia, Saunders, 1963.

Langley, L. L., Cheraskin, E., and Sleeper, R.: Dynamic Anatomy and Physiology, ed. 2, New York, Blakiston-McGraw, 1963.

Lockhart, R. D., Hamilton, G. F., and Fyfe, F. W.: Anatomy of the Human Body (1965 printing with revisions), Philadelphia, Lippincott, 1959.

Manner, H. W.: Elements of Anatomy and Physiology, Philadelphia, Saunders, 1962.

McDowall, R. J. S.: Handbook of Physiology, ed. 43, Philadelphia, Lippincott, 1961.

Memmler, R. L.: The Human Body in Health and Disease, ed. 2, Philadelphia, Lippincott, 1962.

Neter, E., and Edgeworth, D. R.: Medical Microbiology, ed. 4, Philadelphia, Davis, 1962.

Nordmark, M. T., and Rohweder, A. W.: Science

Principles Applied to Nursing, Philadelphia, Lippincott, 1959.

Pelczar, M. J., Jr., and Reid, R. D.: Microbiology, ed. 2, New York, Blakiston-McGraw, 1965.

Riddle, J. T. E.: Elementary Textbook of Anatomy and Physiology Applied to Nursing, Baltimore, Williams & Wilkins, 1961.

Roper, N.: Man's Anatomy, Physiology and Health, Baltimore, Williams & Wilkins, 1963.

Smith, A. L.: Microbiology and Pathology, ed. 8, St. Louis, Mosby, 1964.

———: Principles of Microbiology, ed. 5, St. Louis, Mosby, 1965.

Strand, F. L.: Modern Physiology: The Chemical and Structural Basis of Function, New York, Macmillan, 1965.

Sylvester, P. E.: Applied Anatomy and Physiology for Nurses, Philadelphia, Davis, 1964.

Taylor, N. B., and McPhedran, M.: Basic Physiology and Anatomy, New York, Putnam, 1965.

Wheeler, M. F., and Volk, W. A.: Basic Microbiology, Philadelphia, Lippincott, 1964.

White, L. S., and Nelson, Sister S. L.: Practical Approach to Microbiology for Nurses, ed. 2, Philadelphia, Davis, 1964.

Young, G.: Witton's Microbiology, ed. 3, New York, Blakiston-McGraw, 1961.

Physical Sciences

Arnow, L. E., and Logan, M. C.: Introduction to Physiological and Pathological Chemistry, ed. 6, St. Louis, Mosby, 1961.

Biddle, H. C., and Floutz, V. W.: Chemistry for Nurses, ed. 6, Philadelphia, Davis, 1963.

Bogert, L. J.: Fundamentals of Chemistry, ed. 9, Philadelphia, Saunders, 1963.

Borek, E.: The Atoms Within Us, New York, Columbia, 1961.

Brooks, S. M.: Basic Facts of Body Water and Ions, New York, Springer, 1960.

Flitter, H. H.: An Introduction to Physics in Nursing, ed. 4, St. Louis, Mosby, 1962.

Goostray, S., and Schwenck, J. R.: A Textbook of Chemistry, ed. 8, New York, Macmillan, 1961.

Greenwood, M.: Illustrated Approach to Medical Physics, Philadelphia, Davis, 1963.

Jensen, J. T.: Introduction to Medical Physics, Philadelphia, Lippincott, 1960.

Luros, G. O., and Towne, J. C.: Essentials of Chemistry, ed. 7, Philadelphia, Lippincott, 1966.

Neal, R. E., and Kennelly, R.: Chemistry: With Selected Principles of Physics, New York, Blakiston-McGraw, 1962.

Roe, J. H.: Principles of Chemistry, ed. 9, St. Louis, Mosby, 1963.

Routh, J. I.: Fundamentals of Inorganic, Organic and Biological Chemistry, ed. 5, Philadelphia, Saunders, 1965.

Sackheim, G. I.: Practical Physics for Nurses, ed. 2, Philadelphia, Saunders, 1962.

Snively, W. D.: Sea Within, Philadelphia, Lippincott, 1960.

Statland, H.: Fluids and Electrolytes in Practice, ed. 3, Philadelphia, Lippincott, 1963.

Sykes, G.: Disinfection and Sterilization, Philadelphia, Lippincott, 1965.

Fundamentals of Nursing; Medical-Surgical Nursing

Anderson, M. C.: Basic Patient Care: A Programed Introduction to Nursing Fundamentals, Philadelphia, Saunders, 1965.

Barbata, J. C., Jensen, D. M., and Patterson, W. G.: A Textbook of Medical-Surgical Nursing, New York, Putnam, 1964.

Beal, J. M.: Manual of Recovery Room Care, ed. 2, New York, Macmillan, 1962.

Beeson, P. B., and McDermott, W. (eds.): Cecil-Loeb Textbook of Medicine, ed. 11, Philadelphia, Saunders, 1963.

Beland, I. L.: Clinical Nursing: Pathophysiological and Psychosocial Approaches, New York, Macmillan, 1965.

Blumberg, J. E., and Drummond, E. E.: Nursing Care of the Long-Term Patient, New York, Springer, 1963.

Bordicks, K. J.: Patterns of Shock: Implications for Nursing Care, New York, Macmillan, 1965.

Brunner, L. S., *et al.*: Textbook of Medical-Surgical Nursing, Philadelphia, Lippincott, 1964.

Cady, L. L.: Nursing in Tuberculosis, ed. 2, Philadelphia, Saunders, 1961.

Culver, V. M., and Brownell, K. O.: The Practical Nurse: A Textbook of Nursing, ed. 6, Philadelphia, Saunders, 1964.

deGutierrez-Mahoney, C. G., and Carini, E.: Neurological and Neurosurgical Nursing, ed. 4, St. Louis, Mosby, 1965.

Esau, M., *et al.*: Practical Nursing Today, New York, Putnam, 1957.

Fuerst, E. V., and Wolff, L.: Fundamentals of Nursing, ed. 3, Philadelphia, Lippincott, 1964.

Freedman, M. G., and Hannan, J.: Medical-Surgical Workbook for Practical Nurses, ed. 2, Philadelphia, Davis, 1964.

Garb, S.: Laboratory Tests in Common Use, ed. 3, New York, Springer, 1963.

Ginsburg, F., Brunner, L. S., and Cantlin, V.: Manual of Operating Room Technology, Philadelphia, Lippincott, 1966.

Harmer, B., and Henderson, V.: Textbook of the Principles and Practice of Nursing, ed. 5, New York, Macmillan, 1955.

Havener, W. H., *et al.*: Nursing Care in Eye, Ear, Nose and Throat Disorders, St. Louis, Mosby, 1964.

Hirschberg, G. G., Lewis, L., and Thomas, D.: Rehabilitation: A Manual for the Care of the Disabled and Elderly, Philadelphia, Lippincott, 1964.

Hornemann, G. V.: Basic Nursing Procedures, Albany, Delmar, 1966.

Houghton, M.: Practical Nursing, ed. 9, Baltimore, Williams & Wilkins, 1961.

Hull, E., and Perrodin, C. M.: Medical Nursing, ed. 6, Philadelphia, Davis, 1960.

Johnston, D. F.: Total Patient Care: Foundations and Practice, St. Louis, Mosby, 1964.

Keane, C. B.: Essentials of Nursing: A Medical-Surgical Text for Practical Nurses, Philadelphia, Saunders, 1964.

Kimbrough, R. A.: Textbook of Gynecology, Philadelphia, Lippincott, 1965.

Kreuger, E. A.: Hypodermic Injections, A Programed Unit in Fundamentals of Nursing, Philadelphia, Lippincott, 1966.

Larson, C., and Gould, M.: Calderwood's Orthopedic Nursing, ed. 6, St. Louis, Mosby, 1965.

Leake, M. J.: Simple Nursing Procedures, ed. 4, Philadelphia, Saunders, 1966.

LeMaitre, G. D., and Finnegan, J. A.: The Patient in Surgery, Philadelphia, Saunders, 1965.

MacBryde, C. M.: Signs and Symptoms, ed. 4, Philadelphia, Lippincott, 1964.

Mahoney, R. F.: Emergency and Disaster Nursing, New York, Macmillan, 1965.

Mason, M. A.: Basic Medical-Surgical Nursing, New York, Macmillan, 1959.

Matheney, R. V., *et al.*: Fundamentals of Patient-Centered Nursing, St. Louis, Mosby, 1964.

McClain, M. E., and Gragg, S. H.: Scientific Principles in Nursing, ed. 5, St. Louis, Mosby, 1966.

Modell, W., *et al.*: Handbook of Cardiology for Nurses, ed. 5, New York, Springer, 1966.

Moyer, C. A., Rhoads, J. E., Allen, J. G., and Harkins, H. N.: Surgery: Principles and Practice, ed. 3, Philadelphia, Lippincott, 1965.

Nash, D. F. E.: The Principles and Practice of Surgical Nursing, ed. 3, Baltimore, Williams & Wilkins, 1965.

Newton, K., and Anderson, H. C.: Geriatric Nursing, ed. 4, St. Louis, Mosby, 1966.

Norris, W., and Campbell, D.: A Nurse's Guide to Anesthetics, Resuscitation and Intensive Care, Baltimore, Williams & Wilkins, 1964.

Price, A. L.: The Art, Science and Spirit of Nursing, ed. 3, Philadelphia, Saunders, 1965.

Rapier, D. K., *et al.*: Practical Nursing: A Textbook for Students and Graduates, ed. 2, St. Louis, Mosby, 1962.

Rosenthal, H., and Rosenthal, J.: Diabetic Care in Pictures, ed. 3, Philadelphia, Lippincott, 1960.

Rothweiler, E. L., *et al.*: The Art and Science of Nursing, ed. 6, Philadelphia, Davis, 1959.

Seedor, M. M.: Aids to Diagnosis: A Programed Unit in Fundamentals of Nursing, New York, Teachers College Press, Columbia University, Dist. by Lippincott, 1964.

———: Introduction to Asepsis: A Programed Unit in Fundamentals of Nursing, New York, Teachers College Press, Columbia University, Dist. by Lippincott, 1963.

Shafer, K. N., *et al.*: Medical-Surgical Nursing, ed. 3, St. Louis, Mosby, 1964.

Sister M. Louise: The Operating Room Technician, St. Louis, Mosby, 1965.

Smith, D. W., and Gips, C. D.: Care of the Adult Patient: Medical-Surgical Nursing, ed. 2, Philadelphia, Lippincott, 1966.

Stevens, M. K.: Geriatric Nursing for Practical Nurses, Philadelphia, Saunders, 1965.

Sutton, A. L.: Bedside Nursing Techniques, Philadelphia, Saunders, 1964.

Thorek, P.: Illustrated Preoperative and Postoperative Care, Philadelphia, Lippincott, 1958.

———: Surgical Diagnosis, ed. 2, Philadelphia, Lippincott, 1965.

Tobias, N.: Essentials of Dermatology, ed. 6, Philadelphia, Lippincott, 1963.

Turek, S. L.: Orthopaedics: Principles and Their Application, Philadelphia, Lippincott, 1959.

Willard, H. S., and Spackman, C. S.: Occupational Therapy, ed. 3, Philadelphia, Lippincott, 1963.

Pharmacology and the Administration of Drugs

Bergersen, B. S., and Krug, E. E.: Pharmacology in Nursing, ed. 10, St. Louis, Mosby, 1966.

Boettcher, H. M.: Wonder Drugs: A History of Antibiotics, Philadelphia, Lippincott, 1964.

Cutting, W. C.: Handbook of Pharmacology, ed. 2, New York, Appleton, 1964.

Faddis, M. O., and Grime, H. E.: The Mathematics of Solutions and Dosage, ed. 3, Philadelphia, Lippincott, 1948.

Falconer, M. W., Norman, M. R., and Patterson, H. R.: The Drug, The Nurse, The Patient, ed. 3, Philadelphia, Saunders, 1966.

Falconer, M. W., and Patterson, H. R.: 1966-68 Current Drug Handbook, Philadelphia, Saunders, 1966.

Fitch, G. E.: Arithmetic Review and Drug Therapy for Practical Nurses, New York, Macmillan, 1961.

Fream, W. C.: Arithmetic in Nursing, ed. 3, Baltimore, Williams & Wilkins, 1965.

Garb, S., and Crim, B. J.: Pharmacology and Patient Care, ed. 2, New York, Springer, 1966.

Govoni, L. E., Berzon, F. C., and Fall, M. B.: Drugs and Nursing Implications, New York, Appleton, 1965.

Hart, L. K.: The Arithmetic of Dosages and Solutions: A Programmed Presentation, St. Louis, Mosby, 1965.

Keane, C. B., and Fletcher, S. M.: Drugs and Solutions: A Programed Introduction for Nurses, Philadelphia, Saunders, 1965.

Lipsey, S. I.: Mathematics for Nursing Science: A Programmed Review, New York, Wiley, 1965.

McClain, M. E.: Simplified Arithmetic for Nurses, ed. 3, Philadelphia, Saunders, 1966.

Modell, W. M.: Drugs in Current Use, New York, Springer, 1966.

Musser, R. D., and Shubkagel, B. L.: Pharmacology and Therapeutics, ed. 3, New York, Macmillan, 1965.

Nast, M.: Simplified Drugs and Solutions for Nurses (Including Arithmetic), ed. 3, St. Louis, Mosby, 1964.

Price, G.: Self Study Guide of Mathematics Used in Nursing, New York, Putnam, 1963.

Sackheim, G., and Robins, L.: Programmed Mathematics for Nurses, New York, Macmillan, 1964.

Sister Suzanne Marie: Pharmacology for Practical Nurses, Philadelphia, Saunders, 1963.

Skelley, E. G.: Medications for the Nurse, ed. 2, Albany, Delmar, 1964.

Squire, J. E.: Basic Pharmacology for Nurses, ed. 3, St. Louis, Mosby, 1965.

Weaver, M. E., and Koehler, V. J.: Programmed Mathematics of Drugs and Solutions, Philadelphia, Lippincott, 1964.

Wilson, C. O., and Jones, T. E.: American Drug Index 1966, Philadelphia, Lippincott, 1966.

Maternal and Child Care

Armstrong, I. L., and Browder, J. J.: The Nursing Care of Children, ed. 2, Philadelphia, Davis, 1964.

Benz, G. S.: Pediatric Nursing, ed. 5, St. Louis, Mosby, 1964.

Blake, F. G.: The Child, His Parents and the Nurse, Philadelphia, Lippincott, 1954.

Blake, F. G., and Wright, F. H.: Essentials of Pediatric Nursing, ed. 7, Philadelphia, Lippincott, 1963.

Bleier, I. J.: Maternity Nursing, A Textbook for Practical Nurses, ed. 2, Philadelphia, Saunders, 1966.

Bookmiller, M. M., and Bowen, G. L.: A Textbook of Obstetrics and Obstetric Nursing, ed. 4, Philadelphia, Saunders, 1963.

Brigley, C. M.: Pediatrics for the Practical Nurse, Albany, Delmar, 1965.

Bryant, R. D., and Overland, A. E.: Woodward and Gardner's Obstetric Management and Nursing, ed. 7, Philadelphia, Davis, 1964.

Burnett, C. W. F.: Obstetric Nursing, Philadelphia, Davis, 1964.

Clark, A. L., Hakerem, H. M., Basara, S. C., and Walano, D. A.: Patient Studies in Maternal Child Nursing: A Family-Centered Student Guide, Philadelphia, Lippincott, 1966.

Craig, W. S.: Care of the Newly Born Infant, ed. 2, Baltimore, Williams & Wilkins, 1961.

Davis, M. E., and Rubin, R.: De Lee's Obstetrics for Nurses, ed. 17, Philadelphia, Saunders, 1962.

Fishbein, M.: Birth Defects, Philadelphia, Lippincott, 1963.

Fitzpatrick, E., Eastman, N. J., and Reeder, S.: Maternity Nursing, ed. 11, Philadelphia, Lippincott, 1966.

Geddes, A. K.: Premature Babies: Their Nursing Care and Management, Philadelphia, Saunders, 1960.

Gustafson, S. R., and Coursin, D. B.: The Pediatric Patient, Philadelphia, Lippincott, 1965.

Jaeger, M. A.: Child Development and Nursing Care, New York, Macmillan, 1962.

Karmel, M.: Thank you, Dr. Lamaze: A Mother's Experience in Painless Childbirth, Philadelphia, Lippincott, 1959.

Kessel, I.: The Essentials of Pediatrics for Nurses, ed. 2, Baltimore, Williams & Wilkins, 1963.

Leifer, G.: Principles and Techniques of Pediatric Nursing, Philadelphia, Saunders, 1965.

Marlow, D. R.: Textbook of Pediatric Nursing, ed. 2, Philadelphia, Saunders, 1965.

McPhedran, M. G.: The Maternity Cycle, Philadelphia, Davis, 1961.

Meeks, D., and Kalafatich, A.: Maternal and Child Health, Paterson, N. J., Littlefield, Adams, 1960.

Meering, A. B.: A Handbook for Nursery Nurses, ed. 4, Baltimore, Williams & Wilkins, 1964.

Mitchell, R. M.: Nine Months to Go, Philadelphia, Lippincott, 1960.
Myles, M. F.: A Textbook for Midwives, ed. 5, Baltimore, Williams & Wilkins, 1964.
Nixon, H. H., and O'Donnell, B.: The Essentials of Pediatric Surgery, Philadelphia, Lippincott, 1961.
Sacharin, R. M., and Hunter, M. H. S.: Pediatric Nursing Procedures, Baltimore, Williams & Wilkins, 1964.
Smith, C. S.: Maternal-Child Nursing, Philadelphia, Saunders, 1963.
Thompson, E. D.: Pediatrics for Practical Nurses, Philadelphia, Saunders, 1965.
Wiedenbach, E.: Family Centered Maternity Nursing, New York, Putnam, 1958.
Ziegel, E., and Van Blarcom, C. C.: Obstetric Nursing, ed. 5, New York, Macmillan, 1964.

Psychiatry

Altschul, A.: Psychiatric Nursing, ed. 2, Baltimore, Williams & Wilkins, 1964.
Brown, M. M., and Fowler, G. R.: Psychodynamic Nursing, ed. 3, Philadelphia, Saunders, 1966.
Crawford, A. L., and Buchanan, B. S.: Psychiatric Nursing: A Basic Manual, Philadelphia, Davis, 1961.
French, E. L., and Scott, J. C.: Child in the Shadows: A Manual for Parents of Retarded Children, Philadelphia, Lippincott, 1960.
Hallas, C. H.: Nursing the Mentally Subnormal, ed. 2, Baltimore, Williams & Wilkins, 1963.
Hofling, C. K.: Textbook of Psychiatry for Medical Practice, Philadelphia, Lippincott, 1963.
Hofling, C. K., and Leininger, M. M.: Basic Psychiatric Concepts in Nursing, Philadelphia, Lippincott, 1960.
Kalkman, M. E.: Introduction to Psychiatric Nursing, ed. 2, New York, Blakiston-McGraw, 1958.
Kroger, W. S.: Clinical and Medical Hypnosis, Philadelphia, Lippincott, 1963.
Maddison, D., Day, P., and Leabeater, B.: Psychiatric Nursing, Baltimore, Williams & Wilkins, 1963.
Manfreda, M. L.: Psychiatric Nursing, ed. 7, Philadelphia, Davis, 1964.
Matheney, R. V., and Topalis, M.: Psychiatric Nursing, ed. 4, St. Louis, Mosby, 1965.
Mereness, D., and Karnosh, L. J.: Essentials of Psychiatric Nursing, ed. 6, St. Louis, Mosby, 1962.
Michal-Smith, H.: The Mentally Retarded Patient, Philadelphia, Lippincott, 1956.
Noyes, A. P., Camp, W. P., and van Sickel, M.: Psychiatric Nursing, ed. 6, New York, Macmillan, 1964.
Pearson, M. M.: Strecker's Fundamentals of Psychiatry, ed. 6, Philadelphia, Lippincott, 1963.
Render, H. W., and Weiss, M. O.: Nurse-Patient Relationships in Psychiatry, ed. 2, New York, Blakiston-McGraw, 1959.
Robinson, A. M.: The Psychiatric Aide, ed. 3, Philadelphia, Lippincott, 1964.

Legal Aspects and Career Opportunities in Practical Nursing

Anderson, P. C.: The Dental Assistant, Albany, Delmar, 1965.
Bush, C. H.: Personal and Vocational Relationships for Practical Nurses, ed. 2, Philadelphia, Saunders, 1966.
Cady, E. L.: Law and Contemporary Nursing, Paterson, N. J., Littlefield, Adams, 1961.
Creighton, H.: Law Every Nurse Should Know, Philadelphia, Saunders, 1957.
Cromwell, G. E.: The Nurse in the School Health Program, Philadelphia, Saunders, 1963.
Freeman, R. B.: Public Health Nursing Practice, ed. 3, Philadelphia, Saunders, 1963.
Hayt, E., *et al.*: Law of Hospital and Nurse, New York, Hospital Textbook, 1958.
Lesnik, M. J., and Anderson, B. E.: Nursing Practice and the Law, ed. 2 (1962 printing with revisions), Philadelphia, Lippincott, 1955.
Levison, H.: Textbook for Dental Nurses, ed. 2, Philadelphia, Davis, 1963.
Morison, L. J.: Steppingstones to Professional Nursing, ed. 4, St. Louis, Mosby, 1965.
Morrison, G. A.: In the Dentist's Office: A Guide for Auxiliary Dental Personnel, Philadelphia, Lippincott, 1959.
Parsons, E.: In the Doctor's Office: The Art of the Medical Assistant, ed. 2, Philadelphia, Lippincott, 1956.
Ross, C. F.: Personal and Vocational Relationships in Practical Nursing, ed. 2, Philadelphia, Lippincott, 1965.
Spalding, E. A., and Notter, L. E.: Professional Nursing: Foundations, Perspectives and Relationships, ed. 7, Philadelphia, Lippincott, 1965.
Tyrer, F. H.: Occupational Health Nursing, Baltimore, Williams & Wilkins, 1961.

National Organizations and Agencies Distributing Health Information

The following organizations and agencies have helpful health materials; such as pamphlets, posters and films, which are available upon request.

Some of these materials are free; for others there is a nominal fee. Similar educational aids can also be obtained from local health departments and insurance companies.

American Cancer Society (ACS), 219 East 42nd Street, New York, N. Y. 10017
American Dental Association (ADA), 222 East Superior Street, Chicago, Ill. 60611
American Diabetes Association (ADA), 1 East 45th Street, New York, N. Y. 10017
American Hearing Society (AHS), 919–18th Street, N.W., Washington, D.C. 20006
American Heart Association (AHA), 44 East 23rd Street, New York, N. Y. 10010
American National Red Cross (ARC), 17th and D Streets, Washington, D.C. 20006
American Physical Therapy Association (APTA), 1790 Broadway, New York, N. Y. 10019
Arthritis and Rheumatism Foundation (ARF), 10 Columbus Circle, New York, N. Y. 10019
Leukemia Society, Inc. (LSI), 211 East 43rd Street, New York, N. Y. 10017
Maternity Center Association (MCA), 48 East 92nd Street, New York, N. Y. 10028
Muscular Dystrophy Associations of America (MDAA), 1790 Broadway, New York, N. Y. 10019
National Association for Mental Health (NAMH), 10 Columbus Circle, New York, N. Y. 10019
National Council on Alcoholism (NCA), New York Academy of Medicine Building, 2 East 103rd Street, New York, N. Y. 10029
National Council on the Aging (NCOA), 49 West 45th Street, New York, N. Y. 10036
National Cystic Fibrosis Research Foundation (NCFRF), 521 Fifth Avenue, Room 307, New York, N. Y. 10017
National Dairy Council (NDC), 111 North Canal Street, Chicago, Ill. 60606
National Epilepsy League (NEL), 203 North Wabash Avenue, Chicago, Ill. 60601
National Foundation, 800 Second Avenue, New York, N. Y. 10017. (Formerly, National Foundation for Infantile Paralysis)
National Health Council (NHC), 1790 Broadway, New York, N. Y. 10019
National Hemophilia Foundation (NHF), 175 Fifth Avenue, New York, N. Y. 10010
National Kidney Disease Foundation (NKDF), 342 Madison Avenue, New York, N. Y. 10017
National Multiple Sclerosis Society (NMSS), 257 Park Avenue South, New York, N. Y. 10010
National Safety Council, 425 North Michigan Avenue, Chicago, Ill. 60611
National Society for Crippled Children and Adults, 2023 West Ogden Avenue, Chicago, Ill. 60612
National Society for the Prevention of Blindness (NSPB), 16 East 40th Street, New York, N. Y. 10016
National Tuberculosis Association (NTA), 1790 Broadway, New York, N. Y. 10019
United Cerebral Palsy Associations (UCPA), 321 West 44th Street, New York, N. Y. 10036
United States Department of Health, Education, and Welfare
  Headquarters—Washington, D.C. 20201
    Public Health Service
    Office of Education
    Vocational Rehabilitation
    Social Security Administration
    Food and Drug Administration
    Welfare Administration

Nursing Journals

Listed below are some of the current nursing journals which can be used as sources for health information. The national association sponsoring each is also indicated.

The Journal of Practical Nursing—National Association for Practical Nurse Education and Service, Inc.
American Journal of Practical Nursing—National Federation of Licensed Practical Nurses, Inc.
American Journal of Nursing—American Nurses' Association
Nursing Outlook—National League for Nursing
The Catholic Nurse—National Council of Catholic Nurses of the USA
AORN Journal—Association of Operating Room Nurses
American Association of Industrial Nurses Journal —American Association of Industrial Nurses
Nursing Research—American Nurses' Association and the National League for Nursing

The following periodicals are also valuable health information aids: Nursing Forum, Perspectives in Psychiatric Care, Journal of Psychiatric Nursing, Nursing Science, The Journal of Nursing Education and RN.

Another source of literature containing timely health articles of interest to the practical nurse are magazines such as Today's Health, Parents' Magazine, Reader's Digest and Life.

Lederle Laboratories, Eli Lilly & Co., E. R. Squibb & Sons, Winthrop Laboratories and Wyeth Laboratories are only a few of the many pharmaceutical manufacturers which distribute free drug literature upon request.

GLOSSARY

Abdomen (ab-do′men), that portion of the body lying between the chest and the pelvis.

Abnormal (ab-nor′mal), contrary to normal.

Abrasion (ab-ra′zhun), a scraping or rubbing off of the skin.

Abscess (ab′ses), a local collection of pus in the tissues.

Absorption (ab-sorp′shun), the taking up of fluids or other substances by the skin and the tissues.

Acceleration (ak-sel-er-a′shun), a quickening of rate, as of the pulse or respiration.

Accreditation (ah-kred-i-ta′shun), attaining standards approved by recognized authority.

Acid (as′id), a chemical compound having properties opposed to those of the alkalis.

Acute (ah-kute′), a sudden, poignant illness of short duration but with severe symptoms.

Addiction (ah-dik′shun), a compulsion to use drugs or stimulants habitually.

Adenitis (ad-e-ni′tis), inflammation of a gland.

Adenoids (ad′en-oids), glandular growths at the back of the nose, behind the palate.

Adhesion (ad-he′zhun), the abnormal joining of tissues by a fibrous band, usually resulting from inflammation or injury.

Adipose (ad′i-pose), fatty.

Adolescence (ad-o-les′ens), the period of development between childhood and adulthood.

Aerosol (a′er-o-sol), a solution of a drug or a bacteriocidal solution which can be atomized into a spray form.

After-birth (af′ter-berth), a mass of tissue, consisting of the membranes and the placenta with the attached umbilical cord, which is cast off after the expulsion of the fetus.

Albolene (al′bo-lene), an oily, white substance derived from petroleum.

Albumin (al-bu′min), a protein substance found in animal and vegetable tissues.

Alimentary canal (al-im-en′ta-re kan-al′), the passage leading from the mouth, the stomach and the intestines to the outer opening of the rectum.

Alkali (al′ka-li), a compound which neutralizes acids.

Allergy (al′er-je), a state in which the body is hypersensitive to some protein.

Alleviate (a-le′vi-ate), to lessen or make easier to endure.

Alopecia (al-o-pe′she-ah), loss of hair from skin where it normally appears.

Ambulatory (am′bu-la-to-re), walking or able to walk.

Amenorrhea (ah-men-o-re′ah), absence or abnormal stoppage of menses.

Amnesia (am-ne′se-ah), loss of memory.

Amputation (am-pu-ta′shun), cutting off of a limb or other part of the body.

Analgesic (an-al-je′sik), relieving pain.

Anastomosis (ah-nas-to-mo′sis), the joining together of 2 normally distinct spaces or organs.

Anemia (ah-ne′me-ah), a deficiency of the blood in quality or quantity.

Anesthetic (an-es-thet′ik), a substance which produces loss of feeling or sensation.

Ankylosis (an-ki-lo′sis), abnormal consolidation of a joint which prevents motion.

Anodyne (an′o-din), a medicine that relieves pain.

Anomaly (a-nom′ah-le), a deviation from the normal.

Anorexia (an-o-rek′se-ah), lack or loss of appetite for food.

Anoxia (an-ok′se-ah), a decrease of oxygen below the normal level in body tissues.

Anthelmintic (ant-hel-min′tik), an agent that destroys worms.

Antibody (an′ti-bod-e), a specific blood substance which neutralizes foreign bodies.

Antidote (an′ti-dote), a remedy that will counteract or remove the effect of poison.

Antiemetic (an-ti-e-met′ik), an agent that prevents or relieves nausea and vomiting.

Antipyretic (an-ti-pi-ret′ik), an agent that relieves or reduces fever.

Antiseptic (an-ti-sep′tik), a substance that inhibits the growth of microorganisms without necessarily destroying them.

Antispasmodic (an-ti-spas-mod′ik), an agent that relieves muscular spasm.

Antitoxins (an-te-tok′sins), substances found in the blood and other body fluids which counteract the harmful effect of the toxins or the poisons to which they are allied.

Anuria (an-u′re-ah), total suppression of urine.

Anus (a′nus), the outer opening, or outlet, of the rectum.

Aortitis (a-or-ti′tis), inflammation of the aorta.

Aphagia (ah-fa′je-ah), inability to swallow.

Aphasia (ah-fa′ze-ah), inability to express oneself by speech or writing.

Aphonia (ah-fo′ne-ah), loss of voice.

Apnea (ap′ne-ah), a temporary cessation of breathing.

Apoplexy (ap′o-plek-se), a paralysis commonly referred to as a "stroke," resulting from a cerebral vascular accident.

Appendix (ah-pen′diks), a slender wormlike tube, connected to the large intestines at the lower end of the cecum.

Apprehension (ap-re-hen′shun), anxiety or fear.

Area (a′re-ah), a limited surface.

Arrhythmia (ah-rith′me-ah), absence of rhythm, particularly in relation to the abnormality in the rhythm of the heart.

Artery (ar′ter-e), any one of the vessels through which the blood passes from the heart to all the different parts of the body.

Artificial (ar-ti-fish′al), not natural.

Aseptic (ah-sep′tik), free from disease germs.

Asphyxia (as-fix′e-ah), suffocation.

Aspiration (as-pi-ra′shun), withdrawal of fluid or gas from a cavity by means of suction.

Assimilation (ah-sim-i-la′shun), the process of changing food into living tissue.

Asthma (az′mah), a disease marked by difficulty in breathing due to spasmodic contractions of the bronchial tubes.

Astringent (as-trin′jent), an agent that causes contraction and arrests discharges.

Ataxia (ah-tak′se-ah), failure or irregularity of muscle coordination.

Atomizer (at′om-i-zer), an instrument for throwing a jet of spray.

Atonic (ah-ton′ik), lacking normal tone or strength.

Atresia (ah-tre′ze-ah), a closing or congenital absence of a normal anatomical opening.

Atrophy (a′tro-fe), a decrease in size or wasting away of a cell, tissue, organ or part.

Audiometer (au-de-om′et-er), an instrument to test the acuity of the hearing.

Aura (aw′rah), a subjective sensation experienced by a person prior to a seizure such as an epileptic attack.

Aural (awr′al), pertaining to the ear.

Auscultation (aw-skul-ta′shun), listening to sounds within the body to determine abnormal conditions.

Autopsy (aw′top-se), examination of the organs of a dead body.

Auxiliary (awk-sil′e-a-re), that which assists or helps.

Axilla (ak-sil′ah), the armpit.

Bacteremia (bak-ter-e′me-ah), the presence of bacteria in the blood.

Bacteria (bak-te′re-ah), disease germs or microbes.

Benign (be-nine′), doing no harm; not malignant.

Biliary (bil′e-a-re), pertaining to bile, the liver, the gallbladder and the associated ducts.

Biopsy (bi′op-se), removal of a piece of body tissue for diagnostic examination, usually microscopic.

Blood pressure (blud presh′ur), the pressure of the blood on the elastic walls of the arteries.

Bradycardia (brad-e-kar′de-ah), abnormally slow heart action.

Bright's disease (brites dis-eze′), a kidney disease accompanied by albumin in the urine.

Bronchitis (brong-ki′tis), inflammation of the bronchial tubes.

Bronchoscope (brong′ko-skope), a lighted instrument used for the examination of the interior of the bronchi.

Buccal (buk′al), pertaining to the cheek or mouth.

Buttocks (but′oks), the prominence of muscle and fat on the posterior part of the body at the hip line.

Calculus (kal′ku-lus), an abnormal concretion, usually composed of mineral salts, occurring within the body.

Callosity (kal-os′it-e), a hardening and thickening of the skin.

Callus (kal′us), a callosity; the bony material that makes the union between the ends of fractured bones.

Calorie (kal′o-re), a unit of heat.

Capsule (kap′sul), a small gelatinous case for holding a dose of medicine.

Carbon dioxide (kar′bon di-ok′sid), a colorless gas which is exhaled in respiration.

Carbon monoxide (kar′bon mon-ok′sid), a colorless poisonous gas which is found in coal gas, automobile exhaust, etc.

Carcinoma (kar-sin-o′mah), a cancer.

Cardiac (kar′de-ak), pertaining to the heart.

Cardiograph (kar′de-o-graf), an instrument for recording the action of the heart.

Carrier (kar′e-er), an individual who harbors in his body the specific organisms of a disease without manifesting its symptoms and thus acts as a distributor or transmitter of the infection.

Cast (kast), an appliance to render immovable displaced or injured parts.

Cathartic (kath-ar′tik), a medicine that causes the evacuation of the bowels.

Cavity (kav′it-e), a hollow space within the body or within one of its organs.

Cell (sel), the minute protoplasmic building unit of living matter.

Cephalic (se-fal′ik), pertaining to the head.

Cervical (ser′vi-kal), pertaining to the neck or cervix of any structure.

Chancre (shang′ker), the primary lesion of syphilis.

Chemotherapy (ke-mo-ther′ah-pe), the use of chemical agents to treat disease.

Chest (chest), the thorax; the part of the body which lies between the neck and the abdominal cavity.

Chorea (ko-re′ah), St. Vitus' dance; a nervous disease characterized by involuntary jerking muscular movements.

Ciliated (sil′e-a-ted), provided with a fringe of hairlike processes.

Cirrhosis (sir-ro′sis), chronic inflammation and degeneration of an organ, especially the liver.

Clavicle (klav′i-kil), the collar bone.

Clinical (klin′ik-al), pertaining to instruction at the bedside or actual treatment of the patient, as distinguished from theoretical or experimental.

Coagulation (ko-ag-u-la′shun), the changing of a liquid to a thickened, curdlike form.

Colic (kol′ik), acute abdominal pain.

Colitis (ko-li′tis), inflammation of the colon.

Colon (ko′lon) the main part of the large intestine, extending from the cecum to the rectum.

Colostomy (ko-los′to-me), an artificial opening into the colon.

Colostrum (ko-los′trum), the fluid secreted by the mammary (breast) glands a few days before or after childbirth.

Coma (ko′mah), profound stupor due to disease or injury.

Communicable disease (ko-mun′ni-ka-bil), a disease that can be transmitted from one person to another.

Concentrated (kon′sen-tra-ted), made stronger.

Concurrent (kon-kur′ent), happening at the same time.

Congenital (kon-jen′it-al), existing at or before birth.

Congestion (kon-jest′yun), an abnormal accumulation of blood in a part of the body.

Conscious (kon′shus), mentally awake.

Consistency (kon-sis′ten-se), the degree of firmness or stiffness.

Constipation (kon-stip-a′shun), difficult or infrequent movement of the bowels.

Contagion (kon-ta′jun), the communication of disease from one person to another.

Contaminate (kon-tam′i-nate), to make unsterile or unclean by contact.

Contraindication (kon-trah-in-di-ka′shun), any condition which makes a form of treatment undesirable.

Contusion (kon-tu′zhun), a bruise.

Convalescence (kon-val-es′ens), the return to health after an attack of disease.

Convulsions (kon-vul′shuns), involuntary contractions of the voluntary muscles.

Copulation (kope-u-la′shun), sexual intercourse between the male and the female.

Cornea (kor′ne-ah), the transparent front part of the eye.

Coronary thrombosis (kor′o-na-re throm-bo′sis), a clot in a coronary artery.

Corrosive (ko-ro′siv), destructive to the tissue.

Coryza (ko-ri′zah), a cold in the head with an acute inflammation of the nasal mucous membrane.

Counterirritants (kown-ter-ir′it-ants), agents used to produce a superficial irritation and thus to relieve irritation or inflammation existing elsewhere.

Crisis (kri′sis), the turning point of a disease.

Cyanosis (si-an-o′sis), blueness of the skin due to the deficiency of oxygen and the excess of carbon dioxide in the blood.

Cyst (sist), a sac containing liquid or soft material.

Cystitis (sis-ti′tus), inflammation of the urinary bladder.

Debility (de-bil′i-te), loss or lack of strength.

Decompose (de-com-poze′), to decay; to rot.

Decubitus (de-ku′bi-tus), a bed or pressure sore.

Defecation (def-e-ka′shun), the discharge of fecal matter from the intestines.

Defect (de′fect), an imperfection or failure.

Degeneration (de-jen-er-a′shun), deterioration from a higher to a lower form.

Dehydration (de-hi-dra′shun), the removal of water.

Delirium (de-lir′e-um), a mental disturbance, usually temporary, marked by cerebral excitement, wandering speech, illusions and hallucinations.

Delusion (de-lu′zhun), a false belief that cannot be corrected by reason.
Dementia (de-men′she-ah), deterioration of mental capacity.
Demulcent (de-mul′sent), a bland, soothing medication or application.
Denture (den′tur), an artificial set of teeth.
Deodorant (de-o′der-ant), an agent that destroys unpleasant odors.
Depilatory (de-pil′at-o-re), a preparation for removing superfluous hair.
Depression (de-presh′un), lowered mental and physical activity.
Dermatitis (derm-ah-ti′tis), an inflammatory condition of the skin.
Desquamation (des-kwa-ma′shun), the shedding or scaling of the skin or cuticle.
Detergent (de-ter′jent), a cleansing or purifying agent.
Deviation (de-ve-a′shun), a turning aside.
Diagnosis (di-ag-no′sis), the recognition of a disease by its signs and symptoms.
Diaphoresis (di-ah-fo-re′sis), profuse perspiration.
Diaphragm (di′af-ram), the muscular partition between the thoracic and the abdominal cavities.
Diarrhea (di-ar-e′ah), abnormal frequency and fluidity of discharges from the bowels.
Digestion (di-jest′yun), the process of converting food into materials which can be assimilated and absorbed by the tissues.
Dilatation (dil-ah-ta′shun), a stretching of a part beyond normal dimensions.
Dilute (di-lute′), to make weaker or more fluid by mixture.
Disease (dis-eze′), a condition which is a departure from the normal health of the body or the mind.
Disinfectant (dis-in-fek′tant), an agent that frees from infection by destroying germs.
Disorientation (dis-o-re-en-ta′shun), a state of mental confusion or loss of bearings.
Distention (dis-ten′shun), the state of being enlarged.
Diuresis (di-u-re′sis), increased secretion of urine.
Divergence (di-ver′jens), a spreading apart or deviation from the normal course.
Dorsal (dor′sal), pertaining to the back.
Douche (doosh), a stream of water or other fluid directed against a part of a body or into a body cavity.
Dropsy (drop′se), an abnormal accumulation of serous fluid in the tissues.
Dysentery (dis′en-ter-e), a disorder accompanied by inflammation of the intestines and marked by pain and frequent stools containing blood and mucus.
Dysfunction (dis-funk′shun), abnormal functioning of an organ.
Dysmenorrhea (dis-men-o-re′ah), difficult and painful menstruation.
Dysphagia (dis-fa′je-ah), difficulty in swallowing.
Dyspnea (disp′ne-ah), difficulty in breathing.
Dystrophy (dis′tro-fe), a disorder arising from impaired nutrition, usually referring to muscles.
Dysuria (dis-u′re-ah), difficult or painful urination.

Ecchymosis (ek-i-mo′sis), bleeding into the tissues under the skin.
Eczema (ek′ze-mah), a skin disease, with itching and red scaly patches.
Edema (e-de′mah), swelling due to an accumulation of watery fluid in the tissues.
Elimination (e-lim-in-a′shun), the act of expelling from the body.
Emaciation (e-ma-se-a′shun), a wasting away of the flesh causing extreme leanness.
Embolus (em′bo-lus), any foreign substance or an air bubble brought to a vessel by the blood, and which partially or completely obstructs the flow of blood.
Emesis (em′e-sis), the act of vomiting.
Emetic (e-met′ik), an agent that causes vomiting.
Emollient (e-mol′e-ent), a soothing medicine.
Emphysema (em-fi-se′mah), an inflation or swelling of the tissues due to the presence of air.
Empyema (em-pi-e′mah), collection of pus in a body cavity.
Enteritis (en-ter-i′tis), inflammation of the intestines.
Enucleation (e-nu-kle-a′shun), the surgical removal of the eyeball.
Enuresis (en-u-re′sis), involuntary discharge of urine, usually referring to the hours of sleep.
Environment (en-vir′on-ment), the surroundings.
Epidemic (ep-i-dem′ik), widespread disease in a certain geographical region.
Epidermis (ep-i-der′mis), the outermost layer of the skin.
Epilepsy (ep′il-ep-se), a chronic disease marked by attacks of convulsions.
Epistaxis (ep-e-stak′sis), nosebleed.
Eructation (e-ruk-ta′shun), forceful expulsion of air from the stomach, known commonly as belching.
Eruption (e-rup′shun), a breaking out of the skin due to disease.
Erythema (er-i-the′mah), redness of the skin due to the congestion of the capillaries.
Etiology (e-te-ol′o-je), the sum of knowledge regarding the cause of a disease.

Euphoria (u-fo′re-ah), a general feeling of comfort and well being.

Eustachian tube (u-sta′ke-an tube), the passage from the throat to the middle ear.

Euthanasia (u-thah-na′ze-ah), an easy or painless death, often referred to as mercy death.

Evisceration (e-vis-er-a′shun), the removal of the abdominal organs, or the protrusion of the intestines through an abdominal wound.

Excoriation (eks-ko-re-a′shun), the removal of pieces of skin as a result of scratching or scraping.

Excreta (eks-kre′tah), waste matter discharged from the body, such as feces, urine, vomitus, etc.

Excreted (eks-kre′ted), thrown off, as waste matter, by a normal discharge.

Exhaustion (eks-awst′yun), the loss of vital power.

Expectoration (eks-pek-to-ra′shun), spitting out mucus or other fluid from the lungs and the throat.

Expiration (eks-pi-ra′shun), exhaling air from the lungs; sometimes used to refer to death.

Exudate (eks′u-date), material that has escaped from blood vessels and is deposited in the tissues or on tissue surfaces.

Fahrenheit (far′en-hite), a thermometer scale in which the boiling point of water is 212° and the freezing point is 32°.

Faint (faint), loss of consciousness due to insufficient blood in the brain.

Fatigue (fah-tig′), weariness resulting from overexertion of the body or the mind.

Febrile (fe′bril), pertaining to a fever.

Fecal (fe′kal), pertaining to feces.

Feces (fe′seze), the residue from digested food which is discharged from the intestines.

Fester (fes′ter), to suppurate superficially.

Fetid (fe′tid), having a disagreeable odor.

Fever (fe′ver), abnormally high body temperature.

Fibrous (fi′brus), composed of or containing fibers.

Fimbriated (fim′bre-at-ed), fringed.

Flaccid (flak′sid), weak, lax or lacking muscle tone.

Flatus (fla′tus), gas in the intestines or the stomach.

Flex (fleks), to bend.

Fomite (fo′mite), any object that may harbor or transmit pathogenic organisms without being corrupted itself.

Foreign body (for′in bod′e), any substance lodged in a place where it does not belong.

Formula (for′mu-lah), a prescribed method of preparation.

Fracture (frak′tur), a break in a bone.

Friction (frik′shun), rubbing.

Fumigation (fum-i-ga′shun), the use of disinfecting fumes to destroy living organisms.

Function (funk′shun), the normal action of a part of an organ.

Fusion (fu′zhun), the joining together of two adjacent parts or bodies.

Gait (gate), a manner or style of walking.

Gall (gawl), the bile.

Gangrene (gang′green), the death of a part or a tissue.

Gargle (gar′gul), a solution to rinse the mouth or throat.

Gastric (gas′trik), pertaining to the stomach.

Gavage (gah-vahzh′), passing food into the stomach through a tube.

Geriatrics (jer-e-at′riks), the branch of medicine that deals with old age and its related diseases, including the psychosocial problems of senility.

Germicidal (jer-mi-si′dal), destructive to germs.

Germs (jerms), bacteria; microbes.

Gestation (jes-ta′shun), the period of development of the individual from fertilization to birth.

Gland (gland), an organ by means of which a secretion is produced.

Glossitis (glos-si′tis), inflammation of the tongue.

Glucose (gloo′kose), a form of sugar.

Gluteal (gloo′te-al), pertaining to the buttocks.

Goiter (goi′ter), an enlargement of the thyroid gland, causing a swelling in the front part of the neck.

Graft (graft), a piece of skin or other tissue from one part of the body which is implanted on another part.

Granulation (gran-u-la′shun), the formation of fleshy tissue in healing wounds.

Groin (groin), the lowest part of the abdominal wall, where it joins the thigh.

Gynecology (jin-e-kol′o-je), the science that treats diseases of women, particularly those of the genital organs.

Hallucination (ha-lu-si-na′shun), seeing, hearing or feeling something when there is no objective stimulus.

Heliotherapy (he-le-o-ther′ah-pe), treatment of disease by exposing the body to the sun's rays.

Hematemesis (hem-at-em′e-sis), vomiting of blood.

Hematocrit (he-mat′o-krit), the volume percentage of red blood cells in whole blood.

Hematuria (hem-ah-tu′re-ah), discharge of blood in the urine.

Hemoglobin (he-mo-glo′bin), the coloring matter of the blood.

Hemoptysis (he-mop′ti-sis), expectoration of blood or blood-stained sputum.

Hemorrhage (hem′or-aje), bleeding; an escape of blood from the arteries, veins or capillaries.

Hemorrhoids (hem′or-oids), a dilatation of the veins of the anal region.

Hemothorax (hem-o-tho′raks), presence of blood in the pleural cavity.

Heredity (he-red′it-e), the inheritance of physical or mental characteristics from ancestors.

Herpes (her′peze), fever blisters; cold sores.

Hiccup (hik′up), an involuntary spasmodic contraction of the diaphragm caused by the irritaton of the phrenic nerve, which produces a sharp, inspiratory cough.

Hirsutism (her′sut-izm), abnormal hairiness, particularly in women.

Homeopathy (hom-e-op′ath-e), a system of medical practice which treats disease by the administration of small doses of medications which, if administered to a healthy person, would produce the symptoms of the disease being treated.

Host (host), a plant or animal which harbors or nourishes another organism.

Humidity (hu-mid′it-e), moisture in the atmosphere.

Hydronephrosis (hi-dro-ne-fro′sis), distention of the pelvis and calyces of the kidney with urine, as a result of obstruction of the ureter.

Hydrotherapy (hi-dro-ther′ap-e), the use of water in the treatment of disease.

Hydrothorax (hi-dro-tho′raks), collection of watery fluid in the pleural cavity.

Hygiene (hi′jene), the science and the preservation of health.

Hyperalgesia (hi-per-al-je′ze-ah), increased sensitiveness to pain.

Hyperemia (hi-per-e′me-ah), excessive blood in a part due to local or general relaxation of the arterioles.

Hyperopia (hi-per-o′pe-ah), farsightedness.

Hypertension (hi-per-ten′shun), chronic elevation of blood pressure.

Hypertrophy (hi-per′trof-e), a diseased enlargement of a part or an organ.

Hypnosis (hip-no′sis), an artificially induced passive state resembling a trance.

Hypochondriac (hi-po-kon′dre-ak), a person with a morbid anxiety about his health.

Hypoglycemia (hi-po-gli-se′me-ah), an abnormally low amount of sugar in the blood.

Hypomania (hi-po-ma′ne-a), mania of a mild type.

Hypotaxia (hi-po-tak′se-ah), diminished control over the will or the actions.

Hypotension (hi-po-ten′shun), chronic depression in blood pressure.

Hypothermia (hi-po-ther′me-ah), a low body temperature.

Hysterectomy (his-ter-ek′to-me), the surgical removal of the uterus.

Hysteria (his-ter′e-ah), lack of emotional control or actions.

Idiosyncrasy (id-e-o-sin′krah-se), a personal peculiarity.

Illusion (i-lu′zhun), a false impression or interpretation of a sensory image.

Immobilize (im-mo′bil-ize), to prevent motion.

Immunization (im-u-niz-a′shun), protecton against infection from any particular disease.

Impacted (im-pak′ted), firmly wedged in place.

Incise (in-size′), to cut.

Incontinence (in-kon′tin-ens), inability to refrain from the urge to urinate or defecate.

Incubation (in-ku-ba′shun), the period of a disease between the implanting of the germs and the manifestation of the symptoms of the disease.

Infection (in-fek′shun), the invasion of the body by disease-producing agents with a resulting reaction to their presence and their toxins.

Inflammation (in-flah-ma′shun), a condition resulting from irritation in any part of the body, marked by pain, heat, redness and swelling.

Inhalation (in-hah-la′shun), drawing air, vapor or fumes into the lungs.

Inherent (in-her′ent), belonging to anything as a result of natural circumstances.

Inhibition (in-hi-bish′un), the partial or complete restraint of any process.

Injection (in-jek′shun), forcing a liquid into a part of the body or into a body cavity.

Inoculation (in-ok-u-la′shun), introduction of a virus or disease-producing microorganism into the body to give protection against certain diseases.

Insanity (in-san′i-te), the legal or lay term referring to a mental derangement or disorder.

Insecticide (in-sek′ti-side), an agent that is destructive to insects.

Insomnia (in-som′ne-ah), sleeplessness.

Intellect (in′te-lekt), thinking ability or understanding.

Intermittent (in-ter-mit′ent), occurring at intervals.

Intubation (in-tu-ba′shun), the insertion of a tube, as in inserting a tube into the larynx in diphtheria to introduce air.

Intussusception (in-tus-sus-sep′shun), the telescoping or prolapsing of one part of the intestine into an adjacent part.
Inunction (in-ungk′shun), application or rubbing of an ointment on the skin.
Involuntary (in-vol′un-ta-re), not under the control of the will.
Irrigation (ir-i-ga′shun), washing out by a stream of water or a solution.
Irritant (ir′i-tant), an agent that causes stimulation or undue sensitiveness to any part of the body.
Ischemia (is-ke′me-ah), decrease of blood to a part as a result of the obstruction or constriction of blood vessels.
Isolation (i-so-la′shun), the separation of persons having infectious diseases from others.
Isthmus (is′mus), a narrow structure connecting 2 larger parts.

Jaundice (jawn′dis), a yellowish discoloration of the skin due to bile.
Jejunectomy (je-joo-nek′to-me), excision of part or all of the jejunum.
Jurisprudence (joor-is-proo′dens), the application or study of legal principles.
Juvenile (joo′ve-nile), pertaining to childhood or immaturity.

Keloid (ke′loid), a scar on the skin consisting of dense tissue, found most often in the Negro race.
Keratitis (ker-a-ti′tis), inflammation of the cornea.
Ketosis (ke-to′sis), an increase in ketone bodies in the body tissues and fluids.
Koplik's spots (kop′liks spots), bright red spots in the mouth and throat found in the early stages of measles.
Kyphosis (ki-fo′sis), an abnormal increase in the thoracic curvature of the spine giving a "hunchback" appearance.

Laceration (las-er-a′shun), a wound produced by tearing.
Lacrimal (lak′ri-mal), pertaining to tears.
Lactation (lak-ta′shun), secretion of milk.
Lactose (lak′tose), a sugar found in milk, commonly called "milk sugar."
Lanolin (lan′o-lin), wool fat.
Laryngitis (lar-in-ji′tis), inflammation of the larynx.
Latent (la′tent), a condition that is concealed or not manifest.
Lateral (lat′er-al), pertaining to a side.
Lavage (lah-vahzh), washing out of an organ, such as the stomach or bowel.
Laxative (laks′ah-tiv), a mild cathartic which acts to promote evacuation of the bowel.
Lens (lenz), a transparent crystalline structure in the eye which converges or scatters light rays as they focus images on the retina.
Lentigo (len-ti′go), small brownish pigmented areas on the skin due to an increased amount of melanin, commonly known as freckles.
Lesion (le′zhun), a break in the body tissue, such as a sore or a wound.
Lethargy (leth′ar-je), a condition of sluggishness or mental dullness.
Leukorrhea (lu-ko-re′ah), a whitish or yellowish viscid discharge from the vagina.
Ligate (li′gate), to bind or tie with a ligature.
Liniment (lin′e-ment), an oily preparation for rubbing on the skin.
Lipoma (li-po′mah), a benign tumor made up of fatty tissue.
Local (lo′kal), limited to one part or place; not general.
Lochia (lo′ke-ah), the vaginal discharge occurring a week or two following childbirth.
Lordosis (lor-do′sis), an abnormal increase in the lumbar curvature of the spine, sometimes called "swayback."
Lotion (lo′shun), a liquid used on the skin to soothe, heal or cleanse.
Lubricant (lu′bri-cant), an oily substance that relieves friction.
Lumbar region (lum′bar re′jun), that part of the back between the pelvis and the thorax.
Lumen (lu′men), a tube or channel within a tube or tubular organ.
Lymphoma (lim-fo′mah), any malignant condition of lymphoid tissue.

Malignant (ma-lig′nant), deadly, tending to go from bad to worse.
Malingering (mah-ling′ger-ing), a deliberate feigning or exaggeration of the symptoms of illness or injury, usually to arouse sympathy.
Malpractice (mal-prak′tis), injurious or faulty treatment that results in injury, loss or damage.
Mania (ma′ne-ah), a disordered mental state of extreme excitement.
Margin (mar′jin), a boundary line; an edge.
Massage (mah-sahzh′), applying friction to or stroking and kneading the body tissues for therapeutic measures.
Masticate (mas′ti-kate), to chew food.
Mastitis (mas-ti′tis), inflammation of the breast.
Mastoiditis (mas-toid-i′tis), inflammation of the mastoid bone.
Masturbation (mas-tur-ba′shun), the handling of the genitals to obtain pleasant sensations.

Maturation (mat-u-ra′shun), the process of ripening or becoming fully developed.

Meconium (me-ko′ne-um), dark green or black fecal substance in the intestines of the full grown fetus or newly born infant.

Membrane (mem′brane), a thin layer of tissue covering a part or lining a body cavity.

Menarche (me-nar′ke), the establishment of menstruation.

Meninges (men-in′jeze), the membranes which cover the brain and the spinal cord.

Meningitis (men-in-ji′tis), inflammation of the meninges.

Menopause (men′o-pawz), cessation of menstruation in the human female.

Menorrhagia (men-o-ra′je-ah), an abnormally profuse menstrual flow.

Mental (men′tal), pertaining to the mind.

Metabolism (me-tab′o-lizm), the sum of all the chemical and physical processes involved in the building up and breaking down of protoplasm in living cells.

Metastasis (me-tas′tah-sis), transfer of disease from one body part to another, usually referring to malignant cells or the tubercle bacillus.

Metrorrhagia (me-tro-ra′je-ah), abnormal uterine bleeding occurring at completely irregular intervals.

Microbe (mi′crobe), a minute organism; a germ.

Micturition (mik-tu-rish′un), the passage of urine from the urinary bladder.

Migraine (mi′grane), severe periodic headaches, frequently unilateral, and often accompanied by nausea, vomiting and sensory disturbances.

Mores (mo′reze), fixed customs and habits of a group generally accepted as conducive to social welfare.

Mucus (mu′kus), the viscid secretion of the mucous glands.

Mutism (mu′tizm), refusal or inability to speak.

Myopia (mi-o′pe-ah), nearsightedness.

Myositis (mi-o-si′tis), inflammation of a voluntary muscle.

Narcotics (nar-kot′iks), drugs that produce sleep or stupor and relieve pain at the same time.

Nasal (na′zal), pertaining to the nose.

Nausea (naw′se-ah), an unpleasant, sick sensation in the stomach which often leads to vomiting.

Necrosis (ne-kro′sis), death of tissues, usually in a localized area.

Negativism (neg′ah-tiv-izm), resistance to outside suggestion, in which the person does the opposite of what is considered normal.

Nephritis (ne-fri′tis), inflammation of the kidney.

Neuralgia (nu-ral′je-ah), pain which extends along one or more nerves.

Neurasthenia (nu-ras-the′ne-ah), nervous exhaustion characterized by extreme fatigue and lack of energy.

Neuritis (nu-ri′tis), inflammation of a nerve or nerves.

Neurosis (nu-ro′sis), a mental or psychic disorder characterized by fears, anxieties and compulsions.

Nevus (ne′vus), a congenital circumscribed discolored area of the skin, either vascular or nonvascular.

Nits (nits), the eggs of lice.

Nomenclature (no′men-kla-tur), a classified system of names.

Nutrition (nu-trish′un), the process of using food for growth and development.

Obese (o-bese′), extremely fat.

Obstetrician (ob-ste-trish′un), a physician who specializes in the management of pregnancy, labor and the puerperium.

Oculist (ok′u-list), an old term for ophthalmologist.

Ointment (oint′ment), a greasy semisolid preparation for external use on the body.

Oliguria (ol-ig-u′re-ah), deficient urinary secretion or too infrequent urination.

Onset (on′set), the beginning of an illness when the first symptoms of disease appear.

Oophorectomy (oo′fo-rek′to-me), the surgical removal of an ovary or the ovaries.

Ophthalmologist (op-thal-mol′o-jist), a physician who specializes in the treatment of disorders of the eye.

Opiate (o′pe-ate), a drug containing or derived from opium.

Optician (op-ti′shun), one who grinds lenses and fits eyeglasses.

Optimum (op′tim-um), the most favorable condition.

Optometrist (op-tom′e-trist), one who measures vision and prescribes glasses for visual defects.

Oral (o′ral), pertaining to the mouth.

Orchitis (or-ki′tis), inflammation of the testicles.

Organ (or′gan), a group of body tissues having a particular function.

Orthopedic (or-tho-pe′dik), pertaining to the correction of deformities.

Orthopnia (or-thop′ne-ah), difficult breathing relieved only by sitting or standing erect.

Osseus (os′e-us), bone-like; pertaining to bone.

Osteoarthritis (os-te-o-ar-thri′tis), a chronic degenerative form of joint disease.

Osteoporosis (os-te-o-po-ro′sis), a chronic bone disorder caused by a loss of minerals in the bone.
Otosclerosis (o-to-skle-ro′sis), a spongy bone formation in the labyrinth of the ear.
Ovaritis (o-vah-ri′tis), inflammation of an ovary.
Oxidize (ok′si-dize), to combine or bring about the combination with oxygen.
Oxygen (ok′si-jen), a colorless, odorless gas which is essential to all life and makes up about one fifth of the air.

Pallor (pal′or), absence of skin pigment; paleness.
Palpitation (pal-pi-ta′shun), an unduly rapid or throbbing heartbeat which can be sensed by the patient.
Palsy (pawl′ze), loss of motion (paralysis) in a part of the body.
Papule (pap′ule), a small, solid, circumscribed elevation of the skin.
Paracentesis (par-ah-sen-te′sis), a surgical puncture of a body cavity for the aspiration of fluid.
Paralysis (par-al′i-sis), loss of motion or impairment of sensation in a part.
Parasites (par′ah-sites), plants or animals which live upon or within another organism.
Paresis (pah-re′sis), slight or incomplete paralysis.
Parietal (pah-ri′e-tal), pertaining to the walls of a cavity.
Paroxysm (par-ok′sizm), a sudden periodic attack or recurrence of symptoms of a disease.
Parturition (par-tu-rish′un), the act of giving birth to a child.
Passive (pas′iv), submissive or not produced by active efforts.
Pasteurization (pas′tur-i-za-shun), the destruction of pathogenic bacteria and the inhibitation in the growth of others by heating a solution without altering to any extent the chemical composition of the substance.
Patency (pa′ten-se), the condition of being freely open.
Pediatrics (pe-de-at′rix), the branch of medicine concerned with children's diseases.
Pediculi (pe-dik′u-li), lice.
Pellagra (pel-lag′rah), a deficiency disease or syndrome caused by the lack of niacin.
Percussion (per-kush′un), tapping a part of the body with short, sharp blows to elicit sounds or vibrations which aid in diagnosis.
Peripheral (pe-rif′er-al), pertaining to the outward part or surface.
Peristalsis (per-is-tal′sis), the wavelike contractions of the intestines by which they propel their contents.
Pessary (pes′ah-re), an instrument inserted into the vagina to support the uterus.
Petechiae (pe-te′ke-i), small, nonraised, hemorrhagic areas on the skin which occur in certain severe fevers, such as typhus.
Petrolatum (pet-ro-la′tum), a purified semisolid mixture of hydrocarbons from petroleum, used as a lubricant and a base for ointments.
Pharmaceutical (fahr-mah-su′ti-kal), pertaining to pharmacy or drugs.
Pharyngitis (far-in-ji′tis), inflammation of the pharynx.
Phlebotomy (fle-bot′o-me), incision of a vein.
Phlegm (flem), viscus mucus secreted by the mucous membrane of the nose and mouth.
Phobia (fo′be-ah), a persistent abnormal fear or dread.
Physical (fiz′ik-al), pertaining to the body.
Placebo (plah-se′bo), an inactive or nonmedicinal substance given in place of a medication to gratify a patient without his knowledge of its actual physiological therapeutic value.
Pledget (pled′jet), a small tuft of cotton or wool.
Podiatrist (po-di′ah-trist), one who diagnosis and treats foot disorders.
Poliomyelitis (pol-e-o-mi-e-li′tis), an acute viral disease involving the spinal cord, commonly known as infantile paralysis.
Pollinosis (pol-i-no′sis), an allergic body reaction due to air-borne pollen.
Polymenorrhea (pol-e-men-o-re′ah), abnormally frequent menstruation.
Polyp (pol′ip), a small protruding growth on a pedicle extending from a mucous membrane.
Polyphagia (pol-e-fa′je-ah), an abnormal craving for all kinds of food.
Polyuria (pol-e-u′re-ah), the voiding of an excessive amount of urine.
Postpartum (post-par′tum), after childbirth or delivery.
Poultice (pol′tis), a soft, moist, hot mass applied to the skin.
Premature (pre-mah-tur′), before the proper time.
Presbyopia (pres-be-o′pe-ah), farsightedness associated with the impairment of vision due to the aging process.
Prescription (pre-skrip′shun), a written direction for the preparation and the use of a medicine.
Process (pros′es), a prominence or projection, as of the end of a bone.
Proctoscope (prok′to-skope), an instrument used for inspecting the rectum.
Prognosis (prog-no′sis), judging in advance the probable duration, course and termination of a disease.

Prophylaxis (pro-fi-lak′sis), prevention of disease.

Prosthesis (pros-the′sis), the replacement of a missing part by an artificial substitute.

Prostration (pros-tra′shun), extreme exhaustion.

Psychiatrist (si-ki′ah-trist), a physician who specializes in the treatment of disorders of the psyche or mind.

Psychology (si-kol′o-je), the science that deals with the mental processes and their effects upon behavior.

Psychosis (si-ko′sis), a mental disturbance in which there is a personality disintegration and an escape into unreality.

Ptosis (to′sis), a drooping or sagging of an organ or part from its normal position.

Puberty (pu′ber-te), the period in life when a person becomes sexually able to reproduce.

Pubes (pu′beze), the hairy region found in the lower part of the hypogastric region.

Puncture (punk′tur), a hole made by a pointed object.

Purulent (pur′u-lent), consisting of or secreting pus.

Pus (pus), a yellowish secretion formed in certain kinds of inflammation, consisting of albuminous substances, a thin fluid, and leukocytes or their remains.

Pustule (pus′tule), a small elevation of the skin filled with pus or lymph.

Pyelitis (pi-e-li′tis), inflammation of the pelvis of the kidney.

Pyemia (pi-e′me-ah), the presence of pus forming organisms in the blood.

Pyloric (pi-lor′ik), pertaining to the last portion of the stomach.

Pyogenic (pi-o-jen′ik), producing pus.

Pyrosis (pi-ro′sis), a burning sensation in the stomach and the esophagus, commonly known as heartburn.

Pyuria (pi-u′re-ah), the presence of pus in the urine.

Quack (kwak) one who pretends to have medical skill and knowledge of remedies.

Quarantine (kwor′an-tene), a period of detention or isolation as a result of suspected contagion of a communicable disease.

Quickening (kwik′en-ing), the first movements of the fetus felt in pregnancy, usually occurring from the 16th to the 18th week.

Radiate (ra′de-ate), to diverge or spread from a common central point.

Radium (ra′de-um), a metallic element that gives off rays which are used in treating malignancies.

Rapport (rah-por′), a state of harmony or good relationship between 2 individuals.

Rash (rash), a superficial eruption of the skin.

Reaction (re-ak′shun), action in response to some influence or force.

Rectum (rek′tum), the distal portion of the large intestine between the sigmoid colon and the anal canal.

Recumbent (re-kum′bent), lying down.

Recuperate (re-ku′per-ate), to recover health or gain strength after an illness.

Recurrence (re-kur′ence), the return of symptoms after their remission.

Regurgitation (re-gur-ji-ta′shun), the return of food from the stomach soon after eating, without the ordinary efforts of vomiting.

Relapse (re-laps′), recurrence of former symptoms during convalescence.

Relax (re-laks′), to loosen up or make less stiff.

Remission (re-mish′un), the lessening in severity or subsiding of the symptoms of an illness.

Research (re-surch′), a careful and diligent hunting for facts, theories or laws.

Resection (re-sek′shun), excision of a portion of an organ or structure, such as bone.

Resistance (re-zis′tans), the power of the body to overcome the ill effects of injurious agents, such as pathogenic microorganisms, poisons or irritants.

Retention (re-ten′shun), holding or keeping within the body matter which is usually expelled, as retention of urine.

Rhinitis (ri-ni′tis), inflammation of the mucous membrane lining the nasal cavity.

Rigor mortis (ri′gor mor′tis), the stiffening of muscles after death.

Rubeola (ru-be-o′lah), measles.

Sac (sak), a baglike organ or structure; a pouch.

Sanatorium (san-ah-to′re-um), an institution for the care of the chronically ill, especially those with mental illness or tuberculosis.

Sarcoma (sar-ko′mah), a type of tumor, often malignant, made up of a substance like the embryonic connective tissue.

Saturated (sat′u-ra-ted), pertaining to a solution in which no more of a substance can be dissolved.

Sclerosis (skle-ro′sis), a hardening of a part.

Scoliosis (sko-le-os′is), a lateral curvature of the normally straight vertical line of the spine.

Sebaceous (se-ba′shus), pertaining to sebum, the oily, fatty secretion of the sebaceous glands.

Seborrhea (seb-o-re′ah), an increase in the secretion of the sebaceous glands, causing an oily skin.

Sebum (se'bum), the oily, fatty secretion from the sebaceous glands.
Secrete (se-krete'), to separate from the blood.
Secretion (se-kre'shun), a substance secreted, as urine secreted by the kidneys.
Sedative (sed'ah-tiv), a remedy that has a quieting effect.
Seizure (se-zhur), a sudden attack or recurrence of a disease, as in an attack of epilepsy.
Senescence (sen-es'ens), the process of growing old.
Senile (se'nile), pertaining to old age.
Septum (sep'tum), a dividing wall between 2 cavities.
Serum (se'rum), the clear liquid which separates from the blood after clotting.
Shock (shok), depression of the body functions due to the failure of the circulation.
Smear (smere), a specimen for microscopic study made by spreading infected material on a glass slide.
Soluble (sol'u-bul), capable of being dissolved.
Solution (so-lu'shun), a liquid in which a substance has been dissolved.
Somnambulism (som-nam'bu-lizm), sleep-walking.
Sordes (sor'deze), the foul, dark matter that collects around the teeth and lips in low fevers.
Spasm (spazm), a sudden muscular contraction.
Specialist (spesh'a-list), a physician who devotes his services to a special class of disease.
Specific (spe-sif'ik), definite; particular.
Specimen (spes'i-men), a sample.
Sphincter (sfingk'ter), a ringlike muscle surrounding and closing an opening, as the sphincter muscle of the rectum.
Splint (splint), an appliance for holding parts of the body in place.
Sputum (spu'tum), matter ejected from the respiratory tract through the mouth.
Stasis (sta'sis), a stoppage or stagnation of the flow of fluid in any part of the body.
Sterile (ster'il), the absence of microorganisms.
Stertorous (ster'to-rus), characterized by a snoring sound, as stertorous breathing.
Stethoscope (steth'o-skope), an instrument used to listen to internal body sounds.
Stimulant (stim'u-lant), any agent that produces an increase in the activity of the body or one of its parts.
Stoma (sto'mah), a small opening on a free surface, such as a pore; an artificially created opening between a body cavity and the body's surface.
Stool (stool), feces.
Stricture (strik'tur), an abnormal narrowing of a passage.
Stroke (stroke), a sudden paralysis of one or more parts of the body, also known as apoplexy or cerebral vascular accident.
Stupor (stu'por), reduced responsiveness or partial unconsciousness.
Subacute (sub-ah-kute'), between an acute or chronic state, with some acute features.
Subcutaneous (sub-ku-ta'ne-us), beneath the skin.
Substitute (sub'sti-tute), an article or material with which to replace another.
Suppository (sup-oz'i-to-re), a cone-shaped mass to be introduced into the vagina, the rectum or the urethra.
Suppuration (sup-u-ra'shun), the formation of pus.
Susceptible (sus-sep'ti-bul), having little resistance.
Suture (su'tur), a surgical stitch.
Symptoms (simp'tums), a functional evidence of a disease or of the patient's condition.
Syncope (sin'co-pe), a temporary state of unconsciousness, commonly known as fainting.
Syndrome (sin'drome), a group of symptoms which occur together.
Synthesis (sin'the-sis), an artificial production of a compound.

Tactile (tak'til), pertaining to touch.
Talcum (tal'kum), a dusting powder with a soft mineral base.
Taut (tawt), tightly drawn.
Temperature (tem'per-a-tur), the degree of hotness or coldness of a substance.
Tension (ten'shun), a stretched or strained condition.
Tepid (tep'id), moderately warm.
Terminal (ter'min-al), at the end.
Therapy (ther'ap-e), the treatment of disease.
Thoracotomy (tho-rah-kot'o-me), a surgical incision of the wall of the thoracic cavity.
Thorax (tho'raks), the chest.
Tibia (tib'e-ah), the shinbone.
Tissue (tish'u), a group of similar specialized cells united to perform a special function.
Tolerance (tol'er-ans), the ability to endure the continued use of a drug.
Tone (tone), normal vigor and tension.
Topical (top'e-kal), pertaining to an external or local spot.
Tourniquet (toor'ne-ket), a device such as a bandage, used to stop hemorrhage from an external wound by the compression of one or more blood vessels.
Toxic (tok'sik), pertaining to a poison.

Transection (tran-sek′shun), a cross-section made by cutting across a long axis.

Transmit (trans-mit′), to pass on.

Trauma (traw′mah), a wound or injury.

Tumor (tu′mor), an abnormal new growth of tissue having no physiologic use, which grows independently of its surrounding structures.

Tympanites (tim-pah-ni′tez), distention of the abdomen due to the accumulation of gas.

Ulcer (ul′ser), an open sore on an external or internal surface of the body which causes the gradual disintegration of the tissues.

Umbilicus (um-bil-i′kus), a small scar on the abdomen which marks the former attachment of the umbilical cord to the fetus.

Unconscious (un-kon′shus), a lack of awareness of the environment with an incapability to react to sensory stimuli.

Urea (u-re′ah), the end product of protein metabolism in the body and the chief nitrogenous substance in the urine.

Urinalysis (ur-in-al′is-is), examination of the urine.

Urticaria (ur-ti-ka′re-ah), hives; an allergic reaction of the skin characterized by wheals which are often attended by severe itching.

Vaccination (vak-sin-a′shun), the injection of killed or modified live microorganisms for the purpose of treating or producing immunity to certain infectious diseases.

Valve (valv), a membranous structure in an orifice or passage which allows the passage of contents in one direction only.

Vapor (va′por), steam; a gas given off by a liquid or a solid.

Varicose veins (var′i-kose vanes), enlarged and twisted veins, usually occurring in the legs.

Venipuncture (ven-i-punk′tur), a puncture of a vein.

Venisection (ven-i-sek′shun), an incision of a vein.

Ventilation (ven-til-a′shun), the circulation of air in a room or the supplying of oxygen to the body through the lungs.

Vertigo (ver′ti-go), a whirling sensation of oneself or of objects in the environment.

Viscera (vis′er-ah), the internal body organs, particularly referring to those in the abdominal cavity.

Vitality (vi-tal′it-e), the life force.

Void (void), to empty or cast out as waste matter.

Volatile (vol′ah-til), tending to vaporize rapidly.

Voluntary (vol′un-ta-re), controlled by the will.

Vomitus (vom′i-tus), matter forcibly expelled from the stomach through the mouth.

Vulva (vul′vah), the region of the external female genital organs.

Wean (ween), to substitute another method of feeding for breast feeding of an infant.

Wen (wen), a sebaceous cyst.

Wheal (wheel), a smooth, slightly elevated area on the skin, usually pale in the center with a reddened periphery, which is often attended by severe itching.

Wound (woond), an injury to any body structure caused by physical means.

Xanthosis (zan-tho′sis), a yellowish pigmentation of the skin, often the result of the ingestion of excessive carotene-rich foods, such as carrots and egg yolks.

Xenophobia (zen-o-fo′be-ah), an abnormal fear of strangers.

Xeroma (ze-ro′mah), an abnormal dryness of the conjunctiva.

Xerosis (ze-ro′sis), abnormal dryness of the skin, conjunctiva or mucous membranes.

X-ray (eks′ra), a ray which is able to penetrate most substances, used to make photographic plates of parts of the body and to treat disease.

Zoomania (zo-o-ma′ne-ah), a morbid love of animals.

Zoophobia (zo-o-fo′be-ah), an abnormal fear of animals.

Zoopsia (zo-op′se-ah), a hallucination in which a person thinks he sees animals.

Zygote (zi′gote), the cell resulting from the fusion of 2 mature germ cells, as an unfertilized egg and a mature sperm cell.

Zymocite (zi′mo-site), an organism which causes fermentation.

MEDICAL TERMINOLOGY

Combining Forms and Prefixes

These forms, with a prefix or a suffix, or both, are those most commonly used in making medical words. G indicates those derived from the Greek; L, those from the Latin. Properly, Greek forms should be used only with Greek prefixes and suffixes; Latin, with Latin. Often a vowel, usually a, i or o, is needed for euphony.

A- or **Ab-** (L) *away, lack of:* abnormal, departing from normal.

A- or **An-** (G) *from, without:* asepsis, without infection.

Acr- (G) *an extremity:* acrodermatitis, a dermatitis of the limbs.

Ad- (L) *to, toward, near:* adrenal, near the kidney.

Aden- (G) *gland:* adenitis, inflammation of a gland.

Alg- (G) *pain:* neuralgia, pain extending along nerves.

Ambi- (L) *both:* ambidextrous, referring to both hands.

Ante- (L) *before:* antenatal, occurring or having been formed before birth.

Anti- (G) *against:* antiseptic, against or preventing sepsis.

Arth- (G) *joint:* arthritis, inflammation of a joint.

Auto- (G) *self:* auto-intoxication, poisoning by toxin generated in the body.

Bi- or **Bin-** (L) *two:* binocular, pertaining to both eyes.

Bio- (G) *life:* biopsy, inspection of living organism (or tissue).

Blast- (G) *bud, a growing thing in early stages:* blastocyte, beginning cell not yet differentiated.

Bleph- (G) *eyelids:* blepharitis, inflammation of an eyelid.

Brachi- (G) *arm:* brachialis, muscle for flexing forearm.

Brachy- (G) *short:* brachydactylia, abnormal shortness of fingers and toes.

Brady- (G) *slow:* bradycardia, abnormal slowness of heartbeat.

Bronch- (G) *windpipe:* bronchiectasis, dilation of bronchial tubes.

Bucc- (L) *cheek:* buccally, toward the cheek.

Carcin- (G) *cancer:* carcinogenic, producing cancer.

Cardi- (G) *heart:* cardialgia, pain in the heart.

Cephal- or **Cephalo** (G) *head:* cephalic measurements.

Cheil- (G) *lip:* cheilitis, inflammation of the lip.

Chole- (G) *bile:* cholecyst, the gallbladder.

Chondr- (G) *cartilage:* chondrectomy, removal of a cartilage.

Circum- (L) *around:* circumocular, around the eyes.

Cleid- (G) *clavicle:* cleidocostal, pertaining to clavicle and ribs.

Colp- (G) *vagina:* colporrhagia, vaginal hemorrhage.

Contra- (L) *against, opposed:* contraindication, indication opposing usually indicated treatment.

Cost- (L) *rib:* intercostal, between the ribs.

Counter- (L) *against:* counterirritation, an irritation to relieve some other irritation (e.g., a liniment).

Crani- (L) *skull:* craniotomy, surgical opening in skull.

Crypt- (G) *hidden:* cryptogenic, of hidden or unknown origin.

Cut- (L) *skin:* subcutaneous, under the skin.

Cyst- (G) *sac or bladder:* cystitis, inflammation of the bladder.

Cyto- (G) *cell:* cytology, scientific study of cells; cytometer, a device for counting and measuring cells.

Dacry- (G) *lacrimal glands:* dacryocyst, tear-sac.

Derm- or **Dermat-** (G) *skin:* dermatoid, skinlike.

Di- (L) *two:* diphasic, occurring in two stages or phases.

Dis- (L) *apart:* disarticulation, taking a joint apart.

Dys- (G) *pain or difficulty:* dyspepsia, impairment of digestion.

Ecto- (G) *outside:* ectoretina, outermost layer of retina.
Em- or **En-** (G) *in:* encapsulated, enclosed in a capsule.
Encephal- (G) *brain:* encephalitis, inflammation of brain.
End- (G) *within:* endothelium, layer of cells lining heart, blood and lymph vessels.
Entero- (G) *intestine:* enterosis, falling of intestine.
Epi- (G) *above or upon:* epidermis, outermost layer of skin.
Erythro- (G) *red:* erythrocyte, red blood cell.
Eu- (G) *well:* euphoria, well feeling, feeling of good health.
Ex- or **E-** (L) *out:* excretion, material thrown out of the body or the organ.
Exo- (G) *outside:* exocrine, excreting outwardly (opposite of endocrine).
Extra- (G) *outside:* extramural, situated or occurring outside a wall.

Febri- (L) *fever:* febrile, feverish.

Galacto- (G) *milk:* galactose, a milk-sugar.
Gastr- (G) *stomach:* gastrectomy, excision of the stomach.
Gloss- (G) *tongue:* glossectomy, surgical removal of tongue.
Glyco- (G) *sugar:* glycosuria, sugar in the urine.
Gynec- (G) *woman:* gynecology, science of diseases pertaining to women.

Hem- or **Hemat-** (G) *blood:* hemopoiesis, forming blood.
Hemi- (G) *half:* heminephrectomy, excision of half the kidney.
Hepat- (G) *liver:* hepatitis, inflammation of the liver.
Hetero- (G) *other* (opposite of homo): heterotransplant, using skin from a member of another species.
Hist- (G) *tissue:* histology, science of minute structure and function of tissues.
Homo- (G) *same:* homotransplant, skin grafting by using skin from a member of the same species.
Hydr- (G) *water:* hydrocephalus, abnormal accumulation of fluid in cranium.
Hyper- (G) *above, excess of:* hyperglycemia, excess of sugar in blood.
Hypo- (G) *under, deficiency of:* hypoglycemia, deficiency of sugar in blood.
Hyster- (G) *uterus:* hysterectomy, excision of uterus.

Idio- (G) *self, or separate:* idiopathic, a disease self-originated (of unknown cause).
Im- or **In-** (L) *in:* infiltration, accumulation in tissue of abnormal substances.
Im- or **In-** (L) *not:* immature, not mature.
Infra- (L) *below:* infra-orbital, below the orbit.
Inter- (L) *between:* intermuscular, between the muscles.
Intra- (L) *within:* intramuscular, within the muscle.

Kerat- (G) *horn, cornea:* keratitis, inflammation of cornea.

Lact- (L) *milk:* lactation, secretion of milk.
Leuk- (G) *white:* leukocyte, white cell.

Macro- (G) *large:* macroblast, abnormally large red cell.
Mast- (G) *breast:* mastectomy, excision of the breast.
Meg- or **Megal-** (G) *great:* megacolon, abnormally large colon.
Ment- (L) *mind:* dementia, deterioration of the mind.
Mer- (G) *part:* merotomy, division into segments.
Mesa- (G) *middle:* mesaortitis, inflammation of middle coat of the aorta.
Meta- (G) *beyond, over, change:* metastasis, change in the seat of a disease.
Micro- (G) *small:* microplasia, dwarfism.
My- (G) *muscle:* myoma, tumor made of muscular elements.
Myc- (G) *fungi:* mycology, science and study of fungi.

Necro- (G) *corpse, dead:* necrosis, death of cells adjoining living tissue.
Neo- (G) *new:* neoplasm, any new growth or formation.
Neph- (G) *kidney:* nephrectomy, surgical excision of kidney.
Neuro- (G) *nerve:* neuron, nerve cell.

Odont- (G) *tooth:* odontology, dentistry.
Olig- (G) *little:* oligemia, deficiency in volume of blood.
Oo- (G) *egg:* oocyte, original cell of egg.
Oophor- (G) *ovary:* oophorectomy, removal of an ovary.
Ophthalm- (G) *eye:* ophthalmometer, an instrument for measuring the eye.
Ortho- (G) *straight, normal:* orthograde, walk straight (upright).

Oss- (L) *bone:* osseous, bony.
Oste- (G) *bone:* osteitis, inflammation of a bone.
Ot- (G) *ear:* otorrhea, discharge from ear.
Ovar- (G) *ovary:* ovariorrhexis, rupture of an ovary.

Para- (G) *irregular, around, wrong:* paradenitis, inflammation of tissue in the neighborhood of a gland.
Path- (G) *disease:* pathology, science of disease.
Ped-[1] (G) *children:* pediatrician, child specialist.
Ped-[2] (L) *feet:* pedograph, imprint of the foot.
Per- (L) *through, excessively:* percutaneous, through the skin.
Peri- (G) *around, immediately around* (in contradistinction to para): periosteum, sheath around bone.
Phil- (G) *love:* hemophilic, fond of blood (as bacteria that grow well in presence of hemoglobin).
Phleb- (G) *vein:* phlebotomy, opening of vein for bloodletting.
Phob- (G) *fear:* hydrophobic, reluctant to associate with water.
Pneum- or **Pneumon-** (G) *lung* (pneum—air): pneumococcus, organism causing lobar pneumonia.
Polio- (G) *gray:* poliomyelitis, inflammation of gray substance of spinal cord.
Poly- (G) *many:* polyarthritis, inflammation of several joints.
Post- (L) *after:* postpartum, after delivery.
Pre- (L) *before:* prenatal, occurring before birth.
Pro- (L and G) *before:* prognosis, forecast as to result of disease.
Proct- (G) *rectum:* proctectomy, surgical removal of rectum.
Pseudo- (G) *false:* pseudoangina, false angina.
Psych- (G) *soul or mind:* psychiatry, treatment of mental disorders.
Py- (G) *pus:* pyorrhea, discharge of pus.
Pyel- (G) *pelvis:* pyelitis, inflammation of pelvis of kidney.

Rach- (G) *spine:* rachicentesis, puncture into vertebral canal.
Ren- (L) *kidney:* adrenal, near the kidney.
Retro- (L) *backward:* retroversion, turned backward (usually, of uterus).
Rhin- (G) *nose:* rhinology, knowledge concerning noses.

Salping- (G) *a tube:* salpingitis, inflammation of tube.

[1] **Ped**—from Greek *pais*, child.
[2] **Ped**—from Latin *pes*, foot.

Semi- (L) *half:* semicoma, mild coma.
Septic- (L and G) *poison:* septicemia, poisoned condition of blood.
Somat- (G) *body:* psychosomatic, having bodily symptoms of mental origin.
Sta- (G) *make stand:* stasis, stoppage of flow of fluid.
Sten- (G) *narrow:* stenosis, narrowing of duct or canal.
Sub- (L) *under:* subdiaphragmatic, under the diaphragm.
Super- (L) *above, excessively:* superacute, excessively acute.
Supra- (L) *above, upon:* suprarenal, above or upon the kidney.
Sym- or **Syn** (G) *with, together:* symphysis, a growing together.

Tachy- (G) *fast:* tachycardia, fast-beating heart.
Tens- (L) *stretch:* extensor, a muscle extending or stretching a limb.
Therm- (G) *heat:* diathermy, therapeutic production of heat in tissues.
Tox- or **toxic-** (G) *poison:* toxemia, poisoned condition of blood.
Trache- (G) *trachea:* tracheitis, inflammation of the trachea.
Trans- (L) *across:* transplant, transfer tissue from one place to another.
Tri- (L and G) *three:* trigastric, having three bellies (muscle).
Trich- (G) *hair:* trichosis, any disease of the hair.

Uni- (L) *one:* unilateral, affecting one side.

Vas- (L) *vessel:* vasoconstrictor, nerve or drug that narrows blood vessel.

Zoo- (G) *animal:* zooblast, an animal cell.

Suffixes

-algia (G) *pain:* cardialgia, pain in the heart.
-asis or **-osis** (G) *affected with:* leukocytosis, excess number of leukocytes.
-asthenia (G) *weakness:* neurasthenia, nervous weakness.
-blast (G) *germ:* myeloblast, bone-marrow cell.
-cele (G) *tumor, hernia:* enterocele, any hernia of intestine.
-cid (L) *cut, kill:* germicidal, destructive to germs.
-clysis (G) *injection:* hypodermoclysis, injection under the skin.
-coccus (G) *round bacterium:* pneumococcus, bacterium of pneumonia.

-cyte (G) *cell:* leukocyte, white cell.

-ectasis (G) *dilation, stretching:* angiectasis, dilatation of a blood vessel.

-ectomy (G) *excision:* adenectomy, excision of adenoids.

-emia (G) *blood:* glycemia, sugar in blood.

-esthesia (G) (*noun*) *relating to sensation:* anesthesia, absence of feeling.

-ferent (L) *bear, carry:* efferent, carry out to periphery.

-genic (G) *producing:* pyogenic, producing pus.

-iatrics (G) *pertaining to a physician or the practice of healing* (medicine): pediatrics, science of medicine for children.

-itis (G) *inflammation:* tonsillitis, inflammation of tonsils.

-logy (G) *science of:* pathology, science of disease.

-lysis (G) *losing, flowing, dissolution:* autolysis, dissolution of tissue cells.

-malacia (G) *softening:* osteomalacia, softening of bone.

-oma (G) *tumor:* myoma, tumor made up of muscle elements.

-osis (-asis) (G) *being affected with:* atherosis, arteriosclerosis.

-(o)stomy (G) *creation of an opening:* gastrostomy, creation of an artificial gastric fistula.

-(o)tomy (G) *cutting into:* laparotomy, surgical incision into abdomen.

-pathy (G) *disease:* myopathy, disease of a muscle.

-penia (G) *lack of:* leukopenia, lack of white blood cells.

-pexy (G) *to fix:* proctopexy, fixation of rectum by suture.

-phagia (G) *eating:* polyphagia, excessive eating.

-phasia (G) *speech:* aphasia, loss of power of speech.

-phobia (G) *fear:* hydrophobia, fear of water.

-plasty (G) *molding:* gastroplasty, molding or reforming stomach.

-pnea (G) *air or breathing:* dyspnea, difficult breathing.

-poiesis (G) *making, forming:* hematopoiesis, forming blood.

-ptosis (G) *falling:* enteroptosis, falling of intestine.

-rhythmia (G) *rhythm:* arrhythmia, variation from normal rhythm of heart.

-rrhagia (G) *flowing or bursting forth:* otorrhagia, hemorrhage from ear.

-rrhaphy (G) *suture of:* enterorrhaphy, act of sewing up gap in intestine.

-rrhea (G) *discharge:* otorrhea, discharge from ear.

-sthen (ia) (ic) (G) *pertaining to strength:* asthenia, loss of strength.

-taxia or **-taxis** (G) *order, arrangement of:* ataxia, failure of muscular coordination.

-trophia or **trophy** (G) *nourishment:* atrophy, wasting, or diminution.

-uria (G) *to do with urine:* polyuria, excessive secretion of urine.

INDEX